# INTRODUCTION

This book started with the realization that I did not know the meaning of my name. All I knew was that Menaka (I spell it Maneka) was the name of an apsara in the court of Indra. No one I had encountered knew the meaning of their names either. Like me, they had been named after historical or mythological people. I hunted for a book, but while the libraries are full of information about the gods, I did not come across one book in India which gave the meaning of the name. What does Sarasvati mean? No, not 'learning' even though she is the goddess of that, but 'full of water'. Chandrashekhar does not mean Shiva but one who bears the moon on his forehead. I waited for someone to write a book but the two that emerged listed 'Menaka' as 'apsara'. When my sister announced that a baby was on the way, I decided to compile the dictionary myself. Aaryaman is now almost four years old!

The Vedic rishis believed that the name defined the child's character—its face, figure, temper, morals, tastes and profession. The name Anamika or 'without a name' for instance, would ensure that the child's future was what she wanted to make it—since she was not hedged in by any preordained limitations. Most of us look for phonetically pleasing names without realizing their significance. But Minna means 'fat' and Ambika means 'little mother', Sita means 'furrow', Mina means 'fish' and Draupadi has no meaning other than 'daughter of Drupada'. A number of names which are very common do not have any meaning at all. Anita, Lina, Rina and Tina for instance, come from languages other than Indian. If Roma is of Indian origin it means 'hairy'! The Phul, Sona and Pyar family (Phulvati, Phulrani, Sonalika, Soriam, Pyari) have no roots in Sanskrit, Pali or any of the classical Indian languages. Rishma and Rashmini simply do not exist. Malvika is a combination name that has no meaning. (There is however a plant of the Ipomoea family called Malvika.) My mother's name Amteshwar is a corruption of, I think, Amritesvara or lord of the Amrita. Alternatively it has no meaning at all. Names like Bina are distortions of Vina (the musical instrument), Bihari is not from Bihar, for instance, but from Vihari or roamer. I have left out the local versions of the classical name (Poonam comes from Purnima, Rakhi from Rakshaka, for instance) or the local diminutives or corruptions (e.g. Lacchman or Lakha for Lakshman, Upinder for Upendra, Vanti for Vati). The only exception I have made is for Rima which is a corruption of Hrim—since this happens to be my copy editor's name!

A lot of the names in India are combination names. Two primary names (usually of two gods or of a god and goddess) taken and made into one. For instance Ramakrishna or Radheshyam and in some cases, the conjoining of two gods produces an entirely new deity. I have tried to give as many combinations as possible, especially where there is a historical or mythological person with that compound. However the compounds can be infinite—and a lot of distortion of the primary names takes place in the mixture. Punjab is full of Gurveens, Tarveens, Harleens, Hargurbirinders and Harkirats. Some combinations are unique to certain regions in the country. The suffixes of Jit, Mita and Inder/Indra to the main name are usually from Punjab, Haryana and Rajasthan. Swamy,

Appa, Amma show Tamil Nadu and Karnataka. The nagas or serpents who formed such an integral part of pre-Vedic and Vedic mythology are now confined to south and east India—e.g. Seshan, Nagabhushan, Phenamani. Even Manasa, the goddess of serpents, is a name far more common in Bengal than anywhere else in India.

The entries in this dictionary have been designed so that each entry is divided into three categories:

1. The exact or literal meaning. For instance Menaka means 'daughter of Mena'.

2. The intended meaning or rather, the meaning of the meaning. Menaka's intended meaning is 'of the mountains' because, in Indian mythology, Mena is the consort of Himavan who is the lord of the Himalayas.

3. This is divided into two sub-categories. The first is the locating of the name in mythology, history, literature, botany or ornithology. If the name denotes a person out of mythology, history or literature I have tried to give the name of the mythological consort, the children and the name of the dynasty, as well as the names of Sanskrit Vedic commentators, grammarians and playwrights. I have included the names that come from plants, trees, birds and animals along with their Latin and English names.

The last sub-category is 'another name for—'. In Menaka's case, it is 'another name for Parvati' as Parvati was born a daughter of Himavan in her incarnation as Uma. (The name Parvati also means of the mountains.)

I have read the *Mahabharata*, the *Ramayana*, the *Kathasaritsagara*, the *Panchatantra*, the listings of all the Vedas and Upanishads, books on Sanskrit plants and birds, the catalogues that list the thousand names of each major god, Vedic and Puranic encyclopaedias and the Buddhist and Jaina mythologies and histories and, of course, Sanskrit dictionaries to unearth the meanings of the names in this dictionary. Very often the meaning of the name sounds bizarre unless one knows the context. Aparna which is another name for Parvati in her incarnation as Himavan's daughter means 'leafless'. This is explained by the legend of Parvati fasting to marry Shiva.

One result of this search has been new and unexpected perceptions into the traditional Indian way of life. For instance, what is truth? Or again, what is right and what is wrong? Jaya and Vijaya were the two door-keepers of Vishnu's palace in Vaikuntha. One day they were cursed by Lakshmi to be reborn on the earth as mortals. Vishnu modified the curse on his two devoted servants by saying that if they were killed thrice by him, they could come back to Vaikuntha. Jaya and Vijaya chose to be reborn as the most evil (or what we define as evil within the parameters of morality set by our religion) asuras or anti-gods Hiranyaksha and Hiranyakashipu, Ravana and Kumbhakarna, Shisupala and Dantavaktra so that their deaths at the hands of Vishnu—in his incarnation of Narasimha, Rama and Krishna—became quick and inevitable. So were these asuras good or bad? It was inevitable that Sita be separated from Rama for she had imprisoned a pregnant female parrot and had been cursed by the consort of the parrot to suffer the same fate. So, is Rama to be blamed for listening to the jibes of a washerman or was his action inevitable? Krishna means dark or black and Arjuna fair or white. They are reborn from Nara and Narayana or man and superman/god. Do they represent people or the Eastern philosophy of yin and yang, two opposites that fuse to complete? I find my attitude towards people and current affairs, goals and achievements, and even the pursuit of happiness or rather the diminishing of pain has changed with the unfolding of the history of each mythological character.

I would like to thank all the people who helped me in the preparation of this book. The friends who brought in the odd name in the beginning, those who pitched in to type the manuscript over and over again, the pandits and Sanskrit teachers who corrected my mistakes, the editors at Penguin who put the work into order and spent hours proof-reading and inserting new words till the last minute. I have used the Sanskrit classical style of spelling with diacritical marks, to help in the correct pronunciation of the names.

*New Delhi*
*December 1991*

*Maneka Gandhi*

# Guide to the Use of the Book

## *How to Read an Entry*

1. All Sanskrit words are marked (S).

2. Genders are differentiated as follows—(M) denotes male names and (F) denotes female.

3. The definition of each name is listed in a numbered sequence in the following order: the subdivision marked '1' gives the literal meaning; '2' is the implied or intended meaning and '3' places the name in its specific mythological/literary/botanical context. Some entries do not feature all the subdivisions as these are not required.

4. All books and scriptures referred to in abbreviated form in the entries are expanded in full at the end of the book.

## *Pronunciation*

| | | |
|---|---|---|
| ā | – | f*a*ther |
| ī | – | *ea*gle/pol*i*ce |
| ū | – | r*u*de |
| ṛ | – | mer*ri*ly |
| ṅ | – | ki*n*g |
| ć | – | *ch*ick |
| ćh | – | *chh*ota |
| ñ | – | si*n*ge |
| ṭ | – | *t*omato |
| ṭh | – | an*th*ill |
| ḍ | – | *d*rum |
| ḍh | – | re*dh*aired |
| ṇ | – | no*n*e |
| ś | – | *s*ure |
| ṣ | – | *sh*un |
| ṃ or ṁ | – | nasal sound |

A

**Abādhya** (S) (M) 1. not to be opposed. 2. invincible; ever victorious.

**Abala** (S) (M) 1. powerless. 2. weak. 3. a son of Pānćajañya (*M. Bh.*)

**Abālendu** (S) (M) 1. not the nascent moon. 2. the full moon.

**Abdhiśayana** (S) (M) 1. sleeping on the ocean. 2. another name for Viṣṇu.

**Ābhā** (S) (F) splendour; light; colour; appearance; beauty; reflected image; resemblance; likeness.

**Ābhāsa** (S) (M) splendour; light; colour; reflection.

**Ābhāsvara** (S) (M) 1. shining one. 3. a class of 64 minor deities who are attendants of Śiva (*Ś. Purāṇa*)

**Ābhāta** (S) (M) 1. shining; blazing. 2. appearing; visible.

**Ābhāti** (S) (F) splendour; light.

**Abhaya** (S) (M) 1. without fear. 2. undaunted. 3. a son of Bimbisāra (*M. Bh.*); a son of Idhmajihva (*Bh. Purāṇa*); a son of Dhṛtarāṣṭra (*M. Bh.*); another name for Śiva; the Black Myrobalan tree (*Terminalia chebula*); Khuskhus grass (*Vetiveria zizanioides*)

**Abhayada** (S) (M) 1. giving safety. 3. a Jaina Arhat; a son of Manasyu and father of Sudhanvan.

**Abhayānanda** (S) (M) delighting in fearlessness.

**Abhayaṇkara** (S) (M) one who causes safety.

**Abhayaprada** (S) (M) 1. bestower of safety. 3. an Arhat of the Jainas (*J.S. Koṣa*); another name for Viṣṇu.

**Abhayasinha** (S) (M) fearless lion.

**Abherī** (S) (F) 1. fearless. 3. a rāgiṇī.

**Abhī** (S) (M) fearless.

**Abhibhā** (S) (F) glittering.

**Abhibhava** (S) (M) overpowering; powerful; victorious.

**Abhibhū** (S) (M) 1. to overcome; predominate; surpass; conquer. 3. a king of the nāgas (*M. Bh.*); the son of the king of Kaśī (*M. Bh.*)

**Abhićandra** (S) (M) 1. with a moon-like face. 3. one of the 7 Manus of the Śvetāmbara Jaina sect (*J.S. Koṣa*)

**Ābhidhā** (S) (F) 1. literal meaning. 2. name; word; sound.

**Abhidhyā** (S) (F) of thought; wish; longing; desire.

**Abhidī** (S) (M) radiant.

**Abhidīpa** (S) (M) illuminated.

**Abhidyu** (S) (M) heavenly; bright.

**Abhigīta** (S) (M) praised in song.

**Abhigūrtī** (S) (F) chants of praise.

**Abhihita** (S) (M) 1. expression. 2. word; name.

**Abhijana** (S) (M) 1. of noble descent. 2. ornament of a family.

**Abhijāta** (S) (M) 1. well-born. 2. fit; proper; wise; learned; handsome; noble.

**Abhijaya** (S) (M) conquest; complete victory.

**Abhiji** (S) (M) to conquer completely.

**Abhijit** (S) (M) 1. one who has been conquered; one who has conquered. 2. victorious; conquering completely; born under the constellation Abhijit. 3. a son of Punarvasu (*A. Veda*); a star or 22nd constellation (*J. Śastra*); another name for Viṣṇu.

**Abhijitī** (S) (F) victory.

**Abhijñā** (S) (F) 1. knowing; recollection; skilful; clever. 2. remembrance.

**Abhijñāna** (S) (M) recollection; remembrance; a sign or token of remembrance.

**Abhijvala** (S) (M) blazing forth.

**Abhīka** (S) (M) 1. fearless. 2. a passionate lover.

**Abhikāma** (S) (M) affection; desire.

**Abhikāṅkṣa** (S) (M) wish; desire; longing.

**Abhikhyā** (S) (F) beauty; splendour; fame; glory.

**Abhikhyāna** (S) (M) fame; glory.

**Abhilāṣā** (S) (F) desire; wish; affection.

**Abhilāṣin** (S) (M) (F) one who desires.

**Abhīma** (S) (M) 1. one who causes no fear. 2. one who destroys fear. 3. another name for Viṣṇu.

**Abhimand** (S) (M) gladdening.

**Abhimānī** (S) (M) 1. full of pride. 3. another name for Agni as the eldest son of Brahmā.

**Abhimanyu** (S) (M) 1. with self-respect; heroic; fiery. 3. the son of Arjuna and Subhadrā (*M. Bh.*); son of Manu Ćākṣuṣa and Nadvalā (*R. Taraṅginī*)

**Abhimanyusuta** (S) (M) 1. son of Abhimanyu. 3. another name for Parīkṣit.

**Abhimatijit** (S) (M) 1. one who conquers the ego. 2. subduing enemies.

**Abhimoda** (S) (M) joy; delight.

**Abhimukhī** (S) (F) turned towards; facing.

**Abhinabhas** (S) (M) 1. one whose glory has reached the heavens. 2. renowned; famous; sagacious.

**Abhināmin** (S) (M) 1. one who has a famous name. 2. renowned. 3. a ṛṣi of the 6th Manvantara (*V. Purāṇa*)

**Abhinanda** (S) (M) 1. to rejoice; to celebrate. 2. to praise; to bless; to be glad; delight; pleasure; wish; desire. 3. the first month; another name for the Supreme Being.

**Abhinandana** (S) (M) 1. felicitous. 2. one who pleases; delighting; pleasing all; welcoming. 3. the 4th Jaina Arhat of the present Avasarpinī who was the son of King Nābhi and Marudevī of Ayodhyā (*J. S. Koṣa*); a prince mentioned in the *Skanda* and *Maudgala Purāṇa*.

**Abhinandin** (S) (M) 1. wishing. 2. rejoicing.

**Abhinandita** (S) (M) delighted; made happy; saluted; applauded.

**Abhinātha** (S) (M) 1. lord of desires. 3. another name for Kāma.

**Abhinava** (S) (M) 1. new; young; fresh; modern. 3. a Śākta notable for his great learning and spiritual attainment (7th century) (*R. Taraṅginī*)

**Abhinavan** (S) (M) innovation.

**Abhinīta** (S) (M) 1. well carried. 2. well performed; highly ornamented; proper; suitable; patient; forgiving; evenminded; kind; friendly.

**Abhinīti** (S) (F) 1. that which has already been performed. 2. one who has achieved perfection; gesture; friendship; civility.

**Abhiniveśa** (S) (M) 1. study. 2. affection; devotion; determination.

**Abhipāda** (S) (M) 1. one who steps fearlessly. 3. a ṛṣi (*Ṛg. Veda*)

**Abhipāla** (S) (M) protector.

**Abhiprī** (S) (F) gladdening; refreshing.

**Abhipriti** (S) (F) 1. full of love. 2. that which is pleasing; that which causes pleasure.

**Abhipuṣpa** (S) (M) covered with flowers.

**Abhipuṣpam** (S) (F) an excellent flower.

**Ābhīra** (S) (M) cowherd.

**Abhirāja** (S) (M) 1. supreme king. 2. one who reigns everywhere; to shine; one who is brilliant.

**Abhirakṣā** (S) (F) one who protects.

**Abhirakṣa** (S) (M) one who protects.

**Abhirakṣita** (S) (M) one who is protected.

**Abhirāma** (S) (M) 1. pleasing; delightful; agreeable; beautiful. 3. another name for Śiva.

**Abhiramaṇa** (S) (M) one who delights.

**Abhirāṣṭra** (S) (M) one who conquers kingdoms.

**Abhirata** (S) (M) 1. immersed. 2. one who is immersed in worldly affairs.

**Abhirati** (S) (F) pleasure.

**Abhīrkā** (S) (F) wife of a cowherd.

**Abhīru** (S) (M) 1. not a coward. 2. one who is fearless; strong and powerful. 3. a rājarṣi (*M. Bh.*); another name for Śiva and Bhairava; *Asparagus racemosa*.

**Abhiruća** (S) (M) to be bright; to please.

**Abhirući** (S) (F) 1. delighting in pleasures. 2. deep interest.

**Abhirućira** (S) (M) extremely beautiful; splendid; pleasant; agreeable.

**Abhirūpa** (S) (M) 1. pleasing form. 2. handsome; charming; well-formed; delightful; beloved; favourite; learned; wise; beautiful. 3. another name for Śiva, Viṣṇu, Kāma and the moon.

**Abhisala** (S) (M) convergence.

**Abhisāra** (S) (M) to spread brightness; companion.

**Abhiṣeka** (S) (M) 1. anointing or consecrating. 2. the installation of a king.

**Abhiṣikta** (S) (M) 1. anointed. 2. enthroned.

**Abhisneha** (S) (M) affection; desire.

**Abhiśoka** (S) (M) passionate; loving.
**Abhiśri** (S) (F) 1. surrounded by glory. 2. one who is glorious; worthy; shining; powerful.
**Abhiśri** (S) (M) to spread brightness.
**Abhīṣu** (S) (M) ray of light.
**Abhīṣumat** (S) (M) 1. radiant. 3. another name for the sun.
**Abhiśvarā** (S) (F) 1. invocation. 2. a song or hymn of praise.
**Abhiśyanta** (S) (M) 1. splendid. 3. a son of Kuru and Vāhinī (*M. Bh.*)
**Abhīta** (S) (M) fearless.
**Abhīti** (S) (F) fearlessness.
**Abhivāda** (S) (M) reverential salutation.
**Abhivādakā** (S) (F) 1. one who pays homage. 2. a devotee.
**Abhivibhā** (S) (F) illuminating.
**Abhivīra** (S) (M) 1. surrounded by heroes. 2. a commander.
**Abhivirāja** (S) (M) full of brightness.
**Abhiyuktākṣika** (S) (M) 1. watchful eyed. 2. observant. 3. one of the 49 maruts in the *Brahmāṇḍa Purāṇa*.
**Abhra** (S) (M) 1. water bearing; clouds. 2. the sky.
**Abhragaṅgā** (S) (F) 1. Gaṅgā of the sky. 2. the Ākāśgaṅgā (the celestial Gaṅgā)
**Abhrakāśin** (S) (M) 1. with clouds for shelter. 2. that which is open to the sky; an ascetic.
**Abhrama** (S) (M) one who has no illusions; one who does not blunder; steady; clear.
**Abhramū** (S) (F) 1. steady; clear. 3. the female elephant of the east who is also the mate of Airāvata (*V.D. Ćaritam*)
**Abhramūpriya** (S) (M) 1. lover of the steady. 3. another name for Airāvata, the elephant of the east.
**Abhranāga** (S) (M) 1. celestial elephant. 3. one of the 8 elephants of the quarters (*A. Koṣa*)
**Abhranta** (S) (M) 1. unperplexed. 2. clear; composed.
**Abhrānti** (S) (F) without perplexity; without error.
**Abhraroha** (S) (M) 1. borne by the clouds. 2. Lapis lazuli.
**Abhrayanti** (S) (F) 1. forming clouds. 2. bringing rain. 3. one of the 7 kṛttikās (*T. Samhitā*)
**Abhrottha** (S) (M) 1. cloud born. 3. Indra's thunderbolt (*A. Koṣa*)
**Abhū** (S) (M) 1. unborn; not earthly. 3. another name for Viṣṇu.
**Abhyagni** (S) (M) 1. towards the fire. 3. a son of Aitaśa (*A. Brāhmaṇa*)
**Abhyāvarśini** (S) (M) 1. coming repeatedly. 2. returning. 3. a king who was a descendant of Pṛthu (*M. Bh.*)
**Abhyudaya** (S)/(M) 1. sunrise. 2. elevation; increase; prosperity; happiness; good result.
**Abhyudita** (S) (M) elevated; risen; prosperous.
**Abīr** (S) (M) red powder; the red colour used in Holi festival.
**Abjā** (S) (F) 1. born in water. 2. water lily (*Nymphaea alba*)
**Abja** (S) (M) 1. born in water. 2. a conch; a lotus (*Nelumbium speciosum*). 3. a son of Viśāla; another name for Dhanvantari and the moon.
**Abjayoni** (S) (M) 1. born of the lotus. 3. another name for Brahmā.
**Abjinī** (S) (F) a multitude of lotuses.
**Abjinipati** (S) (M) 1. lord of lotuses. 3. another name for Sūrya.
**Abjit** (S) (M) conquering water.
**Abolī** (S) (F) a flower.
**Aćalā** (S) (F) 1. immovable. 2. the earth. 3. a mother in Skanda's retinue (*Sk. Purāṇa*)
**Aćala** (S) (M) 1. immovable. 2. mountain; rock. 3. the son of King Subala of Gāndhāra and brother of Śakuni (*M. Bh.*); a bull who was an attendant of Skanda (*M. Bh.*); one of the 9 deities of the Jainas.
**Aćalapati** (S) (M) 1. lord of the immovable. 2. lord of the mountains.
**Aćalendra** (S) (M) 1. lord of the immovable. 2. lord of the mountains. 3. the Himālayas.
**Aćaleśvara** (S) (M) 1. god of the immovable. 3. another name for Śiva.
**Aćaṇḍa** (S) (M) 1. not of a hot temper; without anger. 2. gentle; mild.
**Āćārya** (S) (M) 1. teacher. 3. another name for Droṇa, Aśvaghoṣa and Kṛpa.

**Āćāryanandana** (S) (M) 1. son of the teacher. 3. another name for Aśvatthāman.

**Āćāryaputra** (S) (M) 1. son of the teacher. 3. another name for Aśvatthāman.

**Āćāryasuta** (S) (M) 1. son of the teacher. 3. another name for Aśvatthāman.

**Āćāryatanaya** (S) (M) 1. son of the teacher. 3. another name for Aśvatthāman.

**Aććhindra** (S) (M) flawless; uninterrupted; perfect.

**Aććhoda** (S) (M) 1. with clear water. 2. transparent.

**Aććhodā** (S) (F) 1. with clear water. 3. a river; a daughter of the Pitṛs reborn as Satyavatī the mother of Vyāsa, Ćitrāṅgada and Vićitravīrya (*M. Bh.*)

**Aććhuptā** (S) (F) 1. inactive. 3. one of the 16 Jaina vidyādevīs (*J. Koṣa*)

**Aćintya** (S) (M) 1. surpassing thought. 2. incogitable; one who cannot be understood easily. 3. another name for Śiva.

**Aćirā** (S) (F) 1. brief; instantaneous. 2. swift; fast; active; prompt. 3. a queen of Hastināpura and mother of Śāntinātha Jaina Tīrthaṅkara (*J. S. Koṣa*)

**Aćyuta** (S) (M) 1. immovable. 2. firm; solid; imperishable; neverfailing. 3. one of the 24 incarnations of Viṣṇu and Kṛṣṇa (*V. Purāṇa*)

**Aćyutāgraja** (S) (M) 1. elder brother. 2. never failing; more perfect. 3. another name for Balarāma and Indra.

**Aćyutanuja** (S) (M) 1. younger brother of Kṛṣṇa. 3. another name for Bhīma.

**Aćyutaraya** (S) (M) worshipper of the infallible; a devotee of Viṣṇu.

**Aćyutāyu** (S) (M) 1. with an imperishable life. 3. a warrior on the Kaurava side (*M. Bh.*)

**Āḍambara** (S) (M) 1. a great noise; a drum; the roaring of an elephant. 2. the highest degree. 3. an attendant of Skanda given to him by Brahmā (*M. Bh.*)

**Adambha** (S) (M) 1. free from deceit. 2. straightforward. 3. another name for Śiva.

**Ādarśa** (S) (M) 1. principle; ideal; perfection. 2. that which reveals completely; a mirror; a copy; the day of the new moon; mythology. 3. the son of the 11th Manu (*H. Purāṇa*)

**Aḍḍana** (S) (M) shield.

**Ādelika** (S) (M) 1. approaching the target; successful. 2. full of concentration.

**Ādeśa** (S) (M) command; order; advice; instruction; declaration; precept.

**Ādeśvara** (S) (M) 1. lord of command. 3. another name for Skanda.

**Ādevī** (S) (F) devoted to the gods; one who performs meritorious rites.

**Adharma** (S) (M) 1. injustice; unrighteousness. 3. a prajāpati son of Brahmā who was the husband of Himsa or Mṛṣā; an attendant of the sun.

**Adhasaśiras** (S) (M) 1. with the head downward. 3. a sage (*M. Bh.*)

**Adhibhū** (S) (M) 1. superior among beings. 2. a king.

**Adhideva** (S) (M) 1. presiding or tutelary deity. 3. another name for Kṛṣṇa.

**Adhiguṇa** (S) (M) with superior qualities.

**Adhija** (S) (M) superior by birth.

**Adhikara** (S) (M) 1. principal. 2. chief; controller. 3. another name for Śiva.

**Adhikṣita** (S) (M) lord; ruler.

**Adhilokanātha** (S) (M) 1. lord of the lords of the universe. 2. that which is divine; a deity.

**Adhimuhya** (S) (M) 1. above attraction. 3. Śākyamuni in one of his 34 births (*V's B. Samhitā*)

**Adhinātha** (S) (M) supreme lord; a chieftain.

**Adhipa** (S) (M) one who protects; a ruler; a king.

**Adhīra** (S) (M) 1. impatient. 3. a king who became an attendant of Śiva (*P. Purāṇa*)

**Adhirāja** (S) (M) supreme leader; an emperor.

**Adhiratha** (S) (M) 1. charioteer. 3. a prince of Aṅga who was the son of Satyakarmā and the foster father of Karṇa (*M. Bh.*)

**Ādhirathi** (S) (M) 1. one who is on a chariot. 3. son of Adhiratha; another name for Karṇa.

**Adhirohaṅa** (S) (M) ascending.

**Adhirukma** (S) (M) wearing gold.

**Adhīśa** (S) (M) lord; master.

**Adhīśvara** (S) (M) supreme lord; an emperor.

**Ādhīta** (S) (M) 1. learned; reflected or meditated upon. 2. a scholar.

**Adhivāhana** (S) (M) 1. beyond motion; one

who is on a vehicle. 2. very fast. 3. a son of Aṅga.

**Adhivirāja** (S) (M) surpassing in brightness.

**Adhokṣaja** (S) (M) 1. son of the lower regions. 2. universe. 3. another name for Viṣṇu and Kṛṣṇa.

**Adhokśaya** (S) (M) 1. resting on the lower regions. 3. Viṣṇu in his 18th incarnation (*V. Purāṇa*)

**Adhṛgu** (S) (M) 1. knower of the inconsistent. 3. a Ṛg Vedic sage who was a protégé of the aśvins and Indra.

**Adhṛṣyā** (S) (F) 1. invincible. 3. a river (*M. Bh.*)

**Adhṛśya** (S) (M) 1. unassailable; invincible. 2. proud.

**Adhṛta** (S) (M) 1. unrestrained; uncontrolled. 3. another name for Viṣṇu.

**Adhvara** (S) (M) 1. not causing any injury. 2. a sacrifice. 3. a vasu (*A. Koṣa*)

**Adhvaryu** (S) (M) 1. best among the priests. 2. one who knows how to perform yajñas; Ṛg Vedic priests who represent the 5 planets; the priest who performs the ritual.

**Adhyā** (S) (F) 1. beyond perception. 2. the 1st creator. 3. one of the 10 Durgās (*D. Purāṇa*)

**Adhyapāyana** (S) (M) 1. divider; distributor. 3. a disciple of Sumantu who divided the *Atharva Veda* into two parts (*Bhā. Purāṇa*)

**Ādi** (S) (M) 1. beginning. 2. firstborn. 3. a son of the asura Andhaka killed by Śiva (*P. Purāṇa*)

**Ādibuddha** (S) (M) 1. the first seer; the primal Buddha. 2. perceived in the beginning. 3. the chief deity of the northern Buddhists (*A. Koṣa*)

**Ādidaitya** (S) (M) 1. the first demon. 3. another name for Hiraṇyakaśipu.

**Ādideva** (S) (M) 1. the first god. 3. another name for Brahmā, Viṣṇu, Śiva, Gaṇeśa and the sun.

**Ādigadādhara** (S) (M) 1. he who first handled the mace. 3. another name for Viṣṇu.

**Ādikara** (S) (M) 1. the first creator. 3. another name for Brahmā.

**Ādikavi** (S) (M) 1. the first poet. 3. another name for Brahmā and Vālmīki.

**Ādikūrma** (S) (M) 1. the original tortoise. 3. the incarnation of Viṣṇu as the tortoise who lifted the Mandāra mountain from the Ocean of Milk (*M. Bh.*)

**Ādilakṣmana** (S) (M) the primal or only Lakṣmana.

**Ādilakṣmī** (S) (F) 1. the primal Lakṣmī. 3. Lakṣmi as the wife of Ādinārāyaṇa.

**Ādima** (S) (M) beginning; root; original.

**Ādimātā** (S) (F) 1. the primal mother. 3. another name for Manasā.

**Ādimūla** (S) (M) the primal root.

**Ādimūrti** (S) (M) 1. the primal idol. 3. another name for Viṣṇu.

**Adīna** (S) (M) noble minded.

**Ādinārāyaṇa** (S) (M) 1. the first protector of beings. 3. the primal Viṣṇu.

**Ādinātha** (S) (M) 1. the first lord; the Supreme Lord. 3. a Jina.

**Ādīpa** (S) (M) kindled; illuminating.

**Ādirāja** (S) (M) 1. the first king. 3. a son of King Kuru of the Purū dynasty (*M. Bh.*); another name for Manu and Pṛthu.

**Ādiratha** (S) (M) the first chariot.

**Ādiśa** (S) (M) ordered; directed; commanded; pointed out.

**Ādiśakti** (S) (F) 1. the primal energy. 3. another name for Pārvatī and Māyā.

**Ādiśankara** (S) (M) 1. the primal god of welfare. 3. another name for Śiva.

**Ādiśeṣan** (S) (M) 1. the primal residue. 2. the primal serpent, and supporter of the earth.

**Ādisiṁha** (S) (M) 1. the primal lion. 3. a king of Magadha (*H. Koṣa*)

**Ādisiśira** (S) (M) 1. the primal head of religious sacrifice. 3. a disciple of Śākalya, the son of Vyāsa (*Bhā. Purāṇa*)

**Ādīśvara** (S) (M) the original god; the Absolute Reality.

**Ādit** (S) (M) first.

**Āditā** (S) (F) the first root.

**Ādita** (S) (M) the sun.

**Āditeya** (S) (M) 1. son of Aditī. 3. another name for the sun.

**Aditī** (S) (F) 1. freedom. 2. security; safety; immensity; abundance; perfection; creative power; cow; milk; speech. 3. a primal Indian goddess; the daughter of Dakṣa; wife of Kaśyapa, mother of the ādityas, rudras and vasus (*M. Bh.*); the incarnation of Pṛṣnī later reborn as Devakī and the mother of lord Viṣṇu in his incarnation as the dwarf Vāmana (*V. Purāṇa*); another name for the earth.

**Āditya** (S) (M) 1. belonging to Aditī. 3. patronymics of 33 of sage Kaśyapa and Aditī's children of whom the most prominent are Dhātā, Mitra, Aryamā, Rudra, Varuṇa, Sūrya, Bhaga, Vivasvān, Pūṣā, Dakṣa, Śakra, Varuṇa, Aṅśa, Savitā, Tvaṣṭā and Viṣṇu and these 33 are the fathers of the 33 crore devatās of whom the eldest is Indra and the youngest Vāmana (*M. Bh.*)

**Ādityabandhu** (S) (M) 1. friend of the sun. 3. another name for Sākyamuni.

**Ādityabhakta** (S) (M) 1. devotee of the sun. 3. the plant *Cleome viscosa*.

**Ādityagarbha** (S) (M) 1. with the sun as his matrix. 3. a Bodhisattva (*A. Koṣa*)

**Ādityakeśava** (S) (M) 1. the sun and Viṣṇu conjoined. 2. with long shining hair. 3. an idol of Viṣṇu (*M. Bh.*)

**Ādityaketu** (S) (M) 1. sun bannered. 3. a son of Dhṛtarāṣṭra (*M. Bh.*)

**Ādityaprabhā** (S) (M) with the splendour of the sun.

**Ādityanandana** (S) (M) 1. son of the sun. 3. another name for Karṇa.

**Ādityasena** (S) (M) 1. with a glorious army. 2. one who has a powerful army; one who is well protected; a commander. 3. a king of the Gupta dynasty of Magadha (*M. Ćarita*)

**Ādityasūnu** (S) (M) 1. son of the sun. 3. another name for Sugrīva, Yama and Manu.

**Ādityavardhana** (S) (M) 1. one who increases glory. 2. augmented by the sun. 3. the grandfather of Harśavardhana (*K. Sāgara*)

**Ādityavarman** (S) (M) protected by the ādityas.

**Ādityavarṇa** (S) (M) with the colour of the sun.

**Ādityasena** (S) (M) 1. with the sun as master. 2. Sūrya, lord of the ādityas. 3. a Magadha king (*M. Ćarita*)

**Ādityeśa** (S) (M) 1. lord of the ādityas.

3. another name for the sun.

**Ādivaki** (S) (M) 1. the first seer. 3. another name for Brahmā.

**Ādivārāha** (S) (M) 1. the first boar. 3. Viṣṇu in his boar incarnation.

**Admaṇi** (S) (M) fire.

**Adra** (S) (M) 1. hard; rock. 3. a solar dynasty king (*M. Bh.*)

**Adri** (S) (M) 1. hard; rock; mountain; thunderbolt; cloud; the sun. the number 7 (according to the Hindu scriptures, there are 7 main sacred mountains in the universe and the term Adri, apart from meaning a mountain, is also the name of the 7th mountain of the universe – hence, number 7 is one of the construed meanings). 3. a king who was the son of Viśvagāśva and the father of Yuvanāśva (*M. Bh.*); a grandson of Pṛthu (*M. Bh.*); the thunderbolt of Indra (*M. Bh.*)

**Adrigu** (S) (M) 1. one who goes to the mountains. 3. a protégé of the aśvins and Indra (*Ṛg Veda*)

**Adrijā** (S) (F) 1. of the mountain. 3. another name for Pārvatī.

**Adrikā** (S) (F) 1. small mountain. 3. an apsarā who was the mother of Matsya and Satyavatī (M. Bh.)

**Adrindra** (S) (M) 1. lord of the mountains. 3. the Himālaya.

**Adripati** (S) (M) 1. master of the mountains. 3. the Himālaya.

**Adriśa** (S) (M) lord of the mountains.

**Adṛśyantī** (S) (F) 1. invisible. 3. the wife of sage Śakti daughter-in law of Vasiṣṭha and mother of sage Parāśara (*M. Bh.*)

**Adrupa** (S) (M) 1. consuming the earth. 3. a son of Bali.

**Adūra** (S) (M) 1. not far; near; omnipresent. 2. soul.

**Adūṣita** (S) (M) 1. unspotted; irreproachable. 2. without guile.

**Advaita** (S) (M) 1. with no duplicate; sole; unique. 3. an Upaniṣad; another name for Viṣṇu and Brahmā.

**Advaitavādinī** (S) (F) propounder of the uniqueness of the absolute.

**Advaya** (S) (M) 1. without a second; unique.

2. one who does not believe in duality. 3. a Buddha (*A. Koṣa*)

**Advayānanda** (S) (M) 1. absolute bliss. 3. a 15th century founder of a Vaiṣṇava sect in Bengal.

**Advika** (S) (M) unique.

**Advitīya** (S) (M) without a second; unique; matchless.

**Ādyā** (S) (F) 1. first. 2. unparalleled; excellent. 3. goddess Durga; the earth.

**Ādyaśarana** (S) (M) protected by the Absolute; taking shelter in the Absolute.

**Ādyota** (S) (M) 1. surrounded by light. 2. brilliant.

**Agādhi** (S) (M) deep; incogitable; indescribable; unfathomable.

**Agajā** (S) (F) 1. produced on a mountain. 3. another name for Pārvatī.

**Āgama** (S) (M) 1. coming forth; birth. 2. knowledge; wisdom.

**Agarva** (S) (M) free from pride.

**Agasti** (S) (M) 1. thrower of mountains. 3. another name for Agastya; the *Sesbania grandiflora* tree.

**Agastya** (S) (M) 1. thrower of mountains. 2. one who humbles even the mountain. 3. a great sage who, once while travelling south, had found the Vindhya Mountains in his way and, in order to proceed further, had commanded them to lie down, this sage is believed to have been born in a water jar, is considered the son of Pulastya and Havirbhū – a daughter of sage Kardama according to the Purāṇas, the son of Mitra and Varuṇa by Urvaśī, the husband of Lopāmudrā, the father of Idhmavāha, the preceptor of Droṇa, the presenter of Viṣṇu's bow to Rāma, (*V. Rāmāyaṇa*) and is regarded as the first teacher of science to the Dravidian tribes in South India and is believed to have been immortalized as the star Canopus; the *Sesbania grandiflora* tree; another name for Śiva and the star Canopus.

**Agavāha** (S) (M) 1. borne by fire; borne by a mountain; the lord of all the yajñas. 2. all the oblations poured into the fire. 3. a son of Vasudeva (*Bhā. Purāṇa*)

**Agendra** (S) (M) king of the mountains.

**Agha** (S) (M) 1. sinful. 3. an asura follower of Kaṇsa who was the brother of Pūtanā (*Bhā. Purāṇa*)

**Aghaghna** (S) (M) 1. destroyer of sin. 2. one who is virtuous; pious. 3. another name for Viṣṇu.

**Aghamarṣana** (S) (M) 1. destroying sin. 3. a Vedic ṛsi who was the author of the doctrine of time (*M. Bh.*)

**Aghora** (S) (M) 1. not terrible. 3. a worshipper of Śiva and Durgā (*Ś. Purāṇa*); another name for Śiva.

**Āghrikā** (S) (M) 1. one who sprinkles the fat in the oblation. 2. one who participates in religious activities. 3. a son of Viśvāmitra (*M. Bh.*)

**Āghṛṇi** (S) (M) 1. glowing with heat. 3. another name for Pūṣan.

**Āghṛṇīvasu** (S) (M) 1. rich with heat. 3. another name for Agni.

**Agira** (S) (M) 1. the sun. 2. fire. 3. a rākṣasa (*A. Koṣa*)

**Agnajitā** (S) (F) 1. one who has conquered fire. 3. wife of Kṛṣṇa (*Bhāgavata*)

**Agnāyī** (S) (F) 1. fiery. 3. the wife of Agni (*A. Purāṇa*)

**Āgneya** (S) (M) 1. son of Agni. 3. another name for Kārttikeya and Agastya.

**Āgneyī** (S) (F) 1. daughter of fire. 3. a daughter of Agni and the wife of Ūru (*Ś. Brāhmaṇa*); the wife of Kuru, the son of Manu and the mother of Aṅga, Sumanas, Khyāti, Kratu, Aṅgiras and Śibi (*V. Purāṇa*)

**Agni** (S) (M) 1. fire. 2. gold; one of the 5 elements of the universe. 3. a prominent deity of the *Ṛg Veda*, represented as the eldest son of Brahmā in the post Vedic age, the son of sage Aṅgiras as a marut, as also the son of Saṁyu and Satyā, the grandson of Śāṇḍilya who is appointed by Brahmā as the sovereign of the Quarter between the East and the South, represented as also the grandson of Bṛhaspati the twin brother of Indra, the husband of Sudarśanā and Svāhā, the father of Dakṣiṇam, Gārhapatyam, Āhavanīyam (*D. Bhāgavata*), Pāvaka, Pavamāna, Śuci, Dhṛṣṭhadyumna, Subrahmaṇya, Bhṛgu and Nīla the monkey, the preceptor of the gods, protector of ceremonies, men, the head, the summit of the sky, the centre of the earth and the conferer of immortality (*A. Purāṇa*)

**Agnibāhu** (S) (M) 1. the arms of fire. 2. smoke. 3. a son of the first Manu (*H. Purāṇa*); a son of Priyavrata and Kāmyā (*V. Purāṇa*); a seer of the 14th Manvantara (*V. Purāṇa*)

**Agnibha** (S) (M) 1. shining like fire. 2. gold.

**Agnibhaṭṭa** (S) (M) 1. as noble as fire. 3. another name for Agni and the maruts.

**Agnibhū** (S) (M) 1. born of fire. 3. another name for Skanda.

**Agnibhūti** (S) (M) 1. produced from fire. 2. with the lustre of fire. 3. one of the main disciple of Mahāvīra (*J. literature*)

**Agnibīja** (S) (M) 1. the seed of fire. 2. gold.

**Agnidatta** (S) (M) 1. given by fire. 2. given to the fire. 3. one who is born as a result of yajña.

**Āgnīdhra** (S) (M) 1. descendant of fire. 3. a son of Priyavrata and Barhiṣmatī, the husband of Pūrvaćittī and the father of Kuru, Nābhi, Kiṁpuruṣa, Hari, Ilāvrata, Ramyaka, Hirañćaya, Bhadrāśva, Ketumāla (*Bhā. Purāṇa*); a seer of the 14th Manvantara (*M. Ćarita*); a son of Manu Svāyambhuva (*Bhā. Purāṇa*)

**Āgnidhraka** (S) (M) 1. descendant of fire. 2. fire like; shining; glowing. 3. a ṛṣi of the 12th Manvantara (*M. Ćarita*)

**Agnidurgā** (S) (F) 1. Durgā in her fiery form.

**Agnija** (S) (M) 1. born of fire. 2. gold. 3. another name for Kārttikeya and Viṣṇu.

**Agnijvāla** (S) (M) 1. flame of fire. 3. another name for Śiva; the *Woodfordia fruticosa* shrub.

**Āgnika** (S) (M) 1. born of fire. 3. the Common Marking Nut tree (*Semecarpus anacardium*)

**Agnikaṇa** (S) (M) particle of fire; spark.

**Agniketu** (S) (M) 1. fire bannered. 2. with fire as the characteristic feature. 3. a rākśasa friend of Rāvaṇa (*V. Rāmāyaṇa*)

**Agnikumāra** (S) (M) 1. son of Agni. 3. another name for Subrahmaṇya.

**Agnima** (S) (M) 1. torch bearer. 2. leader; elder brother.

**Agnimaśa** (S) (M) 1. stinging like fire. 3. the Intellect tree (*Celastrus paniculata*)

**Agnimitra** (S) (M) 1. friend of fire. 3. a king of the Śuṅga dynasty (150 B.C.) who was the son of Puṣyamitra and a contemporary of Patajali (*M. Bh.*)

**Agnimukha** (S) (M) 1. fire-faced. 3. an asura who was the son of Śurapadma and Maya's daughter and the grandson of Kaśyapa (*Bhā. Purāṇa*); *Plumbago zeylanica*.

**Agnimukhī** (S) (F) 1. fire faced. 3. the Common Marking Nut tree (*Semecarpus anacardium*); the *Gloriosa superba* creeper.

**Agnipā** (S) (M) 1. one who drinks fire. 2. one who protects the fire. 3. the son of the Brāhmin Vedanidhi and the husband of 5 gandharva maidens (*P. Purāṇa*)

**Agnipūrṇa** (S) (M) 1. full of fire. 2. extremely powerful. 3. a solar dynasty king who was the grandson of Dhruva; the son of Sudarśana and the father of Śīghra and Maru (*Bhā. Purāṇa*)

**Agnirājan** (S) (M) 1. glorified by fire. 2. with Agni as king. 3. another name for the vasus.

**Agniruha** (S) (M) 1. fire tree. 3. the Indian Redwood tree (*Soymida febrifuga*)

**Agnisambhava** (S) (M) 1. born of fire. 3. a solar dynasty king who was the son of Upagupta (*V. Rāmāyaṇa*)

**Agniśikha** (S) (M) 1. fire crested. 2. flame of fire; pointed; arrow; lamp. 3. Vararuḉi's father (*K. Sāgara*); saffron (*Crocus sativus*)

**Agnisiṇha** (S) (M) 1. fiery lion. 3. the father of the 7th Black Vasudeva (*J. Literature*)

**Agnīsoma** (S) (M) 1. fire and nectar conjoined. 3. a deity born of the conjunction of Agni and Soma (*Ṛg Veda*)

**Agniśrī** (S) (M) with the brightness of fire.

**Agniṣṭu** (S) (M) 1. devotee of fire. 3. a son of Manu Ćakṣusa and Nadvalā (*A. Purāṇa*)

**Agniṣṭuta** (S) (M) 1. devotee of fire. 2. praised by fire; glorious; illuminating; enlightening; all-consuming. 3. a son of Manu Ćakṣuṣa and Naḍvalā (*A. Purāṇa*)

**Agnisvāmin** (S) (M) lord of fire.

**Agnitejas** (S) (M) 1. with the energy and lustre of fire. 3. a ṛṣi of the 11th Mavantara.

**Agnivallabha** (S) (M) 1. beloved of fire. 3. the

Indian Dammer tree (*Shorea robusta*)

**Agnivardhinī** (S) (F) 1. increasing fire. 3. the Lovage plant (*Carum copticum*)

**Agnivarṁa** (S) (M) 1. fire coloured. 2. red faced; hot; fiery. 3. a character in Kalidāsa's poem *Raghuvaṁśa*; a son of Sudarśana (*Bhā. Purāṇa*)

**Agniveśa** (S) (M) 1. fire clad. 2. one who is as glorious as the fire. 3. a sage who was the disciple of Agastya and the preceptor of Droṇa and Drupada (*M. Bh.*); an authority of medicine in ancient India (*M. Bh.*)

**Agniveśya** (S) (M) 1. surrounded by fire. 2. one who offers an oblation. 3. a sage who was the preceptor of Droṇa and the most learned in Dhanurveda (*M. Bh.*)

**Agnivīrya** (S) (M) 1. with the power of fire. 2. gold.

**Agraha** (S) (M) 1. which cannot be held. 2. an Agni who was the son of the Agni Bhānu and Suprajā (*M. Bh.*)

**Agrajā** (S) (F) 1. born first. 2. elder daughter.

**Agraja** (S) (M) born first; eldest.

**Agrasena** (S) (M) 1. chief warrior. 3. a son of Janamejaya.

**Āgrayaṇa** (S) (M) 1. leader; oblation of first fruit. 2. a form of fire; the first *soma* libation. 3. a son of the agni Bhānu (*M. Bh.*)

**Agrayaṇi** (S) (M) 1. leader. 3. a son of Dhṛtarāṣṭra (*M. Bh.*)

**Agrayī** (S) (F) 1. primal. 3. a wife of Agni, who is also the goddess of fire and the daughter of Dakṣa (*A. Purāṇa*)

**Agreṇī** (S) (M) 1. first; preceding; leader. 3. an agni who was a son of the Agni Bhānu and Niśādevī (*M. Bh.*)

**Agrima** (S) (M) first; foremost; best; excellent; eldest.

**Aha** (S) (M) 1. affirmation. 2. ascertainment. 3. a vasu who was the son of Dharma and Ratidevī (*M. Bh.*); an asura (*M. Bh.*); a sacred pond (*M. Bh.*)

**Ahalyā** (S) (F) 1. agreeable. 3. the daughter of Mudgala, wife of sage Gautama, mother of sage Śatānanda, who according to the Rāmāyaṇa, supposed to have been the first woman created by Brahmā and is one of the 5 women renowned for their chastity and purity (*V. Rāmāyaṇa*)

**Ahaṁyāti** (S) (M) 1. egoless. 3. a son of Saṁyāti (*M. Bh.*)

**Ahan** (S) (M) dawn; morning.

**Ahanā** (S) (F) 1. one who cannot be killed; one who is immortal. 2. one who is born in the day.

**Ahankāra** (S) (M) 1. that which causes the day. 3. another name for the sun.

**Ahanmaṇi** (S) (M) 1. jewel of the day. 2. the sun.

**Ahannātha** (S) (M) 1. lord of the day. 2. the sun.

**Ahanpati** (S) (M) 1. lord of the day. 3. another name for Śiva and the sun.

**Ahanti** (S) (M) indestructible.

**Ahar** (S) (M) 1. defender. 3. day personified as a vasu (*M. Bh.*)

**Ahara** (S) (M) 1. tormentor. 3. a son of Kaśyapa and Danu (*M. Bh.*); a Manu (*H. Purāṇa*)

**Aharbāndhava** (S) (M) 1. friend of the defenders. 2. friend of the day. 3. another name for the sun.

**Aharmaṇi** (S) (M) 1. jewel of the day. 3. another name for the sun.

**Aharpati** (S) (M) 1. lord of the day. 3. another name for the sun and Śiva.

**Ahaskara** (S) (M) 1. producing the day. 3. another name for Sūrya.

**Āhavanīya** (S) (M) 1. to be offered as oblation. 2. perpetual fire; receiver of oblations. 3. an agni (*M. Bh.*)

**Āhavanīyam** (S) (M) 1. offered as an oblation. 3. a son of Agni.

**Ahī** (S) (F) heaven and earth conjoined.

**Ahi** (S) (M) 1. serpent; cloud; water; sun; the number 8. 3. a ṛṣi; another name for Rāhu.

**Ahijit** (S) (M) 1. conquerer of the serpent. 3. another name for Kṛṣna and Indra.

**Ahikā** (S) (M) of heaven and earth; the Silk Cotton tree (*Salmalica malabarica*)

**Ahilocana** (S) (M) 1. serpent eyed. 3. a servant of Śiva (*Ś. Purāṇa*)

**Ahilyā** (S) (F) 1. unploughed. 2. maiden;

pious; sacred.

**Ahima** (S) (M) 1. not cold; hot. 2. cloud; water; traveller.

**Ahimakara** (S) (M) 1. hot rayed. 3. another name for the sun.

**Ahiṁsā** (S) (F) 1. not injuring. 3. a wife of Dharma (*V. Purāṇa*)

**Ahīna** (S) (M) 1. whole; entire; all. 2. serpent. 3. another name for Vāsuki the lord of the serpents.

**Ahīnagu** (S) (M) 1. excellent ray. 3. son of Devānīka (*H. Purāṇa*)

**Ahīndra** (S) (M) 1. lord of serpents. 3. another name for Vāsuki and Indra.

**Ahiratha** (S) (M) 1. having a snake chariot. 3. a Purū dynasty king (*M. Bh.*)

**Ahirbudhnya** (S) (M) 1. one who knows about serpents. 3. a son of Viśvakarman and Surabhī (*V. Purāṇa*); one of the 11 maruts in the Mahābhārata; a rudra (*M. Bh.*)

**Ahīśvara** (S) (M) 1. lord of serpents. 3. another name for Śeṣa.

**Ahitā** (S) (F) 1. hostile; evil. 3. a river (*M. Bh.*)

**Āhlād** (S) (M) causing delight; refreshing.

**Āhlāditā** (S) (F) delighted.

**Āhobala** (S) (M) very powerful.

**Āhovīra** (S) (M) 1. very strong. 3. a sage (*M. Bh.*)

**Āhū** (S) (F) calling; invoking.

**Āhuka** (S) (M) 1. offerer; sacrificer. 3. a Yadu king who was the father of Ugrasena and 99 other sons, the grandfather of Kaṇsa (*M. Bh.*) and great grandfather of Kṛṣṇa (*Bhā. Purāṇa*)

**Ahukā** (S) (F) 1. offerer; sacrificer. 3. another name for Damayantī.

**Ahupathi** (S) (M) 1. follower of prayer. 2. a devotee.

**Āhuta** (S) (M) 1. invoked; invited. 2. called; summoned.

**Āhūtī** (S) (F) 1. calling; summoning; offering. 2. a solemn rite.

**Āhuti** (S) (M) 1. invoking; calling; offering oblations. 3. a king of Jaruthi (*M. Bh.*); a son of Babhru (*M. Bh.*)

**Āhvāna** (S) (M) invocation.

**Aikṣvākī** (S) (F) 1. produced from sugarcane. 2. very sweet. 3. the wife of Suhotra and the mother of Ajamīdha, Sumīdha and Purumīdha (*M. Bh.*)

**Aila** (S) (M) 1. born of intellect; the son of Ilā. 3. a member of the court of Yama (*M. Bh.*); another name for Purūravas.

**Aindradyumni** (S) (M) 1. descendant of Indradyumna. 3. another name for Janaka.

**Aindrī** (S) (F) 1. belonging to the senses. 3. another name for Indrāṇī, consort of Indra; the *Amomum subulatum* herb; *Cucumis prophetarum*.

**Aingini** (S) (F) 1. agitated. 2. inviting; welcoming. 3. consort of Gaṇeśa.

**Airāvata** (S) (M) 1. as fast as the wind. 3. the lord of elephants, the son of Irāvatī, a descendant of Kaśyapa, the steed of Indra and considered to be one of the 8 elephants guarding the universe (*M. Bh.*); a serpent son of Kaśyapa and Kadru whose descendant Ulūpi married Arjuna (*M. Bh.*); an asura killed by Kṛṣṇa (*M. Bh.*)

**Aiśvaryā** (S) (F) wealth; fame; riches; glory.

**Aitareya** (S) (M) 1. unique. 3. a son of sage Māṇḍuki and Itarā and a great scholar of the Vedas (*Sk. Purāṇa*)

**Aiteśvara** (S) (M) 1. lord of the agitated; lord of the fighters. 3. another name for Indra.

**Aiyenar** (Tamil) (M) 1. lord or abode of the mountains. 3. a tutelary deity said to be a son of Viṣṇu or Śiva (*V. Purāṇa*)

**Ajā** (S) (F) 1. not born. 2. one who is self existent. 3. another name for Prākṛtī and Māyā.

**Aja** (S) (M) 1. eternal; driver; mover; instigator; leader of a flock; ram. 3. a solar dynasty king, father of Daśaratha (*M. Bh.*); a son of King Jahnu and father of Uśika (*M. Bh.*); a son of Surabhī (*A. Purāṇa*); a son of Manu Uttama (*V. Purāṇa*); one of the 11 maruts in the *Bhāgavata Purāṇa*; the vehicle of Agni (*A. Purāṇa*); the zodiac sign of Aries; another name for Brahmā, Viṣṇu, Rudra, Indra, Śiva, Kāma, Sūrya and Agni.

**Ajagara** (S) (M) 1. python; a large serpent. 3. a sage (*M. Bh.*); an asura.

**Ajagāva** (S) (M) 1. looking after cattle; that which protects cattle. 3. the bow of Māndhāta and Pṛthu and the Gāṇḍiva of Arjuna

(*V. Purāṇa*); a nāga priest.

**Ajaikapāda** (S) (M) 1. herdsman. 3. one of the 11 maruts in the Mahābhārata; another name for Viṣṇu.

**Ajaikapāla** (S) (M) 1. herdsman; protector of cattle. 2. lord of animals, or one of the 11 rudras born to Sthāṇu (*M. Bh.*); a son of Viśvakarman in charge of protecting all the gold in the world (*M. Bh.*); another name for Viṣṇu.

**Ajaka** (S) (M) 1. a young goat; a kid. 3. an asura son of Kaśyapa and Danu (*M. Bh.*); a descendant of Purūravas; a king of Magadha.

**Ājakāra** (S) (M) 1. protector of cattle. 3. the bull of Śiva (*Ś. Purāṇa*)

**Ajakāśva** (S) (M) 1. horse of the unborn; horse of a god. 3. a Purū king who was the son of Jahnu (*M. Bh.*)

**Ajakāva** (S) (M) 1. bow of the unborn. 3. the bow of Śiva (*A. Koṣa*)

**Ajālā** (S) (F) 1. eternal; birthless and deathless. 3. the daughter of Prākṛtī (*V. Purāṇa*); another name for the earth.

**Ajamīḍha** (S) (M) 1. one who offers goats as a sacrifice. 2. a devotee of the absolute. 3. Purū dynasty king who was the son of Hasti, the husband of Dhūminī, Nīlī and Keśinī and the father of Ṛksa, Duṣyanta, Jahnu, Praja and Rūpiṇa (*M. Bh.*); a lunar dynasty king who was the father of Saṁvaraṇa and husband of Sudevā (*M. Bh.*); a son of Suhotra (*M. Bh.*); another name for Yudhiṣṭhira and Dhritarāṣṭra.

**Ajāmila** (S) (M) 1. indisciplined. 3. a devotee of Viṣṇu (*Bhā. Purāṇa*)

**Ajamukha** (S) (M) 1. goatfaced. 3. a soldier in Skanda's army (*M. Bh.*)

**Ajamukhī** (S) (F) 1. goatfaced. 3. an asura daughter of Kaśyapa and Surasā and the wife of Durvāsas (*Sk. Purāṇa*)

**Ajana** (S) (M) 1. instigator. 3. another name for Brahmā.

**Ajānadeva** (S) (M) a god by birth.

**Ājānī** (S) (F) of noble birth.

**Ajānidha** (S) (M) 1. treasure or ocean of instigation. 3. a seer referred to in a hymn of the *Ṛg Veda*.

**Ajapa** (S) (M) protector of cattle; one who possesses goats; the sacred Barna or the Garlic Pear tree (which provides nourishment to the cattle apart from giving shade) (*Crataeva nurvala*)

**Ajapāla** (S) (M) 1. goatherd. 3. father of Daśaratha.

**Ajapārśva** (S) (M) 1. with sides like a goat; one who possesses many goats. 3. a son of Śvetakarṇa (*M. Bh.*)

**Ajarā** (S) (F) 1. ever young. 3. another name for the river Sarasvatī.

**Ajasra** (S) (M) not to be obstructed.

**Ajāta** (S) (M) unborn; a god.

**Ajātari** (S) (M) 1. having no enemy. 3. another name for Yudhiṣṭhira.

**Ajātaśatru** (S) (M) 1. with no enemy. 2. with no equal adversary. 3. a son of Śamīka; a son of Bimbisāra; father of Arbhaka and grandfather of Udayana (*V. Purāṇa*); a king of Kāśī (*K. Upaniṣad*); a son of the earth (*V. Purāṇa*); a son of Vidhisāra (*V. Purāṇa*); another name for Śiva and Yudhiṣṭhira.

**Ajathyā** (S) (F) the yellow jasmine (*Jasminum humile*)

**Ajavindu** (S) (M) 1. one who has the knowledge of eternity. 3. a Suvīra king (*M. Bh.*)

**Ajayā** (S) (F) 1. one who cannot be conquered; Indian Hemp (*Cannabis sativa*). 3. a friend of Durgā also known as Māyā (*D. Bhāgvata*)

**Ajaya** (S) (M) 1. one who cannot be conquered. 2. invincible. 3. a king of the Bharata dynasty known for his generosity and kindness (*M. Bh.*); another name for Viṣṇu and Agni.

**Ajīgarta** (S) (M) 1. one who has nothing to swallow. 3. a ṛṣī and Śunahśepha's father (*M. Bh.*)

**Ajina** (S) (M) 1. skin of a goat; tiger skin. 3. a son of Havirdhāna and Dhīṣaṇā (*V. Purāṇa*)

**Ajinkya** (S) (M) invincible.

**Ajirā** (S) (F) 1. not slow. 2. agile; quick; rapid. 3. a river (*D. Bhāgavata*); another name for Durgā.

**Ajira** (S) (M) 1. not slow. 2. agile; rapid.

3. the Subramanyā priest at the snake festival of the Pānćavaṁsa Brāhmaṇa.

**Ajīṣa** (S) (M) 1. lord of goats. 3. another name for Śiva.

**Ajita** (S) (M) 1. invincible; irresistible. 3. the ṛṣis of the 14th Manvantara (*A. Koṣa*); the 2nd Arhat of the present Avasarpinī (*J. Literature*); a future Buddha (*B. Literature*); another name for Viṣṇu and Śiva.

**Ajitābha** (S) (M) unconquerable brilliance.

**Ajitanātha** (S) (M) 1. lord of the invincible. 3. the 2nd Jaina Tīrthānkara who was the son of King Jitaśatru and Bijoyā of Ayodhyā (*J. Literature*)

**Ajitapāla** (S) (M) protector of the invincible.

**Ajitātman** (S) (M) 1. one whose soul can never be conquered. 2. pious; chaste; pure.

**Ajodara** (S) (M) 1. goat bellied. 3. a soldier in Skanda's army (*M. Bh.*)

**Ājyapa** (S) (M) 1. drinking clarified butter. 3. sons of Pulastya or Kardama and ancestors of the Vaiśya caste.

**Akalaṅka** (S) (M) 1. without stains. 2. unblemished; flawless.

**Ākālikī** (S) (F) lightning.

**Akalkā** (S) (F) 1. free from impurity. 2. moonlight.

**Akalmāṣa** (S) (M) 1. sinless; pure. 3. a son of the 4th Manu (*H. Purāṇa*)

**Akalpa** (S) (M) ornament; decoration.

**Akaluṣa** (S) (M) unblemished.

**Akāma** (S) (M) 1. without lust. 2. pious; chaste; virtuous.

**Akampana** (S) (M) 1. unshaken. 2. calm; resolute. 3. a rākṣasa son of Sumāli and Ketumatī (*V. Rāmāyaṇa*)

**Akampita** (S) (M) 1. unshaken. 2. calm; resolute; a Jaina or Buddhist saint. 3. chief pupil of Mahāvīra (*J. S. Koṣa*)

**Akaniṣṭha** (S) (M) 1. not young. 2. elder; superior. 3. a class of Buddhist deities (*He. Koṣa*)

**Ākāṅkṣā** (S) (F) desire; wish.

**Akaṇṭaka** (S) (M) free from thorns; troubles, enemies.

**Akapīvata** (S) (M) 1. unshaken. 2. firm; tranquil; resolute. 3. a ṛṣi (*M. Bh.*)

**Ākara** (S) (M) mine; a collection; a treasure; best.

**Akarkkara** (S) (M) 1. handless. 3. a serpent son of Kadru (*M. Bh.*)

**Ākarṣaṇa** (S) (M) attraction; handsome; charming.

**Ākarṣita** (S) (M) attracted; an admirer of beauty.

**Ākaṣa** (S) (M) a touchstone.

**Ākāśa** (S) (M) 1. free or open space. 2. ether; sky; atmosphere; with an open mind; one whose thoughts pervade the sky.

**Ākāśaćamasa** (S) (M) 1. a cup of ether. 2. the moon which is depicted as a cup of nectar in the sky.

**Ākāśadīpa** (S) (F) 1. a lamp in the sky. 2. a lamp lit in honour of Lakṣmī at the Divāli festival.

**Ākāśagaṅgā** (S) (F) the celestial Gaṅgā; the Milky Way.

**Ākāśagarbhī** (S) (M) 1. one whose womb is the sky. 2. boundless; limitless; divine. 3. a Bodhisattva (*B. Ćarita*)

**Ākāśī** (S) (F) 1. all pervading. 2. the atmosphere.

**Akatha** (S) (M) 1. boisterous. 3. a son of Maṅkaṇa and devotee of Śiva (*P. Purāṇa*)

**Akhaṇḍa** (S) (M) 1. without parts. 2. indestructible; divine.

**Ākhaṇḍala** (S) (M) 1. that which cannot be broken. 3. another name for Indra and Śiva.

**Akhila** (S) (M) complete; whole.

**Akhilātman** (S) (M) the universal soul or Brahman.

**Akhilendra** (S) (M) lord of the universe.

**Akhileśa** (S) (M) all pervading god.

**Akhileśvara** (S) (M) lord of all.

**Ākhuga** (S) (M) 1. riding on a rat. 3. another name for Gaṇeṣa.

**Akīla** (S) (M) 1. not fixed; not nailed. 2. wavering.

**Akopa** (S) (M) 1. without anger. 3. a minister of Daśaratha (*V. Rāmāyaṇa*)

**Akra** (S) (M) banner; wall; fence.

**Akrānta** (S) (M) 1. unsurpassed. 2. unconquered.

**Ākrānti** (S) (F) might; valour; force.

**Ākrīḍa** (S) (M) 1. pleasure grove; garden. 3. a son of Kurūtthāma.

**Akṛṣaśāśva** (S) (M) 1. with strong horses. 3. a king of Ayodhyā (*V. Rāmāyaṇa*)

**Akṛṣna** (S) (M) 1. not black. 2. spotless; white; pure. 3. another name for the moon.

**Akṛṣnakarman** (S) (M) free from sins; guiltless.

**Akṛtavraṇa** (S) (M) 1. without a wound. 2. cannot be hurt. 3. a commentator of Purāṇas (*V. Purāṇa*); a companion of Rāma Jāmdagnya (*M. Bh.*)

**Ākṛtī** (S) (F) form; figure; shape; appearance; a constituent part; a vedic metre consisting of 4 lines with 22 syllables each ancient mathematicians substituted Akṛtī for the number 22 which remains one of its meanings.

**Ākṛti** (S) (M) 1. form; shape. 3. a king of Saurāṣtra (*M. Bh.*)

**Ākrodhana** (S) (M) 1. free from anger. 3. a Purū king who was the son of Ayutanāyi and Kāmā (*M. Bh.*)

**Ākroṣa** (S) (M) 1. wild anger. 3. a king of Mahottha (*M. Bh.*)

**Akrūra** (S) (M) 1. not cruel. 2. gentle. 3. a son of Śvaphalka and Nandinī, the husband of Sutanu, the father of Devaka and Upadevaka and an advisor and uncle of Kṛṣṇa (*Bhā. Purāṇa*)

**Akṣa** (S) (M) 1. the soul; knowledge; senses; sky; earth; the *Eleocarpus ganitrus* or Rudrākṣa which is strung to make rosaries; the Bedda Nut tree (*Terminalia belerica*); cube; dice; axle; the beam of a balance; the number 5; snake. 3. son of Rāvaṇa (*V. Rāmāyaṇa*); a son of Nara (*Bhā. Purāṇa*); another name for Garuḍa.

**Akṣaja** (S) (M) 1. direct knowledge or cognition; thunderbolt; diamond. 3. another name for Viṣṇu.

**Akṣaka** (S) (M) 1. sensual. 3. the Chariot tree (*Ougeinia oojeinensis*)

**Akṣakumāra** (S) (M) 1. eternal prince. 3. a son of Rāvaṇa and Mandodarī (*V. Rāmāyaṇa*); a soldier of Skanda's army (*M. Bh.*)

**Akṣalā** (S) (M) 1. unbroken; whole. 3. another name for Śiva.

**Akṣamālā** (S) (F) 1. a rosary of Rudrākṣa seeds (*Eleocarpus ganitrus*). 3. the mother of Vatsa (*Ś. Purāṇa*); another name for Arundhatī.

**Akṣamālin** (S) (M) 1. wearing a rosary of Rudrākṣa seeds (*Eleocarpus ganitrus*). 3. another name for Śiva.

**Akṣamata** (S) (M) 1. rosary. 2. a string of beads which include the Rudrākṣa (*Eleocarpus ganitrus*) the coral, the crystal and the ruby.

**Akṣapāda** (S) (M) 1. follower of knowledge; pursuer of knowledge. 2. learned; wise; enlightened. 3. another name for sage Gautama the founder of the Nyāya philosophy or for a follower of that system.

**Akṣara** (S) (M) 1. imperishable. 2. unalterable. 3. another name for Brahmā, Viṣṇu, Śiva the syllable 'Om', and the final beatitude.

**Akṣasutrā** (S) (F) 1. bearer of knowledge. 3. wife of sage Āpastamba (*Ā. Samhitā*)

**Akṣata** (S) (M) 1. unbroken. 2. whole; Barley (*Hordeum vulgare*) 3. another name for Śiva.

**Akṣāvalī** (S) (F) a string of Akṣa (*Eleocarpus ganitrus*) seeds.

**Akṣaya** (S) (M) 1. undecaying; imperishable; a day which confers undying religious merit. 3. the Supreme Spirit.

**Akṣayā** (S) (F) 1. undecaying. 3. another name for Pṛthvī, the goddess of earth.

**Akṣayiṇī** (S) (F) 1. undecaying. 3. another name for Pārvatī.

**Akṣī** (S) (F) abode; existence; a possession; the eye.

**Akśīna** (S) (M) 1. not failing. 3. a son of Viśvamitra (*M. Bh.*)

**Akṣiṇa** (S) (M) 1. not perishing; not waning; not diminishing. 3. a son of Viṣvamitra (*M. Bh.*)

**Akṣita** (S) (M) 1. undecaying. 2. permanent; unfailing.

**Akṣitāvasu** (S) (M) 1. possessing undecaying wealth. 3. another name for Indra (*Ṛg. Veda*)

**Akṣitī** (S) (F) imperishability.

**Akṣitoti** (S) (M) 1. one who abounds in unending wealth. 3. another name for Indra (*Ṛg. Veda*)

**Akṣobhya** (S) (M) 1. immovable. 2. imperturbable; unassailable. 3. a Buddha (*B. Ćaritā*); a sage (*B. Ćarita*)

**Akṣudra** (S) (M) 1. not small or insignificant. 2. big or important. 3. another name for Śiva.

**Akṣuṇṇa** (S) (M) 1. unconquered. 2. successful.

**Aktu** (S) (M) tinge; ray; light.

**Akula** (S) (M) 1. transcendental. 2. casteless; familyless. 3. another name for Śiva.

**Akuṇṭha** (S) (M) vigorous; everfresh; eternal.

**Akūpārā** (S) (F) 1. unbounded. 2. free; independent. 3. a daughter of sage Aṅgiras (*P. Brāhmaṇa*)

**Akūpāra** (S) (M) 1. unbounded. 2. free; independent; the ocean. 3. the tortoise in the Indradyumna lake, regarded as the 2nd incarnation of Viṣṇu (*M. Bh.*) on which the earth is supposed to rest; an āditya (*A. Koṣa*)

**Akupya** (S) (M) 1. not base. 2. gold; silver.

**Ākūrća** (S) (M) 1. the guileless one. 3. a Buddha (*B. Literature*)

**Ākūtā** (S) (F) 1. not of the earth. 3. another name for Parvati.

**Akutaśćala** (S) (M) 1. not moveable from a cause. 3. another name for Śiva.

**Ākūtī** (S) (F) 1. intention. 3. wish personified as the daughter of Manu Svāyambhuva and Śatarūpā (*V. Samhitā*), the wife of Prajāpati Rući and the mother of Yajña and Dakṣiṇā (*V. Purāṇa*); the wife of Pṛthuśena (*Bhā. Purāṇa*)

**Alageśa** (S) (M) lord of individuals.

**Alaghu** (S) (M) 1. not light. 2. heavy; weighty; serious; solemn. 3. a son of Vasiṣṭha and Urjā (*A. Purāṇa*)

**Alakā** (S) (F) 1. girl; curl; lock of hair. 3. city of Kubera (*M. Bh.*)

**Alakādhipa** (S) (M) 1. lord of Alakā. 3. another name for Kubera.

**Alakanandā** (S) (F) 1. young girl. 3. the celestial Gaṅgā (*A. Koṣa*); a river (*M. Bh.*)

**Alakaprabhā** (S) (M) a glorious girl.

**Alakarāvatī** (S) (F) 1. loving. 2. with adorable hands. 3. wife of King Naravāhanadatta who was emperor of the vidyādharas (*K. Sāgara*)

**Ālakṣya** (S) (M) visible; apparent.

**Alakīśvara** (S) (M) 1. lord of Alakā. 3. another name for Kubera.

**Ālamba** (S) (M) 1. support; receptacle; asylum. 3. a sage in Yudhiṣṭhira's court (*M. Bh.*)

**Alambala** (S) (M) 1. with immeasurable power. 3. an asura son of Jatāsura (*M. Bh.*); another name for Śiva.

**Ālambāyana** (S) (M) 1. one who supports. 3. a comrade of Indra (*M. Bh.*)

**Ālambi** (S) (M) 1. dependable. 3. a son of Kaśyapa (*M. Bh.*)

**Alambuśā** (S) (F) 1. a line not to be crossed. 2. a barrier; the *Sphaeranthus indicus* herb. 3. an apsarā daughter of Kaśyapa and Prādhā who married King Tṛnabindu and was the mother of Ilabilā, Viśālā, Śunyabandhu and Dhūmraketu (*Bhā. Purāṇa*)

**Alambuśa** (S) (M) 1. a line not to be crossed; the palm of the hand with the fingers extended (as once the fingers are extended, the boundary of the palm cannot be stretched any further). 3. son of the rākṣasa Ṛśyaśṛṅga (*M. Bh.*); a king on the Kaurava side (*M. Bh.*); king of the rākṣasas (*M. Bh.*); a son of Jaṭāsura (*M. Bh.*)

**Alamelā** (S) (F) 1. extremely intelligent. 3. another name for Rukminī the consort of Kṛṣṇa.

**Alamelū** (S) (F) 1. very sportive. 2. extremely merry.

**Alaṅkāra** (S) (M) ornament.

**Alaṅkṛta** (S) (M) 1. decorated. 2. adorned.

**Alaṅkṛtī** (S) (M) ornament.

**Ālāpinī** (S) (F) a lute.

**Alarka** (S) (M) 1. furious. 2. a mad dog; an unusual animal; the plant *Calotopis gigantea*. 3. a king of Kāśī and Karuṣā who was a member of Yama's court (*M. Bh.*)

**Alātākṣī** (S) (F) 1. fire eyed. 3. a mother in Skanda's retinue (*M. Bh.*)

**Alāyudha** (S) (M) 1. one whose weapon is a scorpion sting. 3. brother of Bakāsura (*M. Bh.*)

**Alayya** (S) (M) 1. assailant. 3. another name

for Indra.

**Aleśa** (S) (M) 1. not little. 2. much; large.

**Alia** (S) (M) forehead.

**Alin** (S) (F) 1. that which possesses a sting. 3. the zodiac sign of Scorpio.

**Ālinda** (S) (M) the balcony in front of a house.

**Alipriya** (S) (M) 1. beloved of the black bee. 2. the red lotus (*Nymphaea rubra*)

**Aliśā** (S) (F) grand; stately.

**Allā** (S) (F) 1. mother. 2. the Supreme Spirit.

**Alobhin** (S) (M) 1. not wanting or desiring anything. 2. free from greed.

**Āloka** (S) (M) vision; sight; aspect; light; lustre; splendour.

**Alola** (S) (M) 1. unagitated. 2. firm; steady.

**Alolupa** (S) (M) 1. free from desire; unagitated. 2. firm; steady. 3. a son of Dhṛtarāṣṭra (*M. Bh.*)

**Ālopa** (S) (M) a small morsel.

**Alpanā** (S) (F) delighted; glad.

**Alpasāras** (S) (M) a little jewel.

**Alpeśa** (S) (M) 1. the subtle god. 3. another name for Kṛṣṇa.

**Ālūgu** (S) (M) 1. that which divides; that which cuts. 2. blade.

**Āluka** (S) (M) 1. ebony. 3. another name for Śeṣa.

**Amad** (S) (M) 1. without intoxication. 2. sober; grave; serious.

**Amadana** (S) (M) 1. opposed to Kāma. 2. sexless; free of sexual desires. 3. another name for Śiva.

**Amadhya** (S) (M) 1. not indifferent. 2. compassionate; humane; loving. 3. another name for Kṛṣṇa.

**Amahatha** (S) (M) 1. wanting a house. 3. a nāga (*M. Bh.*)

**Amahīyu** (S) (M) 1. not of the earth. 2. celestial; divine. 3. a ṛṣi and part author of *Ṛg Veda* (ix)

**Amalā** (S) (F) 1. spotless. 2. pure; shining. 3. another name for Lakṣmī; Bombay Hemp plant (*Hibiscus cannabinus*)

**Amala** (S) (M) 1. spotless. 2. clean; pure; shining; crystal; the tree (*Emblica officianalis*). 3. another name for Nārāyaṇa.

**Amalagarbha** (S) (M) 1. born of purity. 2. unblemished; flawless; pure; chaste; virtuous. 3. a Bodhisattva (*B. Ćarita*)

**Amalamaṇi** (S) (M) 1. pure jewel. 2. crystal.

**Amalātman** (S) (M) 1. pure minded. 2. pure; chaste; virtuous.

**Amama** (S) (M) 1. without ego. 3. the 12th Jaina arhat of a future Utsarpinī.

**Āmana** (S) (M) friendly disposition; kindness; affection.

**Amanath** (S) (M) 1. property; treasure. 2. extremely wealthy.

**Amanda** (S) (M) not slow; active; merry; bright.

**Amandīpa** (S) (M) sharp witted; the light of peace; the lamp of peace.

**Amanī** (S) (F) 1. road; way. 2. one who shows the path; a leader; a preceptor.

**Amanthu** (S) (M) 1. not slow. 2. sharpwitted; one who takes decisions instantly. 3. a king who was the son of Vīravrata of the family of Priyavrata (*Bhā. Purāṇa*)

**Amānuṣa** (S) (M) 1. non-human. 2. divine; celestial; demonic.

**Amara** (S) (M) 1. immortal; a god; the number 33 (as there are 33 main deities); imperishable. 3. a marut (*H. Purāṇa*); the Rudraksha tree (*Elaeocarpus ganitrus*); the Adamant creeper (*Vitis quadrangularis*)

**Amarabhartṛ** (S) (M) 1. supporter of the gods. 3. another name for Indra.

**Amaraćandra** (S) (M) 1. moon among the gods; immortal moon. 3. a poet of Gujarat (13th century) (*B. Bhārata*)

**Amarāćārya** (S) (M) 1. teacher of the gods. 3. another name for Bṛhaspati.

**Amaradatta** (S) (M) given by the gods.

**Amarādhipa** (S) (M) 1. lord of the gods. 3. another name for Śiva.

**Amaraguru** (S) (M) 1. teacher of the gods. 3. another name for Bṛhaspati.

**Amarajā** (S) (F) daughter of the gods.

**Amaraja** (S) (M) 1. eternally born. 2. of an eternal existence. 3. another name for Bṛhaspati.

**Amarajīta** (S) (M) conquering the gods.

**Amarajota** (S) (M) light of the gods.
**Amarajyotī** (S) (M) eternal light.
**Amaranātha** (S) (M) 1. lord of the gods. 3. another name for Śiva.
**Amarāṅganā** (S) (F) celestial damsel.
**Amarañjaya** (S) (M) conquering the gods.
**Amarapā** (S) (M) 1. lord of the gods. 3. another name for Indra.
**Amarapati** (S) (M) 1. master of the gods. 3. another name for Indra.
**Amaraprabhu** (S) (M) 1. lord of the immortals. 3. one of the 1000 names of Viṣṇu.
**Amaraprīta** (S) (M) immortal love.
**Amararāja** (S) (M) 1. king of the gods. 3. another name for Indra.
**Amararatna** (S) (M) 1. jewel of the gods. 2. crystal.
**Amarasinha** (S) (M) 1. lion of the gods. 3. a 6th century Buddhist lexicographer considered to have been one of the 9 gems of Vikramāditya's court (*B. Literature*)
**Amaraśrī** (S) (M) 1. eternally divine. 3. another name for Indra, Viṣṇu and Śiva.
**Amaratāṭinī** (S) (F) 1. river of deathless beings. 3. the Gaṅgā which is considered the river of immortals.
**Amarāvatī** (S) (F) 1. abode of the eternal. 3. city of Indra (*D. Bhāgavata*)
**Amardita** (S) (M) unsubdued.
**Amarejya** (S) (M) 1. preceptor of the gods. 3. another name for Bṛhaspati.
**Amarendra** (S) (M) 1. lord of the gods. 2. immortal Indra.
**Amareśa** (S) (M) 1. lord of the gods. 3. another name for Rudra-Śiva.
**Amareśvara** (S) (M) 1. lord of the gods. 3. another name for Viṣṇu.
**Amari** (S) (F) 1. eternal 3. couch grass (*Cynodon dactylon*)
**Amarika** (S) (M) 1. one who is deathless. 2. immortal; divine; a god.
**Amarīndra** (S) (M) eternal Indra.
**Amarīśa** (S) (M) lord of the gods.
**Amariṣṇu** (S) (M) desirous of immortality.
**Amarīśvara** (S) (M) 1. lord of the immortals. 3. another name for Viṣṇu, Śiva and Indra.
**Amaropama** (S) (M) like a god.
**Amarottama** (S) (M) 1. the best among gods. 3. another name for Indra.
**Amarṣa** (S) (M) 1. anger; passion; impatience. 3. a prince (*V. Purāṇa*)
**Amartā** (S) (F) immortality.
**Amartya** (S) (M) 1. immortal. 2. divine; a god.
**Amaru** (S) (M) 1. immortal. 3. a king who was the author of *Amaruṣataka*.
**Amaruka** (S) (M) son of an immortal.
**Amarūpam** (S) (M) god-like.
**Amarūttama** (S) (M) the best of the gods.
**Āmas** (S) (M) 1. fine; soft; tender; raw. 2. not dark; not hard; not gross. 3. a son of Kṛṣṇa (*Bhāgavata*); a son of Ghṛtapṛṣṭha (*Bh. Purāṇa*)
**Amati** (S) (F) 1. beyond intellect. 2. that which cannot be perceived; form; shape; splendour; lustre; time.
**Amava** (S) (M) 1. one who cannot be humbled. 2. violent; strong; powerful.
**Amāvasu** (S) (M) 1. deity of the house. 3. a king who was the son of Purūravas and Urvaśī (*M. Bh.*)
**Amāvasya** (S) (F) 1. dwelling together. 2. a moonless night in which neither the sun nor the moon can be spotted as they are considered to be dwelling together.
**Amāya** (S) (M) not cunning; guileless.
**Amaya** (S) (M) 1. immeasurable; boundless. 2. the Costus shrub (*Saussurea lappa*)
**Amayātman** (S) (M) 1. with immense powers of the mind. 3. another name for Viṣṇu.
**Ambā** (S) (F) 1. mother. 2. a good woman. 3. daughter of the king of Kāśī, the sister of Ambikā and Ambālikā, later reborn as Śikhaṇḍi to seek revenge on Bhīṣma (*M. Bh.*); one of the 7 kṛttikās (*T. Samhita*); an apsarā (*A. Koṣa*); a river which is part incarnation of princess Ambā of Kāśī (*M. Bh.*); another name for Durgā.
**Ambaka** (S) (M) eye.
**Ambālā** (S) (F) 1. mother. 2. sensitive; compassionate; loving.
**Ambālī** (S) (F) 1. mother. 2. sensitive; compassionate; loving.
**Ambālikā** (S) (F) 1. mother. 2. one who is sen-

sitive. 3. a daughter of the king of Kāśī, the sister of Ambā and Ambikā, the wife of Vićitravīrya and the mother of Pāṇḍu through sage Vyāsa (*M. Bh.*); Bombay Hemp plant (*Hibiscus cannabinus*)

**Ambara** (S) (M) 1. circumference; sky; atmosphere; ether. 2. saffron (*Crocus sativus*). 3. a kind of perfume.

**Ambaramaṇi** (S) (M) 1. jewel of the sky. 3. another name for the sun.

**Ambaraprabhā** (S) (F) light of the sky.

**Ambarīṣa** (S) (M) 1. lord of the sky. 2. the atmosphere. 3. a rājarṣi son of King Vṛṣāgir and the part author of *Ṛg Veda* (i); son of Nābhāga and descendant of Manu Vaivasvata (*M. Bh.*); an Ikṣvāku king the son of Māndhātā and is regarded as one of the 16 great kings of Bhārata (*M. Bh.*); a nāga who received Balarāma's soul (*M. Bh.*); a son of Pulaha (*V. Purāṇa*); another name for Viṣṇu, Śiva and Gaṇeśa; the Indian Hog Plum (*Spondias pinnata*)

**Ambastha** (S) (M) 1. devotee of the sky; devotee of goddess Ambā; one who resides in water. 3. a warrior on the Pāṇḍava side (*M. Bh.*)

**Āmbasthya** (S) (M) 1. devotee of the mother. 3. an *Aitareya Brāhmaṇa* king whose consecration priest was Nārada.

**Ambava** (S) (M) 1. water like. 2. making a sound like running water.

**Ambayā** (S) (F) mother.

**Ambhaspati** (S) (M) 1. lord of the waters. 3. another name for Varuṇa.

**Ambhassāra** (S) (M) 1. the essence of water. 2. pearl.

**Ambhinī** (S) (F) 1. born of water. 3. the preceptress who transmitted the *Yajur Veda* to Vāćā (*Y. Veda*)

**Ambhoja** (S) (M) 1. born of water. 2. the day lotus (*Nelumbium speciosum*)

**Ambhojinī** (S) (F) 1. an assemblage of lotuses. 2. fragrant; auspicious; venerated; dear to the gods.

**Ambhoruha** (S) (M) 1. born of water. 3. a son of Viśvāmitra (*M. Bh.*)

**Ambhṛṇa** (S) (M) 1. full of water. 2. powerful. 3. a ṛṣi father of Vāća (*Ṛg Veda*)

**Ambī** (S) (F) 1. mother. 2. sensitive; compassionate; loving.

**Ambikā** (S) (F) 1. mother. 2. sensitive; compassionate; loving; a good woman; the harvest in the most productive season; Bombay Hemp (*Hibiscus cannabinus*) 3. a daughter of the king of Kāśī, the sister of Ambā and Ambālikā, the wife of Vićitravīrya and the mother of Dhṛtarāṣṭra through sage Vyāsa (*M. Bh.*); a Matṛ or village goddess who represents a fierce class of yoginīs (*Y. Veda*); a goddess formed from the energies of all the gods to defeat the asuras (*D. Bhāgavata*); a sister of Rudra (*V. Saṃhitā*); a mother in Skanda's retinue (*M. Bh.*); the wife of Rudra Ugraretas (*Bhā Purāṇa*); Jaina deity (*A. Koṣa*); another name for Pārvatī.

**Ambikāpati** (S) (M) 1. lord of Ambikā. 3. another name for Śiva and Rudra.

**Ambikāsuta** (S) (M) 1. son of Ambikā. 3. another name for Dhṛtarāṣṭra.

**Āmbikeya** (S) (M) 1. of Ambikā. 3. a mountain (*M. Bh.*); another name for Gaṇeśa, Kārttikeya and Dhṛtarāṣṭra.

**Ambu** (S) (M) water.

**Āmbuda** (S) (M) 1. one who gives water. 2. a cloud.

**Ambudeśvara** (S) (M) 1. lord of the clouds. 3. another name for Indra.

**Ambudhara** (S) (M) 1. water bearer. 2. a cloud.

**Ambuja** (S) (M) 1. produced in water. 2. the thunderbolt of Indra, the Lotus (*Nelumbo speciosum*); the Sārasa bird (*Ardea nivea*); a conch. 3. another name for the moon; the Indian Oak tree (*Barringtonia acutangula*)

**Ambujabhū** (S) (M) 1. being in a lotus. 3. another name for Brahmā.

**Ambujākṣī** (S) (F) 1. lotus eyed. 2. with beautiful eyes.

**Ambujānanā** (S) (F) 1. lotus faced. 3. a tutelary deity (*Brah. Purāṇa*)

**Ambumaṇi** (S) (M) 1. jewel of water. 2. lotus (*Nelumbo speciosum*); the pearl.

**Ambumatī** (S) (F) 1. containing water. 3. a river (*M. Bh.*)

**Ambunātha** (S) (M) 1. lord of the waters. 2. the ocean. 3. another name for Varuṇa.

**Ambunidhi** (S) (M) 1. store of water. 2. the ocean.

**Ambupa** (S) (M) 1. protector of the water. 3. another name for Varuṇa.

**Ambupadma** (S) (F) 1. lotus of the water. 2. Indian Lotus (*Nelumbo nucifera*)

**Āmbupati** (S) (M) 1. lord of the waters. 2. the ocean.

**Amburāja** (S) (M) 1. lord of the waters. 2. the ocean. 3. another name for Varuṇa.

**Amburuha** (S) (M) 1. born in the water. 2. the Indian lotus (*Nelumbo nucifera*)

**Ambuvāhinī** (S) (F) 1. carrying water. 3. a holy river (*M. Bh.*)

**Ambuvica** (S) (M) 1. living in water. 3. king of Magadha (*M. Bh.*)

**Amini** (S) (M) bailiff; rigid; unalterable.

**Amiṣā** (S) (F) free from guile or deceit.

**Āmiṣa** (S) (M) an object of enjoyment; a pleasing object; a gift.

**Amita** (S) (M) unmeasured; unlimited; boundless; great; immense; infinite.

**Amitābha** (S) (M) 1. of unmeasured splendour. 3. deities of the 8th Manvantara.

**Amitadhvaja** (S) (M) 1. with an immeasurable flag. 2. reigns over a huge territory. 3. a ćakravartin; son of Dharmadhvaja (*V. Purāṇa*); a rākṣasa (*M. Bh.*)

**Amitadyuti** (S) (M) of infinite splendour.

**Amitagati** (S) (M) 1. extremely fast. 3. a vidyādhara (*H. Purāṇa*)

**Amitakratu** (S) (M) of unbounded energy.

**Amitarući** (S) (M) 1. very glorious. 3. a Buddhist deity.

**Amitāsan** (S) (M) 1. with sacred marks. 2. omnipresent. 3. another name for Viṣṇu.

**Amitātman** (S) (M) with an immense mind.

**Amitaujas** (S) (M) 1. with unbounded energy. 2. the almighty. 3. a Pāñćāla king who was part incarnation of Ketumān and an ally of the Pāṇḍavas (*M. Bh.*)

**Amitavikrama** (S) (M) 1. of unbounded valour. 3. another name for Viṣṇu.

**Amitaya** (S) (M) boundless.

**Amitāyuṣ** (S) (M) 1. of infinite age. 2. immortal; divine; a god. 3. a Dhyāni Buddha (*B. Literature*)

**Amiteśa** (S) (M) 1. lord of the infinite. 3. another name for Viṣṇu.

**Amiteśvarī** (S) (F) with unlimited wealth; goddess of the infinite.

**Amiti** (S) (F) 1. immeasurable. 2. boundless; divine.

**Amitojas** (S) (M) of unbounded energy.

**Amitoṣa** (S) (M) ever happy.

**Amitraghāta** (S) (M) 1. slayer of enemies. 3. another name for Bindusāra.

**Amitrajit** (S) (M) 1. conqueror of enemies. 3. a son of Suvarna; a king who was the husband of Malayagandhinī and the father of Vīra (*Sk. Purāṇa*)

**Amitrasāha** (S) (M) 1. one who overcomes enemies. 3. another name for Indra.

**Amiya** (S) (F) 1. full of tenderness. 2. nectar.

**Amlāna** (S) (M) 1. unwithered. 2. fresh; clean; clear; bright; unclouded.

**Ammavaru** (Tamil) (F) 1. the primal mother. 3. tutelary goddess of Madras once regarded the primary Śakti.

**Āmoda** (S) (M) amusement; gladdening; cheering; joy; serenity; pleasure; strong perfume.

**Āmodin** (S) (M) fragrant; famous.

**Āmodinī** (S) (F) fragrant; famous.

**Āmohanikā** (S) (F) fragrance.

**Amoghā** (S) (F) 1. unerring; unfailing; productive; fruitful; the Trumpet flower (*Bignonia suaveolens*). 3. a wife of Śantanu (*M. Bh.*); a mother in Skanda's retinue (*Sk. Purāṇa*); another name for Durgā and the night; the Black Myrobalan tree (*Terminata chebula*)

**Amogha** (S) (M) 1. unerring; unfailing; productive; fruitful. 3. a yakṣa companion of Śiva (*M. Bh.*); a river (*A. Koṣa*); another name for Viṣṇu, Śiva and Skanda.

**Amoghadaṇḍa** (S) (M) 1. unerring in punishing. 2. an unerring judge. 3. another name for Śiva.

**Amoghadarśana** (S) (M) 1. with an unerring eye. 3. a nāga.

**Amoghadarśin** (S) (M) 1. perceiving faultlessly; with unerring perception; a Bodhisattva

(*B. Literature*)

**Amoghākṣī** (S) (F) 1. of unerring eye. 3. Dākṣāyaṇī (*M. Purāṇa*)

**Amoghasiddhi** (S) (M) 1. with unfailing success. 3. the 5th Dhyāni Buddha (*B. Literature*)

**Amoghavajra** (S) (M) 1. the unerring thunderbolt. 3. Buddhist scholar (6th century A.D.) (*B. Literature*)

**Amoghavarṣa** (S) (M) 1. productive year; productive reign. 3. a Ćālukya king.

**Amoghavikrama** (S) (M) 1. of unerring valour. 3. another name for Śiva.

**Amoha** (S) (M) 1. without delusion. 2. that which is errorless; clear; straight.

**Amola** (S) (M) priceless.

**Amolaka** (S) (M) priceless.

**Amprthu** (S) (M) strong and healthy.

**Āmramañjarī** (S) (F) the mango blossom.

**Āmrapāli** (S) (M) guardian of the Mango tree (*Mangifera indica*)

**Amṛtā** (S) (F) 1. beyond death; immortal; nectar like. 2. a goddess. 3. daughter of a king of Magadha who was the wife of Anaśya and the mother of Parīkṣit (*M. Bh.*); a sister of Amṛtodana (*B. Literature*); a digit of the moon (*Brah. Purāṇa*); a Dākṣāyaṇī (*M. Purāṇa*)

**Amṛta** (S) (M) 1. immortal nectar. 2. nectar of immortality; ambrosia; the Supreme Spirit; god; splendour; light; beautiful; anything sweet; gold; the number 4; a ray of the sun. 3. another name for Viṣṇu, Śiva, Dhanvantari, Prajāpati, Indra, the sun and the soul; the Dew Bean (*Phaseolus aconitifolius*); *Aconitum heterophyllum*; Couch grass (*Cynodon dactylon*); the *Gloriosa superba* creeper.

**Amṛtadrava** (S) (M) 1. that which emits nectar. 3. another name for the moon.

**Amṛtadyuti** (S) (M) 1. with immortal rays; nectar rayed. 3. another name for the moon.

**Amṛtāharaṇa** (S) (M) 1. nectar stealer. 3. another name for Garuḍa as incarnation of Viṣṇu.

**Amṛtaka** (S) (M) the nectar of immortality.

**Amṛtakara** (S) (M) 1. nectar rayed. 3. another name for the moon.

**Amṛtākṣara** (S) (M) imperishable.

**Amṛtam** (S) (M) ambrosia produced by the churning of the Ocean of Milk; the collective body of immortals; eternity; heaven; a ray of light; milk; butter; sweetmeat; water; gold; the number 4.

**Amṛtamā** (S) (F) food obtained from the Ocean of Milk.

**Amṛtamālinī** (S) (F) 1. with an everfresh garland. 3. another name for Durgā.

**Amṛtamaya** (S) (M) 1. full of nectar. 2. immortal.

**Amṛtānanda** (S) (M) the delight of immortals.

**Amṛtāṅśu** (S) (M) 1. nectar rayed. 3. another name for the moon.

**Amṛtapā** (S) (M) 1. drinking nectar. 3. a dānava (*M. Bh.*); another name for Viṣṇu.

**Amṛtaprabha** (S) (M) 1. with eternal glory. 3. a vidyadhara (*K. Sāgara*)

**Amṛtāśa** (S) (M) 1. whose soul is immortal; one who drinks nectar. 2. a deity. 3. another name for Viṣṇu.

**Amṛtasū** (S) (M) 1. distilling nectar. 3. another name for the moon.

**Amṛtatejas** (S) (M) 1. with eternal power. 3. a vidyādhara prince (*K. Sāgara*)

**Amṛtavapus** (S) (M) 1. of immortal form. 3. another name for Viṣṇu.

**Amṛteśa** (S) (M) 1. lord of the immortals. 3. another name for Śiva.

**Amṛteśaya** (S) (M) 1. sleeping in nectar. 3. another name for Viṣṇu.

**Amṛteśvara** (S) (M) 1. lord of the immortals. 3. another name for Śiva.

**Amṛtodana** (S) (M) 1. cloud of nectar. 3. a son of Siṇhahanu the uncle of Śākyāmuni (*B. Literature*)

**Amteśvara** (S) (M) 1. eternal god. 2. virtuous; immortal.

**Amūl** (S) (M) 1. without a beginning; without roots. 2. one who does not have anyone to follow; without a superior.

**Amūlya** (S) (M) invaluable.

**Amūrā** (S) (M) wise; intelligent; sharpsighted.

**Amūrta** (S) (M) 1. formless. 3. another name for Śiva.

**Amūrtarajas** (S) (M) 1. with a formless emotion; heavenly emotion; with an indescribable emotion; whose emotions are like those of a god; lofty; universally beneficient. 3. a son of Kuśa and Vaidarbhī.

**Amūrtarayas** (S) (M) 1. with formless power. 2. whose limits of power are indescribable; one who has divine power. 3. a king of Bharata and the father of King Gaya (*M. Bh.*)

**Amūrti** (S) (M) 1. formless. 2. incorporeal; all pervading; omnipresent; a god. 3. another name for Viṣṇu.

**Anā** (Malayalam) (M) elephant.

**Anābhayin** (S) (M) 1. fearless. 3. another name for Indra.

**Anabhiśasta** (S) (M) 1. blameless. 2. one who is faultless; pure.

**Anabhra** (S) (M) cloudless.

**Anabhrā** (S) (F) 1. cloudless. 2. clear in visage and mind.

**Anādṛṣṭi** (S) (M) 1. perfect; beyond check. 3. a Purū dynasty king who was the son of Raudrāśva and Miśrakeśī (*M. Bh.*); one of the 7 great Yādava warriors and son of King Vṛddhasena (*M. Bh.*); a son of Śūra; a son of Ugrasena (*Bhā. Purāṇa*)

**Anādhṛṣya** (S) (M) 1. unchecked; unimpaired. 2. of a free will; without flaw. 3. a Kaurava (*M. Bh.*)

**Anādi** (S) (M) 1. eternal. 2. immortal; divine. 3. another name for Śiva and Kṛṣṇa.

**Anādimadhyaparyanta** (S) (M) 1. extending without beginning, middle or end. 3. another name for Kṛṣṇa.

**Anādinava** (S) (M) faultless; without a beginning; forever new.

**Anadīnidhana** (S) (M) 1. with no beginning or end. 2. eternal. 3. another name for Kṛṣṇa.

**Anādyā** (S) (F) 1. without a beginning. 2. one who has always been there; immortal; divine. 3. an apsarā (*M. Bh.*)

**Anādya** (S) (M) 1. existing from eternity. 3. another name for Kṛṣṇa.

**Anādyanta** (S) (M) 1. without beginning or end. 2. that which is eternal; immortal and divine. 3. another name for Śiva.

**Anāgā** (S) (F) 1. sinless. 3. a river.

**Anāgalammā** (S) (F) 1. formless mother; angry mother. 3. a Coimbatore deity known for her anger.

**Anagha** (S) (M) 1. without sin. 2. innocent; pure; above reproach; perfect. 3. a son of Vaśiṣṭha and Ūrjā who became a ṛṣi of the 3rd Manvantara (*V. Rāmāyaṇa*); a gandharva (*M. Bh.*); a child of Garuḍa (*M. Bh.*); another name for Viṣṇu, Śiva and Skanda.

**Anaghādru** (S) (M) 1. injuring the sinless. 3. son of Bali.

**Anaka** (S) (M) 1. without weakness; thundercloud. 3. a warrior of the Yādava dynasty (*Bhā. Purāṇa*)

**Anakadundubha** (S) (M) 1. at whose birth drums are beaten; whose birth is eagerly awaited. 3. Kṛṣṇa's grandfather (*M. Bh.*)

**Anakadundubhi** (S) (M) 1. son of Anakadundubha; praised all over; kettledrum; like a thundercloud; very powerful. 3. another name for Kṛṣṇa's father, Vasudeva.

**Anākrānta** (S) (M) 1. unassailable. 2. invincible; strong; victorious.

**Analā** (S) (F) 1. composed of fire. 2. without a blemish. 3. a daughter of Dakṣa, wife of Kaśyapa and mother of trees and creepers (*V. Rāmāyaṇa*); a daughter of Rohiṇī and granddaughter of Surabhī (*M. Bh.*); a daughter of Mālyavān and Sundarī, the wife of Viśvavasu and the mother of Kumbhināśī (*V. Rāmāyaṇa*)

**Anala** (S) (M) 1. fire; wind; the number 3. 3. one of the 8 vasus; another name for Agni and Vāyu.

**Analajit** (S) (M) 1. conqueror of fire. 2. pure, blameless and invincible.

**Analapriyā** (S) (F) beloved of fire; wife of Agni.

**Anama** (S) (M) 1. who returns salutations with a blessing. 3. Jaina Tirthaṅkara (*J. S. Koṣa*)

**Anāmaya** (S) (M) 1. free from disease. 2. healthy. 3. another name for Śiva.

**Anāmikā** (S) (F) without a name (since the name of a person reflects the virtues desired, one without a name is considered without limitations of virtues associated with a particular name, therefore one who has all the virtues); ring finger.

**Anamitra** (S) (M) 1. without an enemy. 2. liked by all. 3. a solar dynasty king who was a son of Nighna (*M. Bh.*); Yādava king who was a son of Dhṛṣṭa (*M. Purāṇa*); a son of King Kroṣṭa and Mādrī (*M. Bh.*); father of Manu Ćākṣuṣa (*Br. Purāṇa*); a son of Vṛṣni and father of Sini (*M. Bh.*)

**Anamiva** (S) (M) 1. free from disease. 2. well; happy.

**Anamol** (S) (M) 1. priceless. 2. precious; rare.

**Ānamrā** (S) (F) bent; humble; modest; propitious.

**Ānana** (S) (M) 1. face. 2. appearance; visage.

**Anānata** (S) (M) 1. not bent. 2. arrogant; proud; upright; undefeated. 3. a sage (*Ṛg. Veda*)

**Ānanda** (S) (M) 1. bliss; happiness; joy; enjoyment; pleasure. 3. forest on the top of mount Mahāmeru inhabited by devas, gandharvas, apsarās and mahāṛṣis (*P. Purāṇa*); the previous incarnation of Manu Ćākṣuṣa (*Mā. Purāṇa*); another name for Śiva.

**Ānandabhairava** (S) (M) 1. causing both bliss and fear. 3. a form of Śiva.

**Ānandabhairavī** (S) (F) 1. consort of Śiva. 3. another name for Gaurī.

**Ānandabhuj** (S) (M) 1. enjoying happiness. 2. fortunate.

**Ānandaghana** (S) (M) 1. cloud of joy. 2. consisting of pure joy.

**Ānandagiri** (S) (M) 1. the peak of joy. 2. one who is full of joy and brings happiness to others.

**Ānandalakṣmī** (S) (F) 1. goddess of happiness. 2. always happy.

**Ānandamayī** (S) (F) full of bliss.

**Ānandamohana** (S) (M) 1. delightful. 3. another name for Kṛṣṇa.

**Ānandāmṛta** (S) (M) the nectar of joy.

**Ānandaparṇa** (S) (F) 1. with wings of joy. 2. one who spreads happiness and joy.

**Ānandaprabhā** (S) (F) 1. spreading pleasure. 3. an apsarā (*M. Bh.*)

**Ānandaprada** (S) (M) bestower of pleasure.

**Ānandasāgara** (S) (M) sea of joy.

**Ānandātman** (S) (M) 1. whose essence is happiness; whose soul has attained bliss. 2. one who is always happy and whose soul has attained Mokṣa or salvation.

**Ānandavardhana** (S) (M) 1. increasing joy. 2. one who augments joy. 3. a Sanskṛt critic (9th century A.D.) (*R. Taraṅginī*)

**Ānadhika** (S) (M) having no superior.

**Ānandī** (S) (F) 1. bestower of pleasure. 3. another name for Gaurī.

**Ānandin** (S) (M) blissful; happy; cheerful.

**Ānandita** (S) (M) delighted; happy; blissful.

**Anaṅga** (S) (M) 1. limbless; formless. 2. incorporeal; divine. 3. a king who was the son of Prajāpati Kardama, the father of Atibala and known for his integrity (*M. Bh.*); another name for Kāma; Arabian Jasmine (*Jasminum sambac*)

**Anaṅgada** (S) (M) 1. inspired by Ananga. 2. who inspires love.

**Anaṅgadevī** (S) (F) 1. formless goddess. 2. divine; immortal. 3. a queen of Kāśmira (*R. Taraṅginī*)

**Anangalekhā** (S) (F) 1. a love-letter. 2. a personification of love. 3. a queen of Kāśmira (*R. Taraṅginī*)

**Anangam** (S) (M) 1. not of the body. 2. one who is beyond the body; beyond passion; beyond destruction; divine; immortal; the mind; sky; ether; air.

**Anaṅgāngahara** (S) (M) 1. destroying the body of Kāma. 3. another name for Śiva.

**Anaṅgapāla** (S) (M) 1. protector of the limbless. 2. protector of the gods; religious spiritual; immortal; divine. 3. the founder of Delhi.

**Anaṅgapīḍa** (S) (M) 1. self-restrained. 2. balanced; mature. 3. a king of Kāśmira.

**Anaṅgasuhṛd** (S) (M) 1. friend of Kāma. 2. vasanta or the season of spring; enemy of Anaṅga. 3. another name for Śiva.

**Ananjan** (S) (M) 1. without collyrium. 2. faultless; taintless; the sky; the Supreme Spirit. 3. another name for Viṣṇu.

**Ananmaya** (S) (M) 1. one who cannot be broken. 2. healthy. 3. another name for Viṣṇu.

**Anantā** (S) (F) 1. endless. 2. eternal; divine. 3. a wife of King Janamejaya; another name for Pārvatī, the earth.

**Ananta** (S) (M) 1. endless (sky, cloud). 2. one who is beyond death; immortal; divine; eternal. 3. a nāga also known as Ādiśeṣa, described as a Prajāpati son of Brahmā (*V. Rāmāyaṇa*) but in reality born of Kaśyapa and Kadru, dwelling in Patāla wearing the earth as a grown for his 1000 heads and partially incarnated as Balarāma (*M. Bh.*) and Lakṣmaṇa (*Rāmāyaṇa*); a captain of Skanda (*M. Bh.*); a viśvadeva; the Śravaṇa asterism; the 14th Jaina Arhat; another name for Brahmā, Viṣṇu, Śiva, Kṛṣṇa, Balarāma, Seṣa, Vāsuki and the Supreme Spirit; the Arabian Manna plant (*Alhagi camelorum*); the *Gloriosa Superba* creeper; Couch grass (*Cynodon dactylon*); the *Ichnocarpus frutescens* shrub.

**Anantaćāritra** (S) (M) 1. with eternal character. 2. one who is all pervading, eternal, divine. 3. a Bodhisattva (*B. Literature*)

**Anantadeva** (S) (M) 1. immortal deity. 3. a king of Kāśmira (*R. Taraṅginī*)

**Anantaguṇa** (S) (M) with infinite virtues.

**Anantajit** (S) (M) 1. always victorious. 3. a Jaina Arhat (*J. S. Koṣa)*

**Anantalakṣmī** (S) (F) 1. eternal Lakṣmī. 2. eternally fortunate.

**Anantamati** (S) (M) 1. with an infinite mind; one whose mind is boundless; all pervading. 2. a god. 3. a Bodhisattva.

**Anantanāga** (S) (M) 1. infinite mountain. 2. a very tall mountain. 3. one of the 8 cobras worn by Śiva (*Ś. Purāṇa*)

**Anantanātha** (S) (M) 1. eternal lord; lord of Ananta or Śeṣa the 1000 headed serpent; eternal; divine. 3. the 14th Jaina Tirthankara who was the son of King Siṁhasena and Sujaśā of Ayodhyā (*J.S. Koṣa*); another name for Viṣṇu.

**Anantarāma** (S) (M) ever pleasing.

**Anantarūpa** (S) (M) 1. innumerable forms. 3. another name for Viṣṇu.

**Anantaśakti** (S) (M) 1. of boundless power. 3. another name for the Supreme Spirit.

**Anantaśayan** (S) (M) 1. one who sleeps on the serpent Śeśa. 3. another name for Viṣṇu.

**Anantaśirṣā** (S) (F) 1. with an immortal mind. 2. eternal; divine. 3. Vāsuki's wife.

**Anantaśrī** (S) (M) 1. of boundless magnificence. 3. another name for the Supreme Being.

**Anantavarman** (S) (M) 1. possessed with supreme power. 3. another name for the Supreme Spirit.

**Anantavatān** (S) (M) 1. an endless stretch. 3. one of Brahmā's 4 feet.

**Anantavijaya** (S) (M) 1. endless victory. 2. never defeated. 3. Yudhiṣṭhira's conchshell (*M. Bh.*)

**Anantavikrama** (S) (M) 1. with eternal valour. 3. a Bodhisattva.

**Anantavīrya** (S) (M) 1. with infinite energy. 3. the 23rd Jaina Arhat of a future age (*J. S. Koṣa*)

**Anantyā** (S) (F) 1. endless. 2. eternal; divine; a god.

**Ānantya** (S) (M) 1. endless. 2. eternal; divine; a god.

**Ananyā** (S) (F) 1. without a second. 2. sole; unique; peerless.

**Ananyaja** (S) (M) 1. unique son. 3. another name for Kāma.

**Anāpāna** (S) (M) 1. unattained; cannot be competed with. 3. a son of Aṅga (*M. Bh.*)

**Anapāya** (S) (M) 1. without obstacle. 2. prosperous. 3. another name for Śiva.

**Anapāyaćola** (S) (M) 1. prosperous; Ćola king. 3. a king of Ćola (11th century A.D.) (*Bhā. Purāṇa*)

**Anaraṇya** (S) (M) 1. possessor of eternal power. 3. a king of Ayodhyā and the father of Pṛthu who cursed Rāvaṇa to die at the hands of Rāma (*Br. Purāṇa*)

**Anargha** (S) (M) priceless.

**Anari** (S) (M) enemy less.

**Anarśani** (S) (M) 1. injuring. 3. an asura killed by Indra (*Ṛg Veda*)

**Ānarta** (S) (M) 1. stage; theatre. 2. a king 3. the son of Śaryāti and the grandson of Vaivasvata Manu (*Br. Purāṇa*)

**Anarva** (S) (M) irresistable.

**Anarvaṇa** (S) (M) 1. uncovering; manifesting. 3. another name for Pūṣan, the lord of endowment and enlightenment.

**Anāśa** (S) (M) 1. indestructible; undivided;

sky; the Supreme Being. 3. a brother of Akrūra (*Bhā. Purāṇa*)

**Anāśaya** (S) (M) 1. without any self interest. 2. selfless.

**Anāśin** (S) (M) indestructible; imperishable.

**Anāśu** (S) (M) imperishable; indestructible.

**Anasūri** (S) (M) 1. not unwise. 2. active; alert; energetic; intelligent.

**Anasuyā** (S) (F) 1. without spite or envy. 3. a daughter of Kardama and Devahutī, the wife of ṛṣi Atri, the mother of Dattatreya, Durvāsas and Ćandra (*V. Purāṇa*), who after practising great austerities found miraculous powers and irrigated the earth with the water of the Gaṅgā after a drought (*M. Bh.*); a friend of Śakuntalā (*K. Granthāvali*); a daughter of Dakṣa (*M. Bh.*)

**Anaśvan** (S) (M) 1. without any horses. 3. father of Parīkṣit (*M. Bh.*)

**Anaśvara** (S) (M) imperishable.

**Anaśya** (S) (M) 1. indestructible. 3. husband of Amṛtā (*M. Bh.*)

**Anatā** (S) (F) 1. not bent. 3. a daughter of Atri and Anasuyā and the mother of fruit (*M. Bh.*)

**Anāthapiṇḍa** (S) (M) 1. one who feeds the poor. 3. merchant in whose garden Sākyamuni instructed his disciples (*B. Literature*)

**Ānati** (S) (F) 1. bent. 2. modest; respectful; humble.

**Anaupamyā** (S) (F) 1. without comparison. 2. unique; peerless. 3. wife of Bāṇāsura (*P. Purāṇa*)

**Anava** (S) (M) 1. humane. 2. kind to men. 3. a seer of the 3rd Manvantara (*Br. Purāṇa*)

**Anavadyā** (S) (F) 1. faultless. 3. an apsarā.

**Anavaratha** (S) (M) 1. with an eternal chariot. 3. a son of Madhu and father of Kuruvatsa (*V. Purāṇa*)

**Anavatapta** (S) (M) 1. without heat; without jealousy; without disease; without agony. 3. a nāga king (*B. Literature*); a lake (*V. Rāmāyaṇa*)

**Ānavī** (S) (F) 1. humane. 2. kind to people.

**Anāyuṣā** (S) (F) 1. with a short life. 3. mother of Bala and Vṛtta (*Bhā. Purāṇa*)

**Añćala** (S) (M) part; valley; hamlet; the pallu of a sari.

**Aṇḍaja** (S) (M) 1. born of the egg. 3. another name for Brahmā.

**Aṇḍajeśvara** (S) (M) 1. lord of the eggborn. 3. another name for Garuḍa the king of birds and the vehicle of lord Viṣṇu.

**Āṇḍaka** (S) (M) 1. egg; of an egg. 3. a daitya.

**Aṇḍalā** (T) (F) 1. eggless; partless; petalless 2. whole; perfect. 3. a Tamil poetess of the Bhakti cult and adopted daughter of Periyalvar.

**Andha** (S) (M) 1. blind; dark. 3. a son of Kaśyapa and Kadru (*M. Bh.*)

**Andhaka** (S) (M) 1. blind; lawless. 3. an asura son of Kaśyapa and Diti (*M. Bh.*); a king of the Yadu dynasty and ancestor of Kṛṣṇa (*Bhāgavatā*); an asura son of Śiva and foster son of Hiraṇyākṣa later incarnated as Bhṛngi the head of the asura army (*Vām. Purāṇa*)

**Andhakāghatī** (S) (M) 1. destroyer of Andhaka. 3. another name for Śiva.

**Andhakanipātī** (S) (M) 1. descending on Andhaka. 3. another name for Śiva.

**Andhakāri** (S) (M) 1. enemy of Andhaka. 2. who fights against injustice; ignorance; who stands for all that is fair; correct and just; who is for knowledge and enlightenment. 3. another name for Śiva.

**Andhakaripu** (S) (M) 1. slayer of the asura Andhaka. 3. another name for Śiva.

**Andhakavṛṣṇinātha** (S) (M) 1. lord of the descendants of Andhaka and Vṛṣṇi. 3. another name for Kṛṣṇa.

**Āndhraka** (S) (M) 1. belonging to Āndhra. 3. an Āndhra king who was a member of the Indraprastha court (*M. Bh.*)

**Aṇḍikā** (S) (F) elder sister.

**Androṣa** (S) (M) introverted.

**Anekalaćana** (S) (M) 1. with several eyes. 2. all-seeing; at all times. 3. another name for Śiva.

**Anekakṛta** (S) (M) 1. doing much. 2. creating things. 3. another name for Śiva.

**Anenas** (S) (M) 1. blameless; sinless. 3. a lunar dynasty king who was the son of Āyus and father of Śuddha (*Ṛg Veda*); an Ikṣvāku king who was the son of Kakutstha

(*Bhā. Purāṇa*)

**Anenasya** (S) (M) 1. freedom from sin. 2. chaste; pious; pure.

**Aṅga** (S) (M) 1. limb. 3. a son of Ulmuka and husband of Sunīthā (*M. Bh.*); a lunar dynasty king who was the son of Bali and Sudeṣṇā and father of Veṇa (*Bhā. Purāṇa*)

**Aṅgabhū** (S) (M) 1. born of the limbs. 2. a son.

**Aṅgada** (S) (M) 1. bestower of limbs; with beautiful limbs. 2. armlet. 3. a monkey son of Tārā and Vāli considered to have been the reincarnation of Bṛhaspati and appointed by Rāma as king of Kiṣkindha (*U. Rāmāyaṇa*); a son of Lakṣmaṇa and Ūrmilā (*V. Rāmāyaṇa*); an elephant of the south; a warrior etc.

**Aṅgajā** (S) (F) 1. born of the body. 2. a daughter.

**Aṅgaja** (S) (M) 1. produced from the body. 2. a son; ornamental love. 3. another name for Kāma.

**Aṅgālamma** (S) (F) 1. mother with a form. 3. wife of Vīrabhadra who hauls up the spirits of the dead; an idol of goddess Ambā.

**Aṅgama** (S) (M) 1. that which cannot be pierced. 2. strong; with high integrity.

**Aṅganā** (S) (F) 1. with a beautiful form; a beautiful woman. 2. the zodiac sign of Virgo.

**Aṅganemi** (S) (M) follower of the scriptures.

**Aṅgāra** (S) (M) 1. burning charcoal. 3. a king of the maruts (*H. Purāṇa*); another name for the planet Mars (*M. Bh.*)

**Aṅgarāja** (S) (M) 1. best among beings with a form; king of Aṅga. 2. most handsome. 3. another name for Karṇa.

**Aṅgārakā** (S) (M) 1. charcoal; the planet Mars. 3. an asura who was the father of Aṅgarāvatī (*K. Sāgara*); a descendant of King Jayādratha of Sauvīra (*M. Bh.*); one of the 108 sons of the sun (*M. Bh.*); a rudra (*Ś. Purāṇa*)

**Aṅgāraparṇa** (S) (M) 1. with charcoal wings. 2. Chlerodendron siphonanthus. 3. another name for the gandharva king Ćitraratha.

**Aṅgāras** (S) (M) 1. charcoal. 3. a marut; another name for Mars.

**Aṅgārasetu** (S) (M) 1. destroyer of fire; one who destroys the invincible. 3. the father of Gāndhāra (*M. Bh.*)

**Aṅgāravatī** (S) (F) 1. having fire. 2. that which is hot, destructive and unperishable. 3. a daughter of the asura Angāraka, and mother of Gopālaka, Pālaka and Vāsavadattā who married King Udayana (*K. Sāgara*)

**Āṅgāriṣṭha** (S) (M) 1. one who exists in burning charcoal; knower of the word; with a delicate body. 3. a king of Bhārata (*M. Bh.*)

**Aṅgāritā** (S) (F) 1. a luminous plant; blossom of the Kiṇśuka tree (*Butefrondosa*). 3. a river (*A. Koṣa*)

**Aṅgasvāmi** (S) (M) 1. lord of limbs. 2. who has mastered his body; strong and powerful.

**Aṅgati** (S) (M) 1. one who maintains the sacred fire. 3. another name for Brahmā and Viṣṇu.

**Aṅgavāha** (S) (M) 1. bearer of scriptures. 3. a Vṛṣṇi dynasty king (*M. Bh.*)

**Aṅgeśvara** (S) (M) 1. lord of Aṅga. 3. another name for Karṇa.

**Aṅghāri** (S) (M) 1. enemy of sin. 3. a celestial guard of the Soma.

**Aṅgirā** (S) (F) 1. of indescribable form. 2. celestial; divine. 3. mother of Bṛhaspati (*Mu. Upaniṣad*)

**Aṅgiras** (S) (M) 1. knows the essence of the parts. 2. a knower of Vedāngas or parts of the Vedas; knower of the scriptures. 3. a ṛṣi who was one of the 10 prajāpati sons of Brahmā, born from his mouth, considered a Saptarṣi of the 1st Manvantara, he had several wives of which the more prominent were Śubhā, Smṛtī, Śraddhā, Devasenā and Vasudhā, his prominent sons included Agni, Saṁvarta, Bṛhaspati, Utathya, Sudhanvā and Savya who was an incarnation of Indra, notable among his daughters were Sinīvālī, Kuhū, Rākā, Anumatī, Rāgā, Bhānumatī, Arćiṣmatī, Haviṣmatī, Mahiṣmatī and Mahāmatī and in astronomy he is a star in Ursa major (*M. Bh.*)

**Āṅgirasa** (S) (M) 1. of Aṅgiras. 3. another name for Ćyavana and Bṛhaspati.

**Aṅgoṣin** (S) (M) 1. resonant; praiseworthy. 3. Soma.

**Aṅgśu** (S) (M) with beautiful limbs.

**Aṅgula** (S) (M) 1. finger; thumb; a finger's breadth. 3. another name for Ćāṇakya.

**Aṅgurī** (S) (F) finger; finger ring.

**Āṅgūṣa** (S) (M) 1. praising. 2. a hymn.

**Aṅhati** (S) (F) gift.

**Aṅhiti** (S) (F) gift; donation.

**Anhu** (S) (M) 1. imperishable, invincible. 3. an asura killed by Indra (*Ṛg Veda*)

**Aniha** (S) (M) 1. indifferent. 3. a king of Ayodhyā (*M. Bh.*)

**Anīka** (S) (M) army; front; head, face; splendour, brilliance; form.

**Anīkavidāraṇa** (S) (M) 1. slayer of the army. 2. a warrior. 3. a brother of King Jayadratha of Sindhu (*M. Bh.*)

**Aniketa** (S) (M) 1. homeless. 2. to whom the entire world is home. 3. a yakṣa who became king of the Aṅga dynasty (*A. Purāṇa*)

**Anīla** (S) (M) 1. not blue, fair. 3. a serpent mentioned in the *Ādi Parva*.

**Anila** (S) (M) 1. wind; the god of wind. 3. one of the 8 vasus and son of Dharma and Śvasā, (*Vā. Purāṇa*) the husband of Śivā and father of Manojava and Avijña (*M. Bh.*); a son of Garuḍa (*M. Bh.*); the lunar asterism of Svāti (*P. Samhita*); another name for Viṣṇu and Śiva.

**Anīlābha** (S) (M) not of blue hue; zephyr; fair; bright; white; shining.

**Anilātmaja** (S) (M) 1. son of the wind. 2. strong; swift. 3. another name for Hanumān and Bhīma.

**Anīlavājin** (S) (M) 1. with white horses. 3. another name for Arjuna.

**Ānili** (S) (M) 1. descendant of Anila. 3. another name for Hanumān and Bhīma.

**Animān** (S) (M) 1. immense; unbounded. 2. beyond any boundary; limitless; all pervading; divine.

**Animeṣa** (S) (M) 1. unwinking. 2. vigilant; never tired; all seeing; a god.

**Animiṣa** (S) (M) 1. unwinking. 2. a god. 3. a son of Garuḍa (*M. Bh.*); another name for Śiva and Viṣṇu.

**Animiṣācārya** (S) (M) 1. preceptor of the gods. 3. another name for Bṛhaspati.

**Anina** (S) (M) small.

**Anindā** (S) (F) irreproachable.

**Anindata** (S) (M) who does not speak ill of others; who is not spoken ill of.

**Anindinī** (S) (F) who does not speak ill of others; who is not spoken ill of.

**Aninditā** (S) (F) 1. who is never spoken ill of. 2. virtuous; irreproachable; venerated.

**Anindyā** (S) (F) beyond reproach.

**Anirbāṇa** (S) (M) 1. unextinguished. 2. never dies; immortal; a god.

**Anirjita** (S) (M) unconquered.

**Aniruddha** (S) (M) 1. unobstructed; unopposed. 3. son of Pradyumna and grandson of Kṛṣṇa, the husband of Ūṣā and father of Vajra, a part incarnation of Brahmā and Viṣṇu (*Bhāgavata*); an Arhat and contemporary of Śākyamuni (*J. S. Koṣa*); a Vṛṣṇi (*M. Bh.*)

**Anirviṇa** (S) (M) 1. not weary; not downcast. 2. active; energetic; progressive. 3. another name for Viṣṇu.

**Aniśā** (S) (F) without night; nightless.

**Anīśa** (S) (M) 1. without a superior; paramount; supreme. 3. another name for Viṣṇu.

**Anīśvara** (S) (M) 1. without a superior; paramount. 3. the Supreme Spirit.

**Anita** (S) (M) (F) 1. without guile; not driven. 2. a leader.

**Anitābhā** (S) (P) 1. with guileless charm. 3. a *Ṛg Veda* river.

**Aniteja** (S) (M) of immeasurable splendour.

**Anivartin** (S) (M) 1. does not retreat. 2. brave. 3. another name for Viṣṇu and the Supreme Being.

**Añjaka** (S) (M) 1. decorated; anointed. 3. a son of Vipracitti (*V. Purāṇa*)

**Añjalī** (S) (M) 1. anointed; polished. 2. honoured; received respectfully. 3. a sage and colleague of Śaunaka (*Bhāgavata*)

**Añjali** (S) (M) 1. cupped palms. 2. one who reveres, offers salutations, respects, is humble, modest; mark of respect; the folding of hands to make a hollow for offering oblations to a god, a deity.

**Añjalika** (S) (M) 1. bearer of cupped arrows. 3. one of Arjuna's arrows (*M. Bh.*)

**Añjami** (S) (M) 1. not black. 2. nightless; glorious; bright, illuminating.

**Añjanā** (S) (F) 1. collyrium coloured. 2. grey; swarthy; dusky. 3. daughter of the monkey King Kuñjara and wife of Kesarī (*Br. Purāṇa*); mother of Hanumān through Vāyu, and incarnation of apsara Puñjikāsthalā (*Rāmāyaṇa*)

**Añjana** (S) (M) 1. collyrium. 2. grey in complexion. 3. a fabulous serpent (*Bhāgavata*); elephant of the southwest quarter (*Br. Purāṇa*); a mountain; son of Kṛti and father of Kurujit (*V. Purāṇa*)

**Añjanam** (S) (F) collyrium; paint used as a cosmetic; lampblack; antimony; night; fire.

**Añjanaparvan** (S) (M) 1. part of night; part of fire; bearer of power. 3. a son of Ghaṭotkaća and grandson of Bhīma (*M. Bh.*)

**Añjanavatī** (S) (M) 1. one who has applied collyrium to her eyes. 3. female elephant of the northeast quarter.

**Āñjaneya** (S) (M) 1. of Añjana; son of Añjanā. 2. powerful; fiery. 3. another name for Hanumān.

**Anjañi** (S) (M) 1. son of Anjañā. 3. another name for Hanumān; the Ironwood tree (*Memecylon umbellatum*)

**Añjanīnandana** (S) (M) 1. son of Añjanā. 3. another name for Hanumān.

**Añjasa** (S) (M) 1. not dark. 2. guileless; deceitless; straightforward; honest.

**Añjasī** (S) (F) 1. not dark; not crooked. 2. honest; upright; deceitless. 3. a celestial river (*Ṛg Veda*)

**Añjī** (S) (F) a blessing; who blesses.

**Añjika** (S) (M) 1. blessed; collyrium coloured. 2. black; dark. 3. a son of Yadu (*Bhāgavata*); son of Vipraćittī (*V. Purāṇa*)

**Añjinī** (S) (F) blessed.

**Añjiṣṇu** (S) (M) 1. who eats up darkness. 2. removes darkness; one who shines; is brilliant; illuminating; highly brilliant. 3. another name for the sun.

**Añjiṣṭha** (S) (M) 1. highly brilliant. 3. another name for the sun.

**Añjuli** (S) (M) revered; worshipped.

**Aṅkalammā** (S) (F) 1. goddess with an auspiciously marked body. 3. another name for the goddess Śītaladevī.

**Aṅkati** (S) (M) 1. wind; fire. 2. a Brahmin who maintains the sacred fire. 3. another name for Brahmā.

**Aṇkitā** (S) (F) with auspicious marks.

**Aṇkolikā** (S) (F) 1. an embrace. 2. who personifies love; affection; respect.

**Aṇkolita** (S) (M) who has been embraced; loved; accepted; respected.

**Aṇkura** (S) (M) sprout; shoot; blade; newborn.

**Aṇkuśī** (S) (F) 1. one who exercises restraint. 3. one of the 24 Jaina goddesses.

**Anna** (S) (M) 1. grain. 3. grain which in a mystical sense is considered the coarsest envelope of Viṣṇu, the Supreme Spirit; earth and water.

**Annabhuj** (S) (M) 1. who eats grain. 3. Śiva to whom edible grain is offered as an oblation.

**Annabrahman** (S) (M) Brahmā as represented by food.

**Annadā** (S) (F) 1. one who gives food. 3. another name for Durgā.

**Annada** (S) (M) 1. one who grants food. 3. another name for Śiva.

**Annadeva** (S) (M) lord of food.

**Annalakṣmī** (S) (F) 1. who bestows grain; giver of grain. 3. another name for Lakṣmī.

**Annāmallai** (S) (M) 1. lord of the mountains. 3. another name for Śiva.

**Annamaya** (S) (M) 1. full of food. 2. free from disease; healthy; prosperous.

**Annammā** (Kannada) (F) goddess of food.

**Annapati** (S) (M) 1. lord of food. 3. another name for Savitṛ, Agni and Śiva.

**Annapatnī** (S) (F) goddess of food.

**Annapūrṇā** (S) (F) 1. one who bestows food to the fullest. 3. a goddess who is a form of Durgā (*D. Bhāgavata*)

**Annī** (S) (F) shortened name for Annapurṇā.

**Anniśvarī** (S) (F) 1. goddess of food. 3. Bhairavī, a fearsome form of Durgā.

**Anogopta** (S) (M) 1. not hidden. 2. well-known. 3. a viśvadeva (*M. Bh.*)

**Anokhī** (S) (F) unique; unparalleled.

**Anomā** (S) (F) 1. illustrious. 3. a river (*H. Koṣa*)

**Anṛta** (S) (M) 1. lie; falsehood. 3. a son of

Adharma and Himsā (*V. Purāṇa*)

**Anṛtām** (S) (F) 1. lie. 3. a daughter of Adharma and Hiṁsā and mother of Bhaya and Naraka (*A. Purāṇa*)

**Aṅśa** (S) (M) 1. a share; a part; a day. 3. a sage who was the son of Aditi, one of the 12 ādityas who represents luck in gaining wealth (*M. Bh.*); a king of the Manu dynasty (*M. Bh.*)

**Anśaka** (S) (M) 1. has a share in the property. 2. an heir.

**Ansala** (S) (M) lusty; strong.

**Aṅśala** (S) (M) 1. has a share in the property. 2. an heir.

**Aṅśānśa** (S) (M) 1. part of a part. 2. a minute part; that which is subtle; part incarnation of a deity.

**Aṅśarin** (S) (M) 1. has a share in the property. 2. an heir.

**Aṅśin** (S) (M) 1. has a share in the property. 2. an heir.

**Aṅśrutā** (S) (F) 1. unheard of; unique; whose fame is pearless. 3. wife of Aṅgiras (*M. Bh.*)

**Aṅśrutas** (S) (M) 1. not famous. 3. a son of Kṛṣṇa (*Bhāgavata*); a son of Dyutimat (*M. Bh.*)

**Aṅśu** (S) (M) 1. a ray; filament of the Soma plant; a minute particle; a sunbeam; beam of light; lustre; splendour; brilliance; embellishment; speed. 3. a sage; a protégé of the aśvins in the *Ṛg Veda*.

**Aṅśubāṇa** (S) (M) 1. with rays for arrows. 2. the sun.

**Aṅśudhara** (S) (M) 1. bearer of rays. 3. another name for the sun.

**Aṅśujala** (S) (M) 1. a collection of rays. 2. a blaze of light; brilliant; illuminating; enlightening.

**Aṅśuka** (S) (M) 1. leaf; ray. 2. tender; bright; illuminating; enlightening.

**Aṅśula** (S) (M) 1. radiant; luminous. 2. enlightening; bright. 3. another name for Cāṇakya.

**Aṅśumālā** (S) (F) 1. a garland of rays; a halo. 2. as glorious as the sun.

**Aṅśumālin** (S) (M) 1. garlanded with rays. 2. the sun.

**Aṅśumān** (S) (M) 1. bearer of rays. 2. the sun; the moon; radiant; illuminating; enlightening. 3. a solar dynasty king who was the son of Asamañjas and father of Bhagiratha and Dilīpa (*V. Rāmāyaṇa*); a king of Bhoja who fought on the side of the Pāṇḍavas (*M. Bh.*)

**Anśumat** (S) (M) 1. bearer of rays. 2. luminous; radiant. 3. son of Asamañjas and grandson of Sagara; another name for the sun and moon.

**Anśumatī** (S) (F) 1. bearer of rays. 2. resplendent; glorious; wise. 3. daughter of the gandharva King Dramila (*A. Koṣa*); another name for the Yamunā river (*Bhāgavata*); a shrub (*Desmodium gangeticum*)

**Anśupati** (S) (M) 1. lord of rays. 2. the sun.

**Anśusvāmi** (S) (M) 1. lord of rays. 2. the sun.

**Anśuvāṇa** (S) (M) 1. with rays for arrows. 3. another name for the sun.

**Āntaka** (S) (M) 1. one who causes the end. 2. Yama (lord of death). 3. a rajaṛṣi (*Ṛg Veda*)

**Antakaripu** (S) (M) 1. enemy of Antaka. 3. another name for Śiva.

**Antama** (S) (M) 1. without darkness; next. 2. nearest; intimate.

**Antara** (S) (M) 1. near; related; intimate; interior; soul; heart; surety; guarantee. 3. father of Suyajña (*H. Purāṇa*)

**Antardhāna** (S) (M) 1. with divine insight. 3. a son of King Aṅsa of the Manu dynasty and father of Havirdhāna (*M. Bh.*); a son of Pṛthu (*V. Purāṇa*); a weapon of Kubera (*M. Bh.*)

**Antardhī** (S) (M) 1. with inner perception. 3. a son of Emperor Pṛthu (*A. Purāṇa*)

**Antarhitātman** (S) (M) 1. with a concealed mind; whose mind is deeply concerned for the general welfare; whose soul cannot be read. 3. another name for Śiva.

**Antarikṣa** (S) (M) 1. space; outer space; sky. 3. a son of Murāsura killed by Kṛṣṇa (*Bhāgavata*); a king the son of Ṛṣabha and grandson of Nābhi (*Bhāgavata*)

**Antarjyotiṣ** (S) (M) with an illuminated soul.

**Antarvedī** (S) (M) 1. dwelling in an area that lies between 2 rivers. 2. dwelling in the sacred area between the Gaṅgā and Yamunā rivers.

**Anti** (S) (M) nearness; living in a sacred area; living in a hermitage.

**Antideva** (S) (M) 1. near the gods. 2. spiritual; virtuous.

**Āntikā** (S) (F) elder sister.

**Antinī** (S) (F) living in a hermitage.

**Āntya** (S) (M) who accomplishes (personified as Bhauvana)

**Ānu** (S) (M) living; human.

**Anu** (S) (M) 1. follower. 3. a son of Yayāti and Śarmiṣṭhā.

**Aṇu** (S) (M) 1. minute; an atom. 2. subtle; divine. 3. a son of Digbhraja and husband of Kīrti the daughter of Śuka and Pīvarī (*D. Bhāgavata*); another name for Śiva.

**Anubhā** (S) (F) one who follows glory.

**Aṇubhā** (S) (F) lightning.

**Anubhaj** (S) (M) 1. one who follows worship. 2. spiritual.

**Anubhava** (S) (M) experience; perception.

**Anubhāvya** (S) (M) 1. known through experience. 2. divine truth.

**Anubodha** (S) (M) 1. after thought; reviving the scent of an old perfume. 2. recollection.

**Anućakra** (S) (M) 1. who works according to schedule. 2. organized; punctual; planned. 3. an attendant given to Skanda by Prajāpati Tvaṣṭā (*M. Bh.*)

**Anūćānā** (S) (F) 1. devoted to learning; well behaved. 3. an apsarā (*M. Bh.*)

**Anūćāna** (S) (M) well versed in the Vedas; devoted to learning.

**Anudāra** (S) (M) 1. mean; dishonest. 3. a son of Dhṛtarāṣṭra (*M. Bh.*)

**Anudātta** (S) (M) 1. not raised; not elevated; neutral. 3. a son created by Pāñćajanya (*M. Bh.*)

**Anudeśya** (S) (M) 1. obedient. 2. one who proceeds towards the goal.

**Anudruhyu** (S) (M) 1. follower of motion. 3. a son of Yayāti and Śarmiṣṭhā (*A. Purāṇa*)

**Aṇudrutta** (S) (M) 1. with subtle movement. 2. swift; all pervading; divine.

**Anudvega** (S) (M) free from anxiety.

**Anugā** (S) (F) 1. one who follows behind. 2. a companion. 3. an apsarā (*Bhāgavata*)

**Anugāyas** (S) (M) praised in hymns.

**Anugītā** (S) (F) after song; overtly praised.

**Anugra** (S) (M) 1. not violent. 2. gentle; mild; peace loving; pacifist.

**Anugraha** (S) (M) 1. favour; kindness. 3. the 5th incarnation of Viṣṇu (*V. Purāṇa*)

**Anugya** (S) (M) authority.

**Anuha** (S) (M) 1. without desire. 2. satisfied; contented; tranquil; at peace. 3. a son of Vibhrāja and father of Brahmadatta (*M. Bh.*) (*K. Sāgara*)

**Anuhlāda** (S) (M) 1. who seeks pleasure. 3. a son of Hiraṇyakaṣipu and brother of Prahlāda (*V. Purāṇa*)

**Anuhrāda** (S) (M) 1. following the heart. 3. a son of Hiraṇyakaṣipu (*H. Purāṇa*)

**Anūhu** (S) (M) 1. without desire. 3. an ancient king (*M. Bh.*)

**Anujā** (S) (M) 1. the later born. 2. younger sister.

**Anuja** (S) (M) 1. born later. 2. younger brother.

**Anujyeṣṭha** (S) (M) next to the eldest.

**Anukā** (S) (F) 1. one who follows the earth; backbone; spine; follows the principles of nature; who supports. 3. an apsarā (*Ś. Brāhmaṇa*)

**Ānūka** (S) (M) 1. lying close to. 2. ornament; jewel.

**Anukānkṣā** (S) (F) desire; wish.

**Anukarman** (S) (M) 1. a subsequent action. 3. a viśvadeva (*M. Bh.*)

**Anukarṣa** (S) (M) invoking; summoning by incantation.

**Anūkāśa** (S) (M) reflection of light.

**Anukroṣa** (S) (M) 1. not harsh. 2. tenderness; compassion.

**Anukūla** (S) (M) agreeable; favourably disposed.

**Anulā** (S) (F) 1. not wild. 2. gentle; agreeable. 3. a female Arhat or Buddhist saint (*B. Literature*); a river in Kaśmira (*R. Tarangiṇī*)

**Anulekhā** (S) (F) one who follows destiny.

**Anulī** (S) (F) 1. homage. 2. respected; respectful.

**Anumatī** (S) (F) 1. assent; sanction. 3. approval personified as a goddess (*Ṛg Veda, A. Veda*); the 15th day of the moon personified as a daughter of Aṅgiras and Smṛtī (*V. Purāṇa*); a goddess who is invoked to bestow wealth, inspiration, offspring and longevity (*Bhāgavata*); a goddess present at the time of Skanda's crown-ceremony (*M. Bh.*)

**Anumita** (S) (M) 1. logically established. 2. analytical; precise.

**Anumloćā** (S) (F) 1. very flexible. 2. agreeable. 3. an apsarā (*Purāṇas*)

**Anumodana** (S) (M) approbation; pleasing; causing pleasure.

**Anumoditā** (S) (F) 1. pleased. 2. delighted; applauded.

**Anūnā** (S) (F) 1. not inferior. 2. superior; entire; whole. 3. an apsarā (*H. Purāṇa*)

**Anūna** (S) (M) 1. not inferior. 2. not less; superior; whole; entire.

**Anūnavarćas** (S) (M) full of splendour.

**Anunāyikā** (S) (F) 1. submissive. 2. humble; modest.

**Anunīta** (S) (F) 1. disciplined; obtained. 2. respected; learned; wise.

**Anunīti** (S) (F) 1. supplication. 2. courtesy.

**Anūpa** (S) (M) 1. unequalled; abounding in water. 2. unique. 3. a pond; bank of river; a ṛṣi.

**Anupallavī** (S) (F) 1. like a petal. 2. that which is young; tender; soft; fragrant.

**Anupamā** (S) (F) 1. matchless. 2. peerless; unique; rare. 3. the elephant of the southwest quarter (*Br. Purāṇa*)

**Anupama** (S) (M) 1. incomparable. 2. matchless; rare; precious; ginger (*Zingiber officinale*)

**Aṇupati** (S) (M) 1. lord of the atom; lord of the subtle. 3. another name for Kārtavīrya (*M. Bh.*)

**Anuprabhā** (S) (F) followed by glory.

**Anupradāna** (S) (M) gift; donation.

**Anuprakha** (S) (M) that which pierces.

**Anupriyā** (S) (M) (F) beloved; very dear.

**Anūpya** (S) (M) matchless; incomparable.

**Anurādhā** (S) (F) 1. who bestows welfare. 3. the 17th lunar asterism.

**Anūrādha** (S) (M) who bestows happiness and welfare; born under the Anurādhā asterism.

**Anurāga** (S) (M) attachment; affection; love; passion; red colour.

**Anurāgin** (S) (M) inducing love.

**Anuraj** (S) (M) 1. devoted. 2. beloved; attracted.

**Anurāj** (S) (M) 1. to be brilliant. 2. illuminating; enlightening.

**Anurakti** (S) (F) devotion; affection; love.

**Anurañjana** (S) (M) 1. satisfying. 2. who pleases; who induces attachment; who is loved.

**Anurañjita** (S) (M) pacified; reconciled; satisfied.

**Anuratha** (S) (M) 1. following the chariot. 2. a soldier. 3. a son of Kuruvatsa and father of Puruhotra (*V. Purāṇa*)

**Anurati** (S) (F) love; affection; attachment.

**Anurimā** (S) (F) attached; fond of.

**Anurodha** (S) (M) request.

**Anūrū** (S) (M) 1. thighless. 3. the dawn that precedes Sūrya and is personified as Aruṇa, the charioteer of the sun who is visualized without legs.

**Anuruć** (S) (M) 1. to one's taste. 2. who is liked; interesting; chosen; preferred.

**Anuruddha** (S) (M) 1. soothed; pacified. 3. a cousin of Śākyamuni (*B. Literature*)

**Anurudha** (S) (M) who obeys.

**Anurūpa** (S) (M) 1. one that follows the form. 2. in shape; compatible; agreeable; suitable.

**Anuśā** (S) (M) 1. following desires. 2. seeks desires.

**Anusara** (S) (F) 1. full of desires. 3. a rākṣasa (*M. Bh.*).

**Anuśikha** (S) (M) 1. crested. 2. decorated, embellished; respected. 3. the priest at the snake festival (*P. Brāhmaṇa*)

**Anuṣṇā** (S) (F) 1. not hot. 2. cool; soothing; pacifying. 3. a river (*M. Bh.*); the Blue Lotus (*Nymphaea stellata*)

**Anuśobhin** (S) (M) 1. shining; follows grace. 2. graceful; glorious; dignified; illuminating; enlightening.

**Anuśobhinī** (S) (F) 1. shining; follows grace.

2. bright; dignified; illuminating.

**Anuśrī** (S) (F) glorious; famous.

**Anuśruta** (S) (M) well-known; much heard of; handed down by Vedic tradition.

**Anuśrutaśravas** (S) (M) 1. with Vedic fame, with unparalleled fame. 3. a son of Somāli (*V. Purāṇa*)

**Anuṣṭup** (S) (M) 1. metre; hymn; invocation; praise. 3. an 8 syllabic metre; one of the 7 horses of Sūrya (*V. Purāṇa*)

**Anutaptā** (S) (F) 1. heated; filled with regret. 3. a river (*V. Purāṇa*)

**Anutoṣa** (S) (M) gratification; relief.

**Anutta** (S) (M) invincible.

**Anuttama** (S) (M) 1. having no superior. 2. unsurpassed; highest; best. 3. another name for Viṣṇu and Śiva.

**Anuvāha** (S) (M) 1. following; carrying. 3. one of the 7 tongues of fire.

**Anuvās** (S) (M) to make fragrant.

**Anuvindā** (S) (F) 1. one who finds or discovers. 3. a wife of Kṛṣṇa (*P. Purāṇa*)

**Anuvinda** (S) (M) 1. one who discovers or obtains; one who strives for success. 3. a king of Ujjain (*K. Sāgara*); a son of Dhṛtarāṣṭra (*M. Bh.*); a prince of Avantī, the brother of Kṛṣṇa's wife Mitravindā who fought on the side of the Kauravas (*Bhāgavata*); a Kekaya prince who fought on the side of the Kauravas (*M. Bh.*)

**Anuvitta** (S) (M) found; obtained.

**Anuvrata** (S) (M) 1. devoted; faithful; attached. 3. son of Satyakarman.

**Anuvrindā** (S) (F) 1. surrounded by a crowd. 2. with many friends; moving in a group. 3. a queen of Kṛṣṇa (*Bhāgavata*)

**Anuyātri** (S) (M) follower; a companion.

**Anuyāyin** (S) (M) 1. follower. 3. a son of Dhṛtarāṣṭra (*M. Bh.*)

**Anvāgabhānu** (S) (M) 1. following the sun. 3. a Purū king who was the son of Manasyu and Misrakeśī (*M. Bh.*)

**Anvākṛti** (S) (F) 1. shaping after. 2. one who imitates.

**Anvitā** (S) (F) reached by the mind; connected with; linked to; understood.

**Anviti** (S) (F) following after.

**Anyā** (S) (F) inexhaustible.

**Anyanga** (S) (M) 1. spotless. 2. flawless; pure; virtuous; divine.

**Anyūna** (S) (M) 1. not defective. 2. healthy; whole; entire; complete.

**Āpa** (S) (M) 1. water. 3. one of the 8 vasus and father of Vaitanda, Śrama, Śānta and Svāni (*V. Purāṇa*); a seer of the 10th Manvantara (*Vā. Purāṇa*)

**Apaćita** (S) (M) honoured; respected.

**Apaćiti** (S) (F) 1. honouring; reverence; loss. 2. incurs expenditure. 3. a daughter of Marići (*Vā. Purāṇa*)

**Apādeva** (S) (M) 1. god of water. 3. another name for Varuṇa.

**Apagā** (S) (F) 1. flowing water. 3. a holy river (*M. Bh.*)

**Āpagāsuta** (S) (M) 1. son of the river. 3. another name for Bhīṣma.

**Āpageya** (S) (M) 1. originating from the river; son of the river. 3. another name for Bhīṣma, the son of the sacred Gaṅgā.

**Apaghana** (S) (M) 1. cloudless. 2. a limb of the body.

**Apan** (S) (M) 1. sun. 2. glorious; brilliant; illuminating; enlightening.

**Apakuñja** (S) (M) 1. not hidden. 3. a younger brother of Śeṣanāga.

**Apālā** (S) (F) 1. unguarded. 2. undefended. 3. a daughter of Atri (*Ṛg Veda*)

**Apālāla** (S) (M) 1. fleshless; strawless; huskless. 3. a rākṣasa (*V. Rāmāyaṇa*)

**Apalāśin** (S) (M) free from desire.

**Apālaṣuka** (S) (M) free from desire.

**Apamanyu** (S) (M) free from grief.

**Apāmpati** (S) (M) 1. lord of the waters. 3. another name for the ocean and Varuṇa.

**Apāntaratamas** (S) (M) 1. completely free of darkness. 2. brilliant; enlightening. 3. a sage born of the sound 'bhu' uttered by Viṣṇu and reincarnated as sage Vyāsa (*Ṛg Veda*)

**Āpapati** (S) (M) 1. lord of the waters. 2. the ocean. 3. another name for Varuṇa.

**Apārā** (S) (F) 1. boundless; with no rival or second. 2. inexhaustible; unequalled; divine. 3. a wife of Vasudeva (*Vā. Purāṇa*)

**Aparāditya** (S) (M) 1. not unlike the sun. 2. brilliant; enlightening.

**Aparāhṇaka** (S) (M) 1. born in the afternoon. 2. as brilliant as the afternoon sun.

**Aparājiṣṇu** (S) (M) unconquerable; invincible.

**Aparājitā** (S) (F) 1. never been conquered. 3. a form of Durgā worshipped on Vijayādaśami or Dussera; the Blue Pea plant which serves as an amulet (*Clitoria ternatea*); a yoginī (*M. Bh.*); a river of Śāka Dvīpa (*Bhāgavata*); the northeast quarter.

**Aparājita** (S) (M) 1. undefeated; unsurpassed. 3. a naga son of Kaśyapa and Kadru (*M. Bh.*); a son of Dhṛtarāṣṭra (*M. Bh.*); a Kuru dynasty king (*M. Bh.*); one of the 11 rudras (*A. Purāṇa*); a son of Kṛṣṇa; a class of Jaina divinities (*J. S. Koṣa*); a mythical sword (*Bhāgavata*); another name for Viṣṇu and Śiva (*M. Bh.*)

**Aparānandā** (S) (F) 1. pleasing others. 3. a prominent holy river (*M. Bh.*)

**Aparimāṇa** (S) (M) 1. immeasurable. 2. immense; unlimited.

**Aparimeya** (S) (M) 1. immeasurable. 2. immense; unbounded; unlimited.

**Aparimita** (S) (M) 1. unlimited. 2. immense; unbounded.

**Aparīta** (S) (M) irresistable.

**Āparīta** (S) (M) 1. gladdened. 2. joyous.

**Aparṇā** (S) (F) 1. without leaves. 3. another name for Pārvatī who undertook a penance in order to obtain Śiva as her consort and during the process gave up eating everything including leaves.

**Aparṇeśa** (S) (M) 1. lord of Pārvatī. 3. another name for Śiva.

**Aparokṣa** (S) (M) 1. not beyond sight. 2. visible; manifest.

**Apārthiva** (S) (M) 1. not earthly. 2. subtle; immortal; divine.

**Aparuṣa** (S) (M) free from anger.

**Apaśaṅka** (S) (M) fearless.

**Apaspati** (S) (M) 1. skilful; active. 3. a son of Uttānapāda (*V. Purāṇa*)

**Āpastamba** (S) (M) 1. one who stills water. 3. a sage who was the husband of Akṣasutrā and the father of Gārgī (*Ā. Samhitā*)

**Apasyu** (S) (M) skilful; active.

**Āpava** (S) (M) 1. sheltered from wind. 2. a grove. 3. another name for Vasiṣṭha (*M. Bh.*)

**Apayā** (S) (F) 1. going away; milkless; waterless. 3. a tributary of the river Sarasvatī (*Bhāgavata*)

**Apekṣitā** (S) (F) 1. expected. 2. desired; wanted; required; looked for.

**Āpi** (S) (M) friend; ally; acquaintance.

**Apiguṇa** (S) (M) 1. one with attributes. 2. excellent; virtuous.

**Apija** (S) (M) 1. born after or in addition to. 2. a brother.

**Apīndra** (S) (M) 1. resembling Indra. 2. handsome; virtuous; divine.

**Apnavāna** (S) (M) 1. the arm. 2. one who provides support. 3. a ṛṣi of the line of Bhṛgu (*Ṛg Veda*)

**Āpomūrti** (S) (M) 1. with a water-like form. 2. adaptable; flexible. 3. an idol of the god of water (*A.Veda*); a son of Manu Svāroćiṣa (*H. Purāṇa*); a ṛṣi of the 10th Manvantara (*H. Purāṇa*)

**Āponāptṛ** (S) (M) 1. grandson of the waters. 3. another name for Agni.

**Appayyadikṣita** (S) (M) 1. with thoughts like water or milk. 2. one who is clear; clean; pure; without vice. 3. a reputed Sanskṛt rhetorician (16th century A.D.)

**Appitta** (S) (M) 1. fire. 3. another name for Agni.

**Aprakarṣita** (S) (M) 1. undiminished. 2. irresistable; unequalled.

**Apramaya** (S) (M) imperishable.

**Aprati** (S) (M) 1. without opponents. 2. irresistable; unequalled.

**Apratima** (S) (M) 1. without comparison. 2. unequalled; irresistible; without opponents.

**Apratīpa** (S) (M) 1. not obstinate. 2. flexible; compromising. 3. a king of Magadha (*V. Purāṇa*)

**Apratiratha** (S) (M) 1. a chariot borne warrior who has no rival. 2. a matchless warrior. 3. a ṛṣi considered to be the son of Indra (*Ṛg. Veda*); a son of Rantināra (*V. Purāṇa*)

**Apratirūpa** (S) (M) with matchless beauty.

**Aprativīrya** (S) (M) of irresistible power.

**Apratiyodhin** (S) (M) 1. not having an adversary. 2. irresistible.

**Apratula** (S) (M) 1. cannot be compared. 2. unparalleled.

**Āprītapā** (S) (M) 1. guarding the joyous. 3. another name for Viṣṇu.

**Apriya** (S) (M) 1. not liked. 2. unpopular. 3. a yakṣa (*B. Literature*)

**Apsarā** (S) (F) 1. moving in the water of the clouds. 3. celestial nymphs born of the churning of the Ocean of Milk (*V. Rāmāyaṇa*), who dwell in Svarga, the heaven of Indra and visit the earth in different shapes (*A. Veda*)

**Apsavya** (S) (M) 1. being in the water. 3. another name for Varuṇa.

**Apsuhomya** (S) (M) 1. one who subsists on water alone during the period of offering penance or sacrifice. 3. a sage in the assembly of Yudhiṣṭhira (*M. Bh.*)

**Āpta** (S) (M) 1. achieved the goal. 2. logical; organized; reliable. 3. a serpent of the Kaśyapa dynasty (*M. Bh.*)

**Āpti** (S) (F) 1. fitness; fulfilment; completion. 2. abundance; fortune.

**Aptu** (S) (M) small; tender.

**Āpu** (S) (M) 1. to be pure. 2. flawless; virtuous; divine.

**Apūpa** (S) (M) little; honeycomb; cake.

**Āpūraṇī** (S) (F) 1. one that fulfils. 2. the silkcotton tree (*Bombax celba*)

**Apūrvā** (S) (F) 1. unprecedented. 2. incomparable; new; extraordinary.

**Apūrva** (S) (M) 1. unprecedented; singular. 2. Supreme Soul.

**Āpyas** (S) (M) 1. belonging to water. 3. a vasu (*Ṛg Veda*)

**Ara** (S) (M) 1. swift. 2. speedy; the spoke of an altar. 3. an ocean in Brahmā's world (*Brah. Purāṇa*); the 18th Jaina Arhat of the present Avasarpiṇī (*J. S. Koṣa*)

**Arā** (S) (F) 1. decorative. 3. a daughter of sage Śukra (*U. Rāmāyaṇa*)

**Arabhaṭa** (S) (M) enterprising; courageous.

**Araḍā** (S) (F) 1. languid. 3. a tutelary goddess (*G's Ś. Kalpa*)

**Ārādhaka** (S) (M) worshipper.

**Ārādhanā** (S) (F) worship; adoration; prayer.

**Ārādhitā** (S) (F) 1. one who receives the devotion of others. 2. worshipped.

**Arāga** (S) (M) 1. without passion. 2. cool; calm.

**Ārāgam** (S) (M) 1. assisting; helpful. 3. another name for Kārttikeya.

**Arajā** (S) (F) 1. dustless. 2. clean; pure; virtuous. 3. the daughter of Uśanas (*V. Rāmāyaṇa*); a daughter of ṛṣi Bhārgava (*V. Rāmāyaṇa*)

**Arāli** (S) (M) 1. crooked. 3. a son of Viśvāmitra (*M. Bh.*)

**Aramanas** (S) (M) 1. desire. 2. pleasure; delight; enjoyment; ready to serve; obedient.

**Aramati** (S) (F) 1. piety and devotion conjoined. 3. as a goddess who protects the worshippers of the gods.

**Araṇa** (S) (M) 1. distant. 2. heaven.

**Aranātha** (S) (M) 1. controller of time. 2. a god. 3. the 18th Jaina Tirthankara and the son of King Sudarśana of Hastināpura (*J. S. Koṣa*)

**Araṇī** (S) (F) 1. turning round. 3. removes darkness by sifting the fire; wood of the tree *Ficus religiosa* used for kindling fire.

**Araṇis** (S) (M) 1. turning round. 3. another name for the sun.

**Araṇya** (S) (M) 1. forest. 2. a foreign place; a desert. 3. a son of Manu Raivata (*H. Purāṇa*); an Ikṣvāku king (*Bhāgavata*)

**Araṇyakumāra** (S) (M) prince of the forest.

**Araṇyānī** (S) (F) 1. wilderness. 2. desert; large forest. 3. the goddess of wilderness (*Ṛg. Veda*)

**Arapaćana** (S) (M) 1. to surrender oneself. 3. a mystical collective name of the 5 Dhyāni Buddhas (*B. Literature*)

**Arāru** (S) (M) 1. without mercy. 2. cruel. 3. an asura (*Ṛg. Veda*)

**Ārāti** (S) (F) 1. offering prayer; ceremonial adoration with kindled lamps. 2. sacred; spiritual; venerated.

**Arati** (S) (M) moving quickly; delighted; drowned in love.

**Aravinda** (S) (M) 1. lotus (*Nelumbium speciosum*). 2. fragrant; beautiful; auspicious; dear to the gods.

**Aravindanābha** (S) (M) 1. the lotus navelled. 3. another name for Viṣṇu.

**Aravindinī** (S) (F) 1. an assemblage of lotuses. 2. fragrant; beautiful; auspicious; dear to the gods.

**Arāvinī** (S) (M) 1. making a tinkling sound. 3. a son of Jayaṣena (*V. Purāṇa*)

**Arayannam** (S) (M) 1. lover of nature. 2. living in the forest. 3. the celestial hansa or swan regarded as the son of Dhṛtarāṣṭra and Kaśyapa (*V. Rāmāyaṇa*)

**Arbuda** (S) (M) 1. tumour; 10 million; mountain; foetus. 3. an asura killed by Indra (*Ṛg. Veda*); a nāga (*M. Bh.*); another name for Mount Abu (*M. Bh.*)

**Arbudī** (S) (M) 1. born of a tumour. 3. a Vedic ṛṣi (*Ṛg Veda*)

**Arćā** (S) (M) 1. shining; brilliant; worship. 2. one who is adored; venerated.

**Arćanā** (S) (F) 1. worship; homage paid to deities. 2. respected; propitiated.

**Arćanānas** (S) (M) 1. having a rattling carriage. 2. whose arrival and departure is announced. 3. a sage in the Atri family who married Rathavīti and became the father of Mahāṛṣi Śyāvāśva (*Ṛg Veda*)

**Arćat** (S) (M) 1. shining; praising. 2. brilliant; glorious; praised. 3. a ṛṣi and son of Hiraṇyastūpa (*Nirukta*)

**Arći** (S) (M) 1. ray; flame; one who offers prayers; to whom the prayers are offered. 3. one of the 12 ādityas (*K. Brāhmaṇa*)

**Ārćika** (S) (M) 1. one who prays. 3. a descendant of a ṛṣi (*M. Bh.*); another name for Jamadagni.

**Arćin** (S) (M) 1. shining; devout. 3. Varuṇa's feet.

**Arćis** (S) (F) 1. ray of light; flame. 2. illuminating; enlightening. 3. the wife of Kṛśāśva and mother of Dhūmraketu (*Bhāgavata*)

**Arćiśmat** (S) (M) 1. flaming. 2. brilliant; resplendant. 3. another name for Agni, Viṣṇu and the sun.

**Arćiśmatī** (S) (F) 1. flaming. 2. brilliant; resplendant. 3. a daughter of Angiras (*M. Bh.*)

**Arćita** (S) (M) worshipped.

**Ardana** (S) (M) 1. moving restlessly. 3. another name for Śiva.

**Ardhaćakrin** (S) (M) 1. half a ćakravartin. 3. one of the 9 Black vasudevas of the Jainas (*J. S. Koṣa*)

**Ardhagaṅgā** (S) (F) 1. half the Gaṅgā. 2. as half as the Gaṅgā. 3. another name for the river Kāverī.

**Ardhakāla** (S) (M) 1. half destroyer. 3. Śiva who when conjoined with Śakti – the female form of energy brings about complete destruction.

**Ardhaketu** (S) (M) 1. half bannered. 3. the half or crescent moon that adorns the locks of Śiva and is identified with him; a rudra (*Vā. Purāṇa*)

**Ardhalakṣmīharī** (S) (M) 1. half Lakṣmī and half Viṣṇu. 3. a form of Viṣṇu (*V. Purāṇa*)

**Ardhanārīśvara** (S) (M) 1. lord who is half female. 3. form of Śiva where he is conjoined with Śakti – the female form of energy.

**Ardhendra** (S) (M) one whose half belongs to Indra.

**Ardhendu** (S) (M) crescent moon.

**Ardhendumauli** (S) (M) 1. one whose diadem is the crescent moon. 3. another name for Śiva.

**Ārdra** (S) (M) 1. moist; succulent; green; soft; tender; warm; young. 3. a grandson of Pṛthu (*H. Purāṇa*)

**Areṅu** (S) (M) 1. without dust. 2. pure; not earthly; celestial; a god.

**Argañjan** (S) (M) 1. act of offering. 2. sacred; venerated; devoted.

**Argheśvara** (S) (M) 1. lord of offering. 3. another name for Śiva.

**Arghya** (S) (M) 1. valuable. 2. the act of offering sacred water to propitiate the deities; an oblation; valuable; one who deserves a respectful reception.

**Arha** (S) (M) 1. deserving. 3. another name for Śiva and Indra.

**Arhaṇā** (S) (F) 1. worship. 2. honoured; venerated.

**Arhaṇa** (S) (M) 1. worshipped. 3. an attendant of Viṣṇu (*V. Purāṇa*)

**Arhant** (S) (M) 1. worthy; praised worshipper; without violence. 2. peaceful; mild;

gentle; humane; kind; a Buddha. 3. another name for Śiva.

**Arhantikā** (S) (F) 1. one who worships. 2. has shunned violence. 3. a Buddhist nun (*B. Literature*)

**Arhat** (S) (M) 1. deserving. 2. worthy; respectable. 3. a superior divinity of the Jainas (*J. S. Koṣa*); a Buddhist aspiring for Nirvāṇa (*B. Literature*)

**Arhattama** (S) (M) most deserving.

**Aridamana** (S) (M) suppressor of foes.

**Arihan** (S) (F) killing enemies.

**Ariha** (S) (M) 1. killing enemies. 3. a lunar dynasty king who was a son of Arvaćina and Maryādā and the father of Mahābhauma (*M. Bh.*); a son of Devātithi.

**Arijit** (S) (M) 1. conquering enemies. 3. a son of Kṛṣṇa and Sūbhadrā (*Bhāgavata*)

**Ariktā** (S) (F) 1. not empty. 2. fulfilled; satisfied; abundant.

**Arimardana** (S) (M) 1. destroying enemies. 3. a king of owls (*Panćatantra*); a son of Śvaphalka (*H. Purāṇa*)

**Arimejaya** (S) (M) 1. conqueror of enemies. 3. a Purū king (*A. Purāṇa*)

**Arimejaya** (S) (M) 1. shaking enemies. 3. a son of Śvaphalka; a nāga priest; another name for Kuru.

**Arimdama** (S) (M) 1. suppresses foes. 3. the father of Sanaśruta (*A. Brāhmaṇa*); another name for Śiva.

**Arin** (S) (M) 1. with spokes. 2. discus.

**Ariprā** (S) (F) 1. spotless. 2. clear; faultless; virtuous; divine.

**Ariṣṭā** (S) (F) 1. unhurt; safe; secure. 3. a daughter of Dakṣa, wife of Kaśyapa, and the mother of the gandharvas (*M. Bh.*); another name for Durgā.

**Ariṣṭa** (S) (M) 1. unhurt; secure; safe. 3. an asura son of Bali killed by Kṛṣṇa (*H. Purāṇa*); a son of Manu Vaivasvata (*V. Purāṇa*); an asura servant of Kaṇsa (*Bhāgavata*); the Neem tree (*Azadirachta indica*)

**Ariṣṭahan** (S) (M) 1. slayer of Ariṣṭa. 3. another name for Viṣṇu.

**Ariṣṭamathana** (S) (M) 1. slayer of Ariṣṭa. 3. another name for Viṣṇu.

**Ariṣṭanemi** (S) (M) 1. unbroken felly. 2. felly whose wheel is intact; smooth and uninterrupted journey. 3. a son of Vinatā who was the father of Sumati (*M.Bh.*); the wife of King Sagara (*Rāmāyaṇa*); a son of Kaśyapa (*M. Bh.*); a king in the council of Yama (*M. Bh.*); name assumed by Sahadeva in the Virāta kingdom (*M. Bh.*); the 22 Jaina Tirthaṅkaras of the present Avasarpinī (*A. Koṣa*); a prajāpati who married 4 of Dakṣa's daughters (*Ś. Purāṇa*); a yakṣa who dwells in the chariot of the sun (*Ṛg Veda*); a gandharva (*V. Samhitā*); another name for Kṛṣṇa.

**Ariṣṭuta** (S) (M) 1. praised with zeal. 3. another name for Indra.

**Arisūdana** (S) (M) killing enemies.

**Ārita** (S) (M) praised.

**Ariyappā** (S) (M) eliminating the enemy.

**Arjā** (S) (F) 1. dustless. 2. free from passion; pure; virtuous; divine. 3. a daughter of Uśanas (*Bhāgavata*)

**Arjana** (S) (M) conqueror of the enemy.

**Ārjava** (S) (M) 1. straight. 2. upright; sincere; honest. 3. son of Subala and brother of Śakuni (*M. Bh.*)

**Arjita** (S) (M) 1. acquired. 2. gained; earned. 3. a son of Kṛṣṇa (*Bhāgavata*)

**Arjuna** (S) (M) 1. made of silver; peacock; the tree *Terminalia arjuna*; the White Murdah tree (*Terminalia citrina*); the tree (*Lagerstroemia flos-reginae*); white; clear; bright; the colour of day; lightning; milk; dawn. 2. fair in visage and mind; pure; glorious; illuminating; enlightening. 3. the third Pāṇḍava who was the son of Indra and Kuntī, whose accepted father was Pāṇḍu, regarded as the reincarnation of the sage Nara, equal to Śiva in prowess and as unconquerable as Indra, husband of Draupadī, Ulūpika, Ćitrangadā and Subhadrā, father of Śrutakīrti (from Draupadī), Irāvān (from Ulūpika), Babhruvāhana (from Ćitrangadā) and Abhimanyu (from Subhadrā) (*M. Bh.*); a son of Emperor Nimi (*M. Bh.*); a member of Yama's assembly (*M. Bh.*); a son of Kṛtavīrya (*M. Bh.*)

**Arjunāgraja** (S) (M) 1. elder brother of

Arjuna. 3. another name for Bhīma.

**Arjunapāla** (S) (M) 1. protector of the Arjuna tree; protector of Arjuna. 3. son of Śamīka who guarded the Arjuna tree (*Terminalia arjuna*) (*Bhāgavata*); another name for Kṛṣṇa.

**Arjunapūrvaja** (S) (M) 1. preceding Arjuna. 3. another name for Bhīma.

**Arjunasakhi** (S) (M) 1. friend of Arjuna. 2. with Arjuna as companion. 3. another name for Kṛṣṇa.

**Arjunātmaja** (S) (M) 1. son of Arjuna. 3. another name for Abhimanyu.

**Ārjuni** (S) (M) 1. son of Arjuna. 3. another name for Abhimanyu.

**Arjunī** (S) (M) 1. of fair complexion. 2. shining; glorious; illuminating; enlightening. 3. the Phālguni Nakṣatra considered to be very bright (*Ṛg Veda*)

**Arka** (S) (M) 1. ray; flash of lightning; the sun; fire. 2. crystal; praise; hymn; song; a learned man; an elder brother. 3. another name for Indra; the Red Sandalwood tree (*Pterocarpus santalinus*)

**Arkaja** (S) (M) 1. born of the sun. 3. another name for Karṇa, Yama, Sugrīva and Saturn.

**Arkakara** (S) (M) 1. hand of the sun. 2. a sunbeam.

**Arkanandana** (S) (M) 1. son of the sun. 3. another name of Karṇa and Saturn.

**Arkanayana** (S) (M) 1. sun eyed. 3. an asura (*H. Purāṇa*)

**Arkaprakāśa** (S) (M) light of the sun; as bright as the sun.

**Arkapriya** (S) (M) 1. beloved of the sun. 3. Shoeflower (*Hibiscus rosa chinensis*)

**Arkaputra** (S) (M) 1. son of the sun. 3. another name for Karṇa, Saturn, Yama and Sugrīva.

**Arkaśa** (S) (M) 1. illuminated by the sun. 2. visible; manifest.

**Arkāśmaṇi** (S) (M) 1. jewel of the sun. 2. heliotrope; crystal; sunstone; ruby.

**Arkasutā** (S) (F) 1. daughter of the sun. 3. another name for the river Yamunā.

**Arkatanaya** (S) (M) 1. son of the sun. 3. another name for Saturn, Karṇa, Manu Sāvarṇa and Manu Vaivasvata.

**Ārki** (S) (M) 1. descendant of the sun. 3. another name for Saturn, Yama, Manu, Sugrīva and Karṇa.

**Arkin** (S) (M) 1. radiant with light. 2. shining; bright; praised; worshipped.

**Arkka** (S) (M) 1. the substance; the essence. 2. subtle; divine. 3. an asura reborn as sage Ṛṣika (*M. Bh.*); the plant (*Calotropis gigantea*); another name for the sun.

**Arkkaparṇa** (S) (M) 1. a leaf of the Arkka plant (*Calotropis gigantea*). 3. a gandharva son of Kaśyapa and Munī (*M. Bh.*)

**Ārkṣa** (S) (M) 1. stellar; belonging to the stars; descendant of Ṛkṣa. 3. another name for Saṁvaraṇa.

**Armugam** (S) (M) 1. one who grants emancipation speedily. 3. another name for Kārttikeya.

**Arṇava** (S) (M) ocean; sea; sun; air; stream; flood; wave.

**Ārocana** (S) (M) 1. shining. 2. bright; glorious.

**Arogā** (S) (F) 1. without disease. 3. Dākṣāyāṇī in Vaidyanātha (*M. Purāṇa*)

**Āroga** (S) (M) 1. destroyer; shatterer. 3. one of the 7 suns at the end of a period of the world which in Hindu mythology is termed as Pralaya.

**Ārohī** (S) (F) 1. ascending. 2. growing; evolving; positive; progressive.

**Arokya** (S) (M) very pious.

**Arpaṇā** (S) (F) 1. act of offering. 2. auspicious; sacred; venerated.

**Arpitā** (S) (F) 1. offered. 2. fixed upon; delivered; entrusted; given back; surrendered.

**Arśa** (S) (M) 1. sky; heaven; celestial; of sacred descent. 2. heavenly; venerated; divine.

**Ārṣabhi** (S) (M) 1. like a bull. 3. the first Ćakravartin of Bharata.

**Ārṣṭiṣena** (S) (M) 1. protected by swords. 2. a commander. 3. a sage visited by the Pāṇḍavas (*M. Bh.*)

**Arśya** (S) (M) 1. celestial; of sacred descent. 2. belonging to hermits.

**Ārtaparṇa** (S) (M) 1. son of Ṛtaparna. 3. another name for Sudāsa (*H. Purāṇa*)

**Arthadarśin** (S) (M) 1. one who knows the meaning; knower of the essence; attained salvation or mokṣa. 2. a Buddha.

**Artham** (S) (M) 1. fortune. 3. the golden lotus on the forehead of Viṣṇu from which the goddess Śrī originated.

**Arthanā** (S) (F) request; entreaty.

**Arthapati** (S) (M) 1. lord of wealth. 3. the grandfather of the poet Bāṇa; another name for Kubera (*Kad*)

**Arthasiddhi** (S) (M) 1. acquisition of wealth. 3. a son of Puṣya (*H. Purāṇa*)

**Arthasādhaka** (S) (M) 1. promoting an aim. 2. useful; profitable. 3. a minister of Daśaratha (*V. Rāmāyaṇa*)

**Arthvāna** (S) (M) with a purpose; wealth; full of sense and meaning.

**Ārtimān** (S) (M) 1. suffering from pain; begs for divine mercy for being relieved from suffering. 3. a mantra that eliminates all fear (*M. Bh.*)

**Artikā** (S) (F) elder sister.

**Aru** (S) (M) 1. tawny. 3. the red blossomed Khadira tree (*Acacia catechu*); another name for the sun.

**Arudra** (S) (M) 1. not cruel. 2. soft; gentle; tender; calm.

**Arujā** (S) (F) daughter of the sun; free from disease.

**Arujas** (S) (M) 1. free from disease. 2. brisk; gay. 3. a rākṣasa attendant of Rāvaṇa (*V. Rāmāyaṇa*); Indian Laburnum (*Cassia Fistula*)

**Arūkṣitā** (S) (F) 1. not dry. 2. young; tender; soft; supple.

**Arūkṣṇā** (S) (F) 1. not dry. 2. soft; tender; young.

**Arula** (S) (M) 1. shining as the sun. 2. brilliant; glorious; enlightening.

**Arulamaṇi** (S) (M) jewel of the sun.

**Arumakham** (S) (M) 1. as vigorous as the sun. 3. another name for Kārttikeya.

**Arunā** (S) (F) 1. red. 2. passionate; fecund; life giving. 3. an apsarā daughter of Kaśyapa and Prādhā (*M. Bh.*); a tributary of the river Sarasvatī (*M. Bh.*); the Rosary Pea (*Abrus precatorius*); the Shoeflower (*Hibiscus rosa chinensis*); the Saffron plant (*Crocus sativus*); the Indian Madder Plant (*Rubia cordifolia*); *Aconitum heterophyllum*; *Sphaeranthus indicus*; *Alpinia galanga*.

**Aruṇa** (S) (M) 1. red; gold; saffron; tawny; ruddy. 3. dawn personified as the charioteer of the sun (*M. Smṛti*); one of the 12 ādityas (*Sk. Purāṇa*); a son of Kaśyapa and Vinatā, brother of Garuḍa, husband of Śyenī, the father of Sampāti and Jaṭāyu (*V. Rāmāyaṇa*), and who became the charioteer of the sun (*M. Bh.*); a solar dynasty king who was the father of Triśanku (*D. Bh. Purāṇa*); a ṛṣi born from the flesh of Brahmā (*T. Āraṇyaka*); a dānava born in the dynasty of Vipraćitti (*D. Bh. Purāṇa*); a son of Narakāsura killed by Kṛṣṇa; a son of Kṛṣṇa (*Bhāgavata*); a serpent (*M. Bh.*)

**Aruṇābhā** (S) (F) 1. the red glow of the sun. 2. life giving; passionate; fecund.

**Aruṇāditya** (S) (M) 1. the crimson sun. 3. one of the 12 forms of the sun (*Sk. Purāṇa*)

**Aruṇāgraja** (S) (M) 1. the 1st born of Aruṇa. 3. another name for Garuḍa.

**Aruṇajyotiṣ** (S) (M) 1. as bright as the sun. 3. another name for Śiva.

**Aruṇakamala** (S) (M) 1. the Red lotus (*Nymphaea rubra*). 2. passionate; fecund; fragrant; famous; dear to the gods.

**Aruṇākara** (S) (M) 1. red rayed. 3. another name for the sun.

**Aruṇānśu** (S) (M) with red rays.

**Aruṇānuja** (S) (M) 1. younger brother of Aruṇa. 3. another name for Garuḍa.

**Aruṇapriyā** (S) (F) 1. beloved of the dawn. 3. an apsarā (*H. Purāṇa*)

**Aruṇapriya** (S) (M) 1. beloved of the *Nymphaea rubra*. 3. another name for the sun.

**Aruṇarćis** (S) (M) the rising sun; with a red glow.

**Aruṇasārathī** (S) (M) 1. one whose charioteer is Aruṇa. 3. another name for the sun.

**Aruṇāśva** (S) (M) 1. driving with red horses. 3. another name for the maruts.

**Aruṇāva** (S) (M) 1. the red flavour. 2. immensely protected; well-preserved.

**Arundhatī** (S) (F) 1. fidelity. 3. the morning star Alcor in the Great Bear personified as the wife of Vasiṣṭha and the daughter of Prajāpati Kardama and Devahutī, regarded as the epitome of wifely devotion and considered to sit in Brahmā's assembly (*M. Bh.*); one of the Pleiades (*P. Samhitā*); the daughter of Dakṣa, wife of Dharma and mother of the divisions of the earth (*H. Purāṇa*); another name for the supernatural faculty also called Kuṇḍalinī.

**Arundhatīnātha** (S) (M) 1. lord of Arundhatī. 3. another name for Vasiṣṭha.

**Aruṇeśa** (S) (M) 1. lord of Aruṇa. 3. another name for Sūrya.

**Aruṇī** (S) (F) 1. glowing red; ruddy; red cow; dawn; gold; ruby. 2. passionate; fecund; precious; illuminating; sacred. 3. Aruṇa as a female in Indra's assembly (*H. Purāṇa*)

**Āruni** (S) (M) 1. reddish in complexion. 3. another name for Uddālaka the disciple of Ayodhyadhaumya (*Bhāgavata*); a serpent of the Dhṛtarāṣṭra family (*M. Bh.*); a soldier of the Kaurava army (*M. Bh.*)

**Aruṇikā** (S) (F) 1. tawny red. 2. life giving; passionate; bright.

**Aruṇimā** (S) (F) 1. reddish glow. 2. glow of the dawn which is considered sacred.

**Aruṇodaya** (S) (M) 1. dawn. 2. blooming; awakened.

**Aruṇopala** (S) (M) 1. the stone of the sun. 2. the ruby.

**Arunśu** (S) (M) heals wounds.

**Arūpā** (S) (F) 1. without form. 2. unbounded; immense; divine. 3. a daughter of Dakṣa (*M. Bh.*)

**Aruṣa** (S) (M) 1. without anger; calm; shining; bright; red. 2. another name for the sun.

**Āruṣī** (S) (F) 1. kills. 2. takes lives; killer. 3. a daughter of Manu, wife of Ćyavana and the mother of Aurva (*M. Bh.*)

**Aruṣī** (S) (F) 1. reddish. 2. the dawn; flame; bright; fecund; illuminating; sacred; enlightening.

**Arva** (S) (M) 1. horse. 2. agile; swift. 3. a son of Ṛpunjaya (*V. Purāṇa*); a seer of the 2nd Manvantara (*Ś. Brāhmaṇa*)

**Arvācīna** (S) (M) 1. turned towards; favouring. 3. husband of Maryādā (*M. Bh.*)

**Arvana** (S) (M) 1. running like a horse. 2. swift; quick; agile. 3. a horse of the moon (*A. Koṣa*); another name for Indra.

**Arvantī** (S) (F) mare; nymph.

**Arvavasan** (S) (M) 1. borne by horses. 2. that which is swift. 3. one of the 7 principal rays of the sun (*Ṛg Veda*)

**Arvāvasu** (S) (M) 1. priest of the gods. 2. immersed in religious and spiritual pursuits; venerated. 3. a Brāhmaṇa of the gods (*Kau. Upaniṣad*); a son of Raibhya (*M. Bh.*); an ascetic in the court of Yudhiṣṭhira (*M. Bh.*)

**Arvīndra** (S) (M) lord of horses; lord of wheels; lord of priests.

**Arvuda** (S) (M) 1. priest of hymns. 3. the priest described in the *Kauṣtikī Brāhmaṇas* as a creator of mantras.

**Āryā** (S) (F) 1. honoured; noble; a lady. 2. respected; worshipped. 3. one of the 7 mothers present at the birth of Subrahmaṇya (*M. Bh.*); another name for Bhadrakālī.

**Ārya** (S) (M) 1. honoured; noble; master. 2. kind; auspicious; attached; devoted; dear; excellent; respectable; faithful; worthy; wise and masterly.

**Āryabhaṭā** (S) (M) 1. enterprising; best among the masters; courageous. 3. a famous Indian mathematician and astronomer (5th century A.D.) (*Aryabhatīya*)

**Āryaćetas** (S) (M) of a noble mind.

**Āryadeva** (S) (M) 1. lord of the honoured; noblest. 2. considered the best among Aryans. 3. a Buddhist philosopher and foster son of the king of Simhala who succeeded Nāgārjuna as the head of the Mādhyamika school in Nālandā and was the author of the *Ćatuhśataka*.

**Āryaka** (S) (M) 1. like an Ārya. 2. a person who has all the virtues of an Ārya; honourable; respectable. 3. a serpent advisor of Vāsuki (*M. Bh.*)

**Āryakī** (S) (F) 1. respected; honoured. 3. another name for Durgā (*A. Purāṇa*)

**Āryakumāra** (S) (M) 1. noble prince. 2. noble; virtuous; meritorious.

**Aryaman** (S) (M) 1. companion; playfellow; the sun. 3. an āditya or sovereign principle of the *Ṛg Veda*, represented as a son of Kaśyapa and Aditi, standing for honour, nobility, chivalry and the rules of society, considered the original aristocrat and the source of blue blood, the protector of the family, a main Vedic deity that rules over the cosmic body, considered the embodiment of the sun which is the cosmic eye, supposed to be the chief of the manes and whose path is the Milky Way (*T. Brāhmaṇa*); son of Atri and Anasūyā and the brother of Anatā, he presides over the Nakṣatra Uttarāphālguni (*V.'s B. Samhitā*)

**Āryaman** (S) (M) 1. surrounded by nobles; of noble lineage. 2. belonging to the sun.

**Āryamaṇī** (S) (F) 1. jewel among noble ladies; belonging to the sun. 3. another name for the river Yamunā.

**Āryāmbā** (S) (F) 1. mother of the respectable. 3. mother of Śankarāćārya.

**Āryamik** (S) (M) 1. as meritorious as an Ārya. 2. noble; virtuous.

**Āryamiśra** (S) (M) distinguished among nobles.

**Āryaśūra** (S) (M) 1. brave among the Āryas. 2. honourable. 3. a Buddhist poet and philosopher (*B. Literature*)

**Āryāśva** (S) (M) 1. with devoted horses. 3. a solar dynasty king (*V. Rāmāyaṇa*)

**Āryāvarta** (S) (M) 1. land of the worshipped. 3. a king of the dynasty of Viśvakarmā who was the son of Ṛṣabha and Jayantī (*M. Bh.*); ancient India in the Aryan period (*M. Smṛti*)

**Āryendra** (S) (M) lord of the masters.

**Āryika** (S) (M) masterly; honoured.

**Āśā** (S) (F) 1. wish; desire; space; region; a quarter of the heavens. 3. hope personified as the wife of a vasu (*H. Purāṇa*); daughter-in-law of Manas (*P. Ćandrodaya*)

**Āṣāḍha** (S) (M) 1. brings hope (hope for the rains that provide a respite from the sweltering heat of the month of Jyeṣtha [May–June] the hottest month in the Indian Calendar, thus this hope is provided in the form of the moon of Āṣāḍha [June–July] which heralds the monsoons in India). 2. a sacred staff. 3. a king who was a partial incarnation of the rākṣasa Krodhavaśa (*M. Bh.*); another name for Śiva.

**Āṣāḍhikā** (S) (F) born in the month of Āśāḍha.

**Āśalī** (S) (F) 1. beloved of the world; friend of the heavens. 2. liked by all.

**Asamañjasa** (S) (M) 1. unfit; unbecoming. 2. vascillating. 3. a solar dynasty king who was the son of Sagara and Keśinī and father of Anśumān (*V. Rāmāyaṇa*)

**Asamātī** (S) (M) 1. unequalled. 2. unparalleled; supreme; divine.

**Asambāṇa** (S) (M) 1. with an odd number of arrows. 3. another name for Kāma, who releases arrows in odd numbers.

**Aśan** (S) (M) 1. rock. 2. the firmament; one who is strong yet subtle.

**Āsaṅga** (S) (M) 1. attachment; devotion. 2. attached; devoted; of a loving nature. 3. a son of Śvaphalka (*Bhāgavata*)

**Asaṅgas** (S) (M) 1. not attached. 2. free from worldly ties; a flag; a vessel; not blunt; not obstructed; soul; independant. 3. a son of Yuyudhāna (*H. Purāṇa*); another name for Vasubandhu (*B. Ćarita*)

**Asaṅginī** (S) (F) 1. not attached. 2. not bound; a whirlwind.

**Aśanī** (S) (F) a flash of lightning; thunderbolt.

**Aśaniprabha** (S) (M) 1. as illuminating as a flash of lightning. 3. a rākṣasa (*V. Rāmāyaṇa*)

**Aśanis** (S) (M) 1. flash of lightning. 2. Indra's thunderbolt; missile; fire. 3. a hermit (*M. Bh.*); one of the 9 names of Rudra; another name for Indra.

**Aśaṅka** (S) (M) 1. without doubt. 2. fearless; certain.

**Aśankita** (S) (M) 1. without doubt; without fear. 2. clear; hopeful; fearless. 3. a king of the Bhoja family of Gujarat (*K. Sāgara*)

**Āśāpurṇa** (S) (M) 1. whose desire is fulfilled. 2. fulfilling desires.

**Aśatrus** (S) (M) 1. with no adversaries. 3. another name for the moon.

**Āśāvari** (S) (F) 1. celestial spirit. 3. a raga.

**Aśavijaya** (S) (M) conquering the world; heaven and space.

**Aśavāha** (S) (M) 1. borne by space; the heavens; the world. 2. celestial; heavenly; divine. 3. a son of Kaśyapa and Aditi (*M. Bh.*);

a Vṛṣni prince (*M. Bh.*)

**Asećana** (S) (M) charming; lovely.

**Aśeṣa** (S) (M) 1. without any remainder. 2. whole; entire; complete; perfect; divine.

**Aśiddhārtha** (S) (M) 1. one who has mastered archery. 3. a minister of King Daśaratha (*V. Rāmāyaṇa*)

**Aśikā** (S) (F) 1. dagger. 2. sharp and piercing.

**Asiknī** (S) (F) 1. the dark one. 2. the night. 3. a river now known as Ćenāb (*M. Bh.*); a daughter of Prajāpati Vīraṇa, wife of Dakṣa and the mother of 60 girls who are the mothers of creation (*H. Purāṇa*)

**Asikṛṣṇa** (S) (M) 1. as sharp as a sword. 3. son of solar dynasty King Aśvamedhas (*Bhāgavata*)

**Asiloman** (S) (M) 1. with hair as sharp as the points of swords. 3. a minister of Mahiṣāsura (*D. Bh. Purāṇa*)

**Asīma** (S) (M) endless; limitless.

**Asīman** (S) (M) 1. unlimited. 2. boundless; immense; divine.

**Asira** (S) (F) 1. an arrow. 2. a beam; a ray.

**Āśira** (S) (M) 1. eating everything. 2. a fragrant root; fire; sun; wind; diamond. 3. a rākṣasa (*A. Koṣa*)

**Asīra** (S) (M) 1. milk mixed with Soma. 2. pious; energetic.

**Āśiṣā** (S) (F) 1. blessed. 3. hope personified as the daughter of Bhaga (*H. Purāṇa*)

**Āśiṣa** (S) (M) 1. a blessing. 2. blessed; venerated; highly sought; rare.

**Aśiśira** (S) (M) 1. not cool. 2. hot.

**Āśiṣṭha** (S) (M) 1. very quick. 2. fast; swift; agile; active.

**Āsita** (S) (M) 1. seated; at rest. 2. tranquil; at peace; poised.

**Asitā** (S) (F) 1. not white; unbound. 2. the dark one; the night. 3. a daughter of Vīraṇa and wife of Dakśa (*H. Purāṇa*); an apsarā (*M. Bh.*); another name for the river Yamunā.

**Asita** (S) (M) 1. not white; unbounded. 2. dark coloured; blue; black. 3. the planet Saturn (*V's B. Samhitā*); a son of Bharata (*V. Rāmāyaṇa*); a prominent sage and father of Devala who spread the story of Mahābhārata to the public (*R. Ankuramaṇkā*); a mountain; Common Indigo (*Indigofera tinctoria*); another name for Kṛṣṇa.

**Aśīta** (S) (M) 1. not cold. 2. warm; hot.

**Asitābha** (S) (M) with unrestrained glory; surrounded by light.

**Asitadhanvā** (S) (M) 1. with an unbound bow; with a blue bow. 2. never had to bind his bow and therefore to fight, conquered his enemy without lifting his bow. 3. a Vedic king who wrote the *Veda* of *Asuravidyā*.

**Asitadhvaja** (S) (M) 1. with an unbound flag. 2. has a glorious reign. 3. a son of Kaśyapa and Vinatā (*M. Bh.*)

**Asitāṅga** (S) (M) 1. blue limbed. 3. a form of Śiva.

**Asitāśman** (S) (M) 1. blue stone. 2. the Lapis lazuli.

**Asitotpala** (S) (M) the blue lotus (*Nymphaea stellata*)

**Asjita** (S) (M) 1. bearing victory. 2. always victorious.

**Asketa** (S) (M) master of will; master of the house; destroyer of apparition.

**Askhala** (S) (M) 1. not shaking or slipping. 2. firm; steady. 3. an Agni (*A. Purāṇa*)

**Askol** (S) (M) 1. painted. 3. the painted Spurfowl (*Galloperdix lunulatus*)

**Askran** (S) (M) attacking enemies.

**Āśleṣā** (S) (M) 1. an embrace. 3. the 7th lunar mansion of whose 5 stars are grouped together as if in an embrace (*V.'s B. Samhitā*)

**Aśma** (S) (M) 1. hard as stone; a cloud. 2. the firmament; strong yet subtle. 3. a sage (*Ṛg Veda*)

**Aśmaka** (S) (M) 1. stone; thunderbolt; cloud. 2. rock; precious stone; the firmament. 3. a son of Vasiṣṭha and the wife of King Kalmāṣapāda of Ayodhyā (*M. Bh.*); a king on the Pāṇḍava side (*M. Bh.*); a sage (*M. Bh.*)

**Aśmakadāyāda** (S) (M) 1. stone thrower; attacking with a thunderbolt. 3. a son of King Aśmaka who fought on the side of the Kauravas (*M. Bh.*); another name for Indra.

**Aśmakī** (S) (F) 1. rocky. 2. strong yet subtle. 3. the wife of Prāćinvān of the Purū dynasty and mother of Saṁyāti (*M. Bh.*)

**Āśmana** (S) (M) 1. stone; gem; rock; thunderbolt; cloud; mountain; pervading. 3. another name for Aruṇa.

**Aśmanta** (S) (M) 1. a fireplace. 3. a marutvat (*Vā. Purāṇa*)

**Aśmatī** (S) (F) 1. as hard as rock. 2. strong; tough; unyielding.

**Asmi** (S) (M) (F) am.

**Aśmita** (S) (M) 1. rock born. 2. very hard; tough; strong.

**Aśmuṇḍ** (S) (M) existing; shining.

**Aśnā** (S) (F) 1. eating a lot. 2. voracious. 3. daughter of Bali and mother of a 100 sons (*V. Purāṇa*)

**Aśokā** (S) (F) 1. without sorrow; blossom of the Aśoka tree (*Saraca indica*). 3. one of the 5 arrows of Kāmā (*V. Purāṇa*); a Jaina deity (*A. Koṣa*)

**Aśoka** (S) (M) 1. without sorrow; blossom of the Aśoka tree (*Saraca indica*). 3. a king of Pātaliputra (*M. Bh.*); charioteer of Bhīma (*M. Bh.*); a minister of King Daśaratha (*V. Rāmāyaṇa*); a Kalinga king of the family of the asura Aśva (*M. Bh.*); an emperor of the Maurya dynasty who was the son of Bimbisāra and went on to become a Buddhist monk (269 B.C.) (*B. Literature*)

**Aśokadatta** (S) (M) 1. given without sorrow. 2. happily given. 3. incarnation of the vidyādhara Aśokavega (*K. Sāgara*)

**Aśokakara** (S) (M) 1. eliminating sorrows. 3. a vidyādhara (*K. Sāgara*)

**Aśokarī** (S) (F) 1. enemy of the Aśoka tree. 3. the Kadamba tree (*Anthocephalus cadamba*)

**Aśokavardhana** (S) (M) 1. increasing grieflessness. 3. a king (*Bh. Purāṇa*).

**Aśokavega** (S) (M) 1. whose emotions are without sorrow or suffering. 2. calm; tranquil; blissful. 3. a vidyādhara (*K. Sāgara*)

**Āspada** (S) (M) 1. seat; dignity; authority; power. 3. the 10th lunar mansion.

**Aśpan** (S) (M) 1. an efficient horse rider. 3. another name for the Supreme Spirit who controls time which is personified as a horse.

**Aśrapa** (S) (M) 1. drinking blood. 3. a rākṣasa presiding over the 19th lunar mansion.

**Aśrava** (S) (M) listening to; obedient; compliant.

**Āśravya** (S) (M) 1. much heard of; whom people listen to attentatively. 3. a sage in Indra's assembly (*M. Bh.*)

**Āśrayāśa** (S) (M) 1. consuming that which comes in contact. 3. another name for Agni.

**Aśrī** (S) (F) 1. ill luck; ugliness. 3. the opposing force of Lakṣmī personified as a goddess who when propitiated will take back luck.

**Āśrita** (S) (M) dependant.

**Āśruta** (S) (M) 1. heard. 2. well known.

**Āśrutavrana** (S) (M) 1. with a well-known injury. 3. a son of Dyutimat (*V. Purāṇa*)

**Astā** (S) (F) arrow; missile.

**Aṣṭābhujā** (S) (F) 1. 8 armed. 3. another name for Durgā.

**Aṣṭajīhva** (S) (M) 1. 8 tongued. 3. a soldier of Skanda's army (*M. Bh.*)

**Aṣṭaka** (S) (M) 1. with 8 parts. 2. an octrahedron. 3. 8th day after full moon; a Purū dynasty king who was the son of Ajamīdha and brother of Śunaśepha; a son of Viśvāmitra and Mādhavī the wife of Yayāti (*A. Brāhmaṇa*)

**Aṣṭakarṇa** (S) (M) 1. 8 eared. 3. another name for the 4 headed Brahmā.

**Aṣṭamūrti** (S) (M) 1. 8 faced. 3. a form of Śiva.

**Aṣṭaratha** (S) (M) 1. with 8 chariots. 3. a son of Bhīmaratha (*H. Purāṇa*)

**Aṣṭāvakra** (S) (M) 1. with 8 bends. 3. a great sage born with 8 physical deformities, who was the son of Kāhodara and Sujātā or Uddālaka, the husband of Suprabhā and who cursed the apsarās who had made fun of his physical crookedness and because of this they were reborn as the wives of Kṛṣṇa (*A. Purāṇa*)

**Āsthā** (S) (F) consideration; regard; care; confidence; hope; support; prop.

**Asthūlā** (S) (F) 1. not fat. 2. delicate; thin.

**Asti** (S) (F) 1. existing. 2. present; existence which cannot be denied; an important person. 3. the daughter of King Jarāsandha of Magadha and wife of Kaṇsa (*M. Bh.*)

**Aṣṭika** (S) (M) 1. 8th child. 3. the 8th son of

sage Jaratkaru and Manasādevī.

**Āstīka** (S) (M) 1. believing in existence and god. 3. a sage and son of Jaratkaru (*H. Purāṇa*)

**Āstīkamātā** (S) (F) 1. mother of Āstīka. 3. another name for Manasā.

**Astrita** (S) (M) invincible; gold.

**Astṛti** (S) (F) invincibility.

**Āśu** (S) (M) 1. fast. 2. quick; agile; active.

**Āśuga** (S) (M) 1. swift; fleet. 2. wind; sun; arrow. 3. one of the first five followers of Śākyamuni.

**Aśūla** (S) (M) 1. without thorns. 2. without obstacles; peaceful; tranquil; ever happy. 3. the tree *Vitex alata*.

**Āśumat** (S) (M) 1. mentally agile. 2. quick witted.

**Asurā** (S) (F) 1. incorporeal. 2. spiritual; ghost; demon; spirit. 3. a daughter of Kaśyapa and Prādhā (*M. Bh.*)

**Asura** (S) (M) 1. incorporeal. 2. spiritual; divine; spirit; demon; ghost. 3. opponents of the gods regarded as children of Diti by Kaśyapa (*Ṛg Veda/A. Veda*)

**Asurādhipa** (S) (M) 1. lord of the asuras. 3. another name for Bali.

**Asuratarajasa** (S) (M) 1. frightening the asuras. 3. a son of King Kuśa and Vaidarbhī (*V. Rāmāyaṇa*)

**Asurāyana** (S) (M) 1. devoted to demons. 3. a son of Viśvāmitra (*M. Bh.*)

**Asurendra** (S) (M) 1. lord of the asuras. 3. another name for Vṛtra.

**Āsurī** (S) (M) 1. demonlike; very powerful. 3. a sage and preceptor of sage Panćaśikha and the husband of Kapilā (*M. Bh.*)

**Asūrtarajasa** (S) (M) 1. sphere of darkness; mist or gloom of the unknown; living in darkness; remote. 3. a son of Kuśa (*H. Purāṇa*)

**Āśuśukṣaṇi** (S) (M) 1. shining forth. 3. another name for Agni.

**Āśutoṣa** (S) (M) 1. easily pleased. 3. another name for Śiva.

**Aśva** (S) (M) 1. horse; the number 7. 2. strong; swift; materially successful. 3. a son of Ćitraka (*H. Purāṇa*); a demon reborn as King Aśoka of Kalinga (*M. Bh.*); a sage and father of Vaśa (*Ṛg Veda*); a dānava (*M. Bh.*)

**Aśvadāvan** (S) (M) 1. acceptor of the horse sacrifice. 3. another name for Indra.

**Aśvaghoṣa** (S) (M) 1. neighing. 2. horse voiced. 3. a Sanskṛt poet; a Buddhist patriarch (*B. Literature*)

**Aśvagrīva** (S) (M) 1. horse necked. 3. with a long and strong neck. 3. an asura; a son of Ćitraka; an incarnation of Viṣṇu in horse form; a son of Kaśyapa and Danu (*M. Bh.*)

**Aśvajit** (S) (M) horses by conquest gaining.

**Aśvaketu** (S) (M) 1. horse bannered. 3. a king who had performed the Aśvamedha Yajña and was therefore a ćakravartin; a son of King Gāndhāra who fought on the side of the Kauravas (*M. Bh.*)

**Aśvākiṇī** (S) (F) 1. obtained from the horse. 2. strong; swift. 3. the 1st lunar mansion (*A. Koṣa*)

**Aśvala** (S) (M) 1. one who brings horses. 2. a stableboy. 3. the priest of King Janaka who led the horse for the Aśvamedha Yajña (*Br. Upaniṣhad*)

**Aśvalāyana** (S) (M) 1. causes breath. 2. revives; a god. 3. a son of Viśvāmitra (*M. Bh.*)

**Aśvamedhas** (S) (M) 1. horse sacrifice. 3. a descendant of Bharata (*Ṛg Veda*); a son of King Sahasrānīka (*Bhāgavata*)

**Aśvamedhadatta** (S) (M) 1. obtained from the horse sacrifice. 3. a son of Śatānīka (*M. Bh.*)

**Aśvapati** (S) (M) 1. lord of horses. 3. king of Madra and father of Sāvitrī (*M. Bh.*); a son of Kaśyapa and Danu (*M. Bh.*); a brother-in-law of Daśaratha (*Rāmāyaṇa*); an asura; another name for Indra.

**Aśvarāja** (S) (M) 1. king of horses. 3. another name for the horse Uććaihśravas.

**Aśvarya** (S) (M) not ordinary; marvellous; extraordinary; miraculous; surprising; prodigal.

**Aśvaśanku** (S) (M) 1. phallus of the horse; possesses ten billion horses. 3. a son of Kaśyapa and Danu (*M. Bh.*)

**Aśvasena** (S) (M) 1. one who has an army of horses. 2. commander of an army of horsemen. 3. a son of Kṛṣṇa (*Bhāgavata*); the father of the 23rd Arhat of the present Avasarpinī

(*J. S. Koṣa*); a serpent (*M. Bh.*)

**Aśvaśiras** (S) (M) 1. horse headed. 3. a son of Kaśyapa and Danu (*M. Bh.*)

**Aśvaśīrṣa** (S) (M) 1. horse headed. 3. a form of Viṣṇu (*M. Bh.*)

**Aśvatara** (S) (M) 1. a better horse. 2. a swifter, stronger horse chief of the nāgas (*S. Purāṇa*); a sacred pond in Prayāga (*M. Bh.*). 3. a gandharva (*H. Purāṇa*)

**Aśvattha** (S) (M) the Aśvattha tree (*Ficus religiosa*); lord of the place where the horses rest; holy tree under which the gods sit.

**Aśvatthā** (S) (F) day of the full moon in the month of Āśvina.

**Aśvatthāman** (S) (M) 1. having the strength of a horse. 3. son of Droṇa and Kṛpī (*M. Bh.*); an elephant of the king of Mālavā killed by Bhīma (*M. Bh.*); a ṛṣi in the period of Manu Sāvarṇi (*H. Purāṇa*)

**Aśvatthanārāyaṇa** (S) (M) lord of the Aśvattha tree (*Ficus religiosa*); lord of the place where horses rest.

**Aśvatthi** (S) (M) the Aśvattha tree (*Ficus religiosa*) under which horses are kept.

**Aśvatyama** (S) (M) 1. sees beyond 7 (the number 7 is of tāntric significance and one who sees beyond it is supposed to have attained salvation or mokṣa). 3. a seer of the 8th Manvantara (*H. Purāṇa*)

**Aśvavān** (S) (M) 1. rich in horses. 3. a son of King Kuru and Vāhinī (*M. Bh.*)

**Aśvavatī** (S) (F) 1. rich in horses. 3. an apsarā (*V. Purāṇa*); a river (*M. Bh.*)

**Aśvikā** (S) (F) a little mare.

**Aśvin** (S) (M) 1. mounted on horseback; with horses; cavalier. 3. the collective name of the divine physicians – the twin sons of Sūrya and Sañjña, Satya and Dasra, and parents of Nakula and Sahadeva (*M. Bh.*); the zodiac sign of Gemini (*N. Samhitā*); the Vedic god of agriculture (*Ṛg Veda*)

**Āśvineya** (S) (M) 1. son of the aśvins. 3. another name for Sahadeva.

**Aśvinī** (S) (F) 1. possessing horses. 2. wealthy; a swift mover. 3. the first of the 27 lunar mansions (*B. Samhitā*); the nymph who was the mother of the aśvins (*Ṛg Veda*); another name for a wife of the sun.

**Aśvini** (S) (M) 1. possessing horses. 2. wealthy; moves swiftly. 3. the divine physicians (*Ṛg Veda*); the number two (*Ṛg Veda*); a constellation (*V's B. Samhitā*)

**Aśvinīkumāra** (S) (M) 1. the son of Aśvinī. 3. the 2 sons of Vivasvan and Sañjña in her horse form, named Satya and Dasra, who are the physicians of the gods and the fathers of Nakula and Sahadeva (*Br. Purāṇa*)

**Aśvinīsuta** (S) (M) 1. son of Aśvinī. 3. a son of Sūrya and wife of Sutapas (*Br. Purāṇa*)

**Āṭaka** (S) (M) 1. wanderer. 2. homeless; a sadhu. 3. a serpent of the Kaurava dynasty (*M. Bh.*)

**Aṭala** (S) (M) firm; immoveable; stable; steady.

**Atalas** (S) (M) 1. bottomless. 2. depth cannot be gauged. 3. another name for Śiva.

**Atamas** (S) (M) 1. without darkness. 2. flawless; of a clear mind; virtuous; sinless.

**Atandra** (S) (M) 1. free from lassitude. 2. alert; unwearied.

**Atanu** (S) (M) 1. without body. 2. incorporeal; divine. 3. another name for Kāma.

**Ātapana** (S) (M) 1. causing heat. 3. another name for Śiva.

**Ātāpin** (S) (M) 1. radiating heat. 3. a daitya (*K. Sāgara*)

**Atasa** (S) (M) 1. not gross; air; the soul. 2. subtle; divine.

**Atharvaṇa** (S) (M) 1. place where oblations are made; worshipped by the priests. 2. an attar. 3. a sage born from Brahmā's face who rediscovered Agni from the sea and the husband of Śānti and Ćitti (*A. Veda*); a son of Vasiṣṭha (*Bhāgavata*); the 3rd Veda; another name for Śiva.

**Athileśa** (S) (M) lord of intelligence.

**Āti** (S) (M) the Aśoka tree (*Saraca indica*); swan (*Turdus ginginianus*)

**Atibāhu** (S) (M) 1. long armed. 2. according to *Sāmudrika Śastra* which classifies individuals by studying their physical features, people with long arms were considered to be virtuous leaders and warriors. 3. a ṛṣi of the 14th Manvantara (*H. Purāṇa*); a gandharva son of Kaśyapa and Prādhā and brother of Hāhā, Hūhū and Tumburu (*M. Bh.*)

**Atibalā** (S) (F) 1. very strong. 2. a daughter of Dakṣa.

**Atibala** (S) (M) 1. excessive power. 2. immensely powerful; very strong. 3. a sage responsible for the death of Rāma and Lakṣmana (*U. Rāmāyaṇa*); an attendant given to Skanda by Vāyu (*M. Bh.*)

**Atibhāva** (S) (M) 1. superiority. 2. superior; one who overcomes people; situations; emotions.

**Atibhīma** (S) (M) 1. very strong. 3. a son of the Agni Tapa (*M. Bh.*)

**Atićaṇḍā** (S) (F) 1. very fierce. 3. a minor and intense form of Durgā.

**Atićaṇḍa** (S) (M) very fiery.

**Atidatta** (S) (M) 1. to whom much has been given. 2. on whom love and gifts are showered; fortunate. 3. son of Rājādhideva and brother of Datta (*M. Bh.*)

**Atideva** (S) (M) surpassing the gods.

**Atidhanvan** (S) (M) 1. runs very fast. 3. a ṛṣi who was a descendant of Śunaka (*V. Brāhmaṇa*)

**Atihata** (S) (M) firmly fixed.

**Atikāya** (S) (M) 1. with a gigantic body. 3. a rākṣasa son of Rāvaṇa and gandharvī Ćitrāṅgī (*K. Rāmāyaṇa*)

**Ātikī** (S) (F) 1. overflowing; outdoing; marriageable; strolling about; heavy bodied. 3. a wife of Uṣasti (*Ć. Upaniṣad*)

**Atiloma** (S) (M) 1. very hairy. 3. an asura killed by Kṛṣṇa (*M. Bh.*)

**Atima** (S) (M) proud.

**Atimānita** (S) (M) highly honoured.

**Atimānuṣa** (S) (M) 1. more than human. 2. celestial; divine.

**Atimanyu** (S) (M) 1. extremely zealous. 3. a son of Manu (*H. Purāṇa*)

**Atimāya** (S) (M) 1. emancipated from illusion. 2. beyond illusion; attained salvation or mokśa.

**Atimodā** (S) (F) 1. very fragrant; immensely happy. 2. the jasmine (*Jasminum arboreum*)

**Atināman** (S) (M) 1. renowned. 3. a ṛṣi of the 6th Manvantara (*H. Purāṇa*)

**Atīndra** (S) (M) 1. beyond the senses. 2. incogitable; control over the senses; shuns sensous pleasures; pious; chaste; more powerful; meritorious and virtuous than an average king.

**Atiraktā** (S) (F) 1. very red. 2. passionate; fecund; all consuming; unblemished; sacred. 3. one of the 7 tongues of Agni (*A. Purāṇa*)

**Atiratha** (S) (M) 1. with many chariots. 2. wealthy; great with assets; means. 3. a son of the Purū King Matināra (*M. Bh.*)

**Atirātra** (S) (M) 1. made overnight. 3. a son of Manu Ćākṣuṣa and Nadvalā (*V. Purāṇa*)

**Atiriyā** (S) (F) 1. very dear. 2. loved; eagerly sought after; rare.

**Atirūpa** (S) (M) 1. very beautiful. 3. another name for the Supreme Being.

**Ātiṣa** (S) (M) 1. fire. 2. sacred; glows; is resplendent; all consuming; purifying.

**Atiśakra** (S) (M) superior to Indra.

**Atiṣaṇḍa** (S) (M) 1. very pushy; extremely impotent. 3. a serpent among those who received Balarāma's soul (*M. Bh.*)

**Atiśaya** (S) (M) 1. excellence. 2. meritorious; superior; pre-eminent.

**Atisena** (S) (M) 1. with large army. 2. a king; a commander.

**Atiśī** (S) (M) 1. surpasses. 2. excels; full of fire.

**Atiśṛṅga** (S) (M) 1. surpasses the peak. 2. surpassed perfection; divine. 3. an attendant given to Skanda by Vindhyā (*M. Bh.*)

**Atisthira** (S) (M) 1. very stable. 3. an attendant given to Skanda by Mahāmeru (*M. Bh.*)

**Atisvārya** (S) (M) 1. beyond notes. 3. the 7th note in music which is beyond the 6 notes.

**Atithi** (S) (M) 1. arriving without appointment. 2. a guest. 3. an attendant of Soma; another name for Agni and Suhotra the grandson of Rāma.

**Atithigva** (S) (M) 1. to whom guests should go. 2. guesthouse. 3. another name for King Divodāsa who was a helper of Indra (*Ṛg Veda*)

**Ativarćas** (S) (M) 1. very glorious. 3. an attendant given to Skanda by Himavān (*M. Bh.*)

**Ativiśva** (S) (M) 1. superior to the universe. 2. divine; celestial. 3. a muni (*M. Bh.*)

**Atiyā** (S) (M) to surpass.

**Atiyāma** (S) (M) 1. very black. 2. very dark. 3. an attendant given to Skanda by Varuṇa (*M. Bh.*)

**Atkīla** (S) (M) 1. solidly fixed. 2. an ascetic or hermit who is unwavering in his meditation. 3. a female ṛṣi who was a descendant of Viśvāmitra and author of some Vedic hymns (*Ṛg Veda*)

**Ātmabhava** (S) (M) 1. mind born. 2. created from the mind. 3. another name for Kāma.

**Ātmabhū** (S) (M) 1. creates oneself; self made. 3. another name for Brahmā, Viṣṇu, Śiva and Kāma.

**Ātmādhikā** (S) (F) dearer than one's self.

**Ātmajā** (S) (F) 1. daughter of the soul. 3. another name for Pārvatī.

**Ātmājñāna** (S) (M) 1. self knowledge. 2. attained self realization, salvation or mokṣa.

**Ātmajyoti** (S) (M) 1. the light of the soul. 3. another name for the Supreme Spirit.

**Ātman** (S) (M) 1. soul, principle of life. 3. another name for Kṛṣṇa.

**Ātmananda** (S) (M) rejoicing in the soul.

**Ātmārāma** (S) (M) 1. pervading the soul. 2. omnipresent; the Supreme Spirit.

**Ātmavīra** (S) (M) 1. with a mighty soul. 2. attained mokṣa or salvation.

**Ātmaya** (S) (M) blessed with a long life.

**Ātmodbhavā** (S) (F) 1. born of the soul. 2. a daughter.

**Ātmodbhava** (S) (M) 1. born of the soul. 2. a son. 3. another name for Kāma.

**Atnu** (S) (M) the sun.

**Ātreya** (S) (M) 1. receptacle of glory; crosses the 3 worlds. 3. a sage who was a composer of hymns and had the power to cross planets (*Brahma Purāṇa*)

**Ātreyī** (S) (F) 1. receptacle of glory; crosses the three worlds; belonging to Atri. 3. wife of King Ūru the son of Manu and the mother of Aṅga, Sumanas, Svāti, Kratu, Aṅgiras and Gaya (*A. Purāṇa*); daughter of sage Atri who married Aṅgiras the son of Agni and who later became the Paruṣṇī river (*Br. Purāṇa*); a river (*M. Bh.*)

**Atri** (S) (M) 1. who devours; overcomes; progresses; prosperous and glorified. 3. a mind-born son of Brahmā, a great ṛṣi and the author of a number of Vedic hymns who was the husband of Anasuyā, the father of Dattātreya, Durvāsas and Ćandra (or Soma), the moon, who were the incarnations of Viṣṇu, Brahmā and Śiva, as also the father of Prāćinabarhis; according to the Vedas, represents one of the stars in the Great Bear, and according to the Purāṇas is said to have produced the moon from his eye (*A. Purāṇa*); a son of Śukrāćārya (*M. Bh.*); another name for Śiva.

**Aṭṭahāsa** (S) (M) 1. with loud laughter. 3. a Yaksa; another name for Śiva.

**Aṭṭana** (S) (M) discus.

**Atula** (S) (M) unequalled.

**Atulavikrama** (S) (M) of unequalled valour.

**Atulya** (S) (M) unequalled.

**Atyadbhūta** (S) (M) 1. extremely unique. 3. Indra in the 9th Manvantara (*H. Purāṇa*)

**Atyāditya** (S) (M) 1. surpassing the sun. 2. surpasses the lustre of the sun; glorious; renowned; enlightened.

**Ātyantika** (S) (M) 1. infinite; endless; universal. 2. continual; uninterrupted; whole; flawless.

**Atyarāti** (S) (M) 1. exceedingly envious; maligns. 3. a son of Janatapa (*M. Bh.*)

**Atyūhā** (S) (F) 1. that which is fragrant. 2. the jasmine (*Jasminum villosum*)

**Au** (S) (M) Śiva.

**Aućiti** (S) (F) appropriateness; the soul of good poetry (*Kṣemendra's Oućityavićārćarća*)

**Audambara** (S) (M) 1. surrounded by water. 2. cloud. 3. the king of Udambara and an ally of Yudhiṣṭhira (*M. Bh.*)

**Aukthya** (S) (M) 1. belonging to praise. 2. much praised. 3. a glorifying prayer of the *Sāma Veda*.

**Aurasa** (S) (M) produced by oneself; son.

**Aurddhva** (S) (M) 1. belonging to the upper world; belonging to the stars. 2. celestial being; one who travels the star path. 3. a rāga.

**Aurjitya** (S) (M) (F) energy; vigour; strength.

**Aurva** (S) (M) 1. born of the thigh. 3. a sage of the Bhṛgu family who was the son of Cyavana and Āruṣī and the grandfather of Jamadagni (*M. Bh.*); a son of Vasiṣṭha (*H. Purāṇa*); another name for Agni.

**Aurvaseya** (S) (M) 1. son of Urvaśī.

3. another name for Agastya (*Ṛg Veda*)

**Auśija** (S) (M) 1. born of the dawn. 2. bright as the dawn; renowned; glorious; desirous; zealous. 3. a king who equalled Indra in strength (*M. Bh.*); a sage who was a son of Aṅgiras and a member of Yudhiṣṭhira's court (*M. Bh.*)

**Auśīnarī** (S) (F) 1. belonging to the mountains. 3. a Śūdra girl of Uśīnara from whom was born Kaksivān by Sage Gautama (*M. Bh.*); the wife of Purūravas (*Vikramorvaśīyam*)

**Autathya** (S) (M) 1. knower of the substance. 2. knows the truth; a philosopher; wise; illumined; enlightened. 3. son of Utathya (*M. Bh.*)

**Auttamikā** (S) (M) related to the pious; related to the gods of the sky.

**Auttānapadi** (S) (M) 1. descendant of Uttānapāda. 3. the Dhruva star (*Bhā. Purāṇa*)

**Auvvayar** (S) (F) 1. best among the best. 3. a celebrated Tamil poetess who lived for 240 years.

**Ạvabhā** (S) (F) shining; brilliant.

**Avabhāsita** (S) (M) shining; bright.

**Avabodha** (S) (M) 1. perception; knowledge; awakening. 2. wise; enlightened; a preceptor.

**Avacūḍa** (S) (M) 1. a pendant. 2. ornaments; embellishes; the pendant crest or streamer of a standard.

**Avadāta** (S) (M) clean; clear; pure; blameless; excellent; of white splendour.

**Avadha** (S) (M) inviolable; invulnerable.

**Avadhūteśvara** (S) (M) 1. lord of ascetics. 2. very pious; very chaste. 3. an incarnation of Śiva (*S. Purāṇa*)

**Avagāha** (S) (M) 1. to plunge into; to be absorbed in. 3. a warrior of the Vṛṣṇi dynasty (*M. Bh.*)

**Āvaha** (S) (M) 1. bearer; conveyor. 2. a mediator. 3. a vāyu (*M. Bh.*); one of the 7 tongues of fire.

**Āvāha** (S) (M) 1. invitation; a guest of honour. 3. a son of Śvaphalka (*H. Purāṇa*)

**Avajaya** (S) (M) overcoming; winning by conquest.

**Avajita** (S) (M) won by conquest.

**Avajiti** (S) (F) conquest; victory.

**Avajyuta** (S) (M) 1. illumining. 2. illuminates others; enlightened.

**Avakāśa** (S) (M) visible; manifest; shining. 2. space; opportunity; room. 3. certain verses in the Kātyāvana Srauta-Sūtra.

**Avalokiteśvara** (S) (M) 1. watchful lord. 3. a Bodhisattva (*B. Literature*)

**Avanati** (S) (F) 1. bowing down. 2. humble; modest.

**Avani** (S) (F) 1. on course. 2. the bed of a river; the earth.

**Avanibhūṣaṇa** (S) (M) jewel of the earth; ornament of the world.

**Avanija** (S) (M) 1. son of the earth. 2. a king.

**Avanikānta** (S) (M) beloved of the earth; a king.

**Avanimohana** (S) (M) attracting the world.

**Avanīndra** (S) (M) lord of the earth.

**Avanipāla** (S) (M) protector of the earth.

**Avanīśa** (S) (M) 1. lord of the earth. 2. a king.

**Avanīśvara** (S) (M) 1. god of the earth. 2. a king.

**Avantas** (S) (M) 1. crest. 2. the ornament worn on the head; ornaments; embellishes. 3. a son of Dhṛṣṭa.

**Avantī** (S) (F) 1. endless; modest. 3. the city of Ujjaini which is one of the sacred cities of the Hindus (*M. Bh.*)

**Āvantikā** (S) (F) 1. very modest; coming from Avanti. 3. the daughter of Yaugandharāyaṇa (*M. Bh.*)

**Avantivarman** (S) (M) 1. defending Avanti. 3. a king (*R. Taraṅginī*)

**Avantīvatī** (S) (F) 1. bowed down. 3. wife of Pālakạ (*K. Sāgara*)

**Āvapāka** (S) (M) sinless; spotless; a bracelet of gold.

**Avarā** (S) (F) 1. inferior. 2. youngest. 3. another name for Pārvatī.

**Avarajā** (S) (F) younger sister.

**Avaraja** (S) (M) younger brother.

**Āvaraṇa** (S) (M) 1. cover; shelter. 3. a king of the dynasty of Viśvakarman who was the son of Bharata and Pañcajanī (*Bhā. Purāṇa*)

**Avarīyas** (S) (M) 1. not better. 2. belongs to

common; to the common masses. 3. a son of Manu Sāvarṇa (*H. Purāṇa*)

**Avarodha** (S) (M) 1. obstacle. 2. an obstacle for the enemies. 3. a king of the Bharata dynasty (*A. Brāhmaṇa*)

**Avarokin** (S) (M) shining; brilliant.

**Avas** (S) (M) favour; protection; assistance; pleasure.

**Avaśa** (S) (M) independent; free.

**Āvasathya** (S) (M) 1. being in a house; domestic fire. 3. son of Pavamāna and Sanśatī (*M. Purāṇa*)

**Avasthya** (S) (M) 1. adaptable; suitable. 3. an Agni (*M. Bh.*)

**Avasyu** (S) (M) 1. desirous of helping. 3. another name for Indra.

**Avatansā** (S) (F) garland; ring shaped ornament; earring; crest.

**Avatāra** (S) (M) descent from heaven or a complete incarnation of a god (usually Viṣṇu)

**Avatsāra** (S) (M) 1. presentation. 3. a descendant of Kaśyapa and Praśravaṇa (*M. Bh.*); a seer mentioned in the *Ṛg Veda*.

**Avi** (S) (M) 1. favourable; kindly disposed; protector; lord; air, wind; the wooden Soma strainer; favourite; mountain. 3. another name for the sun.

**Avicala** (S) (M) immovable; steady; firm.

**Avidānta** (S) (M) 1. unsubdued. 3. a son of Śatadhanvan (*H. Purāṇa*)

**Avidoṣa** (S) (M) faultless.

**Avijita** (S) (M) one wno cannot be conquered.

**Avijña** (S) (M) 1. ignorant. 3. son of Anila (*M. Bh.*)

**Avijñāta** (S) (M) 1. not known; incogitable. 3. a son of Anala (*H. Purāṇa*)

**Avijñātagati** (S) (M) 1. with unknown speed. 2. very swift. 3. a son of the vasu Anila; another name for Śiva (*Bhāgavata*)

**Avika** (S) (M) lives in a group; as hard as the earth; sheep; tough and strong; diamond.

**Avikala** (S) (M) unimpaired; entire; perfect; whole; all.

**Aviklava** (S) (M) not confused; not unsteady.

**Avikśipa** (S) (M) 1. unable to distribute. 2. cannot discern between the good and the bad. 3. a son of Śvaphalka (*H. Purāṇa*)

**Avikṣit** (S) (M) 1. undeveloped; not seen before. 3. a king who was the son of Karandhama, the father of Marutta and was considered the equal of Indra (*Ṛg Veda*); a son of King Kuru and Vāhinī (*M. Bh.*)

**Avilasa** (S) (M) free from whims; faithful; constant.

**Avimukta** (S) (M) 1. not loosened; not unharnessed. 3. a Tīrtha near Benaras (*M. Bh.*)

**Avimukteśa** (S) (M) 1. firm; resolute; a god. 3. a form of Śiva (*Ś. Purāṇa*)

**Avināśa** (S) (M) indestructible.

**Avindhya** (S) (M) 1. unmoving; firm; solid. 3. a minister of Rāvaṇa who prevented him from killing Sītā (*V. Rāmāyaṇa*)

**Avinīdevas** (S) (M) 1. not showing respect to the gods. 3. father of Mainda.

**Āvinna** (S) (M) existing; being.

**Avipriya** (S) (M) very dear; very favourable; favourite.

**Avirāga** (S) (M) 1. unceasing. 3. a Prākṛt poet.

**Avirāma** (S) (M) 1. uninterrupted. 2. in succession; continuous.

**Aviratha** (S) (M) 1. continuous. 3. a hermit of the Kardama family who was the son of Ketuman (*H. Purāṇa*)

**Āvirhotra** (S) (M) 1. performing the oblation. 3. a king of the dynasty of Viśvakarmā and the son of Ṛṣabha and Jayantī (*Ṛg Veda*)

**Aviṣa** (S) (M) 1. not poisonous; sky; ocean; king. 3. nectar-like; life giving.

**Aviṣī** (S) (F) 1. not poisonous; heaven; earth; river. 2. nectar-like; life giving.

**Aviśyā** (S) (F) 1. desire; ardour. 2. desirous; full of ardour.

**Avita**(S) (M) protected.

**Avitṛ** (S) (M) protector.

**Āvṛta** (S) (M) path; direction; order; method

**Avyakta** (S) (M) 1. invisible; imperceptible; the universal spirit. 3. another name for Viṣṇu, Śiva, Kāma.

**Avyaya** (S) (M) 1. not liable to change; imperishable; undecaying. 3. a serpent of the family of Dhṛtarāṣṭra (*M. Bh.*); a seer of the 13th Manvantara (*H. Purāṇa*)

**Avyayas** (S) (M) 1. imperishable; undecaying. 3. a son of Manu Raivata (*H. Purāṇa*); a nāga demon (*M. Bh.*); another name for Viṣṇu and Śiva.

**Ayahkāya** (S) (M) 1. iron bodied. 2. very strong. 3. a daitya (*K. Sāgara*)

**Ayahśaṅku** (S) (M) 1. an iron bolt. 3. an asura reborn as a Kekaya prince (*H. Purāṇa*)

**Ayahśiras** (S) (M) 1. iron headed. 3. an asura (*H. Purāṇa*)

**Ayahsthūṇa** (S) (M) 1. with iron pillars. 3. a ṛṣi (*Ś. Brāhmaṇa*)

**Ayāsmaya** (S) (M) 1. made of iron. 3. a son of Manu Svārocisa (*H. Purāṇa*)

**Ayāsya** (S) (M) indefatigable; valiant; agile.

**Āyati** (S) (F) 1. stretching the future; extending the lineage; a descendant. 2. posterity; majesty; dignity; restraint of mind. 3. a daughter of Mahāmeru, the wife of Dhātā and mother of Prāṇa (*V. Purāṇa*)

**Ayāti** (S) (M) 1. no ascetic; spacious; majestic; dignity. 3. a son of King Nahuṣa and brother of Yati and Yayāti (*M. Bh.*)

**Āyatī** (S) (M) coming near; arrival.

**Ayobāhu** (S) (M) 1. iron armed. 2. very strong. 3. a son of Dhṛtarāṣṭra (*M. Bh.*)

**Āyoda** (S) (M) 1. giver of life. 3. a ṛṣi (*Ṛg Veda*)

**Ayodhikā** (S) (F) 1. never quarrels. 2. of calm disposition; sedate; peace-loving.

**Ayodhyā** (S) (M) 1. not to be fought against. 2. irresistible. 3. the city of Rāma on the river Śarayū (*V. Rāmāyaṇa*)

**Ayodhyadhaumya** (S) (M) 1. the irresistable ascetic. 2. an ascetic who cannot be defeated in the field of knowledge. 3. a great sage who was the preceptor of Uddālaka, Upamanyu and Veda (*Ṛg Veda*)

**Ayomukhī** (S) (F) 1. iron faced. 3. a rākṣasī (*V. Rāmāyaṇa*)

**Ayuddha** (S) (M) irresistable; unconquerable.

**Ayudha** (S) (M) does not fight; peace-loving.

**Ayugmanetra** (S) (M) 1. with odd numbered eyes. 3. another name for Śiva who has 3 eyes.

**Ayugū** (S) (F) 1. without a companion. 2. the only daughter.

**Ayuja** (S) (M) without a companion; without an equal.

**Āyus** (S) (M) 1. age; duration of life; man; son; family; lineage; a divine personification presiding over life. 3. fire personified as a son of Purūravas and Urvaśī and father of Nahuṣa by Svarbhāvanavī (*M. Bh.*); the king of frogs whose daughter Suśobhanā married King Parīkṣit (*M. Bh.*)

**Āyuṣmān** (M) 1. one blessed with a long life. 3. a brother of Dhruva (*V. Purāṇa*); a son of Saṁhrāda and grandson of Hiraṇyakaśipū (*A. Purāṇa*); a son of Uttānapāda.

**Āyustejas** (S) (M) 1. energy of life. 3. a Buddha (*B. Literature*)

**Ayuta** (S) (M) 1. unimpeded; unbound; myriad. 3. a son of Rādhikā (*Bhāgavata*)

**Ayutājit** (S) (M) 1. conquerer of many. 3. a king who was the son of Sindhudvīpa and father of Ṛtuparṇa (*Brahma Purāṇa*); a son of Bhajamāna (*V. Purāṇa*)

**Ayutanāyī** (S) (M) 1. judge of many. 2. the head of a province; the leader of a group; a king. 3. a Purū king who was the son of King Bhauma and Suyajña, the husband of Kāmā and father of Akrodhana (*M. Bh.*)

**Ayutāśva** (S) (M) 1. having many horses. 2. the commander of the cavalaries. 3. a son of Sindhudvīpa (*V. Purāṇa*)

**Ayutāyu** (S) (M) 1. with an unlimited age. 3. a son of Jayasena Ārvin (*V. Purāṇa*); a son of Śrutavat (*V. Purāṇa*); a king who was the son of Śrutaśravas and who ruled for 1000 years (*V. Purāṇa*); the father of King Ṛtuparṇa (*Bhā. Purāṇa*)

**Azhagar** (Tamil) (M) 1. the beautiful one. 3. the god of the Azhagirisami temple of Madurai.

B

**Bābhravī** (S) (F) 1. fire-clad; roaming about; victorious; carrying. 2. omnipresent; descendant of sage Babhru. 3. another name for Durgā.

**Babhri** (S) (M) victorious; carrying away.

**Babhru** (S) (M) 1. fire. 2. fierce; brown; tawny; with tawny hair. 3. a descendant of Atri and an author of *Ṛg Veda*; a son of Viśvāmitra (*M. Bh.*); a son of Viśvagarbha (*H. Purāṇa*); a son of Lomapāda (*V. Rāmāyaṇa*); a gandharva (*V. Purāṇa*); a disciple of Śaunaka (*V. Rāmāyaṇa*); a Yādava of the Vṛṣṇi dynasty who was a friend of Kṛṣṇa (*M. Bh.*); a king of Kāśi (*M. Bh.*); a son of King Virāṭa (*M. Bh.*); a son of Druhyu; a constellation (*V's B. Samhitā*); another name for Viṣṇu, Kṛṣṇa and Śiva.

**Bābhru** (S) (F) 1. reddish brown cow. 3. a wife of Yadu.

**Babhrudaivavṛdha** (S) (M) 1. oldest among the fierce gods. 3. a Yādava king who was a disciple of Nārada (*Bhāgavata*)

**Babhrukeśa** (S) (M) brown haired.

**Babhruloman** (S) (M) brown haired.

**Babhrumālin** (S) (M) 1. fire keeper. 3. a sage who was a prominent member of the court of Yudhiṣṭhira (*M. Bh.*)

**Babhrusetu** (S) (M) 1. a bridge of fire. 3. a Gāndhāra king who was the brother of Druhyu and father of Purovasu (*A. Purāṇa*)

**Babhruvāhana** (S) (M) 1. chariot of fire; carring fire; the brown chariot. 3. the son of Arjuna and Chitrāṅgadā and king of Mahodaya (*M. Bh.*)

**Babila** (S) (M) a house; swift.

**Babitā** (S) (F) 1. born in the first quarter of an astrological day. 2. reference here to 'bava' or 'baba' as being that quarter.

**Bābul** (S) (M) father.

**Bachendrī** (S) (F) the sense of speech; tongue.

**Bachharāja** (S) (M) 1. king among the calves. 2. very strong.

**Bachil** (S) (M) 1. one who speaks much. 2. an orator.

**Bādal** (S) (M) cloud.

**Badara** (S) (M) the Jujube tree (*Zizyphus jujuba*)

**Bādarāyaṇa** (S) (M) 1. belonging to the Jujube tree (*Zizyphus jujuba*); a descendant of Viṣṇu. 3. the first teacher to formulate the system of Vedāntic philosophy between 200-450 A.D. (*D. Śastra*); another name for sage Vyāsa.

**Bādarāyaṇī** (S) (F) new; young; pure; perfume.

**Bādarāyaṇi** (S) (M) 1. dwelling on the Jujube tree (*Zizyphus jujuba*). 3. another name for Śuka.

**Badarī** (S) (F) the Jujube Tree (*Zizyphus jujuba*); a source of the Gaṅgā and the neighbouring hermitage of Nara and Nārāyaṇa (*H. Purāṇa*)

**Badarīdāsa** (S) (M) devotee of Viṣṇu.

**Badarīnātha** (S) (M) 1. lord of Badarī. 3. a temple at Badarī (*H. Purāṇa*); another name for Viṣṇu.

**Badarīśaila** (M) 1. the rock of Badarī. 2. the mountain where the badarī or Jujube tree grows.

**Badarīvāsā** (S) (F) 1. dwelling at Badarī. 3. another name for Durgā.

**Baḍavāgni** (S) (M) 1. mare's fire. 3. another name for Agni in the form of submarine fire.

**Baḍavānala** (S) (M) 1. pepper powder. 3. another name for Agni.

**Baddhānanda** 1. bound by pleasure; having pleasure. 2. attached; joyful.

**Baddhānurāga** (S) (M) 1. bound by love. 2. feeling affection.

**Baddharājya** (S) (M) 1. bound to the throne. 2. succeeding to the throne.

**Badhira** (S) (M) 1. deaf. 3. a serpent who was a son of Kaśyapa (*M. Bh.*)

**Bāduli** (S) (M) 1. logician. 2. argumentative. 3. a son of Viśvāmitra (*M. Bh.*)

**Bāgeśrī** (S) (F) 1. prosperity; beauty. 3. a rāga.

**Bagulā** (S) (F) 1. crane. 3. the crane headed village goddess now identified with Durgā.

**Bāhu** (S) (M) 1. arm. 2. the shadow of the sundial; the constellation Ārdrā. 3. a son of Vṛka (*H. Purāṇa*); a son of Vajra (*V. Purāṇa*);

a daitya (*M. Bh.*)

**Bahubala** (S) (M) 1. with great strength. 2. a lion.

**Bahubhujā** (S) (F) 1. many armed. 3. another name for Durgā.

**Bāhubhedin** (S) (M) 1. arm breaker. 3. another name for Viṣṇu.

**Bahudā** (S) (F) 1. giving much. 3. a river now known as Jhelum; a wife of Parīkṣit.

**Bahudama** (S) (M) 1. suppressor of many. 2. strong and powerful. 3. an attendant of Skanda (*M. Bh.*)

**Bahudāmā** (S) (F) 1. suppressor of many. 2. strong and powerful. 3. a mother of Skanda's retinue (*Ś. Purāṇa*)

**Bahudantī** (S) (F) 1. with many teeth; with large teeth; with whom many folk-tales are connected. 3. the mother of Purandara (*H. Purāṇa*)

**Bahudhana** (S) (M) having much wealth.

**Bahudhara** (S) (M) 1. bearer of many. 2. supporting many; a king.

**Bahudhāra** (S) (M) 1. many edged. 2. a diamond. 3. Indra's thunderbolt.

**Bahugandhā** (S) (F) 1. strong scented; very fragrant. 3. a bud of the Ćampaka tree (*Michelia champaka*); the jasmine (*Jasminum auriculatum*); sandalwood; musk.

**Bahugava** (S) (M) 1. owning many cattle. 3. a king of the family of Yayāti (*Bhā. Purāṇa*)

**Bahugraha** (S) (M) 1. holding much; receiving much. 2. a water jar; a minister.

**Bahuguṇa** (S) (M) 1. with many good qualities; many threaded. 2. rope. 3. a gandharva (*M. Bh.*)

**Bahujñāna** (S) (M) 1. possessed with great knowledge. 2. a scholar; a philosopher.

**Bahuhiraṇya** (S) (M) rich in gold.

**Bāhuka** (S) (M) 1. dependant; servile. 2. the arm. 3. name assumed by Nala as the charioteer to King Ṛtuparṇa (*Nalopākhyāna*); a son of Vṛka (*Purāṇas*); a serpent of the Kaurava family (*M. Bh.*); a hero of the Vṛṣnis (*M. Bh.*)

**Bahukalyāṇa** (S) (M) well-wisher of many; extremely illustrious; noble.

**Bahuketu** (S) (M) 1. many peaked. 2. a mountain.

**Bahukṣaṇa** (S) (M) 1. enduring much. 3. another name for a Buddha or a Jaina saint.

**Bahulā** (S) (F) 1. broad; ample; abundant; a cow; cardamoms (*Elettaria cardamomum*); indigo (*indicum*). 3. a mother attending on Skanda (*M. Bh.*); the wife of Uttama who was the son of Uttānapāda (*Mā. Purāṇa*); a river of ancient India (*M. Bh.*); a digit of the moon.

**Bahula** (S) (M) 1. thick; dense; broad; spacious; ample; large; abundant. 3. a Jina born under the Pleiades; the dark half of the month; the month of Kārttika when the moon is near the Pleiades (*A. Koṣa*); a prajāpati (*V. Purāṇa*)

**Bahulāśvan** (S) (M) 1. many horses; a strong horse. 3. a king of the family of Rāma (*Bhā. Purāṇa*)

**Bahulī** (S) (F) 1. manifold; magnified; multiplied. 2. one who has many facets. 3. the full moon in the month of Kārttika (*Pāṇinī*)

**Bahuli** (S) (M) 1. manifold; magnified; multiplied. 2. a versatile person. 3. a son of Viśvāmitra (*H. Purāṇa*)

**Bahulikā** (S) (F) 1. manifold; magnified; multiplied. 2. a multifaceted personality. 3. the Pleiades.

**Bahumānya** (S) (M) esteemed and honoured by many.

**Bahumārgī** (S) (M) follower of many paths; a place where many roads meet.

**Bahumatī** (S) (F) 1. extremely knowledgeable. 2. a scholar.

**Bahumitra** (S) (M) 1. friend of many; with many friends. 2. popular; famous.

**Bahumūlaka** (S) (M) 1. with many origins; with many roots. 2. obtained virtues from many sources. 3. a serpent who was the son of Kaśyapa and Kadru (*M. Bh.*)

**Bahumūlya** (S) (M) 1. high priced. 2. anxiously sought after; precious; rare.

**Bahumurdhan** (S) (M) 1. many headed. 3. another name for Viṣṇu.

**Bahupaṭu** (S) (M) very clever.

**Bahuprada** (S) (M) one who donates much; liberal.

**Bahupriya** (S) (M) dear to many.

**Bahupuṣpā** (S) (F) 1. has many flowers;

decorated with many flowers; many blossomed. 2. respected; venerated. 3. *Erythrina indica*.

**Bahuputra** (S) (M) 1. with many sons; the devil's tree (*Alstonia scholaris*). 3. a prajāpati who was one of the spiritual sons of Brahmā (*Vā. Purāṇa*)

**Bahuputrī** (S) (F) 1. with many sons. 3. another name for Durgā whose blessings are invoked when praying for a son.

**Bahuputrikā** (S) (F) 1. with many daughters. 3. an attendant of Skanda (*M. Bh.*)

**Bahurai** (S) (M) with great riches.

**Bahuratha** (S) (M) 1. one who has many chariots. 2. a king. 3. a king belonging to the Bharata family (*Bhā. Purāṇa*)

**Bahuratnā** (S) (F) rich in gems.

**Bahūrja** (S) (M) 1. full of energy. 2. energetic; strong; powerful.

**Bahurūpā** (S) (F) 1. with many forms. 3. one of the 7 tongues of fire (*A. Koṣa*)

**Bahurūpa** (S) (M) 1. with many forms. 2. vareigated. 3. a son of Medhātithi (*Ṛg Veda*); a rudra who was the son of Kaśyapa and Surabhī (*Purāṇas*); another name for Brahmā, Viṣṇu, Śiva, Kāma, Rudra, the Sun and a Buddha.

**Bahuśakti** (S) (M) very powerful.

**Bāhuśakti** (S) (M) strong armed.

**Bāhuśālin** (S) (M) 1. strong armed. 3. a son of Dhṛtarāṣṭra (*M. Bh.*); a dānava; another name for Śiva.

**Bāhusambhava** (S) (M) 1. born from the arm. 3. another name for a Kṣatriya – a member of the military class which is supposed to have been born from the arm of Brahmā.

**Bahuśasta** (S) (M) excellent; right; happy.

**Bahuśruta** (S) (M) 1. extremely learned; much heard of. 2. well versed in the Vedas.

**Bahusūkta** (S) (M) 1. made of many hymns. 2. a stotra.

**Bahusuvarṇa** (S) (M) rich in gold.

**Bāhusuyaśā** (S) (F) 1. earning fame through the strength of her arms. 2. famous for her valour. 3. the wife of King Parīkśit of the Kuru dynasty and the mother of Bhīmasena (*M. Bh.*)

**Bahuvāśin** (S) (M) 1. controller of many. 3. a son of Dhṛtarāṣṭra (*M. Bh.*)

**Bāhuvata** (S) (M) strong armed.

**Bahuvida** (S) (M) 1. very learned. 2. wise; sagacious; enlightened.

**Bahuvidha** (S) (M) 1. very intelligent; knows many arts. 2. versatile; many faceted; talented. 3. a king of Aṅga (*A. Purāṇa*)

**Bahuvikrama** (S) (M) very powerful.

**Bahuvīrya** (S) (M) very powerful.

**Bāhuvṛkta** (S) (M) 1. surrounded by arms; hailed by arms. 2. a commander; a leader; a preceptor. 3. a sage and descendant of Atri (*V. Rāmāyaṇa*)

**Bahuyojanā** (S) (M) 1. great planner; a vast area of land. 3. a mother of Skanda's retinue (*M. Bh.*)

**Bahvīśvarā** (S) (F) 1. follower of many gods; god of many. 3. a sacred place on the banks of the Narmadā river.

**Bāhyakarṇa** (S) (M) 1. listener; with protruding ears. 2. observer; one with many ambassadors. 3. a serpent son of Kaśyapa and Kadru (*M. Bh.*)

**Bāhyakuṇḍa** (S) (M) 1. out of its hole. 2. emancipated; progressive; enlightened. 3. a serpent son of Kaśyapa (*M. Bh.*)

**Bāhyāśvana** (S) (M) 1. protecting from outside troubles. 3. a king of the Purū dynasty who was the son of King Purujit (*M. Bh.*)

**Baidaujas** (S) (M) 1. without a rhyme. 2. irregular; unbound; free. 3. a son of Viṣṇu and Aditi (*P. Purāṇa*)

**Baijanātha** (S) (M) 1. descendant of the lord of creation. 3. descendant of Bījanātha or Śiva.

**Baira** (S) (M) brave.

**Bajaraṅga** (S) (M) 1. rock-bodied. 2. mighty; powerful. 3. another name for Hanumān.

**Bajraṅgabali** (S) (M) 1. with a rock-like body. 3. another name for Hanumān.

**Bakā** (S) (F) 1. crane. 3. the daughter of the demon Sumāli and maternal aunt of Rāvaṇa (*U. Rāmāyaṇa*)

**Baka** (S) (M) 1. heron; crane (in Hindu mythology, the crane is represented as a bird of great cunning and circumspection);

*Sesbania grandiflora*. 3. a rākṣasa killed by Bhīma (*M. Bh.*); a sage (*M. Bh.*); another name for Kubera.

**Bakajita** (S) (M) 1. conqueror of Baka. 3. another name for Bhīma.

**Bakanakha** (S) (M) 1. with nails as sharp as that of a crane. 3. a son of Viśvāmitra (*M. Bh.*)

**Bakarāja** (S) (M) 1. king of the cranes. 3. another name for Rājadharman the son of Kaśyapa.

**Bakaripu** (S) (M) 1. enemy of Baka. 3. another name for Bhīma.

**Bakasahavāsin** (S) (M) 1. fellow lodger of the heron; living with the cranes. 3. another name for the lotus.

**Bakavata** (S) (M) 1. with the qualities of a heron. 2. very attentive patient; watchful; circumspect.

**Bakavatī** (S) (F) 1. with the qualities of a heron. 2. very attentive; patient; watchful; cautious. 3. a river (*R. Taraṅgiṇī*)

**Bakerukā** (S) (F) 1. a small crane; a branch of a tree bent by the wind. 2. cautious; clever; goal oriented.

**Bakulā** (S) (F) 1. resembling a crane; the blossom of the Bakula tree (*Mimusops elengi*). 2. very attentive; patient; watchful; circumspect.

**Bakula** (S) (M) 1. resembling a crane; the blossom of the Bakula tree – the flowers of this tree are said to blossom when kissed by women. 3. another name for Śiva.

**Bākulamālā** (S) (F) a garland of Bakula blossoms (*Mimusops elengi*)

**Bakuleśa** (S) (M) lord of blossoms.

**Bakulī** (S) (F) 1. lady of the blossoms. 2. nature. 3. a rāgiṇī of rāga Bhairava.

**Bakulikā** (S) (F) small Bakula blossom (*Mimusops elengi*)

**Bakulitā** (S) (F) decorated with Bakula blossoms (*Mimusops elengi*)

**Bakura** (S) (M) 1. horn; thunderbolt; lightening; trumpet used in battle. 2. illuminates; glorifies.

**Bālā** (S) (F) 1. girl; jasmine. 2. young; newly risen; child. 3. mother of Vāli and Sugrīva said to have been formed by the eye dust of Prajāpati (*V. Rāmāyaṇa*)

**Bāla** (S) (M) 1. young; newly risen. 2. simple; pure. 3. another name for the sun.

**Bala** (S) (M) 1. power. 2. strength; energy. 3. force personified as a viśvadeva; a son of Kṛṣṇa (*M. Bh.*); a horse of the moon (*V. Purāṇa*); a Jaina elder brother of Vāsudeva; a demon who was the son of Kaśyapa and Danu (*M. Bh.*); a deva born to Varuṇa from his elder brothers's wife (*M. Bh.*); a son of King Parīkṣit of the Ikṣvāku dynasty (*M. Bh.*); a monkey warrior of Rāma (*M. Bh.*); one of the 2 attendants given to Skanda by Vāyu; a sage and son of Aṅgiras (*M. Bh.*); a viśvadeva (*M. Bh.*); a demon killed by Indra and subsequently turned into a diamond mine (*Ṛg Veda*)

**Balā** (S) (F) 1. force; power; energy. 3. a daughter of Raudrāśva; a deity who executes the orders of the 17th Arhat of the present Avasarpiṇī.

**Balabandhu** (S) (M) 1. having power as a friend. 2. always helped by power; associated with strength. 3. a son of Manu Raivata (*Mā. Purāṇa*); a son of Bhṛgu (*Vā. Purāṇa*)

**Balabhadra** (S) (M) 1. one with power. 2. strong; powerful. 3. another name for Balarāma or of Ananta the serpent identified with him (*Purāṇas*); a descendant of Bharata (*Bhāgavata*)

**Balabhṛt** (S) (M) 1. carrying a lot of strength. 2. powerful; mighty; strong.

**Balaćakravartin** (S) (M) a powerful monarch.

**Bālaćandra** (S) (M) 1. the crescent moon. 2. the young or waxing moon.

**Bālaćarya** (S) (M) 1. behaves like a child. 2. innocent; curious. 3. another name for Skanda.

**Baladā** (S) (F) 1. bestower of strength. 3. a daughter of Raudrāśva (*H. Purāṇa*)

**Balada** (S) (M) 1. bestower of strength. 3. the 1st son of the Agni named Bhānu (*M. Bh.*)

**Bāladeva** (S) (M) a young god.

**Baladeva** (S) (M) 1. lord of strength. 2. the wind. 3. the elder brother of Kṛṣṇa regarded as a nāga (*M. Bh.*)

**Baladeya** (S) (M) bestower of strength.

**Baladhara** (S) (M) bearer of strength.

**Baladhī** (S) (M) **1.** with a powerful intellect. **2.** deep insight; is perceptive. **3.** an ancient hermit and father of Medhāvin (*M. Bh.*)

**Balādhika** (S) (M) surpassing all in strength.

**Balāḍhya** (S) (M) **1.** rich in strength. **2.** a bean.

**Bālāditya** (S) (M) the newly risen sun.

**Baladviṣa** (S) (M) **1.** jealous of strength; enemy of the strong; enemy of Bala. **3.** another name for Indra.

**Bālagaṅgādhara** (S) (M) **1.** the young bearer of the Gaṅgā. **3.** young Śiva.

**Bālagopāla** (S) (M) **1.** the young cowherd. **3.** young Kṛṣṇa.

**Bālagovinda** (S) (M) **1.** the young cowherd. **3.** the boy Kṛṣṇa.

**Balāgra** (S) (M) **1.** first in strength. **2.** best among the powerful.

**Balagupta** (S) (M) protected by strength.

**Balāhaka** (S) (M) **1.** cloud; thundercloud. **3.** a serpent famous in the Purāṇas and a member of Varuṇa's court (*M. Bh.*); a brother of King Jayadratha of Sindhu (*M. Bh.*); a horse of Kṛṣṇa (*M. Bh.*); a daitya; a mountain.

**Balahantṛ** (S) (M) **1.** killer of the powerful; slayer of Bala. **3.** another name for Indra.

**Balajā** (S) (F) **1.** born of power. **2.** Arabian jasmine (*Jasminum sambac*); a pretty woman; the earth. **3.** a river (*Brahma Purāṇa*)

**Balaja** (S) (M) **1.** produced by strength. **2.** grain.

**Balāji** (S) (M) **1.** strong. **3.** another name for Viṣṇu.

**Balajyeṣṭha** (S) (M) whose superiority is based on his strength.

**Balāka** (S) (M) **1.** a mixture of treacle and milk; a kind of crane. **3.** a pupil of Śākyāmuni; a son of Purū and grandson of Jahnu (*Bhā. Purāṇa*); a rākṣasa (*V. Purāṇa*); a son of Vatsapri (*Mā. Purāṇa*)

**Balakara** (S) (M) **1.** bestower of strength. **2.** a strong supporter.

**Balakāśva** (S) (M) **1.** as strong as a horse. **3.** the grandson of Jahnu, son of Aja and the father of Kuśika (*M. Bh.*)

**Bālāki** (S) (M) **1.** as innocent as a child. **3.** a hermit who was a son of Gārgya (*Bhāgavata*)

**Balaki** (S) (M) **1.** of strength. **2.** powerful; strong. **3.** a son of Dhṛtarāṣṭra (*M. Bh.*)

**Balākin** (S) (M) **1.** abounding in cranes. **3.** a son of Dhṛtarāṣṭra (*M. Bh.*)

**Bālakṛṣṇa** (S) (M) the boy Kṛṣṇa; young Kṛṣṇa.

**Balakṛt** (S) (M) obtained by power.

**Balākṣa** (S) (M) strong eyed.

**Balakṣa** (S) (M) **1.** the light half of the month. **2.** blameless; innocent; of white hue.

**Balakṣagu** (S) (M) **1.** white rayed. **3.** another name for the moon.

**Bālakundā** (S) (F) **1.** a young flower. **2.** the jasmine (*Jasminum pubescens*)

**Bālakunda** (S) (M) **1.** a young flower. **2.** the jasmine (*Jasminum pubescens*)

**Balamada** (S) (M) proud of one's power.

**Bālamaṇi** (S) (M) a small jewel.

**Bālāmbikā** (S) (F) **1.** a virgin who is worshipped as mother. **3.** a goddess worshipped by south Indian tāntrics and considered identical to Kanyākumarī.

**Balamitra** (S) (M) **1.** a strong friend; a friend of the strong. **3.** a king who fought with Śatrughna during the horse yajña (*V. Rāmāyaṇa*)

**Bālamodaka** (S) (M) **1.** favourite of children. **3.** the son of King Suratha of Kuṇḍalanagari (*P. Purāṇa*)

**Bālamohana** (S) (M) **1.** attracting children; the youth who attracts. **3.** young Kṛṣṇa.

**Balamukhya** (S) (M) **1.** the chief of an army. **2.** a commander.

**Bālamukunda** (S) (M) **1.** young blossom. **2.** as tender and soft as a young blossom; a child. **3.** young Kṛṣṇa.

**Balar** (S) (M) strength; power; might; army.

**Balanātha** (S) (M) lord of strength.

**Balanćitā** (S) (F) **1.** strongly stretched; carried by power. **3.** Balarāma's lute.

**Balandharā** (S) (F) **1.** possessor of power. **3.** a daughter of the king of Kaśī, the wife of Bhīmasena and mother of Sarvaśa (*M. Bh.*)

**Balāṅgaka** (S) (M) **1.** strong limbed. **2.** the spring season.

**Balānīka** (S) (M) **1.** with a powerful army.

3. a son of King Drupada (*M. Bh.*)

**Bālānuja** (S) (M) 1. the younger brother of Balarāma. 3. another name for Kṛṣṇa.

**Balapati** (S) (M) 1. commander of an army; lord of strength. 3. another name for Indra.

**Balaprada** (S) (M) bestower of strength.

**Balapramathanī** (S) (F) 1. destroyer of the proud; destroyer of power. 3. a form of Durgā (*H. Ć. Ćintāmaṇi*)

**Balaprāṇa** (S) (M) 1. strength and spirit conjoined. 2. powerful and intelligent.

**Balaprasū** (S) (M) 1. creator of strength. 3. mother of Baladeva; another name for Rohiṇī.

**Bālapuṣpikā** (S) (F) 1. the young blossom. 2. the strong scented jasmine (*Jasminum auriculatum*)

**Bālarāja** (S) (M) 1. lord of the rising sun. 2. the Lapiz lazuli.

**Balarāma** (S) (M) 1. abode of strength. 3. the son of Vasudeva and Rohiṇī, the elder brother of Kṛṣṇa, 3rd of the Rāmas, considered the 8th incarnation of Viṣṇu and sometimes as an incarnation of Ananta (*V. Purāṇa*)

**Bālaravi** (S) (M) the morning sun.

**Bālārka** (S) (M) the rising sun.

**Bālāruṇa** (S) (M) early dawn.

**Balaśālin** (S) (M) 1. possessing a great army. 2. powerful.

**Bālasandhyā** (S) (F) 1. early twilight. 2. dawn.

**Bālasarasvatī** (S) (F) the goddess of knowledge.

**Balasena** (S) (M) a strong leader.

**Bālasinha** (S) (M) a young lion.

**Balastha** (S) (M) abode of strength.

**Balasthala** (S) (M) 1. abode of strength. 3. a son of Parijāta (*Bhāgavata*)

**Balasūdana** (S) (M) 1. destroyer of large armies; destroyer of Bala. 3. another name for Indra.

**Bālasūrya** (S) (M) 1. the rising sun. 2. the purple light of dawn. 3. the Lapiz lazuli.

**Balasvāmi** (S) (M) 1. master of power. 3. a warrior of Skanda (*M. Bh.*)

**Balavala** (S) (M) 1. very powerful. 3. an asura killed by Balarāma (*M. Bh.*)

**Balavāna** (S) (M) strong; powerful.

**Balavardhana** (S) (M) 1. increasing strength. 3. a son of Dhṛtarāṣṭra (*M. Bh.*)

**Balavarṇin** (S) (M) strong and looking well.

**Balavata** (S) (M) 1. powerful. 2. intense; prevailing; dense.

**Balavatī** (S) (F) 1. powerful; strong; daughter; small cardamoms. 3. the pious daughter of sage Kaṇva (*P. Purāṇa*)

**Balavikarṇikā** (S) (F) 1. possessed with the rays of power. 3. a form of Durgā (*H. Ć. Ćintāmaṇi*)

**Bālavinaṣṭaka** (S) (M) 1. destroyer of childhood. 2. wisdom; adulthood.

**Balavīra** (S) (M) 1. brave and powerful. 2. a hero.

**Balavīrya** (S) (M) 1. strength and heroism conjoined. 3. a descendant of Bharata (*Ś. Mahātmya*)

**Bālavrata** (S) (M) 1. worshipping the rising sun. 3. another name for the Buddhist saint Manjuśrī (*B. Literature*)

**Bālayani** (S) (M) 1. one liked by the pupil. 3. a teacher mentioned in the *Bhāgavata*.

**Bālayogi** (S) (M) 1. young ascetic. 3. a king of the Aṅga dynasty who was the son of Bali (*A. Purāṇa*)

**Balayukta** (S) (M) endowed with strength.

**Balāyuṣ** (S) (M) 1. living on his own strength. 3. a son of Purūravas and Urvaśī (*P. Purāṇa*)

**Bālendra** (S) (M) Indra in his childlike form.

**Bālendu** (S) (M) 1. the crescent moon. 2. the new or waxing moon.

**Baleśa** (S) (M) the commander of an army; lord of power.

**Bāleśvara** (S) (M) 1. lord of children. 3. another name for Kṛṣṇa.

**Bālhīka** (S) (M) 1. powerful; energetic; a country. 3. a king who was an incarnation of the asura Krodhāvaśa (*H. Purāṇa*); a king of the Ahara dynasty (*M. Bh.*); the 3rd son of King Janamejaya and the grandson of King Kuru (*M. Bh.*); a son of King Pratīpa of the Kuru dynasty and Sunandā of Śibi (*M. Bh.*); the charioteer of Yudhiṣṭhira (*M. Bh.*); the father of Rohiṇī the wife of Vasudeva

(*H. Purāṇa*); a gandharva (*A. Koṣa*)

**Balhīkapuṅgava** (S) (M) 1. bull of the Balhīkas. 3. another name for Śalya.

**Bāli** (S) (M) 1. powerful. 3. a mighty monkey king of Kiṣkindhā who was the son of Indra, half brother of Sugriva, the husband of Tārā, father of Aṅgada, and was slain by Rāma (*V. Rāmāyaṇa*)

**Bali** (S) (M) 1. offering; powerful. 2. gift; tribute; oblation. 3. an emperor of the asuras who was the son of Viroćana, the grandson of Prahlāda and was defeated by Viṣṇu in his Vāmana or dwarf incarnation (*M. Bh.*); Indra in the 8th Manvantara (*Purāṇas*); a hermit of Hastināpura (*M. Bh.*); an incarnation of Śiva as a hermit (*Ś. Purāṇa*); a king of the Yādavas who was the son of Kṛtavarman and the husband of Ćārumatī the daughter of Kṛṣṇa (*Bhāgavata*); the monkey king of Aṇava who was the son of Sutapas and the husband of Sudeṣṇā (*Bhāgavata*)

**Balibandhana** (S) (M) 1. binder of Bali. 3. another name for Viṣṇu.

**Balibhuja** (S) (M) 1. devouring offerings. 2. a deity.

**Balidhvansī** (S) (M) 1. destroying Bali. 3. another name for Kṛṣṇa.

**Balidhvanśin** (S) (M) 1. destroyer of Bali. 3. another name for Viṣṇu.

**Baliman** (S) (M) powerful.

**Balin** (S) (M) 1. powerful. 2. strong; mighty; robust.

**Balinī** (S) (F) powerful; the constellation of Aśvinī.

**Baliśikhā** (S) (M) 1. the best oblation. 3. a serpent son of Kaśyapa and Kadru (*M. Bh.*)

**Baliṣṭha** (S) (M) 1. very powerful. 2. mighty.

**Balivāka** (S) (M) 1. praying at the oblation. 2. an orator; a preacher. 3. a hermit who was a member of Yudhiṣṭhira's court (*M. Bh.*)

**Ballava** (S) (M) 1. cowherd; bull-keeper. 3. name assumed by Bhīma at the court of Virāṭa (*M. Bh.*)

**Balotkaṭā** (S) (F) 1. with a frightening power. 2. very powerful. 3. mother of Skanda's retinue (*Sk. Purāṇa*)

**Balūla** (S) (M) 1. powerful. 2. strong.

**Balya** (S) (M) 1. powerful. 2. strong; mighty.

**Bālya** (S) (M) child-like; the crescent moon.

**Bambhāri** (S) (M) 1. lowes like a cow. 3. one of the 7 tutelary deities of the Soma plant (*Ṛg Veda*)

**Bāṇa** (S) (M) 1. arrow; number 5. 2. a sharp intellect. 3. an asura who was the son of Bali (*V. Purāṇa*); a poet in the court of Harṣavardhana who was the author of *Kādambari* and *Harśa Ćarita* (7th century A.D.); a 1000 armed asura considered the son of Pārvatī, who attacked the gods and was killed by Kṛṣṇa (*Bha. Purāṇa*); a warrior of Skanda (*M. Bh.*); an asura killed by Lakṣmaṇa (*V. Rāmāyaṇa*)

**Bāṇagaṅgā** (S) (F) 1. Gaṅgā like an arrow. 2. a fast moving river. 3. a river flowing past Someśa said to have been produced by Ravaṇa's cleaving a mountain with an arrow (*V. Purāṇa*)

**Bāṇajita** (S) (M) 1. conqueror of Bāṇa; conquering with arrows. 3. another name for Viṣṇu.

**Bāṇaliṅga** (S) (M) 1. an arrow shaped phallus; a pointed stone; knowing the secrets of archery. 3. a white stone found in the river Narmadā and worshipped as the Liṅga of Śiva.

**Banamālin** (S) (M) 1. gardener of the forest. 3. another name for Kṛṣṇa.

**Banārasī** (S) (M) 1. belonging to Benaras. 2. sacred.

**Bāṇaśankara** (S) (M) 1. arrow of Śiva. 2. reaching his target of peace, tranquility and welfare.

**Banaśrī** (S) (F) beauty of the forest.

**Bāṇasutā** (S) (F) 1. daughter of Bāṇa. 3. the wife of Aniruddha (*Bhāgavata*)

**Banavārī** (S) (M) 1. dweller of the forest. 3. another name for Kṛṣṇa.

**Bandana** (S) (M) 1. prayer; chant. 2. sacred; illumined; enlightened; beyond wordly bonds.

**Bandhamoćinī** (S) (F) 1. releasing from bonds. 3. a yoginī (*K. Sāgara*)

**Bandhinī** (S) (F) 1. who binds; bound. 2. imprisoned; bond.

**Bandhitra** (S) (M) 1. binder. 3. another name

for Kāma, the god of love.
**Bandhujīvin** (S) (M) lives on friends; on whom the friends live; deep red like the blossom of the *Pentapetes phoenicea*; a ruby.
**Bandhumān** (S) (M) 1. with many brothers. 2. protected. 3. a king of Videha (*Br. Purāṇa*)
**Bandhumatī** (S) (F) 1. with many brothers. 3. an attendant of Vāsavadattā the wife of Udayana.
**Bandhupāla** (S) (M) protecting his kin.
**Bandhuprabha** (S) (M) 1. light of the family. 3.a vidyadhara.
**Bandhupriyā** (S) (F) dear to friends and relations.
**Bandhurā** (S) (F) wavy rounded; lovely; charming.
**Bandin** (S) (M) praiser; a bard; herald.
**Baneśvara** (S) (M) the Bāṇaliṅga stone; lord of the forest.
**Banhimān** (S) (M) has plenty.
**Banhiṣṭha** (S) (M) found in abundance.
**Bāṇi** (S) (M) 1. speech. 2. articulate; an orator.
**Bāṇibrata** (S) (M) 1. controller of speech; devoted to speech. 2. eloquent; an orator.
**Baṅkimćandra** (S) (M) 1. crooked moon; half moon. 2. charming as well as shrewd. 3. another name for Kṛṣṇa.
**Banśī** (S) (M) 1. flute. 2. sweet-voiced; melodious.
**Baṅśidhara** (S) (M) 1. bearer of flute. 3. another name for Kṛṣṇa.
**Banśika** (S) (M) 1. king of the forest. 2. the lion.
**Banśivinoda** (S) (M) 1. amuses with his flute. 3. another name for Kṛṣṇa.
**Bānsurī** (S) (F) flute.
**Bapannabhaṭṭa** (S) (M) scholar of agriculture.
**Bappā** (S) (M) 1. universal father. 3. the Rāṇā of Mewar who was considered the direct descendant of Rāma.
**Bappaka** (S) (M) 1. good cook. 3. a prince.
**Bapū** (Marathi) (M) the middle child.
**Bapudeva** (S) (M) lord of the body.
**Barayi** (S) (M) 1. lover of the great. 2. admirer; respect; idolizing great things and people.
**Barbarīka** (S) (M) 1. curly haired; wild. 2. savage. 3. the son of Ghaṭotkaća and Maurvī (*M. Bh.*); a form of Śiva.
**Baren** (S) (M) 1. the lust. 3. another name for Indra.
**Barendra** (S) (M) Indra, the best.
**Barhaćandra** (S) (M) 1. the eye of a peacock's tail; the moon of peacock feather. 2. beautiful.
**Barhaketu** (S) (M) 1. with the banner of a peacock's tail. 2. as bright as peacock's feathers. 3. a son of Sagara (*Bhāgavata*); a son of the 9th Manu (*Mā. Purāṇa*)
**Barhaṇa** (S) (M) 1. strong. 2. vigorous; powerful; energetic; active; agile; dazzling the eyes.
**Barhaṇāśva** (S) (M) 1. owner of strong horses; a strong horse. 2. wealthy; swift; strong. 3. a son of King Nikumbha of the Pṛthu dynasty (*Bhāgavata*)
**Barhanetra** (S) (M) 1. the eye of a peacock's tail. 2. beautiful.
**Barhapīḍa** (S) (M) 1. decorated with peacock-feathers; wearing a wreath of peacock-feathers on the head. 2. crested; titled; decorated.
**Barhayitā** (S) (F) as beautiful as the eye on a peacock-feather.
**Barhidhvajā** (S) (F) 1. peacock-bannered. 2. symbolized by a peacock; surrounded by peacocks. 3. another name for Durgā.
**Barhidhvaja** (S) (M) 1. peacock-bannered. 2. symbolized by a peacock; surrounded by peacocks. 3. another name for Skanda whose mount is the peacock.
**Barhin** (S) (M) 1. peacock; a kind of the perfume. 3. a gandharva (*A. Koṣa*)
**Barhiṇā** (S) (F) adorned with peacock-feathers.
**Barhis** (S) (M) 1. that which is plucked up. 2. sacrificial grass; fire; light; splendour. 3. another name for Agni.
**Barhiṣa** (S) (F) 1. sacred Kuśā grass (*Desmostachya bipinnata*); ether; water; fire; sacrifice; light; splendour. 2. the Kuśā grass is considered to be sacred because it serves as a

seat for the gods; sacred; illuminating; renowned; respected; glorious. 3. a son of Bṛhadrāja.

**Barhiṣada** (S) (M) 1. seated on sacred grass. 3. a son of Havirdhana (*Brah. Purāṇa*); a ṛṣi (*V. Rāmāyaṇa*)

**Barhiṣakeśa** (S) (M) 1. grass-haired. 2. fire-haired; blazing. 3. another name for Agni.

**Barhiṣapāla** (S) (M) 1. protector of fire; blazing. 2. worshipped; sacred; venerated; illuminated; enlightening.

**Barhiṣmatī** (S) (F) 1. blazing; provided with sacred grass. 2. pure; pious; sacred; ambitious; a worshipper. 3. a wife of Priyavrata, daughter of Viśvakarman and the mother of Uttama, Tāmasa and Raivata (*Bhāgavata*)

**Barhismukha** (S) (M) 1. with fire for a mouth. 2. a deity to whom sacrifices are offered in fire.

**Barhiṣṭha** (S) (M) 1. dwelling in fire. 2. mightiest; strongest; highest; loudest.

**Barhiyāna** (S) (M) 1. whose mount is the peacock. 3. another name for Skanda.

**Barkhā** (S) (M) 1. rain. 2. moistens; soothes; cools; life giving.

**Bāroṭa** (S) (M) speech.

**Barsāti** (S) (M) 1. protecting from the rain. 2. a shelter; providing shelter and protect.

**Barū** (S) (M) 1. noble. 3. a descendant of Aṅgiras and an author of *Ṛg Veda* (x)

**Baruṇ** (S) (M) 1. lord of water. 2. found in water; the sacred barṇa tree (*Crataeva nurvala*)

**Basabi** (S) (M) resident.

**Basantā** (S) (M) spring.

**Basantī** (S) (F) 1. of the spring. 2. the yellow colour associated with spring and stands for life; excitement and creation.

**Bāsava** (S) (M) 1. bull. 2. strong; virile. 3. a minister of a Jaina king who developed the Vīra-Śaiva system (12th century A.D.) (*J.S. Koṣa*)

**Bāsavarāja** (S) (M) 1. lord of the bulls. 2. decorated with many bulls; extremely strong and virile.

**Bāṣkala** (S) (M) 1. preceptor; teacher; knower of substance. 2. well read; wise; illumined; enlightened. 3. a king of asuras, son of Samhrāda of the Kaśyapa line, a minister of Mahiṣasura and slain by Devī (*D. Bhāgavata*); a disciple of Vyāsa (*M. Bh.*)

**Bāṣpa** (S) (M) 1. tears; steam; vapour. 3. a disciple of Gautama Buddha (*B. Ćarita*)

**Basū** (S) (M) 1. wealth. 2. wealthy.

**Baṭer** (S) (M) the grey quail (*Tetrao coturnix*)

**Battu** (S) (M) 1. boy; lad; stripling; youth; a Brāhmin who reads the scriptures daily. 3. a form of Śiva (*Ś. Purāṇa*)

**Baṭuka** (S) (M) Brāhmin youth.

**Baṭukanātha** (S) (M) 1. lord of boys. 3. a form of Śiva (*A. Koṣa*)

**Bāyabhaṭṭa** (S) (M) 1. knowing the age; an astrologer. 3. a son of Kṛṣṇa and father of Advaita (*Bhāgavata*)

**Beanta** (S) (M) 1. endless. 2. eternal.

**Bekurā** (S) (M) 1. voice; sound; a musical instrument. 2. melodious; harmonious.

**Bekurī** (S) (F) 1. playing a musical instrument. 2. an apsarā.

**Belā** (S) (F) the jasmine creeper (*Jasminum sambac*); wave; time.

**Beman** (S) (M) 1. without interest. 2. disinterested; detached.

**Beṇi** (S) (M) plait of hair.

**Beṇiprasāda** (S) (M) 1. gift of a wreath of flowers. 2. flowers sacred enough to be offered to the lord.

**Bhābāgrahi** (S) (M) 1. perceiving another's emotions. 2. understanding; sensitive; considerate.

**Bhabeśa** (S) (M) lord of existence; lord of the universe; lord of emotions.

**Bhadanta** (S) (M) 1. term of respect applied to a Buddhist mendicant. 3. another name for the poet Aśvaghoṣa.

**Bhadrā** (S) (F) 1. fair; good; beautiful; fortunate; prosperous; happy; gentle. 2. gracious; blessed; auspicious; a cow. 3. the 2nd, 7th and 12th days of the lunar fortnight (*P. Samhitā*); a form of Durgā (*T. Śastra*); a form of goddess known as the Dākśāyaṇī and considered to reside in Bhadreśvara (*V. Purāṇa*); a Buddhist deity (*A. Koṣa*); a vidyādharī (*V. Rāmāyaṇa*); a daughter of

Surabhi (*V. Rāmāyaṇa*); the wife of Vaiśravaṇa (*M. Bh.*); a daughter of Soma and wife of Utathya (*V. Rāmāyaṇa*); a daughter of Raudrāśva and Ghṛtāćī (*H. Purāṇa*); a daughter of Śrutakīrti and wife of Kṛṣṇa (*Bhāgavata*); a river of ancient India (*V. Purāṇa*); the daughter of King Kakṣivāna and the wife of King Vyuṣitāśva of the Purū dynasty (*M. Bh.*); a wife of Kubera (*M. Bh.*); the daughter of the king of Viśāla and wife of Śiśupāla (*M. Bh.*); a wife of Vasudeva (*H. Purāṇa*); a daughter of the king of Kāśi and wife of a grandson of King Sagara (*Br. Purāṇa*); a daughter of Meru and wife of King Āgnidhra (*Bhāgavata*); one of the 4 branches of the celestial Gaṅgā (*A. Koṣa*); a daughter of Rohiṇi (*Bhāgavata*); a wife of Garuḍa (*V. Purāṇa*); a daughter of Meru and wife of Bhadrāśva (*Bhāgavata*); another name for Subhadrā, the sister of Kṛṣṇa, the celestial Gaṅgā and gold.

**Bhadra** (S) (M) 1. blessed; auspicious; gracious; good. 2. fair; happy; prosperous; handsome; fortunate; gentlemanly; excellent. 3. one of the 12 sons of Viṣṇu (*Bhāgavata*); a son of Upaćārumat (*B. Literature*); the sages of the 3rd Manvantara (*Bhāgavata*); a king of Ćedi who fought on the side of the Pāṇḍavas (*M. Bh.*); one of the 4 elephants that support the world (*V. Rāmāyaṇa*); a son of Śraddha and grandson of Svāyambhuva Manu (*Bhāgavata*); a yakṣa who was a minister of Kubera (*M. Bh.*); a sage who was the son of Pramati and father of Upamanyu (*M. Bh.*); a son of Kṛṣṇa and Kālindī (*Bhāgavata*); a son of Vasudeva and Devakī (*Bh. Purāṇa*); another name for Śiva and Mount Meru.

**Bhadrabāhu** (S) (M) 1. auspicious armed. 2. performing ambitious acts. 3. a son of Vasudeva and Rohiṇī (*Bhāgavata*); a king of Magadha (*M. Bh.*); a celebrated Jaina author (*J.S. Koṣa*); a king of the line of Purū (*M. Bh.*)

**Bhadrabalana** (S) (M) 1. strengthening good. 3. another name for Balarāma.

**Bhadrabhuja** (S) (M) 1. whose arms confer prosperity. 2. a god.

**Bhadrabhūṣaṇā** (S) (F) 1. precious ornament. 3. a goddess.

**Bhadraćāru** (S) (M) 1. gentle and beautiful. 3. a son of Kṛṣṇa (*Mā. Purāṇa*); a son of Pradyumna (*Bhā. Purāṇa*)

**Bhadradeha** (S) (M) 1. with an auspicious body. 2. beautiful; handsome. 3. a son of Vasudeva and Devakī (*Bhāgavata*)

**Bhadragupta** (S) (M) 1. collector of good things. 2. knows the secrets of the good; meritorious; virtuous. 3. a Jaina saint (*J. Literature*)

**Bhadrajātika** (S) (M) of noble birth.

**Bhadraka** (S) (M) 1. good; handsome. 2. brave; beautiful; meritorious; virtuous. 3. an Aṅga king (*A. Purāṇa*)

**Bhadrakālī** (S) (F) 1. goddess of welfare; destroyer of ignorance. 3. a mother attending to Skanda (*Sk. Purāṇa*); a form of Durgā (*Bhāgavata*)

**Bhadrakāra** (S) (M) 1. doer of good. 2. meritorious; virtuous. 3. a son of Śiva (*Mā. Purāṇa*); a son of Kṛṣṇa.

**Bhadrakarṇikā** (S) (F) 1. wearing beautiful earrings. 2. listening only to pious talks. 3. a form of goddess known as Dākśāyaṇī who is considered to reside in Gokarṇa (*D. Bhāgavata*)

**Bhadrakāya** (S) (M) 1. with a beautiful body. 3. a son of Kṛṣṇa (*Bhāgavata*)

**Bhadrakṛt** (S) (M) 1. causing prosperity. 3. 24th arhat of the future Utsarpiṇī.

**Bhadrākṣa** (S) (M) whose eyes reflect auspiciousness.

**Bhadrakumbha** (S) (M) 1. auspicious jar. 2. a golden jar filled with water from the Gaṅgā.

**Bhadramanā** (S) (F) 1. kind-hearted; noble-minded. 3. a daughter of Kaśyapa and Krodhavaśā (*V. Rāmāyaṇa*)

**Bhadramanas** (S) (F) 1. noble minded; kindhearted. 3. the mother of Airāvata (*M. Bh.*)

**Bhadramanda** (S) (M) 1. gentle and good. 3. a son of Kṛṣṇa (*V. Purāṇa*)

**Bhadramātā** (S) (F) 1. beautiful mother. 3. daughter of Kaśyapa and Krodhavaśā.

**Bhadramukha** (S) (M) with a handsome face; whose look confers prosperity.

**Bhadramukhī** (S) (F) with a beautiful face.

**Bhadrāṅga** (S) (M) 1. a beautiful body.

3. another name for Balarāma.

**Bhadranidhi** (S) (M) 1. treasure of goodness. 3. a vessel offered to Viṣṇu.

**Bhadrapāla** (S) (M) 1. protector of goodness. 2. meritorious; virtuous. 3. a Bodhisattva.

**Bhadrarūpā** (S) (F) beautiful.

**Bhadraśākha** (S) (M) 1. connoisseur of tasty food. 3. the goat form of Subrahmaṇya (*M. Bh.*)

**Bhadrasāra** (S) (M) 1. essence of goodness; ocean of goodness. 3. a king of Kāśmira and father of Sudharman (*R. Taraṅginī*)

**Bhadraṣaṣṭhī** (S) (F) 1. praising good. 3. a form of Durgā.

**Bhadrasena** (S) (M) 1. with an army of good people. 2. good; virtuous. 3. a son of Vasudeva and Devakī (*Bhāgavata*); a son of Ṛṣabha (*Bhāgavata*); a son of Mahiṣmat (*Bhāgavata*)

**Bhadraśīla** (S) (M) noble in behaviour.

**Bhadrasomā** (S) (F) 1. as noble and beautiful as the moon. 3. a river in Uttarakuru (*Mā. Purāṇa*); another name for the Gaṅgā.

**Bhadraśravas** (S) (M) 1. listening to good things; one about whom good things are said. 3. a king of Saurāṣṭra mentioned in the Purāṇas; a son of Dharma (*Bhā. Purāṇa*)

**Bhadrāśraya** (S) (M) abode of auspiciousness; sandalwood which is used in religious ceremonies and therefore considered sacred.

**Bhadraśreṇya** (S) (M) 1. belonging to a noble family. 3. a Hehaya king (*H. Purāṇa*)

**Bhadrāśva** (S) (M) 1. noble horse; owner of good horses. 3. a king of the Purū dynasty who was the son of Rahovādi and the husband of Kāntimatī (*M. Bh.*); a son of Āgnīdhra and Purvaćitti (*M. Bh.*); a son of Vasudeva and Rohiṇī (*Bhāgavata*); a son of Dhundhumāra (*Bhā. Purāṇa*)

**Bhadrasvapnā** (S) (F) seeing good dreams.

**Bhadratanu** (S) (M) with a beautiful body.

**Bhadrātmaja** (S) (M) 1. son of a noble. 2. meritorious; virtuous.

**Bhadravadana** (S) (M) 1. auspicious faced. 3. another name for Balarāma.

**Bhadravāha** (S) (M) bearer of prosperity.

**Bhadravallī** (S) (F) 1. a beautiful vine. 2. the Arabian jasmine (*Jasminum sambac*)

**Bhadravarman** (S) (M) 1. a gentle warrior. 2. over powering gently and subtly; the Arabian jasmine (*Jasminum sambac*)

**Bhadrāvatī** (S) (F) 1. noble in character. 3. a daughter of Kṛṣṇa (*Bhāgavata*); a wife of Madhu (*M. Bh.*)

**Bhadravinda** (S) (M) 1. achieving good. 3. a son of Kṛṣṇa (*Bhāgavata*)

**Bhadrāyu** (S) (M) leads a good life.

**Bhadreśa** (S) (M) 1. lord of nobles; husband of a noble family; husband of Durgā. 3. another name for Śiva.

**Bhadrika** (S) (M) 1. noble. 3. a king of the Śakyas.

**Bhadrikā** (S) (F) 1. a noble woman. 2. beautiful; meritorious; virtuous; auspicious; an amulet.

**Bhaga** (S) (M) 1. disperser; lord; patron; happiness; fortune; wealth. 3. an āditya who bestowes wealth and presides over love and marriage, the brother of dawn and the regent of the Nakṣatra Uttarā Phalgunī (*V.'s B. Samhitā*); a son of Kaśyapa and Aditi (*Bhāgavata*); the sun in the month of Puṣya (*V.'s B. Samhitā*); the celestial dispenser of boons, husband of Siddhi, the father of Vibhu, Prabhu and Mahimān and a member of Indra's assembly (*M. Bh.*); a rudra (*Ṛg Veda*); another name for the sun and the moon.

**Bhagadā** (S) (F) 1. bestower of wealth and happiness. 3. an attendant of Skanda (*M. Bh.*)

**Bhagadatta** (S) (M) 1. given by good fortune; given by the creator. 3. a king of Prāgjyotiṣapura who was born from a limb of the demon Baṣkala and fought on the side of the Kauravas (*M. Bh.*); a king of Kāmrup.

**Bhagāditya** (S) (M) 1. the sun which bestows wealth; the sun in the month of Puṣya. 3. a Rāṇa of Mewar.

**Bhagaghna** (S) (M) 1. destroying Bhaga. 3. another name for Śiva.

**Bhagālin** (S) (M) 1. bedecked with skulls. 3. another name for Śiva.

**Bhagana** (S) (M) 1. next; of the nature of happiness. 2. happy; joyful.

**Bhagānandā** (S) (F) 1. bestower of happiness; enjoyer of fortune. 3. a mother of

Skanda's retinue (*M. Bh.*)

**Bhagaratha** (S) (M) 1. with a lucky chariot. 2. a fortunate warrior who always wins.

**Bhagata** (S) (M) devotee.

**Bhagavāna** (S) (M) 1. with a great fortune. 2. lord; god.

**Bhāgavant** (S) (M) 1. has a fortune. 2. fortunate; shareholder.

**Bhāgavantī** (S) (F) shareholder; fortunate.

**Bhāgavata** (S) (M) 1. spiritual being; a follower of Viṣṇu. 2. with great fortune; glorious; illustrious; divine; happy; adorable; holy. 3. a king in the 5th lunar dynasty of Magadha (*Bhāgavata*); a Buddha; another name for Viṣṇu, Kṛṣṇa and Śiva.

**Bhagavatī** (S) (F) 1. universal self and nature conjoined; creator. 3. a goddess who is a personification of universal self and nature conjoined; another name for Lakṣmī.

**Bhagavatīprasāda** (S) (M) born from the blessings of goddess Durgā.

**Bhagīratha** (S) (M) 1. with a glorious chariot. 3. the son of Dilīpa (*M. Bh.*) or Anśumān (*Puranas*) he brought down the Gaṅgā river to earth and is now a member of Yama's assembly.

**Bhāgīrathī** (S) (F) 1. of Bhagīratha. 3. another name for the Gaṅgā.

**Bhāgīrathīputra** (S) (M) 1. son of Bhagīrathī. 2. another name for Bhīṣma.

**Bhagnaratha** (S) (M) 1. devoid of chariots. 3. another name for Ćitraratha.

**Bhāguri** (S) (M) thinks himself lucky; desiring happiness.

**Bhāgyā** (S) (F) fate; destiny; fortune; luck; happiness.

**Bhagyalakṣmī** (S) (F) 1. goddess of fortune. 3. another name for Lakṣmī.

**Bhāgyanandana** (S) (M) controller of destiny.

**Bhāgyaśrī** (S) (F) 1. goddess of fortune. 3. another name for Lakṣmī.

**Bhaimā** (S) (F) 1. descendant of Bhīma. 2. daughter of a fearsome warrior; the 11th day in the light half of the month of Māgha. 3. another name for Damayantī.

**Bhaimaseni** (S) (M) 1. son of Bhīmasena. 3. another name for Ghaṭotkaća and Divodāsa.

**Bhaimi** (S) (M) 1. son of Bhīma. 3. another name for Ghaṭotkaća.

**Bhainā** (S) (F) large Grey Babbler Bird; not afraid.

**Bhairava** (S) (M) 1. destroyer of fear; making a terrible sound. 2. formidable; frightening. 3. a nāga of the Kaurava dynasty (*M. Bh.*); a terrible form of Śiva (*Ś. Purāṇa*); a rāga; a chief of Śiva's host (*K. Purāṇa*); a son of Śiva by Tārāvatī the wife of King Ćandraśekhara of Karavirapura (*M. Bh.*); a rāga.

**Bhairavasin** (S) (M) 1. terrible lion. 3. a son of Narasiṁha and the patron of Rućipati (*V. Purāṇa*)

**Bhairavesa** (S) (M) 1. lord of terror. 3. another name for Śiva.

**Bhairavī** (S) (F) 1. terrible; consort of Bhairava. 3. a terrifying form of Kālī (*D. Bhāgavata*); a rāga; one of the 8 Ambās or forms of Devī (*A. Koṣa*); a rāgiṇī; another name for Nirṛti.

**Bhairika** (S) (M) 1. terrible. 3. a son of Kṛṣṇa and Satyabhāmā.

**Bhairon** (S) (M) 1. terrible. 2. fear inducing; awesome; formidable. 3. a village field spirit now identified with Śiva.

**Bhajālanka** (S) (M) 1. with auspicious marks on the forehead. 3. another name for Śiva.

**Bhajamana** (S) (M) 1. praying through heart. 2. praying deeply, sincerely, fervently and with a lot of feeling. 3. a Yādava king who was the son of Satvata and Kauśalyā and the husband of Bāhyakā and Upabāhyakā, the 2 daughters of Sanjaya (*Bhāgavata*)

**Bhajana** (S) (M) 1. devotional song. 2. sacred; venerated.

**Bhākosa** (S) (M) 1. treasure of light. 3. another name for the sun.

**Bhakta** (S) (M) devotee; loyal; honouring; worshipping.

**Bhaktarāja** (S) (M) 1. prince among devotees; king of devotees. 2. best devotee.

**Bhakti** (S) (F) 1. devotion. 2. love; trust; homage; piety. 3. a goddess or devi of Draviḍadeśa and the mother of Jñāna and Vairāgya (*Bhāgavata*)

**Bhālaćandra** (S) (M) 1. with the moon on his forehead. 3. another name for Śiva and Gaṇeṣa.

**Bhālandana** (S) (M) 1. with a pleasing forehead. 3. a king who was the son of Nābhāga (*M. Bh.*)

**Bhālanetra** (S) (M) 1. with an eye on his forehead. 3. another name for Śiva.

**Bhālendra** (S) (M) 1. lord of fortune. 3. another name for Śiva.

**Bhāleśvarī** (S) (F) goddess of forehead.

**Bhalla** (S) (M) 1. auspicious; arrow; spear. 2. sharp; piercing and reaching its mark. 3. another name for Śiva.

**Bhallāṭa** (S) (M) 1. with a large forehead. 2. a bear; one who is fortunate; virtuous; learned. 3. a king of the line of Bharata who was the son of Viśvaksena and the father of Bṛhadāśva.

**Bhallī** (S) (F) 1. a kind of arrow; a small spear. 2. sharp; piercing and reaching its mark.

**Bhaluki** (S) (M) 1. with a large forehead. 2. a bear. 3. a sage who was a member of Yudhiṣṭhira's court (*M. Bh.*); a sage who was a disciple of Lāṅgali.

**Bhāmā** (S) (F) 1. passionate; has splendour. 2. charming; beautiful; famous; loving. 3. a wife of Kṛṣṇa (*Bhāgavata*)

**Bhāma** (S) (M) light; brightness; splendour.

**Bhāmaha** (S) (M) 1. bright. 2. illuminating; enlightening. 3. an important Sanskṛt critic (6th century A.D.)

**Bhāmaṇḍala** (S) (M) 1. sphere of light; garland of rays. 2. illuminating; enlightening; renowned. 3. the sun.

**Bhāminī** (S) (F) 1. shining; radiant. 2. beautiful; glorious; renowned passionate. 3. the wife of King Avikṣit of Vaiśāli and the mother of Marutta (*Bhā. Purāṇa*)

**Bhānavī** (S) (F) 1. descendant of the sun; shining like the sun. 2. sacred; illuminating; glorious; enlightening. 3. a river crossed by Rāma and Lakṣmaṇa (*V. Rāmāyaṇa*); another name for the Yamunā river.

**Bhānavīya** (S) (M) 1. belonging to the sun. 2. sacred; glorious; enlightening.

**Bhandanā** (S) (F) applause; praise; sunrays

**Bhaṇḍāyanī** (S) (M) 1. praising highly. 3. a sage of Indra's court (*M. Bh.*)

**Bhandila** (S) (M) fortune.

**Bhānemi** (S) (M) 1. girdle of light. 3. another name for the sun.

**Bhaṅga** (S) (M) 1. to break; to destroy. 2. destroyer. 3. a serpent of the Takṣaka dynasty (*Bhā. Purāṇa*)

**Bhangakara** (S) (M) 1. destroyer. 3. a son of Avikṣit and grandson of King Kuru (*M. Bh.*)

**Bhānū** (S) (F) 1. appearance; light. 2. beautiful; glorious; virtuous; enlightened. 3. a daughter of Dakṣa, wife of Dharma or Manu and the mother of Bhānu and Āditya (*V. Purāṇa*); the mother of Devarṣabha (*Bhāgavata*); a daughter of Kṛṣṇa (*V. Purāṇa*); mother of Śakuni.

**Bhānu** (S) (M) 1. appearance. 2. light; glory; fame; king; master; lord. 3. an āditya (*Rā. Upaniṣad*); a son of Prativyoma (*Bhāgavata*); a son of Viśvadhara and father of Harinātha (*Rāmāyaṇa*); a son of Kṛṣṇa and Satyabhāmā (*Bhāgavata*); a son of Dyau and the preceptor of Sūrya (*M. Bh.*); a gandharva who was the son of Kaśyapa and Pṛthā (*M. Bh.*); an ancient king who witnessed the battle between Arjuna and Droṇa in Indra's chariot (*M. Bh.*); a Yādava whose daughter married Sahadeva (*M. Bh.*); the king of Ratnapuri and father of Jaina Tirathankara Dharmanātha (*J.S. Koṣa*); another name for an agni called Pānćajanya, Śiva and the sun.

**Bhānućandra** (S) (M) 1. shining moon; sun and moon conjoined. 2. can be fierce as well as soothing.

**Bhānudatta** (S) (M) 1. given by the sun. 2. bright; enlightening; sacred. 3. a brother of Śakuni (*M. Bh.*)

**Bhānudeva** (S) (M) 1. lord of glory; sun, the lord. 3. a Panćāla warrior (*M. Bh.*); another name for Sūrya.

**Bhānujā** (S) (F) 1. daughter of the sun. 3. another name for the Yamunā river.

**Bhānuja** (S) (M) 1. son of the sun. 3. another name for Karṇa and the planet Saturn.

**Bhānukeśara** (S) (M) 1. maned with rays; the lion of light. 3. another name for the sun.

**Bhānukopa** (S) (M) 1. with a blazing anger;

as angry as the sun. 3. an asura who fought against Skanda (*M. Bh.*)

**Bhānumān** (S) (M) 1. as bright as the sun. 3. a king belonging to Rāma's dynasty and the father of King Śakradyumna; a son of Kṛṣṇa and Satyabhāmā (*Bhā. Purāṇa*); a prince of Kaliṅga who fought on the side of the Kauravas (*M. Bh.*)

**Bhānumata** (S) (M) 1. luminous. 2. glorious; splendid; handsome. 3. a son of Kuśadhvaja (*M. Bh.*); a son of Bṛhadaśva (*Bhā. Purāṇa*)

**Bhānumatī** (S) (F) 1. luminous; as intelligent as the sun. 2. glorious; famous; enlightening; beautiful. 3. the wife of Duryodhana (*M. Bh.*); a daughter of Bhānu and wife of Sahadeva (*M. Bh.*); a daughter of Kṛtavīrya, wife of King Ahamyāti and the mother of Sārvabhauma (*H. Purāṇa*); an extremely beautiful daughter of Aṅgiras (*M. Bh.*); a daughter of Vikramāditya (*A. Koṣa*); mother of Śaṁkara.

**Bhānunātha** (S) (M) 1. lord of brightness. 3. another name for Sūrya.

**Bhānupriyā** (S) (F) beloved of the sun.

**Bhānuratha** (S) (M) 1. with a glorious chariot. 3. a son of Bṛhadaśva.

**Bhānusena** (S) (M) 1. splendid leader. 2. with a glorious army. 3. a son of Karṇa (*M. Bh.*)

**Bhānuśrī** (S) (F) as glorious as the sun.

**Bhānuvarman** (S) (M) 1. sun armoured. 2. safeguarded; protected by the sun.

**Bhāradvāja** (S) (M) 1. son of Bharadvāja. 3. another name for Droṇa.

**Bharadvāja** (S) (M) 1. speed and strength; a skylark. 3. a Purāṇic sage considered Saptarṣi, the son of Atri, father of Droṇa, the grandfather of Kubera and considered to sit in the council of Brahmā (*Purāṇas*); the eldest son of the Agni Śaṁyu (*M. Bh.*); a renowned sage and the son of King Bharata of the Purū line (*M. Bh.*); a sage born in the Aṅgiras family and the father of Yavakṛta (*V. Rāmāyaṇa*); an Arhat.

**Bharadvājasuta** (S) (M) 1. son of Bharadvāja. 3. another name for Droṇa.

**Bharadvājatmaja** (S) (M) 1. son of Bharadvāja. 3. another name for Droṇa.

**Bhāradvajī** (S) (F) 1. belonging to Bharadvāja; with speed and strength. 3. a river mentioned in the Purāṇas (*M. Bh.*)

**Bharanda** (S) (M) 1. one who fulfils. 2. master; lord.

**Bharaṇī** (S) (F) 1. one who fulfils. 3. the 2nd constellation with 3 stars.

**Bharaṇyu** (S) (M) 1. striving to fulfil. 2. protector; master; friend; fire. 3. another name for the moon and the sun.

**Bharatā** (S) (F) 1. immersed in pleasures; well maintained. 3. a daughter of Agni Bharata (*M. Bh.*); an apsara (*V. Purāṇa*)

**Bharata** (S) (M) 1. fulfils all desires; well-maintained. 3. a son of Duṣyanta and Śakuntalā, a partial reincarnation of Viṣṇu, the 1st of the 12 ćakravartins, and who ruled the land for 27,000 years; a Manu whom this country is named after (*M. Bh.*); an āditya; a son of Daśaratha and Kaikeyī and the husband of Māṇḍavī (*V. Rāmāyaṇa*); a son of Ṛṣabha and the husband of Panćajanī the daughter of Viśvarūpa (*Bhā. Purāṇa*); a sage and author of *Nāṭyaśāstra* (4th century B.C.); a son of Dhruvasandhi and the father of Asita; various agnis (*V. Rāmāyaṇa*); (*Mā. Purāṇa*); a son of Manu Bhautya (*Mā. Purāṇa*); another name for Rudra.

**Bhārata** (S) (M) 1. descended from Bharata. 3. India; another name for Bhīṣma and Yudhiṣṭhira.

**Bhāratabhuṣana** (S) (M) ornament of India.

**Bharataćārya** (S) (M) 1. teacher of the Bharatas. 3. another name for Kṛpa and Droṇa.

**Bhāratāćāryaputra** (S) (M) 1. son of the teacher. 3. another name for Aśvatthāman.

**Bhāratāgrya** (S) (M) 1. best of the Bharatas. 3. another name for Duryodhana.

**Bhāratapravara** (S) (M) 1. chief of the Bharatas. 3. another name for Yudhiṣṭhira.

**Bhārataräma** (S) (M) 1. lover of India; enjoyer of India; pervader of India. 2. an Indian patriot.

**Bharatarama** (S) (M) Rama and his brother Bharata conjoined.

**Bhārataṛṣabha** (S) (M) 1. bull of the Bharatas. 3. another name for Bhīṣma, Yudhiṣṭhira and Dhṛtarāṣṭra.

**Bhāratasārdula** (S) (M) 1. tiger of the Bharatas; noblest of the Bharatas. 3. another name for Yudhiṣṭhira and Dhṛtarāṣṭra.

**Bhāratasattama** (S) (M) 1. best of the Bharatas. 3. another name for Bhīṣma, Dhṛtarāṣṭra and Yudhiṣṭhira.

**Bhāratasiṁha** (S) (M) 1. lion of the Bharatas. 3. another name for Yudhiṣṭhira.

**Bhārataśreṣṭha** (S) (M) 1. first of the Bharatas. 3. another name for Dhṛtarāṣṭra.

**Bhāratendu** (S) (M) moon of India.

**Bharatha** (S) (M) 1. protector of the world. 2. taking up the responsibilities; a king.

**Bhāratī** (S) (F) 1. descendant of Bharata; well maintained; belonging to India; speech. 2. articulate; meritorious; virtuous. 3. a goddess identified with Sarasvatī (*Ṛg Veda*); a famous Purāṇic river from which fire is considered to have originated (*V. Purāṇa*)

**Bhāravā** (S) (F) 1. a pleasing sound; moving with a steady speed; sacred basil (*Ocimum sanctum*) around which females move in singing the *Samīhagāna*, or a song sung in chorus thus resulting in the emanation of a melodious sound. 2. pleasing; quick reflexes; agile and flexible.

**Bhārava** (S) (M) a bowstring.

**Bhāravi** (S) (M) 1. shining sun. 3. a Sanskṛt poet and author of *Kirātārjuna* (6th century A.D.)

**Bharga** (S) (M) 1. with fulfilled desires; the number 11. 2. radiance; splendour; effulgence. 3. the grandson of Divodāsa, son of Pratardana (*A. Purāṇa*); a son of Veṇuhotra (*H. Purāṇa*); one of Vītihotra's sons (*Bhāgavata*); a son of Vahni (*M. Bh.*); another name for Rudra-Śiva and Brahmā.

**Bhārgabhūmi** (S) (M) 1. radiant object. 3. a king (*V. Purāṇa*)

**Bhārgava** (S) (M) 1. attaining radiance; related to Bhṛgu. 2. archer; preceptor. 3. another name for Śukra regent of the planet Venus and preceptor of the daityas, Paraśurāma, Jamadagni, Mārkaṇḍeya and Śiva.

**Bhārgavaka** (S) (M) 1. radiant. 2. a diamond.

**Bhārgavanandana** (S) (M) 1. son of Bhārgava. 3. another name for Jamadagni.

**Bhārgavapriya** (S) (M) 1. dear to Śukra. 2. a diamond.

**Bhārgavendu** (S) (M) 1. moon of the Bhṛgu family; Venus and moon conjoined. 2. beautiful; aesthetic; passionate; soothing.

**Bhārgavī** (S) (F) 1. descendant of Bhṛgu; Śukra's daughter. 2. radiant; charming; glorious; beautiful. 3. another name for Devayānī, Lakṣmī and Pārvatī.

**Bhāri** (S) (M) 1. lion; one who supports. 2. that which nourishes.

**Bhārimān** (S) (M) 1. supporting; nourishing. 3. another name for Viṣṇu.

**Bharmyaśva** (S) (M) 1. wandering horse. 3. a king of Pāñcāla and father of Mudgala (*Bhāgavata*)

**Bharosā** (S) (M) faith; trust.

**Bhartṛhari** (S) (M) 1. protected by god. 2. a worshipper of god. 3. a famous Sanskṛt poet of the 7th century (*N. Śataka*)

**Bhārū** (S) (F) 1. heavy. 2. takes up responsibilities. 3. a daughter of Dakṣa and Vīraṇī and consort of the viśvadevas (*Ś. Purāṇa*)

**Bharu** (S) (M) 1. bearing the load. 2. lord; master; gold; sea. 3. a son of Kṛṣṇa (*Bhāgavata*); another name for Viṣṇu and Śiva.

**Bharuka** (S) (M) 1. responsible. 2. lifting the load. 3. a solar dynasty king who was the son of Sudeva and the father of Bāhuka (*Bhāgavata*)

**Bhārūpa** (S) (M) 1. with a glorious form. 2. resplendent; shining; brilliant.

**Bhāravi** (S) (M) 1. protected by God. 2. the shining sun. 3. the author of *Kirātārjuna*.

**Bhāsakarṇa** (S) (M) 1. with shining ears. 3. a captain of Rāvaṇa killed by Hanumān (*V. Rāmāyaṇa*)

**Bhāsanta** (S) (M) 1. illuminating; shining; radiant. 2. splendid; beautiful; a star. 3. another name for the sun and the moon.

**Bhāsī** (S) (F) 1. illusory; transluscent; of the nature of light; bright; lustrous. 3. a daughter of Tāmrā and mother of vultures (*H. Purāṇa*); a daughter of Prādhā (*M. Bh.*)

**Bhāsin** (S) (M) shining; brilliant.

**Bhāskara** (S) (M) 1. sun; that which radiates; that which emits light; that which illumines.

2. fire; hero; gold. 3. a son of Kaśyapa and Aditī (*H. Purāṇa*); an astrologer (10th century) (*J. Śāstra*); another name for Śiva.

**Bhāskarāćarya** (S) (M) 1. a teacher as glorious as the sun. 2. illuminating; enlightening; venerated. 3. a master astronomer of ancient India who declared in ancient times that the world was round (*J. Śāstra*)

**Bhāskarapriya** (S) (M) 1. beloved of the sun. 2. the ruby.

**Bhāskari** (S) (M) 1. son of the sun; one who brings glory. 3. a sage (*M. Bh.*); another name for Sugrīva and Saturn.

**Bhasma** (S) (M) 1. ashes. 3. another name for Agni.

**Bhasmapriya** (S) (M) 1. fond of ashes. 3. another name for Śiva.

**Bhasmaśayin** (S) (M) 1. lying on ashes. 3. another name for Śiva.

**Bhasmāsura** (S) (M) 1. a demon; the burnt demon; one who can burn others; born of ashes. 3. an asura who was born of the ashes of Śiva's body.

**Bhāsu** (S) (M) 1. creator of light; born of light. 2. the sun.

**Bhāsura** (S) (M) 1. the shining god; crystal; hero. 2. bright; radiant; splendid; glorious; illuminating; enlightening; sacred; venerated; divine.

**Bhāsvān** (S) (M) 1. full of brightness. 3. another name for Sūrya.

**Bhāsvara** (S) (M) 1. luminous; resplendent. 2. shining; glorious; brilliant; enlightening. 3. one of the 2 attendants given to Skanda by Sūrya (*M. Bh.*); a Buddhist deity (*B. Literature*)

**Bhāsvatī** (S) (F) 1. luminous. 2. splendid; shining. 3. the city of the sun (*K. Sāgara*); a river of ancient India (*Nirukta*); another name of the dawn.

**Bhātī** (S) (F) 1. lovely. 2. liked by all; perceptible; luminous; light; splendour; evidence; perception; knowledge.

**Bhaṭṭaprayāga** (S) (M) 1. a noble confluence. 2. one in whom all virtues conjoin. 3. the spot where the Yamunā joins the Gaṅgā.

**Bhaṭṭara** (S) (M) 1. noble lord. 2. meritorious; virtuous; venerated.

**Bhaṭṭāraka** (S) (M) 1. great lord. 2. sacred; venerable; illuminating; enlightening. 3. another name for the sun.

**Bhaṭṭārikā** (S) (F) 1. noble lady. 2. sacred; virtuous; venerated; a tutelary deity. 3. another name for Durgā.

**Bhaṭṭi** (S) (M) 1. noble. 2. meritorious; virtuous. 3. a Sanskṛt poet in the court of Valabhi (7th century A.D.)

**Bhaṭṭika** (S) (M) 1. noble. 3. the son of Ćitragupta, grandson of Brahmā and the mythical progenitor of copyists (*A. Koṣa*)

**Bhaṭṭinī** (S) (F) noble lady.

**Bhātu** (S) (M) 1. light. 2. the sun.

**Bhaulī** (S) (F) 1. full of feeling. 2. humane; compassionate. 3. a rāga.

**Bhaumā** (S) (F) 1. of the earth. 2. firm; unwavering; fecund. 3. daughter of Satyabhāmā (*Bhā. Purāṇa*)

**Bhauma** (S) (M) 1. of the earth; son of the earth; the planet Mars. 3. the 14th Manu (*V. Purāṇa*); a rākṣasa who was the son of Sinhikā and Vipraćitti and was killed by Paraśurāma (*Br. Purāṇa*); Tuesday the day of the planet Mars (*V. Pañćavinśatikā*); another name for Narakāsura.

**Bhaumana** (S) (M) 1. creating the earth by a will (to create). 2. belongs to the earth. 3. another name for Viśvakarman, the architect of the universe.

**Bhaumendra** (S) (M) lord of the earth.

**Bhaumika** (S) (M) being on the earth.

**Bhaumiratna** (S) (M) 1. jewel of the earth 2. the coral.

**Bhautika** (S) (M) 1. physical; elemental; material; corporeal; the shining one. 2. the pearl. 3. another name for Śiva who is fair in visage.

**Bhautya** (S) (M) 1. made of elements; composed of the earth. 3. a Manu (*H. Purāṇa*)

**Bhauvana** (S) (M) 1. belonging to the world. 3. a deity.

**Bhava** (S) (M) 1. existing; of the nature of existence. 2. feeling; sentiment. 3. one of the 12 sons of Bhṛguvaruṇi and Divyā (*V. Purāṇa*); one of the 11 rudras who was the son of Sthāṇu and grandson of Brahmā (*M. Bh.*); a viśvadeva (*M. Bh.*); a son of Viloman (*V. Purāṇa*); a son of Pratihartṛ (*V. Purāṇa*); a son of Kaśyapa and Surabhī (*M. Bh.*); another name for Śiva and Agni.

**Bhavabhūti** (S) (M) 1. the ashes of Śiva; made of existence. 2. whose existence is felt; welfare; prosperity. 3. a Sanskṛt poet of the Kaśyapa gotra (8th century A.D.)

**Bhavadā** (S) (F) 1. giving life. 3. a mother attending on Skanda (*M. Bh.*)

**Bhavada** (S) (M) 1. giving life; cause of existence. 3. a follower of Skanda (*M. Bh.*)

**Bhavadatta** (S) (M) given by Śiva.

**Bhavadeva** (S) (M) 1. lord of existence. 3. another name for Śiva.

**Bhāvajā** (S) (F) 1. born of the heart. 2. beautiful; sincere; compassionate; sentimental.

**Bhāvaja** (S) (M) 1. born of the heart. 3. another name for Kāma.

**Bhavamoćana** (S) (M) 1. one who releases from a worldly existence. 3. another name for Kṛṣṇa.

**Bhāvanā** (S) (F) 1. feeling. 2. fancy; thought; meditation; conception; imagination.

**Bhāvana** (S) (M) 1. creator; promoter of welfare; pleasing to the heart; forest of rays. 2. manifesting; causing to be; illuminating; imagining. 3. another name for Kṛṣṇa.

**Bhavanāga** (S) (M) 1. serpent of Śiva. 2. serpent of existence. 3. the Kundalini which is personified as a 1000 headed serpent and which when uncoiled results in spiritual enlightenment.

**Bhavānanda** (S) (M) that which delights Śiva; pleasure of life; existence and bliss conjoined.

**Bhavanātha** (S) (M) lord of creation.

**Bhāvaṅgamā** (S) (F) 1. touching the heart. 2. charming; sincere; emotional.

**Bhāvaṅganā** (S) (F) 1. embraced by Śiva; the consort of Śiva. 3. another name for Pārvatī.

**Bhavānī** (S) (F) 1. consort of Bhava. 3. Pārvatī in her pacific and amiable form; a devī of the Śakti cult (*H. Purāṇa*)

**Bhavanikā** (S) (F) living in a castle.

**Bhavānīkānta** (S) (M) 1. beloved of Bhavānī. 3. another name for Śiva.

**Bhavāniprasāda** (S) (M) given by Bhavānī; blessed by Bhavānī.

**Bhavānīśaṇkara** (S) (M) Śiva and Pārvatī conjoined.

**Bhavamanyu** (S) (M) 1. creator of the universe; universally accepted. 3. a Purū king (*V. Purāṇa*)

**Bhavantī** (S) (F) 1. now; existent; becoming. 2. charming; new; a virtuous wife.

**Bhavapuṣpā** (S) (F) 1. flowers offered to Śiva; with a flower-like heart. 2. with a tender, compassionate heart. 3. the blossoms of dhaturā, ćameli, etc. which are offered as an oblation to Śiva.

**Bhavarudra** (S) (M) 1. Śiva and Rudra conjoined; existence and fear conjoined. 2. striving to survive by safeguarding himself from fear; pro-life.

**Bhavasāgara** (S) (M) the ocean of worldly existence.

**Bhavaśekhara** (S) (M) 1. Śiva's crest. 3. another name for the moon.

**Bhavatiga** (S) (M) 1. overcoming worldly existence. 2. attaining salvation or mokṣa.

**Bhavātmaja** (S) (M) 1. the son of Śiva. 3. another name for Gaṇeśa and Kārttikeya.

**Bhavātmajā** (S) (F) 1. daughter of Śiva. 3. another name for Manasā.

**Bhavayavya** (S) (M) 1. living in glory. 2. renowned; glorious; respected. 3. a sage of the *Ṛg Veda* who married Romaṣā the daughter of Bṛhaspati.

**Bhaveśa** (S) (M) 1. lord of worldly existence. 3. another name for Śiva.

**Bhāvikī** (S) (F) emotional; sentimental.

**Bhavika** (S) (M) 1. well-meaning. 2. righteous; pious; happy.

**Bhāvikī** (S) (F) 1. real. 2. natural; full of feeling.

**Bhavila** (S) (M) good.

**Bhavin** (S) (M) living being; man.

**Bhāvinī** (S) (F) 1. inducing emotions. 2. noble; beautiful; illustrious; sensitive; loving. 3. an attendant of Skanda (*M. Bh.*)

**Bhaviṣa** (S) (M) 1. striving to exist; lord of existence. 3. another name for Śiva.

**Bhaviṣṇu** (S) (M) 1. knowing the future. 2. faring well; thriving.

**Bhavitrā** (S) (F) 1. manifested. 2. the earth as the manifest form of nature.

**Bhavitra** (S) (M) the 3 worlds.

**Bhāvuka** (S) (M) 1. sensitive; sentimental; productive; happy; well. 3. a king of the solar dynasty who was a son of Ravīya and father of Ćakroddhata (*Bhāgavata*)

**Bhāvukā** (S) (F) 1. happy; productive; prosperous; with a taste for the beautiful. 3. a demon.

**Bhavyā** (S) (F) 1. magnificent. 2. good; beautiful; calm; tranquil; worthy. 3. another name for Pārvatī.

**Bhavya** (S) (M) 1. magnificent. 2. existing suitable; fit; proper; handsome; beautiful; excellent; pious; true. 3. a ṛṣi of the 9th Manvantara (*V. Purāṇa*); a son of Priyavrata (*H. Purāṇa*); a son of Dhruva and the husband of Śambhu (*V. Purāṇa*); a sage of the Dakṣasāvarni Manvantara (*V. Purāṇa*); *Averrhoa carambola*.

**Bhavyakīrti** (S) (F) 1. with magnificent fame. 2. very wise.

**Bhayā** (S) (F) 1. fear. 3. a demoness who is the sister of Kāla, the wife of Heti the son of Brahmā and the mother of Vidyutkeśa (*V. Purāṇa*); the daughter of Anarta and Nikṛti (*H. Purāṇa*)

**Bhayaṅkara** (S) (M) 1. terrible; horrible. 3. a prince of Sauvīra who was a dependent of Jayadratha (*M. Bh.*); a viśvadeva (*M. Bh.*)

**Bhayaṅkarī** (S) (F) 1. terrifying. 3. a follower of Skanda (*M. Bh.*)

**Bhedī** (S) (F) 1. one who gives out secrets; that which pierces. 3. an attendant of Skanda (*M. Bh.*)

**Bhena** (S) (M) 1. the lord of stars. 3. another name for the sun and the moon.

**Bherisvatā** (S) (F) 1. with a musical instrument. 2. a musician. 3. an attendant of Skanda (*M. Bh.*)

**Bherunda** (S) (M) 1. formidable; terrible. 3. an intense, fear inducing form of Śiva.

**Bherundā** (S) (F) 1. formidable; terrible. 3. an intense, fear inducing form of Kālī; a yakṣinī (*A. Koṣa*)

**Bhettṛ** (S) (M) 1. pierces. 2. breaking; splitting; a conqueror. 3. another name for Skanda.

**Bhikṣita** (S) (M) obtained as alms.

**Bhikṣu** (S) (M) 1. beggar; mendicant; Buddhist monk. 3. a son of Bhoja (*K. Sāgara*)

**Bhīmā** (S) (F) 1. terrible; powerful; tremendous; immense; whip. 3. a form of Durgā (*H. Purāṇa*); an apsara (*V. Rāmāyaṇa*)

**Bhīma** (S) (M) 1. terrible; formidable; tremendous. 3. a gandharva who was the son of Kaśyapa and Munī (*M. Bh.*); the grandson of King Avikṣit, son of Parikṣit and Suyaśā, brother of Janamejaya, husband of Kumārī and the father of Pratiśravas (*M. Bh.*); father of King Divodāsa of Kāśi (*M. Bh.*); father of Damayantī (*Nalopākhyāna*); a son of Dhṛtarāṣṭra (*M. Bh.*); the son of King Īlīna and Rathāntarī (*M. Bh.*); one of the 5 attendants given to Subrahmaṇya by the god called Anśa (*M. Bh.*); a 100 kings in Yama's assembly (*M. Bh.*); a Yādava king who was the father of Andhaka and conqueror of Madhurapuri (*Bhāgavata*); friend of Rāvaṇa (*V. Rāmāyaṇa*); one of the 8 forms of Śiva (*Ś. Purāṇa*); one of the 11 rudras (*Ś. Purāṇa*); the 2nd Pāṇḍava who was the son of Kuntī and Vāyu and noted for his strength and size (*M. Bh.*); a son of Kumbhakarṇa (*V. Rāmāyaṇa*); a vidyādhara (*H. Purāṇa*); a dānava (*V. Rāmāyaṇa*); another name for Śiva.

**Bhīmabala** (S) (M) 1. with enormous strength. 3. a son of Dhṛtarāṣṭra (*M. Bh.*)

**Bhīmabhaṭa** (S) (M) 1. great warrior. 3. a gandharva (*K. Sāgara*)

**Bhīmaćandra** (S) (M) moon of strength.

**Bhīmadhanvā** (S) (M) 1. with a formidable bow. 3. another name for Bhīma.

**Bhīmagupta** (S) (M) protected by Bhīma.

**Bhīmajānu** (S) (M) 1. strong thighed. 3. a king in the assembly of Yama (*M. Bh.*)

**Bhīmaka** (S) (M) 1. terrible. 3. an attendant of Śiva.

**Bhīmikā** (S) (F) 1. terrible. 3. a goddess.

**Bhīmākṣa** (S) (M) 1. terrible- eyed. 3. a rākṣasa killed by King Haryaśvan (*H. Purāṇa*)

**Bhīmanātha** (S) (M) lord of strength.

**Bhīmāṅgada** (S) (M) strong bodied.

**Bhīmapāla** (S) (M) protected by Bhīma, protected by the powerful.

**Bhīmapūrvaja** (S) (M) 1. elder brother of Bhīma. 3. another name for Yudhiṣṭhira.

**Bhīmaratha** (S) (M) 1. with a formidable chariot. 2. with a powerful chariot. 3. a king of Viśvāmitra's family who was the son of Ketumān and the father of Divodāsa (*Bhāgavata*); a son of Dhṛtarāṣṭra (*M. Bh.*); a hero on the Kaurava side (*M. Bh.*)

**Bhīmārikā** (S) (F) 1. enemy of the terrible. 2. powerful; fearless. 3. a daughter of Kṛṣṇa and Satyabhāmā (*Bhāgavata*)

**Bhīmaśara** (S) (M) 1. with terrible arrows. 3. a son of Dhṛtarāṣṭra (*M. Bh.*)

**Bhīmasena** (S) (M) 1. having a formidable army. 2. commander of a formidable army. 3. the second Pāṇḍava and the son of Vāyu and Kuntī (*M. Bh.*); a yakṣa; a gandharva (*M. Bh.*)

**Bhīmasenasuta** (S) (M) 1. son of Bhīma. 3. another name for Ghaṭotkaća.

**Bhīmasenātmaja** (S) (M) 1. son of Bhīma. 3. another name for Ghaṭotkaća.

**Bhīmaśankara** (S) (M) 1. Śiva in his terrible form. 3. Śiva in his intense, fearful and destructive form; a linga.

**Bhīmaśastra** (S) (M) 1. with formidable weapons. 2. highly skilled in the use of weapons. 3. a son of Dhṛtarāṣṭra (*M. Bh.*)

**Bhīmasūnu** (S) (M) 1. son of Bhīma. 3. another name for Ghaṭotkaća.

**Bhīmavega** (S) (M) 1. with a very high speed. 2. quick; swift; active. 3. a son of Dhṛtarāṣṭra (*M. Bh.*)

**Bhīmavegarava** (S) (M) 1. of terrific velocity and sound. 2. moving very fast while pounding his feet. 3. a son of Dhṛtarāṣṭra (*M. Bh.*)

**Bhīmrāja** (S) (M) 1. the king of the powerful. 2. the Racket tailed Drongo (*Dicrurus paradiseus*)

**Bhīru** (S) (M) 1. coward. 3. a son of Maṇibhadra and Puṇyajānī (*H. Purāṇa*)

**Bhīṣaṇa** (S) (M) 1. gruesome. 2. awful. 3. a son of the demon Baka killed by Arjuna; a form of Bhairava.

**Bhiṣaj** (S) (M) 1. medicine; healer; physician. 2. heals; cures. 3. a son of Śatadhanvan (*M. Bh.*)

**Bhīṣma** (S) (M) 1. dreadful. 2. terrible; fear-inducing; forbidding. 3. a son of Śāntanu and Gaṅgā who was renowned for his wisdom, bravery and fidelity to his word and who, after death, lived in heaven as Dyau, one of the 8 vasus (*M. Bh.*). a rākṣasa (*H. Koṣa*); another name for Śiva.

**Bhīṣmahanta** (S) (M) 1. killing Bhīṣma. 3. another name for Śikhaṇḍī.

**Bhīṣmaka** (S) (M) 1. dreadful. 2. terrifying; fear-inducing; forbidding. 3. the king of Vidarbha and father of Rukmiṇī (*M. Bh.*)

**Bhīṣmasū** (S) (F) 1. mother of Bhīṣma. 3. another name for Gaṅgā.

**Bhīṣmasvarāja** (S) (M) 1. king of terrible sounds. 2. not affected by noise around. 3. a Buddha (*B. Literature*)

**Bhogadā** (S) (F) 1. bestower of worldly pleasures. 2. grants enjoyment and happiness. 3. a tutelary goddess of the Piṅgalas (*T. Śastra*)

**Bhoganātha** (S) (M) lord of worldly pleasures.

**Bhogavatī** (S) (F) 1. curving. 2. a female serpent (*M. Bh.*) 3. a mother attending on Skanda (*Sk. Purāṇa*); the city of serpents in the subterranean region (*M. Bh.*); the river Gaṅgā in Pātāla (*M. Bh.*)

**Bhogindra** (S) (M) 1. lord of the curved ones, lord of serpents. 3. another name for Ananta and Patañjali.

**Bhogīśa** (S) (M) 1. lord of serpents. 3. another name for Ananta and Śeṣa.

**Bhogyā** (S) (F) 1. worthy of being enjoyed. 2. an object of enjoyment; a precious stone; money; corn grain.

**Bhojā** (S) (F) 1. bestowing enjoyment. 2. beautiful; liberal. 3. a princess of the Bhojas (*Bhā. Purāṇa*); an exquisite woman of Sauvīra abducted by Sātyakī and then married to him (*Bhā. Purāṇa*); the wife of Vīravrata (*H. Purāṇa*)

**Bhoja** (S) (M) 1. bestowing enjoyment; bountiful; liberal. 2. a king with uncommon qualities. 3. a king of the country of Bhoja near the Vindhya mountains (*H. Purāṇa*); a king of Mālvā (*M. Bh.*); an ancient king of Marttikātava who fought on the side of the Kauravas (*M. Bh.*); a Yadu dynasty king who founded the Bhoja dynasty (*M. Bh.*); a renowned king and a Sanskṛt scholar (11th century A.D.) (*B. Carita*); a follower of Sudāsa who once helped sage Viśvāmitra (*M. Bh.*); a king of Kānyakubja (*R. Taraṅginī*)

**Bhojadeva** (S) (M) 1. fulfiller of desires. 3. a celebrated king of Dhārā who was a patron of learning and an author himself (11th century A.D.) (*M. Smṛti*)

**Bhojanarendra** (S) (M) 1. best among the Bhoja kings. 3. another name for King Bhojadeva of Dhārā.

**Bhojarāja** (S) (M) 1. lord of the generous. 3. another name for King Bhojadeva of Dhārā.

**Bhojarājanyavardhana** (S) (M) 1. increasing the Bhoja dynasty. 3. another name for Kṛṣṇa.

**Bhoktṛ** (S) (M) 1. enjoyer. 2. consumer; eater; possesser; ruler.

**Bholānātha** (S) (M) 1. lord of the innocent. 3. another name for Śiva.

**Bhomirā** (S) (F) 1. originating from the earth. 2. the coral; fecund; life-giving; tolerant.

**Bhoneśa** (S) (M) lord of the universe.

**Bhrāja** (S) (M) 1. shining; glittering. 2. sacred; illuminating; enlightening. 3. a gandharva who protects the Soma; an agni; one of the 7 suns.

**Bhrājasvata** (S) (M) 1. sparkling; glittering. 2. illuminates; enlightens; sacred.

**Bhrājata** (S) (M) 1. shining; glittering. 2. gleaming; glorious; enlightening.

**Bhrājathu** (S) (M) 1. brilliance. 2. splendour; glory; fame; enlightenment.

**Bhrājī** (S) (F) 1. lustre. 2. sheen; splendour; fame; glory.

**Bhrājiṣṇu** (S) (M) 1. desirous of splendour. 2. striving for glory; achievement; renown; shining; splendid; radiant. 3. another name for Viṣṇu and Śiva.

**Bhrājiṣṭha** (S) (M) 1. residing in splendour. 2. splendid; glorious; renowned; enlightened; shining very brightly. 3. a son of Ghṛtapṛṣṭha (*Ṛg Veda*)

**Bhramara** (S) (M) 1. large black bee. 2. wanderer. 3. a Sauvīra prince who was a dependant of Jayadratha (*M. Bh.*)

**Bhramarāmbā** (S) (F) 1. the bee-mother.

3. another name for Pārvatī who was incarnated in the form of a bee to slay an asura (*D. Saptaśati*)

**Bhramarī** (S) (F) 1. dancing around; belonging to a bee; a form of kinetic energy; a magnet or lodestone. 3. a yoginī or female attendant of Durgā (*D. Saptaśati*); a rākṣasī of Kaśyapa's family who was slain by Ganeśa (*M. Bh.*); another name for Durgā.

**Bhrāmarikā** (S) (F) 1. wandering in all directions; honey of the large black bee. 2. a spinning top.

**Bhramī** (S) (F) 1. whirlpool; whirlwind. 3. a daughter of Śiśumāra and wife of Dhruva (*Bhā. Purāṇa*); *Enhydra fluctuans*.

**Bhrāsakarṇa** (S) (M) 1. one possessed with dancing cars. 2. a rapt, attentive listener. 3. a rākṣasa who was the son of Sumāli and Ketumatī (*Bhāgavata*)

**Bhṛgu** (S) (M) 1. born of fire. 3. a prajāpati son of Brahmā, the founder of the Bhārgava line of sages, considered to have been born twice — first from Brahmā's skin and the second time from the Brahmāyajña the fire of Varuṇa, in the first birth was the husband of Khyāti and fathered Lakṣmī, Dhātā, Vidhātā and Kavi, in the second was the husband of Pulomā and Bhūtā from whom he had the 11 rudras, Bhūta, Ćyavana, Śuchi, Śukra, Sāvana and Vajraśīrṣa, was a member of Brahmā's assembly, his race is said to have brought fire to the earth (*Ṛg Veda*); one of the Saptaṛṣis or Seven Sages (*H. Purāṇa*); the father of Dhātṛ and Māndhātṛ (*Purāṇa*); a son of Arthapati and uncle of the poet Bāṇa.

**Bhṛgunandana** (S) (M) 1. son of Bhṛgu. 3. another name for the planet Śukra or Venus.

**Bhṛgunātha** (S) (M) 1. lord of fire. 3. another name for Śiva.

**Bhṛguśārdūla** (S) (M) 1. tiger of the Bhṛgus; noblest of the Bhṛgus. 3. another name for Mārkaṇḍeya and Jamadagni.

**Bhṛguśreṣṭha** (S) (M) 1. the best among Bhṛgus. 3. another name for sage Jamadagni and Paraśurāma.

**Bhṛguttama** (S) (M) 1. best of the Bhṛgus. 3. another name for Jamadagni.

**Bhṛguvāruṇi** (S) (M) 1. of Varuṇa. 3. a ṛsi regarded as the ancestor of the Bhṛgus and part author of *Ṛg. Veda* (ix)

**Bhṛngāra** (S) (M) 1. a vessel of fire; a golden vase of 8 different substances and forms. 2. meritorious; virtuous; venerated.

**Bhṛngarāja** (S) (M) 1. king of black bees. 2. the large black bee. 3. a tutelary deity (*H. Ć. Ćintāmaṇi*); a kind of oblation or sacrifice (*He. Koṣa*), an ayurvedic herb used for darkening the hair (*S. Samhitā*)

**Bhṛngarī** (S) (F) 1. as black as bee; as bright as fire. 2. cloves; gold.

**Bhṛngarīta** (S) (M) 1. the Indian fig tree (*Ficus indica*) 3. an attendant of Śiva (*Ś. Purāṇa*)

**Bhṛngī** (S) (M) 1. 6 footed insect. 3. a 3 footed sage who was a devotee of Śiva (*V. Purāṇa*)

**Bhṛngin** (S) (M) 1. the Indian fig tree (*Ficus indica*) 3. one of Śiva's attendants (*Ś. Purāṇa*)

**Bhūbhṛta** (S) (M) 1. supporter of the earth; supported by the earth. 2. a mountain. 3. another name for Viṣṇu.

**Bhūbhuja** (S) (M) 1. possessor of the earth; enjoyer of the earth. 2. a king.

**Bhūdeva** (S) (M) 1. lord of earth. 2. a divinity on earth.

**Bhudevī** (S) (F) 1. the goddess of the earth. 3. another name for Pṛthvī.

**Bhūdhana** (S) (M) 1. whose property is the earth. 2. a king.

**Bhūdhara** (S) (M) 1. supporter of the earth. 2. mountain; the number 7. 3. another name for Kṛṣṇa, Śiva and Śeṣa.

**Bhūgandhapati** (S) (M) 1. lord of the essence of the earth. 3. another name for Śiva.

**Bhūgarbha** (S) (M) 1. womb of the earth. 2. a tunnel; an underground establishment; who keeps secrets; who is secretive; protects; protected.

**Bhujabalin** (S) (M) strong armed.

**Bhujagarāja** (S) (M) 1. king of serpents. 3. another name for Śeṣa.

**Bhujagāri** (S) (M) 1. enemy of serpents. 2. a peacock. 3. another name for Garuḍa.

**Bhujageśvara** (S) (M) 1. lord of serpents. 3. another name for Śeṣa.

**Bhujaketu** (S) (M) 1. holding a banner; with a victorious arm. 3. a king who fought on the side of the Kauravas (*M. Bh.*)

**Bhujaṅga** (S) (M) 1. black snake. 2. lord; the constellation Āśleṣā; the number 8. 3. a serpent son of Kadru and Kaśyapa (*M. Bh.*); another name for Rāhu.

**Bhujaṅgahan** (S) (M) 1. slayer of serpents. 3. another name for Garuḍa.

**Bhujavīrya** (S) (M) strong armed.

**Bhuji** (S) (M) 1. granting favours. 2. protector; patron. 3. another name for the aśvins and Agni.

**Bhujyu** (S) (M) 1. with a desire to enjoy; can be eaten; a connoisseur; an epicurean. 2. wealthy; rich; edible. 3. a son of Tugra protected by the aśvins (*Ṛg Veda*)

**Bhūkaśyapa** (S) (M) 1. drinker of the earth; tortoise of the earth. 2. above earthly attachments; supporting the earth. 3. the father of Vasudeva and the grandfather of Kṛṣṇa (*Bhāgavata*)

**Bhūman** (S) (M) 1. consisting of all existing things; consisting of existence. 2. the earth.

**Bhūmanyu** (S) (M) 1. universally accepted; devotee of the earth. 3. a son of Bharata and Sunandā, grandson of Duṣyanta and the husband of Puṣkariṇī (*M. Bh.*); a grandson of King Kuru and son of Dhṛtarāṣṭra (*M. Bh.*); a gandharva (*M. Bh.*)

**Bhumat** (S) (M) 1. possessing the earth. 2. a king.

**Bhūmayī** (S) (F) 1. full of existence. 2. produced from the earth. 3. another name for Ćhāyā the wife of the sun (*H. Purāṇa*)

**Bhūmi** (S) (F) 1. earth. 2. of existence; receptacle of existence; object; soil. 3. the earth personified as a goddess who was the daughter of Brahmā and the wife of Mahāviṣṇu (*V. Purāṇa*); the daughter of Śiśumāra, wife of Dhruva and mother of Kalpa and Vatsala (*Bhāgavata*); the wife of King Bhūmipati (*M. Bh.*)

**Bhūmijā** (S) (F) 1. born of the earth. 3. another name for Sītā.

**Bhūmija** (S) (M) 1. born of the earth.

2. produced from the earth.
**Bhūmimitra** (S) (M) 1. friend of the earth. 2. well- wisher of all that exists, of people.
**Bhūminātha** (S) (M) 1. controller of the earth. 2. a king.
**Bhūmīndra** (S) (M) 1. lord of the earth. 2. a king.
**Bhūmiñjaya** (S) (M) 1. conqueror of the earth. 3. a son of Virāta; a warrior of the Kaurava side (*M. Bh.*)
**Bhūmipāla** (S) (M) 1. guardian of the earth; protector of the earth. 2. a king. 3. a king who was a partial incarnation of the asura Krodhavaśa (*M. Bh.*)
**Bhūmipati** (S) (M) 1. lord of the earth; master of the earth. 3. a king mentioned in the *M. Bh.*
**Bhūmiputra** (S) (M) 1. son of the earth. 3. another name for the planet Mars.
**Bhūmiśaya** (S) (M) 1. sleeping on the earth. 2. an ascetic; forsaker of earthly pleasures. 3. a king who gifted a sword to Bharata the son of Duṣyanta (*M. Bh.*)
**Bhūmisena** (S) (M) 1. commander of the earth. 2. an extremely powerful, renowned king. 3. a son of the 10th Manu (*M. Purāṇa*)
**Bhūmīśvara** (S) (M) sovereign of the earth.
**Bhūmitra** (S) (M) 1. friend of the earth. 2. a king.
**Bhūmya** (S) (M) 1. belonging to the earth. 2. terrestrial.
**Bhūnandana** (S) (M) 1. delighting the earth; son of earth. 2. a virtuous person.
**Bhūnāyaka** (S) (M) leader of the earth.
**Bhūnetri** (S) (M) 1. leader of the earth; eye of the earth. 2. a king.
**Bhūpa** (S) (M) 1. protector of the earth. 2. a king.
**Bhūpada** (S) (M) 1. fixed on earth. 2. stable; firm; a tree.
**Bhūpāla** (S) (M) 1. guardian of the earth. 2. a king.
**Bhūpat** (S) (M) 1. lord of the earth. 2. a king. 3. a king of the lunar dynasty of Indraprastha (*M. Bh.*)
**Bhūpati** (S) (M) 1. lord of the earth. 3. a viśvadeva (*M. Bh.*); another name for Rudra and Śiva; a class of gods under Manu Raivata (*Mā. Purāṇa*)
**Bhūpen** (S) (M) 1. lord of the world. 2. a king.
**Bhūpendra** (S) (M) 1. king of kings. 3. an apsarā; another name for Indra.
**Bhūputra** (S) (M) 1. son of the earth. 3. another name for Mars.
**Bhūputrī** (S) (F) 1. daughter of the earth. 3. another name for Sītā.
**Bhūraṇyu** (S) (M) 1. worshipped by the world. 2. quick; eager; restless; active. 3. another name for Viṣṇu and the sun.
**Bhūratna** (S) (F) jewel of the earth.
**Bhūrbhuva** (S) (M) 1. born of the earth; father of the earth. 3. a mind-born son of Brahmā (*Brah. Purāṇa*); another name for the sun.
**Bhūri** (S) (M) 1. much, abundant. 2. important; mighty; great; boundless; infinite; divine; gold. 3. a son of King Somadatta of the Bālhikas (*M. Bh.*); a king of the Kuru dynasty who obtained a place among the viśvadevas (*M. Bh.*); a son of sage Śuka and Pīvarī (*V. Purāṇa*); another name for Brahmā, Viṣṇu, Śiva and gold.
**Bhūribala** (S) (M) 1. very strong. 3. a son of Dhṛtarāṣṭra (*M. Bh.*)
**Bhūrida** (S) (M) one who donates in abundance.
**Bhūridakṣiṇa** (S) (M) 1. bestowing rich presents; liberal. 3. another name for Bhūriśravas.
**Bhūridhāman** (S) (M) 1. possessing great might. 3. a son of the 9th Manu (*H. Purāṇa*)
**Bhūridyumna** (S) (M) 1. possessing great glory. 3. a son of Vīradyumna (*M. Upaniṣad*)
**Bhuridyumna** (S) (M) 1. killer of many; as glorious as fire. 2. a warrior; pious; sacred. 3. a king in the assembly of Yama (*M. Bh.*); a sage and contemporaneous devotee of Kṛṣṇa (*Bhāgavata*); son of Vīradyumna (*M. Bh.*)
**Bhūrihan** (S) (M) 1. slayer of many. 3. a rākṣasa (*M. Bh.*)
**Bhūrijyeṣṭha** (S) (M) 1. eldest among all. 2. greatest; the best. 3. a son of King Vićakṣus (*V. Purāṇa*)
**Bhūrikīrti** (S) (M) 1. very famous; very

learned. 3. a king whose 2 daughters Ćampikā and Sumatī married Lava and Kuśa (*A. Rāmāyaṇa*)

**Bhūriṣeṇa** (S) (M) 1. with many armies. 3. a son of the 10th Manu (*H. Purāṇa*); another name for King Śaryāti (*Bhāgavata*)

**Bhūriśravas** (S) (M) 1. about whom much is heard. 3. a son of King Somadatta of the Bālhikas; the son of King Somada of the Kuru dynasty who helped the Kaurava side (*M. Bh.*); another name for Indra.

**Bhūritejas** (S) (M) 1. very glorious. 3. an ancient king who was a partial incarnation of the asura Krodhavaśa (*M. Bh.*)

**Bhūrivasu** (S) (M) one who has a lot of wealth.

**Bhūṣā** (S) (F) 1. ornament; decoration; one who wears many ornaments. 2. one who is an embellishment; precious; much loved; wealthy.

**Bhūśakra** (S) (M) 1. Indra of the earth. 2. much renowned; powerful; venerated; meritorious king.

**Bhūṣaṇa** (S) (M) 1. ornament; embellishment. 2. that which decorates; adorns.

**Bhūṣṇu** (S) (M) growing; thriving.

**Bhūsura** (S) (M) 1. earth; god. 2. a cow; a Brahmin.

**Bhūtā** (S) (F) 1. present; existing; true, real, past. 3. the 14th day of the dark half of the lunar month; a wife of Bhṛgu.

**Bhūta** (S) (M) 1. existent; essence of the material substance. 2. past; son; a devotee; an ascetic. 3. a son of Vasudeva and Pauravī (*Bhāgavata*); a priest of the gods (*A. Koṣa*); a son-in-law of Dakṣa and the father of various rudras (*Bhāgavata*); name of a yakṣa (*Bhāgavata*)

**Bhutabhāvana** (S) (M) 1. causing the welfare of living beings. 3. another name for Brahmā, Viṣṇu and Śiva.

**Bhūtadamanī** (S) (F) 1. one who slays ghosts. 3. one of the 9 Śaktis of Śiva (*H. Purāṇa*)

**Bhūtadhāman** (S) (M) 1. one who dwells in substance. 2. all pervading; omnipresent. 3. a son of Indra.

**Bhūtādi** (S) (M) 1. originator of all beings. 2. the Supreme Spirit.

**Bhūtajyoti** (S) (M) 1. light of living beings; flame of the 5 essences. 3. the father of Vasu and son of Sumati.

**Bhūtakarman** (S) (M) 1. who acts in accordance with the past; who performs rites to invoke the evil spirits. 3. a warrior on the side of the Kauravas (*M. Bh.*)

**Bhūtaketu** (S) (M) 1. who bears the banner of ascetics; saviour of the ascetics. 3. a son of Manu Dakṣasāvarṇi.

**Bhūtanātha** (S) (M) 1. lord of ascetics; lord of ghosts; lord of essences; lord of existence. 3. another name for Śiva.

**Bhūtānśa** (S) (M) 1. part of existence. 3. a sage and descendant of Kaśyapa who was an author of *Ṛg Veda* (x)

**Bhūtapāla** (S) (M) protector of living beings; protector of spirits; protector of existence.

**Bhūtapati** (S) (M) 1. lord of beings. 3. another name for Kṛṣṇa.

**Bhūtarāja** (S) (M) 1. lord of living beings. 3. another name for Viṣṇu.

**Bhūtasantāpana** (S) (M) 1. tortures living beings; tortures evil spirits. 3. a son of Hiranyākṣa (*Bhā. Purāṇā*)

**Bhūtaśarman** (S) (M) 1. protector of spirits. protector of the existence. 3. a warrior of the Kauravas (*M. Bh.*)

**Bhūtātman** (S) (M) 1. soul of all beings; the Supreme Self; the Universal Self. 3. another name for Brahmā and Viṣṇu.

**Bhūteśa** (S) (M) 1. lord of living beings. 3. another name for Brahmā, Viṣṇu, Śiva and the sun.

**Bhūteśvara** (S) (M) 1. lord of beings. 3. another name for Kṛṣṇa.

**Bhūti** (S) (F) 1. existence; wellbeing; prosperity. 2. wealth; might; power; ashes. 3. the wife of Rući and mother of Manu Bhautya (*H. Purāṇa*)

**Bhūtibhūṣaṇa** (S) (M) 1. adorned with ashes; ornament among the living beings. 3. another name for Śiva.

**Bhūtigaurī** (S) (M) 1. pervades life. 2. omnipresent. 3 another name for Pārvatī the consort of Śiva.

**Bhūtikṛt** (S) (M) 1. causing welfare.

3. another name for Śiva.
**Bhūtinanda** (S) (M) bestower of pleasure.
**Bhūtirāja** (S) (M) lord of existence.
**Bhūtivardhana** (S) (M) 1. increases welfare. 2. a king; a leader; a saint.
**Bhuvā** (S) (F) fire; the earth.
**Bhuva** (S) (M) 1. atmosphere. 3. a son of Pratihartṛ (*V. Purāṇa*); another name for Agni.
**Bhuvadvasu** (S) (M) bestowing wealth.
**Bhuvadvata** (S) (M) 1. bestowing prosperity. 3. another name for the ādityas.
**Bhūvallabha** (S) (M) liked by the universe; universally adored.
**Bhuvanā** (S) (F) 1. omnipresent; the earth. 3. Bṛhaspati's sister, wife of Prabhāsa one of the 8 vasus and the mother of Viśvakarmā (*Br. Purāṇa*)
**Bhuvana** (S) (M) 1. being; the earth; abode. 2. living creature; human. 3. a rūdra (*V. Purāṇa*); a sage (*M. Bh.*)
**Bhuvanaćandra** (S) (M) moon of the earth.
**Bhuvanādhiśa** (S) (M) master of the earth.
**Bhuvanadīpa** (S) (M) light of the earth.
**Bhuvanamatī** (S) (F) 1. owner of the world. 2. princess.
**Bhuvanamātṛ** (S) (F) 1. mother of the earth. 3. another name for Durgā.
**Bhuvanamohana** (S) (M) 1. attractive to the 3 worlds; universally attractive. 3. a name of Kṛṣṇa, kept by Rukmiṇī.
**Bhuvanāṇḍaka** (S) (M) 1. the cosmic egg. 2. the universe.
**Bhuvanapatī** (S) (M) lord of the earth.
**Bhuvanapāvanī** (S) (F) 1. one who makes the earth sacred. 3. another name for the holy Gaṅgā.
**Bhuvanarāja** (S) (M) king of the earth.
**Bhuvanasvara** (S) (M) 1. voice of the earth. 3. a rudra (*Ṛg Veda*)
**Bhuvanatraya** (S) (M) 1. the 3 worlds. 3. on the basis of knowledge, the 3 worlds are earth, atmosphere and heaven, and on the basis of *karmaphala*, or the fruit of Karma, the 3 worlds are hell, earth and heaven.
**Bhuvaneśa** (S) (M) lord of the earth.
**Bhuvaneśānī** (S) (F) mistress of the earth.
**Bhuvaneśī** (S) (F) 1. goddess of the earth. 3. a goddess (*D. Bhāgavata*)
**Bhuvaneśvara** (S) (M) lord of the earth.
**Bhuvaneśvarī** (S) (M) mistress of the earth.
**Bhuvanyu** (S) (M) 1. possessing the earth. 3. another name for the sun, fire and moon.
**Bhuvapati** (S) (M) lord of the atmosphere.
**Bhuvas** (S) (M) 1. air; atmosphere; heaven. 2. second of the 14 worlds; a mind-born son of Brahmā (*Bhā. Purāṇa*)
**Bhuvis** (S) (F) heaven.
**Bibhatsu** (S) (M) 1. averse to loathsome acts. 3. another name for Arjuna who desisted from performing or participating in loathsome deeds (*M. Bh.*)
**Biḍalāksa** (S) (F) 1. cateyed. 3. a rākṣasī.
**Biḍālikā** (S) (F) 1. young cat. 2. a kitten.
**Biḍaujas** (S) (M) 1. light of the people; powerful sovereign. 3. another name for Indra.
**Bidūla** (S) (M) 1. spotted; variegated. 2. one with an unusual, attractive body. 3. the Kachnār tree (*Bauhinia Variegata*)
**Bidyut** (S) (M) 1. lightning; electricity; full of knowledge. 2. effulgent; illumined; enlightened.
**Bījahāriṇī** (S) (F) 1. taking away seed. 3. a daughter of Duḥsaha.
**Bījākṣarā** (S) (F) 1. the seed alphabet; Om. 2. the first syllable of a mantra; the atomic alphabet; profound; omnipotent.
**Bījanātha** (S) (M) 1. lord of the seed. 2. lord of the elements. 3. another name for Śiva and the sun.
**Bījāñjalī** (S) (F) 1. a handful of seed. 2. fecund; life-giving.
**Bījavāhana** (S) (M) 1. carrier of seed. 2. creator. 3. another name for Śiva.
**Bījin** (S) (M) 1. cosmic creator; the owner and giver of seed; progenitor. 3. another name for the sun.
**Bijlī** (S) (F) 1. lightning. 2. bright; glorious; illuminating; enlightening.
**Bikāsa** (S) (M) development; expansion.
**Bila** (S) (M) 1. hole. 2. hollow; opening; cave. 3. another name for Indra's horse Uććaiḥśravas.

**Billa** (S) (M) 1. hole. 2. reservoir.

**Bilvaḍaṇḍin** (S) (M) 1. one who holds a staff made of bilva wood (*Aegle marmelos*) (the fruit, leaves and wood of the Bilva tree are offered to Śiva and therefore considered sacred). 3. another name for Śiva.

**Bilvaka** (S) (M) 1. living in a hole; living in a cave. 3. a serpent son of Kaśyapa and Kadru (*M. Bh.*)

**Bilvamaṅgala** (S) (M) 1. the auspicious bilva tree (*Aegle marmelos*). 3. a friend of Kṛṣṇa (*Bhā. Purāṇa*)

**Bilvanātha** (S) (M) 1. lord of the bilva tree; lord of serpents. 3. another name for Śiva.

**Bilvapāṇḍura** (S) (M) 1. yellow serpent. 3. a serpent son of Kaśyapa (*M. Bh.*)

**Bilvapattrikā** (S) (F) 1. leaf of the bilva tree. 3. a form of goddess known as the Dākṣāyāṇī who resides at the temple of Bilvaka (*D. Bhāgavata*)

**Bilvatejas** (S) (M) 1. energetic serpent. 3. a serpent son of Takṣaka (*M. Bh.*)

**Biman** (S) (M) honoured; respected from the heart.

**Bimbā** (S) (F) 1. disc of the sun or the moon; image; mirror. 2. that which reflects; a preceptor. 3. mother of King Bimbisāra; the wife of King Bālāditya of Kāśmira (*R. Taraṅgiṇī*)

**Bimbaka** (S) (M) the disc of the sun or the moon; round-faced; mirror.

**Bimbeśvara** (S) (M) 1. lord of the sun and the moon; lord of images. 2. a preceptor. 3. a temple founded by princess Bimbā (*R. Taraṅginī*)

**Bimbī** (S) (F) 1. as glorious as the sun or the moon; the fruit of the *Momordica monodelpha* plant; *Coccinia indica*. 3. the mother of King Bimbisāra (*B. Literature*)

**Bimbinī** (S) (F) the pupil of the eye.

**Bimbisāra** (S) (M) 1. the essence of the Absolute. 3. a king of Magadha who was a patron of Gautama Buddha (*B. Ćarita*)

**Bimbita** (S) (M) reflected.

**Biṇā** (S) (F) 1. lute. 2. melodious; harmonious.

**Bindeśvara** (S) (M) 1. lord of creation. 2. the Supreme Lord.

**Bindiyā** (S) (F) 1. a small dot. 3. reference here to a small dot that married Hindu women wear on their forehead as an embellishment and a sign of auspiciousness.

**Bindu** (S) (F) a point; mark; symbol; drop; pearl; truth; alphabet; origin; which connotes; subtle; immeasurable; absolute; divine; the Brahman.

**Bindu** (S) (M) 1. drop; dot; globule; spot. 2. a dot worn on the forehead between the eyebrows. 3. the dot in the alphabet that represents the Anuśvāra which is connected with Śiva and is of mystical importance.

**Bindudeva** (S) (M) 1. lord of the Bindu; lord of alphabets. 3. a Buddhist deity (*B. Literature*); another name for Śiva.

**Binduhṛada** (S) (M) 1. knower of truth. 2. attained salvation or mokṣa. 3. a lake said to have been formed by the drops of the Gaṅgā shaken from Śiva's locks (*V. Purāṇa*)

**Bindumādhava** (S) (M) 1. thinker of the Absolute; lord of the alphabet. 2. well read; wise; illumined; enlightened. 3. a form of Viṣṇu (*V. Purāṇa*)

**Bindumālinī** (S) (F) 1. wearing a garland of pearls. 3. a rāga.

**Bindumat** (S) (M) 1. has pearls; knows the truth; knows the alphabet. 2. wealthy; well-read; wise; enlightened; has attained mokṣa or salvation. 3. a son of Marīći (*Bhā. Purāṇa*)

**Bindumatī** (S) (F) 1. learned; knower of the Absolute. 2. wise; illumined; enlightened; has attained mokṣa or salvation. 3. a wife of Marīći (*Bhāgavata*); a daughter of Śasābindu and wife of Māndhātṛ (*H. Purāṇa*); the wife of King Māndhātā and the mother of Pūrukutsa and Mućukunda (*Bhāgavata*)

**Bindunātha** (S) (M) 1. lord of the Bindu; lord of alphabets; lord of truth. 2. wise; illuminated; enlightened; has attained mokṣa or salvation. 3. another name for Śiva.

**Binduphala** (S) (M) a pearl.

**Bindurekhā** (S) (F) 1. a line of dots; a verse. 2. a poetic composition. 3. a daughter of Ćaṇḍavarman (*K. Sāgara*)

**Bindusāra** (S) (M) 1. an excellent pearl; essence of truth. 3. the son of Ćandragupta Maurya and the father of Emperor Aśoka (*H. Parvan*)

**Bindusāras** (S) (M) 1. concentrated; pious lake; an ocean of alphabets. 2. well read; wise; venerated; enlightened. 3. a sacred lake (*M. Bh.*)

**Binītā** (S) (F) humble.

**Binota** (S) (M) happy.

**Binoy** (S) (M) humility; humble; request.

**Bipin** (S) (M) 1. forest. 2. free; magnificent; providing shelter.

**Bipinćandra** (S) (M) 1. moon of the forest. 3. another name for Kṛṣṇa.

**Biplab** (S) (M) 1. revolution. 2. revolutionary; progressive.

**Bipula** (S) (M) 1. plenty; much; many. 2. strong; manifold.

**Bīrbala** (S) (M) a powerful warrior.

**Biren** (S) (M) 1. lord of warriors. 2. great warrior.

**Bīrendra** (S) (M) 1. lord of warriors. 2. a great warrior.

**Bīreśvara** (S) (M) lord of warriors.

**Bīrju** (S) (M) powerful.

**Bisālā** (S) (F) 1. sprout. 2. bud; young shoot; a child.

**Bisāvatī** (S) (F) 1. abounding in lotus-fibre. 2. garbed in lotuses; fragrant; sacred; auspicious.

**Biśambharnātha** (S) (M) saviour of the universe; lord of the universe.

**Bisinī** (S) (F) 1. a collection of lotus flowers. 2. beautiful; fragrant; auspicious; famous; venerated; dear to the gods.

**Bisvājita** (S) (M) victorious in the world.

**Bittu** (S) (M) 1. seed. 2. fecund; life-giving.

**Boddhavāsara** (S) (M) 1. the day of enlightenment. 3. the 11th day of the light half of the Kārttika month when Viṣṇu awakens from his sleep (*S. Māhātmya*)

**Boddhidharma** (S) (M) 1. follower of Buddhist doctrine; follower of the enlightened path. 3. a Buddhist patriarch (*B. Literature*)

**Boddhṛ** (S) (M) 1. who comprehends; who knows. 2. a preceptor; a seer.

**Bodha** (S) (M) 1. knowledge; awakening. 2. thought; intelligence; understanding; enlightenment. 3. knowledge personified as a son of Buddhi.

**Bodhadiśana** (S) (M) 1. whose intellect is knowledge. 2. profoundly wise; a seer.

**Bodhamaya** (S) (M) 1. consisting of pure knowledge; pervaded with knowledge. 2. learned; wise; enlightened.

**Bodhana** (S) (M) 1. inspiration; awakening. 2. prudent; clever; wise; enlightened. 3. another name for Bṛhaspati.

**Bodhanā** (S) (F) 1. the awakening; the arousing; the enlightening; the inspiring; the intellect. 2. knowledge. 3. the awakening of Durgā; a festival on the 9th day of the dark half of the month Bhadra.

**Bodhāna** (S) (M) 1. arousing; enlightening. 2. clever; exciting; prudent; wise; enlightening. 3. another name for Bṛhaspati.

**Bodhendra** (S) (M) lord of intelligence; lord of enlightenment.

**Bodhi** (S) (F) 1. perfect knowledge; wisdom; enlightenment. 3. the knowledge by which one becomes a Buddha or Jina in the Buddhist and Jaina religions respectively; the Bodhi tree (*Ficus religiosa*); meditating under which Gautama Buddha attained spiritual enlightenment and which since has been called the tree of wisdom.

**Bodhinī** (S) (F) 1. intellect. 2. awakens; knowledge; understanding; perception; wisdom; enlightenment.

**Bodhinmanas** (S) (M) 1. an enlightened mind. 2. awake; attentive; watchful; wise.

**Bodhisattva** (S) (M) 1. whose essence is perfect knowledge. 3. a term used to denote one who has only one stage to cover before the at taining of Buddha or spiritual enlightenment.

**Bogli** (S) (M) the pond-heron.

**Bolin** (S) (M) speaker.

**Bora** (S) (M) brave.

**Bradhna** (S) (M) 1. pale red; yellowish; mighty; ruddy; horse; the world of the sun; great. 2. fecund; life-giving; strong; illuminating; enlightening; sacred. 3. a son of Manu Bhautya (*H. Purāṇa*); another name for the sun.

**Bradhnāśva** (S) (M) 1. as powerful as a horse. 3. a king.

**Brahmā** (S) (M) **1.** creator of the universe. **2.** growth; evolution; prayer. **3.** the one universal spirit represented as the creator and first of the divine Hindu trinity (the other two being Viṣṇu - the sustainer and Śiva - the destroyer), the husband of Sarasvatī, born from the navel of Viṣṇu and creator of the 7 sages or the Saptṛṣis who are considered the prajāpatis or lords of creation and from whom originate all the movables and immovables of the universe and the abode of whom is Mount Mahāmeru (*Bhā. Purāṇa*)

**Brahmabhuti** (S) (M) **1.** created by the absolute; twilight. **2.** soothing and perfect.

**Brahmabīja** (S) (M) **1.** the seed of the Vedas. **3.** the sacred syllable Om.

**Brahmaćāri** (S) (M) **1.** devotee of the Absolute; bachelor. **3.** a gandharva who was the son of Kaśyapa and Prādhā (*M. Bh.*); another name for Śiva and Skanda.

**Brahmadaṇḍa** (S) (M) **1.** the staff of Brahmā. **2.** as just and fair as Brahmā.

**Brahmadatta** (S) (M) **1.** given by Brahmā. **2.** perfect; held sacred. **3.** a prince of the Pāñćālas (*M. Bh.*); the 12th ćakravartin (*A. Koṣa*); the father of Kṛṣṇadatta; a king of Kāmpila who married the hundred daughters of King Kuṣanābha of Kānyakubja (*M. Bh.*); a famous Solar dynasty king of Kāmpilya who was the son of Anūha and Kṛtvī (*Rāmāyaṇa*); the king of Śālva and the father of Hansa and Dībhaka (*H. Purāṇa*); a king of Kāśi (*K. Sāgara*)

**Brahmadeva** (S) (M) **1.** the god Brahmā; the Absolute. **3.** a warrior on the side of the Pāṇḍavās (*M. Bh.*)

**Brahmadhara** (S) (M) **1.** possessing sacred knowledge. **2.** has attained salvation or mokṣa.

**Brahmadhvaja** (S) (M) **1.** a banner of Brahmā; banner of the Absolute. **2.** meritorious; virtuous; venerated; divine; all perfect. **3.** a Buddha (*B. Literature*)

**Brahmadṛśa** (S) (M) **1.** Brahmā's mirror. **2.** preceptor of the Absolute; illuminated; enlightened; attained spiritual bliss and is a vehicle for the attainment of salvation.

**Brahmādya** (S) (M) **1.** beginning with Brahmā. **2.** absolute; the beginning.

**Brahmagandha** (S) (M) **1.** the fragrance of Brahmā. **2.** the fragrance of sacred knowledge.

**Brahmaghoṣa** (S) (M) **1.** the sacred word. **2.** the sacred syllable Om.

**Brahmagiri** (S) (M) the mountain of Brahmā.

**Brahmagupta** (S) (M) **1.** protected by Brahmā. **3.** a son of Brahmā by the wife of the vidyādhara Bhīma; a son of Jiṣṇu.

**Brahmajīta** (S) (M) **1.** winner of Brahmā; controller of self. **2.** perfect; enlightened. **3.** a son of Kālanemi (*B. Purāṇa*)

**Brahmakṛta** (S) (M) **1.** offering prayers; caused by Brahmā, caused by the Absolute. **2.** performed by divinity; perfect.

**Brahmakuṇḍa** (S) (M) a sacred pool; a pool of Brahmā.

**Brahmāmbikā** (S) (F) mother of the Absolute; mother; the Absolute.

**Brahmamūrti** (S) (M) with the form of Brahmā.

**Brahmanābha** (S) (M) **1.** with Brahmā as the navel. **2.** in whose navel the Absolute rests; the Supreme Self. **3.** another name for Viṣṇu.

**Brahmanadī** (S) (F) **1.** river of Brahmā. **3.** another name for the river Sarasvatī which originated from the Kamandalu of Brahmā.

**Brahmānanda** (S) (M) **1.** bliss; absolute pleasure; joy in Brahmā. **2.** illumined; spiritually enlightened.

**Brahmāṇḍa** (S) (M) **1.** Brahmā's egg; the Absolute shell. **2.** the universe. **3.** a Purāṇa.

**Brāhmanī** (S) (F) **1.** consort of Brahmā. **2.** intelligent; wise; enlightened; venerated; sacred. **3.** another name for Sarasvatī.

**Brahmāṇī** (S) (F) **1.** consort of Brahmā. **2.** the personified female energy or Śakti of Brahmā; perfume. **3.** a river; another name for Durgā.

**Brahmanīḍa** (S) (M) **1.** the resting place of Brahmā. **2.** the nest of the Absolute; in whom all the virtues are found.

**Brahmāñjali** (S) (F) **1.** to pray with cupped hands. **2.** venerated; one who venerates; to join the hands while repeating the Vedas.

**Brahmapattra** (S) (M) **1.** Brahmā's leaf. **3.** a leaf of the flame of the forest tree (*Butea frondosa*) which is considered to have

originated from the feet of Brahmā.
**Brahmapitṛ** (S) (M) 1. Brahmā's father. 3. Viṣṇu from whose navel Brahmā is considered to have originated.
**Brahmaprabhā** (S) (M) 1. the light of Brahmā. 2. glory of the Absolute.
**Brahmaprakāśa** (S) (M) 1. the light of Brahmā. 2. light of the Absolute.
**Brahmapri** (S) (M) 1. devotee of Brahmā; knower of the Absolute. 2. delighting in prayer; a preceptor.
**Brahmaputrā** (S) (F) 1. daughter of Brahmā. 3. a river rising from the Tibet side of the Himālayas and falling with the Gaṅgā into the Bay of Bengal; Bulb bearing Yam (*Discorea bulbifera*)
**Brahmāputra** (S) (M) 1. son of Brahmā. 3. a river in Assam.
**Brahmarasa** (S) (M) 1. the essence of Brahmā; the Supreme Essence.
**Brahmarāta** (S) (M) 1. given by Brahmā; absorbed in the Absolute. 3. the father of Yājñavalkya (*M. Bh.*); another name for Śuka.
**Brahmārgha** (S) (M) 1. worthy of Brahmā. 2. as worthy as the Absolute.
**Brahmarūpa** (S) (M) 1. incarnation of the Absolute. 2. the Absolute in its manifest form. 3. another name for Viṣṇu.
**Brahmasambhava** (S) (M) 1. sprung from Brahmā. 2. meritorious; virtuous; venerated; divine. 3. the 2nd Black Vasudeva (*H. Purāṇa*)
**Brahmasaras** (S) (M) 1. the lake of Brahmā. 2. sacred; venerated; divine.
**Brahmasatī** (S) (M) 1. granted by Brahmā. 3. another name for the river Sarasvatī who is considered to be Brahmā's daughter.
**Brahmasāvarṇa** (S) (M) 1. resembles Brahmā. 3. the 10th Manu (*V. Purāṇa*)
**Brahmaśiras** (S) (M) 1. the head of Brahmā; with an Absolute mind. 2. knowing all. 3. a mythical weapon (*M. Bh.*)
**Brahmasū** (S) (M) 1. son of Brahmā. 3. another name for Kāma and Aniruddha.
**Brahmasūnu** (S) (M) 1. son of the Absolute. 3. the 12th king of Bhārata.
**Brahmatejas** (S) (M) 1. the glory of Brahmā. 2. venerated; illuminating; enlightened; divine. 3. a Buddha (*L. Vistara*)
**Brahmavarman** (S) (M) Brahmā's armour.
**Brahmāvarta** (S) (M) 1. the holy land; the land of the Absolute; surrounded by the Absolute. 3. a son of Ṛṣabha (*Bhāgavata*)
**Brahmavṛnda** (S) (F) 1. an assembly of divine beings. 3. the city of Brahmā.
**Brahmayāna** (S) (M) 1. chariot of Brahmā. 3. another name for Nārāyaṇa who is paired with Nara.
**Brahmayaśas** (S) (M) as famous as Brahmā.
**Brahmayuj** (S) (M) 1. harnessed by prayer; attached to the Absolute. 2. pious; devout; blessed.
**Brahmāyuṣ** (S) (M) lives as long as Brahmā.
**Brahmeśaya** (S) (M) 1. dwelling in Brahmā. 3. another name for Kārttikeya who is depicted as the commander of the divine army.
**Brāhmī** (S) (F) 1. holy. 2. the Śakti of Brahmā. 3. the feminine energy of Brahmā personified as Śakti and regarded as one of the 8 divine mothers of creation; the wife of Dhruva and mother of Kalpa; another name for Sarasvatī, Śatarūpā, Durgā and the constellation Rohiṇī; *Enhydra fluctuanes*.
**Brāhmībhūta** (S) (M) 1. essence of Brahmā. 3. another name for Śaṁkarāćārya.
**Brahmiṣṭhā** (S) (F) 1. the highest form of the Absolute. 3. another name for Durgā.
**Brahmottara** (S) (M) 1. treating principally with Brahmā. 3. a Jaina deity (*D. Śastra*)
**Brajamaṇi** (S) (M) 1. brilliant jewel. 2. beautiful; precious; rare; held dear; illuminating.
**Bṛbaduktha** (S) (M) 1. highly praiseworthy. 3. another name for Indra.
**Bṛbutṣka** (S) (M) 1. liberal; praise-worthy. 2. generous; meritorious; virtuous. 3. a Vedic king known for his generosity and interest in architecture (*Ṛg Veda*)
**Bṛgala** (S) (M) 1. fragment. 2. piece; morsel; analytical.
**Bṛhaćchloka** (S) (M) 1. loudly praised. 3. a son of Urukrama (*Bh. Purāṇa*)
**Bṛhadagni** (S) (M) 1. mighty fire. 2. sacred and all consuming. 3. a ṛṣi (*H. Purāṇa*)
**Bṛhadambālikā** (S) (F) 1. a stout mother.

2. strong; voluptuous; courageous. 3. an attendant of Skanda (*M. Bh.*)

**Bṛhadaśva** (S) (M) 1. possesses mighty horses. 2. strong, wealthy and fleet-footed. 3. hermit who taught Yudhiṣṭhira important spells (*M. Bh.*); a king of the Ikṣvāku dynasty who was the son of Śrāvasta and the father of Kuvalayāśva (*M. Bh.*); a gandharva (*M. Bh.*)

**Bṛhadātma** (S) (M) 1. has a great soul. 2. wise; illumined; enlightened. 3. a king of the Aṅga dynasty (*M. Bh.*)

**Bṛhadbala** (S) (M) 1. very strong; with immense power. 3. the son of King Subala of Gāndhāra (*M. Bh.*); a king of Kosala (*H. Purāṇa*)

**Bṛhadbhānu** (S) (M) 1. the great sun. 2. brilliant; glorious; illuminating; enlightening; shining brightly. 3. a son of Sattrāyaṇa considered to be a manifestation of Viṣṇu (*Bhāgavata*); a son of Kṛṣṇa (*Bhāgavata*); a hermit who was very learned in the Vedas (*M. Bh.*); Ceylon Leadwort (*Plumbago zeylanica*); another name for Agni.

**Bṛhadbhās** (S) (M) 1. has great splendour. 3. a grandson of Brahmā (*M. Bh.*)

**Bṛhadbhāsā** (S) (F) 1. has great splendour. 3. a daughter of Sūrya and wife of Agni Bhānu (*M. Bh.*)

**Bṛhadbhaya** (S) (M) 1. feared by many; instilling much fear. 3. a son of the 9th Manu (*Mā. Purāṇa*)

**Bṛhadbrāhmaṇa** (S) (M) 1. great ascetic. 2. illuminating; enlightened; has attained salvation or *mokṣa*. 3. a grandson of Brahmā (*M. Bh.*)

**Bṛhaddanta** (S) (M) 1. has large teeth. 3. a king of Ulūka who fought on the side of the Pāṇḍavas (*M. Bh.*); the brother of King Kśemadhurti who fought on the side of the Pāṇḍavās (*M. Bh.*)

**Bṛhaddhala** (S) (M) 1. has a mighty shield. 2. well protected. 3. the son of King Subala of Gāndhāra (*M. Bh.*); a Yādava king who was the son of Devabhaga and the brother of Vasudeva (*Bhāgavata*)

**Bṛhaddharman** (S) (M) strong supporter.

**Bṛhaddhvaja** (S) (M) 1. with a mighty banner. 2. mighty; powerful; a ruler of kingdoms. 3. a rākṣasa who attained the world of Viṣṇu (*Sk. Purāṇa*)

**Bṛhaddhvani** (S) (F) 1. makes a lot of noise. 3. a king of the family of Bharata (*Bhāgavata*)

**Bṛhaddivā** (S) (F) 1. highly illuminated; celestial. 2. bright; radiant; enlightened. 3. a goddess (*A. Brāhmaṇa*)

**Bṛhadguru** (S) (M) 1. great master. 3. an ancient king (*M. Bh.*)

**Bṛhadikṣu** (S) (M) 1. broadminded; with great insight. 3. a king of the family of Bharata (*Bhāgavata*)

**Bṛhadiṣṭha** (S) (M) 1. much loved. 3. a king of the Purū dynasty (*A. Purāṇa*)

**Bṛhadkāya** (S) (M) large bodied.

**Bṛhadketu** (S) (M) 1. with a very bright banner. 2. bright; glorious; renowned; illuminating. 3. another name for Agni.

**Bṛhadkīrti** (S) (M) 1. far-famed. 3. a grandson of Brahmā (*M. Bh.*)

**Bṛhadphala** (S) (M) 1. with a large fruit. 2. yielding very high profit. 3. a class of Buddhist gods (*B. Literature*)

**Bṛhadrāja** (S) (M) 1. a mighty king. 3. a king (*Pur*)

**Bṛhadratha** (S) (M) 1. with a mighty chariot. 2. a mighty, powerful, heroic warrior. 3. a king of the Aṅga family who was the son of Jayadratha and father of Viśvajīta (*M. Bh.*); a Purū king who was the son of Girīka and the father of Kusāgra (*A. Purāṇa*); the son of King Uparićara of Ćedi and the father of Jarāsandha of Magadha (*M. Bh.*); an agni who was the son of Vasiṣṭha and the father of Praṇīti (*M. Bh.*); another name for Indra.

**Bṛhadsena** (S) (M) 1. a mighty leader; has a large army. 2. a commander. 3. a son of Kṛṣṇa (*Bhāgavata*); a son of Sunakṣatra (*Bhāgavata*)

**Bṛhadsenī** (S) (F) 1. mighty leader; has a large army. 3. Damayantī's nurse (*Nalopākhyāna*)

**Bṛhadtejas** (S) (M) 1. very glorious. 3. another name for the planet Jupiter.

**Bṛhaduktha** (S) (M) 1. loudly praised; extremely famous; originator of many tales. 2. speaks very much; much spoken of. 3. an agni who was the son of Tapas (*M. Bh.*); a son of Devarāta (*V. Purāṇa*); the son of the sage

Pāñćajanya who was transformed to a god who is remembered at the beginning of a sacrifice (*M. Bh.*)

**Bṛhadviṣa** (S) (M) 1. extremely poisonous. 3. a king of the line of Bharata.

**Bṛhadyuti** (S) (F) 1. highly luminous; intensely brilliant. 2. great light; radiance.

**Bṛhajjana** (S) (M) an illustrious man.

**Bṛhajjyoti** (S) (M) 1. very glorious. 3. the son of Aṅgiras and Śubhā (*M. Bh.*)

**Bṛhajjyotiṣ** (S) (M) 1. very bright. 2. shining; glorious; famous; illuminating; enlightening. 3. a grandson of Brahmā (*Bhā. Purāṇa*)

**Bṛhaka** (S) (M) 1. fully grown. 2. massive; mighty adult; mature; evolved. 3. a deva gandharva (*M. Bh.*)

**Bṛhanmanas** (S) (M) 1. broadminded. 3. a grandson of Brahmā (*M. Bh.*); one of the 7 sons of Aṅgiras and Sumanā (*M. Bh.*); a king (*H. Purāṇa*)

**Bṛhanmatī** (S) (F) possesses a lot; immensely intellectual.

**Bṛhanmedhas** (S) (M) 1. highly intelligent. 3. a Yādava king who was the son of Vapuṣmān and the father of Śrideva (*Kū. Purāṇa*)

**Bṛhannala** (S) (M) 1. a large reed; an important person. 2. arm. 3. name assumed by Arjuna at the court of King Virāṭa (*M. Bh.*)

**Bṛhantā** (S) (F) 1. destroyer of the powerful. 2. strong; great. 3. one of the 7 mothers of Skanda (*M. Bh.*)

**Bṛhanta** (S) (M) 1. destroyer of the powerful. 2. large; great. 3. a king who fought on the side of the Pāṇḍavās (*M. Bh.*); a Kaurava warrior who was the brother of Kśemadhurti (*M. Bh.*)

**Bṛhaspati** (S) (M) 1. lord of prayer. 2. lord of devotion; lord of the powerful. 3. a deity who is the chief offerer of sacrifices and the god of wisdom and eloquence, regarded as the grandson of Brahmā, the son of Aṅgiras and Vasudā, the husband of Tārā, the father of Romaṣa, Kaća, Kuśadhvaja and the 6 agnis, of Bharadvāja from his elder brother Utathya's wife Mamatā, grandfather of Devavatī who was re-born as Sīta, the regent of the planet Jupiter and the preceptor of the gods (*Ṛg Veda*); the great grandson of Aśoka (*B. Literature*); a king of Kāśmira (*R. Taraṅginī*)

**Bṛhat** (S) (M) 1. lofty; tall; large; vast; abundant. 2. strong; mighty; clear; loud. 3. a son of Suhotra and father of Ajamīdha (*H. Purāṇa*); a marut (*H. Purāṇa*)

**Bṛhata** (S) (M) 1. large; great. 3. a son of the 9th Manu (*H. Purāṇa*)

**Bṛhatī** (S) (F) 1. heaven and earth (*A. Koṣa*). 2. speech; large; strong; reservoir; a Vedic metre. 3. the lute of Nārada (*A. Koṣa*); the mother of Manu Ćākṣuṣa and wife of Ṛpu (*H. Purāṇa*); one of the 7 horses of the sun (*V. Purāṇa*)

**Bṛhatka** (S) (M) 1. lofty; massive; mighty; abundant. 3. a king and son of the asura Kelaya (*M. Bh.*)

**Bṛhatkarman** (S) (M) 1. performs mighty deeds. 3. a king of Aṅga (*M. Bh.*)

**Bṛhatkāya** (S) (M) 1. huge bodied. 3. a king of Bharata family (*M. Bh.*)

**Bṛhatketu** (S) (M) 1. has a mighty banner; with great brightness. 2. king among kings. 3. another name for Agni.

**Bṛhatkīrti** (S) (M) 1. with infinite fame. 2. renowned. 3. a son of Aṅgiras; an asura.

**Bṛhatkṣatra** (S) (M) 1. with great power; with huge dominion. 3. father of Suhotra (*H. Purāṇa*)

**Bṛhatkukṣi** (S) (F) 1. large bellied. 3. a yoginī.

**Bṛhatphala** (S) (M) 1. bringing large rewards. 3. a class of Buddhist deities.

**Bṛhatputra** (S) (M) 1. son of the great. 2. the great son. 3. a king of the Purū dynasty who was the son of Suhotra and the father of Ajamīdha, Dvimīdha and Pūrumīdha (*A. Purāṇa*)

**Bṛhatsama** (S) (M) 1. considers all as equal. 3. a teacher of the Aṅgiras family; a hymn (*Ṛg Veda*)

**Bṛhatśāstra** (S) (M) 1. knower of many treatises. 2. well-read; learned; wise. 3. a king of the family of Bhagiratha (*V. Rāmāyaṇa*); a Kekaya king who fought on the side of the Pāṇḍavās (*M. Bh.*); a Niṣādha king who fought on the side of the Kauravas (*M. Bh.*)

**Bṛhatsena** (S) (M) 1. has a huge army. 3. a

king of the family of Bharata (*Bhāgavata*); an asura who was a partial incarnation of Krodhavaśa and whose daughter married Kṛṣṇa (*Bhāgavata*); a sage and disciple of Nāradā (*M. Bh.*)

**Bṛhita** (S) (M) 1. strengthened. 2. nourished; cherished. 3. an attendant in Skanda's retinue (*Sk. Purāṇa*)

**Bṛindā** (S) (F) 1. surrounded by many; the sacred basil (*Ocimum sanctum*). 3. another name for Rādhā who was always surrounded by many friends.

**Bṛjabālā** (S) (F) 1. daughter of nature. 2. daughter of Bṛja. 3. another name for Rādhā.

**Bṛjābhūṣaṇa** (S) (M) 1. ornament of nature. 2. the ornament of Bṛja. 3. another name for Kṛṣṇa who spent his childhood in Bṛja, a place near Mathura.

**Bṛjalatā** (S) (F) 1. creeper of Bṛja. 3. a kind of creeper that grows in Bṛja.

**Bṛjamohana** (S) (M) 1. attracts nature; universally attractive. 3. another name for Kṛṣṇa.

**Bṛjanandana** (S) (M) 1. the son of Bṛja. 3. another name for Kṛṣṇa.

**Bṛjarāja** (S) (M) 1. lord of Bṛja. 3. another name for Kṛṣṇa.

**Bṛjanārāyaṇa** (S) (M) 1. lord of Bṛja. 3. another name for Viṣṇu/Kṛṣṇa.

**Bṛjeśa** (S) (M) 1. lord of nature. 2. lord of Bṛja. 3. another name for Kṛṣṇa.

**Bubhutsu** (S) (M) 1. desirous to know all. 2. curious.

**Budbudā** (S) (F) 1. bubble. 2. an ornament resembling a bubble (*M. Bh.*). 3. an apsarā.

**Buddha** (S) (M) 1. enlightened; awakened. 3. the title 'Buddha' was first used for prince Gautama (later known as Śākyāmuni and considered by same to be an incarnation of Viṣṇu), the founder of the Buddhist religion born in Kapilavastu of King Śuddodana and Māyādevī of the Śākya tribe, this title is used to denote successive teachers past and future of this religion (*V. Purāṇa*)

**Buddhaćakṣus** (S) (M) 1. the enlightened eye. 2. eye of the Buddha. 3. one of the 5 sorts of vision.

**Buddhadatta** (S) (M) 1. obtained from enlightenment. 2. given by the Buddha. 3. a minister of Ćaṇḍamahāsena (*K. Sāgara*)

**Buddhadeva** (S) (M) 1. lord of the wise. 2. enlightened, honorific of a king.

**Buddhaghoṣa** (S) (M) 1. voice of knowledge; speech of the enlightened; village of the enlightened. 3. Sanskṛt poet (4th century A.D.)

**Buddhagupta** (S) (M) protected by the Buddha; protected by the wise.

**Buddhaguru** (S) (M) preceptor of the wise; a Buddhist spiritual teacher.

**Buddhajñāna** (S) (M) 1. with the Buddha's knowledge. 2. with intellectual knowledge; who has attained enlightenment.

**Buddhakapālinī** (S) (F) 1. with an enlightened mind. 2. wise; enlightened; venerated; one who has attained mokṣa or salvation. 3. one of the 6 goddesses of magic (*D. Sāstra*)

**Buddhamitra** (S) (M) 1. friend of the wise. 2. friend of the Buddha. 3. the 9th Buddhist patriarch (*B. Literature*)

**Buddhānandi** (S) (M) 1. one who enjoys knowledge. 2. well-read; wise; enlightened. 3. the 8th Buddhist patriarch.

**Buddhapāla** (S) (M) defender of the wise; defender of the Buddha.

**Buddhapālita** (S) (M) 1. protected by the wise; protected by the Buddha. 3. a disciple of Nāgārjuna (*B. Literature*)

**Buddharāja** (S) (M) lord of the wise.

**Buddhasena** (S) (M) leader of the wise.

**Buddhasinha** (S) (M) lion among the wise.

**Buddhi** (S) (F) 1. intelligence; intellect. 2. judgement; reason. 3. intelligence personified as a daughter of Dakṣa and wife of Dharma and mother of Bodha (*M. Bh.*) 3. a wife of Gaṇeśa (*Purāṇas*)

**Buddhidevī** (S) (F) goddess of wisdom.

**Buddhikāmā** (S) (F) 1. desirous of acquiring wisdom. 3. a mother attending Skanda (*M. Bh.*)

**Buddhikārī** (S) (F) 1. bestower of wisdom. 3. another name for Sarasvatī.

**Buddhimatikā** (S) (F) intelligent; wise.

**Buddhiprabha** (S) (M) light of reason.

**Buddhirāja** (S) (M) lord of intellect.

**Buddhisrīgarbha** (S) (M) **1.** the womb of divine wisdom. **3.** a Bodhisattva (*B. Literature*)

**Budha** (S) (M) **1.** intelligent; wise. **3.** a descendant of Soma and father of Purūravas, and identified with the planet Mercury (*M. Bh.*); a descendant of Atri and author of *Ṛg Veda* (v); a son of Vegavat and father of Tṛṇabindu (*Purāṇas*); the son of Ćandra and Tārā the wife of Bṛhaspati (*Ṛg Veda*)

**Budhana** (S) (M) **1.** awaking. **2.** wise; knowing; sage; spiritual guide.

**Budharatna** (S) (M) **1.** jewel among the wise. **3.** jewel of the planet Mercury; the emerald.

**Budhasuta** (S) (M) **1.** son of Budha; son of the wise. **3.** another name for Purūravas.

**Budhila** (S) (M) wise; learned.

**Budrasena** (S) (M) **1.** with an army of the enlightened; commander of the wise. **3.** a Hehaya king (*H. Purāṇa*)

**Budrika** (S) (M) learned; enlightened; a king of the 5th lunar dynasty of Magadha (*M. Bh.*)

**Bukkā** (S) (M) **1.** the heart. **2.** sentimental; loving; sincere.

**Bulā** (S) (F) a nose-ring.

**Bunda** (S) (M) **1.** arrow. **2.** which pierces; reaches its aim unfailingly.

# C

**Ćācharī** (S) (M) 1. moving quickly. 3. a wrestler (*R. Taraṅginī*)

**Ćāha** (S) (M) 1. desire. 2. desired; desirable; charming; loving. 3. the Pintail Snipe (*Gallinago sthenura*)

**Ćāhanā** (S) (F) desire; affection.

**Ćaidya** (S) (M) 1. intelligent. 2. administrator. 3. king of Ćedi; honorifics of Dhṛṣṭaketu and Śiśupāla (*M. Bh.*)

**Ćaitalī** (S) (F) belonging to the mind; with a sharp memory.

**Ćaitanya** (S) (M) 1. consciousness. 2. intelligence; mind; spirit; soul. 3. the founder of one of the 4 principal Vaiṣṇava sects, was born in 1485 in Nadia, Bengal and is believed by his followers to have been a reincarnation of Kṛṣṇa.

**Ćaitra** (S) (M) 1. absorbed in pleasure; as pleasant as the spring. 3. the 2nd spring month (*J. Śāstra*); a son of Budha and grandfather of Suratha (*Brah. Purāṇa*); Buddhist and Jaina mendicants (*He. Koṣa*)

**Ćaitraratha** (S) (M) 1. the chariot of intelligence. 2. the sun. 3. a son of King Kuru and Vāhinī (*M. Bh.*); the grove of Kubera situated on Mount Meru (*H. Purāṇa*)

**Ćaitrasakhā** (S) (M) 1. a friend of spring. 2. inciting a feeling of love. 3. another name for Kāma and Kṛṣṇa.

**Ćaitrī** (S) (F) 1. born in spring. 2. as beautiful, tender and fresh as a new blossom; ever-happy.

**Ćaitya** (S) (M) 1. pertaining to the mind; the individual soul. 3. a stupa built in Jaina or Buddhist places of worship.

**Ćaityaka** (S) (M) 1. abode of conciousness. 2. a temple; a monument; a stupa. 3. a mountain near Magadha worshipped as being sacred and divine (*P. Smṛti*)

**Ćaka** (S) (M) 1. to be content; to shine. 3. a priest at Janamejaya's snake sacrifice (*Tā. Brāhmaṇa*)

**Ćakora** (S) (M) 1. shining; content. 3. the Greek partridge (*Perdis rufa*) fabled to subsist on moonbeams; the Chukor partridge (*Alectoris chukar chukar*)

**Ćakorī** (S) (F) 1. shining; content. 2. the female Greek partridge (*Perdix rufa*); fabled to subsist on moonbeams.

**Ćakra** (S) (M) 1. wheel; disc; circle. 2. a symbol of the sun. 3. the son of Vāsuki (*M. Bh.*); an attendant given to Skanda by Tvaṣṭṛ (*M. Bh.*); the weapon of Mahāviṣṇu (*M. Bh.*)

**Ćakrabandhana** (S) (M) 1. bound in the form of a circle. 2. bearer of a wheel or discus; an emperor; one in authority; a great warrior. 3. another name for Viṣṇu; musk; Jasminum pubescens.

**Ćakrabāndhava** (S) (M) 1. friend of the Ćakra birds. 3. another name for the sun.

**Ćakrabandhu** (S) (M) 1. with a disc. 3. another name for the sun.

**Ćakrabhṛt** (S) (M) 1. discus bearer. 3. another name for Viṣṇu.

**Ćakrabhuj** (S) (M) 1. holding a disc. 3. another name for Viṣṇu.

**Ćakraćāra** (S) (M) 1. going in a circle. 3. a class of superhuman beings.

**Ćakradeva** (S) (M) 1. lord of the discus. 2. with a warchariot for his deity. 3. a warrior of the Vṛṣṇi dynasty (*M. Bh.*); another name for Viṣṇu.

**Ćakradhanuṣ** (S) (M) 1. armed with a bow and a disc. 3. another name for sage Kapila.

**Ćakradhara** (S) (M) 1. bearing a discus. 2. an emperor. 3. another name for Viṣṇu.

**Ćakradhāri** (S) (M) 1. holding the discus. 3. another name for Kṛṣṇa.

**Ćakradharma** (S) (M) 1. the path of the disc. 2. righteous and virtuous. 3. the chief of the vidyādharas who lived in the court of Kubera (*M. Bh.*)

**Ćakradṛśa** (S) (M) 1. round eyed. 3. an asura (*Bhāgavata*)

**Ćakradvāra** (S) (M) 1. the way to the sun. 3. a great mountain on which Agni performed a sacrifice (*M. Bh.*)

**Ćakragadābhṛt** (S) (M) 1. holding disc and mace. 3. another name for Kṛṣṇa (*M. Bh.*)

**Ćakragadādhara** (S) (M) 1. holding disc and mace. 3. another name for Kṛṣṇa (*M. Bh.*)

**Ćakragadāpāṇi** (S) (M) 1. holding disc and

mace. 3. another name for Kṛṣṇa.

**Ćakraka** (S) (M) 1. circular. 2. resembling a wheel. 3. a son of Viśvāmitra (*M. Bh.*)

**Ćakrākārā** (S) (F) 1. disc shaped. 2. circular. 3. another name for the earth.

**Ćakrakī** (S) (M) 1. possessing the disc. 3. another name for Viṣṇu.

**Ćakramanda** (S) (M) 1. one who worships the discus; a slow moving wheel. 2. one who sides with power. 3. a serpent lord who was entrusted by Ananta, the serpent king, to lead the soul of Balarāma to Pātāla (*M. Bh.*)

**Ćakramardikā** (S) (F) 1. destroyer of the disc. 3. wife of Līlāditya (*R. Taraṅgiṇī*)

**Ćakramauli** (S) (M) 1. with a round diadem. 3. a rākṣasa (*V. Rāmāyaṇa*)

**Ćakranemi** (S) (F) 1. felly of a wheel. 2. disc; ring; thunderbolt; responsible for progress. 3. a mother in Skanda's retinue (*M. Bh.*)

**Ćakrapālita** (S) (M) 1. lord of the discus. 3. another name for Viṣṇu.

**Ćakrapāṇi** (S) (M) 1. discus holder. 3. another name for Viṣṇu.

**Ćakrasaṁvara** (S) (M) 1. choosing the disc. 3. a Buddha.

**Ćakrasena** (S) (M) 1. commander of the army. 2. leader; warrior. 3. a son of Tārāćandra and father of Siṁha (*K. Sāgara*)

**Ćakravāka** (S) (M) 1. has a round mouth; the Ruddy Shelduck (*Anas casarca*). 3. likened to the aśvins in the *Ṛg Veda*

**Ćakravāla** (S) (M) 1. circle; mass; assemblage; surrounded by people as a circle by spokes; a leader. 3. one of the mythical range of mountains which encircle the earth and are the limits of light with Mount Meru as the central mountain (*M. Bh.*)

**Ćakravāna** (S) (M) 1. possesser of the Ćakra. 2. worshipper of Viṣṇu. 3. a mountain frequently extolled in the Purāṇas and on which Viśvakarma made the Sudarśana Ćakra (*V. Rāmāyaṇa*)

**Ćakravarman** (S) (M) 1. armoured with the Ćakra. 3. a king of Kāśmira (*R. Taraṅginī*)

**Ćakravartin** (S) (M) 1. whose chariot rolls everywhere. 2. powerful; renowned; emperor. 3. another name for the 12 emperors, beginning with Bharata.

**Ćakravat** (S) (M) 1. with a discus. 2. an emperor. 3. another name for Viṣṇu.

**Ćakravāta** (S) (M) 1. fierce; forceful. 2. whirlwind.

**Ćakrayodhin** (S) (M) 1. discus fighter. 3. a dānava (*V. Purāṇa*)

**Ćakrāyudha** (S) (M) 1. fighting with a discus. 3. another name for Viṣṇu.

**Ćakreśa** (S) (M) 1. lord of the discus. 3. another name for Viṣṇu.

**Ćakreśvara** (S) (M) 1. lord of the discus. 3. another name for Viṣṇu.

**Ćakreśvarī** (S) (F) 1. goddess of the discus. 3. a vidyādevī.

**Ćakrika** (S) (M) discus bearer.

**Ćakrin** (S) (M) 1. with a discus. 2. a king. 3. another name for Kṛṣṇa and Śiva.

**Ćakroddhata** (S) (M) 1. moving the disc upwards. 2. the Supreme Being. 3. a king in the dynasty of Yayāti (*Bhāgavata*)

**Ćakṣaṇa** (S) (M) soothing to the eyes; appearance; aspect.

**Ćakṣaṇī** (S) (F) soothing to the eyes; illuminating.

**Ćakṣas** (S) (M) 1. look; sight. 2. radiance; a teacher. 3. another name for Bṛhaspati, the teacher of the gods.

**Ćākṣīśvara** (S) (M) 1. lord of the eye. 2. all seeing; all knowing; all pervading; divine. 3. another name for Viṣṇu.

**Ćakṣu** (S) (M) 1. eye. 3. another name for the sun god Sūrya who sees beyond the sky, earth, waters, and is the eye of all that exists; a prince (*M. Bh.*); the river now called Oxus (*V. Purāṇa*)

**Ćaksurvardhanikā** (S) (F) 1. refreshing the eyes. 2. beautiful; charming. 3. a river which flows through Śaka Island (*M. Bh.*)

**Ćakṣus** (S) (M) 1. eyes. 3. a tributary of the Gaṅgā which falls on the peak of Mount Malyāvāna, and flows through Ketumālā into the western sea (*D. Bhāgavata*); a king born in the lunar dynasty and the son of king Anudruhyu (*Bhāgavata*); a marut; another name for the sun.

**Ćākṣuṣa** (S) (M) 1. preceptor. 2. seer. 3. a

marut (*Ṛg Veda*); a sage and author of *Ṛg Veda*; a son of Anu (*Bhā. Purāṇa*); a river of ancient India (*Bhā. Purāṇa*); a son of Ṛpu and Bṛhatī (*V. Purāṇa*); a son of Viśvakarmā and Ākritī (*Bh. Purāṇa*); a son of Kakṣeyu; a son of Khanitra (*Bh. Purāṇa*); another name for Agni.

**Ćākṣuṣamanu** (S) (M) **1.** that which is visible. **2.** believer in the perceivable. **3.** the 6th Manu who was the son of Ćākṣusa and Puṣkaraṇī and husband of Nadvalā.

**Ćākṣuṣī** (S) (F) **1.** preceptor; seer. **2.** the faculty of perceiving everything in the 3 worlds (*M. Bh.*)

**Ćākṣuṣya** (S) (M) **1.** pleasing to the eyes. **2.** beautiful; harmonious; *Pandanus odoratissimus cassia absus*.

**Ćalā** (S) (F) **1.** shaking; fickle; lightning. **2.** that which is moving; a sprout; quicksilver; perfume. **3.** the incarnation of goddess Lakṣmī as a mare on the banks of the river Sarasvatī who regained her form after delivering a son who came to be known as Ekavīra the founder of the Hehaya kingdom (*D. Bhāgavata*); the tree *Altingia excelsa*.

**Ćala** (S) (M) **1.** ever moving. **3.** another name for the Supreme Being.

**Ćālaka** (S) (M) **1.** directing and driving. **3.** another name for the Supreme Soul.

**Ćalamā** (S) (F) **1.** ever moving goddess. **3.** goddess Pārvatī who is the personification of kinetic energy.

**Ćalāmeśvara** (S) (M) **1.** lord of Ćalamā. **3.** another name for Śiva.

**Ćalāpati** (S) (M) **1.** lord of the moving. **3.** Viṣṇu as consort of Lakṣmī.

**Ćallalamma** (Telugu) (F) **1.** goddess of buttermilk. **3.** a goddess worshipped in the villages of South India.

**Ćamalammā** (Telugu) (F) **1.** the goddess of the downtrodden. **3.** the Telugu representation of Kālī.

**Ćāmar** (S) (M) **1.** rod with a large tuft of hair; fibre or feathers at the end; animal hair; an army; yak's tail. **2.** this rod was a symbol of authority and was used by kings and Brāhmins in ancient India.

**Ćāmarāja** (S) (M) leader of an army; lord of the ćāmara.

**Ćāmarvāla** (S) (M) **1.** with hair as fine as a yak's tail. **3.** a prince (*M. Bh.*)

**Ćamasa** (S) (M) **1.** a cup; a vessel used for drinking Soma at sacrifices (*Ṛg Veda*); a kind of cake (*A. Koṣa*). **3.** the younger brother of Bharata (*M. Bh.*); a king born in the dynasty of Priyavrata (*Bhāgavata*); a son of Manu (*Bhāgavata*); a son of Ṛṣabha (*Bhāgavata*); a sage (*M. Bh.*)

**Ćamasodbheda** (S) (M) **1.** priest who is in charge of the drinking vessel for Soma at sacrifices. **3.** holy place in Saurāṣṭra which forms a part of the Hindu sacred places (*M. Bh.*)

**Ćamelī** (S) (F) a jasmine flower (*Jasminum grandiflorum*)

**Ćāmīkara** (S) (M) gold.

**Ćampā** (S) (F) soothing; a flower of the Ćampakā tree (*Michelia champaka*)

**Ćampa** (S) (M) **1.** that which soothes. **3.** a king of the Aṅga dynasty (*M. Bh.*)

**Ćampaka** (S) (M) **1.** Ćampaka tree (*Michelia champaka*). **3.** a vidyādhara and husband of Madālasā (*K. Sāgara*); the foster father of Ekavīra (*R. Taraṅginī*)

**Ćampākali** (S) (F) **1.** a bud of the Ćampakā tree (*Michelia champaka*). **2.** tender; young; fragrant; much liked.

**Ćampakaprabhu** (S) (M) **1.** eternally blooming; lord of the Ćampaka tree (*Michelia champaka*). **3.** Kalhaṇa's father (*R. Taraṅginī*)

**Ćampakavatī** (S) (F) **1.** owner of Ćampaka trees; blooms eternally. **2.** fragrant; much liked; fecund; life-giving. **3.** a forest in Magadha (*Hitopadeśa*)

**Ćampāmālinī** (S) (F) a garland of Ćampā flowers (*Michelia champaka*)

**Ćampat** (S) (M) fallen from glory.

**Ćampeśa** (S) (M) **1.** lord of Ćampā a town in Aṅga. **3.** another name for Karṇa.

**Ćampeya** (S) (M) **1.** fruit of the Kovidāra tree (*Bauhinia vareigata*). **3.** a son of Viśvāmitra (*M. Bh.*)

**Ćampikā** (S) (F) **1.** little Champā flower. **3.** a daughter of Bhurikīrtī and wife of Kuśa.

**Ćampū** (S) (M) an elaborate and literary

form of presenting a story in verse and prose.

**Ćamūhara** (S) (M) 1. receptacle; vessel. 2. heaven and earth as the two receptacles of all living beings. 3. a viśvādeva (*M. Bh.*)

**Ćāmuṇḍā** (S) (F) 1. slayer of Ćaṇḍa and Muṇḍa. 2. Ćaṇḍa and Muṇḍa conjoined. 3. a terrific form of Durgā who, as goddess Kālī sprang from the forehead of goddess Ambikā to destroy the asuras Ćaṇḍa and Muṇḍa (*D. Bhāgavata*)

**Ćāmuṇḍarāya** (S) (M) 1. lord of Ćāmuṇḍā. 3. a scholar of Sanskṛt and Kannaḍa who had the statue of Bāhubali built; another name for Śiva.

**Ćāmuṇḍeśvarī** (S) (F) 1. the goddess Ćāmuṇḍī. 3. a form of Durgā.

**Ćāmuṇḍī** (S) (M) 1. slayer of Ćaṇḍa and Muṇḍa. 3. the terrible form of Durgā as one of the 7 mothers who destroyed the demons Ćaṇḍa and Muṇḍa.

**Ćamūrudṛṣ** (S) (F) antelope eyed.

**Ćaṇaka** (S) (M) Chickpea (*Cicer arietinum*); the father of Ćāṇakya (*A. Koṣa*)

**Ćāṇakya** (S) (M) 1. son of Ćanaka. 3. a renowned writer on civil polity, the author of the *Arthaśāstra* and a minister of Ćandragupta Maurya (320 B.C.)

**Ćanalakṣmī** (S) (F) 1. goddess of delight and satisfaction. 3. another name for Lakṣmī.

**Ćanasyā** (S) (F) delighting.

**Ćanćala** (S) (M) 1. playful; fickle; that which moves. 2. wind; lover. 3. an asura.

**Ćanćalā** (S) (F) 1. fickle; restless; moving constantly. 2. lightning; a river. 3. another name for Lakṣmī.

**Ćanćalākṣī** (S) (F) 1. with restless playful eyes. 3. a vidyādhara girl who cursed Rāvaṇa to die (*V. Rāmāyaṇa*)

**Ćanću** (S) (M) 1. renowned; famous; a bird's beak. 3. a son of Harita (*H. Purāṇa*)

**Ćānd** (S) (M) 1. to shine; to gladden. 3. the moon.

**Ćaṇḍā** (S) (F) 1. passionate; angry; wrathful. 3. a female attendant of Durgā (*Brah. Purāṇa*); the wife of Uddālaka (*J. Bhārata*); Chaṇḍā/Chaṇḍī is a tutelary deity of Bengal and Mysore (*H. Purāṇa*); an attendant of the 12th Arhat of the present Avasarpiṇī (*He. Koṣa*); another name for Durgā; Cocklebur (*Xanthium strumarium*).

**Ćaṇḍa** (S) (M) 1. fierce; violent; glowing with passion. 3. an attendant of Yama and Śiva (*A. Koṣa*); one of the 7 clouds enveloping the earth (*M. Purāṇa*); a river (*H. Koṣa*); an asura who was the brother of Muṇḍa and was killed by Durgā (*D. Bhagavata*)

**Ćaṇḍabala** (S) (M) 1. fiercely strong. 3. a prominent monkey of Rāma's army (*M. Bh.*)

**Ćaṇḍabhārgava** (S) (M) 1. Śiva, the fierce. 3. a sage in the dynasty of Ćyavana who was deeply versed in the Vedās (*M. Bh.*)

**Caṇḍaghaṇtā** (S) (F) 1. with passionate bells. 3. another name for Durgā.

**Ćandaharta** (S) (M) 1. destroyer of the disc. 3. a son of Kaśyapa and Simhikā (*M. Bh.*)

**Ćandaka** (S) (M) 1. the shining one; pleasing. 2. the moon; moonlight.

**Ćaṇḍākauśika** (S) (M) 1. passionate love. 3. a son of Kakśīvat.

**Ćaṇḍakauśika** (S) (M) 1. receptacle of glory. 3. place where the idol of Ćaṇḍī is installed; a sage and son of Kakṣivāna who lived in Magadha as the preceptor of the kings (*M. Bh.*)

**Ćandakiraṇa** (S) (F) 1. moonlight. 2. fair; luminous; soothing.

**Ćaṇḍakiraṇa** (S) (M) fierce rayed.

**Caṇḍālikā** (S) (F) 1. of a low caste. 3. another name for Durgā.

**Ćāṇḍālinī** (S) (F) 1. glorious; destroyer of Ćaṇḍa. 3. a tāntric goddess (*T. Śāstra*)

**Ćaṇḍamahāsena** (S) (M) 1. fierce commander of an army. 3. a prominent king of Ujjayinī who was the husband of Aṅgāravatī and father of Vāsavadattā who became the wife of Udayana the emperor of the vidyādharas (*K. Sāgara*)

**Ćaṇḍamuṇḍā** (S) (F) 1. slayer of Caṇḍa and Muṇḍa. 3. another name for Durgā.

**Ćandana** (S) (M) 1. sandalwood (*Pterocarpus santalinus*). 2. fragrant; cool; soothing; auspicious and dear to the gods.

**Ćandanā** (S) (F) 1. sandalwood (*Pterocarpus santalinus*). 2. fragrant; cool; soothing and auspicious 3. a river (*V. Purāṇa*); saffron (*Crocus sativus*); *Ichnocarpus frutescens*.

**Ćaṇḍanāyikā** (S) (F) 1. slayer of Ćaṇḍa. 3. a minor form of Durgā.

**Ćāndanī** (S) (F) 1. moonlight; silver. 2. fair; cool; luminous; soothing.

**Ćandanikā** (S) (F) a small sandalwood tree (*Pterocarpus santalinus*)

**Ćandanin** (S) (M) 1. anointed with sandalwood. 3. another name for Śiva.

**Ćandānśu** (S) (M) 1. hot rayed. 3. another name for the sun.

**Ćaṇḍarudrikā** (S) (F) 1. the glorious fierce goddess. 3. mystical knowledge acquired by worship of the 8 forms of Durgā (*D. Bhāgavata*)

**Ćaṇḍarūpā** (S) (F) 1. terrible in form. 3. a goddess (*Brah. Purāṇa*)

**Ćandasa** (S) (M) moon like.

**Caṇḍaśakti** (S) (M) 1. of impetuous valour. 3. a daitya.

**Ćaṇḍatuṇḍaka** (S) (M) 1. has a powerful beak. 3. a son of Garuḍa (*M. Bh.*)

**Ćaṇḍavatā** (S) (F) 1. violent; passionate. 2. warm. 3. one of the 8 forms of Durgā (*D. Bhāgavata*)

**Ćaṇḍavatī** (S) (F) 1. violent; passionate. 3. a minor form of Durgā (*Brah. Purāṇa*)

**Ćaṇḍavega** (S) (M) 1. moves with a fierce speed. 2. very swift; hot, passionate current. 3. a gandharva (*Bhāgavata*)

**Caṇḍavikrama** (S) (M) 1. of impetuous valour. 3. a prince (*K. Sāgara*)

**Ćaṇḍavīra** (S) (M) 1. passionately brave. 2. extremely brave. 3. a Buddhist deity.

**Ćaṇḍeśvara** (S) (M) 1. lord of Ćaṇḍa. 3. a Tīrtha; an attendant of Śiva; another name for Śiva.

**Ćaṇḍi** (S) (F) 1. the passionate and angry. 3. wife of Uddālaka; another name for Durgā.

**Ćāndī** (S) (M) 1. silver. 2. fair; precious; cooling.

**Ćaṇḍidāsa** (S) (M) 1. devotee of the fierce. 3. the devotee of Durgā.

**Ćaṇḍikā** (S) (F) 1. slayer of Ćaṇḍa; fierce woman. 3. a terrifying form of Pārvatī, who is worshipped under the name of Ćandikādevī and whose idol has twenty hands (*D. Bhāgavata*)

**Ćaṇḍīkusumā** (S) (F) 1. the flower of a passionate woman. 3. the Red Oleander (*Nerium odorum*)

**Ćaṇḍila** (S) (M) 1. passionate; angry; hot. 3. another name for Rudra.

**Ćaṇḍīpati** (S) (M) 1. lord of Ćaṇḍi. 3. another name for Śiva.

**Ćaṇḍogrā** (S) (F) 1. fierce and angry. 3. a minor form of Durgā (*Brah. Purāṇa*)

**Ćandprādyotam** (S) (M) 1. act of lighting. 3. king of Malva and follower of Mahāvīra (*J. Literature*)

**Ćandra** (S) (M) 1. bright; shining; radiant; the moon. 2. glittering; beautiful; fair; water; a red pearl; eye of a peacock's tail; gold; silver; number one. 3. the moon personified as the deity Ćandra created from the Ocean of Milk and the king of Soma (*Ś. Brāhmaṇa*); a prominent asura who was born as Ćandravarman the king of Kamboja (*M. Bh.*); a king of the solar dynasty who was the son of Viśvagandhi and the father of Yuvanāśva (*R. Taraṅginī*); the moon as a child of Atri and Anasuyā who lived with Tārā the consort of Bṛhaspati, had 27 of Dakṣa's daughters as his wives which are the 27 lunar mansions, and is considered to be the king of the stars and medicines (*Brah. Purāṇa*); the herb *Bryonopsis laciniosa*.

**Ćandrabāhū** (S) (M) 1. as mighty as the moon. 3. an asura (*H. Purāṇa*)

**Ćandrabālā** (S) (F) 1. daughter of the moon. 2. a girl as beautiful as the moon; Cardamom (*Elettaria cardamomum*)

**Ćandrabala** (S) (M) power of the moon.

**Ćandrabali** (S) (M) warrior of the moon; as brave as the moon.

**Ćandrabha** (S) (M) 1. as luminous as the moon. 3. an attendant of Skanda (*M. Bh.*)

**Ćandrabhāgā** (S) (F) 1. a piece of the moon. 3. the river now called Ćenab (*M. Bh.*)

**Ćandrabhāla** (S) (M) 1. one who bears the moon on his forehead. 3. another name for Śiva.

**Ćandrabhāna** (S) (M) as lustrous as the moon.

**Ćandrabhānu** (S) (M) 1. radiant moon; sun and moon conjoined. 2. illuminating; enlightening; renowned; venerated. 3. a son of Kṛṣṇa (*Bhāgavata*)

**Ćandrabhāsa** (S) (M) 1. as brilliant as the moon. 2. a sword.

**Ćandrabhūti** (S) (M) 1. born of the moon. 2. silver.

**Ćandrabindu** (S) (F) crescent moon.

**Ćandrācārya** (S) (M) 1. moon among teachers. 3. a Jaina teacher.

**Ćandraćūḍa** (S) (M) 1. moon crested. 3. a Yādava king of a state in Saurāṣṭra; a form of Bhairava (*M. Bh.*); another name for Śiva.

**Ćandradārā** (S) (F) 1. wives of the moon. 3. 27 of Dakṣa's daughters married to Ćandra or the moon and considered to be the 27 lunar mansions.

**Ćandradatta** (S) (M) 1. moon given. 2. fair; cool; soothing; tranquil.

**Ćandradeva** (S) (M) the moon personified as a deity.

**Ćandradhara** (S) (M) 1. holding the moon. 3. another name for Śiva.

**Ćandradīpa** (S) (M) moonlight.

**Ćandradūta** (S) (M) messenger of the moon.

**Ćandradyuti** (S) (M) 1. as bright as the moon. 3. sandalwood.

**Ćandragarbha** (S) (M) 1. one who has the moon as his navel. 2. tranquil; poised; of a cool-temperament. 3. a Buddha (*B. Literature*)

**Ćandragaurī** (S) (F) 1. as fair as the moon. 2 extremely fair; tranquil; soothing.

**Ćandragolikā** (S) (F) moonlight.

**Ćandragomin** (S) (M) 1. possessor of moonlike cows. 2. cows which are fair beautiful and quiet. 3. a grammarian (*G. Mahodadhi*)

**Ćandragupta** (S) (M) 1. moon protected. 3. a son of Rāvaṇa (*K. Rāmāyaṇa*); a minister of Kartavīryārjuna (*Bhāgavata*); a king of the Maurya dynasty who reigned in Paṭaliputra (315 B.C.) (*K. Sāgara*)

**Ćandrahantṛ** (S) (M) 1. destroyer of the moon. 3. an asura who was reborn as King Śunaka (*M. Bh.*)

**Ćandrahāsa** (S) (M) 1. smile of the moon; laughter of the moon. 2. moonlight; a pleasing smile; a glittering sword. 3. a powerful Kerala king and son of King Sudhārmika who was a friend of Kṛṣṇa (*Bhāgavata*); Rāvaṇa's sword given to him by Śiva (*Rāmāyaṇa*); the king of Ćandanāvatī (*J. Aśvamedha*); the bow of Śiva (*Ś. Purāṇa*)

**Ćandrahāsā** (S) (F) 1. with a beautiful smile. 3. a yoginī.

**Ćandrajā** (S) (F) 1. daughter of the moon. 2. a moonbeam.

**Ćandraja** (S) (M) 1. born of the moon. 3. another name for the planet Mercury.

**Ćandrajanaka** (S) (M) 1. father of the moon. 3. another name for the ocean.

**Ćandrajita** (S) (M) 1. conqueror of the moon. 2. surpassing the moon.

**Ćandraka** (S) (M) 1. the crescent moon. 2. the eye on the tail of a peacock; the red mark on the forehead. 3. another name for the moon.

**Ćandrakalā** (S) (F) 1. 1/16th of the moon's disc. 2. the segments of the moon. 3. each segment or crescent of the moon is personified as a goddess (*K. Sāgara*)

**Ćandrakalī** (S) (F) 1. a digit of the moon. 2. progressive.

**Ćandrakānta** (S) (M) 1. as lovely as the moon; loved by the moon. 3. the White Water lily (*Nymphaea alba*); sandalwood (*Pterocarpus santalinus*)

**Ćandrakāntā** (S) (F) 1. as lovely as the moon; beloved of the moon. 2. moonstone; night; moonlight. 3. another name for Rohiṇī, the consort of the moon.

**Ćandrakānti** (S) (F) 1. as brilliant as the moon. 2. silver; moonlight. 3. the 9th day of the waxing moon (*J. Śāstra*)

**Ćandrakeśa** (S) (M) fair haired.

**Ćandraketu** (S) (M) 1. whose banner is the moon. 2. whose fame and glory is renowned and spotless. 3. the son of Śatrughna and Śrutaka (*U. Rāmāyaṇa*); a vidyādhara king (*K. Sāgara*); a son of Lakṣmaṇa (*Rāmāyaṇa*)

**Ćandrākin** (S) (M) 1. wearing the moon. 3. the peacock who has moonlike eyes on its tail.

**Ćandrakiraṇa** (S) (M) moonbeam.

**Ćandrakīrti** (S) (M) **1.** as famous as the moon. **3.** a Buddhist saint; a prince of Ujjayinī (*B. Ćarita*); a teacher of the Mādhyamika-Prasańgikā school of Buddhism at Nālandā (600-650A.D.); a Sūri of the Jainas (*J.S. Koṣa*)

**Ćandrākṛti** (S) (M) **1.** moon shaped. **2.** as beautiful as the moon.

**Ćandrakuṭa** (S) (M) **1.** a peak as luminous as the moon. **3.** a mountain in Assam (*M. Bh.*)

**Ćandralekha** (S) (F) **1.** a digit of the moon. **3.** a daughter of Suśravas.

**Ćandrālī** (S) (F) moonbeam.

**Ćandralocana** (S) (M) **1.** mooneyed. **3.** a dānava.

**Ćandramā** (S) (F) moonbeam.

**Ćandramādhava** (S) (M) **1.** honey of the moon. **2.** the moonbeam.

**Ćandramālā** (S) (F) **1.** garland of the moon. **2.** the aura of the moon; of dazzling beauty. **3.** a river (*M. Bh.*)

**Ćandramallikā** (S) (F) **1.** queen of the moon. **3.** another name for Rohiṇī, the consort of the moon; *Crysanthemum coronarium*.

**Ćandramanas** (S) (M) **1.** sprung from the moon. **3.** one of the 10 horses of the moon (*A. Koṣa*)

**Ćandramāṇek** (S) (M) **1.** jewel of the moon. **2.** the pearl.

**Ćandramaṇī** (S) (M) moonstone.

**Ćandramāsa** (S) (M) **1.** lunar month. **2.** gem of the moon. **3.** the deity of the moon (*J. Śāstra*); a sage and advisor of Jaṭāyu (*V. Rāmāyaṇa*); a vasu.

**Ćandramasī** (S) (F) **1.** lunar. **3.** the constellation Mṛgaśiras; the wife of Bṛhaspati (*H. Purāṇa*)

**Ćandramatī** (S) (F) **1.** as beautiful as the moon. **2.** with an intellect as bright as the moon. **3.** the wife of King Hariśćandra (*M. Bh.*)

**Ćandramauli** (S) (M) **1.** moon crested. **3.** another name for Śiva.

**Ćandramohan** (S) (M) as attractive as the moon.

**Ćandrāmṛta** (S) (M) **1.** essence of the moon's nectar. **2.** nectar like; life giving.

**Ćandramukhā** (S) (F) **1.** moonfaced **2.** beautiful. **3.** a yakṣī considered to live in the Bakula tree (*Mimusops elengi*)

**Ćandramukhī** (S) (F) as beautiful as the moon.

**Ćandramukuta** (S) (M) **1.** moon crested. **3.** another name for Śiva.

**Ćandranābha** (S) (M) **1.** moon navelled. **3.** a dānava.

**Ćandrānana** (S) (M) **1.** moon faced. **3.** a son of King Janamejaya (*M. Bh.*); a king of Kāśmira and brother of Tārāpīda (*R. Taranginī*); a prince of Kānyakubja (*M. Bh.*); a Jina (*V. Ćarita*); another name for Kārttikeya.

**Ćandranātha** (S) (M) **1.** lord of the moon. **3.** another name for Śiva.

**Ćandrāngada** (S) (M) **1.** wearing moon as a bracelet. **2.** wearing bright shining bracelets.**3.** the grandson of Nala and husband of Sīmantinī (*Nalopākhyāna*); the son of King Indrasena (*Sk. Purāṇa*)

**Ćandrāṇī** (S) (F) **1.** wife of the moon. **3.** another name for Rohiṇī, consort of the moon.

**Candranibha** (S) (M) **1.** moonlike. **2.** bright; handsome.

**Ćandrānśu** (S) (M) **1.**moonbeam. **2.** with the lustre of the moon. **3.** another name for Viṣṇu.

**Ćandrapāda** (S) (M) **1.** the feet of the moon. **2.** moonbeam.

**Ćandraparvata** (S) (M) **1.** moon mountain. **2.** lofty; beautiful.

**Ćandrāpīḍa** (S) (M) **1.** eclipsing the moon; torturing the moon. **3.** a son of Janamejaya and Vapustamā and the father of a 100 brave sons (*H. Purāṇa*); a king of Kāśmira.

**Ćandraprabhā** (S) (F) **1.** moonlight. **3.** a female gandharva (*K. Sāgara*); the mother of Somaprabhā (*Ć. Ćarita*)

**Ćandraprabha** (S) (M) **1.** moonlight. **2.** as glorious as the moon. **3.** the 7th Jaina Tīrathańkara whose emblem was a crescent moon (*J. S. Koṣa*); an Arhat of the present Avasarpinī; a Bodhisattva; a yakṣa; *Psoralea corylifolia*.

**Ćandraprabhāva** (S) (M) the effect of the moon; as glorious as the moon.

**Ćandraprakāśa** (S) (M) moonlight.

**Ćandrapramardana** (S) (M) 1. enemy of the moon. 3. a brother of Rāhu (*M. Bh.*)

**Ćandraprava** (S) (M) 1. belonging to the moon. 3. 8th Jaina Tīrathańkara who was the son of King Mahāsena and Queen Lakṣmaṇā of Ćandrapura and whose emblem is the moon.

**Candraratna** (S) (M) 1. jewel of the moon. 2. pearl.

**Ćandrasaćiva** (S) (M) 1. friend of the moon. 3. another name for Kāma.

**Ćandrasena** (S) (M) 1. moon among the warriors; commander of a glorious army. 2. an excellent warrior or leader. 3. a king of Śrī Lankā and the father of Mandodarī and Indumatī by his wife Guṇavatī (*V. Ćarita*); a king of Ujjayanī and a great devotee of Śiva (*Ś. Purāṇa*); a son of King Samudrasena of Bengal who fought on the side of the Pāṇḍavas (*M. Bh.*); a warrior on the side of the Kauravas who was killed by Yudhiṣṭhira (*M. Bh.*)

**Ćandraśarman** (S) (M) 1. protected and sheltered by the moon. 3. a Brāhmin of the Agni Gotra and son-in-law of Devaśarman, later reborn as Akrūra (*P. Purāṇa*)

**Ćandraśekhara** (S) (M) 1. one who wears the moon as his crest jewel. 3. a king who was the son of Pauṣya and the husband of Tārāvatī; another name for Śiva.

**Ćandraśilā** (S) (F) 1. stone of the moon. 2. cool; sedate; soothing and tranquil. 3. the moonstone.

**Ćandraśman** (S) (M) 1. moonstone. 2. cool; sedate; soothing; tranquil.

**Ćandraśrī** (S) (F) 1. divine moon. 2. fair; beautiful; charming; soőthing; tranquil.

**Ćandraśubhra** (S) (F) 1. illumined by the moon. 2. as fair as the moon.

**Ćandrāśva** (S) (M) 1. horse of the moon. 2. the moonlight which precedes the moon. 3. the son of King Kuvalayāśva of the Ikṣvāku dynasty (*M. Bh.*); the son of king Dhundhumāra (*Bhāgavata*)

**Ćandrāsitā** (S) (F) 1. pale white moon; cooled by the moon; a day in the bright half of the month. 3. an attendant of Skanda (*M. Bh.*)

**Ćandrasūrya** (S) (M) 1. sun and moon conjoined. 3. a Buddha (*L. Vistara*)

**Ćandrasūryākṣa** (S) (M) 1. one who has the sun and the moon as eyes. 2. boundless; omnipresent; omniscient; all pervading; divine. 3. another name for Viṣṇu.

**Ćandrasuta** (S) (M) 1. son of the moon. 2. fair; handsome; soothing; tranquil. 3. another name for Mercury.

**Ćandrasvāmī** (S) (M) 1. lord of the moon; 3. a Brāhmin who was the husband of Devamatī and who was brought back to life by worshipping Sūrya (*K. Sāgara*)

**Ćandrata** (S) (M) 1. nectar of the moon. 2. fair; handsome; tranquil; nectar-like. 3. a physician of ancient India (*A. Veda*)

**Ćandratārā** (S) (F) 1. the moon and the stars conjoined. 2. eye catching.

**Ćandravadanā** (S) (F) moon faced.

**Ćandrāvalī** (S) (F) 1. moon like. 3. a gopī and friend of Rādhā the beloved of Kṛṣṇa (*V. Purāṇa*); a yoginī.

**Candravallabha** (S) (M) beloved of the moon.

**Ćandravallabha** (S) (M) 1. beloved of the moon. 3. Indian Redwood tree (*Soymida febrifuge*)

**Ćandravalli** (S) (F) 1. vine of the moon. 3. the Mādhavī creeper (*Hiptage madoblata*)

**Ćandrāvaloka** (S) (M) 1. light of the moon; resembling the moon. 3. a king of Ćitrakūṭanagara and husband of Indīvaraprabhā, the daughter of ṛṣi Kaṇva and apsarā Menakā (*K. Sāgara*)

**Ćandravarman** (S) (M) 1. moon; warrior; protector of the moon. 2. having brilliant armour. 3. the king of Kamboja who was as handsome as Ćandra (the moon) and who fought on the side of the Kauravas (*M. Bh.*)

**Ćandravasā** (S) (F) 1. one whose abode is the moon. 2. peaceful; tranquil. 3. a river (*Bhā. Purāṇa*)

**Ćandrāvatī** (S) (F) 1. lit by the moon. 2. brilliant. 3. the daughter of Sunābha the asura and the wife of Gadā (*H. Purāṇa*); a wife of King Hariśćandra in his previous birth (*Rāmāyaṇa*); a wife of King Dharmasena (*V. Pañcavinśatika*); the daughter of King Ćandragupta (*K. Sāgara*)

**Ćandravijaya** (S) (M) 1. conqueror of the moon. 2. surpassing the moon in all its qualities.

**Ćandravimala** (S) (M) as pure as the moon.

**Ćandravināśana** (S) (M) 1. destroyer of the moon. 3. an asura who was reborn as King Jānakī (*M. Bh.*)

**Ćandreśa** (S) (M) 1. lord of the moon. 3. another name for Śiva.

**Ćandreṣṭa** (S) (M) 1. beloved of the moon. 3. the Kumudinī or the night lotus (*Nelumbium speciosum*) which flowers only at night.

**Ćāndrī** (S) (F) 1. moonlight. 2. fair; cool; soothing. 3. *Psoralea corylifolia*.

**Ćandrikā** (S) (F) 1. moonlight. 2. fair; illuminating; cool; soothing; the Mallikā creeper (*Jasminum sambac*); Garden cress (*Lepidum sativum*); Fenugreek (*Trigonella foenum-graecum*); Cardamom (*Elletaria cardamomum*); *Rauwolfia serpentina*. 3. another name for the Ćandrabhāgā river; another name for Dākṣāyaṇī.

**Ćandrikāmbuja** (S) (F) 1. lotus of the night. 2. the night lotus (*Nelumbium speciosum*)

**Ćandrila** (S) (M) 1. possessing the moon. 3. another name for Śiva.

**Ćandrimā** (S) (F) moonlight.

**Ćandrin** (S) (M) golden.

**Ćandrodaya** (S) (M) 1. moonrise. 2. inspiring love. 3. a brother of the king of Virāṭa (*M. Bh.*)

**Ćandrupā** (S) (F) 1. with the form of the moon. 2. as beautiful as the moon.

**Ćandurī** (S) (M) 1. belonging to the moon. 2. like the moon.

**Ćaṅga** (S) (M) understanding; wise; handsome.

**Ćaṅgadāsa** (S) (M) 1. a wise devotee. 3. a grammarian.

**Ćanna** (S) (M) 1. renowned; famous. 3. the charioteer of Gautama Buddha (*B. Ćarita*)

**Ćāṇūra** (S) (M) 1. with thin thighs. 3. Kṣatriya king who served Yudhiṣṭhira (*M. Bh.*); an asura and attendant of Kaṁsa who was killed by Kṛṣṇa (*Bhāgavata*)

**Ćapalā** (S) (F) 1. fickle; swift; wavering. 2. lightning. 3. another name for Lakṣmī.

**Ćapala** (S) (M) 1. unsteady; moving; fickle; swift. 2. the wind; lightning; quicksilver. 3. a king of ancient India (*M. Bh.*)

**Ćāpdhara** (S) (M) 1. owns a bow. 2. an archer. 3. another name for the zodiac sign of Sagittarius.

**Ćāpin** (S) (M) 1. armed with a bow. 2. an archer. 3. another name for the zodiac sign of Sagittarius.

**Ćaraka** (S) (M) 1. wanderer. 2. a wandering religious student. 3. the incarnation of Śeṣa who came to the earth to alleviate sickness and is supposed to have been the author of *Ćaraka Samhitā*, a medical work (*B. Prakāśa*); the court physician of King Kaniṣka.

**Ćāraṇa** (S) (M) 1. chanter of praises. 3. Ćāranas were the wandering minstrels employed by the royal court to sing the king's praises; a class of bird deities (*M. Smṛti*)

**Ćaraṇa** (S) (M) 1. foot; support. 2. a pillar; behaviour; good or moral conduct.

**Ćaraṇadāsa** (S) (M) 1. devotee of the feet. 2. respectful; servant of god. 3. an author and philosophical poet of ancient India (*Nalopākhyāna*)

**Ćarćikā** (S) (F) 1. repeating a word; smeared with unguents. 2. fragrant; inviting. 3. a tutelary goddess (*H. Ć. Ćintāmaṇi*); another name for Durgā.

**Ćāriman** (S) (M) beauty; movable.

**Ćaraṇī** (S) (F) 1. wandering from place to place; a wanderer. 2. a bird.

**Ćariṣṇu** (S) (M) 1. moving; wandering. 3. a son of Manu Sāvarṇa; a son of Kirtimat and Dhenukā (*Vā. Purāṇa*)

**Ćaritra** (S) (M) 1. character; nature; disposition; behaviour. 3. Tamarind tree (*Tamarindus indica*)

**Ćarmavān** (S) (M) 1. covered with hides. 2. protected; sheltered. 3. a son of King Subala and the brother of Śakuni (*M. Bh.*)

**Ćarmin** (S) (M) 1. covered with hides. 3. an attendant of Śiva; Musa Sapientum.

**Ćarṇapūrṇa** (S) (F) 1. full moon. 2. fair; beautiful; soothing; tranquil.

**Ćarṣaṇi** (S) (F) 1. active; agile; swift. 2. intelligence; moonlight; saffron. 3. Aryaman's daughters by Mātrikā and the progenitors of the human race (*H. Purāṇa*); the wife of Varuṇa and the mother of Bhṛgu (*Var. Purāṇa*); the wife of Kubera (*V. Rāmāyaṇa*)

**Ćāru** (S) (M) 1. agreeable. 2. charming; beautiful; beloved; esteemed. 3. a son of Kṛṣṇa (*H. Purāṇa*); a son of Dhṛtarāṣṭra (*M. Bh.*); another name for Bṛhaspati; saffron (*Crocus sativus*); Himalayan cherry (*Prunus cersoides*)

**Ćārubāhu** (S) (M) 1. beautiful arms. 3. a son of Kṛṣṇa and Rukmiṇī (*H. Purāṇa*)

**Ćārubālā** (S) (F) a beautiful girl.

**Ćārubhadra** (S) (M) 1. an auspicious person; a handsome gentleman. 2. fortunate. 3. a son of Kṛṣṇa and Rukmiṇī (*H. Purāṇa*)

**Ćārućandra** (S) (M) 1. beautiful moon. 3. a son of Kṛṣṇa and Rukmiṇī (*H. Purāṇa*)

**Ćārūćitrā** (S) (F) beautiful picture; one with a beautiful form.

**Ćārūćitra** (S) (M) 1. beautiful picture; one with a beautiful form. 3. a son of Dhṛtarāṣṭrā (*M. Bh.*)

**Ćārudarśanā** (S) (F) beautiful in appearance.

**Ćārudarśana** (S) (M) beautiful in appearance.

**Ćārudatta** (S) (M) 1. born of beauty. 2. extremely handsome. 3. a hero in a Sanskṛt drama (*M. Katikam*)

**Ćārudeha** (S) (M) 1. with a beautiful form. 3. a son of Kṛṣṇa and Rukmiṇī (*Bhāgavata*)

**Ćārudeṣṇa** (S) (M) 1. beautiful gift. 3. a son of Kṛṣṇa and Rukmiṇī (*M. Bh./L. Purāṇa*); the father of Gaṇḍūṣa (*H. Purāṇa*)

**Ćārudhārā** (S) (F) 1. beautiful. 3. another name for Indra's consort Śaćī.

**Ćāruḍhī** (S) (F) 1. with an auspicious mind. 3. a mountain near Mahāmeru (*D. Bhāgavata*)

**Ćārūdhiṣṇya** (S) (M) 1. the altar of beauty. 3. a ṛṣi of the 11th Manvantara (*H. Purāṇa*)

**Ćārūgarbha** (S) (M) 1. a vessel of beauty. 3. a son of Kṛṣṇa and Rukmiṇī (*H. Purāṇa*)

**Ćārugupta** (S) (M) 1. protected by beauty. 3. a son of Kṛṣṇa and Rukmiṇī (*H. Purāṇa*)

**Ćāruhāsan** (S) (M) with a beautiful smile.

**Ćārukesara** (S) (M) 1. of golden beauty. 3. *Crysanthemum Indicum*; *Rosa Alba*.

**Ćārulatā** (S) (F) beautiful vine.

**Ćārulоćanā** (S) (F) with beautiful eyes.

**Ćārumat** (S) (M) 1. intelligent. 3. a Ćakravartin.

**Ćārumatī** (S) (F) 1. with an auspicious intellect. 2. intelligent; wise; enlightened. 3. the daughter of Kṛṣṇa and Rukmiṇī (*H. Purāṇa*)

**Ćārumatsya** (S) (M) 1. beautiful fish. 3. a son of sage Viśvāmitra (*M. Bh.*)

**Ćārumoda** (S) (M) 1. pleasing; joy; gladness. 3. *Jasminum Officianale*.

**Ćārunetrā** (S) (F) 1. with beautiful eyes. 3. an apsarā in the court of Kubera (*M. Bh.*)

**Ćārupāda** (S) (M) 1. with beautiful feet. 3. a son of Namasyu.

**Ćāruśravas** (S) (M) 1. with a beautiful voice. 3. a son of Kṛṣṇa and Rukmiṇī.

**Ćārusāra** (S) (M) 1. the essence of all that is lovely. 2. gold.

**Ćāruśilā** (S) (F) beautiful jewel.

**Ćāruśirṣa** (S) (M) 1. with a beautiful head. 3. a sage of Ālambagotra who was a friend of Indra (*M. Bh.*)

**Ćārutamā** (S) (F) most beautiful.

**Ćāruvāki** (S) (F) 1. sweet tongued. 3. the wife of King Aśoka.

**Ćāruvaktra** (S) (M) 1. beautiful faced. 3. an attendant of Skanda who was devoted to Brāhmins (*M. Bh.*)

**Ćāruvāṅgī** (S) (F) 1. with splendid limbs. 3. a daughter of Kuśambha and the wife of King Bhadraśreṇya (*Br. Purāṇa*)

**Ćāruvardhana** (S) (M) who enhances beauty.

**Ćāruveṇī** (S) (F) 1. a beautiful braid. 3. a river (*M. Bh.*)

**Ćāruveṣa** (S) (M) 1. beautifully attired. 3. a son of Kṛṣṇa and Rukmiṇī (*L. Purāṇa*)

**Ćāruvī** (S) (F) 1. splendour; splendid (*R. Taraṅginī*). 3. another name for Kubera's wife Bhadrā.

**Ćāruvinda** (S) (M) 1. striving for beauty; attaining charm. 3. a son of Kṛṣṇa and Rukmiṇī (*H. Purāṇa*)

**Ćāruyaśas** (S) (M) 1. with charming fame. 3. a son of Kṛṣṇa and Rukmiṇī (*H. Purāṇa*)

**Ćārvāka** (S) (M) 1. sweet tongued. 3. a rākṣasa friend of Duryodhana (*M. Bh.*); a philosopher of ancient India who was an atheist (*R. Tarangini*)

**Ćārvāngī** (S) (F) 1. with a beautiful body. 3. a daughter of Kuśamba and wife of King Bhadraśrenya (*Bh. Purāṇa*)

**Ćāṣa** (S) (M) the Blue Jay (*Coracias benghalensis*)

**Ćāṣavaktra** (S) (M) 1. jay faced. 3. an attendant of Skanda (*M. Bh.*)

**Ćātaka** (S) (M) 1. a mythical Indian bird considered to live on raindrops. 3. a poet; Pied Crested Cuckoo (*Clamator jacobinus serratus*)

**Ćatuhsana** (S) (M) containing the 4 sons, Sanaka, Sananda, Sanātana, Sanatkumāra of Brahmā.

**Ćatura** (S) (M) 1. clever; skilful. 2. quick; swift; beautiful; charming; agreeable.

**Ćaturaṅga** (S) (M) 1. 4 limbed; horse. 2. with beautiful limbs. 3. a king of the Aṅga dynasty who was the son of Hemapāda and the father of Pṛthulākṣa (*A. Purāṇa*); a son of Lomapāda (*M. Purāṇa*)

**Ćaturānana** (S) (M) 1. 4 faced. 3. another name for Brahmā.

**Ćaturānīka** (S) (M) 1. 4 faced. 3. another name for Varuṇa.

**Ćaturaśva** (S) (M) 1. one who owns 4 horses. 3. a sage who was the member of Yama's court (*H. Purāṇa*)

**Ćaturāsya** (S) (M) 1. quadrangular abode. 2. living in a quadrangular abode. 3. a heroic asura who loved the apsarā Rambhā (*K. Rāmāyaṇa*)

**Ćaturbāhu** (S) (M) 1. 4 armed. 3. another name for Viṣṇu and Śiva.

**Ćaturbhuja** (S) (M) 1. 4 armed. 3. another name for Viṣṇu, Kṛṣṇa, Gaṇeśa and Śiva.

**Ćaturdanṣṭra** (S) (M) 1. 4 tusked. 3. an attendant of Skanda (*M. Bh.*); another name for Viṣṇu.

**Ćaturdanta** (S) (M) 1. 4 tusked. 3. another name for Indra's elephant, Airāvata.

**Ćaturgati** (S) (M) 1. 4 legged. 2. has 4 kinds of speed; moving in all the 4 directions at the same time. 3. another name for the tortoise and the Supreme Soul.

**Ćaturikā** (S) (F) clever; skilful.

**Ćaturmukha** (S) (M) 1. 4 faced. 3. another name for Brahmā, Viṣṇu and Śiva.

**Ćaturmūrti** (S) (M) 1. having 4 appearances. 2. with 4 forms; versatile. 3. another name for Brahmā, Viṣṇu, Skanda.

**Ćaturvaktra** (S) (M) 1. 4 faced. 3. a dānava (*H. Purāṇa*); an attendant of Durgā; another name for Brahmā.

**Ćaturveda** (S) (M) 1. the 4 Vedas conjoined; the 4 fold knowledge. 3. the knowledge of Dharma, Artha, Kāma and Mokṣa.

**Ćatuṣkarṇī** (S) (F) 1. 4 eared. 3. a mother in Skanda's retinue (*M. Bh.*)

**Ćatuṣpāṇī** (S) (M) 1. 4 armed. 3. another name for Viṣṇu.

**Ćatuṣpathā** (S) (F) 1. living on a crossroad. 3. an attendant of Skanda (*M. Bh.*)

**Ćatvaravāsinī** (S) (F) 1. living on a crossroad. 3. a mother and attendant of Skanda (*M. Bh.*)

**Ćaudrāyaṇa** (S) (M) 1. a prince who inspires. 3. a prince of Daśapura (*H. Purāṇa*)

**Ćedi** (S) (M) 1. intelligent. 2. pleasant; likeable. 3. a king of the Yaduvanśa and son of Uśika who founded the Ćedi dynasty; a people of Bundelkhand (*Bhāgavata*)

**Ćedija** (S) (M) 1. son of Ćedi. 3. another name for Dhṛṣṭaketu.

**Ćedipati** (S) (M) 1. king of the Ćedis; master of bliss. 3. honorific of Śiśupāla.

**Ćedipuṅgava** (S) (M) 1. bull of the Ćedis; chief of the Ćedis. 3. another name for Dhṛṣṭaketu.

**Ćedirāja** (S) (M) 1. king of Ćedi. 3. another name for Śiśupāla son of Damaghoṣa.

**Ćekitāna** (S) (M) 1. intelligent. 3. an archer of the Vṛṣṇi dynasty who fought on the side of the Pāṇḍavas in the war of Mahābhārata (*M. Bh.*); another name for Śiva.

**Ćelanā** (S) (F) 1. of the nature of consiousness. 3. a daughter of King Ćetaka of Vaiśāli and the wife of King Śreṇika (*P. Purāṇa*)

**Ćenćanna** (S) (M) vivacious.

**Ćeṣṭā** (S) (F) 1. effort; endeavour. 2. motion; movement.

**Ćetaka** (S) (M) 1. thoughtful 3. Rānā Pratāp's horse; a Lićchavī prince of Vaiśāli and the uncle of Jaina Tīrathaṅkara Mahāvira (*M. Ćarita*); *Jasminum grandiflorum*.

**Ćetakī** (S) (F) 1. sentient. 3. Spanish Jasmine (*Jasminum grandiflorum*); Black Myrobalan (*Terminalia chebula*)

**Ćetanā** (S) (F) 1. intelligence. 2. consciousness; mind; knowledge; sense; vitality; life; wisdom; understanding.

**Ćetana** (S) (M) 1. concious; animated; visible; conspicuous; distinguished; elegant; sentient. 2. soul; mind; man.

**Ćetas** (S) (M) 1. intelligence; consciousness; splendour. 2. soul; heart; mind.

**Ćetrāma** (S) (M) pervading the conciousness.

**Ćhabīlā** (S) (M) 1. charming; picturesque. 2. beautiful; splendid; brilliant.

**Ćhāga** (S) (M) 1. moisture; born of moisture. 3. the goat which is supposed to have originated from the moisture present on the shell of the cosmic egg (*Y. Veda*)

**Ćhaga** (S) (M) 1. he goat. 2. the Zodiac sign of Aries. 3. an attendant of Śiva.

**Ćhagala** (S) (M) 1. goat. 3. a sage (*Vā. Purāṇa*)

**Ćhagamukha** (S) (M) 1. with the face of a goat. 3. another name for Subrāhmaṇya (*M. Bh.*)

**Ćhagavaktra** (S) (M) 1. goat faced. 3. a companion of Skanda (*Sk. Purāṇa*)

**Ćhaggan** (S) (M) 1. intelligence; mind; spirit; soul; goat. 2. the Zodiac sign of Aries.

**Ćhailā** (S) (M) a handsome youth.

**Ćhajju** (S) (M) 1. shade. 2. cool; soothing; provides shelter.

**Ćhandā** (S) (F) moon.

**Ćhandaka** (S) (M) 1. charming; hymn like; poetic. 3. Sākyamuni's charioteer (*Divyāvadāna*)

**Ćhandakā** (S) (M) 1. assuming any shape at will. 3. another name for Viṣṇu.

**Ćhandodeva** (S) (M) 1. lord of the hymns; invoker of deities with hymns. 3. another name for sage Mataṅga.

**Ćhandodevī** (S) (F) 1. goddess of the metre. 3. another name for Gāyatrī.

**Ćhattra** (S) (M) 1. parasol; umbrella. 2. with the white parasol symbolizing royal or delegated power. 3. according to the Hindu scriptures, the universe in divided into 7, arranged one above the other like a number of parasols.

**Ćhattradhāra** (S) (M) bearer of the royal umbrella.

**Ćhatraketu** (S) (M) 1. a bright umbrella banner. 2. chief; head. 3. a son of Lakṣmaṇa and Ūrmilā who became the king of Ćandramatī (*U. Rāmāyaṇa*)

**Ćhatramukhā** (S) (F) 1. umbrella faced. 2. many faced. 3. a nāga (*K. Vyūha*)

**Ćhatrapati** (S) (M) 1. lord of the umbrella. 2. whose kingdom shelters the people like an umbrella; an emperor.

**Ćhatravatī** (S) (M) possessing the umbrella of power.

**Ćhatreśa** (S) (M) 1. lord of the umbrella. 3. another name for Śiva.

**Ćhaturhotrī** (S) (M) 1. a litany recited at the new moon. 3. another name for Kṛṣṇa.

**Ćhavi** (S) (F) image; reflection; beauty; splendour; a ray of light.

**Ćhavillākara** (S) (M) (F) 1. of handsome appearance. 3. a historian of Kāśmira (*R. Taraṅginī*)

**Ćhāyā** (S) (F) 1. shade; shadow. 2. colour; lustre; beauty; resemblance; line; reflection. 3. the daughter of Viśvakarmā (*V. Purāṇa*); a substitute wife of Sūrya and mother of Manu, Yama and Yamī, Sāvarṇi, Śani and Tāpanī (*H. Purāṇa*); a form of Durgā known as Kātyāyāni (*A. Koṣa*); a rāga.

**Ćhāyāgrāhī** (S) (F) 1. catching the image. 2. mirror. 3. a rākṣasi who was killed by Hanumān (*V. Rāmāyaṇa*)

**Ćhāyana** (S) (M) moon.

**Ćhāyānātha** (S) (M) 1. lord of Ćhāyā. 3. another name for Sūrya.

**Ćhāyāṅka** (S) (M) 1. marked with the hare. 2. one who is like the moon. 3. another name for the moon.

**Ćhedi** (S) (M) 1. which cuts and breaks. 3. the thunderbolt of Indra.

**Ćhinnamastā** (S) (F) 1. beheaded. 2. she of the split skulls. 3. a tāntric form of Durgā who is depicted as headless (*T. Śāstra*)

**Ćidākāśa** (S) (M) 1. universal soul. 3. Absolute Brahmā.

**Ćidambara** (S) (M) 1. with a heart as vast as the sky. 3. a Sanskṛt poet who stayed at the court of Emperor Veṅkaṭa of Vijayānagara and whose greatest work is the *Rāghavayādavapāṇḍavīya* (16th century A.D.); a pilgrimage centre in Tamil Nādu.

**Ćidānanda** (S) (M) ultimate bliss.

**Ćidātma** (S) (M) 1. pure intelligence. 3. Supreme Spirit.

**Ćidātmata** (S) (M) consisting of pure thought.

**Ćiddhātu** (S) (M) Original Soul.

**Ćidghana** (S) (M) 1. full of knowledge. 3. another name for Brahmā.

**Ćidrūpa** (S) (M) knowledge incarnate.

**Ćidullāsa** (S) (M) 1. thoughts that radiate. 2. has radiant thoughts; wise; spiritually enlightened.

**Ćidvilāsa** (S) (M) 1. one who sports in the knowledge of illusion. 3. a disciple of Śankarāćārya (*Ś. Vijaya*)

**Ćidvilasinī** (S) (M) 1. one who sports in the knowledge of illusion. 2. enlightened and enjoying the thoughts of enlightenment; in a state of eternal bliss.

**Ćihir** (S) (M) the bird Chummum (*Cheer phasianus wallichi*)

**Ćikita** (S) (M) 1. experienced. 2. well read; wise; enlightened.

**Ćikka** (S) (M) a small mouse.

**Ćikṣura** (S) (M) 1. inflicter of pain. 3. the war minister of Mahiṣāsura (*D. Bhāgavata*)

**Ćikura** (S) (M) 1. mountain; hair on the head. 3. the son of Āryaka the serpent king and father of Sumukha (*M. Bh.*)

**Ćitta** (S) (M) 1. knowledge; consciousness. 3. another name for Brahmā.

**Ćiman** (S) (M) curious.

**Ćinmaya** (S) (M) 1. consisting of pure intelligence. 3. the Supreme Spirit.

**Ćinnintammā** (Telugu) (F) village goddess regarded as the head of the household.

**Ćintā** (S) (F) consideration; thought.

**Ćintāmaṇi** (S) (M) 1. gem of thought; gem that fulfils desires. 3. a diamond produced from the Ocean of Milk which is considered to grant all desires (*H. Purāṇa*); a Buddha (*B. Literature*); another name for Brahmā.

**Ćintāmukta** (S) (M) free from worry.

**Ćintan** (S) (M) 1. thought; perception. 2. meditation; mind; intellect.

**Ćintāratna** (S) (M) 1. gem of thought. 3. a fabulous gem considered to grant all desires (*S. Dvatrinśikā*)

**Ćintya** (S) (M) worthy of thought; worthy of being conceived.

**Ćintyadyota** (S) (M) 1. of brightness conceivable only by imagination. 3. a class of deities.

**Ćirājuṣa** (S) (M) favoured with a long life.

**Ćirakāri** (S) (M) 1. making slow progress. 3. a son of Gautama Mahaṛṣi (*M. Bh.*)

**Ćirañjīvan** (S) (M) 1. long lived. 2. infinite. 3. another name for Viṣṇu and Kāma.

**Ćirantaka** (S) (M) 1. eternal. 3. a son of Garuḍa (*M. Bh.*)

**Ćiravāsas** (S) (M) 1. long lived. 2. master of one's own death; one who can die as and when he chooses to. 3. a Kśatriya king born as a reincarnation of the asura Krodhavaśa (*M. Bh.*); a yakṣa in the court of Kubera (*M. Bh.*)

**Ćirāyu** (S) (M) long lived.

**Ćirāyus** (S) (M) 1. long lived. 3. a king of Ćirāyu who was the husband of Dhanapārā and the father of Jīvahara, he had the secret elixir of long life and lived a 1000 years (*K. Sāgara*)

**Ćiriṇī** (S) (M) 1. clothed in bark or rags. 3. a river on the banks of which Vaivasvata Manu performed his penance (*M. Bh.*)

**Ćiriñjīvin** (S) (M) 1. long lived. 3. another name for Viṣṇu; Red Silkcotton tree (*Bombax celba*)

**Ćirjīvaka** (S) (M) 1. long lived. 3. another name for Mārkaṇḍeya, Bali, Vyāsa, Hanumat, Vibhīṣana, Paraśurāma, Kṛpa, Aśvatthāman, Viṣṇu and crow.

**Ćirlabdha** (S) (M) obtained after a long time.

**Ćitadhana** (S) (M) 1. the conscious. 3. another name for Brahmā.

**Ćiṭaka** (S) (M) ornament of the neck; necklace.

**Ćitaparā** (S) (F) 1. beyond the power of thought. 2. incogitable; indescribable. 3. another name for Kāmākṣī.

**Ćitapati** (S) (M) lord of intellect; lord of thought.

**Ćitāyu** (S) (M) 1. descended from thought; born of intellect. 3. a Puru king who was the son of Bhadrāśva (*Agni Purāṇa*)

**Ćitrā** (S) (F) 1. beautiful; wonderful; conspicuous. 2. picture; anything bright that strikes the eye; ornament; constellation; sky; painting; heaven; worldly illusion. 3. an apsarā (*M. Bh.*); a daughter of Gada; a river; the 14th lunar mansion;another name for Subhadra.

**Ćitra** (S) (M) (F) 1. picture; conspicuous. 2. excellent; distinguished; various; bright. 3. son of Dhṛtarāṣṭra (*M. Bh.*); a king of elephants with whom Subrahmaṇya played (*M. Bh.*); warriors of the Kauravas (*M. Bh.*); a hero of the Ćedi kingdom who fought on the side of the Pāṇḍavas (*M. Bh.*); a gandharva; a Dravida king (*P. Purāṇa*); the herb *Cucumis trigonus*; Ceylon Leadwort (*Plumbago zeylanica*); Asoka tree (*Saraca indica*)

**Ćitrabāhu** (S) (M) 1. with a speckled arm. 3. a son of Dhṛtarāṣṭra (*M. Bh.*); a gandharva.

**Ćitrabāṇa** (S) (M) 1. owner of variegated arrows. 3. a son of Dhṛtarāṣṭra (*M. Bh.*)

**Ćitrabarha** (S) (M) 1. with a variegated tail. 3. a son of Garuḍa (*M. Bh.*)

**Ćitrabarhin** (S) (M) 1. with a variegated tail. 2. a peacock. 3. a son of Garuḍa (*M. Bh.*)

**Ćitrabhānu** (S) (M) 1. of variegated lustre; the beautiful sun. 2. multicoloured; shining; lit. 3. another name for Agni, Bhairava, Śiva, the aśvins and the sun.

**Ćitrabhūta** (S) (M) painted; decorated.

**Ćitraćāpa** (S) (M) 1. owner of a vareigated bow. 3. a son of Dhṛtarāṣṭra (*M. Bh.*)

**Ćitradarśī** (S) (M) 1. seeing clearly; with bright observation. 3. a sage who was the son of Kuśika.

**Ćitradeva** (S) (M) 1. a strange deity. 3. an attendant of Subrahmaṇya who loved Brāhmins (*M. Bh.*)

**Ćitradharman** (S) (M) 1. follower of various customs; follower of strange customs. 2. one of various customs; an arrangement of various hues. 3. reincarnation of the asura Virūpākṣa who was invited by the Pāṇḍavas to help them in the Māhābhārata war (*M. Bh.*)

**Ćitragu** (S) (M) 1. owner of brindled cows; knower of the wonderful. 3. a son of Kṛṣṇa (*Bhāgavata*)

**Ćitragupta** (S) (M) 1. secret picture; protected by the wonderful. 3. the scribe of the gods who was born from the body of Brahmā (*Tithyāditya*); one of Yama's attendants who records the doings of men (*M. Bh.*); the 16th Arhat of the future Utsarpinī (*J. S. Koṣa*)

**Ćitrai** (Tamil) (F) 1. the spring. 2. the month of April.

**Ćitrajyotī** (S) (F) 1. wonderfully glorious. 2. shining brilliantly.

**Ćitraka** (S) (M) 1. painted; spotted. 2. tiger; leopard; bright; beautiful; brave; powerful. 3. a son of Dhṛtarāṣṭra (*M. Bh.*); a son of Vṛṣṇi (*Vā. Purāṇa*); a nāga.

**Ćitrakaṇṭha** (S) (M) 1. with a speckled throat. 2. pigeon. 3. the horse of King Vikramāditya known for his bravery.

**Ćitrakarman** (S) (M) performer of extraordinary acts.

**Ćitrakeṣī** (S) (F) 1. having wonderful hair. 3. an apsarā and consort of King Vatsa (*Bhāgavata*)

**Ćitraketu** (S) (M) 1. owner of a beautiful banner. 3. a gandharva who was reborn as the asura Vṛtrāsura (*Bhāgavata*); a son of Garuḍa (*M. Bh.*); a Pāncāla prince who fought on the side of the Pāṇḍavas (*M. Bh.*); a son of Śiśupāla (*Bhāgavata*); the king of the Sūrasenas and a devotee of Viṣṇu and Śiva (*Bhā. Purāṇa*); another name for Lakṣmaṇa, Kṛṣṇa, Vasiṣṭha, Devabhāga.

**Ćitrākṣa** (S) (M) 1. speckle eyed. 2. with strange eyes; with beautiful eyes. 3. a son of Dhṛtarāṣṭra (*M. Bh.*); a serpent lord (*M. Bh.*); a Draviḍa king.

**Ćitrakuṇḍala** (S) (M) 1. owns radiant earrings. 3. a son of Dhṛtarāṣṭra (*M. Bh.*)

**Ćitrakūṭa** (S) (M) 1. wonderful peak. 3. a mountain of a district where Rāma and Lakṣmaṇa first spent their exile (*V. Rāmāyaṇa*)

**Ćitralatā** (S) (F) 1. wonderful vine. 3. an apsarā (*B. Rāmāyaṇa*); Indian Madder (*Rubia cordifolia*)

**Ćitralekhā** (S) (F) 1. beautiful outline; picture. 2. portrait; digit of the moon. 3. an apsarā who danced at the assembly of the Pāṇḍavas (*M. Bh.*); a companion of Uṣā the daughter of the demon Bāṇa (*Bhāgavata*); a daughter of Kumbhāṇḍa (*Bhāgavata*)

**Ćitrālī** (S) (F) a wonderful lady; friend of the strange.

**Ćitramanas** (S) (M) 1. with a bright intellect. 3. a horse of the moon (*Va. Purāṇ*)

**Ćitramāyā** (S) (F) worldly illusion; strange manifestation.

**Ćitramayī** (S) (F) 1. full of wonders. 2. like a picture.

**Ćitramukha** (S) (M) 1. bright-faced. 3. a Vaiśya sage who became a Brāhmin by his penances (*M. Bh.*)

**Ćitranātha** (S) (M) 1. excellent lord. 3. a son of Dhṛṣṭa (*M. Purāṇa*)

**Ćitrāṅga** (S) (M) 1. with a multicoloured body. 2. antelope; vermilion. 3. a warrior killed by Śatrughna during Rāma's Aśvamedha Yajña (*Rāmāyaṇa*); a son of Dhṛtarāṣṭra (*M. Bh.*); Ceylon Leadwort (*Plumbago zeylanica*)

**Ćitrāṅgadā** (S) (F) 1. with wonderful limbs. 2. with bejewelled arms. 3. an apsarā (*M. Bh.*); a wife of Arjuna who was the daughter of King Ćitravāhana of Manālur and the mother of Babhruvāhana (*M. Bh.*); a daughter of Viśvakarmā (*M. Bh.*)

**Ćitrāṅgada** (S) (M) 1. decorated with wonderful bracelets. 2. with bejewelled arms. 3. a son of King Śāntanu and Satyavatī (*M. Bh.*); a gandharva (*K. Sāgara*); a king of Kaliṅga (*M. Bh.*); a king of Daśārṇa who was killed by Arjuna (*M. Bh.*); a deer in the *Panćatantra*; a vidyādhara; a divine recorder of men's deeds.

**Ćitrāṅgadāsuta** (S) (M) 1. son of Ćitrāngadā. 3. another name for Babhruvāhana.

**Ćitrāṅgī** (S) (F) 1. with a vareigated body. 2. with a charming body. 3. the daughter of King Bhadraśreṇya of the Hehayas and the wife of Durmada (*M. Bh.*); Indian Madder (*Rubia cordifolia*)

**Ćitrapakṣa** (S) (M) 1. with speckled wings. 3. the Northern Painted Partridge (*Francolinus pictus pallidus*)

**Ćitrapuṣpī** (S) (F) 1. variegated blossom. 3. the *Hibiscus cannabinus*.

**Ćitraraśmi** (S) (M) 1. with variegated rays. 3. a marut (*H. Purāṇa*)

**Ćitraratha** (S) (M) 1. with a bright chariot. 3. a gandharva who was the son of sage Kaśyapa and a friend of the Pāṇḍavas (*M. Bh.*); a minister of Daśaratha who belonged to the Sūta dynasty (*V. Rāmāyaṇa*); a king of Sālva (*Br. Purāṇa*); a king of the dynasty of Bharata who was the son of King Gaya (*Bhāgavata*); a prince of Pānćāla who fought on the side of the Pāṇḍavas (*M. Bh.*); an Aṅga king and the husband of Prabhāvatī (*M. Bh.*); a yādava king who was the son of Uśaṅkhu and father of Śūra (*M. Bh.*); the son of Vīrabāhu and a friend of Rāma who married Hemā the daughter of Kuśa (*Rāmāyaṇa*); river of Purāṇic fame (*M. Bh.*); the king of the gandharvas (*A. Veda*); a descendant of Aṅga and son of Dharmaratha (*H. Purāṇa*); a son of Kṛṣṇa (*Bhāgavata*); a vidyādhara (*A. Koṣa*); another name for the Polar Star and the sun; a son of Uṣadgu.

**Ćitrarathī** (S) (F) 1. with a bright chariot. 3. a form of Durgā.

**Ćitraratī** (S) (F) granter of excellent gifts.

**Ćitrarekhā** (S) (F) 1. picture; a wonderful line. 3. an apsarā who was skilled in the art of painting (*A. Veda*); a daughter of Kuṣmāṇḍa (*Bhāgavata*)

**Ćitrarepha** (S) (M) 1. bright passion. 2. fire; heat; splendour. 3. a son of Medhātithi (*Bhāgavata*)

**Ćitrarūpa** (S) (M) 1. with a vareigated form. 3. an attendant of Śiva (*D. Bhāgavata*)

**Ćitraśarāsana** (S) (M) 1. wearer of a variegated armour. 3. a son of Dhṛtarāṣṭra (*M. Bh.*)

**Ćitrasenā** (S) (F) 1. with a bright spear. 3. an apsarā who danced in the court of Kubera (*M. Bh.*); a mother in Skanda's retinue (*M. Bh.*); a river (*M. Bh.*)

**Ćitrasena** (S) (M) 1. with a bright spear. 2. commander of a wonderful army. 3. a gandharva who was the son of Viśvāvasu and husband of Sandhyāvalī and Ratnāvalī and who became a friend of the Pāṇḍavas and instructed Arjuna in music and dancing (*M. Bh.*); a son of Dhṛtarāṣṭra who was with Duryodhana in the game of dice (*M. Bh.*); a son of the 13th Manu; a son of Gada; a divine recorder of the deeds of men; a Purū prince who was the son of Parīkṣit and grandson of Avīkṣit (*M. Bh.*); a minister of Jarāsandha (*M. Bh.*); a king of Abhisāra who fought on the side of the Kauravas (*M. Bh.*); a brother of Suśarmā the king of Tṛgārta (*M. Bh.*); a warrior of Pānćāla (*M. Bh.*); a son of Karṇa killed by Nakula (*M. Bh.*); a brother of Karṇa killed by Yudhamanyu (*M. Bh.*); a serpent who helped Arjuna (*M. Bh.*); a king of the dynasty of Vaivasvata Manu (*Bhā. Purāṇa*); the 13th Manu (*H. Purāṇa*); another name for Parīkṣit.

**Ćitraśikhaṇḍī** (S) (M) 1. bright crested. 3. the son of Aṅgiras (*M. Bh.*); another name for the Saptṛṣis, Viśvāmitra and the planet Jupiter.

**Ćitraśilā** (S) (F) 1. of strange character; stony. 3. a Purāṇic river (*M. Bh.*)

**Ćitraśrī** (S) (F) with divine beauty.

**Ćitrāśvā** (S) (M) 1. a painted horse. 2. with wonderful horses. 3. another name for Satyavān (*M. Bh.*)

**Ćitrasiras** (S) (M) 1. with a bright head. 3. a gandharva (*H. Purāṇa*)

**Ćitrasvana** (S) (M) 1. clear voiced. 3. a rākṣasa (*Bhāgavata*)

**Ćitravāhā** (S) (F) 1. with an extraordinary current. 3. a river of ancient India (*M. Bh.*)

**Ćitravāhana** (S) (M) 1. with decorated vehicles. 3. a king of Maṇipura and the father of Ćitrāṅgada (*M. Bh.*)

**Ćitravāja** (S) (M) 1. owning wonderful riches. 3. another name for the maruts.

**Ćitravalayā** (S) (F) 1. with a painted bracelet. 3. a goddess mentioned in the *Brahma Purāṇa*.

**Ćitravarmā** (S) (M) 1. with painted armour. 3. a son of Dhṛtarāṣṭra (*M. Bh.*); a Panćāla prince who was the son of Sućitra who fought on the side of the Pāṇḍavas (*M. Bh.*); the father of Sīmantinī (*Sk. Purāṇa*)

**Ćitravasu** (S) (M) with many treasures; rich in shining stars.

**Ćitrvatī** (S) (F) 1. decorated. 3. a daughter of Kṛṣṇa (*H. Purāṇa*)

**Ćitravegika** (S) (M) 1. moving with an unusual velocity. 3. a serpent of the family of Dhṛtarāṣṭra (*M. Bh.*)

**Ćitrayodhin** (S) (M) 1. fighting in many ways. 3. another name for Arjuna.

**Ćitrāyudha** (S) (M) 1. various weapons. 3. a son of Dhṛtarāṣṭra (*M. Bh.*); a king of Siṁhapuri who was defeated by Arjuna (*M. Bh.*); a warrior of Ćedi who fought on the side of the Pāṇḍavas (*M. Bh.*)

**Ćitreśa** (S) (M) 1. lord of Ćitrā. 2. wonderful lord. 3. the moon.

**Ćitriṇī** (S) (F) 1. endowed with marks of excellence. 2. brightly ornamented; with various talents.

**Ćitriśa** (S) (M) 1. lord of Ćitra; wonderful lord. 3. another name for the moon.

**Ćitritā** (S) (F) 1. variegated; painted. 2. decorated; decorated with ornaments.

**Ćitropaćitra** (S) (M) 1. brightly coloured. 2. vareigated. 3. a son of Dhṛtarāṣṭra (*M. Bh.*)

**Ćitrotpala** (S) (M) 1. with various lotus flowers. 3. a river of Purāṇic fame (*M. Bh.*)

**Ćitrūpa** (S) (M) 1. of the form of conciousness. 2. wise; intelligent; goodhearted. 3. another name for the Supreme Spirit.

**Ćittā** (S) (F) thoughtful; intellectual; spiritual.

**Ćitta** (S) (M) 1. thought; mind. 2. intellect; reason.

**Ćittabhoga** (S) (M) 1. fully conscious; enjoyer of mind. 2. wise; intelligent; thoughtful.

**Ćittahārin** (S) (M) one who captures the heart.

**Ćittaja** (S) (M) 1. born of the heart. 3. another name for Kāma, the lord of love.

**Ćittanātha** (S) (M) 1. lord of the soul. 3. the Supreme Being.

**Ćittapara** (S) (M) 1. beyond reason. 3. the Supreme Spirit.

**Ćittaprabha** (S) (M) the light of the soul.

**Ćittaprasāda** (S) (M) 1. gift of mind. 2. gladdening the mind; pleases the heart; charming.

**Ćittaprasādana** (S) (M) 1. gladdening the mind. 2. pleasing the heart; charming.

**Ćittaprasanna** (S) (M) 1. mentally happy. 2. cheerful; making others happy.

**Ćittarañjana** (S) (M) 1. pleasing the mind.

2. charming; loving.

**Ćittavata** (S) (M) 1. with a heart. 2. understanding; kindhearted.

**Ćittāyu** (S) (M) 1. the son of the heart. 2. born of the mind. 3. a king of the Purū dynasty who was the son of Bhadrāśva (*A. Purāṇa*)

**Ćitti** (S) (F) 1. thought. 2. devotion; thinking; understanding. 3. the wife of Atharvan and (*Bhāgavata*); mother of Dadhyać (*Bh. Purāṇa*)

**Ćittin** (S) (M) 1. thinker. 2. intelligent; wise.

**Ćitvana** (S) (M) 1. glance. 2. a look.

**Ćitvata** (S) (M) 1. endowed with mind. 2. wise; reasonable; logical.

**Ćityadyotā** (S) (F) 1. brightness conceived by imagination; enlightening the mind. 3. a class of deities (*D. Bhāgavata*)

**Ćivarin** (S) (M) 1. wearing rags. 2. lives austerely in accordance with the guidelines of religion. 3. another name for Buddhist and Jaina monks.

**Cokṣa** (S) (M) pure; clean; agreeable; pleasant.

**Ćola** (S) (M) 1. a long robe. 3. a righteous ruler of Kanćipura who gave his name to the kingdom and dynasty (*P. Purāṇa*)

**Ćūḍābhikṣuṇī** (S) (F) 1. a female ascetic who has a crest on the head; best among the ascetics. 3. a Buddhist goddess (*B. Literature*)

**Ćuḍakā** (S) (F) 1. forming the crest. 3. an apsarā.

**Ćūḍākaraṇa** (S) (M) 1. crest ceremony. 2. a particular ceremony in which ascetics and kings tie a lock of hair into a crest.

**Ćūḍālā** (S) (F) 1. with a lock of hair on the crown of the head. 3. the saintly wife of King Śikhidhvaja (*Yogavāśiṣṭha*)

**Ćūḍāmaṇī** (S) (M) 1. jewel worn on the crest. 2. excellent; best; Rosary Pea (*Abrus precatorius*)

**Ćūḍaratna** (S) (M) 1. jewel of the crest. 2. excellent; best.

**Ćūlin** (S) (M) 1. wearing an ornament on the crown. 3. a sage and spiritual father of Brahmadatta by the apsarā Somadā (*V. Rāmāyaṇa*)

**Ćumbā** (S) (F) 1. kiss. 2. adorable person.

**Ćumban** (S) (F) 1. kiss. 2. adorable person.

**Ćummum** (S) (M) 1. adorable. 3. the bird *Cheer phasianus wallichi*.

**Ćunanda** (S) (M) 1. perception. 2. learning. 3. a Buddhist mendicant (*L. Vistara*)

**Ćunću** (S) (M) 1. renowned. 3. a Hehaya king who was the grandson of Rohitāśva, the son of Harita and the father of King Vijaya (*Br. Purāṇa*)

**Ćuṇḍa** (S) (M) 1. perceptor. 2. to perceive; learn; understand. 3. a pupil of Śākyamuni (*M. Bh.*)

**Ćunnī** (S) (F) a small ruby.

**Ćupka** (S) (M) the Wooded Sandpiper (*Tringa glareola*)

**Ćyavana** (S) (M) 1. moving. 2. active; agile. 3. a celebrated sage of the Bhārgava dynasty who was the son of Bhṛgu and Pulomā and the husband of Sukanyā the daughter of King Śaryāti and was restored to youth and beauty by the aśvins (*A. Brāhmaṇa*); a son of Suhotra (*Bhāgavata*); a sage of the 2nd Manvantara (*H. Purāṇa*)

D

**Dabhīti** (S) (M) 1. injurer. 3. a hermit praised in the *Ṛg Veda*.

**Dadhića** (S) (M) 1. sprinkling milk or curd. 3. a ṛṣi son of Bhṛgu, made of the essences of the world and having a huge body (*Ku. Purāṇa*); the father of Sārasvata by the river Sarasvatī (*Vā. Purāṇa*) who discarded his life so that Indra could make a thunderbolt out of his bones to kill Vṛtrāsura (*M. Bh.*)

**Dadhijā** (S) (F) 1. daughter of milk; born of curd. 3. the goddess Lakṣmī who is considered to be the daughter of the sea and born from the Ocean of Milk.

**Dadhikṛā** (S) (M) 1. born from the Ocean of Milk. 2. fast in motion. 3. a divine horse who personifies the morning sun.

**Dadḥimukha** (S) (M) 1. milk-faced. 3. a nāga son of Kaśyapa and Kadru (*M. Bh.*); a yakṣa (*M. Bh.*); the brother-in-law of the monkey Sugrīva and general of his army (*V. Rāmāyaṇa*)

**Dadhinadī** (S) (F) 1. river of curd. 3. a river of ancient India (*M. Bh.*)

**Dadhipūraṇa** (S) (M) 1. living on milk. 2. full of milk. 3. a nāga (*M. Bh.*)

**Dadhivāhana** (S) (M) 1. with a chariot of milk. 2. curd-carrier. 3. a king of Bhāratā (*M. Bh.*); a prince who was the son of Anga and father of Divaratha (*M. Bh.*); a king of Ćampā (*M. Bh.*)

**Dadhivaktra** (S) (M) 1. milk faced. 3. the uncle of Sugrīva (*Rāmāyaṇa*)

**Dadhyān** (S) (M) 1. milk vendor. 2. bringer of milk. 3. a hermit to whom Indra taught the art of preparing rice in a particular manner for oblation (*Ṛg Veda*)

**Dagdharatha** (S) (M) 1. with a burnt chariot. 3. a gandharva (*M. Bh.*)

**Daha** (S) (M) 1. blazing. 2. very bright. 3. one of the 11 rudras, the son of Sthāṇu and grandson of Brahmā (*M. Bh.*); an attendant given to Skanda by the god Anśa (*M. Bh.*)

**Dahadahā** (S) (F) 1. blazing; destroying enemies. 3. a mother in Skanda's retinue (*M. Bh.*)

**Dahana** (S) (M) 1. burning; destroying. 3. a rudra; an attendant of Skanda (*Sk. Purāṇa*); another name for Agni, the lord of fire.

**Dahanapriyā** (S) (F) 1. beloved of fire. 3. the wife of Agni (*H. Koṣa*)

**Dahanolkā** (S) (F) firebrand.

**Dahati** (S) (M) 1. one who burns. 2. destroyer. 3. an attendant of Skanda given by the god Anśa (*M. Bh.*)

**Dahragni** (S) (M) 1. small fire. 3. Agāstya in a former birth.

**Daitya** (S) (M) 1. demon. 3. a class of demons who are sons of Kaśyapa and Diti (*M. Smṛti*); *Caesaria esculenta*.

**Daityadvīpa** (S) (M) 1. refuge of daityas. 3. a son of Garuḍa (*M. Bh.*)

**Daityahan** (S) (M) 1. slayer of daityas. 3. another name for Śiva.

**Daityanāśana** (S) (M) 1. destroyer of daityas. 3. another name for Viṣṇu.

**Daityaniṣudana** (S) (M) 1. destroyer of daityas. 3. another name for Indra.

**Daityapati** (S) (M) 1. lord of the daityas. 3. another name for Vṛtra.

**Daityāri** (S) (M) 1. enemy of the daityas. 3. another name for Kṛṣṇa.

**Daityasenā** (S) (F) 1. one who has an army of demons. 3. a daughter of Prajāpati, the sister of Devasenā and the wife of the asura Keśi (*M. Bh.*)

**Daityendra** (S) (M) 1. lord of the daityas. 3. another name for Vṛtra.

**Daivarāti** (S) (M) 1. of Devarata. 3. another name for Janaka.

**Daivya** (S) (M) 1. divine; glorious. 3. a messenger of the asuras (*T. Samhitā*)

**Ḍākinī** (S) (F) 1. witch. 3. a female magician attendant of Kālī (*Brah. Purāṇa*)

**Dakṣa** (S) (M) 1. able; talented. 2. fit; energetic; perfect; fire; gold. 3. an aditya identified with Prajāpati and the father of Kṛttikā (*T. Samhita*); a prajāpati born of the right thumb of Brahmā, the husband of Aśikni, the father of Satī who married Śiva, and was killed by Śiva (*D. Purāṇa*), to be later reborn as the mindborn son of the 10 Praćetases and Marīśa, the father of 24 daughters by Prasūti, as also of 60 daughters by Aśikni who became the lunar mansions and the mothers of gods, demons, men and animals (*V. Purāṇa*); a son of Garuḍa (*M. Bh.*); the bull of Śiva (*A. Koṣa*)

**Dakṣakanyā** (S) (F) **1.** an able daughter. **3.** daughter of Dakṣa; another name for Durgā.

**Dakṣaketu** (S) (M) **1.** with a golden banner. **3.** a son of Manu Dakṣasāvarṇa (*H. Purāṇa*)

**Dakṣakratuhara** (S) (M) **1.** able minded Śiva. **3.** another name for Śiva.

**Dakṣānila** (S) (M) a perfect breeze; a cold southern breeze.

**Dakṣapati** (S) (M) lord of the perfect; lord of the faculties.

**Dakṣāri** (S) (M) **1.** Dakṣa's foe. **2.** enemy of the perfect. **3.** another name for Śiva.

**Dakṣasāvarṇi** (S) (M) **1.** resembling gold; golden coloured. **2.** with a perfect nature. **3.** the 9th Manu (*V. Purāṇa*)

**Dakṣayana** (S) (M) coming from Dakṣa.

**Dakṣāyaṇi** (S) (F) **1.** coming from Dakṣa. **2.** gold; golden ornament; daughter of a perfect being. **3.** any daughter of Dakṣa; another name for the goddess Durgā.

**Dākṣāyaṇinyā** (S) (F) **1.** obtained from Dakṣa. **2.** gold; golden ornament; daughter of a perfect being. **3.** the Dākṣāyāṇi Aditi (*Mā Purāṇa*)

**Dakṣayaṇinya** (S) (M) **1.** obtained from Dakṣa. **2.** gold; golden ornament **3.** another name for the sun.

**Dakṣeśa** (S) (M) **1.** lord of Dakṣa. **3.** another name for Śiva.

**Dakṣeyu** (S) (F) **1.** striving for perfection; perfect. **3.** a daughter of Dakṣa and the mother of parrots (*V. Purāṇa*)

**Dāksi** (S) (M) son of Dakṣa; golden son; son of a perfect being.

**Dakṣiṇā** (S) (F) **1.** a donation to an officiating priest or god. **2.** fit; able; righthanded; towards the south; a prolific cow. **3.** the daughter of Ruči and Ākūti, the wife of Yajñapuruṣa (*V. Purāṇa*); the mother of a class of devas called the Yamas, as also of Phaladā – the god who awards the fruit of all actions, and reborn later as Suśilā a friend of Rādhā (*M. Bh.*); an idol of Durgā with its right side prominent (*D. Purāṇa*); the wife of Suyayña, the mother of Suyama and a previous incarnation of Lakṣmī (*Bhā Purāṇa*)

**Dakṣiṇa** (S) (M) right; the sense of direction; clever; fit; able; towards the south; candid; sincere.

**Dakṣiṇakālika** (S) (F) **1.** protectress of the south. **3.** a form of Durgā worshipped by the tāntrics (*T. Śastra*)

**Dakṣinam** (S) (M) **1.** right fire. **3.** a son of Agni.

**Dakṣināmūrti** (S) (M) **1.** the idol of the so· **3.** a tāntric form of Śiva (*T. Śastra*); a co (17th century).

**Dala** (S) (M) **1.** petal. **2.** fragment; ‹ ṗ. **3.** the son of the Ikṣvāku King Parī ‹a and Suśobhanā (*M. Bh.*)

**Daladhiśvara** (S) (M) lord of petals; leader of the group.

**Dalajā** (S) (F) **1.** produced from petals. **2.** honey.

**Dalajita** (S) (M) winning over a group.

**Dalakamala** (S) (M) lotus (*Nelumbo speciosum*)

**Dalakosā** (S) (F) treasure of petals; the jasmine flower.

**Dalamodaka** (S) (M) petal honey.

**Dalapati** (S) (M) **1.** leader of a group. **2.** master of petals. **3.** a prince.

**Dalbha** (S) (M) **1.** wheel. **3.** a ṛṣi (*M. Bh.*)

**Dalbhaghoṣa** (S) (M) **1.** sound of the whe ascetic; a person living in a grass hut. **3.** a s (*M. Bh.*)

**Dalbhya** (S) (M) **1.** belonging to wheels. **2.** a ascetic. **3.** a sage of Naimisaraṇya who was a member of Yudhiṣṭhira's court (*M. Bh.*)

**Dalmi** (S) (M) **1.** tearing. **3.** Indra's thunderbolt; another name for Indra.

**Dāmā** (S) (F) **1.** one who suppresses. **2.** wealthy; self-restrained. **3.** an attendant of Skanda (*M. Bh.*)

**Dama** (S) (M) **1.** wealth; house; home; self-restraint. **3.** a brother of Damayantī (*Nalopākhyāna*); a son of Dakṣa (*Bhā. Purāṇa*); a son of Marutta (*V. Purāṇa*); a mahāṛṣi (*M. Bh.*)

**Damaćandra** (S) (M) **1.** suppressing moon.

3. a mighty king who was a friend of Yudhiṣṭhira (*M. Bh.*)

**Damaghoṣa** (S) (M) 1. with a restrained voice. 3. a Ćedi prince and the father of Śiśupāla (*M. Bh.*)

**Dāmagranthi** (S) (M) 1. tied by a rope. 3. name assumed by Nakula in the court of Virāṭa (*M. Bh.*)

**Dāman** (S) (M) 1. rope; girdle; chaplet; wreath. 3. a friend of Kṛṣṇa.

**Damana** (S) (M) 1. subduing; taming. 2. overpowering; self controlled. 3. a son of Vasudeva and Rohiṇī (*H. Purāṇa*); a son of Bharadvāja (*Sk. Purāṇa*); a brother of Damayantī and son of King Bhīma; the son of King Paurava who fought on the side of the Kauravas (*M. Bh.*); a hermit who blessed King Bhīma to have children (*M. Bh.*); *Artemisia sieversiana*.

**Damanaka** (S) (M) 1. subduer; brave; powerful; four periods of time; six short syllables. 2. conqueror; a victor. 3. *Artemisia indica*; a daitya killed by Viṣṇu in his Matsya incarnation (*Sk. Purāṇa*)

**Damasvaśrī** (S) (F) 1. Dama's sister. 3. another name for Damayantī.

**Damati** (S) (M) subduer; conqueror.

**Damāya** (S) (M) 1. to control oneself. 3. a son of Marutta.

**Damayantī** (S) (F) 1. subduing men; self-restrained. 3. the daughter of King Bhīma of Vidarbha, the wife of King Nala, considered to be the most noble of Indian heroines (*Nalopākhyāna*); a daughter of Pramloća; a king of jasmine.

**Damayitri** (S) (M) 1. tamer or subduer. 3. another name for Viṣṇu and Śiva.

**Dambara** (S) (M) 1. self restrained. 3. an attendant given to Skanda by Brahmā (*M. Bh.*)

**Dambha** (S) (M) 1. pride. 2. deceit; ego. 3. an asura son of Vipraćitti and the father of Śankhaćuḍa (*D. Bh. Purāṇa*)

**Dambhodbhava** (S) (M) 1. born of deceit; son of pride. 3. a mighty emperor of the world subdued by Nara and Nārāyaṇa (*M. Bh.*)

**Dambholi** (S) (M) 1. weapon of the proud; a subduing weapon; Indra's thunderbolt. 3. a ṛṣi of the 1st Manvantara (*H. Purāṇa*)

**Dambholipāṇi** (S) (M) 1. holds a thunderbolt in his hand. 3. another name for Indra.

**Damin** (S) (M) self controlled.

**Dāmodara** (S) (M) 1. with a rope around the waist. 3. the 9th Arhat of the past Utsarpinī (*J. Literature*); a king of Kāśmira (*R. Taraṅginī*); a river held sacred by the Sāntāls (*A. Koṣa*); another name for Kṛṣṇa.

**Damoṣ** (S) (M) 1. bound. 2. wealthy; fortunate. 3. a sage in the assembly of Yudhiṣṭhira (*M. Bh.*)

**Damoṣṇīṣa** (S) (M) 1. desirous of wealth. 3. an ancient sage (*M. Bh.*)

**Damunas** (S) (M) 1. subduer; head of the family. 3. another name for Agni.

**Damya** (S) (M) tamable.

**Damyasārathī** (S) (M) 1. guide of those who can restrain themselves. 3. a Buddha (*B. Literature*)

**Dānaṇḍadā** (S) (F) 1. donates generously. 3. an apsarā or gāndharvi (*K. Vyuha*)

**Dānapati** (S) (M) 1. lord of generosity; munificent. 3. a daitya (*H. Purāṇa*); another name for Akrūra.

**Dānasāgara** (S) (M) ocean of generosity.

**Dānaśūra** (S) (M) 1. hero among the donors. 3. a Bodhisattva (*K. Sāgara*)

**Dānava** (S) (M) 1. of Danu; valiant; victor; conqueror. 3. dānavas are a class of demons described as the children of Kaśyapa and Danu and often identified with the daityas (*M. Bh.*)

**Dānavapati** (S) (M) 1. king of the dānavas. 3. another name for Indra.

**Dānavendra** (S) (M) 1. lord of the danavas. 3. another name for Vṛtra.

**Dānavīra** (S) (M) hero among the donors; an extremely generous man.

**Danāyus** (S) (F) 1. suppressed. 3. a daughter of Dakṣa; the wife of Kaśyapa and mother of Bala, Vikṣara, Vīra and Vrata (*M. Bh.*)

**Daṇḍa** (S) (M) 1. stick; staff; club. 3. punishment personified as the son of Dharma and Kriyā; a son of Ikṣvāku who was a partial incarnation of the asura Krodhahanta; the son of King Vidaṇḍa and brother of King Daṇḍadhara of Magadha (*M. Bh.*); an attendant of the sun (*M. Bh.*); a Ćedi warrior on the side of the Pāṇḍavas (*M. Bh.*); a rākṣasa son of Sumāli and Ketumatī (*U. Rāmāyaṇa*); another name for Yama, Śiva and Viṣṇu.

**Danḍabāhu** (S) (M) **1.** one who takes law in his own hands. **2.** punishing with his arms; just; a judge; an executioner. **3.** a warrior of Skanda (*M. Bh.*)

**Danḍadhāra** (S) (M) **1.** carrying a staff; punisher. **3.** a Magadha king who was a partial incarnation of the asura Krodhavardhana (*M. Bh.*); a son of Dhṛtarāṣṭra (*M. Bh.*); a Pāñćāla warrior on the side of the Pāṇḍavas (*M. Bh.*); another name for Yama.

**Danḍagaurī** (S) (F) **1.** goddess of punishment. **3.** an apsarā (*M. Bh.*)

**Danḍaka** (S) (M) **1.** a small staff; a pole; handle; beam; staff of a banner. **3.** a son of Ikṣvāku (*H. Purāṇa*)

**Dānḍakidakya** (S) (M) **1.** one who uses the staff amicably; good administrator. **2.** a stern ruler. **3.** a prince of the Tṛgarta tribe (*V. Purāṇa*)

**Danḍamukha** (S) (M) **1.** leader of a column. **2.** punishing by word of mouth; leader of an army; a general.

**Danḍanāyaka** (S) (M) **1.** chief justice. **2.** hero among the rod wielders; a judge. **3.** an attendant of the sun (*V's B. Samhitā*)

**Danḍapāṇi** (S) (M) **1.** staff handed. **2.** holding a staff in his hands. **3.** the leader of Śiva's troops (*Sk. Purāṇa*); the father of Buddha's wife Gopā (*L. Vistara*); the grandfather of Kṣemaka (*Bhāgavata*); a King who was the son of Vibhīnara and the father of Nimi (*Bhāgavata*); the son of King Paundraka of Kāśi (*P. Purāṇa*)

**Danḍasena** (S) (M) **1.** with an army of staffs. **2.** whose army wields staffs; a commander of executioners. **3.** a son of Viṣvakṣeṇa (*H. Purāṇa*)

**Danḍaśrī** (S) (M) **1.** best among the staffs. **2.** best judge; best administrator.

**Danḍavata** (S) (M) carrying a staff; with a large army; prostrating the body in a straight line; one who does not bow before anyone; full of self-respect; a leader; a commander.

**Danḍavīrya** (S) (M) power of the staff; possessed with ruling power; the general of an army.

**Danḍin** (S) (M) **1.** carrying a staff. **2.** a class of sannyāsins who carry a staff in their hands. **3.** an order of ascetics founded by Sankarāćārya (*Ś. Vijaya*); a son of Dhṛtarāṣṭra (*M. Bh.*); a god worshipped as an attendant of the sun (*A. Purāṇa*); a Sanskṛt critic of the Gupta reign (6th century A.D.) (*A. Koṣa*); another name for Yama and Manjuśrī.

**Daṇśa** (S) (M) **1.** sting; bite. **2.** wrathful; jealous; doesn't forgive and forget enemies. **3.** a rākṣasa who was turned into a beetle (*M. Bh.*)

**Danṣtranivāsin** (S) (M) **1.** teeth dweller; surrounded by teeth. **2.** the tongue. **3.** a yakṣa.

**Danṣtrin** (S) (M) **1.** bearer of teeth; tusked. **3.** another name for Śiva.

**Dantā** (S) (F) **1.** tamed; mild; having teeth. **3.** an apsarā (*M. Bh.*)

**Dānta** (S) (M) **1.** subdued; tamed; tooth. **2.** mild; patient. **3.** the Indian fig tree (*Ficus indica*); the son of King Bhīma of Vidarbha (*M. Bh.*)

**Dantadhvaja** (S) (M) **1.** tusk-bannered. **3.** a son of Manu Tāmasa (*Vām. Purāṇa*)

**Dantamukha** (S) (M) **1.** with a tooth on the face; tusked. **3.** an asura killed by Skanda (*Sk. Purāṇa*)

**Dantapattraka** (S) (M) **1.** with teeth like petals. **2.** the Jasmine flower.

**Dantavaktra** (S) (M) **1.** tusked; tooth protruding out of mouth. **2.** fierce; terrible. **3.** a Karūṣa king who was an incarnation of Viṣṇu's doorkeeper Vijaya who was killed by Kṛṣṇa and returned to Vaikunṭha; another name for Gaṇeśa.

**Dānti** (S) (F) patience; self restraint.

**Dantin** (S) (M) **1.** tusked. **3.** another name for Gaṇeśa.

**Dantivaktra** (S) (M) **1.** elephant faced. **3.** another name for Gaṇeśa.

**Danu** (S) (F) **1.** noisy; high-pitched. **2.** growler. **3.** a daughter of Dakṣa, the wife of Kaśyapa and the mother of the 100 dānavas (*M. Bh.*)

**Danu** (S) (M) **1.** noisy; high-pitched; one who shouts. **3.** a son of Śrī who was changed into a monster by Indra (*Rāmāyaṇa*); a king who was the father of Rambha and Karambha (*M. Purāṇa*)

**Dānu** (S) (M) 1. liberal; courageous. 2. prosperity; contentment. 3. air; wind.

**Danuja** (S) (M) born of Danu; a dānava.

**Danujadviṣa** (S) (M) 1. enemy of the dānava. 3. another name for Indra.

**Dāraka** (S) (M) 1. breaking; splitting. 3. Kṛṣṇa's charioteer.

**Darbha** (S) (M) sacrificial grass used in oblations (*Saccharum cylindricum*)

**Darbhi** (S) (M) 1. with sacrificial grass. 2. an ascetic. 3. a hermit who is supposed to have brought the 4 oceans to his bath in Kurukṣetra (*M. Bh.*)

**Dardura** (S) (M) 1. big; terrible; with caves. 3. a mountain personified by a deity in the court of Kubera (*M. Bh.*)

**Dari** (S) (M) 1. splitting; opening. 2. moving slowly. 3. a nāga born in the family of Dhṛtarāṣṭra (*M. Bh.*)

**Daridra** (S) (M) 1. roving; strolling; poor. 3. a Yayāti king who was the son of Dundubhi and father of Vasu (*Bhāgavata*)

**Darpa** (S) (M) 1. pride; arrogance. 3. pride personified as the son of Adharmā and Śrī (*M. Bh.*); a Yayāti king (*Bhāgavata*)

**Darpada** (S) (M) 1. pride inducer; creator of pride. 3. another name for Śiva.

**Darpahan** (S) (M) 1. destroyer of ego. 3. another name for Śiva.

**Darpahara** (S) (M) 1. eliminator of ego. 3. another name for Śiva.

**Darpaka** (S) (M) 1. pride. 3. another name for Kāma.

**Darpaṇa** (S) (M) 1. inducing vanity. 2. a mirror.

**Darpanārāyaṇa** (S) (M) 1. shielding men from vanity. 3. a king (*Kathārṇava*)

**Darpaṇikā** (S) (F) a small mirror.

**Darśa** (S) (M) 1. looking at; worth looking at. 3. the day of the new moon personified as the son of Dhātṛ (*Bhāgavata*); another name for Kṛṣṇa.

**Darśana** (S) (M) seeing; philosophy; showing; observing; discernment; vision; audience.

**Darśanapāla** (S) (M) protector of vision; a philosopher; a scholar of philosophy.

**Darśanī** (S) (F) 1. worth looking at. 3. another name for goddess Durgā.

**Darśanīya** (S) (M) 1. worth seeing. 2. visible; beautiful; worthy of being seen.

**Darśanojjvalā** (S) (F) 1. of brilliant aspect; fair to look at. 2. the Jasmine.

**Darśata** (S) (M) 1. making things visible. 2. glowing; visible; conspicuous; beautiful. 3. another name for the sun and the moon.

**Darśataśrī** (S) (F) of noticeable beauty.

**Darśayāminī** (S) (F) a night that is worth seeing; night of the new moon.

**Dāru** (S) (M) liberal.

**Dāruka** (S) (M) 1. a small piece of wood. 2. breaking; splitting. 3. an incarnation of Śiva (*Ś. Purāṇa*); the charioteer of Mahiṣāsura (*D. Bh. Purāṇa*); a son of Garuḍa (*M. Bh.*); the charioteer of Kṛṣṇa (*M. Bh.*)

**Dāruki** (S) (M) 1. a small piece of wood; breaking; splitting. 3. Pradyumna's charioteer (*Bhā. Purāṇa*)

**Dāruṇa** (S) (M) as hard as wood.

**Dārvan** (S) (M) 1. the hood of a snake. 3. a son of Uśīnara (*Bhā. Purāṇa*)

**Dārvanda** (S) (M) a peacock.

**Darvarīka** (S) (M) 1. wind. 3. another name for Indra.

**Darvi** (S) (M) 1. wooden ladle. 2. the hood of a snake. 3. a son of Uśīnara (*V. Purāṇa*)

**Daśabāhu** (S) (M) 1. 10 armed. 3. that form of Śiva in which he performs the tāṇḍava or the cosmic dance.

**Daśabala** (S) (M) 1. possessing 10 powers. 3. a Buddha (*B. Literature*)

**Daśadhanuṣ** (S) (M) 1. 10 bowed. 2. owner; 10 bows; a perfect archer. 3. an ancestor of Śākyamuni (*D. Śastra*)

**Daśadyu** (S) (M) 1. equivalent to 10 heavens; very powerful. 3. a hermit (*Ṛg Veda*)

**Daśagrīva** (S) (M) 1. 10 necked. 3. a rākṣasa (*M. Bh.*); a son of Damaghoṣa (*G. Purāṇa*)

**Daśaharā** (S) (F) 1. eliminator of 10; destroyer of 10. 2. taking away 10 sins. 3. another name for the Gaṅgā.

**Daśajyoti** (S) (M) 1. 10 flamed. 2. whose

glory spreads in 10 directions. 3. a son of Suhṛt (*M. Bh.*); a son of Subhrāj (*M. Bh.*)

**Daśakandhara** (S) (M) 1. ten necked. 3. another name for Rāvaṇa.

**Daśakaṇṭha** (S) (M) 1. 10 necked. 3. another name for Rāvaṇa.

**Daśakaṇṭhajita** (S) (M) 1. conquering the 10 necked one. 3. Rāma, who conquered the 10 headed Rāvaṇa.

**Daśaketu** (S) (M) with 10 banners.

**Daśamālika** (S) (F) with 10 garlands.

**Daśamukha** (S) (M) 1. 10 faced. 3. another name for Rāvaṇa.

**Daśamukharipu** (S) (M) 1. enemy of the 10 faced one. 2. enemy of Rāvaṇa. 3. another name for Rāma.

**Daśānana** (S) (M) 1. 10 faced. 3. another name for Rāvaṇa.

**Dāśanandinī** (S) (F) 1. daughter of a fisherman. 3. another name for Satyavatī.

**Daśarāja** (S) (M) 1. master of the 10 directions. 2. master of the universe. 3. the foster father of Śāntanu's wife Satyavatī (*M. Bh.*)

**Daśaratha** (S) (M) 1. with 10 chariots. 3. the Ikṣvāku king of Ayodhyā and the son of Aja and Indumatī or Ilabilā, husband of Kauśalyā, Kaikeyī and Sumitrā, and father of Śāntā, Rāma, Bharata, Lakṣmana and Śatrughna (*V. Rāmāyaṇa*); a son of Navaratha (*Bhā. Purāṇa*); son of Suyaśas (*H. Purāṇa*)

**Dāśarathi** (S) (M) 1. of Daśaratha. 3. patronymic of Rāma and Lakṣmaṇa (*V. Rāmāyaṇa*); the 8th black Jaina Vasudeva (*J. S. Koṣa*)

**Daśardhabāṇa** (S) (M) 1. 5 arrowed. 3. another name for Kāma.

**Daśārha** (S) (M) 1. destroyer of 10, eliminator of 10. 2. taking away 10 sins. 3. a warrior tribe and its Yadu dynasty king (*Bhāgavata*); another name for Kṛṣṇa.

**Dāśarhābhartā** (S) (M) 1. chief of the Dāśarhās. 3. another name for Kṛṣṇa.

**Daśarhādhipa** (S) (M) 1. lord of the Daśarha tribe. 3. another name for Kṛṣṇa.

**Daśarhakulavardhana** (S) (M) 1. increasing the Daśarha tribe. 3. another name for Kṛṣṇa.

**Daśarhanandana** (S) (M) 1. son of the Daśarha tribe. 3. another name for Kṛṣṇa.

**Daśarhanātha** (S) (M) 1. lord of the Daśarha tribe. 3. another name for Kṛṣṇa.

**Daśarhasiṁha** (S) (M) 1. lion of the Daśarha tribe. 3. another name for Kṛṣṇa.

**Daśarhavīra** (S) (M) 1. hero of the Daśarha tribe. 3. another name for Kṛṣṇa.

**Daśārṇa** (S) (M) 1. 10 lakes. 3. a country and its king (*M. Bh.*)

**Daśārṇeyu** (S) (M) 1. master of 10 lakes. 3. a son of Raudrāśva (*H. Purāṇa*)

**Daśarūpa** (S) (M) 1. the 10 forms. 3. the 10 forms of Viṣṇu.

**Daśaśarman** (S) (M) protecting 10; with 10 joys.

**Daśāśva** (S) (M) 1. with 10 horses. 3. a son of Ikṣvāku (*M. Bh.*)

**Daśāsya** (S) (M) 1. ten mouthed. 3. another name for Rāvaṇa.

**Daśāsyajit** (S) (M) 1. conqueror of Rāvaṇa. 3. another name for Rāma.

**Daśavājin** (S) (M) 1. with 10 horses. 3. another name for the moon.

**Daśavara** (S) (M) 1. with 10 faces. 3. an asura attendant of Varuṇa (*M. Bh.*)

**Dāśeyī** (S) (F) 1. fisherman's daughter. 3. another name for Satyavatī.

**Dāsī** (S) (F) 1. servant; devotee. 3. an important river of ancient India (*M. Bh.*); the *Leea aequata* shrub.

**Dasmata** (S) (M) desirable; acceptable.

**Dasmaya** (S) (M) beautiful.

**Dasra** (S) (M) 1. accomplishing wonderful deeds; giving marvellous aid. 3. one of the twins known as the Aśvinikumāras who were the divine physicians (*A. Veda*)

**Dasrasū** (S) (F) 1. mother of the aśvins. 3. another name for Sanjñā.

**Dāśu** (S) (M) worshipping; sacrificing.

**Dāśūra** (S) (M) holy; pious.

**Dāśūrī** (S) (M) devout; pious.

**Dasyu** (S) (M) 1. outcast. 3. a class of demons slain by Indra.

**Datta** (S) (M) 1. given; granted. 2. presented. 3. a sage in the 2nd Manvantara (*H. Purāṇa*); the 7th Jaina Vasudeva (*H. Koṣa*); the 8th

Tirthaṅkara of the past Utsarpinī.

**Dattātman** (S) (M) 1. given the soul. 2. with total concentration of the mind; performing his duty sincerely. 3. a viśvadeva (*M. Bh.*)

**Dattādatta** (S) (M) 1. given and received; transaction. 2. a businessman.

**Dattādevī** (S) (F) 1. goddess of gifts. 3. the wife of Samudragupta and mother of Ćandragupta II.

**Dattāmitra** (S) (M) 1. given to a friend. 3. the Sauvira prince Sumitra (*Bhā. Purāṇa*)

**Dattātreya** (S) (M) 1. given by Atri. 3. a famous Purāṇic hermit, and the son of Atri and Anasūyā, considered an incarnation of Mahāviṣṇu, his penance caused Brahmā, Viṣṇu and Śiva to partially incarnate themselves as his sons Soma, Datta and Durvāsas (*M. Bh./H. Purāṇa/V. Purāṇa*); another name for the 3 headed divinity of Viṣṇu, Śiva and Brahmā.

**Datti** (S) (F) a gift.

**Dattoli** (S) (M) 1. given the heart. 2. fully engrossed. 3. a son of Pulastya and Prīti (*V. Purāṇa*)

**Dattra** (S) (M) Indra's gift.

**Dattravat** (S) (M) rich in gifts.

**Dāva** (S) (M) 1. wild fire. 3. another name for Agni.

**Dayā** (S) (F) 1. compassion; sympathy; pity. 3. compassion personified as the daughter of Dakṣa and mother of Abhaya (*Bhā. Purāṇa*)

**Dāyāda** (S) (M) to whom the transaction is made; son; inheritor.

**Dāyādī** (S) (F) to whom the inheritance is given; daughter; heiress.

**Dayākara** (S) (M) 1. showing compassion. 2. compassionate. 3. another name for Śiva.

**Dayākūrća** (S) (M) 1. store of compassion. 3. another name for Buddha.

**Dayāla** (S) (M) compassionate; tender; merciful.

**Dayānidhi** (S) (M) treasure house of mercy.

**Dayanīta** (S) (M) compassionate conduct.

**Dayānvitā** (S) (F) surrounded by mercy; full of mercy.

**Dayārāma** (S) (M) pervaded with mercy.

**Dayāsāgara** (S) (M) ocean of compassion.

**Dayāśaṅkara** (S) (M) Śiva the compassionate.

**Dayāvatī** (S) (F) full of mercy.

**Dayāvīra** (S) (M) heroically compassionate.

**Dayitā** (S) (F) worthy of compassion; beloved; cherished; dear.

**Dayita** (S) (M) worthy of compassion; cherished; beloved; dear.

**Dehabhṛt** (S) (M) 1. of the body; bearer of a body. 2. corporeal. 3. another name for Śiva.

**Dehabhuj** (S) (M) 1. possessing a body. 3. another name for Śiva.

**Dehaja** (S) (M) 1. born of a body. 2. child. 3. another name for Kāma.

**Deheśvara** (S) (M) 1. lord of the body. 2. the soul.

**Dehinī** (S) (F) 1. of the body. 2. corporeal; bearer of a body. 3. another name for the earth.

**Deśaka** (S) (M) one who directs; ruler; guide; perceptor.

**Deśākhya** (S) (M) 1. famous in land. 2. internal. 3. a rāga.

**Deśapālī** (S) (F) 1. protected by the country. 2. belonging to the country; a native. 3. a rāga.

**Deśaraj** (S) (M) king of a country; produced in the right country; of genuine descent.

**Deśarāja** (S) (M) king of a country.

**Deśkārī** (S) (F) 1. done by country. 3. a rāginī.

**Deśnā** (S) (F) gift; offering.

**Deśtrī** (S) (F) 1. pointer; indicator. 3. an apsarā (*Ṛg Veda*)

**Deva** (S) (M) 1. light; divine; deity; playing divinely; a god. 3. a class of gods which includes the maruts, apsarās, vidyādharas, tuśitas, gandharvas, nāgas, kinnaras, guhyakas, anilas, aśvins, rudras, adityas, vasus, visvadevas, etc. there are 33 crore, devas presided over by 33 presiding spirits with Indra as the chief (*Vedas/Purāṇas*); the 22nd Jaina Arhat of the future Utsarpinī (*J.S. Koṣa*); a title of honour; the Kadamba tree (*Anthocephalus cadamba*); *Momordica balsamina*.

**Devabāhu** (S) (M) 1. the arm of the gods. 3. a son of Hṛdika (*Bhāgavata*); a ṛṣi (*H Purāṇa*)

**Devabala** (S) (M) with the strength of the gods.

**Devabālā** (S) (F) 1. daughter of the gods. 3. Jelly Leaf (*Sida rhombofolia*)

**Devabali** (S) (M) oblation to the gods.

**Devabandhu** (S) (M) 1. a friend of the gods. 2. belonging to the gods. 3. a Yayāti king (*Bhā. Purāṇa*); a son of Śūra and brother of Vasudeva (*Bhāgavata*); a ṛṣi who was the son of Śruta (*K. Sāgara*)

**Devabhakta** (S) (M) devotee of the gods.

**Devabhaga** (S) (M) 1. a portion of the gods. 3. a brother of Vasudeva (*Bh. Purāṇa*)

**Devabhrāja** (S) (M) 1. luminous like a god. 3. a son of Mahya and grandson of Vivasvata (*M. Bh.*)

**Devabhrātā** (S) (M) 1. brother of the gods. 3. an effulgent devata who was the son of Ravi and father of Subhrāta (*M. Bh.*)

**Devabhūti** (S) (M) 1. an image of the gods. 3. the last prince of the Śuṅga dynasty (*V. Purāṇa*)

**Devabodha** (S) (M) with divine knowledge.

**Devabodhi** (S) (M) inspired by god.

**Devaćandra** (S) (M) moon among the gods.

**Devaććanda** (S) (M) divine necklace; a bright necklace; a necklace of pearls.

**Devaćitta** (S) (M) the will of the gods.

**Devadarśa** (S) (M) 1. preceptor of the divine. 2. preceptor of heaven; observer of the gods. 3. a teacher in the line of Vyāsa who was the disciple of Kabandha (*M. Bh.*)

**Devadarśana** (S) (M) 1. familiar with the gods. 3. another name for sage Nārada.

**Devadāsa** (S) (M) slave of the gods.

**Devadattā** (S) (F) 1. given by the gods. 3. the mother of Gautama Buddha's cousin Devadatta (*B. Literature*)

**Devadatta** (S) (M) 1. god given. 3. one of the 5 vital airs; a cousin of Gautama Buddha (*B. Literature*); a son of Uruśravas and father of Agniveśya (*Bh. Purāṇa*); a son of King Jayadatta (*K. Sāgara*); a son of Haridatta (*K. Sāgara*); the father of Utathya (*M. Bh.*); the conchshell of Arjuna (*M. Bh.*); a nāga (*Bhāgavata*)

**Devadeva** (S) (M) 1. lord of the gods. 3. another name for Kṛṣṇa.

**Devadeveśvara** (S) (M) 1. lord of the gods. 3. another name for Kṛṣṇa.

**Devadhānī** (S) (F) 1. divine abode. 3. Indra's city (*Bh. Purāṇa*)

**Devadharman** (S) (M) performing heavenly deeds.

**Devādhipa** (S) (M) 1. lord of the gods. 2. a king identified with the asura Nikumbha (*M. Bh.*); another name for Indra.

**Devādhipati** (S) (M) 1. lord of the gods. 3. another name for Śiva.

**Devadīpa** (S) (M) lamp of the gods; the eye.

**Devadundubhi** (S) (M) 1. drum of the gods. 3. the sacred basil with red flowers (*Ocimum sanctum*); another name for Indra.

**Devadūta** (S) (M) messenger of the gods.

**Devadyumna** (S) (M) 1. glory of the gods. 3. a king of the Bharata dynasty who was the son of Devatajita and the father of Parameṣṭhin (*Bhā. Purāṇa*)

**Devadyuti** (S) (M) 1. with heavenly lustre. 3. a ṛṣi (*P. Purāṇa*)

**Devagaṇeśvara** (S) (M) 1. lord of the divine people. 2. lord of the gaṇas. 3. another name for Indra.

**Devagarbhā** (S) (F) 1. the womb of the gods. 2. divine child. 3. a river of ancient India (*Bhā. Purāṇa*)

**Devagarbha** (S) (M) 1. the womb of the gods. 2. divine child. 3. a ṛṣi (*P. Purāṇa*)

**Devagāyana** (S) (M) a divine song; celestial songster; a gandharva.

**Devaghoṣa** (S) (M) voice of the gods; village of the gods; the abode of godly virtues.

**Devagirī** (S) (F) 1. divine knowledge. 3. a rāgiṇī.

**Devago** (S) (F) 1. divine protectress. 3. a form of Śakti (*T. Śastra*)

**Devagopa** (S) (M) shepherd of the gods; guarded by the gods.

**Devaguhya** (S) (M) 1. hidden by the gods. 3. father of Sārvabhauma (*Bhāgavata*)

**Devagupta** (S) (M) guarded by the gods.

**Devaguru** (S) (M) 1. preceptor of the gods. 2. father of the gods. 3. another name for Kaśyapa and Bṛhaspati.

**Devahans** (S) (M) 1. divine duct. 3. the White-winged Wood Duck (*Cairina scutulata*)

**Devahavis** (S) (M) oblation to the gods.

**Devahavya** (S) (M) 1. sacrificing to the gods. 3. a sage who is a member of Indra's assembly (*M. Bh.*)

**Devahotra** (S) (M) 1. making oblations to the gods. 3. a maharṣi who was the father of Yogeśvara and considered a partial incarnation of Viṣṇu (*H. Purāṇa*)

**Devahṛada** (S) (M) divine heart; divine pool.

**Devahū** (S) (M) invoking the gods.

**Devahūtī** (S) (F) 1. invocation of the gods. 3. a daughter of Manu Svāyambhuva, wife of Prajāpati Kardama, and the mother of Kapila (*Bh. Purāṇa*)

**Devaja** (S) (M) 1. born of the gods. 3. a son of Saṅyama (*Ṛg Veda*)

**Devajāmi** (S) (F) sister of the gods.

**Devajapa** (S) (M) 1. meditating on the gods. 3. a vidyādhara (*K. Sāgara*)

**Devajayā** (S) (F) wife of the gods.

**Devajuṣṭa** (S) (M) agreeable to the gods.

**Devajūta** (S) (M) attached to the gods; inspired by the gods.

**Devajūti** (S) (M) 1. attached to the gods. 3. an āditya (*T. Samhitā*)

**Devaka** (S) (M) 2. heavenly; godly; celestial. 3. a Yayāti king who was the son of Ugrasena's brother Āhuka and the father of Kṛṣṇa's mother Devakī (*M. Bh.*); a king whose daughter married Vidura (*M. Bh.*); a son of Yudhiṣṭhira and Pauravī (*M. Bh.*); a son of Akrūra (*Bha. Purāṇa*)

**Devakalaśa** (S) (M) receptacle of the gods.

**Devakalpa** (S) (M) god like.

**Devakāma** (S) (M) striving for divinity; loving the gods; pious.

**Devakanćanā** (S) (F) 1. divine gold. 3. the tree *Bauhinea purpurea*.

**Devakānta** (S) (M) beloved of the gods.

**Devakanyā** (S) (F) celestial maiden.

**Devakī** (S) (F) 1. divine; glorious; pious. 3. the daughter of Devaka, wife of Vasudeva, the mother of Kṛṣṇa and the reincarnation of Aditī the wife of Kaśyapa (*Bhāgavata*)

**Devakīnandana** (S) (M) 1. son of Devakī. 3. another name for Kṛṣṇa.

**Devakīputra** (S) (M) 1. son of Devakī. 3. another name for Kṛṣṇa.

**Devakirī** (S) (F) 1. tongue of the gods. 3. a rāginī in music regarded as the wife of Megharāja.

**Devakīrti** (S) (M) with heavenly fame.

**Devakīsūnu** (S) (M) 1. son of Devakī. 3. another name for Kṛṣṇa.

**Devakoṣa** (S) (M) receptacle of the gods.

**Devakrī** (S) (F) 1. myth. 3. a rāga.

**Devakṣatra** (S) (M) 1. domain of the gods. 3. a Yayāti king who was the son of Devarāta (*H. Purāṇa*)

**Devakṣema** (S) (M) assistant of the gods.

**Devakulyā** (S) (F) 1. divine pitcher; belonging to the gods. 3. another name for the holy Gaṅgā, the river of the gods personified as the daughter of Pūrṇiman and the granddaughter of Marīćī (*Bhāgavata*); the wife of Udgītha (*Bhā. Purāṇa*)

**Devakumāra** (S) (M) son of a deva.

**Devakusuma** (S) (F) divine flower; cloves.

**Devalā** (S) (F) 1. attached to the gods; music personified. 3. the daughter of Āhuka and sister of Dhṛti and Ugrasena (*Bhā. Purāṇa*); a rāginī.

**Devala** (S) (M) 1. attached to the gods. 2. an attendant to an idol. 3. a descendant of Kaśyapa and an author of *Ṛg Veda* (ix); a son of Muni Asita and the husband of Ekaparṇā (*M. Bh.*); a ṛṣi who was the son of Pratyūṣa (*H. Purāṇa*); an elder brother of ṛṣi Dhaumya and the father of Suvarćalā who married Śvetaketu (*M. Bh.*); the father of Saṅnatī (*H. Purāṇa*); a son of Viśvāmitra (*H. Purāṇa*); a son of Kṛṣtāśva and Dhīṣaṇā (*Bhāgavata*)

**Devalatā** (S) (F) 1. divine vine. 2. the Double jasmine (*Jasminum sambac*)

**Devalekhā** (S) (F) a divine line; with a divine outline; a celestial beauty.

**Devamadana** (S) (M) gladdening or inspiring the gods.

**Devamadhu** (S) (M) divine honey; nectar.

**Devamālā** (S) (F) 1. divine garland. 3. an apsarā (*M. Bh.*)

**Devamāṇaka** (S) (M) 1. jewel of the gods. 3. the jewel on Viṣṇu's breast (*A. Koṣa*)

**Devamaṇi** (S) (F) jewel of the gods.

**Devamaṇi** (S) (M) 1. jewel among the gods. 3. another name for Śiva.

**Devamañjara** (S) (M) 1. divine jewel. 3. the jewel on Viṣṇu's breast (*A. Koṣa*)

**Devamata** (S) (M) 1. approved by the gods. 3. a ṛṣi (*M. Bh*)

**Devamatī** (S) (F) 1. godly minded. 2. meritorious; virtuous; venerated.

**Devamātrā** (S) (F) 1. equivalent to a god. 3. a mother in Skanda's retinue (*M. Bh.*)

**Devamātṛ** (S) (F) 1. mother of the gods. 3. another name for Dākṣāyāṇī (*H. Purāṇa*)

**Devamaya** (S) (M) consisting of the gods; the abode of all virtues.

**Devamāyī** (S) (F) divine illusion.

**Devamidha** (S) (M) 1. god begotten. 3. the grandfather of Vasudeva (*M. Bh.*); a descendant of Nimi and Janaka (*Rāmāyaṇa*)

**Devamīdhusa** (S) (M) 1. bestowed by the gods; divinely liberal. 3. son of Śūra.

**Devamiśra** (S) (M) a godly mixture; connected with the gods.

**Devamitrā** (S) (F) 1. friend of the gods. 3. a mother in Skanda's retinue (*M. Bh.*)

**Devamitra** (S) (M) 1. a friend of the gods. 3. the father of Viṣṇumitra (*M. Bh.*)

**Devamuni** (S) (M) 1. divine sage. 3. a son of Iraṇmadā and the part author of *Ṛg Veda* (x)

**Devanābha** (S) (M) celestial navel; the origin of celestial beings; the supreme god.

**Devanadī** (S) (F) 1. river of the gods. 3. a river personified as a deity in Varuṇa's court (*M. Bh.*); another name for the Gaṅgā.

**Devanāṅganā** (S) (F) divine woman.

**Devanaman** (S) (M) bowing before the gods.

**Devanandā** (S) (F) 1. joy of the gods. 3. an apsarā (*S. Dvātrinśika*)

**Devānanda** (S) (M) joy of the gods.

**Devanandin** (S) (M) 1. amusing the gods. 3. Indra's doorkeeper (*A. Koṣa*)

**Devanātha** (S) (M) 1. lord of the gods. 3. another name for Śiva.

**Devanāyaka** (S) (M) leader of the gods.

**Devānīka** (S) (M) 1. an army of gods. 3. a king belonging to the solar dynasty of Rāma, who was the son of Kṣhemadhanvan and the father of Ṛkṣa (*Rāmāyaṇa*); the son of the 11th Manu (*H. Purāṇa*)

**Devanirmita** (S) (M) 1. made by god. 2. perfect; god's creation.

**Devānna** (S) (M) food offered to the gods; sacred; auspicious.

**Devānśa** (S) (M) a partial incarnation of the gods.

**Devanta** (S) (M) 1. killer of the gods. 3. a son of Hṛdika (*Bhā. Purāṇa*)

**Devāntaka** (S) (M) 1. killer of the gods. 3. a rākṣasa who was the son of Rudraketu and was slain by Gaṇapati (*P. Purāṇa*)

**Devajanman** (S) (M) 1. born of the gods. 2. the child of the gods. 3. another name for Yudhiṣṭhira (*M. Bh.*)

**Devānućara** (S) (M) follower of the gods.

**Devapāda** (S) (M) the feet of the god.

**Devapāla** (S) (M) 1. defender of the gods. 3. a mountain (*Bh. Purāṇa*)

**Devapālita** (S) (M) protected by the gods.

**Devapaṇḍita** (S) (M) scholar of heavenly rites; a divine scholar.

**Devapāṇi** (S) (M) 1. god handed; hand of the gods. 2. assisting the gods; helpful to the gods. 3. a class of asuras (*M. Smriti*)

**Devapatha** (S) (M) 1. the path of the gods. 3. another name for the Milky Way or the Akāś Gaṅgā.

**Devāpi** (S) (M) 1. friend of the gods. 3. a lunar dynasty king who became a sage, was the son of King Pratīpa and is supposed to be still alive (*M. Bh.*); a Ćedi warrior on the side of the Pāṇḍavas (*M. Bh.*)

**Devaprabha** (S) (M) 1. with divine splendour. 3. a gandharvī (*K. Sāgara*)

**Devaprasāda** (S) (M) given by the gods.

**Devapratha** (S) (M) 1. custom of the gods. 2. follower of the customs of the gods; virtuous; meritorious; venerated. 3. a Yayāti dynasty king (*Bhāgavata*)

**Devapratimā** (S) (F) image of the gods; an idol.

**Devapriya** (S) (M) 1. dear to the gods. 3. another name for Śiva; and for Kārttikeya as the consort of Devasena; *Wedelia calendulacea.*

**Devapūjita** (S) (M) 1. worshipped by the gods. 3. another name for Kṛṣṇa and Bṛhaspati.

**Devapūjya** (S) (M) 1. honoured by the gods. 3. another name for Bṛhaspati the preceptor of the gods and the planet Jupiter.

**Devapuṣpa** (S) (M) flower of the gods.

**Devārādhanā** (S) (F) worship of the gods.

**Devarāja** (S) (M) 1. king of the gods. 3. a king in the assembly of Yama (*M. Bh.*); a Buddha; another name for Indra.

**Devarakṣitā** (S) (F) 1. protected by the gods. 3. a daughter of Devaka and sister of Devakī, the mother of Kṛṣṇa.

**Devaraktadanṣī** (S) (F) 1. favoured by gods. 3. a rāgiṇī.

**Devarāma** (S) (M) 1. absorbed in divine deeds. 2. meritorious; virtuous; venerated.

**Devāraṇya** (S) (M) the garden of the gods.

**Devarāta** (S) (M) 1. delighting in the gods; attached to the gods. 2. pious; religious; god given. 3. a Mithilā king Śunahśepa after coming into the family of Viśvāmitra (*A. Brāhmaṇa*); a king who was the son of Suketu and descendant of Nimi (*Rāmāyaṇa*); the son of Karambhi (*Purāṇas*); the father of Yājñavalkya (*Bhā. Purāṇa*)

**Devaratha** (S) (M) vehicle of the gods.

**Devarati** (S) (F) 1. delight of the gods. 3. an apsarā (*K. Sāgara*)

**Devārćaka** (S) (M) devotee of the gods.

**Devārha** (S) (M) worthy of the gods.

**Devarṣabha** (S) (M) 1. a bull among the gods. 2. a powerful god. 3. a son of Dharma and Bhānu (*Bhā Purāṇa*)

**Devārpaṇa** (S) (M) offering to the gods.

**Devarṣi** (S) (M) 1. a ṛṣi among the gods. 3. another name for Nārada.

**Devarūpā** (S) (F) 1. of divine form. 3. an apsarā (*K. Sāgara*)

**Devarya** (S) (M) 1. divine belief. 3. the last Jaina Arhat of the present Avasarpinī.

**Devasakha** (S) (M) friend of the gods.

**Devaśakti** (S) (M) with divine strength.

**Devasarasa** (S) (M) pool of the gods.

**Devaśarman** (S) (M) 1. with the gods as refuge. 3. a minister of King Jayapīda of Kāśmira (*R. Taraṅginī*); a muni who was the husband of Rući and father of Vipula (*M. Bh.*); an Arhat (*J.S. Koṣa*)

**Devasattva** (S) (M) with a godly nature.

**Devasāvarṇi** (S) (M) 1. god like. 3. the 13th Manu (*Bhā. Purāṇa*)

**Devaśekhara** (S) (M) 1. divine diadem. 3. *Artemisia sieversiana*.

**Devasenā** (S) (F) 1. with an army of gods. 3. a daughter of Prajāpati Dakṣa and wife of Subrahmaṇya (*M. Bh.*)

**Devasena** (S) (M) 1. with an army of gods. 3. a king of Śrāvastī (*K. Sāgara*); the husband of Kīrtisenā (*M. Bh.*); a Buddhist Arhat; another name for Skanda.

**Devasiddhi** (S) (M) a divine achievement; as perfect as the gods.

**Devaśilpa** (S) (M) a divine work of art.

**Devaśilpin** (S) (M) 1. divine artist. 3. another name for Tvaṣṭṛ.

**Devasinha** (S) (M) 1. god-lion. 3. another name for Śiva.

**Devāśīśa** (S) (M) blessing of the gods.

**Devāśiṣṭa** (S) (M) 1. taught by the gods; follows the ways of gods. 2. pious; divine.

**Devaśiśu** (S) (M) divine child.

**Devasmita** (S) (F) 1. with a divine smile. 3. a heroine of *Kathāsaritsāgara*.

**Devasoma** (S) (M) the drink of the gods.

**Devaśravas** (S) (M) 1. with divine reknown. 3. a son of Yama (*Ṛg Veda*); a son of Viśvāmitra (*M. Bh.*); a Yayāti king who was the son of Śūra and brother of Vasudeva (*Bhāgavata*)

**Devaśreṣṭha** (S) (M) 1. best among the gods. 3. a son of the 12th Manu (*H. Purāṇa*)

**Devaśrī** (S) (F) 1. divine goddess. 3. another name for Lakṣmī.

**Devaśrīgarbha** (S) (M) 1. creator of the gods and glory. 3. a Bodhisattva (*B. Ćarita*)

**Devaśrū** (S) (M) known to the gods.

**Devaśruta** (S) (M) 1. with divine knowledge. 3. the 6th Jaina Arhat of the future Utasarpiṇī (*J. S. Koṣa*); another name for Nārada.

**Devasthalī** (S) (M) the abode of the gods; the temple of the gods.

**Devasthāna** (S) (M) 1. the abode of the gods. 3. a ṛṣi who was a friend of the Pāṇḍavas (*M. Bh.*)

**Devaśūra** (S) (M) divine hero.

**Devāsuri** (S) (M) connected with the gods and demons.

**Devāśva** (S) (M) 1. divine horse. 3. another name for Uccaiśravas.

**Devasvāmin** (S) (M) 1. lord of the gods. 3. a Brahmin (*K. Sāgara*)

**Devatājita** (S) (M) 1. conquering the god. 3. a son of Sumati and grandson of Bharata (*M. Bh.*)

**Devatāras** (S) (M) released by the gods; godlike.

**Devatarū** (S) (M) 1. tree of the gods. 3. the 5 sacred trees of paradise (*Bhā. Purāṇa*)

**Devatātman** (S) (M) 1. with a divine soul. 3. another name for Śiva; *Ficus religiosa.*

**Devātideva** (S) (M) 1. surpassing all the gods. 3. another name for Śiva, Viṣṇu and Śākyamuṇi.

**Devātithi** (S) (M) 1. guest of the gods. 3. a ṛṣi and part author of *Ṛg Veda* (viii); a Purū king who was the son of Akrodhana and Karambhā and the husband of Maryādā (*M. Bh.*)

**Devātman** (S) (M) 1. divine soul. 3. the Bodhi tree (*Ficus religiosa*)

**Devavaćanā** (S) (F) 1. with divine speech. 3. a gandharvī (*M. Bh.*)

**Devavadha** (S) (M) weapon of the gods.

**Devavāha** (S) (M) 1. with a divine chariot. 3. a Yayāti king (*Bhāgavata*)

**Devavaktra** (S) (M) 1. the mouth of the gods. 3. another name for Agni, the lord of fire considered to receive oblations on behalf of the gods.

**Devavallabha** (S) (M) 1. beloved of the gods. 3. the tree *Ochrocarpus longifolius*.

**Devavāṇi** (S) (F) divine voice.

**Devavardhaki** (S) (M) 1. divine architect. 3. another name for Viśvakarman.

**Devavardhana** (S) (M) 1. supported by the gods. 3. a son of Devaka (*V. Purāṇa*)

**Devavarman** (S) (M) 1. with the armour of the gods. 2. extremely powerful; protected by the gods,

**Devavarṇinī** (S) (F) 1. describer of the gods. 3. a daughter of Bharadvāja (*Rāmāyaṇa*); the wife of Viśravas and mother of Kubera (*Rāmāyaṇa*)

**Devavarṣa** (S) (M) divine year.

**Devavarya** (S) (M) 1. best of the gods. 3. another name for Śiva.

**Devavata** (S) (M) 1. surrounded by the gods. 2. guarded by the gods. 3. another name for Akrūra (*V. Purāṇa*); the 12th Manu (*H. Purāṇa*)

**Devavatī** (S) (F) 1. owned by the gods. 3. the daughter of the gandharva Maṇimaya; wife of the rākṣasa Sukeśa and mother of Mālyavān, Sumāli and Māli (*U. Rāmāyaṇa*); the daughter of the daitya Mandaramāli (*Rāmāyaṇa*)

**Devavāyu** (S) (M) 1. heavenly wind. 2. life giving; swift. 3. the 12th Manu (*H. Purāṇa*)

**Devaveśman** (S) (M) home of the gods; a temple.

**Devavī** (S) (M) 1. gratifying the gods. 2. a priest; devotee; a worshipper of the gods.

**Devavid** (S) (M) knowing the gods.

**Devavīti** (S) (F) 1. enjoyment for the gods. 2. pleasing the gods. 3. a daughter of Meru and wife of Ketumāla, the son of Agnidhra (*Bhā. Purāṇa*)

**Devavrata** (S) (M) 1. the favourite food of the gods; a religious vow. 2. follower of the religious path. 3. a Brāhmin born as a bamboo from which Kṛṣṇa made his flute (*P. Purāṇa*); another name for Bhīṣma and Skanda.

**Devāvṛdha** (S) (M) 1. as old as the gods. 3. the father of Babhru (*M. Bh./H.Purāṇa*); a warrior on the side of the Kauravas (*M. Bh.*)

**Devayaji** (S) (M) 1. worshipper of the gods. 3. a warrior of Skanda (*M. Bh.*)

**Devayājin** (S) (M) 1. sacrificing to the gods. 2. one invested with god like qualities. 3. a dānava (*H. Purāṇa*); an attendant of Skanda (*M. Bh.*)

**Devayāna** (S) (M) leading to the gods; the vehicle of a god.

**Devayānī** (S) (F) 1. chariot of the gods. 2. one invested with divine power; divine affluence.

3. a daughter of Śukrāćarya and Ūrjasvatī, the wife of Yayāti and mother of Yadu and Turvasu (*H. Purāṇa*); a wife of Skanda.

**Devayaśas** (S) (M) divine glory.

**Devayoṣā** (S) (F) the wife of a god.

**Devāyudha** (S) (M) 1. weapon of the gods. 3. another name for Indra.

**Devāyukta** (S) (M) attached to the gods; yoked by the gods; a devotee; a worshipper of the gods.

**Devejya** (S) (M) 1. teacher of the gods. 3. another name for Bṛhaspati.

**Devendra** (S) (M) 1. chief of the gods. 3. another name for Indra.

**Deveśī** (S) (F) 1. chief of the goddesses. 3. another name for Durgā.

**Deveśita** (S) (M) sent by the gods.

**Deveṣṭha** (S) (M) 1. best among the gods. 3. the tree *Commiphora mukul*.

**Deveśu** (S) (M) divine arrow.

**Deveśvara** (S) (M) 1. lord of the gods. 3. a pupil of Śankarāćārya; another name for Śiva.

**Devī** (S) (F) 1. divine; deity; goddess; queen; lady. 3. the ultimate sāttvika force responsible for the creation of the worlds, who appears in various forms of which the 5 main are Durgā, Lakṣmī, Sarasvatī, Sāvitrī and Rādhā, the 6 partial forms are Gaṅgā, Tulasī, Manasādevī, Devasenā, Maṅgalāćaṇḍikā, Bhūmī, the Anśalakāladevis are also parts of this ultimate sāttvika force or Mahādevī, she is known by 108 names; a nymph beloved of the sun (*A. Koṣa*); the mother of the 18th Arhat of the present Avasarpinī (*H. Koṣa*); *Bryonopsis laciniosa*; *Cucumis trigonos*; Black myrobalan (*Terminalia chebula*); Velvet Leaf (*Cissampelos pareira*); *Clematis triloba*; *Desmodium gangeticum*; Common Flax (*Linum usitatissimum*)

**Devīdāsa** (S) (M) slave of the goddess.

**Devīdatta** (S) (M) given by the goddess.

**Devikā** (S) (F) 1. minor deity; minor goddess. 2. god like. 3. a class of goddess of an inferior order – Aṇumatī, Rākā, Sinīvālī, Kuhū and Dhātṛ; the daughter of Śaibya king Govāsana, the wife of Yudhiṣṭhira and mother of Yaudheya (*M. Bh.*); Ash coloured Fleabane (*Vernonia cinerea*)

**Devikādevī** (S) (F) 1. invested with divine quantities. 3. a wife of Yudhiṣṭhira and mother of Yaudheya (*M. Bh.*); a river (*M. Bh.*)

**Devikī** (S) (F) derived from the goddess.

**Devila** (S) (M) 1. attached to the gods. 2. righteous; pious; venerated.

**Devin** (S) (M) resembling a god.

**Devinā** (S) (F) resembling a goddess.

**Deviprasāda** (S) (M) gift of the goddess.

**Deviśa** (S) (M) 1. chief of the gods. 2. another name for Brahmā, Viṣṇu, Śiva and Indra.

**Deviśī** (S) (F) 1. chief of the goddesses. 3. another name for Durgā and Devakī, the mother of Kṛṣṇa.

**Devya** (S) (M) divine power.

**Dhāma** (S) (M) 1. ray; strength; splendour; majesty. 2. light; house; place of pilgrimage. 3. a ṛṣi who protected Gaṅgā Mahādvāra (*M. Bh.*)

**Dhamadhamā** (S) (F) 1. making a noise. 2. a blowhorn. 3. an attendant of Skanda (*M. Bh.*)

**Dhāmādhipa** (S) (M) 1. lord of rays. 3. another name for Sūrya.

**Dhāmakeśin** (S) (M) 1. ray haired. 3. another name for Sūrya.

**Dhāman** (S) (M) 1. ray; light; abode. 2. majesty; glory; splendour; strength; house. 3. a ṛṣi of the 4th Manvantara (*H. Purāṇa*)

**Dhamanī** (S) (F) 1. pipe; tube. 3. wife of Hrāda and mother of Vātāpi and Ilvala.

**Dhāmanidhi** (S) (M) 1. treasure of splendour. 3. another name for Sūrya.

**Dhāmavat** (S) (M) owner of a house; powerful; strong.

**Dhanadā** (S) (F) 1. wealth bestowing. 2. prize giving; giving booty or treasure (*Ṛg Veda*). 3. a mother in Skanda's retinue (*Sk. Purāṇa*); a tāntric deity (*T. Śastra*)

**Dhanada** (S) (M) 1. wealth bestowing. 3. another name for Kubera.

**Dhanadeśvara** (S) (M) 1. wealth giving lord. 3. another name for Kubera.

**Dhanādhipa** (S) (M) 1. lord of wealth. 3. another name for Kubera.

**Dhanādhipati** (S) (M) 1. wealth giving lord. 3. another name for Kubera.

**Dhanādhyakṣa** (S) (M) 1. lord of wealth. 3. another name for Kubera.

**Dhanagopta** (S) (M) 1. guarding treasure. 3. another name for Kubera.

**Dhanajita** (S) (M) wealth; winner.

**Dhanaka** (S) (M) 1. avarice. 3. a son of Durmada.

**Dhanalakṣmī** (S) (F) 1. the goddess of wealth. 3. another name for goddess Lakṣmī.

**Dhanandadā** (S) (F) 1. granting wealth. 3. a Buddhist deity.

**Dhanañjaya** (S) (M) 1. fire. 2. *Plumbago zeylanica; Terminalia arjuna*. 3. a nāga (*M. Bh.*); a king of Kalinga; another name for Arjuna and Agni.

**Dhanañjaya** (S) (M) 1. conqueror of wealth. 2. victorious. 3. a king of Kaliṅga (*Kathārṇeva*); a nāga who was the son of Kaśyapa and Kadru and a member of Varuṇa's court (*M. Bh.*); the army given to Skanda by Śiva (*M. Bh.*); a Sanskṛt critic in the court of King Muñja (11th century); a Brāhmin devotee of Viṣṇu (*P. Purāṇa*); another name for Arjuna and Kuṇḍalini.

**Dhanañjayasuta** (S) (M) 1. son of Arjuna. 3. another name for Babhruvāhana.

**Dhanapāla** (S) (M) guardian of wealth; king.

**Dhanapati** (S) (M) 1. lord of wealth. 3. another name for Kubera.

**Dhanaśrī** (S) (F) 1. goddess of wealth. 3. a rāgiṇī.

**Dhanavanta** (S) (M) possessing wealth.

**Dhanavardhana** (S) (M) increasing wealth.

**Dhanavat** (S) (M) 1. containing wealth. 2. the sea.

**Dhanavatī** (S) (F) containing wealth.

**Dhanāyuṣ** (S) (M) 1. with a rich life. 3. a son of Purūravas (*M. Bh.*)

**Dhaneśa** (S) (M) 1. lord of wealth. 3. another name for Kubera.

**Dhaneśvara** (S) (M) 1. lord of wealth. 3. another name for Kubera.

**Dhaneśvarī** (S) (F) 1. goddess of wealth. 3. another name for the wife of Kubera.

**Dhanin** (S) (M) 1. wealthy. 3. a messenger of the asuras (*M. Bh.*); another name for Kubera.

**Dhanīrāma** (S) (M) 1. with Rāma as one's wealth. 2. one who is deeply religious.

**Dhaniṣṭhā** (S) (F) 1. residing in wealth; extremely wealthy. 3. a constellation.

**Dhanu** (S) (M) 1. bow. 3. the zodiac sign of Sagittarius.

**Dhanurgraha** (S) (M) 1. holding a bow. 3. a son of Dhṛtarāṣṭra (*M. Bh.*)

**Dhanuhastā** (S) (F) 1. with a bow in hand. 2. archer. 3. an attendant of the ultimate sāttvika force which is personified as Devī.

**Dhanurāja** (S) (M) 1. king of archers. 3. an ancestor of Śākyamuṇi (*M. Bh.*)

**Dhanurdhara** (S) (M) 1. bearer of a bow. 3. the zodiac sign of Sagittarius; a son of Dhṛtarāṣṭra (*M. Bh.*); another name for Śiva.

**Dhanurvaktra** (S) (M) 1. bow mouthed. 3. an attendant of Skanda (*M. Bh.*)

**Dhanurvedin** (S) (M) 1. knower of the bow. 2. well versed in archery. 3. another name for Śiva.

**Dhanuṣa** (S) (M) 1. bow. 3. a ṛṣi (*M. Bh.*)

**Dhanuṣākṣa** (S) (M) 1. bow eyed. 3. a sage (*M. Bh.*)

**Dhanuṣmatī** (S) (F) 1. armed with a bow. 3. the tutelary deity in the family of Vyāghrapāda (*Brahma Purāṇa*)

**Dhanva** (S) (M) 1. with a bow. 3. a king of Kāśi who was the father of Dhanvantari (*M. Bh.*)

**Dhanvantari** (S) (M) 1. moving in a curve. 3. the physician of the gods; founder of Āyurveda produced at the churning of the ocean, later incarnated as King Divodāsa of Benaras.

**Dhanvanyā** (S) (F) treasure of the jungle; an oasis.

**Dhanvin** (S) (M) 1. armed with a bow. 3. a son of Manu Tāmasa (*H. Purāṇa*); another name for Śiva, Arjuna and Viṣṇu.

**Dhanyā** (S) (F) 1. virtuous. 2. good; bestowing wealth. 3. Dhruva's wife (*V. Purāṇa*)

**Dhanyamālā** (S) (F) 1. auspicious garland. 2. virtuous; meritorious. 3. the foster mother of Atikāya.

**Dhanyarāja** (S) (M) 1. king of grain. 3. Barley (*Hordeum vulgare*)

**Dharā** (S) (F) 1. bearer; supporter. 2. the

earth; a mass of gold. 3. one of the 8 forms of Sarasvatī (*Purāṇas*); a wife of Kaśyapa (*H. Purāṇa*); the wife of the vasu named Droṇa (*V. Purāṇa*); another name for the earth.

**Dhara** (S) (M) 1. bearing; supporting. 3. the king of the tortoises (*A. Koṣa*); the father of Padmapāṇi (*H. Koṣa*); a vasu son of Dharma and Dhūmrā (*M. Bh.*); a king who was a friend of Yudhiṣṭhira (*M. Bh.*)

**Dharābhuja** (S) (M) earth enjoyer; a king.

**Dhāraṇa** (S) (M) 1. bearing. 2. holding; keeping; resembling. 3. a king in the family of Ćandravatsa (*M. Bh.*); a serpent son of Kaśyapa (*M. Bh.*); another name for Śiva.

**Dhāraṇī** (S) (F) 1. holding; bearing possessing. 2. a mystical verse used to assuage pain (*A. Veda*). 3. a daughter of Svadhā (*D. Bh. Purāṇa*); the wife of Agnimitra (*M. Bh./Rāmāyaṇa*); the earth personified as the wife of Dhruva (*M. Bh./Rāmāyaṇa*)

**Dharaṇīdhara** (S) (M) 1. supporting the earth. 2. tortoise; a king. 3. one of the 10 elephants that support the earth (*M. Bh.*); the father of Śaśidhara (*R. Taraṅginī*); a Bodhisattva (*B. Ćarita*); the father of Vāsudeva (*Bhagavata*); another name for Viṣṇu, Kṛṣṇa and Śeṣa.

**Dharaṇija** (S) (M) born of the earth.

**Dharaṇisutā** (S) (F) 1. daughter of the earth. 3. another name for Sitā, the consort of Rāma.

**Dharāpati** (S) (M) 1. lord of the earth. 3. another name for Viṣṇu.

**Dharbaka** (S) (M) 1. superficial. 3. a son of Ajātaśatru (*V. Purāṇa*)

**Dharendra** (S) (M) 1. king of the earth. 3. another name for the Himalayas.

**Dharma** (S) (M) 1. path of life; religion. 2. established; law; justice; practice; duty; observance; right. 3. justice personified as born from the right breast of Yama (*M. Bh.*); the father of Sāma, Kāma, Harṣa, Yudhiṣṭhira and Vidura (*M. Bh.*); as a prajāpati, the husband of 13 daughters of Dakṣa apart from 10 other wives each of whom originated a family of ṛṣis, and the father of, among others Hari, Kṛṣṇa and Nārāyana – the last being an incarnation of Mahaviṣṇu (*H. Purāṇa*); the 15th arhat of the present Avasarpinī (*J. S. Koṣa*); a son of Aṇu and father of Ghṛtas (*H. Purāṇa*); a son of Gandhara and father of Dhrita (*V. Purāṇa*); a son of Hehaya and father of Netra (*Bhāgavata*); a son of Pṛthuśravas.

**Dharmābhimukhā** (S) (F) 1. turned towards religion. 2. religious; virtuous. 3. an apsarā (*K. Vyuha*)

**Dharmabhṛt** (S) (M) 1. bearer of religion. supports and practices religion; virtuous. 3. a ṛṣi (*V. Rāmāyaṇa*)

**Dharmaćandra** (S) (M) 1. moon of Dharma. 2. deeply religious; virtuous; venerated.

**Dharmaćara** (S) (M) observer of Dharma.

**Dharmaćārin** (S) (M) 1. observing Dharma. 2. virtuous; moral. 3. the deity in the Bodhi tree (*Ficus religiosa*); another name for Śiva.

**Dharmada** (S) (M) 1. bestower of Dharma. 3. a follower of Skanda (*M. Bh.*)

**Dharmadatta** (S) (M) 1. given by Dharma. 3. the previous incarnation of King Daśaratha as a Brāhmin of Karavīra (*Sk. Purāṇa*)

**Dharmadeva** (S) (M) god of justice.

**Dharmadhara** (S) (M) 1. supporter of Dharma. 3. a Bodhisattva (*B. Literature*)

**Dharmadhātu** (S) (M) 1. made of the different metals of law. 3. a Buddhist deity.

**Dharmadhṛt** (S) (M) 1. one who makes Dharma realized; carrier of Dharma. 2. a judge; a preacher. 3. a son of Śvaphalka (*H. Purāṇa*)

**Dharmadhvaja** (S) (M) 1. Dharma bannered. 2. extremely virtuous; religious; venerated. 3. a king of Mithilā who was the son of Kuśadhvaja (*V. Purāṇa*); another name for the sun.

**Dharmāditya** (S) (M) 1. sun of Dharma. 2. extremely virtuous; religious; venerated. 3. a Buddhist king.

**Dharmadravī** (S) (F) 1. with virtuous waters. 3. another name for the Gaṅgā.

**Dharmaghoṣa** (S) (M) the voice of Dharma.

**Dharmagopa** (S) (M) protector of Dharma.

**Dharmaja** (S) (M) 1. son of Dharma. 3. another name for Yudhiṣṭhira.

**Dharmākara** (S) (M) 1. mine of Dharma. 3. the 99th Buddha.

**Dharmakāya** (S) (M) 1. law body. 3. a god of the Bodhi tree; a Buddhist or Jaina Saint.
**Dharmaketu** (S) (M) 1. justice bannered. 3. a Bhārgava king who was the son of Suketu and father of Satyaketu (*H. Purāṇa*); a Buddha (*L. Vistara*); a Jaina saint (*J.S. Koṣa*)
**Dharmamatī** (S) (M) 1. with a religious mind. 3. a god of the Bodhi tree (*Ficus religiosa*) (*L. Vistara*)
**Dharmamitra** (S) (M) a friend of Dharma.
**Dharmāmṛta** (S) (M) nectar of Dharma.
**Dharman** (S) (M) 1. bearer of Dharma, supporter of Dharma. 3. a son of Bṛhadraja and father of Kṛtañjaya (*V. Purāṇa*)
**Dharmanābha** (S) (M) 1. the centre of Dharma. 3. another name for Viṣṇu.
**Dharmanandana** (S) (M) 1. son of Dharma. 3. a Bhārgava king (*Bhāgavata*); another name for Yudhiṣṭhira.
**Dharmanātha** (S) (M) lord of Dharma.
**Dharmandhū** (S) (M) 1. well of Dharma. 2. deeply religious; venerated.
**Dharmanetra** (S) (M) 1. Dharma eyed. 3. a son of Tanṣu and father of Duṣamanta (*H. Purāṇa*); a son of Suvrata (*Bhāgavata*); a son of Dhṛtarāṣṭra (*M. Bh.*); a Hehaya king who was the son of Hehaya and the father of Kṛti (*Br. Purāṇa*); a son of Suvrata (*Bh. Purāṇa*)
**Dharmāṅga** (S) (M) 1. whose body is Dharma; receptacle of Dharma. 3. another name for Viṣṇu.
**Dharmāṅgada** (S) (M) 1. ornamented by Dharma. 3. a king who was the son of Priyaṅkara (*Purāṇas*)
**Dharmanitya** (S) (M) constant in Dharma.
**Dharmapāla** (S) (M) 1. guardian of Dharma. 3. a minister of King Daśaratha (*A. Purāṇa*)
**Dharmaprabhāsa** (S) (M) light of Dharma; extremely virtuous; religious; venerated.
**Dharmaprabhava** (S) (M) 1. speaking the truth. 3. another name for Yudhiṣṭhira.
**Dharmaprakāśa** (S) (M) light of Dharma.
**Dharmapriya** (S) (M) 1. loving Dharma. 3. a gandharva prince (*K. Vyuha*)
**Dharmaputra** (S) (M) 1. son of Dharma. 3. son of the 11th Manu; another name for Yudhiṣṭhira who was the son of Dharma and Kuntī.
**Dharmarāja** (S) (M) 1. lord of Dharma. 3. a Buddha; a king of Gauḍadeśa who revived the Vedic rites (*Bh. Purāṇa*); a king of herons; another name for Yama and Yudhiṣṭhira.
**Dharmarājan** (S) (M) 1. Dharma, the king. 2. a virtuous king. 3. another name for Yudhiṣṭhira.
**Dharmāraṇya** (S) (M) 1. grove of Dharma. 3. a Brāhmin devotee of the sun (*M. Bh.*)
**Dharmaratha** (S) (M) 1. the chariot of Dharma. 3. an Aṅga king who was the great-grandfather of Lomapāda and the son of Diviratha (*A. Purāṇa*); a son of Sagara.
**Dharmasakhā** (S) (M) 1. friend of Dharma. 3. a Kekaya king (*Sk. Purāṇa*)
**Dharmasārathi** (S) (M) 1. charioteer of Dharma. 3. a son of Tṛkakuda (*Bhāgavata*)
**Dharmasāvarṇi** (S) (M) 1. resembling Dharma. 3. the 11th Manu (*V. Purāṇa*)
**Dharmasetu** (S) (M) 1. barrier of Dharma. 3. a son of Āryaka (*Bhāgavata*)
**Dharmaśila** (S) (M) follower of Dharma.
**Dharmasindhu** (S) (M) ocean of Dharma.
**Dharmasiṁha** (S) (M) lion of Dharma; one who guards; protects and practices Dharma deeply.
**Dharmāśoka** (S) (M) 1. Aśoka the dutiful. 3. another name for Emperor Aśoka.
**Dharmasthavira** (S) (M) stable in Dharma; one who practices his dharma firmly.
**Dharmasuta** (S) (M) 1. son of Dharmā. 3. another name for Yudhiṣṭhira.
**Dharmavāhana** (S) (M) 1. vehicle of Dharma. 3. another name for Śiva.
**Dharmavardhana** (S) (M) 1. increasing Dharma. 3. another name for Śiva.
**Dharmavarman** (S) (M) 1. warrior for Dharma; shield of justice. 3. another name for Kṛṣṇa.
**Dharmavarṇa** (S) (M) 1. colour of Dharma. 2. clad in Dharma; extremely virtuous; religious.
**Dharmavatī** (S) (M) 1. possessing Dharma. 3. a wife of Dharmadeva and the mother of Dharmavratā who married Marīci (*K. Sāgara*)

**Dharmavīra** (S) (M) hero of Dharma; a champion of Dharma; one who fights for religious causes.

**Dharmavivardhana** (S) (M) 1. promoter of Dharma. 3. a son of Aśoka.

**Dharmavratā** (S) (F) 1. acting according to Dharma. 3. a daughter of Dharma and Dharmavatī and wife of sage Marīći (*V. Purāṇa*)

**Dharmayaśas** (S) (M) glory of Dharma.

**Dharmayoni** (S) (M) 1. the source of Dharma. 3. another name for Viṣṇu.

**Dharmayu** (S) (M) 1. one who lives for Dharma. 3. a Purū king who was the son of Raudrāśva and Miśrakeśi (*M. Bh.*)

**Dharmayūpa** (S) (M) a pillar of Dharma.

**Dharmendra** (S) (M) 1. lord of Dharma. 3. another name for Yama and Yudhiṣṭhira.

**Dharmeśa** (S) (M) 1. lord of Dharma. 3. another name for Yama.

**Dharmeśvara** (S) (M) god of Dharma.

**Dharmiṇī** (S) (F) 1. religious; virtuous; pious. 2. a kind of perfume.

**Dharmiṣṭha** (S) (M) staying in Dharma; very virtuous and righteous.

**Dharmottara** (S) (M) entirely devoted to Dharma.

**Dharśanātman** (S) (M) 1. with a violent nature. 3. another name for Śiva.

**Dhārtarāṣṭra** (S) (M) 1. son of Dhṛtarāṣṭra. 3. another name for Duryodhana.

**Dharuṇa** (S) (M) 1. bearing; supporting; holding. 3. another name for Brahmā.

**Dhātā** (S) (M) 1. establisher. 2. creator; founder; supporter. 3. one of the 12 ādityas (*M. Bh.*); a son of Bhṛgu and Khyāti and the husband of Āyati (*V. Purāṇa*); another name for Brahmā.

**Dhātaki** (S) (M) 1. resembling the creator. 3. a son of Vītihotra (*M. Bh.*)

**Dhātreyikā** (S) (F) 1. supporter; nurse; confidante. 3. a maid of Draupadī (*M. Bh.*)

**Dhātṛ** (S) (M) 1. establisher. 2. creator; founder; supporter. 3. a divine being who personifies these functions and was later identified with Brahmā or Prajāpati (*M. Bh.*); one of the 12 ādityas and brother of Vidhatṛ (*M. Bh.*); a son of Brahmā (*M. Bh.*); a son of Bhṛgu and Khyāti (*V. Purāṇa*); fate in a personified form (*K. Prakāśa*); one of the 49 winds (*Vah. Purāṇa*); a ṛṣi in the 4th Manvantara (*H. Purāṇa*)

**Dhātṛputra** (S) (M) 1. Dhatṛ's son. 3. Sanatkumāra, the son of the creator or Brahmā.

**Dhaumra** (S) (M) 1. grey; smoke; spring; well; a rivulet. 3. an ancient ṛṣi (*M. Bh.*)

**Dhaumya** (S) (M) 1. smoky; grey. 3. a ṛṣi who was the brother of Upamanyu (*M. Bh.*); a son of Vyāghrapāda (*M. Bh.*); a brother of Devala and family priest of the Pāṇḍavas (*M. Bh.*); a pupil of Vālmīki (*V. Rāmāyaṇa*)

**Dhāvak** (S) (M) 1. runner. 2. quick; swift; flowing. 3. a poet who composed Ratnāvali for King Śrīharṣa.

**Dhavala** (S) (M) 1. dazzling white. 2. handsome; beautiful. 3. rāga; one of the elephants of the quarters (*V. Rāmāyaṇa*)

**Dhavalaćandra** (S) (M) white moon.

**Dhavalapakṣa** (S) (M) 1. white winged. 2. the light half of the mouth.

**Dhāvita** (S) (M) whitish; washed; purified; clean.

**Dhenā** (S) (F) 1. milch cow. 2. any beverage made of milk. 3. the wife of Bṛhaspati (*T. Āraṇyaka*)

**Dhenū** (S) (F) 1. cow. 3. the earth as a life supporting cow; the feminine gender of any species.

**Dhenukā** (S) (F) 1. milch cow. 3. the wife of Kīrtimat the son of Aṅgiras (*V. Purāṇa*); a celestial river (*V. Purāṇa*)

**Dhenuka** (S) (M) 1. calf. 2. a coital posture mentioned in the *Kāmasūtra*. 3. an asura slain by Balarāma (*Bhāgavata*); a son of Durdama (*V. Purāṇa*)

**Dhenukārī** (S) (M) 1. enemy of Dhenuka. 3. another name for Balarāma.

**Dhenumatī** (S) (F) 1. possessing the earth. 2. that which yields nourishment. 3. the wife of Devadyumna (*Bhāgavata*); another name for the river Gomatī.

**Dhīlatī** (S) (F) daughter.

**Dhīmān** (S) (M) 1. possessed with wisdom;

wise. 3. a son of Purūravas (*M. Bh.*)

**Dhīmant** (S) (M) 1. possessed with wisdom. 2. one who is wise; intelligent; learned. 3. another name for Bṛhaspati.

**Dhīmat** (S) (M) 1. possessed with wisdom. 2. one who is intelligent; wise; learned; sensible. 3. a son of Virāj (*V. Purāṇa*); a ṛṣi of the 4th Manvantara (*V. Purāṇa*); a son of Purūravas (*M. Bh.*); another name for Bṛhaspati; a Bodhisattva.

**Dhīra** (S) (M) 1. patient; tolerant; intelligent; wise; skilful. 3. a saffron (*Crocus sativus*); South Indian Redwood (*Dalbergia sissoo*); *Luvunya scandens*; *Tinospora cordifolia*.

**Dhīradhi** (S) (M) 1. a mine of tolerance. 3. a Brāhmin devotee of Śiva (*P. Purāṇa*)

**Dhīraja** (S) (M) 1. treasure of tolerance; born of tolerance; creator of tolerance. 3. an attendant of Śiva (*A. Koṣa*)

**Dhīraṇa** (S) (M) delighting in devotion.

**Dhīrćetas** (S) (M) a patient mind; one who is strongminded; courageous.

**Dhīreśa** (S) (M) lord of tolerance.

**Dhīroṣṇin** (S) (M) 1. fiery and brave. 3. a viśvadeva (*M. Bh.*)

**Dhīṣaṇā** (S) (F) 1. Soma vessel. 2. knowledge; intelligence; speech; praise; hymn; goddesses. 3. The goddess of abundance and the divine guardian of the sacred fire (*Ṛg Veda*); the wife of Havirdhāna, daughter of Agni (*H. Purāṇa*) and the mother of Śukra, Gaya, Vraja, Ajina and Prāćinabarhis (*V. Purāṇa*); the wife of Kṛśāśva and mother of Vedaśira, Devala, Vāyuna and Manu (*Bhāgavata*)

**Dhiṣaṇa** (S) (M) 1. wise. 3. another name for Bṛhaspati.

**Dhītā** (S) (F) bird-born; a daughter.

**Dhīti** (S) (F) 1. thought; idea. 3. wisdom; reflection; intention; devotion; prayer.

**Dhītika** (S) (M) 1. thoughtful; wise. 3. a Buddhist patriarchal saint (*L. Vistara*)

**Dhīyāmpati** (S) (M) 1. lord of the thoughts. 2. the soul. 3. another name for Manjughoṣa.

**Dhṛṣaj** (S) (M) bold; a hero.

**Dhṛṣamāṇ** (S) (M) 1. confident; bold. 3. a king of the Bharata dynasty.

**Dhṛṣita** (S) (M) bold; brave; daring.

**Dhṛṣṇi** (S) (M) a ray of light.

**Dhṛṣṇu** (S) (M) 1. fierce; violent. 2. bold; courageous; strong. 3. a son of Manu Vaivasvata (*M. Bh./H. Purāṇa*); a son of Manu Sāvarṇa (*H. Purāṇa*)

**Dhṛṣṭa** (S) (M) 1. bold; brave; confident; audacious. 3. a son of Manu Vaivasvata (*Bhāgavata*); a son of Kunti; a son of Bhajamana (*H. Purāṇa*)

**Dhṛṣṭadyumna** (S) (M) 1. glorified by bravery. 3. a son of King Drupada and brother of Draupadī who after death became a part of the fire god (*H. Purāṇa*)

**Dhṛṣṭaka** (S) (M) bold; brave; audacious.

**Dhṛṣṭakarma** (S) (M) 1. one who performs brave deeds. 3. a Yayāti king (*Bhāgavata*)

**Dhṛṣṭaketu** (S) (M) 1. marked by boldness. 3. a king of Ćedi who was the son of Śiśupāla and the reincarnation of Anuhlāda the son of Hiraṇyakaśipu (*M. Bh.*); a king of Mithilā and son of Sudhṛti (*V. Purāṇa*); a son of Sukumāra (*H. Purāṇa*); a son of Dhṛṣṭadyumna (*H. Purāṇa*); a Kekaya king (*Bhāgavata*); a son of Manu (*H. Purāṇa*); a Yayāti king (*Bhāgavata*)

**Dhṛṣṭaśarman** (S) (M) 1. protector of the brave; one who performs. 3. a son of Śvaphalka (*H. Purāṇa*)

**Dhṛṣṭi** (S) (M) 1. bold. 3.a son of Hiraṇyakaśipu (*V. Purāṇa*); a minister of King Daśaratha (*V. Rāmāyaṇa*)

**Dhṛṣṭokta** (S) (M) 1. one whose bravery is much spoken of; one who is stubborn in speech. 3. a son of Arjuna Kārtavīrya.

**Dhṛta** (S) (M) 1. held; borne. 2. maintained; fixed upon; pledged. 3. a son of the 13th Manu (*H. Purāṇa*); a descendant of Druhyu son of Dharma (*V. Purāṇa*)

**Dhṛtadakṣa** (S) (M) of calm and constant mind.

**Dhṛtadevā** (S) (F) 1. goddess of constancy. 3. a daughter of King Devaka, the wife of Vasudeva, and mother of Vipṛṣṭha (*Bhāgavata*)

**Dhṛtadevī** (S) (F) 1. goddess of constancy. 3. a daughter of Devala.

**Dhṛtadhiti** (S) (M) 1. constant in splendour. 2. fire.

**Dhṛtaka** (S) (M) 1. bearer of constancy. 3. a

Buddhist patriarch (*B. Literature*); Vṛka (*V. Purāṇa*)

**Dhṛtaketu** (S) (M) **1.** constant flagbearer. **3.** a son of the 9th Manu; a king of the Bhṛgu family (*Bhāgavata*)

**Dhṛtarājan** (S) (M) ornament bearer.

**Dhṛtarāṣṭra** (S) (M) **1.** powerful king. **3.** a nāga (*A. Veda*); a king of the gandharvas; a son of the daitya Bali (*H. Purāṇa*); a king of Kāśī; the eldest son of Vyāsa who was the husband of Gāndhārī and the father of the hundred Kauravas (*M. Bh.*); a son of Janamejaya.

**Dhṛtarāṣṭraja** (S) (M) **1.** son of Dhṛtarāṣṭra. **3.** another name for Duryodhana.

**Dhṛtarāṣṭrī** (S) (F) **1.** supporter of the nation. **3.** a daughter of Kaśyapa and Tāmrā and mother of Krauñćī, Bhāsī, Śyeṇī, Dhṛtarāṣṭrī and Śukī (*V. Rāmāyaṇa*) and the mother of swans, geese and other waterbirds (*B. Tatakash*)

**Dhṛtārćis** (S) (M) **1.** of constant splendour. **3.** another name for Viṣṇu.

**Dhṛtasaṇdhi** (S) (M) **1.** supporter of alliance. **2.** keeping faith. **3.** a son of Susandhi and father of Bharata (*M. Bh.*)

**Dhṛtasena** (S) (M) **1.** supporter of the army; one who holds the army; a commander. **3.** a king on steady mind; the side of the Kauravas (*M. Bh.*)

**Dhṛtātman** (S) (M) steady mind; steady, calm; firm.

**Dhṛtavarman** (S) (M) **1.** wearing armour. **3.** the brother of King Suvarṇa of Tṛgartta and a Kaurava warrior (*M. Bh.*)

**Dhṛtavatī** (S) (F) **1.** steady; calm. **3.** a river (*M. Bh.*)

**Dhṛtavrata** (S) (M) **1.** maintaining law. **2.** devoted; attached; faithful. **3.** a son of Dhṛti; a Yayāti king (*Bhāgavata*); another name for Rudra.

**Dhṛti** (S) (F) **1.** firmness. **2.** resolution; constancy; will; command; satisfaction; joy; resolution. **3.** personified as the daughter of Dakṣa who was the wife of Dharma and mother of Niyama (*V. Purāṇa*); a goddess who is the wife of Kapila (*Purāṇas*); one of the 16 digits of the moon (*V. Purāṇa*); the wife of Rudra Manu (*V. Purāṇa*)

**Dhṛti** (S) (M) **1.** patience. **2.** virtue; resolution. **3.** the son of Vijaya and father of Dhṛtavrata (*H. Purāṇa*); a son of king Vītahavya of Videha and the father of Bahulāśva (*M. Bh.*); a son of Babhru (*M. Bh.*); a viśvadeva (*M. Bh.*)

**Dhṛtimat** (S) (M) **1.** steadfast; resolute. **2.** one who is calm; patient. **3.** a form of Agni (*M. Bh.*); a son of Manu Raivata (*H. Purāṇa*); a ṛṣi in the 13th Manvantara (*H. Purāṇa*); a son of Yavīnara (*H. Purāṇa*); a grandson of Aṅgiras.

**Dhṛtimatī** (S) (F) **1.** steadfast; resolute. **3.** a river of ancient India (*M. Bh.*)

**Dhṛtvan** (S) (M) **1.** resolute; steadfast. **2.** the sky; the sea; clever; virtuous. **3.** another name for Viṣṇu and Brahmā.

**Dhruva** (S) (M) **1.** firm; fixed; constant; permanent; eternal. **3.** the polar star personified as the son of Uttānapāda and Sunītī and the grandson of Manu (*G. Sutra*); a son of Vasudeva and Rohiṇī (*Bhāgavata*); a son of Nahuṣa and brother of Yayāti (*M. Bh.*); a son of Dharma and Dhumrā, who is also one of the 8 vasus (*M. Bh.*); a son of Rantinara (*V. Purāṇa*); a Kaurava warrior (*M. Bh.*); the serpent holding the earth (*T. Ārāṇyaka*); the syllable Om (*Rā. Upaniṣad*); another name for Brahmā, Viṣṇu and Śiva.

**Dhruvadevī** (S) (F) **1.** goddess of the poles. **2.** a stable goddess; unshakeable; firm. **3.** the wife of Ćandragupta (*A. Koṣa*)

**Dhruvaka** (S) (M) **1.** stable; firm. **2.** that which is unchangeable; a post; a stake. **3.** an attendant of Skanda (*M. Bh.*)

**Dhruvākṣara** (S) (M) **1.** the eternal syllable. **3.** Om as Viṣṇu.

**Dhruvaratnā** (S) (F) **1.** imperishable jewel. **3.** a mother attending on Skanda (*M. Bh.*)

**Dhruvasaṁdhi** (S) (M) **1.** one who is firm in alliance. 3 a king of Kosala; the son of Susaṇdhi, the husband of Manoramā and Lilāvatī and the father of Sudarśana and Śatrujita; a son of Puṣya.

**Dhruvāśva** (S) (M) with firm horses.

**Dhruvi** (S) (M) firmly fixed.

**Dhūlikā** (S) (F) pollen of flowers.

**Dhūmaketu** (S) (M) 1. smoke-bannered. 2. fire; a comet. 3. a yakṣa (*K. Sāgara*); another name for the sun.

**Dhumala** (S) (M) 1. brownish-red; purple; smoke coloured. 3. *Alpinia galanga*.

**Dhūmalekhā** (S) (F) 1. line of smoke. 2. one who is dark in visage. 3. a daughter of a yakṣa (*K. Sāgara*)

**Dhūmapāla** (S) (F) 1. protector of vapour. 3. a river (*M. Bh.*)

**Dhūmavarṇa** (S) (M) 1. smoke coloured. 2. grey or dark complexioned. 3. the father of the 5 daughters married to Yadu (*Bhāgavata*); a nāga chief (*H. Purāṇa*)

**Dhūmin** (S) (M) 1. smoking. 2. steaming. 3. one of the 7 tongues of Agni (*G. Sutra*)

**Dhūminī** (S) (F) 1. smoky. 2. one dark in visage. 3. the wife of King Ajamīḍha and the mother of Ṛkṣa (*M. Bh.*)

**Dhūmorṇā** (S) (F) 1. smoke covered. 2. fire; that which is sacred; all consuming; life giving. 3. the wife of Yama (*M. Bh.*); the wife of sage Mārkaṇḍeya (*M. Bh.*)

**Dhūmrā** (S) (F) 1. smoky. 2. vapourous. 3. a daughter of Dakṣa who was the wife of Dharma and the mother of Dhruva and Dhara (*M. Bh.*); another name for Durgā.

**Dhūmra** (S) (M) 1. smoky. 2. grey; purple; dim. 3. an attendant of Skanda (*M. Bh.*); a dānava (*H. Purāṇa*); a hermit in the court of Indra (*M. Bh.*); another name for Śiva; *Attingia elcelsa*.

**Dhūmrakeśa** (S) (M) 1. dark haired. 3. a son of Pṛthu and Arćis (*Bhāgavata*); a son of Bharata and Pānćajanī (*Bhāgavata*); a dānava (*Bhāgavata*)

**Dhūmraketu** (S) (M) 1. grey bannered. 3. a son of Bharata (*M. Bh.*); a rakṣasa; a son of Tṛṇabindu (*Bhā. Purāṇa*); a son of Pṛthu and Arćis (*Bh. Purāṇa*)

**Dhūmrākṣa** (S) (M) 1. grey eyed. 2. dark eyed. 3. a son of Hemaćandra and the grandson of Tṛṇabindu (*Bhā. Purāṇa*); a rākṣasa who was the son of Sumāli and Ketumatī and a minister of Rāvaṇa (*V. Rāmāyaṇa*); a Niṣāda king (*Sk. Purāṇa*); an Ikṣvāku king (*M. Bh.*)

**Dhūmraloćana** (S) (M) 1. grey eyed. 3. a general of the asura Śumbha (*Mā. Purāṇa*)

**Dhūmraśikha** (S) (M) 1. with a smoky plait of hair. 3. a rākṣasa (*K. Sāgara*)

**Dhūmrāśva** (S) (M) 1. with grey horses. 3. a son of Sućandra, the grandson of Hemaćandra, and the father of Sṛñjaya (*V. Rāmāyaṇa*)

**Dhūmravarṇa** (S) (F) 1. smoke coloured. 3. one of the 7 tongues of Agni.

**Dhūmravarṇa** (S) (M) 1. smoke coloured. 3. a son of Ajamīdha and Dhūminī (*H. Purāṇa*)

**Dhuna** (S) (M) obsession; tune; ruling passion.

**Dhundhī** (S) (M) 1. hazy. 2. obscure; sought after.

**Dhundhu** (S) (M) 1. roaring. 2. boisterous; obsessed. 3. an asura son of Madhu and Kaitabhā who was slain by Kuvalāśva (*M. Bh.*)

**Dhundhumāra** (S) (M) 1. slayer of Dhundhu. 3. a son of Triśaṅku and father of Yuvanāśva (*Rāmāyaṇa*); another name for Kuvalayāśva.

**Dhundhumat** (S) (M) 1. roaring. 2. boastful. 3. an asura killed by Gaṇeśa (*G. Purāṇa*)

**Dhundīrāja** (S) (M) 1. king of the obscure. 3. Gaṇeśa who is considered to be complex in character and therefore difficult to understand.

**Dhuni** (S) (M) 1. roaring. 2. loud sounding; boisterous. 3. a son of the vasu Āpa (*Bhāgavata*); a demon slain by Indra (*Ṛg Veda*)

**Dhuninātha** (S) (M) 1. lord of the roaring. 2. lord of the rivers; the ocean.

**Dhūpa** (S) (M) sun; perfume; incense; frankincensce.

**Dhūpāla** (S) (M) fragrant.

**Dhūpanravan** (S) (M) fragrant; shining; prince.

**Dhūrai** (S) (M) chief; yoke; head; leader; one charged with important duties.

**Dhuraṇdhara** (S) (M) 1. bearing a yoke. 2. chief; leader. 3. a rākṣasa (*Rāmāyaṇa*); another name for Śiva.

**Dhūri** (S) (M) 1. axis; yoke; pivot. 3. the son of the vasu Āpa (*Bhāgavata*)

**Dhūrjaṭi** (S) (M) 1. the pivotal ascetic. 3. another name for Śiva.

**Dhūśulyā** (S) (F) 1. soil coloured. 2. muddy. 3. a river of ancient India (*M. Bh.*)

**Dhūtaka** (S) (M) 1. agitator. 2. stirrer; destroyer. 3. a serpent in the Kaurava family (*M. Bh.*)

**Dhutī** (S) (F) 1. splendour; light; lustre. 2. majesty. 3. the goddess who protected Arjuna (*M. Bh.*)

**Dhūti** (S) (M) 1. agitator. 2. shaker. 3. an āditya (*V. Purāṇa*)

**Dhvajavatī** (S) (F) 1. decorated with banners. 2. a queen. 3. a divine attendant of a Bodhisattva (*L. Vistara*); the daughter of sage Harimedhās who lived in the sky as an attendant of the sun (*M. Bh.*)

**Dhvana** (S) (M) 1. making a sound. 3. a wind (*T. Āraṇyaka*)

**Dhvanamodin** (S) (M) delighting by its sound.

**Dhvani** (S) (M) 1. sound. 2. thunder; noise; tune; voice. 3. a son of the vasu Āpa (*V. Purāṇa*); a viśvadava (*V. Purāṇa*)

**Dhvanya** (S) (M) 1. suggested meaning. 3. a son of Lakṣmaṇa (*Rāmāyaṇa*)

**Dhvaṣanti** (S) (M) 1. brightened. 3. a Ṛg Vedic hermit (*Ṛg Veda*)

**Dhyāna** (S) (M) meditation; reflection; contemplation; discernment; intuition.

**Dhyānayogī** (S) (M) one who is proficient in meditation.

**Dhyāneśa** (S) (M) lord of meditation.

**Dhyānibuddha** (S) (M) a spiritual Buddha.

**Dībhaka** (S) (M) 1. destroyer. 3. a son of King Brahmadatta of Śālva who was killed by Balarāma (*Bh. Purāṇa*)

**Diddā** (S) (F) 1. eyeball. 3. a celebrated princess of Kaśmira (*R. Taraṅginī*)

**Didhi** (S) (F) firmness; stability; brightness.

**Dīdhiti** (S) (F) firm; stable; devotion; inspiration; religious reflection.

**Dīdhitimat** (S) (M) shining; brilliant; the sun.

**Ḍīdivī** (S) (F) 1. shining; bright; risen as a star. 3. another name for Bṛhaspati.

**Didyotiṣu** (S) (M) wishing to shine.

**Didyu** (S) (M) weapon; arrow; missile.

**Didyudyuta** (S) (F) 1. shining; missile. ?. thunderbolt of Indra (*Ṛg Veda*); an apsara.

**Digadhipa** (S) (M) 1. lord of a direction. 3. regent of a quarter of the sky (*M. Bh.*)

**Digambara** (S) (M) 1. sky clad. 3. another name for Śiva and Skanda; a Jaina and Buddhist sect (*B. Literature*)

**Digambarī** (S) (M) 1. consort of Digambara. 2. sky clad. 3. another name for Durgā.

**Digaṅganā** (S) (F) 1. maiden of the quarter. 3. quarter of the sky identified as a young virgin (*Bhāgavata*)

**Digbhrāja** (S) (M) 1. fire of the sky. 2. the sun. 3. father of Aṇu.

**Digīśa** (S) (M) 1. lord of a direction. 3. the regent of a quarter of the sky (*M. Bh.*)

**Digīśvara** (S) (M) 1. god of a direction. 3. the regent of a quarter of the sky (*M. Bh.*)

**Digjaya** (S) (M) the conquerer of all directions; wearing the sky as a garment.

**Digvāsas** (S) (M) 1. sky clad. 3. another name for Śiva.

**Digvastra** (S) (M) 1. sky clad. 2. bearing the sky as a garment. 3. another name for Śiva.

**Digvijaya** (S) (M) 1. victorious in all directions; victory over several countries. 3. a chapter in the *Mahābhārata* describing the victories of Yudhiṣṭhira.

**Dikkanyā** (S) (F) 1. maiden of a quarter; 3. quarter of the sky deified as a young virgin (*B. Śatakam*)

**Dikkārin** (S) (M) 1. elephant of the quarter. 3. a mythical elephant that supports a quarter of the earth (*Bh. Purāṇa*)

**Dikpāla** (S) (M) 1. protector of a direction. 3. regent of a quarter of the sky (*R. Taraṅginī*)

**Dīkṣā** (S) (F) 1. initiation. 2. consecration; dedication. 3. initiation personified as the wife of Soma, Rudra, Ugra and Rudra Vāmadeva (*Purāṇas*)

**Dīkṣapāla** (S) (M) 1. guardian of initiation. 3. another name for Agni and Viṣṇu.

**Dīkṣin** (S) (M) initiated; consecrated.

**Dīkṣita** (S) (M) initiated; consecrated.

**Dilīpa** (S) (M) 1. one who gives, accepts and protects. 2. a king who donates generously, receives taxes as revenue and protects his subjects. 3. an Ikṣvāku king regarded as among the noblest, the son of Anśuman, the husband of Sudakṣinā and the father of Bhagiratha and Raghu (*V. Rāmāyaṇa*); a nāga of the Kaśyapa family (*M. Bh.*)

**Dimbeśvarī** (S) (F) 1. goddess of creation. 3. another name for Durgā.

**Ḍimbha** (S) (M) 1. newborn. 2. a boy; a young shoot.

**Dīnabandhu** (S) (M) a friend of the poor; Supreme Spirit.

**Dinabandhu** (S) (M) 1. friend of the day. 2. the sun.

**Dinādhinātha** (S) (M) 1. lord of the day. 2. the sun.

**Dinādhīśa** (S) (M) 1. god of the day. 2. the sun.

**Dinajyotiṣ** (S) (M) illuminating the day; Sūrya or sunshine.

**Dinakara** (S) (M) 1. that which causes the day. 3. the sun; an āditya (*Rā. Upaniṣad*)

**Dinakarātmajā** (S) (F) 1. daughter of Dinakara. 3. the river Yamunā who is considered to be the daughter of the sun.

**Dinakṣaya** (S) (M) 1. day decline. 2. the evening.

**Dinamaṇi** (S) (M) 1. day jewel. 2. the sun.

**Dinānātha** (S) (M) 1. day lord. 2. the sun.

**Dīnānātha** (S) (M) 1. saviour of the poor. 3. a king who was a famous Vaiśṇava (*P. Purāṇa*)

**Dinānta** (S) (M) 1. day end. 2. the evening; dusk.

**Dinapati** (S) (M) 1. day lord. 2. the sun.

**Dinaprabhā** (S) (F) day's splendour; the sunshine.

**Dinarāja** (S) (M) 1. day lord. 2. the sun.

**Dinārambha** (S) (M) 1. daybreak. 2. the dawn.

**Dinaratna** (S) (M) 1. day jewel. 2. the sun.

**Dīndayāla** (S) (M) being kind to the poor.

**Dineśa** (S) (M) 1. day lord. 2. the sun.

**Dineśvara** (S) (M) 1. day lord. 2. the sun.

**Dinkaradeva** (S) (M) 1. lord of the sun. 3. another name for Sūrya.

**Diṅnāga** (S) (M) 1. mountain of a direction; elephant of a direction. 3. one of the 4 mountains that stand for and guard the 4 directions (*M. Bh.*); a Buddhist author (*L. Vistara*)

**Dīpā** (S) (F) illuminated; that which illuminates; enlightens.

**Dīpa** (S) (M) 1. that which illuminates, enlightens. 2. light; lamp; lantern.

**Dīpaka** (S) (M) 1. lamp. 2. kindling; inflaming; illuminating. 3. a rāga; a son of Garuḍa (*M. Bh.*); another name for Kāma; saffron (*Crocus sativus*)

**Dīpakalikā** (S) (F) the flame of a lamp.

**Dīpakarṇī** (S) (M) 1. with shining ears. 2. one who digests what he hears. 3. a king who was the husband of Śaktimatī and the father of Sātavāhana (*K. Sāgara*)

**Dīpākṣī** (S) (F) bright-eyed.

**Dīpālī** (S) (F) a row of lights.

**Dīpamālā** (S) (F) 1. garland of lights. 2. a row of lights.

**Dīpana** (S) (F) 1. illuminating; passion. 2. that which kindles, in flames. 3. an attendant of Devī (*T. Śastra*); Fetid Cassia (*Cassia occidentalis*)

**Dīpanī** (S) (F) 1. exciting; animating; stimulating; illuminating. 2. a tonic. 3. Lovage (*Carum copticum*)

**Dīpāñjali** (S) (F) a lamp for praying; a lamp held in the palm which is waved around the idol at the time of worship.

**Dīpaṅkara** (S) (M) 1. light causer. 3. a mythical Buddha.

**Dīpaṅkura** (S) (M) the flame of the lamp.

**Dīpapuṣpa** (S) (M) 1. with illuminated flowers. 3. Yellow Champa (*Michelia champaka*)

**Dīpāvalī** (S) (F) a row of lights.

**Dīpavatī** (S) (F) 1. containing lights. 3. a mythical river (*K. Purāṇa*)

**Dīpen** (S) (M) lord of the lamp; the light of the lamp.

**Dīpikā** (S) (F) 1. a small lamp. 2. light; lamp; lantern; moonlight. 3. a rāgiṇī; Fire plant (*Plumbago rosea*)

**Dīpin** (S) (M) inflaming; exciting; illuminating.

**Dīpita** (S) (M) inflamed; illuminated; manifested; excited.

**Diprā** (S) (F) radiant; flaming; shining.

**Dīpśikhā** (S) (F) the flame of a lamp.

**Dīpta** (S) (M) 1. illuminated. 2. blazing; hot; flaming; shining; bright; brilliant. 3. the son of the 3rd Manu (*V. Purāṇa*); *Gloriosa superba*.

**Dīptāgni** (S) (M) 1. blazing fire. 3. another name for sage Agastya.

**Dīptaketu** (S) (M) 1. bright bannered. 3. a son of Manu Dakṣasāvarni (*Bhā. Purāṇa*)

**Dīptakīrti** (S) (M) 1. bright famed. 3. the family of Purūravas (*M. Bh.*); another name for Skanda.

**Dīptanśu** (S) (M) 1. bright rayed. 3. another name for the sun.

**Dīptaroman** (S) (M) 1. bright haired. 3. a viśvadeva (*M. Bh.*)

**Dīptaśakti** (S) (M) 1. bright power; owner of a glittering spear. 3. another name for Skanda.

**Dīptaśikha** (S) (M) 1. bright flamed. 3. a yakṣa (*K. Sāgara*)

**Dīptatapas** (S) (M) of glowing piety.

**Dīptatejas** (S) (M) radiant with glory.

**Dīptavarṇa** (S) (M) 1. flame coloured. 3. another name for Skanda.

**Dīptavīrya** (S) (M) of fiery strength.

**Dīpti** (S) (M) 1. light; splendour; beauty. 3. a viśvadeva (*M. Bh.*)

**Dīpti** (S) (F) brightness; light; illuminating; enlightening.

**Dīptiketu** (S) (M) 1. bright bannered. 3. a son of Manu Dakṣasāvarni (*Bhāgavata*)

**Dīptimān** (S) (M) 1. bright; shining. 3. a seer of the 8th Manvantara (*H. Purāṇa*); a son of Kṛṣṇa.

**Dīptopala** (S) (M) 1. brilliant gem. 3. the white topaz.

**Dīrgha** (S) (M) 1. lofty. 2. long; high; tall; deep. 3. a king of Magadha (*M. Bh.*); another name for Śiva.

**Dīrghabāhu** (S) (M) 1. long armed. 3. an attendant of Śiva (*H. Purāṇa*); a dānava (*H. Purāṇa*); the son of Dhṛtarāṣṭra (*M. Bh.*); a son of Dilīpa (*Purāṇas*)

**Dīrghabhuja** (S) (M) 1. long armed. 3. an attendant of Śiva (*Ś. Purāṇa*)

**Dīrghadanṣtra** (S) (M) 1. long toothed. 3. father of Śrutā (*K. Sāgara*)

**Dīrghadarśana** (S) (M) 1. far seeing. 2. provident; sagacious; wise.

**Dīrghajangha** (S) (M) 1. with long thighs. 3. a yakṣa who was the elder brother of Puṣpadatta (*K. Sāgara*); a guhyaka (*Bhāgavata*); a servant of Padmapāṇi (*B. Literature*)

**Dīrghajihvā** (S) (F) 1. long tongued. 3. a rākṣasi; (*M. Bh./Rāmāyaṇa*); a mother in Skanda's retinue (*M. Bh.*)

**Dīrghajihva** (S) (M) 1. long tongued. 3. a dānava son of Kaśyapa and Danu (*M. Bh.*)

**Dīrghakaṇṭha** (S) (M) 1. long necked. 3. a dānava (*H. Purāṇa*)

**Dīrghaloćana** (S) (M) 1. long eyed. 3. a son of Dhṛtarāṣṭra (*M. Bh.*)

**Dīrghamukha** (S) (M) 1. long faced. 3. a yakṣa (*T. Āraṇyaka*)

**Dīrgharoma** (S) (M) 1. long haired. 3. a son of Dhṛtarāṣṭra (*M. Bh.*)

**Dīrgharoman** (S) (M) 1. long haired. 3. an attendant of Śiva (*H. Purāṇa*)

**Dīrghaṣravas** (S) (M) 1. with far reaching fame. 3. a son of Dīrghatamas (*Ṛg Veda*)

**Dīrghaśruta** (S) (M) with far reaching knowledge; renowned; respected.

**Dīrghatamas** (S) (M) 1. with a lot of anger. 3. a ṛṣi who was the son of Bṛhaspati, the father of Kakṣivat; Aṅga, Vaṅga, Kaliṅga, Pundra and Śuhma by King Bali's wife Sūdeṣṇā (*M. Bh.*)

**Dīrghatapas** (S) (M) 1. long penance. 2. absorbed in pious deeds for a long time. 3. the father of Dhanvantari (*H. Purāṇa*)

**Dīrghayajña** (S) (M) 1. performing a long yajña. 3. a king of Ayodhyā (*M. Bh.*)

**Dīrghikā** (S) (F) 1. a tall girl; an oblong lake. 3. a daughter of Viśvākarman (*Purāṇas*)

**Diśā** (S) (F) region; direction; the point of the compass.

**Diśaćakṣus** (S) (M) 1. purveyor of the skies. 2. with an all encompassing view. 3. a son of Garuḍa (*M. Bh.*)

**Diśāpāla** (S) (M) 1. guardian of a direction. 2. a regent of a quarter of the sky.

**Diṣṇu** (S) (M) liberal.

**Diṣṭa** (S) (M) 1. settled; directed. 2. appointed; assigned; fixed. 3. a son of Manu Vaivasvata (*Purāṇas*)

**Diṣṭi** (S) (F) direction; good fortune; happiness; auspicious juncture.

**Ditakiraṇa** (S) (M) 1. hot rayed. 3. another name for the sun.

**Ditaujas** (S) (M) glowing with energy.

**Diti** (S) (F) 1. glow. 2. brightness; light; splendour; beauty. 3. a daughter of Dakṣa; the wife of Kaśyapa and the mother of the daityas (*M. Bh.*) and the maruts (*V. Purāṇa*)

**Ditija** (S) (M) 1. son of Diti. 3. another name for Vṛtra.

**Ditijaguru** (S) (M) 1. preceptor of the daityas. 3. the planet Venus.

**Ditijarati** (S) (M) 1. enemy of the daityas. 3. another name for Viṣṇu.

**Ditikara** (S) (M) bringing glow; irradiating, illuminating.

**Ditimat** (S) (M) 1. possessed with a glow. 2. bright; splendid; brilliant. 3. a son of Kṛṣṇa (*Bhāgavata*)

**Divākara** (S) (M) 1. day maker. 2. the sun. 3. an āditya (*Rā. Upaniṣad*); a rākṣasa (*V. Purāṇa*)

**Divāmaṇi** (S) (M) 1. day jewel. 3. another name for the sun.

**Divapaṭi** (S) (M) 1. day lord. 3. another name for the sun.

**Divaratha** (S) (M) 1. chariot of the day. 3. a Bharata king who was the son of Bhumanya (*M. Bh.*); a king who was the son of Dadhivāhana (*M. Bh.*); another name for the sun.

**Divasabhartṛ** (S) (M) 1. day lord. 3. another name for the sun.

**Divasakara** (S) (M) 1. day maker. 2. another name for the sun.

**Divasamukha** (S) (M) 1. day break. 3. another name for the dawn.

**Divasanātha** (S) (M) 1. day lord. 3. another name for the sun.

**Divasapati** (S) (M) 1. day lord. 3. the Indra of the 13th Manvantara (*H. Purāṇa/Bhāgavata*); another name for Indra, Nahuṣa and Viṣṇu.

**Divaseśvara** (S) (M) 1. day lord. 3. another name for the sun.

**Divaspati** (S) (M) 1. lord of the day. 3. another name for Indra.

**Divaukasa** (S) (M) 1. sky dweller. 3. a yakṣa (*Vā. Purāṇa*)

**Divavasu** (S) (M) treasure of the sky; the sun.

**Divi** (S) (M) the Blue Jay (*Coracias benghalensis*)

**Divigamana** (S) (M) 1. sky travelling. 2. a planet; a star.

**Divijā** (S) (F) born of the sky; heaven born; celestial; a goddess.

**Divija** (S) (M) 1. born of the sky; heaven-born. 2. celestial; a god.

**Divijāta** (S) (M) 1. born of the sky; born of heaven. 3. a son of Purūravas (*V. Purāṇa*)

**Divikṣaya** (S) (M) heaven dwelling.

**Diviratha** (S) (M) 1. sky chariot. 2. the sun. 3. another name for the vasus, ādityas and rudras.

**Diviyaj** (S) (M) praying to heaven.

**Diviyoni** (S) (M) 1. sky born. 3. another name for Agni.

**Divodāsa** (S) (M) 1. heaven's devotee. 2. seeking the heavens; religious; pious. 3. the son of Vadhryaśva (*Ṛg Veda*); the father of Sudāsa (*Ṛg Veda*); a Kāśi king who was the son of Bhīmaratha and the founder of the Indian school of medicine (*M. Bh.*); the father of Pratārdana (*M. Bh.*); a descendant of Bhīma (*K. Sāgara*); another name for sage Bharadvāja (*Ṛg Veda*)

**Divoja** (S) (M) descended from heaven.

**Divolkā** (S) (F) 1. fallen from the sky. 2. a meteor.

**Divyā** (S) (F) 1. divine; celestial; heavenly; charming; beautiful. 3. an apsarā (*Ṛg Veda*); asparagus race mosus; Barley (*Hordeum vulgare*); Indian Pennywort (*Hydrocotyle asiatica*); Black Myrobalan (*Terminalia Chebula*)

**Divyaćakṣus** (S) (M) with a divine eye.

**Divyadarśana** (S) (M) of divine appearance.

**Divyadeha** (S) (M) with a divine body.

**Divyadevī** (S) (F) divine goddess.

**Divyagandhā** (S) (F) 1. with divine fragrance. 3. *Amomum subulatum*; Jew's Mallow (*Corchorus olitorius*)

**Divyagāyana** (S) (M) 1. divine songster. 2. a gandharva (*A. Koṣa*)

**Divyagovṛṣabhadhvaja** (S) (M) 1. with the banner of the celestial bull. 3. another name for Śiva.

**Divyājyotī** (S) (F) divine light.

**Divyakarmakṛt** (S) (M) 1. performer of divine deeds. 3. a viśvadeva (*M. Bh.*)

**Divyakṛiti** (S) (F) of divine form; beautiful.

**Divyanārī** (S) (F) 1. celestial maiden. 2. an apsarā.

**Divyāṅganā** (S) (F) celestial woman; apsarā.

**Divyāṅśu** (S) (M) 1. with divine rays. 2. the sun.

**Divyaprabhāva** (S) (M) with celestial power.

**Divyaratna** (S) (M) 1. a divine jewel. 2. a fabulous Ćintāmaṇi gem that grants all the desires of its possessor (the Pārasa stone or the philosopher's stone)

**Divyasānu** (S) (M) 1. of divine eminence. 3. a viśvadeva (*M. Bh.*)

**Divyāstrī** (S) (F) celestial woman; an apsarā.

**Divyayamunā** (S) (F) 1. the divine Yamunā. 3. a river in Kāmarūpa (*M. Bh.*)

**Divyendu** (S) (M) moonlight.

**Doraisvāmi** (S) (M) 1. lord of celestial grass. 2. sacred; venerated; dear to the gods.

**Doṣā** (S) (F) 1. night. 2. full of shortcomings. 3. night personified as the wife of Puṣpārṇa and the mother of Pradoṣa, Niśitha and Vyuṣṭa (*Bhāgavata*)

**Doṣa** (S) (M) 1. evening. 3. personified as one of the 8 vasus and the husband of night (*Br. Purāṇa*)

**Doṣahari** (S) (M) 1. enemy of sin. 3. the Asoka tree (*Saraca indica*)

**Doṣakara** (S) (M) 1. night maker. 2. the moon.

**Doṣaramaṇa** (S) (M) 1. beloved of the night. 2. the moon.

**Drākṣārāmeśvara** (S) (M) 1. the lord of the vineyard. 3. another name for Śiva.

**Dramila** (S) (M) 1. born in Dramila. 3.another name for Ćāṇakya.

**Drāpa** (S) (M) 1. matted hair; mud; heaven; sky. 3. Śiva with his hair matted.

**Drauṇayani** (S) (M) 1. son of Droṇa. 3. another name for Aśvatthāman.

**Drauṇī** (S) (M) 1. son of Droṇa. 3. another name for Aśvatthāman.

**Draupada** (S) (M) 1. son of Drupada. 3. another name for Dhṛṣṭadyumna.

**Draupadeya** (S) (M) 1. belonging to Drupada. 3. patronymic of the 5 sons of Draupadī – Prativindhya, Sutasoma, Śrutakīrti, Śatānīka and Śrutasena (*M. Bh.*)

**Draupadī** (S) (F) 1. daughter of Drupada. 3. another name for Kṛṣṇā who was the wife of the Pāṇḍu princes.

**Drava** (S) (M) 1. flowing; liquid; property. 2. practical; wealthy; juice; essence. 3. a viśvadeva (*M. Bh.*)

**Draviḍa** (S) (M) 1. property owner. 2. a landlord; wealthy. 3. a king of the family of Priyavrata (*Bhāgavata*); a gandharva who was the father of Kaṅsa and Anśumatī (*M. Bh.*); a son of Kṛṣṇa (*Bh. Pu.*)

**Draviṇa** (S) (M) 1. moveable property. 3. a son of the vasu Dhara (*M. Bh./V. Purāṇa*); a son of Pṛthu (*Bhāgavata*); a mountain (*Bhāgavata*)

**Draviṇādhipati** (S) (M) 1. lord of wealth. 3. another name for Kubera.

**Draviṇaka** (S) (M) 1. son of a wealthy person. 3. a son of Agni (*Bhāgavata*)

**Draviṇaratha** (S) (M) 1. with a chariot of wealth. 2. extremely wealthy. 3. an Aṅga king who was the son of Dadhivāhana and the father of Dharmaratha (*A. Purāṇa*)

**Draviṇeśvara** (S) (M) 1. lord of wealth. 3. another name for Kubera.

**Dṛḍha** (S) (M) 1. hard; strong; solid; massive. 3. a son of the 13th Manu (*H. Purāṇa*); a son of Dhṛtarāṣṭra (*M. Bh.*)

**Dṛḍhabhakti** (S) (M) firm in devotion.

**Dṛḍhaćyuta** (S) (M) 1. departed from firmness. 2. adaptive; flexible. 3. a son of Agastya (*Bhāgavata*)

**Dṛḍhadasyu** (S) (M) 1. resolute against enemies. 3. a son of Dṛḍhaćyuta also called Idhmavāha (*Bhāgavata*)

**Dṛḍhadhana** (S) (M) 1. with secure wealth. 3. another name for Gautama Buddha.

**Dṛḍhadhanus** (S) (M) 1. with a strong bow. 3. an ancestor of Gautama Buddha (*V. Purāṇa*)

**Dṛḍhadhanvā** (S) (M) 1. with a strong bow. 3. a king of the Purū dynasty (*M. Bh.*)

**Dṛḍhahanu** (S) (M) strong jawed.

**Dṛḍhahasta** (S) (M) **1.** strong handed. **3.** a son of Dhṛtarāṣṭra (*M. Bh.*)

**Dṛḍhākṣa** (S) (M) strong eyed.

**Dṛḍhakṣatra** (S) (M) **1.** having strong prowess. **3.** a son of Dhṛtarāṣṭra.

**Dṛḍhamatī** (S) (F) strong willed; resolute.

**Dṛḍhanemi** (S) (M) **1.** firm in beliefs. **2.** an idealist; a strong follower of morals. **3.** a king of the Purū dynasty who was the son of Satyadhṛti and father of Supārśva (*Bhāgavata*)

**Dṛḍhanetra** (S) (M) **1.** strong eyed. **2.** sure of vision; observation; conclusion. **3.** a son of Viśvāmitra (*V. Rāmāyaṇa*)

**Dṛḍhāṅga** (S) (M) **1.** strong bodied; hard. **2.** a diamond.

**Dṛḍhapāda** (S) (M) **1.** firm footed. **3.** another name for Brahmā.

**Dṛḍharatha** (S) (M) **1.** with a strong chariot. **3.** a son of Dhṛtarāṣṭra (*M. Bh.*); a son of Jayadratha and the present Avasarpinī (*He. Koṣa*); a king who should be remembered at dawn and sunset (*M. Bh.*)

**Dṛḍharući** (S) (M) with firm tastes; with unshakeable glory.

**Dṛḍhasaṇdha** (S) (M) **1.** firm in keeping engagements. **3.** a son of Dhṛtarāṣṭra (*M. Bh.*)

**Dṛḍhasena** (S) (M) **1.** with a strong army. **3.** a Yayāti king on the side of the Pāṇḍavas (*M. Bh.*)

**Dṛḍhāśva** (S) (M) **1.** with strong horses. **3.** a son of Dhundhumāra; a son of Kāśya; an Ikṣvāku king who was a son of Kuvalayāśva (*M. Bh.*)

**Dṛḍhasyu** (S) (M) **1.** violent against the impious. **3.** a son of Agastya.

**Dṛḍhavajra** (S) (M) **1.** with a strong thunderbolt. **3.** a king of the asuras (*Purāṇas*)

**Dṛḍhavarman** (S) (M) **1.** with strong armour; a firm warrior. **3.** a king of Prayāga; a son of Dhṛtarāṣṭra (*M. Bh.*)

**Dṛḍhavrata** (S) (M) **1.** staunch believer in faith. **3.** a sage of South India (*M. Bh.*)

**Dṛḍhāyudha** (S) (M) **1.** with strong weapons. **3.** a son of Dhṛtarāṣṭra (*M. Bh.*); another name for Śiva.

**Dṛḍheṣudhi** (S) (M) with a strong quiver.

**Dṛḍheyu** (S) (M) **1.** with a strong will. **3.** one of the 7 sages of the west (*M. Bh.*)

**Dṛgbhū** (S) (F) **1.** eye born. **2.** thunderbolt; the sun.

**Driḍhā** (S) (F) **1.** firm. **2.** fixed; stronghold; fortress. **3.** a Buddhist goddess.

**Driḍha** (S) (M) **1.** firm. **2.** fixed; hard; solid; strong; steady; resolute; persevering. **3.** a son of the 13th Manu (*H. Purāṇa*); a son of Dhṛtarāṣṭra (*M. Bh.*)

**Driḍhabuddhi** (S) (M) firm minded.

**Driḍhāyu** (S) (M) **1.** living a stable life. **3.** a son of Purūravas and Urvaśī (*M. Bh.*); one of the 7 sages of the South (*M. Bh.*); a son of the 3rd Manu Sāvarṇa (*Sk. Purāṇa*)

**Dṛmbhika** (S) (M) **1.** powerful. **2.** one who makes others afraid. **3.** a demon slain by Indra (*V. Purāṇa*)

**Droṇā** (S) (F) **1.** saviour of society. **3.** the daughter of Siṁhahanu (*B. Ćarita*)

**Droṇa** (S) (M) **1.** a bowl. **2.** wooden vessel; bucket; trough; Soma vessel; altar shaped like a trough; saviour of society. **3.** one of the 8 vasus who was the husband of Abhimatī and father of Harṣa (*Bhāgavata*); the son of Bharadvāja and military preceptor of Pāñćāla and general of the Kaurava army, was the husband of Kṛpi and the father of Aśvatthāman (*M. Bh.*); a son of Mandapala and Jaritā.

**Droṇāćārya** (S) (M) Droṇa, the preceptor.

**Droṇahanta** (S) (M) **1.** destroying Droṇa. **3.** another name for Dhṛṣṭadyumna.

**Droṇaputra** (S) (M) **1.** son of Droṇa. **3.** another name for Aśvatthāman.

**Droṇasūnu** (S) (M) **1.** son of Droṇa. **3.** another name for Aśvatthāman.

**Droṇodana** (S) (M) **1.** donated by Droṇa. **3.** a son of Siṁhahanu and uncle of Buddha (*L. Vistara*)

**Dṛṣadvata** (S) (M) **1.** stone like. **2.** that which is hard; firm; resolute. **3.** the father of Vārangī (*M. Bh.*)

**Dṛṣadvatī** (S) (F) **1.** stone like. **2.** that which is hard, firm, resolute. **3.** a river flowing into the Sarasvatī (*Ṛg Veda*); the mother of Aṣṭaka and wife of Viśvāmitra (*H. Purāṇa*); the mother of Pratardana (*H. Purāṇa*); the wife of Divodaśa (*H. Purāṇa*); the wife of Nṛpa and mother of Śibi Auśinara (*H. Purāṇa*); the mother of Prasenajit (*H. Purāṇa*); another name for Durgā.

**Dṛṣālu** (S) (M) **1.** full of light. **3.** another name for the sun.

**Dṛṣāṇa** (S) (M) **1.** seer; light, brightness; a spiritual teacher. **3.** a ṛṣi (*K. Upaniṣad*)

**Dṛśikā** (S) (F) good looking.

**Dṛśika** (S) (M) good looking; worthy to be seen; splendid.

**Dṛṣtasāra** (S) (M) of tried strength.

**Dṛṣtavīrya** (S) (M) of tried strength.

**Dṛṣtavīrya** (S) (M) of tried strength.

**Dṛṣṭiguru** (S) (M) **1.** lord of sight. **3.** another name for Śiva.

**Druha** (S) (M) son.

**Druhī** (S) (F) daughter.

**Druhina** (S) (M) **1.** who hurts asuras. **3.** another name for Brahmā, Viṣṇu and Śiva.

**Druhyu** (S) (M) **1.** one who loves nature. **3.** a son of Yayāti and Devayānī and brother of Yadu; a son of king Matīnara (*M. Bh.*)

**Druma** (S) (M) **1.** a tree. **3.** a king who was the incarnation of the asura Śibi (*M. Bh.*); the leader of the kinnaras who sits in the court of Kubera and sings (*M. Bh.*)

**Drumasena** (S) (M) **1.** with an army of trees. **2.** ascetic. **3.** a king who was a partial incarnation of the asura Garviṣṭha (*M. Bh.*); a warrior on the side of the Kauravas (*M. Bh.*)

**Druminīmila** (S) (M) **1.** with eyelashes like trees. **2.** one who is a lover of nature. **3.** a dānava king of Śaubha (*H. Purāṇa*); a son of Ṛṣabha (*Bhāgavata*); the husband of Kalāvatī and father of Nārada (*Brah. Purāṇa*)

**Drupada** (S) (M) **1.** firm footed. **2.** a wooden pillar, a column. **3.** a king of the Pañćālas who was the son of Pṛṣata and father of Dhṛṣṭadyumna, Śikhaṇḍin and Draupadī (*M. Bh.*)

**Druti** (S) (F) **1.** softened. **3.** the wife of Nakṣa and mother of Gaya (*Bhāgavata*)

**Dūdha** (S) (M) voice; milk.

**Dūdhanātha** (S) (M) lord of the voice; lord of milk.

**Dukul** (S) (M) **1.** resting at a shore. **2.** the Nepal Maroonbacked Imperial pigeon (*Ducula badia insignis*)

**Dulā** (S) (F) **1.** shaking. **3.** one of the 7 kṛttikās (*T. Samhitā*)

**Dūlāla** (S) (M) loveable youth.

**Dulārī** (S) (F) loveable.

**Dulī** (S) (M) **1.** happy. **3.** a sage (*A. Koṣa*)

**Dulī** (S) (F) a female tortoise.

**Dulīćandra** (S) (M) happy moon.

**Duliduha** (S) (M) **1.** collector of pleasures. **3.** a king of ancient India (*M. Bh.*)

**Dumatī** (S) (F) **1.** with bright intellect. **3.** a river (*A. Koṣa*)

**Dundhā** (S) (F) **1.** roaring; noisy; boisterous. **3.** a rākṣasi (*M. Bh.*)

**Dundu** (S) (M) **1.** flautist. **2.** a musician. **3.** another name for Vasudeva.

**Dundubha** (S) (M) **1.** born of kettledrum. **2.** the non poisonous watersnake. **3.** another name for Śiva.

**Dundubhī** (S) (F) **1.** born of a kettledrum; a throw of dice. **3.** a gandharvi (*M. Bh.*)

**Dundubhi** (S) (M) **1.** a large kettledrum; son of Dundu. **3.** a son of Andhaka and grandson of Aṇu (*Purāṇas*); an asura who was the son of Māyā, the brother of Māyāvi, the brother in law of Rāvana and was killed by Balin (*V. Rāmāyaṇa*); another name for Kṛṣṇa and Varuṇa.

**Dundubhīśvara** (S) (M) **1.** lord of drums. **3.** a Buddha (*B. Literature*)

**Dūra** (S) (M) **1.** difficult. **3.** vital breath or Prāṇa regarded as a deity (*Ṛg Veda*)

**Durabādhana** (S) (M) **1.** without an obstacle. **2.** one who cannot be stopped. **3.** another name for Śiva.

**Durādhana** (S) (M) **1.** difficult to withstand. **3.** son of Dhṛtarāṣṭra (*M. Bh.*)

**Durādhara** (S) (M) **1.** difficult to be withstood. **2.** irresistable; invincible. **3.** a son of Dhṛtarāṣṭra (*M. Bh.*)

**Durāpa** (S) (M) **1.** inaccessible. **3.** a dānava.

**Durārihan** (S) (M) **1.** slaying wicked enemies. **3.** another name for Viṣṇu.

**Durāsada** (S) (M) **1.** dangerous to be approached. **2.** difficult to be found; unparalleled. **3.** a son of Bhasmāsura (*G. Purāṇa*); another name for Śiva.

**Dūrbā** (S) (M) sacred grass; this grass is offered at worship.

**Durdama** (S) (M) **1.** difficult to subdue. **3.** a son of Vasudeva and Rohiṇī (*H. Purāṇa*); a son of Bhadraśreṇya (*H. Purāṇa*); a son of the gandharva Viśvavasu (*V. Purāṇa*)

**Durdamana** (S) (M) **1.** difficult to subdue. **3.** a son of Śatānīka (*Bhāgavata*)

**Durdharā** (S) (F) **1.** difficult to withstand. **2.** irresistable; insatiable; difficult. **3.** Ćandragupta's wife (*H. Purāṇa*)

**Dūrdarśin** (S) (M) **1.** farsighted. **2.** seer. **3.** a minister of Ćitravarṇa.

**Durdhara** (S) (M) **1.** difficult to withstand. **2.** irresistable; unrestrainable; quicksilver. **3.** a son of Dhṛtarāṣṭra (*M. Bh.*); one of Śambara's generals (*H. Purāṇa*)

**Durdharṣa** (S) (M) **1.** difficult to be assaulted. **2.** inviolable; inaccessible; invincible; dangerous. **3.** a son of Dhṛtarāṣṭra (*M. Bh.*); rākṣasa (*Rāmāyaṇa*); name of a mountain (*M. Bh.*)

**Durdharṣakumāra** (S) (M) **1.** inviolable youth. **3.** a Bodhisattva (*B. Literature*)

**Dūrepaśyā** (S) (F) **1.** far sighted. **3.** an apsarā (*M. Bh.*)

**Durgā** (S) (F) **1.** difficult to approach; the inaccessible or terrifying goddess. **3.** goddess of the universe worshipped in 64 different forms of which Pārvatī the daughter of Himavān and wife of Śiva is one (*T. Āraṇyaka*)

**Durga** (S) (M) **1.** difficult to approach. **2.** impassable, unattainable. **3.** a rākṣasa slain by the goddess Durgā (*Sk. Purāṇa*); *Commiphora mukul.*

**Durgādāsa** (S) (M) devotee of Durgā.

**Durgādatta** (S) (M) given by Durgā.

**Durgama** (S) (M) **1.** difficult to travel over. **2.** unattainable; impassable; difficult to traverse. **3.** a son of Vasudeva and Pauravī (*V. Purāṇa*); an asura born in the dynasty of Hiraṇyākśa, was the son of Taru and to fight whom the devas prayed to Devi who annihilated him and was consequently called Durgā (*Sk. Purāṇa*)

**Durgatināśini** (S) (F) **1.** eliminating distress. **3.** another name for Durgā.

**Durgāvallabha** (S) (M) **1.** beloved of Durgā. **3.** another name for Śiva.

**Durgavatī** (S) (F) **1.** owning a fort. **3.** a queen of Jabalpura.

**Durgī** (S) (F) **1.** one who lives in a fort. **3.** another name for Durgā.

**Durgilā** (S) (F) owning a fort.

**Duritākṣaya** (S) (M) **1.** one whose sins have been eliminated. **2.** sinless. **3.** a son of King Mahāvīrya (*Bhāgavata*)

**Dūritāri** (S) (F) **1.** enemy of sin. **3.** a Jaina goddess (*J. Koṣa*)

**Durjaya** (S) (M) **1.** difficult to conquer. **2.** invincible; irresistable. **3.** a dānava son of Kaśyapa and Danu (*M. Bh.*); a rākṣasa (*M. Bh.*); a son of Dhṛtarāṣṭra (*M. Bh.*); a son of King Suvira of the Ikṣvāku dynasty (*M. Bh.*); a son of Supratīka (*Va. Purāṇa*); another name for Viṣṇu; a son of Supratīka (*Var. Purāṇa*)

**Durlabha** (S) (M) **1.** difficult to be obtained. **2.** extraordinary; eminent; dear; rare; *Fagonia cretica.*

**Dūrlabhaka** (S) (M) **1.** difficult to be obtained. **2.** rare, precious. **3.** a king of Kāśmira (*R. Taraṅginī*)

**Durmada** (S) (M) **1.** false pride; illusion, unclear conception. **3.** a son of Dhṛtarāṣṭra (*M. Bh.*); a son of Dhṛta and the father of Praćetas (*Purāṇas*); a son of Bhadrasena and the father of Dhanaka (*Purāṇas*); a son of Vasudeva and Pauravī; a son of the gandharva King Haṅsa, and Unmadā (*K. Sāgara*); a son of the asura Maya (*Ā. Rāmāyaṇa*)

**Durmarṣa** (S) (M) **1.** difficult to manage. **2.** unmanageable; insupportable; unforgettable. **3.** an asura (*Bhāgavata*)

**Durmarṣaṇa** (S) (M) **1.** unmanageable. **3.** a son of Dhṛtarāṣtra (*M. Bh.*); a son of Śṛnjaya and Rāṣṭrapāli (*Bhāgavata*); another name for Viṣṇu.

**Durmukha** (S) (M) **1.** with a foul mouth. **2.** abusive. **3.** a Pāñćāla prince (*A. Brāhmaṇa*); a son of Dhṛtarāṣṭra (*M. Bh.*); a nāga; a rākṣasa member of Rāvaṇa's court (*M. Bh.*); a yakṣa (*Br. Purāṇa*); a general of Mahiṣa asura (*D. Bhāgavata*); a king in the assembly of Yudhiṣṭhira (*M. Bh.*); an astronomer (*A. Koṣa*)

**Duruktī** (S) (F) 1. harsh speech. 3. harsh speech personified as the daughter of Krodha and Hinsā and the wife of Kali (*Bhāgavata*)

**Dūrvā** (S) (M) 1. celestial grass (*Panicum dactylon*). 3. a prince who was the son of Nṛpañjaya and father of Timi (*Bhāgavata*)

**Dūrvā** (S) (F) 1. Panic grass (*Panicum dactylon*). 3. wife of Dhṛṣṭaketu.

**Dūrvākṣī** (S) (F) 1. ruining dūrvā grass (*Panicum dactylon*). 3. wife of Vṛka.

**Durvāra** (S) (M) 1. irresistible. 3. a son of King Suratha of Kuṇḍalanagara (*P. Purāṇa*)

**Durvāraṇa** (S) (M) 1. destroyer of troubles. 3. a messenger of Jalandhara (*P. Purāṇa*)

**Durvartu** (S) (M) irresistible.

**Durvāsas** (S) (M) 1. badly clad. 3. a sage who was the son of sage Atri and Anasūyā and thought to be a partial incarnation of Śiva (*Rāmāyaṇa*)

**Durvigāha** (S) (M) 1. cannot be pierced. 2. unpierceable. 3. a son of Dhṛtarāṣṭra (*M. Bh.*)

**Durvimoćana** (M) 1. difficult to be set free. 3. a son of Dhṛtarāṣṭra (*M. Bh.*)

**Durviroćana** (S) (M) 1. unmanageable. 3. a son of Dhṛtarāṣṭra (*M. Bh.*)

**Durviṣa** (S) (M) 1. cannot be obtained by simple rites. 3. another name for Śiva.

**Durviṣaha** (S) (M) 1. difficult to be supported. 2. intolerable; irresistible. 3. a son of Dhrtarāṣṭra (*M. Bh.*); another name for Śiva.

**Duryodhana** (S) (M) 1. invincible. 3. the eldest son of Dhṛtarāṣṭra and Gāndhārī and the leader of the Kauravas (*M. Bh.*); the son of Suvīra, the grandson of Durjaya who was the husband of Narmadā and father of Sudarśanā who married Agnideva (*M. Bh.*)

**Dūṣaṇa** (S) (F) 1. full of vices. 3. the wife of Bhavana and mother of Tvaṣṭri (*Bhāgavata*)

**Dūṣaṇa** (S) (M) 1. full of vices. 3. a rākṣasa general of Rāvaṇa (*M. Bh.*); a daityā slain by Śiva (*Ś. Purāṇa*)

**Dūṣaṇāri** (S) (M) 1. enemy of vice. 3. another name for Rāma.

**Duśćyavana** (S) (M) 1. unshaken. 3. another name for Indra.

**Duśkāla** (S) (M) 1. destroyer of time. 3. another name for Śiva.

**Duṣkarṇa** (S) (M) 1. listening to evil. 3. a son of Dhṛtarāṣṭra (*M. Bh.*)

**Duṣparājaya** (S) (M) 1. difficult to conquer. 3. a son of Dhṛtarāṣṭra (*M. Bh.*)

**Duśpradharṣa** (S) (M) 1. not to be attacked. 2. cannot be attacked, difficult to fight with. 3. a son of Dhṛtarāṣṭra (*M. Bh.*)

**Duśpradharṣana** (S) (M) 1. difficult to tame. 3. a son of Dhṛtarāṣṭra (*M. Bh.*)

**Duśpraharśa** (S) (M) 1. one who rejoices in evil deeds. 3. a son of Dhṛtarāṣṭra (*M. Bh.*)

**Dusśaha** (S) (M) 1. difficult to tolerate. 3. a son of Dhṛtarāṣṭra (*M. Bh.*)

**Dusśalā** (S) (F) 1. difficult to praise. 3. princes Dusśalā considered to be peerless, was the only daughter of Dhṛtarāṣṭra and Gāndhārī and the wife of King Jayadratha of Sindhū (*M. Bh.*)

**Dusśala** (S) (M) 1. difficult to shake. 2. firm; resolute. 3. a son of Dhṛtarāṣṭra (*M. Bh.*)

**Dusśāsana** (S) (M) 1. difficult to overcome. 3. a son of Dhṛtarāṣṭra who attempted to disrobe Draupadī after the Pāṇḍavas lost her to the Kauravas in a game of dice (*M. Bh.*)

**Dusṭara** (S) (M) difficult to resist; unconquerable; irresistable; excellent.

**Duṣyanta** (S) (M) 1. destroyer of evil. 3. a lunar dynasty emperor who was the son of Śanturodha, the husband of Śakuntalā and the father of Bharata (*M. Bh.*); a son of King Ajamīdha and Nīlī (*M. Bh.*)

**Duvasvatī** (S) (F) offering worship; enjoying worship.

**Dvādaśakara** (S) (M) 1. 12 rayed. 3. another name for Kāttikeya and Bṛhaspati.

**Dvādaśabhuja** (S) (M) 1. 12 handed. 3. a warrior of Skanda (*M. Bh.*)

**Dvādaśākṣa** (S) (M) 1. 12 eyed. 3. a Buddha; another name for Vyāsa and Skanda.

**Dvadaśātman** (S) (M) 1. appearing in 12 forms. 3. another name for Sūrya.

**Dvaimātura** (S) (M) 1. with 2 mothers. 2. another name for Gaṇeśa.

**Dvāpara** (S) (M) 1. the dice personified as a god. 3. the earlier form of Śakuni.

**Dvāparā** (S) (F) 1. born in the epoch of

Dvāpara. 3. a friend of Kāli (*M. Bh.*)

**Dvārakā** (S) (F) 1. with many gates. 3. Kṛṣṇa's capital on the west coast of Gujarāt supposed to have been submerged by the sea.

**Dvārakādāsa** (S) (M) 1. devotee of Dvārakā. 2. Kṛṣṇa's devotee since Dvārakā is associated with Kṛṣṇa.

**Dvārakānātha** (S) (M) 1. lord of Dvārakā. 3. another name for Kṛṣṇa.

**Dvārakāprasāda** (S) (M) 1. one who makes Dvāraka happy. 3. Kṛṣṇa.

**Dvārakeśa** (S) (M) 1. lord of Dvārakā. 3. another name for Kṛṣṇa.

**Dvārika** (S) (M) 1. door-keeper. 3. one of the 18 attendants of Sūrya (*A. Koṣa; H. Koṣa*)

**Dvibāhuka** (S) (M) 1. 2 armed. 3. an attendant of Śiva (*H. Purāṇa*)

**Dvidhātu** (S) (M) 1. of 2 parts. 3. another name for Gaṇeśa who is part human and part elephant.

**Dvija** (S) (M) twice born; a bird; a Brāhmin.

**Dvijapati** (S) (M) 1. lord of the twice born. 3. Ćandra which was born once from Atri's eye and then from the Ocean of Milk.

**Dvijarāja** (S) (M) 1. lord of the twice born. 3. another name for Ćandra, Garuḍa and Ananta.

**Dvijavāhana** (S) (M) 1. having a bird as a mount. 3. another name for Viṣṇu and Kṛṣṇa.

**Dvijeśa** (S) (M) 1. lord of the twice born. 3. another name for Ćandra or the moon.

**Dvijeśvara** (S) (M) 1. lord of the twice born. 2. a Brāhmin. 3. another name for Ćandra or the moon and Śiva.

**Dvimidha** (S) (M) 1. with 2 kinds of intellect. 2. one who knows the present as well as the future. 3. a Purū king who was the son of Hastin, the grandson of Suhotra and the brother of Ajamīdha and Purūmīdha (*A. Purāṇa*)

**Dvimūrdhan** (S) (M) 1. 2 headed. 3. a son of Hiranyākṣa (*A. Purāṇa*)

**Dvīpendra** (S) (M) 1. lord of the island. 3. another name for Rudra.

**Dvita** (S) (M) 1. existing in 2 forms. 2. one who practices the life of a sannyāsin or an ascetic while living in a house-hold. 3. a sage who was the son of Gautama (*V. Rāmāyaṇa*)

**Dvivaktra** (S) (M) 1. 2 faced. 3. a dānava (*H. Purāṇa*)

**Dvivida** (S) (M) 1. knower of 2 types of truth. 2. one who knows the empirical as well as the transcendal reality. 3. a monkey in the army of Rāma (*M. Bh.*)

**Dvividāri** (S) (M) 1. destroyer of Dvivida. 3. another name for lord Viṣṇu.

**Dviyodha** (S) (M) 1. fighting with 2. 2. a skilled warrior. 3. Kṛṣṇa's charioteer (*Bhā. Purāṇa*)

**Dyau** (S) (M) 1. bright. 2. heaven; illuminating sky; space. 3. a vasu also called Āpa (*S. Brāhmaṇa*)

**Dyota** (S) (M) light; brilliance.

**Dyotanā** (S) (F) 1. illuminating. 2. enlightening; shining.

**Dyotani** (S) (F) brightness; splendour.

**Dyućara** (S) (M) 1. walking through the heavens. 3. a vidyādhara (*K. Sāgara*)

**Dyudhāman** (S) (M) with one's abode in heaven; a god.

**Dyudhunī** (S) (F) heavenly Gaṅgā; the Ākāśagaṅgā or the Milky Way.

**Dyujaya** (S) (M) conqueror of heaven.

**Dyukṣā** (S) (F) of heaven; celestial.

**Dyukṣa** (S) (M) of heaven; celestial.

**Dyumaṇi** (S) (M) 1. sky jewel. 3. another name for Śiva and the sun.

**Dyumat** (S) (M) 1. bright; brilliant. 2. strong; splendid; excellent. 3. a son of Vasiṣṭha (*Bhāgavata*); a son of Divodāsa (*Bhāgavata*); a son of Manu Svārocíśa (*Bhāgavata*); a Bhārgava king (*Bhāgavata*)

**Dyumatsena** (S) (M) 1. with an excellent army. 3. a king of Śālva and father of Satyavān (*M. Bh.*)

**Dyumayī** (S) (F) 1. full of brightness. 3. a daughter of Tvaṣṭṛ and the wife of Sūrya.

**Dyumna** (S) (M) 1. splendour. 2. inspiration; glory; majesty; power. 3. a son of Manu and Naḍvalā (*Bhāgavata*)

**Dyumnahūtī** (S) (F) inspired invocation.

**Dyumni** (S) (M) 1. inspired. 2. majestic; strong; powerful. 3. a prince (*V. Purāṇa*)

**Dyumnika** (S) (M) 1. inspired. 2. majestic; powerful. 3. a son of Vaśiṣṭha (*Ṛg Veda*)

**Dyuniśa** (S) (M) day and night; one invested with day like, night-like virtues.

**Dyupati** (S) (M) 1. sky lord; a god. 3. another name for Indra and the sun.

**Dyuratna** (S) (M) 1. sky jewel. 3. another name for the sun.

**Dyutana** (S) (M) shining; bright.

**Dyuti** (S) (M) 1. splendour; brightness; lustre. 2. majesty. 3. a son of Manu Tāmasa (*H. Purāṇa*)

**Dyutikara** (S) (M) 1. illuminating. 2. bright; handsome. 3. another name for the Dhruva star.

**Dyutimān, Dyutimat** (S) (M) 1. heavenly; bright. 2. resplendant; majestic. 3. a Madra king whose daughter Vijayā married Sahadeva (*M. Bh.*); a son of the Ikṣvāku king Madirāśva and the father of King Suvīra (*M. Bh.*); a hermit of the family of Bhṛgu who was the son of Prāṇa (*V. Purāṇa*); a Śālva prince and father of Ṛćika (*M. Bh.*); a ṛṣi under Manu Dākṣasāvarṇi (*Bhāgavata*); a son of Manu Svāyambhuva (*H. Purāṇa*)

**Dyutita** (S) (M) illuminated; clear; bright; shining.

**Dyuvadhū** (S) (F) celestial woman; an apsarā.

E

**Edha** (S) (M) **1.** a type of wood; sacred; holy. **3.** fuel used for the sacred fire (*Ṛg Veda*)

**Edhā** (S) (F) prosperity; happiness.

**Edhas** (S) (M) **1.** sacred wood; happiness. **3.** wood used for the sacrificial fire.

**Edhatu** (S) (M) **1.** born of wood; having semen; fire. **2.** man; prosperity; happiness.

**Edhita** (S) (M) **1.** grown. **2.** increased; progressed; evolved.

**Eḍi** (S) (M) **1.** healing. **3.** a follower of Skanda (*M. Bh.*); a medicinal plant (*Cassia tora*)

**Egattalā** (Tamil) (F) the non-Aryan tutelary goddess of Madrās.

**Eha** (S) (M) **1.** desirous. **2.** desired. **3.** another name for Viṣṇu.

**Ehimāyā** (S) (M) **1.** an all pervading intellect. **3.** another name for the viśvādevas.

**Eila** (S) (M) **1.** son of Ila the earth. **3.** another name for Purūravas.

**Eilvila** (S) (M) **1.** son of Ilvilā. **3.** another name for Kubera.

**Ekā** (S) (F) **1.** one and only. **2.** alone; peerless; matchless; firm; unique. **3.** another name for Durgā.

**Eka** (S) (M) **1.** one; only. **2.** peerless; matchless; firm; unique. **3.** another name for Viṣṇu and the Supreme Being.

**Ekabaṇdhu** (S) (M) one friend.

**Ekabhakta** (S) (M) one who worships one deity.

**Ekabhakti** (S) (F) the worship of one deity.

**Ekaćakra** (S) (M) **1.** one wheel. **3.** the chariot of the sun; a demon who was the son of sage Kaśyapa and Danu (*M. Bh.*)

**Ekaćandra** (S) (F) **1.** the only moon. **2.** the best one. **3.** a mother in the retinue of Skanda (*M. Bh.*)

**Ekāćāriṇī** (S) (F) a woman devoted to a single man; obedient; a loyal chaste woman.

**Ekachit** (S) (M) with one mind; one with concentration; poise.

**Ekaćūda** (S) (M) **1.** single crested. **3.** a follower of Skanda (*M. Bh.*)

**Ekadā** (S) (M) the 1st one; giver of one; the seers who guide their pupils to know the only reality, the Absolute.

**Ekadanta** (S) (M) **1.** single tusked. **3.** another name for Gaṇeśa.

**Ekādaśī** (S) (M) (F) the 11th day; After a new moon or full moon considered sacred to Viṣṇu.

**Ekadeha** (S) (M) **1.** with one body. **2.** elegantly formed. **3.** another name for the planet Mercury.

**Ekadeva** (S) (M) **1.** the only God. **3.** Supreme Being.

**Ekadhanā** (S) (M) (F) **1.** a portion of wealth. **2.** one who has a portion of wealth.

**Ekādhipati** (S) (M) sole monarch.

**Ekadyū** (S) (M) **1.** supreme sky. **3.** a sage mentioned in a hymn of the *Ṛg Veda*.

**Ekāgra** (S) (M) **1.** concentrated. **2.** calm; stable; attentive; tranquil.

**Ekahans** (S) (M) **1.** the only swan. **2.** soul.

**Ekaja** (S) (M) (F) born alone; the only child.

**Ekajata** (S) (M) **1.** with a single twisted lock of hair. **3.** a warrior of Skanda (*M. Bh.*)

**Ekajatā** (S) (F) **1.** with a single twisted lock of hair. **3.** a tāntric goddess; a rākṣasi in the castle of Rāvaṇa.

**Ekajyotis** (S) (M) **1.** the sole light. **3.** another name for Śiva.

**Ekāk** (S) (M) once; alone.

**Ekākini** (S) (F) lonely; alone.

**Ekākṣa** (S) (M) **1.** single eyed. **2.** one with an excellent eye. **3.** a soldier of Skanda (*M. Bh.*); another name for Śiva.

**Ekākṣara** (S) (M) **1.** imperishable; the single syllable. **3.** the letter Om.

**Ekakuṇḍala** (S) (M) **1.** one earringed. **3.** another name for Balarāma, Kubera and Śeṣa who wore only one earring.

**Ekalā** (S) (M) solitary.

**Ekalavya** (S) (M) **1.** one with concentrated knowledge. **3.** the son of Hiraṇyadhanuṣ, a king of foresters, who sacrificed his thumb and skill for his Guru Dronāćārya and who epitomizes steadfastedness and courage (*M. Bh.*); a king who fought on the side of the Pāṇḍavas during the Mahābhārata (*M. Bh.*); a brother of Śatrughna who was abandoned in infancy and later adopted by the Niṣādha tribe of which he became the king (*M. Bh.*)

**Ekalinga** (S) (M) **1.** with one liṅga; the supreme phallus. **3.** another name for Śiva.

**Ekama** (S) (M) **1.** one. **2.** unique; peerless. **3.** the Absolute.

**Ekamatī** (S) (F) concentrated.

**Ekāmbara** (S) (M) **1.** with a single dress. **2.** the sky as his dress. **3.** a Jaina sect (*J. Literature*)

**Ekamevādvitīyam** (S) (M) **1.** the only one without a second. **3.** the Supreme Being – the one eternally existing entity, having no second.

**Ekāmranātha** (S) (M) **1.** the only lord of the mango. **2.** bestower of the fruit of one's deeds. **3.** the deity of Śiva at Kāñjivaram.

**Ekamukha** (S) (M) (F) **1.** single faced; with one mouth. **2.** the best kind of Rudrākṣaphala or the fruit of the Rudrākṣa tree (*Guazuma ulmifolia*) which is considered extremely auspicious.

**Ekanai** (S) (M) the only leader.

**Ekānanśā** (S) (F) **1.** new moon. **3.** another name for Subhadrā, the wife of Arjuṇa and the sister of Kṛṣṇa and for Durgā.

**Ekānaṅgā** (S) (F) **1.** lover. **3.** the daughter of Yaśodā and foster sister of Kṛṣṇa (*Bhāgavata*)

**Ekanātha** (S) (M) the only master.

**Ekanāyaka** (S) (M) **1.** sole leader. **3.** another name for Śiva as leader of the gods.

**Ekāṅga** (S) (M) **1.** single bodied. **2.** unique; rare; the only one. **3.** another name for Viṣṇu and the planets Mercury and Mars.

**Ekaṅgikā** (S) (F) **1.** made of sandalwood. **2.** fair; frequent; auspicious; dear to the gods.

**Ekānśa** (S) (M) the single part; portionless; whole; one.

**Ekāntā** (S) (F) lovely; devoted to one.

**Ekāntikā** (S) (F) devoted to one aim.

**Ekantin** (S) (M) (F) **1.** devoted to one object. **3.** another name for a follower of Viṣṇu.

**Ekapāda** (S) (M) **1.** one footed. **3.** another name for Śiva and Viṣṇu.

**Ekaparṇā** (S) (F) **1.** single leafed; living on a single leaf. **3.** the daughter of Himavāna and Menā, the sister of Durgā, Aparṇā and Ekapātalā and the wife of sage Devala (*H. Purāṇa*)

**Ekapāt** (S) (M) **1.** with a single garment. **3.** a demon son of sage Kaśyapa and Danu (*M. Bh.*); another name for Viṣṇu.

**Ekapātalā** (S) (F) **1.** living on a single leaf. **3.** the daughter of Himavāna and Menā; the sister of goddess Durgā and the wife of sage Jaigiśavyā (*H. Purāṇa*)

**Ekapiṅga** (S) (M) **1.** one eyed. **3.** another name for Kubera.

**Ekapuruṣa** (S) (M) **1.** the sole being. **3.** Supreme Being.

**Ékarāja** (S) (M) **1.** sole monarch. **3.** the herb *Eclipta alba.*

**Ekarāya** (S) (M) sole monarch.

**Ekasarga** (S) (M) closely attentive; concentrated.

**Ekaśṛṅga** (S) (M) **1.** one horned. **3.** a Saptpitṛ in Brahmā's court (*M. Bh.*)

**Ekāṣṭakā** (S) (F) **1.** a collection of 8. **2.** the time for consecration; the 8th day after the full moon in the month of Māgha (January-February). **3.** a Vedic deity who was the wife of Prajāpati and mother of Indra and Soma (*Ś. Brāhmaṇa*)

**Ekata** (S) (M) **1.** first; single. **3.** the son of Mahāṛṣī Gautama and brother of Dvita and Tṛta (*V. Purāṇa*)

**Ekatāla** (S) (M) **1.** a single beat. **2.** rhythmic; melodious; musical harmony.

**Ekātan** (S) (M) closely attentive; concentrated.

**Ekātma** (S) (M) one universal soul.

**Ekātvachā** (S) (M) **1.** one who keeps repeating the same thing. **2.** parrot. **3.** a follower of Skanda (*M. Bh.*)

**Ekavaktrā** (S) (F) **1.** one faced. **3.** a mother of Skanda (*M. Bh.*)

**Ekavaktra** (S) (M) **1.** one faced. **3.** a dānava (*H. Purāṇa*)

**Ekāvalī** (S) (F) **1.** a string of pearls. **3.** the daughter of King Raibhya and Rukmarekhā and wife of Ekavīra (*Bhi. Purāṇa*)

**Ekavīra** (S) (M) **1.** outstandingly brave. **3.** the founder of the Hehaya line of kings (*Ṛg Veda / A. Veda*)

**Ekavīrā** (S) (F) 1. outstandingly brave. 3. a daughter of Śiva (*M. Bh.*)

**Ekayāna** (S) (M) that doctrine following which one can be successful in life i.e. the doctrine of unity; worldly wisdom.

**Ekayaṣṭī, Ekyaṣṭikā** (S) (M) a single string of pearls.

**Ekayāvan** (S) (M) the wise one.

**Ekdak** (S) (M) identical.

**Ekendra** (S) (M) 1. the sole lord. 3. the Supreme Being.

**Ekeśa** (S) (M) 1. the sole god. 3. the Supreme Being.

**Ekeśvara** (S) (M) 1. the sole god. 3. the Supreme Being.

**Ekiśā** (S) (F) one goddess; the primal goddess.

**Ekiśa** (S) (M) one god; the primal god.

**Ekodarā** (S) (M) 1. born of the same womb. 2. a sister.

**Ekśikā** (S) (F) eye.

**Ektā** (S) (M) 1. unity. 2. union. 3. the son of Maharṣi Gautama (*V. Samhitā*)

**Elā** (F) 1. born of Ila; the earth. 3. cardamom; the cardamom creeper (*Elettaria cardamomum*)

**Elāparṇa** (S) (M) leaves of the Elā creeper (*Elettaria cardamomum*)

**Elāputra** (S) (M) 1. of the cardamom creeper. 3. a serpent son of Kaśyapa and Kadru (*M. Bh.*)

**Ellu** (S) (M) sesame seed (*Sesamum indicum*), considered divine as it is said to be born of sage Kaśyapa.

**Elokṣī** (S) (F) with hair as thick as the cardamom creeper.

**Elu** (Malayalam) (M) seven.

**Emūṣa** (S) (M) 1. the lifter. 3. the boar who raised up the earth when it was only one span in breadth (*Ś. Brāhmaṇa*)

**Eṇa** (S) (M) 1. doe; marked; spotted. 2. a black antelope. 3. another name for the zodiac sign of Capricorn.

**Eṇākṣi** (S) (F) doe eyed.

**Eṇavāda** (S) (M) 1. one who speaks of deer; one with a spotted speech. 2. eloquent; truthful. 3. a poet mentioned in the *Ṛg Veda*.

**Eṇī** (S) (F) a deer; spotted; a flowing stream.

**Eṇīpadā** (S) (F) with deer like feet; that which is fleet footed.

**Entilaka** (S) (M) 1. marked. 3. another name for Ćandra.

**Eraka** (S) (F) 1. a hard grass. 3. a grass which turned into a club when plucked by Kṛṣṇa; a nāga of the Kaurava family (*M. Bh.*)

**Eśa** (S) (M) 1. desirable. 3. another name for Viṣṇu.

**Eśā** (S) (F) wish; desire; aim.

**Eśaṇa** (S) (M) desire; wish; aim.

**Eṣaṇikā** (S) (F) fulfilling desire; a goldsmith's balance.

**Eṣikā** (S) (M) 1. one that reaches the aim. 2. an arrow; a dart.

**Eṣitā** (S) (M) desired.

**Etā** (S) (F) shining; flowing.

**Eta** (S) (M) 1. shining; painted; dappled. 2. kind of spotted deer. 3. the steed of the maruts (*Ṛg Veda/T. Samhitā*)

**Etahā** (S) (F) shining.

**Etapātra** (S) (M) 1. dappled leaves. 3. a nāga king who is depicted in both reptile and human form (*Purāṇas*)

**Etaśa** (S) (M) 1. shining; dappled horse. 3. a horse of the sun (*Ṛg Veda*); a sage extolled in the *Ṛg Veda*; a sage whom Indra helped against Sūrya (*Ṛg Veda*)

**Etī** (S) (F) arrival.

**Ettan** (S) (M) breath.

**Evāvāda** (S) (M) 1. truthful. 3. a singer mentioned in the *Ṛg Veda*.

**Evyāmarut** (S) (M) 1. protected by the maruts. 3. a hymn of the *Ṛg Veda*; a sage (*Ṛg Veda*)

**Evyāvān** (S) (M) 1. possessed with swiftness; swift. 2. granting desires. 3. another name for Viṣṇu.

G

**Gabhasti** (S) (F) 1. ray; light. 2. moonbeam; sunbeam. 3. another name for Svāhā the wife of Agni.

**Gabhastimata** (S) (M) 1. containing light. 3. another name for Sūrya.

**Gadā** (S) (M) 1. mace. 2. a mace of iron wielded only by the very strong (*M. Bh.*) 3. a demon son of Kaśyapa and Diti who was killed by Viṣṇu and whose bones were made into a club by Viśvakarman (*H. Purāṇa*)

**Gada** (S) (M) 1. sentence. 3. a brother of Balarāma and the son of Vasudeva and Rohiṇī (*H. Purāṇa*)

**Gadābhṛt** (S) (M) 1. one who wields a mace. 3. another name for Viṣṇu.

**Gadādevī** (S) (F) 1. mace lady. 3. Viṣṇu's mace personified as a beautiful woman.

**Gadādhara** (S) (M) 1. one who wields a mace. 3. another name for Viṣṇu.

**Gadāgada** (S) (M) 1. Gada and Agada conjoined. 3. the 2 Aśvins regarded as the physicians of the gods (*A. Koṣa*)

**Gadāgraja** (S) (M) 1. holding a mace. 3. another name for Kṛṣṇa (*M. Bh.*)

**Gaḍayitnu** (S) (M) 1. covering. 2. cloud. 3. another name for Kāma.

**Gādhi** (S) (M) 1. one who seeks knowledge. 2. one who stands. 3. the father of sage Viśvāmitra (*M. Bh./Rāmāyaṇa*); the son of Kuṣambha (*Rāmāyaṇa*); the father of sage Jamadāgni and grandfather of sage Paraśurāma (*M. Bh./Rāmāyaṇa*)

**Gādhija** (S) (M) 1. son of Gādhi. 3. another name for sage Viśvāmitra.

**Gādhinandana** (S) (M) 1. son of Gādhi. 3. another name for sage Viśvāmitra.

**Gādhirāja** (S) (M) 1. King Gādhi. 3. another name for Gādhi the king of Kauśambhi who is supposed to have been the incarnation of Indra.

**Gadin** (S) (M) 1. armed with a club. 3. another name for Kṛṣṇa.

**Gagana** (S) (M) 1. the moving one. 2. the sky; the heaven.

**Gaganadhvaja** (S) (M) 1. banner of the sky. 2. the sun.

**Gaganadīpikā** (S) (F) 1. lamp of the sky. 3. another name for the sun.

**Gaganaghōṣa** (S) (M) 1. the noise of the sky. 2. thunder.

**Gaganakuṇḍā** (S) (F) 1. pool of the sky. 2. *Jasminum pubescens*.

**Gaganāṅganā** (S) (F) 1. celestial damsel. 3. an apsarā (*Purāṇas*)

**Gaganamūrdha** (S) (M) 1. with a sky like forehead. 2. one with a large forehead. 3. a famous asura who was the son of sage Kaśyapa and Danu and who was later reborn as a Kekaya king (*M. Bh./H. Purāṇa*)

**Gaganasindhu** (S) (F) 1. ocean of the sky. 3. another name for the Ākāśgaṅgā or celestial Gaṅgā.

**Gaganasparśana** (S) (M) 1. touching the sky. 3. a marut.

**Gaganātmaja** (S) (M) 1. descendant of heaven. 3. another name for Soma or the divine nectar.

**Gaganavihārī** (S) (M) 1. wandering in the sky. 3. another name for Sūrya.

**Gaganamaṇi** (S) (M) 1. jewel of the sky. 3. another name for Sūrya.

**Gaganecara** (S) (M) (F) 1. moving through the air. 2. birds, planets and heavenly spirits.

**Gaganeśvara** (S) (M) 1. lord of the sky. 3. another name for Garuḍa.

**Gahininātha** (S) (M) 1. lord of mysteries. 3. a saint of the Nātha cult (*D. Śastra*)

**Gaja** (S) (M) 1. the origin and the goal; elephant. 3. one of the 8 elephants of the quarters; a monkey king who fought on the side of Rāma (*M. Bh.*); a son of Subala and younger brother of Śakuni (*M. Bh.*); an asura; an attendant of the sun.

**Gajadanta** (S) (M) 1. with the tusk of an elephant. 3. another name for Gaṇeśa.

**Gajagāmanī** (S) (F) with a gait as graceful as an elephant.

**Gajagatī** (S) (F) a gait as graceful as an elephant.

**Gajakarṇa** (S) (M) 1. elephant eared. 3. a yakṣa in Kubera's court (*M. Bh.*); another name for Śiva.

**Gajakūrmāśin** (S) (M) 1. one who devours an elephant and a tortoise. 3. another name for Garuḍa, the mount of Viṣṇu.

**Gajalakṣmī** (S) (F) Lakṣmī who is as graceful as an elephant.

**Gajamukha** (S) (M) 1. elephant faced. 3. another name for Gaṇeśa.

**Gajamuktā** (S) (F) pearl found on the foreheads of elephants, snakes and crocodiles.

**Gajānanā** (S) (M) 1. elephant faced. 3. another name for Gaṇeśa.

**Gajapati** (S) (M) 1. lord of elephants. 3. another name for Airāvata, the elephant of Indra.

**Gajarāja** (S) (M) 1. lord of elephants. 3. another name for Airāvata the elephant of Indra.

**Gajāri** (S) (M) 1. enemy of elephants. 2. lion. 3. another name for Śiva.

**Gajarūpa** (S) (M) 1. in the image of an elephant. 3. another name for Gaṇeśa.

**Gajaśiras** (S) (M) 1. elephant headed. 3. a warrior of Skanda (*M. Bh.*); a dānava (*H. Purāṇa*)

**Gajaskandha** (S) (M) 1. with shoulders like an elephant. 3. a dānava.

**Gajaṣya** (S) (M) 1. elephant faced. 3. another name for Gaṇeśa.

**Gajavadana** (S) (M) 1. elephant faced. 3. another name for Ganeśa.

**Gajendra** (S) (M) 1. lord of elephants. 3. a Pāṇḍyan king called Indrāyumna who was reborn as an elephant (*Bhāgavata*); another name for Airāvata, the elephant of Indra.

**Gajeṣṭha** (S) (M) 1. best among elephants. 3. another name for Airāvata; the creeper *Pueraria tuberosa*.

**Gajnan** (S) (M) root of a lotus.

**Gajodara** (S) (M) 1. elephant bellied. 3. an attendant of Skanda.

**Gajrā** (S) (F) garland of flowers.

**Gālava** (S) (M) 1. to worship. 3. a celebrated sage who was the son of Viśvāmitra (*Br. Upaniṣad*); a pupil of Viśvāmitra (*Vā. Purāṇa*); a seer of the 8th cycle of creation (*H. Purāṇa*); a grammarian (*Nirukta /Pāṇinī*); the tree *Sympolocos crataegoides*.

**Gamati** (S) (F) with a flexible mind.

**Gambhārī** (S) (F) 1. sky reaching. 2. the Gumhar tree (*Gmelina arborea*)

**Gambhīra** (S) (M) 1. deep; serious; considerate; patient; thoughtful; grave; influential. 3. a son of Manu Bhautya (*V. Purāṇa*)

**Gambhīrikā** (S) (F) 1. deep. 3. a river.

**Gamin** (S) (F) with a graceful gait.

**Gaṇa** (S) (M) 1. troop. 3. the demi god attendants of Śiva and Sūrya who are invoked to protect children.

**Gaṇā** (S) (F) 1. assembly; troop. 3. a female attendant of Skanda (*M. Bh.*)

**Gaṇādhīpati** (S) (M) 1. lord of the gaṇas. 3. another name for Śiva and Gaṇeśa.

**Gaṇadhyaksa** (S) (M) 1. leader of the ganas. 3. another name for Śiva.

**Gaṇaka** (S) (M) 1. one who calculates. 2. a mathematician; an astrologer. 3. a collection of 8 stars.

**Gaṇanātha** (S) (M) 1. lord of the ganas. 3. another name for Śiva and Gaṇeśa.

**Gaṇanāyikā** (S) (F) 1. consort of the lord of the ganas. 3. another name for goddess Pārvatī and Gaṇeśanī.

**Gaṇaparvata** (S) (M) 1. mountain of the ganas. 3. another name for Mount Kailāśa also called the mountain of silver.

**Gaṇapati** (S) (M) 1. leader of the gaṇas. 3. another name for Gaṇeśa.

**Gaṇapatihṛdayā** (S) (F) 1. the heart of Gaṇapati. 3. a Buddhist tantric elephant-headed goddess (*B. Literature*)

**Gaṇarupā** (S) (F) 1. of the form of ganas. 3. a flower of the Madār tree (*Erythrina suberosa*) which is offered to Śiva.

**Gaṇavatī** (S) (F) 1. followed by attendants. 3. the mother of Divodāsa.

**Gaṇḍā** (S) (F) 1. knot; a cheek. 3. a servant of the Saptarṣis or the 7 Seers (*M. Bh.*)

**Gaṇḍakaṇḍu** (S) (M) 1. scratching the cheek. 3. a yakṣa in the court of Kubera (*M. Bh.*)

**Gaṇḍakī** (S) (F) 1. obstacle. 3. a north Indian river flowing into the Gaṅgā (*M. Bh.*)

**Gandhā** (S) (F) fragrant.

**Gandhadhārin** (S) (M) 1. possessing perfumes. 3. another name for Śiva.

**Gandhajā** (S) (F) consisting of fragrant perfume.

**Gandhalatā** (S) (F) **1.** fragrant creeper. **3.** another name for the Priyangu creeper (*Aglaia odorotissima*)

**Gandhāli** (S) (F) **1.** perfumed. **3.** *Paederia foetida.*

**Gandhālikā, Gandhakālī** (S) (F) **1.** fragrant. **3.** an apsara; another name for goddess Pārvatī and Satyavatī, the mother of Vyāsa.

**Gandhamāda** (S) (M) **1.** delighting with perfume. **3.** a son of Śvaphalka (*Bh. Purāṇa*)

**Gandhamādana** (S) (M) **1.** intoxicating with fragrance. **3.** one of the 4 mountains enclosing the central region of the world and on which dwell Indra, Kubera and the yakṣas, part of the Rudra Himālayas it is east of Meru on the Kailāśa range and is watered by the river Mandākinī, is also the home of healing herbs including the herb Sañjīvinī which was brought by Hanumān to restore Lakṣmaṇa to life during the war between Rāma and Rāvaṇa (*V. Rāmāyaṇa*); a monkey general who was the ally of Rāma and was the son of Kubera (*V. Rāmāyaṇa*); a king in the assembly of Kubera (*M. Bh.*); the large black bee (*A. Koṣa*)

**Gandhamadanī** (S) (F) **1.** intoxicating fragrance. **3.** the tree *Caesaria esculenta.*

**Gandhamālin** (S) (M) **1.** with fragrant garlands. **3.** a nāga.

**Gandhamohinī** (S) (F) with an enchanting fragrance; the bud of the Ćampaka tree (*Michelia ćampaka*)

**Gandhapālin** (S) (M) **1.** protector of fragrance. **3.** another name for Śiva.

**Gandhaphalī** (S) (F) **1.** with fragrant fruit. **3.** another name for the Priyangu creeper (*Aglaia odorotissima*)

**Gandhapuṣpam** (S) (F) **1.** fragrance and flowers conjoined; collective name for the flowers and sandalwood offered at worship. **3.** Aśoka tree (*Saraca indica*); *Pandanus odoratissimus.*

**Gāndhāra** (S) (M) **1.** fragrance. **2.** a country which is now Kandāhar in Afghanistan· 3rd of the 7 primary notes of music personified as a son Rāga Bhairava (*M. Bh.*); a gem.

**Gandharāj** (S) (M) **1.** king of fragrance. **2.** the Cape Jasmine (*Gardinia jasminoides*). **3.** another name for Ćitraratha the chief of the gandharvas.

**Gāndhārapati** (S) (M) **1.** lord of Gāndhāra. **3.** another name for Śakuni.

**Gāndhārī** (S) (F) **1.** from Gāndhāra. **3.** the daughter of King Subala of Gāndhāra, the wife of King Dhṛtarāṣṭra and mother of the 100 Kauravas (*M. Bh.*); the wife of King Ajamīdha of the Purū dynasty (*M. Bh.*); a vidyādevī (*M. Bh.*); a rāgiṇī.

**Gandhārikā** (S) (F) **1.** preparing perfume. **3.** the herb *Hedychium spicatum.*

**Gandhārin** (S) (M) **1.** fragrant. **3.** another name for Śiva.

**Gāndhārīputra** (S) (M) **1.** son of Gāndhārī. **3.** another name for Duryodhana.

**Gandharva** (S) (M) **1.** celestial musician. **3.** gandharvas are the sons of sage Kaśyapa and Aristhā, who are both musicians and dancers and guardians of the Soma juice (*A. Purāṇa*); a king born in the dynasty of Janamejaya (*Bhāgavata*); a sage of ancient India; the Blackheaded Cuckoo (*Coracina melanoptera*); another name for Sūrya.

**Gandharvasenā** (S) (F) **1.** army of gandharvas. **3.** the daughter of the gandharva Dhanavāhana who lived on Mount Kailāśa (*M. Bh.*)

**Gandharvavatī** (S) (F) **1.** one who is as learned in the arts as the gandharvas. **3.** the queen of Kāmarupa or Assam (*M. Bh.*)

**Gāndharvī** (S) (F) **1.** speech of a gandharva. **3.** the granddaughter of sage Kaśyapa and Krodhavaśā, the daughter of Surabhī and the mother of horses (*M. Bh.*); another name for Durgā; a seductive water-nymph who haunts the banks of rivers (*T. Śastra*)

**Gandhasoma** (S) (M) **1.** with perfumed juice. **3.** the White Water lily (*Nymphaea alba*)

**Gandhavadhu** (S) (F) **1.** fragrant maiden. **3.** *Hedychium spicatum.*

**Gandhavajrā** (S) (F) **1.** with a perfumed thunderbolt. **3.** a goddess.

**Gandhavallī** (S) (F) **1.** fragrant creeper. **3.** the Jelly Leaf (*Sida rhombofolia*)

**Gandhavaruṇī** (S) (F) **1.** with perfumed juice.

3. *Alpinia galanga*.

**Gandhavatī** (S) (F) 1. sweetly scented. 2. wine. 3. the earth; the city of Vāyu situated on Mount Mahāmeru; another name for Satyavatī.

**Gandheśa** (S) (M) lord of fragrance.

**Gāndhinī** (S) (F) 1. fragrant. 3. another name for Pṛthvī; *Caesaria esculenta*.

**Gandhotamā** (S) (F) 1. the best fragrance. 3. another name for wine.

**Gāndinī** (S) (F) 1. one who gives a cow daily. 3. the daughter of the king of Kāsī, the wife of Śvaphalka, the mother of Akrūra and known for donating one cow to the Brāhmins every day.

**Gāṇḍīra** (S) (M) 1. hero. 3. son of Varutha and father of Gāndhāra; a species of cucumber.

**Gāṇḍīva** (S) (M) 1. illuminator of the earth; conquering the earth. 2. a magical bow which no weapon can damage. 3. the famous bow of Arjuna made by Brahmā which could fight 100,000 people at the same time (*M. Bh.*)

**Gaṇendra** (S) (M) 1. lord of a troop. 3. a Buddha.

**Gaṇeśa** (S) (M) 1. lord of the gaṇas. 3. the son of Śiva and Pārvatī having the head of an elephant, is the god who removes all obstacles from the paths of men, is worshipped at the commencement of any action, is the leader of the attendants of Śiva and occupies the most prominent place among the gods connected with Śiva, is considered to contain the entire universe in his belly and is the husband of Ṛddhi and Siddhi.

**Gaṇeśagītā** (S) (F) 1. song of Gaṇeśa. 3. a work of the Gaṇapatyas which is an interpretation of the *Bhāgavata* in which Gaṇeśa's name is substituted for Kṛṣṇa as the Supreme Deity.

**Gaṇeśanī** (S) (F) 1. consort of Gaṇesa. 3. the Śakti or female form of energy of Gaṇeśa, personified as his consort Gaṇeśani.

**Gaṇeśvara** (S) (M) 1. lord of the gaṇas. 3. another name for Gaṇeśa, Viṣṇu and Śiva.

**Gaṅgā** (S) (F) 1. the swift flowing. 3. the holy Gaṅgā river which washes away the sins of people, is personified as a goddess, the consort of Śiva, and the mother of Kārttikeya, was brought down from the heavens by King Bhagīratha in the form of a river that originated from Viṣṇu's feet and coursing through Śiva's hair flowed from the heavens to the earth, where she became the wife of King Śāntanu and the mother of Bhīṣma (*M. Bh.*)

**Gaṅgābhrit** (S) (M) 1.carrying the Gaṅgā. 3. another name for Śiva and the ocean.

**Gaṅgādāsa** (S) (M) 1. devotee of Gaṅgā. 3. son of Santoṣā.

**Gaṅgādatta** (S) (M) 1. given by Gaṅgā. 3. the 8th son of Gaṅgā and Śāntanu, also known as Bhīṣma (*M. Bh.*)

**Gaṅgādhara** (S) (M) 1. holding the Gaṅgā. 3. another name for Śiva and the ocean.

**Gaṅgāhṛday** (S) (F) the heart of the Gaṅgā; a sacred place near Kurukṣetra.

**Gaṅgaja** (S) (M) 1. son of Gaṅgā. 3. another name for Bhīṣma and Kārttikeya.

**Gaṅgājala** (S) (M) water of the Gaṅgā; the water of the Gaṅgā is held sacred by the Hindus because it is considered to wash away all sins.

**Gaṅgākṣetra** (S) (M) land through which the Gaṅgā flows.

**Gaṅgāla, Gaṅgola** (M) 1. of the Gaṅgā. 3. another name for beryl.

**Gaṅganātha** (S) (M) 1. lord of Gaṅgā. 3. another name for Śiva.

**Gaṅgāṅginī** (S) (F) daughter of Gaṅgā.

**Gaṅgāputra** (S) (M) 1. son of Gaṅgā. 3. another name for Bhīṣma and Kārttikeya.

**Gaṅgāsāgara** (S) (M) the sea of Gaṅgā; that point where the river Gaṅgā enters the ocean.

**Gaṅgāsuta** (S) (M) 1. son of Gaṅgā. 3. another name for Bhīṣma.

**Gaṅgeśa** (S) (M) 1. lord of Gaṅgā. 3. another name for Śiva.

**Gaṅgeśvara** (S) (M) 1. lord of Gaṅgā. 3. a liṅga.

**Gāṅgī** (S) (F) 1. of Gaṅgā; like the Gaṅgā; as sacred as the Gaṅgā river. 3. another name for Durgā.

**Gāṅgikā** (S) like the Gaṅgā; one who is as pure, sacred and pious as the Gaṅgā river.

**Gaṅgodaka** (S) (M) water of the Gaṅgā river.
**Gaṅgotrī** (S) (F) **1.** the mouth of the Gaṅgā river. **3.** a place held sacred by the Hindus.
**Gaṅgu** (S) (F) **1.** where Gaṅgā flows. **2.** alluvial land. **3.** a tutelary lunar goddess.
**Gāṅgeya** (S) (M) **1.** of Gaṅgā. **3.** another name for Bhīṣma; Nut grass (*Cyperus rotundis*)
**Gaṇikā** (S) (F) **1.** female elephant. **3.** Common White Jasmine (*Jasminum officianale*)
**Gaṇikārikā** (S) (F) **1.** made by the gaṇas. **3.** the creeper *Oxystelma esculentum*.
**Gaṇin** (S) (M) who has attendants.
**Gaṇita** (S) (M) **1.** numbered; regarded; mathematics. **3.** a viśvādeva who records time (*K. Upaniṣad*)
**Gañjan** (S) (M) (F) surpassing; excelling; conquering.
**Gañmānya** (S) (M) (F) distinguished; honoured; respected.
**Gannikā** (S) (F) **1.** counted of value. **3.** the Jasmine blossom (*Jasminum officianale*)
**Gara** (S) (M) **1.** fluid. **3.** a friend of Indra who was the author of a mantra or chant (*P. Brāhmaṇa*)
**Garbha** (S) (M) **1.** inner womb. **2.** the bed of a river; fire. **3.** a son of King Bharata (*A. Purāṇa*)
**Garbhagṛha** (S) (F) **1.** the inner house. **2.** the inner sanctum of a temple which enshrines the main deity and is regarded as the container of the seed.
**Garbhaka** (S) (M) a chaplet of flowers worn in the hair.
**Gārdabhi** (S) (M) **1.** an ass. **2.** dungbeetle; scarab. **3.** a son of Viśvāmitra.
**Garga** (S) (M) **1.** bull. **3.** a sage who descended from Viṣṇu, became the preceptor of the Yādavas, discovered some principles of astronomy and was the chief astronomer in the court of King Pṛthu (*Ṛg Veda*)
**Gārgī** (S) (F) **1.** churn; a vessel for holding water. **3.** a Brahmavādinī or learned woman born in the Garga family (*M. Bh.*)
**Gārgya** (S) (M) **1.** of the family of Garga. **3.** a sage who was a son of Viśvāmitra (*M. Bh./Rāmāyaṇa*)
**Gārhapati** (S) (M) **1.** one who protects the house. **3.** one of the 3 sacred fires (*A. Veda/V. Samhita/S. Brahmaṇa*); a Saptpitṛ (*M. Bh.*); another name for Agni.
**Gārhapatyam** (S) (M) **1.** householder's fire. **3.** a son of Agni.
**Garimā** (S) (F) **1.** grace; divinity; greatness; sublimity. **3.** one of the 8 siddhis acquired by yoga.
**Gariman** (S) (M) **1.** heaviness. **3.** one of the 8 siddhis of Śiva.
**Gariṣṭha** (S) (M) **1.** heaviest; most venerable; greatest. **2.** abode of greatness. **3.** a sage who was a devotee of Indra and sat in his assembly (*M. Bh.*); an asura.
**Garteśa** (S) (M) **1.** master of a cave. **3.** another name for Manjuśrī.
**Garuḍa** (S) (M) **1.** bearer of a heavy load. **3.** the king of birds who is the son of Kaśyapa and Vinatā, the brother of Aruṇa and Sumati, the husband of 4 daughters of Dakṣa (*Bhāgavata*), the father of Sampāti, Kapota and Mayūra and the vehicle of Viṣṇu; a son of Kṛṣṇa; an attendant of the 16th Arhat of the present Avasarpiṇī.
**Garuḍadhvaja** (S) (M) **1.** with Garuḍa as his banner. **3.** another name for Viṣṇu and Kṛṣṇa (*M. Bh.*)
**Garuḍāgraja** (S) (M) **1.** brother of Garuḍa. **3.** another name for Aruṇa the charioteer of Sūrya.
**Garuiṣtha** (S) (M) **1.** extremely proud. **3.** an asura.
**Garula** (S) (M) **1.** carrier of the great. **3.** another name for Garuḍa.
**Garutmat** (S) (M) **1.** winged. **2.** one who protects against poison. **3.** another name for Garuḍa; who is considered to live on snakes.
**Gārutmata** (S) (M) **1.** sacred to Garuḍa. **2.** emerald.
**Garvarī** (S) (F) **1.** haughty. **3.** another name for Durgā.
**Garviṣtha** (S) (M) **1.** extremely proud. **3.** an asura.
**Gati** (S) (F) **1.** power of understanding; speed. **2.** gait. **3.** motion personified as a daughter of Kardama and Devahūtī and wife of Pulaha (*Bhāgavata*)

**Gāthā** (S) (M) story; song; verse.

**Gāthikā** (S) (F) song.

**Gāthin** (S) (M) 1. story teller; a singer. 3. the son of Kuśika and the father of Viśvāmitra (*A. Brāhmaṇa*)

**Gāthina** (S) (M) 1. son of Gathin. 3. another name for Viśvāmitra (*A. Brāhmaṇa*)

**Gatitālin** (S) (M) 1. with a musical gait. 3. a warrior of Skanda (*M. Bh.*)

**Gātra** (S) (M) 1. body; corporeal. 3. a seer of the 3rd cycle of creation (*H. Purāṇa*); a sage who was the son of sage Vasiṣṭha (*V. Purāṇa*); the husband of Ūrjjā and the father of seven sages (*A. Purāṇa*)

**Gātragupta** (S) (M) 1. with a protected body. 3. a son of Kṛṣṇa and Lakṣmanā.

**Gātravat** (S) (M) 1. with a handsome body. 3. a son of Kṛṣṇa and Lakṣmanā.

**Gātravatī** (S) (F) 1. with a handsome body. 3. a daughter of Kṛṣṇa and Lakṣmanā.

**Gātravinda** (S) (M) 1. bodied; acquiring a body. 3. a son of Kṛṣṇa and Lakṣmanā.

**Gātū** (S) (M) 1. song; singer; gandharva. 2. the Indian Cuckoo (*Cuculus Scolopaceus*). 3. a descendant of Atri.

**Gauhar** (S) (M) 1. cow like. 2. white; one who has taken the colour of the cow; the pearl.

**Gaunārda** (S) (M) 1. celebrated bringer of light; that which is illuminating; enlightening. 3. another name for Patañjali the author of *Mahābhāṣya*.

**Gaura** (S) (M) 1. cow coloured. 2. that which is fair; beautiful; red or white in visage; a species of ox (*Bos gauras*). 3. mountain of gold, north of Kailāśa where Bhagiratha performed his austerities (*Bhā. Purāṇa*); another name for Śiva; the Button tree (*Anogeissus latifolia*); saffron (*Crocus sativus*); the Indian Beech tree (*Pongamia glabra*); another name for the moon, Śeṣa, the planet Jupiter, Ćaitanya.

**Gauradāsa** (S) (M) servant of Śiva.

**Gauramukha** (S) (M) 1. moon faced. 2. son of sage Śamīka (*Bhā. Purāṇa*)

**Gaurāṅga** (S) (M) 1. fair; cow coloured. 3. another name for Viṣṇu, Kṛṣṇa, Śiva and sage Ćaitanya.

**Gaurangī** (S) (F) 1. fair; cow coloured. 3. Cardomum (*Elettaria cardamomum*)

**Gauraprabhā** (S) (M) 1. moonlight. 3. Vyāsa's grandson and the son of Śuka and Pīvarī (*D. Bh. Purāṇa*)

**Gaurapṛstha** (S) (M) 1. mountain of the moon. 3. a sage who worships Yama in his court (*M. Bh.*)

**Gauraśiras** (S) (M) 1. one with a moon like head. 3. a sage who worships Indra in his court (*M. Bh.*)

**Gaurava** (S) (M) glory; dignity; prestige; respect; regard; gravity.

**Gauravāhana** (S) (M) 1. vehicle of Gaura; vehicle of the white. 3. the vehicle of Śiva; a king who was present at the investiture sacrifice of Yudhiṣṭhira (*M. Bh.*)

**Gaureśa** (S) (M) 1. lord of Gaurī. 3. a royal sage who was a member of Yama's assembly (*M. Bh.*); another name for Śiva and Varuṇa.

**Gaurī** (S) (F) 1. cow coloured; fair. 2. that which is yellow; fair; brilliant; beautiful; the Mallikā creeper (*Jasminum sambac*); the Sacred Basil plant (*Ocimum sanctum*). 3. the consort of Varuṇa (*M. Bh.*); a female attendant of Pārvatī (*M. Bh.*); a river of ancient India (*M. Bh.*); another name for the earth and Pārvatī.

**Gaurīhṛdayavallabha** (S) (M) 1. beloved of Gaurī's heart. 3. another name for Śiva.

**Gaurija** (S) (M) 1. son of Pārvatī. 3. another name for Kārttikeya.

**Gaurikā** (S) (F) 1. like Gauri. 3. another name for Śiva.

**Gaurīkānta** (S) (M) 1. beloved of Gaurī. 3. another name for Śiva.

**Gaurīnātha** (S) (M) 1. lord of Gaurī. 3. another name for Śiva.

**Gaurīprasanna** (S) (M) 1. one who pleases Gaurī. 3. another name for Śiva.

**Gaurīputra** (S) (M) 1. son of Gaurī. 3. another name for Kārttikeya.

**Gaurisa** (S) (M) 1. lord of Gaurī. 3. a ṛṣi of Yama's assembly (*M. Bh.*); another name for Śiva.

**Gaurīśaṅkara** (S) (M) 1. Gaurī and Śiva conjoined. 3. Mount Everest the tallest peak of the Himālayas (*M. Bh./Rāmāyaṇa*); the Himālayan Pear plant (*Purāṇas*)

**Gauriśikhara** (S) (M) 1. with a yellow crest. 3. a monkey king who helped Rāma with 60,000 monkeys (*M. Bh.*); the son of Subala and the younger brother of Śakuni (*M. Bh.*)

**Gauśra** (S) (M) 1. the time of cattle grazing. 2. daybreak. 3. a teacher of the *K. Brāhmaṇa.*

**Gautama** (S) (M) 1. remover of darkness. 3. a sage who was the husband of Ahalyā; a Brāhmin in the court of Yudhiṣṭhira (*M. Bh.*); a sage of great erudition and father of Ekata, Dvita and Trita (*M. Bh.*); another name for Śākyamuni, Droṇa, the historical Buddha.

**Gautamī** (S) (F) 1. dispeller of darkness. 3. the teachings of Gautama Buddha; another name for the rivers Godāvarī and Gomatī, goddess Durgā, and Kṛpi the wife of Droṇa.

**Gavah** (S) (F) 1. the moving ones. 2. the stars of heaven.

**Gavākṣa** (S) (M) 1. bull's eye. 2. window. 3. a monkey king who helped Rāma with 60,000 monkeys (*M. Bh.*); a brother of Śakuni (*M. Bh.*)

**Gavala** (S) (M) Wild buffalo; buffalo horn.

**Gavalagaṇa** (S) (M) 1. possessing many buffaloes. 2. a cowherd. 3. the father of Sañjaya (*M. Bh.*)

**Gavalagaṇi** (S) (M) 1. son of Gavalagaṇa. 3. another name for Sañjaya.

**Gavamṛita** (S) (M) nectar of the cow; milk; nectar of light.

**Gavasīra** (S) (M) 1. mixed with milk. 3. another name for Soma or the nectar of the gods.

**Gavaṣṭhira** (S) (M) 1. steady light. 2. a deity which emits light. 3. a sage who was a descendant of Atri (*Ṛg Veda*)

**Gavaya** (S) (M) 1. made of milk. 3. a monkey chief who helped Rāma (*M. Bh.*)

**Gavendra** (S) (M) 1. lord of oxen; bull. 3. another name for Viṣṇu.

**Gaveṣin** (S) (M) 1. seeking. 3. a son of Ćitraka and brother of Pṛthu.

**Gaveṣṭhin** (S) (M) 1. seeking cattle. 3. a dānava (*H. Purāṇa*); father of Śumbha.

**Gaviṣṭha** (S) (M) 1. abode of light. 2. Sūrya as the emitter of light. 3. an asura who was incarnated as King Drumasena (*M. Bh.*)

**Gavīṣvara** (S) (M) 1. lord of oxen. 3. another name for Viṣṇu.

**Gaya** (S) (M) 1. worth going to; worth having. 2. wealth; household; offspring; sky. 3. a sacred place in Bihar near the Gaya mountains where Buddha is supposed to have performed his penance (*B. Literature*); a king who was the son of Āyus and Svarbhānu and the grandson of Purūravas (*H. Purāṇa*); a king of the Pṛthu line (*H. Purāṇa*); a king who was the descendant of Dhruva (*A. Purāṇa*); a king who was also a royal sage and son of Amūrtarayas (*M. Bh.*); an asura (*M. Bh.*); a son of Ūru and Agneyī; a son of Havirdhāna and Dhīśaṇā; a monkey follower of Rāma; a son of Naklṣa and Druti; a Manu.

**Gāyaka** (S) (M) 1. singer. 2. wealthy; with offspring. 3. a warrior of Skanda (*M. Bh.*)

**Gayan** (S) (M) where objects move; the sky.

**Gayand** (S) (M) tusker; an elephant.

**Gāyanti** (S) (F) 1. of Gaya. 3. wife of King Gaya the royal sage.

**Gāyantikā** (S) (F) 1. singing. 3. a Himalayan cave.

**Gayāparvata** (S) (M) the mountain of Gaya, the sacred mountain of Gaya on which is situated Brahmāsaras or the pool of Brahmā.

**Gayāplata** (S) (M) 1. able to go. 2. that which is traversable. 3. the son of Plati and the composer of 2 hymns of the *A. Brāhmaṇa.*

**Gayāprasāda** (S) (M) the blessing of Gaya, the blessing of the sacred place of pilgrimage – Gaya.

**Gayāśiras** (S) (M) the peak of the Gaya mountain.

**Gāyatrī** (S) (F) 1. 3 phased verse. 2. a collection of 38-lettered Anuṣṭupa hymns; a Vedic mantra; a hymn to the sun. 3. one of the 7 horses of the sun; another name for Sarasvatī the consort of Brahmā and the mother of the Vedas; Black Catechu tree (*Acacia catechu*)

**Gāyatriṇī** (S) (F) one who sings hymns of the *Sāma Veda.*

**Geṣṇā** (S) (F) singer.

**Geyarājan** (S) (M) 1. king of songs. 3. a ćakravartin.

**Ghanajñānī** (S) (F) 1. deeply wise; profoundly wise. 3. another name for Durgā.

**Ghanāmbu** (S) (M) 1. cloud water. 3. another name for rain.

**Ghanāñjanī** (S) (F) 1. with collyrium as black as the clouds. 3. another name for Durgā.

**Ghanarām** (S) (M) 1. dependant on clouds; abode of clouds. 2. a garden.

**Ghanaśyāma** (S) (M) 1. as dark as a cloud. 3. another name for Kṛṣṇa who is of a dark visage.

**Ghanaśravas** (S) (M) 1. of pervading fame. 3. an attendant of Skanda (*M. Bh.*)

**Ghanavāhana** (S) (M) 1. with clouds as vehicles. 3. another name for Śiva and Indra.

**Ghanāvallī, Ghanavallikā** (S) (F) 1. creeper of the clouds. 2. lightning.

**Ghansara** (S) (M) 1. fragrant; auspicious; sacred. 2. camphor (*Cinnamonum comphora*).

**Ghaṇṭa** (S) (F) 1. bell. 2. objects used in Hindu rituals especially for Śiva (*Ś. Purāṇa*). 3. a Brāhmin of the Vasiṣṭha family who helped Indrayumna (*Rāmāyaṇa*)

**Ghaṇṭadhara** (S) (M) 1. one who holds a bell. 3. an asura who was a member of Varuṇa's court (*M. Bh.*)

**Ghaṇṭākarṇa** (S) (M) 1. bell eared. 3. an attendant of Skanda and Śiva (*Ś. Purāṇa*); a demon who attained salvation through the worship of Viṣṇu (*H. Purāṇa*)

**Ghaṇṭeśvara** (S) (M) 1. lord of the bells. 3. a son of Mangala or Mars and Medhā (*Brah. Purāṇa*)

**Ghaṇṭin** (S) (M) 1. one who sounds like a bell. 3. another name for Śiva.

**Gharbharaṇ** (S) (M) to be embedded in one's heart.

**Gharman** (S) (M) 1. cauldron. 2. the cauldron used for boiling milk for the sacrifice. 3. a king of the Aṅga dynasty (*M. Bh.*)

**Ghoṣā** (S) (F) 1. noisy; resounding. 2. a proclamation; fame. 3. an ascetic daughter of King Kakṣīvān famed for her knowledge of the *Ṛg Veda*; the climber *Luffa echinata*.

**Ghoṣavatī** (S) (F) 1. resounding. 2. resonant. 3. the famous viṇā or lute of the emperor Udayana (*K. Sāgara*)

**Ghoṣiṇī** (S) (F) 1. famed; proclaimed; noisy. 3. the female attendants of Rudra (*Sk. Purāṇa*)

**Ghaṭaja** (S) (M) 1. born from a pitcher. 3. another name for sage Agastya who is considered to have been born in a water jar.

**Ghaṭajānuka** (S) (M) 1. with pot-shaped knees. 3. a sage who was a prominent member of Yudhiṣṭhira's assembly (*M. Bh.*)

**Ghaṭakarpara** (S) (M) 1. of pitcher. 2. a collection of weapons. 3. one of the 9 great poets of Sanskṛt, said to have been one of the 9 gems of Vikramāditya's court.

**Ghaṭin** (S) (M) 1. with a waterjar. 3. the zodiac sign of Aquarius; another name for Śiva.

**Ghaṭodara** (S) (M) 1. pot bellied. 3. an attendant of Varuṇa; a rākṣasa (*M. Bh.*); another name for Gaṇeśa.

**Ghaṭotkacha** (S) (M) 1. pot headed. 3. the son of Bhīma the Pāṇḍava prince and Hiḍimbā (*M. Bh.*)

**Ghṛta** (S) (M) 1. clarified butter. 2. used for the sacrificial fire. 3. a king of the Aṅga dynasty who was the son of Gharman and the father of Viduṣa (*M. Bh.*)

**Ghṛtācī** (S) (F) 1. abounding in clarified butter; full of water. 3. a beautiful apsarā who was the mother of Śuka by Vyāsa, Droṇācārya by sage Bharadvāja and a 100 daughters by sage Kuśanābha (*M. Bh.*); *Amomum subulatum*.

**Ghṛtapas** (S) (M) 1. one who drinks ghee. 3. a sage who lived on ghee and was a disciple of Brahmā (*Bhā. Purāṇa*)

**Ghṛtapṛṣṭha** (S) (M) 1. whose back is brilliant with clarified butter. 3. a son of Priyavrata and Barhiṣmatī; another name for Agni.

**Ghṛtavatī** (S) (F) 1. composed of clarified butter. 3. a river of ancient India (*M. Bh.*)

**Ghugharī** (S) (F) bracelet of jingling bells.

**Ghūrṇikā** (S) (F) 1. one who whirls. 3. the foster mother of Devayānī the daughter of Śukra (*M. Bh.*)

**Gīra** (S) (F) 1. speech; voice; language; word; song; vedic hymn. 3. another name for Sarasvatī.

**Gīradevī** (S) (F) 1. the goddess of speech. 2. one who is learned; wise. 3. another name for the goddess Sarasvatī.

**Gīrapati** (S) (M) 1. lord of speech; consort of Sarasvatī. 3. another name for Brahmā and Bṛhaspati the preceptor of the gods.

**Gīratha** (S) (M) 1. learned. 3. another name for Bṛhaspati.

**Giri** (S) (M) 1. mountain; honorific title given to ṛṣis; number 8; cloud; ball. 3. a son of Śvaphalka.

**Giribālā** (S) (M) 1. daughter of the mountain. 3. another name for Pārvatī.

**Giribāndhava** (S) (M) 1. friend of mountains. 3. another name for Śiva.

**Giribhū** (S) (F) 1. originating from the mountain. 3. another name for the holy Gaṅgā and Pārvatī.

**Giridhara, Giridhārī** (S) (M) 1. holder of the mountain. 3. another name for Kṛṣṇa who in order to save the people of Vrindāvana from the deluge which Indra released in anger, lifted the Govardhana mountain on his finger to serve as an umbrella.

**Giridhvaja** (S) (M) 1. with the mountain as its banner. 3. Indra's thunderbolt.

**Girigaṅgā** (S) (F) Gaṅgā that comes from the mountains.

**Girijā** (S) (F) 1. daughter of the mountain. 3. Black myrobalan tree (*Terminalia chebula*); *Bauhinia vareigata* tree; the Cotton Teal bird (*Nettopus coromandelianus*); another name for Pārvatī the daughter of Himāvana and Menā and the consort of Śiva.

**Girijambā** (S) (F) 1. daughter of the mountain. 3. another name for Pārvatī.

**Girijānātha** (S) (M) 1. lord of Pārvatī. 3. another name for Śiva.

**Girijāpati** (S) (M) 1. lord of Pārvatī. 3. another name for Śiva.

**Girijāprasāda** (S) (M) given by the blessing of Pārvatī.

**Girijāvallabha** (S) (M) 1. beloved of Pārvatī. 3. another name for Śiva.

**Girijāvara** (S) (M) 1. consort of Pārvatī. 3. another name for Śiva.

**Girijvara** (S) (M) 1. best among the rocks. 3. Indra's thunderbolt.

**Girika** (S) (M) 1. the heart of the gods. 3. a nāga chief; an attendant of Śiva.

**Girikā** (S) (F) 1. summit of a mountain. 3. the daughter of the river Śaktimatī and the wife of Uparićara and the wife of Vasu (*M. Bh.*)

**Girikarṇī** (S) (F) 1. lotus of the mountain. 3. a lotus (*A. Koṣa*)

**Girikarṇikā** (S) (F) 1. having mountains for-seed vessels. 2. the earth. 3. the Arabian Manna plant (*Alhagi camelorum*); the Blue Pea (*Clitoria ternatea*); the Wild Guava (*Careya arborea*)

**Girīkṣita** (S) (M) 1. living on the mountain. 3. another name for Śiva.

**Girilāla** (S) (M) 1. son of the mountain lord. 3. another name for Gaṇeśa and Kārttikeya.

**Girimallikā** (S) (F) creeper of the mountain; a flower (*Wrightia antidysenterica*)

**Girimāna** (S) (M) 1. like a mountain. 2. a powerful elephant.

**Girinandana** (S) (M) 1. son of the lord of the mountain. 3. another name for Kārttikeya and Gaṇeśa.

**Girinandinī** (S) (F) 1. daughter of the mountain. 3. another name for Pārvatī and Gaṅgā.

**Girināthа** (S) (M) 1. lord of the mountains. 3. another name for Śiva.

**Girīndra** (S) (M) 1. lord of speech. 3. another name for Śiva.

**Girindra** (S) (M) 1. lord of the mountains; the highest mountain. 3. another name for Śiva.

**Girindramohinī** (S) (F) 1. beloved of the lord of the mountain. 3. another name for Pārvatī.

**Giripati** (S) (M) 1. lord of the mountain. 3. another name for Śiva.

**Girirāj** (S) (M) 1. king of the mountains. 3. another name for Himavān.

**Girisā** (S) (F) 1. lady of the mountains. 3. another name for Pārvatī.

**Girīśa** (S) (M) 1. lord of speech. 3. another name for Bṛhaspati.

**Giriśa** (S) (M) 1. lord of the mountain. 3. another name for Rudra/Śiva and Himavān.

**Girīṣmā** (S) (F) summer.

**Girisutā** (S) (F) 1. daughter of the mountain.

3. another name for Pārvatī.

**Girivara** (S) (M) **1.** excellent mountain. **3.** another name for Kṛṣṇa after he held Mount Govardhana.

**Girni** (S) (F) praise; celebrity.

**Gita** (S) (M) (F) song; lyric; poem.

**Gītā** (S) (F) **1.** song; lyric; poem. **3.** a religious book of the Hindus consisting of a sermon given by Kṛṣṇa to Arjuna during the war of Mahabharata.

**Gītālī** (S) (F) lover of song.

**Gītāñjali** (S) (F) devotional offering of a hymn.

**Gītapriya** (S) (M) **1.** one who loves music. **3.** an attendant of Skanda (*M. Bh.*); another name for Śiva.

**Gītāśrī** (S) (F) the divine Gītā.

**Gītavidyādhara** (S) (M) **1.** scholar of the art of music. **3.** a gandharva who was a great musician (*H. Purāṇa*)

**Gīti** (S) (F) song.

**Gītikā** (S) (F) a short song.

**Go** (S) (M) (F) **1.** cow; bull; ox; bullock. **2.** ray; thunderbolt; moon; sun; heaven. **3.** a wife of sage Pulastya and mother of Vaiśravaṇa (*M. Bh.*); a daughter of Kakutstha and wife of Yayāti; another name for Gaurī.

**Gobhānu** (S) (M) **1.** king of cattle. **3.** a king who was the grandson of Turvasu of the Purū dynasty (*A. Purāṇa*); another name for Śiva.

**Godā** (S) (M) **1.** one who gives cows. **3.** a follower of Skanda (*M. Bh.*)

**Godāvarī** (S) (F) **1.** granting water. **2.** that which bestows prosperity. **3.** a river in south India which originates from Brahmagiri in Nāsik and by bathing in which one attains the kingdom of Vāsukī (*Kādambarī*)

**Godila** (S) (M) **1.** harbour. **3.** a yakṣa servant of Vaiśravaṇa (*K. Sāgara*)

**Godhārin** (S) (M) **1.** one who keeps cows; cowherd. **3.** another name for Kṛṣṇa.

**Godhikā** (S) (F) Sita's lizard (*Sitana ponticeriana*); emblem of the goddess Gaurī.

**Godhvaja** (S) (M) **1.** with the moon as his banner. **3.** another name for Śiva.

**Gogana** (S) (M) a multitude of rays.

**Gojā** (S) (F) born amidst rays; born of milk; born in the earth.

**Gokanyā** (S) (M) **1.** a maiden who looks after cows. **3.** a nymph of Vṛndāvana (*Bhāgavata*)

**Gokarṇā** (S) (F) **1.** cow eared. **3.** the mother of Karṇa's serpent missile Aśvasena (*M. Bh.*)

**Gokarṇa** (S) (M) **1.** cow eared. **3.** a place in north Kerala sacred to Śiva where Yama practiced austerities to become a Lokapāla (*M. Bh.*); an incarnation of Śiva; an attendant of Śiva; a muni; a king of Kāśmira (*R. Taraṅginī*)

**Gokarneśvara** (S) (M) **1.** lord of Gokarṇa. **3.** a king of Kāśmīra (*R. Taraṅginī*); a statue of Śiva.

**Gokarṇi** (S) (M) **1.** cow eared. **3.** a follower of Skanda (*Sk. Purāṇa*) *Clematis triloba*

**Gokirātikā** (S) (F) **1.** grating sound. **3.** the Sārikā (*Paradisca tristis*) or Indian Myna bird (*A. Koṣa*)

**Gokula** (S) (M) **1.** herd of cows. **3.** the district on the banks of the river Yamunā near Mathurā where Kṛṣṇa spent his boyhood (*Bhāgavata*)

**Golā** (S) (F) **1.** circle; sphere; celestial globe. **3.** another name for goddess Durgā and the river Godāvarī.

**Golakī** (S) (M) **1.** globe; ball. **2.** water jar. **3.** a woman who sprang from the face of Brahmā in Kṛta Yuga (*U. Rāmāyaṇa*)

**Golap** (S) (M) mooing of the cow.

**Goloka** (S) (M) **1.** cows' world. **3.** the paradise of Kṛṣṇa situated on mountain Meru on which dwells the wish fulfilling cow Surabhī (*Purāṇas*)

**Gomadhī** (S) (F) **1.** wealthy in cows. **3.** another name for river Gomatī.

**Goman** (S) (M) rich in herds.

**Gomateśvara** (S) (M) **1.** lord of the Gomant mountain. **3.** another name for Kṛṣṇa.

**Gomatī** (S) (F) **1.** rich in cattle; milky. **3.** a river personified as a goddess supposed to be the incarnation of Kauśikī the sister of Viśvāmitra and the wife of sage Ṛcīka (*Sk. Purāṇa*)

**Gomeda** (S) (F) **1.** one who respects cows. **2.** the beryl; a gem brought from the Himalayas and the river Indus which is used

to purify water.
**Gomin** (S) (M) 1. owner of cattle. 3. an attendant of the Buddha (*B. Literature*)
**Gomukha** (S) (M) 1. cow faced. 3. the son of Mātali (*M. Bh.*); an asura (*M. Bh.*); an attendant of Śiva; a son of King Vatsa; an attendant of the 1st Arhat of present Avasarpinī.
**Gonanda** (S) (M) 1. son of a cow. 3. a follower of Skanda (*M. Bh.*).
**Gopā** (S) (M) 1. herdsman; guardian; protector of cows. 2. *Ichnocarpus frutescens*.
**Gopabālā** (S) (F) daughter of a cowherd.
**Gopajā** (S) (F) daughter of a cowherd.
**Gopāla** (S) (M) 1. protector of cows. 2. a cowherd. 3. another name for Kṛṣṇa.
**Gopāladāsa** (S) (M) a devotee of Kṛṣṇa.
**Gopālaka** (S) (M) 1. protector of cows. 3. son of Angāraka.
**Gopālī** (S) (F) 1. protector of cows. 2. a cowherdess. 3. an apsarā who danced for Arjuna (*M. Bh.*); a follower of Skanda (*M. Bh.*); *Ichnocarpus frutescens*; the Monkeybread tree (*Adansonia digitata*); another name for Rādhā.
**Gopānandana** (S) (M) 1. son of a cowherd. 3. another name for Kṛṣṇa.
**Goparasā** (S) (F) made of the water of the earth; nourished by the earth.
**Gopati** (S) (M) 1. owner of cows. 2. leader; chief; sun. 3. a gandharva who was the son of Kaśyapa and Muni (*M. Bh.*); the son of Emperor Śibi (*M. Bh.*); an asura (*M. Bh.*); another name for Viṣṇu, Śiva, Kṛṣṇa and Varuṇa.
**Gopendra** (S) (M) 1. lord of cowherds. 3. another name for Kṛṣṇa.
**Gopeśa** (S) (M) 1. chief of the herdsmen. 3. another name for Kṛṣṇa.
**Gopī** (S) (F) 1. herdswoman. 3. milkmaid and friend of Kṛṣṇa; *Ichnocarpus frutescens*.
**Gopīćandana** (S) (M) sandal of the herdswoman; white clay from Dvārakā used to mark the body before worship.
**Gopīćandra** (S) (M) 1. the moon of the Gopīs. 3. another name for Kṛṣṇa.
**Gopījanapriya** (S) (M) 1. beloved of the gopīs. 3. another name for Kṛṣṇa.
**Gopikā** (S) (F) 1. herdswoman. 2. one who protects the herd. 3. another name for Rādhā.
**Gopīkṛṣṇa** (S) (M) Kṛṣṇa and Rādhā conjoined.
**Gopila** (S) (M) 1. protector of cows. 2. a king.
**Gopīnātha** (S) (M) 1. lord of the Gopīs. 3. another name for Kṛṣṇa.
**Gopita** (S) (M) hidden; guarded; preserved; the Water Wagtail (*Motacilla indica*) regarded as a bird of augury.
**Goputra** (S) (M) 1. son of a cow. 2. a young bull. 3. another name for Karṇa.
**Gorakhanātha** (S) (M) 1. lord of senses; master of senses; one who has control over his senses; cowherd. 3. a sage of the Nātha cult where Śiva is the Ādinatha or the supreme source of perfection.
**Gorala** (S) (M) likeable.
**Gormā** (S) (F) 1. worth considering. 3. another name for Pārvatī.
**Goroćanā** (S) (F) 1. yellow pigment. 3. a beautiful and virtuous woman.
**Gośālaka** (S) (M) 1. master of the cowherds. 3. a contemporary and competitor of Mahāvīra.
**Gośarya** (S) (M) 1. dawn. 3. a protégé of the aśvins.
**Gostanī** (S) (M) 1. a dug of a cow; a cluster of blossoms. 3. a follower of Skanda (*M. Bh.*)
**Gosvāmī** (S) (M) 1. lord of cows. 3. head of a Vaiṣnava cult; another name for Kṛṣṇa.
**Gotama** (S) (M) 1. best among the wise. 3. a Vedic ṛṣi who was the son of Rāhugaṇa to whom the finest verses in the *Ṛg Veda* have been attributed (*Ṛg/A. Veda*); the gotra (lineage) to which Buddha belonged.
**Gotra** (S) (M) 1. herd of cows; lineage. 2. that which moves the earth. 3. a son of Vasiṣtha.
**Gotrabhid** (S) (M) 1. opening the cowpens of the sky. 3. another name for Indra.
**Govardhana** (S) (M) 1. increasing cows. 3. a mountain of Gokula believed to be a form of Kṛṣṇa.
**Govāsana** (S) (M) 1. covered with ox hides. 3. a king of Śibi whose daughter married Yudhiṣṭhira (*M. Bh.*)
**Govinda** (S) (M) 1. master of the mountain.

3. another name for Kṛṣṇa.

**Govindadatta** (S) (M) 1. given by Kṛṣṇa. 3. a Brāhmin known for his piety (*K. Sāgara*)

**Govraja** (S) (M) 1. dust that ensues from the feet of moving cows; sunset; an atom; sundust. 3. a soldier of Skanda (*M. Bh.*)

**Govṛṣabhadhvaja** (S) (M) 1. bull-bannered. 3. another name for Śiva.

**Govṛṣāṅka** (S) (M) 1. marked by the bull. 3. another name for Śiva.

**Govṛṣottamavāhana** (S) (M) 1. with the supreme bull as his vehicle. 3. another name for Śiva.

**Graharāja** (S) (M) 1. lord of planets. 3. another name for the sun and Jupiter.

**Graharājan** (S) (M) 1. king of planets. 3. another name for the sun.

**Grahin** (S) (M) 1. of planets. 3. the woodapple fruit (*Feronia Limonia*)

**Grahīśa** (S) (M) 1. lord of the planets. 3. another name for the sun and Saturn.

**Grāmadevatā** (S) (M) tutelary god of the village.

**Grāmadruma** (S) (M) a village tree; it is regarded as sacred and worshipped by the villagers.

**Grāmaghóṣin** (S) (M) 1. the sound of the village. 2. the voice of men. 3. another name for Indra.

**Grāmakālī** (S) (F) 1. the Kāli of the village. 3. the protective deity of the village and forest and in the same class as the nāgas.

**Grāmakūṭa** (S) (M) the village mountain; the noblest man in the village.

**Grāmaṇī** (S) (F) ladies of the village; a class of 12 celestial beings who attend in pairs to Sūrya and Śiva (*H. Purāṇa*)

**Grāmapāla** (S) (M) guardian of the village.

**Granthika** (S) (M) 1. one who ties the knots; composer. 2. an astrologer; narrator. 3. name assumed by Nakula at the Virāta palace (*M. Bh.*)

**Gṛdhra** (S) (M) 1. desiring eagerly. 3. a son of Kṛṣṇa (*Bh. Purāṇa*); a ṛṣi of the 14th Manvantara; a rākṣasa.

**Gṛdhu** (S) (M) 1. libidinous. 3. another name for Kāma.

**Gṛdhukalākeli** (S) (M) 1. desirous of amorous play; frolicsome. 3.another name for Kāma.

**Gṛhadevī** (S) (F) 1. goddess of the household. 3. a rākṣasi who protects the house.

**Gṛhakanyā** (S) (F) 1. daughter of the house. 3. Aloe (*Aloe vera*)

**Gṛhalakṣmī** (S) (F) the Lakṣmī of the house; the guardian goddess of a house who is invoked for prosperity and happiness.

**Gṛhanāyaka** (S) (M) 1. lord of the house. 2. one who seizes. 3. another name for the sun and Saturn.

**Gṛhapati** (S) (M) 1. lord of the house. 2. lord of the planets. 3. a sage who was the son of Viśvānara and Śućiṣmatī; another name for Sūrya and Agni.

**Gṛhiṇī** (S) (F) 1. mistress of the house. 3. Asfoetida (*Ferula narthex*); *Fagonia cretica*.

**Gṛhīta** (S) (M) taken up; understood and accepted.

**Gṛtsamada** (S) (M) 1. associated with ghee. 2. sacrificial wood. 3. a sage who was the son of Vītahavya; a great friend of Indra and the father of Kućeta (*M. Bh.*); a king of the Bhārgava dynasty and the son of King Suhotra (*Bhāgavata*); a son of Indra by Mukundā (*Bhāgavata*)

**Gṛtsapati** (S) (M) 1. full of clarified butter. 3. a son of King Kapila of the Purū dynasty (*A. Purāṇa*)

**Guḍapuṣpa** (S) (F) 1. sweet flower. 3. *Bassia latifolia*.

**Guḍiyā** (S) (F) doll.

**Guggul** (S) (M) 1. fragrant. 3. the Indian Bdellium (*Commiphora mukul*) which is an aromatic gum resin forming the base of perfumes and medicines.

**Guha** (S) (M) 1. secret one. 3. a king of the Niṣādas and friend of Rāma (*V. Rāmāyaṇa*); another name for Kārttikeya; the creeper *Uraria lagopoides*.

**Guhamāyā** (S) (M) 1. secret power; secret illusion. 3. another name for Kārttikeya.

**Guhapriyā** (S) (F) 1. liking secret places. 3. Indra's daughter.

**Guhavāhana** (S) (M) 1. Skanda's vehicle.

3. the peacock.

**Guheśvara** (S) (M) 1. lord of caverns. 2. the secret one. 3. an attendant of Śiva; another name for Kārttikeya and Śiva.

**Guhyaka** (S) (M) 1. concealed; hidden; secret. 3. a class of half- man half-horse demigods who are the attendants of Kubera, exercise their powers from caves, and carry Kubera's palace from place to place (*M. Smṛti/H. Purāṇa*); a yakṣa who was present at the marriage of Draupadī (*M. Bh.*)

**Guhyakādhipati** (S) (M) 1. lord of the guhyakas. 3. another name for Kubera.

**Guhyakālī** (S) (F) 1. the mysterious Kālī. 3. a form of Durgā.

**Guhyeśvarī** (S) (F) 1. mystic deity. 3. another name for Prajña the female energy of the Ādibuddha.

**Gulāl** (S) (F) auspicious powder.

**Gulikā** (S) (F) ball; anything round; a pearl.

**Gulmiṇī** (S) (F) clustering; a creeper.

**Guṇadhāra** (S) (M) bearer of attributes.

**Guṇāḍhya** (S) (M) 1. rich in virtues. 3. the author of the *Bṛhatkathā*.

**Guṇajā** (S) (F) 1. daughter of virtue. 3. the Priyaṅgu creeper (*Aglaia odoratissima*)

**Guṇajña** (S) (M) knower of virtues.

**Guṇakali** (S) (F) 1. possessing virtues. 3. a rāgiṇī of rāga Malkaus.

**Guṇākara** (S) (M) 1. a mine of virtues. 3. another name for Śiva and Śākyamuni.

**Guṇākeśī** (S) (M) 1. with tied hair. 3. the daughter of Mātali who was his equal in bravery (*M. Bh.*)

**Guṇaketu** (S) (M) 1. flag of virtue. 3. a Buddha (*L. Vistara*)

**Guṇalakṣmī** (S) (F) Lakṣmī the virtuous.

**Guṇamaya** (S) (M) (F) endowed with virtues.

**Guṇamukhyā** (S) (M) 1. superior among the virtuous. 3. an apsarā who danced for Arjuna (*M. Bh.*)

**Guṇanidhi** (S) (M) treasure of virtues.

**Guṇarāśi** (S) (M) 1. with a great number of virtues. 3. a Buddha (*L. Vistara*); another name for Śiva.

**Guṇaratna** (S) (M) 1. jewel of virtues. 3. a Jaina writer (15th century)

**Guṇasāgara** (S) (M) 1. ocean of virtue. 3. another name for Brahmā.

**Guṇaśarman** (S) (M) 1. abode of qualities. 3. a character in the Purāṇas who was the son of the Brāhmin Adityaśarman and well versed in all the arts and sciences.

**Guṇaśekhara** (S) (M) crested with virtues.

**Guṇaśraja** (S) (M) virtuous; excellent.

**Guṇasundarī** (S) (F) 1. made beautiful with virtues. 3. another name for the Supreme Being.

**Guṇāvarā** (S) (F) 1. better in qualities. 2. one who is meritorious; virtuous. 3. an apsarā who danced for Arjuna (*M. Bh.*)

**Guṇāvaraṇ** (S) (M) 1. on the path of virtue. 3. a Buddhist aćarya who travelled to China (*B. Literature*)

**Guṇavata** (S) (M) virtuous.

**Guṇavatī** (S) (F) 1. virtuous. 3. the mother of Mandodarī (*V. Rāmāyaṇa*); the wife of Sāmba the son of Kṛṣṇa; a river of ancient India; the mother of Divodāsa (*M. Bh.*)

**Guṇavinā** (S) (F) virtuous.

**Guṇayukta** (S) (M) endowed with virtue.

**Guṇćā** (S) (F) blossom; flowerbud.

**Guṇćakā** (S) (F) bunch of flowers.

**Guṇḍrā** (S) (M) Nut grass (*Cyperus rotundis*); *Aglaia odoratissima*.

**Guṇḍū** (Tamil) (M) (F) plump; round; circle.

**Guṇeṣa** (S) (M) 1. lord of virtues. 3. a mountain.

**Guṇeśvara** (S) (M) 1. lord of virtues. 3. another name for the Supreme Being and the Ćitrakūta mountain.

**Guṇgla** (S) (M) the Openbilled Stork.

**Guṇidatta** (S) (M) given by a virtuous man.

**Guṇin** (S) (M) endowed with virtues.

**Guṇitā** (S) (F) proficient; virtuous.

**Gunja** (S) (M) 1. well woven. 3. a flower worn by Kṛṣṇa in his garland (*Bhāgavata*); a ṛṣi (*K. Sāgara*)

**Guñjan** (S) (F) humming; a cluster of blossoms.

**Gunjika** (S) (M) 1. humming; reflection; meditation. 3. the Rosary Pea (*Abrus precar-*

*torius*)

**Guṇṇikā** (S) (F) well woven; a garland, a necklace.

**Guṇóttama** (S) (M) endowed with excellent qualities.

**Guptaka** (S) (M) 1. protected. 3. a king of Sauvīra.

**Gupti** (S) (F) preserving; protecting.

**Gurnikā** (S) (F) 1. wife of a preceptor. 3. a companion of Devayānī.

**Gūrti** (S) (F) approval; praise.

**Guru** (S) (M) 1. teacher; master; priest; spiritual guide. 3. another name for Bṛhaspati and Droṇa; Cowage (*Mucuna prurita*)

**Gurućaraṇa** (S) (M) (F) at the feet of the guru.

**Gurudā** (S) (M) (F) given by the guru.

**Gurudāṅkar** (S) (M) 1. given by the gods. 3. another name for Viṣṇu.

**Gurudara** (S) (M) 1. intellectual hegemony. 3. a son of Garuḍa (*V. Purāṇa*)

**Gurudāsa** (S) (M) servant of the guru.

**Gurūdatta** (S) (M) 1. given by the guru. 3. another name for sage Dattātreya.

**Gurudéva** (S) (M) (F) the divine guru.

**Gurudīpa** (S) (M) (F) lamp of the guru.

**Gurumel** (S) (M) to be one with the guru.

**Gurumīta** (S) (M) (F) friend of the guru.

**Gurumukha** (S) (M) (F) face of the preceptor; facing the preceptor; one who follows the guru; in the image of the guru.

**Gurumūrtī** (S) (M) idol of guru; one who tries to follow the path shown by the guru.

**Gurunāma** (S) (M) (F) name of the guru.

**Gurunātha** (S) (M) 1. lord of the spiritual teachers. 3. another name for the Supreme Being.

**Guruprasāda** (S) (M) (F) the blessing of the guru.

**Guruputra** (S) (M) 1. son of the teacher. 3. another name for Aśvatthāman.

**Gururāja** (S) (M) 1. lord of the spiritual teachers. 3. another name for Bṛhaspati.

**Gururatna** (S) (M) 1. jewel among teachers; Bṛhaspati's jewel. 3. topaz.

**Guruśaraṇa** (S) (M) (F) in the guru's protection.

**Gurusimran** (S) (M) in remembrance of the guru.

**Gurusutā** (S) (M) 1. son of the teacher. 3. another name for Aśvatthāman.

**Guruttama** (S) (M) 1. the best teacher. 3. another name for Viṣṇu.

**Guruvaćana** (S) (M) (F) word or promise of the guru.

**Guruvīra** (S) (M) (F) a warrior of the guru.

**Guṣaṇa** (S) (M) the eye of a peacock's tail.

**Guṭikā** (S) (F) small ball; a pearl; a cocoon of the silkworm.

**Gutsaka** (S) (M) a cluster of blossoms.

**Gvālipa** (S) (M) 1. proud. 3. a saint after whom the city of Gwalior is named (8th century)

# H

**Hahā** (S) (M) 1. exclamation of surprise. 3. a gandharva who was the son of Kaśyapa and Prādhā and who lived in Kubera's assembly (*M. Bh.*)

**Hāha** (S) (M) 1. water; sky; blood; meditation; auspiciousness; moon; heaven; battle; pride; horse; knowledge. 3. another name for Viṣṇu and Śiva.

**Hāhāgiri** (S) (M) 1. the mountain of heaven. 3. a Jaina monk (*J.S. Koṣa*); another name for Mount Meru.

**Haiḍimba** (S) (M) 1. son of Hiḍimbā. 3. another name for Ghaṭotkaća.

**Haiḍimbi** (S) (M) 1. son of Hiḍimbā. 3. another name for Ghaṭotkaća.

**Haihaya** (S) (M) 1. of the horse. 3. a king who was the greatgrandson of Yadu, the son of Vatsa and the founder of the Haihaya dynasty (*M. Bh.*); Arjuna Kārtavīrya who had a 1000 arms (*M. Bh./Rāmāyaṇa*)

**Haimā** (S) (F) 1. of the snow; golden. 3. another name for Pārvatī and Gaṅgā.

**Haima** (S) (M) 1. snow; frost; dew; golden. 3. another name for the Himālaya mountains; another name for Śiva; Yellow Jasmine (*Jasminum bignoniaceum*)

**Haimavatī** (S) (F) 1. one who has snow. 3. a wife of Viśvāmitra (*M. Bh.*); a wife of Kṛṣṇa who cremated herself with him when he died (*M. Bh.*); a wife of Kauśika (*M. Bh.*); another name for Pārvatī as the daughter of Himavān; another name for the river Śatadru; Black Myrobalan (*Terminalia chebula*); *Berberis asiatica*.

**Haimī** (S) (F) 1. golden. 3. *Hedychium spicatum*.

**Hairaṇyagarbha** (S) (M) 1. relating to Hiraṇyagarbha. 3. another name for Vasiṣṭha.

**Hairaṇyavatī** (S) (F) 1. possessing gold. 3. a river that flows along a Purāṇic region known as Hiraṇmāya (*M. Bh.*)

**Hakeśa** (S) (M) lord of sound.

**Hākinī** (S) (F) female demon like the Dākini.

**Halā** (S) (F) 1. a female friend. 3. another name for the earth, liquor and water.

**Hala** (S) (M) 1. plough. 3. another name for King Śālivāna.

**Halabhṛt** (S) (M) 1. carrying a plough. 3. another name for Kṛṣṇa's brother Balarāma.

**Haladhara** (S) (M) 1. holding a plough. 3. another name for Balarāma.

**Haladharanuja** (S) (M) 1. younger brother of the ploughman. 3. another name for Kṛṣṇa (*M. Bh.*)

**Halāyudha** (S) (M) 1. plough weaponed. 3. a Sanskṛt poet whose major work was *Kavirahasya* (10th century A.D.); another name for Balarāma.

**Halika** (S) (M) 1. ploughman. 3. a serpent of the Kaśyapa dynasty (*M. Bh.*)

**Halīkṣaṇa** (S) (M) a fast moving animal; a lion.

**Halimā** (S) (F) 1. full of poison. 3. a Saptamatṛ of Skanda (*M. Bh.*)

**Halīmaka** (S) (M) 1. poison spewing. 3. a nāga of the Vāsuki family (*M. Bh.*)

**Halin** (S) (M) 1. ploughman. 3. a ṛṣi; another name for Balarāma.

**Halipriyā** (S) (F) 1. beloved of Viṣṇu. 3. the Kadamba tree (*Anthocephalus cadamba*)

**Hansa** (S) (M) 1. swan; gander; duck; flamingo; goose; the Bar-headed Goose (*Anser indicus*); an ascetic; a pure person; the individual soul; the Supreme Soul. 3. a reincarnation of Viṣṇu in Kṛta Yuga (*V. Purāṇa*); a gandharva who was a son of Kaśyapa and Ariṣṭā; a minister of Jarāsandha (*M. Bh.*); a son of Vasudeva; a horse of the moon; another name for Sūrya, Kāma, Śiva and Viṣṇu.

**Hansaćūḍa** 1. the crest of the swan. 3. a yakṣa who worships Kubera in his assembly (*M. Bh.*)

**Hansadhvaja** (S) (M) 1. with the swan as his banner. 3. a king of Ćampānagari who was a great devotee of Viṣṇu (*Bhāgavata*)

**Hansagāminī** (S) (F) 1. as graceful as a swan. 3. another name for Brahmāṇī the consort of Brahmā.

**Hansaja** (S) (M) 1. son of a swan. 3. a warrior of Skanda (*M. Bh.*)

**Hansakāya** (S) (M) 1. a group of swans. 3. a

Kṣatriya who was present at the investiture yajña of Yudhiṣṭhira (*M. Bh.*)

**Hansakūṭa** (S) (M) 1. abode of the swan. 3. a peak of the Himālaya.

**Hansanāḍa** (S) (M) 1. the cry of the swan. 3. a vidyādhara.

**Hansanāḍinī** (S) (F) chattering like a swan; a woman with a slender waist; large hips; a gait as graceful as an elephant's and the voice of a cuckoo.

**Hansanandinī** (S) (F) daughter of a swan.

**Hansapādā** (S) (F) 1. the foot of the swan. 3. an apsarā (*V. Purāṇa*)

**Hansapadikā** (S) (F) 1. with the feet of the Hansa. 3. the first wife of Duṣyanta.

**Hansarāja** (S) (M) king of swans.

**Hansaratha** (S) (M) 1. with the swan as his chariot. 3. another name for Brahmā.

**Hansāruḍha** (S) (M) 1. mounted on a swan. 3. another name for Brahmā and Varuṇa.

**Hansavāhana** (S) (M) 1. with the swan as his vehicle. 3. another name for Brahmā.

**Hansavaktra** (S) (M) 1. the beak of a swan. 3. a warrior of Skanda (*M. Bh.*)

**Hansaveṇī** (S) (F) 1. with a braid like a swan. 2. with a beautiful braid. 3. another name for Sarasvatī, the goddess of learning.

**Hansī** (S) (F) 1. swan. 3. a daughter of Bhāgiratha and wife of sage Kautsa (*M. Bh.*)

**Hansikā** (S) (F) 1. swan. 3. a daughter of Surabhī who is said to support the southern region.

**Hansin** (S) (M) 1. containing the universal soul. 3. another name for Kṛṣṇa.

**Hansinī** (S) (F) swan; goose.

**Hanspāla** (S) (M) 1. lord of the swan. 3. another name for Brahmā.

**Hanugiri** (S) (M) the mountain of Hanumān.

**Hanumān/Hanumaṇt/Hanumat/Hanut** (S) (M) 1. heavy jawed. 3. son of Vāyu, the maruta god of wind and Añjanā the apsarā, and the leader of Rāma's army (*V. Rāmāyaṇa*)

**Hanumeśa** (S) (M) 1. lord of Hanumān. 3. another name for Rāma.

**Hanuṣa** (S) (M) 1. anger; wrath. 3. a rākṣasa.

**Hara** (S) (M) 1. seizer; destroyer; divisor. 3. a dānava who was the son of Kaśyapa and Danu and was reborn as King Subāhu (*M. Bh.*); a rudra (*Ś. Purāṇa*); another name for Śiva and Agni.

**Haraćūḍāmaṇi** (S) (M) 1. the crest gem of Śiva. 3. another name for Ćandra.

**Haradeva** (S) (M) 1. the lord of Śiva. 3. the asterism Śravaṇa with 3 stars; another name for Kṛṣṇa.

**Haradikā** (S) (M) 1. king and soul of love. 2. Brahmā, the sun and Viṣṇu. 3. a Kṣatriya king who was the son the of asura Aśvapati (*M. Bh.*); another name for Kṛtavarman as the son of Hṛdikā of the Yadu dynasty.

**Haragaurī** (S) (M) Śiva and Pārvatī conjoined.

**Haragovinda, Hargobinda** (S) (M) Śiva and Kṛṣṇa conjoined.

**Harahāra** (S) (M) 1. Śiva's necklace. 3. another name for Śeṣa.

**Haraka** (S) (M) 1. one who takes away; a rogue; a divisor; a thief. 3. another name for Śiva.

**Harakalpa** (S) (M) 1. the sacred precept of Śiva. 3. a son of Vipraćitti and Siṁhī (*Vā. Purāṇa*)

**Haramālā** (S) (F) garland of Śiva.

**Haramanas** (S) (M) the soul of Śiva; the soul of God.

**Haramohana** (S) (M) attracting Śiva.

**Haranārāyaṇa** (S) (M) Viṣṇu and Śiva conjoined.

**Haranétra** (S) (M) 1. the eye of Śiva. 2. all seeing; omniscient; ommipresent; the number 3.

**Harapriyā** (S) (F) 1. beloved of Śiva. 3. another name for Pārvatī.

**Hararūpa** (S) (M) with the form of Śiva.

**Harasakha** (S) (M) 1. Śiva's friend. 3. another name for Kubera.

**Haraśekharā** (S) (F) 1. the crest of Śiva. 3. another name for the river Gaṅgā

**Harasiddha** (S) (M) eternal Śiva.

**Haraśringārā** (S) (F) 1. ornament of Śiva. 3. a rāgiṇī; the tree *Nyctantes arbor-tristes*.

**Harasūnu** (S) (M) 1. son of Śiva. 3. another name for Kārttikeya.

**Harasvarūpa** (S) (M) in the image of Śiva; in the image of God.

**Haratejas** (S) (M) 1. Śiva's energy. 2. quicksilver.

**Harava** (S) (M) 1. painful to Śiva. 2. causing harm to the Supreme Spirit. 3. an asura born from the teardrops of Brahmā (*Sk. Purāṇa*)

**Hārāvalī** (S) (F) garland of pearls.

**Haravīra** (S) (M) a warrior of god.

**Harendra** (S) (M) Indra the tawny; Indra and Śiva conjoined.

**Hareṇu** (S) (M) 1. a creeper which serves as a village boundary; respectable. 3. the Garden Pea (*Pisum sativum*); another name for Lankā.

**Hareśvara** (S) (M) Śiva and Viṣṇu conjoined.

**Hari** (S) (M) 1. yellow; tawny; green. 2. the Zodiac sign of Leo; a parrot; a cuckoo; a peacock; a horse; a horse of Indra; a man; a ray of light; wind; fire; the moon; the sun; Indra; Brahmā; Viṣṇu and Śiva. Vāyu; Yama; Śukra. 3. a warrior of Skanda (*M. Bh.*); a warrior who fought on the side of the Pāṇḍavas (*M. Bh.*); an asura who was the son of Tārakākṣa who had the boon of being able to revive the dead (*M. Bh.*); a group of attendants of Rāvaṇa (*M. Bh.*); a powerful bird born in the dynasty of Garuḍa (*M. Bh.*); a sect of golden coloured horses (*M. Bh.*); a daughter of Kaśyapa and Krodhavaśā who was the mother of lions and monkeys (*V. Rāmāyaṇa*); a son of Dharma by the daughter of Dakṣa (*D. Bhāgavata*); a group of devas (*Bhāgavata*); the Sanskṛt poet Bhartṛhari; another name for King Akampana who was as powerful and proficient in war as Indra.

**Harī** (S) (F) 1. fawn-coloured; reddish brown; tawny. 3. name of the mother of monkeys (*M. Bh.*)

**Hariakṣa** (S) (M) 1. the pivot of Viṣṇu; the eye of Viṣṇu; the eye of the lion. 3. another name for the lion; Kubera and Śiva.

**Hariakṣva** (S) (M) 1. fair coloured. 3. another name for Sūrya.

**Harial** (S) (M) green coloured; the common green pigeon (*Crocopus phoenicopterus*)

**Hariaṅka** (S) (M) 1. in the lap of Viṣṇu. 3. a king of Aṅga who was the son of King Ćampā and father of King Bṛhadratha (*A. Purāṇa*)

**Hariaśva** (S) (M) 1. horse of Viṣṇu. 3. the 5000 sons born to Dakṣa and Asiknī (*Br. Purāṇa*); a king of the solar dynasty of Ayodhyā who married Mādhavī the daughter of Yayāti (*M. Bh.*); the father of King Sudeva of Kāśi (*M. Bh.*)

**Haribabhru** (S) (M) 1. Viṣṇu the great. 3. a sage who was a member of Yudhiṣṭhira's assembly (*M. Bh.*)

**Haribālā** (S) (F) daughter of Viṣṇu.

**Haribhadrā** (S) (F) 1. tawny and beautiful; a beautiful golden colour; as beautiful, auspicious and praiseworthy as Viṣṇu. 3. a daughter of Kaśyapa and Krodhā, the wife of sage Pulaha and the mother of monkeys.

**Haribhadra** (S) (M) 1. as beautiful, auspicious and praiseworthy as Viṣṇu. 3. a distinguished Jaina writer who composed critical commentaries in Sanskṛt (*J.S. Koṣa*)

**Haribhajana** (S) (M) a hymn to Viṣṇu.

**Haribhakta** (S) (M) a devotee of Viṣṇu.

**Harićandana** (S) (M) 1. the sandal of Hari; yellow moonlight. 3. the yellow sandalwood tree (*Santalum album*) as one of the 5 trees of paradise; saffron (*Crocus sativus*); the filament of a lotus (*Nelumbium speciosum*); moonlight.

**Harićāpa** (S) (M) 1. Indra's bow. 2. the rainbow.

**Harićarana** (S) (M) at the feet of Viṣṇu.

**Haridāsa** (S) (M) 1. servant of Viṣṇu. 3. a monkey king who was the son of Pulaha and Śvetā (*Br. Purāṇa*)

**Haridaśva** (S) (M) 1. the 10 incarnations of Viṣṇu; with fallow horses. 3. another name for the sun.

**Haridatta** (S) (M) 1. the blessing of Viṣṇu; given by Viṣṇu. 3. a dānava.

**Haridhāma** (S) (M) 1. the abode of Viṣṇu. 3. a sage who chanted the Kṛṣṇamantra and so was reborn as the gopī Raṅgaveṇī (*P. Purāṇa*)

**Haridhana** (S) (M) the treasure of Viṣṇu.

**Haridhrava** (S) (M) the Yellow Water Wagtail (*Motacilla indica*)

**Haridra** (S) (M) 1. yellow. 3. turmeric (*Curcuma longa*); *Aconitum ferox; Berberis asiatica*; the Yellow Sandal tree; a deity.

**Haridrāgaṇapati, Haridrāgaṇeśa** (S) (M) Gaṇeśa who is offered turmeric by his devotees.

**Hāridraka** (S) (M) 1. timid snake. 3. a nāga born in Kaśyapa's dynasty (*M. Bh.*)

**Haridru** (S) (M) 1. free of the gods. 3. the Devadāra tree (*Pinus deodara*)

**Harigaṅgā** (S) (F) 1. the Gaṅgā of Viṣṇu. 3. the river Gaṅgā which flows from the foot of Viṣṇu.

**Harihara** (S) (M) Viṣṇu and Śiva conjoined.

**Harihaya** (S) (M) 1. with golden horses; the horse of Viṣṇu. 3. another name for Indra, Sūrya, Skanda and Gaṇeśa.

**Hārija** (S) (M) the horizon.

**Harijaṭā** (S) (F) 1. fire haired. 3. a rākṣasa woman who guarded Sītā in the Aśoka grove (*V. Rāmāyaṇa*)

**Harikāntā** (S) (F) 1. dear to Viṣṇu. 3. another name for Lakṣmī.

**Harikānta** (S) (M) dear to Indra; as beautiful as a lion.

**Harikeśa** (S) (M) 1. with yellow hair. 3. one of the 7 principal rays of the sun; a yakṣa; a son of Śyāmaka; another name for Viṣṇu, Śiva, Savitṛ.

**Harikīrtana** (S) (M) devotional hymns to Viṣṇu.

**Harikṛṣṇa** (S) (M) Kṛṣṇa and Viṣṇu conjoined.

**Harilāla** (S) (M) son of Viṣṇu.

**Harilīna** (S) (M) (F) engrossed and merged in Viṣṇu.

**Harimālā** (S) (F) garland of Viṣṇu.

**Harimaṇi** (S) (M) 1. Viṣṇu's gem. 2. the sapphire.

**Harimat** (S) (M) 1. with bay horses. 3. another name for Indra.

**Harimbhara** (S) (M) bearing the yellow thunderbolt.

**Harimedhas** (S) (M) 1. an oblation to Viṣṇu. 3. a saintly king and father of Dhvajavatī (*M. Bh.*); another name for Viṣṇu-Kṛṣṇa.

**Harimitra** (S) (M) 1. with Viṣṇu as his friend. 3. a Brāhmin who had his āśrama on the banks of the Yamunā (*P. Purāṇa*)

**Hariṇa** (S) (M) 1. yellowish white. 2. deer; antelope; gazelle; goose; wearing a garland of pearls; attractive. 3. a nāga of Airāvata's family (*M. Bh.*); another name for Viṣṇu, Śiva and the sun.

**Hariṇākṣa** (S) (M) 1. doe eyed. 3. another name for Śiva.

**Hariṇākṣī** (S) (F) doe eyed.

**Harināma** (S) (M) the name of Viṣṇu.

**Hariṇāṅka** (S) (M) 1. marked like a deer; camphor. 3. another name for Ćandra.

**Hariṇeśa** (S) (M) 1. deer-lord. 2.lion.

**Harinetra** (S) (M) 1. the eye of Viṣṇu. 3. another name for the white lotus (*Nelumbium speciosum*)

**Hariṇī** (S) (F) 1. gazelle; doe; green; Yellow Jasmine (*Jasminum humile*); a golden image. 3. an apsarā; a yakṣiṇī; one of the 4 kinds of beautiful women; the mother of Viṣṇu; the daughter of Hiraṇyakaśipu and wife of the asura Viśvapati (*M. Bh.*); Indian Madder (*Rubia cordifolia*)

**Harinmaṇi** (S) (F) 1. green gem. 2. the emerald.

**Hariom** (S) (M) 1. lord of the Om. 3. another name for Brahmā.

**Haripāla** (S) (M) 1. defending Viṣṇu. 2. the lion.

**Haripiṇḍā** (S) (F) 1. with the limbs of Viṣṇu; lion limbed. 3. a female attendant of Skanda (*M. Bh.*)

**Hariprasāda** (S) (M) the blessing of Viṣṇu.

**Haripṛīta** (S) (M) (F) beloved of Viṣṇu.

**Haripriyā** (S) (F) 1. dear to Viṣṇu. 3. another name for Lakṣmī, the earth, Tulasī or the Sacred Basil plant (*Ocimum sanctum*) and the Kadamba tree (*Anthocephalus cadamba*); *Gloriosa superba* creeper; Khuskhus Grass (*Vetiveria zizanioides*); *Pentapetes phoenicea*; *Wedelia calendulacea*.

**Harirāja** (S) (M) king of lions.

**Harirāma** (S) (M) Viṣṇu and Rāma conjoined.

**Harirudra** (S) (M) Viṣṇu and Śiva conjoined.

**Hariśa** (S) (M) 1. short form of Śiva and

Viṣṇu conjoined. 3. a monkey king.

**Hariśankara** (S) (M) Śiva and Viṣṇu conjoined.

**Hariśara** (S) (M) 1. with Viṣṇu for an arrow. 3. another name for Śiva.

**Hariśćandra** (S) (M) 1. with golden splendour; merciful as the moonlight; full of patience; Viṣṇu and moon conjoined. 3. the son of Triśanku, a king of a solar race, lord of the 7 islands and known for his adherance to truth (*M. Bh.*); a Sanskṛt poet (9th century A.D.)

**Harisena** (S) (M) 1. lion like commander. 3. a son of the 10th Manu; the 10th Jaina ćakravartin.

**Harisiddi** (S) (F) 1. achieving Hari; the proof of Hari; acquiring the supernatural powers of Hari. 3. a goddess.

**Hariśipra** (S) (M) 1. ruddy cheeked. 3. another name for Śiva.

**Hariśmaṇī** (S) (M) 1. green gem; gem of Viṣṇu. 2. the emerald.

**Hariśrāvā** (S) (F) 1. praising Hari. 3. a river (*M. Bh.*)

**Hariśrī** (S) (F) beautifully golden; blessed with Soma.

**Harisuta** (S) (M) 1. son of Viṣṇu. 3. another name for Arjuna.

**Harita** (S) (M) 1. horse of the sun. 2. lion; sun; yellow; pale red; green; verdant; tawny; gold. 3. a king who was the son of Rohita and the grandson of Hariśćandra (*Bhāgavata*); a king of Haritavarṣa in the island of Śālmali who was the son of Vapusman and the grandson of Svāyambhuva Manu (*M. Purāṇa*); a son of Yadu by a nāga woman called Dhūmravarṇā who founded a kingdom in the nāga island (*H. Purāṇa*); a great sage whose discourse on eternal truths in Yudhiṣṭhira's assembly is known as the *Hāritagītā* (*M. Bh.*); a son of Kaśyapa; a son of Yuvanāśva (*Bh. Purāṇa*); an author on codes of conduct (*M. Bh.*); Turmeric (*Curcuma longa*); Couch grass (*Cynodon dactylon*); another name for Viṣṇu.

**Hārita** (S) (M) 1. green; descendant of Harita; a moderate wind. 3. a son of Viśvāmitra.

**Haritaka** (S) (M) yellow green.

**Haritālikā** (S) (F) 1. bringer of greenery; goddess of fertility. 3. 4th day of the bright half of the month of Bhādra (August-September) personified as a goddess of pleasure.

**Haritāśva** (S) (M) 1. with tawny horses. 3. a king born in the solar dynasty whose ability in music was superior to that of all the gods (*K. Rāmāyaṇa*)

**Harītī** (S) (F) 1. tawny; verdant; green. 3. the goddess of Rājagṛha and mother of the yakṣas (*K. Sāgara*)

**Hariturañgam** (S) (M) 1. a horse like the wind, or of the wind. 3. another name for Indra.

**Harivāhana** (S) (M) 1. vehicle of Viṣṇu; with bay horses. 3. another name for Garuḍa.

**Harivallabha** (S) (F) 1. beloved of Viṣṇu. 3. another name for Lakṣmī and Tulasī or the Sacred Basil plant (*Ocimum sanctum*); Shoeflower (*Hibiscus rosa chinensis); Pterospermum suberifolium*.

**Harivana** (S) (M) Indra of the bay horses.

**Harivanśa** (S) (M) 1. of the family of Viṣṇu. 3. a celebrated work by Vyāsa which is a supplement to the *Mahābhārata*.

**Harivarṇa** (S) (M) 1. of the colour of Viṣṇu. 2. green. 3. a sage who wrote a mantra or a chant in the *Panćavimśa Brāhmaṇa*.

**Hārivāsa** (S) (M) 1. with the perfume of Hari. 3. a deity.

**Harivatsa** (S) (M) 1. beloved of Viṣṇu. 3. another name for Arjuna.

**Harmut** (S) (M) 1. bearing the unbreakable. 3. the tortoise that upholds the earth; another name for Sūrya.

**Harmyā** (S) (F) house; palace; mansion.

**Harośit** (S) (M) (F) very happy; joyful.

**Harṣa** (S) (M) 1. joy; delight. 3. one of the 3 sons of Dharmā, brother of Śama and Kāma and husband of Nandā (*M. Bh.*); a Sanskṛt poet who wrote one of the 5 main epic poems and was a member of the court of King Jaićanda of Kannauj (12th century A.D.); King Harṣavardhana ruler of north India who is remembered mainly as a Sanskṛt poet and author of *Ratnāvali*; a son of Kṛṣṇa; an asura (7th century A.D.)

**Harṣada** (S) (M) delighted.
**Harsaka** (S) (M) 1. gladdening; delighting. 3. a son of Citragupta.
**Harṣalā** (S) (F) glad.
**Harṣala** (S) (M) glad; a lover.
**Harṣamana** (S) (M) full of joy; delighted.
**Harṣamaya** (S) whose essence is joy.
**Harṣana** (S) (M) 1. causing delight. 3. one of the 5 arrows of Kāma (*Ś. Purāṇa*)
**Harṣaviṇā** (S) (F) a lute that delights.
**Harṣavardhana** (S) (M) one who increases joy.
**Harṣendu** (S) (M) the moon of joy.
**Harṣī** (S) (M) (F) happy; joyful.
**Harṣitā** (S) (M) (F) full of joy.
**Harṣoda** (S) (M) creating joy.
**Harṣula** (S) (M) 1. disposed to be cheerful. 2. a lover; a deer. 3. a Buddha.
**Harṣumatī** (S) (F) filled with joy.
**Haryakṣa** (S) (M) 1. yellow eyed. 2. lion; the zodiac sign of Leo. 3. an asura; a son of Pṛthu; another name for Kubera and Śiva.
**Haryalā** (S) (M) 1. desired; precious; pleasant. 2. deer. 3. a ṛṣi (*Ṛg. Veda*)
**Haryaṅga** (S) (M) 1. golden bodied. 3. a son of Campa.
**Haryaśva** (S) (M) 1. with bay horses. 3. a solar dynasty king of Ayodhyā and husband of Mādhavī (*M. Bh.*); father of King Sudeva of Kāśī; another name for Indra and Śiva.
**Haryavana** (S) (M) 1. joyful lion; protected by lions. 3. a son of Kṛta.
**Hasamukha** (S) (M) smiling.
**Hasana** (S) (M) 1. laughing. 3. an attendant of Skanda (*M. Bh.*)
**Hasantī** (S) (F) 1. one that delights. 3. the Mallikā Jasmine (*Jasminum sambac*)
**Hasaratha** (S) (M) a chariot that delights.
**Hāsavatī** (S) (F) 1. full of laughter. 3. a tantra deity.
**Hasikā** (S) (F) abloom; smiling; causing laughter.
**Hāsinī** (S) (F) 1. delightful. 3. an apsara of Alakāpuri who danced in Kubera's assembly (*M. Bh.*)
**Hasita** (S) (M) 1. delighting; delighted. 3. the bow of Kāma (*K. Sāgara*)
**Hasrā** (S) (F) 1. laughing woman. 3. an apsarā (*Ṛg Veda*)
**Hasta** (S) (M) 1. hand. 3. a constellation.
**Hastakamalā** (S) (F) 1. with lotus in hand. 3. another name for Lakṣmī.
**Hastāmalaka** (S) (M) 1. seeing the world in its totality. 3. a disciple of Śrī Śankara (*Ś. Vijaya*)
**Hastibhadra** (S) (M) 1. with a superior trunk; with a hood as wide as a palm. 3. a nāga of the Kaśyapa dynasty (*M. Bh.*)
**Hastikarṇa** (S) (M) 1. elephant eared. 3. an attendant of Śiva; a rākṣasa; a nāga.
**Hastikaśyapa** (S) (M) 1. elephant and tortoise conjoined. 3. a sage who was a contemporary of Kṛṣṇa (*M. Bh.*)
**Hastimalla** (S) (M) 1. with strong hands. 3. another name for Airāvata, Gaṇeśa and Śaṅkha.
**Hastimukha** (S) (M) 1. elephant faced. 3. another name for Gaṇeśa.
**Hastin** (S) (M) 1. having hands; elephant. 3. a lunar dynasty king who was the son of Suhotra and Suvarṇā of the Ikṣvāku dynasty, the husband of Yaśodharā, the father of Vikaṇṭha and the builder of the city of Hastināpura (*M. Bh.*); a son of Dhṛtarāṣṭra; a son of Kuru.
**Hastipada** (S) (M) 1. with elephant feet. 3. a nāga of the Kaśyapa dynasty (*M. Bh.*)
**Hastisomā** (S) (F) 1. ambrosia handed. 3. a river mentioned frequently in the Purāṇas.
**Hasumatī** (S) (F) always laughing.
**Hāṭakeśa** (S) (M) 1. lord of gold. 3. another name for Śiva.
**Hāṭakeśvara** (S) (M) 1. lord of gold. 3. another name for Śiva as the prime deity of the Nāgara Brāhmins of Gujarat.
**Hāṭāki** (S) (F) a river formed by the conjoining of Śiva and Pārvatī.
**Haṭhavilāsinī** (S) (F) 1. one who enjoys according to her own desire. 3. another name for Pārvatī.
**Hatiṣa** (S) (M) with no desire.
**Hatitoṣa** (S) (M) not afraid of troubles.
**Havaldār** (H) (M) to whom the responsibility is given; a constable.

**Havana** (S) (M) 1. calling; invocation; the sacrifice. 3. one of the 11 rudras (*M. Bh.*); another name for Agni.

**Havighna** (S) (M) 1. sacrificial. 3. an ancient king held and remembered both in the morning and evening (*M. Bh.*)

**Havirbhū** (S) (F) 1. a place of sacrifice. 3. a daughter of Devahutī and Kardama who married sage Pulatsya and was the mother of Agastya and Viśravas (*Bhāgavata*)

**Havirbhuj** (S) (M) 1. eating the oblation. 3. another name for Agni and Śiva.

**Havirdhāna** (S) (M) 1. one whose wealth is the sacrifice. 3. a grandson of Emperor Pṛthu and son of Antardhāna and Śikhaṇḍinī (*V. Purāṇa*)

**Havirdhānī** (S) (F) 1. whose wealth is the oblation. 3. another name for the cow Kāmadhenu.

**Havirgandhā** (S) (M) 1. giving the sacrifice fragrance. 3. the Śami tree (*Prosopis spicigera*)

**Havirvarṣa** (S) (M) 1. an area of sacrifice. 3. a son of Āgnīdhra.

**Haviṣkṛta** (S) (M) 1. preparing the oblation. 3. a sage who was a descendant of Aṅgiras and the author of a mantra or a chant in the *Panćaviṁśa Brāhmaṇa*.

**Haviṣman** (S) (M) 1. sacrificial. 3. a sage who was a member of the assembly of Indra (*M. Bh.*)

**Haviṣmata** (S) (M) 1. believing in sacrifices. 3. a sage who was a descendant of Aṅgiras and author of a mantra or chant in the *Panćavimśa Brāhmaṇa*; a seer of the 6th, 10th and 11th cycles of creation (*H. Purāṇa*)

**Haviṣmatī** (S) (F) 1. offering in sacrifices. 3. a daughter of Aṅgiras (*M. Bh.*)

**Haviṣravas** (S) (M) 1. sounding like the fire. 3. a Kuru king of the lunar dynasty (*M. Bh.*)

**Havya** (S) (M) 1. to be invoked. 3. a son of Manu Svāyambhuva (*H. Purāṇa*); a son of Atri (*V. Purāṇa*)

**Havyaghna** (S) (M) 1. destroyer of the sacrifice. 3. another name for Agni.

**Havyavāhana** (S) (M) 1. oblation bearer. 3. a ṛṣi under Manu Sāvarna; another name for Agni.

**Havyavāhinī** (S) (F) 1. oblation bearer. 3. the tutelary deity of the Kapila family.

**Hayāgrīva** (S) (M) 1. with a horse's neck. 3. an asura who was the son of Kaśyapa and Danu; a king of the Videha dynasty (*M. Bh.*); an asura who guarded the kingdom of Narakāsura (*M. Bh.*); an incarnation of Viṣṇu as a celestial horse (*V. Purāṇa*); a saintly king (*M. Bh.*); a tāntra deity.

**Hayamukhī** (S) (F) 1. horse faced. 3. a rākṣasī.

**Hayānanā** (S) (F) 1. horse faced. 3. a yoginī.

**Hayapati** (S) (M) 1. lord of horses. 2. king.

**Hayaśiras** (S) (M) 1. horse's head. 3. an incarnation of Viṣṇu (*V. Purāṇa*)

**Hāyatī** (S) (F) flame.

**Hayavāhana** (S) (M) 1. driving horses. 3. another name for Revanta, the son of the sun.

**Hayi** (S) (F) wish; desire.

**Hélā** (S) (F) moonlight; without any difficulty; ease; passion; coquetry.

**Héli** (S) (M) 1. embrace. 3. the sun as all pervasive.

**Hemā** (S) (F) 1. golden; the earth. 2. handsome. 3. an apsarā wife of Maya (*H. Purāṇa*); a river.

**Hema** (S) (M) 1. gold. 2. a dark horse. 3. the father of Sutapas; a Buddha; Ironwood tree (*Mesua ferrea*)

**Hemabala** (S) (M) power of gold; the pearl.

**Hemabhā** (S) (F) 1. looking like gold. 3. the palace of Rukmiṇī.

**Hemabhojam** (S) (M) golden lotus (*Nymphaea alba*)

**Hemaćandra** (S) (M) 1. golden moon. 3. a celebrated Jaina scholar (*J. S. Koṣa*); the son of King Viśāla and the father of Sućandra (*Bhāgavata*)

**Hemadhanvan** (S) (M) 1. with a golden bow. 3. a son of the 11th Manu.

**Hemādri** (S) (M) 1. golden mountain. 3. another name for the mountain Sumerū.

**Hemaguha** (S) (M) 1. golden cave. 3. a nāga born in the Kaśyapa dynasty (*M. Bh.*)

**Hemakānta** (S) (M) 1. bright as gold. 3. the son of King Kuśaketu of Vaṅga (*Sk. Purāṇa*)

**Hemakeli** (S) (M) 1. golden sport. 3. another

name for Agni.

**Hemakeśa** (S) (M) 1. with golden hair. 3. another name for Śiva.

**Hemaketakī** (S) (M) the Golden Screwpine; the fragrant Ketāki plant (*Pandanus odoratissimus*)

**Hemākṣi** (S) (F) golden eyed.

**Hemalatā** (S) (F) 1. golden vine. 3. the Yellow Jasmine (*Jasminum humile*)

**Hemamalā** (S) (F) 1. golden garland. 3. one of Yama's wives.

**Hemamālī** (S) (M) 1. wearing a golden garland. 3. a son of King Drupada (*M. Bh.*); gardener of Vaiśravaṇa (*P. Purāṇa*)

**Hemamālin** (S) (M) 1. garlanded with gold. 3. another name for Sūrya.

**Hemāmālinī** (S) (F) garlanded with gold.

**Hemāmbikā** (S) (F) 1. golden mother. 3. a form of Durgā whose shrine is at Pālaghat.

**Heman** (S) (M) 1. golden yellow. 2. the Jasmine blossom (*Jasminum pubescens*); the Saffron flower (*Crocus sativus*); gold; golden ornament. 3. another name for the planet Mercury.

**Heman** (S) (M) made of gold.

**Hemanātha** (S) (M) 1. lord of gold. 3. another name for Śiva.

**Hemanetra** (S) (M) 1. golden eyed. 3. a yakṣa who worships Kubera in his assembly (*M. Bh.*)

**Hemāṅga** (S) (M) 1. golden bodied. 2. a Brāhmin; a lion; the Ćampaka tree (*Michelia champaka*). 3. another name for Garuḍa, Viṣṇu, Brahmā and Mount Meru.

**Hemāṅgadā** (A) (F) 1. golden bracelet. 3. an apsarā (*M. Bh.*)

**Hemāṅginī** (S) (F) golden bodied.

**Hemāni** (S) (F) 1. made of gold. 2. as precious as gold. 3. another name for Pārvatī, the consort of Śiva.

**Hemanta** (S) (M) winter.

**Hemantī** (S) (F) of winter.

**Hemanya** (S) (M) gold bodied.

**Hemaprabhā** (S) (F) golden light.

**Hemapuṣpakā** (S) (F) 1. with golden flowers. 3. the flower of the Ćampaka tree (*Michelia champaka*); the Yellow Jasmine (*Jasminum humile*)

**Hemapuṣpam** (S) (M) 1. golden flowered. 3. Aśoka tree (*Saraca indica*)

**Hemapuṣpikā** (S) (F) 1. with small golden flowers. 3. the Yellow Jasmine (*Jasminum humile*)

**Hemarāginī** (S) (F) 1. coloured gold. 3. Turmeric (*Curcuma longa*)

**Hemarāja** (S) (M) lord of gold.

**Hemaratha** (S) (M) 1. with a golden chariot. 3. a king of the solar dynasty and grandson of Ćitraratha, son of Kśema and father of Satyaratha (*Bhāgavata*)

**Hemaśaṅkha** (S) (M) 1. with a golden conch shell. 3. another name for Viṣṇu.

**Hemasāvarṇi** (S) (M) 1. golden coloured. 3. father of Svāyamprabha (*Rāmayaṇa*)

**Hemaśikha** (S) (M) 1. gold crested. 3. Prickly Poppy (*Argemone mexicana*)

**Hemavarṇā** (H) (F) golden complexioned.

**Hemavarṇa** (S) (M) 1. golden complexioned. 3. the son of King Rocamāna who fought on the side of the Pāṇḍavas (*M. Bh.*); a son of Garuḍa; a Buddha.

**Hemavatī** (S) (F) 1. possessing gold. 3. the Prickly Poppy (*Argemone mexicana*); another name for Pārvatī.

**Hemāvatī** (S) (F) 1. possessing gold. 2. a mountain stream. 3. another name for Pārvatī.

**Hemavatīnandana** (S) (M) 1. son of Pārvatī; son of Hemavatī. 3. another name for Gaṇeśa and Kārttikeya.

**Hemayūthikā** (S) (F) 1. gold woven. 3. the Yellow Jasmine (*Jasminum humile*)

**Hemendra** (S) (M) 1. lord of gold. 3. another name for Indra.

**Heraka** (S) (M) 1. spy. 3. an attendant of Śiva.

**Herambā** (S) (F) 1. consort of Ganeśa the boastful. 3. another name for Gaṇeśaṇi.

**Heramba** (S) (M) 1. son of wealth. 2. boastful. 3. another name for Gaṇeśa.

**Heti** (S) (M) 1. flame. 3. another name for Agni.

**Hiḍimbā** (S) (F) 1. instigator. 3. a wife of the Pāṇḍava prince Bhīma and the mother of Ghaṭotkaća (*M. Bh.*)

**Hijjalā** (S) (F) 1. well wisher of water. 3. a

goddess of the Indian Oak tree (*Barringtonia acutangula*)

**Hilmoćikā** (S) (F) 1. destroyer of sins. 3. *Enhydra fluctuans*.

**Hima** (S) (M) 1. snow. 2. winter; night. 3. a year as mentioned in scriptures (*V. Purāṇa*); Nut gram (*cyperus rotundis*); Himalayan Cherry (*Prunus cerasoides*)

**Himā** (S) (F) 1. snow. 2. winter; night. 3. an apsarā who lives in the mountains (*A. Veda/V. Samhitā*)

**Himābja** (S) (M) the Blue Lotus (*Nymphaea stellata*)

**Himāćala** (S) (M) abode of snow; the Himālaya mountain.

**Himādri** (S) (M) peak of snow; the Himālaya mountain.

**Himadyuti** (S) (M) 1. of cool radiance. 2. the moon.

**Himajā** (S) (F) 1. daughter of snow; daughter of Himavāna. 3. another name for Pārvatī; Black Myrobalan (*Terminalia chebula; Hedychium spicatum*)

**Himajyotī** (S) (M) 1. with snowlike light. 3. another name for Ćandra.

**Himakara** (S) (M) 1. snow handed; causing cold. 2. white. 3. another name for the moon.

**Himakiraṇa** (S) (M) 1. cold-rayed. 2. the moon.

**Himambū** (S) (M) water of snow; dew.

**Himānī** (S) (F) 1. glacier; snow; avalanche. 3. another name for Pārvatī.

**Himānśu** (S) (M) 1. cool rayed. 3. another name for Ćandra.

**Himaraśmi** (S) (F) 1. white light; cool rayed. 3. moonlight; moon.

**Himaratī** (S) (M) 1. enemy of snow. 2. fire. 3. Ceylon Leadwort (*Plumbago zeylanica*); another name for the sun.

**Himaśaila** (S) (M) 1. snow mountain. 3. another name for the Himālaya.

**Himaśailajā** (S) (F) 1. born of Himālaya; born of snow. 3. another name for Pārvatī.

**Himaśveta** (S) (F) as white as snow.

**Himasutā** (S) (F) 1. daughter of snow; daughter of Himavāna. 2. fair; peaceful; calm. 3. another name for Pārvatī.

**Himavāllūka** (S) (M) ice like in appearance.

**Himavāna, Himavata** (S) (M) 1. cold; of white; having snow. 3. the great mountain range on the northern borders personified as a divine soul called Himavāna who is married to Menā and is the father of Pārvatī; another name for Ćandra.

**Himośra** (S) (M) 1. white rayed. 3. another name for Ćandra.

**Hiṁsra** (S) (M) 1. cruel; destructive; savage fierce. 3. a sage who was the son of Kuśika; another name for Bhīma and Śiva.

**Hinā** (S) (F) fragrance; the Myrtle vine (*Lawsonia inermis*) commonly known as mehndi.

**Hīnadośa** (S) (M) without fault.

**Hiṅgula** (S) (M) 1. vermilion. 2. auspicious; sacred.

**Hingulājā** (S) (F) 1. of vermilion. 3. a goddess.

**Hiṅkara** (S) (M) 1. chanting of hymns. 2. the invocation of a deity.

**Hinsā** (S) (F) injury personified as the wife of Adharma and daughter of Lobha and Niṣkriti.

**Hīra** (S) (M) quintessence; a diamond; thunderbolt; lion.

**Hīrā** (S) (F) 1. diamond. 3. another name for Lakṣmī.

**Hīraka** (S) (M) diamond.

**Hīral** (S) (M) 1. bearer of diamonds. 2. very wealthy.

**Hirañćaya** (S) (M) 1. deer footed. 3. a son of Āgnīdhra.

**Hiraṅga** (S) (M) 1. diamond bodied. 2. as hard as a diamond. 3. the thunderbolt of Indra.

**Hiraṇya** (S) (M) 1. gold. 2. most precious. 3. another name for Viṣṇu.

**Hiraṇyā** (S) (F) 1. golden. 3. one of the 7 tongues of fire.

**Hiraṇyabāhu** (S) (M) 1. golden armed. 2. very strong. 3. a nāga born in Vāsuki's dynasty (*M. Bh.*)

**Hiraṇyabindu** (S) (F) 1. golden spot. 2. fire; a sacred pool near the Himālayas a dip in which is considered to wash away all sins.

**Hiraṇyābja** (S) (M) 1. golden lotus (*Nymphaea alba*)

**Hiraṇyadā** (S) (F) 1. giving gold. 3. another name for the earth.
**Hiraṇyadanta** (S) (M) 1. gold toothed. 3. a teacher mentioned in the *Aitereya Brāhmaṇa*.
**Hiraṇyadhanuṣ** (S) (M) 1. with a golden bow. 3. a king of forest tribes and father of Ekalavya.
**Hiraṇyagarbha** (S) (M) 1. the golden womb. 3. another name for Brahmā and Kṛṣṇa.
**Hiraṇyahasta** (S) (M) 1. golden handed. 3. the son of Princess Vadhṛmatī, given by the aśvins who became a sage and married the daughter of King Madirāśva (*M. Bh.*); another name for Sāvitṛ.
**Hiraṇyakaśipu** (S) (M) 1. covered with gold. 3. a son of Viśvāmitra who was a Brahmavādin (*M. Bh.*); a son of Kaśyapa and Diti, the brother of Hiraṇyākṣa and the father of Prahlāda (*V. Purāṇa/M. Bh./Bhāgavata*)
**Hiraṇyakeśa** (S) (M) 1. golden haired. 3. another name for Viṣṇu.
**Hiraṇyākṣa** (S) (M) 1. golden eyed. 3. a son of Kaśyapa and Diti and the brother of Hiraṇyakaśipu (*V. Purāṇa/Bhāgavata/M. Bh.*)
**Hiraṇyamaya** (S) (M) 1. full of gold. 2. a particular region in the Jambu island to the south of Mount Nīla and the north of Mount Niśādha (*Bhāgavata*)
**Hiraṇyanābha** (S) (M) 1. with a golden navel. 3. a solar dynasty king who was the father of Puṣya (*Bhāgavata*); a son of a child of Śṛñjaya who lived for a 1000 years (*M. Bh.*); a Kośalā prince (*P. Upaniṣad*)
**Hiraṇyaretas** (S) (M) 1. having gold as seed. 3. son of Priyavrata who was king of Kuśa island (*Bhāgavata*); an aditya; another name for Śiva and Agni.
**Hiraṇyaroman** (S) (M) 1. with golden hair. 3. a king of Vidharbha who was suzerain of the southern regions (*H. Purāṇa*); a seer of the 5th cycle of creation (*Bhāgavata/ Mā. Purāṇa*)
**Hiraṇyastūpa** (S) (M) 1. golden pillar. 3. a great sage who was the son of Aṅgiras (*Ṛg Veda*)
**Hiraṇyava** (S) (M) golden ornament; property of a god.
**Hiraṇyavāha** (S) (M) 1. bearing gold. 2. another name for Śiva and the river Śona.
**Hiraṇyavakṣā** (S) (F) 1. chest of gold. 3. the earth personified as the goddess Vasundharā who conceals the treasures of the world in her bosom (*A. Veda*)
**Hiraṇyāvarman** (S) (M) 1. with golden armour. 3. a king of Daśārna whose daughter married Śikhandī (*M. Bh.*)
**Hiraṇyina** (S) (M) of gold.
**Hīren** (S) (M) 1. lord of gems. 2. attractive pearls.
**Hīreśa** (S) (M) king of gems.
**Hiriśipra** (S) (M) 1. golden checked. 3. another name for Agni and Indra.
**Hīru** (S) (M) as hard as a diamond.
**Hita** (S) (M) 1. welfare. 2. beneficial; good; wholesome; friendly; auspicious; kind.
**Hitaiśi** (S) (M) well wisher.
**Hitaṣa** (S) (M) 1. the oblation eater. 3. another name for Agni.
**Hiteṣin** (S) (M) benevolent.
**Hiteśvara** (S) (M) god of welfare; caring for others.
**Hiyā** (S) (F) heart.
**Hlādini** (S) (F) 1. lightning. 3. the thunderbolt of Indra; a river which is a tributary of the Gaṅgā; the tree *Boswellia serrata*.
**Holikā** (S) (F) 1. lighting the ceremonial fire. 3. a sister of Hiraṇyakaśipu (*Bhāgavata*)
**Homa** (S) (M) 1. oblation. 3. a king of the Bharata dynasty who was the son of Kṛsadratha and the father of Sutapas (*Bhāgavata*); Black Catechu tree (*Acacia catechu*)
**Honna** (S) (M) to possess.
**Hośang** (S) (M) to be one's own self.
**Hotrā** (S) (F) 1. invocation. 2. invocation which is used in ritual. 3. one of Agni's wives (*Ṛg Veda/A. Veda*)
**Hotravāhana** (S) (M) 1. with the chariot of invocation. 3. a saintly king who was the grandfather of Ambā (*M. Bh.*)
**Hradā** (S) (F) lake; pond.
**Hṛāda** (S) (M) 1. sound; noise; roar; reality. 3. a son of Hiraṇyakaśipu (*V. Purāṇa*); a nāga who helped carry the body of Balarāma to

Pātāla (*M. Bh.*)

**Hradinī** (S) (F) 1. pond like. 2. very happy. 3. a tributary of the Gaṅgā which flows eastwards.

**Hrādodara** (S) (M) 1. lake-bellied. 3. a daitya (*M. Bh.*)

**Hrasvaroman** (S) (M) 1. shorthaired. 3. a king of Videha and son of Svarṇaroman (*Bh. Purāṇa*)

**Hṛććhaya** (S) (M) 1. dwelling in the heart; conscience. 3. another name for Kāmā.

**Hṛdambhoja** (S) (M) with a lotus-like heart.

**Hṛdaya** (S) (M) heart.

**Hṛdayagandhā** (S) (F) 1. fragrance of the heart. 2. love; kindness; affection. 3. Spanish Jasmine (*Jasminum grandiflorum*); the Woodapple tree (*Aegle marmelos*)

**Hṛidayaja** (S) (M) 1. born of the heart. 2. son.

**Hṛdayanārāyaṇa** (S) (M) 1. lord of the heart. 3. another name for Viṣṇu.

**Hṛdayaṅgam** (S) (M) 1. entered into the heart. 2. beautiful; beloved; cherished.

**Hṛdayeśa** (S) (M) lord of the heart.

**Hṛdayeśvara** (S) (M) lord of the heart; beloved.

**Hṛdi** (S) (M) 1. heart. 3. a Yādava prince (*Bhāgavata*)

**Hṛdika** (S) (M) 1. of heart. 2. friendship. 3. a Yādava who was the father of Kṛtavarman (*M. Bh.*)

**Hṛdīkātmaja** (S) (M) 1. son of Hṛdīka. 3. another name for Kṛtavarman.

**Hṛdya** (S) (M) 1. agreeable; desired. 3. a sage who lives in the assembly of Indra (*M. Bh.*); Caraway (*Carum carvi*)

**Hrdyānanda** (S) (M) joy of the heart.

**Hrdyanātha** (S) (M) lord of the heart.

**Hṛdvilāsinī** (S) (F) 1. diverting the heart. 3. Turmeric (*Curcuma longa*)

**Hreśa** (S) (M) to be delighted; to be glad.

**Hṛī** (S) (F) 1. modesty. 3. shyness personified as a daughter of Dakṣa and wife of Dharmā; one of the 16 daughters of Svāyambhuva Manu and Śatarūpā and a worshipper of Brahmā in his assembly (*Bhāgavata*)

**Hrim** (S) (M) 1. one who takes away; wealth. 3. a mantra or a holy chant representing Maya the power of illusion and Bhuvanesvarī, the dispeller of sorrow (*V. Samhitā*)

**Hrīmān** (S) (M) 1. dispeller of sorrow; wealthy. 3. a viśvadeva (*H. Purāṇa*)

**Hrīniṣeva** (S) (M) 1. relinquisher of wealth. 3. a saintly king of the asura dynasty who relinquished his kingdom (*M. Bh.*)

**Hṛsīkeśa** (S) (M) 1. controlling the senses. 3. Kṛṣṇa with his senses controlled (*M. Bh.*)

**Hṛṣu** (S) (M) 1. glad; happy. 3. another name for Agni, the sun and moon.

**Hūhū** (S) (M) 1. in attentive response. 3. a gandharva who was the son of Kaśyapa and Prādhā (*H. Purāṇa/M. Bh.*)

**Hulās** (S) (M) jubilation.

**Humbādevī** (S) (F) goddess of jubilation.

**Humkārā** (S) (F) 1. roaring. 3. a yoginī.

**Huṇda** (S) (M) 1. giver of pain. 2. one who tortures; tiger. 3. an asura son of Vipraćitti who abducted Aśokasundarī the sister of Kārttikeya (*P. Purāṇa*)

**Hurditya** (S) (M) joyous; happy.

**Hutabhu** 1. created by the oblation. 3. another name for Agni.

**Hutabhuj** (S) (M) 1. oblation eater. 3. another name for Agni.

**Hutabhuk** (S) (M) 1. oblation eater. 3. another name for Agni.

**Hutapriyā** (S) (F) 1. beloved of fire. 3. another name for Svāhā, the wife of Agni.

# I

**Ibha** (S) (F) elephant; the number 8.

**Ibhāna** (S) (M) **1.** elephant faced. **3.** another name for Gaṇeśa.

**Ibhānan** (S) (M) **1.** elephant faced. **3.** another name for Gaṇeśa.

**Ibhī** (S) (F) female elephant.

**Ibhya** (S) (M) possessor of many attendants.

**Iććhā** (S) (F) desire; ambition; aim.

**Iććhaka** (S) (M) **1.** granting desires. **3.** the Citron tree (*Citrus medica*)

**Iććhavasu** (S) (M) **1.** possessing all wealth wished for. **3.** another name for Kubera.

**Iććhāvatī** (S) (F) one who desires.

**Iḍā** (S) (F) **1.** this moment. **2.** intelligence; insight; the earth as the primal giver of food. **3.** the daughter of Vāyu who was the wife of Dhruva and mother of Utkala (*Bhāgavata*); a daughter of Manu Vaivasvata (*T. Samhitā*)

**Iḍā** (S) (M) **1.** a stream of praise; a period of time; libation. **3.** one of sage Kardama's sons (*V. Purāṇa*); another name for Agni.

**Iḍāspati** (S) (M) **1.** lord of refreshment. **3.** another name for Pūṣan, Viṣṇu, and Parjanya, the god of rain.

**Iḍaviḍa/Ilavilā/Ilibila** (S) (F) **1.** knower of libation; having insight. **2.** scholar; praise. **3.** the daughter of the royal sage Tṛṇabindu and Alambuṣā, wife of Viśravas and the mother of Kubera (*V. Purāṇa*)

**Iḍavida, Ilavilā** (S) (M) **1.** knower of libation; one who has insight. **3.** a son of Daśaratha.

**Iddham** (S) (M) **1.** shining; glowing; blazing. **2.** sunshine; light; heat.

**Iḍenya** (S) (M) to be praiseworthy.

**Idhabodha** (S) (M) of illuminative insight.

**Idhma** (S) (M) sacrificial fuel; the fuel used for a yajña.

**Idhmajīhva** (S) (M) **1.** fuel tongued. **2.** one who brings fuel for the sacrifice. **3.** a son of Priyavrata and Surūpā and the grandson of Svāyambhuva Manu (*M. Bhāgavata*)

**Idhmavāha** (S) (M) **1.** carrier of fuel. **2.** one who carries wood for the sacrifice. **3.** a son of Dṛḍacyuta; a son of Lopāmudrā and Agastya who was the equivalent of a 1,000 sons in strength (*V. Rāmāyaṇa*)

**Iḍikā** (S) (F) **1.** belonging to Iḍa. **3.** another name for Pṛthvī or the earth.

**Īḍitri** (S) (F) one who praises.

**Īhā** (S) (F) wish; desire; effort; activity.

**Īhitā** (S) (F) desired.

**Ijyā** (S) (F) sacrifice; image; gift; donation; worship.

**Ijya** (S) (M) **1.** worthy of worship. **2.** a teacher; deity; god. **3.** another name for Bṛhaspati as the teacher of the gods; another name for the Supreme Being, Viṣṇu and the planet Jupiter.

**Ijyaśīla** (S) (M) performing the sacrifice repeatedly.

**Īkṣa** (S) (F) sight.

**Īkṣaṇa** (S) (M) sight.

**Īkṣeṇya** (S) (F) deserving to be seen.

**Īkṣita** (S) (F) visible; seen.

**Ikṣu** (S) (F) **1.** sweetness. **2.** Sugarcane (*Saccharum officinarum*)

**Ikṣuda** (S) (M) that which gives sweetness; sweet tongued.

**Īkṣudā** (S) (F) **1.** granting wishes; bringing sweetness. **3.** a river (*M. Bh.*)

**Īkṣugandhā** (S) (F) **1.** smelling as sweet as sugarcane; that which is fragrant. **3.** *Saccharum spontaneum*.

**Ikṣulā** (S) (F) **1.** bringer of sweetness; granting wishes. **2.** one of the prongs of Śiva's trident (*Ś. Purāṇa*). **3.** a holy river (*M. Bh.*)

**Ikṣulatā** (S) (F) creeper of sweetness.

**Ikṣumatī/Ikṣumālinī/Ikṣumālavī** (F) **1.** one who has sugarcane; one who is sweet. **3.** a river which flowed near Kurukśetra and was inhabited by the serpent lord Takṣaka (*M. Bh.*)

**Ikṣura** (S) (M) sugarcane; a fragrant grass called Khas (*Vetiveria zizanioides*); *Polytoca barbata* grass.

**Ikṣusamudra** (S) (M) **1.** the sea of syrup. **3.** one of the 7 seas of the mythical world (*A. Koṣa*)

**Ikṣuvāri** (S) (F) **1.** sugarcane juice; the sea of syrup. **3.** one of the 7 seas of the world (*A. Koṣa*)

**Ikṣvāku** (S) (M) 1. one who attracts desire. 2. one who brings wishes to effect. 3. the son of Manu Vaivasvata, the grandson of Vivasvāna who founded the solar dynasty and ruled at Ayodhyā and the ancestor of Rāma (*M. Bh./Ṛg Veda/Bhāgavata/H. Purāṇa/ Rāmāyaṇa*)

**Ikvāla, Ekvāl** (S) (M) prosperity; good fortune.

**Ilā** (S) (F) 1. earth; speech; prayer; refreshment; recreation; vital spirit; offering; stream of praise. 2. mother; teacher; priestess. 3. a daughter of Manu Vaivasvata and Śraddhā, the sister of Ikṣvāku, the wife of Budha and the mother of Purūravas (*Bhāgavata*); the goddess of the earth who, with Sarasvatī and Mahī, forms the trinity which bestows delight; a river which pays homage to Kārttikeya (*M. Bh.*); a daughter of Dakṣa and wife of Kaśyapa; a wife of Vasudeva; a wife of the rudra Ṛtadhvaja; another name for Durgā.

**Ilābilā** (S) (F) the praised one; protector of the earth; the 5 stars on the head of the constellation Orion.

**Ilācandra** (S) (M) moon of the earth.

**Ilādhara** (S) (M) upholder of the earth; mountain.

**Ilākṣi** (S) (F) eye of the earth; the axis of the earth; centre of the earth.

**Ilānko** (S) (M) surface of the earth.

**Ilāspada** (S) (M) foot of the earth; an ancient bathing ghat considered holy and a dip in which is considered to ward off ill-luck.

**Ilāspati** (S) (M) lord of the earth.

**Ilāvarta** (S) (M) 1. surrounding the earth. 2. cloud over the earth. 3. a king in the line of Priyavrata (*Bhāgavata*); a son of Svāyambhuva Manu.

**Ilavila** (S) (M) 1. protector of earth. 3. a son of Daśaratha (*V. Rāmāyaṇa*)

**Ilāvṛta** (S) (M) protector of speech; one of the 9 divisions of the earth (*M. Bh./Mā. Purāṇa*); a son of Āgnīdhra.

**Ilī** (S) (M) a small sword; a knife.

**Ilībiśa** (S) (M) 1. one who throws knives at the enemy. 3. an asura conquered by Indra (*Ṛg Veda*)

**Ilīkā** (S) (F) small earth; diminutive form of earth.

**Ilikā** (S) (F) of earth; transitory; corporeal.

**Īlila, Īlina** (S) (M) 1. possessing high intelligence. 3. a sword of Indra (*H. Purāṇa*); a king of the Purū dynasty who was the son of King Taṁsu, husband of Rathāntarī and the father of King Duṣyanta (*M. Bh.*)

**Ilinā** (S) (F) 1. possessing high intelligence. 3. a daughter of Medhātithi (*H. Purāṇa*); Yama's daughter (*V. Purāṇa*)

**Iliśā, Ileśā** (S) (F) queen of the earth.

**Ilūṣa** (S) (M) 1. covering the earth; a wanderer. 3. the father of Kavaṣa (*H. Purāṇa*)

**Ilvakā, Ilvika** (S) (F) 1. protector of the earth. 3. the 5 stars at the head of the constellation Orion (*J. Śastra*)

**Ilya** (S) (M) a mythical tree of paradise.

**Īnakānta** (S) (M) beloved of the sun; the sunstone.

**Īnākṣi** (S) (F) sharp eyed.

**Iṇan** (S) (M) sun; lord; master; king.

**Inas** (S) (M) 1. able; strong; bold; wild; glorious; powerful; mighty. 3. an aditya; another name for Sūrya.

**Indalī** (S) (F) to attain power.

**Indambara** (S) (M) 1. with precious clothing. 3. the Blue Lotus (*Nymphaea stellata*)

**Indeśvara** (S) (M) 1. lord of the moon. 3. a pilgrimage centre.

**Indirā** (S) (F) 1. bestower of prosperity; bestower of power; powerful. 3. another name for Lakṣmī.

**Indirālaya** (S) (M) 1. abode of Indira. 3. another name for the Blue Lotus (*Nymphaea stellata*) from which Lakṣmī emerged at the time of creation.

**Indīvara** (S) (M) 1. best among the precious. 2. blessing. 3. the Blue Lotus (*Nymphaea stellata*); another name for Viṣṇu.

**Indīvarākṣa** (S) (M) 1. lotus eyed. 3. a gandharva who was the son of Nalanābha the chief of the vidyādharas (*M. Purāṇa*)

**Indīvaraprabhā** (S) (F) 1. the light of the blue lotus. 3. a daughter of sage Kaṇva (*M. Bh.*)

**Indīvarasena** (S) (M) 1. the army of Viṣṇu. 3. the son of King Parityāgasena of Irāvati (*K. Sāgara*)

**Indīvariṇī** (S) (F) a collection of blue lotuses.

**Indīya** (S) (M) knowledgeable; of the river Narmadā; the planet Mercury.

**Indra** (S) (M) 1. god of the atmosphere and sky. 2. excellent; first; chief; symbol of generous heroism. 3. the deity who fights the demons and is subordinate to Brahmā, Viṣṇu and Śiva in the pantheon but chief of all the other deities (*Ṛg Veda/A. Veda/M. Smṛti/ M. Bh./Rāmāyaṇa*); the plant *Holarrhena antidysenterica*.

**Indrabālā** (S) (F) daughter of Indra.

**Indrabala** (S) (M) with the strength of Indra.

**Indrabhā** (S) (F) light of Indra.

**Indrabha** (S) (M) 1. with the glory of Indra. 3. a son of Dhṛtarāṣtra (*M. Bh.*)

**Indrabhaginī** (S) (F) 1. sister of Indra. 3. another name for Pārvatī.

**Indrabhaṭṭārikā** (S) (F) honoured by Indra.

**Indrabhūti** (S) (M) 1. image of Indra. 3. one of the 11 Gaṇādhipas of the Jainas (*J.S. Koṣa*); the main disciple of Mahāvira (*J. Literature*)

**Indraćāpa** (S) (M) 1. bow of Indra. 3. another name for the rainbow.

**Indradamana** (S) (M) 1. conqueror of Indra. 3. a king known for his generosity towards Brāhmins (*M. Bh.*); an asura.

**Indradatta** (S) (M) gift of Indra.

**Indradevī** (S) (F) 1. as sacred as Indra. 3. a wife of King Meghavāhana.

**Indradhvaja** (S) (M) 1. Indra's banner. 3. a Tathāgata; a nāga.

**Indrādu** (S) (M) desired by Indra.

**Indradyumna** (S) (M) 1. the light, lustre and splendour of Indra. 3. a king of the Pāṇḍya country from the Svāyambhuva Manu dynasty (*M. Bh.*); a king who was a contemporary of Kṛṣṇa and killed by him (*M. Bh.*); a sage who blessed Yudhiṣṭhira during his exile (*M. Bh.*); the father of King Janaka of Mithilā (*Rāmāyaṇa*); a king of the Ikṣvāku dynasty (*M. Bh.*); a king of the Kṛta yuga who was a devotee of Viṣṇu (*Sk. Purāṇa*); a lake near Mount Gandhamādana visited by the Pāṇḍavas (*M. Bh.*); the son of Sumati and grandson of King Bharata (*M. Bh.*)

**Indraghoṣa** (S) (M) 1. the voice of Indra; one who praises Indra. 3. a deity.

**Indragiri** (S) (M) 1. the mountain of Indra. 3. another name for the mountain Mahendra.

**Indrāgnī** (S) (M) Indra and Agni conjoined; the Indrāgni deity is the embodiment of heroism.

**Indragopa** (S) (M) protected by Indra.

**Indragupta** (S) (M) protected by Indra; Khuskhus grass (*Vetiveria zizanioides*)

**Indraguru** (S) (M) 1. teacher of Indra. 3. another name for sage Kaśyapa.

**Indrahūti** (S) (F) invocation of Indra.

**Indraja** (S) (M) 1. born of Indra. 3. another name for Vālin.

**Indrajāla** (S) (M) 1. the net of Indra. 2. hypnotism, the science of magic. 3. the weapon of Arjuna (*M. Bh.*)

**Indrajālin** (S) (M) 1. of the net of Indra. 2. a sorcerer. 3. a Bodhisattva (*L. Vistara*)

**Indrajit** (S) (M) 1. conqueror of Indra. 3. another name for Meghanāda the son of King Rāvaṇa of Lankā (*U. Rāmāyaṇa*); a dānava; a king of Kāśmira (*R. Tarangiṇī*)

**Indrakarman** (S) (M) 1. performing Indra's deeds. 3. another name for Viṣṇu.

**Indrakārmuka** (S) (M) rainbow.

**Indraketu** (S) (M) Indra's banner.

**Indrakīla** (S) (M) 1. banner of Indra. 3. a mountain situated between the Himālayas and the Gandhamādana mountain, the deity of which is a devotee of Kubera (*M. Bh.*)

**Indrākṣī** (S) (F) 1. eyes like Indra. 3. a tutelary goddess.

**Indramantrin** (S) (M) 1. advisor of Indra. 3. another name for sage Bṛhaspati.

**Indramedin** (S) (M) one whose ally is Indra.

**Indramohinī** (S) (F) 1. one to whom Indra is attracted. 3. an apsarā in Indra's court (*M. Bh.*)

**Indrāṇī** (S) (F) 1. consort of Indra. 3. the female form of Indra's energy personified as the daughter of Pulomān, the consort of Indra, the mother of Jayanta and Jayantī, also called Śaći and Aindrī and considered the epitome of beauty and voluptuousness (*A. Veda/Sk. Purāṇa*); *Amomum subulatum*.

**Indranīla** (S) (M) 1. as blue as Indra. 2. the sapphire.

**Indranīlikā** (S) (F) as blue as Indra.

**Indrānuja** (S) (M) 1. younger brother of Indra. 3. another name for Viṣṇu.

**Indrapālita** (S) (M) 1. protected by Indra. 3. a king (*V. Purāṇa*)

**Indrapramati** (S) (M) 1. knowledge of Indra; protected by Indra. 3. a disciple of sage Vyāsa (*M. Bh.*)

**Indrapriya** (S) (M) dear to Indra.

**Indrapurohitā** (S) (F) 1. the priest of Indra. 3. the asterism Puṣya.

**Indrapūṣan** (S) (M) Indra and Pūṣan conjoined; the Indrapūṣan deity is invoked to give assistance in battle.

**Indrarājan** (S) (M) Indra, the king; having Indra as king.

**Indraśakti** (S) (F) 1. the energy of Indra. 3. the feminine form of Indra's energy personified as his consort Indrāṇī.

**Indrāsana** (S) (M) throne of Indra.

**Indrasārathi** (S) (M) 1. the charioteer of Indra. 3. another name for Mātali the charioteer of Indra; another name for Vāyu.

**Indrasāvarṇi** (S) (M) 1. Indra's complexion. 2. one with the complexion of Indra. 3. the 14th Manu (*H. Purāṇa*)

**Indrasenā** (S) (F) 1. the army of Indra; the best warrior. 3. Draupadī in her previous incarnation (*M. Bh.*); a daughter of King Nala and Damayantī (*S. Samhitā*); a princess of Aṅga who married sage Ṛṣyaśṛṅga (*M. Bh.*)

**Indrasena** (S) (M) 1. the army of Indra; the best warrior. 3. a son of King Nala (*M. Bh.*); a son of King Parīkṣit (*M. Bh.*); the charioteer of Yudhiṣṭhira (*M. Bh.*)

**Indrasoma** (S) (M) 1. Indra and Soma conjoined. 3. Indrasoma who discovered the sun, supported the heavens, filled the sea with water and gave milk to the cows and the function of whom is to perform heroic deeds for man and invest him with heroic strength (*M. Bh.*)

**Indrasunu** (S) (M) 1. son of Indra. 3. another name for Jayanta; the White Murdah (*Terminalia citrina*)

**Indrāsura** (S) (M) Indra the brave.

**Indrasuras** (S) (M) the tree of Indra; the Arjuna tree (*Terminalia arjuna*)

**Indrasuta** (S) (M) 1. son of Indra. 3. another name for the monkey king, Valin, Arjuna and Jayanta.

**Indrasvat** (S) (M) accompanied by Indra.

**Indratā** (S) (F) the power and dignity of Indra.

**Indratan** (S) (M) as strong as Indra.

**Indratāpa** (S) (M) 1. the penance of Indra. 2. offering sacrifices and penances to Indra. 3. an asura who was a devotee of Varuṇa (*M. Bh.*)

**Indratejas** (S) (M) 1. the strength of Indra. 3. the thunderbolt of Indra.

**Indravadana** (S) (M) 1. the face of Indra. 2. one with the beauty of Indra.

**Indravāhana** (S) (M) 1. the vehicle of Indra. 2. with Indra as the vehicle; one who is carried by Indra. 3. another name for King Kakutṣṭha of the Ikṣvāku dynasty who made Indra his vehicle while fighting the asuras.

**Indravajra** (S) (M) the thunderbolt of Indra.

**Indrāvaraja** (S) (M) 1. the younger brother of Indra. 3. another name for Viṣṇu, Kṛṣṇa and Śiva.

**Indravarman** (S) (M) 1. protected by Indra. 3. a king of Mālava who fought on the side of the Pāṇḍavas (*M. Bh.*)

**Indravaruṇa, Indravāruṇī** (S) (M) 1. Indra and Varuṇa conjoined. 3. the deity Indravaruṇa which represents kingly and heroic power and from which comes the bestowal of protection, prosperity, fame and many horses (*Ṛg Veda*); a wild gourd (*Cucumis colocynthis*) considered the favourite plant of both Indra and Varuṇa; another name for Indra's special wine, Soma.

**Indravaṣṇu, Indraviṣṇu** (S) (M) 1. Indra and Viṣṇu. 3. the deity in which Viṣṇu in his Vedic solar form conjoined with Indra and which is invoked to provide shelter, bestow wealth and accept sacrifice (*Ṛg Veda*)

**Indravāyu** (S) (M) Indra and Vāyu conjoined.

**Indrāyaṇī** (S) (F) 1. wife of Indra. 3. the feminine form of Indra's energy, personified as his consort Śaći (*Sk. Purāṇa*)

**Indrāyatana** (S) (M) depending on Indra.

**Indrayava** (S) (M) one whose friend is Indra.

**Indrāyudha** (S) (M) **1.** weapon of Indra. **2.** the rainbow.

**Indrayumna** (S) (M) **1.** one who can stop Indra. **3.** a Pāṇḍyan king who was incarnated as the elephant Gajendra.

**Indrejya** (S) (M) **1.** teacher of Indra; excellent teacher. **3.** another name for Bṛhaspati.

**Indresita** (S) (M) sent by Indra.

**Indreśvara** (S) (M) **1.** lord of the senses. **3.** a form of the Śivaliṅga.

**Indriṇika** (S) (M) desired by Indra.

**Indrota** (S) (M) **1.** one who lives near Indra. **2.** promoted by Indra. **3.** a sage who was the son of sage Śuka and also known as Śaunaka (*M. Bh.*); the son of Atithigva mentioned in the *Ṛg Veda* as a bestower of gifts.

**Indu** (S) (F) **1.** a bright drop. **3.** the moon; Soma; camphor (*Cinnamonum camphora*)

**Indubha** (S) (M) with the light of the moon; the water lily (*Nymphaea alba*); a group of lotuses.

**Indubhava** (S) (M) **1.** creating the moon. **3.** another name for Śiva.

**Indubhavā** (S) (F) **1.** coming from the moon. **3.** a river.

**Indubhṛt** (S) (M) **1.** with the crescent on his forehead. **3.** another name for Śiva.

**Indubhūṣana** (S) (M) **1.** with the moon as an ornament. **2.** whose ornament is the moon. **3.** another name for Śiva.

**Indugiri** (S) (M) **1.** mountain of the moon. **2.** silver; fair; cool; soothing. **3.** another name for Indra's mountain known as Rajata.

**Indujā** (S) (F) **1.** daughter of the moon. **3.** another name for the river Narmadā.

**Induja** (S) (M) **1.** son of the moon. **3.** another name for Budha or the planet Mercury.

**Indujanaka** (S) (M) **1.** father of the moon. **3.** another name for the ocean and sage Atri.

**Indukakṣā** (S) (F) the radiating circle of the moon; the orbit of the moon.

**Indukalā** (S) (F) a digit of the moon.

**Indukalikā** (S) (F) a small piece of the moon; the Indian Screwpine (*Pandanus odoratissimus*)

**Indukamala** (S) (M) **1.** moon like lotus. **2.** the White Lotus (*Nelumbium speciosum*)

**Indukamalā** (S) (F) **1.** the blossom of the moon like lotus. **2.** the blossom of the white lotus (*Nelumbium speciosum*)

**Indukānta** (S) (M) **1.** beloved of the moon. **2.** the moonstone.

**Indukāntā** (S) (F) **1.** beloved of the moon. **2.** night.

**Indukara** (S) (M) **1.** hand of the moon. **2.** a moonbeam.

**Indukarman** (S) (M) **1.** act of moon. **2.** performing pious deeds. **3.** another name for Viṣṇu.

**Indukārmuka** (S) (M) encircling the moon; the rainbow.

**Indukesarin** (S) (M) **1.** golden moon. **3.** a king (*K. Sāgara*)

**Induketu** (S) (M) **1.** moon bannered. **3.** the banner of Indra (*L. Vistara*)

**Indukiriṭa** (S) (M) **1.** moon crested. **3.** another name for Śiva.

**Indukṣaya** (S) (M) **1.** fall of the moon. **2.** the period just after full moon when the moon wanes.

**Indukukṣa** (S) (M) the belly of the moon.

**Indukūṭa** (S) (M) the mountain of the moon.

**Indulekhā** (S) (F) **1.** a digit of the moon. **3.** the 2nd day after the new moon.

**Indumaṇi** (S) (M) **1.** gem of the moon. **2.** moonstone.

**Indumat** (S) (M) **1.** respected by the moon. **3.** another name for Agni.

**Indumatī** (S) (F) **1.** the full moon; full of the moon. **2.** fair; tranquil; soothing; healing. **3.** the daughter of King Ćandrasena of Siṁhala and Guṇavātī who was the wife of Aja and sister of King Bhoja (*Raghuvanśa*); the mother of Nahuṣa (*Bhāgavata*); the wife of Raghu (*V. Rāmāyaṇa*); a river.

**Indumauli** (S) (M) **1.** moon crested. **3.** another name for Śiva.

**Indumitra** (S) (M) **1.** friend of the moon. **3.** a grammarian (*A. Koṣa*)

**Indumukhī** (S) (M) **1.** with a face like the

moon. 2. a face as beautiful as the moon.

**Indunandana** (S) (M) 1. son of the moon. 3. another name for the planet Mercury.

**Indupāla** (S) (M) 1. gem of the moon. 2. the moonstone; ocean.

**Induputra** (M) 1. son of the moon. 3. another name for the planet Mercury.

**Induratna** (S) (F) 1. jewel of the moon. 2. the pearl.

**Induśekhara** (S) (M) 1. moon crested. 3. a kinnara; another name for Śiva.

**Induvadanā** (S) (F) with a moon like face; with a beautiful face.

**Ineśa** (S) (M) 1. a strong king. 3. another name for Viṣṇu.

**Inganam** (S) (M) knowledge.

**Ingida** (S) (M) 1. granting knowledge. 3. a plant used in magic rites to ensure the destruction of enemies (*A. Veda*)

**Ingur** (S) (M) 1. the sacred colour. 2. the colour vermilion which is considered auspicious and sacred.

**Inikā** (S) (F) little earth.

**Inodaya** (S) (M) sunrise.

**Iṇu** (S) (M) 1. charming. 3. a gandharva (*K. Sāgara*)

**Inukānta** (S) (M) 1. beloved of the sun. 2. the sunstone.

**Īpsā** (S) (F) desire; wish.

**Īpsitā** (S) (F) wished for; desired.

**Irā** (S) (F) 1. speech; the earth; refreshment; nourishment; water. 3. a daughter of Dakṣa, a wife of sage Kaśyapa and the mother of grass (*A. Purāṇa*); an attendant of Kubera (*M. Bh.*); an apsarā (*M. Bh.*); another name for Sarasvatī.

**Īra** (S) (M) wind.

**Īraiśa** (S) (M) 1. lord of the earth. 3. another name for Varuṇa, Viṣṇu and Gaṇeśa.

**Īrajā** (S) (M) 1. born of the wind. 3. another name for Hanumān, the son of the wind god Vāyu.

**Īrajā** (S) (F) daughter of the wind; primal water.

**Irāja** (S) (M) 1. son of the primal waters. 3. another name for Kāma.

**Īrāmā** (S) (F) 1. happiness of the earth. 3. a river that sage Mārkaṇḍeya is supposed to have seen in the stomach of the child Kṛṣṇa (*M. Bh.*)

**Iranmada** (S) (M) 1. delighting in drink. 2. lightning. 3. another name for Agni (*A. Purāṇa*)

**Īrāputra** (S) (M) 1. born of the wind. 3. another name for Hanumān, the son of the wind god, Vāyu.

**Irāvaja** (S) (M) 1. born of water. 3. another name for Kāma.

**Irāvān** (S) (M) 1. possessing water or milk. 2. ocean; cloud; king. 3. the son of Arjuna and Ulūpi (*M. Bh.*)

**Irāvata** (S) (M) 1. full of water. 2. cloud.

**Irāvatān** (S) (M) 1. resembling water or milk. 2. satiating; comforting; refreshing. 3. the son of Arjuna and Ulūpi (*M. Bh.*)

**Irāvatī** (S) (F) 1. full of water or milk. 2. clouds. 3. the granddaughter of sage Kaśyapa, the daughter of Kadru and the wife of King Parīkṣita (*V. Rāmāyaṇa*); a river (*M. Bh.*); another name for Durgā as the consort of Rudra (*Bh. Purāṇa*); a daughter of Suśravas.

**Iremut** (S) (M) full of wind; thunder.

**Īri** (S) (M) 1. son of the wind. 3. a king who worships Yama (*M. Bh.*); another name for Hanumān, son of the wind god, Vāyu.

**Īrijayā** (S) (F) victorious wind.

**Irikā** (S) (F) a diminutive form of earth.

**Irimbiṭhi** (S) (M) 1. the path of the wind. 3. a sage of the family of Kaṇva (*M. Bh.*)

**Īrimpu** (Malayalam) (M) purifying wind; iron.

**Īriśa, Īreśa** (S) (M) 1. lord of the earth. 3. another name for Viṣṇu, Varuṇa and Gaṇeśa.

**Irith** (S) (M) of wind; scent.

**Īrma** (S) (M) 1. of the nature of wind. 2. moves constantly; instigates everything. 3. another name for Sūrya.

**Irmaṇḍa** (S) (M) 1. delighting in drinking. 2. a flash of lightning. 3. another name for Agni.

**Irya** (S) (M) 1. powerful; energetic; active. 3. another name for Pūṣan and the aśvins.

**Iśa** (S) (M) 1. god; lord of the universe. 2. fertile; performing pious deeds; one who impels; swift; powerful; venerated; all pervading; divine. 3. one of the 13 principal Upaniṣads; the month of the aśvins (September-October); a sage (*H. Purāṇa*); another name for the viśvadevas or universal gods; a rudra; another name for Śiva.

**Iśā** (S) (F) faculty; power; dominion.

**Iṣā** (S) (F) 1. pole of a plough. 3. another name for Durgā.

**Iśadatta** (S) (M) 1. acquired through pious deeds. 3. a son of Atri and Anasuyā (*V. Rāmāyaṇa*)

**Iśan** (S) (M) bestowing wealth.

**Iśāṇā** (S) (F) 1. sovereign. 3. another name for Durgā.

**Iśāna** (S) (M) 1. sovereign; lord. 3. a rudra; another name for Śiva, Viṣṇu, Agni, and Sūrya; the Śami tree (*Prosopis spicigera*)

**Iśānadeva** (S) (M) sovereign; lord; guardian of the north-east.

**Iśānam** (S) (M) light, splendour.

**Iśanī** (S) (F) 1. ruling; possessing. 3. the wood from the Śami tree (*Prosopis spicigera*) which, when rubbed, produces fire; another name for Durgā.

**Iśānikā** (S) (F) belonging to the north-east.

**Iśat** (S) (M) superiority; greatness.

**Iśayu** (S) (M) fresh; strong; powerful.

**Iśī** (S) (F) 1. goddess. 3. another name for Durgā.

**Iśik** (S) (M) desirable; the Silkcotton tree (*Salmalia malabarica*)

**Iṣikā** (S) (F) a painter's brush; the pen used for writing auspicious things.

**Iṣir** (S) (M) 1. powerful; strong; quick; active; refreshing. 3. another name for Agni.

**Iśitā** (S) (F) 1. desired. 2. superiority; greatness. 3. one of the 8 attributes of Śiva (*M. Bh.*)

**Iṣita** (S) (M) desired.

**Iṣma** (S) (M) 1. pervaded with desire; desire provoking; impetuous. 3. the spring season; another name for Kāma.

**Iṣmin** (S) (M) 1. as swift as the spring; speedy; impetuous. 2. like the wind.

**Iśrita** (S) (M) owner; master; lord of the universe.

**Iṣṭā** (S) (F) that which is worshipped through a sacrifice; the Śami tree (*Prosopis spicigera*)

**Iṣṭagandha** (S) (M) fragrant.

**Iṣṭaka, Iṣṭika** (S) (M) a brick used in preparing the ceremonial altar.

**Iṣṭara** (S) (F) that which is desired more; dearer.

**Iṣṭaraśmi** (S) (M) 1. desiring light. 3. a king mentioned in the *Ṛg Veda* and known for the number of yajñas or sacrifices he performed.

**Iṣṭāśva** (S) (M) 1. a desired horse. 3. a king mentioned in the *Ṛg Veda* and known for the number of yajñas or sacrifices he performed.

**Iṣṭu** (S) (F) wish; desire.

**Iṣu** (S) (M) 1. quivering. 2. an arrow; the number 5; a ray of light.

**Iṣuka** (S) (M) arrow.

**Iṣukā** (S) (F) 1. arrow like; arrow. 3. an apsarā (*M. Bh.*)

**Iṣupa** (S) (M) 1. quiver. 3. a serpent reborn as King Nagnajita (*M. Bh.*)

**Iṣupada** (S) (M) 1. the target of an arrow. 3. an asura born to Kaśyapa and Danu who was later reborn as the heroic king, Nagnajita (*M. Bh.*)

**Iśva** (S) (M) spiritual teacher.

**Iśvara** (S) (M) 1. capable of mastering; ruler; the Supreme Being. 3. a rudra; another name for Śiva and Kāma.

**Iśvaraćandra** (S) (M) the moon among gods; the greatest god.

**Iśvarāgitā** (S) (F) 1. song of the lord. 3. the 1st 11 chapters of the *Kurma Purāṇa* which are devoted to Śiva as the supreme deity.

**Iśvarakāntā** (S) (F) 1. beloved of the gods. 3. another name for Durgā.

**Iśvaraprasāda** (S) (M) given by the gods.

**Iśvarī** (S) (F) 1. best among the divine. 2. consort of Iśvara. 3. *Rauwolfia serpentina*; *momordica balsamina*; *Bryonopsis laciniosa*; another name for Pārvatī the consort of Iśvara or Śiva.

**Iṣvasa** (S) (M) arrow shooter; an archer.

**Iṣya** (S) (M) effecting wishes; the spring season.

**Iṭa** (S) (M) 1. to wander; a kind of reed. 3. a ṛṣi who was a protégé of Indra (*Ṛg Veda*)

**Itanta, Idhanta** (M (S) 1. shining; bright; sharp; clean; wonderful. 3. a sage (*K. Brāhmaṇa*)

**Itar** (S) (M) another.

**Itarā** (S) (F) 1. another. 3. the mother of Aitareya.

**Itiśa** (S) (M) such a lord.

**Itkila** (S) (F) full of fragrance; perfume.

**Ivīlaka** (S) (M) 1. wealthy son. 3. the son of Lambodara (*V. Purāṇa*)

**Īya** (S) (F) pervading.

**Īyam** (Malayalam) (M) lead.

**Iyenar** (Tamil) (M) tutelary village god who is the guardian of the fields and the herds.

## J

**Jabākusuma** (S) (F) **1.** flower of meditation; flower of barley. **2.** beloved of Kṛṣṇa; the shoeflower (*Hibiscus rosa sinensis*)

**Jabālā** (S) (F) **1.** possessing a herd of goats; a young cowherdess. **3.** the mother of sage Satyakāmā (*M. Bh.*)

**Jābāli** (S) (M) **1.** possessing a herd of goats. **2.** a goatherd. **3.** an ancient sage who was the son of Viśvāmitra, the author of a law book and the priest of Daśaratha (*P. Purāṇa*); the son of sage Ṛtadhvaja (*M. Bh.*); a hermit who performed penance on the Mandara mountain and was a devotee of Kṛṣṇa for which he was reborn as the cowherdess Ćitrangadā (*Bhāgavata*); a hermit who was the sometime consort of the apsara Rambhā (*Sk. Purāṇa*)

**Jabbar** (S) (M) barley grower; a peasant.

**Jādhava** (S) (M) a descendant of Jadu (or Yadu); a yādava.

**Jagaćakṣu** (S) (M) **1.** eye of the universe. **3.** the Supreme Being.

**Jagaćandra** (S) (M) **1.** moon of the universe. **3.** a Jaina Sūrī (*J.S. Koṣa*)

**Jagaćitra** (S) (M) wonder of the universe.

**Jagad** (S) (M) universe; world.

**Jagadambā** (S) (F) **1.** mother of the world. **3.** a form of Durgā (*D. Bh. Purāṇa*)

**Jagadambikā** (S) (F) **1.** little mother of the universe. **3.** a form of Durgā (*D. Bh. Purāṇa*)

**Jagadānanda** (S) (M) **1.** pleasure of the universe. **2.** pleasing and satiating the world.

**Jagadātman** (S) (M) **1.** soul of the universe. **3.** another name for the Supreme Spirit.

**Jagadāya** (S) (M) **1.** life of the universe. **2.** the wind.

**Jagadāyu** (S) (M) **1.** life spring of the universe. **2.** the wind.

**Jagadbala** (S) (M) strength of the universe.

**Jagadeva** (S) (M) **1.** lord of the world. **3.** the Supreme Being.

**Jagadgaurī** (S) (F) **1.** fairest of the universe. **3.** another name for Manasā Devī and Pārvatī.

**Jagadgurū** (S) (M) **1.** guru of the universe; preceptor of the world. **3.** another name for Brahmā, Viṣṇu, Śiva and Rāma.

**Jagadhātrī** (S) (F) **1.** sustainer of the universe. **3.** another name for Pārvatī and Sarasvatī.

**Jagadhratu** (S) (M) **1.** abode of the universe. **2.** the creator of the universe. **3.** another name for Brahmā.

**Jagadīpa** (S) (M) **1.** lamp of the universe. **3.** another name for Sūrya.

**Jagadīśa** (S) (M) **1.** lord of the universe. **3.** another name for Brahmā.

**Jagadīśvara** (S) (M) **1.** god of the universe. **3.** another name for Śiva and Indra.

**Jagajīva** (S) (M) living force of the world; soul of the world.

**Jagamohana** (S) (M) **1.** one who attracts the world. **3.** another name for Kṛṣṇa.

**Jagan** (S) (M) world; universe.

**Jaganmaṇi** (S) (M) jewel of the world.

**Jaganmātā** (S) (F) **1.** mother of the world. **3.** another name for Durgā and Lakṣmī.

**Jagannātha** (S) (M) **1.** lord of the world. **3.** an idol of Viṣṇu at Puri; a Sanskṛt critic who is known as Panḍitarāja or king of scholars (16th century A.D.) (*R. Gangādhara*); another name for Viṣṇu, Kṛṣṇa and Dattātreya.

**Jagannetra** (S) (M) **1.** eye of the world. **3.** another name for Sūrya and Ćandra.

**Jagannidhi** (S) (M) receptacle of the world.

**Jagannivāsa** (S) (M) **1.** abode of the world; one who pervades the world. **3.** another name for Viṣṇu and Kṛṣṇa.

**Jaganu** (S) (M) living being; fire.

**Jagaprīta** (S) (M) beloved of the world.

**Jāgara** (S) (M) armour.

**Jagarūpa** (S) (M) form of the world.

**Jagat** (S) (M) **1.** moving; alive. **2.** the world; people.

**Jagatādhāra** (S) (M) **1.** the abode of the world. **2.** time; wind; air. **3.** another name for Viṣṇu, Śeṣa and Lakṣmaṇa.

**Jagatasvāmī** (S) (M) **1.** lord of the universe. **3.** another name for Viṣṇu.

**Jagatdīpa** (S) (M) **1.** lamp of the universe. **3.** another name for Sūrya.

**Jagatgaurī** (S) (F) **1.** beauty of the world.

3. another name for Manasā.

**Jagatguru** (S) (M) 1. preceptor of the world; father of the world. 2. the Supreme Deity. 3. another name for Śiva, Nārada, Brahmā and Viṣṇu.

**Jagatī** (S) (F) 1. of the universe; heaven and hell conjoined. 3. a Vedic metre (*Ṛg Veda*); another name for the earth.

**Jagati** (S) (M) 1. bestowed with speed. 3. one of the 7 horses that draw the chariot of Sūrya (*V. Purāṇa*)

**Jagatīdhara** (S) (M) 1. earth-supporter. 2. mountain. 3. a Bodhisattva.

**Jagatīpati** (S) (M) 1. lord of the earth. 2. a king.

**Jagatjita** (S) (M) victor of the world.

**Jagatjīva** (S) (M) being of the world; a living being.

**Jagatkāraṇa** (S) (M) the cause of the universe.

**Jagatnārāyaṇa** (S) (M) 1. lord of the universe. 3. another name for Viṣṇu.

**Jagatnātha** (S) (M) 1. lord of the world. 3. another name for Viṣṇu, Dattātreya and Śiva.

**Jagatpatī** (S) (M) 1. master of the universe. 3. another name for Brahmā, Śiva, Viṣṇu, Agni.

**Jagatpitṛ** (S) (M) 1. father of the universe. 3. another name for Śiva.

**Jagatprabhu** (S) (M) 1. cause of the universe. 2. one through whom the world has been brought into existence. 3. a Jaina Arhat; another name for Brahmā, Viṣṇu and Śiva.

**Jagatprakāśa** (S) (M) light of the universe.

**Jagatprāṇa** (S) (M) 1. breath of the universe. 2. the wind. 3. another name for Rāma.

**Jagavanta** (S) (M) one to whom the world belongs.

**Jagavī** (S) (F) born of the world.

**Jageśa** (S) (M) 1. lord of the world. 3. another name for Viṣṇu.

**Jagiśa** (S) (M) lord of the world.

**Jagmi** (S) (M) 1. pervading the world. 2. the wind.

**Jagnu** (S) (M) 1. carrier of the world. 2. the fire.

**Jāgravi** (S) (M) 1. watchful. 2. bright. 3. another name for Agni and the sun.

**Jāgṛti** (S) (F) awakening.

**Jāgṛvi** (S) (M) 1. watchful; attentive; not extinguishable. 2. fire; Soma; a king.

**Jāguri** (S) (M) one who wakes others up; one who has risen up; one who leads; conducts.

**Jāhnavī** (S) (F) 1. ear born. 3. the daughter of Jahnu (*Bhāgavata*); another name for the river Gaṅgā.

**Jāhnavīputra** (S) (M) 1. son of Gaṅgā. 3. another name for Bhīṣma.

**Jahnu** (S) (M) 1. ear. 2. a good listener. 3. a king and sage who was the son of Ajamīdha and Keśinī, ancestor of the Kuśikas and who drank up the waters of the Gaṅgā but on the prayers of Bhagiratha discharged them from his ears because of which the river is regarded as his daughter (*M. Bh.*); a ṛṣi of the 4th Manvantara (*H. Purāṇa*); another name for Viṣṇu.

**Jahnukanyā** (S) (M) 1. daughter of Jahnu. 3. another name for Gaṅgā.

**Jahnutanayā** (S) (M) 1. daughter of Jahnu. 3. another name for Gaṅgā.

**Jāhuṣa** (S) (M) 1. leftover; young animal. 3. a king of the Ṛg Vedic period and protégé of the aśvins (*Ṛg Veda*); a son of Puṣpavat.

**Jai** (S) (M) 1. conqueror; victor. 2. a kind of flute. 3. an attendant of Viṣṇu (*Bhāgavata*); a son of Aṅgiras (*Ṛg Veda*); a son of Dhṛtarāṣṭra (*M. Bh.*); a son of Yuyudhāna (*H. Purāṇa*); a son of Kṛṣṇa (*Bhāgavata*); a son of Kanka (*H. Purāṇa*); a son of Vatsara and Svarvīṭhī (*H. Purāṇa*); a son of Purūravas and Urvaśi (*M. Bh.*); 11th ćakravartin of ancient Bhārat; name of Yudhiṣṭhira at Virāṭa's court (*M. Bh.*); one of the 7 flagsticks of Indra's banner (*Ṛg Veda*); the 3rd, 8th and 13th days of each half-month (*V's. B. Samhitā*); Aśoka in a former birth (*Divyāvadana*); a dānava (*M. Bh.*); Yellow Jasmine (*Jasminum humile*); another name for Indra, the sun and Arjuna.

**Jaibhūṣaṇa** (S) (M) ornament of victory.

**Jaićandra** (S) (M) 1. moon among victors. 2. always victorious. 3. a king of Kānyakubja (*Rāmāyaṇa*); a king of Gauḍa (*R. Taraṅginī*)

**Jaideva** (S) (M) 1. lord of victory. 3. a king of Gujarat (738 A.D.) (*I. Tantra*); a Sanskṛt poet who was the author of the *Gītagovinda* (13th century A.D.) (*Ćandrāloka*)

**Jaidhara** (S) (M) 1. bearer of victory. 3. Saṁkara's great-grandfather (*M. Bh.*)

**Jaidharman** (S) (M) 1. victorious in religion. 2. one who is ever victorious. 3. heroes from the Kaurava side (*M. Bh.*)

**Jaidhvaja** (S) (M) 1. flag of victory. 3. a son of Arjuna Kārtavīrya and the father of Talajangha (*V. Purāṇa*)

**Jaidhvani** (S) (M) a shout of victory.

**Jaidurgā** (S) (F) 1. Durgā the victorious. 3. a form of Durgā (*T. Śastra*)

**Jaidvala** (S) (M) 1. powerful. 3. name assumed by Sahadeva at the court of Virāṭa (*M. Bh.*)

**Jaigata** (S) (M) victorious.

**Jaighoṣa** (S) (M) shout of victory.

**Jaigiśavyā** (S) (M) 1. victorious lord. 3. a hermit who was the husband of Ekapātalā (*M. Bh.*)

**Jaigopāla** (S) (M) 1. Gopāla, the victor. 3. another name for Kṛṣṇa.

**Jaigupta** (S) (M) protected by victory.

**Jaijaivantī** (S) (F) 1. full of victory. 2. a song of victory. 3. a rāga.

**Jaikara** (S) (M) mine of victory.

**Jaikīrti** (S) (M) glory of victory.

**Jaikṛta** (S) (M) causing victory.

**Jailekhā** (S) (F) 1. a record of victory. 2. has been victorious many times.

**Jaimālā** (S) (F) garland of victory.

**Jaimalla** (S) (M) victorious fighter.

**Jaimān** (S) (F) victorious.

**Jaimaṅgala** (S) (M) 1. auspicious victory; victory and welfare conjoined. 2. a royal elephant.

**Jaimati** (S) (M) 1. victorious mind. 3. a Bodhisattva (*B. Ćarita*)

**Jaimini** (S) (M) 1. desiring victory; striving for victory. 3. a celebrated sage and philosopher who was a member of the council of Yudhiṣṭhira, a pupil of Vyāsa, founder of the *Pūrva Mimānsa*, co-author of the work *Jaya* which is the original of the *Mahābhārata* and the narrator of his work the *Brahmāṇḍa Purāṇa* to Hiraṇyanābha at Naimiṣaraṇya (*M. Bh.*); the priest of King Subāhu of the Ćolas (*P. Purāṇa*)

**Jaināraāyaṇa** (S) (M) Viṣṇu, the victor.

**Jainabhakti** (S) (M) 1. devoted to Jainism. 3. a Jaina Sūrī (*J.S. Koṣa*)

**Jainendra** (S) (M) lord of the Jainas; a religion which worships the Jinas.

**Jaipāla** (S) (M) 1. guardian of victory. 2. a king. 3. another name for Brahmā and Viṣṇu; *croton tiglium*.

**Jaipīḍa** (S) (M) victory and torture combined; one who attains victory by torturing others.

**Jaiprabhā** (S) (F) the light of victory.

**Jaipriyā** (S) (F) 1. beloved of victory. 3. an attendant of Skanda (*M. Bh.*)

**Jaipriya** (S) (M) 1. beloved of victory. 3. a Pāṇḍava hero (*M. Bh.*)

**Jairāja** (S) (M) victorious ruler.

**Jairāma** (S) (M) victorious Rāma.

**Jairasa** (S) (M) the essence of victory.

**Jaiśekhara** (S) (M) the crest of victory.

**Jaisena** (S) (M) 1. with a victorious army. 3. a prince of Magadha who was a member of the council of Yudhiṣṭhira (*M. Bh.*); a king of Avantī who was the father of Mitravindā who married Kṛṣṇa (*Bhāgavata*); the father of Ćandamahāsena (*M. Bh.*)

**Jaiśīlā** (S) (F) 1. character of victory. 2. one to whom victory comes habitually.

**Jaisinha** (S) (M) 1. victorious lion; lion among the victors. 3. a king of Kāśmira (*R. Taraṅginī*)

**Jaisinharāja** (S) (M) a king like a victorious lion.

**Jaiśīṣa** (S) (M) 1. a cheer of victory; victorious head. 2. best among the victors.

**Jaiskandha** (S) (M) 1. shoulder of victory; with victorious shoulders. 2. one very strong. 3. a minister of King Yudhiṣṭhira (*M. Bh.*)

**Jaiṣṇava** (S) (M) desirous of victory.

**Jaistambha** (S) (M) column of victory.

**Jaisudhā** (S) (F) nectar of victory; the sweet taste of victory.

**Jaitāṅga** (S) (M) 1. victorious over body; who has mastered his senses. 2. who has overcome worldly attachments.

**Jaitra** (S) (M) 1. leading to victory. 3. a son of Dhṛtarāṣṭra (*M. Bh.*)

**Jaitrāma** (S) (M) 1. abode of victory. 3. the chariot of King Hariśćandra (*M. Bh.*); the conch of Dhṛṣṭhadyumna (*M. Bh.*)

**Jaitvatī** (S) (F) 1. bearer of victory. 2. victorious. 3. a daughter of Uśinara.

**Jaivāha** (S) (M) carrier of victory.

**Jaivāhinī** (S) (F)1. victorious army; an army of victors. 3. Indra's wife.

**Jaivala** (S) (M) 1. giving life. 3. name assumed by Sahadeva at the court of Virāṭa (*M. Bh.*)

**Jaivanta** (S) (M) long lived.

**Jaivantī** (S) (F) long lived; being victorious.

**Jaivata** (S) (M) 1. being victorious. 2. winning.

**Jaivatī** (S) (F) 1. being victorious. 2. winning.

**Jaivātrika** (S) (M) 1. long lived; one for whom long life is desired. 2. son. 3. another name for the moon.

**Jaivīra** (S) (M) victorious warrior.

**Jāja** (S) (M) warrior; powerful.

**Jājali** (S) (M) 1.with the power of judgement. 3. a hermit who reared birds on his head (*M. Bh.*)

**Jājhara** (S) (M) 1. eliminator of power. 2. very powerful; a warrior.

**Jalā** (S) (F) 1. full of water. 3. a tributary of the Yamunā river (*M. Bh.*)

**Jala** (S) (M) 1. water. 3. the deity of water who was a luminary in the court of Brahmā (*M. Bh.*)

**Jalabālā** (S) (F) 1. maiden of water; daughter of the water. 2. nymph. 3. another name for Lakṣmī.

**Jalabālikā** (S) (F) 1. maiden of water; daughter of the waters. 2. lightning as the daughter of cloud.

**Jalabhuṣaṇa** (S) (M) 1. ornament of the water. 2. the lotus (*Nelumbium speciosum*); the wind.

**Jalada** (S) (M) 1. giving water. 2. raincloud; ocean.

**Jaladeva** (S) (M) 1. with water as its deity. 3. the constellation of Āṣāḍha.

**Jaladevatā** (S) (M) (F) god of water; goddess of water.

**Jaladhara** (S) (M) 1. holding water. 2. ocean; with a voice as musical as thunder. 3. a Buddha (*S. Puṇḍarikā*); Chariot tree (*Ougeinia oojeinensis*)

**Jaladhi** (S) (M) 1. living in water; treasure of water. 2. a crocodile; the ocean. 3. the black crocodile born from the ear of Rudra and which is the carrier of Varuṇa (*M. Bh.*)

**Jaladhijā** (S) (F) 1. daughter of the ocean. 3. another name for Lakṣmī.

**Jalādhipa** (S) (M) 1. lord of the waters. 3. another name for Varuṇa.

**Jalagambu** (S) (M) 1. essence of water. 3. a son of Sūrya (*Bhā. Purāṇa*)

**Jalahāsinī** (S) (F) 1. smile of water. 3. a wife of Kṛṣṇa (*Bhāgavata*)

**Jalajā** (S) (F) 1. born of water. 2. the lotus (*Nelumbium speciosum*). 3. Sweet Flag (*Acorus calamus*); another name for Lakṣmī.

**Jalaja** (S) (M) 1. born of the water. 2. a conchshell; the lotus (*Nelumbium speciosum*). 3. another name for the moon.

**Jalajākṣi** (S) (F) lotus eyed.

**Jalajātā** (S) (F) 1. born of the water. 2. a lotus (*Nelumbium speciosum*)

**Jalajinī** (S) (F) a group of lotuses.

**Jalakānta** (S) (F) 1. beloved of water. 2. the ocean; the wind.

**Jalakaraṅka** (S) (M) 1. embraced by water; born in water. 2. a conchshell; lotus (*Nelumbium speciosum*); cloud; wave.

**Jalakusumā** (S) (F) 1. flower of water. 2. the lotus (*Nelumbium speciosum*)

**Jalalatā** (S) (F) creeper of water; a wave; a watervine.

**Jalāmbara** (S) (M) 1. water clad. 2. the ocean. 3. Rāhulabhadra in a former birth (*S. Prābhāsa*)

**Jalāmbikā** (S) (F) 1. mother of water. 2. a well.

**Jalamūrti** (S) (M) Śiva in the form of water.

**Jalānćala** (S) (M) 1. water clad. 2. a spring; a fountain.

**Jalandhamā** (S) (F) **1.** water blower. **3.** a daughter of Kṛṣṇa (*Bhā. Purāṇa*)

**Jalandhama** (S) (M) **1.** water blower. **3.** an attendant of Skanda (*M. Bh.*); a dānava (*Sk. Purāṇa*)

**Jalandharā** (S) (F) **1.** water bearer. **3.** a daughter of Kāśirāja and the sister of Duryodhana's wife Bhānumatī (*M. Bh.*)

**Jalandhara** (S) (M) **1.** water bearer. **3.** an asura who was the husband of Vṛndā and was produced by the contact of a flash from Śiva's eye with the ocean (*Bhāgavata*)

**Jalanidhi** (S) (M) **1.** treasure of water. **2.** ocean.

**Jalanīlī** (S) (F) **1.** as blue as water. **2.** a water nymph.

**Jalāntaka** (S) (M) **1.** containing water. **3.** a son of Kṛṣṇa (*H. Purāṇa*)

**Jalapadmā** (S) (F) Water Lotus (*Nelumbium speciosum*)

**Jalapati** (S) (M) **1.** lord of the waters. **3.** another name for Varuṇa.

**Jalapriyā** (S) (F) **1.** dear to water. **3.** the Ćātaka bird; another name for Dākṣāyāṇī.

**Jalapuṣpā** (S) (F) Water Lily (*Nymphaea alba*)

**Jalarākṣasī** (S) (F) **1.** demon of the waters. **3.** a rākṣasī who tried to swallow Hanumān; a mother of nāgas.

**Jalārka** (S) (M) **1.** sun in water. **2.** the image of the sun in water.

**Jalārṇavā** (S) (F) ocean of water.

**Jalasa** (S) (M) **1.** water like. **2.** appeasing; healing; happiness.

**Jalasandha** (S) (M) **1.** confluence of waters. **3.** a son of Dhṛtarāṣṭra.

**Jalasandhi** (S) (M) **1.** confluence of waters. **2.** a place where 2 rivers meet. **3.** a warrior who fought on the side of the Kauravas (*M. Bh.*); a son of Dhṛtarāṣṭra (*M. Bh.*)

**Jalāśaya** (S) (M) **1.** reposing on water. **2.** a pond. **3.** another name for Viṣṇu.

**Jalaukas** (S) (M) **1.** living near water. **3.** a king of Kāśmira (*R. Taraṅginī*)

**Jalavāhana** (S) (M) **1.** water carrier. **3.** Gautama Buddha in a previous birth (*S. Prābhāsa*)

**Jalavālikā** (S) (F) **1.** encircled by water. **2.** lightning.

**Jalavīrya** (S) (M) **1.** power of water. **3.** a son of Bharata (*M. Bh.*)

**Jalelā** (S) (F) **1.** goddess of water. **3.** a mother attending on Skanda (*M. Bh.*)

**Jalendra** (S) (M) **1.** lord of the waters. **3.** a Jina; another name for Varuṇa.

**Jaleśvara** (S) (M) **1.** god of waters. **2.** ocean. **3.** another name for Varuṇa.

**Jaleyu** (S) (M) **1.** inhabitant of water; living in water. **3.** a son of Raudrāśva and the apsarā Miśrakeśī (*M. Bh.*)

**Jalīndra** (S) (M) **1.** lord of the waters. **2.** the ocean. **3.** another name for Varuṇa and Mahādeva.

**Jallatā** (S) (F) **1.** a streak of water. **2.** a wave.

**Jalpa** (S) (M) **1.** talk; discussion; discourse. **3.** a ṛṣi (*M. Purāṇa*)

**Jāmā** (S) (F) daughter.

**Jamadagni** (S) (M) **1.** consuming fire. **3.** a sage and descendant of Bhṛgu who was the son of Ṛćīka and Satyavatī, the husband of Reṇukā, the father of Paraśurāma, a luminary of the court of Brahmā and is considered the embodiment of Kṣatriya majesty (*Ṛg Veda/A. Veda/V. Samhitā*)

**Jamagha** (S) (M) **1.** consumer of sins; destroyer of sins. **3.** a king of the family of Yayāti (*Bhāgavata*)

**Jamālin** (S) (M) **1.** connoisseur. **3.** Mahāvira's son-in-law and the founder of schism I of the Jaina church (*J.S. Koṣa*)

**Jaman** (S) (M) connoisseur.

**Jambakā** (S) (M) **1.** possessor of water. **3.** another name for Varuṇa.

**Jambālini** (S) (F) **1.** maiden of water. **3.** a river (*A. Koṣa*)

**Jāmbavat** (S) (M) **1.** possessing the Jambu fruit; the fruit of the Roseapple tree (*Eugenia jambolana*). **3.** a monkey chief of extraordinary might born from the yawn of Brahmā and who witnessed all the incarnations of Viṣṇu from Matsya to Kṛṣṇa (*Rāmāyaṇa*); the son of Pitāmaha, the father of Jāmbavatī and a minister of Sugrīva.

**Jāmbavatī** (S) (M) **1.** daughter of Jāmbavata.

3. a wife of Kṛṣṇa and mother of Sāmba (*D. Bh. Purāṇa*)

**Jambha** (S) (M) 1. tooth; tusk; jaws; yawn. 3. several demons conquered by Kṛṣṇa (*Bhā. Purāṇa*); a son of Hiraṇyakaśipu (*Bhāgavata*); the father-in-law of Hiraṇyakaśipu (*Bhāgavata*); a daitya who snatched the Amṛta from the hands of Dhanvantari (*A. Purāṇa*); Indra's thunderbolt (*M. Bh.*); the Bergamot tree (*Citrus bergamia*)

**Jambhabhedin** (S) (M) 1. destroyer of Jambha. 3. another name for Indra.

**Jambhaka** (S) (M) 1. yawning; crushing; devouring. 3. an attendant of Śiva (*H. Purāṇa*); a king conquered by Kṛṣṇa (*M. Bh.*)

**Jambhalā** (S) (F) 1. yawning. 3. a rākṣasi by meditating on whom women became pregnant (*A. Koṣa*)

**Jambhālikā** (S) (F) yawning; a song.

**Jambhārati** (S) (M) 1. enemy of Jambha. 3. another name for Indra.

**Jambu** (S) (F) 1. Roseapple tree (*Eugenia jambolana*); an island covered on 3 sides by the ocean (i.e. Bhārata or India) which stands on the southern side of Mahāmeru mountain and bears flowers and fruit throughout the year. 3. a fabulous river flowing down from Mount Meru which is formed by the juice of the Jambu tree that stands on the top (*M. Bh.*)

**Jambudhvaja** (S) (M) 1. having the Jambu tree as a flag. 3. a nāga (*A. Koṣa*); another name for Mount Meru.

**Jambukā** (S) (F) 1. a seedless grape. 3. an attendant of Durgā (*M. Bh.*)

**Jambūka** (S) (M) 1. jackal. 3. an attendant of Skanda (*M. Bh.*); the Screwpine (*Pandanus tectorius*); another name for Varuṇa.

**Jambūkésvara** (S) (M) 1. lord of the jackals. 3. a liṅga or idol of Śiva in Mysore.

**Jambuki** (S) (M) 1. jambu coloured. 2. purple; indigo; the amethyst.

**Jambumālikā** (S) (M) 1. garlanded with jambu fruit. 3. a Śudra sage (*U. Rāmāyaṇa*)

**Jambumālin** (S) (M) 1. garlanded with jambu fruit. 3. a rākṣasa who was the son of Prahasta (*V. Rāmāyaṇa*)

**Jambumaṇi** (S) (M) jambu coloured jewel; the sapphire.

**Jambumatī** (S) (F) 1. rich in Jambu trees. 3. an apsarā.

**Jambūnada** (S) (M) 1. coming from the Jambu river; gold. 3. a golden mountain in Uśīrabīja (*M. Bh.*); a son of Janamejaya (*M. Bh.*)

**Jāmbūnadaprabhā** (S) (M) 1. of golden splendour. 3. a Buddha (*S. Puṇḍarīka*)

**Jambūnadī** (S) (F) 1. the Jambu river. 3. one of the 7 arms of the celestial Gaṅgā (*M. Bh.*)

**Jamburudra** (S) (M) 1. lord of the Jambu tree. 3. a nāga (*Ś. Purāṇa*)

**Jambūsvāmin** (S) (M) 1. lord of the Jambu tree. 3. the pupil of Mahāvira's pupil Sudharman (*J.S. Koṣa*)

**Jambuvadinī** (S) (F) 1. Jambu faced. 3. a goddess who lives on the banks of the Jambu river and bestows health, wealth, happiness and a long life (*T. Śastra*)

**Jamī** (S) (F) 1. consort of Yama. 3. the consort of the lord of death, who is the goddess of femininity and maternity (*T. Śastra*)

**Jāmī** (S) (F) 1. daughter-in-law. 3. an apsarā.

**Jamunā** (S) (F) 1. of Yama. 3. another name for the river Yamunā personified as the sister of Yama (*G. Purāṇa*)

**Janabālikā** (S) (F) 1. daughter of the people; very bright. 2. lightning.

**Janaćakṣus** (S) (M) 1. eye of all creatures. 2. the sun.

**Janaćandra** (S) (M) moon among people.

**Janadeva** (S) (M) 1. god of men. 3. a Janaka king who ruled over Mithilā (*M. Bh.*)

**Janādhinātha** (S) (M) 1. lord of men. 2. a king. 3. another name for Viṣṇu and Yama.

**Janādhipa** (S) (M) lord of men.

**Jānaka** (S) (M) 1. knower. 3. a Buddha.

**Janaka** (S) (M) 1. producing; causing; progenitor; father. 3. a king of Mithilā whose actual name was Śiradhvaja and who was a descendant of Viṣṇu, the father of Sītā and the personification of all virtues (*V. Rāmāyaṇa*); a king of Videha or Mithilā who was the son of Mithi and the father of Udāvasu (*Ś. Brāhmaṇa*)

**Janaki** (S) (M) 1. causing; producing. 3. a

Kşatriya king who was in previous birth, an asura called Ćandravināsa.

**Jānakī** (S) (F) 1. daughter of Janaka. 3. another name for Sītā.

**Jānakīnātha** (S) (M) 1. lord of Jānakī. 3. another name for Rāmā.

**Janamejaya** (S) (M) 1. causing men to tremble; victorious from birth. 3. a king of the solar dynasty who was the son of Parīkşit and Madrāvatī, the great-grandson of Rāma, the husband of Vapustamā and Kāśyā, the father of Śatānīka, Śaṅkukarṇa, Ćandrapīda and Sūryapiḍa, conductor of the Sarpaśatra or snake sacrifice which was stopped at the intervention of Āstika and to whom the *Mahābhārata* was related by Vyāsa (*M. Bh.*); a prominent member of Yama's assembly who conquered the world in 3 days and was then defeated by Māndhātā (*M. Bh.*); a king who was the incarnation of the asura Krodhavaśa (*M. Bh.*); a son of King Kuru and Vāhinī (*M. Bh.*); a son of King Kuru and Kauśalyā (*M. Bh.*); a serpent in the council of Varuṇa (*M. Bh.*); a king and son of King Durmukha who helped Yudhiṣṭhira in the great battle of Mahābhārata (*M. Bh.*)

**Janamohinī** (S) (F) infatuating men.

**Janasaha** (S) (M) 1. subduing men. 3. another name for Indra.

**Jananātha** (S) (M) lord of men; a king.

**Jananī** (S) (M) 1. mother; tenderness; compassion. 3. Indian Madder (*Rubia cordifolia*)

**Janapadī** (S) (F) 1. living place of people. 3. an apsarā who was the consort of Śaradvān and the mother of Kṛpa and Kṛpī (*M. Bh.*)

**Janapadin** (S) (M) country ruler; a king.

**Janapālaka** (S) (M) protector of men.

**Janapati** (S) (M) lord of men.

**Janapriya** (S) (M) 1. dear to men. 3. the Drumstick tree (*Moringa oleifera*); another name for Śiva.

**Janarājan** (S) (M) king of men.

**Janārdana** (S) (M) 1. exciting people. 2. one who makes the asuras tremble. 3. another name for Viṣṇu and Kṛṣṇa.

**Janārdhana** (S) (M) 1. exciting people. 3. another name for Viṣṇu and Kṛṣṇa.

**Janaśruta** (S) (M) famous among people.

**Janaśrutī** (S) (F) folklore.

**Janatapa** (S) (M) 1. inflaming men. 3. father of Atyarāti.

**Janāv** (S) (M) protecting men.

**Jaṇḍakara** (S) (M) 1. bestower of light. 3. one of the 18 Vināyakas who stays near the sun and carries out the orders of Yama (*Śukasaptati*)

**Janendra** (S) (M) lord of men.

**Janeśa** (S) (M) lord of men.

**Janeṣṭhā** (S) (F) 1. desired by men. 3. the Spanish jasmine (*Jasminum grandiflorum*)

**Janeśvara** (S) (M) god of men.

**Jangari** (S) (M) 1. fast; swift. 3. a son of Viśvāmitra (*M. Bh.*)

**Janghabandhu** (S) (M) 1. strong thighed; speedy. 3. a sage who was a member of Yudhiṣṭhira's assembly (*M. Bh.*)

**Jangi** (S) (M) warrior.

**Jānguli** (S) (F) 1. with knowledge of poisons. 3. the Buddhist deity who is a version of the goddess Manasā (*S. Puṇḍarikā*); another name for Durgā.

**Janhitā** (S) (F) one who thinks of the welfare of men.

**Janiṣṭha** (S) (M) desired by people.

**Janita** (S) (M) born.

**Janmādhipa** (S) (M) 1. lord of birth. 3. another name for Śiva.

**Janmajyeṣṭha** (S) (M) the 1st born.

**Janmakīla** (S) (M) 1. birth pillar. 3. another name for Viṣṇu.

**Janmavīra** (S) (M) 1. a warrior by birth. 3. another name for Abhimanyu the son of Arjuna.

**Jantu** (S) (M) 1. born. 2. a living being. 3. a king of the Purū dynasty who was the son of King Somaka and father of Vṛṣatanu (*M. Bh./H. Purāṇa*)

**Jantumatī** (S) (F) 1. full of living beings; the one who conceives. 3. the earth.

**Janu** (S) (M) the soul.

**Janujā** (S) (F) born; a daughter.

**Jānujaṅgha** (S) (M) 1. knee and thigh conjoined. 3. a king who should be remembered every morning and evening (*M. Bh.*)

**Janya** (S) (M) born.

**Janyu** (S) (M) 1. born. 2. creature; fire. 3. another name for Brahmā.

**Japā** (S) (F) 1. repetition of the names of the deities. 2. recitation of god's name on a rosary. 3. the Shoe flower (*Hibiscus rosa chinensis*)

**Jāpaka** (S) (M) 1. reciter. 2. meditator. 3. a sage who is constantly engaged in the Gāyatrī mantra (*M. Bh.*)

**Japana** (S) (M) 1. muttering prayers. 3. a brother of Śunaśśepha.

**Japendra** (S) (M) 1. lord of reciters. 3. another name for Śiva.

**Japeśa** (S) (M) 1. lord of reciters. 3. another name for Śiva.

**Jarā** (S) (F) 1. old age. 2. Gṛhadevī or goddess of the household. 3. the rākṣasi wife of the King Bṛhadratha of Magadha and mother of Jarāsandha (*M. Bh.*); a rakṣasī.

**Jara** (S) (M) 1. old age. 3. a son of Vasudeva and Tūrī; the hunter who accidently killed Kṛṣṇa (*H. Purāṇa*)

**Jarābhiru** (S) (M) 1. afraid of old age. 3. another name for Kāma.

**Jarāsandha** (S) (M) 1. born in halves but joined by Jarā. 3. a king of Magadha and Ćedi, the son of Bṛhadratha and a rākṣasi called Jarā, the father-in-law of Kaṁsa and enemy of Kṛṣṇa, and was killed by Bhīma (*M. Bh.*); a son of Dhṛtarāṣṭra (*M. Bh.*); the father of King Jayatsena who fought on the side of the Kauravas (*M. Bh.*)

**Jaratkarū** (S) (F) 1. wearing out the body. 3. another name for Manasā the goddess who was the daughter of Kaśyapa and was incarnated as the sister of Vāsuki, the wife of sage Jaratkaru and the mother of Āstika (*Brahma Purāṇa*)

**Jaratkaru** (S) (M) 1. wearing out the body. 3. a Purānic sage who was born in the Yāyāvara dynasty, married the sister of Vāsuki and was the father of Āstika (*Brahma Purāṇa*)

**Jarāyu** (S) (F) 1. viviparous. 3. an attendant of Skanda (*M. Bh.*)

**Jaritā** (S) (F) 1. old; decayed. 3. a Sarṅgikā bird who had 4 sons by ṛṣi Mandapāla.

**Jaritāri** (S) (M) 1. enemy of old age. 3. Mandapāla and Járitā's eldest son.

**Jaritṛi** (S) (M) a singer of hymns; a worshipper; an invoker.

**Jarjarānanā** (S) (F) 1. old faced. 2. with a wrinkled face. 3. a mother in Skanda's retinue (*M. Bh.*)

**Jarṇu** (S) (M) 1. waning. 3. another name for the moon.

**Jārul** (S) (F) queen of flowers; the Crepe Myrtle (*Lagerstroemia indica*)

**Jarūtha** (S) (M) 1. making old. 3. a demon conquered by Agni (*Ṛg Veda*)

**Jasalinā** (S) (M) (F) abode of fame.

**Jasamita** (S) (M) immensely famous.

**Jasapāla** (S) (M) protected by fame.

**Jasaprīta** (S) (M) desiring fame.

**Jasarāja** (S) (M) lord of fame.

**Jasarānī** (S) (F) queen of fame.

**Jasavanta** (S) (M) having fame.

**Jasavīra** (S) (M) famous warrior.

**Jasundhi** (S) (M) the Aśoka tree (*Jonesia aśoka*)

**Jasuri** (S) (M) 1. starved. 3. Indra's thunderbolt (*Ṛg Veda*)

**Jaṭā** (S) (M) matted hair; twisted hair; uncombed hair.

**Jaṭāćira** (S) (M) wearing a plait of hair as a garment.

**Jatādhara** (S) (M) 1. bearer of twisted locks. 2. an ascetic. 3. an attendant of Skanda (*M. Bh.*); a Buddha; another name for Śiva.

**Jaṭādhārin** (S) (M) 1. wearing twisted hair. 3. another name for Śiva.

**Jaṭākara** (S) (M) 1. sprung from twisted hair. 2. spring; fountain.

**Jaṭālikā** (S) (F) 1. with twisted hair. 3. a mother in Skanda's retinue (*M. Bh.*)

**Jātarūpa** (S) (F) beautiful; brilliant; golden.

**Jaṭāsana** (S) (M) 1. sitting on matted hair. 3. another name for Brahmā.

**Jaṭāśaya** (S) (M) 1. network of roots. 2. the ocean.

**Jaṭāśaṅkara** (S) (M) Śiva, with matted hair.

**Jaṭāśila** (S) (M) a stone of matted hair; a massive stone.

**Jaṭāsura** (S) (M) 1. demon with twisted locks of hair. 3. a king who was a member of Yudhiṣṭhira's assembly (*M. Bh.*); a rākṣasa killed by Bhīma (*M. Bh.*); another rākṣasa who was the father of Alambuṣa (*M. Bh.*)

**Jātaveda** (S) (M) 1. all-possessor; knowing all created beings. 3. the son of Purūravas born from the fire (*Bhāgavata*); another name for Agni.

**Jātavedas** (S) (M) 1. with tufts of twisted hair. 3. another name for Agni.

**Jaṭāyu** (S) (M) 1. full of twisted hair. 2. fibrous; a bird. 3. the king of vultures, the son of Aruṇa and Śyenī and the younger brother of Sampāti, was mortally wounded by Rāvaṇa while trying to rescue Sītā (*V. Rāmāyaṇa*); a Purānic bird descended from Viṣṇu; *Commiphora Mukul.*

**Jāṭhara** (S) (M) 1. hard; firm; womb; child. 3. a warrior of Skanda (*M. Bh.*); an erudite Brāhmin scholar of Vedic lore (*M. Bh.*); a mountain on the eastern side of Mahāmeru.

**Jatī** (S) (F) 1. birth. 3. Spanish Jasmine (*Jasminum grandiflorum*); the Malati creeper (*Hiptage madoblata*)

**Jaṭi** (S) (M) 1. ascetic. 3. a warrior of Skanda (*M. Bh.*); another name for Śiva.

**Jatikayāna** (S) (M) 1. vehicle of ascetics. 3. a sage and part author of the *Atharva Veda* (vi)

**Jaṭilā** (S) (F) 1. complex; having twisted hair. 3. a woman skilled in Vedic knowledge who was born in the dynasty of Gautama (*M. Bh.*)

**Jaṭila** (S) (M) 1. complex; having uncombed hair. 2. a lion. 3. name assumed by Śiva when disguised as a Brahmaćārin or ascetic (*M. Bh.*); Sweet Flag (*Acorus calamus*)

**Jatin** (S) (M) 1. wearing twisted hair. 2. an ascetic. 3. an attendant of Skanda (*M. Bh.*); another name for Śiva.

**Jaṭindhara** (S) (M) 1. a true state; bearing the lineage. 3. physician of Śuddhodana in a previous birth.

**Jatūkarṇa** (S) (M) 1. with patient ears. 3. a sage who was a member of the council of Yudhiṣṭhira (*M. Bh.*); a sage who was one of the 28 transmitters of the Vedas (*V. Purāṇa*); another name for Śiva.

**Jātūkarṇā** (S) (F) 1. with patient ears. 3. Bhavabhūti's mother (*Kaṇvādi*)

**Jātusthira** (S) (M) ever solid; never yielding.

**Jāṭya** (S) (M) of a noble family; pleasing; beautiful; best.

**Javāhara** (S) (M) jewel.

**Javana** (S) (M) 1. swift. 3. one of Skanda's attendants (*M. Bh.*)

**Javānila** (S) (M) swift wind; a hurricane.

**Javin** (S) (M) swift; a horse; a deer.

**Javiṣṭha** (S) (M) quickest.

**Jāvitrī** (S) (F) spice; mace (*Myristica fragrans*)

**Jayā** (S) (F) 1. victory; victorious. 3. Pārvatī who was the daughter of Dakṣa and the wife of Śiva (*M. Purāṇa*); a daughter of the hermit Gautama (*Bhāgavata*); a handmaiden of Durgā who was the wife of the gaṇa Puṣpadanta (*K. Sāgara*); the mother of the 12th Arhat of the present Avasarpinī (*He. Koṣa*); a maid of Pārvatī who was the daughter of the prajāpati Kṛṣāśva (*M. Bh.*); a tutelary deity (*Brahmā Purāṇa*); a Śakti (*Ś. Purāṇa*); a yoginī (*He. Koṣa*)

**Jaya** (S) (M) 1. victory; victorious. 3. a son of Dhṛtarāṣṭra (*M. Bh.*); a king in the court of Yama (*M. Bh.*); name assumed by Yudhiṣṭhira in the court of Virāṭa (*M. Bh.*); a nāga born in the family of Kaśyapa (*M. Bh.*); a warrior who fought on the side of the Kauravas (*M. Bh.*); a warrior of Pāñćāla who fought on the side of the Pāṇḍavās (*M. Bh.*); a attendant of Skanda given to him by Vāsuki (*M. Bh.*); gatekeeper of Vaikuṇṭha – Viṣṇu's palace – who was reborn as Hiraṇyākṣa (*Bhāgavata*); the father of the rākṣasa Virādha who was killed by Rāma (*V. Rāmāyaṇa*); the original *Mahābhārata*; Black Myrobalan (*terminalia chebula*); Couch grass (*Cynodon dactylon*); another name for Mahāviṣṇu, Bhīma and the sun.

**Jayadā** (S) (M) 1. causing victory. 3. a tutelary deity of Vāmadeva's family (*Br. Purāṇa*)

**Jayadatta** (S) (M) 1. given by victory. 3. a son of Indra (*A. Koṣa*); a tutelary deity of Vāmadeva's family (*Br. Purāṇa*); a king (*K. Sāgara*); a Bodhisattva; a son of Indra.

**Jayadbala** (S) (M) 1. of victorious power.

3. name assumed by Sahadeva at the Virāṭa court (*M. Bh.*)

**Jayadevī** (S) (F) 1. goddess of victory. 3. a Buddhist deity.

**Jayadratha** (S) (M) 1. with victorious chariots. 3. a Sindhu- Sauvīra king who was the son of Bṛhatkāya, the husband of Duśśala, a suitor for the hand of Draupadī who being rejected fought on the Kaurava side (*M. Bh.*); a son of Bṛhanmanas (*H. Purāṇa*); a king in the court of Yama (*V. Purāṇa*); the 10th Manu (*H. Purāṇa*)

**Jayalakṣmī** (S) (F) goddess of victory.

**Jayalalitā** (S) (F) 1. as beautiful as victory. 3. the goddess of victory; the fickle Lakṣmī.

**Jayanā** (S) (F) 1. bestower of victory. 2. the armour for cavalry. 3. a daughter of Indra (*A. Koṣa*)

**Jayanandinī** (S) (F) 1. daughter of victory. 3. daughter of Lakṣmī.

**Jayanī** (S) (F) 1. one who brings victory. 3. a daughter of Indra (*A. Koṣa*)

**Jayānīka** (S) (M) 1. an army of victors. 3. a grandson of Drupada (*M. Bh.*); a brother of the king of Virāṭa (*M. Bh.*)

**Jayanta** (S) (M) 1. victorious in the end. 2. the moon. 3. a son of Indra and Śacī (*H. Purāṇa*); a rudra (*M. Bh.*); a son of Dharma (*Bhāgavata*); the father of Akrūra (*M. Purāṇa*); a gandharva (*K. Sāgara*); name assumed by Bhīma at Virāṭa's court (*M. Bh.*); a minister of Daśaratha (*V. Rāmāyaṇa*); the father of Vikramāditya (*K. Sāgara*); one of the 12 adityas (*M. Bh.*); name of Kṛṣṇa's birthright (*H. Purāṇa*); a mountain (*H. Purāṇa*); another name for Mahāviṣṇu, Śiva and Skanda.

**Jayantī** (S) (F) 1. victorious in the end. 2. a flag. 3. a daughter of Indra and the wife of Śukra (*A. Koṣa*); the wife of King Ṛṣabha and the mother of 300 children (*Bhāgavata*); a yoginī; Kṛṣṇa's birthnight (*H. Purāṇa*); a river (*M. Bh.*); *Curcuma longa*; another name for Durgā and Dākṣāyāṇī.

**Jayāpīda** (S) (M) 1. garland or chaplet of victory. 3. husband of Kamalā (*R. Taraṅginī*)

**Jayarata** (S) (M) 1. absorbed in victory. 3. a prince of Kaliṅga who fought on the side of the Kauravas (*M. Bh.*); Sanskṛt poet of Kāśmira (12th century) (*R. Taraṅginī*)

**Jayaratha** (S) (M) a chariot of victory.

**Jayasena** (S) (M) 1. a victorious army. 3. the father of Caṇḍamahāsena (*M. Bh.*); a prince of Magadha who was a member of the council of Yudhiṣṭhira (*M. Bh.*); a king of Avantī who was the father of Mitravindā who became a wife of Kṛṣṇa (*Bhāgavata*)

**Jayāṣṇava** (S) (M) one who has tasted victory.

**Jayaśrī** (S) (F) 1. goddess of victory. 3. a nāga virgin (*K. Vyuha*); a sword (*R. Taraṅginī*)

**Jayāśva** (S) (M) 1. horse of victory. 3. a son of King Drupada (*M. Bh.*); a brother of the king of Virāṭa (*M. Bh.*)

**Jayāsvāmin** (S) (M) the master of victory; lord of Lakṣmī.

**Jayātmaja** (S) (M) 1. son of the victorious; son of Arjuna. 3. another name for Abhimanyu.

**Jayatsena** (S) (M) 1. conqueror of the army. 2. with victorious armies. 3. a king of Magadha who was the son of Jarāsandha and a friend of the Pāṇḍavas (*M. Bh.*); a king of the Purū dynasty, the son of King Sarvabhauma and Sunandā, the husband of Suśravas and the father of Arvācīna (*H. Purāṇa*); name assumed by Nakula in the court of Virāṭa (*M. Bh.*); a son of Dhṛtarāṣṭra (*M. Bh.*); an attendant of Skanda (*M. Bh.*)

**Jayatsenā** (S) (F) 1. with victorious armies. 3. a mother in Skanda's retinue (*M. Bh.*)

**Jayendra** (S) (M) 1. lord of victory. 3. a king of Kāśmira (*R. Taraṅginī*); another name for Indra.

**Jayeśvara** (S) (M) 1. lord of victors. 3. a form of Śiva.

**Jayin** (S) (M) conqueror.

**Jayiṣṇu** (S) (M) desiring victory.

**Jayitā** (S) (F) victorious.

**Jayitri** (S) (F) victorious.

**Jehila** (S) (M) 1. follower. 3. a Jaina Sūri.

**Jeman** (S) (M) having victory; one who is victorious.

**Jenya** (S) (M) of noble origin; true.

**Jetaśrī** (S) (F) 1. goddess of gains. 3. a rāga.

**Jetṛ** (S) (M) 1. victorious. 3. a son of

Madhuććandas (*Ṛg Veda*); a prince who had a grove near Śrāvastī (*B. Literature*)

**Jetva** (S) (M) to be gained.

**Jhājha** (S) (M) **1.** noisy. **3.** the father of asura Sunda and grandfather of Marīća (*V. Rāmāyaṇa*); a musical instrument.

**Jhālā** (S) (F) a girl; the heat of the sun.

**Jhambāri** (S) (F) **1.** enemy of darkness. **3.** fire; Indra's thunderbolt; another name for Indra.

**Jhankāriṇī** (S) (F) **1.** producing a tinkling sound. **2.** a bell; a woman wearing anklets. **3.** another name for Durgā and the Gaṅgā.

**Jharjhara** (S) (M) **1.** flow. **2.** making a sound like that of filling water. **3.** a son of Hiraṇyākṣa (*Bhāgavata*)

**Jharnā** (S) (F) **1.** flowing down. **2.** spring; fountain; a streamlet.

**Jhaṣodari** (S) (F) **1.** feeding on fish. **2.** a fisherwoman. **3.** another name for Satyavatī.

**Jhaṣudharū** (S) (F) **1.** catching fish. **2.** a fisherwoman. **3.** another name for Satyavatī.

**Jhaṭā** (S) (F) daughter; fighter; girl; splendour; brilliance.

**Jhaṭalikā** (S) (F) light; lustre; splendour.

**Jhaṭi** (S) (F) **1.** glittering; shining; producing glitter. **2.** the White jasmine (*Jasminum pubescens*)

**Jhilli** (S) (M) **1.** worm. **3.** a Yādava of the house of Vṛṣṇi who was a minister of Kṛṣṇa in Dvārakā; a warrior of the Vṛṣṇis who fought bravely in the great battle.

**Jhillikā** (S) (F) light; moth; sunshine.

**Jhilmil** (S) (F) sparkling.

**Jhilmit** (S) (M) partially visible.

**Jhinka** (S) (M) moth.

**Jhūmarī** (S) (F) **1.** ornament of the forehead. **3.** a rāgiṇī.

**Jighatsu** (S) (F) **1.** hungry. **3.** a demon (*A. Veda*)

**Jigīśā** (S) (F) desire to be victorious.

**Jigīśu** (S) (M) striving to conquer.

**Jījābāi** (S) (F) **1.** victorious woman. **3.** Śivaji's mother.

**Jīmūta** (S) (M) **1.** cloud. **2.** nourisher; the sun; mountain; sustainer; enjoyer. **3.** a king of the vidyādharas and hero of the play *Nāgānanda* (*K. Sāgara*); a king of the family of Yayāti (*Bhāgavata*); a wrestler at the court of Virāṭa (*M. Bh.*); a hermit who received treasure from the Himālayas; the horse of King Vasumanas; an ancient sage (*M. Bh.*); another name for Indra.

**Jīmūtaketu** (S) (M) **1.** cloud flag. **3.** a vidyādhara prince (*K. Sāgara*); another name for Śiva.

**Jīmūtavāhana** (S) (M) **1.** with a chariot of clouds. **3.** a vidyādhara who was the son of Jīmūtaketu, the husband of Malayavatī and the emperor of the vidyādharas (*K. Sāgara*); a son of Śalivāhana (*K. Sāgara*); another name for Indra.

**Jina** (S) (M) **1.** victor. **3.** a Buddha; an Arhat or the chief saint of the Jainas (*J. Literature*); a son of Yadu (*Ku. Purāṇa*); another name for Viṣṇu.

**Jinabhadra** (S) (M) **1.** rightly victorious. **3.** a famous Jaina author (*J. S. Koṣa*); a Jaina Sūri (*J. S. Koṣa*)

**Jinabhakti** (S) (M) **1.** worshipping victory. **3.** a Jaina Sūri (*H. Koṣa*)

**Jinaćandra** (S) (M) **1.** moon among victors. **3.** 8 Jaina Sūris (*S. Veda*)

**Jinadatta** (S) (M) **1.** giving victory. **3.** a Jaina Sūri (*H. Koṣa*)

**Jinadeva** (S) (M) **1.** lord of victory. **3.** an Arhat (*P. Ćhatraprabandha*)

**Jinadhāra** (S) (M) **1.** bearing victory. **3.** a Bodhisattva (*L. Vistara*)

**Jinahansa** (S) (M) **1.** the swan of victory. **3.** a Jaina Sūri.

**Jinaharṣa** (S) (M) **1.** pleasure of victory. **3.** a Jaina Sūri (*V. Samgraha*)

**Jinakīrti** (S) (M) **1.** the fame of victory. **3.** a Jaina Sūri (*M. Stava*)

**Jinakuśala** (S) (M) **1.** perfectly victorious. **3.** a Jaina Sūri (*Ć. Vandana*)

**Jinalabdhi** (S) (M) **1.** receiver of victory. **3.** a Jaina Sūri (*J. Literature*)

**Jinalābha** (S) (M) **1.** finder of victory. **3.** a Jaina Sūri (*A. Prabodha*)

**Jinamāṇikya** (S) (M) **1.** jewel of victory. **3.** a Jaina Sūri (*Su. Purāṇa*)

**Jinandhara** (S) (M) **1.** abode of victory. **3.** a Bodhisattva (*H. Koṣa*)

**Jināṅkura** (S) (M) **1.** seed of victory. **3.** a Bodhisattva (*H. Koṣa*)

**Jinapadma** (S) (M) **1.** lotus of victory. **3.** a Jaina Sūri (*He. Koṣa*)

**Jinapati** (S) (M) **1.** master of victory. **3.** a Jaina Sūri (*J. Literature*)

**Jinaprabha** (S) (M) **1.** light of victory. **3.** a Jaina Sūri (*J.S. Koṣa*)

**Jinaprabodha** (S) (M) **1.** inspiring of victory. **3.** a Jaina Sūri (*P. Prabodha*)

**Jinaputra** (S) (M) **1.** son of a victor. **3.** a Bodhisattva (*H. Koṣa*)

**Jinarāja** (S) (M) **1.** king of the victors. **3.** a Jaina Sūri (1591-1643)

**Jinaratna** (S) (M) **1.** jewel of victory. **3.** a Jaina Sūri.

**Jinasamudra** (S) (M) **1.** ocean of victory. **3.** a Jaina Sūri (*J. Literature*)

**Jinasaukhya** (S) (M) **1.** pleasure of victory. **3.** a Jaina Sūri (*J. S. Koṣa*)

**Jinaśekhara** (S) (M) **1.** best among the victors. **3.** the founder of the 2nd subdivision of the Kharataragaććā of the Jaina community (*K. gaććha*)

**Jinasinha** (S) (M) **1.** lion among victors. **3.** the founder of the 3rd subdivision of the Kharataragaćća of the Jaina community (*J. S. Koṣa*); a Jaina Sūri (*J. S. Koṣa*)

**Jinavaktra** (S) (M) **1.** with a victorious face. **3.** a Buddha (*L. Vistara*)

**Jinavallabha** (S) (M) **1.** beloved of victors. **3.** a Jaina author (*J. S. Koṣa*)

**Jinavardhana** (S) (M) **1.** promoter of victory. **3.** the founder of the 5th subdivision of the Kharataragaćća of the Jaina community (*K. gaććha*)

**Jindurāja** (S) (M) conquering old age.

**Jinendra** (S) (M) **1.** lord of victors. **3.** a Buddha (*H. Koṣa*); Jaina saint (*P. Caritra*)

**Jineśa** (S) (M) **1.** lord of victors (*K. Stotra*) **3.** an Arhat of the Jainas (*K. Stotra*); 2 Jaina Sūris (*P. Ćhatraprabandha*)

**Jinodaya** (S) (M) **1.** victorious. **3.** a Jaina Sūri (*H. Koṣa*)

**Jinorasa** (S) (M) **1.** essence of victory. **3.** a Bodhisattva (*H. Koṣa*)

**Jinottama** (S) (M) **1.** best among victors. **3.** a Jaina Sūri.

**Jiṣṇu** (S) (M) **1.** victorious. **3.** a Ćedi warrior who fought on the side of the Pāṇḍavas (*M. Bh.*); the son of Manu Bhautya (*H. Purāṇa*); another name for Viṣṇu, Kṛṣṇa, Indra, Arjuna and the sun.

**Jita** (S) (M) conquered.

**Jitamanyu** (S) (M) **1.** one who has subdued anger. **3.** another name for Viṣṇu.

**Jitamitra** (S) (M) **1.** one who has conquered his enemies. **3.** another name for Viṣṇu.

**Jitāri** (S) (M) **1.** one who has conquered his enemies. **3.** the father of the Arhat Sambhava; a son of Avīkṣit and the grandson of King Kuru (*M. Bh.*)

**Jitaśatru** (S) (M) **1.** conqueror of enemies. **3.** the father of the Arhat Ajita (*He. Koṣa*); a Buddha (*L. Vistara*)

**Jitātmā** (S) (M) **1.** conqueror of the soul. **3.** a viśvadeva (*M. Bh.*)

**Jitātmana** (S) (M) **1.** conqueror of the self. **3.** a viśvadeva (*M. Bh.*)

**Jitavatī** (S) (F) **1.** one who has acquired victory; best among women. **3.** a daughter of King Uśinara who was considered the most beautiful woman in the world (*M. Bh.*)

**Jitavrata** (S) (M) **1.** winning by vows. **3.** a son of Havirdhāna (*Bh. Purāṇa*)

**Jitendra** (S) (M) conqueror of the senses.

**Jitī** (S) (F) obtaining victory.

**Jittana** (S) (M) **1.** conqueror of body. **2.** the zodiac sign of Gemini.

**Jituma** (S) (M) **1.** full of victory. **2.** the zodiac sign of Gemini.

**Jitvan** (S) (M) victorious.

**Jitvarī** (S) (F) **1.** best among the victorious. **3.** another name for the city of Benaras.

**Jityā** (S) (F) victorious.

**Jīva** (S) (M) **1.** a living being; alive. **2.** the principle of life; the personal soul. **3.** the Puṣya constellation; one of the 8 maruts; another name for Bṛhaspati, Karṇa and the earth; *Dendrobium fimbriatum*.

**Jīvabhūta** (S) (M) endowed with life.

**Jīvadeva** (S) (M) lord of the soul.

**Jīvaja** (S) (M) born alive.

**Jīvala** (S) (M) 1. inspiring; animating; full of life; carries victory. 3. the tree *Lannea grandis*; a charioteer of King Ṛtuparṇa of Ayodhyā and a friend of Nala (*Nalopākhyāna*)

**Jīvana** (S) (M) 1. life; giving life; wind; son. 3. another name for Śiva and the sun.

**Jīvanātha** (S) (M) lord of life.

**Jīvanadhara** (S) (M) bearer of life.

**Jīvanikāya** (S) (M) the system of life; one who is endowed with life.

**Jīvanta** (S) (M) 1. long lived. 2. *Prosopis spicigera*.

**Jīvantikā** (S) (F) 1. bestower of long life. 2. *Tinospora corolifolia*.

**Jīvapriya** (S) (M) 1. beloved of living beings. 3. Black Myrobalan (*Terminalia chebula*)

**Jīvapuṣpā** (S) (F) flower of life.

**Jīvarāja** (S) (M) 1. lord of life. 3. a Jaina Tīrthaṅkara (*J. S. Koṣa*)

**Jīvaratna** (S) (M) jewel of life.

**Jīvatha** (S) (M) 1. long lived; virtuous. 2. life; breath; tortoise; peacock; cloud.

**Jīvavijaya** (S) (M) conqueror of life.

**Jīvikā** (S) (F) 1. the source of life. 2. water; occupation.

**Jīvinī** (S) (M) 1. one who lives really. 2. the sun; a Brāhmin; praise.

**Jīviteśa** (S) (M) 1. lord of the living. 3. Yama; the sun; the moon.

**Jīviteśvara** (S) (M) 1. god of the living. 3. another name for Śiva.

**Jñāna** (S) (M) knowledge.

**Jñānaćakṣus** (S) (M) eye of knowledge; intellectual vision.

**Jñānaćandra** (S) (M) moon of knowledge.

**Jnanadarpaṇa** (S) (M) 1. mirror of knowledge. 3. a Bodhisattva.

**Jñānadarsana** (S) (M) 1. supreme knowledge. 3. a Bodhisattva.

**Jñānadarśana** (S) (M) 1. supreme knowledge. 3. a Bodhisattva.

**Jñānadatta** (S) (M) given by knowledge.

**Jñānadeva** (S) (M) lord of knowledge.

**Jñānadīpa** (S) (M) lamp of knowledge.

**Jñānagamya** (S) (M) 1. attainable by understanding. 3. another name for Śiva.

**Jñānagarbha** (S) (M) 1. filled with knowledge. 3. a Bodhisattva.

**Jñānakara** (S) (M) 1. mine of knowledge. 3. a Buddha.

**Jñānaketu** (S) (M) with the marks of intelligence.

**Jñānakīrti** (S) (M) 1. with famed knowledge. 3. a Buddhist teacher.

**Jñānamaya** (S) (M) 1. full of knowledge. 3. another name for Śiva.

**Jñānamūrti** (S) (M) knowledge personified.

**Jñānamūrti** (S) (M) a symbol of knowledge.

**Jñānanghanāćārya** (S) (M) teacher of pure intellect.

**Jñānapāraga** (S) (M) 1. with celebrated knowledge. 3. a sage who was the son of Kuśika.

**Jñānapāvana** (S) (M) 1. purifying knowledge. 3. a Tīrtha.

**Jñānaprabha** (S) (M) 1. brilliant with knowledge. 3. a Bodhisattva.

**Jñānaprakāśa** (S) (M) light of knowledge.

**Jñānarāja** (S) (M) lord of knowledge.

**Jñānasāgara** (S) (M) 1. ocean of knowledge. 3. a Jaina Sūri.

**Jñānavajra** (S) (M) 1. thunderbolt of knowledge. 3. a Buddhist author.

**Jñānavata** (S) (M) 1. endowed with knowledge. 3. a Bodhisattva.

**Jñānavatī** (S) (F) endowed with knowledge.

**Jñānavibhūtigarbha** (S) (M) 1. filled with superhuman knowledge. 3. a Bodhisattva.

**Jñānbhāskara** (S) (M) sun of knowledge.

**Jñāneśa** (S) (M) lord of knowledge.

**Jñāneśvara** (S) (M) lord of knowledge.

**Jñānin** (S) (M) endowed with knowledge.

**Jñānolka** (S) (M) meteor of knowledge.

**Jñānottama** (S) (M) with supreme knowledge.

**Jñānśrī** (S) (M) 1. with divine knowledge. 3. a Buddhist author.

**Jñāta** (S) (M) 1. known; comprehended; understood. 3. a sage who was the son of Kuśika; family of Mahāvīra.

**Jñātaputra** (S) (M) 1. son of the Jñāta family.

3. another name for Mahāvīra.

**Jñātanandana** (S) (M) 1. son of the Jñāta family. 3. another name for Mahāvīra.

**Jvalana** (S) (M) 1. flaming. 3. another name for Agni.

**Joganātha** (S) (M) 1. lord of yoga. 3. another name for Śiva.

**Jogarāja** (S) (M) 1. lord of ascetics. 3. another name for Śiva.

**Jogendra** (S) (M) 1. king of yogis. 3. another name for Śiva.

**Jogeśa** (S) (M) 1. lord of yogis. 3. another name for Śiva.

**Jogiā** (S) (M) 1. the colour worn by ascetics. 2. the colour saffron. 3. a rāga.

**Jogū** (S) (F) praising.

**Jośa** (S) (M) approval; pleasure; satisfaction; a bud.

**Joṣā** (S) (F) woman.

**Jośikā** (S) (F) cluster of buds; a young woman.

**Jośita** (S) (M) pleased.

**Jośyā** (S) (F) delightful.

**Jotiṅga** (S) (M) 1. absorbed in penance. 2. an ascetic who subjects himself to severe penances. 3. another name for Śiva.

**Jugala** (S) (M) pair.

**Jugalakiśora** (S) (M) 1. a pair of adolescents. 3. a form of Kṛṣṇa with adolescent Rādhā and Kṛṣṇa conjoined.

**Jugnu** (S) (M) glow worm; firefly; ornament.

**Jūhī** (S) (F) jasmine flower (*Jasminum pubescens*)

**Juhū** (S) (M) 1. a tongue. 2. a flame. 3. a king of the family of Yayāti (*Bhāgavata*); another name for Brahmā and the sun.

**Jūrṇī** (S) (F) firebrand; glowing fire's blaze.

**Juśka** (S) (M) 1. lover; worshipper; meritorious. 3. one of the 3 Kāśmiri Turuśka kings (*R. Taraṅginī*)

**Juṣṭa** (S) (M) loved; pleased; welcomed; propitious; served; worshipped.

**Juṣṭi** (S) (F) love; service.

**Jutikā** (S) (F) a kind of camphor.

**Jūvas** (S) (M) quickness.

**Jvāla** (S) (M) flame; blaze; light; torchglow; shine.

**Jvālā** (S) (F) 1. flame. 2. blaze; light; torchglow; shine. 3. a daughter of Takṣaka, the wife of King Ṛkṣa and the mother of Matīnara (*M. Bh.*); the wife of King Nīladhvaja who made Gaṅgā curse Arjuna (*M. Bh.*)

**Jvālājihvā** (S) (M) 1. tongue of fire. 3. an attendant given to Skanda by Agni; a warrior of Skanda (*M. Bh.*); a dānava (*H. Purāṇa*)

**Jvālāliṅga** (S) (M) 1. flame marked with a blazing phallus. 3. a sanctuary of Śiva.

**Jvālāmukhā** (S) (F) 1. flame faced. 3. a tutelary deity of Lomaśa's family located in the hills of north east Punjab (*T. Śastra*)

**Jvalanā** (S) (F) 1. flaming; shining. 3. a daughter of Takṣaka and wife of Ṛćeyu (*H. Purāṇa*)

**Jvālanmaṇi** (S) (M) a burning jewel; a highly glittering jewel.

**Jvālantaśikharā** (S) (F) 1. flame tufted. 3. a gandharva virgin (*K. Vyuha*)

**Jvālāprasāda** (S) (M) gift of fire; passionate; sacred; all consuming.

**Jvālāvaktra** (S) (M) 1. flame mouthed. 3. an attendant of Śiva (*Brahma Purāṇa*)

**Jvālin** (S) (M) 1. flaming. 3. another name for Śiva.

**Jvālitā** (S) (F) lighted; blazing; shining; flaming.

**Jvālitrī** (S) (F) lighted; shining; flaming.

**Jvalkā** (S) (M) a large flame.

**Jyāmagha** (S) (M) 1. great; superior; winning battles. 3. a king born in the Ikṣvāku dynasty, the husband of Śaibya and the father of Vidarbha (*M. Bh.*)

**Jyāyas** (S) (M) superior; greater; stronger.

**Jyeṣṭhā** (S) (F) 1. eldest sister. 3. the 18th lunar mansion of 3 stars (*T. Brāhmaṇa*); a deity of inauspicious things considered the elder sister of Lakṣmī because she preceded Lakṣmī from the Ocean of Milk (*P. Purāṇa*); a star considered to bring luck (*V's B. Saṁhitā*); a yoginī or fierce village goddess (*D. Bh. Purāṇa*); another name for Gaṅgā.

**Jyeṣṭha** (S) (M) 1. eldest. 2. pre-eminent;

best; greatest; chief. 3. the 16th lunar mansion sacred to Indra (*A. Veda*); the middle finger (*A. Koṣa*); a hermit versed in the *Sāma Veda* (*M. Bh.*)

**Jyeṣṭhāghni** (S) (M) 1. the oldest fire. 2. slaying the eldest. 3. a lunar mansion (*A. Veda/T. Brāhmaṇa*)

**Jyeṣṭhilā** (S) (F) 1. elder. 2. superior; greater. 3. a river that lives in the palace of Varuṇa (*M. Bh.*)

**Jyotā** (S) (F) the brilliant one.

**Jyotī** (S) (F) 1. brilliant; flame like. 2. the light of the sun; dawn; fire; lightning; brightness of the sky; light of heaven; light as a divine principle of life and source of intelligence; Fenugreek (*Trigonella foenum-graecum*)

**Jyoti** (S) (M) 1. flame. 2. brilliant; passionate; sacred; all consuming. 3. a son of the vasu named Aha (*M. Bh.*); one of the 2 attendants given to Skanda by Agni (*M. Bh.*)

**Jyotika** (S) (M) 1. with a flame. 2. brilliant. 3. a famous serpent who was the son of Kaśyapa and Kadru (*M. Bh.*)

**Jyotindra** (S) (M) lord of light.

**Jyotiprakāśa** (S) (M) the light of the flame.

**Jyotiranikā** (S) (F) with a shining face.

**Jyotirasa** (S) (M) 1. the essence of light. 2. a gem.

**Jyotiratha** (S) (M) 1. chariot of light. 2. the Pole Star. 3. a river that joins the river Śoṇa (*M. Bh.*); a nāga (*B. Literature*)

**Jyotirbhāga** (S) (M) womb of light; possessing light.

**Jyotirbhāsin** (S) (M) brilliant with light.

**Jyotirhastā** (S) (F) 1. fire handed. 3. another name for Durgā.

**Jyotirlekhā** (S) (F) 1. a line of light. 2. studded with rows of stars. 3. a daughter of a yakṣa (*K. Sāgara*)

**Jyotirmaya** (S) (M) 1. consisting of light. 3. another name for Viṣṇu and Śiva.

**Jyotirmukha** (S) (M) 1. bright faced. 3. one of Rāma's monkey followers (*V. Rāmāyaṇa*)

**Jyotirvasu** (S) (M) 1. the deity of light. 3. a king born in the family of Purūravas who was the son of Sumati and the father of Pratīka (*Bhāgavata*)

**Jyotiṣa** (S) (M) 1. full of light; luminous. 2. fire; the sun; astrology as the study of the luminous objects of the sky i.e. stars and planets. 3. a son of Manu Svāroćiṣa (*H. Purāṇa*); a marut (*H. Purāṇa*)

**Jyotiṣka** (S) (M) 1. luminous. 3. a luminous weapon of Arjuna (*M. Bh.*); a bright peak of Meru (*M. Bh.*); a serpent son of Kaśyapa and Kadru (*M. Bh.*); a class of deities of light including the sun, moon, planets, stars and constellations; Intellect tree (*Celastrus paniculata*)

**Jyotiṣmān** (S) (M) 1. possessor of light. 3. a king of Kuśadvīpa (*M. Bh.*)

**Jyotiṣmat** (S) (M) 1. possessing light. 3. a son of Manu Svāyambhuva (*H. Purāṇa*); a son of Manu Sāvarṇa (*V. Purāṇa*); the 3rd foot of Brahmā (*Ć. Upaniṣad*); a mountain (*Bhāgavata*)

**Jyotiṣmatī** (S) (F) luminous; brilliant; shining; celestial; belonging to the world of light; Intellect tree (*Celastrus paniculata*); Black Liquorice (*Cardiospermum halicacabum*)

**Jyotiṣprabha** (S) (M) 1. brilliant with light. 3. a Buddha (*B. Literature*); a Bodhisattva (*B. Literature*)

**Jyotsnā** (S) (F) 1. moonlight. 2. a moonlit night; light; splendour. 3. one of Brahmā's bodies; one of the 16 digits of the moon; another name for Durgā; the annual *Trichosanthes cucumerina*.

**Jyotsnākalī** (S) (F) 1. a piece of the moon; moonlight. 3. the daughter of the moon and wife of Varuṇa's son Puśkara; the 2nd daughter of Ćandra who married the Sun (*M. Bh.*)

**Jyotsnāpriya** (S) (M) 1. beloved of moonlight; one who loves the moonlight. 2. the Ćakora bird (*Alectoris chukar chukar*)

**Jyotsneśa** (S) (M) 1. lord of moonlight. 3. the moon.

**Jyotsnī** (S) (F) a moonlit night.

## K

**Kā** (S) (M) **1.** creator. **2.** prajāpati. **3.** a dakṣa (*M. Bh.*); another name for Viṣṇu.

**Kabandha** (S) (M) **1.** cloud; comet; water; belly; barrel. **3.** a disciple of Sumanta the earliest teacher of the *Atharva Veda*; a demon who was an incarnation of a gandharva called Viśvavasu, who attacked Rāma and Lakṣmana and was released from his curse by them (*V. Rāmāyaṇa*); another name for Śiva who presides over the cosmic sacrifice; another name for Rāhu.

**Kabandhin** (S) (M) **1.** bearing vessels of water. **2.** the clouds. **3.** another name for the maruts.

**Kāberī** (S) (F) **1.** full of water. **2.** harlot; courtesan. **3.** a river in south India.

**Kabilabarhiṣa** (S) (M) **1.** brown lion. **3.** a king of Vṛṣṇivanśa (*M. Bh.*)

**Kabūtarī** (S) (F) pigeon.

**Kaća** (S) (M) **1.** hair; beauty; brilliance; cloud. **3.** the eldest son of Bṛhaspati known for his beauty (*M. Bh./Bhāgavata/R. Taraṅginī*)

**Kaćaṅgala** (S) (M) **1.** from whose body the clouds emerge. **2.** the ocean.

**Kaćapa** (S) (M) **1.** cloud drinker. **2.** leaf.

**Kaććhanīra** (S) (M) **1.** water near the banks. **3.** a serpent (*M. Bh.*)

**Kaććhapa** (S) (M) **1.** inhabiting a marsh; tortoise. **3.** one of the 9 treasures of Kubera (*A. Koṣa*)

**Kaćeśvara** (S) (M) **1.** deity of beauty. **3.** a temple.

**Kāćima** (S) (M) **1.** abode of clouds; where clouds rest. **2.** a tree; a sacred tree that grows near a temple.

**Kadalī** (S) (F) **1.** the banana tree (*Musa sapientum*). **3.** the sacred river on the banks of which Rāma lived (*V. Rāmāyaṇa*)

**Kadalīgarbhā** (S) (F) **1.** born from a plantain tree. **3.** the daughter of sage Maṅkaṇaka and the wife of King Dṛdhavarman (*K. Sāgara*)

**Kadalika** (S) (M) made of banana skin; banner; flag.

**Kadalīvana** (S) (M) **1.** garden of plantain trees. **3.** Hanumān's garden on the banks of the Kuberapuṣkariṇī river (*Rāmāyaṇa*)

**Kadambā** (S) (F) group; cloud; the Kadambā tree (*Adina cordifolia*)

**Kādambā** (S) (M) group; cloud; a particular kind of flower (*Adina cordifolia*)

**Kādambakī** (S) (F) flowers of Kadambā (*Adina cordifolia*); to transform into flowers of the Kadambā.

**Kadambānila** (S) (M) **1.** fragrant breeze; accompanied by fragrant breezes. **2.** the rainy season.

**Kādambarī** (S) (F) **1.** coming from the Kadambā tree (*Adina cordifolia*). **2.** female cuckoo; wine distilled from the flowers of the Kadambā tree. **3.** a river in Jambudvīpa (*A. Koṣa*); a Sanskṛt work by Bāṇabhaṭṭa (*Kādambarī*); a daughter of Ćitraratha and Madirā (*Kādambarī*); the heroine of the prose romance by this name composed by Bāṇa; another name for Sarasvatī.

**Kadambavāyu** (S) (M) breeze flowing through the Kadambā tree (*Adina cordifolia*); a fragrant breeze; scented with the blossoms of the Kadambā tree.

**Kādambinī** (S) (F) **1.** a garland of clouds. **3.** a daughter of Takṣaka.

**Kadhapriyā** (S) (F) ever loved; ever friendly.

**Kadhmor** (S) (M) **1.** killing enemies. **3.** a saintly king who should be remembered in the morning (*M. Bh.*)

**Kadītula** (S) (M) sword; scimitar.

**Kadru** (S) (F) **1.** tawny; brown. **2.** a Soma vessel; the earth in a personified form. **3.** a daughter of Dakṣa, wife of Kaśyapa and the mother of serpents (*M. Bh.*)

**Kāgni** (S) (M) a little fire.

**Kāhalā** (S) (F) **1.** mischievous. **2.** a young woman; a kind of musical instrument. **3.** an apsarā (*M. Bh.*); Varuṇa's wife.

**Kāhali** (S) (M) **1.** mischievous. **3.** another name for Śiva.

**Kāhinī** (S) (F) mischievous; young.

**Kāhodara** (S) (M) **1.** making a sound in water. **3.** a sage who was the son of Uddālaka and the father of Aṣṭāvakra.

**Kāhola** (S) (M) bringing water; drinking water.

**Kaikasī** (S) (F) 1. growing plants in water. 2. grows in water; vertebra; rib. 3. the daughter of Sumāli and Ketumatī, the wife of Viśravas and the mother of Rāvaṇa, Kumbhakaraṇa and Vibhīṣana (*V. Rāmāyaṇa*)

**Kaikeyī** (S) (F) 1. princess of the Kekayas. 3. a wife of King Daśaratha of Ayodhyā and the mother of Bharata (*V. Rāmāyaṇa*); the wife of King Ajamīdha of the Purū dynasty (*M. Bh.*); another name for Sudeṣna the wife of the king of Virāṭa.

**Kailāsa** (S) (M) 1. a mountain placed in the Himālaya range; a type of temple. 3. a serpent belonging to the Kaśyapa family (*M. Bh.*); a mountain where Mahāviṣṇu performed penance to please Śiva; the mountain where Śiva and Kubera reside.

**Kailāsanātha** (S) (M) 1. lord of Mount Kailāśa. 3. another name for Śiva and Kubera.

**Kailāsanilaya** (S) (M) 1. residing on Kailāsa. 3. another name for Kubera.

**Kailāsapati** (S) (M) 1. master of Mount Kailāśa. 3. another name for Śiva.

**Kaileśvarī** (S) (F) 1. goddess of water. 2. the family goddess. 3. another name for Durgā.

**Kairava** (S) (M) water born; the White Lotus (*Nelumbium speciosum*)

**Kairavī** (S) (F) moonlight.

**Kairaviṇī** (S) (F) water born; the White Lotus plant (*Nelumbium speciosum*)

**Kaiśika** (S) (M) 1. hairlike; fine as a hair; love; passion. 3. a rāga; a son of Vidarbha and brother of Kratha.

**Kaiṭabha** (S) (M) 1. water born. 2. lightning; thunder. 3. an asura who was killed by Viṣṇu (*D. Bh. Purāṇa/Bhāgavata*)

**Kaiṭabhajit** (S) (M) 1. conqueror of Kaiṭabha. 3. another name for Viṣṇu.

**Kaitaka** (S) (M) 1. coming from the Kevra tree (*Pandanus odoratissimus*). 3. another name for Ulūka.

**Kaitava** (S) (M) 1. gambler. 2. deceitful. 3. another name for Ulūka the son of Śakuni (*M. Bh.*)

**Kaivalya** (S) (M) emancipation; bliss.

**Kājal** (S) (F) kohl; collyrium

**Kajjala** (S) (M) cloud; collyrium.

**Kajjalī** (S) (F) collyrium.

**Kajrī** (S) (F) collyrium coloured; cloud like; a folksong of Uttar Pradesh sung in the monsoon.

**Kāka** (S) (M) 1. crow; Adam's apple; neck. 3. a son of Kaṇsa (*Bhāgavata*)

**Kākalī** (S) (F) voice of the cuckoo; a musical instrument.

**Kākalikā** (S) (F) 1. with a low and sweet voice. 3. an apsarā (*V. Purāṇa*)

**Kakanda** (S) (M) gold.

**Kākāsyā** (S) (F) 1. crow faced. 3. a Buddhist goddess.

**Kākati** (S) (F) 1. cawing like a crow. 3. a tutelary goddess form of Durgā (*T. Śastra*)

**Kākavaktra** (S) (M) 1. crow faced. 3. a Buddhist goddess.

**Kākavarṇa** (S) (M) 1. formed like a crow; crow coloured; with the nature of a crow. 3. a king and son of Śiśunāga (*V. Purāṇa*)

**Kākī** (S) (F) 1. female crow. 3. one of the 7 mothers of Skanda (*M. Bh.*); the original mother of crows personified as a daughter of Kaśyapa and Tāmrā (*H. Purāṇa*)

**Kākila** (S) (M) worn around the neck; a jewel.

**Kākinī** (S) (F) 1. a small coin equal to 20 cowries. 3. a goddess (*T. Śastra*)

**Kakkula** (S) (M) 1. Bakula tree (*Mimusops elengi*). 3. a Buddhist bhikṣu (*L. Vistara*)

**Kākodara** (S) (M) 1. eaten by a crow. 2. serpent.

**Kakṣaka** (S) (M) 1. living in the forest. 3. a serpent born in the family of Vāsuki (*M. Bh.*)

**Kakṣapa** (S) (M) 1. water drinker. 2. tortoise. 3. one of the 9 treasures of Kubera (*A. Koṣa*)

**Kakṣasena** (S) (M) 1. warrior of the forest. 3. the son of Parīkṣit and a member in the court of Yama (*M. Bh.*)

**Kakṣeyu** (S) (M) 1. held in the armpit. 2. overpowered; embraced. 3. the son of Raudrāśva born of a nymph called Miśrakeśī (*V. Purāṇa/H. Purāṇa*)

**Kakṣī** (S) (F) of jungle; perfume; fragrant earth.

**Kakṣīvān** (S) (M) 1. furnished with a girth. 2. one with large arms; a king. 3. a keeper of the forest (*M. Bh.*); a ṛṣi who was the son of

Dirghatamas and Uśija and the husband of the 10 daughters of Rājasvaṇaja (*Ṛg Veda*); the son of Maharṣi Gautama (*Purāṇas*)

**Kakṣīvant** (S) (M) **1.** furnished with a girth. **3.** a ṛṣi mentioned frequently in the *Ṛg Veda* who was the son of Uśija and Dirghatamas and the husband of Vṛćayā (*Ṛg Veda*)

**Kakṣivatasutā** (S) (F) **1.** daughter of Kakṣivant. **3.** a female sage Ghoṣā daughter of sage Kakṣivant and sister of Bhadra (*Ṛg Veda*)

**Kakubha** (S) (F) **1.** peak; summit; quarter of the heavens; splendour; beauty. **2.** a wreath of ćampaka flowers (*Michelia champaka*). **3.** a rāgiṇī (*Kavyādarśa*)

**Kakubjaya** (S) (M) victorious over the quarters.

**Kakuda** (S) (F) **1.** summit. **2.** symbol of royalty. **3.** a daughter of Dakṣa and wife of Dharma (*T. Samhitā*)

**Kakudman** (S) (M) possessor of peak; high; lofty.

**Kakudmi** (S) (F) **1.** mountain daughter. **3.** a river (*P. Purāṇa*); another name for Revatī the wife of Balarāma.

**Kakudmin** (S) (M) **1.** peaked; mountain. **2.** humped. **3.** a king of the Ānartas (*H. Purāṇa*); another name for Viṣṇu.

**Kakuha** (S) (M) **1.** reached the peak. **2.** the seat of a chariot; chief; pre-eminent; lofty; high. **3.** a Yādava prince (*Bhāgavata*)

**Kakuṇḍa** (S) (M) **1.** peak. **2.** chief; symbol of royalty.

**Kakuñjala** (S) (M) striving for water; the Ćātaka bird (*Clamator jacobinus serratus*); a bud of the Ćampaka tree (*Michelia champaka*)

**Kakutstha** (S) (M) **1.** residing on the mountain peak. **3.** the son of King Saṣāda of the Ikṣvāku dynasty (*M. Bh.*); Rāma as he was born in the dynasty of Kakutstha.

**Kalā** (S) (F) **1.** a small point; a digit of the moon; art; an atom. **2.** a small part of anything; skill; ingenuity. **3.** a daughter of Devahūti, the wife of Marīći and the mother of Kaśyapa and Purṇimā (*Bhāgavata*); a daughter of Dakṣa (*M. Purāṇa*)

**Kāla** (S) (M) **1.** time; fate; dark blue; black; death; the Supreme Spirit as a destroyer; the Indian cuckoo. **3.** a son of Hṛāda (*H. Purāṇa*); a brother of King Prasenajit (*B. Ćarita*); a future Buddha; a serpent lord; a mountain (*V. Rāmāyaṇa*); a rakṣasa (*Rāmāyaṇa*); another name for Śiva, Rudra, Yama and Saturn.

**Kālabandhaka** (S) (M) **1.** conqueror of time. **2.** death. **3.** an adviser of Mahiṣāsura (*D. Bhāgavata*)

**Kalabhāṣin** (S) (M) with a pleasing voice.

**Kālabhīti** (S) (M) **1.** of whom death is afraid. **2.** immortal; long lived. **3.** a devotee of Śiva and son of Māmti, who performed penance for a 1000 years for the sake of a son (*Ś. Purāṇa*)

**Kalābhṛt** (S) (M) **1.** bearing digits. **3.** another name for the moon.

**Kālabrāhmaṇa** (S) (M) **1.** a Brāhmaṇ who is beyond time and death. **3.** a Brāhmin who defeated time and death with his penance (*Sk. Purāṇa*)

**Kāladantaka** (S) (M) **1.** black toothed. **3.** a serpent born in the dynasty of Vāsuki (*M. Bh.*)

**Kalādhara** (S) (M) **1.** with digits. **3.** another name for the moon and Śiva.

**Kaladhūta** (S) (M) silver.

**Kāladvija** (S) (M) **1.** victor of death. **3.** a serpent (*Sk. Purāṇa*)

**Kālaghaṭa** (S) (M) **1.** present time; pitcher of time. **3.** a Brāhmin scholar in the Vedas who was a member of the assembly of the serpent yajña (*M. Bh.*)

**Kalāguru** (S) (M) **1.** lord of the digits. **3.** another name for the moon.

**Kalahansa** (S) (M) **1.** the black swan; an excellent king; the Supreme Spirit; a rare breed of swan. **3.** a type of hans; another name for Brahmā.

**Kalahapriyā** (S) (F) **1.** quarrelsome. **3.** a prostitute who attained svarga by observing the Kārttikavrata (*P. Purāṇa*)

**Kalahapriya** (S) (M) **1.** quarrelsome. **3.** another name for Nārada.

**Kālahara** (S) (M) **1.** destroyer of death. **3.** another name for Kṛṣṇa.

**Kālakā** (S) (F) **1.** blue; black. **2.** pupil of the eye; a female crow; flawed gold; fragrant earth. 3. an attendant of Skanda (*M. Bh.*); the daughter of Dakṣa and mother of the Kālakeyas (*D. Bh. Purāṇa*); an attendant of the 4th Arhat (*J.S. Koṣa*); a vidyadhari (*K. Sāgara*); a river (*M. Bh.*); another name for Durgā.

**Kālakākṣa** (S) (M) 1. black eyed. 3. an asura killed by Garuḍa (*M. Bh.*); a warrior of Skanda (*M. Bh.*)

**Kālakāmukha** (S) (M) 1. dark faced. 2. inauspicious faced; a species of ape. 3. a rākṣasa brother of Prahasta, and Rāvaṇa's minister (*V. Rāmāyaṇa*)

**Kālakānja** (S) (M) a galaxy of time bearers; the galaxy of stars.

**Kālakanyā** (S) (F) daughter of time; daughter of death.

**Kālakarṇī** (S) (F) 1. black eared. 3. a yoginī; another name for Lakṣmī.

**Kālakavi** (S) (M) 1. physician of death; poet of death. 3. another name for Agni.

**Kālakavṛkṣīya** (S) (M) 1. tree of time. 3. a sage in the assembly of Indra (*M. Bh.*)

**Kalakeli** (S) (M) 1. frolicsome. 3. another name for Kāma.

**Kālakendra** (S) (M) 1. lord of the black ones. 3. a prince of the dānavas (*Rāmāyaṇa*)

**Kālaketu** (S) (M) 1. comet of death. 3. an asura emperor and son of Kaśyapa and Danu (*M. Bh.*)

**Kālakeya** (S) (M) 1. of Kālakā. 3. an asura (*H. Purāṇa*); a dānava race (*M. Bh.*)

**Kālakīrti** (S) (M) 1. with timeless fame; with deathless fame. 3. a Kṣatriya king who was born from the limb of Suparṇa the younger brother of the asura Mayūra (*M. Bh.*)

**Kālakunja** (S) (M) 1. abode of time. 3. another name for Viṣṇu.

**Kālakūṭa** (S) (N) 1. potion of death. 3. the virulent poison that came up during the churning of the ocean of milk and which was swallowed by Śiva upon the request of Brahmā and retained in his throat (*M. Bh.*)

**Kalāl** (S) (M) wine seller.

**Kalamālī** (S) (F) dispelling darkness; splendid; sparkling.

**Kalamesi** (S) (M) 1. dark fleeced. 2. Caraway (*Curum carvi*); *Psoralea corylifolia*; Garden Cress (*Lepidum sativum*)

**Kālamūrti** (S) (M) time personified.

**Kālanābha** (S) (M) 1. black navelled. 3. a rākṣasa (*H. Purāṇa*); a son of Hiraṇyakṣa (*Bhāgavata*); a son of Vipraćitti and Siṇhikā (*H. Purāṇa/V. Purāṇa*)

**Kalānaka** (S) (M) 1. a digit of the moon. 3. attendants of Śiva (*Ś. Purāṇa*)

**Kālanara** (S) (M) 1. dark hero. 3. a son of Sabhānara (*Bh. Purāṇa*)

**Kālanātha** (S) (M) 1. lord of time. 3. another name for Śiva.

**Kalānātha** (S) (M) 1. lord of the digits. 3. another name for the moon.

**Kalāndikā** (S) (F) bestower of art and/or skills; wisdom; intelligence.

**Kālanemi** (S) (M) 1. felly of the wheel of time. 3. a great asura, who in later years was born as Kaṇsa, son of King Ugrasena; a son of Yajñasena of Mālava (*K. Sāgara*); a rākṣasa who was killed by Hanumān (*Ā. Rāmāyaṇa*)

**Kalānidhi** (S) (M) 1. with a treasure of digits; treasure of arts or skills. 3. another name for the moon.

**Kālañjagiri** (S) (M) 1. the black mountain; a mountain where saints live. 3. a mountain at Medhāvika tīrtha.

**Kālañjara** (S) (M) 1. destroyer(s) of death; an assembly of sages. 3. a mountain in Bundelkhand.

**Kālañjarī** (S) (F) 1. dwelling in the Kālanjara mountain. 3. another name for Pārvatī.

**Kālañjaya** (S) (M) 1. conqueror of time or death. 3. another name for Kṛṣṇa.

**Kālāṅkura** (S) (M) the bud of time; scion of the family.

**Kalāpa** (S) (M) 1. intelligent; a quiver of arrows; a peacock's tail; totality; ornament. 3. a sage who was worshipped by Yudhiṣṭhira at the end of the Rājasūya yajña (*M. Bh.*); another name for the moon.

**Kalāpaka** (S) (M) 1. one who has many feathers; possessed with skills; a band; a bundle; an ornament; a single string of pearls; bearing a quiver of arrows; a peacock. 3. a sage (*M. Bh.*); another name for the moon.

**Kālaparvata** (S) (M) **1.** the mountain of time. **3.** a mountain beside the sea near Laṅkā (*M. Bh.*); a mountain seen by Arjuna on his way to Śiva with Kṛṣṇa during their dream journey (*M. Bh.*)

**Kālapatha** (S) (M) **1.** the course of time. **3.** a son of Viśvāmitra (*M. Bh.*)

**Kalāpin** (S) (M) peacock (*Pavo cristatus*); Indian cuckoo (*Cuculus scolopaceus*)

**Kalāpinī** (S) (F) as blue as the peacock's tail; the night.

**Kālapraṣṭha** (S) (M) **1.** black backed. **3.** a serpent (*M. Bh.*)

**Kalāpriya** (S) (M) lover of art.

**Kalāpūrṇa** (S) (M) **1.** perfect in arts; the totality of the digits. **3.** another name for the moon.

**Kālarāja** (S) (M) lord of death.

**Kālarātri** (S) (F) **1.** dark night; night of death. **3.** the devī presiding over the night on the eve of death (*M. Bh./Rāmāyaṇa*)

**Kālāri** (S) (M) **1.** enemy of death. **3.** another name for Kṛṣṇa.

**Kalaśa** (S) (M) **1.** a pitcher; a churn; the pinnacle of a temple. **3.** a serpent born of the family of Kaśyapa (*M. Bh.*)

**Kalaśabhū** (S) (M) **1.** pitcher born. **3.** another name for Agastya.

**Kālaśaila** (S) (M) **1.** dark mountain. **3.** a range of mountains in the Uttarākhaṇḍa in ancient India (*M. Bh.*)

**Kālaśapotaka** (S) (M) **1.** destroyer of peacocks. **3.** a serpent (*M. Bh.*)

**Kālaśinha** (S) (M) **1.** black lion; lion of time. **3.** a Prākṛt poet.

**Kalaśodara** (S) (M) **1.** pot bellied. **3.** an attendant of Skanda's retinue (*M. Bh.*); a daitya.

**Kalatra** (S) (M) **1.** a royal citadel. **3.** the 7th lunar mansion.

**Kalāvaka** (S) (M) sparrow.

**Kalāvata** (S) (M) **1.** with digits. **3.** another name for the moon.

**Kalāvatī** (S) (F) **1.** with digits; moonlight. **2.** well versed in the 64 arts. **3.** a daughter of the king of Kāśī and wife of King Daśārha of Mathura (*M. Bh.*); a tāntric ceremony in which Durgā enters the body of the novice (*T. Śastra*); the lute of the gandharva Tumburu (*A. Koṣa*); a daughter of apsarā Alambuṣā (*K. Sāgara*); a rāga.

**Kālavega** (S) (M) **1.** speed of time. **3.** a serpent born in the Vāsuki dynasty (*M. Bh.*)

**Kalavinkā** (S) (F) a sparrow (*Passer indicus*); the Indian cuckoo (*Cuculus scolopaceus*)

**Kālayavana** (S) (M) **1.** as horrible as death. **2.** horrible for time and religion. **3.** the king of the Yavana tribe (*H. Purāṇa*); an asura born out of the effulgence of Gargāćārya who was killed by Kṛṣṇa (*V. Purāṇa*); a prince of the Yavanas (*V. Purāṇa*)

**Kālayogi** (S) (M) **1.** reigning over time. **3.** another name for Śiva.

**Kaldhūta** (S) (M) completely white; silver.

**Kalehikā** (S) (F) **1.** black sandalwood. **3.** an attendant of Skanda (*M. Bh.*)

**Kalendu** (S) (M) **1.** digit of the moon. **3.** the moon on the 2nd day of the month (*V's B. Samhitā*)

**Kalhaṇa** (S) (M) **1.** knower of meaning. **2.** knowing; alliteration; sound; reader. **3.** a historian of Kāśmira and author of *Rāja Taraṅginī*.

**Kalhara** (S) (M) water lily (*Nymphaea alba*)

**Kalī** (S) (F) bud.

**Kālī** (S) (F) **1.** blackness; destroyer of time. **2.** night; a succession of black clouds. **3.** goddess Durgā in her terrible form representing eternal time, both giving life and taking it and worshipped as the tutelary deity of Bengal (*D. Bh. Purāṇa*); the daughter of Dakṣa and the mother of the asuras (*M. Bh.*); one of the 16 vidyādevīs; one of the 7 tongues of fire (*M. Upaniṣad*); a sister of Yama (*H. Purāṇa*); a wife of Bhīma (*Bhāgavata*); a river (*Bhāgavata*); a Śakti (*M. Bh.*); another name for Satyavatī, the mother of Vyāsa; Bedda Nut (*Terminalia belerica*)

**Kali** (S) (M) **1.** the period of sin. **3.** the son of Kaśyapa and Munī (*A. Veda*); the lord of Kalīyuga – a period where sin predominates, considered to thrive on gambling, drinking, gold, women and murder (*A. Brāhmaṇa*); another name for Śiva and Sūrya.

**Kālićarana** (S) (M) devotee of Kālī.

**Kālīḍāsa** (S) (M) **1.** servant of Kāli. **3.** a

famous dramatist who was one of the 9 gems of the court of King Vikramāditya of Ujjainī (4th century A.D.) (*K. Granthāvali*)

**Kalijan** (S) (M) men of art; skilled men. blessed; happy; fortunate; excellent; auspicious; beautiful.

**Kālikā** (S) (F) **1.** dark blue; black. **2.** a flaw in gold; a multitude of clouds; fog; a kind of fragrant earth. **3.** mother of Skanda's retinue (*M. Bh.*); an attendant of the 4th Arhat (*J.S. Koşa*); a vidyādharī (*K. Sāgara*); a kinnarī (*M. Bh.*); another name for Durgā.

**Kalikā** (S) (F) **1.** 1/16th of the moon; bud. **2.** progressive; tender; fragrant; the herb *Tephrosia purpurea*.

**Kālika** (S) (M) **1.** beyond death. **2.** long lived. **3.** an attendant given to Skanda by Pūṣaṇ (*M. Bh.*); a species of heron (*Ardea jaculator*)

**Kalīkaṇṭha** (S) (F) **1.** with a pleasing voice. **2.** dove; the Indian cuckoo (*Cuculus scolopaceus*). **3.** an apsarā (*B. Rāmāyaṇa*)

**Kalila** (S) (M) unpierceable; deep.

**Kālimā** (S) (F) blackness; darkness; the mother Kāli.

**Kalimuttu** (S) (M) **1.** remover of sins. **2.** pious; faultless.

**Kalinda** (S) (M) **1.** bestower of arts and skills. **2.** giving blossoms; the sun. **3.** the mountain from which the river Yamunā begins its journey (*M. Bh.*); an attendant of Skanda (*M. Bh.*); Bedda Nut (*Terminalia belerica*)

**Kalindakanyā** (S) (F) **1.** daughter of Kalinda. **3.** another name for the river Yamunā.

**Kālindī** (S) (F) **1.** belonging to Kalinda; the Yamunā river which begins its journey from Mount Kalinda. **3.** a wife of Asita and mother of Sagara; a wife of Kṛṣṇa (*Bhāgavata*); Wild Guava (*Careya arborea*)

**Kaliṅga** (S) (M) **1.** one who knows the arts and the skills. **2.** one who pervades the blossom. **3.** a warrior of Skanda (*M. Bh.*); a daitya who conquered heaven and was finally killed by Devī (*H. Purāṇa*); another name for Śrutāyus, the king of Kaliṅga and a member of Yudhiṣṭhira's court; Sizzling tree (*Albizzla lebbeck*); *Holarrhena antidysenterica*.

**Kalinī** (S) (F) **1.** carrier of blossoms; pea plant; pulse. **2.** a watermelon; a vessel; red flowers. **3.** a daughter of Sūrya; a wife of Kṛṣṇa (*Bhā. Purāṇa*); the wife of Asita and mother of Sagara; another name for the river Yamunā.

**Kalita** (S) (M) known; understood.

**Kalivināśinī** (S) (F) **1.** one who destroys the Kaliyuga. **3.** a goddess (*Br. Purāṇa*)

**Kāliya** (S) (M) **1.** of time; of death. **3.** a 1000 headed serpent son of Kaśyapa and Kadru who was killed by Kṛṣṇa (*Bhāgavata*)

**Kalki** (S) (M) **1.** destroyer of sins. **3.** the 10th incarnation of Viṣṇu portrayed as mounted on a white horse with a drawn sword as the liberator of the world and destroyer of the wicked.

**Kālkṛta** (S) (M) **1.** decided by time; fixed; peacock. **3.** another name for the Supreme Spirit and the sun.

**Kalli** (S) (F) ornament for the wrist.

**Kallola** (S) (M) **1.** joy; a huge wave. **2.** surge; billow; happiness; pleasure.

**Kallolinī** (S) (F) **1.** always happy. **2.** a surging stream; a river. **3.** a river (*V. Rāmāyaṇa*)

**Kalmali** (S) (M) **1.** dispelling darkness. **2.** splendour; brightness.

**Kalmāṣa** (S) (M) **1.** speckled with black. **2.** variegated. **3.** a rākṣasa (*A. Koṣa*); a form of Agni (*H. Purāṇa*); an attendant of the sun (*A. Koṣa*); Sākyamuni in a previous birth (*M.Bh./ Rāmāyaṇa*); a nāga (*M. Bh.*)

**Kalmāṣakaṇṭha** (S) (M) **1.** with a speckled neck. **3.** Śiva whose neck turned black when he drank up the Kālakuta or the poison obtained from the churning of the Ocean of Milk.

**Kalmāṣapāda** (S) (M) **1.** black footed. **2.** with speckled feet. **3.** another name for Mitrasaha, a famous king of the Ikṣvāku dynasty and son of Sudāsa.

**Kalmāṣī** (S) (F) **1.** having black spots. **2.** speckled; variegated. **3.** the cow of Jamadagni that grants all desires (*Purāṇas*); another name for the Yamunā river.

**Kalmeṣikā** (S) (F) variegated.

**Kalpa** (S) (M) **1.** fit; proper; able; competent; perfect. **2.** the 1st astrological mansion; a day in the life of Brahmā equivalent to 4,320,000,000 years; grants wishes; ritual;

determination; opinion. 3. a son of Dhruva and Brāhmī; another name for Śiva.

**Kalpaka** (S) (M) 1. of a certain standard. 2. rite; ceremony. 3. Śiva's garden (*Ś. Purāṇa*)

**Kalpalatā** (S) (F) 1. a wish granting creeper. 3. a creeper of Indra's paradise that grants all wishes.

**Kalpanā** (S) (F) imagination; doing; decoration; composition; idea.

**Kalpanātha** (S) (M) lord of perfection; lord of time.

**Kalpataru** (S) (F) 1. a wish granting tree. 3. one of the 5 trees of Paradise that fulfils all desires (*Pañćatantra*)

**Kalpavata** (S) (M) 1. as perfect as time. 2. perfect. 3. a son of Vasudeva (*Bhāgavata*)

**Kalpavatī** (S) (F) competent.

**Kalpavṛkṣa** (S) (M) 1. tree of life; a wish granting tree. 3. a tree in Devaloka (*M. Bh.*)

**Kalpeśa** (S) (M) lord of perfection.

**Kalpita** (S) (M) imagined; fit; proper.

**Kālskandha** (S) (M) the shoulder of death.

**Kālu** (S) (M) 1. black complexioned. 3. the father of the 1st Sikh Guru, Guru Nānak.

**Kalvik** (S) (M) sparrow.

**Kalyā** (S) (F) 1. praise; eulogy. 3. another name for the mother of Vyāsa.

**Kālya** (S) (M) timely; pleasant; agreeable; auspicious.

**Kalyāṇa** (S) (M) 1. welfare; benefit; virtue; good fortune; beautiful; agreeable; excellent; happy; beneficial; prosperous; propitious. 3. a sage (*P. Brāhmaṇa*); a rāga which forms the basis for all the other rāgas; a gandharva (*A. Koṣa*)

**Kalyāṇamitra** (S) (M) 1. a friend of virtue. 3. another name for Buddha.

**Kalyāṇaśarman** (S) (M) 1. master of virtue. 3. a commentator on Varāhamihira's *Bṛhat Samhitā*.

**Kalyāṇavarman** (S) (M) soldier of virtue; a virtuous soldier.

**Kalyāṇavata** (S) (M) full of virtue.

**Kalyāṇavatī** (S) (F) 1. full of virtue. 3. a princess (*K. Sāgara*)

**Kalyāṇī** (S) (F) 1. beneficial. 2. lucky; excellent; propitious; a sacred cow. 3. a follower of Skanda (*M. Bh.*); a rāgiṇī; Dākṣāyaṇī in Malaya (*M. Bh.*); another name for Pārvatī; Indian Senna (*Cassia augustifolia*); *Teramnus labialis*.

**Kalyāṇin** (S) (M) beneficial; happy; lucky; auspicious; prosperous; virtuous; illustrious.

**Kamā** (S) (F) beauty; radiance; loveliness.

**Kāmā** (S) (F) 1. desired; loved. 3. a daughter of Pṛthūśravas and the wife of King Ayutanāyi (*M. Bh.*)

**Kāma** (S) (M) 1. desire; wish; longing; love; affection; enjoyment; pleasure. 3. the god of love (*A. Veda*); the husband of Rati (*H. Purāṇa*); reincarnated as Pradyumna the son of Kṛṣṇa and Rukmiṇī and the father of Aniruddha (*M. Bh.*)

**Kāmabāṇa** (S) (M) 1. an arrow of the god of love. 2. Arabian jasmine (*Jasminum sambac*)

**Kāmaćārī** (S) (F) 1. following one's own desires. 2. unrestrained. 3. a mother of Skanda's retinue (*M. Bh.*)

**Kāmaćārini** (S) (F) 1. moving at will. 3. Dākṣāyaṇī in Mount Mandāra.

**Kāmadā** (S) (F) 1. granting desires. 3. a follower of Skanda (*M. Bh.*)

**Kāmada** (S) (M) 1. granting desires. 3. another name for the sun and Skanda.

**Kāmadeva** (S) (M) 1. Kāma, the god. 3. the god of love Kāma, who is said to have been the son of Sahiṣṇu and Yaśodharā (*V. Purāṇa*)

**Kāmadhenu** (S) (F) 1. the desire granting cow. 3. the mythical cow of Vasiṣṭha which satisfies all desires (*Brah. Purāṇa*); the mother of cattle (*K. Sāgara*)

**Kāmaduhā** (S) (F) 1. which grants desires. 3. a mythical cow that grants all desires (*Brah. Purāṇa*); a river flowing from Mount Kumuda (*V. Samhitā*)

**Kāmadyū** (S) (F) 1. granter of wishes. 3. the daughter of Purumitra and wife of Vimada (*Ṛg Veda*)

**Kāmaja** (S) (M) 1. born of love; son of Kāma. 3. another name for Aniruddha.

**Kāmajit** (S) (M) 1. conqueror of desire. 3. another name for Śiva and Kārttikeya.

**Kāmakalā** (S) (F) 1. the art of love.

3. another name for Rati.

**Kāmakāntā** (S) (F) beloved of Kāma; the jasmine (*Jasminum sambac*)

**Kāmākhyā** (S) (F) 1. giver of desires. 3. another name for Durgā.

**Kāmākṣī** (S) (F) 1. with voluptuous eyes. 3. a tantric goddess (*T. Śastra*); another name for Durgā; Indian Bead (*Canna indica*)

**Kamalā** (S) (F) 1. born of a lotus. 2. spring; desirous; beautiful; excellent; wealth. 3. another name for Lakṣmī; the mother of Prahlāda (*P. Purāṇa*); a follower of Skanda (*M. Bh.*); the daughter of Reṇu; wife of Jayāpīḍa (*R. Taraṅginī*); another name for Dākṣāyāṇī.

**Kamala** (S) (M) 1. lotus (*Nelumbo speciosum*). 2. pale red; rose coloured. 3. a pupil of Vaiśampāyana; an asura (*G. Purāṇa*); another name for Brahmā; *Nymphaea rubra*; *Nelumbo nucifera*.

**Kamalabhava** (S) (M) 1. sprung from the lotus. 3. another name for Brahmā.

**Kamalabhū** (S) (M) 1. born of the lotus. 3. another name for Brahmā.

**Kamalabuddhi** (S) (M) 1. with lotus like intelligence. 3. a philosopher who was a student of Buddhapālita of the Mādhyamika philosophy (*L. Vistara*)

**Kamaladeva** (S) (M) 1. lord of the lotus. 3. another name for Viṣṇu.

**Kamalādevī** (S) (F) 1. lady of the lotus. 3. the wife of King Lalitāditya and mother of King Kuvalayāpīḍa (*M. Bh.*)

**Kamalagarbha** (S) (M) 1. offspring of a lotus. 3. another name for Brahmā.

**Kamalāhāsa** (S) (M) smiling like a lotus.

**Kamalaja** (S) (M) 1. born of the lotus. 3. another name for Brahmā and the lunar asterism of Rohiṇī.

**Kamalākānta** (S) (M) 1. beloved of Kamalā. 3. another name for Viṣṇu.

**Kamalākara** (S) (M) a mass of lotuses.

**Kamalākṣa** (S) (M) 1. lotus eyed. 3. a great warrior who fought against the Pāṇḍavas (*M. Bh.*); a son of Tarakāsura (*M. Purāṇa*)

**Kamalākṣī** (S) (F) 1. lotus-eyed. 3. a mother in Skanda's retinue (*M. Bh.*)

**Kamalalakṣmī** (S) (F) Lakṣmī of the lotus.

**Kamalālayā** (S) (F) 1. abiding in a lotus. 3. another name for Lakṣmī.

**Kamalalocanā** (S) (F) lotus eyed.

**Kamalamaya** (S) (M) consisting of lotus flowers.

**Kamalanābha** (S) (M) 1. lotus navelled. 3. another name for Viṣṇu.

**Kamalanayana** (S) (M) lotus eyed.

**Kamalanayanī** (S) (F) lotus eyed.

**Kamalanetra** (S) (M) lotus eyed.

**Kamalāpati** (S) (M) 1. husband of Kamalā. 3. another name for Viṣṇu.

**Kamalāsana** (S) (M) 1. with a lotus flower as a seat. 3. another name for Brahmā; Bastard Teak (*Butea monosperma*)

**Kāmalatā** (S) (F) creeper of love; sensous; exotic; exquisite.

**Kamalekṣaṇā** (S) (F) lotus eyed.

**Kamaleśa** (S) (M) 1. lord of Kamalā. 3. another name for Viṣṇu.

**Kamaleśvara** (S) (M) 1. lord of Kamalā. 3. another name for Viṣṇu.

**Kamalī** (S) (F) a collection of lotuses; water; the sārasa crane (*Grus antigone*)

**Kāmālī** (S) (F) 1. full of desire. 2. extremely passionate. 3. another name for Reṇukā.

**Kamalikā** (S) (F) a small lotus.

**Kamalinī** (S) (F) 1. lotus plant; a collection of lotuses. 2. beautiful; fragrant; auspicious; dear to the gods.

**Kamalodaya** (S) (M) the rising of a lotus; the unfurling of a lotus.

**Kamalottama** (S) (M) 1. the best flower. 2. Wild Saffron (*Carthamus tinctorius*)

**Kāmamālin** (S) (M) 1. the gardener of desires. 3. another name for Gaṇeśa.

**Kamana** (S) (M) 1. one who is desirous. 2. desired; beautiful. 3. another name for Kāma and Brahmā; *Saraca indica*.

**Kāmanā** (S) (F) desire.

**Kāmāndaka** (S) (M) 1. with bound desires. 3. a sage who was the preceptor of King Aṅgiras (*M. Bh.*)

**Kāmāndakā** (S) (F) 1. with bound desires. 3. a Buddhist priestess (*B. Literature*)

**Kāmāndaki** (S) (F) with bound desires.

**Kāmaṅga** (S) (M) 1. love bodied. 2. Mango tree (*Mangifera indica*)

**Kāmāṅganāśana** (S) (M) 1. destroying the body of Kāma. 3. another name for Śiva.

**Kāmapāla** (S) (M) 1. gratifier of human desires. 3. a Yādava dependant on Kṛṣṇa (*Bhāgavata*); another name for Viṣṇu, Śiva and Balarāma (*V. Purāṇa*)

**Kāmarāja** (S) (M) lord of desire.

**Kāmarekhā** (S) (F) line of love.

**Kāmarūpa** (S) (M) 1. of the form of love. 2. beautiful; pleasing.

**Kāmasakha** (S) (M) 1. friend of Kāma. 2. the season of spring which is considered to inflame passions.

**Kāmasenā** (S) (F) 1. warrior of love. 3. wife of Nidhipati.

**Kāmāśrama** (S) (M) the abode of love.

**Kāmasū** (S) (F) 1. gratifying wishes. 3. another name for Rukmiṇī.

**Kāmata** (S) (M) 1. following one's desires. 2. unrestrained. 3. a king of Kamboja and member of the court of Yudhiṣṭhira (*M. Bh.*); a serpent born in Dhṛtarāṣṭra's family (*M. Bh.*)

**Kamatha** (S) (M) 1. tortoise; water-jar; porcupine; bamboo. 3. a sage (*M. Bh.*); an asura (*G. Purāṇa*); Spiny Bamboo (*Bambusa arundinacea*)

**Kāmavallabha** (S) (M) 1. love's favourite. 3. another name for moonlight, the season of spring, the Mango tree (*Mangifera indica*) and the Cinnamon tree (*Cinnamomum tamala*)

**Kāmavīrya** (S) (M) 1. displaying heroism at will. 3. another name for Garuḍa.

**Kāmāyakā** (S) (F) 1. desired abode. 3. the forest in which the Pāṇḍavas stayed for the 12 years of their exile (*M. Bh.*)

**Kāmāyanī** (S) (F) 1. the mirror of love. 3. Jayaśankara Prasad's work which contains 125,000 couplets.

**Kāmāyuṣ** (S) (M) 1. one who lives as long as he desires. 3. another name for Garuḍa.

**Kambala** (S) (M) 1. a small worm. 3. a serpent of the Kaśyapa family (*M. Bh.*)

**Kambara** (S) (M) 1. of variegated colour. 3. a Tamil poet.

**Kamboja** (S) (M) 1. shell; elephant. 3. a country and its inhabitants (*M. Bh.*)

**Kāmbojinī** (S) (F) 1. she-elephant. 3. an attendant of the Devī.

**Kambu** (S) (M) conchshell; variegated; elephant; bracelet made of shell.

**Kambugrīva** (S) (M) 1. conchshell necked. 2. according to the *Samudrika Śastra*, a neck marked with 3 lines like that on a shell is considered to be a sign of great fortune. 3. a son of the King Sudhanvā of Madra (*K. Sāgara/ M. Bh.*)

**Kāmeṣṭha** (S) (M) 1. desired by Kāma. 2. Mango tree (*Mangifera indica*)

**Kāmeśvara** (S) (M) 1. lord of desire. 3. another name for the Supreme Being, Śiva, Kāma and Kubera.

**Kāmeśvarī** (S) (F) 1. consort of Kāmeśvara. 3. another name for Pārvatī and Rati.

**Kāmika** (S) (M) desired; wished for.

**Kāmini** (S) (F) 1. desirable. 2. beautiful; loving; *Berberis asiatica*.

**Kāminiṣa** (S) (M) 1. ruling the god of love. 2. Drumstick tree (*Moringa oleifera*)

**Kāmitā** (S) (F) desired; wished for.

**Kāmmā** (S) (F) lovable.

**Kāmoda** (S) (M) 1. one who grants wishes. 3. a rāga.

**Kāmodī** (S) (F) 1. that which excites. 2. a musical note that excites. 3. a rāgiṇī of the Dīpaka rāga; a goddess who, upon its churning, emerged out of the Ocean of Milk.

**Kampa** (S) (M) 1. tremor. 2. earthquake. 3. a Vṛṣṇi prince who became a viśvadeva after his death (*M. Bh.*)

**Kampana** (S) (M) 1. trembling. 2. unsteady. 3. a king and member of the court of Yudhiṣṭhira (*M. Bh.*); a kind of weapon (*M. Bh.*)

**Kamrā** (S) (F) 1. desirable; beautiful. 2. loving.

**Kāmuka** (S) (M) passionate.

**Kāmukā** (S) (F) 1. desired. 3. Madhāvī Creeper (*Hiptage madoblata*)

**Kāmunā** (S) (F) desired; the flower *Hedchium ellipticum*.

**Kāmyā** (S) (F) 1. beautiful; desirable; amiable; striving. 3. a celestial woman.

**Kaṇā** (S) (F) atom; small; sand.

**Kanā** (S) (F) girl; maid; eye.

**Kaṇabhaksa** (S) (M) 1. atom destroyer. 3. another name for the sage Kaṇāda.

**Kāṇabhuti** (S) (M) 1. with one eye. 3. a yakṣa (*K. Sāgara*)

**Kaṇāda** (S) (M) 1. inventor of the atom. 3. a son of Dhīmaraṇa (*P. Ćandrodaya*); a famous sage of ancient India who was also called Kaṇabhakṣa and Pippalāda (*S. Samgraha*); a rāgiṇī.

**Kanadeva** (S) (M) 1. youthful god. 3. a Buddhist patriarch (*B. Literature*)

**Kanaka** (S) (M) 1. gold; sandalwood; the ironwood tree (*Mesua ferrea*); Flame of the Forest tree (*Butea frondosa*); the Variegated Bauhinia (*Bauhinia variegata*); the Thornapple (*Datura stramonium*). 3. a forest near the southern base of Mahāmeru where Hanumān was born (*M. Bh.*)

**Kaṇakā** (S) (F) 1. born of sand. 3. another name for Sītā.

**Kanakadatta** (S) (M) 1. given by gold; a golden gift. 2. very precious.

**Kanakadhvaja** (S) (M) 1. with a golden banner. 3. a son of Dhṛtarāṣṭra (*M. Bh.*)

**Kanakādri** (S) (M) 1. golden mountain. 3. another name for the Mount Meru.

**Kanakakānta** (S) (M) one who loves gold.

**Kanakākṣa** (S) (M) 1. golden eyed. 3. a soldier of Skanda (*M. Bh.*)

**Kanakakuṇḍalā** (S) (F) 1. wearing golden earrings. 3. the mother of the yakṣa Harikeśa (*M. Bh.*)

**Kanakalatā** (S) (F) a golden vine.

**Kanakamañjarī** (S) (F) golden blossom.

**Kanakamaya** (S) (M) consisting of gold; golden.

**Kanakāmbarā** (S) (F) clad in gold; golden; a flower (*Crossandra infundibuliformis*)

**Kanakāmbujam** (S) (M) golden lotus.

**Kanakamudrā** (S) (F) golden ring; gold coin.

**Kanakāñgada** (S) (M) 1. a golden bracelet. 3. a son of Dhṛtarāṣṭra (*M. Bh.*); a gandharva (*B. Rāmāyaṇa*)

**Kanakaparvata** (S) (M) 1. golden mountain. 3. another name for Mount Meru.

**Kanakapīḍa** (S) (M) 1. one who wins gold. 3. an attendant of Skanda (*M. Bh.*)

**Kanakaprabhā** (S) (F) 1. with the lustre of gold; as bright as gold. 2. *Bauhinia variegata*; *Jasminum bignoniaceum*.

**Kaṇakarāja** (S) (M) 1. lord of Sītā. 2. Rāma.

**Kanakarasa** (S) (M) fluid gold; essence of gold; composed of the essence of gold; person with a golden heart and mind; a golden stream.

**Kanakarekhā** (S) (F) 1. a line of gold. 3. the daughter of the king of Kanakapurī (*K. Sāgara*)

**Kanakaśakti** (S) (M) 1. with golden power. 2. the golden speared one. 3. another name for Kārttikeya.

**Kanakasundarī** (S) (F) as beautiful as gold.

**Kanakavāhinī** (S) (F) 1. golden stream. 3. a river (*R. Taranginī*)

**Kanakāvalī** (S) (F) golden chain.

**Kanakavallī** (S) (F) golden creeper.

**Kanakavarṇa** (S) (N) 1. of golden colour. 3. a king supposed to have been the former incarnation of Śākyamuni (*M. Bh.*)

**Kanakavarṣa** (S) (M) 1. shower of gold. 3. the king of Kanakapurī (*R. Taranginī*)

**Kanakavatī** (S) (F) 1. possessing gold. 2. golden. 3. a follower of Skanda (*M. Bh.*)

**Kanakāyus** (S) (M) 1. a golden life. 3. a son of King Dhṛtarāṣṭra (*M. Bh.*)

**Kanakendu** (S) (M) golden moon.

**Kanakvī** (S) (F) a small kite.

**Kanala** (S) (M) shining; bright.

**Kaṇam** (S) (F) the black soiled earth; sand.

**Kānana** (S) (F) 1. forest. 2. grove. 3. the mouth of Brahmā.

**Kānanabālā** (S) (F) forest maiden.

**Kańća** (S) (M) shining.

**Kāńćana** (S) (M) 1. that which shines. 2. gold; money; wealth; the filament of a lotus (*Nelumbium speciosum*); the Iron wood tree (*Mesua ferrea*); Yellow Ćampaka (*Michelia champaka*); *Ficus glomerata*; *Bauhinia variegata*. 3. one of the 2 warriors given by

Mahāmeru to Skanda (*M. Bh.*); a Purū king (*M. Bh.*); a son of Nārāyaṇa (*V. Purāṇa*); the 5th Buddha.

**Kāñćanābhā** (S) (F) golden splendour.

**Kāñćanādri** (S) (M) 1. golden mountain. 3. another name for Mount Meru.

**Kāñćanagaurī** (S) (F) 1. as fair as gold. 3. another name for Pārvatī.

**Kāñćanagiri** (S) (M) 1. golden mountain. 3. another name for Mount Meru.

**Kāñćanaka** (S) (M) golden; the variegated Bauhinia (*Bauhinia vareigata*)

**Kāñćanākṣa** (S) (M) 1. golden eyed. 3. a warrior of Skanda (*M. Bh.*); a dānava (*H. Purāṇa*)

**Kāñćanākṣī** (S) (F) 1. golden eyed. 3. a river which flows through Naimiṣāraṇya and is a part of the river Sarasvatī (*M. Bh.*)

**Kāñćanamālā** (S) (F) 1. garland of gold. 3. an attendant of Vāsavadattā; the wife of Udayana; the daughter of Kṛkin and the wife of Aśoka's son Kuṇāla (*K. Vyuha*); an apsarā.

**Kāñćanaprabhā** (S) (F) 1. as bright as gold. 3. a vidyādhara princess (*K. Sāgara*)

**Kāñćanaprabha** (S) (M) 1. as bright as gold. 3. a son of Bhīma and the father of Suhotra (*H. Purāṇa*)

**Kāñćanavega** (S) (M) 1. with golden passion. 3. a vidyādhara (*K. Sāgara*)

**Kañćapi** (S) (F) 1. connoisseur of glory. 3. the lute of Sarasvatī (*Purāṇas*)

**Kañćāra** (S) (M) 1. shining. 3. another name for the sun.

**Kāñćī** (S) (F) 1. shining. 2. waistband with bells. 3. a pilgrimage centre in South India.

**Kanćuka** (S) (M) armour.

**Kanćukita** (S) (M) furnished with armour.

**Kandalā** (S) (F) the flower of the Kandalī tree (*Rhizophora mucronata*); deer; lotus seed; a flag; a banner.

**Kandala** (S) (M) gold; war; battle; a new shoot; a sprig.

**Kandalāyana** (S) (M) 1. one who brings forth in abundance. 3. an ancient sage.

**Kandalī** (S) (M) *Rhizophora mucronata*; a sweet sound; deer; lotus (*Nelumbo speciosum*); plantain tree.

**Kandalīkusuma** (S) (F) the flower of the Kandalī tree (*Rhizophora mucronata*)

**Kandalin** (S) (M) covered with Kandalī flowers (*Rhizophora mucronata*)

**Kandan** (S) (M) knower; cloud; garlic; radish; camphor.

**Kandarā** (S) (F) 1. lute. 2. cave; hollow. 3. a mother of Skanda's retinue (*M. Bh.*)

**Kandarpā** (S) (F) 1. inflamer. 3. a divine woman attending on the 15th Arhat (*J.S. Koṣa*)

**Kandarpa** (S) (M) 1. inflamer. 3. another name for Kāma.

**Kandarpabālā** (S) (F) daughter of Kāma, the inflamer.

**Kandarpaketu** (S) (M) a banner of passion.

**Kandarpamātṛ** (S) (F) 1. mother of Kāma. 3. another name for Lakṣmī.

**Kandharā** (S) (F) water bearer; a cloud.

**Kandiri** (S) (F) root like; the Sensitive Plant (*Mimosa pudica*)

**Kaṇḍu** (S) (M) 1. itching. 3. a sage who was the husband of apsarā Pramloćā and the father of Māriṣā (*M. Bh.*)

**Kāṇḍulā** (S) (F) 1. itching. 2. an itching in various bodily parts which induces sexual desires. 3. a rāgiṇī.

**Kaṇḍūti** (S) (F) 1. sexual desire. 3. a follower of Skanda (*M. Bh.*)

**Kaṅgana** (S) (F) a bracelet.

**Kaṅganīla** (S) (M) 1. resembling a bracelet. 3. a nāga (*V. Purāṇa*)

**Kānhā** (S) (M) 1. the adolescent. 3. another name for Kṛṣṇa.

**Kanhaiya** (S) (M) 1. the adolescent. 3. another name for Kṛṣṇa.

**Kanī** (S) (F) girl.

**Kaṇići** (S) (F) creeper with blossoms.

**Kaṇika** (S) (M) 1. a grain; an atom; an ear of corn; heart of wheat. 3. a minister of Dhṛtarāṣṭra (*M. Bh.*)

**Kaṇikā** (S) (F) an atom; small; diminutive.

**Kanikā** (S) (F) girl.

**Kaṇikarāja** (S) (M) lord of the atom.

**Kānīna** (S) (M) 1. born of a young wife. 3. another name for Meghanāda, Vyāsa and Karṇa.

**Kanīna** (S) (F) youthful; the pupil of the eye; the little finger.

**Kanīnaka** (S) (M) youth; the pupil of the eye; a boy.

**Kaniṣka** (S) (M) 1. small. 3. a king who supported Buddhism (1st century A.D.) (*B. Literature*)

**Kaniṣṭhā** (S) (F) the little finger; the youngest.

**Kaniṣṭha** (S) (M) 1. the youngest. 3. a class of deities of the 14th Manvantara (*V. Purāṇa*)

**Kanitā** (S) (F) iris of the eye.

**Kañja** (S) (M) 1. produced from water; produced from the head. 2. a lotus; hair. 3. another name for Brahmā.

**Kañjabāhu** (S) (M) 1. lotus armed; with hairy arms. 3. an asura (*H. Purāṇa*)

**Kañjaka** (S) (M) 1. water and earth born. 2. Eastern Hill Mynah (*Gracula religiosa*)

**Kañjam** (S) (M) lotus; ambrosia; nectar.

**Kañjana** (S) (M) 1. produced from water. 3. another name for Kāma.

**Kañjanābha** (S) (M) 1. lotus navelled. 3. another name for Viṣṇu.

**Kañjāra** (S) (M) 1. the sun; a hermit; belly; peacock; elephant. 3. another name for Brahmā.

**Kañjarī** (S) (F) musical instrument; a bird.

**Kañjasū** (S) (M) 1. from a lotus. 3. another name for Kāma.

**Kañjavadana** (S) (M) lotus faced.

**Kañji** (S) (M) crooked.

**Kañjira** (S) (F) tambourine.

**Kaṅka** (S) (M) 1. scent of the lotus; heron. 3. one of the 7 famous archers of the Vṛṣṇi dynasty (*M. Bh.*); name assumed by Yudhiṣṭhira in the palace of the king of Virāṭa (*M. Bh.*); a son of Surasa; a bird; another name for Yama; a son of Ugrasena (*M. Bh.*)

**Kaṅkā** (S) (F) 1. scent of the lotus. 3. a daughter of Ugrasena and sister of Kaṅka (*Bhāgavata/V. Purāṇa*)

**Kaṅkāla** (S) (M) skeleton; a collection of bones.

**Kaṅkālin** (S) (M) 1. with a necklace of bones. 3. a yakṣa.

**Kaṅkālinī** (S) (F) 1. with a necklace of bones. 3. another name for Durgā.

**Kaṅkaṇā** (S) (F) 1. a bracelet. 2. an ornament; a crest. 3. a mother in the retinue of Skanda (*M. Bh.*)

**Kaṅkaṇīkā** (S) (M) 1. an ornament of bells. 3. a serpent (*V. Purāṇa*)

**Kaṅkaṇikā** (S) (F) a small bell; a tinkling ornament.

**Kāṅkṣā** (S) (F) wish; desire; inclination.

**Kāṅkṣiṇī** (S) (F) one who desires.

**Kāṅkṣitā** (S) (M) wished; desired; longed for.

**Kannakī** (S) (F) 1. chaste and devoted wife. 3. another name for Sītā.

**Kannikā** (S) (F) maiden.

**Kaṇsa** (S) (M) 1. vessel of bell-metal. 2. with a metal like body. 3. the son of King Ugrasena of Mathurā and maternal uncle of Kṛṣṇa (*M. Bh./Bhāgavata/V. Purāṇa*)

**Kaṅsakeśinisūdana** (S) (M) 1. destroyer of Kaṅsa and Keśin. 3. another name for Kṛṣṇa.

**Kaṅsanisūdana** (S) (M) 1. destroyer of Kaṅsa. 3. another name for Kṛṣṇa.

**Kaṇsārāti** (S) (M) 1. slayer of Kaṇsa. 3. another name for Kṛṣṇa.

**Kaṇsavatī** (S) (F) 1. made of metal. 3. the sister of Kaṇsa.

**Kāntā** (S) (F) beloved; perfume; the earth.

**Kānta** (S) (M) 1. beloved. 2. the spring; a jewel. 3. a son of Dharmanetra; another name for Kṛṣṇa, Kārttikeya and the moon; *Aglaia odoratissima*; *Amomum subulatum*; *Mimordica balsamina*.

**Kaṇṭaka** (S) (M) 1. thorn. 3. the horse of Śākyamuni (*L. Vistara*); another name for Makara, the symbol of Kāma.

**Kaṇṭakin** (S) (M) 1. thorny; prickly; *acacia catechu*; bamboo; *Zizyphus jujuba*; Amaranth (*amaranthus tricolor rubra*). 3. a mother of Skanda's retinue (*M. Bh.*)

**Kaṇṭakinī** (S) (M) 1. full of thorn. 2. a porcupine (*Solanum jacquini*). 3. a follower of Skanda (*M. Bh.*)

**Kaṇṭārikā** (S) (M) 1. thorn like; Prickly Pear (*Opuntia dillenii*). 3. an ancient sage and founder of a gotra in which the pre-eminent Brahmadatta was born (*K. Sāgara*)

**Kaṇṭhaka** (S) (M) 1. of neck. 2. an ornament

for the neck; a one-stringed necklace. 3. the horse of Śākyamuni (*L. Vistara*)

**Kaṇṭhamaṇi** (S) (M) a jewel of the neck; a jewel worn on the throat; a dear object.

**Kaṇṭhekāla** (S) (M) 1. black necked. 3. another name for Śiva.

**Kānti** (S) (F) 1. glory; beauty; wish; decoration; a digit of the moon. 3. another name for Lakṣmī; Garden Pea (*Pisum sativum*)

**Kāntida** (S) (M) giving beauty; adorning.

**Kāntimān** (S) (M) 1. lovely. 3. another name for Kāma and the moon.

**Kantu** (S) (M) 1. love. 2. mind; heart; a granary. 3. another name for Kāma.

**Kānupriyā** (S) (F) beloved of Kṛṣṇa.

**Kaṇva** (S) (M) 1. talented; praised. 2. honoured; intelligent. 3. a sage of the Kaśyapa family; the son of Medhātithi, father of Indīvaraprabhā by the apsara Menakā, the foster father of Śakuntalā and one of the 24 ṛṣis associated with the Gāyatrī mantra (*Ṛg Veda*); a king of the Purū dynasty who was the son of Prītiratha and the father of Medhātithi (*A. Purāṇa*)

**Kaṇvaka** (S) (M) 1. son of a talented person. 3. a son of Śūra (*H. Purāṇa*)

**Kaṇvala** (S) (M) a lotus.

**Kaṇvalajita** (S) (M) 1. winner of the lotus. 3. another name for Viṣṇu.

**Kanvar** (S) (M) a prince.

**Kaṇvasutā** (S) (F) 1. daughter of Kaṇva. 3. another name for Śakuntalā.

**Kanyā** (S) (F) 1. daughter; maiden. 3. the zodiac sign of Virgo; *Aloe vera*; Bulb bearing Yam (*Dioscorea bulbifera*); *Capparis sepiaria*; another name for Durgā.

**Kanyakā** (S) (F) 1. the smallest; girl; maiden; daughter; the virgin goddess. 3. the zodiac constellation Virgo; another name for Durgā.

**Kanyākumārī** (S) (F) 1. the eternal virgin. 3. the daughter of Dakṣa (*M. Bh.*); a devotee of Śiva who sat in meditation on the southernmost shore of India and in whose memory a pilgrimage centre has been established there (*Purāṇas*); the child that escaped from Kaṇsa at the time of Kṛṣṇa's birth (*P. Purāṇa*); *Amomum subulatum*; another name for Durgā.

**Kanyalā** (S) (F) girl.

**Kanyanā** (S) (F) maiden; girl.

**Kanyāratna** (S) (F) a gem of a girl.

**Kapālabhṛt** (S) (M) 1. bearing a skull. 3. another name for Śiva.

**Kapālaketu** (S) (M) 1. with a skull for a banner. 3. another name for a comet.

**Kāpalamālā** (S) (F) 1. with a garland of skulls. 3. an attendant of Devī.

**Kapālamālin** (S) (M) 1. with a garland of skulls. 3. another name for Śiva.

**Kapālaśiras** (S) (M) 1. skull headed. 3. another name for Śiva.

**Kāpālī** (S) (M) 1. skull carrier. 2. one with a skull. 3. one of the 11 rudras who was the son of Sthāṇu and the grandson of Brahmā (*M. Bh.*); a son of Kṛṣṇa and Yaudhiṣṭhirī (*H. Purāṇa*); another name for Śiva.

**Kāpālika** (S) (M) 1. one who eats in a skull. 3. a member of a Śaivā sect.

**Kapālinī** (S) (F) 1. consort of Kapālī. 3. another name for Durgā.

**Kāpardi** (S) (M) 1. shell (conch). 2. as white as a conch shell; fair in visage. 3. another name for Śiva.

**Kapardikā** (S) (F) a small shell (*Cypraea moneta*)

**Kapardin** (S) (M) 1. cowrie shell. 3. Śiva whose hair is braided like a cowrie shell; one of the 11 rudras (*A. Purāṇa*); a yakṣa; another name for Rudra and Pūṣaṇ.

**Kapardinī** (S) (F) 1. whose hair is braided like a cowrie shell. 3. a goddess (*Brahma Purāṇa*)

**Kapaṭa** (S) (M) 1. deceit. 3. a demon who was the son of Kaśyapa and Danu (*M. Bh.*)

**Kaphinī** (S) (F) 1. phlegmatic. 3. a river.

**Kapi** (S) (M) 1. monkey. 2. the sun; *Emblica officinalis*. 3. another name for Viṣṇu and Kṛṣṇa.

**Kāpī** (S) (F) 1. of Kṛṣṇa. 3. a river (*M. Bh.*)

**Kapidhvaja** (S) (M) 1. with a monkey banner. 3. another name for Arjuna.

**Kapiketana** (S) (M) 1. with a monkey as a symbol. 3. another name for Arjuna.

**Kapilā** 1. monkey coloured. 2. a brown cow; perfume; tawny. 3. a fabulous cow of Indra celebrated in the Purāṇas (*M. Bh.*); a daughter of Dakṣa and wife of Kaśyapa (*M. Bh.*); the mother of Panćaśikha (*M. Bh.*); the consort of Puṇḍarīka an elephant of a quarter (*A. Koṣa*); a holy place of Kurukṣetrā (*M. Bh.*); a river of ancient India (*M. Bh.*); the Śīśam tree (*Dalbergia sissoo*)

**Kapila** (S) (M) 1. monkey coloured. 2. brown; tawny; reddish; the sun. 3. a sage who was the son of Kardama and Devahutī, an incarnation of Viṣṇu, a great exponent of the Sāṅkhya philosophy and on whose teachings the entire *Yoga Śāstra* is based (*D. Bhāgavata*); son of an agni named Bhānu who is supposed to be an incarnation of sage Kapila (*M. Bh.*); a sage who was the father of Śālihotra (*M. Bh.*); one of the 7 serpent kings who are said to hold the earth in place (*M. Bh.*); a son of Viśvāmitra (*M. Bh.*); Viṣṇu in his 5th incarnation as the lord of all Siddhis (*M. Bh./Bhāgavata*); a form of Agni (*M. Bh.*); a serpent lord (*M. Bh.*); a mountain (*M. Bh.*); *Aloe vera*; another name for Viṣṇu, Śiva and Sūrya.

**Kapiḷadhārā** (S) (F) 1. with brown waves. 2. muddy. 3. another name for the Gaṅgā.

**Kapilākṣa** (S) (M) 1. sun eyed. 2. whose eyes glow; with piercing and bright eyes. 3. *Cucumis trigonus*; another name for Indra.

**Kapilāñjana** (S) (M) 1. using a brown collyrium. 3. another name for Śiva.

**Kapilapati** (S) (M) 1. lord of the brown. 2. lord of the brown coloured i.e. Indian. 3. another name for Drupada (*M. Bh.*)

**Kapilāśva** (S) (M) 1. with brown horses. 3. the son of King Kuvalāśva (*M. Bh.*); another name for Indra.

**Kapileya** (S) (M) 1. brown coloured. 3. a son of Viśvāmitra (*A. Brahmāṇa*)

**Kapilī** (S) (F) 1. with tawny waves. 3. a river in modern Nowgong which is in Assam.

**Kapīndra** (S) (M) 1. lord of monkeys. 3. another name for Viṣṇu, Jāmbavata, Sugrīva and Hanumān.

**Kapiñjalā** (S) (F) 1. with brown water. 2. Francoline partridge. 3. a river of ancient India (*M. Bh.*)

**Kapiñjala** (S) (M) 1. with brown water. 2. Baluchistan Grey Partridge (*Francolinus pondicerianus mecranensis*); the Pied Crested Cuckoo which is supposed to drink water only from the clouds. 3. a son of ṛṣi Śvetaketu (*M. Bh.*); a vidyādhara (*K. Sāgara*)

**Kapipati** (S) (M) 1. lord of apes. 3. another name for Hanumān.

**Kapiprabhu** (S) (M) 1. master of monkeys. 3. another name for Rāma.

**Kapisā** (S) (F) 1. monkey coloured. 2. brown; reddish. 3. the mother of the Piśāćas; a river (*M. Bh.*)

**Kapiśa** (S) (M) 1. lord of monkeys. 2. brown; reddish brown; incense. 3. another name for Śiva and the sun; *Altingia excelsa*.

**Kapiśāñjana** (S) (M) 1. using a brown collyrium. 3. another name for Śiva.

**Kapiskandha** (S) (M) 1. monkey shouldered. 2. a soldier who leaps like a monkey. 3. a soldier of Skanda (*M. Bh.*); a dānava (*H. Purāṇa*)

**Kapīśvara** (S) (M) 1. lord of monkeys. 3. another name for Sugrīva.

**Kapivaktra** (S) (M) 1. monkey faced. 3. another name for Nārada.

**Kapota** (S) (M) 1. Indian Ring Dore (*Columba risoria*); Blue Rock Pigeon (*Columba neglecta*). 3. a sage who was the husband of Ćitrāṅgadā and the father of Tumburu and Suvarćas (*K. Purāṇa*); a son of Garuḍa (*M. Bh.*)

**Kapotaroman** (S) (M) 1. having hair like feathers of a pigeon. 2. a blond. 3. the son of Emperor Śibi and a member of Varuṇa's court (*M. Bh.*)

**Kapṛtha** (S) (M) 1. increasing pleasure. 3. another name for Indra.

**Kapūri** (S) (M) camphor.

**Karabha** (S) (M) 1. trunk of an elephant. 2. anything useful. 3. a king who was a dependant of Emperor Jarāsandha (*M. Bh.*)

**Karabhājana** (S) (M) 1. one born like an elephant. 2. an elephant. 3. a son of Ṛṣabhadeva who was a yogī of divine wisdom (*Bhāgavata*)

**Karabhin** (S) (M) 1. with a trunk; elephant. 3. the son of Śakuni (*M. Purāṇa*)

**Karabhorū** (S) (F) one whose thighs resemble the trunk of an elephant.

**Karaćūra** (S) (M) gold.

**Karajāla** (S) (M) a stream of light.

**Karakaṣa** (S) (M) 1. harsh. 2. hard; firm; a sword. 3. a soldier who fought on the side of the Kauravas (*M. Bh.*)

**Karakaṣaka** (S) (M) 1. harsh. 2. hard; firm; a sword. 3. a brother of the king of Ćedi who fought on the side of the Pāṇḍavas (*M. Bh.*)

**Karakāyu** (S) (M) 1. having a hard life. 3. a son of Dhṛtarāṣṭra (*M. Bh.*)

**Karālā** (S) (F) 1. terrible; opening; wide; tearing. 2. formidable. 3. one of the 7 tongues of Agni; another name for Durgā.

**Karāla** (S) (M) 1. terrible; wide; opening; tearing. 2. great; large; lofty; uneven. 3. a gandharva (*M. Bh.*); a rākṣasa (*D. Bh. Purāṇa*); another name for Janaka.

**Karāladanta** (S) (M) 1. with large teeth. 3. a great sage who was a member of Indra's court (*M. Bh.*)

**Karālajanaka** (S) (M) 1. Janaka the great. 3. another name for King Janaka of Mithilā whose preceptor was sage Vasiṣṭha (*M. Bh.*)

**Karālākṣa** (S) (M) 1. with frightening eyes. 3. a soldier of Skanda (*M. Bh.*)

**Karālī** (S) (F) 1. the terrible. 3. Durgā in her destructive form.

**Karālī** (S) (F) 1. frightening. 2. destructive; fear inducing. 3. one of Agni's 7 tongues of fire (*M. Upaniṣad*)

**Karālikā** (S) (F) 1. that which tears. 2. sword. 3. another name for Durgā.

**Karambhā** (S) (F) 1. mixed. 2. fennel; *foeniculum vulgare*; *Asparagus racemosus*. 3. a princess of Kaliṅga, the wife of King Akrodhana of the Purū dynasty and the mother of Devātithi (*M. Bh.*); *Aglaia odoratissima*; *Capparis zeylanica*.

**Karambha** (S) (M) 1. mixture. 2. coarsely ground oats; gruel. 3. sacrificial offering to Pūṣan made of barley and sesame (*Ṛg Veda*); a son of Śakuni and the father of Devarāṭa (*H. Purāṇa*); the father of the asura, Mahiṣa (*Rāmāyaṇa*); a brother of Rambha (*H. Purāṇa*)

**Karandhama** (S) (M) 1. clapping of hands. 3. a king of the Ikṣvāku dynasty and the father of Avīkṣit who was a prominent member of Yama's court (*M. Bh.*)

**Karañja** (S) (M) 1. born of hand; the tree (*Pongamia glabra*). 2. obtained by toil; difficult to obtain; precious.

**Karañjanilayā** (S) (F) 1. wind of the Karañja tree (*Pongamia glabra*). 3. the daughter of Dakṣa, the wife of Kaśyapa, the mother of all trees and who is believed to stay in the Karañja tree (*M. Bh.*); another name for Analā.

**Karapagam** (S) (M) hands and feet.

**Karaṭa** (S) (M) 1. with the temple of an elephant. 3. another name for Gaṇeśa.

**Karatoya** (S) (M) 1. with flowing water. 3. a holy river that started at the time of Pārvatī's marriage to Śiva and which worships Varuṇa (*M. Bh.*)

**Karavinda** (S) (M) 1. possessed by hand. 2. doing; causing; creator.

**Karavirī** (S) (F) 1. strong armed. 2. a good cow; the oleander flower (*Nerium odorum*). 3. another name for Aditī.

**Karavira** (S) (M) 1. strong armed. 2. sword; scimitar; thumb. 3. a daitya (*A. Koṣa*); a serpent (*M. Bh.*); a mountain on the south of Mahāmeru (*Bhāgavata*); a forest near Dvārakā (*H. Purāṇa*); the Oleander tree (*Nerium odorum*)

**Karavirākṣa** (S) (M) 1. the tip of the sword. 3. a demon who fought against Rāma (*V. Rāmāyaṇa*)

**Karbura** (S) (M) 1. variegated. 2. gold; a venomous leech. 3. a rākṣasa (*A. Koṣa*)

**Karburī** (S) (F) 1. golden; lioness; tigress. 3. another name for Durgā.

**Kardama** (S) (M) 1. covered with mud. 2. slime; dirt; clay; filth; shade. 3. a prajāpati son of Brahmā born from his shadow, reborn as the son of Pulaha and Kṣamā and the grandson of Brahmā, was the husband of Devahūti the daughter of Svāyambhuva Manu, and the father of sage Kapila and 9 daughters who married Marīći (*Bhāgavata*); a sage who sits in the court of Brahmā (*M. Bh.*); a sage who was the grandson of Virāja and the father of Anaṅga (*M. Bh.*); a serpent (*M. Bh.*); a kind of rice produced in the marsh.

**Kareṇu** (S) (M) elephant.

**Kareṇumatī** (S) (F) 1. like a female elephant. 3. the daughter of King Śiśupāla of Ćedi, the wife of Nakula and the mother of Niramitra (*M. Bh.*)

**Kārikā** (S) (F) a collection of verses on philosophy.

**Karikṛṣṇa** (S) (M) black elephant.

**Karimukha** (S) (M) 1. elephant faced. 3. another name for Gaṇeśa.

**Kārin** (S) (M) doing; accomplishing; rejoicing; praising; jubiliant.

**Karīndra** (S) (M) 1. lord of elephants. 2. war elephant; the largest elephant. 3. the elephant of Indra.

**Karīṣa** (S) (M) 1. dry cow dung. 3. a son of Viśvāmitra (*M. Bh.*)

**Karīṣa** (S) (M) 1. lord of elephants. 3. another name for Airavata.

**Kariṣini** (S) (M) 1. abounding in dung. 3. a river (*M. Bh.*)

**Kariśmā** (S) (F) miracle.

**Kariśṇī** (S) (F) goddess of elephants; goddess of wealth.

**Kariṣṇu** (S) (M) doing; accomplishing.

**Karka** (S) (M) 1. white; crab; good; excellent; fire; mirror; water-jar; beauty. 3. the zodiac sign of Cancer.

**Karkandhu** (S) (M) 1. crab like; whitish; the jujube tree (*Zizyphus jujuba*). 3. a protégé of the aśvins (*V. Samhitā/Ś. Brāhmaṇa*); a saintly king mentioned in the *Ṛg Veda*.

**Karkara** (S) (M) 1. harsh. 2. hard; firm; a bone; hammer; mirror. 3. a prominent serpent (*M. Bh.*)

**Karkarī** (S) (F) a lute.

**Karkaṣa** (S) (M) 1. harsh. 2. hard; firm; rough; sword; scimitar.

**Karki** (S) (M) 1. of crab. 3. the zodiac sign of Cancer; the son of sage Āpastamba and Akasūtrā (*V. Samhitā*)

**Karkoṭa** (S) (M) 1. abode of sword. 2. the sugarcane plant. 3. a principal serpent of Pātāla (*V. Purāṇa*); helper of Nala (*R. Taraṅginī*)

**Karma** (S) (M) 1. fate; destiny; duty; action. 2. the purple Moorhen (*Porphyrio porphyrio*)

**Karmaćandra** (S) (M) 1. moon of destiny. 2. attaining destiny; successful.

**Karmajit** (S) (M) 1. victorious over his destiny. 3. a king of the family of Arjuna who was the son of Bṛhatsena and the father of Śrutañjaya (*Bhāgavata*)

**Karmakara** (S) (M) 1. servant. 3. another name for Yama.

**Karmanāśā** (S) (F) 1. one who destroys fate or action. 2. one who destroys the merit of works. 3. river between Kāśī and Vihāra (*Bh. Purāṇa*)

**Karmaṇya** (S) (M) 1. clever in work. 2. skilful; diligent.

**Karmaśa** (S) (M) 1. one who does his duty. 3. a son of Pulaha (*V. Purāṇa*)

**Karmaśīla** (S) (M) dutiful.

**Karmaśreṣṭha** (S) (M) 1. excellent in work. 3. a son of Pulaha and Gati (*V. Purāṇa/Bhāgavata*)

**Karmaśūra** (S) (M) brave in action; assiduous.

**Karmātman** (S) (M) one whose character is action.

**Karmasākṣī** (S) (M) 1. witnessing the performance of duty; standing as a witness to duty. 3. another name for Sūrya.

**Karmavajra** (S) (M) one whose power lies in work.

**Karmavira** (S) (M) brave in action.

**Karmendra** (S) (M) lord of action.

**Karmiṣṭhā** (S) (F) extremely diligent.

**Kārmuka** (S) (M) 1. bow. 2. rainbow. 3. the zodiac sign of Sagittarius; *Acacia ferruginea*.

**Karṇa** (S) (M) 1. ear. 2. skilful; clever; the rudder of a ship; handle of a vessel; an instrument of action; document; field. 3. the eldest son of Kuntī and Sūrya, the adopted son of the charioteer Adhiratha and Rādhā, who joined sides with the Kauravas and became the king of Aṅga and is the epitome of valour and generosity (*M. Bh.*); a son of Dhṛtarāṣṭra (*M. Bh.*); the younger brother of Ghaṇṭā (*M. Bh.*); another name for the Supreme

Being.

**Karṇadhārā** (S) (F) 1. having large ears. 3. an apsarā (*K. Vyuha*)

**Karṇadhāra** (S) (M) 1. one who holds others by the ear. 2. a leader; pilot; helmsman; sailor

**Karṇādi** (S) (M) 1. of ear. 2. performing according to the scriptures. 3. a gaṇa (*Pāṇinī*)

**Karṇajit** (S) (M) 1. conqueror of Karṇa. 3. another name for Arjuna.

**Karṇaka** (S) (M) 1. belonging to the ear. 2. prominence on the side (as in case of the ear); listening carefully.

**Karṇamotī** (S) (F) 1. pearls of the ear. 3. Pārvatī with pearls in her ears; Durgā in her form as Ćāmuṇḍā (*T. Śastra*)

**Karṇamukha** (S) (M) having Karṇa as the leader.

**Karṇanirvaha** (S) (M) 1. dependant on the ears. 2. one who listens religiously. 3. a sage (*M. Bh.*)

**Karṇānuja** (S) (M) 1. Karṇa's younger brother. 3. another name for Yudhiṣṭhira.

**Karṇapiśāćī** (S) (F) 1. witch of the ear. 3. a tantric goddess who, when properly invoked is considered to whisper the future of people in the ear of her devotees (*J. Śastra*)

**Karṇapravaraṇā** (S) (F) 1. one who whispers in the ears. 3. a follower of Skanda (*M. Bh.*)

**Karṇaprayāga** (S) (M) 1. ear shaped confluence. 3. the confluence of the rivers Gaṅgā and Piṇḍur.

**Karṇapūra** (S) (F) 1. that which fulfils the ears. 2. ornament of flowers worn round the ears; a blue lotus flower (*Nymphaea stellata*). 3. the father of Kavićandra and the author of *Alamkāra Kaustubha*.

**Karṇapuṣpa** (S) (M) 1. flower of the ear. 2. an earring; the Blue Amaranth (*Amaranthus caudatus*)

**Karṇāri** (S) (M) 1. enemy of Karṇa. 3. another name for Arjuna.

**Karṇaśravas** (S) (M) 1. heard by the ears. 2. famous. 3. a sage of the Aṅgiras family and seer of mantras or chants (*P. Brāhmaṇa*); a sage who was a member of the court of Yudhiṣṭhira (*M. Bh.*)

**Karṇasū** (S) (M) 1. father of Karṇa. 3. another name for Sūrya.

**Karṇāṭa** (S) (M) 1. name of a people. 3. a rāga; a kind of Mimosa.

**Karṇāveśṭa** (S) (M) 1. an earring. 3. a Kśatriya king who was the incarnation of the asura Krodhavaśa (*M. Bh.*).

**Karṇavīra** (S) (M) 1. whose glory has come to be heard. 2. a well known warrior.

**Karṇī** (S) (F) 1. with ears. 2. a good listener. 3. Kaṇsa's mother (*Bhāgavata*)

**Karṇi** (S) (M) arrow.

**Karṇikā** (S) (F) 1. creeper. 2. heart of a lotus; earring. 3. an apsarā who sang and danced at the birth celebrations of Arjuna (*M. Bh.*); *Rosa alba*; *Crysanthemum indicum*.

**Karṇikācala** (S) (M) 1. the central mountain. 3. another name for Mount Meru.

**Karṇikāra** (S) (M) 1. the pericarp of a lotus. 2. as soft as a lotus; very soft.

**Karṇiki** (S) (M) judge; examiner; elephant.

**Karṇini** (S) (M) 1. arrow; missile; steersman. 3. one of the 7 principal ranges of mountains dividing the universe (*A. Koṣa/He. Koṣa*)

**Karṇotpala** (S) (M) 1. ear-lotus. 2. a lotus flower that ornaments the ears.

**Kārpanī** (S) (F) gladness.

**Karpūra** (S) (M) camphor.

**Karpūratilakā** (S) (F) 1. one who applies camphor on the forehead. 3. another name for Jayā, a friend of Durgā.

**Karpūratilaka** (S) (M) 1. one who applies camphor on the forehead. 2. with a white spot on forehead. 3. an elephant (*Hitopadeśa*)

**Karpūrī** (S) (F) scented with camphor.

**Karṣin** (S) (M) 1. one who attracts. 3. another name for Kāma.

**Karṣṇā** (S) (F) 1. black. 2. belonging to the dark half of the month; that which belongs to Kṛṣṇa.

**Karṣṇi** (S) (M) 1. black. 3. a gandharva (*M. Bh.*); another name for Kāma and Abhimanyu; *Asparagus racemosus*.

**Kārta** (S) (M) 1. to encompass; to spin; to cut; to destroy. 3. a viśvadeva (*M. Bh.*); a son of Dharmanetra (*H. Purāṇa*)

**Kartāra** (S) (M) lord of all creation.

**Kārtaśvara** (S) (M) 1. gold. 3. an asura who once became the emperor of the world (*M. Bh.*)

**Kārtavīrya** (S) (M) 1. of destructive ability. 2. of great valour. 3. son of Kritavīrya; the 1000 armed Arjuna who was the king of the Hehayas, father of a 100 sons, ruled at Mahiṣmatī for 86,000 years, was one of the emperors of the world in Bhāratavarṣa and was killed by Paraśurāma (*Br. Purāṇa*)

**Kārtik** (S) (M) 1. one who bestows courage and happiness. 3. which belongs to the month of Kārttika.

**Kartṛ** (S) (M) 1. doer. 2. maker; creator; author. 3. another name for Brahmā, Viṣṇu and Śiva.

**Kārttika** (S) (M) 1. one who gives courage and happiness. 3. the month of October-November when the full moon is near the Pleiades.

**Kārttikeya** (S) (M) 1. one who bestows courage. 2. brave; vital; energetic. 3. the son of Śiva and Pārvatī known as the god of war because he led the army of gaṇas against the demons, the foster son of Gaṅgā and the 6 Kṛttikās or Pleiades, also known as Skanda, Subrahmaṇya and Kumāra (*M. Bh.*); the planet Mars.

**Kārttikī** (S) (F) 1. the full moon night in the Kārttika month. 2. pious; holy.

**Kāru** (S) (M) poet.

**Karuṇā** (S) (F) 1. compassion. 2. tenderness; mercy.

**Karuṇa** (S) (M) 1. compassionate. 2. tender; a Jaina ascetic. 3. another name for the Supreme Being.

**Karuṇākara** (S) (M) mine of compassion.

**Karuṇāmallī** (S) (F) 1. the vine of compassion. 3. the jasmine (*Jasminum sambac*)

**Karuṇāmaya** (S) (M) consisting of compassion.

**Karuṇānidhi** (S) (M) store of compassion.

**Karuṇāśankara** (S) (M) Śiva, the compassionate.

**Karundhaka** (S) (M) 1. one who guides society. 2. a leader. 3. a son of Śūra and a brother of Vasudeva (*V. Purāṇa*)

**Karuṇeśa** (S) (M) 1. lord of mercy. 3. another name for the moon.

**Karuṇeśvara** (S) (M) 1. god of mercy. 3. a liṅga.

**Kāruṇyā** (S) (F) merciful: compassionate; praiseworthy.

**Karūṣa** (S) (M) 1. dry. 2. hard. 3. a tribe; a son of Manu Vaivasvata who was the founder of a tribe which is named after him (*M. Bh.*); a yakṣa who became a lord of a Manvantara (*D. Bhāgavata*)

**Karutthāma** (S) (M) 1. perfect in duty. 2. master. 3. a son of Duṣyanta and father of Ākrīḍa (*H. Purāṇa*)

**Karvara** (S) (M) 1. variegated. 2. tiger. 3. a rākṣasa (*A. Koṣa*)

**Karvarī** (S) (F) 1. variegated. 2. tigress; night. 3. another name for Durgā.

**Kāśa** (S) (M) 1. appearance. 2. *Saccharum spontaneum*. 3. a son of Suhotra and father of Kāśirāja; an attendant of Yama.

**Kāśageśa** (S) (M) sugarcane; a sweet grass (*Saccharum spontaneum*)

**Kaṣaku** (S) (M) 1. fire. 3. another name for the sun.

**Kāsāra** (S) (M) pond.

**Kaṣāya** (S) (M) 1. saffron colour. 2. the garment of an ascetic; Button tree (*Anogeissus latifolia*)

**Kāṣāyin** (S) (M) 1. wearing a saffron garment. 3. a sage (*Br. Upaniṣad*); a Buddhist monk.

**Kaśerū** (S) (F) 1. backbone. 2. the root of the grass (*Scirpus kysoor*). 3. one of the 9 divisions of Bhāratavarṣa; the beautiful daughter of Prajāpati Tvaṣṭṛ who married Kṛṣṇa (*M. Bh.*)

**Kaśeruka** (S) (M) 1. backbone; spine. 3. a yakṣa who was a member of Kubera's assembly (*M. Bh.*)

**Kaśerumata** (S) (M) 1. a backbone. 2. straight; upright. 3. an asura who was killed by Kṛṣṇa (*M. Bh.*); a Yavana king (*Bhāgavata*)

**Kāśī** (S) (F) 1. shining; splendid; a clenched hand. 3. an old and most sacred pilgrimage centre of India which has the famous Viśvanatha temple whose Śivaliṅga is considered to have been installed by Brahmā

(*Rāmāyaṇa*); a prince of the family of Bharata who was the son of Suhotra and grandfather of Dhanvantari (*H. Purāṇa*); a son of Kaviprajāpati (*M. Bh.*); the wife of Sudeva and the mother of Supārśva; another name for the sun.

**Kāśika** (S) (M) 1. the shining one. 3. the city of Benaras; a famous charioteer on the Pāṇḍava side (*M. Bh.*)

**Kāśin** (S) (M) 1. shining. 2. appearing like a conqueror.

**Kāśīnātha** (S) (M) 1. lord of Kāśī. 3. another name for Śiva.

**Kāśīpati** (S) (M) 1. lord of Kāśī. 3. another name for Divodāsa Dhanvantari a king of Benaras, the author of certain medical works and the teacher of Ayurveda.

**Kāśīrāja** (S) (M) 1. king of Kāśī. 3. the king of Kāśī and the father of Ambā, Ambikā and Ambālikā (*M. Bh.*)

**Kāśīrāma** (S) (M) 1. abode of Kāśī; living at Kāśī. 2. seeking deliverance at Kāśī.

**Kāśīśa** (S) (M) 1. lord of Kāśī. 3. another name for Śiva and Divodāsa.

**Kāśiṣṇu** (S) (M) shining; brilliant.

**Kāśīvara** (S) (F) 1. lord of Kāśī. 3. another name for Śiva.

**Kāśīviśvanātha** (S) (M) 1. universal lord of Kāśī; the idol of Kāśī. 3. another name for Śiva.

**Kāśmari** (S) (M) the Coomb tree (*Gmelina arborea*)

**Kāśmīra** (S) (M) grape; coming from Kāśmīr; *Costus speciosus*.

**Kāṣṭha** (S) (M) 1. a piece of wood. 3. an attendant of Kubera (*M. Bh.*)

**Kāṣṭhā** (S) (F) 1. the path of the wind; top; summit; cardinal point; a quarter of the world; a 16th of the moon; form; appearance; water; the sun. 3. a daughter of Dakṣa, the wife of Kaśyapa and the mother of the solidungulous quadripeds (*Bhā. Purāṇa*)

**Kastūra** (S) (M) musk; the Malabar whistling thrush (*Myophonus horsfieldii*)

**Kastūrī** (S) (F) scented with musk.

**Kasturīgandhī** (S) (F) 1. fragrant with musk. 3. another name for Kālī and Satyavatī.

**Kasturikā** (S) (F) musk.

**Kaśu** (S) (M) 1. an iron spear. 3. a Ćedi prince mentioned in the *Ṛg Veda* for his liberality.

**Kāsū** (S) (F) spear; lance; light; lustre; understanding.

**Kāśvī** (S) (F) shining; beautiful.

**Kāśya** (S) (M) 1. hard grass (*Saccharum spontaneum*); dried grass. 3. a kind of grass belonging to the Kāśīs; the king of Kāśī (*Ś. Brāhmaṇa*); the father of Kaśyapa and ancestor of Kāśirāja Dhanvantari (*H. Purāṇa*); the son of Suhotra (*Bhāgavata*); the son of Senājita (*Bhāgavata*); a king of Kāśī who was the father of Ambā, Ambikā and Ambālikā (*M. Bh.*); a sage (*M. Bh.*)

**Kāśyapa** (S) (M) 1. son of Kaśyapa. 3. a priest of Vasudeva and a friend of the Pāṇḍavas (*M. Bh.*); a son of Kaśyapa who was a member of Indra's assembly (*M. Bh.*); one of the 5 agnis (*M. Bh.*)

**Kaśyapa** (S) (M) 1. one who drinks water; one with black teeth; a tortoise. 3. chief of the prajāpatis, the son of Marīći, the grandson of Brahmā, husband of 21 wives and the father of all living beings in the world (*Ś. Brāhmaṇa*); a serpent who was present at Arjuna's birth (*M. Bh.*); a class of semi divine beings; that regulate the course of the sun (*V. Purāṇa*); the Water Lily (*Nymphaea esculenta*)

**Kaśyapeya** (S) (M) 1. belonging to Kaśyapa. 3. a patronymic of the 12 ādityas, Garuḍa and Aruṇa the sun.

**Kāśyapī** (S) (F) 1. belonging to Kaśyapa. 3. another name for the earth which was given as a gift to Kaśyapa by Paraśurāma.

**Kaṭaka** (S) (M) a bracelet of gold; the ring ornamenting an elephant's tusk.

**Katama** (S) (M) best; excessively handsome.

**Katamarāja** (S) (M) 1. best king. 2. king among the best.

**Kataprū** (S) (M) 1. gambler. 3. a vidyadhara; a rakṣasa; another name for Śiva.

**Kaṭha** (S) (M) 1. distress. 3. a sage who was a founder of a branch of *Yajur Veda* which is named after him.

**Kathaka** (S) (M) 1. reciting; narrating. 3. a

soldier of Skanda (*M. Bh.*)

**Kaṭhamarda** (S) (M) **1.** dispelling distress. **3.** another name for Śiva.

**Kathita** (S) (M) **1.** well recited; one about whom much is said. **2.** praised by all.

**Kati** (S) (M) **1.** how many? **2.** one possessed with many qualities. **3.** a sage who was the son of Viśvāmitra and the ancestor of Katyāyana (*Ṛg Veda*)

**Kātumbi** (S) (M) water purifier.

**Kātunga** (S) (M) **1.** seeker of the highest position. **3.** another name for King Dilīpa.

**Kaṭvaku** (S) (M) **1.** distressing speech. **2.** one who speaks of sad things. **3.** a son of Vaivasvata Manu who constructed Ayodhyā and was an ancestor of Ikṣvāku (*H. Purāṇa*)

**Kātyāyana** (S) (M) **1.** one who desires. **3.** a descendant of Kati; a grammarian who wrote a commentary on Pāṇini's work; a sage who lived in Indra's assembly (*M. Bh.*)

**Kātyāyanī** (S) (F) **1.** dressed in red. **3.** a wife of Yājñavalkya (*Rāmāyaṇa*); another name for Pārvatī.

**Kaukulikā** (S) (F) **1.** belonging to the universe. **2.** one who considers the universe as his family. **3.** a mother of Skanda (*M. Bh.*)

**Kaulīna** (S) (M) from a noble family.

**Kaumarī** (S) (F) **1.** the virgin. **2.** a rāgiṇī. **3.** another name for Pārvatī as the virgin goddess and the consort of Kārttikeya.

**Kaumodakī** (S) (M) **1.** festive; moon like; made of lilies. **3.** the club of Kṛṣṇa given to him by Varuṇa (*H. Purāṇa/Bhāgavata/M. Bh.*)

**Kaumudī** (S) (F) **1.** moonlight personified as the wife of Candra; festivity. **3.** full moon day in the month of Kārttika.

**Kauṇakutsya** (S) (M) **1.** despised due to drinking blood. **3.** a noble Brāhmin (*M. Bh.*)

**Kauṇapā** (S) (M) **1.** feeding on corpses. **3.** a serpent of the family of Vāsuki (*M. Bh.*)

**Kauṇapāśana** (S) (M) **1.** feeding on corpses. **3.** a serpent born in the Kaurava family (*M. Bh.*)

**Kauṇḍinya** (S) (M) **1.** one who lives by priesthood. **3.** a hermit who lived in the palace of Yudhiṣṭhira (*M. Bh.*)

**Kaunteya** (S) (M) **1.** son of Kuntī. **3.** another name for the Paṇḍavas; White Murdah (*Terminalia citrina*)

**Kaupodakī** (S) (M) **1.** made of lilies. **3.** the mace of Kṛṣṇa (*H. Purāṇa*)

**Kauravanandana** (S) (M) **1.** son of the Kurus. **3.** another name for Bhīsma, Yudhiṣṭhira and Duryodhana.

**Kauravanātha** (S) (M) **1.** lord of the Kauravas. **3.** another name for Yudhiṣṭhira and Dhṛtarāṣṭra.

**Kauravarāja** (S) (M) **1.** king of the Kauravas. **3.** another name for Dhṛtarāṣṭra.

**Kauravaśārdula** (S) (M) **1.** tiger of the Kurus; noblest of the kurus. **3.** another name for Bhīṣma and Yudhiṣṭhira.

**Kauravaśreṣṭha** (S) (M) **1.** best of the Kauravas. **3.** another name for Yudhiṣṭhira and Dhṛtarāṣṭra.

**Kauravendra** (S) (M) **1.** lord of the Kauravas. **3.** another name for Dhṛtarāṣṭra, Janamejaya and Duryodhana.

**Kauraveya** (S) (M) **1.** of the Kauravas. **3.** another name for Bhūriśravas, Yudhiṣṭhira and Duryodhana.

**Kauravya** (S) (M) **1.** of the Kuru clan. **3.** a noble serpent born of Airāvata who was the father of Ulūpi (*M. Bh.*); another name for Bhīṣma.

**Kauśa** (S) (M) silken; skill.

**Kauśala** (S) (M) **1.** welfare. **2.** well being; happiness; prosperity. **3.** Skanda in his goat faced incarnation (*M. Bh.*)

**Kausalā** (S) (F) **1.** from Kosala. **3.** a wife of Kṛṣṇa.

**Kauśalikā** (S) (F) **1.** present. **2.** offering.

**Kausalya** (S) (F) **1.** skill; welfare; cleverness; from Kosala. **3.** a wife of King Daśaratha and mother of Rāma (*V. Rāmāyaṇa*); the wife of the king of Kāśī and mother of Ambā, Ambikā, Ambālikā (*M. Bh.*); the wife of a Yādava king and mother of Keśin (*D. Bhāgavata*); the wife of King Janaka of Mithilā (*V. Rāmāyaṇa*); mother of Dhriṭarāṣṭra and Pāṇḍu; wife of Purū and mother of Janamejaya (*M. Bh.*)

**Kausalyānandavardhana** (S) (M) **1.** increasing joy and prosperity. **3.** another name for Pāṇḍu.

**Kauśikā** (S) (F) 1. drinking vessel; silk. 2. receptacle; cup. 3. a goddess sprung from the body of Pārvatī (*H. Purāṇa*)

**Kauśika** (S) (M) 1. knower of hidden treasure; a son of Kuśika; owl; sheathed; one who catches snakes; the sentiment of love. 3. a hermit who lived in the palace of Yudhiṣṭhira (*M. Bh.*); a son of Vasudeva; a rāga; an asura; a minister of Jarāsandha (*M. Bh.*); a king of the Purū dynasty who was the son of Kapila and the brother of Gṛtsapati who designed the 4 castes (*A. Purāṇa*); another name for Indra, Śiva and Viśvāmitra; *Commiphora mukui*; Indian Dammer tree (*Shorea robustea*); Arabian Jasmine (*Jasminum sambac*)

**Kauśikāćārya** (S) (M) 1. master of secrets. 3. another name for King Ākṛti who ruled over Saurāśtra (*M. Bh.*)

**Kauśikī** (S) (F) 1. sheathed; hidden; silken; covered. 3. Viśvāmitra's sister Satyavatī who turned into the Gomatī river beside which stood the hermitage of Viśvāmitra and which is now known as the Kosi and falls in Bihar (*H. Purāṇa*); another name for Durgā.

**Kauśtubha** (S) (M) 1. a heavenly jewel. 2. a diamond; a pearl. 3. a precious stone mentioned in the *Agni Purāṇa* as having originated from the Ocean of Milk and worn on the breast by Viṣṇu (*M. Bh.*)

**Kaustubhabhūsaṇa** (S) (M) 1. wearing the Kaustubha jewel. 3. another name for Kṛṣṇa.

**Kauṭilya** (S) (M) 1. crooked thinker. 3. writer of a renowned work on civil polity called the *Arthaśastra* and an advisor to King Ćandragupta.

**Kauṭiryā** (S) (F) 1. living in a hut. 3. another name for Durgā.

**Kautsa** (S) (M) 1. of the family of Kutsa. 2. that which is crooked; a hymn composed by Kutsa. 3. a sage and disciple of Varatantu who was given 14 crore gold coins by Emperor Raghu (*Raghuvanśa*)

**Kautukā** (S) (F) causing curiosity or admiration; giving pleasure.

**Kavaća** (S) (M) 1. armour. 3. a sage in the court of Indra (*M. Bh.*)

**Kavaćin** (S) (M) 1. covered with armour. 3. a son of Dhṛtarāṣṭra (*M. Bh.*); another name for Śiva.

**Kāvalī** (S) (F) bangle.

**Kavana** (S) (M) water.

**Kavaṣa** (S) (M) 1. shield. 3. a sage who was the son of Ilūṣa and the author of several hymns of the *Ṛg Veda* (*A. Brāhmaṇa*); an author of a *Dharmaśāstra*.

**Kavela** (S) (M) 1. water born. 2. a lotus flower.

**Kāverī** (S) (F) 1. full of water; a courtesan; turmeric. 3. a daughter of Yuvanāśva and wife of Jahnu changed into a holy river of south India and whose devī is a worshipper of Varuṇa (*Sk. Purāṇa*); a rāga; *Curcuma longa*.

**Kavi** (S) (M) 1. omniscient; knows medicine; a poet. 2. clever; wise; skilful; sensible; a physician; a surgeon; a singer. 3. a brother of Bhṛgu and Aṅgiras and the adopted son of Brahmā (*M. Bh.*); an agni who is the 5th son of Bṛhaspati (*Ṛg Veda*); a sage and son of Manu (*M. Bh.*); the youngest son of Śraddhādeva Manu and Śraddhā (*H. Purāṇa*); a son of Vaivasvata Manu (*V. Purāṇa*); another name for Brahmā, Śukra, the sun and sage Vālmīki.

**Kavibhūṣana** (S) (M) jewel among poets.

**Kavijyeṣṭha** (S) (M) 1. oldest of poets. 3. another name for Vālmīki.

**Kavikā** (S) (F) poetess.

**Kavikratu** (S) (M) of a poet's wisdom; wise.

**Kavīndra** (S) (M) prince among poets.

**Kavindu** (S) (M) 1. moon among poets. 3. another name for Vālmīki.

**Kavirāja** (S) (M) 1. chief of physicians; chief of poets. 2. wise; intelligent. 3. a Sanskṛt poet (12th century)

**Kaviratha** (S) (M) 1. with an excellent chariot. 3. a son of Ćitraratha.

**Kavīśa** (S) (M) 1. lord of poets; best physician. 3. a sage (*V. Rāmāyaṇa*); another name for Śukra.

**Kavīśvara** (S) (M) lord among poets.

**Kavitā** (S) (F) poem.

**Kavitara** (S) (M) 1. the great poet. 3. another name for Varuṇa who is supposed to be the god of oceans and oceans are forever singing songs by way of their tides.

**Kavitva** (S) (M) poetic ability; intelligence.

**Kāvya** (S) (M) 1. poem; intelligence; wisdom; prophetic inspiration. 2. endowed with the qualities of a sage or poet; descended from a sage; prophetic; inspired. 3. a son of Kavi Prajāpati (*M. Bh.*)

**Kāvyamātā** (S) (F) 1. mother of the poet; mother of the physician. 2. mother of an intelligent one. 3. the mother of Śukra the preceptor of the daityas (*V. Purāṇa*)

**Kayādhū** (S) (F) 1. removing illusion. 2. bestowing wisdom. 3. a wife of Hiraṇyakaśipu and the mother of Prahlāda (*Bhā. Purāṇa*)

**Kāyanavarman** (S) (M) 1. protector of duty. 3. a king of Kāmarūpa and husband of Gandharvavatī (*R. Taraṅginī*)

**Kedāra** (S) (M) 1. field; meadow. 3. peak of the Himālaya mountain (*M. Bh.*); a sacred place in Kurukṣetra and one of the 12 liṅga centres (*A. Koṣa*); a constellation (*V's. B. Samhitā*); a rāga; another name for Śiva.

**Kedārāja** (S) (M) 1. lord of the mountain. 3. Himalayan Cherry (*Prunus cerasoides*)

**Kedāranātha** (S) (M) 1. lord of meadows; lord of fields; lord of Mount Kedāra. 3. another name for Śiva.

**Kedāreśa** (S) (M) 1. lord of Mount Kedāra. 3. the statue of Śiva in Kāśī.

**Kedāreśvara** (S) (M) 1. lord of Mount Kedāra. 3. the statue of Śiva in Kāśī.

**Kekāralohita** (S) (M) 1. with fragrant red hair. 3. a great serpent (*K. Sāgara*)

**Kekārava** (S) (M) 1. cry of a peacock. 3. an asura (*M. Bh.*)

**Kekāvala** (S) (M) peacock.

**Kekaya** (S) (M) 1. full of water. 2. a place where there are many rivers, ponds and springs. 3. a king of the solar dynasty and father of Sudeṣna, Kīćaka and Upakīćaka (*M. Bh.*); a king who was the son of Śibi and the founder of the Kekaya dynasty (*Bhāgavata*); another name for Dhṛṣṭaketu.

**Kekayī** (S) (F) 1. princess of the Kekaya tribe. 3. wife of Daśaratha and mother of Bharata.

**Kelakā** (S) (F) 1. playful; sportive; knower of arts. 2. a dancer; a musician; a dancer who dances on the edge of a sword.

**Kelasa** (S) (M) crystal.

**Kelika** (S) (M) 1. sporting; sportive. 2. Asoka tree (*Saraca indica*)

**Kelikilā** (S) (F) 1. sport; amusement. 3. another name for Rati.

**Kenāti** (S) (F) 1. surpassing all. 3. another name for Rati, the wife of Kāma.

**Kerkhi** (S) (M) a gold necklace.

**Kesara** (S) (M) a hair of the brow; mane; saffron; the filament of any flower; Saffron (*Crocus sativus*); Ironwood tree (*Mesua ferrea*); *Mimusops elengi*.

**Kesarāj** (S) (M) 1. lord of hair. 3. *Eclipta alba; Wedelia calendulacea*.

**Kesarin** (S) (M) 1. lion; having a mane; of yellow complexion. 3. a forest king of the Mahāmeru mountain and the husband of Keśinī the mother of Hanumān (*V. Rāmāyaṇa*); the tree *Ochrocarpus longifolius*.

**Kesarini** (S) (F) saffron coloured; a lioness.

**Keśaṭa** (S) (M) 1. being richly endowed; an arrow of Kāma. 3. another name for Viṣṇu.

**Keśava** (S) (M) 1. long haired; slayer of Keśi. 3. the father of Brahmā and uncle of Maheśvara; another name for Viṣṇu and Kṛṣṇa.

**Keśavara** (S) (M) 1. having beautiful hair. 2. saffron (*Crocus sativus*); *Ochrocarpus longifolius*.

**Keśayanti** (S) (M) 1. long haired. 3. an attendant of Skanda (*M. Bh.*)

**Keśayantrī** (S) (F) 1. long haired. 3. a mother in Skanda's retinue (*M. Bh.*)

**Keśihā** (S) (M) 1. destroying Keśi. 3. another name for Kṛṣṇa.

**Keśihan** (S) (M) 1. slayer of Keśin. 3. another name for Kṛṣṇa.

**Keśihantā** (S) (M) 1. slayer of Keśin. 3. another name for Kṛṣṇa.

**Keśikā** (S) (F) 1. long haired. 3. the mother of Jahnu (*V. Purāṇa*); *Asparagus racemosus*.

**Keśin** (S) (M) 1. long haired. 2. lion. 3. an asura who was the son of Kaśyapa and Danu (*M. Bh.*); an asura who fought Kṛṣṇa and was killed by him (*Bhā. Purāṇa*); a son of Vasudeva and Kauśalyā (*Bhā. Purāṇa*); Bombay Hemp (*Hibiscus cannabinus*); Common Indigo (*Indigofera tinctoria*); another name for Rudra.

**Keśini** (S) (F) **1.** long haired. **3.** an apsarā who was the daughter of Kaśyapa and Prādhā and the mother of Hanumān (*M. Bh.*); the wife of King Ajamīdha and mother of Jahnu, Vraja and Rupinā (*A. Purāṇa*); the wife of Sudhanva the son of Aṅgiras (*M. Bh.*); a wife of King Sagara and the mother of Asamañjas (*V. Rāmāyaṇa*); the wife of Viśravas (*Bhā. Purāṇa*); a servant of Pārvatī (*A. Koṣa*); a maid of Damayantī (*Nalopākhyāna*); another name for Durgā.

**Keśinivadan** (S) (M) **1.** destroyer of Keśin. **3.** another name for Kṛṣṇa.

**Keśisūdana** (S) (M) **1.** slayer of Keśin. **3.** another name for Kṛṣṇa.

**Keśto, Keśut** (S) (M) **1.** son of Kesari. **3.** another name for Hanumān.

**Ketaka** (S) (M) banner; flag; gold ornament worn in the hair; the Ketaki flower (*Pandanus odoratissimus*)

**Ketakī** (S) (F) **1.** golden. **3.** the Ketakī flower (*Pandanus odoratissimus*) worn on Śiva's head.

**Ketana** (S) (M) **1.** house; flag; banner. **2.** sign; symbol; invitation.

**Ketita** (S) (M) called; summoned.

**Ketu** (S) (M) **1.** brightness; comet; the 9th planet; meteor; lamp; flame; form; intellect; flag; banner; leader. **3.** a dānava son of Kaśyapa and Danu who became a planet (*M. Bh.*); a king of Bharata's dynasty (*Bhāgavata*); the son of Ṛṣabha (*Bhā. Purāṇa*); a son of Agni (*R. Anukramaṇikā*); the 4th Manu (*A. Veda*); a sage (*M. Bh.*); another name for Śiva.

**Ketubha** (S) (M) cloud.

**Ketubhūta** (S) (M) **1.** having a symbol. **2.** a banner.

**Ketumāla** (S) (M) **1.** a garland of light. **3.** the grandson of Priyavrata (*M. Bh.*); a son of Āgnidhra (*V. Purāṇa*); a holy place in Jambūdvīpa where the people are equal to gods (*M. Bh.*)

**Ketumālin** (S) (M) **1.** garlanded with light. **3.** a dānava (*H. Purāṇa*)

**Ketumat** (S) (M) **1.** bright. **2.** splendid; with intellect. **3.** a king who fought on the side of the Paṇḍavas and was known for his valour (*M. Bh.*); the son of Dhanvantari and the father of Bhīmaratha (*Bhā. Purāṇa*); the son of Ekalavya who fought on the side of the Kauravas (*M. Bh.*); a son of Kṣema and father of Suketu (*H. Purāṇa*); a king who fought on the side of the Kauravas (*M. Bh.*); the regent of the western part of the world (*A. Purāṇa*); a king of the Purū dynasty (*M. Bh.*); a yakṣa (*A. Koṣa*); a mountain; the palace of Sudattā, one of Kṛṣṇa's wives (*H. Purāṇa*)

**Ketumatī** (S) (F) **1.** endowed with brightness. **3.** the wife of Sumālin and the mother of Prahasta a minister in Rāvaṇa's court (*V. Rāmāyaṇa*)

**Keturatna** (S) (M) a bright jewel; Rahu's favourite; beryl; Lapis lazuli.

**Ketuśṛṅga** (S) (M) **1.** horn bannered; with shining horns. **3.** a king of ancient India (*M. Bh.*)

**Ketutārā** (S) (M) comet.

**Ketuvarman** (S) (M) **1.** flag shooter. **2.** one whose flag flies everywhere. **3.** a ćakravartin; a prince of Trigarta (*M. Bh.*)

**Ketuvīrya** (S) (M) **1.** with the strength of a leader. **3.** a king of Magadha; a dānava (*H. Purāṇa*)

**Kevala** (S) (M) **1.** alone; absolute; exclusive. **2.** pure; whole; perfect.

**Kevalī** (S) (F) **1.** one who has attained the absolute. **3.** a Jaina who has achieved pure, absolute knowledge (*J. Literature*)

**Kevalin** (S) (M) seeker of the absolute.

**Kevikā** (S) (F) flower of the *Pandanus odoratissimus*.

**Keya** (S) (M) speed.

**Keyūra** (S) (M) armlet.

**Keyūraka** (S) (M) **1.** one who wears an armlet. **3.** a gandharva (*Kādambarī*)

**Keyūradharā** (S) (F) **1.** one who wears an armlet. **3.** an apsarā (*K. Vyuha*)

**Keyūrin** (S) (F) with an armlet.

**Khaḍga** (S) (M) **1.** sword. **2.** scimitar; a rhino

horn. 3. a warrior of Skanda (*M. Bh.*)

**Khaḍgahastā** (S) (F) 1. sword-handed. 3. an attendant of Devī.

**Khaḍgin** (S) (M) 1. armed with a sword. 3. another name for Śiva.

**Khādi** (S) (M) brooch or ring worn by the maruts.

**Khadira** (S) (M) 1. heavenly; celestial; Black Catechu tree (*Acacia catechu*). 3. another name for Indra and the moon.

**Khadirikā** (S) (F) 1. the Lājvantī creeper (*Mimosa pudica*). 3. another name for Indra and the moon.

**Khadyota** (S) (M) 1. light of the sky; firefly. 3. another name for the sun.

**Khaga** (S) (M) 1. moving in the air. 2. sun; planet; air; wind; bird. 3. a serpent born in the family of Kaśyapa (*M. Bh.*); another name for Śiva.

**Khagādhirāja** (S) (M) 1. lord of the birds. 3. another name for Garuḍa.

**Khagaṇa** (S) (M) 1. moving through space. 3. a king born in the family of Rāma who was the son of Vajranābha and the father of Vidhṛti (*V. Purāṇa*)

**Khagaṅgā** (S) (F) the celestial Gaṅgā.

**Khagañja** (S) (M) 1. best among birds. 3. the father of Gokarneśvara (*Bhā. Purāṇa*)

**Khagāsana** (S) (M) 1. seat of the sun. 3. the mountain Udaya (*M. Bh.*); Viṣṇu whose seat is a bird.

**Khagendra** (S) (M) 1. lord of birds. 3. another name for Garuḍa.

**Khageśa** (S) (M) 1. lord of birds. 3. another name for Garuḍa.

**Khageśvara** (S) (M) 1. lord of birds. 3. another name for Garuḍa.

**Khajit** (S) (M) 1. conquering heaven. 3. a Buddha (*B. Literature*)

**Khalā** (S) (F) 1. mischievous. 3. a daughter of Raudrāśva.

**Khalin** (S) (M) 1. one who possesses threshing floors. 3. another name for Mahāviṣṇu and Śiva.

**Khalu** (S) (F) 1. indeed! verily! 3. a river of ancient India (*M. Bh.*)

**Khamūrti** (S) (M) a celestial person.

**Khanaka** (S) (M) 1. miner; digger. 3. a messenger sent by Vidura to the Pāṇḍavas to save them from the burning house (*M. Bh.*)

**Khanḍakhanḍā** (S) (F) 1. found in pieces. 3. a female attendant of Skanda (*M. Bh.*)

**Khanḍaparaśu** (S) (M) 1. cutting one's foes with an axe. 3. the weapons of Śiva and Viṣṇu (*M. Bh.*); another name for Śiva and Rāhu.

**Khāṇḍava** (S) (M) 1. sugar candy; sweetmeat. 3. a forest in Kurukṣetra sacred to Indra.

**Khāndikya** (S) (M) 1. that which cuts. 3. a Kśatriya king (*H. Purāṇa*); another name for Janaka.

**Khanḍinī** (S) (F) 1. made of parts; having continents. 3. the earth.

**Khaninetra** (S) (M) 1. with eyes like a mine of jewels. 3. the eldest son of King Vivinśa of the solar dynasty (*M. Bh.*)

**Khaṇjana** (S) (M) bird; a dimple.

**Khapagā** (S) (F) 1. stream of the heavens. 3. another name for the Gaṅgā.

**Khapūra** (S) (M) full of space; filler of the skies; the betel nut tree.

**Khara** (S) (M) 1. an ass; hard; harsh; rough; sharp; solid; dense; cutting; thorny. 3. a rākṣasa who was a son of Viśravas and Rākā (*V. Rāmāyaṇa*)

**Kharag** (S) (M) sword.

**Kharajaṅghā** (S) (F) 1. solid shanked; strong thighed. 3. a mother in the retinue of Skanda (*M. Bh.*)

**Kharakarṇī** (S) (F) 1. ass eared. 3. a mother of the retinue of Skanda (*M. Bh.*)

**Kharānsu** (S) (M) 1. sharp rayed. 3. another name for the sun.

**Kharapuṣpā** (S) (F) pungent flower; a sharp leaved variety of ocimum.

**Khararoman** (S) (M) 1. with rough hair. 3. a nāga chief.

**Kharī** (S) (F) 1. mule. 3. a mother of the retinue of Skanda (*M. Bh.*)

**Kharikā** (S) (F) powered musk.

**Kharjūrī** (S) (F) reaching the skies; the Wild Date tree (*Phoenix sylvestris*)

**Kharu** (S) (M) 1. white; horse; pride. 3. another name for Kāma and Śiva.

**Khaśā** (S) (F) 1. pervading the air. 2. a kind

of perfume. 3. a wife of Kaśyapa (*V. Purāṇa*) and mother of the yakṣas and rākṣasas.

**Khasama** (S) (M) 1. resting in the air. 3. a Buddha.

**Khasarpaṇa** (S) (M) 1. gliding through the air. 3. a Buddha.

**Khaśaya** (S) (M) 1. resting in the air. 3. a Jina.

**Khatilaka** (S) (M) 1. ornament of the sky. 3. another name for the sun.

**Khatū** (S) (F) an ornament worn on the wrist or ankle.

**Khaṭvānga** (S) (M) 1. leg of the cot; with a skull headed club. 3. a weapon of Śiva (*G's. Dharmaśastra*); another name for the Ikṣvāku dynasty King Dilīpa (*Bhā. Purāṇa*); an attendant of Devī.

**Khaṭvāngādhari** (S) (M) 1. bearing the Khaṭvānga club. 3. another name for Śiva.

**Khayāli** (S) (M) one who moves in the sky.

**Khela** (S) (M) 1. sport. 3. another name for Vivasvata in whose honour games were held.

**Khelī** (S) (F) 1. moving in the sky. 2. arrow; bird; sun; song; hymn.

**Khevanarāja** (S) (M) the best rower.

**Khila** (S) (M) 1. wasteland. 2. desert; bare soil; a hymn added to the collection. 3. another name for Vāyu, Śiva and Brahmā.

**Khilāvan** (S) (M) 1. one who plays in the sky; an arrow. 3. another name for the sun.

**Khokhun** (S) (M) boy.

**Kholka** (S) (M) sky meteor.

**Khullanā** (S) (F) 1. small. 3. a tutelary deity of Bengal (*T. Śastra*)

**Khullana** (S) (M) small; little.

**Khuśila** (H) (M) happy; pleasant.

**Khuśirāma** (H) (M) one who lives happily.

**Khuśmana** (H) (M) with a happy mind.

**Khuśvanta** (H) (M) bearer of happiness.

**Khyāna** (S) (M) perception; knowledge.

**Khyāta** (S) (M) 1. pervading the sky; celebrated; named; called. 3. an attendant of Skanda (*M. Bh.*)

**Khyāti** (S) (F) 1. declaration; view; perception; idea; knowledge; celebrity; glory; hymn of praise. 3. a daughter of Dakṣa, the wife of Bhṛgu and the mother of Dāta, Vidhātā and Lakṣmī (*A. Purāṇa*); a daughter of King Kuru and Āgneyi (*V. Purāṇa*); one of the 9 daughters of Kardama and Devahūtī (*D. Bh. Purāṇa*); another name for Lakṣmī.

**Kīćaka** (S) (M) 1. hollow bamboo. 3. the chief of the army of King Virāṭa (*M. Bh.*); the son of Kekaya and Mālavī who was killed in the palace of Virāṭa by Bhīma (*M. Bh.*); a rākṣasa (*A. Koṣa*); Wild Tobacco (*Lobelia nicotianaefolia*)

**Kīkaṭa** (S) (M) 1. horse. 3. a king born in the dynasty of Priyavrata who was a son of King Bharata (*Bhāgavata*); a son of Ṛṣabha (*Bhā. Purāṇa*); a son of Śaṅkāta (*M. Bh.*); a tribe (*Bhā. Purāṇa*)

**Kiki** (S) (F) Bluejay (*Coracias garrulus*)

**Kīla** (S) (M) 1. flame. 3. another name for Agni.

**Kilāla** (S) (F) 1. nectar; wine. 3. a sweet heavenly drink akin to Amṛta (*A. Veda*)

**Kilāta** (S) (M) 1. dwarf. 3. an asura priest (*A. Koṣa*)

**Kīli** (S) (F) 1. parrot. 3. a parrot said to be the offspring of Kaśyapa and Śuki (*Rāmāyaṇa*)

**Kilkita** (S) (M) Pied Kingfisher (*Ceryle rudis leucomelanura*)

**Kiṁćaṇaka** (S) (M) 1. very small. 3. a nāga.

**Kiṁdatta** (S) (M) 1. given what?; one who has been given very little. 3. a sacred well of the *Mahābhārata*.

**Kiṁkara** (S) (M) 1. what to do?; servant. 3. one of Śiva's attendants (*K. Sāgara*); Kāla's stick which strikes down living beings (*M. Bh.*); a race of Ćākṣasas who built Indraprastha for the Pāṇḍavas (*M. Bh.*)

**Kiṁnara** (S) (M) 1. what sort of man? 2. unmanly; a singer. 3. a sect of demi-gods and celebrated musicians attached to Kubera, portrayed as horse headed with rest of their bodies in human shape, holding vīṇās in their hands (*A. Purāṇa*); the attendant of the 15th Arhat of the present Avasarpiṇī; the son of Vibhīṣaṇa (*V. Rāmāyaṇa*)

**Kiṁnarī** (S) (F) 1. female singer. 3. a singer in Indra's court (*V. Rāmāyaṇa*)

**Kimpunā** (S) (F) 1. small and pious. 3. a river in Devaloka which worships Varuṇa (*M. Bh.*)

**Kiṁpuruṣa** (S) (M) 1. what man? 2. a very

small man; a dwarf. 3. one of the 9 sons of Āgnidhra (*V. Purāṇa*)

**Kiṁśuka** (S) (F) 1. a very small parrot; which parrot? 3. the parrot shaped; odourless blossoms of *Butea frondosa*; Intellect Tree (*Celastrus paniculata*)

**Kīnāśa** (S) (M) 1. cultivator of the soil. 2. ploughman. 3. a rākṣasa (*Ṛg Veda*); another name for Yama.

**Kindama** (S) (M) 1. conqueror of the proud. 3. a sage who was killed while in the form of a deer by King Pāṇḍu (*M. Bh.*)

**Kiṇjalā** (S) (F) brook.

**Kiṇjalka** (S) (M) blossom of a lotus; Ironwood tree (*Mesua ferrea*)

**Kiñjata** (S) (M) blossom.

**Kiṅkana** (S) (M) 1. lotus bud; bell. 3. a king of the lunar dynasty and the son of King Mahābhoja (*Bhāgavata*)

**Kinkiṇa** (S) (M) 1. small drum. 3. son of Bhajamāna (*Bh. Purāṇa*)

**Kiṅkiṇā** (S) (F) 1. a small bell. 3. a tantric goddess.

**Kiṅkira** (S) (M) 1. horse; Indian cuckoo (*Cuculus scolopaceus*); black bee. 3. another name for Kāma.

**Kiṅkirāta** (S) (M) 1. parrot; Indian cuckoo (*Cuculus scolopaceus*). 3. another name for Kāma.

**Kiraṇa** (S) (M) 1. dust; very minute particle of dust. 2. ray or beam of light; a sun or moon beam.

**Kiraṇamālin** (S) (M) 1. garlanded with rays. 2. bright; illuminating; enlightening. 3. another name for the sun.

**Kiraṇamaya** (S) (M) 1. full of rays; consisting of rays. 2. radiant; brilliant; enlightening. 3. another name for the sun.

**Kiraṇamayī** (S) (F) full of rays.

**Kiraṇapāṇi** (S) (M) 1. ray handed. 3. another name for the sun.

**Kiraṇapati** (S) (M) 1. lord of rays. 3. another name for the sun.

**Kirāta** (S) (M) 1. cave dwellers. 3. hunters of a mountain tribe; Śiva in his form as a warrior of the Kirāta tribe (*M. Bh.*)

**Kirātī** (S) (F) 1. from the mountain. 3. another name for Pārvatī and the Gaṅgā.

**Kirika** (S) (M) sparkling; beaming.

**Kīriṇ** (S) (M) 1. one who praises. 2. a poet; a writer; a speaker.

**Kirīṭa** (S) (M) 1. crown; diadem. 2. crest; tiara.

**Kirīṭabhṛt** (S) (M) 1. wearing a diadem. 3. another name for Arjuna.

**Kirīṭin** (S) (M) 1. one who wears a crown. 3. a warrior of Skanda (*M. Bh.*); another name for Arjuna and Indra; White Murdah (*Terminalia citrina*)

**Kirīṭitanayātmaja** (S) (M) 1. grandson of Arjuna. 3. another name for Parīkṣit.

**Kirmī** (S) (F) an image of gold.

**Kirmīra** (S) (M) 1. of variegated colour. 3. a rākṣasa who was a friend of Hiḍimba (*M. Bh.*)

**Kīrtana** (S) (M) praise; praising; repeating.

**Kīrtenya** (S) (M) worthy of praise.

**Kīrti** (S) (F) 1. fame; renown; glory. 3. a daughter of Śuka the son of Vyāsa and Pīvari and the wife of prince Aṇu the son of King Brahmadatta (*D. Bhāgavata*); a daughter of Dakṣa and Prasūti and a wife of Dharma (*V. Purāṇa*); the goddess of fame and reputation (*M. Bh.*)

**Kīrtibhāj** (S) (M) 1. famous. 3. another name for Droṇāćārya.

**Kīrtibhuṣaṇa** (S) (M) one whose ornament is fame.

**Kīrtida** (S) (F) 1. one who bestows fame. 3. Rādhā's mother (*Bhā. Purāṇa*)

**Kīrtideva** (S) (M) lord of light; lord of fame.

**Kīrtidhara** (S) (M) bearer of fame; famous.

**Kīrtidharmā** (S) (M) 1. one to whom fame comes naturally. 3. a Kṣatriya who fought on the side of the Pāṇḍavas (*M. Bh.*)

**Kīrtimālinī** (S) (F) 1. garlanded with fame. 3. an attendant of Skanda (*Sk. Purāṇa*)

**Kīrtimān** (S) (M) 1. famous. 3. the 1st son of Vasudeva and Devakī (*Bhā. Purāṇa*); a son of Vīrajas the mindborn son of Brahmā and the father of Kardama (*M. Bh.*); the son of Uttānapāda and Sūnṛtā (*H. Purāṇa*); a son of Aṅgiras (*V. Purāṇa*); a viśvadeva (*M. Bh.*)

**Kīrtimanta** (S) (M) 1. famous. 3. the eldest son of Vasudeva and Devakī (*V. Purāṇa*)

**Kīrtimaya** (S) (M) 1. consisting of fame. 2. famous.

**Kīrtimukha** (S) (M) 1. with a famous face. 3. a gaṇa born from the hair of Śiva (*Ś. Purāṇa*)

**Kīrtiratha** (S) (M) 1. one who has fame as a chariot. 2. one who travels in the chariot of fame. 3. a prince of Videha and son of Prasiddhaka (*V. Rāmāyaṇa*)

**Kīrtisena** (S) (M) 1. with a glorious army. 3. a nephew of Vāsuki and the husband of Śrutārtha (*K. Sāgara*)

**Kīrtita** (S) (M) famous; celebrated.

**Kisalaya** (S) (M) 1. sprout. 2. a young shoot.

**Kiṣeṇrāj** (S) (M) the Hairchested Drongo (*Corvus hottentottus*)

**Kiṣku** (S) (M) the forearm; handle of an axe.

**Kiśni** (S) (M) 1. killer of enemies. 2. a good administrator.

**Kiśora** (S) (M) 1. adolescent; colt. 2. youth. 3. another name for Kṛṣṇa and the sun.

**Kiśorī** (S) (F) maiden; adolescent.

**Kiśorīlāla** (S) (M) 1. beloved of maidens. 3. another name for Kṛṣṇa.

**Kiṣṭikumāra** (S) (M) prince of saviours.

**Kīṭaka** (S) (M) 1. worm like. 3. a king born from an aspect of the asura Krodhavaśa (*M. Bh.*)

**Kitava** (S) (M) 1. gambler. 3. another name for Śakuni.

**Kiyā** (S) (F) the cooing of a bird.

**Kiyedha** (S) (M) 1. abounding in; containing much. 3. another name for Indra.

**Kodaṇḍin** (S) (M) 1. armed with a bow. 3. another name for Śiva.

**Koel** (S) (M) the Indian cuckoo (*Cuculus scolopaceus*)

**Kohala** (S) (M) 1. spirituous barley. 2. one that intoxicates. 3. a musical instrument (*A. Koṣa*); a Brahmin scholar (*Va. Purāṇa*); a sage who invented drama (*M. Bh.*)

**Kohi** (S) (M) Shahin falcon (*Falco peregrinator*)

**Kokā** (S) (M) (F) 1. cuckoo; Ruddy Shelduck (*Anas casarca*); Wild Date tree (*Phoenix sylvestris*). 3. an attendant of Skanda (*M. Bh.*); the earlier name of the river Śoṇa

(*Ś. Brāhmaṇa*); another name for Viṣṇu.

**Kokabandhu** (S) (M) 1. friend of the Ruddy Shelduck. 3. another name for the sun.

**Kokanada** (S) (M) 1. the voice of the cuckoo; the red water lily (*Nymphaea rubra*); reed of a flower. 3. a Kṣatriya king who was a minor ally of Arjuna (*M. Bh.*); a warrior of Skanda (*M. Bh.*)

**Kokila** (S) (M) Indian cuckoo (*Cuculus Scolopaceus*); firebrand.

**Kokiladevī** (S) (F) 1. goddess of the cuckoo. 2. with a sweet sound. 3. a goddess (*T. Śastra*)

**Kokilaka** (S) (M) 1. Indian cuckoo (*Cuculus scolopaceus*). 3. a warrior of Skanda (*M. Bh.*)

**Kola** (S) (M) 1. hog; embrace; a weapon. 3. a son of Ākrīḍa; another name for Śiva and the Planet Saturn.

**Kolāhala** (S) (M) 1. loud noise; chaos. 3. a rāga.

**Kolambī** (S) (F) Śiva's lute.

**Komala** (S) (M) 1. tender; soft; delicate. 2. sweet; handsome; beautiful.

**Komri** (S) (M) the Grey Junglefowl (*Gallus sonnerati*)

**Koṅkaṇā** (S) (F) 1. living on the western shores. 3. the mother of Paraśurāma (*A. Koṣa*)

**Kooñj** (S) (M) Demoiselle Crane (*Ardea virgo*)

**Kopana** (S) (M) 1. angry; passionate. 3. an asura (*H. Purāṇa*)

**Kopavega** (S) (M) 1. impetuosity of passion; passionate; full of anger. 3. a hermit who served Yudhiṣṭhira (*M. Bh.*)

**Kośin** (S) (F) bud; the mango tree (*Mangifera indica*)

**Koṣṭhakoṭi** (S) (M) 1. store house consisting of 10 million rooms. 3. an attendant of Śiva (*A. Koṣa*)

**Koṣṭhavān** (S) (M) 1. store house; a vessel of grain. 3. a mountain which is the overlord of many mountains (*M. Bh.*)

**Koṭarā** (S) (F) 1. hollow of a tree. 3. an attendant of Skanda (*M. Bh.*); the mother of Bāṇa (*Bhā. Purāṇa*); another name for Durgā.

**Koṭaraka** (S) (M) 1. hollow of a tree. 2. one who lives in the hollow of a tree. 3. a serpent from the Kaśyapa family (*M. Bh.*)

**Kotavī** (S) (M) 1. naked woman. 2. a form of Durgā; the tutelary deity of the daityas.

**Koṭijit** (S) (M) 1. conquering millions. 3. another name for Kālidāsa.

**Koṭikāśya** (S) (M) 1. abode of millions. 3. a king of Tṛgarta and son of Suratha who was a follower of Jayadratha (*M. Bh.*)

**Kotira** (S) (M) 1. horned. 3. another name for Indra.

**Koṭīśa** (S) (M) 1. pointed harrow; lord of millions. 3. a serpent born in the family of Vāsuki (*M. Bh.*)

**Koṭiśrī** (S) (F) 1. goddess of millions. 3. another name for Durgā.

**Kotisthā** (S) (F) 1. goddess of millions. 3. tutelary deity of the Ćyavana family (*Br. Purāṇa*)

**Koṭīśvara** (S) (M) lord of millions.

**Koṭṭa** (S) (M) fort.

**Koṭṭeśvarī** (S) (F) 1. goddess of the fort. 3. another name for Durgā.

**Kovida** (S) (M) knowledgeable; wise.

**Krakaća** (S) (M) 1. a saw. 3. a priest (*Ś. Vijaya*)

**Krama** (S) (M) 1. order. 2. sequence; course; custom; succession.

**Kramajit** (S) (M) 1. In succession; succeeding. 3. a Kṣatriya king and constant follower of Yudhiṣṭhira (*M. Bh.*)

**Kramaṇa** (S) (M) 1. a step; the foot; a horse. 3. a son of Bhajamāna (*H. Purāṇa*)

**Kramapa** (S) (M) 1. step by step. 3. a son of Pulaha and Kṣamā (*A. Purāṇa*)

**Kramu** (S) (M) 1. going; proceeding. 2. the Betel-nut tree (*Areca catechu*). 3. a river in Plakṣadvīpa (*V. Purāṇa*)

**Krānti** (S) (F) 1. revolution; the sun's course; surpassing. 2. going; proceeding; overcoming.

**Krāntivīra** (S) (M) brave warrior.

**Kratha** (S) (M) 1. suffocated; to hurt; to injure. 3. a Kṣatriya king who was an incarnation of Krodhavaśa (*M. Bh.*); a king defeated by Bhīma (*M. Bh.*); a son of Vidarbha and brother of Kaiśika (*M. Bh.*); a warrior on the side of the Kauravas (*M. Bh.*); a warrior of Skanda (*M. Bh.*); a yakṣa who fought with Garuḍa (*M. Bh.*); a demon reborn as King Sūryākṣa (*H. Purāṇa*); a son of Dhṛtarāṣṭra (*M. Bh.*); a hermit (*M. Bh.*)

**Krathana** (S) (M) 1. one who is in danger of suffocation. 3. a nāga son of Dhṛtarāṣṭra (*M. Bh.*); an asura (*H. Purāṇa*)

**Kratu** (S) (M) 1. plan; resolution; power; intention; wisdom; sacrifice. 2. intelligence; ability; determination; will; purpose; design; desire; enlightenment; worship; the month of Āṣāḍha. 3. one of the 6 mindborn sons of Brahmā and a prajāpati (*M. Smṛti*); a viśvadeva (*V. Purāṇa*); a son of Kṛṣṇa (*Bh. Purāṇa*); a son of Ūru and Āgneyī (*H. Purāṇa*); another name for Viṣṇu.

**Kratubhuj** (S) (M) 1. one who eats the sacrificial oblation. 2. a god; a deity.

**Kratudhvansī** (S) (M) 1. destroyer of Dakṣa's sacrifice. 3. another name for Śiva.

**Kratukaraṇa** (S) (M) 1. perfect in oblation. 3. a sacrificial offering (*Ā. Śrauta Sūtra*)

**Kratumata** (S) (M) 1. wise; having power. 2. intelligent; prudent; vigorous. 3. a son of Viśvāmitra (*Bhā. Purāṇa*)

**Kratumaya** (S) (M) endowed with wisdom.

**Kratupati** (S) (M) lord of sacrifice; lord of wisdom.

**Kratvāmagha** (S) (M) 1. gift of wisdom. 2. constituting a reward gained through intelligence.

**Kratvaṅga** (S) (M) 1. pot of sacrifice. 2. a utensil used in sacrifices.

**Krauḍa** (S) (M) 1. belonging to a hog; coming from a hog. 3. the incarnation of Viṣṇu as a boar.

**Krauñća** (S) (M) 1. curlew; osprey; snipe; heron. 3. the emblem of the 5th Arhat of the present Avasarpiṇī (*He. Koṣa*); a mountain range in North Assam said to have been split by Kārttikeya (*V. Purāṇa*); an asura killed by Kārttikeya (*Vām. Purāṇa*)

**Krauñćī** (S) (F) 1. curlew; snipe; heron. 3. a daughter of Kaśyapa and Tāmrā and the mother of curlews (*V. Rāmāyaṇa*)

**Krīḍana** (S) (M) 1. playing. 3. another name for the wind.

**Kriti** (S) (F) 1. action; creation. 3. a wife of Saṁhrāda and mother of Panćajana (*Bh. Purāṇa*)

**Kriya** (S) (M) literary composition; energy; ability; accomplishment; act; instruction; knowledge; worship; the zodiac sign of Aries.

**Kriyā** (S) (F) 1. performance; work; action. 3. religious action personified as a daughter of Dakṣa and wife of Dharma (*M. Bh.*); or as a daughter of Kardama and wife of Kratu (*Bh. Purāṇa*)

**Kriyāvidhi** (S) (M) 1. a rule of action; method of doing. 2. accomplished person/method.

**Kṛkaneyu** (S) (M) 1. one who shouts repeatedly; one who wins again and again. 2. a cock. 3. a son of Raudrāśva (*M. Bh.*)

**Kṛkavākudhvaja** (S) (M) 1. with a cock for his banner. 3. another name for Kārttikeya.

**Kṛmī** (S) (F) 1. silkworm; ant; lac-insect. 3. a wife of Uśīnara and mother of Kṛmi (*H. Purāṇa*); a river (*M. Bh.*)

**Kṛmi** (S) (M) 1. silkworm; ant; lac-insect. 3. a king of the dynasty of Aṅga and the son of King Uśīnara (*A. Purāṇa*); the brother of Rāvaṇa (*V. Rāmāyaṇa*); a serpent lord.

**Kṛmilāśva** (S) (M) 1. with worms; having snakes. 3. a king of the Purū dynasty who was the son of King Bāhyāśvana (*M. Bh.*)

**Kṛmīśa** (S) (M) 1. lord of serpents. 3. a yakṣa (*Divyāvadāna*); hell (*V. Purāṇa*)

**Kroḍakāntā** (S) (F) 1. dear to Saturn. 3. another name for the earth.

**Kroḍāṅka** (S) (M) a tortoise.

**Krodhā** (S) (F) 1. angry. 3. passion personified as a child of Lobha and Nikṛti (*V. Purāṇa*); a daughter of Dakṣa and wife of Kaśyapa (*M. Bh.*); a dānava (*M. Bh.*)

**Krodha** (S) (M) 1. anger. 3. an asura born to Kaśyapa and Kalā (*M. Bh.*); a son of Brahmā born from his eyebrow (*V. Samhitā*)

**Krodhanā** (S) (F) 1. an angry woman; bad tempered. 2. a passionate woman; vixen. 3. a mother in Skanda's retinue (*M. Bh.*); a yoginī; another name for Durgā.

**Krodhana** (S) (M) 1. bad tempered. 3. an important hermit in the palace of Indra (*M. Bh.*); a son of Kauśika and pupil of Garga (*H. Purāṇa*); a son of Ayuta and father of Devātithi (*Bhā. Purāṇa*); an attendent of Skanda (*M. Bh.*)

**Krodhavaśā** (S) (F) 1. the power of passion. 2. passionate. 3. a daughter of Dakṣa and wife of Kaśyapa whose asura children guarded the lotus lake of Kubera (*M. Bh.*)

**Krodhavaśa** (S) (M) 1. the power of anger. 3. a follower of Indrajit (*M. Bh.*); a rākṣasa (*M. Bh.*)

**Krośanā** (S) (F) 1. crying. 3. a mother in Skanda's retinue (*M. Bh.*)

**Kroṣṭa** (S) (M) 1. crying; calling out. 3. a son of Yadu (*H. Purāṇa*)

**Kroṣṭu** (S) (M) 1. one who cries; jackal. 3. a son of Yadu and father of Vṛjinīvata (*Bhā. Purāṇa*)

**Kroṣṭukī** (S) (F) 1. jackal. 3. a daughter of Krodhavaśā and mother of the yellow apes (*M. Bh.*)

**Kṛpa** (S) (M) 1. beauty; splendour; appearance; pity; tenderness; compassion; kindness; favour. 3. a powerful king of ancient India who practiced strict vegetarianism (*M. Bh.*); the son of sage Śaradvata and Janapadī, the twin brother of Kṛpi, brought up by King Śāntanu, a member of the Hastināpura council, a master of archery and the preceptor of the Kauravas and Pāṇḍavas (*M. Bh.*); one of the 10 Ćirañjīvīs or immortals (*M. Bh.*); a friend of Indra (*Ṛg Veda*); a river (*M. Bh.*)

**Kṛpā** (S) (F) compassion; favour; kindness; pity.

**Kṛpādvaita** (S) (M) 1. unrivalled in compassion. 3. a Buddha (*B. Ćarita*)

**Kṛpāla** (S) (M) kind; gentle.

**Kṛpāṇa** (S) (M) sword; dagger; scimitar.

**Kṛpāṇaka** (S) (M) sword; dagger; scimitar.

**Kṛpānanda** (S) (M) one who pleases with his kindness; one who takes delight in kindness.

**Kṛpānīla** (S) (M) 1. dwelling in splendour. 3. another name for Agni (*Ṛg Veda*)

**Kṛpāsāgara** (S) (M) ocean of compassion.

**Kṛpāśankarā** (S) (M) Śiva, the merciful.

**Kṛpī** (S) (F) 1. beautiful. 3. the daughter of sage Śaradvata and apsarā Janapadī, the sister of Kṛpa, the wife of Droṇa and the mother of Aśvatthāman (*M. Bh.*)

**Kṛpīṭayoni** (S) (M) 1. wood born. 3. another

name for Agni.

**Kṛśa** (S) (M) 1. lean. 3. a hermit and friend of sage Śṛṅgi (*M.Bh./Ṛg Veda*); a serpent of the family of Airāvata (*M. Bh.*); a sage endowed with divine powers (*M. Bh.*)

**Kṛṣadratha** (S) (M) 1. one who pulls the chariot. 3. the son of Titīkṣa and nephew of Emperor Śibi (*Bhāgavata*)

**Kṛṣaka** (S) (M) 1. farmer. 3. a sage who stood guard over Soma (*A. Veda*)

**Kṛśāluretas** (S) (M) 1. with thin seed. 3. another name for Śiva.

**Kṛśaṇ** (S) (M) 1. mother of pearl. 2. pearl; gold; form; yielding pearls.

**Kṛśaṇa** (S) (F) pearl; gold; form; shape.

**Kṛśaṇćandra** (S) (M) 1. moon and pearl conjoined. 3. another name of Vasudeva.

**Kṛṣāṅgā** (S) (F) 1. slender. 2. bean bodied; 3. an apsarā; another name for the Priyaṅgu creeper; *Aglaia odoratissima*; *Capparis zeylanica*.

**Kṛṣāṅga** (S) (M) 1. thin. 3. another name for Śiva.

**Krśāngī** (S) (F) 1. slender. 3. an apsarā.

**Kṛśaṇin** (S) (M) decorated with pearls.

**Kṛśānu** (S) (M) 1. archer. 3. a divine being identified with Rudra; a sage (*Ṛg Veda*); a gandharva; another name for Viṣṇu and Agni.

**Kṛśāśva** (S) (M) 1. with lean horses. 3. a prajāpati who married Jayā and Suprabhā the daughters of Dakṣa and had a 100 sons in the form of a 100 arrows that Viśvāmitra gave Rāma and Lakṣmaṇa (*V. Rāmāyaṇa*); a king of the solar dynasty (*Bhāgavata*); a king who served Yama in his court (*M. Bh.*)

**Kṛśeyu** (S) (M) 1. striving to be slender. 2. one who is body conscious. 3. a king of the Purū dynasty (*M. Bh.*)

**Kṛṣi** (S) (F) ploughing; the cultivation of the soil personified; the earth.

**Kṛṣivala** (S) (M) 1. farmer; tiller. 3. a sage who lived in Indra's court (*M. Bh.*)

**Kṛṣṇā** (S) (F) 1. dark; night. 2. pupil of the eye; a dark blossomed and dark blossomed plant; a kind of perfume. 3. the daughter of King Drupada who married the 5 Pāṇḍava brothers and was known as Draupadī or Pānćālī (*M. Bh.*); a river in South India (*Bhā. Purāṇa*); a female attendant of Skanda (*M. Bh.*); one of the 7 tongues of Agni (*A. Purāṇa*); a yoginī; another name for Durgā.

**Kṛṣṇa** (S) (M) 1. black; dark blue. 2. the dark half of the lunar month. 3. the 9th incarnation of Viṣṇu as a great hero and teacher, the son of Vasudeva and Devakī of the Yādava clan, born on the Aṣṭami day in the month of Sinha (Leo), and was fostered by a herdsman named Nanda and his wife Yaśodā in Gokula and Vṛndāvana (*H. Purāṇa*); the Buddhist chief of the black demons – the enemies of Buddha and the white demons (*B. Literature*); an attendant in Skanda's retinue (*M. Bh.*); a king of the nāgas (*M. Bh.*); the father of Dāmodara and uncle of Malhaṇa (*V. Purāṇa*); a son of Śuka and Pīvarī (*V. Purāṇa*); an adopted son of Asamañjas (*V. Purāṇa*); a son of Arjuna (*M. Bh.*); an asura (*H. Purāṇa*); Caraway (*Carumcarvi*); Common Graperine (*Vitis vinifera*); *Luffa acutangula*; *Ichnocarpus frutescens*.

**Kṛṣṇāćala** (S) (M) 1. black mountain. 3. one of the 9 principal ranges that separate the 9 divisions of the world (*A. Koṣa*)

**Kṛṣṇadvaipāyana** (S) (M) 1. loved by Kṛṣṇa; black islander. 3. another name for Vyāsa.

**Kṛṣṇagupta** (S) (M) 1. protected by Kṛṣṇa. 3. another name for Pradyumna.

**Kṛṣṇakānta** (S) (M) beloved of Kṛṣṇa.

**Kṛṣṇakarṇī** (S) (F) 1. black eared. 3. a female attendant of Skanda (*M. Bh.*)

**Kṛṣṇakeśa** (S) (M) 1. black haired. 3. an attendant in Skanda's retinue (*M. Bh.*)

**Kṛṣṇamitra** (S) (M) friend of Kṛṣṇa; friend of the night.

**Kṛṣṇan** (S) (F) 1. blackness. 2. lead; the centre of the pupil of the eye.

**Kṛṣṇanada** (S) (M) 1. black river. 3. a Sanskṛt poet who wrote on the theme of Nala (13th century A.D.); author of *Sahrdayanana Kavya*.

**Kṛṣṇanetra** (S) (M) 1. black eyed. 3. another name for Śiva.

**Kṛṣṇāṅgī** (S) (F) 1. black bodied. 2. a kind of parrot. 3. an apsarā (*V. Purāṇa*)

**Kṛṣṇāntara** (S) (M) the lodestone.

**Kṛṣṇānubhautika** (S) (M) **1.** one who has realized Kṛṣṇa; one with dark experiences. **3.** a sage (*M. Bh.*)

**Kṛṣṇaparvata** (S) (M) **1.** black mountain. **3.** a mountain in Kuśa island very dear to Viṣṇu (*M. Bh.*)

**Kṛṣṇapingā** (S) (F) **1.** dark brown. **3.** another name for Durgā.

**Kṛṣṇasārathi** (S) (M) **1.** with Kṛṣṇa as a charioteer. **3.** another name for Arjuna; White Murdah (*Terminalia citrina*)

**Kṛṣṇātreya** (S) (M) **1.** the dark Atreya; the dark complexioned Brāhmin of the Atreya family. **3.** a sage who grasped the whole of Ayurveda (*M. Bh.*)

**Kṛṣṇavallī** (S) (F) **1.** dark leaved. **3.** another name for Tulasī (*Ocimum sanctum*); *Ichnocarpus frutescens*.

**Kṛṣṇavarṇā** (S) (F) **1.** black. **3.** an attendant of Skanda (*M. Bh.*)

**Kṛṣṇāvartamāna** (S) (M) **1.** surrounded by blue flames. **3.** another name for Agni.

**Kṛṣṇaveṇī** (S) (F) **1.** with dark blue braids. **3.** a river in South India from where Agni is supposed to have emerged (*M. Bh.*)

**Kṛṣṇī** (S) (F) dark night.

**Kṛṣṇika** (S) (M) related to Kṛṣṇa; of blackness. **3.** Black Mustard (*Brassica nigra*)

**Kṛṣṇiya** (S) (M) **1.** black. **3.** a man protected by the 2 aśvins (*A. Veda*)

**Kṛta** (S) (M) **1.** accomplished; proper; good. **3.** a king of Janaka's dynasty who was the son of Vijaya and the father of Śunaka (*Bhāgavata*); one of the 7 sons of Vasudeva (*Bhā. Purāṇa*); one of the 4 ages (*M. Smṛti*); a viśvadeva (*M. Bh.*)

**Kṛtabhuj** (S) (M) **1.** accomplished. **2.** done; made; obtained; gained. **3.** a son of Saṁnati and a pupil of Hiraṇyanābha (*Bhā. Purāṇa*); a son of Kṛtaratha and the father of Vibudha (*V. Purāṇa*); a son of Jaya and father of Haryavana (*Bhā. Purāṇa*); a son of Ćyavana and father of Uparićara (*Vā. Purāṇa*); a viśvadeva (*M. Bh.*); a son of Vasudeva (*Bhā. Purāṇa*)

**Kṛtaćetas** (S) (M) **1.** with an accomplished intelligence. **3.** a sage (*M. Bh.*)

**Kṛtadhvaja** (S) (M) **1.** with the flag of achievement. **3.** a king of Janaka's dynasty (*Bhā. Purāṇa*); a son of Dharmadhvaja (*Bhā. Purāṇa*)

**Kṛtadyuti** (S) (F) **1.** with accomplished glory. **3.** a queen of King Ćitraketu (*Bhāgavata*)

**Kṛtāgni** (S) (M) **1.** possessing fire. **3.** a king of the Yadu dynasty who was the brother of Kṛtavīrya (*M. Bh.*); a son of Kanaka.

**Kṛtahasta** (S) (M) **1.** with accomplished hands. **2.** dextrous.

**Kṛtaka** (S) (M) **1.** made. **2.** artificial; adopted. **3.** a son of Vasudeva (*Bhā. Purāṇa*); a son of Ćyavana (*Bhā. Purāṇa*)

**Kṛtakāma** (S) (M) **1.** accomplisher of desires. **2.** one whose desires are satisfied.

**Kṛtakarman** (S) (M) **1.** accomplisher of acts. **2.** skilful; clever; the Supreme Spirit.

**Kṛtakṣaṇa** (S) (M) **1.** one who makes time; one who utilizes time; successful. **3.** a king of Videha who was a member of Yudhiṣṭhira's court (*M. Bh.*)

**Kṛtalakṣaṇa** (S) (M) with the mark of accomplishment.

**Kṛtamālā** (S) (F) **1.** one who makes garlands. **3.** the river in which Mahāviṣṇu appeared as a fish (*Bhā. Purāṇa*)

**Kṛtamukha** (S) (M) with a well made face; skilled; clever.

**Kṛtāñjali** (S) (M) one who stands in a reverent posture.

**Kṛtānta** (S) (M) **1.** the end of action. **3.** another name for Yama, the lord of death.

**Kṛtaparva** (S) (M) **1.** the golden age of the world; one who enjoys festivals. **3.** a king of the Yadu dynasty (*Bhā. Purāṇa*)

**Kṛtāratha** (S) (M) **1.** with ready chariots. **3.** a grandson of Maru.

**Kṛtāśrama** (S) (M) **1.** painstaking; laborious. **2.** one who has led his life in accordance with the kind prescribed in the Hindu scriptures. **3.** a sage in the assembly of Yudhiṣṭhira (*M. Bh.*)

**Kṛtasthalā** (S) (F) **1.** abode of action. **3.** an apsarā.

**Kṛtāśva** (S) (M) **1.** accomplished of horses. **2.** one who has many horses, a good rider. **3.** a sage who married 2 of Dakṣa's daughters

(*D. Bhāgavata*)

**Kṛtavāka** (S) (M) 1. accomplished in speech. 3. a sage and admirer of Yudhiṣṭhira (*M. Bh.*)

**Kṛtavarman** (S) (M) 1. successful warrior. 3. a king of the Vṛṣṇi dynasty who was the son of Dhānaka and the brother of Kṛṣṇa's grandfather (*M. Bh.*); father of the 13th Arhat of the present Avasarpiṇī (*He. Koṣa*); son of Hṛdīka (*H. Purāṇa*); a son of Kanaka (*M. Bh.*)

**Kṛtavega** (S) (M) 1. that which moves fast. 3. a sage in the court of Yama (*M. Bh.*).

**Kṛtavīrya** (S) (M) 1. accomplished warrior. 2. strong; powerful. 3. the son of Kanaka, father of Kārtavīrya and a member of the court of Yama (*M. Bh.*); the father-in-law of solar King Ahaṁyati and the father of Bhānumatī (*M. Bh.*)

**Kṛtāyuṣa** (S) (M) 1. master of age. 2. one who lives as long as one wishes. 3. a brother of Kṛtāgni (*H. Purāṇa*)

**Kṛteyu** (S) (M) 1. controller of an age. 2. master of an era; one who lives long; immortal. 3. a king of the Aṅga dynasty (*M. Bh.*); a son of Raudrāśva (*V. Purāṇa*)

**Kṛtī** (S) (F) 1. accomplishment; creation. 2. magic; enchantment; making; performing; the act of doing. 3. the wife of Saṁhrāda and mother of Pañćajana (*Bhā. Purāṇa*)

**Kṛti** (S) (M) 1. creation. 3. a sage who belonged to the order of Vedavyāsa (*V. Purāṇa*); a pupil of Hiraṇyanābha (*Vā. Purāṇa*); a king of Śūkradeśa who gave a 100 elephants to Yudhiṣṭhira (*M. Bh.*); a son of Nahuṣa (*H. Purāṇa*); a king in the court of Yama (*M. Bh.*); a viśvadeva (*M. Bh.*); another name for Viṣṇu.

**Kṛtikara** (S) (M) 1. practicing magic. 3. another name for Rāvaṇa.

**Kṛtimān** (S) (M) 1. creator; sculptor. 3. a son of Yavīnara.

**Kṛtin** (S) (M) 1. active; skilful; expert; clever; pure; pious; satisfied; happy; successful; lucky; wise; learned; virtuous; blessed. 3. a son of Ćyavana and father of Uparićara (*Bhā. Purāṇa*); a son of Saṇnatimat (*Bhā. Purāṇa*)

**Kṛtirāta** (S) (M) 1. creating; presenting actions. 3. a prince (*Bh. Purāṇa*)

**Kṛtnu** (S) (M) 1. working well. 2. an accomplished worker; one who performs one's duty nicely; skilful; clever; mechanic; artist. 3. a ṛṣi (*Ṛ Ankuramaṇika*)

**Kṛtsna** (S) (M) entire; whole.

**Kṛtsnakarā** (S) (F) 1. one who does all. 2. a perfect performer. 3. an apsarā (*K. Vyuha*)

**Kṛtsnavid** (S) (M) omnicient.

**Kṛttikā** (S) (F) 1. covered with stars. 3. the Pleiades constellation which is made of 6 stars with Agni as its regent and these 6 stars or Kṛttikās are supposed to have been nymphs who became the nurses of Kārttikeya (*Sk. Purāṇa*) who then merged to form the Kṛttikā stars of Pleiades.

**Kṛttivāsas** (S) (M) 1. covered with a skin. 3. another name for Rudra-Śiva.

**Kṛttivāśasā** (S) (F) 1. covered with skin. 3. another name for Durgā.

**Kṛtvī** (S) (F) 1. accomplished. 3. the daughter of sage Śuka, the wife of Anuha of the Ajamīdha family and the mother of Brahmadatta (*H. Purāṇa*)

**Kṛtyā** (S) (F) 1. action. 2. achievement; right; proper; magical rites. 3. female deity; a rākṣasi (*M. Bh.*); a river (*M. Bh.*)

**Kṛtya** (S) (M) action; achievement.

**Kṛtyakā** (S) (F) 1. full of achievements. 3. an enchantress who is the cause of destruction worshipped by Tāntrikas (*T. Śastra*)

**Kṛvi** (S) (M) 1. cloud. 3. another name for Rudra.

**Krumu** (S) (F) 1. zigzag. 3. a river mentioned in the *Ṛg Veda* and which is now Kurum a tributary of the Indus.

**Krūrā** (S) (F) 1. cruel; pitiless. 3. a wife of Kaśyapa, and mother of the asuras, she is also known as Krodhā (*M. Bh.*)

**Krūradantī** (S) (F) 1. with cruel teeth. 2. one who chews/exterminates everything; goddess of destruction. 3. another name for Durgā.

**Kruradṛśa** (S) (M) 1. with a cruel aspect. 3. another name for the planet Saturn.

**Krūrākṛti** (S) (M) 1. with a cruel appearance. 3. another name for Rāvaṇa.

**Krūrākṣa** (S) (M) 1. evil eyed. 3. a minister of the owl King Arimardana (*Pañćatantra*)

**Kṣā** (S) (F) 1. earth. 2. that which is patient; enduring; hearing.

**Kṣama** (S) (M) 1. of earth. 2. patient; enduring; bearing; submissive; adequate; fit.

**Kṣamā** (S) (F) 1. of earth; patience; the number one. 2. mercy. 3. patience personified as a daughter of Dakṣa, wife of Pulaha and the mother of Kardama, Urvarīyān and Sahiṣṇu (*V. Purāṇa*); another name for Durgā and the earth.

**Kṣamābhuj** (S) (M) 1. one who enjoys the earth. 2. patient; prince; a king.

**Kṣamaka** (S) (M) 1. merciful. 3. a king of the Purū dynasty (*A. Purāṇa*)

**Kṣamākara** (S) (M) 1. patient; indulgent. 3. a yakṣa (*K. Sāgara*)

**Kṣamāmatī** (S) (F) with a merciful mind.

**Kṣamāmitra** (S) (M) 1. friend of the earth. 2. patient; forgiving; capable.

**Kṣaman** (S) (M) earth; soil; ground.

**Kṣamāpati** (S) (M) 1. lord of the earth; lord of mercy. 2. a king.

**Kṣamātanaya** (S) (M) 1. son of the earth. 3. the planet Mars (*V's B. Saṃhitā*)

**Kṣamāvarta** (S) (M) 1. surrounded by patience. 3. a son of Devala (*V. Purāṇa*)

**Kṣamāvatī** (S) (F) 1. one who is compassionate; enduring; forbearing; tame. 3. the wife of Nidhipati (*M. Bh.*)

**Ksamyā** (S) (F) of the earth; terrestrial.

**Kṣaṇadā** (S) (F) 1. bestower of moments; bestower of leisure. 2. one who bestows life; night; water.

**Kṣānti** (S) (F) 1. forbearance; patience. 2. endurance; indulgence; the state of saintly abstraction. 3. a river (*V. Purāṇa*)

**Kṣantu** (S) (M) patient; enduring.

**Kṣapā** (S) (F) night.

**Kṣapāćara** (S) (M) 1. one who wanders at night. 3. another name for the moon.

**Kṣapākara** (S) (M) 1. that which causes night. 2. the moon.

**Kṣapākarasekhara** (S) (M) 1. wearing the moon on his head. 3. another name for Śiva.

**Kṣapaṇa** (S) (M) 1. fasting. 2. a religious mendicant; a Jaina or Buddhist mendicant.

**Kṣapaṇaka** (S) (M) 1. fasting. 2. a religious mendicant; especially a Jaina mendicant who wears no garments. 3. an author supposed to have lived at the court of King Vikramāditya (*K. Granthāvali*)

**Kṣapānātha** (S) (M) 1. lord of the night. 3. another name for the moon.

**Kṣapāramaṇa** (S) (M) 1. night lover. 3. another name for the moon.

**Kṣāpāvāna** (S) (M) earth protector.

**Kṣapendra** (S) (M) 1. king of the night. 3. another name for the moon.

**Kṣapeśa** (S) (M) 1. lord of the night. 3. another name for the moon.

**Kṣāra** (S) (M) 1. ashes. 3. another name for Agni.

**Kṣaragna** (S) (M) supreme soul.

**Kṣatradeva** (S) (M) 1. lord of warriors. 3. the son of Śikhaṇḍi who was a famous archer (*M. Bh.*)

**Kṣātradharman** (S) (M) 1. religious warrior. 3. a son of Dhṛṣṭhadyumna (*M. Bh.*)

**Kṣatrañjaya** (S) (M) 1. conqueror of warriors. 3. a son of Dhṛṣṭhadyumna (*M. Bh.*)

**Kṣatriyāṇī** (S) (F) wife of a noble warrior.

**Kṣaya** (S) (M) dwelling; dominion.

**Kṣayadvīra** (S) (M) 1. ruling. 2. governing men; granting heroic sons. 3. another name for Indra, Rudra and Pūṣan.

**Kṣayana** (S) (M) a place of tranquil water; a dwelling.

**Kṣayata** (S) (M) to possess; to have power over to rule; to govern; to be the master.

**Kṣemā** (S) (F) 1. safety; security; welfare; peace. 2. tranquillity; bliss; final emancipation. 3. an apsarā (*M. Bh.*); another name for Durgā.

**Kṣema** (S) (M) 1. safely; security; welfare; peace. 2. tranquillity; bliss; final emancipation. 3. a king who was an incarnation of Krodhavaśa and fought on the side of the Pāṇḍavas (*M. Bh.*); a son of Śući and father of Suvrata (*Bhā. Purāṇa*); a son of Dharma and Śānti (*V. Purāṇa*); a son of Titikṣā (*Bhā. Purāṇa*)

**Kṣemadarśi** (S) (M) 1. seer of security. 3. a king of Kośala (*M. Bh.*)

**Kṣemadhanvan** (S) (M) 1. with the bow of prosperity. 3. a famous archer who fought on the side of the Kauravas (*M. Bh.*); a son of Manu Sāvarṇa (*H. Purāṇa*); a son of Puṇḍarīka (*Bhā. Purāṇa*)

**Kṣemadhṛti** (S) (M) 1. bearer of security. 3. a Kṣatriya king who was an incarnation of Krodhavaśa and fought on the side of the Kauravas (*M. Bh.*)

**Kṣemāgirī** (S) (F) 1. mountain of security. 2. that which is full of security. 3. another name for goddess Bhadrakālī.

**Kṣemaka** (S) (M) 1. one who brings security. 2. a kind of perfume. 3. last descendant of Parīkṣit in the Kaliyuga (*V. Purāṇa*); a rākṣasa who was killed before Kāśī was built by King Divodāsa (*H. Purāṇa*); a serpent son of Kaśyapa and Kadru (*M. Bh.*); a king in the court of Yudhiṣṭhira (*M. Bh.*); an attendant of Śiva (*A. Koṣa*); a son of Niramitra (*M. Purāṇa*); a nāga (*M. Bh.*)

**Kṣemakara** (S) (M) 1. conferring peace and prosperity. 3. a mythical Buddha (*B. Literature*)

**Kṣemamaya** (S) (M) full of peace and or prosperity.

**Kṣemaṁkarā** (S) (F) 1. conferring peace and prosperity. 3. another name for Durgā.

**Kṣemamūrti** (S) (M) 1. symbol of peace and prosperity. 3. a son of Dhṛtarāṣṭra (*M. Bh.*)

**Kṣemaṅkara** (S) (M) 1. conferring peace, security, happiness. 3. a king of Trigarta (*M. Bh.*); a mythical Buddha; a son of Brahmadatta.

**Kṣemaṅkarī** (S) (F) 1. conferring peace; security; happiness. 3. another name for Durgā.

**Kṣemaśarma** (S) (M) 1. warrior of peace. 3. a warrior who fought on the side of the Kauravas (*M. Bh.*)

**Kṣemavāha** (S) (M) 1. carrier of prosperity. 3. a warrior of Skanda (*M. Bh.*)

**Kṣemavṛddhi** (S) (M) 1. increasing peace and prosperity. 3. a minister of King Sālva (*M. Bh.*)

**Kṣemendra** (S) (M) 1. lord of peace. 3. a celebrated Kāśmīra poet (11th century)

**Kṣemyā** (S) (F) 1. goddess of welfare. 3. another name for Durgā.

**Kṣemya** (S) (M) 1. resting; at ease; giving peace. 2. healthy; prosperous; auspicious. 3. a father of Ketumat; a son of Ugrayudha and father of Suvīra (*H. Purāṇa*); another name for Śiva.

**Kśetrapāla** (S) (M) 1. protector of the fields. 3. a 3-eyed deity presumed to be a portion of Śiva, the protector of villages and cities and each eye of which represents Sāttva, Rajasa and Tamasa (*Mā. Purāṇa*); the guardian of the Śaiva temples of South India.

**Kṣetrin** (S) (M) 1. owning land. 3. the soul.

**Kṣipaṇu** (S) (M) 1. thrown; moving. 2. archer; missile; air; wind.

**Kṣipra** (S) (M) 1. springing; elastic; quick; speedy. 3. a son of Kṛṣṇa.

**Kṣiprā** (S) (F) 1. fast. 3. a river in Ujjain (*M. Bh.*)

**Kṣiprahasta** (S) (M) 1. swift handed. 3. a rākṣasa; another name for Agni.

**Kṣipreṣu** (S) (M) 1. with quick arrows. 3. another name for Rudra.

**Kṣīrabdhijā** (S) (F) 1. born of the Ocean of Milk. 2. amṛta or any other precious objects produced at the churning of the Ocean of Milk. 3. another name for Lakṣmī.

**Kṣīraja** (S) (M) 1. born of milk. 2. nectar; pearl. 3. another name for Śeṣa and the moon.

**Kṣīrajā** (S) (F) 1. born of milk. 3. another name for Lakṣmī.

**Kṣīrapāna** (S) (M) 1. to drink milk. 2. vessel out of which milk is drunk; milk drinkers. 3. another name for the Uśīnaras (*Pāṇinī*)

**Kṣīrasāgarā** (S) (F) the sea of milk.

**Kṣīraśukla** (S) (M) as fair as milk.

**Ksīravatī** (S) (F) 1. made of milk. 3. a river (*M. Bh.*)

**Kṣīrin** (S) (F) 1. milky; with plenty of milk. 3. a tree from which milk flows unceasingly and from which we get cloth, ornaments, etc. (*M. Bh.*); Prickly Poppy (*Argemone mexicana*)

**Kṣīrodijā** (S) (F) 1. produced from the Ocean of Milk. 3. another name for Lakṣmī.

**Kṣitāditi** (S) (F) 1. the Aditī of the earth. 3. another name for Devakī the mother of Kṛṣṇa.

**Kṣitendra** (S) (M) 1. lord of the earth. 2. a

ruler; a king.

**Kṣiti** (S) (F) abode; dwelling; habitation; the earth; settlements; colonies; soil of the earth; races of men.

**Kṣitibhū** (S) (F) 1. born of the earth. 3. another name for Sītā.

**Kṣitibhuj** (S) (M) 1. enjoyer of the earth. 2. a king; a ruler.

**Kṣitideva** (S) (M) 1. god of the earth. 3. another name for Brahmā.

**Kṣitigarbha** (S) (M) 1. produced in the earth. 3. a Bodhisattva.

**Kṣitijā** (S) (F) 1. born of the earth. 3. another name for Sītā.

**Kṣitija** (S) (M) 1. son of the earth. 2. tree; earthworm; the horizon; snail. 3. another name for the demon Naraka and the planet Mars.

**Kṣitikampana** (S) (M) 1. an earthquake. 3. a captain of the army of Skanda (*M. Bh.*)

**Kṣitikṣita** (S) (M) 1. ruler of the earth. 2. a king.

**Kṣitilavabhuj** (S) (M) 1. possessing only a small tract of the earth. 2. a petty prince.

**Kṣitinātha** (S) (M) lord of the earth.

**Kṣitīndra** (S) (M) lord of the earth.

**Kṣitipati** (S) (M) master of the earth.

**Kṣitipuruhūta** (S) (M) 1. the Indra of the earth. 2. a king.

**Kṣitiputra** (S) (M) 1. son of the earth. 3. the demon Naraka (*Kā. Purāṇa*)

**Kṣitīśa** (S) (M) lord of the earth.

**Kṣitīśvara** (S) (M) 1. god of the earth. 2. a king. 3. a king of Kānyakubja.

**Kṣityāditī** (S) (F) 1. the Aditī of the earth. 3. another name for Devakī the mother of Kṛṣṇa (*Bhā. Purāṇa*)

**Kṣobhaka** (S) (M) 1. that which shakes; that which agitates. 3. a mountain in Kāmākhyā sacred to Durgā (*Kā. Purāṇa*); one of the 5 arrows of Kāma; another name for Śiva and Viṣṇu.

**Kṣoṇā** (S) (F) 1. immovable. 3. another name for the earth.

**Kṣoṇī** (S) (F) 1. immovable; stable. 3. the earth.

**Kṣoṇideva** (S) (M) earth god.

**Kṣubhā** (S) (F) 1. weapon. 3. the deity which presides over punishment.

**Kṣudhi** (S) (M) 1. hungry. 3. a son of Kṛṣṇa (*Bh. Purāṇa*)

**Kṣumā** (S) (F) 1. arrow. 2. Common Flax (*Linum usitatissimum*)

**Kṣūnu** (S) (F) fire.

**Kṣupa** (S) (M) 1. shrub; bush. 3. a king who was the son of Prasandhi, the grandson of Vaivasvata Manu and the father of Ikṣvāku (*M. Bh.*); a son of Kṛṣṇa and Satyabhāmā (*H. Purāṇa*); a prajāpati born from the sneeze of Brahmā (*Br. Purāṇa*)

**Kṣurakarṇī** (S) (M) 1. with sharp ears. 3. an attendant of Skanda (*M. Bh.*)

**Kubera** (S) (M) 1. slow; lazy. 3. the chief of evil beings with the patronymic Vaiśravaṇa, Kubera who performed penance in Laṅkā to be a Lokapāla and the custodian of wealth – both of which were granted to him by Brahmā, is the son of Viśravas and Īlibilā, the husband of Bhadrā, the father of Nalakubara, the lord of the oceans which yield him extreme wealth, the lord of the yakṣas, the regent of the Northern Quarters, a special friend of Śiva, considered to live on Mount Gandhamādana with his capital as Alakā and among the Jainas considered the attendant of the 19th Arhat of the present Avasarpiṇī (*J.S. Koṣa*); the great grandfather of the author Bāṇabhatta (*Kādambari*); a prince of Devarāṣṭra.

**Kuberabandhu** (S) (M) 1. friend of Kubera. 2. one who is wealthy.

**Kubha** (S) (M) 1. zigzag; jar. 3. a river mentioned in the *Ṛg Veda* which is now the Kabul river.

**Kubhināsā** (S) (F) 1. jar nosed. 2. one with extremely wide nostrils. 3. a wife of the gandharva Aṅgāraparṇa (*M. Bh.*); a rākṣasī and mother of Lavaṇa (*V. Rāmāyaṇa*)

**Kubjā** (S) (F) 1. hunch backed. 3. a widow who was incarnated as Tilottamā the apsarā (*Bhā. Purāṇa*)

**Kucandana** (S) (M) the fragrance of the earth.

**Kucelu** (S) (M) 1. one who wears dirty

clothes. 3. another name for Sudāmā a classmate of Kṛṣṇa (*Bhāgavata*)

**Kuḍāyikā** (S) (F) 1. one who lives under the earth. 3. a rāga.

**Kudhara** (S) (M) 1. that which supports the earth. 2. a mountain.

**Kuha** (S) (M) 1. deceiver. 3. a prince of Sauvīra (*M. Bh.*); another name for Kubera.

**Kuhara** (S) (M) 1. cavity; hollow; ear; throat. 3. a king of Kaliṅga who was an incarnation of the asura Krodhavaśa (*M. Bh.*)

**Kuhārīta** (S) (F) the song of the Kokila or Indian Cuckoo (*Cuculus scolopaceus*)

**Kuhāvatī** (S) (F) 1. one who owns the Zizyphus tree (*Zizyphus jujuba*); bearer of a song. 3. another name for Durgā.

**Kuhū** (S) (F) 1. the cry of the Kokila or Indian Cuckoo (*Cuculus scolopaceus*). 3. the new moon night personified as the daughter of Aṅgiras and Śraddhā (*V. Purāṇa*)

**Kuhupāla** (S) (M) 1. lord of the moon. 3. the king of turtles who is supposed to uphold the world; another name for Śiva.

**Kujā** (S) (F) 1. daughter of the earth. 3. another name for Durgā, Sītā and the horizon.

**Kuja** (S) (M) 1. born from the earth. 2. tree. 3. the gana who wears the rudrākṣa māla (*Ś. Purāṇa*); another name for the daitya Naraka conquered by Kṛṣṇa (*Bhā. Purāṇa*); another name for the planet Mars.

**Kujambha** (S) (M) 1. destroyer. 3. a son of Prahlāda.

**Kujapa** (S) (M) one whose protector is Mars.

**Kujṛmbha** (S) (M) 1. with a wide yawn. 2. lazy. 3. an asura (*Mā. Purāṇa*)

**Kuka** (S) (M) crow pheasant.

**Kukīla** (S) (M) 1. a bolt of the earth. 2. a mountain.

**Kukkuṭikā** (S) (F) 1. hen. 3. a female attendant of Skanda (*M. Bh.*)

**Kukṣi** (S) (M) 1. the abdomen; the interior; a bay; a gulf; the sheath of a sword. 3. a son of Priyavrata and Kāmyā (*A. Purāṇa*); a son of Ikṣvāku and father of Vikukṣi (*Bhā. Purāṇa*); an asura who was reborn as King Pārvatīya (*M. Bh.*); another name for Bali (*V. Rāmāyaṇa*)

**Kukṣijā** (S) (F) 1. born from the womb. 3. a daughter of Priyavrata and Kāmyā (*M. Bh.*)

**Kukubhā** (S) (F) female personification of music or rāgiṇīs.

**Kukudmi** (S) (M) 1. mountain; humped bull. 3. the father of Revatī (*D. Bh. Purāṇa*); the son of King Anarta (*D. Purāṇa*)

**Kukura** (S) (M) 1. dog; a species of deer. 3. a king of the lunar dynasty and the founder of the Kukura dynasty (*M. Bh.*); a sage at the court of Yudhiṣṭhira (*M. Bh.*); a son of Andhaka (*M. Bh.*)

**Kulabhūṣaṇa** (S) (M) ornament of the family.

**Kuladeva** (S) (M) the deity of the family.

**Kuladevī** (S) (F) 1. the family goddess. 3. another name for Durgā.

**Kuladīpa** (S) (M) light of the family.

**Kuladīpaka** (S) (M) lamp of the family.

**Kulaja** (S) (M) well born; of a noble family.

**Kulamaṇi** (S) (M) the jewel of the family.

**Kulambā** (S) (F) deity of the family.

**Kulampunā** (S) (F) 1. one who makes the family pious. 2. the virtue of the family. 3. a river that ought to be remembered daily (*M. Bh.*)

**Kulānanda** (S) (M) joy of the family.

**Kulanārī** (S) (F) 1. a woman of a good family. 2. one who is virtuous.

**Kulāṅganā** (S) (F) highborn woman.

**Kulapati** (S) (M) head of the family.

**Kulasundarī** (S) (F) 1. maiden of the family. 3. a deity (*Br. Purāṇa*)

**Kulatilaka** (S) (M) 1. glory of the family. 2. one who brings honour to his family.

**Kulavīra** (S) (M) one who fights for the honour of his family.

**Kuleśvarī** (S) (F) 1. family goddess. 3. another name for Durgā.

**Kulika** (S) (M) 1. well born. 3. a serpent of the Kadru family (*M. Bh.*); one of the 8 chiefs of the nāgas having a half moon on his face and of a dusky brown visage (*M. Bh.*)

**Kulīn** (S) (M) highborn; of a good family.

**Kulīra** (S) (M) crab; the zodiac sign of Cancer.

**Kuliśa** (S) (M) 1. axe. 2. the thunderbolt of Indra. 3. a river supposed to be in the middle region of the sky (*Ṛg Veda*); another name for a diamond.

**Kuliśāsana** (S) (M) 1. one who commands with his axe. 3. another name for Śākyāmuni.

**Kuliśaya** (S) (M) that which is as hard as thunderbolt.

**Kulīśvara** (S) (M) 1. family god. 3. another name for Śiva.

**Kullūka** (S) (M) 1. land covered with high mountains. 3. a celebrated commentator on Manu (*D. Śastra*)

**Kulyā** (S) (F) 1. virtuous. 2. well born; presiding over a river as a deity.

**Kulya** (S) (M) 1. well born. 2. respectable; canal. 3. a sage who was a disciple of Vyāsa (*Bhā. Purāṇa*)

**Kumāra** (S) (M) 1. child; boy; youth; prince. 3. a son of Agni who is the author of some Ṛg Vedic hymns; the attendant of the 12th Arhat of the present Avasarpiṇī (*J.S. Koṣa*); one of the 9 names of Agni (*R. Aṅkuramaṇikā*); a king who fought on the side of the Pāṇḍavas (*M. Bh.*); a son of Garuḍa (*Gar. Purāṇa*); a prajāpati (*Vā. Purāṇa*); a son of Bhavya; *Crataeva nurvala*; Yellow Champaka (*Michelia champaka*); another name for the Sindhu river; another name for Skanda.

**Kumāradarśana** (S) (M) 1. he who sees Skanda. 3. a prince of the gandharvas (*H. Purāṇa*)

**Kumāradāsa** (S) (M) 1. devotee of Skanda. 3. Sanskṛt poet who wrote *Jānakīharaṇam* (7th century A.D.)

**Kumāradatta** (S) (M) 1. given by Kārttikeya. 3. a son of Nidhipati (*K. Sāgara*)

**Kumāradevī** (S) (F) 1. goddess of children. 3. a Liććhavi princess who was the wife of Ćandragupta I.

**Kumāradhara** (S) (M) 1. bearer of children; borne of Skanda. 3. a river with its source in the Brahmarasas, considered to bestow intelligence and wealth upon those who bathe in it (*M. Bh.*)

**Kumāragupta** (S) (M) protected by Skanda.

**Kumāraka** (S) (M) 1. youth; the pupil of the eye. 3. a serpent of the Kauravya dynasty (*M. Bh.*)

**Kumārapāla** (S) (M) 1. protected by Skanda; protector of children. 3. a king of Gujarat who made Jainism the state religion.

**Kumārapita** (S) (M) 1. father of Skanda. 3. another name for Śiva.

**Kumārasū** (S) (M) 1. father of Skanda. 3. another name for Agni.

**Kumāreśa** (S) (M) 1. lord of youths. 3. another name for Kārttikeya.

**Kumārī** (S) (F) 1. daughter; maiden; the Jasmine (*Jasminum pubescens*); gold. 3. a princess of the Kekaya kingdom who was the wife of the Purū King Bhīmasena and the mother of Pratiśravas (*M. Bh.*); the wife of the serpent Dhanañjaya (*M. Bh.*); a daughter of Vasudeva and Rohiṇī (*Bhā. Purāṇa*); the central part of the universe (*V's. B. Samhitā*); a river of ancient India (*M. Bh.*); another name for Durgā, Dākṣāyaṇī, Sītā and the Śyāmā bird (*Copsychus malabaricus indicus*); *Aloe vera*; *Crysanthemum indicum*; *Rosa alba*.

**Kumārikā** (S) (F) 1. virgin; girl; the Jasmine (*Jasminum sambac*). 3. another name for Durgā and Sītā.

**Kumārila** (S) (M) 1. intelligent youth. 3. a renowned teacher of the Mimāmsā philosophy.

**Kumbha** (S) (M) 1. jar; pitcher; the zodiac sign of Aquarius. 3. the father of the 19th Arhat of the present Avasarpiṇī; one of the 34 rebirths of Śākyāmuni; one of the 3 sons of Prahlāda (*M. Bh.*); son of Kumbhakarṇa and Vajrajvālā (*V. Rāmāyaṇa*); a mantra pronounced over a weapon (*V. Rāmāyaṇa*); *Commiphora mukul*.

**Kumbhadhara** (S) (M) pitcher; the zodiac sign of Aquarius.

**Kumbhaja** (S) (M) 1. son of a pitcher. 3. another name for Agastya.

**Kumbhaka** (S) (M) 1. pot; pitcher; the protuberance on an elephant's forehead. 3. a warrior of Skanda (*M. Bh.*);

**Kumbhakarṇa** (S) (M) 1. pot eared. 3. a son of Viśravas and Puṣpotkaṭā and the brother of Rāvaṇa (*V. Rāmāyaṇa*)

**Kumbhaketu** (S) (M) 1. pot-bannered. 3. a

son of Śambara.

**Kumbhamātā** (S) (F) 1. goddess of pots. 3. tutelary goddess of a village represented by a pot.

**Kumbhanābha** (S) (M) 1. pot navelled. 3. a son of Bali (*V. Rāmāyaṇa*)

**Kumbhāṇḍa** (S) (M) 1. one for whom the earth is as light as a pot. 3. a minister of Bāṇāsura and the father of Ćitralekhā (*Bhā. Purāṇa*)

**Kumbhāṇḍakodara** (S) (M) 1. pot bellied. 3. a warrior of Skanda (*M. Bh.*)

**Kumbhahanu** (S) (M) 1. with a pot shaped chin. 3. a rākṣasa (*V. Rāmāyaṇa*)

**Kumbharetas** (S) (M) 1. born in a pot. 2. a flame in a pot. 3. an agni who was the son of Bharadvāja and Vīrā (*M. Bh.*)

**Kumbharī** (S) (F) 1. enemy of Aquarius; destroyer of pitchers; one who hates the harlots. 3. a form of Durgā (*A. Koṣa*)

**Kumbhasambhava** (S) (M) 1. born of a pot. 3. another name for Agastya and Nārāyaṇa.

**Kumbhaśravas** (S) (M) 1. pot eared. 3. an attendant of Skanda (*M. Bh.*)

**Kumbhavaktra** (S) (M) 1. pot faced. 3. an attendant of Skanda (*M. Bh.*)

**Kumbhayonī** (S) (F) 1. pot born. 3. an apsarā (*M. Bh.*)

**Kumbhayoni** (S) (M) 1. pot born. 3. another name for Agastya, Droṇa, Vasiṣṭha.

**Kumbhikā** (S) (F) 1. a small waterjar. 3. a mother of Skanda's retinue (*M. Bh.*); Water lettuce (*Pistia stratiotes*); *Ochrocarpos longifolius*.

**Kumbhinādī** (S) (F) 1. one who sounds like a pitcher. 3. a daughter of the rākṣasa Sumāli and Ketumatī (*M. Bh.*)

**Kumbhināśa** (S) (M) 1. jar-nosed; poisonous snake. 3. an asura (*M. Bh.*)

**Kumbhināśi** (S) (F) 1. one who feeds on poison. 2. venomous. 3. a daughter of Viśvavasu and Analā and the mother of Lavaṇāsura by the rākṣasa Madhu (*V. Rāmāyaṇa*); the wife of the gandharva Aṅgāraparṇa (*M. Bh.*)

**Kumbhinī** (S) (F) 1. shaped like a jar. 3. another name for the earth.

**Kumbhīra** (S) (M) 1. crocodile of the Gaṅgā. 3. a yakṣa (*M. Bh.*)

**Kumbhodara** (S) (M) 1. pot bellied. 3. an attendant of Śiva (*K. Granthāvali*)

**Kuṁkum** (S) (M) (F) saffron (*Crocus sativus*); red; pollen; red sandalwood paste applied on the forehead.

**Kumuda** (S) (M) 1. pleasure of the earth; the white water lily (*Nymphaea alba*); the red lotus (*Nymphaea rubra*); camphor. 3. one of the 15 attendants given by Brahmā to Skanda (*M. Bh.*); one of the 4 mountains surrounding the Mahāmeru (*V. Purāṇa*); a great elephant born in the dynasty of Supratīka (*M. Bh.*); a monkey attendant of Sugrīva (*M. Bh.*); a warrior who fought with Skanda (*M. Bh.*); a son of Garuḍa (*M. Bh.*); an attendant of Skanda (*M. Bh.*); the elephant of the South West Quarter (*A. Koṣa*); a particular comet (*V.s B. Samhitā*); a serpent (*M. Bh.*); a daitya; a son of Gada and Bṛhatī (*H. Purāṇa*); another name for Viṣṇu.

**Kumudadi** (S) (M) 1. given by the pleasure of earth; one who gives the white water lily. 3. a Vedic scholar of the line of Vyāsa's disciples (*V. Purāṇa*); another name for Viṣṇu.

**Kumudaka** (S) (M) 1. one who gives the white water lily. 3. another name for Viṣṇu.

**Kumudākṣa** (S) (M) 1. lotus eyed; red eyed. 3. an attendant of Viṣṇu (*M. Bh.*); a serpent (*M. Bh.*)

**Kumudamaṇi** (S) (M) 1. jewel among water lilies. 3. one of the 4 attendants given by Brahmā to Skanda (*M. Bh.*)

**Kumudanātha** (S) (M) 1. lord of the white water lily. 3. another name for the moon.

**Kumudapati** (S) (M) 1. lord of the white water lily. 3. another name for the moon.

**Kumudapuṣpā** (S) (F) 1. white water lily. 3. a gandharvī.

**Kumudasundarī** (S) (F) as beautiful as the white water lily (*Nymphaea alba*)

**Kumudavatī** (S) (F) 1. abounding in water lilies. 3. the daughter of the serpent king Kumuda, the wife of Kuśa and the mother of Atithi (*Bhā. Purāṇa*); the wife of the Kirāta King Vimarṣaṇa (*Ś. Purāṇa*); the wife of Pradyumna (*Bhā. Purāṇa*)

**Kumudeśa** (S) (M) 1. lord of the white water lily. 3. another name for the moon.

**Kumudikā** (S) (F) one who bears or wears water lilies.

**Kumudinī** (S) (F) an assemblage of white water lilies.

**Kunābhi** (S) (M) 1. having the earth for a navel. 3. the collective treasures of Kubera (*M. Bh.*)

**Kunadika** (S) (M) 1. one who pleases the earth. 2. pleaser of the earth. 3. a warrior of Skanda (*M. Bh.*)

**Kuṇāla** (S) (M) 1. lotus; the Painted Snipe bird. 3. a son of Emperor Aśoka named after the eyes of a Himālayan bird.

**Kunālikā** (S) (F) the Indian Cuckoo (*Cuculus scolopaceus*)

**Kunda** (S) (M) 1. musk; jasmine (*Jasminum pubescens*); Oleander (*Nerium odorum*); the number 9. 3. one of Kubera's 9 treasures; another name for Viṣṇu.

**Kuṇḍa** (S) (M) 1. bowl; pot; spring; well. 3. one of the 5 attendants given by Dhātā to Skanda (*M. Bh.*); a son of Dhṛtarāṣṭra (*M. Bh.*); a Brāhmin known for his learning (*M. Bh.*); one of Kubera's 9 treasures; a nāga (*M. Bh.*); a guhyaka; another name for Viṣṇu and Śiva.

**Kuṇḍabhedin** (S) (M) 1. pot breaker. 3. a son of Dhrtarāṣṭra (*M. Bh.*)

**Kundadanta** (S) (M) 1. with jasmine like teeth. 3. a Videha Brāhmin who studied with sage Vasiṣṭha (*Yogavāśiṣṭha*)

**Kuṇḍadhāra** (S) (M) 1. pot bearer. 3. a nāga (*M. Bh.*); a son of Dhṛtarāṣṭra.

**Kuṇḍaja** (S) (M) 1. pot born. 3. a son of Dhṛtarāṣṭra (*M. Bh.*)

**Kuṇḍaka** (S) (M) 1. a pot. 3. a son of Dhṛtarāṣṭra (*M. Bh.*)

**Kuṇḍala** (S) (M) 1. earring. 3. a serpent of the Kaurava dynasty (*M. Bh.*).

**Kuṇḍalī** (S) (F) 1. round; circle. 3. a child of Garuḍa (*M. Bh.*); a son of Dhṛtarāṣṭra (*M. Bh.*); a river (*M. Bh.*)

**Kuṇḍalin** (S) (M) 1. decorated with earrings. 3. another name for Śiva and Varuṇa.

**Kuṇḍalinī** (S) (F) 1. decorated with earrings. 3. a Śakti or form of Durgā; *Tinospora cordifolia.*

**Kuṇḍam** (S) (M) altar; grinding stone.

**Kundamālā** (S) (F) a garland of Jasmine flowers.

**Kundan** (S) (M) pure; sparkling; fine; purified; glittering; gold.

**Kundanikā** (S) (F) jasmine.

**Kuṇḍapāyin** (S) (M) drinking out of pitchers.

**Kuṇḍareśvara** (S) (M) 1. lord of vegetation. 3. a Liṅga (*Sk. Purāṇa*)

**Kundarikā** (S) (F) 1. olibanum; the plant *Boswellia thurifera*. 3. a female attendant of Skanda (*M. Bh.*)

**Kuṇḍaśāyin** (S) (M) 1. resting in a pot. 3. a son of Dhṛtarāṣṭra.

**Kuṇḍaśin** (S) (M) 1. panderer. 3. a son of Dhṛtarāṣṭra.

**Kuṇḍavāsinī** (S) (F) 1. living in a pitcher. 3. Gautama's tutelary deity (*B. Purāṇa*)

**Kuṇḍika** (S) (M) 1. round pot. 3. a son of Dhṛtarāṣṭra (*M. Bh.*)

**Kuṇḍina** (S) (M) 1. furnished with a pitcher; born of a pitcher. 3. a son of Dhṛtarāṣṭra (*M. Bh.*); another name for Śiva.

**Kundinī** (S) (F) an assemblage of jasmines.

**Kuṇḍira** (S) (M) strong; powerful.

**Kuṇḍodara** (S) (M) 1. pot bellied. 3. a son of Dhṛtarāṣṭra (*M. Bh.*); a son of King Janamejaya (*M. Bh.*); a serpent (*M. Bh.*)

**Kungabihāri** (S) (M) 1. living in the woods. 3. another name for Kṛṣṇa.

**Kuni** (S) (M) 1. with a crooked arm; whitlow. 3. a sage and father of ṛṣī (*Vā. Purāṇa*); father of Jaya (*Bh. Purāṇa*)

**Kuṇi** (S) (M) 1. with a withered arm. 3. a son of Jaya (*Bhā. Purāṇa*); a ṛṣi (*Vā. Purāṇa*); another name for Garga (*M. Bh.*)

**Kuṇigarga** (S) (M) 1. saint with a withered arm. 3. a sage (*Vā. Purāṇa*)

**Kūṇika** (S) (M) 1. horn. 3. a prince of Ćampā (*H. Purāṇa*)

**Kuninda** (S) (M) 1. administrator. 3. a sage who possessed a divine conch (*M. Bh.*)

**Kuñjā** (S) (F) bower; arbour; shrub or jungle.

**Kuñja** (S) (M) 1. bower; living in a bush,

shrub or jungle. 3. a sage (*V. Purāṇa*); Indian Lotus (*Nelumbo nucifera*)

**Kuñjakiśore** (S) (M) 1. youth of the woods. 3. another name for Kṛṣṇa (*Bhā. Purāṇa*)

**Kuñjala** (S) (M) 1. living in shrubs. 2. koel or Indian cuckoo (*Cuculus scolopaceus*); sour gruel. 3. an attendant of Skanda.

**Kuñjalatā** (S) (F) forest creeper.

**Kuñjara** (S) (M) 1. dwelling in forests. 2. an elephant; the number 8. 3. a monkey who was the father of Añjanā (*V. Rāmāyaṇa*); a prince of Sauvīra and follower of Jayadratha (*M. Bh.*); a serpent (*M. Bh.*); *Ficus religiosa*.

**Kuñjavihārī** (S) (M) 1. one who sports in the forest. 3. another name for Kṛṣṇa.

**Kuñjeśvara** (S) (M) 1. lord of the forest. 3. another name for Kṛṣṇa.

**Kuñjikā** (S) (F) 1. belonging to the bower. 3. Nutmeg flower (*Nigella sativa*)

**Kuñjita** (S) (M) hidden in the forest.

**Kunśa** (S) (M) to shine; to speak.

**Kunśī** (S) (F) shining.

**Kuntaka** (S) (M) necklace.

**Kuntala** (S) (F) plough; spear; perfume; barley; a lock of hair; *Pavonia odorata*.

**Kuntanātha** (S) (M) 1. lord of vegetation. 3. the 17th Jaina Tīrathaṅkara whose emblem was a goat (*J.S. Koṣa*)

**Kunteśa** (S) (M) 1. master of Kuntī. 3. another name for Pāṇḍu.

**Kunthu** (S) (M) 1. one who hurts. 3. the 6th Jaina ćakravartin or emperor in Bhāratavarṣa (*J.S. Koṣa*); the 17th Arhat of the present Avasarpiṇī (*J.S. Koṣa*)

**Kuntī** (S) (F) 1. spear; lance. 3. the sister of Kṛṣṇa's father, the daughter of King Śūrasena, foster daughter of Śūrasena's nephew Kuntibhoja, wife of King Pāṇḍu, the mother of the Pāṇḍavas and the supposed incarnation of Siddhi (*M. Bh.*); a rākṣasī; a river (*V. Purāṇa*)

**Kunti** (S) (M) 1. spear; lance. 3. a son of Vidarbha and father of Dhṛṣṭa (*H. Purāṇa*); a son of Supārśva and grandson of Sampati (*Mā. Purāṇa*); a son of Kṛṣṇa (*Bhā. Purāṇa*); a son of Dharmanetra (*V. Purāṇa*); a grandson of Dharma (*Bh. Purāṇa*); a people; *Commiphora mukul*.

**Kuntibhoja** (S) (M) 1. bearer of spears. 3. a king of the Yadu dynasty and fosterfather of Kuntī (*M. Bh.*)

**Kuntīnandana** (S) (M) 1. son of Kuntī. 3. another name for Yudhiṣṭhira.

**Kuntīsuta** (S) (M) 1. son of Kuntī. 3. another name for Karṇa.

**Kupata** (S) (M) excellent.

**Kupatha** (S) (M) 1. follower of a bad path. 3. an asura son of Kaśyapa and Danu (*M. Bh.*)

**Kupati** (S) (M) lord of the earth.

**Kupendra** (S) (M) 1. lord of anger. 3. another name for Śiva.

**Kuppusvāmi** (S) (M) 1. lord of anger. 3. another name for Śiva.

**Kuraṅgākṣī** (S) (F) fawn eyed; beautiful.

**Kuraṅgī** (S) (F) 1. spot in the moon; deer. 3. a daughter of Prasenajit (*K. Sāgara*)

**Kurannu** (Malayalam) (M) 1. monkey. 3. the children of Harī the daughter of Kaśyapa and Marīći (*V. Rāmāyaṇa*)

**Kuraparvata** (S) (M) 1. spotted mountains. 3. a mountain that encirles Mahāmeru (*D. Bhāgavata*)

**Kūrćāmukha** (S) (M) 1. with a brush like face. 2. one who has a beard. 3. a son of Viśvāmitra (*M. Bh.*)

**Kurćika** (S) (M) a painter's brush.

**Kūrdanā** (S) (F) the full moon day in the month of Ćaitra; a festival held in honour of Kāma.

**Kurīra** (S) (F) ornament of the head.

**Kurīrin** (S) (M) crested; a peacock.

**Kūrma** (S) (M) 1. tortoise; turtle. 2. the earth considered as a tortoise swimming on water. 3. the 2nd incarnation of Viṣṇu as a tortoise (*N. Purāṇa*); the son of Gṛtsamada (*R. Ankuramanikā*); a serpent son of Kadru (*M. Bh.*)

**Kūrmapṛṣṭha** (S) (M) 1. tortoise shell. 3. a yakṣa (*Brahma Purāṇa*)

**Kūrmāvatāra** (S) (M) 1. the tortoise incarnation. 3. the 2nd incarnation of Viṣṇu as a tortoise (*N. Purāṇa*)

**Kuru** (S) (M) 1. attached. 3. a king of Dhruva's dynasty who was the grandfather of

Veṇa and the great grandfather of Emperor Pṛthu (*V. Purāṇa*); a famous king of the Purū dynasty who was the son of Saṁvaraṇa and Tapatī, the husband of Saudāminī and after whom the Kaurava dynasty was named (*M. Bh.*); a people and a country considered to be the ancient home of the Aryans; a son of Āgnidhra and grandson of Priyavrata (*V. Purāṇa*); a king and brother of Rantideva; a king of the Uttānapāda dynasty (*V. Purāṇa*); a sage; Nut Grass (*Cyperus rotundis*)

**Kurūdvaha** (S) (M) 1. elevating the Kurus. 3. another name for Dhṛtarāṣṭra, Bhīṣma and Yudhiṣṭhira.

**Kurujita** (S) (M) 1. conquering the Kurus. 3. a king of Janaka's dynasty and the son of Aja (*Bhā. Purāṇa*)

**Kurukuladhāma** (S) (M) 1. delight of the Kuru family. 3. another name for Duryodhana.

**Kurukulaśreṣṭha** (S) (M) 1. pre-eminent in the Kuru family. 3. another name for Bhīṣma and Yudhiṣṭhira.

**Kurukullā** (S) (M) 1. belonging to the Kuru race. 3. a Buddhist deity (*B. Literature*)

**Kurukulodvara** (S) (M) 1. elevating the Kuru family. 3. another name for Bhīṣma and Yudhiṣṭhira.

**Kurumukhya** (S) (M) 1. leader of the Kurus. 3. another name for Bhīṣma, Duryodhana and Yudhiṣṭhira.

**Kurumuni** (Tamil) (M) 1. short hermit. 3. another name for Agastya.

**Kurunandana** (S) (M) 1. son of the Kurus. 3. another name for Bhīṣma, Dhṛtarāṣṭra, Duryodhana and Yudhiṣṭhira.

**Kuruṇḍi** (S) (M) 1. resident of the land ot Kurus. 3. a ṛṣi in the 3rd Manvantara (*V. Purāṇa*)

**Kuruntika** (S) (M) resident of the land of the Kurus.

**Kurupāṇḍavāgrya** (S) (M) 1. first of the Kurus and Pāṇḍavas. 3. another name for Yudhiṣṭhira.

**Kurupati** (S) (M) 1. leader of the Kurus. 3. another name for Bhīṣma and Yudhiṣṭhira.

**Kurupravīra** (S) (M) 1. hero of the Kurus. 3. another name for Yudhiṣṭhira, Janamejaya and Duryodhana.

**Kurupṛthānāpati** (S) (M) 1. son of Pṛthā of the Kurus. 3. another name for Karṇa.

**Kurupuṅgava** (S) (M) 1. bull of the Kurus; chief of the Kurus. 3. another name for Yudhiṣṭhira and Duryodhana.

**Kururāja** (S) (M) 1. lord of the Kurus. 3. another name for Yudhiṣṭhira and Dhṛtarāṣṭra.

**Kurusattama** (S) (M) 1. best of the Kurus. 3. another name for Yudhiṣṭhira, Janamejaya and Duryodhana.

**Kurusiṁha** (S) (M) 1. lion of the Kurus. 3. another name for Duryodhana.

**Kuruśreṣṭha** (S) (M) 1. best among the Kurus. 3. another name for Bhīṣma, Arjuna, and Dhṛtarāṣṭtra.

**Kuruttama** (S) (M) 1. best of the Kurus. 3. another name for Yudhiṣṭhira and Duryodhana.

**Kuruvanśavardhana** (S) (M) 1. increasing the line of the Kurus. 3. another name for Dhṛtarāṣṭra.

**Kuruvardhana** (S) (M) 1. increasing the Kurus. 3. another name for Yudhiṣṭhira.

**Kuruvatsa** (S) (M) 1. power of the Kurus. 3. a son of Anavaratha.

**Kuruvīra** (S) (M) 1. hero of the Kurus. 3. another name for Yudhiṣṭhira and Karṇa.

**Kuruvṛddha** (S) (M) 1. eldest of the Kurus. 3. another name for Dhṛtarāṣṭra.

**Kuruvṛṣbha** (S) (M) 1. bull of the Kurus. 3. another name for Yudhiṣṭhira.

**Kuruyodha** (S) (M) 1. warrior of the Kurus. 3. another name for Karṇa.

**Kuśa** (S) (M) 1. the sacred grass *Poa cynosuroides* or *Desmostachhupa bipinnata*. 2. this grass is primarily used in sacred ceremonies. 3. a sage who was the son of Brahmā, the husband of Vaidarbhī and the father of Kuśāmbha, Kuśanābha, Asurtarajasa and Vasu (*H. Purāṇa*); a king of the Kuru dynasty who was the son of Suhotra and Girīkā (*A. Purāṇa*); a son of Rāma and the king of Kuśāvatī (*V. Rāmāyaṇa*); a sage who was an ancestor of Viśvāmitra (*V. Rāmāyaṇa*); a son of Lava the king of Kāśmira (*R. Taraṅginī*); a son of Vidarbha (*K. Granthāvali*); a great division of the world

(*Bhā. Purāṇa*); a son of vasu Uparićara (*H. Purāṇa*); the founder of Kuśasthali (*Sk. Purāṇa*)

**Kuśadhārā** (S) (F) 1. with sharp waves. 3. a river of ancient India (*M. Bh.*)

**Kuśadhvaja** (S) (M) 1. grass flag. 3. a Brāhmin and son of Bṛhaspati (*U. Rāmāyaṇa*); a brother of King Janaka (*V. Rāmāyaṇa*); a prince and son of Hrasvaroman (*Brahma Purāṇa*)

**Kuśagra** (S) (M) 1. the sharp edge of a blade of Kuśa grass. 2. sharp; shrewd. 3. a son of Bṛhadratha (*H. Purāṇa*)

**Kuśaketu** (S) (M) 1. grass bannered. 3. another name for Brahmā.

**Kuśākṣa** (S) (M) sharp eyed.

**Kuśala** (S) (M) 1. one who brings the sacred grass; skilled; efficient; right; good; happy; clever; auspicious; proficient; skill; strategy; efficiency. 3. another name for Śiva.

**Kuśalin** (S) (M) healthy; clever; prosperous; auspicious.

**Kuśāmbha** (S) (M) 1. son of Kuśa. 3. a son of sage Kuśa, the father of Śakra and Gādhi, the grandfather of Viśvāmitra and the builder of Kauśāmbhi (*Br. Purāṇa*); a son of Uparićaravasu (*H. Purāṇa*)

**Kuśanābha** (S) (M) 1. with kuśā grass in his navel. 2. chaste. 3. a son of sage Kuśa and Vaidharbhī, husband of Ghṛtāćī and the father of a 100 daughters (*V. Rāmāyaṇa*)

**Kuśanetra** (S) (M) 1. grass eyed. 3. a daitya (*M. Bh.*)

**Kuśaśārdula** (S) (M) 1. tiger in the sacrificial grass. 3. another name for Bhīma.

**Kuśāśva** (S) (M) 1. fast horse. 3. an Ikṣvāku king who was the son of King Sahadeva and the father of Somadatta (*V. Rāmāyaṇa*)

**Kuśāvarta** (S) (M) 1. surrounded by kuśā grass; passage of the Gaṅgā. 2. pious. 3. a son of King Ṛṣabha (*Bh. Purāṇa*); another name for Śiva.

**Kuśeśaya** (S) (M) 1. one who rests on the kuśā grass. 3. one of the 6 great mountains of the Kuśa island (*M. Bh.*)

**Kuṣidin** (S) (M) 1. moneylender. 3. a sage of the order of Vyāsa's disciples (*Bhāgavata*)

**Kuśika** (S) (M) 1. with squint eyes. 3. a monarch of the Purū dynasty who was the father of Gādhi and the grandfather of Viśvāmitra (*M. Bh./Ṛg Veda*); a sage (*M. Bh.*); Indian Dammer Tree (*Shorea robusta*); Bedda Nut (*Terminalia belerica*)

**Kuśīlava** (S) (M) 1. bard. 3. another name for Vālmīki.

**Kuśin** (S) (M) 1. furnished with kuśa grass. 3. another name for Vālmīki.

**Kuṣmāndaka** (S) (M) 1. pumpkin gourd (*Beninkasa cerifera*). 3. an attendant of Śiva (*M. Bh.*); a serpent (*M. Bh.*)

**Kūṣmāṇḍinī** (S) (F) 1. born from a pumpkin. 3. a goddess (*H. Purāṇa*)

**Kuśodakā** (S) (F) 1. water purified by kuśā. 3. Dākṣāyāṇī in Kuśādvīpa.

**Kuṣṭha** (S) (M) 1. found on earth; dwelling on earth. 3. a herb (*Costus speciosus*) which grew along with Soma on the peaks of the Himālayas and was described as the best and all healing (*A. Veda*)

**Kustubha** (S) (M) 1. sea; ocean. 3. another name for Viṣṇu.

**Kustumbaru** (S) (M) 1. the coriander plant (*Coriandrum sativum*). 3. one of Kubera's rākṣasa attendants (*M. Bh.*); a rākṣasa in Kubera's court (*M. Bh.*)

**Kusumā** (S) (F) 1. flower like. 2. a blossom; Ringworm Plant (*Cassia obtusifolia*); Yellow Champaka (*Michelia champaka*)

**Kusuma** (S) (M) 1. flower. 2. a form of fire. 3. an attendant of the 6th Arhat of the present Avasarpinī; one of the 5 attendants given by Dhātā to Skanda (*M. Bh.*)

**Kusumabāṇa** (S) (M) 1. flower arrowed. 3. another name for Kāma.

**Kusumaćandra** (S) (F) moon among flowers; the kuṁkuma or the saffron flower.

**Kusumākara** (S) (M) 1. treasure of flowers. 2. a garden; nosegay; the spring season.

**Kusumaketu** (S) (M) 1. flower bannered. 3. a kiṇnara.

**Kusumalakṣmaṇa** (S) (M) 1. with flowers as a symbol. 3. another name for Pradyumna.

**Kusumalatā** (S) (F) a blossoming creeper.

**Kusumanaga** (S) (M) 1. flower mountain. 3. a

mountain.

**Kusumāñjali** (S) (F) an offering of flowers.

**Kusumaśekhara** (S) (M) **1.** best among flowers. **2.** a chaplet of flowers.

**Kusumaśreṣṭha** (S) (M) the best flower.

**Kusumavatī** (S) (F) **1.** with flowers. **3.** another name for Pāṭaliputra.

**Kusumāyudha** (S) (M) **1.** one who has flowers as his weapons. **3.** another name for Kāma.

**Kusumbha** (S) (M) outward affection; water pot of a sage; gold; Safflower (*Carthamus tinctorius*); Saffron (*Crocus sativus*)

**Kusumbhaparvata** (S) (M) **1.** golden mountain. **3.** a mountain surrounding Mahāmeru (*D. Bhāgavata*)

**Kusumeśa** (S) (M) **1.** lord of flowers. **3.** another name for Kāma.

**Kusumeśu** (S) (M) **1.** with an arrow of flowers. **3.** the bow of Kāma.

**Kusumitā** (S) (F) decorated with flowers; made of flowers.

**Kusummayā** (S) (F) consisting of flowers.

**Kusumoda** (S) (M) sea of flowers.

**Kusumojjvala** (S) (M) brilliant with blossoms.

**Kusumujvala** (S) (M) brilliant with blossoms.

**Kūṭa** (S) (M) **1.** the bone on the forehead; highest; most excellent; heap. **3.** a constellation (*V's B. Samhitā*); another name for Agastya.

**Kuta** (S) (M) **1.** to spread. **3.** one of the 18 attendants of the sun.

**Kūtamohana** (S) (M) **1.** bewildering cheats. **3.** another name for Skanda.

**Kutanu** (S) (M) **1.** deformed. **3.** a form of Kubera with 3 legs.

**Kutha** (S) (M) **1.** a painted cloth; sacrificial grass (*Poa cynosuroides*); wealth. **3.** Śākyāmuni in one of his 34 births.

**Kuṭhāra** (S) (M) **1.** spade; axe. **3.** a serpent of Dhṛtarāṣṭra's family who was among those that received Balarāma when he went into the sea (*M. Bh.*)

**Kuthodarī** (S) (F) **1.** wealthy; with a large stomach. **3.** a daughter of Nikumbha (*K. Purāṇa*)

**Kuthumi** (S) (M) **1.** dressed in sacrificial grass (*Poa cynosuroides*). **3.** a teacher and author of a law book.

**Kuṭilā** (S) (F) **1.** curved. **2.** curled; bent; flowing in curved lines. **3.** a river.

**Kuṭilageśa** (S) (M) **1.** lord of rivers. **2.** the ocean.

**Kuṭimukha** (S) (M) **1.** curved face. **3.** an attendant of Kubera (*M. Bh.*)

**Kutsa** (S) (M) **1.** from where? why? lightning; thunderbolt. **3.** a ṛṣī who was the author of several hymns of the *Ṛg Veda* and a sometime friend of Indra who helped him to defeat the demon Śuṣṇa and win the sun (*Ṛg Veda*); a descendant of Aṅgiras (*Ṛg Veda*)

**Kuvala** (S) (M) **1.** one who enriches knowledge. **2.** water lily (*Nymphaea alba*); pearl; water.

**Kuvalaya** (S) (M) **1.** the Blue Lotus (*Nymphaea stellata*). **2.** the orb.

**Kuvalayadhṛs** (S) (F) **1.** blue lotus eyed. **2.** with beautiful eyes.

**Kuvalayāditya** (S) (M) **1.** lord of the Blue Lotus (*Nymphaea stellata*). **3.** a prince (*R. Taraṅginī*); another name for the sun.

**Kuvalayapīda** (S) (M) **1.** gentle as the lotus. **3.** a daitya who changed into an elephant and became the vehicle of Kaṅsa; a king (*R. Taraṅginī*)

**Kuvalayāśva** (S) (M) **1.** with blue horses. **3.** the prince Dhundhumāra (*V. Purāṇa*); the prince Pratardana (*M. Purāṇa*)

**Kuvalayavatī** (S) (F) **1.** possessing Blue Lotuses (*Nymphaea stellata*). **3.** a princess (*K. Sāgara*)

**Kuvalayeśa** (S) (M) lord of the earth; ruler of waters; lord of the water lilies.

**Kuvalayiṇī** (S) (F) abounding in water lilies.

**Kuvalayitā** (S) (F) decorated with water lilies.

**Kuvaleśaya** (S) (M) **1.** one who rests in the Blue Lotus (*Nymphaea stellata*). **3.** another name for Viṣṇu.

**Kuvam** (S) (M) **1.** producer of the earth. **3.** another name for the sun.

**Kuvara** (S) (M) **1.** astringent in flavour. **2.** fragrant. **3.** a gandharva.

**Kuvarānī** (S) (F) **1.** lady of the lotuses. **2.** princess.

**Kuvaya** (S) (M) 1. the Barn Owl. 2. causing a bad harvest. 3. a rākṣasa slain by Indra; an asura mentioned in the *Ṛg Veda*.

**Kuvīrā** (S) (F) 1. warrior of the earth; brave woman. 3. a river (*M. Bh.*)

**Kvaṇa** (S) (M) 1. to sound; to tinkle; to hum. 2. to sound as a musical instrument; to blow a flute.

L

**Labdha** (S) (M) acquired; obtained.

**Labdhakīrti** (S) (M) one who has acquired fame.

**Labdhasiddhi** (S) (M) one who has attained perfection.

**Labdhavarṇa** (S) (M) 1. one who has gained a knowledge of letters. 2. learned; wise; famous; celebrated.

**Labdhodaya** (S) (M) one who has attained prosperity.

**Labdhudaya** (S) (M) 1. one who has attained prosperity. 2. born; sprung.

**Lābha** (S) (M) 1. profit; perception. 2. advantage; gain.

**Lābukī** (S) (F) a kind of lute.

**Lagadāćārya** (S) (M) 1. most beautiful; most handsome. 3. an astronomer.

**Laghat** (S) (M) the wind.

**Laghiman** (S) (M) 1. lightness. 3. a siddhi in which one can assume lightness at will.

**Laghu** (S) (M) 1. light; small; subtle; swift; soft; low; gentle; lovely; pure; young. 3. the Nakṣatrās or the constellations Hasta, Puṣya and Aśvinī.

**Laghuga** (S) (M) 1. moving quickly. 3. another name for Vāyu.

**Laghupuṣpā** (S) (F) delicate flower; flower of the Kadamba tree (*Anthocephalus indicus*)

**Laghuvī** (S) (F) delicate; small.

**Laharī** (S) (F) wave.

**Lajjā** (S) (F) 1. modesty. 3. a daughter of Dakṣa and the wife of Dharmā and mother of Vinaya (*V. Purāṇa*)

**Lajjakā** (S) (F) modest; the Wild Cotton tree (*Gossypium stocksii*)

**Lajjanā** (S) (F) modest; the Wild Cotton tree (*Gossypium stocksii*)

**Lajjāsīlā** (S) (F) of modest character.

**Lajjavantī** (S) (F) shy; modest; the Touch-me-not plant (*Mimosa pudica*)

**Lajjāvatī** (S) (F) full of modesty.

**Lajjinī** (S) (M) shy; modest; the touch-me-not plant (*Mimosa pudica*)

**Lajjitā** (S) (F) coy; modest; bashful.

**Lakhan/Lakka/Lakke** (H) (M) 1. one who accomplishes the target; one with auspicious marks. 3. colloquial short forms of Lakṣmaṇa.

**Lakhpati** (S) (M) 1. a millionaire. 3. consort of Lakṣmī and the lord of lakhs; another name for Viṣṇu.

**Lākinī** (S) (F) 1. one who takes and gives. 3. a tāntric goddess.

**Lākṣā** (S) (F) lac; a red dye used by women of ancient India for feet and lips; the lac plant; lac obtained from cochineal.

**Lakṣa** (S) (M) mark; aim; target; 100,000.

**Lakṣaka** (S) (M) ray of beauty.

**Lākṣakī** (S) (F) 1. relating to or made of/or dyed with lac. 3. another name for Sītā.

**Lakṣamaṇā** (S) (F) 1. with auspicious marks; accomplisher of target. 3. a wife of Kṛṣṇa (*M. Bh.*); a daughter of Duryodhana; an apsarā; a Buddhist Devī; the mother of the 8th Arhat of the present Avasarpiṇī; another name for Sumitrā, a wife of Daśaratha and the mother of Lakṣmaṇa.

**Lakṣaṇa** (S) (M) with an auspicious mark.

**Lakṣaṇā** (S) (M) 1. aim; object; view. 3. the daughter of Duryodhana and wife of Śamba (*M. Bh.*); an apsarā who danced for Arjuna (*M. Bh.*); the daughter of King Bṛhatsena of Madra and mother of 10 sons (*Bhā. Purāṇa*)

**Lakṣaṇya** (S) (M) 1. serving as a mark with auspicious marks; accomplisher of aim. 2. one who is successful.

**Lakṣaprasādan** (S) (M) 1. accomplisher of target. 2. one who is successful; a diviner.

**Lakṣin** (S) (M) with auspicious marks.

**Lakṣitā** (S) (F) seen; beheld; marked; distinguished.

**Lakṣmaṇa** (S) (M) 1. with auspicious marks; accomplisher of target. 2. lucky; fortunate. 3. the son of King Daśaratha and Sumitrā of Ayodhyā, half-brother of Rāma, husband of Sītā's sister Ūrmilā, the father of Aṅgada and Ćandraketu, accompanied Rāma into exile and is considered the embodiment of loyalty (*V. Rāmāyaṇa*); a son of Duryodhana who was a great archer (*M. Bh.*); the Sārasa crane (*Ardea Sibirica*)

**Lakṣmaṇya** (S) (M) 1. son of Lakṣmaṇa; visible far and wide. 3. another name for

Dhvanya.

**Lakṣmī** (S) (F) 1. fortune; prosperity; success; beauty; splendour; lustre; charm; the wife of a hero; pearl; turmeric. 3. the consort of Mahāviṣṇu, the goddess of fortune, prosperity and success, depicted as emerging from a lotus standing in the Ocean of Milk and the more prominent of her incarnations on the earth include Tulasī, Rādhā, Sītā and Vedavatī (*D. Bh. Purāṇa*); the daughter of Dakṣa and wife of Dharma (*M. Bh.*); a digit of the moon; *Curcuma longa*; *Prosopis spicigera*; *Aphanamixis polystachya*.

**Lakṣmīćandra** (S) (M) 1. the moon of Lakṣmī. 3. another name for Viṣṇu.

**Lakṣmīdāsa** (S) (M) 1. devotee of Lakṣmī. 3. another name for Viṣṇu.

**Lakṣmīdeva** (S) (M) 1. lord of Lakṣmī. 3. another name for Viṣṇu.

**Lakṣmīdhara** (S) (M) 1. possessor of Lakṣmī. 3. another name for Viṣṇu.

**Lakṣmīgṛha** (S) (F) 1. the home of Lakṣmī. 2. the Red Lotus plant (*Nymphaea rubra*)

**Lakṣmīkānta** (S) (M) 1. beloved of Lakṣmī. 3. another name for Viṣṇu.

**Lakṣmīlāla** (S) (M) 1. beloved of Lakṣmī. 3. another name for Viṣṇu.

**Lakṣmīnārāyaṇa** (S) (M) Viṣṇu and Lakṣmī conjoined.

**Lakṣmīnātha** (S) (M) 1. lord of Lakṣmī. 3. another name for Viṣṇu.

**Lakṣmīndra** (S) (M) 1. lord of Lakṣmī. 3. another name for Viṣṇu.

**Lakṣmīprasāda** (S) (M) 1. given by Lakṣmī. 2. the ruby.

**Lakṣmīpuṣpa** (S) (M) 1. flower of Lakṣmī. 2. clove; ruby.

**Lakṣmīputra** (S) (M) 1. the son of Lakṣmī. 3. another name for Lava, Kuśa and Kāma.

**Lakṣmīramaṇa** (S) (M) 1. beloved of Lakṣmī. 3. another name for Viṣṇu.

**Lakṣmīśa** (S) (M) 1. lord of Lakṣmī. 2. prosperous; the mango tree (*Mangifera indica*). 3. another name for Viṣṇu.

**Lakṣmīsahaja** (S) (M) 1. brother of Lakṣmī. 3. a horse of Indra; another name for the moon.

**Lakṣmīśaja** (S) (M) 1. produced with Lakṣmī. 3. another name for the moon.

**Lakṣmīsakha** (S) (M) 1. companion of Lakṣmī. 3. another name for Viṣṇu.

**Lakṣmīśankara** (S) (M) pacifier of Lakṣmī; Śiva and Lakṣmī conjoined.

**Lakṣmīvata** (S) (M) fortunate; wealthy; handsome; beautiful; the Breadfruit tree.

**Lakṣmīvinaya** (S) (M) good fortune; modest conduct.

**Lāla** (H) (M) red; heart; son.

**Lalantikā** (S) (F) a long necklace.

**Lalāṭa** (S) (M) the forehead.

**Lalāṭākṣa** (S) (M) 1. with an eye in the forehead. 3. another name for Śiva.

**Lālāti** (S) (F) forehead.

**Lalāṭikā** (S) (F) an ornament of the forehead.

**Lālavihārī** (S) (M) 1. bearer of a red mark; one who dwells in the hearts. 3. another name for Kṛṣṇa.

**Lālila** (S) (M) 1. beautiful; looked after with affection. 3. another name for Agni.

**Lālimā** (S) (F) 1. reddish glow; redness. 2. aurora; blush; roseate; beautiful; lovely; charming; an ornament for the forehead; the best of its kind; sign; banner; symbol.

**Lalita** (S) (M) (F) 1. lovely; desirable; pleasing; soft; gentle; graceful; wanton; voluptuous; sporting. 3. a rāga.

**Lalitā, Lalithā** (S) (F) 1. woman; lovely; desirable. 2. a woman. 3. the Fairy Bluebird (*Irena puella*); a rāga; a form of Durgā; a river; a gopī.

**Lalitaćandra** (S) (M) beautiful moon.

**Lalitāditya** (S) (M) 1. beautiful sun. 3. an ancient Kāśmira king (*R. Taranginī*)

**Lalitakā** (S) (F) 1. favourite daughter. 3. an ancient holy Tirtha of Brahmā (*M. Bh.*)

**Lalitaka** (S) (M) beautiful; favourite.

**Lalitakiśor** (S) (M) 1. beautiful youth; lovely youth. 3. another name for Kṛṣṇa.

**Lalitakumāra** (S) (M) 1. beautiful youth. 3. another name for Kṛṣṇa.

**Lalitaloćanā** (S) (F) 1. with beautiful eyes. 3. a daughter of the vidyādhara Vāmadatta (*K. Sāgara*)

**Lalitamohana** (S) (M) 1. handsome; attractive. 3. another name for Kṛṣṇa.

**Lalitāṅga** (S) (M) with a beautiful body.

**Lalitāṅgī** (S) (F) with a beautiful body.

**Lalitasyā** (S) (F) loveliness; charm; grace.

**Lālitya** (S) (M) loveliness; charm; beauty; grace.

**Lallan** (S) (M) 1. child. 3. the Śala (*Shorea robusta*) and Piyāla (*Buchanania latifolia*) trees.

**Lāllī** (S) (F) blush; radiance; prestige; sweetness.

**Lālukā** (S) (F) necklace.

**Lamaka** (S) (M) lover; a gallant.

**Lambā** (S) (F) 1. great; large; spacious; tall; pendulous. 3. a daughter of Dakṣa and Asiknī and the wife of Dharma (*H. Purāṇa*); a mother attending Skanda (*M. Bh.*); another name for Durgā and Lakṣmī.

**Lambakeśaka** (S) (F) 1. long haired. 3. a sage (*G. Sutra*)

**Lambākṣa** (S) (M) 1. long eyed. 3. a sage.

**Lambana** (S) (M) 1. great; large; spacious; tall; pendulous; a long necklace. 3. a son of Jyotiṣmat (*V. Purāṇa*); another name for Śiva.

**Lambapayodharā** (S) (F) 1. large breasted. 3. a mother of Skanda (*M. Bh.*)

**Lambhit** (S) (M) procured; cherished.

**Lambinī** (S) (F) 1. hanging down. 3. a mother of Skanda (*M. Bh.*)

**Lambodara** (S) (M) 1. big bellied. 2. large; great; a glutton. 3. another name for Gaṇeśā.

**Lambodarī** (S) (F) 1. consort of Lambodara. 3. another name for Gaṇeśanī.

**Lambūṣā** (S) (F) 1. a hanging ornament. 2. a necklace of 7 strings.

**Langapriyā** (S) (F) 1. adorable. 3. the Kadambā tree (*Anthrocephalus indicus*)

**Lāṅgala** (S) (M) 1. a plough. 2. the Coconut tree (*Cocos nucifera*). 3. a son of Suddhoda and grandson of Śākya (*Bh. Purāṇa*)

**Lāṅgali** (S) (F) 1. the plough carrier. 3. a celebrated Purāṇic river which worships Varuṇa in the form of a goddess (*M. Bh.*)

**Lāṅgalin** (S) (M) 1. one who carries a plough. 3. another name for Balarāma.

**Lāṅgaliśā** (S) (F) 1. the pole of the plough. 3. another name for Durgā.

**Laṅghati** (S) (F) 1. flowing with speed. 3. a celebrated Purāṇic river which worships Varuṇa in the form of a goddess who sits in his court (*M. Bh.*)

**Laṇiban** (S) (M) 1. the phlegmatic humour. 3. another name for Śiva.

**Laṅkālakṣmī** (S) (F) 1. the goddess of Laṅkā. 3. the goddess of Laṅkā who was the incarnation of Vijayalakṣmī or the goddess of victory and was released from her curse by Hanumān (*K. Rāmāyaṇa*)

**Laṅkānātha** (S) (M) 1. lord of Laṅkā. 3. another name for Rāvaṇa and Vibhīṣaṇa.

**Laṅkāpati** (S) (M) 1. master of Laṅkā. 3. another name for Rāvaṇa and Vibhīṣaṇa.

**Laṅkāri** (S) (M) 1. enemy of Laṅkā. 3. another name for Rāma.

**Laṅkeśa** (S) (M) 1. lord of Laṅkā. 3. another name for Rāvaṇa and Vibhīṣaṇa.

**Laṅkiṇī** (S) (F) 1. belonging to Laṅkā. 3. the tutelary goddess of Laṅkā (*V. Rāmāyaṇa*)

**Lapitā** (S) (F) 1. spoken; speech; voice. 3. the wife of sage Mandapāla (*M. Bh.*)

**Lasā** (S) (F) saffron; turmeric.

**Lasadanśu** (S) (M) 1. with flashing rays. 2. the sun.

**Lāsaka** (S) (M) 1. a dancer; a peacock; one who frolics. 3. another name for Śiva.

**Laṣita** (S) (M) wished; desired.

**Lastakin** (S) (M) a bow.

**Latā** (S) (F) 1. vine; a string of pearls; a slender woman; the Madhavi creeper (*Hiptage madoblata*); the Priyaṅgu creeper. 3. an apsarā who was set free from a curse by Arjuna (*M. Bh.*); a daughter of Meru and wife of Ilāvṛta (*Bh. Purāṇa*)

**Latabāṇa** (S) (M) 1. creeper arrowed. 3. another name for Kama.

**Laṭabhā** (S) (F) handsome; beautiful.

**Laṭākara** (S) (M) a collection of pearls.

**Latāmaṇi** (S) (F) coral.

**Latāparṇa** (S) (M) 1. the leaf of the vine. 3. another name for Viṣṇu.

**Latāveṣṭa** (S) (M) 1. surrounded by creepers. 3. a 5 coloured mountain on the southern side of Dvārakā (*H. Purāṇa*)

**Latikā** (S) (F) ornament of the forehead; the vermilion dot on the forehead; a string of pearls; a small creeper.

**Laṭkan** (S) (M) (F) an ornament of the hair; lace; the Lorikeet bird (*Loriculus vernalis*)

**Lauheyī** (S) (F) 1. copper coloured. 3. an apsarā.

**Lauhi** (S) (M) 1. made of metal. 3. a son of Aṣṭaka.

**Lauhita** (S) (M) 1. made of metal; red. 3. the trident of Śiva.

**Lauhitya** (S) (M) 1. red. 3. a sacred place constructed by Rāma, bathing in the pond of which one turns golden (*M. Bh.*)

**Lava** (S) (M) 1. a particle. 2. a piece; tiny. 3. a twin son of Rāma and Sītā and the brother of Kuśa (*V. Rāmāyaṇa*)

**Lavalī** (S) (F) 1. a vine. 2. Custard apple (*Annona reticulate*)

**Lavalikā** (S) (F) a tiny vine.

**Lavalīna** (S) (F) devoted; engrossed.

**Lavama** (S) (M) 1. clove. 2. small. 3. one of the 7 oceans which surrounded the dvīpas or the islands in concentric belts.

**Lavaṇā** (S) (F) lustrous; beautiful.

**Lavaṇa** (S) (M) 1. handsome; lovely; salt; saline. 3. a son of a demon called Madhu who was killed by Śatrughna (*D. Bhāgavata*); a king of the Hariśćandra dynasty who conducted the Rajasūya yajña; a demon who lived on the island of Ramaṇīyaka (*M. Bh.*); a grandson of Hariśćandra (*V. Purāṇa*); Intellect tree (*Celastrus paniculata*)

**Lavanākara** (S) (M) 1. salt mine. 2. treasure of grace and beauty.

**Lavaṇāśva** (S) (M) 1. horse of salt. 3. the ocean; a sage who blessed Yudhiṣṭhira (*M. Bh.*)

**Lavaṇātaka** (S) (M) 1. destroyer of the demon Lavaṇa. 3. another name for Śatrughna.

**Lavaṅgalatā** (S) (F) beautiful creeper; the clove vine (*Limonia scandens*)

**Lavaṅgi** (S) (F) 1. of the clove plant. 3. an apsarā.

**Lavaṅika** (S) (M) handsome; beautiful; salty.

**Lavaṇīśa** (S) (M) 1. lord of the sea. 3. another name for Varuṇa.

**Lavaṇodaka** (S) (M) 1. containing salt water. 3. another name for the ocean.

**Lāvaṇyā, Laboṇyā** (S) (F) lustrous; beautiful.

**Lāvaṇya** (S) (M) beauty; lustre.

**Lāvaṇyalakṣmī** (S) (F) goddess of beauty.

**Lavaṇyālaya** (S) (M) 1. sea of salt; sea of beauty; abode of beauty. 3. another name for the ocean.

**Lāvaṇyamaya** (S) (M) 1. consisting of salt water. 2. handsome; beautiful; charming.

**Lāvaṇyamayī** (S) (F) consisting of beauty; full of charm.

**Lāvaṇyavata** (S) (M) 1. bearing charm. 2. handsome; beautiful; charming.

**Lavarāja** (S) (M) 1. king of the moment. 3. a sage (*R. Taraṅginī*)

**Lavitra** (S) (M) 1. the subtle one; plucking; wool; hair. 3. another name for Śiva.

**Laya** (S) (M) 1. deep concentration; fusion; rest. 3. a Purāṇic king who was a member of the court of Yama (*M. Bh.*); another name for the Supreme Being.

**Lekha** (S) (M) 1. document. 2. a deity; god. 3. a set of 8 celestial beings of the Raivatā Manvantara (*Purāṇas*)

**Lekhā** (S) (F) 1. line. 2. lightning; streak; a figure; a mark; the crescent moon; the crest; horizon.

**Lekhābhra** (S) (M) 1. as bright as light. 2. shining.

**Lekharāja** (S) (M) 1. lord of the gods. 3. another name for the Supreme Being.

**Lekharṣabha** (S) (M) 1. bull of the gods; best of gods. 3. another name for Indra.

**Lelāyamānā** (S) (F) 1. flickering. 3. one of the 7 tongues of fire (*M. Upaniṣad*)

**Lelihāna** (S) (M) 1. darting out the tongue. 2. a serpent. 3. another name for Śiva.

**Lepākṣī** (S) (F) with painted eyes.

**Leśa** (S) (M) 1. a small portion. 2. a small song. 3. a son of King Suhotra.

**Libnī** (S) (F) a manuscript of the gods.

**Libujā** (S) (F) vine.

**Likhita** (S) (M) 1. drawn; fainted; delineated.

3. a sage whose hands were cut off by King Sudyumna but which grew back due to his penance (*M. Bh.*); a sage and author of works of law (*M. Bh.*)

**Lilā** (S) (F) 1. play; pleasure; amusement; ease; beauty; charm; grace; play of universal energy. 3. a yoginī.

**Lilādhara** (S) (M) 1. playful. 3. the consort of Lilāvatī; another name for Viṣṇu.

**Lilādhya** (S) (M) 1. the abode of pleasure. 3. a son of Viśvāmitra (*M. Bh.*)

**Lilambuja** (S) (M) lovely lotus.

**Lilāvatāra** (S) (M) 1. pleasure incarnate. 3. the earthly descent of Viṣṇu as Kṛṣṇa.

**Lilāvatī** (S) (F) 1. playful; beautiful; graceful; charming. 3. the wife of the demon Maya; a well-known work by Bhāskaraćārya; the wife of King Dhruvasandhi of Kosala (*Bh. Purāṇa*); the wife of Avīkṣita; another name for Durgā.

**Limpa** (S) (M) 1. smearing; anointing. 3. one of Śiva's attendants.

**Linā** (S) (F) 1. absorbed; united with. 2. merged; engrossed.

**Liṅga** (S) (M) mark; sign; symbol; badge; the genital organ of Śiva worshipped in the form of a phallic idol.

**Lingadhārinī** (S) (F) 1. wearing the badge of Śiva. 3. Dākṣāyāṇi in Naimiṣa.

**Lipi** (S) (F) alphabet; manuscript; document; anointing; writing.

**Lipikā** (S) (F) 1. alphabet; manuscript. 2. writing; anointing.

**Lipsita** (S) (M) desired.

**Lobha** (S) (M) 1. greed; cupidity. 3. avarice personified as a son of Dambha and Māyā; a spiritual son of Brahmā born from his lip (*M. Purāṇa*)

**Loćamastaka** (S) (M) 1. with a flexible head. 2. humble; well mannered.

**Loćanā** (S) (F) 1. eye. 2. illuminating; brightening. 3. a Buddhist goddess (*B. Literature*)

**Loćanānanda** (S) (M) delight of the eye.

**Loha** (S) (M) 1. red; iron. 3. an asura who attacked the Pāṇḍavas and was blinded (*Sk. Purāṇa*)

**Lohajavaktra** (S) (M) 1. with the face of a goat. 3. another name for Skanda.

**Lohajit** (S) (M) 1. that which conquers iron. 2. a diamond.

**Lohakārī** (S) (F) 1. blacksmith. 3. a tāntric goddess (*T. Śastra*)

**Lohamekhala** (S) (M) 1. an iron ornament for the waist. 3. a follower of Skanda (*M. Bh.*)

**Lohamukha** (S) (M) 1. with an iron mouth. 3. a follower of Skanda (*M. Bh.*)

**Lohamuktikā** (S) (F) a red pearl.

**Lohita** (S) (M) 1. red; copper; the planet Mars. 3. a king who was conquered by Arjuna (*M. Bh.*); a serpent who is a member of the court of Varuṇa (*M. Bh.*); another name for the river Brahmaputra.

**Lohitā** (S) (F) 1. red. 2. ruby. 3. one of 7 tongues of fire (*G. Sūtra*)

**Lohitaćandana** (S) (M) red powder; saffron; red sandalwood.

**Lohitagātra** (S) (M) 1. red limbed. 3. another name for Skanda.

**Lohitagrīva** (S) (M) 1. red necked. 3. another name for Agni (*M. Bh.*)

**Lohitākṣa** (S) (M) 1. red eyed. 3. a sage who took part in the Sarpāṣatra yajña of King Janamejaya (*M. Bh.*); an attendant of Skanda given to him by Brahmā (*M. Bh.*); the Indian Cuckoo (*Cuculus varius*) (*A. Koṣa*); another name for Viṣṇu.

**Lohitākṣī** (S) (F) 1. red eyed. 3. a follower of Skanda (*M. Bh.*)

**Lohitamukti** (S) (F) ruby.

**Lohitāṅga** (S) (M) 1. red bodied. 3. the trident of Śiva (*S. Purāṇa*); another name for Mars.

**Lohitārāṇī** (S) (F) 1. red crossing. 3. an ancient river of Purāṇic fame (*M. Bh.*)

**Lohitāśva** (S) (M) 1. with red horses. 3. another name for Agni and Śiva.

**Lohitāyanī** (S) (F) 1. red. 3. the daughter of Lohitārāṇī and a foster mother of Subrahmaṇya (*M. Bh.*)

**Lohitikā** (S) (F) the ruby.

**Lohityā** (S) (F) 1. rice. 3. the Purāṇic name for the river Brahmaputra (*V's B. Saṃhitā*), whose goddess is a devotee of Varuṇa and sits in his court (*H. Purāṇa*); an apsara.

**Lohottama** (S) (M) 1. the best metal. 2. gold.

**Loka** (S) (M) heaven; world; people.

**Lokabandhu** (S) (M) 1. friend of the world. 3. another name for Śiva and the sun.

**Lokaćakṣus** (S) (M) 1. the eye of the world. 3. another name for the sun.

**Lokāćara** (S) (M) 1. one who roams in all the 3 worlds. 2. one who acts in accordance to the customs of the world.

**Lokādhipa** (S) (M) lord of the world.

**Lokādhipati** (S) (M) master of the world.

**Lokādhyakṣa** (S) (M) president of the world.

**Lokādi** (S) (M) 1. creator of the world. 3. another name for Brahmā.

**Lokadvāra** (S) (M) the gateway of heaven.

**Lokajananī** (M) (F) 1. mother of the world. 3. another name for Lakṣmī.

**Lokajita** (S) (M) 1. one who conquers the world; winning heaven. 3. another name for Buddha.

**Lokajyeṣṭha** (S) (M) 1. most distinguished among men. 3. another name for Buddha.

**Lokakāra** (S) (M) 1. creator of the world. 3. another name for Śiva.

**Lokākṣi** (S) (M) 1. eye of the world. 3. a sage.

**Lokāloka** (S) (F) 1. glory of the world; one who enlightens the people. 3. a mythical golden mountain that surrounds the earth and acts as a boundary to the 3 worlds (*A. Veda*)

**Lokamātrī** (S) (F) 1. mother of the world. 3. another name for Lakṣmī.

**Lokamaheśvara** (S) (M) 1. lord of the world. 3. another name for Kṛṣṇa.

**Lokanādu** (S) (M) master of the world.

**Lokanātha** (S) (M) 1. lord of the 3 worlds. 3. a Buddha; another name for Brahmā, Viṣṇu, Śiva and the sun.

**Lokanetra** (S) (M) 1. eye of the world. 2. one who surveys, checks and guides the world. 3. another name for Śiva.

**Lokapāla** (S) (M) 1. guardian of the world; the guardian of the 8 directions of the world. 3. title of Indra, Agni, Yama Sūrya, Pavana, Kubera, Soma and Varuṇa.

**Lokapati** (S) (M) 1. master of the world. 2. lord of the 3 worlds. 3. another name for Brahmā and Viṣṇu.

**Lokapitāmaha** (S) (M) 1. progenitor of the world. 3. another name for Brahmā.

**Lokapradipa** (S) (M) 1. light of the world. 3. a Buddha.

**Lokarakṣa** (S) (M) 1. protector of the people. 2. a king.

**Lokarāma** (S) (M) one who delights the world.

**Lokarañjana** (S) (M) delight of the people.

**Lokasvāmī** (S) (M) 1. lord of the people. 2. lord of the 3 worlds.

**Lokātman** (S) (M) the soul of the universe.

**Lokavidhi** (S) (M) 1. creator of the world. 3. another name for Brahmā.

**Lokavya** (S) (M) (F) one who deserves heaven.

**Lokāyana** (S) (M) 1. father of the world. 3. another name for Viṣṇu.

**Lokendra** (S) (M) lord of the 3 worlds.

**Lokeśa** (S) (M) 1. lord of the world. 3. a Buddha; another name for Brahmā.

**Lokeśvara** (S) (M) 1. lord of the world. 3. a Buddha; another name for Brahmā.

**Lokin** (S) (M) one who has conquered the next world; one who possesses a world.

**Loksādhaka** (S) (M) one who creates worlds.

**Lolā** (S) (F) 1. fickle; vibrating; changing; beautiful. 2. lightning. 3. the mother of the daitya Madhu; a yoginī; another name for Lakṣmī and Dākṣāyāṇī in Utpalavartaka.

**Lolitā** (S) (F) agitated; tremulous; fickle.

**Lomaharṣaṇa** (S) (M) 1. hair raising; thrilling. 3. the father of Sūta who related the Purāṇic tales and a member of the court of Yudhiṣṭhira (*M. Bh.*)

**Lomapāda** (S) (M) 1. with hairy feet. 3. the king of Aṅga who adopted the daughter of King Daśaratha (*K. Rāmāyaṇa*); a Yadu king who was the son of Vidarbha and the ancestor of the Ćedi dynasty (*P. Purāṇa*)

**Lomaśa** (S) (M) 1. hairy. 3. a great sage and storyteller whose tales form episodes in the Purāṇas; Sweet Flag (*Acorus calamus*)

**Lomaśā** (S) (M) 1. hairy. 3. an attendant of Durgā.

**Lopāmudrā** (S) (F) 1. with an imperceptible form. 3. the daughter of the king of Vidarbha, the wife of sage Agastya, the embodiment of wifely devotion and the supposed authoress of a part of the *Ṛg Veda*.

**Lotikā** (S) (F) 1. Sorrel (*Oxalis pussilla*). 2. light reddish-brown.

**Lubdhaka** (S) (M) 1. hunter. 3. the star Sirius.

**Lumbikā** (S) (F) a kind of musical instrument.

**Lumbinī** (S) (F) 1. grove. 3. the grove where Buddha was born (*B. Literature*)

**Lūṇadoṣa** (S) (M) 1. sinless. 3. an attendant of Śiva (*A. Koṣa*)

**Lūnaduṣkṛta** (S) (M) one whose sins have been destroyed.

**Lūṇakarṇa** (S) (M) with pierced ears.

**Luśa** (S) (M) 1. saffron. 3. a hermit and worshipper of Indra who composed hymns for the *Ṛg Veda*.

**Mabala** (S) (M) 1. pondering over troubles before solving them; boastful; deceiver. 3. another name for Śiva.

**Maćakruka** (S) (M) 1. churner; agitator. 3. a yakṣa guardian of the sacred spot which lies at the entrance to Kurukṣetra.

**Mada** (S) (M) 1. rapture; excitement; intoxication; passion; pride; hilarity; musk; wine; honey. 3. a son of Brahmā born of his pride (*V. Purāṇa*); a dānava (*H. Purāṇa*); a servant of Śiva (*Bhā. Purāṇa*); intoxication personified as a beast created by Ćyavana (*M. Bh.*); the 7th lunar mansion; another name for Kāma and Soma.

**Madālambe** 1. dependant upon intoxication. 2. excited; inspired; arrogant. 3. the mother of Bāsava the bull.

**Madālasā** (S) (F) 1. lazy with intoxication. 2. languid; indolent. 3. the daughter of the gandharva Viśvavasu and the wife of Kuvalayāśva (*Purāṇas*); the daughter of the rākṣasa Bhramaraketu; a vidyādharī and wife of Ćampaka (*D. Bh. Purāṇa*); the wife of King Ṛtadhvaja of Kāśī and the mother of Alarka.

**Madana** (S) (M) 1. passion; love; intoxicating; exhilarating; delighting; spring; Common Emetic Nut (*Randia dumetorum*); the *Vangueria spinosa* tree. 3. another name for Kāma.

**Madanabāṇa** (S) (M) 1. arrow of Kāma. 3. one of the 5 arrows of Kāma.

**Madanāditya** (S) (M) the sun of passion; Kāma or the god of love.

**Madanadviṣa** (S) (M) 1. enemy of Kāma. 3. another name for Śiva.

**Madanagopāla** (S) (M) 1. herdsman of love. 2. the attractive cowherd. 3. another name for Kṛṣṇa.

**Madanalekhā** (S) (F) 1. a love letter; a sequence of love. 3. the daughter of King Pratāpamukha of Varāṇasī (*K. Sāgara*)

**Madanam** (S) (M) delighting; intoxicating.

**Madanamanćukā** (S) (F) 1. erotically aroused. 3. a daughter of Madanavega and Kaliṅgasenā (*K. Sāgara*)

**Madanamañjarī** (S) (F) 1. bud of love. 3. a daughter of the yakṣa prince Dundubhi (*K. Sāgara*)

**Madanamohana** (S) (M) 1. one who attracts; love. 3. another name for Kṛṣṇa and Kāma (*Bha. Purāṇa*)

**Madanapāla** (S) (M) lord of love.

**Madanarekhā** (S) (F) 1. the path of Kāma. 3. the mother of Vikramāditya (*S. Dvātriṇśikā*)

**Madanavega** (S) (M) 1. with the speed of love. 2. sexual arousal. 3. the king of the vidyādharas (*K. Sāgara*)

**Madanī** (S) (F) vine; musk.

**Madanikā** (S) (F) 1. aroused; excited. 3. an apsarā who was the daughter of Menakā (*K. Sāgara*)

**Madapati** (S) (M) 1. lord of the soma. 3. another name for Viṣṇu and Indra.

**Madaprada** (S) (M) intoxicating.

**Madarāga** (S) (M) 1. intoxicated with passion. 3. another name for Kāma.

**Madavallabha** (S) (M) 1. passionate. 3. a gandharva.

**Madayantī** (S) (F) 1. exciting. 3. the wife of King Kalmāṣapāda (*M. Bh.*); Arabian Jasmine (*Jasminum sambac*); another name for Durgā.

**Madayantikā** (S) (F) 1. exciting. 2. the Arabian Jasmine (*Jasminum sambac*)

**Madayatī** (S) (F) 1. exciting; Arabian Jasmine (*Jasminum sambac*). 3. the wife of Mitrasaha (*K. Sāgara*)

**Mādayiṣṇu** (S) (M) delighting; intoxicating.

**Mādayitnu** (S) (M) 1. intoxicating. 3. another name for Kāma.

**Maderu** (S) (M) 1. very intoxicating. 2. worthy of praise.

**Madeśa** (S) (M) 1. lord of intoxication. 3. another name for Śiva.

**Mādhavā** (S) (F) 1. full of intoxication; verdal. 2. relate to the spring; exotic; exciting. 3. an apsarā sent by Indra to destroy the meditation of Viṣṇu (*Bhā. Purāṇa*)

**Mādhava** (S) (M) 1. vernal; relating to the spring; that which belongs to the descendants of Madhu i.e. the Yadavas. 3. a son of the 3rd Manu (*P. Purāṇa*); a ṛṣi under Manu Bhautya

(*T. Samhitā*); son of King Vikrama of Tāladhvaja (*P. Purāṇa*); a son of Yadu and Dhūmravarṇā (*Bhā. Purāṇa*); the 2nd month of spring; Butter tree (*Bassia latifolia*); another name for Kṛṣṇa, Śiva and Indra.

**Mādhavabhaṭṭa** (S) (M) **1.** learned Madhava. **3.** real name of Kavirāja.

**Mādhavaćandra** (S) (M) **1.** the moon of the Mādhavas. **3.** another name for Kṛṣṇa.

**Mādhavāćrya** (S) (M) **1.** the learned Mādhava. **3.** a celebrated scholar and brother of Sāyaṇa.

**Mādhavadāsa** (S) (M) devotee of Kṛṣṇa.

**Mādhavadeva** (S) (M) divine Kṛṣṇa.

**Mādhavanandana** (S) (M) **1.** son of the Mādhavas. **3.** another name for Kṛṣṇa.

**Mādhavapriyā** (S) (F) **1.** beloved of Mādhava. **3.** another name for Rādhā.

**Mādhavarāja** (S) (M) **1.** lord of the Mādhavas. **3.** another name for Kṛṣṇa.

**Mādhavaśrī** (S) (F) vernal beauty.

**Mādhavī** (S) (F) **1.** sweet; intoxicating drink; the date flower; honey-sugar; Sacred Basil (*Ocimum sanctum*); a woman of the race of Madhu. **3.** the Dākṣāyāṇī in Śrīśaila (*M. Bh.*); the daughter of King Yayāti (*M. Bh.*); a follower of Skanda (*M. Bh.*); a rāgiṇī; Fennel(*Foeniculum capillaceum*); *Hiptage madoblata*; another name for Durgā and Subhadrā.

**Mādhavika** (S) (M) **1.** one who collects honey. **2.** a creeper (*Gaertnera racemosa*); *Hiptage madoblata*.

**Mādhavīlatā** (S) (F) spring creeper; *Hiptage madoblata*; *Gaertnera racemosa*.

**Madhu** (S) (F) anything sweet; mead; Soma; honey; butter; nectar; sugar; water.

**Madhu** (S) (M) **1.** sweet. **2.** delicious; charming; delightful; honey; nectar; sugar; wine. **3.** the 2 asuras killed by Viṣṇu and Śatrughna (*M. Bh.*); a sage under Manu Ćākṣuṣa (*Mā. Purāṇa*); a son of the 3rd Manu (*H. Purāṇa*); a son of Vṛṣa; a son of Arjuna Kārttavīrya (*H. Purāṇa*); a son of Bindumat (*H. Purāṇa*); a son of Devakṣatra (*H. Purāṇa*); a king in the court of Yama (*M. Bh.*); the Aśoka tree (*Saraca indica*); another name for the 1st month of the year known in the Indian calendar as Ćaitra, in the English calendar as the months of March-April and is the season of spring; Butter tree (*Bassia latifolia*)

**Madhubālā** (S) (F) sweet maiden.

**Madhubhadra** (S) (M) a sweet gentleman; softspoken; handsome.

**Madhućandra** (S) (M) sweet moon.

**Madhuććandasa** (S) (M) **1.** one who speaks sweetly. **3.** the 51st of Viśvāmitra's 101 sons (*A. Brāhmaṇa*)

**Madhudhārā** (S) (F) stream of honey.

**Madhudhvaja** (S) (M) **1.** honey bannered. **3.** a king (*V. Purāṇa*)

**Madhudīpa** **1.** lamp of spring. **3.** another name for Kāma.

**Madhudivā** (S) (F) **1.** excited by honey; inspired by wine; excited by the spring. **3.** a sacred river (*M. Bh.*)

**Madhudviṣa** (S) (M) **1.** foe of Madhu. **3.** another name for Viṣṇu (*Bhā. Purāṇa*)

**Madhugandhikā** (S) (F) sweet smelling.

**Madhuhana** (S) (M) **1.** destroyer of Madhu. **3.** another name for Viṣṇu.

**Madhuja** (S) (M) **1.** made of honey. **2.** sugar.

**Madhujā** (S) (F) **1.** made of honey. **2.** a honeycomb; the earth.

**Madhujit** (S) (M) **1.** conqueror of Madhu. **3.** another name for Viṣṇu and Kṛṣṇa.

**Madhuka** (S) (M) **1.** honey coloured; sweet; mellifluous; melodious. **2.** the Aśoka tree (*Saraca indica*)

**Madhukaṇṭha** (S) (M) sweet voiced; the Indian Cuckoo (*Cuculus scolopaceus*) (*Ś. Brāhmaṇa*)

**Madhukara** (S) (M) **1.** honey-maker. **2.** the bee; the Mango tree (*Mangifera indica*)

**Madhukaśā** (S) (F) **1.** whip of sweetness; dew. **3.** the whip used by the aśvins to sweeten the Soma juice; the daughter of the maruts who could bestow immortality (*Ṛg Veda*)

**Madhukṛta** (S) (M) **1.** maker of honey. **2.** the bee.

**Madhukṣa** (S) (M) **1.** maker of honey. **2.** the bee.

**Madhukulyā** (S) (F) **1.** a stream of honey. **3.** a river in Kuśa dvīpa (*Bhā. Purāṇa*)

**Madhukumbhā** (S) (F) 1. pitcher of honey. 3. a mother attending on Skanda (*M. Bh.*)
**Madhukūṭa** (S) (M) mountain of sweetness.
**Madhula** (S) (M) sweet; an intoxicating drink.
**Madhūlikā** (S) (F) 1. sweetness. 2. a kind of bee; citron; liquorice; Black Mustard (*Brassica nigra*). 3. a follower of Skanda (*M. Bh.*); *Clematis triloba*.
**Madhumādhavī** (S) (F) a spring flower abounding in honey.
**Madhumakṣika** (S) (M) 1. honey fly; the honey bee. 2. beautiful; the sweet jasmine.
**Madhumallī** (S) (F) the vine of spring; the Mālati blossom (*Jasminum grandiflorum*)
**Madhumatha** (S) (M) 1. destroyer of Madhu. 3. another name for Viṣṇu.
**Madhumatī** (S) (F) 1. rich in honey; intoxicated by the spring. 2. sweet; pleasant; agreeable. 3. the daughter of the asura Madhu and the wife of Haryaśva (*H. Purāṇa*); an attendant of Lakṣmī (*Pañćatantra*); a river (*H. Purāṇa*)
**Madhumaya** (S) (M) consisting of honey.
**Madhumiśra** (S) (M) mixed with honey.
**Madhumītā** (S) (F) sweet friend.
**Madhunandī** (S) (M) 1. enjoyer of spring. 3. a king (*V. Purāṇa*)
**Madhupa** (S) (M) 1. drinking sweetness. 2. a bee.
**Madhuparka** (S) (M) 1. a mixture of honey and milk. 3. a son of Garuḍa (*M. Bh.*)
**Madhupati** (S) (M) 1. master of spring; chief of the race of Madhu. 3. another name for Kṛṣṇa (*Bh. Purāṇa*)
**Madhupratikā** (S) (F) with a sweet mouth; having the qualities of a yoginī.
**Madhupriya** (S) (M) 1. fond of honey or nectar. 3. another name for Balarāma.
**Madhupuṣpa** (S) (M) 1. a spring flower; with sweet flowers. 2. the Aśoka tree; Sizzling tree (*Albizzia lebbeck*); the Bakula tree (*Mimusops elengi*); the Śirīṣa tree (*Albizzia stipulata*)
**Madhupuṣpā** (S) (F) a spring flower; rain.
**Madhura** (S) (M) 1. sweet. 2. pleasant; charming; delightful; melodious. 3. a tutelary deity of the race of Vandhula; an attendant of Skanda (*M. Bh.*); a gandharva (*S. Puṇḍarikā*); *Asparagus racemosus*; *Luvunya scandens*.
**Madhurākṣī** (S) (F) beautiful eyed.
**Madhuranātha** (S) (M) 1. lord of all that is sweet. 3. another name for Kṛṣṇa.
**Madhurapriyadarśana** (S) (M) 1. of sweet and friendly aspect. 3. another name for Śiva.
**Madhurasvarā** (S) (F) 1. sweet voiced. 3. an apsarā (*M. Bh.*)
**Madhurasvara** (S) (M) 1. sweet voiced. 3. a gandharva (*S. Puṇḍarikā*)
**Mādhurī** (S) (F) 1. sweetness; loveliness; charm. 2. mead; wine; treacle; syrup; the double Jasmine blossom (*Jasminum sambac*); Fennel (*Foeniculum capillaceum*); a kind of musical instrument.
**Mādhurīlatā** (S) (F) vine of sweetness.
**Madhurimā** (S) (F) sweetness; charm; comeliness.
**Madhuriman** (S) (M) sweetness; charm.
**Madhuripu** (S) (M) 1. enemy of Madhu. 3. another name for Viṣṇu.
**Madhurtu** (S) (F) spring season.
**Madhuruha** (S) (M) 1. with a sweet body. 3. a son of Ghṛtapṛṣṭha (*Bhā. Purāṇa*)
**Mādhurya** (S) (M) sweetness; tender affection; charm; exquisite beauty.
**Madhusakha** (S) (M) 1. friend of spring. 3. another name for Kāma.
**Madhuśakta** (S) (M) 1. lover of honey. 3. an asura.
**Madhusārathi** (S) (M) 1. with spring for a charioteer. 3. another name for Kāma.
**Madhuśrī** (S) (F) 1. the beauty of spring. 3. one of the 2 queens of spring (*K. Granthāvali*)
**Madhusūdana** (S) (M) 1. destroyer of Madhu. 3. another name for Viṣṇu.
**Madhusyanda** (S) (M) 1. the sweet offspring. 3. a son of Viśvāmitra (*V. Rāmāyaṇa*)
**Madhutana** (S) (M) 1. with an exotic body. 2. intoxicating; sweet.
**Madhutraya** (S) (M) mixture of 3 sweet things.
**Madhuvāhini** (S) (F) 1. carrying sweetness. 3. a river (*M. Bh.*)
**Madhuvalli** (S) (M) sweet citron (*Citrus*

*aurantium*); kind of grape.

**Madhuvantī** (S) (F) 1. endowed with nectar. 3. a rāga.

**Madhuvaraṣa** (S) (M) 1. intoxicated. 2. a bull.

**Madhuvarṇa** (S) (M) 1. honey coloured. 3. a soldier of Skanda (*M. Bh.*)

**Madhuvatī** (S) (F) with an intoxicating beauty.

**Madhuvidyā** (S) (F) 1. sweet knowledge. 2. a mystical lore of the devas.

**Madhuvratā** (S) (F) 1. fasting for spring; absorbed in sweetness. 2. the queen bee.

**Mādhva** (S) (M) 1. born of the spring; born of honey. 2. beautiful; intoxicating. 3. the founder of a sect of Vaiṣṇavas in south India believing in the Dvaita doctrine.

**Mādhvāćārya** 1. preceptor of the Mādhva doctrine. 3. the author of *Sarvadarśanasamgraha* and founder of a Vaiṣṇava sect.

**Madhvakṣa** (S) (M) 1. with honey coloured eyes. 3. another name for Agni.

**Madhvijā** (S) (F) 1. born of honey. 2. an intoxicating drink.

**Madhyamdina** (S) (M) 1. midday. 2. the time near noon personified as a son of Puṣpārṇa and Prabhā (*Bhā. Purāṇa*)

**Madin** (S) (M) 1. intoxicating; exhilarating. 2. lovely; delightful.

**Madirā** (S) (F) 1. intoxicating; nectar; wine; spirituous liquor. 3. one of the 7 wives of Vasudeva (*M. Bh.*); the mother of Kādambarī; another name for the wife of Varuṇa and the goddess of wine (*V. Purāṇa*); another name for Durgā (*H. Purāṇa*)

**Madirāja** (S) (M) 1. lord of the intoxicated; lord of the proud. 3. the father of Bāsava, the bull.

**Madirākṣa** (S) (M) 1. with intoxicating eyes. 3. a king of the Ikṣvāku dynasty who was the son of King Daśāśva and the father of Dyutimān and Sumadhyā (*M. Bh.*); a brother of King Virāṭa of Matsya (*Bhā. Purāṇa*); a brother of Śatānīka (*M. Bh.*)

**Madirāśva** (S) (M) 1. an intoxicated horse. 3. a king who was the son of Daśāśva and the grandson of Ikṣvāku (*Bhā. Purāṇa*)

**Madirāvatī** (S) (F) with intoxicating beauty.

**Madirekṣaṇā** (S) (F) with intoxicating eyes.

**Madrā** (S) (F) 1. belonging to the Madra dynasty. 3. a wife of sage Atri and the mother of Soma (*Br. Purāṇa*); a daughter of Raudrāśva (*H. Purāṇa*)

**Madra** (S) (M) 1. name of a people. 3. the country northwest of Hindustan and the name of its king (*Ś. Brāhmaṇa*); a son of Śibi.

**Madrādhipa** (S) (M) 1. lord of Madra. 3. another name for Śalya.

**Madraja** (S) (M) 1. son of Madra. 3. another name for Śalya.

**Madraka** (S) (M) 1. belonging to the Madra dynasty. 3. a Kṣatriya king who was a partial incarnation of the demon Krodhavaśa (*M. Bh.*)

**Mādraka** (S) (M) 1. of Madra. 3. another name for Śalya.

**Madravatī** (S) (F) 1. princess of the Madras. 3. the wife of Parīkṣit and mother of Janamejaya (*M. Bh.*); the 2nd wife of Pāṇḍu and the mother of Nakula and Sahadeva (*M. Bh.*); the wife of Sahadeva (*M. Bh.*); the wife of Kroṣṭu; a wife of Kṛṣṇa (*Bhā. Purāṇa*)

**Mādreya** (S) (M) 1. son of Mādrī. 3. another name for Sahadeva.

**Mādrī** (S) (F) 1. a princess of Madra. 3. *Aconitum heterophyllum*; a wife of Pāṇḍu and mother of Nakula and Sahadeva; (*M. Bh.*); a wife of Kroṣṭa; a wife of Kṛṣṇa (*H. Purāṇa*)

**Mādrinandana** (S) (M) 1. son of Mādrī. 3. another name for Nakula and Sahadeva.

**Mādrīputra** (S) (M) 1. son of Mādrī. 3. another name for Sahadeva.

**Madura** (S) (M) a bird.

**Madvan** (S) (M) 1. intoxicating. 2. gladdening. 3. another name for Śiva.

**Māgadha** (S) (M) 1. of Magadha. 3. a sage of the 14th manvantara (*H. Purāṇa*); a son of Yadu (*H. Purāṇa*)

**Māgadhī** (S) (F) of Magadha; Common White Jasmine (*Jasminum officianale*); a river (*V. Rāmāyaṇa*)

**Magan** (S) (M) absorbed; engrossed.

**Magaran** (S) (M) 1. following a path. 2. the wind.

**Maghā** (S) (F) 1. gift; reward; wealth. 3. the 10th Nakṣatra or constellation, regarded as a wife of the moon (*A. Veda*); the wife of Śiva (*M. Bh.*)

**Magha** (S) (M) 1. gift; reward; wealth; power. 3. another name for Indra.

**Māgha** (S) (M) 1. rewarding. 2. the month of December/January. 3. the author of *Siśupālavadha* (7th century A.D.)

**Maghavan** (S) (M) 1. bountiful; liberal. 3. the 3rd ćakravartin in Bhārata; a dānava; another name for Indra.

**Māghavat** (S) (M) belonging to Indra.

**Māghī** (S) (F) giving gifts; the day of the full moon in the month of Māgha (December/January/February)

**Māghonī** (S) (F) liberality; the east.

**Māghyā** (S) (F) born in the month of Māgha; the blossom of Jasmine (*Jasminum pubescens*)

**Magundī** (S) (F) 1. female magician. 3. a mythical being whose daughters are female demons (*A. Veda*)

**Māhā** (S) (F) great; cow.

**Mahābāhu** (S) (M) 1. long armed. 3. a son of Dhṛtarāṣṭra (*M. Bh.*); a dānava (*H. Purāṇa*); a rākṣasa (*V. Rāmāyaṇa*); another name for Viṣṇu (*M. Bh.*)

**Mahābala** (S) (M) 1. exceedingly strong. 2. wind. 3. a Buddha; one of the 10 gods of anger (*D. Śastra*); a follower of Skanda (*M. Bh.*); Indra in the 4th Manvantara (*M. Purāṇa*); a nāga; Gamboge tree (*Garcinia morella*); Common Indigo (*Indigofera tinctoria*); Jelly Leaf (*Sida rhombofolia*)

**Mahabaleśvara** (S) (M) 1. lord of the strong ones. 3. another name for Śiva; a liṅga.

**Mahābalī** (S) (M) 1. extremely powerful. 3. the giant Bali; another name for Śiva.

**Mahabhāgā** (S) (F) 1. highly fortunate; pure; holy. 3. the Dākṣāyaṇī in Mahālaya.

**Mahabhāgin** (S) (M) exceedingly fortunate.

**Mahābhairava** (S) (M) 1. extremely angry. 3. a form of Śiva (*Ś. Purāṇa*)

**Mahabhāsura** (S) (M) 1. extremely brilliant. 3. another name for Viṣṇu.

**Mahābhaṭa** (S) (M) 1. great warrior. 3. a dānava (*K. Sāgara*)

**Mahābhaṭṭārikā** (S) (F) 1. great warrior. 3. another name for Durgā.

**Mahābhauma** (S) (M) 1. the great son of the earth. 2. the great Mars. 3. a king of the Purū dynasty who was the son of Ariha, the husband of Suyajñā and the father of Ayutanāyi (*M. Bh.*)

**Mahābhaya** (S) (M) 1. very dreadful. 3. a rākṣasa who was the son of Adharma and Nirṛti (*M. Bh.*)

**Mahābhijana** (S) (M) of noble birth.

**Mahābhikṣu** (S) (M) 1. great monk. 3. another name for Gautama Buddha.

**Mahābhīma** (S) (M) 1. very powerful. 3. one of Śiva's attendants (*A. Koṣa*); another name for Śāntanu (*A. Koṣa*)

**Mahābhīmā** (S) (F) 1. very powerful. 3. another name for Pārvatī.

**Mahabhiṣa** (S) (M) 1. very frightening. 3. a king of the race of Ikṣvāku (*Bhā. Purāṇa*)

**Mahabhīṣma** (S) (M) 1. very dreadful. 3. a king of the Ikṣvāku dynasty also known as Śāntanu (*K. Sāgara*)

**Mahābhiśu** (S) (M) very brilliant.

**Mahābhogā** (S) (F) 1. causing great enjoyment. 3. another name for Durgā.

**Mahābhoja** (S) (M) 1. great monarch. 3. Yādava king (*Bhā. Purāṇa*)

**Mahābhūṣana** (S) (M) costly ornament.

**Mahābīja** (S) (M) 1. with much seed. 3. another name for Śiva (*M. Bh.*)

**Mahābuddhi** (S) (F) 1. extremely intelligent. 3. an asura (*K. Sāgara*)

**Mahāćaṇḍā** (S) (F) 1. very fierce. 3. an attendant of Durgā; another name for a form of Durgā known as Ćāmuṇḍa.

**Mahāćaṇḍa** (S) (M) 1. extremely violent; passionate. 3. one of Yama's 2 servants (*A. Koṣa*); one of Śiva's attendants.

**Mahāćandra** (S) (M) great moon.

**Mahāćārya** (S) (M) 1. great preceptor. 3. another name for Śiva.

**Mahāćūḍā** (S) (F) 1. great crested. 3. a mother attending on Skanda.

**Mahādaitya** (S) (M) 1. the great daitya. 3. the grandfather of Ćandragupta II.

**Mahādanṣtra** (S) (M) 1. large toothed.

2. tiger. 3. a vidyādhara (*K. Sāgara*)

**Mahadāyudha** (S) (M) a great weapon.

**Mahādevā** (S) (F) 1. the great deity. 3. a daughter of Devaka (*V. Purāṇa*)

**Mahādeva** (S) (M) 1. the great deity. 3. one of the 8 forms of Rudra or Śiva (*M. Bh.*); a mountain (*K. Sāgara*); another name for Rudra or Śiva.

**Mahādevī** (S) (F) 1. the great deity; the chief wife of a king; the consort of Mahādeva. 3. the Dākṣāyāṇī in the Śālagrāma (*A. Koṣa*); another name for Pārvatī (*M. Bh.*); another name for Lakṣmī (*M. Bh.*)

**Mahadguṇa** (S) (M) possessing the qualities of the great.

**Mahādharma** (S) (M) 1. follower of a great religion. 3. a prince of the kinnaras.

**Mahādhātu** (S) (M) 1. the great metal. 3. another name for gold and Śiva (*M. Bh.*)

**Mahādhipati** (S) (M) 1. lord of understanding. 3. a tāntric deity.

**Mahādhṛti** (S) (M) 1. very patient; very compassionate. 3. a king of the solar dynasty (*Bhā. Purāṇa*)

**Mahādhvani** (S) (M) 1. making a loud noise. 3. a dānava (*H. Purāṇa*)

**Mahādruma** (S) (M) 1. a great tree. 2. *Ficus religiosa*. 3. a son of Bhavya (*V. Purāṇa*)

**Mahādyotā** (S) (F) 1. extremely shiny. 2. glorious. 3. a tāntric goddess (*B. Literature*)

**Mahādyuti** (S) (M) 1. of great splendour. 3. a son of the yakṣa Maṇibhadra and Puṇyajanī (*M. Bh.*); a king of ancient India (*M. Bh.*)

**Mahādyutikara** (S) (M) 1. extremely glorious. 3. another name for the sun.

**Mahāgaja** (S) (M) 1. great elephant. 3. an elephant that supports the earth.

**Mahāgaṇapati** (S) (M) 1. great leader of the gaṇas. 3. another name for Śiva.

**Mahāgaṅgā** (S) (F) the great Gaṅgā.

**Mahāgarta** (S) (M) 1. the great pit. 3. another name for Śiva.

**Mahāgaurī** (S) (F) 1. the great Gaurī. 3. one of the 9 forms of Durgā (*D. Purāṇa*); a prominent river in India (*M. Bh.*)

**Mahāghasa** (S) (M) 1. great eater. 3. one of Śiva's attendants (*A. Koṣa*)

**Mahāghoṣā** (S) (F) 1. loud sounding. 3. a tāntric deity (*B. Literature*)

**Mahāghoṣa** (S) (M) 1. loud sounding. 3. a Bodhisattva.

**Mahāghoṣeśvara** (S) (M) 1. lord of the loud sounding ones. 3. a king of the yakṣas (*B. Literature*)

**Mahāgiri** (S) (M) 1. a large mountain. 3. a dānava (*H. Purāṇa*)

**Mahāgīta** (S) (M) 1. overtly praised. 2. a great singer. 3. another name for Śiva.

**Mahāgrīva** (S) (M) 1. long necked. 3. one of Śiva's attendants (*H. Purāṇa*); another name for Śiva.

**Mahāguṇa** (S) (M) with excellent qualities.

**Mahāhansa** (S) (M) 1. the great haṇsa. 3. another name for Viṣṇu.

**Mahāhanu** (S) (M) 1. large jawed. 3. an attendant of Śiva (*H. Purāṇa*); a nāga of the family of Takṣaka (*M. Bh.*); a dānava (*H. Purāṇa*)

**Mahāhanus** (S) (M) 1. large jawed. 3. a son of Vasudeva and Rohiṇī (*M. Purāṇa*)

**Mahāhaya** (S) (M) 1. with a great horse; a horse of the sun; a great horse. 3. a king of the Yayāti dynasty (*Bhā. Purāṇa*)

**Mahaja** (S) (M) 1. highborn. 2. of noble descent.

**Mahājambha** (S) (M) 1. a great yawn. 2. having a big yawn. 3. an attendant of Śiva.

**Mahājānu** (S) (M) 1. large kneed. 3. one of Śiva's attendants (*A. Koṣa*)

**Mahājaṭa** (S) (M) 1. a long braid. 2. wearing long braid. 3. another name for Śiva.

**Mahājavā** (S) (F) 1. extremely fast; fleet flooted. 3. a mother attending on Skanda (*M. Bh.*)

**Mahājayā** (S) (F) 1. extremely victorious. 3. another name for Durgā.

**Mahājaya** (S) (M) 1. extremely victorious. 3. one of the 2 attendants given to Skanda by Vāsuki (*M. Bh.*); a nāga (*M. Bh.*)

**Mahājihva** (S) (M) 1. long tongued. 3. a daitya (*H. Purāṇa*); another name for Śiva.

**Mahājñānagītā** (S) (F) 1. singer of the great knowledge. 3. a tāntric deity.

**Mahājñānavatī** (S) (F) 1. great possessor of knowledge. 3. another name for Manasā.

**Mahājñānayutā** (S) (F) 1. great possesser unbounded knowledge. 3. another name for Manasā.

**Mahājñānin** (S) (M) 1. great preceptor. 3. another name for Śiva.

**Mahājuna** (S) (M) 1. great victor. 3. a descendant of Parīkṣit and king of the lunar dynasty of Indraprastha (*M. Bh.*)

**Mahājuṣakā** (S) (F) a celestial flower.

**Mahājvāla** (S) (M) 1. a big flame; blazing greatly. 3. another name for Śiva.

**Mahājyotiṣ** (S) (M) 1. great splendour. 3. another name for Śiva.

**Mahaka** (S) (M) 1. eminent; a tortoise. 3. another name for Viṣṇu.

**Mahākaććha** (S) (M) 1. with vast shores. 2. the sea. 3. another name for Varuṇa.

**Mahākalā** (S) (F) the night of the new moon.

**Mahākāla** (S) (M) 1. lord of death; lord of time. 3. a form of Śiva in his destructive aspect (*M. Bh.*); one of Śiva's attendants (*H. Purāṇa*); one of the 9 treasures of the Jainas (*J.S. Koṣa*); a mythical mountain (*K. Vyuha*); a liṅga in Ujjayinī (*K. Sāgara*); another name for Viṣṇu.

**Mahākālī** (S) (F) 1. consort of Mahākāla. 3. goddess Durgā in her terrifying form (*M. Bh.*); a goddess who executed the commands of the 5th Arhat of the present Avasarpiṇī (*J.S. Koṣa*); one of the 16 Jaina vidyādevis (*J.S. Koṣa*); one of Durgā's attendants (*D. Purāṇa*)

**Mahākambu** (S) (M) 1. stark naked. 3. another name for Śiva.

**Mahākāntā** (S) (F) 1. very pleasing. 3. another name for the earth.

**Mahākānta** (S) (M) 1. very pleasing. 3. another name for Śiva.

**Mahākāntiki** (S) (M) with great splendour: the full moon in the month of Kārttika.

**Mahākapāla** (S) (M) 1. large headed. 3. a minister of the rākṣasa Dūṣaṇa (*V. Rāmāyaṇa*); an attendant of Śiva (*A. Koṣa*)

**Mahākāpi** (S) (M) 1. great ape. 3. an attendant of Śiva; one of the 34 incarnations of Buddha (*B. Jātakas*)

**Mahākapota** (S) (M) 1. great cheeked. 3. an attendant of Śiva.

**Mahākara** (S) (M) 1. with large hands; having great rays. 3. a Buddha (*L. Vistara*)

**Mahākarman** (S) (M) accomplishing great works.

**Mahākarṇa** (S) (M) 1. large eared. 3. a nāga (*H. Purāṇa*); another name for Śiva.

**Mahākarṇī** (S) (F) 1. large eared. 3. a follower of Skanda (*M. Bh.*)

**Mahākaśī** (S) (F) 1. of the great sky. 3. a tutelary goddess of the Mātaṅgajas.

**Mahākātyāyana** (S) (M) 1. the great sage. 3. a disciple of the Buddha.

**Mahākavi** (S) (M) 1. great poet. 3. another name for Śukra.

**Mahākāya** (S) (M) 1. great bodied. 2. very tall; an elephant. 3. a follower of Skanda (*M. Bh.*); an attendant of Śiva (*M. Bh.*); a king of the Garuḍas; another name for Viṣṇu and Śiva.

**Mahākāyika** (S) (M) 1. great bodied; omnipresent. 3. another name for Viṣṇu.

**Mahākeśa** (S) (M) 1. with strong hair. 3. another name for Śiva.

**Mahāketu** (S) (M) 1. with a great banner. 3. another name for Śiva.

**Mahākhyāta** (S) (M) greatly renowned.

**Mahākīrti** (S) (M) highly renowned.

**Mahākoṣa** (S) (M) 1. the great treasure. 2. the great phallus. 3. another name for Śiva.

**Mahākrama** (S) (M) 1. wide striding. 3. another name for Viṣṇu.

**Mahākrodha** (S) (M) 1. with great wrath. 3. another name for Śiva.

**Mahākrūrā** (S) (F) 1. extremely cruel. 3. a yoginī (*T. Śastra*)

**Mahākṣa** (S) (M) 1. large eyed. 3. another name for Śiva.

**Mahākulīna** (S) (M) highly noble; highly born.

**Mahākumāra** (S) (M) the heir apparent.

**Mahākuṇḍa** (S) (M) 1. great pond. 3. an attendant of Śiva.

**Mahākūrma** (S) (M) 1. great tortoise. 3. another name for Viṣṇu.

**Mahākuśa** (S) (M) 1. great grass; of sharp intellect. 3. a ćakravartin.

**Mahālakṣmī** (S) (F) 1. the great Lakṣmī. 3. in actuality Mahālakṣmī is the Śakti or feminine energy of Nārāyaṇa but is sometimes identified with Durgā or Sarasvatī; Dākṣāyaṇī in Karavīra (*K. Sāgara*)

**Mahālīlāsarasvatī** (S) (F) 1. the ever sporting goddess. 3. a form of the goddess Tārā (*T. Śastra*)

**Mahallikā** (S) (F) 1. a female attendant. 3. a daughter of Prahlāda (*Bhā. Purāṇa*)

**Mahāmaitra** (S) (M) 1. great friend; friend of many. 3. a Buddha.

**Mahāmāli** (S) (M) 1. protector of many; great gardener. 3. a hero of Rāvaṇa's army (*V. Rāmāyaṇa*)

**Mahāmalla** (S) (M) 1. great wrestler. 3. another name for Kṛṣṇa.

**Mahāmanas** (S) (M) 1. high minded; with a great mind. 2. noble; virtuous. 3. a grandson of King Janamejaya of the Aṅga dynasty and father of Uśīnara (*A. Purāṇa*)

**Mahāmānasī** (S) (F) 1. with a noble intellect. 3. a Jaina goddess (*J.S. Koṣa*)

**Mahāmānasikā** (S) (F) 1. high minded. 2. noble; virtuous. 3. one of the 16 Jaina vidyādevīs (*J.S. Koṣa*)

**Mahāmaṇi** (S) (M) 1. a precious gem. 3. another name for Śiva.

**Mahāmaṇićūḍa** (S) (M) 1. crested with a precious gem. 3. a nāga.

**Mahāmaṇidhara** (S) (M) 1. great bearer of jewels. 2. the ocean. 3. a Bodhisattva.

**Mahamaṇiratna** (S) (M) 1. best among jewels. 3. a fabulous mountain (*K. Vyuha*)

**Mahāmantrā** (S) (F) 1. a great spell. 3. a Buddhist goddess.

**Mahāmantrānusāriṇī** (S) (F) 1. follower of the great spell. 3. one of the 5 Buddhist tutelary goddesses (*B. Literature*)

**Mahāmarakata** (S) (M) a great emerald.

**Mahāmārī** (S) (F) 1. great destroyer. 3. a form of Durgā.

**Mahāmatī** (S) (F) 1. great intellect. 3. a particular lunar day personified as a daughter of Aṅgiras (*M. Bh.*)

**Mahāmati** (S) (M) 1. great minded. 2. extremely intelligent; very clever. 3. the planet Jupiter; a king of the yakṣas; a Bodhisattva; a son of Sumati (*K. Sāgara*); a son of sage Aṅgiras (*M. Bh.*)

**Mahāmātṛ** (S) (F) 1. the great mother. 3. each deity of a class of deities who are a personification of the Śakti or female energy of Śiva.

**Mahāmāya** (S) (M) 1. the great illusion. 3. an asura (*K. Sāgara*); a vidyādhara; another name for Viṣṇu and Śiva.

**Mahāmayī** (S) (M) 1. the consort of Mahāmāyā. 3. a wife of Śuddhodana; another name for Durgā.

**Mahāmayūrī** (S) (F) the great peahen said to protect against poison; one of the 5 amulets and one of the 5 tutelary goddesses of the Buddhists.

**Mahamedhā** (S) (F) 1. great intelligence. 3. another name for Durgā.

**Mahāmegha** (S) (M) 1. a dense cloud. 3. another name for Śiva.

**Mahāmeru** (S) (M) Meru, the great.

**Mahāmohā** (S) (F) 1. great infatuation. 3. another name for Durgā.

**Mahāmukha** (S) (M) 1. large mouthed. 3. a warrior of King Jayadratha (*M. Bh.*); a Jina (*J.S. Koṣa*); another name for Śiva.

**Mahāmūlya** (S) (M) very costly; a ruby.

**Mahāmuni** (S) (M) 1. great sage. 3. a ṛṣi of the 5th Manvantara (*V. Purāṇa*); another name for Vyāsa and Agastya; another name for a Buddha or a Jina.

**Mahāmūrti** (S) (M) 1. large bodied. 3. another name for Viṣṇu.

**Mahān** (S) (M) 1. great. 2. mighty; powerful; abundant. 3. a king of the Purū dynasty who was the son of Matināra (*M. Bh.*); the son of Agni Bhārata who was a prajāpati (*M. Bh.*)

**Mahānāda** (S) (M) 1. loud sounding. 2. a great drum; lion; elephant; camel. 3. a rākṣasa and uncle of Rāvaṇa (*V. Rāmāyaṇa*); another name for Śiva.

**Mahānadī** (S) (F) 1. a great river. 3. a river of Bengal; another name for the Gaṅgā.

**Mahānāga** (S) (M) 1. great serpent; great elephant. 3. one of the elephants that support the earth.

**Mahānanda** (S) (M) 1. great bliss. 2. mokṣa or the final emancipation. 3. a disciple of Buddha; a king of Madra (*Mā. Purāṇa*)

**Mahānandin** (S) (M) 1. very pleasing. 3. a Magadha king who was the son of Nandivardhana (*M. Purāṇa*)

**Mahānārāyaṇa** (S) (M) 1. the great Nārāyaṇa. 3. another name for Viṣṇu.

**Mahānaṭa** (S) (M) 1. great dancer. 3. another name for Śiva.

**Mahānāyaka** (S) (M) 1. great chief. 2. a great gem in the centre of a string of pearls.

**Mahānetra** (S) (M) 1. large eyed. 3. another name for Śiva.

**Mahānidhi** (S) (M) a great treasure house.

**Mahānīla** (S) (M) 1. dark blue; sapphire. 3. a mountain (*H. Purāṇa*); a nāga (*H. Purāṇa*); a tāntra (*K. Sāgara*)

**Mahāninnāda** (S) (M) 1. loud sounding. 3. a nāga (*B. Literature*)

**Mahāniśā** (S) (F) 1. the greatest of the nights. 3. another name for Durgā.

**Mahānṛtya** (S) (M) 1. great dancer. 3. another name for Śiva.

**Mahānta** (S) (M) great.

**Mahānurāga** (S) (M) great love.

**Mahāpāda** (S) (M) 1. with large feet. 3. another name for Śiva.

**Mahāpadma** (S) (M) 1. the great lotus; the Indian Lotus (*Nelumbium nucifera*). 3. the founder king of the Nanda dynasty who was the son of Mahānandī; an elephant in Ghaṭotkaća's army (*M. Bh.*); one of the 8 elephant guardians of the world (*M. Bh.*); one of the 9 cobras worn by Śiva; a son of Nanda; a dānava (*H. Purāṇa*); a kinnara; one of the 9 treasures of Kubera; another name for Nārada.

**Mahāpāla** (S) (M) 1. great protector; protector of many. 2. a king.

**Mahāpāriṣadeśvara** (S) (M) 1. great leader of a community. 3. a follower of Skanda (*M. Bh.*)

**Mahāpārśva** (S) (M) 1. with thick sides. 3. a heroic warrior of Rāvaṇa (*A. Purāṇa*); a mountain (*M. Bh.*)

**Mahāpāśa** (S) (M) 1. having a large noose. 3. an officer of Yama; a nāga.

**Mahāpaurava** (S) (M) 1. the great citizen. 3. a king (*V. Purāṇa*)

**Mahāpavitra** (S) (M) 1. greatly purifying. 3. another name for Viṣṇu.

**Mahāprabhā** (S) (F) 1. of great splendour. 3. another name for the river Narmadā.

**Mahāprabhu** (S) (M) 1. great lord. 3. another name for Viṣṇu, Śiva and Indra.

**Mahāprajāpatī** (S) (F) 1. great lord of life and creatures. 3. the foster mother and aunt of Buddha and the 1st woman to embrace his doctrines.

**Mahāpraṇāda** (S) (M) 1. great giver of life. 3. a ćakravartin.

**Mahāpratāpa** (S) (M) very dignified; majestic.

**Mahāpratibhāna** (S) (M) 1. very learned; with great intellect. 3. a Bodhisattva (*B. Literature*)

**Mahāpratisarā** (S) (F) 1. greatly expanded. 2. a great leader. 3. one of the 5 Buddhist tutelary goddesses.

**Mahāpuṇyā** (S) (F) 1. extremely auspicious. 2. very purifying; very good; beautiful. 3. a river.

**Mahāpūrṇa** (S) (M) 1. absolutely complete. 2. perfect; whole; satisfied. 3. a king of the Garuḍas (*Gar. Purāṇa*)

**Mahāpūta** (S) (M) exceedingly pure.

**Mahārāja** (S) (M) 1. great king. 3. a particular class of Buddhist divine beings who are the guardians of the earth and the heavens against the demons; a Jina (*J.S. Koṣa*); another name for Viṣṇu, Kubera and the moon.

**Mahārajana** (S) (M) 1. of great splendour. 2. śafflower; gold.

**Mahārajat** (S) (M) 1. better than silver. 2. gold.

**Mahārajika** (S) (M) 1. the princely one. 3. another name for Viṣṇu.

**Mahārakṣā** (S) (F) 1. great saviour; goddess of protection. 3. one of the 5 Buddhist tutelary goddesses.

**Mahārāma** (S) (M) great Rāma.

**Mahārānī** (S) (F) great queen.

**Mahāratha** (S) (M) 1. great warrior; great charioteer. 3. a rākṣasa; a son of Viśvamitra.

**Mahāratna** (S) (M) most precious of all jewels.

**Mahāraudra** (S) (M) 1. very terrible. 3. a rākṣasa who was a friend of Ghaṭotkaća (*M. Bh.*)

**Mahāraudrī** (S) (F) 1. consort of Rudra. 3. a form of Durgā (*H. Ć. Ćintāmaṇi*)

**Mahārava** (S) (M) 1. very noisy. 3. a king of the Yadu dynasty (*Bhā. Purāṇa*); a daitya (*H. Purāṇa*)

**Mahārṇava** (S) (M) 1. the great ocean. 3. another name for Śiva.

**Mahāroman** (S) (M) 1. with many branches; very hairy. 3. a king of the solar dynasty who was the son of Kṛtirāta and father of Svarṇaroman (*Bhāgavata*); a son of Ikṣvāku; another name for the ocean.

**Maharṣi** (S) (M) 1. a great saint. 3. another name for Śiva.

**Mahārta** (S) (M) 1. very truthful. 3. a rāṇā of Mewar.

**Mahārukhā** (S) (F) of pleasing appearance.

**Mahārūpa** (S) (M) 1. great in form. 3. another name for Śiva.

**Mahaśa** (S) (M) 1. one who does not smile. 3. a son of Kṛṣṇa (*Bhā. Purāṇa*)

**Mahāsādhvī** (S) (F) 1. supremely chaste woman. 3. another name for Sītā.

**Mahāsahasrapramardinī** (S) (F) 1. destroyer of 1000 greats. 3. one of the 5 Buddhist tutelary goddesses (*B. Literature*)

**Mahāśakti** (S) (M) 1. very powerful. 3. a son of Kṛṣṇa (*Bh. Purāṇa*); another name for Śiva and Kārttikeya.

**Mahāśakuni** (S) (M) 1. great owl; very intelligent. 3. a ćakravartin.

**Mahāśāla** (S) (M) 1. great householder; possessor of a large house. 2. very strong; very wealthy. 3. a king of the Aṅga dynasty who was the son of Janamejaya and the father of Mahāmanas (*H. Purāṇa*)

**Mahāsammata** (S) (M) 1. highly honoured. 3. according to the Buddhists, the name of the 1st king of the present age of the world.

**Mahāśaṅkha** (S) (M) 1. great conch. 3. a crocodile celebrated in the Purāṇas, the husband of Saṅkhinī who was the mother of the maruts in the Svāroćiṣa Manvantara; a nāga who revolves with the sun in the month of Mārgaśirṣa (*Bhā. Purāṇa*)

**Mahāsārathi** (S) (M) 1. great charioteer. 3. another name for Aruṇa.

**Mahāsatya** (S) (M) 1. the great truth. 3. another name for Yama.

**Mahāsena** (S) (M) 1. with a large army. 3. the father of the 8th Arhat of the present Avasarpiṇī; a prince of Ujjayinī; another name for Śiva and Skanda.

**Mahāsenareśvara** (S) (M) 1. lord of those possessing a large army. 2. the commander of commanders. 3. the father of the 8th Arhat of the present Avasarpiṇī.

**Mahāsetāvatī** (S) (F) 1. extremely fair complexioned. 2. very beautiful. 3. one of the 5 Buddhist tutelary goddesses.

**Mahāśila** (S) (M) 1. great rock. 3. a son of Janamejaya.

**Mahāsinha** (S) (M) 1. a great lion; with the bearing of a lion. 3. another name for Yudhiṣṭhira.

**Mahāsinhatejas** (S) (M) 1. with the glory of a great lion. 3. a Buddha.

**Mahāśiras** (S) (M) 1. large headed. 3. a sage in the assembly of Yudhiṣṭhira (*M. Bh.*); the 6th Black Vasudeva (*A. Koṣa*); a nāga in the court of Varuṇa; a dānava (*M. Bh.*)

**Mahāśirśa** (S) (M) 1. big headed. 3. one of Śiva's attendants (*A. Koṣa*)

**Mahāsmṛti** (S) (F) 1. great tradition. 3. another name for Durgā.

**Mahāsoṇa** (S) (M) 1. very golden. 3. the king of Ćandrapuri and the father of the 17th Jaina Tīrthankara Ćandraprabha (*J.S. Koṣa*)

**Mahāśrī** (S) (F) 1. the great divinity. 3. a Buddhist goddess; another name for Lakṣmī.

**Mahāśruti** (S) (M) 1. the great Vedic scholar; very learned. 3. a gandharva (*H. Purāṇa*)

**Mahāśubhra** (S) (M) extremely white; silver.

**Mahāsudhā** (S) (F) the great nectar.

**Mahāśuklā** (S) (F) 1. extremely white. 2. eternally pure; eternally white. 3. another name for Sarasvatī.

**Mahāśukta** (S) (M) 1. the great pearl. 3. the composer of the hymns of the 10th maṇḍala of the *Ṛg Veda*.

**Mahāsundarī** (S) (F) 1. supreme beauty. 3. another name for the tantric goddess Tārā.

**Mahāsura** (S) (M) 1. great demon. 3. an asura who fought against Skanda (*Sk. Purāṇa*)

**Mahāśva** (S) (M) 1. great horse. 3. a king in Yama's assembly (*M. Bh.*)

**Mahāśvana** (S) (M) 1. great dog. 3. a follower of Skanda (*M. Bh.*)

**Mahasvat** (S) (M) glorious; giving pleasure; gladdening; great; splendid.

**Mahāśvetā** (S) (F) 1. very white. 3. a consort of the sun; the earth goddess; another name for Durgā and Sarasvatī.

**Mahasvin** (S) (M) glorious; brilliant; splendid.

**Mahātapas** (S) (M) 1. very austere; great penance. 3. a sage (*Vār. Purāṇa*); another name for Viṣṇu and Śiva.

**Mahātattvā** (S) (F) 1. the great principle. 2. the intellect. 3. one of Durgā's attendants (*A. Koṣa*)

**Mahātejas** (S) (M) 1. of great splendour; hero; fire. 3. a king of the Garuḍas; a warrior of Skanda (*M. Bh.*); another name for Skanda.

**Mahāthilya** (S) (M) 1. extremely skilful. 2. absolutely still. 3. a disciple of Buddha.

**Mahatī** (S) (F) 1. greatness. 3. Nārada's lute (*Bhāgavata*)

**Mahātman** (S) (M) 1. great soul. 2. meritorious; virtuous; noble; wise; eminent; powerful. 3. a son of Dhīmat (*V. Purāṇa*); the Supreme Spirit.

**Mahatpati** (S) (M) 1. great lord. 3. another name for Viṣṇu.

**Mahatrū** (S) (M) 1. greatest of the great. 3. another name for Śiva.

**Mahattara** (S) (M) 1. oldest; mightiest; strongest. 2. great star; chief. 3. a son of Agni Pāñćajanya (*M. Bh.*); a son of Kaśyapa (*M. Bh.*)

**Mahattārī** (S) (F) 1. great star. 3. a form of the Buddhist goddess Tārā.

**Mahātuṣita** (S) (M) 1. greatly satisfied; very pleased. 3. another name for Viṣṇu.

**Mahātyāgin** (S) (M) 1. extremely generous. 2. great renouncer. 3. another name for Śiva.

**Mahāugha** (S) (M) 1. with a strong current. 3. a son of Tvaṣṭṛ.

**Mahaujas** (S) (M) 1. very powerful. 3. a king invited by the Pāṇḍavas to take part in the great war of Mahābhāratā (*M. Bh.*); another name for Skanda.

**Mahāvādi** (S) (M) 1. great disputant. 3. another name for the poet Aśvaghoṣa.

**Mahavakṣas** (S) (M) 1. broad chested. 3. another name for Śiva.

**Mahāvali** (S) (M) 1. very brave; a great warrior. 3. a king of the 3rd lunar dynasty of Indraprastha (*M. Bh.*)

**Mahāvallī** (S) (F) 1. the great creeper. 2. the Mādhavi creeper (*Hiptage madoblata*)

**Mahāvāṇī** (S) (F) 1. the great speech. 2. transcendant word. 3. another name for Sarasvatī.

**Mahāvarāha** (S) (M) 1. great boar. 3. Viṣṇu in his boar incarnation.

**Mahāvāyu** (S) (M) 1. great wind. 2. gale.

**Mahāvegā** (S) (F) 1. moving swiftly. 3. a mother attending on Skanda (*M. Bh.*)

**Mahāvega** (S) (M) 1. moving swiftly. 3. another name for Garuḍa.

**Mahāvibhūti** (S) (F) 1. great might; great splendour. 3. another name for Lakṣmī.

**Mahāvidyā** (S) (F) 1. great knowledge; great science or art. 3. another name for Lakṣmī.

**Mahāvidyeśvarī** (S) (F) 1. goddess of great knowledge. 3. a form of Durgā (*A. Koṣa*)

**Mahāvikrama** (S) (M) 1. very valorous. 2. lion. 3. a nāga.

**Mahāvikramin** (S) (M) 1. very brave. 3. a Bodhisattva.

**Mahāvila** (S) (M) 1. great veil. 2. the sky.

**Mahāvīra** (S) (M) 1. great hero; sacrificial fire. 2. warrior; archer; lion; white horse; the Indian cuckoo. 3. a son of Priyavrata and Surūpā (*D. Bhāgavata*); a king who was an incarnation of the asura Krodhavaśa (*M. Bh.*); the thunderbolts of Indra, Viṣṇu and Hanumān; another name for Vardhamāna the 24th and last Tīrathankara of the present

Avasarpinī and the most celebrated Jaina teacher of the present age who is supposed to have flourished in Bihar (6th century A.D.); another name for Hanumān and Garuḍa.

**Mahāvīrya** (S) (M) 1. of great strength. 3. Indra in the 4th Manvantara (*M. Purāṇa*); a Buddha; a Jina (*J.S. Koṣa*); Bulb bearing Yam (*Dioscorea bulbifera*); another name for Brahmā.

**Mahāviṣṇu** (S) (M) the great Viṣṇu.

**Mahāvīta** (S) (M) 1. completely detached. 3. a son of Savana (*V. Purāṇa*)

**Mahāyakṣa** (S) (M) 1. the great yakṣa. 3. a servant of the 2nd Arhat of the present Avasarpinī; a class of Buddhist deities.

**Mahāyakṣī** (S) (F) 1. expert in illusionary magic. 3. a tāntric deity (*T. Śastra*)

**Mahāyaśas** (S) (F) 1. very famous. 3. a mother in Skanda's retinue (*M. Bh.*)

**Mahāyaśas** (S) (M) 1. very famous. 2. very glorious; renowned. 3. the 4th Arhat of the past Utsarpinī (*J.S. Koṣa*); a mother attending on Skanda (*M. Bh.*)

**Mahāyati** (S) (M) a great ascetic.

**Mahāyogin** (S) (M) 1. great ascetic. 3. Viṣṇu or Śiva when worshipped by Buddhists (*B. Literature*)

**Mahayya** (S) (M) to be gladdened; to be delighted.

**Mahelikā** (S) (F) woman.

**Mahendra** (S) (M) 1. Indra, the great; an Indra among kings. 3. the father of princess Pātalī; the younger brother of Aśoka; a holy mountain of great Purāṇic importance; a range of mountains (*Bhā. Purāṇa*)

**Mahendragupta** (S) (M) protected by Indra.

**Mahendrāṇī** (S) (F) consort of Mahendra.

**Mahendrapāla** (S) (M) protected by Indra.

**Mahendravarman** (S) (M) armoured by Indra.

**Maheśa** (S) (M) 1. great lord. 2. god. 3. an incarnation of Śiva (*S. Samhitā*); a Buddhist deity.

**Maheśanī** (S) (F) 1. great lady; consort of Maheśa. 3. another name for Pārvatī.

**Maheṣu** (S) (M) a great arrow.

**Maheśvara** (S) (M) 1. great lord. 2. chief. 3. titles of the 4 Lokapālas (*A. Koṣa*); another name for Śiva, Kṛṣṇa and Indra.

**Maheśvarī** (S) (F) 1. great goddess. 3. Dākṣāyāṇī in Mahākāla (*M. Bh.*); another name for Durgā; a river.

**Maheśvāsa** (S) (M) 1. great archer. 3. another name for Śiva.

**Mahī** (S) (F) 1. great world; earth; heaven and earth conjoined. 3. a divine being associated with Iḍā and Sarasvatī (*Ṛg Veda*); a river (*M. Bh.*); the number 1.

**Mahībhuj** (S) (M) 1. earth enjoyer. 3. a king.

**Mahīcandra** (S) (M) moon of the earth.

**Mahīdāsa** (S) (M) 1. devotee of the earth. 3. a preceptor who is believed to be the author of *Aitareya Brāhmaṇa*; a son of Itarā (*T. Āraṇyaka*)

**Mahīdhara** (S) (M) 1. supporting the earth. 2. mountain. 3. the number 7; a commentator on Vedas; another name for Viṣṇu.

**Mahīja** (S) (M) 1. son of the earth. 3. another name for the planet Mars.

**Mahījit** (S) (M) 1. conqueror of the earth. 3. a king of Mahiṣmatī (*P. Purāṇa*)

**Mahikā** (S) (F) dew; frost.

**Mahikānśu** (S) (M) 1. with [illegible] .ays. 3. another name for the moon.

**Mahīkṣatra** (S) (M) possessing great power.

**Mahīksita** (S) (M) 1. earth ruler. 2. a king.

**Mahimā** (S) (F) 1. greatness; majesty; glory. 2. might; power.

**Mahimabhaṭṭa** (S) (M) 1. warrior of glory. 3. a Sanskṛt critic and scholar of logic (11th century A.D.)

**Mahiman** (S) (M) 1. greatness. 2. power; might; dignity. 3. an āditya who was the son of Bhaga and Siddhi (*Bhā. Purāṇa*)

**Mahimati** (S) (M) 1. high minded. 3. another name for Indra.

**Māhin** (S) (M) 1. giving delight. 2. joyous; great; exalted; mighty.

**Mahināśa** (S) (M) 1. destroyer of the great demon. 3. a form of Śiva or Rudra (*Bh. Purāṇa*)

**Mahīnātha** (S) (M) lord of the earth.

**Mahīndra** (S) (M) great Indra of the earth.

**Mahīpa** (S) (M) 1. protector of the earth. 3. a king.

**Mahīpāla** (S) (M) 1. protector of the earth. 2. a king.

**Mahīpati** (S) (M) 1. lord of the earth. 2. a king.

**Mahīputra** (S) (M) 1. son of the earth. 2. the planet Mars.

**Mahīputrī** (S) (F) 1. daughter of the earth. 3. another name for Sītā.

**Mahir** (S) (M) expert; proficient.

**Mahira** (S) (M) 1. proficient. 3. another name for Indra and the sun.

**Mahiradhvaja** (S) (M) 1. mark of the earth. 2. banner; flag.

**Mahīraṇa** (S) (M) 1. warrior of the earth. 3. a viśvadeva and the son of Dharma (*H. Purāṇa*)

**Mahīratha** (S) (M) 1. chariot of the earth. 3. a king and follower of sage Kaśyapa (*P. Purāṇa*)

**Mahiṣa** (S) (M) 1. mighty; buffalo. 2. great; powerful; lord of the earth. 3. the king of the asuras and sometime emperor of the world who was killed by Devī (*D. Bhāgavata*); another name for the sun.

**Mahiṣadā** (S) (F) 1. master of the earth; given by the buffalo. 3. a follower of Skanda (*M. Bh.*)

**Mahiṣadhvaja** (S) (M) 1. with a buffalo emblem. 3. another name for Yama.

**Mahiṣaga** (S) (M) 1. riding on a buffalo. 3. another name for Yama.

**Mahiṣaghna** (S) (M) 1. destroyer of Mahiṣa. 3. another name for Śiva.

**Mahiṣaghnī** (S) (F) 1. slayer of the demon Mahiṣa. 3. another name for Durgā.

**Mahiṣākṣa** (S) (M) 1. with the eyes of a bull. 3. an asura (*Sk. Purāṇa*)

**Mahiṣamardinī** (S) (F) 1. crusher of Mahiṣa. 3. another name for Durgā.

**Mahiṣānanā** (S) (F) 1. buffalo faced. 3. a follower of Skanda (*M. Bh.*)

**Mahiṣārdana** (S) (M) Kārttikeya as the destroyer of the demon Mahiṣa.

**Mahiṣāsura** (S) (M) 1. the asura Mahiṣa. 3. the demon Mahiṣa from whom Mysore is said to take its name (*Vam. Purāṇa*)

**Mahiṣavāhana** (S) (M) 1. buffalo vehicled. 3. another name for Yama.

**Mahiṣayamana** (S) (M) 1. tamer of buffaloes. 3. another name for Yama.

**Mahiṣī** (S) (F) 1. queen; consort; of high rank; female buffalo. 3. the 15th day of the light half of the month Taiśa; another name for the Gaṅgā.

**Mahiṣmān** (S) (M) 1. rich in buffaloes. 3. a king of the Hehaya family who built the city Māhiṣmatī (*Br. Purāṇa*); a king of the Vṛṣṇi dynasty who was the son of Kuṇti (*Bhā. Purāṇa*)

**Mahiṣmat** (S) (M) 1. rich in buffaloes. 3. a king of the Hehaya family (*Br. Purāṇa*); a king of the Vṛṣṇi dynasty (*Bhāgavata*)

**Mahiṣmatī** (S) (F) 1. rich in buffaloes. 3. a particular lunar day personified by a daughter of Aṅgiras (*M. Bh.*)

**Mahīsuta** (S) (M) 1. son of the earth. 2. the planet Mars.

**Mahīsutī** (S) (F) 1. daughter of the earth. 3. another name for Sītā.

**Mahitā** (S) (F) 1. flowing on the earth; greatness. 3. a river (*Bhā. Purāṇa*)

**Mahita** (S) (M) 1. honoured; celebrated. 3. the trident of Śiva (*Ś. Purāṇa*)

**Mahīyā** (S) (F) happiness; exultation.

**Mahīyu** (S) (M) 1. happy. 2. joyous.

**Mahodara** (S) (M) 1. big bellied. 3. a son of Viśvāmitra (*V. Rāmāyaṇa*); a nāga son of Kaśyapa and Kadru (*M. Bh.*); a son of Dhṛtarāṣṭra (*M. Bh.*); an army chief of Rāvaṇa (*U. Rāmāyaṇa*); a friend of Ghaṭotkaća (*Sk. Purāṇa*); a son of Rāvaṇa (*V. Rāmāyaṇa*); a minister of Rāvaṇa's grandfather Sumālin (*V. Rāmāyaṇa*); a son of Viśravas and Puṣpotkaṭā (*V. Rāmāyaṇa*); a rākṣasa (*V. Rāmāyaṇa*)

**Mahodarī** (S) (F) 1. big bellied. 3. an attendant of Durgā (*K. Sāgara*); a daughter of Maya (*V. Purāṇa*)

**Mahodarya** (S) (M) 1. liberal; meritorious. 3. a king worthy of being remembered every morning (*M. Bh.*)

**Mahodaya** (S) (M) 1. greatly risen. 2. respected; eminent. 3. a son of Vasiṣṭha (*V. Rāmāyaṇa*)

**Mahoka/Mahaka** (S) (M) **1.** eminent. **3.** another name for Viṣṇu.

**Maholkā** (S) (F) great firebrand; great meteor.

**Mahotpala** (S) (F) **1.** the great lotus. **2.** Indian Lotus (*Nelumbium nucifera*). **3.** Dākṣāyaṇī in Kamalākśa.

**Mahotsāha** (S) (M) **1.** with great energy. **3.** another name for Śiva.

**Mahottama** (S) (M) **1.** best among the great. **2.** perfume.

**Mahu** (S) (M) **1.** diver-bird; cormorant; a galley or vessel of war. **3.** a son of Śvaphalka (*Bhāgavata*)

**Mahulī** (S) (F) **1.** enchanting voice. **3.** a rāga.

**Mahuratā** (S) (F) **1.** moment; instant. **3.** a daughter of Dakṣa, the wife of Dharma, and the mother of all auspicious moments of time (*H. Purāṇa*)

**Mahya** (S) (M) **1.** highly honoured. **3.** a tribe.

**Mainā** (S) (F) intelligence; the Common Indian Starling (*Sturnus vulgaris*)

**Maināka** (S) (M) **1.** son of Menā. **3.** a mountain situated north of Kailāsa where Bhagīratha offered penance to bring Gaṅgā to the earth, personified as the son of Himavān and Menā and the father of Krauńća.

**Mainda** (S) (M) **1.** giver of art. **3.** a monkey who was the son of Avinīdevas and a leader of Rāma's army (*M. Bh.*); a monkey demon killed by Kṛṣṇa (*M. Bh.*)

**Mairava** (S) (M) belonging to Mount Meru.

**Maithila** (S) (M) **1.** of Mithilā. **3.** another name for Janaka.

**Maithilī** (S) (F) **1.** of Mithilā. **3.** another name for Sītā.

**Maitra** (S) (M) **1.** friendly. **2.** amicable; kind. **3.** a preceptor (*A. Koṣa*)

**Maitrāvaruṇa** (S) (M) **1.** Varuṇa, the friend. **3.** another name for the sages Vasiṣṭha and Agastya when they were reborn as sons of Mitra and Varuṇa (*D. Bhāgavata*)

**Maitrāyaṇa** (S) (M) **1.** of Mitra; friendly. **3.** another name for Agni.

**Maitrāyaṇī** (S) (F) **1.** of Mitra; friendly. **3.** the mother of Pūrṇa.

**Maitreya** (S) (M) **1.** friendly; benevolent. **3.** a sage of great brilliance who was the son of Divodāsa and the father of Somapa (*Bhāgavata*); a Bodhisattva and the future Buddha.

**Maitreyī** (S) (F) **1.** friendly. **3.** the wife of sage Yājñavalkya who was one of the most learned and virtuous women in ancient India.

**Maitrī** (S) (F) **1.** friendship; benevolence; goodwill. **3.** goodwill personified as the daughter of Dakṣa and Prasūtī, the wife of Dharma and the mother of Abhaya (*Bhā. Purāṇa*); an Upaniṣad (*M. Upaniṣad*)

**Maitribala** (S) (M) **1.** one whose strength is benevolence; popular; supported by many; a Buddha. **3.** a king regarded an an incarnation of Gautama Buddha.

**Majjala** (S) (M) **1.** bathing; immersing; sinking. **3.** a soldier of Skanda (*M. Bh.*)

**Majjara** (S) (M) my love.

**Majman** (S) (M) greatness; majesty.

**Mākali** (S) (M) **1.** the moon. **3.** the charioteer of Indra (*Ṛg Veda*)

**Mākanda** (S) (M) **1.** the Mango tree (*Mangifera indica*); Yellow Sandalwood (*Santalum album*). **3.** a city beside the Gaṅgā.

**Makara** (S) (M) **1.** a kind of sea creature sometimes confused with crocodile, shark, dolphin, regarded as the emblem of Kāma. **3.** one of the 9 treasures of Kubera; the zodiac sign of Capricorn.

**Makaradhvaja** (S) (M) **1.** makara bannered. **3.** a son of Hanumān and a crocodile (*A. Rāmāyaṇa*); a son of Dhṛtarāṣṭra (*M. Bh.*); another name for Kāma.

**Makarākṣa** (S) (M) **1.** with the eyes of the makara. **3.** a rākṣasa who was the son of Khara (*V. Rāmāyaṇa*)

**Makarānana** (S) (M) **1.** makara faced. **3.** an attendant of Śiva (*A. Koṣa*)

**Makaranda** (S) (M) honey; nectar; Jasmine (*Jasminum pubescens*); the Indian cuckoo (*Cuculus scolopaceus*); the filament of a lotus; a fragrant species of mango; a pleasure garden; bee; pollen; fragrance.

**Makarandapāla** (S) (M) **1.** protector of nectar. **3.** the father of Trivikrama (*A. Koṣa*)

**Makarandikā** (S) (F) **1.** nectar like; a metre

in music. 3. a daughter of a vidyādhara (*K. Sāgara*)

**Makarāṅka** (S) (M) 1. with the makara for a symbol. 2. the ocean. 3. another name for Kāma.

**Makaraketana** (S) (M) 1. crocodile bannered. 3. another name for Kāma.

**Makaraketu** (S) (M) 1. with a makara as his banner. 3. another name for Kāma.

**Makaravāhana** (S) (M) 1. with a makara for his vehicle. 3. another name for Varuṇa.

**Makarī** (S) (F) 1. she crocodile. 3. a river of Purāṇic fame (*M. Bh.*)

**Makha** (S) (M) cheerful; active; a feat; a festival; a sacrificial oblation.

**Makhaghna** (S) (M) 1. destroying Dakṣa's sacrifice. 3. another name for Śiva.

**Mākhan** (S) (M) an oblation; butter.

**Makhasvāmin** (S) (M) lord of sacrifice.

**Makhatrātṛ** (S) (M) 1. protector of oblation. 3. the protector of Visvāmitra's sacrifice. another name for King Rāma.

**Makheśa** (S) (M) 1. lord of sacrifice. 3. another name for Viṣṇu.

**Mākī** (S) (F) heaven and earth conjoined.

**Makṣarin** (S) (M) 1. ascetic. 2. a religious mendicant. 3. another name for the moon.

**Makṣikā** (S) (F) bee.

**Makṣopeta** (S) (M) 1. surrounded by bees. 3. a daitya who whirls around with an āditya known as Viṣṇu in the month of Kārttika (*Bhā. Purāṇa*)

**Maksūdana** (S) (M) one who performs the sacrifice.

**Makula** (S) (M) a bud.

**Makura** (S) (M) mirror; a bud; the Indian Medlar (*Mimosops elengi*); Arabian Jasmine (*Jasminum sambac*)

**Mālā** (S) (F) 1. necklace; rosary; garland; wreath; row; line; streaks. 3. a river (*M. Bh.*)

**Maladā** (S) (F) 1. that which brings fortune. 3. a wife of sage Atri (*Br. Purāṇa*)

**Mālādevī** (S) (F) 1. goddess of garlands. 3. a form of Lakṣmī worshipped in Jabalpur.

**Mālādhara** (S) (M) 1. wearing a garland. 2. crowned.

**Mālādharī** (S) (F) 1. wreathed; garlanded. 3. a rākṣasī (*B. Literature*)

**Malahā** (S) (F) 1. destroying dirt. 3. a daughter of Raudrāśva (*H. Purāṇa*)

**Mālākara** (S) (M) 1. garland maker; gardener; florist. 3. a son of Viśvakarman by Ghṛtācī (*Brahma Purāṇa*)

**Mālāmantra** (S) (M) 1. the garland hymn. 2. sacred text written in the form of a garland.

**Mālāṅka** (S) (M) 1. garlanded. 3. a king (*A. Koṣa*)

**Mālāsikā** (S) (F) 1. garlanded. 3. a rāgiṇī.

**Mālaśrī** (S) (F) 1. beautiful garland. 3. a rāga.

**Mālatī** (S) (F) 1. Spanish Jasmine (*Jasminum grandiflorium*); bud; blossom; maid; virgin; moonlight; night; Velvet Leaf (*Cissampelos pareira*); *Hiptage madoblata*. 3. a river.

**Mālatikā** (S) (F) 1. made of Jasmine. 3. a mother attending on Skanda (*M. Bh.*)

**Mālatīmādhava** (S) (M) 1. lord of Jasmine. 3. a celebrated drama by Bhavabhūti.

**Mālatimālā** (S) (F) a garland of Jasmine blossoms.

**Mālava** (S) (M) 1. horse keeper. 3. a country in central India and its people; a rāga.

**Mālāvatī** (S) (F) 1. garlanded. 2. crowned. 3. the wife of Kuśadhvaja; the wife of Upabarhaṇa.

**Mālavi** (S) (F) 1. princess of the Mālavas. 3. the wife of King Aśvapati of Madra and progenitress of the Mālavas (*M. Bh.*); a rāgiṇī.

**Mālavikā** (S) (F) 1. of Mālava; *Ipomoea turpethum*. 3. the heroine of a drama by Kālidāsa (*A. Koṣa*)

**Malaya** (S) (M) 1. fragrant; Sandalwood tree (*Santalum album*); rich in sandalwood trees. 3. a mountain in South India, personified by a deity in Kubera's assembly and considered one of the 7 chief mountains of India (*M. Bh.*); a mountain range on the west coast abounding in sandalwood; a mountain just above Kailāsa (*M. Bh.*); the garden of Indra (*M. Bh.*); a son of Garuḍa (*M. Bh.*); a son of Ṛṣabha (*Bhā. Purāṇa*); a son of King Ṛṣabhadeva (*Bhā. Purāṇa*); Himālayan Cherry (*Prunus cerasoides*)

**Malayadhvaja** (S) (M) 1. with a sandalwood

tree; banner. 3. a Pāṇḍya king who fought on the side of the Pāṇḍavas (*M. Bh.*); a son of Merudhvaja (*K. Sāgara*)

**Malayagandhinī** (S) (F) 1. scented with sandalwood. 3. a companion of Umā (*A. Koṣa*); a vidyādharī (*A. Koṣa*)

**Malayagiri** (S) (M) the Malaya mountains (*V. D. Ćaritam*)

**Malayaketu** (S) (M) with the banner/glory of the Sandalwood tree.

**Malayānila** (S) (M) 1. fragrant breeze. 2. sandalwood scented breeze.

**Malayaprabha** (S) (M) 1. with the glory of the sandalwood tree. 3. a king of Kurukṣetra (*K. Sāgara*)

**Malayavāsinī** (S) (F) 1. dwelling on the Malaya mountains. 3. another name for Durgā.

**Malayavatī** (S) (F) very fragrant.

**Malhāra** (S) (M) 1. that which gives rain. 3. a classical music rāga of the monsoons.

**Mālī** (S) (M) 1. fragrant. 3. a demon who was the son of Sukeśa and Devavatī, the husband of Vasudhā and the father of Anila, Anala, Hara and Sampāti (*V. Rāmāyaṇa*)

**Mālīdeva** (S) (M) god of fragrance.

**Mālikā** (S) (F) the mogra or double jasmine; daughter; necklace; intoxicating drink; *Hibiscus mutabilis*.

**Mālin** (S) (M) 1. garlanded; gardener. 2. crowned; florist. 3. a son of the rākṣasa Sukeśa (*V. Rāmāyaṇa*)

**Mālinī** (S) (F) 1. fragrant; sweet smelling; Spanish Jasmine (*Jasminum grandiflorum*); a female gardener. 3. a rākṣasī and mother of Vibhīṣaṇa by Viśravas (*M. Bh.*); name assumed by Draupadī in the court of Virāṭa (*M. Bh.*); the daughter of Sukaru and wife of Śvetakarṇa (*H. Purāṇa*); the wife of Priyavrata (*H. Purāṇa*; the wife of Prasenajit (*B. Literature*); an apsarā (*M. Bh.*); wife of Rući and mother of Manu Raućya (*Mā. Purāṇa*); one of the 7 Mātris of Skanda (*M. Bh.*); an attendant of Durgā; another name for Durgā and the Gaṅgā.

**Mālkausa** (S) (M) 1. garland bearer. 3. a rāga.

**Mālkirata** (S) (M) connoisseur of Jasmine.

**Malla** (S) (M) 1. wrestler. 3. the 21st Arhat of the future Utsarpinī (*J.S. Koṣa*); an asura.

**Mallaga** (S) (M) 1. interested in wrestling. 3. a son of Dyutimat (*M. Bh.*)

**Mallapa** (S) (M) 1. the father of wrestlers. 3. another name for Viṣṇu.

**Mallapriya** (S) (M) 1. beloved of wrestlers. 2. one who is fond of wrestling. 3. another name for Kṛṣṇa.

**Mallārī** (S) (F) 1. enemy of wrestlers. 3. a rāgiṇī.

**Mallāri** (S) (M) 1. enemy of the asura Malla. 3. another name for Kṛṣṇa.

**Mallārjuna** (S) (M) 1. handsome wrestler. 3. a king (*Bhā. Purāṇa*)

**Malleśa** (S) (M) 1. lord of wrestlers. 3. another name for Śiva.

**Malli** (S) (M) 1. having; holding; possessing. 3. the 19th Arhat of the present Avasarpinī; *Jasminum sambac*.

**Malligandhī** (S) (F) smelling like jasmine.

**Mallikā** (S) (F) Arabian Jasmine (*Jasminum sambac*); queen; garland; necklace; daughter.

**Mallikārjuna** (S) (M) 1. white spotted; as white as jasmine. 3. a form of Śiva; a liṅga consecrated to Śiva at Śrīśaila (*Ś. Purāṇa*); the guru of Venkaṭa.

**Mallinātha** (S) (M) 1. lord of possession. 3. a poet and commentator who was the father of Kumārasvāmin and Viśveśvara (14th century); the 19th Jaina Tīrthaṅkara whose emblem is the water jar.

**Malūka** (S) (F) the Sacred Basil (*Ocimum sanctum*)

**Mālyapiṇḍaka** (S) (M) 1. resembling a garland. 3. a serpent born in the family of Kaśyapa (*M. Bh.*)

**Mālyavān** (S) (M) 1. garland bearer. 2. one who is wreathed; crowned. 3. an attendant of Śiva (*V. Rāmāyaṇa*); the son of the demon Sukeśa and brother of Māli and Sumālin (*Rāmāyaṇa*); a golden mountain situated between Meru and Mandāra (*M. Bh.*); a mountain situated in Kiṣkindhā where the fight of Bāli and Sugrīva took place (*M. Bh.*)

**Mālyavat** (S) (M) 1. crowned with garlands. 3. a son of Sukeśa; one of Śiva's attendants; a mountain.

**Mālyavatī** (S) (F) 1. crowned with garlands. 3. a river (*V. Rāmāyaṇa*)

**Māmalladevi** (S) (F) 1. goddess of warriors. 3. the mother of Sriharṣa.

**Māmamī** (S) (F) 1. mine. 3. a Buddhist devī.

**Māmarāja** (S) (M) self praised.

**Mamatā** (S) (F) 1. sense of ownership; motherly love. 3. the wife of Litathya, sister-in-law of Bṛhaspati and mother of sage Bharadvāja (*M. Bh.*); the wife of Utathya; mother of sage Dīrghatamas (*Ṛg Veda*)

**Mammaṭa** (S) (M) 1. theoritician. 3. the author of *Kāvyaprakāśa*.

**Māmti** (S) (M) 1. affectionate; loving. 3. the disciple of Gautama and the guru of Ātreya (*Br. Upaniṣad*); a devotee of Śiva who was the father of Kālabhīti (*Sk. Purāṇa*)

**Māmukhi** (S) (F) 1. face less. 3. a Buddhist devī.

**Mana** (S) (M) 1. Indian Spikenard (*Nardostachys jatamansi*). 3. a son of Śambara (*H. Purāṇa*)

**Māna** (S) (M) 1. opinion; dwelling; measure; likeness; resemblance; notion; idea; purpose; pride; respect; honour. 3. the father of Agastya.

**Manabhava** (S) (M) 1. mind born. 3. another name for Kāma.

**Mānadā** (S) (F) 1. giving honour. 3. a digit of the moon.

**Manadatta** (S) (M) given by thought; absorbed in thought.

**Managarvā** (S) (F) 1. with a proud mind. 2. full of pride. 3. an apsarā who was reborn as the monkey Añjanā and became the mother of Hanumān (*V. Rāmāyaṇa*)

**Manahar** (S) (M) 1. wooing the heart. 2. attractive; fascinating; charming.

**Manaharaṇ** (S) (M) 1. one who woos the heart. 2. lovely; attractive.

**Manaja** (S) (M) 1. born of the mind. 3. another name for Kāma.

**Manajit** (S) (M) 1. one who has conquered thought; one who has won the mind. 3. Indian Madder (*Rubia cordifolia*)

**Manajña/Manojña** (S) (F) princess; pleasing; agreeable; beautiful; charming.

**Manākā** (S) (F) 1. according to the mind. 2. a loving woman; a female elephant; the rosary bead; Elephant's Ears (*Alocasia indica*)

**Manakānta** (S) (M) dear to the mind.

**Manakara** (S) (M) fulfiller of wishes.

**Manal** (S) (M) a bird; the Himālayan Monal Pheasant (*Lopophorus impeyanus*)

**Maṇikarṇika** (S) (M) 1. jewelled earring. 3. one of the 5 pilgrimage centres in Benaras.

**Manmathā** (S) (F) 1. destroying the mind. 2. agitating; suffusing with love. 3. another name for Dākṣāyāṇī.

**Manmatha** (S) (M) 1. churning the mind. 2. passion; desire. 3. another name for Kāma.

**Manmathakara** (S) (M) 1. causing love. 3. an attendant of Skanda (*M. Bh.*)

**Manamathānanda** (S) (M) love's joy.

**Manamohana** (S) (M) 1. winning the heart. 3. another name for Kṛṣṇa.

**Manamohinī** (S) (F) attracting the heart.

**Manana** (S) (M) meditation; reflection; thought; intelligence; understanding.

**Manāṅka** (S) (M) 1. marked with heart. 2. one who is affectionate; compassionate.

**Mananyā** (S) (F) deserving praise.

**Manāpa** (S) (M) 1. gaining the heart. 2. attracting; beautiful.

**Manapati** (S) (M) 1. lord of the heart. 3. another name for Viṣṇu.

**Manaprīta** (S) (M) 1. dear to the heart. 2. joy; delight; mental satisfaction.

**Manaprītī** (S) (F) 1. dear to the heart. 2. delight; gladness.

**Manapriya** (S) (M) 1. dear to the heart. 2. joy; delight; mental satisfaction.

**Manaratha** (S) (M) 1. wish; desire. 3. a king.

**Manarūpa** (S) (M) according to the mind.

**Manas** (S) (M) 1. intellect; intelligence; perception. 3. father in law of Āśā (*H. Purāṇa*)

**Manasā** (S) (F) 1. conceived in the mind. 2. mental power; mind; heart. 3. a goddess who is the daughter of Kaśyapa, sister of Anantanāga, wife of Jaratkaru, mother of Āstīka, the protector of men from serpents and is the tutelary deity of snakes and fertility

(*K. Vyuha*); a kinnarī.

**Mānasa** (S) (M) **1.** conceived in the mind. **2.** soul; mental powers; spiritual mind; heat. **3.** a form of Viṣṇu (*P. Purāṇa*); a serpent of the family of Vāsuki (*M. Bh.*); a serpent of the family of Dhṛtarāṣṭra (*M. Bh.*); a lake on the peak of Mount Kailāśa frequented by the devotees of Śiva (*M. Bh.*); a son of Vapuṣmat (*M. Bh.*); a sacred lake on Mount Kailāsa.

**Manasā** (S) (F) intention.

**Manasādevī** (S) (F) **1.** goddess of mental powers. **3.** a devī born of the mind of Kaśyapa who was also known as Jaratkarū (*K. Vyuha*)

**Mānasāra** (S) (M) **1.** ocean of pride. **2.** extremely proud. **3.** a king of Mālava.

**Manasārāma** (S) (M) absorbed in meditation.

**Mānasavega** (S) (M) swift as thought.

**Mānasī** (S) (F) **1.** mental or spiritual adoration. **3.** a kinnarī; a vidyādevī.

**Manasi** (S) (M) with a sound mind.

**Manasiddhī** (S) (F) **1.** control of the mind; one who attains all desires. **3.** a goddess (*V. D. Ćaritam*)

**Manasija** (S) (M) **1.** born of the heart. **2.** love. **3.** another name for Kāma and the moon.

**Manaskānta** (S) (M) dear to the heart.

**Manastāla** (S) (M) **1.** deep thinker. **3.** the lion which is the vehicle of Durgā.

**Manastokā** (S) (F) **1.** mental satisfaction. **2.** mentally satisfied. **3.** another name for Durgā.

**Manasukha** (S) (M) agreeable to the heart.

**Manasvī** (S) (F) **1.** that which controls the mind. **2.** intelligence; high mindedness; one with a sound mind.

**Manasvin** (S) (M) **1.** one who controls the mind. **2.** intelligent; clever; wise. **3.** a son of Devala (*V. Purāṇa*); a nāga.

**Manasvinī** (S) (F) **1.** one who controls the mind. **2.** noble; proud; high minded; virtuous. **3.** a daughter of Dakṣa, wife of Dharma and the mother of Ćandra (*M. Bh.*); the wife of Mṛkandu; *Momordica balsamina*; another name for Durgā.

**Manasyu** (S) (M) **1.** wishing; desiring. **3.** a Purū king who was the son of Pravīra and Śūrasenī and the husband of Sauvīrī (*M. Bh.*); a son of Mahānta (*V. Purāṇa*)

**Manatoṣa** (S) (M) mental satisfaction.

**Māṇava** (S) (M) **1.** youth; lad; a pearl ornament of 16 strings. **3.** one of the 9 treasures of the Jainas.

**Mānavāćārya** (S) (M) **1.** father of mankind. **3.** another name for Manu.

**Mānavadeva** (S) (M) god among men.

**Mānavapati** (S) (M) **1.** lord of men. **2.** a prince.

**Manavarā** (S) (F) pleasant to the mind.

**Mānavasu** (S) (M) rich in devotion; loyal; faithful.

**Mānavendra** (S) (M) **1.** lord of men. **3.** another name for Indra.

**Mānāvī** (S) (F) **1.** wife of Manu; daughter of man. **3.** a goddess executing the demands of the 11th Arhat of the present Avasarpiṇī; a prominent river of ancient India (*M. Bh.*); a vidyādevī; *Jasminum auriculatum*.

**Māṇavikā** (S) (F) damsel; maiden.

**Manāyī** (S) (F) Manu's wife.

**Manāyu** (S) (M) **1.** zealous. **2.** devoted.

**Mandā** (S) (F) **1.** slow; pot; vessel; inkstand. **3.** a digit of the moon (*A. Koṣa*); another name for Dākṣāyaṇī.

**Mandagā** (S) (M) **1.** moving slowly. **3.** a son of Dyutimat (*V. Purāṇa*); another name for the planet Saturn.

**Mandaka** (S) (M) **1.** speed breaker. **3.** a son of the yakṣa Maṇibhadra and Puṇyajanī (*H. Purāṇa*)

**Mandakānti** (S) (M) **1.** with a soft lustre. **3.** another name for the moon.

**Māṇḍakarṇi** (S) (M) **1.** performing slowly; hearing slowly. **2.** hard of hearing. **3.** a sage who lived only on air for 10,000 years (*V. Rāmāyaṇa*)

**Mandākinī** (S) (F) **1.** that which moves slowly; the Milky Way. **3.** a branch of the Gaṅgā which flows through Kedāranātha (*M. Bh.*); a holy river which flows near the Ćitrakūṭa mountain (*M. Bh.*); a Purāṇic river arising from the Kedāra mountains (*M. Bh.*); one of the 2 wives of Viśravas and the mother of Kubera (*P. Purāṇa*); the celestial Gaṅgā (*M. Bh.*); Kubera's park (*M. Bh.*)

**Mandālaka** (S) (M) 1. with loving eyes. 3. a serpent of the family of Takṣaka (*M. Bh.*)

**Maṇḍana** (S) (M) adorning; ornament; decoration.

**Mandanā** (S) (F) gay; cheerful.

**Mandānila** (S) (M) gentle breeze; zephyr.

**Maṇḍanmiśra** (S) (M) 1. honourable ornament. 3. husband of Sarasavāṇi.

**Mandanum** (S) (M) praise.

**Mandapāla** (S) (M) 1. protector of praise. 3. a sage (*M. Bh.*)

**Mandarā** (S) (F) 1. slow. 2. large; firm. 3. a wife of Viśvakarmā and the mother of Nala the monkey (*V. Rāmāyaṇa*)

**Mandāra** (S) (M) 1. large; thick; firm; slow. 2. a pearl chain of 8 strings. 3. the eldest son of Hiraṇyakaśipu (*M. Bh.*); a son of the sage Dhaumya and the husband of Śamīkā (*G. Purāṇa*); a sage extolled in the *Śiva Purāṇa*; a sacred mountain which served as a stick for churning the Ocean of Milk (*M. Bh.*); a vidyādhara (*K. Sāgara*); one of the 5 trees of Paradise; Indian Coral tree (*Erythrina indica*)

**Mandāradeva** (S) (M) 1. lord of the Indian Coral tree (*Erythrina indica*); coming from Mount Mandāra. 3. a king of the vidyādharas; another name for Śiva.

**Mandaradevī** (S) (F) 1. coming from Mount Mandāra. 3. a sister of Mandāradeva (*K. Sāgara*); another name for Durgā.

**Mandāralakṣmī** (S) (F) 1. goddess of the Indian Coral tree (*Erythrina indica*). 3. the wife of King Siṁhadhvaja (*K. Sāgara*)

**Mandāramālā** (S) (F) 1. a garland of coral flowers. 3. an apsarā who was the daughter of Vasu (*K. Sāgara*)

**Mandaramāli** (S) (M) 1. garlanded with pearl chains. 3. a daitya.

**Mandarāvatī** (S) (F) bearer of coral flowers.

**Mandārikā** (S) (F) the Indian Coral tree (*Erythrina indica*)

**Mandavāhinī** (S) (F) 1. gently flowing. 3. a river (*M. Bh.*)

**Māṇḍavī** (S) (F) 1. able administrator. 3. Dākṣāyaṇī in Māṇḍavya (*M. Bh.*); a daughter of Kuṣadhvaja, the wife of Bharata, the mother of Śūrasena and Subāhu and the cousin of Sītā (*U. Rāmāyaṇa*)

**Māṇḍavikā** (S) (F) of administration; of people.

**Mandayu** (S) (M) gay; cheerful; happy.

**Māndhana** (S) (M) rich in honour.

**Māndhara** (S) (M) honourable.

**Māndhārī** (S) (F) bearer of honour.

**Māndhātā** (S) (M) 1. respected; honoured; revered. 3. an eminent Ikṣvāku king who was the son of Yuvanāśva (*M. Bh.*)

**Māndhatṛ** (S) (M) 1. bearer of respect; thoughtful; pious. 3. a royal ṛṣi of the solar dynasty who was the son of Yuvanāśva and the husband of Bindumatī (*D. Bh. Purāṇa*); a king and son of Madanapāla the patron of Viśveśvara.

**Mandin** (S) (M) 1. delighting; exhilarating. 3. another name for Soma.

**Mandirā** (S) (F) of temple; a slow sound; sacred; venerated; melodious; metallic cymbals producing a musical sound.

**Mandiramaṇi** (S) (M) 1. jewel of the temple. 3. another name for Śiva.

**Mandiṣṭha** (S) (M) most exhilarating.

**Maṇḍita** (S) (M) adorned; decorated.

**Maṇḍitṛ** (S) (F) 1. that which adorns. 2. an ornament.

**Mandodaka** (S) (M) 1. slow flowing water. 3. the mythical lake situated on Mount Kailāśa and said to be the source of the Gaṅgā – the counterpart of the celestial river Mandākinī (*D. Ćarita*)

**Mandodarī** (S) (F) 1. narrow waisted; one who can digest secrets. 3. an incarnation of the apsarā Madhurā, the daughter of Maya, the favourite wife of Rāvaṇa, the mother of Meghanā, Atikāya and Akṣakumāra (*V. Rāmāyaṇa*) and regarded as one of the 5 chaste women; a mother attending on Skanda (*D. Bh. Purāṇa*); a princess of Siṁhala and wife of King Ćārudeṣṇa of Madra (*D. Bh. Purāṇa*)

**Mandrā** (S) (F) pleasant; agreeable; charming; low voiced.

**Mandu** (S) (M) 1. pleased. 2. joyful; cheerful.

**Māṇḍūkeya** (S) (M) 1. son of a frog. 3. a ṛṣi.

**Māṇḍūkya** (S) (M) 1. son of a frog. 3. one of the 13 principal Upaniṣads.

**Manendra** (S) (M) lord of the mind.

**Mangalā** (S) (F) 1. auspicious; lucky. 2. a faithful wife; Couch Grass (*Cynodon dactylon*); the white and blue flowering Dūrvā grass (*Panicum dactylon*); the Karañja blossom (*Pongamia glabra*); Spanish Jasmine (*Jasminum grandiflorum*). 3. the mother of the 5th Arhat of the present Avasarpinī (*J.S. Koṣa*); another name for Umā, Durgā and the Dākṣāyaṇī as worshipped in Gayā.

**Maṅgala** (S) (M) 1. happiness; felicity; welfare; bliss; auspiciousness. 3. a king belonging to the race of Manu; a chief of the Ćālukyas; a Buddha (*B. Literature*); another name for Agni and the planet Mars.

**Maṅgalaćaṇḍī** (S) (F) 1. goddess of welfare. 3. a form of Durgā (*A. Koṣa*)

**Mangalaćaṇḍikā** (S) (F) 1. goddess of welfare. 3. a tutelary deity of the Vedas who is a form of Durgā and worshipped by Paramaśiva (*D. Bhāgavata*)

**Mangalapāṇi** (S) (M) with auspicious hands.

**Mangalāvatī** (S) (F) 1. bestowed with luck. 3. a daughter of Tumburu (*K. Sāgara*)

**Mangalāvrata** (S) (M) 1. devoted to Mangalā; devoted to Umā. 3. another name for Śiva.

**Maṅgalī** (S) (F) 1. auspicious. 2. scented with jasmine.

**Maṅgalya** (S) (M) 1. pious; pure; beautiful; bringing luck. 2. gold; sandalwood. 3. a nāga.

**Maṅgalyā** (S) (F) 1. auspicious. 2. Sandalwood (*Santalum album*); Wood Apple (*Ferronia elephantum*); *Prosopis spicigera*; *Aglaia odoratissima*. 3. another name for Durgā.

**Maṅgammā** (S) (F) 1. enticing heart. 2. beautiful; that which charms the heart.

**Maṅhana** (S) (M) gift; present.

**Manhayu** (S) (M) liberal.

**Manhiṣtha** (S) (M) 1. granting according to the wishes; granting abundantly. 2. generous; liberal.

**Maṇi** (S) (M) 1. jewel; gem; ornament; crystal; pearl; magnet. 3. a son of Yuyudhāna (*M. Bh.*); the king of the kiṇnaras (*K. Vyuha*); a serpent of the family of Dhṛtarāṣṭra (*M. Bh.*); a sage and member of Brahmā's court (*M. Bh.*); an attendant given to Skanda by Ćandra (*M. Bh.*); a nāga son of Kaśyapa and Kadru (*Br. Purāṇa*)

**Maṇibandhana** (S) (M) ornament of pearls.

**Maṇibhadra** (S) (M) 1. jewelled person; jewel among people. 2. gem of a person. 3. a brother of Kubera; the king of the yakṣas, the tutelary deity of merchants and travellers and worshipped in the temple of Tāmralipti (*M. Bh.*); a lunar dynasty king who was the husband of Kavikā and whose 7 sons were freed from their curse by Rāma (*K. Rāmāyaṇa*); an attendant of Śiva (*Ś. Purāṇa*)

**Maṇibhava** (S) (M) 1. born of a jewel. 3. one of the 5 Dhyāni Buddhas.

**Maṇibhūmi** (S) (F) a mine of pearls.

**Maṇibīja** (S) (M) 1. with jewelled seeds. 2. the Pomegranate tree (*Punica granatum*)

**Manīća** (S) (M) hand; pearl; flower.

**Maṇićara** (S) (M) 1. jewel eater. 2. eater of pomegranate seeds. 3. a prince of the yakṣas (*V. Rāmāyaṇa*)

**Maṇićūḍā** (S) (F) 1. jewel crested. 3. a kiṇnarī (*K. Vyuha*)

**Maṇićūḍa** (S) (M) 1. jewel crested. 3. a vidyādhara; a nāga.

**Maṇidara** (S) (M) 1. living in a jewelled cave. 3. a chief of the yakṣas (*K. Sāgara*)

**Maṇidhanu** (S) (M) 1. jewelled bow. 2. the rainbow.

**Maṇidhāriṇī** (S) (F) 1. bearer of jewels. 2. bejewelled; ornamented. 3. a kinnarī.

**Maṇidīpa** (S) (M) a jewelled lamp; a jewel that shines.

**Maṇidvīpa** (S) (M) 1. the island of jewels. 3. the abode of Devī far beyond Kailāsa (*D. Bhāgavata*)

**Maṇigaṇa** (S) (M) a group of jewels; pearls.

**Maṇigrīva** (S) (M) 1. jewel necked. 3. a son of Kubera and the brother of Nalakūbara (*Ṛg Veda*)

**Maṇihāra** (S) (M) a string of jewels.

**Maṇijalā** (S) (F) 1. with crystal clear water.

3. a river (*M. Bh.*)

**Māṇikā** (S) (F) 1. of jewels. 2. a particular weight.

**Mānika** (S) (M) highly honoured and esteemed.

**Maṇika** (S) (M) jewel; gem.

**Maṇikam** (S) (M) collyrium.

**Māṇikāmbā** (S) (F) 1. mother of jewels. 3. the mother of Viṭṭhala.

**Maṇikaṇṭha** (S) (M) 1. jewel necked. 2. the Blue Jay (*Coracias benghalensis*). 3. a nāga.

**Maṇikāra** (S) (M) jeweller; lapidary.

**Maṇikarṇa** (S) (M) jewel eared.

**Maṇikarṇikā** (S) (F) 1. jewelled earring. 3. a daughter of Ćandraghoṣa; a sacred pool in Benaras (*R. Upaniṣad*)

**Maṇiketu** (S) (M) 1. with a jewelled banner. 3. a comet (*Var. Purāṇa*)

**Maṇikusuma** (S) (M) 1. jewelled flower. 3. a Jina (*J.S. Koṣa*)

**Maṇikuṭṭikā** (S) (F) 1. inlaid with jewels. 3. a follower of Skanda (*M. Bh.*)

**Māṇikya** (S) (M) ruby.

**Māṇikyaćandra** (S) (M) moon among rubies.

**Māṇikyāditya** (S) (M) sun among rubies.

**Māṇikyādri** (S) (M) 1. mountain of rubies. 3. a mountain (*M. Bh.*)

**Māṇikyamaya** (S) (M) made of rubies.

**Māṇikyavāćakara** (S) (M) 1. with a ruby like speech. 2. a great orator. 3. poet and devotee of Śiva from Tamil Nadu who became a minister of the Pāṇḍya king (8th century) (*M. Bh.*)

**Maṇilāla** (S) (M) jewel of a son.

**Maṇimālā** (S) (F) 1. a necklace of jewels. 2. beautiful; lustrous. 3. another name for Lakṣmī.

**Maṇimān** (S) (M) 1. jewelled. 3. a king who was a partial incarnation of the asura Vṛtra and who fought on the side of the Pāṇḍavas (*M. Bh.*); a serpent of the court of Varuṇa (*M. Bh.*); a yakṣa friend of Kubera (*M. Bh.*); an attendant of Śiva (*Bhā. Purāṇa*); a mountain (*M. Bh.*); another name for the sun.

**Maṇimaṇḍita** (S) (M) adorned with jewels.

**Maṇimañjarī** (S) (F) cluster of jewels.

**Maṇimat** (S) (M) 1. adorned with jewels. 3. a servant of Śiva (*Bh. Purāṇa*); a rākṣasa (*M. Bh.*); a nāga (*M. Bh.*); a yakṣa (*M. Bh.*); another name for the sun.

**Maṇimaya** (S) (M) 1. made of jewels. 3. the father of Devavatī and father-in-law of Sukeśa (*U. Rāmāyaṇa*)

**Maṇināga** (S) (M) 1. jewelled serpent; jewelled elephant; jewelled mountain. 3. a serpent son of Kaśyapa and Kadru (*M. Bh.*); a sacred bathing place (*M. Bh.*)

**Maṇinanda** (S) (M) born of the jewel.

**Maṇīndra** (S) (M) 1. chief of jewels. 2. the diamond.

**Maṇingā** (S) (F) 1. treasure of jewels. 3. a river.

**Māninī** (S) (F) 1. resolute; self respecting. 3. a daughter of Vidūrastha and wife of Rājyavardhana (*Mā. Purāṇa*); the daughter of sage Tṛṇabindu and the mother of Viśravas (*Mā. Purāṇa*); an apsarā (*V. Purāṇa*)

**Maṇipadma** (S) (M) 1. jewelled lotus. 3. a Bodhisattva.

**Maṇiprabhā** (S) (F) 1. splendour of a jewel. 3. an apsarā (*K. Vyuha*)

**Maṇipurapati** (S) (M) 1. lord of Maṇipura. 3. another name for Babhravāhana.

**Maṇipureśvara** (S) (M) 1. lord of Maṇipura. 3. another name for Babhruvāhana.

**Maṇipuṣpaka** (S) (M) 1. jewel and flower conjoined. 3. the conch of Sahadeva (*M. Bh.*)

**Maṇipuṣpeśvara** (S) (M) 1. lord of jewels and flowers. 3. an attendant of Śiva (*K. Sāgara*)

**Maṇirāga** (S) (M) with the colour of a jewel.

**Maṇirāja** (S) (M) 1. king of jewels. 2. the diamond.

**Maṇirāma** (S) (M) existing in jewels.

**Maṇiratna** (S) (F) jewel.

**Maṇirоćanī** (S) (F) 1. one who likes jewels. 3. a kinnarī (*K. Vyuha*)

**Manīṣa** (S) (M) 1. lord of the mind. 2. profound thinker; wise.

**Maṇīṣā** (S) (F) thought; reflection; consideration; wisdom; intelligence; conception; idea; prayer; hymn; desire; wish; request; reflection; intellect.

**Maṇiśaṅkara** (S) (M) the jewelled Śiva.

**Maṇisānu** (S) (M) 1. jewel ridged. 3. another

name for Mount Meru.

**Manisara** (S) (M) string of jewels; a necklace.

**Manīṣī** (S) (F) desired by heart.

**Manīṣikā** (S) (F) understanding; intelligence.

**Maṇiśilā** (S) (F) a jewelled stone.

**Manīṣin** (S) (M) 1. thoughtful. 2. intelligent; wise; prudent; devout; sagacious.

**Manīṣitā** (S) (F) wisdom.

**Manīṣita** (S) (M) desired; wished; wish.

**Manīṣkā** (S) (F) wisdom; intelligence.

**Maṇiskandha** (S) (M) 1. with jewelled shoulders. 3. a serpent of the family of Dhṛtarāṣṭra (*M. Bh.*)

**Maṇisraj** (S) (F) a garland of jewels.

**Maṇiśringa** (S) (M) 1. jewel horned. 3. another name for Sūrya.

**Maniṣṭhakā** (S) (F) the little finger.

**Maṇīśvara** (S) (M) lord of jewels.

**Manita** (S) (M) honoured; respected; known; understood.

**Manīvaka** (S) (M) 1. jewel tongued. 3. a son of Bhavya (*V. Purāṇa*)

**Maṇīvaka** (S) (M) 1. with pearl like words; with flowery speech. 3. a son of Bhavya and grandson of Priyavrata (*V. Purāṇa*)

**Maṇivakra** (S) (M) 1. jewel faced. 3. a son of the vasu Āpa.

**Maṇivara** (S) (M) 1. best jewel. 2. the diamond. 3. a yakṣa who was the son of Rajatanātha and the father of the guhyakas (*Br. Purāṇa*)

**Maṇivarman** (S) (M) a jewelled talisman.

**Maṇiyā** (S) (F) glass bead.

**Mañjā** (S) (F) a cluster of blossoms.

**Mañjarī** (S) (F) 1. a cluster of blossoms. 2. spring; stalk of a flower; a flowerbud; a shoot; a sprout; a sprig; blossom; vine; pearl; Mango tree (*Mangifera indica*)

**Mañjarikā** (S) (F) 1. a small cluster of blossoms. 2. a small pearl; the Tulasī plant.

**Mañjava** (S) (M) swift as thought.

**Mañjī** (S) (F) a cluster of blossoms.

**Mañjimān** (S) (F) 1. bearer of blossoms. 2. beauty; elegance.

**Mañjirā** (S) (F) 1. anklet. 2. an ornament for the foot. 3. a river (*A. Koṣa*)

**Mañjira** (S) (M) a cymbal; an anklet.

**Mañju** (S) (F) 1. attracting the heart. 2. beautiful; lovely; charming; pleasant; sweet.

**Mañjudeva** (S) (M) lord of beauty.

**Mañjugati** (S) (F) 1. having a graceful gait. 2. the flamingo.

**Manjughoṣā** (S) (F) 1. with a sweet sound. 3. an apsarā (*A Koṣa*)

**Mañjughoṣa** (S) (M) 1. with a sweet voice. 2. the dove (*Streptopelia chinensis*)

**Mañjukeśin** (S) (M) 1. with beautiful hair. 3. another name for Kṛṣṇa.

**Mañjulā** (S) (F) 1. taking the heart. 2. beautiful; pleasing; lovely; charming; a bower; an arbour; a spring. 3. a river of Purāṇic fame (*M. Bh.*)

**Mañjulatā** (S) (F) vine of beauty.

**Mañjulikā** (S) (F) beautiful.

**Mañjumaṇi** (S) (M) 1. beautiful gem. 2. the topaz.

**Mañjumatī** (S) (F) 1. with a lovely heart. 2. loving; compassionate; humane.

**Mañjunaśī** (S) (F) 1. connoisseur of beauty. 2. a beautiful woman. 3. the wife of Indra; another name for Durgā.

**Mañjunātha** (S) (M) 1. lord of beauty; lord of ice. 3. another name for Śiva.

**Mañjuprāṇa** (S) (M) 1. beautiful soul. 3. another name for Brahmā.

**Mañjūṣaka** (S) (M) celestial flower.

**Manjuśrī** (S) (F) 1. divine beauty. 3. another name for Lakṣmi.

**Mañjuśrī** (S) (M) 1. divine beauty. 3. a celebrated Bodhisattva considered the epitome of wisdom.

**Mañjutara** (S) (F) most lovely.

**Mankaṇa** (S) (M) 1. a part of the mind. 3. a sage who was the son of Vāyubhagavān and Sukanyā, the father of 7 sons by Sarasvatī Devī and a daughter named Kadalīgarbhā by the apsara Menakā.

**Maṅkaṇaka** (S) (M) 1. partially thoughtful. 3. a ṛṣi (*M. Bh.*); a yakṣa (*M. Bh.*)

**Maṅki** (S) (M) 1. governed by thought. 3. a Vaiṣṇavite sage who was the son of Kauṣtikī and the husband of Surupā and Virupā (*P. Purāṇa*); a great sage (*M. Bh.*)

**Maṅkśa** (S) (M) 1. longing. 2. to long for; to desire.

**Maṅkura** (S) (M) 1. that which reflects the mind. 2. a mirror.

**Manmandira** (S) (M) 1. a temple of ego. 2. arrogance. 3. another name for Rāvaṇa.

**Mannata** (S) (M) 1. with a devoted mind. 2. a vow to a deity.

**Mannitha** (S) (M) 1. heart. 2. chosen.

**Manobhāvanā** (S) (F) 1. feeling of the heart. 2. sentiment; emotion.

**Manobhirāma** (S) (M) 1. pleasing to the mind. 2. delightful; charming; beautiful.

**Manobhū** (S) (M) 1. born of the mind. 2. love. 3. another name for Kāma.

**Manodāhin** (S) (M) 1. influencing the heart. 3. another name for Kāma.

**Manodarī** (S) (F) 1. pleasing to the heart. 3. the wife of Dārukāsura (*Ś. Purāṇa*)

**Manodatta** (S) (M) given by the mind.

**Manodhara** (S) (M) one who bears the mind.

**Manogati** (S) (F) 1. the heart's course. 2. wish; desire.

**Manoharā** (S) (F) 1. winning the heart. 2. that which steals the heart. 3. the wife of the vasu Soma; an apsarā in the court of Kubera (*M. Bh.*); a kinnarī; wife of Dhara and mother of Śiśira (*H. Purāṇa*); Yellow Jasmine.

**Manohara** (S) (M) 1. winning the heart. 2. that which steals the heart; *Jasminum pubescens*. 3. another name for Kṛṣṇa.

**Manoharī** (S) (F) 1. that which steal the heart; Spanish Jasmine (*Jasmine grandiflorum*). 3. the wife of Varćasvin and mother of Śiśira; an apsarā; a kinnarī.

**Manohārikā** (S) (F) one who steals the heart.

**Manoja** (S) (M) 1. born of the mind. 2. love. 3. another name for Kāma.

**Manojāta** (S) (M) born of the mind.

**Manojavā** (S) (F) 1. with the speed of thought; born of the mind. 3. one of the 7 tongues of Agni (*M. Upaniṣad*); a mother attending on Skanda (*M. Bh.*); a river (*V. Purāṇa*)

**Manojava** (S) (M) 1. with the speed of thought; born of the mind. 3. son of the vasu Anila and his wife Śivā (*M. Bh.*); Indra during the Manvantara of Manu Ćākṣusa (*V. Purāṇa*); a follower of Skanda (*M. Bh.*); a son of the rudra Īśāna; a son of Medhātithi (*Bhā. Purāṇa*)

**Manojñā** (S) (F) 1. agreeable to the mind. 2. pleasant; charming; beautiful; a princess.

**Manojñasvara** (S) (M) 1. with a pleasing voice. 3. a gandharva (*S. Puṇḍarikā*)

**Manojū** (S) (M) as swift as thought.

**Manojvalā** (S) (F) as fair as thought; *Jasminum auriculatum*.

**Manojyotis** (S) (M) 1. whose light is the intellect. 2. extremely intelligent.

**Manokāmanā** (S) (F) hearts desire.

**Manomātrā** (S) (M) 1. one who can change forms according to will. 3. another name for Śiva and Viṣṇu.

**Manomohinī** (S) (F) attracting the heart.

**Manonīta** (S) (M) 1. carried by the mind. 2. chosen; approved.

**Manorāga** (S) (M) 1. the colour of the heart. 2. affection; passion.

**Manoramā** (S) (F) 1. gratifying the mind. 2. pleasing; beautiful; charming. 3. the daughter of the vidyādhara Indīvara, the wife of Svāroćiṣa and the mother of Vijaya; an apsarā who was the daughter of Kaśyapa and Prādhā (*M. Bh.*); a branch of the Sarasvatī river (*M. Bh.*); the wife of King Dhruvasandhi of Kosala; a gandharvī; Musk Jasmine (*Jasminum pubescens*)

**Manorañjana** (S) (M) pleasing to the mind.

**Manoratha** (S) (M) 1. chariot of the mind. 2. wish; cherished desire. 3. a calf created by Kṛṣṇa.

**Manoritā** (S) (F) 1. of the mind. 2. desire; wish.

**Manota** (S) (M) 1. born of the mind. 3. the hymn of *Ṛg Veda* (vi) and the deity to whom it is dedicated.

**Manotī** (S) (F) 1. daughter in mind. 2. vow of offering to a deity.

**Manotṛ** (S) (M) 1. one who possesses the mind. 2. an inventor; a discoverer.

**Manovallabhā** (S) (F) heart's beloved.

**Manovatī** (S) (F) 1. desired by the mind. 3. the daughter of the vidyādhara Ćitrāṅgada; the daughter of the asura Sumāya; the city of

Brahmā on Mount Mahāmeru (*D. Bh. Purāṇa*); an apsarā.

**Manovindā** (S) (F) amusing to the mind.

**Manoyoni** (S) (M) 1. born of the mind. 3. another name for Kāma.

**Manta** (S) (M) 1. thought. 3. one of the 12 methods of realization.

**Mantha** (S) (M) 1. churning; agitating. 3. another name for the sun.

**Manthāna** (S) (M) 1. that which shakes. 3. Śiva as one who shakes the universe; an asura in the army of Tārakāsura (*M. Purāṇa*)

**Mantharā** (S) (F) 1. slow; broad; indolent; curved; crooked; an obstacle. 3. the humpbacked slave of Kaikeyī who is supposed to have been an incarnation of the gāndharvī Dundubhī (*M. Bh.*); a daughter of Viroćana (*V. Rāmāyaṇa*)

**Manthinī** (S) (F) 1. that which churns. 2. a butter vat. 3. a mother attending on Skanda (*M. Bh.*)

**Mantikā** (S) (F) 1. thoughtful. 3. an Upaniṣad.

**Mantra** (S) (M) 1. instrument of thought. 2. vedic hymn; sacred verse; spell; charm. 3. the 5th lunar mansion; another name for Viṣṇu and Śiva.

**Mantramālā** (S) (F) 1. a garland of hymns. 2. a collection of prayers and magical verses. 3. a river (*Ṛg Veda*)

**Mantramūrti** (S) (M) 1. lord of spells. 3. another name for Śiva.

**Mantraṇā** (S) (F) counsel; advice; deliberation.

**Mantrapāla** (S) (M) 1. protector of hymns. 3. a minister of King Daśaratha (*V. Rāmāyaṇa*)

**Mantreśvara** (S) (M) 1. lord of spells. 3. another name for Śiva.

**Mantrin** (S) (M) 1. the knower of hymns. 2. wise; eloquent; clever in counsel; minister.

**Mantriṇī** (S) (F) the queen of chess; the 12th lunar mansion.

**Mantu** (S) (M) 1. advisor. 2. ruler; arbiter; man; mankind.

**Mantuṅga** (S) (M) high in honour.

**Manū** (S) (F) 1. of the mind. 2. desirable. 3. an apsara born of Kaśyapa and Prādhā (*M. Bh.*)

**Manu** (S) (M) 1. thinking; wise; intelligent. 3. the man par excellence or the representative man and father of the human race (*Ṛg Veda*), the name Manu is applied to 13 successive mythical progenitors and sovereigns of the earth, each of whom headed a period of time or Antara known as Manvantara, the 1st Manu was Svāyambhuva or 'self-existent' who produced 10 prajāpatis, the 1st being Marīći or light, the next 6 Svāroćiṣa, Auttami, Tāmasa, Raivata, Ćākṣuṣa and Vaivasvata or sunborn, the last is regarded as the progenitor of the human race and the 8th Manu (*V. Purāṇa*); Sāvarṇi as the 1st of the future Manus; a rudra; an agni (*M. Bh.*); the number 14; the son of the agni Pāñćajanya (*M. Bh.*)

**Manuga** (S) (M) 1. follower of wishes. 3. a son of Dyutimat (*Bhā. Purāṇa*)

**Manuja** (S) (M) 1. son of Manu. 2. man.

**Manujā** (S) (F) 1. daughter of man. 2. woman.

**Manujanātha** (S) (M) lord of man.

**Manujendra** (S) (M) 1. lord of men. 2. a king.

**Manujeśvara** (S) (M) 1. lord of men. 2. a king.

**Manujottama** (S) (M) best among men.

**Manujyeṣṭha** (S) (M) best of men; eldest among men; a sword.

**Manupati** (S) (M) 1. master of man. 2. a king.

**Manurāj** (S) (M) 1. king of men. 3. another name for Kubera.

**Mānuṣī** (S) (F) woman; humane.

**Manuṣkulāditya** (S) (M) the sun of the family of Manu.

**Manuśreṣṭha** (S) (M) 1. best among men. 3. another name for Viṣṇu.

**Mānyā** (S) (F) to be respected; worthy of honour.

**Manyantī** (S) (F) 1. honourable. 3. the daughter of Agni Manyu (*Bhā. Purāṇa*)

**Mānyavatī** (S) (F) 1. honoured; esteemed. 3. the daughter of Bhīmarāja and wife of Avīkṣit (*Mā. Purāṇa*)

**Manyu** (S) (M) 1. mind; spirit; mood; temper; zeal; passion; rage; anger. 3. anger personified as a rudra; a king of the Purū dynasty and the son of Bharadvāja (*M. Bh.*); the author of some of the hymns of *Ṛg Veda* (x); a

Vedic god produced from the 3rd eye of Śiva (*M. Bh.*); a king and son of Vitatha (*Bhā. Purāṇa*); another name for Agni (*Ṛg Veda*)

**Manyumān** (S) (M) **1.** spiritual; thoughtful; zealous; passionate; angry. **3.** the son of the agni Bhānu (*M. Bh.*)

**Manyumata** (S) (M) spirited; ardent; passionate; vehement.

**Māpatya** (S) (M) **1.** not a child. **2.** an adult. **3.** another name for Kāma.

**Māra** (S) (M) **1.** destroyer; passion. **3.** a form of Śiva (*Ś. Purāṇa*); an enemy of Buddha and Buddhism; another name for Kāma.

**Mārābhibhu** (S) (M) **1.** overthrower of Māra. **3.** a Buddha (*H. Koṣa*)

**Māraćitta** (S) (M) **1.** destroyer of desires. **3.** a Buddhist deity (*B. Literature*)

**Mārajit** (S) (M) **1.** conqueror of Māra. **3.** the Buddha who overcame Māra, the chief enemy of Buddhists; another name for Śiva.

**Marakata** (S) (M) the emerald; with properties of an emerald.

**Mārakkā** (S) (F) **1.** death. **3.** the goddess Mariamma who is a form of Pārvatī.

**Marāla** (S) (M) soft; mild; tender.

**Marālī** (S) (F) female swan.

**Marālikā** (S) (F) small swan.

**Maranda** (S) (M) nectar.

**Marandaka** (S) (M) **1.** the abode of nectar. **2.** flower.

**Mārāṅka** (S) (M) marked by love.

**Marasurāma** (S) (M) **1.** that which consists of love. **3.** the festival of Vaisakha.

**Māravat** (S) (M) full of love.

**Marāyin** (S) (M) destroying enemies.

**Mardana** (S) (M) **1.** crushing; grinding. **3.** a chief of the vidyadharas.

**Mārdavā** (S) (F) softness; kindness.

**Mārḍika** (S) (M) mercy; pity; compassion.

**Mārgamarṣi** (S) (M) **1.** preceptor of the path. **3.** a son of Viśvāmitra (*M. Bh.*)

**Mārgaṇapriyā** (S) (F) **1.** lover of research; one who loves inquiry. **3.** a daughter of Kaśyapa and Prādhā (*M. Bh.*)

**Mārgapālī** (S) (F) **1.** protecting the roads. **3.** a goddess (*P. Purāṇa*)

**Mārgavatī** (S) (F) **1.** follower of the path; bearer of the path. **3.** the goddess of paths and the protector of travellers (*K. Sāgara*)

**Mārgin** (S) (M) showing the way; pioneer.

**Mārgita** (S) (M) sought; desired; required.

**Māri** (S) (F) **1.** of death; of love. **3.** a form of Durgā as the goddess of death.

**Mariammā** (S) (F) **1.** mother of death; mother of love. **3.** a form of Pārvatī (*G. Purāṇa*)

**Mārića** (S) (M) **1.** glowing; the pepper plant. **3.** the son of Śunda and Tāṭakā, the brother of Subāhu and the uncle of Rāvaṇa who transformed himself into a golden deer to lure Rāma away from Sītā in order to let Rāvaṇa abduct her (*V. Rāmāyaṇa*); a dānava (*U. Rāmāyaṇa*)

**Mārići** (S) (F) **1.** ray of light. **3.** a Buddhist goddess; the wife of Parjañya (*V. Purāṇa*); an apsarā (*M. Bh.*)

**Marići** (S) (M) **1.** a ray of light. **3.** a mindborn son of Brahmā and Prājāpati, regarded as the 1st of the 10 lords of creation, as the husband of Kalā he was the father of Kaśyapa and Pūrṇiman, as the husband of Ūrṇā he fathered sons reborn as the 6 elder brothers of Kṛṣṇa and as the husband of Sambhūtī he was the father of Paurṇamāsa; a king who was the son of Samrāj and the father of Bindumat; a son of the Tīrathaṅkara Ṛṣabha (*J. Literature*): a son of Śankarāćārya; a star in the Great Bear constellation; Kṛṣṇa as a marut (*Bhā. Purāṇa*); a daitya (*V. Rāmāyaṇa*); a maharṣi (*V. Purāṇa*)

**Marićikā** (S) (F) mirage.

**Marićimat** (S) (M) **1.** with rays; radiant; shining. **3.** another name for the sun.

**Māriṣā** (S) (F) **1.** worthy; respectable. **3.** a nymph born of trees and moonlight (*V. Purāṇa*); the mother of Dakṣa (*H. Purāṇa*); the wife of Śūra (*Bhā. Purāṇa*); a river of Purāṇic fame (*M. Bh.*); a daughter of Kaṇḍu (*M. Bh.*)

**Mārisa** (S) (M) respectable; worthy.

**Māriya** (S) (M) belonging to Kāma.

**Mārjani** (S) (F) **1.** that which cleans. **2.** washing; purifying; a broom. **3.** an attendant of

Durgā (*S. Koṣa*)

**Mārjāra** (S) (M) 1. cleaning itself; a cat. 3. a son of Jāmbavān (*V. Rāmāyaṇa*)

**Mārjārakarṇī** (S) (F) 1. cat eared. 3. another name for Ćāmuṇḍā.

**Mārjārī** (S) (M) 1. cat; peacock. 3. a son of Sahadeva (*M. Bh.*)

**Marka** (S) (M) 1. the mind; eclipse; the vital breath. 3. a son of Śukra, the purohita of the asuras (*M. Bh.*); a yakṣa; another name for Vāyu.

**Mārkaṇḍeya** (S) (M) 1. winning over death. 3. a sage and descendant of the line of Bhṛgu, the son of Mṛkaṇḍu and Vedaśiras, the husband of Dhūmorṇā and a great devotee of Śiva (*M. Bh.*); a sage and son of the author of *Mārkaṇḍeya Purāṇa* (*M. Bh.*)

**Mārkaṇḍeyī** (S) (F) 1. winning over death. 3. the wife of Rajas (*V. Purāṇa*)

**Markatamaṇi** (S) (M) the emerald.

**Mārmika** (S) (M) 1. having a deep insight into; knowing the essence. 2. very intelligent; perceptive.

**Marmit** (S) (M) 1. the vanquisher of Kāma. 3. another name for Śiva.

**Marṣa** (S) (M) patience; endurance.

**Marṣaṇa** (S) (M) 1. enduring. 2. patient; forgiving.

**Mārṣaka** (S) (M) honourable; respectable.

**Mārṣṭhī** (S) (F) 1. dwelling in cleanliness. 2. washing; ablution; purification. 3. the wife of Duḥsaha (*V. Purāṇa*)

**Mārtaṇḍa** (S) (M) 1. sprung from an egg. 2. bird; bird in the sky. 3. an āditya; another name for the sun or the god of the sun.

**Maru** (S) (M) 1. desert; mountain; rock. 3. an Ikṣvāku king who was the son of Śīghra, the father of Prasūśruta who became immortal by his yogic power (*Bhā. Purāṇa*); a Videha king of the Nimi dynasty (*Bhā. Purāṇa*); a warrior of Narakāsura killed by Kṛṣṇa (*M. Bh.*); a son of Haryaśva (*V. Rāmāyaṇa*); a vasu (*H. Purāṇa*)

**Marudeva** (S) (M) 1. lord of the desert. 3. the father of the Arhat Ṛṣabha (*J. Literature*)

**Marudevī** (S) (F) 1. consort of Marudeva. 3. a queen of Ayodhyā and mother of Jaina Tīrathaṅkara Ṛṣabhadeva (*J. Literature*)

**Marudhanvan** (S) (M) 1. with a bow of rock. 2. an invincible bow; one who is ever victorious. 3. the father-in-law of the vidyādhara Indīvara (*M. Purāṇa*)

**Marudvartmana** (S) (M) 1. the path of the clouds. 2. the sky.

**Maruga** (S) (M) 1. living in a desert; a peacock; a deer, an antelope. 3. another name for Kārttikeya.

**Marūka** (S) (M) from wilderness; a peacock; deer; antelope.

**Mārulā** (S) (F) 1. rock born; born due to the blessings of Śiva; a kind of duck. 3. a poetess.

**Marula** (S) (M) 1. rock born; born due to blessings of Śiva; a kind of duck. 3. one of the 5 ascetics who were said to have sprung from the 5 heads of Śiva and who founded the Vara-Śaiva sect (*K. Sāgara*)

**Marupati** (S) (M) 1. lord of the desert. 3. another name for Indra.

**Marur** (S) (M) 1. killer; a tiger. 3. another name for Rāhu.

**Marut** (S) (M) 1. the flashing or shining one; wind; air; breeze; breath. 3. maruts are the storm gods and the companions of Indra, in the Vedas they are depicted as the sons of Rudra and Pṛṣṇi, in later literature they are the sons of Diti and are led by Mātariśvan (*Ṛg Veda*); the god of wind, the father of Hanumān and the regent of the northwest quarter (*M. Bh.*)

**Māruta** (S) (M) 1. breath; wind; air; belonging to the maruts; belonging to the wind; a son of the maruts. 3. another name for Viṣṇu and Rudra.

**Maruṭā** (S) (F) with a high forehead.

**Mārutantavya** (S) (M) 1. pervading in the wind. 2. one who is very popular. 3. a son of Viśvāmitra (*M. Bh.*)

**Marutapāla** (S) (M) 1. protector of the maruts. 3. another name for Indra.

**Marutapati** (S) (M) 1. lord of maruts. 3. another name for Indra.

**Marutaputra** (S) (M) 1. son of the wind god. 3. another name for Bhīma and Hanumān.

**Mārutāśana** (S) (M) 1. feeding on the wind

alone. **2.** one who does not consume anything; everfasting. **3.** one of Skanda's attendants (*Brah. Purāṇa*); a dānava (*H. Purāṇa*)

**Mārutātmaja** (S) (M) **1.** son of the wind. **3.** another name for Agni, Bhīma and Hanumān.

**Mārutī** (S) (F) consort of Marut; the northwest quarter; the constellation Svāti.

**Māruti** (S) (M) **1.** son of the wind. **3.** another name for Hanumān, Bhīma and Dyutāna.

**Marutta** (S) (M) **1.** wind; gale. **3.** a king who was the son of Karandhama, a member of Yama's assembly and considered one of the 5 great emperors (*M. Bh.*); a sage of ancient India (*M. Bh.*)

**Maruttama** (S) (M) as swift as the maruts.

**Maruttaruṇī** (S) (F) **1.** wind virgin. **3.** a vidyādharī (*H. Purāṇa*)

**Marutvān** **1.** lord of the winds. **3.** another name for Indra.

**Marutvat** (S) (M) **1.** attended by the maruts; a cloud. **3.** a son of Dharma by Marutvatī (*Bhā. Purāṇa*); another name for Indra and Hanumān.

**Marutvatī** (S) (F) **1.** attended by the maruts. **3.** a daughter of Dakṣa and wife of Dharma (*H. Purāṇa*)

**Maryā** (S) (F) mark; limit; boundary.

**Maryādā** (S) (F) **1.** containing clear marks. **2.** frontier; limit; boundary; rule of morality; propriety of conduct; a ring used as an amulet. **3.** wife of Devātithi (*M. Bh.*); wife of Arvācīna (*M. Bh.*)

**Maśāl** (S) (M) torch.

**Masāra** (S) (M) sapphire; emerald.

**Māśī** (S) (F) **1.** bean coloured. **2.** dark complexioned. **3.** the wife of Sūra.

**Maskarin** (S) (M) one who moves; a wanderer; a vagabond; a religious mendicant; the moon.

**Masmā** (S) (F) **1.** not ink. **2.** fair complexioned. **3.** 2 princesses (*R. Taraṅginī*)

**Masṛṇita** (S) (M) softened; smoothed.

**Mastaka** (S) (M) **1.** head; skull; top; summit. **3.** a form of Śiva (*S. Saṁgraha*)

**Mata** (S) (M) **1.** thought; understood; honoured; desired; liked. **3.** a son of Śambara (*H. Purāṇa*)

**Mātali** (S) (M) **1.** charioteer. **3.** Indra's charioteer who was the son of Śamīka and Tapasvinī (*K. Granthāvali*)

**Mātali** (S) (F) **1.** mother's friend. **3.** an attendant of Durgā.

**Mātalisārathi** (S) (M) **1.** with Mātali as his charioteer. **3.** another name for Indra.

**Matallī** (S) (F) anything excellent.

**Matallikā** (S) (F) anything excellent of its kind.

**Mātaṅga** (S) (M) **1.** roaming at will; a cloud. **2.** the chief or best of its kind; an elephant; the Bodhi tree (*Ficus religiosa*). **3.** the servant of the 7th and 24th Arhat of the present Avasarpinī (*H. Koṣa*); a preceptor who was the guru of Śabarī (*V. Rāmāyaṇa*); a sage (*V. Rāmāyaṇa*); a nāga (*M. Bh.*); a dānava (*H. Purāṇa*)

**Mātaṅgī** (S) (F) **1.** roaring at will; an elephant. **3.** the daughter of Krodhavaśā and Kaśyapa and the mother of elephants (*V. Rāmāyaṇa*); one of the 10 Mahāvidyās; the mother of Vasiṣṭha (*V. Rāmāyaṇa*); a form of Durgā (*A. Koṣa*)

**Mataṅginī** (S) (F) **1.** roaming at will. **3.** a daughter of Mandāra (*H. Purāṇa/K. Sāgara*)

**Mātariśvan** (S) (M) **1.** growing in the firestick. **3.** Agni or a divine messenger of Vivasvata who brought down the hidden fire to the Bhṛgus and is identified with Vāyu (*Ṛg Veda*); a son of Garuḍa (*Ṛg Veda*); a ṛṣi; another name for Śiva.

**Māṭhara** (S) (M) **1.** traveller; churner. **3.** a demigod deputed by Indra to serve Sūrya (*Bh. Purāṇa*)

**Mathin** (S) (M) **1.** churning stick. **2.** wind; thunderbolt.

**Mathita** (S) (M) **1.** produced by churning. **3.** a decendant of Yama and the author of *Ṛg Veda* (x)

**Māthura** (S) (M) **1.** coming from Mathurā. **3.** a son of Citragupta.

**Mathurā** (S) (F) **1.** the city of Mathurā. **3.** the birthplace of Kṛṣṇa.

**Mathurānātha** (S) (M) **1.** lord of the city of Mathurā. **3.** another name for Kṛṣṇa.

**Mathureśa** (S) (M) **1.** lord of Mathurā. **3.** another name for Kṛṣṇa.

**Mati** (S) (F) **1.** devotion; prayer; worship; hymn; thought; intention; wish; opinion; notion; perception; intelligence; memory. **3.** opinion personified as the daughter of Dakṣa and the wife of Soma or as the wife of Viveka or as the wife of Dharma (*M. Bh.*)

**Matigarbha** (S) (M) **1.** filled with intelligence. **2.** extremely intelligent.

**Matila** (S) (M) **1.** intelligent. **3.** a king (*M. Bh.*)

**Matimat** (S) (M) **1.** wise. **3.** a son of Janamejaya (*M. Bh.*)

**Matinãra** (S) (M) **1.** possessing intellect. **3.** a Purū king who was the son of Kṛteyu, the father of Santurodha and Pratiratha and the grandfather of Duṣyanta (*M. Bh.*)

**Matīśvara** (S) (M) **1.** lord of the mind. **2.** wisest of all. **3.** another name for Viśvakarman.

**Matkulikā** (S) (F) **1.** born in a family of drunkards. **3.** a follower of Skanda (*M. Bh.*)

**Matkuṇikā** (S) (F) **1.** insect; bug. **3.** a mother attending on Skanda (*H. Purāṇa*)

**Mātṛ** (S) (F) **1.** with true knowledge; mother. **2.** the earth; water. **3.** the personified energies of the principal deities; the Mātṛs who are closely connected with the worship of Śiva and were attendants to his son Skanda (*M. Bh.*); the 13 wives of Kaśyapa are also called Mātṛs (*M. Bh.*); another name for Durgā, Lakṣmī and Dākṣāyaṇī.

**Mātṛćeta** (S) (M) one who knows and honours the mother.

**Mātṛdatta** (S) (M) **1.** given by the Mātṛs. **2.** given by the divine mothers.

**Mātṛkā** (S) (F) **1.** divine mother. **3.** the wife of Aryaman (*Bhā. Purāṇa*)

**Mātṛnandana** (S) (M) **1.** joy of the Mātṛs; son of Mātṛs. **3.** another name for Skanda.

**Matṛviṣṇu** (S) (M) Lakṣmī and Viṣṇu conjoined.

**Matsya** (S) (M) **1.** fish; the zodiac sign of Pisces. **3.** a pupil of Devamitra; the 1st incarnation of Mahāviṣṇu (*V. Purāṇa*); another name for Virāta who was found with his sister Satyavatī or Matsyā in the body of a fish.

**Matsyā** (S) (F) **1.** of a fish. **3.** another name for Satyavatī.

**Matsyagandhā** (S) (F) **1.** smelling like a fish. **3.** another name for Satyavatī.

**Matsyakāla** (S) (M) **1.** destroyer of fish; fish eater. **3.** a Purū king born to Girikā (*M. Bh.*)

**Matsyanārī** (S) (F) **1.** mermaid. **3.** another name for Satyavatī.

**Matsyapati** (S) (M) **1.** king of Matsya. **3.** another name for Virāta.

**Matsyarāja** (S) (M) **1.** lord of Matsya. **3.** another name for Virāta.

**Matsyāvatāra** (S) (M) **1.** fish incarnation. **3.** the 1st incarnation of Viṣṇu (*V. Rāmāyaṇa*)

**Matsyendranātha** (S) (M) **1.** lord of the fish. **3.** the founder of the Nātha order of yogins and whose 2 sons were the founders of Jainism (*J.S. Koṣa*)

**Matsyodarī** (S) (F) **1.** born of a fish. **3.** another name for Satyavatī.

**Matta** (S) (M) **1.** intoxicated. **2.** excited; proud. **3.** a demon who was the son of Mālyavan and Sundarī (*A. Purāṇa*)

**Matthara** (S) (M) **1.** traveller; a churner; a Brāhmin. **3.** a disciple of Paraśurāma; an attendant of the sun (*M. Bh.*); another name for Vyāsa.

**Maudgalya** (S) (M) **1.** of Mudgala; with pleasant speech. **3.** a mahāṛṣi who cursed Rāvaṇa (*K. Rāmāyaṇa*)

**Mauli** (S) (M) **1.** the head; chief. **2.** foremost; best; diadem; crown.

**Maulimālikā** (S) (F) a chaplet.

**Maulimaṇi** (S) (M) crest gem.

**Mauliratna** (S) (M) crest gem.

**Mauñjāyana** (S) (M) **1.** winner of the sacred thread. **2.** chaste; pious. **3.** a mahāṛṣi in the court of Yudhiṣṭhira (*M. Bh.*)

**Maurvī** (S) (F) **1.** girdle made of Mūrvā or bowstring hemp. **2.** a bowstring. **3.** a wife of Ghaṭotkaća.

**Maurvikā** (S) (F) bow string.

**Māvella** (S) (M) **1.** a good speaker. **3.** a son of Uparićaravasu of Ćedi (*M. Bh.*)

**Māyā** (S) (F) **1.** wealth; illusion. **2.** unreality; phantom; art; wisdom; compassion; sympathy. **3.** illusion sometimes identified with Durgā, sometimes regarded as a daughter of Anṛta and Nirṛti and the mother of Mṛtyu or as a daughter of Adharma (*Purāṇas*); the mother of Gautama Buddha (*B. Literature*); one of the 9 Śaktis of Viṣṇu (*Bhā. Purāṇa*); another name for Lakṣmī (*A. Koṣa*)

**Maya** (S) (M) **1.** illusion; architect. **2.** a builder. **3.** a dānava who served the devas and the asuras, as their architect and builder, the son of Kaśyapa and Danu, the husband of the apsarā Hemā, the father of Māyāvi and Dundubhi and the father of Mandodarī and Somaprabhā and Svayamprabhā (*Bhā. Purāṇa*)

**Mayabaṭṭu** (S) (M) **1.** possessed of illusory wind. **2.** with a false pride. **3.** a king of the Śabaras (*K. Sāgara*)

**Māyādevī** (S) (F) **1.** goddess of illusion; goddess of wealth. **3.** the mother of Gautama Buddha; the wife of Pradyumna (*V. Purāṇa*)

**Māyādhara** (S) (M) **1.** possessing illusion; possessing wealth. **3.** a king of the asuras killed by Purūravas (*K. Sāgara*)

**Māyāmṛga** (S) (M) **1.** illusory deer. **3.** the golden deer which was a form of Mārīća (*V. Rāmāyaṇa*)

**Māyaṇa** (S) (M) **1.** detached from wealth. **3.** the father of Mādhava and Sāyaṇa.

**Mayanka** (S) (M) **1.** deer marked. **3.** another name for the moon.

**Māyāpati** (S) (M) **1.** lord of illusion. **3.** another name for Viṣṇu.

**Māyārati** (S) (F) **1.** Māyā and Rati combined. **2.** one who loves wealth. **3.** a wife of Pradyumna (*Bhā. Purāṇa*)

**Mayas** (S) (M) refreshment; enjoyment; pleasure; delight.

**Mayāsura** (S) (M) the asura Maya.

**Māyāvāṇi** (S) (M) **1.** with a magical voice. **3.** a vidyādhara (*B. Rāmāyaṇa*)

**Māyāvatī** (S) (F) **1.** with illusory powers. **3.** an incarnation of Rati and wife of Pradyumna (*H. Purāṇa*); the wife of a vidyādhara (*H. Purāṇa*)

**Māyāvin** (S) (M) **1.** lord of illusion. **3.** an asura who was the son of Maya and Hemā (*K. Rāmāyaṇa*)

**Mayeśvara** (S) (M) **1.** lord of illusion. **3.** another name for the asura Maya.

**Mayil** (Malayalam) (M) peacock.

**Māyin** (S) (M) **1.** illusionary; skilled in the art of enchantment. **3.** the Supreme Being as the illusionist who created the universe (*Ṛg Veda*); another name for Brahmā, Śiva, Agni and Kāma.

**Māyu** (S) (M) lowing; roaring; bellowing; magician; celestial musician; a deer.

**Mayūkha** (S) (M) **1.** ray of light. **2.** brightness; lustre; a flame.

**Mayūkhamālin** (S) (M) **1.** wreathed with rays. **3.** another name for the sun.

**Mayūkheśa** (S) (M) **1.** lord of rays. **3.** another name for the sun.

**Mayūkhin** (S) (M) radiant; brilliant.

**Mayūra** (S) (M) **1.** peacock. **3.** an asura who fought against Skanda (*Sk. Purāṇa*); Celery (*Apium graveolen*)

**Mayūradhvaja** (S) (M) **1.** peacock bannered. **3.** a king of Ratnanagara who was blessed by Kṛṣṇa (*Bhā. Purāṇa*); another name for Kārttikeya.

**Mayūraja** (S) (M) **1.** born of a peacock. **3.** the king of the kinnaras (*H. Purāṇa*); another name for Kubera.

**Māyurāja** (S) (M) **1.** lord of sorcery. **3.** a son of Kubera.

**Mayūraketu** (S) (M) **1.** peacock bannered. **3.** another name for Kārttikeya.

**Mayūrākṣa** (S) (M) peacock eyed.

**Mayūrāṅkī** (S) (F) with peacock marks; a jewel.

**Mayūraratha** (S) (M) **1.** with a peacock as a vehicle. **3.** another name for Skanda.

**Mayūravarman** (S) (M) protector of peacocks.

**Mayūrī** (S) (F) peahen.

**Māyūrika** (S) (F) **1.** with peacock feathers. **3.** a rāgiṇī; Bombay Hemp (*Hibiscus cannabinus*)

**Māyus** (S) (M) **1.** detached from life. **2.** a good warrior. **3.** a son of Purūravas (*M. Bh.*)

**Mećaka** (S) (M) **1.** the eye of the peacock's tail. **2.** a gem; a cloud; the colour deep blue.

**Mećakagala** (S) (M) **1.** blue necked. **2.** peacock. **3.** another name for Śiva.

**Meda** (S) (M) 1. fat; the *Sphaeranthus indicus* herb; a mixed caste. 3. a serpent of the clan of Airāvata (*M. Bh.*)

**Medhā** (S) (F) 1. intelligence; wisdom; prudence. 3. wisdom personified as the daughter of Dakṣa and Prasūti and the wife of Dharma (*V. Purāṇa*); a form of the Dākṣāyāṇī in Kāśmīra; a form of Sarasvatī; a sister of Agni (*A. Veda*)

**Medhāćakra** (S) (M) the circle of wisdom; yoga.

**Medhādhṛti** (S) (M) 1. bearer of wisdom. 3. a ṛṣi of the 9th Manvantara.

**Medhājit** (S) (M) 1. victor of intelligence. 3. another name for sage Kātyāyana.

**Medhanī** (S) (F) 1. of intelligence. 3. the consort of Brahmā.

**Medhas** (S) (M) 1. sacrifice; sacrificial animal; broth. 3. a ṛṣi (*V. Saṃhitā*); a son of Priyavrata (*Bhā. Purāṇa*); a son of Manu Svāyambhuva (*H. Purāṇa*)

**Medhātithi** (S) (M) 1. the guest of wisdom; the host of wisdom. 2. very wise. 3. one of the 7 sages under Manu Sāvarṇa (*H. Purāṇa*); a son of Priyavrata and Surūpā and the king of Plakṣadvīpa (*Purāṇas*); a sage who was the son of Kaṇva and the father of Duṣyanta and Pravīra (*M. Bh.*); a sage who was the father of Arundhatī and the father-in-law of Vasiṣṭha (*K. Purāṇa*); a river which is the birthplace of Agni (*M. Bh.*); the father of Kaṇva (*M. Bh.*); a son of Manu Svāyambhuva (*H. Purāṇa*)

**Medhāvat** (S) (M) intelligent; wise.

**Medhāvī** (S) (M) 1. intelligent; wise. 3. a sage who was the son of Bāladhi (*M. Bh.*)

**Medhāvikīrti** (S) (F) with the fame of wisdom.

**Medhāvin** (S) (M) 1. learned man. 3. a king who was the son of Sutapas and the father of Nṛpañjaya (*V. Purāṇa*); a son of Bhavya (*M. Purāṇa*)

**Medhavinī** (S) (F) 1. learned. 3. a wife of Brahmā (*A. Veda*)

**Medhira** (S) (M) wise; intelligent.

**Medhyā** (S) (F) 1. full of sap; vigorous; mighty; strong; fresh; clean; pure; wise; intelligent. 3. a holy place on the west coast; the river that flows through it is believed to be the place of origin of Agni (*M. Bh.*); Black Catechu tree (*Acacia catechu*); Intellect tree (*Celastrus paniculata*); *Prosopis spicigera*.

**Medhyātithi** (S) (M) 1. host of intelligence. 3. a ṛṣi and part author of *Ṛg Veda* (viii)

**Medinī** (S) (F) 1. fertile. 2. the earth. 3. another name for the earth goddess.

**Medinīja** (S) (M) 1. son of the earth. 3. another name for Mars.

**Medinīpati** (S) (M) 1. master of the earth. 2. a king.

**Medinīśa** (S) (M) 1. lord of the earth. 2. a king.

**Megha** (S) (M) 1. sprinkler. 2. cloud; mass. 3. a rāga; a rākṣasa; the father of the 5th Arhat of the present Avasarpiṇī.

**Meghabhūti** (S) (M) 1. cloud born. 2. a thunderbolt.

**Meghaćintaka** (S) (M) 1. anxious for rain clouds. 3. another name for the Ćataka or the Pied Crested Cuckoo (*Clamator jacobinus serratus*)

**Meghadahunna** (S) (M) 1. music of the clouds; sound of the clouds. 3. a king of the solar race who was a descendant of Lava; a rāga.

**Meghaḍambara** (S) (M) 1. cloud drum. 2. the thunder.

**Meghadīpa** (S) (M) 1. light of the cloud. 2. the lightning.

**Meghadūta** (S) (M) 1. cloud messenger. 3. a poem by Kālidāsa.

**Meghadvāra** (S) (M) 1. cloud gate. 2. heaven; sky.

**Meghahāsa** (S) (M) 1. laugh of the clouds. 2. one who laughs loudly. 3. a son of Rāhu (*Br. Purāṇa*)

**Meghajā** (S) (F) 1. born of the clouds. 2. water; a large pearl.

**Meghajanaka** (S) (M) father of the clouds.

**Meghajyoti** (S) (M) 1. light of the clouds. 2. a flash of lightning.

**Meghakarṇā** (S) (F) 1. cloud eared. 3. a mother in Skanda's retinue (*M. Bh.*)

**Meghamālā** (S) (F) 1. a garland of clouds. 3. a mother attending on Skanda (*H. Purāṇa*)

**Meghamāla** (S) (M) 1. crowned with clouds. 3. a rākṣasa captain of the army of Khara

(*V. Rāmāyaṇa*); one of the 2 attendants given to Skanda by Mahāmeru (*M. Bh.*); a son of Kalki (*K. Purāṇa*); a mountain.

**Meghamālin** (S) (M) **1.** cloud wreathed. **3.** an attendant of Skanda (*M. Bh.*); an asura (*S. Mahātmya*)

**Meghamallārikā** (S) (F) **1.** instigator of clouds. **3.** a rāga.

**Meghamañjari** (S) (F) cloud blossom.

**Meghanā** (S) (F) **1.** the rumbling of clouds. **2.** thunder.

**Meghanādā** (S) (F) **1.** with the sound of clouds. **2.** the thunder. **3.** a yoginī (*Bhā. Purāṇa*)

**Meghanāda** (S) (M) **1.** noise of the clouds. **2.** the thunder. **3.** a son of Rāvaṇa and Mandodarī also called Indrajit (*V. Rāmāyaṇa*); one of Skanda's attendants (*M. Bh.*); a daitya (*V. Rāmāyaṇa*); another name for Varuṇa.

**Meghanādajita** (S) (M) **1.** conqueror of Meghanāda. **3.** another name for Lakṣmaṇa.

**Meghānanda** (S) (M) rejoicing in clouds; a peacock.

**Meghanīla** (S) (M) **1.** a blue cloud. **3.** a gaṇa of Śiva (*H. Purāṇa*)

**Meghapravāha** (S) (M) **1.** flowing like the clouds. **3.** an attendant of Skanda (*H. Purāṇa*)

**Meghapṛṣṭha** (S) (M) **1.** supported by the clouds. **2.** very powerful. **3.** the son of Ghṛtapṛṣṭha (*Bhā. Purāṇa*)

**Meghapuṣpa** (S) (M) **1.** cloud flower. **2.** the rainwater. **3.** one of the 4 horses of Viṣṇu-Kṛṣṇa (*M. Bh.*)

**Megharāga** (S) (M) **1.** the essence of clouds. **3.** a rāga.

**Megharāja** (S) (M) **1.** lord of the clouds. **3.** a Buddha (*L. Vistara*); another name for Viṣṇu.

**Megharaṅgikā** (S) (F) **1.** cloud coloured. **2.** dark complexioned. **3.** a rāga.

**Megharañjanī** (S) (F) **1.** one who delights the clouds. **3.** a rāga.

**Megharatha** (S) (M) **1.** with a cloud chariot. **3.** a vidyādhara (*H. Purāṇa*)

**Megharavā** (S) (F) **1.** cloud noise. **2.** the thunder. **3.** a mother attending on Skanda (*M. Bh.*)

**Megharekhā** (S) (F) a row of clouds.

**Meghasandhi** (S) (M) **1.** confluence of clouds. **3.** a prince of Magadha and the grandson of Jarāsandha (*M. Bh.*)

**Meghaśarman** (S) (M) **1.** best among the clouds. **3.** a Brāhmin and devotee of Sūrya in the court of Śantanu (*Bh. Purāṇa*)

**Meghaśvanā** (S) (F) **1.** one who sounds like the clouds. **3.** a mother of Skanda (*M. Bh.*)

**Meghasvara** (S) (M) **1.** one who sounds like the clouds. **2.** the thunder. **3.** a Buddha (*B. Literature*)

**Meghasvararāja** (S) (M) **1.** lord of thunder. **3.** a Buddha.

**Meghasvāti** (S) (M) **1.** conjoined of clouds and the star arcturus. **3.** a king (*Purāṇas*)

**Meghavāhana** (S) (M) **1.** cloud vehicled. **3.** a king and dependant of Jarāsandha (*M. Bh.*); another name for Śiva and Indra.

**Meghavāhinī** (S) (F) **1.** riding on a cloud. **3.** a mother of Skanda (*M. Bh.*)

**Meghavahni** (S) (M) **1.** cloud fire. **2.** the lightning.

**Meghavalī** (S) (F) a row of clouds.

**Meghavarṇa** (S) (M) **1.** cloud coloured. **2.** dark complexioned. **3.** a son of Ghaṭotkaća (*M. Bh.*); Black Plum (*Eugenia jambolana*)

**Meghavāśas** (S) (M) **1.** clad in clouds. **3.** an asura in Varuṇa's court (*M. Bh.*)

**Meghavega** (S) (M) **1.** with the speed of clouds. **2.** very swift; agile. **3.** a brave warrior in the Kaurava army (*M. Bh.*)

**Meghayantī** (S) (F) **1.** one who makes the weather cloudy; one who is responsible for creating the clouds **3.** one of the 7 kṛttikās (*A. Veda*)

**Meghayāti** (S) (M) **1.** cloud bearer. **3.** a king (*V. Purāṇa*)

**Mehula** (S) (M) rain.

**Mekalā** (S) (F) **1.** knower of the self; of the ṛṣi Mekala; girdle. **3.** another name for the river Narmadā.

**Mekala** (S) (M) **1.** knower of the self. **3.** a ṛṣi and father of the river Narmadā (*V. Purāṇa*); another name for the mountain Amarakaṇṭaka in the Vindhyas which is the source of the Narmadā.

**Mekhalā** (S) (F) 1. girdle. 2. belt; the slope of a mountain; the line drawn around an altar. 3. another name for the river Narmadā.

**Mekhalāla** (S) (M) 1. wearing a girdle. 3. another name for Śiva-Rudra (*H. Purāṇa*)

**Mekhalin** (S) (M) 1. wearing a girdle; wearing a sacred thread; a brahmaćārin. 3. another name for Śiva.

**Menā** (S) (F) 1. intellect; speech; woman. 3. the daughter of Mahāmeru and wife of Himavān (*V. Rāmāyaṇa*), who according to the *Viṣṇu Purāṇa* is the mind born daughter of Svadhā and the mother of Maināka, Gaṅgā and Pārvatī, according to the *Rāmāyaṇa*, the mother of Umā or Pārvatī and Gaṅgā both of which were married to Śiva, and according to the *Vāmana Purāṇa*, the mother of Rāgiṇī, Kuṭilā, Kālī or Umā and Sunābha; an apsarā daughter of King Vṛṣṇāśva, the mother of Śakuntalā by sage Viśvāmitra and the mother of Pramadvarā by the gandharva Viśvavasu (*Ṛg Veda*)

**Mena** (S) (M) 1. one who knows. 3. Vṛṣṇāśva who was the father of Menā or Menakā (*Shadvinsa Brāhmaṇa*)

**Menādhava** (S) (M) 1. lover of intellect; the husband of Menā. 3. another name for Himavān.

**Menajā** (S) (F) 1. daughter of Menā. 3. another name for Pārvatī.

**Menākā** (S) (F) 1. born of the mind; of the mountains; of woman. 3. one of the 6 prominent celestial maidens and an apsarā of extraordinary beauty, the daughter of King Vṛṣṇāśva according to the *Ṛg Veda*, according to the *Viṣṇu Purāṇa*, the mind born daughter of Svadhā, mother of Maināka, Gaṅgā and Pārvatī, the mother of Śakuntalā by sage Viśvāmitra and the mother of Pramadvarā by the gandharva Viśvavasu.

**Menākātmajā** (S) (F) 1. daughter of Menākā. 3. another name for Pārvatī.

**Menāvatī** (S) (F) 1. possessed with intellect. 3. another name for Pārvatī.

**Mendha** (S) (M) 1. wise; learned. 3. a Sanskṛt poet and the author of *Hastipāka* (5th century A.D.)

**Menī** (S) (F) thunderbolt; speech.

**Menitā** (S) (F) wise; intelligent.

**Meru** (S) (M) 1. high; principle; union. 2. the central bead in a rosary, the main gem of a necklace. 3. a fabulous mountain regarded as the Olympus of Hindu mythology, all the planets revolve around it, the Gaṅgā falls from heaven on its summit, the whole mountain is covered with gems, its summit is the residence of Brahmā and its 4 quarters are guarded by the regents, it is a place of meeting for all the divine beings (*Purāṇas*)

**Merudevī** (S) (F) 1. goddess of the Meru mountain. 3. one of the 9 daughters of Mahāmeru, wife of King Nābhi and the mother of Ṛṣabha who was an incarnation of Viṣṇu (*Bhā. Purāṇa*)

**Merudhāman** (S) (M) 1. dweller of the mountain Meru. 3. another name for Śiva (*M. Bh.*)

**Merudhvaja** (S) (M) 1. having a high flag. 2. a renowned ruler. 3. a ćakravartin (*K. Sāgara*)

**Meruka** (S) (M) incense.

**Merukuta** (S) (M) 1. the summit of Meru. 3. a Buddha.

**Merunanda** (S) (M) 1. one who pleases the mountain. 2. pleaser of mountains; pleaser of the masses; a son of Svāroćiṣa (*M. Purāṇa*)

**Meruprabhā** (S) (F) 1. shining like the Meru mountain; of great splendour. 2. extremely charming.

**Merusāvarṇi** (S) (M) 1. with high thoughts; like the Meru. 3. the 11th Manu and father of Svayamprabhā (*V. Rāmāyaṇa*)

**Meruśrī** (S) (F) 1. loftiest among the beautiful. 2. the most beautiful; with the beauty of Meru. 3. a nāgakanyā (*K. Vyuha*)

**Meruśrigarbha** (S) (M) 1. as high in glory as the Meru. 3. a Boddhisattva (*B. Literature*)

**Meṣa** (S) (M) 1. goat; ram; sheep. 3. Indra in his form as a goat which he assumed to drink the Soma of sage Medhātithi (*Ṛg Veda*); a soldier of Skanda (*M. Bh.*); the zodiac sign of Aries.

**Meṣahṛt** (S) (M) 1. sheep thief. 3. a son of Garuḍa (*M. Bh.*)

**Meva** (S) (M) to worship; praise.

**Mevalāla** (S) (M) a praiseworthy son; a

devoted son.

**Mīḍhuṣa** (S) (M) 1. bountiful. 3. a son of Indra and Paulomī (*Ṛg Veda*)

**Mīḍhuṣī** (S) (F) 1. liberal; bountiful. 3. Śakti or the feminine energy of Īśāṇa personified as his consort.

**Mīḍhuṣṭama** (S) (M) 1. most liberal. 3. another name for the sun.

**Mīḍhvān** (S) (M) 1. bestowing richly; bountiful; liberal. 3. another name for Śiva.

**Mihikā** (S) (F) mist; fog; snow.

**Mihikānśu** (S) (M) 1. mist rayed. 2. the moon.

**Mihira** (S) (M) 1. causing heat, light and rain. 2. the sun; the moon; cloud; wind; air; a sage.

**Mihirakula** (S) (M) 1. born in the solar dynasty. 3. a king (*R. Taraṅginī*)

**Mihirāṇa** (S) (M) 1. born of the sun; having sun as one of the testides. 3. another name for Śiva.

**Milana** (S) (M) union; meeting; contract.

**Milāp** (S) (M) embrace.

**Milikā** (S) (F) desiring union.

**Milinda** (S) (M) 1. wanting an encounter. 2. the bee which looks for an encounter with the flowers. 3. the King Menander (*B. Literature*)

**Mīnā** (S) (F) 1. a gem; a goblet of wine; a fish; multi coloured glass; a stick. 3. a daughter of Ūṣā, a wife of Kaśyapa and the mother of fish (*Purāṇas*); the zodiac sign of Pisces (*V. Rāmāyaṇa*)

**Mīnaketana** (S) (M) 1. fish bannered. 3. another name for Kāma.

**Mīnākṣī** (S) (F) 1. fish eyed; a species of Dūrvā grass. 3. a daughter of Kubera (*Bh. Purāṇa*); an incarnation of Pārvatī as the daughter of the Pāṇḍya king of Madurai; a yakṣiṇī.

**Mīnālī** (S) (F) 1. fish catcher. 2. a fisherwoman. 3. another name for Satyavatī.

**Mīnaratha** (S) (M) 1. with a fish shaped chariot. 3. a king (*V. Purāṇa*)

**Mīnāti** (S) (F) 1. fish like. 2. voluptuous; having a tendency towards fatness.

**Mīneśvara** (S) (M) 1. lord of the fish. 3. another name for Śiva.

**Minna** (S) (M) fat.

**Mīra** (S) (F) 1. the ocean; the sea; limit; boundary. 3. a renowned saint poetess and devotee of Kṛṣṇa.

**Mirata** (S) (M) a mirror.

**Miśī** (S) (F) Dill (*Anethum panmori*); a species of sugarcane; *Nardostachys jatamansi*.

**Miśraka** (S) (M) 1. mixed; various; manifold. 3. Indra's garden of paradise (*M. Bh.*)

**Miśrakeśī** (S) (F) 1. with hair of mixed colours. 3. a beautiful apsarā born of Kaśyapa and Prādhā, the wife of Raudrāśva and the mother of 10 sons (*M. Bh.*); the wife of King Vatsaka the brother of Vasudeva (*M. Bh.*)

**Misri** (S) (M) 1. mixed; sweet. 3. a serpent who was among those that carried Balarāma's soul to Pātāla (*M. Bh.*)

**Mitā** (S) (F) one who has been measured and gauged; tried and tested; a friend.

**Mita** (S) (M) 1. one who has been measured; which is frugal; little; short; brief; firm; founded; established. 2. a friend. 3. a ṛṣi of the 3rd Manvantara (*V. Purāṇa*)

**Mitadhvaja** (S) (M) 1. with a strong flag. 3. a king of Videha and son of Dharmadhvaja Janaka (*Bhā. Purāṇa*)

**Mitāli** (S) (F) friendship.

**Miṭhāī** (H) (F) sweetmeat.

**Mithi** (S) (M) 1. knowledged; truthful. 3. the son of King Nimi, considered to be the epitome of perfection and the founder of Mithilā (*V. Rāmāyaṇa*)

**Mithilādhipa** (S) (M) 1. lord of Mithilā. 3. another name for Janaka.

**Mithileśa** (S) (M) lord of Mithilā.

**Mithileśvara** (S) (M) 1. lord of Mithilā. 3. another name for Janaka.

**Mithu** (S) (M) 1. falsely; wrongly. 3. a dānava (*Brahma Purāṇa*)

**Mithuna** (S) (M) forming a pair; a small statue at the entrance of a temple; the zodiac sign of Gemini; honey and clarified butter.

**Mithyā** (S) (F) 1. false; wrong. 3. untruth personified as the wife of Adharma (*K. Purāṇa*)

**Mitī** (S) (F) friend.

**Miti** (S) (M) correct perception.

**Mitrā** (S) (F) 1. friend. 2. companion; associate. 3. a queen of Hastināpura and mother of Jaina Tīrathaṅkara Arahātha (*J.S. Koṣa*); the mother of Maitreya and Maitreyī (*Bhā. Purāṇa*); a companion of Pārvatī (*M. Bh.*)

**Mitra** (S) (M) 1. friend; companion; associate. 3. an āditya and one of the 12 Suryās born of Kaśyapa and Aditi, the father of Utsarga, a member of the court of Indra, the deity of the constellation Anurādhā, generally evoked with Varuṇa and Aryaman and described in the *Ṛg Veda* as the sustainer of the earth and the sky and the beholder of all with an unblinking eye; a follower of Lākuliṣa who founded the Paśupata cult; a son of Vasiṣṭha (*Purāṇas*); a marut (*H. Purāṇa*)

**Mitrabāhu** (S) (M) 1. helped by friends. 3. a son of the 12th Manu (*H. Purāṇa*); a son of Kṛṣṇa (*H. Purāṇa*)

**Mitradeva** (S) (M) 1. lord of friends. 3. the brother of King Suśarmā of Trigarta (*M. Bh.*); a son of the 12th Manu (*H. Purāṇa*); another name for the sun.

**Mitradharman** (S) (M) 1. with faith in friends. 3. a rākṣasa (*V. Rāmāyaṇa*); a son of Divodāsa (*V. Purāṇa*); a son of Agni Pāñćajanya.

**Mitraghna** (S) (M) 1. killer of friends. 3. a rākṣasa (*V. Rāmāyaṇa*); a son of Divodāsa (*V. Purāṇa*)

**Mitragupta** (S) (M) protected by friends.

**Mitrajña** (S) (M) 1. knower of friends; knower of the sun. 3. a son of the agni Pāñćajanya (*M. Bh.*)

**Mitrajit** (S) (M) 1. winning friends. 3. a son of Suvarṇa (*V. Purāṇa*)

**Mitrakṛt** (S) (M) 1. friend maker. 3. a son of the 12th Manu (*H. Purāṇa*)

**Mitrasāha** (S) (M) 1. indulgent towards friends. 3. a king (*M. Bh.*)

**Mitrasakhā** (S) (M) 1. a friend of friends; a friend of the sun. 3. a king of the solar race also known as Kalmāṣapāda (*M. Bh.*)

**Mitrasena** (S) (M) 1. with an army of friends; with an army as glorious as the sun. 3. a king in the army of the Kauravas (*M. Bh.*); a gandharva (*H. Purāṇa*); a son of the 12th Manu (*H. Purāṇa*); a grandson of Kṛṣṇa (*H. Purāṇa*); a king of the Draviḍa country (*H. Purāṇa*); a Buddhist monk.

**Mitravāha** (S) (M) 1. attracting friends. 2. sun charioted. 3. a son of the 12th Manu (*H. Purāṇa*)

**Mitravān** (S) (M) 1. having friends. 2. one who knows the sun. 3. a son of the agni Pāñćajanya (*M. Bh.*); an ascetic and devotee of Śiva (*P. Purāṇa*)

**Mitravardhana** (S) (M) 1. cherished by friends. 3. a son of the agni Pāñćajanya (*M. Bh.*)

**Mitravarman** (S) (M) warrior among friends; as protective as the sun.

**Mitrāvaruṇa** (S) (M) 1. Mitra and Varuṇa conjoined. 3. together Mitra and Varuṇa are the lords of truth and light upholding religious rites and the rules of the world, conjoined they become the deity bestowing plentiful rain (*Ṛg Veda*)

**Mitravat** (S) (M) 1. having friends. 3. a son of the 12th Manu (*M. Purāṇa*); a son of Kṛṣṇa (*H. Purāṇa*)

**Mitravatī** (S) (F) 1. with friends. 3. a daughter of Kṛṣṇa (*H. Purāṇa*)

**Mitravindā** (S) (F) 1. possessor of companions. 3. a princess of Avantī who was first cousin and wife of Kṛṣṇa (*Bhā. Purāṇa*); a river (*Bh. Purāṇa*)

**Mitravinda** (S) (M) 1. possessor of friends. 3. a son of the 12th Manu (*H. Purāṇa*); a son of Kṛṣṇa (*H. Purāṇa*); a deva (*M. Bh.*); an agni (*M. Bh.*)

**Mitrayu** (S) (M) 1. friendly. 2. attractive; prudent. 3. a son of Divodāsa and the father of Ćyavana (*H. Purāṇa*)

**Mitrodaya** (S) (M) sunrise.

**Mitula** (S) (M) 1. measured. 2. limited; moderate.

**Mituṣī** (S) (F) with limited desires.

**Moda** (S) (M) 1. pleasure; enjoyment; joy; fragrance. 3. a serpent of the clan of Airāvata (*M. Bh.*); a rākṣasa (*M. Bh.*)

**Modaka** (S) (M) 1. pleasing; delighting. 2. a sweetmeat.

**Modakara** (S) (M) 1. one who accomplishes joy; full of joy, delighted. 3. a ṛṣi (*V. Rāmāyaṇa*)

**Modakī** (S) (F) 1. pleasing; delighting. 2. a sweetmeat.
**Modayantikā** (S) (F) rejoicing; delighting; the Arabian Jasmine (*Jasminum sambac*)
**Modinī** (S) (F) 1. glad; cheerful. 3. *Jasminum Sambac.*
**Moha** (S) (M) 1. infatuation; confusion ignorance. 3. a son of Brahmā born of his lustre (*Bhā. Purāṇa*)
**Mohaka** (S) (M) 1. causing infatuation. 2. attractive. 3. a son of Suratha (*P. Purāṇa*)
**Mohanā** (S) (F) 1. infatuating. 2. beautiful. 3. a wife of Sugrīva (*P. Purāṇa*)
**Mohana** (S) (M) 1. infatuating. 2. confusing; bewildering. 3. one of the 5 arrows of Kāma (*K. Sāgara*); another name for Śiva and Kṛṣṇa.
**Mohanadāsa** (S) (M) devotee of Kṛṣṇa.
**Mohanalāla** (S) (M) the youthful Kṛṣṇa.
**Mohanī** (S) (F) 1. infatuating. 2. charming. 3. one of the 9 Śaktis of Viṣṇu (*A. Koṣa*); an apsarā (*P. Ratra*); a rākṣasī (*A. Veda*)
**Mohantara** (S) (M) very infatuating.
**Mohī** (S) (M) 1. deluded. 3. another name for Kāma.
**Mohin** (S) (M) 1. deluding; fascinating. 2. confusing; perplexing; illusive.
**Mohinī** (S) (F) 1. fascinating; the jasmine blossom. 3. the female form assumed by Mahāviṣṇu during the war of the devas and the asuras for the Amṛta (*Bhā. Purāṇa*); a daughter of Rukmāṅgada (*V. Purāṇa*); an apsarā (*P. Rātra*)
**Mohita** (S) (M) 1. infatuated. 2. bewitched; intoxicated by love.
**Mohonā** (S) (F) endearing.
**Mokṣa** (S) (M) 1. salvation; final emancipation. 3. another name for Mount Meru.
**Mokṣadvāra** (S) (M) 1. gate of emancipation. 3. another name for the sun.
**Mokṣin** (S) (M) free; liberated.
**Mokṣita** (S) (M) set free; liberated.
**Molinā** (S) (F) a tree that grows from a root.
**Monā** (S) (F) alone.
**Moṇa** (S) (M) dry fruit; a kind of fly; a snake-carrying basket.
**Monal** (S) (M) bird.
**Mora** (S) (M) peacock.
**Morara** (S) (M) peacock.
**Moraćandrikā** (S) (F) 1. the moon of the peacock. 2. the moon like eye at the end of a peacock's tail.
**Morikā** (S) (F) peahen; postern gate.
**Mornī** (S) (F) peahen.
**Motī** (S) (M) pearl.
**Motiā** (S) (M) jasmine.
**Mṛdā** (S) (F) 1. compassionate. 2. the earth; clay. 3. another name for Pārvatī.
**Mṛḍa** (S) (M) 1. compassionate; gracious. 3. another name for Śiva.
**Mṛdākara** (S) (M) a thunderbolt.
**Mṛdaṅgaketu** (S) (M) 1. drum-bannered. 3. another name for Yudhiṣṭhira.
**Mṛḍānī** (S) (F) 1. consort of Mṛḍa. 3. another name for Pārvatī.
**Mṛḍanīśvara** (S) (M) 1. lord of Pārvatī. 3. another name for Śiva.
**Mṛdānta** (S) (M) (F) passing through a constellation.
**Mṛdinī** (S) (F) good earth; soil.
**Mṛdu** (S) (F) soft; delicate; tender; pliant; gentle; mild; a vine with red grapes; the Guava tree (*Psidium guyava*)
**Mṛdūbhāva** (S) (M) softness; mildness.
**Mṛdugāmin** (S) (M) with a gentle gait.
**Mṛdugir** (S) (M) soft voiced.
**Mṛdukā** (S) (F) 1. soft; tender. 3. an apsarā (*K. Vyuha*)
**Mṛdula** (S) (M) 1. soft; tender; mild. 2. water.
**Mṛdura** (S) (M) 1. water born; an aquatic animal. 3. a son of Śvaphalka (*H. Purāṇa*)
**Mṛdūtpāla** (S) (M) the Soft Lotus (*Nymphaea cyanea*)
**Mṛduvāta** (S) (M) a gentle breeze.
**Mṛduvid** (S) (M) 1. gentle. 3. a son of Śvaphalka (*H. Purāṇa*)
**Mṛdvaṅgī** (S) (F) soft bodied; delicate.
**Mṛdvikā** (S) (F) softness; gentleness; mildness; a vine; a bunch of red grapes (*Vitis vinifera*)
**Mṛgad** (S) (M) 1. animal devourer. 2. a tiger.
**Mṛgadhara** (S) (M) 1. with deer like marks.

2. the moon.

**Mṛgādhipa** (S) (M) 1. lord of animals. 2. the lion.

**Mṛgādhirāja** (S) (M) 1. lord of animals. 2. the lion.

**Mṛgadṛśa** (S) (M) 1. fawn eyed. 2. the zodiac sign of Capricorn.

**Mṛgaja** (S) (M) 1. son of the moon. 3. another name for Mercury.

**Mṛgākṣī** (S) (F) 1. deer eyed. 2. Bitter Cucumber (*Citrullus colocynthis*); *Cucumis trigonos*.

**Mṛgalakṣaṇa** (S) (M) deer marked; the moon.

**Mṛgalāñćana** (S) (M) 1. son of the moon. 3. another name for the planet Mercury.

**Mṛgaloćanā** (S) (F) doe eyed.

**Mṛgaloćana** (S) (M) doe eyed; the moon.

**Mṛgamandā** (S) (F) 1. moving like a fawn. 2. fleet footed. 3. a daughter of Kaśyapa who was the progenitress of lions (*M. Bh.*)

**Mṛganayanā** (S) (F) fawn eyed.

**Mṛganetrā** (S) (F) 1. fawn eyed. 2. born under the constellation Mṛga or Capricorn.

**Mṛganetra** (S) (M) 1. fawn eyed. 2. born under the constellation Mṛga or Capricorn.

**Mṛgāṅganā** (S) (F) doe.

**Mṛgāṅka** (S) (M) 1. deer marked. 2. the moon; the wind; camphor.

**Mṛgāṅkabandhu** (S) (M) 1. friend of the moon. 3. another name for Kāma.

**Mṛgāṅkalekhā** (S) (F) 1. a line of the moon. 3. a daughter of the king of the vidyādharas (*K. Sāgara*)

**Mṛgāṅkamauli** (S) (M) 1. moon crested. 3. another name for Śiva.

**Mṛgāṅkavatī** (S) (F) 1. possessor of the moon. 3. the daughter of an ancient king called Śrībimbakī (*H. Purāṇa*)

**Mṛgapiplu** (S) (M) 1. deer marked. 2. the moon.

**Mṛgaprabhu** (S) (M) 1. lord of beasts. 2. the lion.

**Mṛgāra** (S) (M) 1. knower of animals. 2. knower of the zodiac sign of Capricorn; an astrologer. 3. a sage and author of *Atharva Veda* (iv); a minister of Prasenajit (*M. Bh.*)

**Mṛgarāja** (S) (M) 1. king of beasts. 2. the lion; the zodiac sign of Leo. 3. another name for the moon.

**Mṛgarājinī** (S) (F) 1. lioness. 3. a gāndharvī

**Mṛgaratha** (S) (M) 1. with a chariot drawn by deer. 3. a king of Ayodhyā and the father of the Jaina Tīrathankara Sumatinātha.

**Mṛgāri** (S) (M) enemy of deer; the lion.

**Mṛgaripu** (S) (M) 1. enemy of deer. 2. the lion; the zodiac sign of Leo.

**Mṛgāśana** (S) (M) 1. one who eats deer. 3. the lion.

**Mṛgaśīrṣa** (S) (M) 1. born under the constellation Mṛgasiras. 3. a nāga (*K. Vyūha*)

**Mṛgasya** (S) (M) 1. the zodiac sign of Capricorn. 3. another name for Śiva.

**Mṛgaṭaṅka** (S) (M) 1. deer marked. 3. another name for the moon.

**Mṛgavadhū** (S) (M) fawn; doe.

**Mṛgavāhana** (S) (M) 1. deer vehicled. 3. another name for Vāyu.

**Mṛgavatī** (S) (F) 1. possessor of deer. 3. the mythical progenitress of antelopes and bears (*V. Rāmāyaṇa*); the Dākṣāyāṇī on the Yamuṇā (*K. Sāgara*)

**Mṛgavyādha** (S) (M) 1. deer hunter. 3. name assumed by Śiva when he went to test Paraśurāma's devotion; one of the 11 rudras (*M. Bh.*); a marut (*M. Bh.*); the dog star Sirius.

**Mṛgayā** (S) (F) the chase personified as an attendant of Revanta.

**Mṛgayu** (S) (M) 1. living on hunting. 2. a hunter. 3. another name for Brahmā.

**Mṛgekṣaṇā** (S) (F) deer eyed.

**Mṛgendra** (S) (M) 1. king of beasts. 2. the lion; the zodiac sign of Leo.

**Mṛgī** (S) (F) 1. doe. 3. the mother of deer, and the daughter of Kaśyapa and Tāmrā (*M. Bh.*)

**Mṛgīndra** (S) (M) 1. lord of animals. 2. the lion; the tiger; the zodiac sign of Leo; the moon.

**Mṛgīśṇā** (S) (F) doe eyed.

**Mṛgottamā** (S) (F) 1. the most beautiful deer. 2. the constellation Mṛgasiras.

**Mṛkaṇḍu** (S) (M) 1. conqueror of death. 3. the father of sage Mārkaṇḍeya (*M. Purāṇa*)

**Mṛkṣiṇī** (S) (F) 1. tearing up. 2. a rain cloud; a torrent.

**Mṛṇāla** (S) (M) 1. liable to be crushed. 2. the root of a lotus; the lotus fibre.

**Mṛṇālī** (S) (F) lotus stalk.

**Mṛṇālikā** (S) (F) a lotus root.

**Mṛṇālin** (S) (M) 1. a lotus. 2. fragrant; tender; sacred; venerated; dear to the gods.

**Mṛṇalinī** (S) (F) 1. a collection of lotuses. 2. fragrant; tender; sacred; venerated; dear to the gods.

**Mṛṇmaya** (S) (M) made of the earth.

**Mṛṣā** (S) (F) 1. lie; falsehood. 3. the wife of Adharma and the mother of Dambha and Māyā (*Bhā. Purāṇa*)

**Mṛṣaṇā** (S) (F) 1. deliberation. 2. reflection; thought.

**Mṛtaṇḍa** (S) (M) 1. illuminating; glorious; enlightening. 3. the father of the sun (*A. Koṣa*)

**Mṛtsā** (S) (F) good earth; fragrant soil.

**Mṛtsnā** (S) (F) 1. good earth. 2. excellent soil; fertile and fragrant earth.

**Mṛttikā** (S) (F) 1. earth; clay. 2. loam.

**Mṛtyū** (S) (F) 1. death. 3. the goddess of death born of Brahmā or Māyā (*M. Bh.*)

**Mṛtyu** (S) (M) 1. death. 3. death personified as a son of Adharma by Nirṛti, sometimes reckoned as a son of Brahmā or Kālī and one of the 11 rudras.

**Mṛtyuṁjaya** (S) (M) 1. overcoming death. 3. another name for Śiva.

**Mṛtyuvañćana** (S) (M) 1. one who cheats death. 3. another name for Śiva.

**Mućilinda** (S) (M) 1. the tree *Pterospermum suberifolium*. 3. a nāga who sheltered the Buddha in a storm; a ćakravartin; a mountain.

**Mućira** (S) (M) 1. generous. 2. liberal; virtuous; the wind; a deity.

**Mućukunda** (S) (M) 1. *Pterospermum suberifolium*; cloud. 3. a king of the solar dynasty who was the son of Māndhātṛ and is listed among those kings who should be remembered morning and evening (*M. Bh.*); a son of Yadu (*H. Purāṇa*); a daitya.

**Mudā** (S) (F) 1. delight; happiness. 3. joy personified as a daughter of Tuṣṭi (*Bhā. Purāṇa*)

**Mudābhāja** (S) (M) 1. desirer of happiness. 3. a son of Prajāti (*V's B. Samhitā*)

**Mudānvita** (S) (M) 1. pleased; delighted. 2. filled with joy.

**Mudāvarta** (S) (M) 1. surrounded by happiness. 3. a Hehaya king (*M. Bh.*)

**Mudāvatī** (S) (F) 1. filled with joy. 3. a daughter of King Vidūratha (*M. Bh.*)

**Muddayā** (S) (M) (F) to be happy; to delight.

**Muditā** (S) (F) 1. happy; joyous; glad. 3. the wife of the agni Saha (*M. Bh.*)

**Mudgala** (S) (M) 1. ever happy; enchanting; a bean eater; a species of grass; a hammer. 3. a serpent of the family of Takṣaka (*M. Bh.*); a sage Purāṇic fame who was known for never being provoked into anger (*M. Bh.*); a ṛṣī and an author of *Ṛg Veda (x)*; a disciple of Śākalya (*V. Purāṇa*); a son of Viśvāmitra (*M. Bh.*)

**Mudgara** (S) (M) 1. hammer. 3. a nāga (*M. Bh.*)

**Mudgarapiṇḍaka** (S) (M) 1. with hammer like knobs. 3. a serpent born to Kaśyapa and Kadru (*M. Bh.*)

**Mudī** (S) (F) happy; moonshine.

**Muditapuṣpā** (S) (F) 1. happy flower. 3. a gandharvī (*K. Vyuha*)

**Mudra** (S) (M) joyous; glad.

**Mudrā** (S) (F) posture; sign; seal; signatory.

**Mugdhā** (S) (F) young; beautiful; innocent; artless; tender.

**Mugdhākṣī** (S) (F) fair eyed.

**Mugdhamaya** (S) (M) full of happiness.

**Mugdhānana** (S) (M) with a lovely face.

**Mugdhavadhū** (S) (F) young and lovely.

**Mugdhendu** (S) (M) the lovely moon; the new moon.

**Muhira** (S) (M) 1. bewilderer. 3. another name for Kāma.

**Muhūrtā** (S) (F) 1. moment; instant. 3. a space of time personified as the daughter of Dakṣa, the wife of Dharma or Manu and the mother of the Muhūrtas (*H. Purāṇa*)

**Muhūrta** (S) (M) 1. moment; instant. 3. a period of 48 minutes personified as the children of Muhūrtā and Dharma or Manu

(*H. Purāṇa*)

**Mūka** (S) (M) 1. silent. 3. a serpent of the family of Takṣaka (*M. Bh.*); an asura killed by Arjuna (*M. Bh.*)

**Mūkakarṇi** (S) (M) 1. deaf. 3. a follower of Skanda (*M. Bh.*)

**Mūkāmbikā** (S) (F) 1. the silent mother. 3. a shrine of a form of Durgā in north Cannore on the Mālābar coast in which only the lower portion of the goddess head is depicted.

**Mukeśa** (S) (M) 1. lord of liberation. 2. another name for Śiva.

**Mukhaćandra** (S) (M) 1. moon face. 2. with a face like the moon.

**Mukhaja** (S) (M) 1. born of the mouth. 2. a Brāhmin who is considered to have been born from the mouth of Brahmā.

**Mukhakamala** (S) (M) 1. lotus face. 2. with a face like a lotus.

**Mukhamaṇḍī** (S) (F) 1. having a filled mouth. 3. a mother attending on Skanda (*H. Purāṇa*)

**Mukhanivāsinī** (S) (F) 1. dwelling in the mouth. 3. another name for Sarasvatī.

**Mukhara** (S) (M) 1. talkative; verbose. 3. a serpent of the family of Kaśyapa (*M. Bh.*)

**Mukhaśrī** (S) (F) 1. beautiful face. 2. with a beautiful face.

**Mukhendu** (S) (M) 1. moon like face. 2. with a face as lovely as the moon.

**Mukta** (S) (M) 1. freed; emancipated; delivered; opened; a pearl. 3. a sage under Manu Bhautya (*M. Bh.*); a river (*V. Purāṇa*)

**Muktabandhanā** (S) (F) 1. released from bonds. 2. the Arabian Jasmine (*Jasminum sambac*)

**Muktābhā** (S) (F) with a pearly lustre; the Double Jasmine (*Jasminum sambac*)

**Muktabuddhī** (S) (F) with an emancipated mind.

**Muktaćetas** (S) (M) with a liberated soul.

**Muktaguṇa** (S) (M) qualities of a pearl.

**Muktālatā** (S) (F) a string of pearls.

**Muktāli** (S) (F) pearl necklace.

**Muktāmbarī** (S) (F) 1. freed of clothes; wearing clothes of pearls. 3. a rāga.

**Muktānanda** (S) (M) the joy of liberation.

**Muktāphala** (S) (M) 1. the fruit of the Lavali plant; Custard Apple (*Annona reticulata*) 2. camphor; a pearl. 3. a king of the Śabaras (*K. Sāgara*)

**Muktāphalaketu** (S) (M) 1. with a banner of pearls. 3. a king of the vidyādharas (*K. Sāgara*)

**Muktapīḍa** (S) (M) 1. crowned with pearls. 3. a king (*R. Taraṅginī*)

**Muktapuṣpa** (S) (M) pearl flower; *Jasminum multiflorum*.

**Muktāratna** (S) (M) pearl gem.

**Muktāsena** (S) (M) 1. with a free army. 3. a king of the vidyādharas (*K. Sāgara*)

**Muktāsraj** (S) (M) a chaplet of pearls.

**Muktāvalī** (S) (F) 1. a pearl necklace. 3. the wife of Ćandraketu (*K. Sāgara*)

**Mukteśa** (S) (M) lord of emancipation.

**Mukti** (S) (F) 1. liberation; freedom. 3. freedom personified as the wife of Satya (*H. Purāṇa*)

**Muktikā** (S) (F) a pearl.

**Mukula** (S) (M) 1. bud. 2. covered; body; soul; closed; hidden. 3. a king of the Purū dynasty who was a son of King Bāhyāśva and the father of Pañćāśva (*A. Purāṇa*); *Mimusops elengi*.

**Mukulikā** (S) (F) a small blossom; a low humming made to a put a child to sleep.

**Mukulita** (S) (M) full of blossoms.

**Mukunda** (S) (M) 1. precious stone; one who liberates. 3. one of the 9 treasures of Kubera (*Mā. Purāṇa*); another name for Viṣṇu-Kṛṣṇa.

**Mukundā** (S) (F) 1. a gem; one who liberates. 3. the wife of ṛṣi Vāćaknavī (*Bhā. Purāṇa*)

**Mukundapriya** (S) (M) 1. one who enjoys gems; a devotee of Viṣṇu. 3. the son of Gadādhara and father of Rāmānanda.

**Mukura** (S) (M) 1. mirror; bud. 2. a bud; a blossom; Indian Medlar tree (*Mimusops elengi*); the double Jasmine (*Jasminum sambac*)

**Mukuṭa** (S) (M) diadem; crown; crest; point.

**Mukuṭā** (S) (F) 1. wearing a crown. 3. a mother attending on Skanda (*M. Bh.*)

**Mukuṭeśvara** (S) (M) 1. lord of the crown. 3. a king (*M. Bh.*)

**Mukuteśvarī** (S) (M) 1. queen of the crowns.

3. the Dākṣāyāṇī in Mukuṭa (*M. Bh.*)
**Mukuṭopala** (S) (M) 1. jewel of the crown. 2. the crest gem.
**Mūlaka** (S) (M) 1. rooted in; springing from. 3. a son of Kumbhakarṇa killed by Sītā (*Ā. Rāmāyaṇa*); a prince and son of Aśmaka (*M. Bh.*)
**Mūlakarāja** (S) (M) the original king.
**Mūlarāja** (S) (M) lord of creation; the original root.
**Mūlatanī** (S) (F) 1. the root bodied. 2. the original body. 3. another name for Gaurī.
**Mumuću** (S) (M) 1. striving to be free. 3. a sage of South India (*M. Bh.*)
**Muṇḍa** (S) (M) 1. bald; blunt; head; thinker. 3. a daitya (*H. Purāṇa*); an asura (*D. Bh. Purāṇa*); another name for Rāhu.
**Muṇḍaka** (S) (M) 1. born of the head; dwelling on the head. 3. one of the 18 principal Upaniṣads (*M. Upaniṣad*)
**Muṇḍāmālinī** (S) (F) 1. garlanded with heads. 3. a form of Durgā (*Mā. Purāṇa*)
**Mundarī** (S) (F) ring.
**Muṇḍavedāṅga** (S) (M) 1. one whose head knows everything. 3. a serpent of the family of Dhṛtarāṣṭra (*M. Bh.*)
**Muṇḍī** (S) (F) 1. bald. 3. a mother in Skanda's retinue (*M. Bh.*)
**Mūngā** (S) (M) the coral gem.
**Muni** (S) (M) 1. sage; ascetic; moved by impulse. 2. seer; monk; devotee; one who is inspired. 3. the son of a vasu named Ahar (*M. Bh.*); a son of Kuru and Vāhinī (*M. Bh.*); a son of King Dyutimat (*Mā. Purāṇa*); the 7 stars of the Ursa Major (*M. Bh.*); a Buddha or Arhat (*J.S. Koṣa*); another name for Vyāsa, Agastya and Bharata; *Artemisia sieversiana*.
**Munī** (S) (F) 1. ascetic; inspired. 3. a daughter of Dakṣa and wife of Kaśyapa and mother of the yakṣas and gandharvas.
**Munia** (S) (F) a small girl.
**Munićandra** (S) (M) moon among ascetics.
**Munikumāra** (S) (M) a young ascetic.
**Munilakṣmī** (S) (F) 1. the treasure of an ascetic. 2. knowledge.
**Muniratna** (S) (M) 1. jewel among sages. 2. chaste; pious; enlightened.
**Munīndra** (S) (M) 1. chief of munis. 2. a Buddha; a Jina. 3. another name for Śiva, Śākyamuni and Bharata.
**Munipuṣpakā** (S) (F) 1. the flower of ascetics. 2. the blossom of *Agati grandiflora*.
**Muniputra** (S) (M) son of a muni; *Artemesia indica*.
**Muniśa** (S) (M) 1. chief of the munis. 2. a Buddha or a Jina. 3. another name for Vālmīki.
**Munisuvrata** (S) (M) 1. a fasting ascetic. 3. the 12th Arhat of the past and 20th Tīrthaṅkara of the present Avasarpinī (*H. Koṣa*)
**Muniśvara** (S) (M) 1. lord of ascetics. 3. another name for Viṣṇu and Buddha.
**Munivara** (S) (M) 1. best among munis. 3. another name for Vasiṣṭha as one of the stars of the Great Bear.
**Munivatī** (S) (F) 1. sage like. 3. a kinnarī (*K. Vyuha*)
**Munivīrya** (S) (M) 1. power of asceticism. 3. a viśvadeva (*K. Sāgara*)
**Muñja** (S) (M) 1. a species of grass (*Saccharum sara*). 3. a sage in the court of Yudhiṣṭhira (*M. Bh.*); a king of Dhārā; the girdle of a Brāhmin.
**Muñjakeśa** (S) (M) 1. with grass like hair. 3. a king who was an incarnation of an asura called Nićandra (*M. Bh.*); another name for Viṣṇu and Śiva.
**Muñjaketu** (S) (M) 1. grass bannered. 3. a king and member of Yudhiṣṭhira's court (*M. Bh.*)
**Muñjasūnu** (S) (M) 1. son of Muñja. 3. another name for Dāśaśarman.
**Munnu** (S) (M) three.
**Mupanāra** (S) (M) 1. not a small being. 2. a great person.
**Murā** (S) (F) 1. merciless; a fragrant plant. 3. the wife of Nanda and mother of Ćandragupta (*V. Purāṇa*)
**Mura** (S) (M) 1. merciless. 2. terrible; horrible; destroyer. 3. an asura born of Kaśyapa and Diti and killed by Kṛṣṇa (*Bhā. Purāṇa*); an asura born of a part of Brahmā and killed by Ekādaśī – a form of Devī (*P. Purāṇa*); the

son of Tālajaṅgha (*P. Purāṇa*); a Yādava king whose daughter married Ghaṭotkaća (*M. Bh.*)

**Murada** (S) (M) 1. destroyer of Mura. 3. the discus of Viṣṇu; another name for Kṛṣṇa.

**Murajā** (S) (F) 1. a great drum (*M. Bh.*) 3. Kubera's wife.

**Murajaka** (S) (M) 1. a drum. 3. one of Śiva's attendants (*K. Sāgara*)

**Murajit** (S) (M) 1. conqueror of Mura. 3. another name for Kṛṣṇa.

**Muralī** (S) (F) 1. flute; pipe. 2. melodious; harmonious; sweet; enchanting.

**Muralīdhara** (S) (M) 1. flute bearer. 3. another name for Kṛṣṇa.

**Muralikā** (S) (F) a small flute.

**Muramathana** (S) (M) 1. slayer of Mura. 3. another name for Kṛṣṇa.

**Murandalā** (S) (F) 1. encompassing. 3. a river of ancient India (*A. Koṣa*); another name for the Narmadā river.

**Murāri** (S) (M) 1. enemy of Mura. 3. another name for Kṛṣṇa.

**Mūrćana** (S) (M) 1. stupifying. 3. one of the 5 arrows of Kāma.

**Mūrdhagata** (S) (M) 1. going up. 2. one who grows, ascends, progresses and rules over people. 3. a ćakravartin (*Divyāvadāna*)

**Mūrdhaja** (S) (M) 1. born of the head. 3. a ćakravartin (*Divyāvadāna*)

**Mūrdhana** (S) (M) forehead; head; summit; chief.

**Mūrdhanavata** (S) (M) 1. dweller of the summit. 2. top; headed; chief. 3. a gandharva (*T. Āranyaka*)

**Mūrdhanyā** (S) (F) 1. highest; pre-eminent. 3. mother of Vedaśiras (*V. Purāṇa*)

**Mūrdheśvara** (S) (M) the highest god.

**Murita** (S) (M) 1. slayed; bound; encompassed; entwined. 3. a son of Yadu and a king of the lunar race.

**Mūrjā** (S) (F) 1. born of bondage; born of destruction. 3. a wife of Kubera (*M. Bh.*)

**Mūrkhalikā** (S) (F) an arrow in the form of a bird's heart.

**Murmurā** (S) (F) 1. ember. 3. a river from which Agni the lord of fire originated (*M. Bh.*)

**Murmura** (S) (M) 1. an ember. 3. a horse of the sun (*M. Bh.*); another name for Kāma.

**Mūrtaya** (S) (M) 1. substantial; material; incarnate; embodied. 3. a son of Kuśa (*V. Rāmāyaṇa*)

**Mūrti** (S) (F) 1. material form; idol; statue. 2. embodiment; incarnation; image. 3. a daughter of Dakṣa, wife of Dharma and the mother of Nara and Nārāyaṇa (*Bhā. Purāṇa*)

**Mūrti** (S) (M) 1. statue; idol. 2. embodiment; incarnation. 3. a ṛṣi in the 10th Manvantara (*Bhā. Purāṇa*); a son of Vasiṣṭha (*V. Purāṇa*)

**Muru** (S) (M) 1. detached. 3. a Yādava king whose daughter married Ghaṭotkaća (*M. Bh.*); a daitya (*M. Bh.*); another name for Vasiṣṭha.

**Murugesa** (S) (M) 1. lord of the detached; lord of the peacocks. 3. another name for Kārttikeya.

**Mūṣakāda** (S) (M) 1. eater of rats. 3. a serpent son of Kaśyapa and Kadru and member of Varuṇa's court (*M. Bh.*)

**Muṣakaratha** (S) (M) 1. rat vehicled. 3. another name for Gaṇeśa.

**Musala** (S) (M) 1. iron rod; pestle. 2. mace; club. 3. a son of Viśvāmitra (*M. Bh.*)

**Musalapāṇi** (S) (M) 1. club handed. 3. another name for Balarāma.

**Musalāyudha** (S) (M) 1. club armed. 3. another name for Balarāma.

**Musalin** (S) (M) 1. armed with a club. 3. another name for Balarāma.

**Muṣṭika** (S) (M) 1. handful; with a fist. 3. an asura who was a servant of Kaṁsa and killed by Balarāma (*M. Bh.*)

**Muthu** (S) (M) nice; gentle.

**Mutya** (S) (M) a pearl.

# N

**Nābha** (S) (M) **1.** nave; navel; central point; king. **3.** a son of Śruta and the father of Sindhudvīpa (*Bhā. Purāṇa*); a son of Manu Vaivasvata and an author of *Ṛg Veda* (x) (*T. Samhitā*); another name for Śiva.

**Nabha** (S) (M) **1.** expanding; the sky; atmosphere; the month Srāvaṇa. **3.** the son of Manu Svāroćiṣa; a sage of the 6th Manvantara (*H. Purāṇa*); a demon who was the son of Vipraćitti and Sinhikā; a son of Nala and the father of Puṇḍarīka (*Bhā. Purāṇa*); the city of the sun.

**Nabhaćakṣus** (S) (M) **1.** eye of the sky. **3.** another name for the sun.

**Nabhaćamaṣa** (S) (M) **1.** goblet of the sky. **3.** another name for the moon.

**Nabhaćarī** (S) (F) **1.** celestial; aerial. **2.** a god; a vidyādhara; bird; cloud; wind.

**Nabhaćyuta** (S) (M) fallen from the sky.

**Nabhadana** (S) (M) **1.** donated by the heavens. **2.** heavenly; celestial. **3.** a descendant of Virūpa and the author of *Ṛg Veda* (x)

**Nābhāga** (S) (M) **1.** moving in the sky. **2.** a bird. **3.** a son of Manu Vaivasvata and father of Ambarīṣa; a son of Yayāti and the father of Aja (*Bhā. Purāṇa*); a brother of Ikṣvāku (*M. Bh.*)

**Nābhāgāriṣṭa** (S) (M) **1.** dweller of the sky. **3.** a son of Manu Vaivasvata (*M. Bh.*)

**Nābhāka** (S) (M) **1.** belonging to the sky. **3.** a ṛṣi of the Kaṇva family and an author of *Ṛg Veda* (viii)

**Nabhakānti** (S) (M) splendour of the sky.

**Nabhaketana** (S) (M) **1.** sky banner. **3.** another name for the sun.

**Nabhanū** (S) (F) **1.** follower of the sky. **2.** one who moves towards the sky; a spring.

**Nabhanyā** (S) (F) **1.** springing forth from the heavens. **2.** ethereal; celestial; heavenly.

**Nabhanyu** (S) (M) **1.** springing forth from the heavens. **2.** ethereal; celestial; heavenly.

**Nabhapāntha** (S) (M) **1.** walking the skies. **3.** another name for the sun.

**Nabhaprāṇa** (S) (M) **1.** the breath of the sky. **2.** the wind.

**Nabhas** (S) (M) **1.** sky; mist; clouds; vapour. **2.** sun; sky; the month of the rainy season; a rope of lotus fibre.

**Nābhasa** (S) (M) **1.** vapoury; misty; of sky. **2.** sky; celestial; heavenly; divine; the ocean. **3.** a ṛṣi of the 10th Manvantara; a dānava (*H. Purāṇa*)

**Nabhasad** (S) (M) **1.** sky dweller. **2.** ethereal; celestial; heavenly; divine; a god; planet.

**Nabhasadīpa** (S) (M) **1.** light of the sky. **3.** another name for the moon.

**Nabhasaras** (S) (M) **1.** sky lake. **2.** the clouds.

**Nabhasarit** (S) (F) **1.** sky river. **3.** the Ākāśgaṅgā or the celestial Gaṅgā, commonly known as the Milky Way.

**Nabhasindhu** (S) (F) **1.** river of the sky. **2.** the Ākāśgaṅgā or the celestial Gaṅgā, commonly known as the Milky Way.

**Nabhasthala** (S) (M) **1.** residing in the sky. **3.** another name for Śiva.

**Nabhasvān** (S) (M) **1.** bearer of the sky. **3.** a son of Narakāsura (*Bhā. Purāṇa*)

**Nabhasvat** (S) (M) **1.** bearer of the sky; young. **2.** the wind. **3.** a son of Naraka Bhauma (*Bhāgavata*)

**Nabhaśvata** (S) (M) **1.** born of the sky. **2.** young; wind; air.

**Nabhaśvātī** (S) (F) **1.** born of the sky. **2.** lightning; thunder.

**Nabhasvatī** (S) (F) **1.** bearer of the sky; young. **2.** the wind. **3.** the wife of Antardhāna and the wife of Havirdhāna.

**Nabhasya** (S) (M) **1.** of the sky. **2.** vapour; misty; the ocean; the rainy season. **3.** a ṛṣi of the 10th Manvantara (*H. Purāṇa*); a son of Manu Svāroćiṣa; another name for Śiva.

**Nābhi** (S) (M) **1.** nave; navel; central point. **2.** sovereign; lord. **3.** a grandson of Priyavrata and father of Ṛṣabha (*J.S. Koṣa*); the father of the 1st Arhat of the present Avasarpinī (*J. S. Koṣa*)

**Nābhigupta** (S) (M) **1.** hidden in the navel. **3.** a son of Hiraṇyaretas.

**Nābhija** (S) (M) **1.** navel born. **3.** another name for Brahmā.

**Nābhijanmā** (S) (M) **1.** born of the navel. **3.** another name for Brahmā.

**Nabhīta** (S) (M) fearless.

**Nabhoda** (S) (M) **1.** one who has arisen from the sky. **2.** a cloud. **3.** a viśvadeva (*M. Bh.*)

**Nabhodhvaja** (S) (M) **1.** banner of the sky. **2.** a cloud.

**Nabhoga** (S) (M) **1.** travelling in the sky. **2.** a planet.

**Nabhogaja** (S) (M) **1.** elephant of the sky. **2.** a cloud.

**Nabhoja** (S) (M) born of the sky.

**Nabhomaṇī** (S) (M) **1.** jewel of the sky. **3.** another name for the sun.

**Nabhoreṇu** (S) (F) **1.** sky dust. **2.** the mist.

**Nabhorūpa** (S) (M) **1.** form of the sky. **2.** beyond any shape; ethereal. **3.** a mythical being (*V. Samhitā*)

**Nabhovīthī** (S) (M) the path of the sun.

**Nabhoyoni** (S) (M) **1.** skyborn. **3.** another name for Śiva.

**Nābhya** (S) (M) **1.** central; of the navel. **3.** another name for Śiva.

**Naćika** (S) (M) **1.** not experienced. **3.** a son of Viśvāmitra (*M. Bh.*)

**Naćiketa** (S) (M) **1.** not conscious. **2.** fire. **3.** an ancient sage who was the son of Uddālaka (*Kau. Upaniṣad*)

**Naḍa** (S) (M) **1.** a brook; a river; a stream; a species of Reed (*Arundo tibialis*). **3.** a nāga.

**Naḍāgiri** (S) (M) **1.** grass mountain. **3.** an elephant endowed with the powers of discrimination (*K. Sāgara*)

**Nadal** (S) (M) **1.** of a river. **2.** fortunate.

**Naḍantikā** (S) (F) **1.** reed destroying. **3.** a river of ancient India (*V. Purāṇa*)

**Nadanu** (S) (M) **1.** noisy. **2.** battle; cloud; lion.

**Nadīdhara** (S) (M) **1.** bearer of the river. **3.** another name for Śiva.

**Nadīja** (S) (M) **1.** from a river. **3.** a king (*M. Bh.*); Kadamba tree (*Anthocephalus cadamba*); another name for Bhīṣma.

**Nāḍījangha** (S) (M) **1.** hollow-thighed. **3.** a kite who was a friend of Brahmā; a stork who lives eternally.

**Nadīkānta** (S) (M) **1.** loving rivers. **2.** the ocean.

**Nadīna** (S) (M) **1.** lord of rivers. **3.** a son of Sahadeva and father of Jagatsena (*H. Purāṇa*); another name for Varuṇa.

**Nadvalā** (S) (F) **1.** a quantity of reeds. **3.** a daughter of Prajāpati Vairāja and wife of Manu Ćākṣuṣa.

**Naga** (S) (M) **1.** not moving. **2.** mountain; the number 7.

**Nāga** (S) (M) serpent; elephant.

**Nāgabala** (S) (M) **1.** with the strength of elephants. **3.** another name for Bhīma; *Plectronia parviflora*.

**Nāgabhaginī** (S) (F) **1.** sister of a snake. **3.** another name for Manasā.

**Nāgabhuṣaṇa** (S) (M) **1.** decorated with snakes. **3.** another name for Śiva.

**Nāgaćūḍa** (S) (M) **1.** serpent crested. **3.** another name for Śiva.

**Nāgadatta** (S) (M) **1.** given by serpents. **3.** a son of Dhṛtarāṣṭra (*M. Bh.*); a king of Āryavarta.

**Nāgadeva** (S) (M) **1.** lord of snakes. **3.** another name for Vāsuki.

**Nagadhipa** (S) (M) **1.** lord of mountains. **3.** another name for Mount Kailāsa and Śiva.

**Nāgadhipa** (S) (M) **1.** lord of snakes. **3.** another name for Śiva.

**Nagaja** (S) (M) mountain born.

**Nāgakumāra** (S) (M) **1.** prince of the serpents. **3.** a class of deities guarding Kubera's treasures.

**Nāgamātṛ** (S) (F) **1.** mother of serpents. **3.** another name for the goddess Manasā.

**Nāgamitrā** (S) (F) **1.** friend of the serpents. **3.** a Buddhist disciple of Rahulamitra of Nālandā; another name for Śiva.

**Nāgammā** (Tamil) (F) **1.** mother of snakes. **3.** a poetess.

**Nagamūrdhana** (S) (M) **1.** peak of a mountain. **2.** the mountain crest.

**Naganaćaraya** (S) (M) **1.** preceptor of mountains. **2.** minstrel.

**Naganadī** (S) (F) mountain river.

**Naganāmana** (S) (F) mark of a mountain; the Sacred Basil plant (*Ocimum sanctum*)

**Nāgānanda** (S) (M) joy of the serpents.

**Naganandinī** (S) (F) **1.** mountain born.

3. another name for Pārvatī.

**Nāganikā** (S) (F) serpent maiden.

**Nāgāñjanā** (S) (F) elephant.

**Nāgantaka** (S) (M) 1. destroyer of serpents. 3. another name for Garuḍa.

**Nāgapāla** (S) (M) protector of serpents.

**Nagapati** (S) (M) 1. lord of the mountains. 3. another name for the Himālaya.

**Nāgapurādhipa** (S) (M) 1. lord of Nāgapura (*Hāstinapura*). 3. another name for Paṇḍu.

**Nāgapurasiṁha** (S) (M) 1. lion of Nāgapura. 3. another name for Paṇḍu.

**Nāgapuṣpikā** (S) (F) flower of the mountains; the Yellow Jasmine (*Jasminum bignoniaceum*); *Crinum asiaticum.*

**Nāgarāja** (S) (M) lord of serpents; a large elephant.

**Nāgāri** (S) (M) 1. enemy of serpents. 3. a prominent child of Garuḍa (*Bhā. Purāṇa*); another name for Garuḍa.

**Nagarin** (S) (M) lord of a town.

**Nagariṇī** (S) (F) civic; civilized; urban.

**Nāgaripu** (S) (M) 1. enemy of serpents. 3. another name for Garuḍa.

**Nāgārjuna** (S) (M) 1. best among the snakes; a white snake. 3. an ancient Buddhist teacher of the rank of a Bodhisattva; a minister of King Ćirāyuṣ.

**Nagasata** (S) (M) 1. mountain of truth. 2. a holy mountain. 3. the mountain where King Pāṇḍu performed his penance (*M. Bh.*)

**Nāgasena** (S) (M) 1. with an army of elephants; the ruler of the nāgas. 3. a great Buddhist philosopher; a king of Āryāvarta.

**Nāgāśraya** (S) (M) living in mountains.

**Nāgaśrī** (S) (F) 1. the wealth of the serpents. 3. wife of King Dharmadatta of Kosala.

**Nagavāhana** (S) (M) 1. bearer of mountains. 3. another name for Śiva.

**Nāgavārika** (S) (M) 1. feeding on snakes; a better elephant. 2. a peacock; the royal elephant; hierarchically the chief person in a royal court. 3. another name for Garuḍa.

**Nāgavīthī** (S) (F) 1. a row of serpents; the moon's path; the serpent's path. 3. a daughter of Dharma and Yāmī (*V. Purāṇa*)

**Nagendra** (S) (M) 1. mountain lord. 3. another name for the Himālaya.

**Nāgendra** (S) (M) 1. lord of serpents. 3. another name for Vāsuki.

**Nāgendrī** (S) (F) 1. daughter of the mountain lord; daughter of the serpent lord; daughter of the king of elephants; coming through the Himālayas. 3. a river of ancient India (*S. Māhatmya*)

**Nageṣa** (S) (M) 1. lord of the mountains. 3. another name for Mount Kailāsa and Śiva.

**Nāgeśa** (S) (M) 1. lord of the serpents; lord of the elephants. 2. a large and noble elephant. 3. another name for Patañjali.

**Nāgeśvarī** (S) (M) 1. goddess of the serpents; goddess of the mountains; goddess of the elephants. 3. another name for Manasā.

**Nāgijā** (S) (F) 1. daughter of the serpent. 3. the blossom of *Mesua roxburghii*.

**Nāgilā** (S) (F) best among serpents; best among elephants.

**Naginā** (S) (F) obtained from a mountain; jewel; gem.

**Nagna** (S) (M) 1. naked; bare; new. 2. a mendicant. 3. another name for Śiva.

**Nagnajit** (S) (M) 1. conqueror of mendicants. 3. a Kṣatriya king of Gāndhāra who was born from a part of the asura Iśupāda (*M. Bh.*); an asura disciple of Prahlāda (*Bhā. Purāṇa*); a prince of the Gāndhāras and the father of one of Kṛṣṇa's wives (*M. Bh.*)

**Nāgnajitī** (S) (F) 1. one who conquers mendicants. 3. the daughter of Nagnajit and a wife of Kṛṣṇa (*M. Bh.*)

**Nāgrāndhakara** (S) (M) 1. destroyer of serpents. 2. a peacock. 3. another name for Kārttikeya.

**Nahnābhai** (H) (M) 1. younger brother. 3. another name for Rāmakṛṣṇa the son of Dāmodara.

**Nahuṣa** (S) (M) 1. fellow creature; man. 3. a lunar dynasty king the son of Āyuṣ and Indumatī, the husband of Aśokasundarī the daughter of Śiva and the father of Yayāti (*P. Purāṇa*); a serpent demon who was the son of Kaśyapa and Kadru (*M. Bh.*); a marut (*Vām. Purāṇa*); a son of Manu and part author of *Ṛg Veda* (ix); another name for

Viṣṇu and Kṛṣṇa.

**Naidhruvā** (S) (F) **1.** near perfection; nearing eternity. **3.** another name for Pārvatī.

**Naidhruva** (S) (M) **1.** near perfection. **3.** the grandson of Kaśyapa and the son of sage Avatsara (*Vā. Purāṇa*)

**Naigameya** (S) (M) **1.** goat faced. **3.** a form of Skanda also considered his son and playfellow (*V. Purāṇa*)

**Naiguta** (S) (M) destroyer of enemies.

**Naikabāhū** (S) (F) **1.** many armed. **3.** another name for Pārvatī.

**Naikadriṣ** (M) **1.** many eyed. **3.** a son of Viśvamitra.

**Naikarupa** (S) (M) taking many forms.

**Naimā** (S) (F) **1.** belonging to one. **2.** striving for the absolute.

**Naimiṣa** (S) (M) **1.** momentary; transient. **3.** a sacred pilgrimage spot and forest where an army of asuras was destroyed in a trice (*V. Rāmāyaṇa*)

**Naimlocanī** (S) (F) **1.** with twinkling eyes. **3.** the city of Varuṇa situated on the western mountain Manasottara.

**Naināhhirāma** (S) (M) **1.** pleasing to the eye. **2.** beautiful.

**Naināra** (S) (M) **1.** preceptor; observer. **3.** an author.

**Nainasukha** (S) (M) delightful to the eye.

**Nainikā** (S) (F) pupil of the eye.

**Nairañjana** (S) (M) **1.** pure; pleasing; spotless. **3.** a river that falls into the Gaṅgā in Magadha (*Ś. Purāṇa*)

**Nairṛti** (S) (M) **1.** lord of the southwest. **3.** a rākṣasa who was one of the ancient guards of the world (*M. Bh.*)

**Naiṣadha** (S) (M) **1.** king of the Niṣadhas. **3.** another name for Nala.

**Nāk** (S) (M) night.

**Nāka** (S) (M) **1.** where there is no pain. **2.** vault of heaven; sky; firmament; the sun. **3.** a mythical weapon of Arjuna (*M. Bh.*)

**Nākanadī** (S) (F) **1.** river of heaven. **3.** the Ākāśgaṅgā or the celestial Gaṅgā also known as the Milky Way.

**Nākanārī** (S) (F) **1.** heavenly woman. **2.** an apsarā.

**Nākanātha** (S) (M) **1.** lord of the sky. **3.** another name for Indra.

**Nākanāyaka** (S) (M) **1.** leader of the sky. **3.** another name for Indra.

**Nākapāla** (S) (M) guardian of the sky.

**Nākapati** (S) (M) **1.** lord of the sky. **3.** another name for Indra.

**Nākavanitā** (S) (F) **1.** heavenly woman. **2.** an apsarā.

**Nākeśa** (S) (M) **1.** lord of the sky. **3.** another name for Indra.

**Nakhaka** (S) (M) **1.** shaped like a talon. **2.** curved. **3.** a serpent lord (*R. Taraṅginī*)

**Nākin** (S) (M) **1.** dwelling in the sky. **2.** a god.

**Nakra** (S) (M) **1.** crocodile. **3.** the zodiac sign of Capricorn.

**Nakraketana** (S) (M) **1.** crocodile bannered. **3.** another name for Kāma.

**Nakṣa** (S) (M) **1.** to come near; to arrive at; to attain. **3.** the son of Pṛthusena and Ākūti, the husband of Druti and the father of Gaya (*Bhā. Purāṇa*)

**Nakṣatra** (S) (M) **1.** heavenly body; a constellation; a lunar mansion; a pearl. **3.** in the Vedas the Nakṣatras are considered the abode of the gods and in the later Hindu scriptures, they are depicted as the daughters of Dakṣa and the wives of the moon (*M. Bh.*)

**Nakṣatraja** (S) (M) **1.** born of the stars; the son of the stars. **3.** another name for the planet Mercury.

**Nakṣatramālā** (S) (F) **1.** a garland of stars. **2.** a necklace of 27 pearls.

**Nakṣatranandana** (S) (M) **1.** son of the stars. **3.** another name for planet Mercury.

**Nakṣatranātha** (S) (M) **1.** lord of the constellations. **3.** another name for the moon.

**Nakṣatranemi** (S) (M) **1.** the axis of the constellations; the centre of the constellations; the pole star. **3.** another name for Viṣṇu and the moon.

**Nakṣatrarāja** (S) (M) **1.** lord of the constellations. **3.** a Bodhisattva; another name for the moon.

**Nakṣatrin** (S) (M) **1.** holding the stars. **2.** fortunate; lucky. **3.** another name for Viṣṇu.

**Nakta** (S) (M) **1.** night. **3.** a son of Pṛthuśena

and Ākūti (*Bhā. Purāṇa*); a son of Pṛthu (*V. Purāṇa*)

**Naktamukhā** (S) (F) **1.** preface of the night. **2.** the evening.

**Naktī** (S) (F) night.

**Nākuja** (S) (M) **1.** born of an anthill. **3.** another name for Vālmiki.

**Nakula** (S) (M) **1.** of the colour of an Ichneumon. **2.** a son; a musical instrument; the Bengal Mongoose (*Viverra ichneumon*) **3.** a son of the aśvins and Mādrī, the brother of Sahadeva and the 4th of the Pāṇḍu princes known for his beauty (*M. Bh.*); another name for Śiva.

**Nakulānuja** (S) (M) **1.** younger brother of Nakula. **3.** another name for Sahadeva.

**Nakulī** (S) (F) **1.** a female mongoose; the *Salmalia malabarica*; Saffron (*Crocus sativus*). **3.** a wife of Śiva (*A. Koṣa*)

**Nākuli** (S) (M) **1.** son of Nakula. **3.** another name for Śatanīka.

**Nala** (S) (M) **1.** stem; any hollow pipe; stem of a flower; lotus; nectar; a species of Reed (*Amphidonax karka*). **3.** a divine being mentioned with Yama; a king of the Niṣadhas who was the son of Vīrasena and the husband of Damayantī (*M. Bh.*); a son of Niṣadha and the father of Nabha (*H. Purāṇa*); a son of Sudhanvan and father of Uktha; a son of Yadu (*V. Purāṇa*); a monkey chief who was the son of Tvaṣṭṛ (*V. Rāmāyaṇa*); a hermit who lived in the court of Indra (*M. Bh.*); a daitya (*Br. Purāṇa*)

**Naladā** (S) (F) **1.** the nectar of a flower; Spikenard (*Nardostachys jatamans*). **3.** a daughter of Raudrāśva (*H. Purāṇa*); an apsarā (*A. Veda*)

**Nālāgiri** (S) (M) **1.** lotus plucker. **2.** an elephant. **3.** an elephant associated with Gautama Buddha; the elephant of Pradyota.

**Nālakinī** (S) (F) **1.** a multitude of lotuses. **2.** a lotus lake.

**Nalakūbara** (S) (M) **1.** with a carriage of reeds; beautiful; fragrant; agreeable. **3.** a son of Kubera and the husband of Rambhā and Somaprabhā (*M. Bh.*)

**Nalamī** (S) (F) fragrant nectar; the lute of Śiva.

**Nalandā** (S) (M) nectar of a flower.

**Nalapriyā** (S) (F) **1.** beloved of King Nala. **3.** another name for Queen Damayantī.

**Nalasetu** (S) (M) **1.** reed bridge. **3.** the bridge constructed by the monkey Nala for Rāma to Laṅkā (*V. Rāmāyaṇa*)

**Nalatantu** (S) (M) **1.** made of lotus threads. **3.** a son of Viśvāmitra (*M. Bh.*)

**Naleśa** (S) (M) king of flowers.

**Nālika** (S) (M) arrow; spear; limb; Lotus flower (*Nelumbium nucifera*)

**Nalina** (S) (M) the Lotus (*Nelumbium speciosum*); the Water Lily (*Nymphaea alba*); the Indian crane; the Indigo plant (*Indigofera tinctoria*); water.

**Nalinanābha** (S) (M) **1.** lotus navelled. **3.** another name for Viṣṇu.

**Nalināsana** (S) (M) **1.** lotus throned. **3.** another name for Brahmā.

**Nalinī** (S) (F) **1.** the Lotus (*Nelumbium speciosum*); Water Lily (*Nymphaea alba*); a multitude of lotuses. **2.** beautiful; fragrant; sacred; dear to the gods. **3.** a wife of Ajamīdha and the mother of Nīla (*Bhā. Purāṇa*); a tributary of the Gaṅgā (*Bhā. Purāṇa*)

**Nalinīnandana** (S) (M) **1.** a lotus bud. **3.** a garden of Kubera (*V. Rāmāyaṇa*)

**Nalinīruha** (S) (M) **1.** born of a lotus. **3.** another name for Brahmā.

**Nāman** (S) (M) name; form; mark; renowned; of a great name.

**Namana** (S) (M) **1.** bending; bowing. **2.** offering homage.

**Namasita** (S) (M) **1.** revered. **2.** virtuous; auspicious; sacred.

**Namasyu** (S) (M) **1.** bowing. **2.** worshipping; deferential. **3.** a king of Yayāti's family (*Bhā. Purāṇa*); a son of Pravīra (*Bha. Purāṇa*)

**Namata** (S) (M) **1.** bending; bowing. **2.** paying homage.

**Nameśa** (S) (M) **1.** lord of obeisance. **2.** worshipped; a divine being.

**Nāmgiri** (S) (M) sacred mountain.

**Nāmi** (S) (M) **1.** of great renown. **3.** another name for Viṣṇu.

**Namināthu** (S) (M) **1.** bowing before the

master. **2.** a devotee. **3.** the 21st Jaina Tirthaṅkara whose emblem is a lotus (*J.S. Koṣa*)

**Namitā** (S) (F) **1.** bowed; bent down. **2.** one who worships; a devotee; humble; modest; submissive.

**Namita** (S) (M) **1.** bowed; bent down. **2.** one who worships; a devotee; humble; modest; submissive.

**Namrāṅga** (S) (M) **1.** bowed posture. **2.** humble; modest; submissive.

**Namratā** (S) (F) **1.** bowing; humility; submissiveness; meekness. **2.** humble; modest; submissive.

**Namuća** (S) (M) **1.** not loose. **2.** taut; firm; fixed. **3.** a sage of ancient India (*M. Bh.*)

**Namūći** (S) (M) **1.** not loose. **2.** taut; firm; fixed. **3.** a rākṣasa son of Kaśyapa and Danu, killed by Indra and the aśvins (*Ṛg Veda*); an army captain of Hiranyākṣa (*P. Purāṇa*); another name for Kāma.

**Namūćighna** (S) (M) **1.** slayer of Namući. **3.** another name for Indra.

**Namūćisudana** (S) (M) **1.** conqueror of Namūći. **3.** another name for Indra.

**Nāmvara** (S) (M) renowned.

**Namyā** (S) (F) **1.** to be bowed to; venerable. **2.** the night.

**Namya** (S) (M) to be bowed to; venerable.

**Nanagābhu** (S) (M) **1.** born of light. **3.** a king of the family of Yayāti (*Bhā. Purāṇa*)

**Nānaka** (S) (M) **1.** without darkness. **2.** griefless; fearless; happy; a coin; anything stamped with an impression. **3.** the founder of Sikhism and the 1st of the 10 Gurus.

**Nāṇaka** (S) (M) coin; anything with an impression.

**Nānakī** (S) (F) sister of Nānaka.

**Nandā** (S) (F) **1.** delight; prosperity; happiness. **3.** felicity personified as a wife of Harṣa (*M. Bh.*); a daughter of Vibhīṣana; the mother of the 10th Arhat of the present Avasarpinī (*J.S. Koṣa*); a river flowing near Kubera's city Alakā (*Bh. Purāṇa*); the 6th day of the light half of the month (*V's B. Saṃhitā*); an apsarā (*H. Purāṇa*); another name for Durgā.

**Nanda** (S) (M) **1.** joy; delight; happiness; a flute; a son; number 9. **3.** one of Yudhiṣṭhira's drums (*M. Bh.*); one of Kubera's 9 gems (*A. Koṣa*); one of Skanda's attendants (*A. Koṣa*); a nāga born in the family of Kaśyapa (*A. Koṣa*); an attendant of Dakṣa (*Bhā. Purāṇa*); a son of Dhṛtarāṣṭra (*M. Bh.*); a stepbrother and disciple of Gautama Buddha (*B. Literature*); a son of Vasudeva (*M. Bh.*); the foster father of Kṛṣṇa (*M. Bh.*); a leader of the Sātvatas (*Bhā. Purāṇa*); a king of Pāṭaliputra; an ancestor of Durgā (*M. Bh.*); a devotee and attendant of Viṣṇu (*M. Bh.*); a Buddhist deity; another name for Viṣṇu (*M. Bh.*); Indian Mahogany (*cedrela Toona*); Couchgrass (*Cynodon dactylon*); Malay Apple (*Eugenia jambos*)

**Nandabhadra** (S) (M) **1.** delightful person. **3.** a devotee of Kapileśvara (*Ś. Purāṇa*)

**Nandādevī** (S) (F) **1.** goddess of happiness. **3.** a lofty Himālayan peak.

**Nandagopa** (S) (M) **1.** cowherd Nanda. **3.** another name for the cowherd Nanda.

**Nandaka** (S) (M) delighting; rejoicing; gladdening; the deity of weapons (*M. Bh.*); Kṛṣṇa's sword (*M. Bh.*)

**Nandakin** (S) (M) **1.** possessor of the Nandaka sword. **3.** another name for Kṛṣṇa.

**Nandakiśora** (S) (M) **1.** son of Nanda. **3.** another name for Kṛṣṇa.

**Nandakumāra** (S) (M) **1.** son of Nanda. **3.** another name for Kṛṣṇa.

**Nandalāla** (S) (M) **1.** son of Nanda. **3.** another name for Kṛṣṇa.

**Nandana** (S) (M) **1.** rejoicing; gladdening. **2.** a son; a type of temple. **3.** an attendant of Skanda given to him by the aśvins (*M. Bh.*); a son of Hiraṇyakaśipu who became a gaṇa of Śiva (*Ś. Purāṇa*); a Buddhist (*L. Vistara*); another name for Viṣṇu and Śiva.

**Nandanā** (S) (F) **1.** gladdening; a daughter. **3.** a divine garden of the gods (*M. Bh.*); Indra's paradise (*A. Veda*); another name for Durgā.

**Nandanamālā** (S) (F) **1.** garland of delight. **3.** a garland worn by Kṛṣṇa (*Bhā. Purāṇa*)

**Nandanta** (S) (M) **1.** rejoicing; gladdening. **2.** a son; a friend; a king.

**Nandantī** (S) (F) **1.** delighting. **2.** a daughter.

**Nandapāla** (S) (M) 1. guardian of the Nanda. 2. guardian of one of Kubera's 9 gems called 'Nanda'. 3. another name for Varuṇa.

**Nandarānī** (S) (F) 1. the wife of Nanda. 3. another name for Yaśodā.

**Nandathu** (S) (M) joy; delight; happiness.

**Nandayantī** (S) (F) bestowing joy.

**Nandī** (S) (F) 1. happiness. 3. joy personified as a daughter of heaven, the wife of Kāma and the mother of Harṣa (*Bhā. Purāṇa*); another name for Durgā (*D. Purāṇa*); the city of Indra.

**Nandi** (S) (M) 1. the happy one. 3. the chief of the attendants of Śiva (*Vām. Purāṇa*); a gandharva (*M. Bh.*); Indian Mahogany (*Cedrela toona*); Wax Flower (*Ervatamia coronaria*); Portia tree (*Thespesia populnea*); another name for Viṣṇu and Śiva.

**Nandighoṣa** 1. the music of joy. 3. Arjuna's chariot (*M. Bh.*)

**Nandigupta** (S) (M) 1. protected by happiness. 3. a king of Kāsmira (*R. Taraṅginī*)

**Nandikā** (S) (F) 1. pleasure giving. 3. Indra's pleasure ground.

**Nandika** (S) (M) 1. pleasure giving. 3. one of Śiva's attendants; a pupil of Gautama Buddha; the tree *Cedrela toona*.

**Nandikara** (S) (M) 1. causing joy. 3. another name for Śiva.

**Nandikeśvara** (S) (M) 1. one who pleases the god. 3. the chief of Śiva's gaṇas or attendants and his bull (*Vām. Purāṇa*)

**Nandil** (S) (M) delighted; glad.

**Nandin** (S) (M) 1. son; delightful. 3. one of the 9 north Indian kings whose empire was annexed by Samudragupta; one of Kubera's attendants (*M. Bh.*); a place held sacred by the Jainas; an attendant of Śiva (*Ś. Purāṇa*); Śiva's bull (*Ś. Purāṇa*)

**Nandinī** (S) (F) 1. delightful; a daughter. 3. a Mātṛ attending on Śiva (*M. Bh.*); a fabulous cow owned by Vasiṣṭha and was the mother of Surabhī (*M. Bh.*); another name for Durgā, Gaṅgā and the river Bāṇanāsa; Garden Cress (*Lepidum sativum*)

**Nandirudra** (S) (M) Śiva in a joyful or serene form.

**Nandīśa** (S) (M) 1. lord of pleasure; lord of the bulls. 3. the chief attendant of Śiva (*Vām. Purāṇa*); another name for Śiva.

**Nandisena** (S) (M) 1. with an army of bulls. 3. one of the 4 attendants of Skanda given to him by Brahmā (*M. Bh.*)

**Nandīśvara** (S) (M) 1. lord of happiness; lord of the bulls. 3. the chief attendant of Śiva; an attendant of Kubera.

**Nanditā** (S) (F) one who pleases.

**Nandivardhana** (S) (M) 1. enhancing pleasure; a son; a friend; the day of the full moon. 3. a king of the solar dynasty, the son of Vīrada and the father of Suketu (*Bhā. Purāṇa*); a prince who was the son of Udāvasu (*V. Purāṇa*); a son of Janaka (*V. Purāṇa*); a son of Udayāśva; a son of Rājaka (*Bh. Purāṇa*); a brother of Mahāvira; the conch of Sātyaki (*M. Bh.*); another name for Śiva.

**Nandivega** (S) (M) 1. with the speed of Nandi. 2. with the speed of Śiva's bull Nandin. 3. a Kṣatriya family into which King Sama was born (*M. Bh.*)

**Naṅhasa** (S) (M) a god who is kind to his worshipper.

**Nanja** (S) (M) 1. consumer of poison. 3. another name for Śiva.

**Naṅsa** (S) (M) acquisition.

**Nāntra** (S) (M) 1. praise; eulogy. 3. a sage; another name for Śiva.

**Naoraṅga** (S) (M) the Indian Pitta (*Corvus brachyurus*)

**Naparājit** (S) (M) 1. not yielding. 3. another name for Śiva.

**Naparājita** (S) (M) 1. not yielding. 3. another name for Śiva.

**Napāt** (S) (M) 1. descendant. 2. son offspring; path of the gods. 3. a viśvadevā (*V. Purāṇa*)

**Naptā** (S) (M) 1. unfulfilled; unsatisfied. 3. a viśvadeva concerned with offerings to the manes or ancestors (*M. Bh.*)

**Nara** (S) (M) 1. man; male; eternal spirit pervading the universe. 3. always associated with Nārāyaṇa, in poetry they are the sons of Dharma and Mūrti or Ahinsa and the emanations of Viṣṇu who became great hermits and lived in Badarikāśrama performing penance to Brahmā for a 1000 years and were later reborn as Arjuna and Kṛṣṇa (*M. Bh.*); a class of mythical beings like the gandharvas and the kinnaras (*M. Bh.*); a son of Manu Tāmasa (*Bhā. Purāṇa*); a son of Viśvāmitra (*H. Purāṇa*); a son of Gaya and the father of Virāj (*V. Purāṇa*); a son of Sudhṛti and father of Kevala (*V. Purāṇa*); one of the 10 horses of the moon (*A. Koṣa*); a gandharva who stayed in the palace of Kubera (*M. Bh.*); 2 kings of Kāśmira (*R. Taraṅginī*); another name for Arjuna.

**Narā** (S) (F) **1.** woman. **3.** wife of Uśīnara and mother of Nara (*Agni Purāṇa*)

**Narabhu** (S) (M) **1.** father of man; born of man. **3.** another name for Indra.

**Naraćandra** (S) (M) moon among men.

**Nārada** (S) (M) **1.** one who gives knowledge to men. **2.** a messenger. **3.** a ṛṣi son of Brahmā born from his lap, one of the 10 prajāpatis, considered a messenger between the gods and men, in later mythology depicted as a friend of Kṛṣṇa and regarded as the inventor of the Vīnā or the lute; a son of Viśvāmitra (*M. Bh.*)

**Naradattā** (S) (F) **1.** given by man. **3.** a goddess executing the commands of the 20th Arhat of the present Avasarpinī (*L. Vistara*); one of the 16 vidyādevīs (*J.S. Koṣa*)

**Naradeva** (S) (M) the god of men.

**Narādhārā** (S) (F) **1.** supporting men. **3.** another name for the earth.

**Narādhipa** (S) (M) lord of men.

**Nāradin** (S) (M) **1.** telling tales. **2.** providing knowledge through tales. **3.** a son of Viśvāmitra (*M. Bh.*)

**Narahari** (S) (M) **1.** man lion. **3.** another name for Viṣṇu.

**Naraka** (S) (M) **1.** hell. **3.** hell personified as a son of Anṛta and Nirṛti (*M. Bh.*); a demon son of Hiraṇyākṣa and Bhūmi who was slain by Kṛṣṇa (*V. Purāṇa*); a rākṣasa son of Kaśyapa and Danu, slain by Indra, upon being reborn, stayed in the palace of Varuṇa (*Bhā. Purāṇa*)

**Narakajit** (S) (M) **1.** conqueror of Naraka. **3.** a son of Vipraćitti (*V. Purāṇa*); another name for Viṣṇu and Kṛṣṇa.

**Narakantaka** (S) (M) **1.** destroyer of Naraka. **3.** another name for Viṣṇu.

**Narakesarin** (S) (M) **1.** lion among men. **3.** Viṣṇu in his 4th incarnation as the man lion.

**Nāram** (S) (M) **1.** of Nara. **2.** water.

**Naran** (S) (M) **1.** belongs to men. **2.** that which is human.

**Naranārāyaṇa** (S) (M) **1.** Nara and Nārāyaṇa conjoined. **3.** another name for Kṛṣṇa and Arjuna conjoined.

**Naranātha** (S) (M) **1.** lord of men; controller of men. **2.** a king.

**Naranāyaka** (S) (M) leader of men.

**Nāranga** (S) (M) **1.** orange coloured; having a human form; a living being; a twin. **2.** an orange tree (*Citrus aurantium*)

**Narānta** (S) (M) **1.** destroyer of men. **3.** a son of Hṛdika (*H. Purāṇa*)

**Narāntaka** (S) (M) **1.** killer of men. **3.** a captain in the army of Rāvaṇa (*V. Rāmāyaṇa*); the son of the asura Rudraketu who was killed by Gaṇapati (*G. Purāṇa*)

**Narapāla** (S) (M) protector of men; king.

**Nararāja** (S) (M) **1.** king of men. **3.** another name for Kubera.

**Narāśaṅsa** (S) (M) **1.** the desire of men. **3.** another name for Agni.

**Naraśārdūla** (S) (M) **1.** lion among men. **2.** very powerful; courageous; brave; a great warrior; a leader among men.

**Narasiṁha** (S) (M) **1.** lion among men. **2.** extremely powerful; courageous; brave; a great warrior; a leader among men. **3.** Viṣṇu in his 4th incarnation (*Purāṇas*); the father of King Bhairava.

**Naravāhana** (S) (M) **1.** with men as the vehicle. **2.** that which is drawn or borne by men. **3.** the successor of Śālivāhana; a minister of King Kṣemagupta (*R. Taraṅginī*); another name for Kubera.

**Naravāhanadatta** (S) (M) **1.** given by Kubera. **3.** a vidyādhara emperor who was the son of King Udayana and Vāsavadattā and the husband of Madanamañćukā and Alaṅkārāvatī.

**Naravarman** (S) (M) **1.** protector of men. **3.** a Mālava prince (12th century) (*R. Taraṅginī*)

**Naravīra** (S) (M) hero among men.

**Nārāyaṇa** (S) (M) 1. the son of the original man. 3. the incarnation of Viṣṇu, regarded as a Kaśyapa, the son of Dharma, the brother of Nara with whom he performed a penance for 1000 years, reborn as Kṛṣṇa and in the Jaina scriptures depicted as the 8th of the 9 Black Vasudevas; a son of prince Bhūmitra of the Kāṇvayānas; son of Narahari; a son of Ajāmila (*Bhā. Purāṇa*)

**Nārāyaṇadāsa** (S) (M) a devotee of Nārāyaṇa.

**Nārāyaṇi** (S) (M) 1. belonging to Viṣṇu or Kṛṣṇa. 3. a son of Viśvāmitra (*M. Bh.*)

**Nārāyaṇī** (S) (F) 1. belonging to Nārāyaṇa, Viṣṇu or Kṛṣṇa. 3. the army of Kṛṣṇa that was given to Duryodhana to fight the Mahābhārata war (*M. Bh.*); another name for Durgā, Lakṣmī, Gaṅgā and Gaṇḍakī; *Aspargus racemosus*.

**Narbadeśvara** (S) (M) 1. lord of the Narmadā river. 3. another name for Śiva.

**Nardana** (S) (M) 1. roarer. 2. celebrating; praising aloud. 3. a serpent lord.

**Narendra** (S) (M) lord of men.

**Narendradeva** (S) (M) divine lord of men.

**Narendrāditya** (S) (M) 1. sun among the lords of men. 2. with qualities that shine forth even among the lords of men. 3. 2 kings of Kāśmira (*R. Taraṅginī*)

**Narendranātha** (S) (M) 1. king among lords of men. 2. king of kings.

**Nareśa** (S) (M) king of men.

**Nārī** (S) (F) 1. woman. 3. a daughter of Meru and wife of Agnīdhra's son Nābhi (*Bhā. Purāṇa*)

**Nārikavaća** (S) (M) 1. women as armour; protected by women. 3. the solar dynasty king Mūlaka who was the son of Aśmaka (*Purāṇas*)

**Nārikera** (S) (M) the Coconut tree (*Cocos nucifera*)

**Nāriratna** (S) (M) 1. a jewel of a woman. 2. beautiful; meritorious; virtuous.

**Nāristhā** (S) (F) 1. dear to a woman. 3. the Arabian Jasmine (*Jasminum sambac*)

**Nariṣyanta** (S) (M) 1. detached from women. 3. a king who was the son of Marutta, the husband of Indrasenā and the father of Dama (*Mā. Purāṇa*); the son of Manu Vaivasvata and the brother of Ikṣvāku (*Bhā. Purāṇa*)

**Narmadā** (S) (F) 1. pleasure giver. 3. a river personified as the wife of Purukutsa, the mother of Trasadasyu, a reincarnation of Tapatī and daughter of the sun and depicted as a goddess who lives in the palace of Varuṇa (*Ś. Purāṇa*); a gandharvī (*V. Rāmāyaṇa*)

**Narmadeśvara** (S) (M) 1. lord of Narmadā. 3. another name for Śiva.

**Narmadyuti** (S) (F) bright with joy; happy; merry.

**Narman** (S) (M) joke; wit; humour; jest; play; sport.

**Narmaṭa** (S) (M) 1. a potsherd. 2. a broken piece of earthenware. 3. another name for the sun.

**Narottama** (S) (M) 1. best among men. 3. another name for Viṣṇu and the Buddha.

**Nartakī** (S) (F) dancer.

**Naruṇa** (S) (M) 1. leader of men. 3. another name for Pūṣan.

**Narya** (S) (M) manly; strong; powerful; heroic.

**Nāsatya** (S) (M) 1. helpful; of the nose. 2. kind; friendly; breath. 3. an aśvin (*M. Bh.*)

**Nāsikā** (S) (F) 1. nostril. 3. the mother of the 2 aśvins (*M. Bh.*)

**Nasīka** (S) (M) 1. perishable. 3. the grandson of Lomapāda (*Bhā. Purāṇa*)

**Nāśīra** (S) (M) 1. at the head; at the top. 2. a champion who advances at the head of the army.

**Natā** (S) (F) 1. bowed; curved. 3. daughter of Śuki and mother of Vinatā.

**Nāṭakī** (S) (F) 1. dancer. 3. the court of Indra (*A. Koṣa*)

**Naṭanārāyaṇa** (S) (M) 1. the dance of Viṣṇu. 3. a rāga.

**Naṭarāja** (S) (M) 1. lord of the cosmic dance. 3. another name for Śiva.

**Natāri** (S) (M) 1. subduing enemies. 3. another name for Kṛṣṇa.

**Naṭavara** (S) (M) 1. best among dancers. 3. another name for Kṛṣṇa.

**Naṭeśa** (S) (M) 1. lord of the Naṭas or dancers. 3. another name for Śiva.

**Naṭeśvara** (S) (M) 1. lord of the Naṭas or dancers. 3. another name for Śiva.

**Nāthan** (S) (M) 1. controller; protector; patron lord. 2. one who protects. 3. another name for Kṛṣṇa.

**Nathin** (S) (M) protected.

**Natī** (S) (F) modesty; humility.

**Nāṭikā** (S) (F) 1. consisting of dancers and/or actors. 3. a rāgiṇī.

**Naubandhana** (S) (M) 1. ship anchorage. 3. the highest peak of the Himālayas to which Manu moored his ship during the great deluge (*M. Bh.*)

**Naudīśvara** (S) (M) 1. pleasing to the god. 2. victor. 3. another name for Śiva.

**Naukarṇī** (S) (F) 1. the helm of a ship. 3. a Mātṛ attending on Skanda (*M. Bh.*)

**Naunihāl** (S) (M) 1. new crop. 2. child.

**Nava** (S) (M) 1. new; fresh; young; praised; celebrated. 3. a son of Uśīnara and Navā (*H. Purāṇa*); a son of Viloman (*V. Purāṇa*)

**Navajā** (S) (M) 1. recently born. 2. new moon.

**Navajāta** (M) fresh; new.

**Navajyota** (S) (M) 1. new light. 2. the fresh light; 1st light of day.

**Navala** (S) (M) new; novel.

**Navamallikā** (S) (F) 1. the new creeper; the Jasmine (*Jasminum sambac*). 3. a daughter of King Dharmavardhana of Śrāvastī.

**Navamī** (S) (F) the 9th; the 9th day of a lunar half month.

**Navana** (S) (M) 1. the act of praising. 2. laudation.

**Navāṅgī** (S) (F) 1. new body. 2. with a fresh body; a refreshing and exquisite woman.

**Navanidhi** (S) (M) 1. the 9 treasures. 3. another name for the 9 fabled treasures of Kubera.

**Navanīta** (S) (M) 1. new butter. 2. fresh butter; mild; soft; gentle. 3. one of the 6 aspects of Gaṇeśa.

**Navanna** (S) (M) new fruits; the 1st fruit.

**Navapallava** (S) (M) new shoot.

**Navaraṅga** (S) (M) of a new design; novel.

**Navaratha** (S) (M) 1. with 9 chariots. 3. the son of Bhīmaratha and father of Daśaratha (*V. Rāmāyaṇa*)

**Navaratna** (S) (M) 9 gems (pearl, ruby, topaz, diamond, emerald, lapiz lazuli, coral, sapphire and Gomedha)

**Navaśakti** (S) (M) 1. with 9 faculties. 3. another name for Viṣṇu and Śiva.

**Navasara** (S) (M) a pearl ornament.

**Navateja** (S) (M) new energy.

**Navatidhanuṣa** (S) (M) 1. with 90 bows. 3. an ancestor of Gautama Buddha.

**Navavrata** (S) (M) 1. new duties. 2. taking up new duties.

**Navendra** (S) (M) 1. the new Indra. 2. the young Indra.

**Navikā** (S) (F) new; fresh; young.

**Navīna** (S) (M) new; novel.

**Navīnā** (S) (F) new; fresh; young.

**Navīnaćandra** (S) (M) new moon.

**Naviṣṭha** (S) (M) newest; youngest.

**Naviṣṭhi** (S) (F) 1. song of praise. 2. a hymn.

**Navīyā** (S) (F) new; a young.

**Navodita** (S) (M) 1. newly risen. 2. new born. 3. another name for the sun.

**Navya** (S) (M) 1. worth praising. 2. laudable.

**Naya** (S) (M) 1. wisdom; doctrine. 2. conduct; behaviour; good; management; prudence; maxim. 3. a son of Dharma and Kriyā (*Purāṇas*); a son of the 13th Manu (*H. Purāṇa*)

**Nayaćakṣuṣ** (S) (M) the eye of prudence.

**Nayajā** (S) (F) daughter of wisdom.

**Nāyaka** (S) (M) 1. leader. 2. lord; principal; the central gem of a necklace. 3. another name for Gautama Buddha.

**Nayanā** (S) (F) 1. of eye. 2. the pupil of the eye.

**Nayana** (S) (M) leading; directing; an eye; prudent conduct; polity.

**Nayanādhyakṣa** (S) (M) lord of the eye.

**Nayanadīpa** (S) (M) light of the eye.

**Nayanaprīti** (S) (F) delighting the eye.

**Nayanatārā** (S) (F) 1. star of one's eye. 2. beloved; very dear to one.

**Nayanotsava** (S) (M) 1. festival to the eye. 2. a lovely sight; a lamp.

**Nayat** (S) (M) leading; guiding.

**Nayavatī** (S) (F) 1. bearer of prudence. 2. one who is prudent.

**Nayiṣṭha** (S) (M) 1. leading in the best way. 3. a son of Manu Vaivasvata (*V. Purāṇa*)

**Nediṣṭha** (S) (M) 1. nearest. 3. a son of Manu Vaivasvata (*V. Purāṇa*)

**Nehā** (S) (F) 1. loving. 2. affectionate.

**Neka** (S) (M) good; virtuous.

**Nekaćandra** (S) (M) 1. the moon of virtuosity. 2. a highly virtuous person.

**Nekarāma** (H) (M) the gentle lord.

**Nemaćandra** (S) (M) half moon.

**Nemi** (S) (M) 1. the felly of a wheel; edge; rim. 2. with many edges; a thunderbolt. 3. the 22nd Arhat of the present Utsarpiṇī (*J.S. Koṣa*); the real name of Daśaratha (*V. Rāmāyaṇa*); a ćakravartin; Chariot tree (*Ougenia oojeninensis*)

**Nemićakra** (S) (M) 1. felly of the wheel. 3. a prince who was a descendant of Parīkṣit and the ruler of Hastināpura (*Bhā. Purāṇa*)

**Neminātha** (S) (M) 1. lord of the thunderbolt. 3. the 22nd Tirathaṅkara whose emblem is a conchshell (*J.S. Koṣa*)

**Netṛ** (S) (M) 1. leader. 2. leading; guiding; bringer; offerer; leader of an army; hero of a drama. 3. another name for Viṣṇu.

**Netra** (S) (M) 1. eye. 2. leader; guide. 3. a son of Dharma and the father of Kuntī (*Bhā. Purāṇa*); a son of Sumati (*M. Purāṇa*)

**Netrakoṣa** (S) (M) 1. treasure of the eye. 2. the eyeball; the bud of a flower.

**Netramatī** (S) (F) 1. having eyes. 2. observant; with discriminatory powers; wise. 3. a south Indian river.

**Netrāmuṣa** (S) (M) 1. capturing the eye. 2. beautiful; unusual.

**Netrayoni** (S) (M) 1. of the eye. 3. the moon because it was produced from the eye of Atri.

**Netravatī** (S) (F) 1. having eyes. 2. observant; with discriminatory powers; wise. 3. another name for Lakṣmī.

**Niagha** (S) (M) 1. sinless. 2. flawless; virtuous; divine.

**Nibāraṇa** (S) (M) removal.

**Nibhā** (S) (F) resembling; like; similar.

**Nibhṛta** (S) (M) 1. firm. 2. immovable; fixed; quiet; modest; mild; gentle.

**Niboddhri** (S) (F) knowing; wise.

**Nićandra** (S) (M) 1. leading moon. 2. foremost among the moons; a moon like leader. 3. a rākṣasa (*M. Bh.*)

**Nićāya** (S) (M) to honour; worship; observe; perceive.

**Nićikā** (S) (F) 1. consisting of parts. 2. consists of all parts; constitutes a whole; perfect; an excellent cow.

**Nīćitā** (S) (F) 1. covered; full of; flowing down. 3. a holy river of ancient India (*M. Bh.*); another name for the Gaṅgā.

**Nićūla** (S) (M) 1. overcoat; the tree *Barringtonia acutangula*; Chairbottom cane (*Calamus rotang*). 3. a poet and contemporary of Kālidāsa (*K. Granthāvali*)

**Nidāgha** (S) (M) 1. scorching heat. 2. summer. 3. a sage and son of Pulastya (*V. Purāṇa*)

**Nidarśin** (S) (M) seeing; pleasing; familiar.

**Niddhā** (S) (F) 1. having a treasure; determined. 2. giving; endeavouring.

**Nidhāna** (S) (M) abode of treasure.

**Nidhinātha** (S) (M) 1. guardian of treasure. 3. another name for Kubera.

**Nidhipa** (S) (M) 1. lord of treasure. 3. another name for Kubera.

**Nidhipati** (S) (M) 1. master of treasure. 3. another name for Kubera.

**Nidhiprabhu** (S) (M) 1. lord of treasure. 3. another name for Kubera.

**Nidhiśvara** (S) (M) 1. god of treasure. 3. another name for Kubera.

**Nīdhra** (S) (M) 1. the circumference of a wheel. 3. another name for the moon; the lunar mansion Revatī.

**Nidhrti** (S) (M) 1. established; appointed. 3. a son of Vṛṣni (*Agni Purāṇa*)

**Nidhruva** (S) (M) 1. constant. 2. persevering; faithful. 3. a sage of the Kaśyapa dynasty, the son of sage Vatsāra, the husband of Sumedhas, the father of Kuṇḍapāyin and part author of *Ṛg Veda* (ix)

**Nidhyāna** (S) (F) intuition; sight.

**Nidhyāti** (S) (F) meditation; reflection.

**Nidī** (S) (F) to shine upon; to bestow.

**Nidrālu** (S) (M) 1. sleepy; drowsy. 3. another name for Viṣṇu.

**Nighna** (S) (M) 1. docile; obedient. 3. a king of Ayodhyā, the son of Anāraṇya and the father of Anamitra and Raghuttama (*P. Purāṇa*)

**Nigu** (S) (M) pleasing; charming.

**Nihāl** (S) (M) 1. satisfied. 2. contented; happy.

**Nīhāra** (S) (M) 1. mist. 2. fog; dew.

**Nīhārarañjana** (S) (M) 1. delighting in dew. 3. another name for the moon.

**Nīhārikā** (S) (F) 1. misty. 3. the Milky Way.

**Nikāma** (S) (M) 1. desire; wish; pleasure. 3. an agni (*Ṛg Veda*)

**Nikara** (S) (M) 1. collection. 2. mass; gift; treasure; the best of anything. 3. a treasure of Kubera (*M. Bh.*)

**Nikaṣa** (S) (M) touchstone.

**Nikaṣā** (S) (M) 1. tried on a touchstone. 2. the streak of gold made on the touchstone. 3. the mother of Rāvaṇa (*Rāmāyaṇa*)

**Nīkāśa** (S) (M) appearance; look; mein.

**Nikāśa** (S) (M) horizon.

**Nikaṣāya** (S) (M) to serve as a touchstone.

**Nikharvata** (S) (M) 1. possessing treasure. 3. a rākṣasa in Rāvaṇa's camp (*V. Rāmāyaṇa*)

**Nikhila** (S) (M) complete; all; whole; entire.

**Nikṛti** (S) (F) 1. baseness; dishonesty; wickedness. 3. one of the 8 vasus (*H. Purāṇa*); a daughter of Adharma and Lobha (*M. Bh.*)

**Nikṣa** (S) (M) kiss.

**Nikṣubhā** (S) (F) 1. not excitable. 3. an apsarā consort of Sūrya and mother of men who married into the Bhoja family (*Bh. Purāṇa*)

**Nikumbha** (S) (M) 1. pot like. 2. resembles a pot. 3. a dānava of the Hiraṇyakaśipu dynasty and father of Sunda and Upasunda (*M. Bh.*); the son of Haryaśva and father of Saṁhatāśva (*H. Purāṇa*); a son of Kumbhakarṇa and Vajramālā (*V. Rāmāyaṇa*); an attendant of Śiva (*H. Purāṇa*); a viśvādeva (*A. Koṣa*); a warrior on the side of the Kauravas (*M. Bh.*); a form of Gaṇapati (*A. Koṣa*)

**Nikumbhila** (S) (M) 1. a place where oblations are offered. 3. a form of Bhadrakālī (*V. Rāmāyaṇa*)

**Nikunja** (S) (M) 1. an abode; a bush. 2. the abode of love; beautiful; enchanting; hidden in a bush; secretive; mysterious; enchanting.

**Nīlā** (S) (F) 1. blue; the Indigo plant (*Indigofera tinctoria*). 3. a daughter of Kaśyapa and Keśinī (*Br. Purāṇa*); a Gopikā who was a friend of Kṛṣṇa.

**Nīla** (S) (M) 1. dark blue; indigo; sapphire; the Ceylon Hill Mynah (*Gracula ptilogenys*); the Indian Fig tree (*Ficus indica*). 3. one of the 9 treasures of Kubera; a prince of Mahiṣmatī; a son of Yadu (*H. Purāṇa*); a son of Ajamīdha; a monkey chief attending on Rāma said to be the son of Agni (*M. Bh.*); a serpent of the family of Kaśyapa and Kadru (*M. Bh.*); a king of the Hehaya dynasty who was a partial rebirth of the asura Krodhavaśa and who fought on the side of the Kauravas (*M. Bh.*); the king of Anūpadeśa who fought on the Pāṇḍava side (*M. Bh.*); a mountain.

**Nīlābha** (S) (M) 1. of bluish hue. 3. another name for moon.

**Nīlābja** (S) (M) Blue Lotus (*Nymphaea stellata*)

**Nīlaćandra** (S) (M) blue moon.

**Nīlaććhada** (S) (M) 1. blue winged. 3. another name for Garuḍa.

**Nīlāda** (S) (M) 1. bestower of blue; bestower of water. 2. cloud. 3. a yakṣa.

**Nīladaṇḍa** (S) (M) 1. with a dark blue staff. 3. one of the 10 Buddhist gods of anger.

**Nīladhvaja** (S) (M) 1. blue bannered. 2. with a blue banner. 3. a prince of Mahiṣmatī.

**Nīlādri** (S) (M) blue peak.

**Nīlagala** (S) (M) 1. blue necked. 3. another name for Śiva.

**Nīlagandhikā** (S) (F) the blue ruby.

**Nīlagaṅgā** (S) (F) 1. blue river. 3. a river with pure blue water and considered as pious as Gaṅgā.

**Nīlagrīva** (S) (M) 1. blue necked. 3. another name for Śiva.

**Nīlaja** (S) (M) 1. produced in the blue mountains. 2. blue steel.

**Nīlakamala** (S) (M) Blue Water lily (*Nympaea stellata*)

**Nīlakaṇṭha** (S) (M) 1. blue necked; a peacock; the Indian Roller (*Coracias* *benghalensis*). 3. another name for Śiva.

**Nīlākṣā** (S) (F) blue eyed.

**Nīlākṣa** (S) (M) blue eyed.

**Nīlakuntalā** (S) (F) 1. blue earrings; with blue earrings; with a blue lock of hair. 3. a friend of Durgā.

**Nīlalohita** (S) (M) 1. red and blue. 3. another name for Śiva and Kārttikeya.

**Nīlama** (S) (M) of dark blue colour; emerald; sapphire; indigo; blue topaz.

**Nīlamādhava** (S) (M) blue Kṛṣṇa.

**Nīlamaṇi** (S) (F) blue gem; sapphire.

**Nīlāmbara** (S) (M) 1. dressed in blue. 3. another name for the planet Saturn and Balarāma.

**Nīlanīraja** (S) (F) Blue Water lily (*Nymphaea alba*)

**Nīlāñjanā** (S) (F) antimony; lightning.

**Nīlāñjasā** (S) (F) 1. blue hued lightning. 3. an apsarā.

**Nīlapadma** (S) (M) Blue Lotus (*Nymphaea stellata*) or Blue Water lily (*Nymphaea alba*)

**Nīlapakṣman** (S) (M) with black eyelashes.

**Nīlaratna** (S) (M) 1. blue gem. 2. sapphire.

**Nīlāruṇa** (S) (M) the first light of dawn.

**Nīlāśoka** (S) (M) the blue blossomed Aśoka tree.

**Nīlavajra** (S) (M) 1. with a blue thunderbolt. 3. an attendant of Śiva (*H. Purāṇa*)

**Nīlavastrā** (S) (F) 1. blue clad. 3. another name for Durgā.

**Nīlavastra** (S) (M) 1. blue clad. 3. another name for Balarāma.

**Nilaya** (S) (M) place of refuge.

**Nīlī** (S) (F) 1. Indigo (*Indigofera tinctoria*); antimony. 3. a goddess; the 2nd wife of King Ajamīdha and the mother of Duṣyanta and Parameṣṭhī (*M. Bh.*); a rāgiṇī; a river (*M. Bh.*)

**Nīlībha** (S) (M) 1. with a blue hue. 2. moon; cloud; bee.

**Nīlīmā** (S) (F) blue.

**Nilimpa** (S) (M) 1. to anoint; to become invisible; a yakṣa. 3. a class of supernatural beings; a troop of maruts (*T. Āranyaka*)

**Nilimpikā** (S) (F) little cow.

**Nīlinī** (S) (F) 1. the Indigo plant (*Indigofera tinctoria*); a type of Convulvulus with blue blossoms. 3. a wife of Śunaśśepa and mother of Śānti (*A. Purāṇā*)

**Nīloda** (S) (M) 1. with blue water. 2. river.

**Nīlopala** (S) (M) sapphire.

**Nīlotpala** (S) (M) Blue Lotus (*Nymphaea stellata*)

**Nīluppala** (S) (M) 1. blue gem. 2. Lapiz lazuli.

**Nimā** (S) (F) 1. to measure to adjust. 3. the mother of Kabir.

**Nimala** (S) (M) spotless; clean; pure; bright.

**Nīmāy** (S) (M) 1. adjusted; ascetic. 3. the childhood name of sage Ćaitanya.

**Nimbū** (S) (M) lemon; the Common Lime (*Citrus acida*)

**Nimeṣa** (S) (M) 1. moment; eye wink. 3. a son of Garuḍa (*M. Bh.*)

**Nimeya** (S) (M) 1. to be measured; measurable. 2. one whose character is known.

**Nimī** (S) (M) 1. the winking of an eye. 2. a moment. 3. a son of sage Dattātreya (*M. Bh.*); a son of Ikṣvāku (*Bh. Purāṇa*); the 21st Jaina Arhat of the present Avasarpinī (*J.S. Koṣa*); son of Bhajamāna (*V. Purāṇa*); a son of Daṇḍapāṇi (*Bh. Purāṇa*); a king of Vidarbha whose daughter married sage Agastya (*M. Bh.*); a dānava (*H. Purāṇa*)

**Nimiṣā** (S) (F) the twinkling of an eye.

**Nimiṣa** (S) (M) 1. twinkling of an eye. 3. a son of Garuḍa (*M. Bh.*); another name for Viṣṇu.

**Nimīśvara** (S) (M) 1. lord of the moment. 3. the 16th Arhat of the past Utsarpinī (*J.S. Koṣa*)

**Nimita** (S) (M) fixed; erected; raised.

**Nimitta** (S) (M) token; omen; mark; sign; cause.

**Nimittaka** (S) (M) kissing; a kiss.

**Nimloćā** (S) (F) 1. the setting of the sun. 3. an apsarā (*K. Sāgara*)

**Nimrući** (S) (M) 1. sunset. 3. a king of the Yādava dynasty who was the son of Bhoja and the father of Kinkaṇa and Vṛṣṇi.

**Nimruktī** (S) (F) sunset.

**Nīnā** (S) (F) ornamented; slender.

**Nināda** (S) (M) gentle murmur; humming; sound.

**Ninādita** (S) (M) full of sound; resonant.

**Niṅga** (S) (M) knower of secrets; a mark; a symbol; the Śivaliṅga (*Ś. Purāṇa*)

**Ninī** (S) (F) to offer as sacrifice; to accomplish.

**Nipā** (S) (F) to guard; to watch over.

**Nīpa** (S) (M) **1.** situated; low; deep. **3.** a Puru king who was the husband of Kirtimat (*M. Bh.*); a son of Kṛtin and father of Ugrāyudha (*Bh. Purāṇa*)

**Nipāka** (S) (M) intelligent; wise; chief.

**Nīpātithi** (S) (M) **1.** arriving at the foot of the mountains. **3.** a descendant of Kaṇva and the author of *Ṛg Veda* (viii)

**Nipuṇa** (S) (M) adept; proficient; skilful; kindly; complete; perfect; clever; adroit; sharp; efficient.

**Nīrā** (S) (F) consisting of water; juice; liquor.

**Nirabhilāṣa** (S) (M) without any desire; above all desires.

**Nirabhimāna** (S) (M) without pride; free from pride.

**Nirabhra** (S) (M) free from clouds.

**Nīrada** (S) (M) **1.** water giver. **2.** cloud.

**Niradāna** (S) (M) **1.** accepting; missing. **3.** a Buddha (*B. Literature*)

**Nīradhauta** (S) (M) washed with water; polished; purified; bright; clean.

**Nirādhi** (S) (M) free from anxiety.

**Nīradindu** (S) (M) clouded moon.

**Nirāga** (S) (M) free from passion.

**Niragha** (S) (M) **1.** free from sins. **2.** innocent; sinless.

**Nīrāj** (S) (M) to illuminate; irradiate.

**Nīrajā** (S) (F) **1.** water born. **2.** water lily; pearl.

**Niraja** (S) (M) **1.** free from dust; free from passion. **3.** another name for Śiva.

**Nīrājākṣi** (S) (F) **1.** lotus eyed. **2.** beautiful.

**Nīrājana** (S) (M) **1.** offering of light. **2.** act of offering light to the deity.

**Nīrājitā** (S) (F) **1.** illuminated. **2.** shone upon consecrated.

**Nirālā** (S) (M) unique.

**Nirāmayā** (S) (M) **1.** free from illness. **2.** healthy; wholesome; pure. **3.** an ancient river (*M. Bh.*)

**Nirāmiṣa** (S) (M) free from convetuousness.

**Niramitra** (S) (M) **1.** free from enemies. **3.** a son of Nakula and Kareṇumatī (*M. Bh.*); a son of the king of Trigarta (*M. Bh.*); a son of Ayutāyuṣ (*M. Bh.*); a sage considered as Śiva's son (*M. Bh.*)

**Nirañjana** (S) (M) **1.** without collyrium; without a blackspot. **2.** spotless; pure; unpainted; devoid of passion. **3.** an attendant of Śiva; another name for Śiva.

**Nirañjanā** (S) (F) **1.** spotless. **2.** pure; the day of full moon. **3.** another name for Durgā.

**Nirāntaka** (S) (M) free from end; free from all that brings the end; free from fear and pain; another name for Śiva.

**Nirantara** (S) (M) without any gap; perpertual.

**Nirāpada** (S) (M) without difficulties.

**Nirapāya** (S) (M) imperishable.

**Nirargala** (S) (M) unimpeded; free, irresisted.

**Nirasa** (S) (M) without anger.

**Nirāśanka** (S) (M) without any doubt; free from any doubt; fearless.

**Nirata** (S) (M) engrossed; absorbed; pleased; satisfied.

**Niratyaya** (S) (M) secure; free from danger.

**Nīrava** (S) (M) free from sound; quiet; silent; still.

**Niravadya** (S) (M) flawlessness; excellence.

**Niravaśeṣa** (S) (M) **1.** without a remainder. **2.** whole; complete.

**Niravinda** (S) (M) **1.** without shine; not glowing; dull. **2.** smoky; dusky. **3.** a mountain (*M. Bh.*)

**Niravyalīka** (S) (M) not causing pain; harmless; sincere.

**Niraya** (S) (M) hell personified as a son of Bhaya and Mṛtyu (*Bh. Purāṇa*)

**Nirbha** (S) (F) to shining forth; appearance; progress.

**Nirbhāsitā** (S) (F) illumined.

**Nirbhaya** (S) (M) **1.** fearless. **3.** a son of the 13th Manu (*H. Purāṇa*)

**Nirbhī** (S) (M) fearless.

**Nirbhīka** (S) (M) fearless.

**Nireka** (S) (M) without an equal; superior; pre-eminent.

**Nirgahana** (S) (M) knowing no difficulties.

**Nirguṇḍi** (S) (F) the root of a lotus.

**Nirikṣā** (S) (F) unseen; not seen before; expectation; hope.

**Niriṅga** (S) (M) immovable; not flickering; still.

**Nirjara** (S) (M) young; fresh; not becoming old; immortal; gold; a gold.

**Nirjarī** (S) (F) not becoming old; young; fresh; immortal; ambrosia.

**Nirjaya** (S) (M) conquest; complete victory.

**Nirjetṛ** (S) (M) conqueror.

**Nirjhara** (S) (M) **1.** cascade. **2.** mountain; torrent; waterfall; elephant. **3.** a horse of the sun.

**Nirjita** (S) (M) conquered; subdued; gained; won.

**Nirjvara** (S) (M) healthy.

**Nirlepa** (S) (M) **1.** unsmeared. **2.** stainless; sinless. **3.** another name for Śiva.

**Nirlipta** (S) (M) **1.** undefiled. **3.** another name for Kṛṣṇa.

**Nirlobha** (S) (M) free from greed.

**Nirmada** (S) (M) without intoxication; sober; quiet; humble; modest.

**Nirmala** (S) (M) **1.** not dirty; spotless; clean; pure; bright; shining; sinless. **3.** another name for Skanda.

**Nirmalendu** (S) (M) full moon; bright moon.

**Nirmama** (S) (M) **1.** unselfish. **3.** the 25th Arhat of the future utsarpinī; another name for Śiva.

**Nirmantu** (S) (M) faultless; innocent.

**Nirmanyu** (S) (M) free from anger.

**Nirmatsara** (S) (M) without envy; unselfish.

**Nirmārṣṭi** (S) (F) **1.** washing; ablution. **3.** a wife of Dusśaha (*Ma. Purāṇa*)

**Nirmita** (S) (M) created; built; fashioned.

**Nirmoha** (S) (M) **1.** free from illusion. **3.** a son of the 5th Manu (*H. Purāṇa*); a ṛṣi of the 13th Manvantara; another name for Śiva (*P. Purāṇa*)

**Nirmoka** (S) (M) **1.** setting free. **2.** sky. **3.** a son of the 8th Manu (*Bh. Purāṇa*); a ṛṣi under the 13th Manu (*Bh. Puraoa*)

**Nirmokṣa** (S) (M) liberation.

**Nirmuta** (S) (M) **1.** ever rising; ever growing. **2.** a tree; the sun.

**Nirodha** (S) (M) restraint; constraint; control.

**Niroṣa** (S) (M) without anger.

**Nirṛti** (S) (F) **1.** calamity; evil; destruction. **3.** the wife of Adharma and mother of Bhaya, Mahābhaya and Antaka (*M. Bh.*)

**Nirṛti** (S) (M) **1.** death; destruction. **3.** a deva who is the guardian of the southwestern quarter and the son of Śthāṇu (*A. Purāṇa*); a rudra (*M. Bh.*); one of the 8 vasus (*H. Purāṇa*)

**Niruja** (S) (M) healthy; wholesome.

**Nīrulatā** (S) (M) a water vine; a vine that grows in water.

**Nirunmāda** (S) (M) tree from pride; humble.

**Nīrūpa** (S) (M) formless; air; wind; ether; a god.

**Nirupadhi** (S) (M) guileless; honest; secure.

**Nirupama** (S) (M) unparalled; fearless; unequalled; incomparable.

**Nirūpita** (S) (M) seen; considered; appointed; elected; chosen.

**Nīruppala** (S) (M) **1.** water stone; a stone as clear as water. **2.** a crystal.

**Nirutsuka** (S) (M) **1.** without curiosity; not curious; tranquil. **3.** a son of Manu Raivata; a ṛṣi of the 13th Manvantara (*H. Purāṇa*)

**Niruttara** (S) (M) without an answer; having no superior.

**Nīruvindhyā** (S) (F) **1.** water from the Vindhya mountain. **3.** a river.

**Nirvā** (S) (F) blowing like wind; refreshing; exhilarating.

**Nirvala** (S) (M) **1.** guide less; sacred; pious. **2.** the sacred Barna tree.

**Nirvāṇī** (S) (F) **1.** goddess of bliss. **3.** a deity who executes the commands of the 16th Arhat of the present Avasarpinī (*J.S. Koṣa*)

**Nirvāṇin** (S) (M) **1.** one who has attained nirvāṇa or final emancipation. **3.** the 2nd Arhat of the past Utsarpinī (*J.S. Koṣa*)

**Nirvara** (S) (M) without a superior; unique; excellent.

**Nirvāta** (S) (M) sheltered; calm.

**Nirvighna** (S) (M) unobstructed.

**Nirvikāra** (S) (M) unchangeable.

**Nirviśaṅka** (S) (M) fearless; doubtless.

**Nirvṛta** (S) (M) emancipated; contented; satisfied; happy; tranquil; at rest.

**Nirvṛti** (S) (M) 1. complete happiness; bliss; emancipation. 3. a son of Vṛṣṇi.

**Nirvyagra** (S) (M) unconfused; calm.

**Nirvyāja** (S) (M) free from deceit; pure.

**Nirvyaṅga** (S) (M) without any deformity.

**Nirvyūha** (S) (M) without formation; turret, a crest ornament.

**Niryūhā** (S) (F) prominence; chaplet; crest; pinnacle; head.

**Niśā** (S) (F) 1. night; vision; dream. 3. a wife of Agni Bhānu (*M. Bh.*)

**Niśācarapati** (S) (M) 1. lord of the wanderer of the night. 2. lord of the moon. 3. another name for Śiva.

**Niṣāda** (S) (M) 1. to sit. 2. a low caste; the last note of the musical gamut. 3. a king said to have sprung from the thigh of Vena.

**Niṣādanareśa** (S) (M) 1. king of the Niṣādas or forest hunters. 3. a king who was an incarnation of the daityas Kālakeya and Krodhahanta (*M. Bh.*); another name for Nala.

**Niṣadha** (S) (M) 1. hunter. 2. place where hunting is done. 3. a mountain range north of the Himālaya; the grandson of Kuśa and son of Aditi; a king of Bharata's dynasty who was the son of Janamejaya (*M. Bh.*)

**Niṣadhāśva** (S) (M) 1. one with mountain horses. 3. a son of Kuru (*Bh. Purāṇa*)

**Niśādi** (S) (F) twilight.

**Niśāhāsa** (S) (M) 1. smiling in the night. 2. the White Water Lily flower (*Nymphaea alba*)

**Niśājala** (S) (F) 1. water of the night. 2. dew.

**Niśākānta** (S) (M) 1. beloved of night. 3. another name for the moon (*K. Sāgara*)

**Niśākara** (S) (M) 1. one who makes the night. 3. a ṛṣi who foretold the future for Sampāti (*V. Rāmāyaṇa*); another name for the moon.

**Niśalya** (S) (M) free from pain; happy; painless; one who doesn't cause pain to others.

**Nisamā** (S) (F) matchless.

**Niśāmaṇi** (S) (M) 1. jewel of night. 3. another name for the moon.

**Niśamanya** (S) (M) uncommon; extraordinary.

**Niśāmukha** (S) (M) 1. the face of the night. 2. twilight.

**Niśānātha** (S) (M) lord of night; another name for the moon.

**Nisaṅga** (S) (M) absence of attachment; moving freely; unselfish.

**Niṣangin** (S) (M) 1. having a sword or quiver. 3. a son of Dhṛtarāṣṭra (*M. Bh.*)

**Niśanka** (S) (M) free from fear or risk.

**Niśankara** (S) (M) 1. creator of night. 3. another name for the moon.

**Niśānta** (S) (M) 1. night close. 2. daybreak; tranquil; calm; quiet.

**Niśāpati** (S) (M) 1. lord of night. 3. another name for the moon.

**Niśāpuṣpa** (S) (F) 1. night flower. 3. the White Water lily (*Nymphaea alba*)

**Niśaṭha** (S) (M) 1. not false. 2. honest. 3. the son of Balarāma and Revatī who became a viśvadeva after his death (*M. Bh.*); a king in the court of Yama (*M. Bh.*)

**Niśatru** (S) (M) free from enemies.

**Niśćalā** (S) (F) 1. immovable; fixed. 3. another name for the earth.

**Niśćala** (S) (M) 1. immovable; fixed; steady; calm. 3. *Desmodium gangeticum*.

**Niśćara** (S) (M) 1. to come forth; appear; rise. 3. a ṛṣi of the 2nd Manvantara (*H. Purāṇa*)

**Niśćint** (S) (M) without anxiety, worry, care; carefree.

**Niśćinta** (S) (M) free from anxiety, worry and care.

**Nisćirā** (S) (F) 1. coming forth; appearing. 3. a river glorified in the Purāṇas.

**Niśćyavana** (S) (M) 1. imperishable. 2. fire. 3. a ṛṣi of the 2nd Manvantara; (*H. Purāṇa*) the 2nd son of Bṛhaspati (*M. Bh.*); a ṛṣi of the 2nd Manvantara (*H. Purāṇa*)

**Niśeṣa** (S) (M) 1. lord of night. 2. another name for the moon.

**Niśī** (S) (F) exciting; strengthening.

**Nisidh** (S) (F) gift; oblation.

**Nisiman** (S) (M) unbounded; infinite; grand.

**Niśītā** (S) (F) night.

**Nisita** (S) (M) sharpened; sharp; excited; eager; prepared; iron; steel.

**Niśītha** (S) (M) **1.** born of night; one of the 3 sons of Doshā or night (*Bh. Purāṇa*). **3.** a king of Dhruva's dynasty who was the son of Puspārṇa and Prabhā (*Bhāgavata*)

**Niṣkā** (S) (F) **1.** undeceitful; pure; honest. **2.** a golden ornament for the neck; a golden vessel. **3.** 6th of a pound of gold (*M. Smṛti*)

**Niṣkaitava** (S) (M) undeceitful; honest; pure.

**Niṣkaivalya** (S) (M) pure; emancipation; absolute; release.

**Niṣkalaṅka** (S) (M) **1.** flawless; immaculate. **3.** another name for Śiva.

**Niṣkāma** (S) (M) selfless.

**Niṣkāmuka** (S) (M) free from worldly desires.

**Niṣkaṇṭaka** (S) (M) **1.** free from thorns; unhurt; secure. **3.** another name for Śiva.

**Niṣkarūṣa** (S) (M) free from dirt.

**Niṣkaṣāya** (S) (M) **1.** free from dirt. **3.** the 13th Arhat of the future Utsarpiṇī.

**Niṣkleśa** (S) (M) free from pain; free from quarrel.

**Niṣkṛti** (S) (M) **1.** restoration; atonement; complete development; cure. **3.** an agni who was the son of Bṛhaspati (*M. Bh.*)

**Niṣkupita** (S) (M) **1.** without anger. **3.** a marut (*V. Purāṇa*)

**Niṣkumbha** (S) (M) **1.** *Croton polyandrum*. **2.** a visvādeva.

**Niṣkuṭikā** (S) (F) **1.** a pleasure grove near a house. **3.** a Mātṛ attending Skanda (*Sk. Purāṇa*)

**Niṣṇā** (S) (F) clever; skilful.

**Niśoka** (S) (M) free from sorrow.

**Niṣpāra** (S) (M) boundless; unlimited.

**Niṣpatti** (S) (M) to originate from; to issue from.

**Niṣpraćāra** (S) (M) not spread; concentrated.

**Niṣprakampa** (S) (M) **1.** without quiver. **2.** immovable. **3.** a ṛṣi of the 13th Manvantara (*H. Purāṇa*)

**Niṣpratīpa** (S) (M) unopposed.

**Niṣpulāka** (S) (M) **1.** free from chaff. **2.** tree of all impurity; pure. **3.** the 14th Arhat of the future Utsarpinī (*J.S. Koṣa*)

**Niśreṇī** (S) (M) **1.** ladder. **3.** the wild date tree (*Phoenix sylvestris*)

**Niśreyasa** (S) (M) **1.** having no better. **2.** best; ultimate bliss. **3.** another name for Śiva.

**Nissangha** (S) (M) without attachment; absolute concentration; detached from worldly things.

**Niṣṭhā** (S) (F) firmness; faith; determination; loyalty; fidelity; devotion.

**Niṣṭhānaka** (S) (M) **1.** speaking loud; roar. **3.** a nāga who was the son of Kaśyapa and Kadru (*M. Bh.*)

**Niṣṭhurika** (S) (M) **1.** cruel; severe; hard; rough. **3.** a nāga who was born in the Kaśyapa dynasty (*M. Bh.*)

**Niṣṭigrī** (S) (F) **1.** thundering and raining. **3.** Indra's mother (*K. Sāgāra*)

**Nistula** (S) (M) matchless; incomparable.

**Nistuṣa** (S) (M) free from chaff; pure.

**Niśumbha** (S) (M) **1.** killing; slaughter. **3.** an asura who was the son of Kaśyapa and Diti and the brother of Śumbha (*H. Purāṇa*)

**Nisūna** (S) (M) **1.** son of the bright ones. **3.** an asura killed by Kṛṣṇa (*M. Bh.*)

**Nisvana** (S) (M) **1.** sound; voice; soundless; noiseless. **3.** another name for Agni.

**Nītā** (S) (F) led; guided; well behaved; modest; correct.

**Nitalākṣa** (S) (M) **1.** with an eye in the forehead. **3.** another name for Śiva.

**Nitambhū** (S) (M) **1.** carrying the earth; remover of the darkness of earth; suffocating the earth. **3.** a great sage (*M. Bh.*)

**Nitambinī** (S) (F) with beautiful hips.

**Nīthā** (S) (F) carried; red; way; stratagem.

**Nītha** (S) (M) **1.** leader. **3.** a king of the Vṛṣṇi dynasty (*M. Bh.*)

**Nīti** (S) (M) policy; moral code; guidance; management; conduct; prudence.

**Nītigotra** (S) (M) **1.** knower of policy; knower of moral code. **2.** managing a dynasty; politician; preceptor. **3.** a king of the Bhṛgu dynasty (*Bhāgavata*)

**Nītikā** (S) (F) moral person; a guide; a leader.

**Nītila** (S) (M) bearer of moral code; the

forehead.
**Nitilākṣa** (S) (M) **1.** with an eye of Nīti. **3.** Śiva with the 3rd eye.
**Nītin** (S) (M) having knowledge of law; moralist; policy maker.
**Nītīndra** (S) (M) lord of policy; king.
**Nityā** (S) (F) **1.** eternal. **2.** constant and indispensable. **3.** a tāntric Śakti; another name for Durgā and Manasā.
**Nitya** (S) (M) **1.** perpetual; eternal; invariable. **2.** sea; ocean.
**Nityagati** (S) (M) **1.** moving constantly. **2.** wind. **3.** another name for Vāyu.
**Nityamaya** (S) (M) consisting of eternity; eternal.
**Nityānanda** (S) (M) eternal happiness.
**Nityanātha** (S) (M) **1.** eternal lord. **3.** another name for Śiva.
**Nityapāda** (S) (M) lord of Nityā.
**Nityapriya** (S) (M) **1.** eternally pleasing. **3.** another name for Śiva.
**Nityasiddha** (S) (M) ever perfect.
**Nityaśrī** (S) (F) with eternal beauty.
**Nityasundarī** (S) (F) eternally beautiful.
**Nityayauvanā** (S) (F) **1.** ever youthful. **3.** another name for Draupadī.
**Nityayūj** (S) (M) ever attached; with the mind always concentrated.
**Nityayukta** (S) (M) **1.** always active; always energetic. **3.** a Bodhisattva.
**Nīva** (S) (F) to become fat.
**Nivaha** (S) (M) **1.** bringing; multitude; heap; killing. **3.** one of the 7 winds and one of the 7 tongues of fire.
**Nivān** (S) (M) **1.** reigned; bound. **2.** reined horse. **3.** one of the 10 horses of the moon.
**Nivāta** (S) (M) **1.** unhurt; compact; safe; secure. **2.** sheltered from the wind; an impenetrable coat of mail.
**Nivātakavaća** (S) (M) **1.** with impenetrable armour. **3.** the grandson of Hiraṇyakaśipu (*Bhā. Purāṇa*)
**Nivatha** (S) (M) calm; sheltered; safe.
**Nivedana** (S) (M) announcement; dedication; offering.
**Nivedin** (S) (M) **1.** requesting; announcing; proclaiming; offering; delivering. **3.** another name for Śiva.
**Niveditā** (S) (F) offered to god.
**Nivida** (S) (M) instruction; information; invocation.
**Nivīta** (S) (M) **1.** adorned with. **3.** the sacred thread worn as a garland round Brahmā's neck.
**Nivrānśu** (S) (M) rays of the moon.
**Niyama** (S) (M) fasten; restrain; grant; govern; control; determine.
**Niyantraṇa** (S) (M) control; restraint; definition.
**Niyatāyu** (S) (M) **1.** with a limited age. **3.** the son of Śrutāyu (*M. Bh.*)
**Niyati** (S) (F) **1.** fate; destiny; restraint; religious duty. **3.** the daughter of Meru and wife of Vidhātā, she was the mother of Prāṇa, and became a goddess after her death, she sits at Brahmā's court (*M. Bh.*); another name for Durgā (*D. Purāṇa*)
**Niyudha** (S) (M) warrior.
**Niyutsā** (S) (F) **1.** warrior. **3.** the wife of Praṣṭāva and mother of Vibhu (*M. Bh.*)
**Nodhas** (S) (M) **1.** seer of 9 fold devotion. **3.** a ṛṣi of the *Ṛg Veda* (*Ṛg Veda*)
**Nṛćakṣus** (S) (M) **1.** the eye of men. **3.** a king of the Yayāti dynasty (*M. Bh.*)
**Nṛdeva** (S) (M) king of men.
**Nṛga** (S) (M) **1.** originating from men. **3.** a king of the dynasty of Vaivasvata Manu who was the son of Kṣupa and the younger brother of Ikṣvāku (*M. Bh.*); a grandson of Oghavat; a son of Uśīnara; a son of Manu (*M. Bh.*); the father of Sumati (*M. Bh.*)
**Nṛgaćandra** (S) (M) **1.** moon among men. **3.** the son of Rantinara (*M. Bh.*)
**Nṛgadeva** (S) (M) god among men.
**Nṛgajit** (S) (M) conqueror of men.
**Nṛgamanas** (S) (M) king to men.
**Nṛgamaṇi** (S) (M) jewel among men.
**Nṛgamithuna** (S) (M) **1.** pair of men. **2.** twin. **3.** zodiac sign of Gemini.
**Nṛgapāla** (S) (M) protector of men.
**Nṛgapati** (S) (M) king of men.
**Nṛgaṣada** (S) (M) **1.** dwelling among men.

3. father of Kaṇva.

**Nṛgasinha** (S) (M) 1. lion among men. 3. Viṣṇu and his 4th incarnation (*H. Purāṇa*)

**Nṛgasoma** (S) (M) moon among men.

**Nṛgātama** (S) (M) most manly; strongest among men.

**Nṛgavara** (S) (M) best among men; sovereign; chief.

**Nṛkesarin** (S) (M) 1. lion among men. 3. great men; man-lion; Viṣṇu in his 4th incarnation.

**Nṛpa** (S) (M) protector of men; king.

**Nṛpadīpa** (S) (M) a lamp among kings; a king as radiant and illuminating as the glow of lamp.

**Nṛpamana** (S) (M) saluted by men.

**Nṛpāṅganā** (S) (F) 1. of a king. 2. princess; queen.

**Nṛpañjaya** (S) (M) 1. conqueror of men. 3. a son of Suvīra (*H. Purāṇa*); a son of Medhāvin (*Bh. Purāṇa*)

**Nṛpavallabha** (S) (M) dear to a king.

**Nṛśad** (S) (M) 1. using man as vehicle; hounting on men; worshipped by men. 3. a sage who was the father of Kaṇva (*Ṛg Veda*)

**Nṛsoma** (S) (M) moon among men; illustrious; great.

**Nṛt** (S) (M) truth; the sacred thread round the neck.

**Nṛtu** (S) (M) 1. dancing. 2. lively; active. 3. another name for Indra and the maruts.

**Nṛtyapriyā** (S) (M) 1. fond of dancing. 2. peacock. 3. a Mātṛ attending Skanda (*Sk. Purāṇa*)

**Nu** (S) (M) praise; eulogium; weapon; time.

**Nukrī** (S) (F) the bird, Indian Courser (*Cursorius coromandelicus*)

**Nūpura** (S) (F) 1. ornament for the toes and ankles; anklet. 3. a descendant of Ikṣvāku (*M. Bh.*)

**Nūpurottamā** (S) (F) 1. with the best anklets. 2. best dancer. 3. a kinnarī (*H. Purāṇa*)

**Nūtana** (S) (M) young; fresh; new; curious; strange; modern.

**Nuti** (S) (F) praise; worship; reverence.

**Nyagrodha** (S) (M) 1. growing downward. 2. Banyan tree (*Ficus indica*). 3. a son of Ugrasena who was killed by Balarāma (*Bhā. Purāṇa*); a son of Kṛṣṇa (*Bh. Purāṇa*)

**Nyāma** (S) (M) restraining; controlling.

**Nyāṅku** (S) (M) 1. antelope. 3. a ćakravartin (*M. Bh.*)

**Nyāyāćāryā** (S) (M) teacher of the moral law; teacher of syllogism; the correct.

**Nyāyavid** (S) (M) knowing the law; knowing the logic; logician; attaining truth through syllogism.

**Nyāyikā** (S) (F) logician.

O

**Ob, Obal** (S) (M) 1. phallus. 3. the Śivaliṅga or the male organ which represents Śiva.

**Obaleśa** (S) (M) 1. lord of the liṅga. 3. another name for Śiva.

**Obaleśvara** (S) (M) 1. lord of the liṅga. 3. another name for Śiva.

**Obbana** (Tamil) (M) 1. lord of the liṅga. 3. another name for Śiva.

**Odana** (S) (M) food; boiled rice; grain cooked with milk; cloud.

**Odatī** (S) (F) 1. refreshing. 2. the dawn.

**Ogaṇa** (S) (M) wave; assembled; united.

**Ogha** (S) (M) 1. stream; current; swift; flood. 2. uninterrupted tradition. 3. a musical concert.

**Ogharatha** (S) (M) 1. with a swift chariot. 3. the son of Oghavāna (*M. Bh.*)

**Oghavāna** (S) (M) 1. conqueror of the current. 3. a grandson of King Nṛga and father of Ogharatha and Oghavatī (*M. Bh.*); a warrior who fought on the side of the Kauravas in the Mahābhārata (*M. Bh.*)

**Oghavatī** (S) (F) 1. possessing current. 2. a stream that flows rapidly. 3. daughter of King Oghavāna and wife of Sudarśana the son of Agni; one of the 7 Sarasvatī rivers of the world, Oghavatī was brought to the Kurukṣetra and Bhīṣma lay on his bed of arrows at her banks (*M. Bh.*)

**Oha** (S) (M) vehicle; bringing near; excellence; true knowledge; meditation.

**Ohabrahman** (S) (M) a true Brāhmin; having knowledge; meditating.

**Ohas** (S) (M) vehicle; praise; idea; true notion.

**Oja** (S) (M) to increase; virility; to grow in lustre and vigour.

**Ojal** (S) (M) having splendour; vision.

**Ojas** (S) (M) 1. virility; energy; power; strength; splendour. 2. water; light; appearance. 3. a son of Kṛṣṇa (*Bh. Purāṇa*); a yakṣa (*Bh. Purāṇa*)

**Ojasīn** (S) (M) strong; powerful.

**Ojasvī** (S) (M) (F) brave; bright; splendid.

**Ojasvin** (S) (M) 1. brave; bright; energetic; vigorous; shining; powerful. 3. a son of Manu Bhautya (*V. Purāṇa*)

**Ojasvinī** (S) (F) brave; bright; energetic; vigorous; shining; powerful.

**Ojasyā** (S) (M) possessing virility; strong; powerful.

**Ojāyita** (S) (M) made virile; on whom courage has been bestowed; courageous.

**Ojiṣṭha** (S) (M) 1. residing in virility; best among the powerful. 2. powerful; vigorous; strongest. 3. a sage (*Bhā. Purāṇa*)

**Ojobalā** (S) (F) 1. having power. 3. a deity of the Bodhi tree.

**Ojodā** (S) (M) one who gives strength.

**Ojopati** (S) (M) 1. master of power. 3. a deity of the Bodhi tree.

**Okāb** (H) (M) Tawny Eagle (*Aquila rapax*)

**Okas** (S) (M) house; shelter; refuge.

**Okithak** (S) (M) 1. speaker; preacher. 3. a Brāhman who studies the prayers of the *Sāma Veda* (*S. Veda*)

**Om** (S) (M) (F) creation; development and destruction; essence of life; the sacred syllable which is the seed of all mantras; assent; so be it; the sound is a combination of 'A' which signifies Viṣṇu, 'U' for Śiva and 'M' signifying Brahmā, the sound is called 'Praṇava' (essence of life) or 'Brahman' (ultimate essence)

**Oma** (S) (M) life giving; friend; helper; protector.

**Omalā** (M) (F) bestower of the Om; the sacred word for the earth; bestower of birth, life and death; earth.

**Oman** (S) (M) life giving; protection; favour; friend; protector.

**Omasvata** (S) (M) friendly; favourable.

**Omeśa** (S) (M) lord of the Om.

**Omeśvara** (S) (M) 1. lord of the sacred word. 2. Om. 3. another name for Śiva.

**Omīśā** (S) (F) goddess of the sacred syllable; goddess of birth, life and death.

**Omkāra** (S) (M) 1. the syllable Om. 3. a liṅga.

**Omkārā** (S) (F) 1. the syllable Om; an auspicious beginning. 3. a Buddhist Śakti.

**Omkaranātha** (S) (M) 1. lord of the Om.

3. the deity at Māndhātā; another name for Śiva.

**Ompati** (S) (M) master of the Om.

**Ompatu** (Malayālam) (M) master of the Om; 9.

**Omprakāśa** (S) (M) the light from of Om; the sacred light; the light spread by the sacred syllable Om.

**Omvatī** (S) (F) possessing the power of the Om; sacred.

**Oṇi** (S) (M) 1. protection; shelter. 2. heaven and earth conjoined. 3. a vessel used in distilling Soma (*Ṛg Veda*)

**Opaśa** (S) (M) support; pillar; ornament of the head.

**Oṣadhi** (S) (F) 1. light containing; medicine; herb; medicinal herbs. 3. plants that possess a healing power (*Ṛg Veda*); a tutelary goddess whose shrine is at Uttarakuru (*Ma. Purāṇa*)

**Oṣadhinātha** (S) (M) 1. lord of herbs. 3. another name for the moon.

**Oṣadhipati** (S) (M) 1. lord of herbs. 3. another name for the moon.

P

**Paćata** (S) (M) 1. cooked; boiled. 3. another name for sun, fire and Indra.

**Padāti** (S) (M) 1. pedestrian; foot soldier. 3. a son of Janamejaya (*Bhā. Purāṇa*)

**Padmā** (S) (F) 1. the lotus; hued one. 3. the mother of Munisuvrata; a daughter of Bṛhadratha and wife of Kalki (*V. Purāṇa*); a devī (*D. Purāṇa*); another name for goddess Manasā and Lakṣmī.

**Padma** (S) (M) 1. Lotus (*Nelumbium speciosum*); a thousand billion. 3. the sacred lotus flower said to have arisen from the navel of Viṣṇu, it supports Brahmā and represents creation; one of the 9 treasures of Kubera (*M. Bh.*); the 9th Jaina ćakravartin of Bhārata; one of the 8 serpents worn by Śiva and who is a son of Kaśyapa and Kadru (*M. Bh.*); a king in the court of Yama (*M. Bh.*); a king of Kāśmira; a soldier of Skanda (*M. Bh.*); an attendant of Skanda (*M. Bh.*); a mythical Buddha; an elephant (*Rāmāyaṇa*); a nāga (*M. Bh.*)

**Padmabālā** (S) (F) daughter of the lotus.

**Padmabandhu** (S) (M) 1. friend of the lotus. 3. another name for the sun.

**Padmabhāsa** (S) (M) 1. with the brilliance of the lotus. 3. another name for Viṣṇu.

**Padmabhava** (S) (M) born of the lotus.

**Padmabhū** (S) (M) born of the lotus.

**Padmabhūta** (S) (M) 1. of the lotus. 3. another name for Brahmā.

**Padmadhara** (S) (M) lotus bearer.

**Padmādhīśa** (S) (M) 1. lord of the lotus. 3. another name for Viṣṇu.

**Padmagandha** (S) (M) smelling like a lotus; fragrant.

**Padmagarbha** (S) (M) 1. the calyx of a lotus. 2. one who is born from a lotus; sprung from a lotus. 3. a Buddha (*L. Vistara*); a Bodhisattva; another name for Brahmā, Viṣṇu, Śiva and the sun.

**Padmagṛhā** (S) (F) 1. lotus housed; living in a lotus. 3. another name for Lakṣmī.

**Padmahāsan** (S) (M) 1. lotus smile. 3. another name for Viṣṇu.

**Padmajā** (S) (F) 1. born of a lotus. 3. another name for Lakṣmī.

**Padmaja** (S) (M) 1. born of a lotus. 3. another name for Brahmā.

**Padmakarā** (S) (F) 1. with a lotus in hand. 3. another name for Śrī.

**Padmakara** (S) (M) 1. with a lotus in hand. 3. another name for the sun.

**Padmakesara** (S) (M) filament of a lotus.

**Padmaketana** (S) (M) 1. lotus bannered. 3. a son of Garuḍa (*M. Bh.*)

**Padmākṣa** (S) (M) 1. lotus eyed. 3. the son of Ćandrahāsa and Ćampakamālinī (*A. Koṣa*); another name for Viṣṇu; Himālayan Cherry (*Prunus cerasoides*)

**Padmalānćanā** (S) (F) 1. marked by lotuses. 2. surrounded by lotuses. 3. another name for Lakṣmī, Sarasvatī and Tārā.

**Padmalāñćana** (S) (M) 1. lotus marked; a king. 3. another name for Brahmā, Kubera and the sun.

**Padmālayā** (S) (F) 1. living in a lotus. 3. another name for Lakṣmī.

**Padmālaya** (S) (M) 1. dwelling in a lotus. 3. another name for Brahmā.

**Padmaloćana** (S) (M) lotus eyed.

**Padmamālin** (S) (M) 1. garlanded with a lotus. 3. a rākṣasa (*Rāmāyaṇa*)

**Padmamālinī** (S) (F) 1. lotus garlanded. 3. another name for Lakṣmī.

**Padmamayī** (S) (F) made of lotus flowers.

**Padmamihira** (S) (M) 1. lotus sun. 2. the sun, that makes the lotus bloom; one who delights the nobles. 3. a historian of Kāśmira (*R. Taraṅginī*)

**Padmanā** (S) (F) 1. lotus faced. 3. another name for Lakṣmī and Sarasvatī.

**Padmanābha** (S) (M) 1. lotus navelled. 3. a son of Dhṛtarāṣṭra (*M. Bh.*); the 1st Arhat of the future Utsarpinī; a nāga of Naimiśāraṇya (*M. Bh.*); another name for Viṣṇu.

**Padmanābhi** (S) (M) 1. lotus navelled. 3. another name for Viṣṇu.

**Padmānana** (S) (M) lotus faced.

**Padmanandana** (S) (M) 1. arisen from a lotus. 3. another name for Brahmā.

**Padmanandin** (S) (M) rejoicing in the lotus.

**Padmanetra** (S) (M) 1. lotus eyed. 3. a future Buddha.

**Padmanidhi** (S) (M) 1. abounding in lotuses. 2. a treasure worth a 1000 billion. 3. one of the 9 treasures of Kubera (*Panćatantra*)

**Padmāñjali** (S) (F) an offering of lotuses.

**Padmapāṇi** (S) (M) 1. lotus handed. 3. another name for Brahmā, Viṣṇu and the Bodhisattva Avalokiteśvara.

**Padmaprabhā** (S) (F) 1. with a light of the lotus. 2. lotus coloured. 3. a daughter of Mahādanṣtra (*K. Sāgara*)

**Padmaprabha** (S) (M) 1. with the light of the lotus. 2. lotus coloured; shining like a lotus. 3. the 6th Arhat of the present Avasarpinī (*J.S. Koṣa*); a future Buddha (*L. Vistara*)

**Padmapriyā** (S) (F) 1. one who loves lotuses. 3. another name for Manasā.

**Padmarāga** (S) (M) 1. lotus hued. 2. a ruby.

**Padmaratha** (S) (M) 1. with a lotus chariot. 3. another name for Rāma.

**Padmarati** (S) (F) lover of lotuses.

**Padmaratna** (S) (M) 1. lotus jewelled. 3. a Buddhist patriarch.

**Padmarūpā** (S) (F) 1. with the beauty of a lotus. 3. another name for Lakṣmī.

**Padmasaugandhikā** (S) (F) as fragrant as the lotus; abounding in lotuses.

**Padmaśekhara** (S) (M) 1. lotus crested. 3. a king of the gandharvas (*K. Sāgara*)

**Padmasnuṣā** (S) (F) 1. dwelling in the lotus. 3. another name for Gaṅgā, Lakṣmī and Durgā.

**Padmaśrī** (S) (F) 1. divine lotus; as beautiful as a lotus. 3. a Bodhisattva (*B. Literature*)

**Padmavarṇā** (S) (F) 1. lotus clothed; lotus coloured. 3. another name for Lakṣmī.

**Padmavarṇa** (S) (M) 1. lotus coloured. 3. a son of Yadu (*H. Purāṇa*)

**Padmāvatī** (S) (F) 1. full of lotus flowers. 3. a wife of Aśoka (*Bhā. Purāṇa*); a mother in Skanda's retinue (*M. Bh.*); a Jaina deity (*J.S. Koṣa*); a wife of King Śṛgāla (*H. Purāṇa*); a wife of Yudhiṣṭhira (*R. Taraṅginī*); a wife of Jayadeva; a wife of Virabāhu; a river which is an incarnation of Mahālakṣmī; the wife of Emperor Udayana; a mother in Skanda's train (*M. Bh.*); a daughter of King Satyaketu of Vidarbha who was the wife of Ugrasena and the mother of Kansa (*P. Purāṇa*); the queen of Rajagraha and mother of Jaina Tirathankara Munisuvrata; a Jaina deity; another name for Lakṣmī and Manasā.

**Padmaveśa** (S) (M) 1. dressed in lotus petals. 3. a king of the vidyādharas.

**Padmayoni** (S) (M) 1. lotus born. 3. a Buddha (*L. Vistara*); another name for Brahmā.

**Padmeśa** (S) (M) 1. lord of the lotus. 3. another name for Brahmā and Viṣṇu.

**Padmeśaya** (S) (M) 1. sleeping in a lotus. 3. another name for Viṣṇu.

**Padmin** (S) (M) lotus like; one who plucks the lotus; one who likes the lotus; elephant.

**Padminī** (S) (F) lotus (*Nelumbium speciosum*); an assemblage of lotuses.

**Padminikā** (S) (F) a multitude of lotuses.

**Padminīkantā** (S) (M) 1. beloved of lotuses. 3. another name for the sun.

**Padminiśa** (S) (M) 1. lord of lotuses. 3. another name for the sun.

**Padmodbhavā** (S) (F) 1. sprung from a lotus. 3. another name for Manasā.

**Padmodbhava** (S) (M) 1. sprung from a lotus. 3. another name for Brahmā.

**Padmottara** (S) (M) 1. the best lotus. 2. beyond comparison; the best. 3. a Buddha; wild saffron (*Carthamus tinctorius*)

**Padvāya** (S) (M) leader; guide.

**Pahāḍī** (S) (F) hillock; a rāgiṇī.

**Paila** (S) (M) 1. son of Pīlā. 3. a disciple of Vyāsa; a teacher of the *Ṛg Veda*.

**Paināka** (S) (M) 1. belonging to Pināka. 3. belonging to Rudra-Śiva (*V. Rāmāyaṇa*)

**Paiṭhaka** (S) (M) 1. one who does not leave his seat. 3. an asura killed by Kṛṣṇa (*M. Bh.*)

**Pājas** (S) (M) 1. firmness; vigour; strength; glitter; sheen; brightness. 2. heaven and earth.

**Pajasvati** (S) (F) firm; strong; brilliant.

**Pajrahoṣin** (S) (M) 1. with rich or fat oblations. 2. to whom many oblations are offered; divine. 3. another name for Indra and Agni.

**Pajriya** (S) (M) 1. fat; stout; strong. 3. another name for Kakṣīvat.

**Pāka** (S) (M) **1.** simple; ignorant; young; child. **3.** a daitya slain by Indra (*M. Bh.*)

**Pākadviṣ** (S) (M) **1.** destroyer of Pāka. **3.** another name for Indra.

**Pakal** (Malayalam) (M) day.

**Pākaśāsana** (S) (M) **1.** punisher of Pāka. **2.** instructor of the ignorant. **3.** another name for Indra.

**Pākaśāsani** (S) (M) **1.** son of Indra. **3.** another name for Jayanta and Arjuna (*M. Bh.*)

**Pakṣaććhid** (S) (M) **1.** cutter of wings. **3.** another name for Indra.

**Pakṣaja** (S) (M) **1.** produced in half a month. **3.** another name for the moon.

**Pakṣālikā** (S) (F) **1.** full of feathers. **3.** a mother attending on Skanda (*M. Bh.*)

**Pakṣālu** (S) (M) **1.** feathered. **2.** a bird.

**Pakṣarāja** (S) (M) **1.** lord of birds. **3.** another name for Garuḍa and Jatāyu.

**Pakṣila** (S) (M) **1.** full of feathers; full of examples; full of logic. **3.** another name for the sage Vātsyāyana.

**Pakṣīndra** (S) (M) **1.** king of birds. **3.** another name for Garuḍa and Jaṭāyu.

**Pakṣiṇī** (S) (F) day of the full moon; a female bird.

**Pakṣman** (S) (M) eyelashes; filament of a flower; leaf; wing.

**Paktha** (S) (M) **1.** cook. **3.** a king who was a protégé of the aśvins (*Ṛg Veda*)

**Pāla** (S) (M) **1.** guardian; protector; keeper; herdsman; king. **3.** a nāga belonging to Vāsuki's race (*M. Bh.*)

**Pālaka** (S) (M) **1.** protector; prince; sovereign. **3.** a son of Aṅgāraka.

**Pālakāpya** (S) (M) **1.** involved in the work of protection. **3.** an ancient sage.

**Palakṣa** (S) (M) white.

**Palakṣī** (S) (F) white.

**Palālā** (S) (F) **1.** a stalk; a straw. **3.** one of the 7 mothers of Skanda (*M. Bh.*)

**Palāśa** (S) (M) **1.** leaf; petal; foliage. **2.** green. **3.** the Bastard Teak (*Butea monosperma*)

**Palāśapattra** (S) (M) **1.** a leaf of the *Butea frondosa*. **3.** a nāga.

**Palāśarañjana** (S) (M) **1.** liking green. **2.** the spring.

**Palāśinī** (S) (F) **1.** covered with foliage. **3.** a river (*M. Bh.*)

**Palījaka** (S) (M) **1.** disturber. **3.** a demon (*A. Veda*)

**Pālin** (S) (M) **1.** protecting; guarding; keeping. **2.** a son of Pṛthu (*H. Purāṇa*)

**Pālita** (S) (M) **1.** grey; aged. **2.** mouse. **3.** a king (*H. Purāṇa*)

**Pālitā** (S) (F) **1.** guarded; protected. **2.** cherished. **3.** a mother in Skanda's retinue (*M. Bh.*)

**Pallava** (S) (M) sprout; shoot; spray; bud; blossom.

**Pallavāstra** (S) (M) **1.** with blossoms for weapons. **3.** another name for Kāma.

**Pallavī** (S) (F) sprouting; a young shoot.

**Pallavikā** (S) (F) resembling a blossom; a scarf.

**Panasa** (S) (M) **1.** resident of a tree; Breadfruit tree (*Artocarpus integrifolia*) **2.** monkey. **3.** a commander of Rāma's monkey army (*Rāmāyaṇa*)

**Panasyu** (S) (M) worthy of admiration; glorious.

**Paṇava** (S) (M) **1.** a small drum; a cymbal. **3.** a prince (*V. Purāṇa*)

**Paṇavin** (S) (M) **1.** possessing a small drum. **3.** another name for Śiva.

**Panāyya** (S) (M) praiseworthy.

**Pañćabāhu** (S) (M) **1.** 5 armed. **3.** an attendant of Śiva (*H. Purāṇa*)

**Pañćabāṇa** (S) (M) **1.** 5 arrowed. **3.** another name for Kāma.

**Pañćaćakṣus** (S) (M) **1.** five eyed. **3.** a buddha.

**Pañćaćīra** (S) (M) **1.** one who wears 5 sacred clothes. **3.** another name of the Buddhist saint Mañjuśrī.

**Pañćaćūḍā** (S) (F) **1.** 5 crested. **3.** an apsarā (*V. Rāmāyaṇa*)

**Pañćaḍākinī** (S) (F) **1.** the 5th dākini; with 5 deities of energy. **3.** an attendant of the devī (*D. Bh. Purāṇa*)

**Pañćadhanuṣ** (S) (M) **1.** 5 bowed. **3.** a Purū king who was the son of Sṛñjaya and the father of Somadatta (*A. Purāṇa*)

**Pañćahasta** (S) (M) 1. 5 handed. 3. a son of Manu (*V. Purāṇa*)

**Pañćahāva** (S) (M) 1. performer of 5 sacrifices. 3. a son of Manu Rohita (*H. Purāṇa*)

**Pañćaja** (S) (M) 1. born of 5. 3. an asura who lived in a conch and was killed by Kṛṣṇa; this conch later came to be known as Kṛṣṇa's Panćajanya conch (*Bhāgavata*); another name for Asamañjas who was the son of Sagara and Keśinī.

**Pañćajanā** (S) (F) 1. bearer of 5 sons. 3. a daughter of Viśvarūpa and wife of Bharata (*Bhā. Purāṇa*)

**Pañćajana** (S) (M) 1. the 5 classes of beings. 2. the 5 classifications are men, gods, apsarās, gandharvās and manes; king; prince. 3. a demon slain by Kṛṣṇa (*M. Bh.*); a son of Saṁhṛāda and Kriti (*Bhā. Purāṇa*); a prajāpati whose daughter Aśiknī married Dakṣa (*Bhāgavata*); a son of Sagara and Keśinī (*H. Purāṇa*); the son of Sṛñjaya and father of Somadatta (*H. Purāṇa*)

**Pañćajanendra** (S) (M) lord of men; king; prince.

**Pañćajanī** (S) (F) 1. made of 5 elements. 3. a daughter of Viśvarupa and wife of Ṛṣabha, she was the mother of Sumati, Rāṣṭrabhṛt, Sudarśana, Āvarana and Dhūmraketu (*Bhāgavata*)

**Pāñćajanya** (S) (M) 1. born of 5. 2. containing the 5 races of men. 3. an agni born of the parts of 5 sages (*M. Bh.*); the conch of Śiva; the conch of Kṛṣṇa.

**Pañćajñāna** (S) (M) 1. possessing 5 fold knowledge. 3. a Buddha.

**Pañćaka** (S) (M) 1. consisting of 5 elements. 3. an attendant of Skanda given to him by Indra (*M. Bh.*); a son of Nahuṣa; one of the first 5 disciples of Gautama Buddha (*B. Literature*)

**Pañćākṣa** (S) (M) 1. 5 eyed. 3. an attendant of Śiva (*Ś. Purāṇa*)

**Pañćāla** (S) (M) consisting of 5; surrounded by 5 rivers; a style of singing; a warrior tribe of the north; a ṛṣi (*M. Bh.*); a nāga; another name for Śiva.

**Pāñćāla** (S) (M) 1. of the Pāñćālas. 3. another name for Dhṛṣṭadyumna and Drupada.

**Pāñćāladāyāda** (S) (M) 1. possessing Pāñćāla. 3. another name for Dhṛṣṭadyumna.

**Pāñćālakulavardhana** (S) (M) 1. increasing the Pāñćāla family. 3. another name for Dhṛṣṭadyumna.

**Pāñćālamukhya** (S) (M) 1. leader of the Pāñćālas. 3. another name for Dhṛṣṭadyumna.

**Pāñćālaputra** (S) (M) 1. son of Pāñćāla. 3. another name for Dhṛṣṭadyumna.

**Pāñćālarāja** (S) (M) 1. lord of Pāñćāla. 3. another name for Dhṛṣṭadyumna and Drupada.

**Pāñćālī** (S) (F) 1. princess of the Pāñćālas. 2. companion of 5; a doll. 3. a rāga; another name for Draupadī.

**Pāñćālikā** (S) (F) princess of Pāñćāla; doll.

**Pañćālika** (S) (M) 1. spices; pepper; dry ginger. 3. belonging to a yakṣa son of Kubera worshipped as a vigour giving deity in some parts of India.

**Pāñćālya** (S) (M) 1. of Pāñćāla. 3. another name for Dhṛṣṭadyumna and Drupada.

**Panćama** (S) (M) the 5th note of classical music; dextrous; clever; beautiful; brilliant.

**Pañćamara** (S) (M) 1. 5th among the mortals; slayer of 5. 2. the 5th spoke in the wheel of time. 3. a son of Balarāma (*Bhā. Purāṇa*)

**Panćamukha** (S) (M) 1. 5 faced. 3. another name for Śiva.

**Panćamūla** (S) (M) 1. 5 rooted. 3. an attendant of Durgā.

**Pañćānana** (S) (M) 1. 5 faced. 2. very fierce; lion. 3. another name for Śiva.

**Pañćānanī** (S) (F) 1. consort of Pañćānana. 3. another name for Durgā.

**Pañćanātha** (S) (M) lord of the 5; the 5 elements of existence.

**Panćārćis** (S) (M) 1. with 5 rays. 3. another name for Mercury.

**Pañćaśara** (S) (M) 1. 5 arrowed. 3. another name for Kāma.

**Pañćaśikha** (S) (M) 1. 5 crested. 3. an attendant of Śiva (*K. Sāgara*); a ṛṣi in the court of Janaka (*M. Bh.*); a gandharva.

**Pañćāśva** (S) (M) 1. with 5 horses. 3. a Purū king.

**Pañćāsya** (S) (M) **1.** 5 faced; lion. **3.** a form of Śiva.

**Pañćavaktrā** (S) (F) **1.** 5 faced. **3.** another name for Durgā.

**Pañćavaktra** (S) (M) **1.** 5 faced. **3.** an attendant of Skanda (*M. Bh.*); another name for Śiva.

**Panćavallabhā** (S) (F) **1.** loved by 5. **3.** another name for Draupadī.

**Pañćavīra** (S) (M) **1.** with 5 warriors. **3.** a viśvadeva (*M. Bh.*)

**Pañćayāma** (S) (M) **1.** with 5 courses. **3.** a son of Ātapa and grandson of Vibhāvasu and Uṣā (*Bh. Purāṇa*)

**Pañćāyatana** (S) (M) **1.** one who makes 5 kinds of effort; one who performs 5 kinds of penance. **3.** an idol of Śiva in Kāśi also called Omkāra.

**Pāñćika** (S) (M) **1.** with the length of 5; with 5 essences. **2.** the 5 essences of existence. **3.** the leader of the yakṣas.

**Paṇḍā** (S) (F) wisdom; knowledge; learning.

**Pāṇḍa** (S) (M) **1.** white; yellow. **3.** a son of Kaṇva and Āryavatī who married Sarasvatīputrī and became the father of 17 sons who will be the future originators of races (*Bh. Purāṇa*)

**Paṇḍaka** (S) (M) **1.** weakling. **3.** a son of Manu Sāvarṇa (*H. Purāṇa*)

**Pāṇḍalameghā** (S) (F) **1.** pale cloud. **3.** a nāga maid (*K. Vyuha*)

**Pāṇḍarā** (S) (F) **1.** pale. **2.** white; white yellow. **3.** a Buddhist Śakti or female energy; Jasmine blossom.

**Pāṇḍara** (S) (M) **1.** pale. **2.** white; white-yellow. **3.** a nāga of of Airāvata's race (*M. Bh.*)

**Pāṇḍava** (S) (M) **1.** son of Pāṇḍu. **3.** a mountain (*L. Vistara*); another name for Yudhiṣṭhira, Bhīma, Arjuna, Nakula, Sahadeva; White Murdah (*Terminalia citrina*)

**Pāṇḍavabhīla** (S) (M) **1.** protector of the Pāṇḍavas (*M. Bh.*). **3.** another name for Kṛṣṇa.

**Pāṇḍavanandana** (S) (M) **1.** son of the Pāṇḍavas. **3.** another name for Yudhiṣṭhira and Janamejaya.

**Pāṇḍavānīka** (S) (M) the army of the Pāṇḍavās.

**Paṇḍavaśreṣṭha** (S) (M) **1.** first of the Pāṇḍavas. **3.** another name for Yudhiṣṭhira.

**Pāṇḍaveya** (S) (M) **1.** of the Pāṇḍavas. **3.** another name for Yudhiṣṭhira and Janamejaya.

**Pandhārinātha** (S) (M) **1.** the lord of Pandhārpura. **3.** another name for Vithoba (*Bhā. Purāṇa*)

**Paṇḍitaka** (S) (M) **1.** wise; learned. **2.** pedantic. **3.** a son of Dhṛtarāṣṭra (*M. Bh.*)

**Paṇḍitarāja** (S) (M) king of learned men.

**Pāṇḍu** (S) (M) **1.** pale. **2.** white. **3.** a son of Vyāsa by the wife of Vićitravīrya, he was the brother of Dhṛtarāṣṭra and Vidura and the husband of Kuntī and Mādrī; he fathered the 5 Pāṇḍavas (*M. Bh.*); a son of Dhātṛ by Āyatī (*V. Purāṇa*); an attendant of Śiva; the 2nd son of Janamejaya (*M. Bh.*); a serpent lord.

**Pāṇḍuka** (S) (M) **1.** pale; yellow white. **3.** one of the 9 treasures of the Jainas (*J.S. Koṣa*); a son of Janamejaya (*M. Bh.*)

**Pāṇḍuputra** (S) (M) son of Pāṇḍu; any one of the Pāṇḍava princes (*M. Bh.*)

**Pāṇḍurā** (S) (F) **1.** yellow lady. **3.** a Buddhist deity (*G's Dharmasāstra*)

**Pāṇḍura** (S) (M) **1.** pale; white; yellow white. **3.** an attendant of Skanda (*M. Bh.*); Button tree (*Anogeissus latifolia*); *Holarrhena antidysenterica*.

**Pāṇḍurangā** (S) (F) **1.** white coloured. **3.** a goddess.

**Pāṇḍuśarmilā** (S) (F) **1.** wife of the sons of Pāṇḍu. **3.** another name for Draupadī.

**Pāṇḍya** (S) (M) **1.** born of Pāṇḍu. **3.** a people and country in South India (*M. Bh.*); a son of Akriḍa; a king of Vidarbha (*M. Bh.*)

**Pāṇīhatā** (S) (F) **1.** created by hand. **3.** a lake created by the gods for Gautama Buddha (*L. Vistara*)

**Pāṇika** (S) (M) **1.** the hand. **3.** an attendant of Skanda (*M. Bh.*)

**Pāṇikarṇa** (S) (M) **1.** hands and ears conjoined. **2.** one who believes in action and is a good listener. **3.** another name for Śiva.

**Pāṇikūrćcas** (S) (M) **1.** knower of hands. **2.** one who understands hand signs; one who understands gestures. **3.** an attendant of

Skanda (*M. Bh.*)

**Pāṇimān** (S) (M) 1. with hands. 2. skilled. 3. a nāga at Varuṇa's court (*M. Bh.*)

**Pāṇinī** (S) (M) 1. with beautiful hands. 2. skilled. 3. the most eminent of all Sanskṛt grammarians, he was the grandson of Devala and the son of Dākṣī.

**Pāṇipraṇayin** (S) (M) loved; resting in the hand.

**Paniṣṭha** (S) (M) very wonderful.

**Paniṣṭhi** (S) (F) admiration; praise.

**Panita** (S) (M) admired; praised.

**Pāṇitaka** (S) (M) 1. one who walks on his hands. 3. one of Skanda's attendants given to him by a deva named Pūṣan (*M. Bh.*)

**Pānīya** (S) (M) to be commended; to be defended or cherished.

**Pāñjari** (S) (F) 1. impression of full hand. 3. another name for the Narmadā river.

**Paṅkaja** (S) (M) 1. born of mud; lotus (*Nelumbium nucifera*). 3. another name for Brahmā.

**Paṅkajākṣī** (S) (F) lotus-eyed.

**Paṅkajamālin** (S) (M) 1. wearing a lotus crown. 3. another name for Viṣṇu.

**Paṅkajinī** (S) (F) abounding in lotuses.

**Paṅkajit** (S) (M) 1. destroying sin. 3. a son of Garuḍa (*M. Bh.*)

**Paṅkti** (S) (M) 1. row; line; numbers 5 and 10. 3. a horse that draws the chariot of Sūrya (*V. Purāṇa*)

**Paṅktigrīva** (S) (M) 1. 10 necked. 3. another name for Rāvaṇa.

**Paṅktiratha** (S) (M) 1. with 10 chariots. 3. another name for Daśaratha.

**Pannā** (S) (F) emerald.

**Pannaga** (S) (M) 1. serpent. 3. another name for Vāsuki.

**Pannagāśana** (S) (M) 1. destroying serpents. 3. another name for Garuḍa.

**Pannageśa** (S) (M) 1. lord of the creeping ones; lord of serpents. 3. another name for Śiva.

**Pānśućandana** (S) (M) 1. with a yellow mark on the forehead; sandalwood mark on the forehead. 3. another name for Śiva.

**Pānśujālika** (S) (M) 1. one who rubs dust on the body. 3. another name for Viṣṇu.

**Pānśula** (S) (M) 1. covered with sandalwood dust. 2. dusty; sandy. 3. Śiva's staff; another name for Śiva; Screwpine (*Pandanus tectorius*)

**Panū** (S) (F) admiration.

**Pāṇyā** (S) (F) admired; astonishing; glorious; praiseworthy; excellent.

**Pāpabhakṣaṇa** (S) (M) 1. devouring the evil. 3. another name for Kālabhairava, a son of Śiva.

**Pāpaghnī** (S) (F) 1. destroying sin. 3. a river.

**Pāpamoćana** (S) (M) liberating from sin.

**Papī** (S) (M) 1. drinker. 3. another name for the sun and the moon.

**Papīhā** (S) (M) Common Hawk-Cuckoo (*Eudynamys scolopacea*)

**Papu** (S) (M) protector.

**Papuri** (S) (M) bountiful; liberal; abundant.

**Para** (S) (M) 1. far; remote; another; adversary. 3. a son of Viśvāmitra (*M. Bh.*); a king of Kosala; the Supreme Being.

**Pāra** (S) (M) 1. bringing across; fulfilling; beyond. 3. a son of Pṛthuśena and father of Nīpa (*H. Purāṇa*); a son of Samara and father of Pṛthu (*H. Purāṇa*); a son of Aṅga and father of Diviratha (*H. Purāṇa*); a sage (*Ma. Purāṇa*)

**Parabrahman** (S) (M) 1. beyond the absolute. 2. the Supreme Spirit.

**Parāga** (S) (M) the pollen of a flower; fragrant; powder; fame; celebrity.

**Pāragata** (S) (M) 1. one who has crossed over safely; pure; holy. 3. a Jaina Arhat.

**Parahan** (S) (M) 1. one who kills others. 2. killer of enemies. 3. an ancient king of Bhārata (*M. Bh.*)

**Pāraj** (S) (M) gold.

**Pāraka** (S) (M) carrying over; saving; delivering; satisfying; pleasing.

**Parākrama** (S) (M) 1. to march forward. 2. to excel; to show courage. 3. a chief of the vidyādharas (*K. Sāgara*); a Kaurava warrior (*M. Bh.*); another name for Viṣṇu.

**Paramā** (S) (F) that which is transcendent; the perfect woman.

**Paramabhāśvara** (S) (M) very radiant.

**Paramādvaita** (S) (M) **1.** without a second. **2.** the highest beings. **3.** another name for Viṣṇu.

**Paramahansa** (S) (M) supreme ascetic.

**Paramajīta** (S) (M) winning perfection; supreme hero.

**Paramajñā** (S) (M) **1.** holding supreme power. **3.** another name for Indra.

**Paramaka** (S) (M) highest; best; greatest.

**Paramakrodhin** (S) (M) **1.** eternally angry; very angry. **3.** a viśvadeva (*M. Bh.*)

**Paramākṣara** (S) (M) **1.** the supreme syllable. **2.** the sacred syllable Om. **3.** another name for Brahmā.

**Paramānanda** (S) (M) supreme bliss.

**Paramāṅganā** (S) (F) a supreme woman; an excellent or beautiful woman.

**Paramaṇi** (S) (M) excellent jewel.

**Paramanyu** (S) (M) **1.** beyond thought; beyond anger. **3.** a son of Kakśeyu (*M. Bh.*)

**Paramaprabha** (S) (M) supreme light.

**Paramāra** (S) (M) **1.** beyond death. **3.** a son of ṛṣi Śaunaka.

**Paramarāja** (S) (M) supreme monarch.

**Paramātmikā** (S) (F) possessing a supreme soul; the supreme; the highest; the greatest.

**Paramekṣu** (S) (M) **1.** desiring supreme things. **3.** a son of Anu (*V. Purāṇa*)

**Parameśa** (S) (M) **1.** supreme lord. **3.** another name for Viṣṇu and the Supreme Being.

**Parameṣṭhaja** (S) (M) **1.** son of Brahmā. **3.** another name for Nārada.

**Parameṣṭhin** (S) (M) **1.** highest; chief; principal. **3.** another name for Agni, Prajāpati, Brahmā, Śiva, Viṣṇu, Garuḍa and Manu Ćākṣusa; a king of Pānćāla who was the son of Ajamīdha (*M. Bh.*); a son of Indradyumna and the father of Pratīhāra (*V. Purāṇa*)

**Parameṣṭhiputra** (S) (M) **1.** son of Brahmā. **3.** another name for Nārada.

**Parameśvara** (S) (M) **1.** supreme god. **2.** king. **3.** another name for Viṣṇu and Indra.

**Parameśvarī** (S) (F) **1.** supreme goddess. **3.** another name for Durgā.

**Parāṅgada** (S) (M) **1.** giving form to another. **3.** another name for Śiva.

**Parantapa** (S) (M) **1.** destroying foes. **2.** hero. **3.** a son of Manu Tāmasa (*H. Purāṇa*); a king of Magadha.

**Pārapāra** (S) (M) **1.** beyond the beyond; the absolute; abode of the ocean. **3.** another name for Viṣṇu.

**Parapauravatantava** (S) (M) **1.** wearing human clothes. **3.** son of Viśvāmitra.

**Parāpurañjaya** (S) (M) **1.** winner of the heart of the ocean. **2.** very popular; born in an ocean. **3.** a Hehaya prince.

**Parapuṣṭā** (S) (F) **1.** female cuckoo. **3.** a daughter of a king of Kauśāmbi (*K. Sāgara*)

**Pāras** (S) (M) the philosopher's stone, (a stone supposed to change iron and other such metals into gold by touch)

**Parāśa** (S) (M) iron.

**Parāśara** (S) (M) **1.** crusher. **2.** destroyer. **3.** the grandson of Vasiṣṭha and son of Śakti and Adriṣyantī, he was the father of Vyāsa by Satyavatī (*V. Purāṇa*); a son of Kuṭumi (*V. Purāṇa*); a serpent of the family of Dhṛtarāṣṭra (*M. Bh.*)

**Pāraśava** (S) (M) **1.** made of iron. **3.** a mine in which pearls are found (*V's B. Samhitā*); another name for Vidura (*M. Bh.*)

**Pārāśarya** (S) (M) **1.** abode of protection; a refuge to enemies. **3.** a sage who was a member of Yudhiṣṭhira's court (*M. Bh.*); the Mādhavi creeper (*Hiptage madoblata*); another name for Vyāsa.

**Paraspā** (S) (M) protector.

**Paraśu** (S) (M) made of iron; thunderbolt; hatchet; axe.

**Paraśući** (S) (M) **1.** very pure; sacred; holy. **3.** a son of Manu Auttama (*M. Purāṇa*)

**Paraśudhara** (S) (M) **1.** axe holder. **3.** another name for Ganeśa.

**Paraśuhastā** (S) (F) **1.** with an axe in hand. **3.** an attendant of the devī (*Ś. Purāṇa*)

**Paraśurāma** (S) (M) **1.** Rāma with the axe. **3.** the 6th avatāra of Viṣṇu born as the son of Jamadagni and Reṇukā (*Bhā. Purāṇa*)

**Paravāṇi** (S) (M) **1.** judge. **3.** Kārttikeya's peacock.

**Parāvasu** (S) (M) **1.** keeping off wealth. **3.** a sage who was the grandson of Viśvāmitra; a son of Raibhya; a gandharva.

**Pārāvata** (S) (M) 1. coming from a distance. 2. pigeon; turtledove. 3. a nāga of the Airāvata family (*M. Bh.*)

**Pārāvatākṣa** (S) (M) dove eyed.

**Pārāvatasavarṇa** (S) (M) 1. dove coloured. 3. the horses of Dhṛṣṭadyumna (*M. Bh.*)

**Pārāvatī** (S) (F) 1. coming from a distance. 2. a song peculiar to cowherds. 3. a river (*H. Purāṇa*)

**Pārayiṣṇu** (S) (M) successful; victorious.

**Parāyus** (S) (M) 1. reaching the highest age. 3. another name for Brahmā.

**Pāreraka** (S) (M) 1. one that pierces. 2. sword; scimitar.

**Pareśa** (S) (M) 1. highest lord. 3. another name for Brahmā.

**Pareṣṭi** (S) (M) with the highest worship.

**Paribarha** (S) (M) 1. with many feathers; surroundings; wealth; property; royal insignia. 3. a son of Garuḍa (*M. Bh.*)

**Pāribhadra** (S) (M) 1. the noble coral tree. 2. as noble as the coral; as auspicious as the Coral Jasmine tree (*Nyctantes arbor tristis*). 3. a son of Yajñabāhu (*Bh. Purāṇa*)

**Paribhrāj** (S) (M) to shed brilliance all around.

**Paribodha** (S) (M) reason.

**Paribṛdha** (S) (M) firm; strong; solid; superior; lord.

**Paridhi** (S) (M) circumference; boundary; enclosure; fence; the ocean; the halo around the sun and moon; the circumference of a circle.

**Paridvīpa** (S) (M) 1. crossing many islands. 2. one who travels a lot. 3. a son of Garuḍa (*Bhā. Purāṇa*)

**Parigha** (S) (M) 1. iron rod. 2. chain used to close doors; a line of clouds crossing the sun at sunrise or sunset. 3. an attendant of Skanda given to him by the deva Anṣa (*M. Bh.*)

**Parighrā** (S) (F) to cover with kisses.

**Parigīta** (S) (M) sung; celebrated; declared.

**Pārijāta** (S) (M) 1. born; the Coral Jasmine (*Nyctantes arbor tristis*). 3. one of the 5 trees of paradise produced at the churning of the ocean (*M. Bh.*); a serpent of the family of Airāvata (*M. Bh.*); a ṛṣi (*M. Bh.*)

**Parijātaka** (S) (M) 1. of the Coral Jasmine tree. 3. a sage who was a member of the court of Yudhiṣṭhira (*M. Bh.*)

**Parijetṛ** (S) (M) victor; conqueror.

**Parijman** (S) (M) 1. surrounding; omnipresent. 2. fire; the moon.

**Parijñana** (S) (M) perception; knowledge; experience; discrimination.

**Parijvāl** (S) (M) surround by flames; to burn brightly; to blaze.

**Parijvān** (S) (M) 1. fully incited; surrounded by invocations. 3. another name for the moon, fire and Indra.

**Parīkṣit** (S) (M) 1. well examined; fully perceived; tested; dwelling; surrounding; extending. 3. a celebrated king of the lunar race who was the son of Abhimanyu and Uttarā and father of Janamejaya (*M. Bh.*); a son of Avīkṣit of the Kuru dynasty (*M. Bh.*); a son of Anaśvan and Amṛtā of the Kuru race and the father of Bhīmasena by Suvaśā (*M. Bh.*); an Ikṣvāku king who was the husband of Suśobhanā and the father of Śala, Bala and Dala (*M. Bh.*); a king of Ayodhyā (*M. Bh.*); a son of Kuru (*H. Purāṇa*); another name for Agni, heaven and earth.

**Pārīkṣit** (S) (M) 1. son of Parīkṣit. 3. another name for Janamejaya.

**Parikūṭa** (S) (M) 1. barrier; trench. 3. a nāga (*M. Bh.*)

**Parimala** (S) (M) fragrance; perfume.

**Parimāṇa** (S) (M) quality; bounty; plenty.

**Parimantrita** (S) (M) well advised; surrounded by praises; charmed; enchanted; consecrated.

**Parimita** (S) (M) measured; regulated.

**Parimohana** (S) (M) extremely fascinating; beguiling; alluring; fascinating.

**Parimugdha** (S) (F) bewitchingly lovely; extremely lovely.

**Parīṇāha** (S) (M) 1. circumference; width. 3. another name for Śiva.

**Parīndana** (S) (M) present; gift.

**Pārīndra** (S) (M) 1. lord of all around. 2. lion.

**Parinirmita** (S) (M) 1. formed; created. 3. another name for Viṣṇu.

**Pariniṣṭhā** (S) (F) dwelling at the top; highest point; complete knowledge; complete accomplishment.

**Pariṇitā** (S) (F) led around; complete; a married woman.

**Pariṇuta** (S) (M) praised; celebrated.

**Paripati** (S) (M) lord of all around.

**Pāriplava** (S) (M) 1. moving to and fro. 2. agitated. 3. a king of the Bharata race who was the son of Nṛćakṣus and the grandson of Nala and the father of Medhāvi (*Bhāgavata*)

**Pariprita** (S) (M) full of love; gratified; delighted.

**Paripūrnasahasraćandrāvati** (S) (F) 1. possessing a thousand moons; 3. another name for Indra's wife.

**Parisambhu** (S) (M) to arise; spring from; be produced from.

**Parisatya** (S) (M) the pure truth.

**Pariśobhitā** (S) (F) 1. adorned. 2. beautiful. 3. an apsarā and a gandharvī (*K. Sāgara*)

**Parisraja** (S) (F) a garland.

**Pariśruta** (S) (M) 1. well heard of. 2. famous; celebrated. 3. an attendant of Skanda (*M. Bh.*)

**Parisuta** (S) (M) impelled to come forth; elicited by the gods.

**Pariśvanga** (S) (M) 1. an embrace; touch. 3. a son of Devaki (*Bh. Purāṇa*)

**Paritoṣa** (S) (M) delight.

**Parivaha** (S) (M) 1. carrying around. 2. one that carries everything away. 3. the wind that courses over the Gaṅgā river; a tongue of Agni.

**Parivarta** (S) (M) 1. revolving; stirring; an abode; spot; place. 3. a son of Duhsaha and grandson of Mṛtyu (*M. Purāṇa*); another name for Kūrma the 2nd incarnation of Viṣṇu.

**Pariveśa** (S) (M) 1. circumference; situation; surrounding. 2. circlet; that which surrounds and protects; winding round. 3. the disc of the sun and moon; the halo around them (*K. Sāgara*)

**Parivita** (S) (F) 1. extremely free; extremely liked; extremely useless. 3. the bow of Brahmā (*Ṛg Veda*)

**Parivyādha** (S) (M) 1. surrounded by hunters. 3. a sage in the west (*M. Bh.*)

**Pariyaṇga** (S) (M) 1. with a strong body. 3. a maharṣi who was the son of Marīći and Ūrṇā (*Bhāgavata*)

**Pāriyātra** (S) (M) 1. Western Vindhya range. 3. a son of Ahīnagu a descendant of Rāma (*Bhāgavata*)

**Parjanya** (S) (M) 1. cloud; rain; raincloud. 3. personified; one of the 12 ādityas (*H. Purāṇa*); a prajāpati who was the father of Hiraṇyaroman; a gandharva (*M. Purāṇa*)

**Parmāḍi** (S) (M) 1. the absolute beginning. 3. a prince of Karṇāṭa (*R. Taraṅginī*)

**Paramāṅganā** (S) (F) excellent woman.

**Paramasukha** (S) (M) ultimate bliss.

**Parṇa** (S) (M) 1. leaf; feather; full of leaves; surrounded by leaves; surrounded by feathers. 2. Flame of the Forest (*Butea frondosa*); which represents royalty and holiness.

**Parnāda** (S) (M) 1. feeding on leaves. 3. a sage who was a member of the court of Yudhiṣṭhira (*M. Bh.*)

**Parṇāmaṇi** (S) (M) jewel among the leaves; a kind of musical instrument made of Parnawood.

**Parṇāśā** (S) (F) 1. feeding on leaves. 2. *Cedrela toona*. 3. a river personified by an apsarā of Varuṇa's court (*M. Bh.*)

**Parṇini** (S) (F) 1. winged; plumed; leafy. 3. an apsarā (*H. Purāṇa*)

**Parokṣa** (S) (M) 1. beyond observation. 2. mysterious. 3. a king of the lunar race (*Bhāgavata*)

**Parokṣi** (S) (F) beyond perception; mysterious; undiscernible.

**Parparīka** (S) (M) 1. braided. 3. another name for Agni and the sun.

**Pārṣada** (S) (M) 1. associate; companion; attendant of a god; spectator. 3. another name for Dhṛṣṭadyumna.

**Pārṣada** (S) (M) 1. son of Pṛṣata. 3. another name for Drupada.

**Pārṣata** (S) (M) 1. son of Pṛṣata. 3. another name for Drupada.

**Parśava** (S) (M) bearer of an axe; a warrior armed with an axe.

**Pārśṇikṣeman** (S) (M) 1. the basis of enquiry.

3. a viśvādeva (*M. Bh.*)

**Parśupāṇi** (S) (M) 1. axe holder. 3. another name for Gaṇeśa.

**Pārśva** (S) (M) 1. the rib region; side; flank. 2. the side horse on a chariot; heaven and earth. 3. the 23rd Jaina Arhat of the present Avasarpinī and his servant; an ancient Buddhist teacher (*B. Literature*)

**Pārśvanātha** (S) (M) 1. lord who is always beside his devotees; lord of the chariot horses. 3. the 23rd Jaina Tirathankara.

**Pārtha** (S) (M) 1. son of Pṛthā; son of the earth; prince; king. 3. metronymic of the 3 elder Pāṇḍavas specially of Arjuna (*M. Bh.*); a king of Kāśmira (*R. Taraṅginī*); White Murdah (*Terminalia citrina*)

**Pārthasārathi** (S) (M) 1. Arjuna's charioteer. 3. another name for Kṛṣṇa (*V. Purāṇa*)

**Pārthiva** (S) (M) 1. of the earth; royal; earthen. 2. prince; king; warrior; Indian Valerian (*Valeriana wallichii*)

**Pārthivendra** (S) (M) greatest of lords of the earth; lord of mortals.

**Pārthivī** (S) (F) 1. daughter of the earth. 3. another name for Sitā and Lakṣmī (*Bhā. Purāṇa*)

**Paru** (S) (M) limb; member; mountain; ocean; sky; paradise.

**Pāru** (S) (M) the sun; fire.

**Parućchepa** (S) (M) 1. preceptor of practical knowledge. 3. a ṛṣi who was the son of Divodāsa and part author of *Ṛg. Veda* (i)

**Pārul** (S) (F) practical; beautiful; gracious.

**Paruṣa** (S) (M) 1. keen; sharp; violent; harsh; an arrow. 3. a rākṣasa (*V. Rāmāyaṇa*)

**Paruṣṇī** (S) (F) 1. violent; severe. 3. a river now called Rāvi.

**Parvadhi** 1. container of time periods. 3. another name for the moon.

**Parvaṇī** (S) (F) the period of the change of the moon; day of the full moon.

**Parvata** (S) (M) 1. rocky; rugged. 2. mountain; the number 7. 2. rock; stone. 3. a ṛṣi who was the nephew of Nārada (*V. Purāṇa*); a son of Paurṇamāsa; (*M. Purāṇa*); a minister of King Purūravas; a vasu (*H. Purāṇa*)

**Parvatacyut** (S) (M) 1. shaking mountains. 3. another name for the maruts.

**Parvataja** (S) (M) born of the mountains; mountain born.

**Parvatarāj** (S) (M) king of the mountains; the highest mountain.

**Parvatarājakanyā** (S) (F) 1. daughter of the king of mountains. 3. another name for Pārvatī.

**Parvatavāsinī** (S) (F) 1. dwelling in mountains. 3. another name for Durgā (*D. Bh. Purāṇa*)

**Parvateṣṭha** (S) (M) 1. dwelling in the mountains. 3. another name for Indra (*M. Bh.*)

**Parvateśvara** (S) (M) 1. lord of the mountains. 3. a king of Vindhyā (*P. Purāṇa*)

**Parvateya** (S) (M) 1. belonging to the mountains. 3. a king who was also a ṛṣi (*M. Bh.*)

**Pārvatī** (S) (F) 1. of the mountains. 2. mountain stream. 3. the wife of Śiva who was the daughter of Himavata the king of the mountains and Menā, she is the reincarnation of Satī – an aspect of Mahāmāya or the eternal Śakti, she is known by different names and worshipped in different forms, the more prominent of which are Kālī; Gaurī, Umā, Īśvarī, Aparṇa, Ćaṇḍikā, Bhavānī, Durgā, Bhairavi, Ambikā, Dākṣāyaṇī, Girijā, Kātyāyānī, Rudrāṇī and Ćāmuṇḍā; Cashewnut (*Anacardium occidentale*); *Lannea grandis*; *Woodfordia fruticosa*; Common Flax (*Linum usitatissimum*)

**Pārvatīnandana** (S) (M) 1. son of Pārvatī. 3. another name for Gaṇeśa and Kārttikeya.

**Pārvatīnātha** (S) (M) 1. lord of Pārvatī. 3. another name for Śiva.

**Pārvatīpati** (S) (M) 1. husband of Pārvatī. 3. another name for Śiva.

**Pārvatīya** (S) (M) 1. belonging to the mountains. 3. a king mentioned in the *Mahābhārata* (*M. Bh.*)

**Parviṇī** (S) (F) festival; a holiday.

**Parvita** (S) (M) 1. surrounded; encompassed. 2. veiled; covered. 3. the bow of Brahmā (*Ṛg Veda*)

**Paryaṅka** (S) (M) 1. bed. 2. litter; a particular mode of sitting. 3. a mountain regarded as the son of Vindhya (*Ṛg Veda*)

**Paryetṛ** (S) (M) subduer; conqueror.

**Pāśa** (S) (M) 1. noose; chain; tie; bond. 3. a divine weapon of Varuṇa unequalled in swiftness (*M. Bh.*)

**Pāśadhara** (S) (M) 1. holding a noose. 3. another name for Varuṇa.

**Pāṣaka** (S) (M) an ornament for the feet.

**Pāśāsinī** (S) (F) 1. controller of thirst. 3. a river (*M. Bh.*)

**Pāśin** (S) (M) 1. with a noose. 3. a son of Dhṛtarāṣṭra; another name for Varuṇa and Yama.

**Pastyā** (S) (F) 1. dwelling. 3. a goddess of household affairs (*Ṛg Veda*)

**Paśubhartā** (S) (M) 1. master of beasts; protecting animals. 3. another name for Śiva.

**Paśudā** (S) (F) 1. giver of cattle. 3. a mother in Skanda's retinue (*M. Bh.*)

**Paśunātha** (S) (M) 1. lord of cattle. 3. another name for Śiva.

**Paśupā** (S) (M) 1. herdsman. 3. another name for Pūṣan.

**Pāśupata** (S) (M) 1. sacred to Śiva. 3. the arrow used on Śiva's bow called Pināka (*K. Granthāvali*)

**Paśupati** (S) (M) 1. lord of animals; lord of the soul. 3. the later incarnation of Rudra-Śiva (*Ś. Purāṇa*)

**Paśurāja** (S) (M) 1. king of beasts. 2. lion.

**Paśusakha** (S) (M) 1. friend of animals. 3. the husband of Gaṇḍā the maid of the Saptarṣis (*M. Bh.*)

**Paśyat** (S) (M) visible; conspicuous.

**Pataga** (S) (M) 1. one who flies in the sky. 2. bird. 3. another name for the sun.

**Patagapati** (S) (M) 1. lord of birds. 3. another name for Garuḍa.

**Patageśvara** (S) (M) 1. lord of birds. 3. another name for Garuḍa and Jaṭāyu.

**Patākin** (S) (M) 1. bearing flags; standard bearer. 3. a soldier of the Kaurava army (*M. Bh.*)

**Pāṭalā** (S) (F) 1. pale red. 2. pink. 3. a form of Durgā; a form of Dākṣāyaṇī; the trumpet flower (*Bignonia suaveolens*)

**Pātāla** (S) (M) 1. descent. 3. one of the 7 regions under the earth and the abode of the nāgas (*M. Bh.*); the attendant of the 14th Arhat of the present Avasarpinī; a monkey of Kiśkindhā (*P. Purāṇa*)

**Pātālaketu** (S) (M) 1. with the flag of the nether regions. 3. a daitya (*Bhā. Purāṇa*)

**Pātālarāvaṇa** (S) (M) 1. making a noise under the earth. 3. a king of the rākṣasas who was the nephew of Malyavān (*K. Rāmāyaṇa*)

**Pāṭalāvatī** (S) (M) 1. of a pale red. 3. a holy river of North India (*M. Bh.*); another name for Durgā.

**Pāṭalī** (S) (F) 1. the trumpet flower (*Bignonia suaveolens*). 3. a daughter of King Mahendravarman.

**Pāṭalopala** (S) (M) red gem; ruby.

**Patana** (S) (M) 1. fall; descent. 2. what flies or falls. 3. a rākṣasa (*M. Bh.*)

**Pataṅga** (S) (M) 1. flying. 2. the sun; kite; butterfly; bee. 3. one of the 7 suns; a ṛṣi who was part author of *Ṛg Veda* (x); a mountain near Mahāmeru; another name for Kṛṣṇa (*Bhā. Purāṇa*)

**Pataṅganā** (S) (F) butterfly.

**Patangī** (S) (F) 1. flying. 3. a wife of Tārkṣa and mother of the flying animals.

**Pātaṅgi** (S) (M) 1. son of the sun. 3. another name for Saturn.

**Patangikā** (S) (F) small bird; a little bee.

**Patañjali** (S) (M) 1. one who should be worshipped. 3. a celebrated grammarian and author of *Mahābhāṣya*; a philosopher and propounder of yoga.

**Patara** (S) (M) 1. with a skin; a ray of sunlight. 3. the 3rd of the 7 suns; another name for Varuṇa.

**Patatri** (S) (M) 1. bird. 3. a warrior on the side of the Kauravas (*M. Bh.*)

**Pāṭava** (S) (M) clever; sharp; dextrous.

**Paṭavāsaka** (S) (M) 1. scented powder. 3. a serpent of the family of Dhṛtarāṣṭra (*M. Bh.*)

**Paṭeśvarī** (S) (F) 1. goddess of clothes. 3. another name for Durgā.

**Pātha** (S) (M) path; fire; sun.

**Pāthamañjarī** (S) (F) 1. decorating the path. 2. one who makes the path easy. 3. a rāgiṇī.

**Patharvan** (S) (M) 1. horse of the path. 2. a preceptor who moves from place to place.

3. a rajarṣī well versed in the *Ṛg Veda* (*Ṛg Veda*)

**Pāthas** (S) (M) spot; place; water; air.

**Pāthaspati** (S) (M) 1. lord of water. 3. another name for Varuṇa.

**Pathikṛt** (S) (M) 1. preparing the way. 3. another name for Agni.

**Pāthinātha** (S) (M) lord of direction.

**Pāthoja** (S) (M) 1. waterborn. 2. Lotus (*Nelumbo nucifera*)

**Pāthojinī** (S) (F) a collection of lotus plants.

**Pāthonātha** (S) (M) 1. lord of water. 3. another name for Varuṇa.

**Pāthoruha** (S) (M) 1. growing in water; water grown. 2. lotus.

**Pathuṣa** (S) (M) 1. eating everything in the way. 3. a rākṣasa of the army of Rāvana (*M. Bh.*)

**Pāthya** (S) (M) 1. heavenly. 3. a ṛṣi (*Ṛg Veda*)

**Pathyā** (S) (F) 1. of path; way; road. 3. the goddess of travellers and paths (*K. Sāgara*); *Mimordica balsamina*; Black Myrobalan (*Terminalia chebula*)

**Pātṛ** (S) (M) defender; protector.

**Pātrī** (S) (F) 1. vessel. 2. small furnace; competent; worthy; protector. 3. another name for Durgā.

**Paṭṭadevī** (S) (F) 1. turbaned woman. 2. the main queen of a king.

**Pattradevī** (S) (F) 1. plumed lady; lady of leaves. 3. a Buddhist deity; another name for Dhanalakṣmī.

**Pattralekhā** (S) (F) decorated with lines of fragrant spices.

**Pattrapati** (S) (M) 1. lord of feathers. 3. another name for Garuda.

**Pattrapuṣpā** (S) (F) flowers and leaves conjoined; made up of flowers and leaves; the Sacred Basil plant (*Ocimum sanctum*)

**Pattrorṇa** (S) (M) 1. with woven silk garments. 3. a king at the court of Yudhiṣṭhira (*M. Bh.*)

**Paṭu** (S) (M) sharp; intense; keen; strong; violent; clever; skilful.

**Paṭul** (S) (M) yellow coloured.

**Paṭumatī** (S) (F) with a clever mind.

**Paṭurūpa** (S) (M) very clever.

**Paṭuśa** (S) (M) 1. clever. 3. a rākṣasa (*M. Bh.*)

**Paulastya** (S) (M) 1. descended from Pulastya. 3. another name for Kubera and Rāvaṇa.

**Paulastyatanaya** (S) (M) 1. son of Pulastya. 3. another name for Rāvaṇa.

**Paulomī** (S) (F) 1. daughter of Puloman. 3. the wife of Indra; the wife of Bhṛgu (*Vā. Purāṇa*)

**Paulomīpati** (S) (M) 1. lord of Paulomī. 3. another name for Indra.

**Paulomīśa** (S) (M) 1. lord of Paulomī. 3. another name for Indra.

**Pauṇḍarīka** (S) (M) consisting of lotus flowers.

**Pauṇḍra** (S) (M) 1. sugarcane of a straw colour. 2. pale. 3. the conch shell of Bhīma (*M. Bh.*); a country and its king who is regarded as a son of Vasudeva.

**Pauṇḍraka** (S) (M) 1. straw coloured. 3. a son of Nikumbha (*A. Rāmāyaṇa*); a king of Kārūśa killed by Kṛṣṇa (*Bhāgavata*); Yama's buffalo (*Vām. Purāṇa*)

**Paundramatsyaka** (S) (M) 1. yellow fish. 3. a king who was the son of the rākṣasa Vīra and Danāyus (*M. Bh.*)

**Paura** (S) (M) 1. filler; increaser. 3. a ṛṣi and part author of *Ṛg Veda* (v); another name for Soma, Indra and the aśvins.

**Pauralikā** (S) (F) 1. pleasant to citizens. 3. a rāga.

**Paurava** (S) (M) 1. born of the Purū dynasty. 3. a king who was a commander of the Kaurava army (*M. Bh.*); a king of Aṅga (*M. Bh.*); a son of Viśvāmitra (*M. Bh.*)

**Pauravī** (S) (F) 1. descended from Purū. 3. a wife of Vasudeva (*Bhāgavata*); a wife of Yudhiṣṭhira and mother of Devaka (*Bhāgavata*); a rāga.

**Paurṇamāsa** (S) (M) 1. the day of full moon. 2. related to the full moon. 3. a son of Marīći and Sambhūti and the father of Virajas and Parvata (*V. Purāṇa*)

**Paurṇamī** (S) (F) day of full moon.

**Pauruṣeya** (S) (M) 1. of men; manly. 2. strong; powerful. 3. a rākṣasa who travels with the sun in the month of Jyeṣṭha (*Bhāgavata*)

**Pauṣajit** (S) (M) **1.** one who has won over cold. **2.** unaffected by cold. **3.** a sage in the line of Vyāsa's disciples (*Bhā. Purāṇa*)

**Pauṣpinji** (S) (M) **1.** with a cool temperament. **3.** a sage in the line of Vyāsa's disciples (*Bhā. Purāṇa*)

**Pauśṭī** (S) (F) **1.** strong; satisfied; voluptuous. **3.** the wife of King Purū and the mother of Pravīra, Īśvara and Raudrāśva (*M. Bh.*)

**Pauṣya** (S) (M) **1.** of the asterism Puṣya. **3.** the king of Karavīrapura who was the son of Pūṣan and the father of Ćandraśekhara (*K. Purāṇa*)

**Pava** (S) (M) **1.** purification. **2.** air; wind. **3.** a son of Nahuṣa (*M. Bh.*)

**Pavākā** (S) (F) **1.** purifier. **2.** storm; whirlwind.

**Pāvaka** (S) (M) **1.** purifier. **2.** pure; clear; bright; shining; fire. **3.** an agni said to be the son of Agni Abhimānin and Svāhā (*M. Bh.*); Ceylon Leadwort (*Plumbago zeylanica*)

**Pāvakārćis** (S) (F) a flash of fire.

**Pāvakī** (S) (F) **1.** purifying. **3.** the Vedic name of Sarasvatī; the wife of Agni (*M. Bh.*)

**Pāvaki** (S) (M) **1.** a son of fire. **3.** another name for Skanda, Sudarśana and Viṣṇu.

**Pavamāna** (S) (M) **1.** purified. **2.** flowing clear; the wind personified. **3.** an agni who was the son of Agni and Svāhā (*V. Purāṇa*); a son of Vijitāśva who was the reincarnation of an agni (*Bhāgavata*); the son of Antardhāna and Śikhaṇḍinī; a mountain near Meru (*D. Bh. Purāṇa*)

**Pavana** (S) (M) **1.** breeze; air; the number 5. **3.** wind personified as a god; the regent of the north west region; a son of Manu Uttama (*Bh. Purāṇa*)

**Pāvana** (S) (M) **1.** purifying; holy. **2.** fire; incense. **3.** a son of Kṛṣṇa and Mitravindā (*Bhāgavata*); a viśvādeva (*M. Bh.*); another name for Vyāsa.

**Pavanaja** (S) (M) **1.** son of the wind. **3.** another name for Hanumān.

**Pavanatanaya** (S) (M) **1.** son of the wind. **3.** another name for Bhīma.

**Pavanātmaja** (S) (M) **1.** son of the wind. **3.** another name for Bhīma.

**Pāvanī** (S) (F) **1.** holy; pure; purifying. **2.** Sacred Basil (*Ocimum sanctum*); water; the Rudrākṣa seed. **3.** another name for the goddess Gaṅgā.

**Pāvanta** (S) (M) holiness; purity; sanctity.

**Pavayitṛ** (S) (M) purifier.

**Pavi** (S) (M) **1.** of fire; lightning; brightness; sheen; arrow; thunderbolt; speech; fire. **3.** the golden tyre on the wheel of the aśvins' chariot (*Ṛg Veda*)

**Pavinasa** (S) (M) **1.** with a nose like a spearhead. **3.** a demon (*A. Veda*)

**Pāvīrāvī** (S) (F) daughter of lightning; thunder.

**Pavitṛ** (S) (M) purifier.

**Pavitra** (S) (M) **1.** purifying; filtering. **2.** honey; water; butter; Kusa grass. **3.** another name for Viṣṇu; *Curcuma longa*; *Prosopis spicigera*; *Desmostachya bipinnata*.

**Pavitrā** (S) (F) **1.** pure; holy; sacred; beneficient. **2.** Sacred Basil (*Ocimum sanctum*); Saffron; the Pippala tree. **3.** a river (*M. Bh.*)

**Pavitrakīrti** (S) (M) of flawless renown.

**Pavitrapāṇi** (S) (M) **1.** holding purity. **2.** holding Darbha grass in the hand. **3.** a ṛṣi (*M. Bh.*)

**Pavitrapati** (S) (M) lord of purity.

**Pavitravāṇi** (S) (M) **1.** pure speech. **3.** a sage in the court of both Yudhiṣṭhira and Indra (*M. Bh.*)

**Pavitravatī** (S) (F) **1.** cleansing; purifying. **3.** a river (*Bhā. Purāṇa*)

**Pāyala** (S) (F) **1.** of the foot. **2.** anklet; strength.

**Payas** (S) (M) milk; water; rain; juice; power.

**Payaspati** (S) (M) **1.** lord of milk. **3.** another name for Viṣṇu.

**Payasya** (S) (M) **1.** made of milk. **3.** a son of Aṅgiras (*M. Bh.*)

**Payodā** (S) (F) **1.** giver of water; milk giver. **3.** a mother in Skanda's retinue (*M. Bh.*)

**Payoda** (S) (M) **1.** milk giving; water giving. **2.** cloud. **3.** a son of Yadu (*Bhā. Purāṇa*)

**Payodhi** (S) (M) **1.** water receptacle. **2.** the ocean.

**Payoṣṇī** (S) (F) **1.** milky. **3.** a holy river starting from the Vindhya mountains (*M. Bh.*)

**Pāyu** (S) (M) guard; protector.

**Pēdarī** (S) (F) 1. with a protruding stomach. 2. grinder; coverer. 3. a female deity (*J.S. Koṣa*)

**Pedhāla** (S) (M) 1. one who hides. 3. the 8th Arhat of the future Utsarpiṇī (*J.S. Koṣa*)

**Pedu** (S) (M) 1. protection. 2. coverer. 3. a man protected by the aśvins.

**Pehlaj** (S) (M) first born.

**Pelavā** (S) (F) delicate; fine; soft; tender.

**Perantālu** (S) (F) goddess of virginity.

**Peru** (S) (M) 1. drinking; rescuing; swelling. 2. the sun; fire; ocean.

**Peruka** (S) (M) 1. rescuer. 3. a king who gave refuge to Bharadvāja (*Ṛg Veda*)

**Peśala** (S) (M) 1. adorned; decorated; beautiful; charming; soft; tender. 3. another name for Viṣṇu.

**Peśalākṣa** (S) (M) with beautiful eyes.

**Peśanī** (S) (F) well formed; beautiful.

**Peṣī** (S) (M) 1. pounding. 2. thunderbolt.

**Pesvara** (S) (M) going; moving; splendid.

**Phāla** (S) (M) 1. ploughshare. 2. pointed portion of the plough. 3. another name for Balarāma and Śiva.

**Phalādhyakṣa** (S) (M) lord of the fruit.

**Phalāhārī** (S) (F) 1. eating fruits. 3. another name for Durgā.

**Phalaka** (S) (M) plank; shield; sky; a plank used in the construction of a chariot or in the extraction of the Soma juice; pericarp of the lotus.

**Phalakapāṇi** (S) (M) armed with a shield.

**Phalakāvana** (S) (F) 1. heavenly forest. 2. a place that has been consecrated by the prayers and sacrifices of devotees. 3. a forest sacred to Sarasvatī.

**Phalakṛṣṇa** (S) (F) 1. with black fruit. 3. the Caraunda plant (*Carissa carandas*) (*M. Bh.*)

**Phalamaṇi** (S) (M) jewel.

**Phalamdā** (S) (F) 1. giving fruit. 3. a female gandharva (*H. Purāṇa*)

**Phalārāma** (S) (M) consisting of fruits; orchard.

**Phalavatī** (S) (F) 1. fruitful. 2. successful. 3. a twig of a thorn tree; a fruit bearing plant.

**Phalgu** (S) (M) 1. small; red. 2. spring; a red powder made from wild ginger considered holy by the Hindus; Fig tree (*Ficus oppositifolia*); Wild Champaka (*Bauhinia tomentosa*). 3. a holy river in Gayā (*M. Bh.*)

**Phalguna** (S) (M) 1. red. 2. of the month of Phālguna; the Hindu month of February-March when the Phālguna constellation is ascendant. 3. another name for Arjuna who was born during this period; another name for the Arjuna tree (*Terminalia arjuna*); another name for Indra.

**Phālgunī** (S) (M) 1. the full moon day of the month of Phālguna. 3. another name for Abhimanyu.

**Phālgunya** (S) (M) 1. moonlight. 3. another name for the planet Jupiter.

**Phalgutantra** (S) (M) 1. to govern well. 3. another name for the king of Ayodhyā and father of King Sāgara.

**Phalin** (S) (M) fruitful; bearing fruit.

**Phalinī** (S) (F) 1. fruitful. 3. another name for the Priyaṅgu creeper; *Aglaia odoratissima*; Bottle Gourd (*Lagenaria vulgaris*)

**Phalodaka** (S) (M) 1. fruit juice. 3. a yakṣa who was a member of the court of Kubera.

**Phalyā** (S) (F) flower; bud.

**Phaṇa** (S) (M) hood; ornament; the expanded hood of a serpent.

**Phaṇadhara** (S) (M) 1. possessing serpents. 3. another name for Śiva.

**Phaṇādhara** (S) (M) 1. bearing a serpent. 3. another name for Śiva.

**Phaṇamaṇi** (S) (M) jewel in the hood of the serpent.

**Phāṇḍin** (S) (M) 1. hooded. 3. a serpent lord.

**Phaṇibhuj** (S) (M) 1. eating serpents; living on serpents. 2. peacock. 3. another name for Garuḍa.

**Phaṇibhūṣana** (S) (M) 1. decorated with serpents. 3. another name for Śiva.

**Phanikesa** (S) (M) 1. lord of the hooded ones. 3. another name for Viṣṇu who reclines on the coiled form of Śeṣa.

**Phaṇin** (S) (M) 1. hooded. 2. serpent. 3. another name for Rāhu (the planet Saturn);

another name for Patañjali.

**Phaṇinātha** (S) (M) 1. lord of the hooded ones. 3. another name for Śiva.

**Phaṇīndra** (S) (M) 1. lord of hoods. 3. another name for Śeṣa the lord of serpents; another name for Patañjali.

**Phaṇipati** (S) (M) 1. hooded. 3. a huge serpent (*B. Śatakam*); another name for the serpent Śeṣa.

**Phaṇipriya** (S) (F) 1. beloved of the hooded ones. 2. wind.

**Phaṇīśvara** (S) (M) 1. king of the hooded ones. 3. another name for Śiva; another name for Vāsuki.

**Phāṇita** (S) (M) raw sugar; juice of the sugarcane.

**Pharendra** (S) (M) lord of the scatterers; the Kewra plant (*Pandanus odoratissimus*)

**Phena** (S) (M) 1. foam. 3. a king belonging to the race of Uśīnara and who was the father of Sutapas (*H. Purāṇa*); *Acacia rugata*.

**Pheṇapa** (S) (M) 1. one who drinks foam; foam drinking. 3. a member of the Bhṛgu family who described the greatness of cows to Yudhiṣṭhira and lived on the froth of cows milk alone (*M. Bh.*)

**Pheṇavāhin** (S) (M) 1. foam bearing. 2. the ocean. 3. Indra's thunderbolt.

**Phullāmbikā** (S) (F) woman; a bloom; a woman in full bloom.

**Phullanalini** (S) (F) a lotus in full bloom.

**Phullarā** (S) (F) 1. blooming woman; woman full of grace. 3. the wife of Kālaketu (*Kau. Upaniṣad*)

**Phullendu** (S) (M) full moon.

**Piććhala** (S) (M) 1. slippery. 3. a nāga of the Vāsuki family (*M. Bh.*)

**Piććhilā** (S) (F) 1. slimy; slippery. 3. a river of North India (*M. Bh.*)

**Piću** (S) (M) 1. cotton; a grain; a weight; fat; thick; heavy. 3. one of the 8 faces of Bhairava (*S. Samhitā*); an asura.

**Pićuvaktrā** (S) (F) 1. with thick lips. 3. a yoginī (*H. Koṣa*)

**Piho** (S) (M) the Pheasant tailed Jacana (*Tringa chirurgus*)

**Pikānanda** (S) (M) 1. the cuckoo's joy. 3. another name for spring.

**Pikī** (S) (F) Indian Cuckoo (*Cuculus varius*)

**Pikkā** (S) (F) a weight approximately equal to the weight of 13 pearls; a string of 13 pearls.

**Pilā** (S) (F) 1. stopping. 3. an apsarā.

**Pilak** (S) (F) yellow coloured; Golden Oriole.

**Pilpilā** (S) (F) 1. impelling again and again; inciting again and again. 3. another name for Lakṣmī.

**Pilu** (S) (M) 1. arrow; flower; stem of the plant; atom; insect; elephant. 3. a rāga; Wild Guava (*Careya arborea*)

**Pināka** (S) (M) 1. a staff; a bow. 3. bow of Rudra-Śiva (*K. Granthāvali*)

**Pinākadhṛk** (S) (M) 1. bearer of Pināka. 3. another name for Śiva.

**Pinākagopta** (S) (M) 1. preserver of Pināka. 3. another name for Śiva.

**Pinākahasta** (S) (M) 1. Pināka handed. 3. another name for Śiva.

**Pinākapāṇi** (S) (M) 1. holding the Pināka. 3. another name for Śiva.

**Pinākasena** (S) (M) 1. armed with the Pināka. 3. another name for Skanda.

**Pinākāvasa** (S) (M) 1. controlling the Pināka. 3. another name for Rudra.

**Pinākin** (S) (M) 1. armed with the Pināka. 3. one of the 11 rudras who was the son of Sthāṇu and grandson of Brahmā (*M. Bh.*); another name for Rudra-Śiva.

**Pinākinī** (S) (F) 1. bow shaped; with the bow. 3. a river (*H. Purāṇa*)

**Piṇḍāraka** (S) (M) 1. gatherer; unites; assembles; join. 2. cowherd; buffalo herdsman. 3. a nāga of the Kaśyapa family (*M. Bh.*); a son of Vasudeva and Rohinī.

**Piṇḍasektṛ** (S) (M) 1. a vessel for oblations. 3. a serpent of the family of Takṣaka (*M. Bh.*)

**Piṇḍinī** (S) (F) 1. receiving oblations. 3. an apsarā (*Bhā. Purāṇa*)

**Piṅgā** (S) (F) 1. yellow. 2. bowstring; yellow pigment; tawny; turmeric; saffron. 3. another name for Durgā.

**Piṅgadṛśa** (S) (M) 1. yellow eyed. 3. another name for Śiva.

**Piṅgajaṭa** (S) (M) 1. with yellow braided hair. 3. another name for Śiva.

**Piṅgākṣa** (S) (M) 1. yellow eyed. 3. rākṣasa; a bird who was the son of Droṇa (*Mā. Purāṇa*); another name for Agni and Śiva.

**Piṅgākṣī** (S) (F) 1. tawny eyed. 3. a deity presiding over the family; a mother in Skanda's retinue (*H. Purāṇa*)

**Piṅgalā** (S) (F) 1. of yellow hue; golden; fiery; reddish brown. 3. the elephant of the south quarter; another name for Lakṣmī.

**Piṅgala** (S) (M) 1. of yellow hue; reddish-brown; tawny; yellow; golden. 2. fire; lion. 3. a demi-god attendant of the sun (*M. Bh.*); a king of the yakṣās and a friend of Śiva (*M. Bh.*); a nāga son of Kaśyapa and Kadrū (*M. Bh.*); an attendant of Śiva (*K. Sāgara*); a sage (*M. Bh.*); a Jaina treasure (*J.S. Koṣa*); a dānava (*K. Sāgara*)

**Piṅgalaka** (S) (M) 1. redbrown; tawny. 3. a yakṣa.

**Piṅgalākṣa** (S) (M) 1. tawny eyed; with red-brown eyes. 3. another name for Śiva.

**Piṅgalarāja** (S) (M) 1. king of the Piṅgala state. 3. a yakṣa who acts as Śiva's pilot (*M. Bh.*)

**Pingalavarman** (S) (M) 1. with yellow armour. 3. father of Suvarṇaśiras.

**Piṅgaleśvarī** (S) (F) 1. goddess of the Piṅgala state. 3. a form of Dākṣāyaṇī (*A. Koṣa*)

**Piṅgekṣana** (S) (M) 1. yellow eyed. 3. another name for Śiva.

**Piṅgeśvara** (S) (M) 1. the yellow deity. 3. an attendant of Pārvatī (*D. Purāṇa*)

**Piñjalā** (S) (F) 1. confused. 3. a river of Purāṇic fame (*M. Bh.*)

**Piñjaraka** (S) (M) 1. yellow; golden. 2. gold. 3. a son of Kaśyapa and Kadrū (*M. Bh.*)

**Pippala** (S) (M) 1. the sacred Fig tree (*Ficus religiosa*). 3. a son of Mitra and Revatī (*Bh. Purāṇa*); a sage of the Kaśyapa race (*P. Purāṇa*)

**Pippalāda** (S) (M) 1. eating the fruit of the Pippala tree. 3. an ancient teacher of the *Atharva Veda*.

**Pippalāyana** (S) (M) 1. living under a Fig tree. 2. sensual. 3. a son of Ṛṣabhadeva and Jayantī (*Bhā. Purāṇa*)

**Pippaleśa** (S) (M) lord of the Pippala tree (*Ficus religiosa*)

**Pipru** (S) (M) 1. mark; spot; mole. 3. a demon conquered by Indra (*Ṛg Veda*)

**Piśācā** (S) (F) 1. of yellow colour; corpse like in appearance; a ghost. 3. a daughter of Dakṣa and mother of the Piśācas (*V. Purāṇa*)

**Piśāca** (S) (M) 1. of yellow colour. 2. corpse like in appearance; a ghost. 3. a class of yellow demons personified as the children of Krodhā, during the Mahābhārata many of these were reborn as kings.

**Piśaṅga** (S) (M) 1. yellow bodied; red brown; tawny. 3. a serpent of Dhṛtarāṣṭra's family (*M. Bh.*)

**Piśaṅgaka** (S) (M) 1. red brown; tawny. 3. an attendant of Viṣṇu (*Br. Purāṇa*)

**Piśuna** (S) (M) 1. slanderous; betrayer. 2. cotton; crow. 3. a sage who was the son of Kuśika; another name for Nārada

**Piśunā** (S) (F) 1. informing against; betraying. 2. saffron. 3. a river described as the Mandākinī (*Rāmāyaṇa*)

**Pītadīptā** (S) (F) 1. yellow light; of yellow hue. 3. a Buddhist deity.

**Pitāmaha** (S) (M) 1. grandfather. 3. another name for Bhīṣma and Brahmā.

**Pītāmbara** (S) (M) 1. dressed in yellow. 3. another name for Viṣṇu and Kṛṣṇa.

**Pītāruṇa** (S) (M) yellowish red; mid dawn.

**Pītaśam** (S) (M) 1. yellow stone. 2. topaz.

**Pītāśman** (S) (M) yellow stone; topaz.

**Pītavāsas** (S) (M) 1. dressed in yellow. 3. another name for Viṣṇu.

**Pītayūthī** (S) (F) an assemblage of yellow; yellow jasmine.

**Pīṭha** (S) (M) 1. seat; pedestal. 3. a demon killed by Kṛṣṇa (*M. Bh.*); a minister of Kaṅsa (*H. Purāṇa*)

**Piṭhara** (S) (M) 1. pot; boiler; pan used for cooking. 3. a daitya who was a member of Varuṇa's court (*M. Bh.*)

**Piṭharaka** (S) (M) 1. boiler. 3. a serpent of the Kaśyapa family (*M. Bh.*)

**Pītikā** (S) (F) saffron; Yellow Jasmine (*Jasminum humile*); honey; turmeric.

**Pīvanārī** (S) (F) 1. fat; strong; robust; voluptous. 3. the wife of Vedaśiras (*H. Purāṇa*); a princess of Vidarbha (*Mā. Purāṇa*)

**Pīvarā** (S) (F) 1. fat; stout. 3. a daughter of the gandharva Huhu (*K. Sāgara*)

**Pīvara** (S) (M) 1. fat; thick; dense; large. 3. a ṛṣi under Manu Tāmasa (*Mā. Purāṇa*); a son of Dyutimat (*V. Purāṇa*)

**Pīvarī** (S) (F) 1. fat. 3. the wife of Śuka the son of Vyāsa and the mother of Kṛṣṇa, Gauraprabha, Bhūri, Devaśruta and Kīrti (*M. Purāṇa*)

**Pīvatī** (S) (F) 1. swelling; overflowing; exuberant; abounding; increasing. 2. acceptor of scripture. 3. a mind born daughter of Dharma who was the wife of Śuka and mother of goddess Kīrtimatī (*M. Bh.*)

**Pīyūṣa** (S) (M) 1. nectar. 2. the 1st milk of a cow. 3. nectar produced at the churning of the Ocean of Milk.

**Pīyūṣabhānu** (S) (M) 1. nectar rayed. 3. another name for the moon.

**Pīyūṣadyuti** (S) (M) 1. nectar rayed. 3. another name for the moon.

**Pīyūṣakaṇikā** (S) (F) nectar drop.

**Plakṣa** (S) (M) Fig tree (*Ficus religiosa*); *Ficus infectoria*.

**Plakṣajātā** (S) (F) 1. rising near the fig tree. 3. a tributary of the Gaṅgā believed to be an incarnation of Sarasvatī (*M. Bh.*)

**Plakṣavatī** (S) (F) 1. surrounded by fig trees. 3. a river (*M. Bh.*); another name for the Sarasvatī river.

**Plavaga** (S) (M) 1. going by leaps and bounds. 3. the charioteer of the sun; a son of the sun (*Bhā. Purāṇa*)

**Poṣita** (S) (M) nourished; protected; cherished.

**Potaka** (S) (M) 1. a young animal; the site of a house. 3. a nāga of the family of Kaśyapa (*M. Bh.*)

**Poṭalapriyā** (S) (M) 1. fond of the Poṭala mountain. 3. a Buddha.

**Potrī** (S) (F) 1. purifier. 3. another name for Durgā.

**Potriratha** (S) (F) 1. hog-vehicled. 3. a female divinity; another name for Māyā.

**Prabāhu** (S) (M) 1. with strong arms. 3. a warrior of the Kauravas (*M. Bh.*)

**Prabala** (S) (M) 1. strong; powerful; mighty. 3. a son of Kṛṣṇa; an attendant of Viṣṇu (*Bhā. Purāṇa*); a daitya (*K. Sāgara*); *Paederia foetida*.

**Prabālaka** (S) (M) 1. powerful; strong. 3. a yakṣa of the court of Kubera (*M. Bh.*)

**Prabhā** (S) (F) 1. light; splendour; radiance. 3. light personified variously as the wife of the sun or as wife of Kalpa and mother of Prātar, Madhyam and Sāya or as a form of Durgā in the disc of the sun (*H. Purāṇa*); a devī in the court of Brahmā (*M. Bh.*); an apsarā (*M. Bh.*); a daughter of Svarbhānu who married Āyus and was the mother of Nahuṣa (*Br. Purāṇa*); a wife of King Puṣpārṇa (*Bhāgavata*)

**Prabhadrā** (S) (F) 1. very noble; very gentle; charming; beautiful. 3. the wife of Karṇa's son (*M. Bh.*)

**Prabhāgaćandra** (S) (M) a part of the moon.

**Prabhākānta** (S) (M) 1. beloved of light. 3. another name for the moon.

**Prabhākara** (S) (M) 1. one who creates light; light maker. 3. a sage of the race of Atri who was the husband of the 10 daughters of Ghṛtāćī and Raudrāśva; a serpent of Kaśyapa's race (*M. Bh.*); a son of Jyotiṣmat (*V. Purāṇa*); another name for Śiva, the sun and the moon (*V. Purāṇa*)

**Prabhāna** (S) (M) light; splendour; radiance.

**Prabhañjana** (S) (M) 1. crushing; destroying. 2. wind; storm; tempest. 3. a son of King Ćitravāhana of Manipura (*M. Bh.*); a king and father of Putātmā (*Sk. Purāṇa*)

**Prabhāñjanasuta** (S) (M) 1. son of the god of wind. 3. another name for Bhīma.

**Prabhāñjani** (S) (M) 1. born of wind. 3. another name for Hanumān and Bhīma.

**Prabhānu** (S) (M) 1. the brightest sun. 2. the sun at noon. 3. a son of Kṛṣṇa and Satyabhāmā (*Bhāgavata*)

**Prabhāpāla** (S) (M) 1. protector of light. 3. a Bodhisattva.

**Prabhāsa** (S) (M) 1. splendour. 2. beauty; radiance. 3. a vasu son of Dharma and Prabhātā and the husband of the sister of Bṛhaspati (*V. Purāṇa*); an attendant of Skanda.

**Prabhāsana** (S) (M) 1. illuminating. 3. a

place of pilgrimage near Dvārakā (*Bhā. Purāṇa*)

**Prabhātā** (S) (F) **1.** goddess of dawn. **3.** a wife of Dharma and mother of the vasus Pratyūṣa and Prabhāsa (*M. Bh.*)

**Prabhāta** (S) (M) **1.** shone forth. **2.** morning; dawn; sunrise. **3.** a son of Sūrya and Prabhā (*V. Purāṇa*)

**Prabhātī** (S) (F) the song of the morning.

**Prabhāva** (S) (M) **1.** cause of existence. **2.** prominent; excelling; distinguished; source; origin; majesty; dignity; mighty; power; strength; splendour; beauty. **3.** a son of Manu Svāroćiṣa (*M. Purāṇa*)

**Prabhāvalī** (S) (F) **1.** shining. **2.** graceful; radiant. **3.** a rāga.

**Prabhāvatī** (S) (F) **1.** luminous; radiant. **2.** splendid. 3. the daughter of Vajranābha and wife of Pradyumna (*Bhā. Purāṇa*); the daughter of Suvīra and wife of Marutta (*M. Purāṇa*); the mother of the 19th Arhat of the present Avasarpinī (*J.S. Koṣa*); a wife of Sūrya; a mother in Skanda's retinue (*M. Bh.*); a wife of King Ćitraratha of Aṅga (*M. Bh.*); a Buddhist deity (*L. Vistara*); an apsarā (*V. Purāṇa*)

**Prabhāvyuha** (S) (M) **1.** circle of light. **2.** origin of light. **3.** a Buddhist deity (*L. Vistara*)

**Prabhu** (S) (M) **1.** effector; creator. **2.** mighty; powerful; rich; abundant; eternal; master; lord; king; god. **3.** a son of Kardama (*H. Purāṇa*); a son of Śuka and Pīvarī (*M. Purāṇa*); a son of Bhaga and Siddhi (*Bh. Purāṇa*); a soldier of Skanda (*M. Bh.*); another name for God.

**Prabhudāsa** (S) (M) slave of the gods; a devotee.

**Prabhūta** (S) (M) come forth; arisen; appeared.

**Prabhūti** (S) (F) arisen; well being; welfare; success; riches.

**Prabodha** (S) (M) awakening; consciousness; knowledge; understanding.

**Prabodhaćandra** (S) (M) the moon of knowledge.

**Prabodhana** (S) (M) **1.** awaking; arousing. **3.** a Buddha.

**Prabodhika** (S) (M) awaking others; one who awakens; dawn; daybreak.

**Prabuddha** (S) (M) awakened; roused; expanded; come forth; known; understood; enlightened; wise; appeared.

**Praćakṣas** (S) (M) **1.** one who tells; one who illumines. **3.** another name for Bṛhaspati.

**Praćaṇḍa** (S) (M) **1.** violent. **2.** furious; passionate; terrible; fiery; fierce. **3.** a son of Vatsaprī and Sunandā (*Mā. Purāṇa*); a dānava (*K. Sāgara*)

**Praćaṇḍikā** (S) (F) **1.** very fiery. **3.** a form of Durgā (*D. Purāṇa*)

**Praćaṇḍogrā** (S) (F) **1.** with a burning anger. 3. a yoginī (*D. Purāṇa*)

**Praćayikā** (S) (F) gatherer; one who gathers flowers.

**Praćetas** (S) (M) **1.** with an awakened mind. **2.** wise; clever; happy; delighted. **3.** the 10 sons of Prāćīnabarhis (*M. Bh.*); a son of Durmada (*Bh. Purāṇa*); a son of Duryāman (*V. Purāṇa*); another name for Agni, Varuṇa.

**Praćetṛ** (S) (M) charioteer.

**Prāćikā** (S) (F) **1.** driving. **2.** a female falcon.

**Prācīna** (S) (M) ancient; eastern; former; prior; preceding; the ancient fire; Velvet Leaf (*Cissampelos pareira*)

**Prāćīnabarhis** (S) (M) **1.** eastern bed of Kuśā grass; eastern light. **3.** a prajāpati who was the son of Havirdhāna and Dhīṣaṇā and the husband of Savarṇā; he fathered the 10 Praćetas (*V. Purāṇa*)

**Prāćīnvān** (S) (M) **1.** gathering; collecting. **3.** a king who was the son of Janamejaya and Anantā and the husband of Aśmakī, he was the father of Saṁyāti and Manasyu (*M. Bh.*)

**Prāćīpati** (S) (M) **1.** lord of the east. **3.** another name for Indra.

**Praćīrṇa** (S) (M) to come forth; to appear.

**Praćodikā** (S) (F) **1.** inflamer. **3.** the daughter of Niyojikā and granddaughter of Duhsaha (*M. Purāṇa*)

**Pradānaśūra** (S) (M) **1.** hero in giving. **2.** liberal. **3.** a Bodhisattva.

**Pradātṛ** (S) (M) **1.** giver; bestower. **3.** a viśvādeva; another name for Indra.

**Pradatta** (S) (M) **1.** bestowed; given. **3.** a

gandharva (*Rāmāyaṇa*)

**Prādhā** (S) (F) 1. extremely distinguished. 2. supreme; eminent. 3. a daughter of Dakṣa and mother of apsarās and gandharvas (*M. Bh.*)

**Pradhānā** (S) (F) 1. chief; most important; original; source; intellect; understanding. 3. a Śakti.

**Pradhī** (S) (F) great intelligence.

**Pradhi** (S) (M) the disc of the moon; felly of a wheel.

**Pradīpa** (S) (M) 1. to blaze forth; immensely illuminating. 2. light; lamp; lantern.

**Pradīpikā** (S) (F) one that illuminates; torch; a small lamp.

**Pradīpti** (S) (F) light; lustre; radiance.

**Pradoṣa** (S) (M) 1. deteriorating; the 1st part of the night. 3. evening personified as a son of Dakṣa or as a son of Doṣā (*M. Bh.*); a son of Puṣpārṇa and Prabhā and grandson of Dhruva (*Bhāgavata*)

**Pradoṣaka** (S) (M) born in the evening.

**Pradveśi** (S) (F) 1. one who hates. 3. the wife of Dīrghatamas (*Ṛg Veda*)

**Pradyota** (S) (M) 1. light; radiance. 3. a yakṣa in the court of Kubera (*M. Bh.*); a son of King Śunaka; a king of Magadha (*V. Purāṇa*)

**Pradyotana** (S) (M) 1. full of light. 3. a king of Ujjayinī; another name for the sun.

**Pradyumna** (S) (M) 1. extremely mighty; the pre-eminently mighty one. 3. the god of love reborn as the son of Kṛṣṇa and Rukminī, he was the father of Aniruddha; a son of Manu and Naḍvalā (*Bhā. Purāṇa*)

**Pradyuta** (S) (M) lighted; to begin to shine.

**Prāgahi** (S) (M) 1. beholder of knowledge. 3. a teacher of yajñas.

**Pragalbhā** (S) (F) 1. bold; confident. 3. another name for Durgā.

**Pragati** (S) (F) progress.

**Praghasā** (S) (F) 1. devourer. 3. a mother in Skanda's retinue (*M. Bh.*); a rākṣasī (*V. Rāmāyaṇa*)

**Praghoṣa** (S) (M) 1. sound; noise. 3. a son of Kṛṣṇa (*Bhāgavata*)

**Prāghuṇa** (S) (M) guest.

**Pragīta** (S) (M) singing; reciting; well-sung; highly praised; lyric; song.

**Prāgītya** (S) (M) celebrity; excellence.

**Prāgra** (S) (M) the highest point; summit.

**Praguṇa** (S) (M) full of qualities; straight; honest; upright; efficient; right.

**Praharaṇa** (S) (M) 1. striking; removing. 2. the verse spoken while throwing grass into the sacrificial fire. 3. a son of Kṛṣṇa (*Bhāgavata*)

**Prahāsa** (S) (M) 1. laughter. 2. appearance; display; splendour of colours. 3. an attendant of Śiva (*M. Bh.*); a minister of Varuṇa (*Rāmāyaṇa*); a serpent of the family of Dhṛtarāṣṭra (*M. Bh.*); a soldier of Skanda (*M. Bh.*); a rākṣasa (*V. Rāmāyaṇa*); another name for Śiva.

**Prahasantī** (S) (F) 1. laughing; smiling. 3. Jasmine (*Jasminum officianale*)

**Prahasita** (S) (M) 1. laughing; cheerful. 3. a king of the kinnaras; a Buddha.

**Prahasta** (S) (M) 1. with long hands. 3. a minister of Rāvaṇa who was the son of Sumālī and Ketumatī (*V. Rāmāyaṇa*)

**Praheti** (S) (M) 1. one that strikes. 2. missile; weapon. 3. a demon who travels with the sun in the month of Vaiśākha (*Bhāgavata*); the father of the sun; a king of rākṣasas.

**Prahlāda** (S) (M) 1. delight; joy; happiness. 3. the son of Hiraṇyakaśipu and Kayādhu who was a devotee of Viṣṇu (*Bhā. Purāṇa*); the chief of the asuras and crowned emperor of the demons in Pātāla, he was the son of Viroćana (*M. Bh.*); a serpent in the court of Varuṇa (*M. Bh.*); a prajāpati (*M. Bh.*)

**Prahvala** (S) (M) of magnificent form; a beautiful body.

**Praja** (S) (M) 1. propagation; birth; offspring; man. 3. a son of Ajamīdha.

**Prajādhara** (S) (M) 1. supporting creatures. 3. another name for Viṣṇu.

**Prajādhyakṣa** (S) (M) 1. surveyer of creation. 3. another name for the sun, Kardama and Dakṣa.

**Prajāgara** (S) (M) 1. watchman; guardian. 3. another name for Viṣṇu.

**Prajāgarā** (S) (F) 1. fully awake; attentive. 3. an apsarā (*M. Bh.*)

**Prajākara** (S) (M) creator of people; potent; a symbol.

**Prajaktā** (S) (F) mother of the people; goddess of creation.

**Prajānātha** (S) (M) 1. lord of creation. 3. another name for Brahmā, Manu and Dakṣa.

**Prajaṅgha** (S) (M) 1. with strong thighs. 3. a rākṣasa in Rāvaṇa's army (*V. Rāmāyaṇa*)

**Prajāpāla** (S) (M) 1. protector of creatures. 2. king. 3. another name for Kṛṣṇa.

**Prajāpatī** (S) (F) 1. lord of the people; lord of creation. 3. the sister of Mahāmāyā and foster mother of Gautama Buddha (*B. Literature*)

**Prajāpati** (S) (M) 1. lord of creation; father; king. 3. time personified; the first 10 or 21 lords created by Brahmā; the father of Ūṣas the goddess of dawn and one who encompasses all the 33 crore gods in himself; another name for Viṣṇu, Śiva, Agni, Sāvitṛ, Soma and the sun.

**Prajas** (S) (M) 1. born; produced; to produce; to bring forth. 3. a son of Manu Auttami (*Ṛg Veda*)

**Prajāsṛj** (S) (M) 1. creator of beings. 3. another name for Brahmā and Kaśyapa.

**Prajāti** (S) (M) 1. generation; production; delivery. 3. a prince (*Ma. Purāṇa*)

**Prajāvatī** (S) (F) 1. having many children. 2. mother. 3. the wife of Priyavrata (*Bhā. Purāṇa*); a tutelary deity of the Sumantus (*Var. Purāṇa*)

**Prajavin** (S) (M) swift; fleet.

**Prajeśa** (S) (M) lord of creatures.

**Prajeśvara** (S) (M) 1. lord of creatures. 2. king.

**Prajina** (S) (M) 1. moving; swift. 2. wind; air.

**Prajit** (S) (M) conquering; defeating.

**Prajivin** (S) (M) 1. exuberant with life; lively. 3. a minister of Meghavarṇa the king of crows.

**Prajñā** (S) (F) 1. wisdom; intelligence; knowledge; discrimination. 3. wisdom personified as the goddess of arts and eloquence; a form of Sarasvatī.

**Prajñāćakṣuṣa** (S) (M) 1. with an eye of wisdom. 2. one who possesses inner wisdom; blind. 3. another name for Dhṛtarāṣṭra.

**Prajñāćandra** (S) (M) the moon of wisdom.

**Prajñadeva** (S) (M) god of wisdom.

**Prajñāditya** (S) (M) sun of wisdom.

**Prajñāgupta** (S) (M) protected by knowledge; wise.

**Prajñākāya** (S) (M) 1. with a body of wisdom. 3. another name for Manjuśrī.

**Prajñākośa** (S) (M) store of wisdom.

**Prajñākūṭa** (S) (M) 1. mountain of wisdom. 3. a Bodhisattva.

**Prajñāna** (S) (M) intelligent; wise; clever.

**Prajñāsagara** (S) (M) ocean of wisdom.

**Prajñasahāya** (S) (M) with wisdom as companion.

**Prajñāvarman** (S) (M) armoured by knowledge.

**Prajñendra** (S) (M) lord of wisdom.

**Prajvālā** (S) (F) inflamed; flame; light.

**Prakālana** (S) (M) 1. to urge; to incite; driving on. 3. a serpent of the family of Vāsuki (*M. Bh.*)

**Prakāma** (S) (M) intense desire; fulfilment of desire; joy; delight.

**Prākara** (S) (M) 1. doing well; friendship; respect. 3. a son of Dyutimat.

**Prakarṣaka** (S) (M) 1. harasser. 3. another name for Kāma.

**Prakāśa** (S) (M) 1. visible; light; clearness; brightness; splendour; lustre; fame; renown; glory; appearance; sunshine. 3. a sage of the family of Bhṛgu who was the son of Tāmasa (*M. Bh.*); the messengers of Viṣṇu; another name for Manu Raivata (*H. Purāṇa*)

**Prakāśāditya** (S) (M) sun among the enlightened; sunlight.

**Prakāśakarman** (S) (M) 1. bestowing light. 3. another name for the sun.

**Prakāśātman** (S) (M) 1. enlightened soul. 2. brilliant in nature. 3. another name for Śiva and the sun.

**Prakāśavat** (S) (M) 1. possessing light. 2. bright; brilliant; shining. 3. one of Brahmā's feet (*Bhā. Purāṇa*)

**Prakaśendra** (S) (M) 1. lord of light. 3. the father of Kṣemendra.

**Prakāśikā** (S) (F) one who enlightens; one that illuminates; bright; shining; illuminating; brilliant; celebrated; renowned.

**Prakāśinī** (S) (F) throwing light; making visible.

**Praketa** (S) (M) perception; intelligence; knowledge; appearance.

**Prakhyā** (S) (F) look; appearance; brightness; splendour; renown; fame; celebrity.

**Prakīrti** (S) (F) highly celebrated; very famous; renowned; celebration; declaration.

**Prakoṣṇā** (S) (M) **1.** ever prepared. **2.** sensuous. **3.** an apsarā (*V. Purāṇa*)

**Prākṛta** (S) (M) **1.** original; natural. **3.** a yakṣa (*M. Bh.*)

**Prākṛtī** (S) (F) **1.** original; primary substance. **3.** nature as the personified will of the Supreme Spirit (*Ṛg Veda*)

**Prakula** (S) (M) a handsome or excellent body.

**Pralamba** (S) (M) **1.** hanging down. **2.** pendant; garland of flowers round the neck. **3.** a daitya slain by Balarāma and Kṛṣṇa (*M. Bh.*); a dānava son of Kaśyapa and Danu (*M. Bh.*)

**Pralambaghna** (S) (M) **1.** slayer of Pralamba. **3.** another name for Balarāma and Kṛṣṇa.

**Pralambahan** (S) (M) **1.** destroyer of Pralamba. **3.** another name for Balarāma and Kṛṣṇa.

**Prālambikā** (S) (F) one that hangs down. golden necklace; a pearl ornament.

**Pralambodara** (S) (M) **1.** with a portruding belly. **3.** a king of the kinnaras.

**Pralayānśu** (S) (M) **1.** frosty rayed. **3.** another name for the moon.

**Pramā** (S) (F) basis; foundation; true knowledge.

**Pramadā** (S) (F) **1.** joyous enchanting; wanton; dissolute; mad; intoxicated. **2.** handsome; woman. **3.** the zodiac sign of Virgo.

**Pramada** (S) (M) **1.** joy; delight; pleasure. **3.** a son of Vasiṣṭha (*Bh. Purāṇa*); a dānava (*H. Purāṇa*)

**Pramadvarā** (S) (F) **1.** inattentive; careless. **2.** proud of one's beauty. **3.** the daughter of Menakā and the gandharva Viśvāvasu, she was the wife of Ruru and mother of Śunaka (*M. Bh.*)

**Pramagandha** (S) (M) **1.** with an enticing smell. **3.** a king of the Kīkaṭas (*Ṛg Veda*)

**Pramahas** (S) (M) of great might and splendour.

**Pramandanī** (S) (F) **1.** with a swan's gait. **3.** an apsarā (*A. Veda*)

**Pramandhu** (S) (M) **1.** crusher of thought; crusher of protection. **3.** a yakṣa (*Sk. Purāṇa*)

**Pramanthu** (S) (M) **1.** tormentor. **3.** a son of Vīravrata and the younger brother of Manthu (*Bhā. Purāṇa*)

**Pramardana** (S) (M) **1.** crushing; devastating. **3.** an attendant of Śiva; a vidyādhara (*K. Sāgara*); another name for Viṣṇu.

**Pramat** (S) (M) wise; prudent.

**Pramaṭaka** (S) (M) **1.** wise; thought out. **3.** a sage (*M. Bh.*)

**Pramāthā** (S) (F) **1.** pain. **2.** mare like. **3.** the wife of Kṣupa and mother of Vīra (*M. Purāṇa*)

**Pramatha** (S) (F) **1.** one who harasses; torments. **3.** an attendant of Skanda given to him by Yama (*M. Bh.*); a class of attendants of Śiva; a son of Dhṛtarāṣṭra (*M. Bh.*)

**Pramathādhipa** (S) (M) **1.** head of the Pramathas. **3.** another name for Śiva.

**Pramathapati** (S) (M) **1.** lord of the Pramathas. **3.** another name for Śiva.

**Pramathin** (S) (M) **1.** harassing; destroying. **3.** a brother of Dūṣana who was an associate of Rāvaṇa (*V. Rāmāyaṇa*); a rākṣasa friend of Ghaṭotkaća (*M. Bh.*); a son of Dhṛtarāṣṭra (*M. Bh.*)

**Pramathinī** (S) (F) **1.** exciting; tormenting. **3.** an apsarā (*M. Bh.*)

**Pramati** (S) (M) **1.** wise; prudent; intelligent; provider; protector. **3.** a sage who was the son of Ćyavana and Sukanyā and the husband of Pratāpī and the father of Ruru (*M. Bh.*); a minister of Vibhīṣaṇa (*V. Rāmāyaṇa*); a sage in the 10th Manvantara (*H. Purāṇa*); a son of Janamejaya (*Rāmāyaṇa*); a son of Prānśu (*Bh. Purāṇa*)

**Pramikā** (S) (F) **1.** highest; best; greatest. **2.** one who fulfils desires and thereby gives desired form to devotees by fulfilling their ambition.

**Pramīlā** (S) (F) **1.** lassitude; enervation; exhaustion from indolence. **3.** the leader of the Strirājya who married Arjuna (*M. Bh.*)

**Pramita** (S) (M) limited; moderate; measured out.

**Pramitī** (S) (F) right perception; wisdom; prudence.

**Pramloćā** (S) (F) 1. with shy eyes. 3. an apsarā who was the consort of sage Kaṇḍu.

**Pramoda** (S) (M) 1. joy; delight; gladness. 3. pleasure personified as a child of Brahmā born from his neck (*M. Purāṇa*); a serpent of the family of Airāvata (*M. Bh.*); a soldier of Skanda (*M. Bh.*)

**Pramodana** (S) (M) 1. one who delights. 3. another name for Viṣṇu.

**Pramodita** (S) (M) 1. delighted; glad. 3. another name for Kubera.

**Pramohinī** (S) (F) 1. enticing; infatuating. 3. a gandharva maiden.

**Pramući** (S) (M) 1. released; liberated. 3. a sage of south India (*M. Bh.*)

**Prāṇa** (S) (M) 1. the breath of life; spirit; vitality; vigour; energy; power. 3. a marut; the son of Dhātā and Āyati and the grandson of Bhṛgu (*V. Purāṇa*); a son of the vasu Soma and Manoharā (*M. Bh.*); a ṛṣi in the 2nd Manvantara (*H. Purāṇa*); a son of Vasu Dhara (*H. Purāṇa*); a son of Dhatṛ; a son of Vidhātṛ (*Bh. Purāṇa*); another name for Brahmā and Viṣṇu.

**Prāṇada** (S) (M) 1. life giving. 3. another name for Brahmā and Viṣṇu; Black Myrobalan (*Terminalia chebula*); *Dendrobium fimbriatum*.

**Praṇāda** (S) (M) 1. roar. 3. a Ćakravartin.

**Prāṇādhika** (S) (M) dearer than life.

**Prāṇaka** (S) (M) 1. living being. 2. one who gives life; giver of breath. 3. the son of an agni called Prāna (*M. Bh.*)

**Prāṇanārāyaṇa** (S) (M) 1. lord of life. 3. a king of Kāmarūpa (*A. Koṣa*)

**Prāṇanātha** (S) (M) 1. lord of life. 3. another name for Yama.

**Prāṇatī** (S) (F) bending; salutation; reverence; obeisance.

**Praṇava** (S) (M) the mystical syllable Om.

**Prāṇavatī** (S) (F) full of life; living; strong; powerful.

**Praṇaya** (S) (M) leader; guidance; conduct; affection; love.

**Praṇayin** (S) (M) beloved; dear; intimate; friend; favourite.

**Praṇayinī** (S) (F) beloved; worshipper; devotee.

**Praṇayitā** (S) (F) animated; kept alive.

**Prāṇeśa** (S) (M) 1. lord of life; lord of breath. 3. a marut (*Bhā. Purāṇa*)

**Prāṇeśvarī** (S) (F) goddess of life; very dear in life; beloved.

**Praṇetṛ** (S) (M) leader; guide.

**Pranidhi** (S) (M) 1. spy. 3. the son of an agni called Pāñćajanya (*M. Bh.*)

**Praṇidhi** (S) (M) 1. request; solicitation; prayer. 3. a son of Bṛhadratha (*M. Bh.*)

**Praṇitā** (S) (F) 1. led forward; conducted; advanced; promoted; produced; performed; executed; finished; written; composed; established. 2. a cup used for sacrifices; holy water. 3. a river (*A. Koṣa*)

**Praṇita** (S) (M) fire consecrated by prayer; agreeable; pleasing.

**Praṇiti** (S) (F) conduct; leading; guidance.

**Prāñjala** (S) (M) straight; upright; honest; sincere.

**Prāñjalī** (S) (F) upright; respectful; joining the hollowed open hands as a mark of respect.

**Praṇoda** (S) (M) 1. driving; directing. 2. one who drives; directs; leads.

**Praṇmaṇi** (S) (M) 1. leading jewel; jewel among the leaders. 3. another name for Nārāyaṇa and Brahmā.

**Prānśu** (S) (M) 1. high; tall; long; strong; intense. 3. a son of Manu Vaivasvata (*H. Purāṇa*); a son of Vatsaprī (*Purāṇas*)

**Prānśunṛga** (S) (M) 1. strongly praised; noblest among men. 3. a Manu (*D. Bh. Purāṇa*)

**Praṇuta** (S) (M) praised; celebrated; lauded.

**Prapakṣa** (S) (M) 1. extremity of a wing; in an army. 3. a son of Kṛṣṇa (*V. Purāṇa*)

**Prapālin** (S) (M) 1. protector. 3. another name for Balarāma.

**Prapanćikā** (S) (M) 1. multiplying; amplifying; manifestation. 3. a yoginī.

**Prapāṭikā** (S) (F) 1. one who manifests.

2. multiplying into many forms. 3. young shoot or sprout.

**Praphulla** (S) (M) blooming; blossoming; covered with blossoms; shining; cheerful; pleased.

**Prapitāmaha** (S) (M) **1.** paternal grandfather. **3.** another name for Bhīṣma.

**Prāpti** (S) (M) (F) **1.** achievement; advent; occurrence; arrival; discovery obtainment. **3.** the wife of Śama who was a son of Dharma (*M. Bh.*); a daughter of Jarāsandha (*H. Purāṇa*); a wife of Kansa (*Bhāgavata*)

**Prarādhya** (S) (M) satisfied.

**Prārthanā** (S) (F) prayer.

**Praruja** (S) (M) **1.** shining forth; likable. **2.** exciting; seductive; handsome; graceful; to break. **3.** a deva who guards the amṛta (*M. Bh.*); a rākṣasa (*M. Bh.*)

**Prāśā** (S) (F) ardent desire.

**Prasāda** (S) (M) **1.** clearness; brightness; purity; free gift; calmness; propitiatory offering; food presented to an idol; favour. **3.** kindness personified as a son of Dharma and Maitri (*Bhā. Purāṇa*)

**Prasādhikā** (S) (M) adorning; beautifying; accomplishing.

**Prāsahā** (S) (F) **1.** force; power. **2.** powerful. **3.** the wife of Indra.

**Prasāha** (S) (M) overpowering; defeating; force; power.

**Prasala** (S) (M) **1.** cool; tranquil. **2.** the cold season; winter.

**Praśama** (S) (M) **1.** peaceful; calm; cool; reposed; pacified; healing; tranquillity; autumn. **3.** a son of Ānakadundubhi (*Bh. Purāṇa*)

**Praśamī** (S) (F) **1.** calmed; tranquil. **3.** an apsarā (*M. Bh.*)

**Praśan** (S) (M) successful; winner.

**Prasandhi** (S) (M) **1.** expert negotiator. **2.** peace maker. **3.** a son of Vaivasvata Manu and the father of Kṣupa (*M. Bh.*)

**Prasaṇga** (S) (M) adherance; attachment; devotion; union; connection; context.

**Prasannā** (S) (F) pleasing; propitiating.

**Prasanna** (S) (M) clear; bright; pure; distinct; true; placid; tranquil; soothed; pleased.

**Prasannateyu** (S) (M) **1.** eternally happy. **3.** a son of Raudraśva (*Ś. Purāṇa*)

**Prasanneyu** (S) (M) **1.** always pleased. **3.** a son of Raudraśva (*Ś. Purāṇa*)

**Praśānta** (S) (M) calm; quiet.

**Praśastā** (S) (F) **1.** praised; happy; consecrated. **2.** clear; calm. **3.** a holy river (*M. Bh.*)

**Praśasti** (S) (F) fame; praise; glorification.

**Prasatta** (S) (M) satisfied; pleased; bright; pure; clean.

**Prasatti** (S) (F) satisfaction; clearness; brightness; purity.

**Prasavitrī** (S) (F) **1.** impeller; vivifier. **3.** daughter of Suryā.

**Prasena** (S) (M) **1.** with an expert army. **3.** a king who was the son of Nighna; a king of Ujjayinī; a son of Karṇa (*M. Bh.*)

**Prasenajit** (S) (M) **1.** conqueror of an expert army. **2.** a great warrior. **3.** the father of Suyajñā (*M. Bh.*); the father of Reṇukā (*Br. Purāṇa*); a king of Śrāvastī who was a contemporary of Gautama Buddha.

**Prasiddhaka** (S) (M) **1.** accomplished; celebrated; famous. **3.** a king of Janaka's line who was the son of Maru and father of Kīrttiratha (*Bhā. Purāṇa*)

**Prasiddhī** (S) (F) fame; accomplishment; success; attainment.

**Praskaṇva** (S) (M) **1.** son of Kaṇva. **3.** a king who was the son of Medhātithi (*Bhāgavata*); a son of Kaṇva (*M. Bh.*)

**Praśravana** (S) (M) **1.** streaming forth; well; spring; spout. **3.** the mouth of the Sarasvatī river.

**Praśravas** (S) (M) **1.** loud sounding. **3.** the maruts (*Ṛg Veda*)

**Praśraya** (S) (M) **1.** resting place. **2.** modesty; respect; affection; relaxation. **3.** civility personified as a son of Dharma and Hrī (*M. Bh.*); a king of the family of Manu (*Bhāgavata*)

**Praśṛta** (S) (M) **1.** modest; well behaved; hidden. **2.** expanded. **3.** a demon killed by Garuḍa (*M. Bh.*); a son of Ānakadundubhi (*Bh. Purāṇa*)

**Prastava** (S) (M) hymn of praise; chant; song.

**Prastha** (S) (M) 1. expanding; expanse; plain. 3. a monkey (*Rāmāyaṇa*)

**Prastharoman** (S) (M) 1. with expanding hair. 3. son of Svarṇaroman.

**Prāśu** (S) (M) very quick or speedy.

**Praśući** (S) (F) extremely pure.

**Prasūna** (S) (M) 1. born; produced. 2. blossom.

**Praśūśruka** (S) (M) 1. knowing the scripture. 3. a son of Maru (*V. Purāṇa*)

**Praśūśruta** (S) (M) 1. knower of scriptures. 3. a king who was a descendant of Rāma (*Bhāgavata*); a son of Maru (*Rāmāyaṇa*)

**Prasūta** (S) (M) born; produced; a flower; the primordial essence.

**Prasūti** (S) (F) 1. coming forth; appearance. 2. child; offspring. 3. a daughter of Svāyambhuva Manu and the wife of Dakṣa (*D. Bh. Purāṇa*)

**Prasvāpiṇī** (S) (F) 1. inducing to sleep. 2. making others sleep. 3. a daughter of Satrājit and wife of Kṛṣṇa (*Bhā. Purāṇa*)

**Prasvāra** (S) (M) the great syllable; the syllable Om.

**Pratāna** (S) (M) branching out; a shoot; tendril.

**Pratanu** (S) (M) of delicate body; delicate; slender; small; minute.

**Pratāpa** (S) (M) 1. heat; warmth; splendour; brilliance; majesty; glory; power; strength; energy. 3. a Sauvira prince (*M. Bh.*)

**Pratapamukha** (S) (M) 1. with a shining face. 3. king of varanasi (*K. Sāgara*)

**Pratāpavat** (S) (M) 1. full of splendour; majestic; glorious. 3. an attendant of Skanda (*H. Purāṇa*); another name for Śiva.

**Pratāpī** (S) (F) 1. brilliant; majestic; powerful; glorious. 3. the wife of Pramatī and the mother of Ruru (*D. Bh. Purāṇa*)

**Prātara** (S) (M) 1. glorious; shining. 3. the dawn; morning personified as the son of Puṣpārṇa and Prabhā (*Bh. Purāṇa*); a son of the āditya Dhātā and his wife Rākā (*Bhāgavata*)

**Pratardana** (S) (M) 1. piercing; destroying. 3. a Purū king who was the son of Divodāsa and Mādhavī (*M. Bh.*); a rākṣasa (*Rāmāyaṇa*)

**Prātaśćandra** (S) (M) the moon in the morning.

**Pratayankara** (S) (M) causing a deluge.

**Prathita** (S) (M) 1. spread; extended; known; celebrated. 3. another name for Manu Svāroćiṣa and Viṣṇu.

**Prathu** (S) (M) 1. widespead. 2. omnipresent. 3. another name for Viṣṇu.

**Prati** (S) (M) 1. near to; in comparison with; towards. 3. a son of Kuśa (*Bhā. Purāṇa*)

**Pratibāhu** (S) (M) 1. with tethered arms. 3. father of Subahu (*B. Literature*)

**Pratibhā** (S) (F) image; light; splendour; appearance; intelligence; understanding; thought; idea; wit.

**Pratibhānakūṭa** (S) (M) 1. mountain of understanding. 3. a Bodhisattva.

**Pratibhānu** (S) (M) 1. as glorious as the sun; an image of the sun. 3. a son of Kṛṣṇa and Satyabhāmā (*Bhāgavata*)

**Pratibhāvatī** (S) (M) (F) full of understanding; splendid; bright; intelligent; bold; ready witted.

**Pratibuddha** (S) (M) 1. awakened; awake; illuminated; enlightened; celebrated; great; prosperous. 2. the dawn.

**Pratićyā** (S) (F) 1. from the west; with foresight. 3. a wife of Pulastya (*M. Bh.*)

**Pratidriṣṭa** (S) (M) visible; conspicuous; famous; celebrated.

**Pratiha** (S) (M) 1. to receive auspicious knowledge; to go towards the sky. 3. husband of Suvarćalā (*Bh. Purāṇa*)

**Pratihāra** (S) (M) 1. door-keeper. 2. guardian; watchman. 3. a king who was the son of Parameṣṭhī and the father of Pratihartṛ (*V. Purāṇa*)

**Pratihartṛ** (S) (M) 1. averter; one who draws back. 3. the son of Pratihāra and Suvarćalā and the husband of Stuti (*Bhāgavata*)

**Pratijñā** (S) (F) agreement; vow; promise.

**Pratijnā** (S) (F) acknowledgement; agreement; promise; vow; declaration.

**Prātikā** (S) (F) 1. symbolic; an image; beautiful. 2. the Chinese Rose (*Hibiscus rosa sinesis*)

**Pratika** (S) (M) 1. look; appearance; image; symbol; portion. 2. member; limb. 3. a son of

Vasu and father of Oghavat (*Bhāgavata*); a son of Maru (*V. Purāṇa*)

**Pratikāma** (S) (M) desired; beloved.

**Pratikāmin** (S) (M) 1. messenger; servant. 3. the charioteer of Duryodhana (*M. Bh.*)

**Pratikṣatra** (S) (M) 1. respected by all warriors. 3. a king of the family of Paraṣurāma (*Bhā. Purāṇa*); a son of Anenas (*H. Purāṇa*); a son of Śamin (*H. Purāṇa*); a descendant of Atri (*Ṛg Veda*)

**Pratimā** (S) (F) image; likeness; symbol; idol.

**Pratimāćandra** (S) (M) a reflection of the moon.

**Pratimāna** (S) (M) model; image; idol; resemblance.

**Pratinava** (S) (M) ever new; new; young; fresh.

**Pratīpa** (S) (M) 1. contrary; opposite; opponent against the stream. 3. the lunar dynasty king who was the father of Śāntanu and grandfather of Bhīśma (*M. Bh.*)

**Pratipāda** (S) (M) 1. demonstration; proof; explanation. 3. a king of the Bharata race who was the son of Gandhamādana (*Bhāgavata*)

**Pratīra** (S) (M) 1. shore; bank. 3. a son of Manu Bhautya (*Mā. Purāṇa*)

**Pratiratha** (S) (M) 1. equal adversary. 3. a Purū king who was the son of King Antibhāra (*Bhā. Purāṇa*); a son of Matināra and father of Kaṇva (*H. Purāṇa*); a son of Vajra and father of Śućāru (*H. Purāṇa*)

**Pratirupā** (S) (F) 1. image; likeness; agreeable; beautiful. 3. a daughter of Meru (*Bh. Purāṇa*)

**Pratirūpa** (S) (M) 1. image; likeness; agreeable. 3. an asura who once ruled the world (*M. Bh.*)

**Pratiskandha** (S) (M) 1. like a shoulder. 2. strong. 3. an attendant of Skanda (*M. Bh.*)

**Pratiśravas** (S) (M) 1. incomparable in fame; well heard of. 3. the son of King Bhīmasena and Kumārī and a descendant of Parīkṣit (*M. Bh.*)

**Pratiśruta** (S) (M) 1. promised; accepted; echoing. 3. a son of Ānakadundubhi (*Bh. Purāṇa*)

**Pratiśruti** (S) (F) answer; promise; assent.

**Pratiṣṭha** (S) (M) 1. well established. 2. steadfast; famous. 3. the father of Supārśva.

**Pratiṣṭhā** (S) (F) 1. steadfastness; stability. 2. base; foundation; support; pre-eminence; fame; celebrity. 3. a mother in Skanda's retinue (*M. Bh.*)

**Pratīta** (S) (M) 1. recognized; known; appeared; manifest; wise. 3. a viśvadeva (*M. Bh.*)

**Pratithī** (S) (M) 1. born on an auspicious day. 3. a ṛṣi (*M. Bh.*)

**Pratīvāha** (S) (M) 1. leading. 3. a son of Śvaphalka (*H. Purāṇa*)

**Prativedin** (S) (M) experienced; knowledgeable.

**Prativindhya** (S) (M) 1. near the Vindhya mountains. 2. ruler of a part of the Vindhyās. 3. a son of Yudhiṣṭhira and Draupadī (*M. Bh.*)

**Pratoṣa** (S) (M) 1. complete satisfaction; gratification. 3. a son of Manu Svāyambhuva (*Ṛg Veda*)

**Prātṛ** (S) (F) 1. dawn; morning. 3. the daughter of Dhātṛ and Rākā (*Ṛg Veda*)

**Pratulya** (S) (M) 1. uncomparable. 2. unique. 3. another name for Kārttikeya.

**Pratuṣ** (S) (M) delighted; to delight in.

**Pratvakṣas** (S) (M) 1. energetic; vigorous; strong. 3. another name for the maruts and Indra.

**Pratyagadhāman** (S) (M) radiant within; self-illuminating.

**Pratyagāsapati** (S) (M) 1. lord of the western quarter. 3. another name for Varuṇa.

**Pratyagraha** (S) (M) 1. fresh; new; young; pure. 3. a son of Vasu Uparićara and the king of the Ćedis (*M. Bh.*)

**Pratyaṅga** (S) (M) 1. secondary parts of the body. 3. a king of Bhārata (*M. Bh.*)

**Pratyaṅgirā** (S) (F) 1. *Acacia sirissa*. 3. a tāntric form of Durgā.

**Pratyātmika** (S) (M) of unique soul; original; peculiar.

**Pratyūṣa** (S) (M) 1. every morning. 2. dawn. 3. a vasu son of Dharma and Prabhātā and father of sage Devala (*M. Bh.*)

**Pravā** (S) (F) 1. blowing forth. 3. a daughter of Dakṣa (*Vā. Purāṇa*)

**Pravaha** (S) (M) 1. bearing along; carrying.

3. one of the 7 winds around the planets; one of the 7 tongues of fire; a soldier of Skanda (*M. Bh.*)

**Pravāhana** (S) (M) 1. bearing down. 3. a king of Pañćāla (*H. Purāṇa*)

**Pravāhita** (S) (M) 1. flowing. 3. a ṛṣi of the 3rd Manvantara (*V. Purāṇa*)

**Pravālaka** (S) (M) 1. with shoots; coral like. 2. as red as coral. 3. a yakṣa (*M. Bh.*)

**Pravan** (S) (M) to vanquish; to conquer.

**Pravarā** (S) (F) 1. best. 2. best among women. 3. a river of Purāṇic fame (*M. Bh.*)

**Pravara** (S) (M) 1. chief; best; principal; eldest; eminent; excellent. 3. a messenger of the gods (*H. Purāṇa*); a dānava (*H. Purāṇa*); a minister of Kṛṣṇa (*V. Purāṇa*)

**Pravarasena** (S) (M) with the best army.

**Pravasara** (S) (M) 1. emancipated; released. 3. a Buddha (*B. Literature*)

**Pravasu** (S) (M) 1. full of wealth; wealthy. 3. a son of Īlina and Rathantarī (*M. Bh.*)

**Praveka** (S) (M) most excellent; principal; chief.

**Pravepana** (S) (M) 1. tremulous. 3. a serpent of the Takṣaka family (*M. Bh.*)

**Pravilasena** (S) (M) 1. chief of the prominent. 3. a king (*V. Purāṇa*)

**Pravīṇa** (S) (M) 1. skilful; clever. 3. a son of the 14th Manu (*H. Purāṇa*)

**Pravira** (S) (M) yellow sandalwood.

**Pravīra** (S) (M) 1. surpassing heroes. 2. prince; hero; chief. 3. a son of Prāćinvat and grandson of Purū; a son of Haryaśva; a son of Dharmanetra (*H. Purāṇa*); a Purū king who was the son of Santurodha (*A. Purāṇa*); a son of Purū and Pauṣṭī who was the husband of Sūraṣenī and the father of Manasyu (*M. Bh.*)

**Pravīrabāhu** (S) (M) 1. strong armed. 3. a rākṣasa (*V. Rāmāyaṇa*)

**Pravīravara** (S) (M) 1. best of heroes. 3. an asura (*K. Sāgara*)

**Pravitṛ** (S) (M) protector; patron; friend.

**Prayāga** (S) (M) 1. place of sacrifice; confluence; meeting place. 3. the confluence of the 3 holy rivers Gaṅgā, Jamunā and Sarasvatī (*A. Purāṇa*)

**Prayas** (S) (M) pleasure; enjoyment; delight.

**Prayuj** (S) (M) impulse; motive.

**Prayuta** (S) (M) 1. conjoined; mingled with. 3. a gandharva son of Kaśyapa and Muni (*M. Bh.*)

**Prayutsu** (S) (M) 1. warrior; ascetic. 2. ram; air; wind. 3. another name for Indra.

**Prekṣā** (S) (F) beholding; seeing; viewing.

**Premā** (S) (F) beloved; love; affection; kindness.

**Prema** (S) (M) love; affection.

**Premadhara** (S) (M) full of love.

**Premaja** (S) (M) born of love.

**Premajita** (S) (M) one who wins love.

**Premalatā** (S) (F) the vine of love.

**Premāmṛta** (S) (M) the nectar of love.

**Preman** (S) (M) love; affection; kindness; favour.

**Premānanda** (S) (M) the joy of love.

**Premanidhi** (S) (M) pleasure of love.

**Premasāgara** (S) (M) ocean of love.

**Premāvatī** (S) (F) full of love.

**Premendra** (S) (M) 1. lord of love. 3. another name for Kāma.

**Premin** (S) (M) loving; affectionate.

**Preraṇā** (S) (F) direction; command.

**Preṣṭhā** (S) (F) dearest; most beloved.

**Pretvan** (S) (M) 1. moving along. 2. wind; air. 3. another name for Indra.

**Priaṅka** (S) (M) 1. with a beautiful mark. 2. deer; bee; saffron.

**Prīṇa** (S) (M) pleased; satisfied.

**Prīṇana** (S) (M) pleasing; gratifying; soothing.

**Prīṇita** (S) (M) pleased; gratified; delighted.

**Prīta** (S) (M) pleased; delighted; joyful; glad.

**Prītī** (S) (F) 1. pleasure; joy; affection; love; satisfaction. 3. joy personified as a daughter of Dakṣa and as one of the 2 wives of Kāma (*H. Purāṇa*); a digit of the moon (*K. Sāgara*); a wife of sage Pulastya and the mother of Dattoli (*V. Purāṇa*)

**Prītijuṣā** (S) (F) 1. loving; beloved. 3. the wife of Aniruddha (*M. Purāṇa*)

**Priyā** (S) (F) 1. beloved; dear. 3. a daughter of Dakṣa (*V. Purāṇa*); Arabian Jasmine

(*Jasminum sambac*); Kadamba tree (*Anthocephalus cadamba*)

**Priya** (S) (M) beloved; dear.

**Priyadarśana** (S) (M) **1.** pleasant to behold. **3.** a prince of the gandharvas (*K. Granthāvali*); a son of Vāsuki (*K. Sāgara*); a soldier of Skanda (*M. Bh.*); a son of King Drupada (*M. Bh.*)

**Priyadarśikā** (S) (F) good looking.

**Priyadarśin** (S) (M) **1.** pleasant to look at. **2.** looking with kindness. **3.** another name for Aśoka.

**Priyadarśinī** (S) (F) dear to the sight.

**Priyadattā** (S) (F) **1.** given with love. **3.** a mystical name for the earth.

**Priyadhanva** (S) (M) **1.** fond of the bow. **3.** another name for Śiva.

**Priyaka** (S) (M) **1.** loving. **2.** a deer; a bee. **3.** a soldier of Skanda (*M. Bh.*); Indian Kino tree (*Pterocarpus marsupium*); Kadamba tree (*Anthocephalus cadamba*)

**Priyakāriṇī** (S) (F) **1.** doer of pleasing acts. **3.** the mother of Mahāvira (*J.S. Koṣa*)

**Priyālā** (S) (F) **1.** bestowing pleasure. **2.** a vine; a bunch of grapes; Butter tree (*Bassia latifolia*); Common Grape vine (*Vitis vinifera*)

**Priyam** (S) (M) beloved.

**Priyamadhu** (S) (M) **1.** fond of wine. **3.** another name for Balarāma.

**Priyambū** (S) (M) **1.** fond of water. **2.** the mango tree.

**Priyamdadā** (S) (F) **1.** giving what is pleasant. **3.** a gandharvī.

**Priyamedha** (S) (M) **1.** with pleasant wisdom. **3.** a ṛṣi and part author of *Ṛg Veda* (viii); a descendant of Ajamīdha (*Bhā. Purāṇa*)

**Priyamitra** (S) (M) **1.** dear friend. **3.** a mythical Ćakravartin.

**Priyamukhā** (S) (F) **1.** with a lovely face. **3.** a gandharvī.

**Priyamvada** (S) (M) **1.** sweet tongued. **3.** a gandharva (*K. Granthāvali*); Spanish Jasmine (*Jasminum grandiflorum*)

**Priyaṅkara** (S) (M) **1.** showing kindness. **2.** attracting regard; amiable. **3.** a dānava (*K. Sāgara*)

**Priyarañjana** (S) (M) **1.** good looking. **2.** pleasant; loving.

**Priyaśiṣyā** (S) (F) **1.** beloved pupil. **3.** an apsarā (*M. Bh.*)

**Priyaśravas** (S) (M) **1.** loving glory. **2.** one whose glory is pleasant to the ears. **3.** another name for Kṛṣṇa (*Bhā. Purāṇa*)

**Priyatama** (S) (M) most beloved; dearest.

**Priyatara** (S) (M) dearer.

**Priyātman** (S) (M) **1.** dear to soul. **2.** agreeable; pleasant.

**Priyavarćas** (S) (F) **1.** one who loves strength. **3.** an apsarā of the court of Kubera (*Sk. Purāṇa*)

**Priyavrata** (S) (M) **1.** fond of obedience. **3.** the eldest son of Svāyambhuva Manu and Śatarūpā and the husband of Baṛhismatī and the father of Samrat, Kukṣi and 10 other sons.

**Pṛṣad** (S) (M) **1.** spotted; variegated. **2.** tiger; antelope.

**Pṛṣadaśva** (S) (M) **1.** with piebald horses. **3.** a son of Anaranya and father of Haryaśva (*V. Purāṇa*); a son of Virūpa (*Bh. Purāṇa*); another name for the maruts, Vāyu and Śiva.

**Pṛṣadhra** (S) (M) **1.** like an antelope. **3.** a warrior on the side of the Pāṇḍavas; a son of Vaivasvata Manu (*H. Purāṇa*); a son of King Drupada (*M. Bh.*)

**Pṛṣadvarā** (S) (F) **1.** best among spotted antelopes. **3.** a daughter of Menakā and wife of Ruru (*K. Sāgara*)

**Pṛśanī** (S) (F) tender; gentle.

**Pṛṣata** (S) (M) **1.** spotted; vareigated. **2.** speckled; a drop of water; spot. **3.** a Pānćāla king who was the father of Drupada (*M..Bh.*)

**Pṛṣatāśva** (S) (M) **1.** spotted horse. **2.** wind; air. **3.** a solar dynasty king who was the son of Ambarīṣa (*Bhāgavata*)

**Pṛṣatātmaja** (S) (M) **1.** son of Pṛṣata. **3.** another name for Drupada.

**Pṛṣatī** (S) (F) **1.** dappled cow. **3.** the daughter of Priśata (*A. Veda*)

**Pṛśṇī** (S) (F) **1.** dappled cow. **2.** the earth; cloud; milk; the starry sky; a ray of light. **3.** a mother of the maruts (*M. Bh.*); the wife of Savitṛ (*Bh. Purāṇa*); the wife of King Sutapas who in a former birth was Devakī the mother of Kṛṣṇa (*Bhā. Purāṇa*)

**Pṛśni** (S) (M) 1. dappled; speckled; spotted; small; thin. 3. the father of Śvaphalka (*H. Purāṇa*); a sage (*M. Bh.*)

**Pṛśnibhadra** (S) (M) 1. propitious to the earth. 3. another name for Kṛṣṇa.

**Pṛśnidhara** (S) (M) 1. earth bearer. 3. another name for Kṛṣṇa.

**Pṛśnigarbha** (S) (M) 1. the womb of the earth. 3. another name for Viṣṇu and Kṛṣṇa (*M. Bh.*)

**Pṛśniśṛṅga** (S) (M) 1. with a vareigated crest. 3. another name for Viṣṇu and Gaṇeśa.

**Pṛṣṭhaja** (S) (M) 1. backbone. 3. a form of Skanda (*M. Bh.*)

**Pṛṣṭi** (S) (F) rib; a ray of light; touch.

**Pṛtanāja** (S) (M) hero.

**Pṛthā** (S) (F) 1. extended; enlarged; fat; voluptous; robust; stout. 3. a daughter of Sūra who was adopted by Kunti and became the wife of Pāṇḍu, she mothered Karna, Yudhiṣṭhira, Arjuna and Bhīma (*M. Bh.*)

**Pṛthabhū** (S) (M) 1. son of Pṛthā. 3. another name for Yudhiṣṭhira.

**Pṛthāja** (S) (M) 1. son of Pṛthā. 3. another name for Arjuna; White Murdah (*Terminalia citrina*)

**Pṛthāpati** (S) (M) 1. husband of Pṛthā. 3. another name for Pāṇḍu.

**Pṛthasūnu** (S) (M) 1. son of Pṛtha. 3. another name for Yudhiṣṭhira (*M. Bh.*)

**Pṛthāśva** (S) (M) 1. with large horses. 3. a king in the court of Yama (*M. Bh.*)

**Pṛthavinandana** (S) (M) son of the earth.

**Pṛthī** (S) (M) 1. of earth; large. 2. material; ruler of lower animals. 3. a mythical personage said to have been the 1st anointed sovereign of men, he is enumerated among the ṛṣis; a man protected by the aśvins (*Ṛg Veda*)

**Pṛthikā** (S) (F) jasmine.

**Pṛthīśa** (S) (M) lord of the world.

**Pṛthu** (S) (M) 1. broad; wide; expansive; large; great; important; ample. 2. fire. 3. a son of Prastāra; an emperor of great virtue who was the son of Vena and who was a partial incarnation of Mahāviṣṇu his rule is considered a golden period of Bhārata, he was the husband of Arćis and the father of Vijitāśva, Haryakṣa, Dhūmrakeśa, Vṛka and Draviṇa; a son of Anaraṇya and father of Triśaṅkhu; a viśvādeva (*V. Purāṇa*); a dānava (*H. Purāṇa*); a son of Anenas (*M. Bh.*); a son of Ćitraka (*H. Purāṇa*); a son of Ćitraratha (*Bh. Purāṇa*); a son of Pāra (*H. Purāṇa*); a son of Rućaka (*Bh. Purāṇa*); a son of Vaṭeśvara and the father of Viśākhadatta; a Saptaṛṣi (*H. Purāṇa*); another name for Śiva (*M. Bh.*); Nutmeg flower (*Nigella sativa*)

**Pṛthudāna** (S) (M) 1. one who donates a lot. 3. a son of Śaśabindu (*V. Purāṇa*)

**Pṛthūdara** (S) (M) 1. broad bellied. 3. a yakṣa.

**Prithudarbha** (S) (M) 1. large grass. 3. a king of Aṅga (*A. Purāṇa*)

**Pṛthugrīva** (S) (M) 1. broadnecked. 3. a rākṣasa (*Ṛg Veda*)

**Pṛthuhara** (S) (M) 1. annihilator of earthly beings. 3. another name for Śiva.

**Pṛthujaya** (S) (M) 1. victorious far and wide. 3. a son of Śaśabindu and grandson of Ćitraratha (*V. Purāṇa*)

**Pṛthukarman** (S) (M) 1. whose deeds have travelled. 3. a son of Śaśabindu (*V. Purāṇa*)

**Pṛthukīrti** (S) (F) 1. one whose fame has reached far. 3. a daughter of Śura (*H. Purāṇa*)

**Pṛthukīrti** (S) (M) 1. one whose fame has reached far. 3. a son of Śaśabindu (*V. Purāṇa*)

**Pṛthula** (S) (M) broad; expanded; fat; robust; stout.

**Pṛthulākṣa** (S) (M) 1. large eyed. 3. an Aṅga king who lived in the court of Yama (*M. Bh.*); the son of Ćaturaṅga (*Bhā. Purāṇa*)

**Pṛthulāśva** (S) (M) 1. large horse. 2. one who has strong horses. 3. an Ikṣvāku king who was the son of Pṛthu and the father of Adra (*Br. Purāṇa*)

**Pṛthumat** (S) (M) 1. abounding in importance. 2. very important.

**Pṛthupājas** (S) (M) far shining; resplendent.

**Pṛthurukma** (S) (M) 1. with a lot of gold. 3. a son of Parājit (*V. Purāṇa*)

**Pṛthuśekhara** (S) (M) 1. broad crested. 2. mountain.

**Pṛthuśeṇa** (S) (M) 1. with an extensive army.

3. a son of Rućirāśva (*H. Purāṇa*); a son of Vibhu (*Bhā. Purāṇa*)

**Pṛthuśiras** (S) (F) 1. large headed. 3. a daughter of Puloman (*H. Purāṇa*)

**Pṛthuśravas** (S) (M) 1. one whose fame has reached far and wide. 2. far famed. 3. a son of Śaśabindu (*V. Purāṇa*); a son of Raghu (*Bhā. Purāṇa*); a son of the 9th Manu (*M. Purāṇa*); an attendant of Skanda; the elephant of the north quarter; a Ṛg Vedic king protected by Indra; king whose daughter Kāmā married King Ayutanāyī (*M. Bh.*); a sage who was a friend of Yudhiṣṭhira (*M. Bh.*); a soldier of Skanda (*M. Bh.*); a serpent who helped carry the soul of Balarāma (*M. Bh.*)

**Pṛthuśrī** (S) (M) with great fortune.

**Pṛthutama** (S) (M) greatest; broadest; widest; largest.

**Pṛthutara** (S) (M) greater; larger; wider; broader.

**Pṛthuvaktrā** (S) (F) 1. wide mouthed. 3. a mother in Skanda's retinue (*M. Bh.*)

**Pṛthuvastrā** (S) (F) 1. with many clothes. 3. a mother in the Skanda's retinue (*M. Bh.*)

**Pṛthuvega** (S) (M) 1. with great speed. 3. a king in the court of Yama (*M. Bh.*)

**Pṛthuyaśas** (S) (M) 1. far famed. 3. a son of Śaśabindu (*V. Purāṇa*)

**Pṛthvī** (S) (F) 1. the broad and extended one. 2. the earth. 3. daughter of Pṛthu (*Ṛg Veda*); the queen of Benaras and mother of Jaina Tirathankara Suparśvanātha (*J.S. Koṣa*); *Amomum subulatum*; Nutmeg flower (*Nigella sativa*); Horse Purslane (*Trianthema port ulacastrum*)

**Pṛthvīćandra** (S) (M) 1. moon of the earth. 3. a king of the Trigartas (*R. Taraṅginī*)

**Pṛthvīdhara** (S) (M) 1. supporter of the earth. 2. mountain. 3. a demon.

**Pṛthvīgarbha** (S) (M) 1. centre of the earth; womb of the earth. 3. a Bodhisattva; another name for Gaṇeśa.

**Pṛthvīja** (S) (M) born of the earth; the planet Mars.

**Pṛthvīkṣit** (S) (M) 1. ruling over the earth. 2. king.

**Pṛthvīñjaya** (S) (M) 1. earth conqueror. 3. a son of Virāṭa (*M. Bh.*); a dānava (*M. Bh.*)

**Pṛthvīpāla** (S) (M) protector of the earth.

**Pṛthvīpati** (S) (M) 1. lord of the earth. 2. king. 3. another name for Yama.

**Pṛthvīra** (S) (M) warrior of the earth.

**Pṛthvīrāja** (S) (M) lord of the earth.

**Pṛthvīśa** (S) (M) 1. lord of the earth. 2. king.

**Pṛthvīvaraloćana** (S) (M) 1. one who has roamed all over the earth. 3. a Bodhisattva (*K. Vyuha*)

**Puććhāṇḍaka** (S) (M) 1. carrying eggs on the tail. 3. a serpent of the Takṣaka family (*M. Bh.*)

**Pudgala** (S) (M) 1. anything living; handsome; beautiful. 2. the body; the soul; the ego. 3. another name for Śiva.

**Pudgalapati** (S) (M) 1. master of the living. 2. prince; king.

**Pūjā** (S) (F) worship; honour; adoration; respect; reverence; veneration.

**Pūjitā** (S) (F) 1. honoured; adorned; worshipped. 2. goddess.

**Pukharāja** (S) (M) 1. king of jewels. 2. topaz.

**Pula** (S) (M) 1. extended wide; living being. 3. an attendant of Śiva (*Ś. Purāṇa*)

**Pulaha** (S) (M) 1. creator of living beings; lord of animals. 3. a prajāpati who was the father of butterflies, lions, tigers, lambs, wolves and kinnaras; a star (*H. Purāṇa*); another name for Śiva.

**Pulaka** (S) (M) 1. a thrill of joy. 2. gem. 3. a gandharva; a nāga.

**Pulakeśin** (S) (M) rejoicing; happy; thrilling.

**Pulasti** (S) (M) of a head wearing the hair straight.

**Pulastya** (S) (M) 1. with straight hair. 3. a prajāpati born from the ear of Brahmā and who was married to Prīti, Haviṛbhū, Sandhyā and Pratīćyā (*A. Veda*); another name for Śiva.

**Pulina** (S) (M) the bank of a river; islet.

**Pulindī** (S) (F) 1. wild; mountaineer. 3. a rāga.

**Pulomā** (S) (F) 1. to be thrilled. 3. the daughter of the demon Vaiśvānara and wife of Bhṛgu (*H. Purāṇa*)

**Pulomajā** (S) (F) 1. daughter of Puloman. 3. another name for Indrāṇī.

**Pulomajit** (S) (M) 1. conqueror of Puloman. 3. another name for Indra.

**Puloman** (S) (M) 1. thrilled in rapture. 3. a demon whose daughter married Indra and who was destroyed by him (*M. Bh.*)

**Punāna** (S) (M) clear; bright; purified.

**Punću** (S) (M) 1. of pious form; pentagon. 3. a solar dynasty king who was the son of Harita and the father of Vijaya (*Br. Purāṇa*)

**Puṇḍarīkā** (S) (F) 1. lotus like. 3. a daughter of Vasiṣṭha and wife of Prāṇa (*V. Purāṇa*); an apsarā (*M. Bh.*)

**Puṇḍarīka** (S) (M) 1. Lotus flower (*Nelumbo nucifera*); white umbrella; a mark on the forehead; tiger; white. 3. the elephant of the south east quarter (*K. Granthāvali*); a Brāhmin worshipped as the god Vithoba; the son of Śvetaketu and Lakṣmī (*K. Vyuha*); a king of the race of Rāma who was the son of Niśādha and the father of Kṣemadhanvā (*Bhā. Purāṇa*); a son of Nabhas (*H. Purāṇa*); a nāga (*M. Bh.*)

**Puṇḍarīkākṣa** (S) (M) 1. lotus eyed. 3. another name for Viṣṇu/Kṛṣṇa.

**Puṇḍarīkamukha** (S) (M) 1. lotus faced. 3. an eminent serpent king.

**Puṇḍarīkanayana** (S) (M) 1. lotus eyed. 3. another name for Viṣṇu/Kṛṣṇa (*M. Bh.*)

**Puṇḍarīsrajā** (S) (F) a garland of lotuses.

**Puṇḍarīyaka** (S) (M) 1. lotus faced. 3. a viśvadeva (*M. Bh.*)

**Puṇḍra** (S) (M) 1. mark; sign. 2. a line made with ashes on the forehead. 3. the son of the daitya Bāli (*M. Bh.*); a son of Vasudeva.

**Pūnīśa** (S) (M) lord of the pious.

**Punītā** (S) (F) sacred; pious; holy.

**Punīta** (S) (M) holy; pious; sacred; cleaned; purified.

**Puñjarāja** (S) (M) lord of a multitude.

**Puñjikāsthalā** (S) (F) 1. abode of hail. 3. an apsarā who was the maid of Bṛhaspati and was later reborn as Añjanā the mother of Hanumān (*V. Samhitā*)

**Pūnkhitaśara** (S) (M) 1. armed with feathered arrows. 3. another name for Kāma.

**Puṇyā** (S) (F) 1. virtue; good work; meritorious act; purity. 2. holy basil. 3. a daughter of Kratu and Saṁnati (*V. Purāṇa*)

**Puṇya** (S) (M) 1. holy; auspicious; fair; good; right; meritorious; pure; sacred. 3. a son of sage Dīrghatamas.

**Puṇyabala** (S) (M) 1. the strength of goodness. 3. one of the 10 forces of a Bodhisattva.

**Puṇyadarśana** (S) (M) of virtuous appearance.

**Puṇyagandhin** (S) (M) 1. of virtuous fragrance. 2. virtuous; famous; sweet scented; fragrant; *Michelia champaka*; Common White Jasmine (*Jasminum officianale*)

**Puṇyajana** (S) (M) 1. good; honest. 3. a rākṣasa (*V. Purāṇa*); another name for the yakṣas.

**Puṇyajaneśvara** (S) (M) 1. lord of the yakṣas. 3. another name for Kubera.

**Puṇyajanī** (S) (F) 1. meritorious. 3. the wife of Manibhadra who was an attendant of Śiva (*Br. Purāṇa*)

**Puṇyajita** (S) (M) gained by virtue.

**Puṇyakīrti** (S) (M) 1. famous for virtues. 2. with celebrated virtues. 3. a man whose shape was assumed by Viṣṇu.

**Puṇyakṛt** (S) (M) 1. doer of meritorious acts. 3. a viśvādeva (*M. Bh.*)

**Puṇyalakṣmīka** (S) (M) 1. virtuous wealth; with a wealth of virtues. 2. auspicious; prosperous.

**Puṇyālankṛta** (S) (M) adorned by virtue.

**Puṇyamahas** (S) (M) of pure glory.

**Puṇyamitra** (S) (M) 1. a friend of virtue. 3. a Buddhist patriarch.

**Puṇyanāman** (S) (M) 1. with a pious name. 3. a soldier of Skanda (*M. Bh.*)

**Puṇyanātha** (S) (M) lord of virtue.

**Puṇyanidhi** (S) (M) 1. treasure of virtue. 3. a king of the lunar race (*Sk. Purāṇa*)

**Puṇyasena** (S) (M) 1. commander of virtues. 2. with an army of pious people.

**Puṇyaślokā** (S) (F) 1. well spoken of. 3. another name for Sītā and Draupadī.

**Puṇyaśloka** (S) (M) 1. well spoken of. 3. another name for Nala, Yudhiṣṭhira and Kṛṣṇa.

**Puṇyaśravas** (S) (M) 1. much heard of virtues. 2. famous for virtues. 3. a sage who was reborn as Nanda the cowherd's niece Lavangā (*P. Purāṇa*)

**Puṇyaśrīgarbha** (S) (M) 1. womb of virtue. 3. a Bodhisattva (*B. Literature*)

**Puṇyātman** (S) (M) pure souled; virtuous.

**Puṇyatoya** (S) (M) 1. holy water. 3. the river in the stomach of Bālamukunda.

**Puṇyavardhana** (S) (M) increasing virtue.

**Puṇyavarman** (S) (M) 1. armoured with virtue. 3. a king of Vidarbha.

**Puṇyavatī** (S) (F) 1. full of virtues. 2. righteous; virtuous; honest; fortunate; happy; blessed; beautiful.

**Puṇyavrata** (S) (M) 1. with a vow to virtue. 2. virtuous.

**Puradviṣ** (S) (M) 1. enemy of a city; enemy of a fortress; enemy of the asura Tripura. 3. another name for Śiva.

**Purahan** (S) (M) 1. slayer of Pura. 3. another name for Śiva.

**Purajit** (S) (M) 1. conqueror of fortresses; conqueror of pura. 3. the son of Aja and father of Ariṣṭanemi; another name for Śiva.

**Puralā** (S) (F) 1. abode of cities. 2. guardian of fortresses; protector of fortresses. 3. another name for Durgā.

**Puramālinī** (S) (F) 1. garlanded with castles. 2. one near which many cities are situated. 3. a river (*M. Bh.*)

**Purandarā** (S) (F) 1. destroyer of strong holds. 3. another name for Gaṅgā.

**Purandara** (S) (M) 1. destroyer of strongholds. 3. Indra in the Vaivasvata Manvantara; another name for Indra, Agni and Śiva.

**Purandhi** (S) (F) 1. woman; liberality; munificence. 3. kindness shown by gods to men; personified as a goddess of abundance and liberality.

**Pūraṇi** (S) (F) 1. fulfilling; completing; satisfying. 3. one of the 2 wives of the deity Ayenār; another name for Durgā; Red Silk Cotton tree (*Bombax ceiba*)

**Purañjana** (S) (M) 1. life; soul. 3. another name for Varuṇa.

**Purañjanī** (S) (F) understanding; intelligence.

**Purañjaya** (S) (M) 1. conqueror of the city. 3. a warrior on the side of the Kurus; a son of Śṛñjaya and father of Janamejaya; a son of Bhajamāna; a son of Śaśada (*V. Purāṇa*); a son of Medhāvin; a son of the elephant Airāvata (*H. Purāṇa*); a king of Ayodhyā.

**Purāri** (S) (M) 1. enemy of Pura. 3. another name for Viṣṇu.

**Puraśāsana** (S) (M) 1. chastiser of the asura Tripura. 3. another name for Śiva.

**Purāvasu** (S) (M) 1. 1st treasure. 3. another name for Bhīṣma.

**Purāvatī** (S) (F) 1. surrounded by cities; proceeding; going ahead. 3. a river (*M. Bh.*)

**Puravī** (S) (F) 1. eastern. 2. living; inviting. 3. a rāgiṇī.

**Pūrayitri** (S) (M) 1. one who fulfils or satisfies. 3. another name for Viṣṇu and Śiva.

**Purlā** (S) (F) 1. abode of cities. 3. another name for Durgā.

**Purṇā** (S) (F) 1. complete. 2. abundant; content. 3. a digit of the moon; a river (*V. Purāṇa*)

**Pūrṇa** (S) (M) 1. complete; entire. 2. full; abundant; rich; content; strong; capable; auspicious. 3. a serpent of the family of Vāsuki (*M. Bh.*); a gandharva son of Kaśyapa and Prādhā (*M. Bh.*)

**Pūrṇabhadra** (S) (M) 1. perfectly gentle. 3. the father of the yakṣa Harikeśa (*M. Bh.*); a serpent son of Kaśyapa (*M. Bh.*); the son of the yakṣa Ratnabhadra and the father of an attendant of Śiva.

**Pūrṇaćandra** (S) (M) 1. full moon. 3. a Bodhisattva.

**Pūrṇamāsa** (S) (M) full moon; personified as a son of Dhātṛ and Anumati (*Bh. Purāṇa*); a son of Kṛṣṇa (*V. Purāṇa*)

**Pūrṇāmṛtā** (S) (F) 1. full of nectar. 3. a digit of the moon.

**Pūrṇāmṛta** (S) (M) full of nectar.

**Pūrṇamukha** (S) (M) 1. with a perfect face. 3. a serpent of the family of Dhṛtarāṣṭra (*M. Bh.*)

**Pūrṇānanda** (S) (M) 1. supremely happy. 3. the Supreme Being.

**Pūrṇāngada** (S) (M) 1. perfect bodied. 3. a serpent of the family of Dhṛtarāṣṭra (*M. Bh.*)

**Pūrṇārtha** (S) (M) one whose wishes have

been realized.

**Pūrṇaśakti** (S) (F) 1. perfect energy. 3. a form of Rādhā (*Bhā. Purāṇa*)

**Pūrṇaśrī** (S) (M) with fortune.

**Pūrṇāyuṣ** (S) (M) 1. with a perfect life. 3. a gandharva son of Kaśyapa and Prādhā (*M. Bh.*)

**Pūrṇendu** (S) (M) the full moon.

**Pūrṇimā** (S) (F) the night or day of full moon.

**Pūrṇiman** (S) (M) 1. complete; fully satisfied. 3. a brother of Kaśyapa and son of Marići and Kalā (*V. Rāmāyaṇa*)

**Pūrṇodarā** (S) (F) 1. with satiated appetite. 3. a deity (*A. Koṣa*)

**Pūrṇotsangha** (S) (M) 1. far advanced in pregnancy. 3. a king (*M. Bh.*)

**Purobhū** (S) (M) 1st born; excelling; in front; superior.

**Purośana** (S) (M) 1. builder of a city. 3. a minister of Duryodhana.

**Purojava** (S) (M) 1. excelling in speed. 3. a son of Medhātithi; a son of the vasu Prāṇa and Urjjaṣvatī (*Bhāgavata*)

**Purojyotiṣ** (S) (M) preceded by radiance.

**Puroratha** (S) (M) 1. one whose chariot is in front. 2. pre-eminent; superior.

**Purovasu** (S) (M) 1. preceded by wealth. 2. very wealthy. 3. an Aṅga king who was the son of Babhrusetu (*A. Purāṇa*)

**Pūrpati** (S) (M) lord of a city.

**Purū** (S) (M) 1. much; many; people; abundant; every. 2. the pollen of a flower; heaven; paradise. 3. a son of Vasudeva and Sahadevā (*Bhā. Purāṇa*); a son of Madhu (*V. Purāṇa*); a son of Manu Cākṣuṣa and Naḍvalā (*H. Purāṇa*); a celebrated king of the Lunar dynasty who was the son of Yayāti and Śarmiṣṭhā and the husband of Pauṣṭi, he was the father of Pravīra or Janamejaya, Īśvara and Raudrāsva (*M. Bh.*); the charioteer of Arjuna (*M. Bh.*); a son of Jahnu (*Bhā. Purāṇa*); a mountain.

**Purucchepa** (S) (M) 1. throwing with great speed. 3. a sage who was the son of Divodāśa (*Ṛg Veda*)

**Purudanśas** (S) (M) 1. abounding in mighty deeds. 2. protecting all; residing in the hearts of everyone; having many virtues; having the support of many people. 3. another name for Indra.

**Purudaya** (S) (M) abounding in compassion.

**Purūdvāha** (S) (M) 1. abounding in religion. 2. very religious. 3. a son of the 11th Manu.

**Puruhotra** (S) (M) 1. abounding in ritual. 3. a son of Anu (*Bhā. Purāṇa*)

**Puruhutā** (S) (F) 1. invoked by many. 3. a form of Dākṣāyaṇī (*M. Purāṇa*)

**Puruhūta** (S) (M) 1. invoked by many. 3. another name for Indra.

**Puruja** (S) (M) 1. born of Purū. 2. born in the Purū dynasty. 3. a son of Suśānti.

**Purujit** (S) (M) 1. conquering many. 3. a brother of Kuntibhoja who fought on the side of the Pāṇḍavas; a son of Rućaka (*Bhā. Purāṇa*); a son of Ānaka (*Bhā. Purāṇa*); another name for Viṣṇu (*Bhā. Purāṇa*)

**Purukṛpā** (S) (F) 1. abounding in mercy. 2. compassionate.

**Purukṛtvan** (S) (M) achieving great deeds.

**Purukutśa** (S) (M) 1. abused by many. 3. a son of King Māndhātā and Bindumatī (*H. Purāṇa*); a descendant of Ikṣvāku (*Ś. Brāhmaṇa*)

**Purumandra** (S) (M) delighting many.

**Purumantu** (S) (M) full of wisdom.

**Purumedha** (S) (M) full of wisdom.

**Purumīdha** (S) (M) 1. full of wisdom. 3. a Purū king who was the son of Bṛhatputra and the brother of Ajamīḍha (*Bhā. Purāṇa*)

**Purumīlha** (S) (M) 1. met by many. 3. a son of Suhotra (*M. Bh.*); a son of Hastin (*H. Purāṇa*)

**Purumitra** (S) (M) 1. friend of many. 3. a warrior on the Kuru side (*M. Bh.*); a son of Dhṛtarāṣṭra (*M. Bh.*)

**Purupriyā** (S) (F) dear to many.

**Purūravas** (S) (M) 1. crying loudly. 2. overtly praised. 3. a famous king of the lunar race who was the son of Buddha and Īlā and the husband of the apsarā Urvaśī, he was the father of Āyus and the ancestor of Purū, Duṣyanta, Bharata, Kuru, Dhṛtarāṣṭra and Pāṇḍu.

**Puruṣa** (S) (M) 1. person. 2. the pupil of the

eye; the concious principle; man; the Supreme Being; the spirit. 3. a son of Manu Ćākṣuṣa (*Bh. Purāṇa*); one of the 18 attendants of the sun (*Bhā. Purāṇa*)

**Puruṣādya** (S) (M) 1. 1st among men. 3. another name for Viṣṇu and Ṛṣabha the 1st Arhat.

**Puruṣakesarin** (S) (M) 1. lion among men; man-lion. 3. Viṣṇu's 4th incarnation.

**Puruṣanti** (S) (M) 1. large gift. 3. a sage protected by the aśvins (*Ṛg Veda*)

**Puruṣapati** (S) (M) 1. lord of men. 3. another name for Rāma.

**Puruṣapuṇḍarīka** (S) (M) 1. lotus among men. 3. the 6th Jaina Black Vasudeva.

**Puruṣasinha** (S) (M) 1. lion among men. 3. the 5th Jaina Black Vasudeva (*J. Literature*)

**Puruṣavara** (S) (M) 1. best among men. 3. another name for Viṣṇu.

**Puruṣćandra** (S) (M) moon among men.

**Purusena** (S) (M) with a large army; commander of many.

**Puruṣendra** (S) (M) 1. lord of men. 2. king.

**Puruṣottama** (S) (M) 1. best among men. 2. the highest being. 3. the 4th Jaina Black Vasudeva; another name for Kṛṣṇa and Viṣṇu.

**Puruṣṭuta** (S) (M) 1. highly lauded. 3. another name for Śiva.

**Puruvāsa** (S) (M) dwelling in all; omnipresent.

**Purūvī** (S) (F) 1. fulfiller. 2. one that satiates; eastern. 3. a rāgiṇī.

**Puruviśruta** (S) (M) 1. much renowned. 3. a son of Vasudeva (*Bhā. Purāṇa*)

**Puruyaśas** (S) (M) 1. perfection; much renowned. 2. very famous. 3. a king of Panćāla who was the son of Bhūriyaśas (*Sk. Purāṇa*)

**Pūrvābhirāmā** (S) (F) 1. ancient giver of pleasures. 3. a river (*M. Bh.*)

**Pūrvaćittī** (S) (F) 1. foreboding. 3. an apsarā (*M. Bh.*)

**Pūrvapālin** (S) (M) 1. ancient protector. 3. another name for Indra.

**Pūṣā** (S) (F) 1. nourishing; cherishing. 3. a digit of the moon.

**Pūṣan** (S) (M) 1. nourisher; protector. 3. a Vedic deity originally connected with the sun and associated with the moon as protector of the universe, he is regarded as the keeper of flocks and bringer of prosperity, in later times he is an āditya and regent of the Nakṣatra Revatī.

**Pūṣanā** (S) (F) 1. nourisher; protector. 3. a mother in Skanda's retinue (*M. Bh.*)

**Pūṣānuja** (S) (M) 1. son of Puṣān. 3. another name for Parjañya.

**Puṣkala** (S) (M) 1. much; copious; abundant; rich; magnificent; full; complete; powerful; excellent; best; loud; purified. 3. a son of Varuṇa (*M. Bh.*); an asura; (*H. Purāṇa*); a soldier of Rāvaṇa (*P. Purāṇa*); a son of Bharata and Māṇḍavī and grandson of Daśaratha (*V. Rāmāyaṇa*), he was the husband of Kāntimatī; a ṛṣi (*Bhā. Purāṇa*); a Buddha (*L. Vistara*); another name for Śiva (*M. Bh.*)

**Puṣkarā** (S) (F) 1. lotus like. 3. one of the 8 wives of Śiva.

**Puṣkara** (S) (M) 1. Blue Lotus (*Nelumbium speciosum*). 2. sky; heaven; sun; a night of new moon falling on Monday, Tuesday or Saturday; arrow; the blade of a sword. 3. a general of Varuṇa (*M. Bh.*); a son of Kṛṣṇa (*Bhā. Purāṇa*); the brother of Nala; a son of Bharata (*V. Purāṇa*); a son of Vṛka and Dūrvākṣī (*M. Bh.*); a son of Varuṇa and husband of the daughter of Soma (*M. Bh.*); a sage who was the preceptor of Paraśurama (*M. Bh.*); an asura (*H. Purāṇa*); a Buddha (*L. Vistara*); a place of pilgrimage in Rājasthan; another name for Kṛṣṇa and Śiva.

**Puṣkaraćūda** (S) (M) 1. lotus crested. 3. one of the 4 elephants that support the earth (*Bhā. Purāṇa*)

**Puṣkarākṣa** (S) (M) 1. lotus eyed. 3. a king who was the son of King Sućandra (*Br. Purāṇa*); another name for Viṣṇu.

**Puṣkaranābha** (S) (M) 1. lotus navelled. 3. another name for Viṣṇu.

**Puṣkarasraj** (S) (F) lotus wreath.

**Puṣkarāvatī** (S) (F) 1. abounding in lotuses; consisting of lotuses. 3. a form of Dākṣāyaṇī (*M. Purāṇa*)

**Puṣkarekṣaṇa** (S) (M) 1. lotus eyed. 3. another name for Viṣṇu.

**Puṣkariṇī** (S) (F) 1. lotus pond. 3. the wife of

Ćākṣuṣa and mother of Manu; the wife of Emperor Bhumanyu (*M. Bh.*); the wife of King Ulmuka (*Bhā. Purāṇa*); another name for Viṣṇu.

**Puṣpā** (S) (F) **1.** flower like. **2.** flower; blossom.

**Puṣpa** (S) (M) **1.** flower; blossom. **2.** perfume; topaz. **3.** a son of Śliṣṭi (*H. Purāṇa*); a son of Śankha (*H. Purāṇa*); a serpent of the family of Kaśyapa (*M. Bh.*); the vehicle of Kubera (*A. Koṣa*)

**Puṣpabhūti** (S) (M) the essence of flowers.

**Puṣpadanta** (S) (M) **1.** flower toothed; the sun and moon conjoined. **2.** one with shining and hard teeth. **3.** an attendant of Śiva (*M. Bh.*); an attendant of Viṣṇu (*Bhā. Purāṇa*); the 9th Jaina Arhat of the present Avasarpiṇī (*J.S. Koṣa*); the elephant of the northwest quarter (*Bhā. Purāṇa*); an attendant given to Skanda by Pārvatī (*M. Bh.*); a vidyādhara; a nāga (*V. Rāmāyaṇa*); another name for Śiva (*A. Koṣa*)

**Puṣpadantī** (S) (F) **1.** flower toothed. **3.** a rākṣasī.

**Puṣpadhanuṣ** (S) (M) **1.** with a bow of flowers. **3.** another name for Kāma.

**Puṣpadhanvan** (S) (M) **1.** armed with a bow of flowers. **3.** another name for Kāma.

**Puṣpadhara** (S) (M) bearing flowers.

**Puṣpadhāraṇa** (S) (M) **1.** flower bearer; embellished with flowers. **3.** another name for Kṛṣṇa.

**Puṣpahāsa** (S) (M) **1.** smiling like flowers. **2.** a flower garden. **3.** another name for Viṣṇu.

**Puṣpajā** (S) (F) **1.** born of a flower; daughter of flowers. **2.** nectar. **3.** a river rising in the Vindhya mountains (*Mā. Purāṇa*)

**Puṣpaja** (S) (M) **1.** born from a flower. **2.** nectar.

**Puṣpajāti** (S) (F) **1.** born of flowers. **3.** a river rising in the Malaya mountains (*V. Purāṇa*)

**Puṣpaketana** (S) (M) **1.** flower bannered. **2.** one who is characterised by flowers. **3.** another name for Kāma.

**Puṣpaketu** (S) (M) **1.** flower bannered. **2.** characterized by flowers. **3.** a Buddha.

**Puṣpaloćana** (S) (M) **1.** flower like eyes. **2.** one whose eyes are as beautiful as a flower.

**Puṣpam** (S) (M) **1.** topaz eyed. **2.** with eyes as brilliant as a topaz; flower; blossom; topaz.

**Puṣpamañjari** (S) (F) flower blossom; the Blue Lotus (*Nelumbium Speciosum*)

**Puṣpāmbu** (S) (M) **1.** water of flowers. **2.** honey; nectar.

**Puṣpamitra** (S) (M) **1.** friend of flowers. **3.** a king and father of Agnimitra (*Bhā. Purāṇa*)

**Puṣpānana** (S) (M) **1.** flower faced. **3.** a yakṣa in the court of Kubera (*M. Bh.*)

**Puṣpāṅganā** (S) (F) flower bodied.

**Puṣpāṅgī** (S) (F) flower bodied.

**Puṣpapīḍa** (S) (M) **1.** chaplet of flowers. **3.** a gandharva; another name for Kāma.

**Puṣparāga** (S) (M) flower hued; topaz.

**Puṣpareṇu** (S) (F) **1.** the dust of flowers. **2.** pollen.

**Puṣpārṇa** (S) (M) **1.** flower stream. **3.** a king of the family of Dhruva and husband of Prabhā (*Bhāgavata*); a son of Vatsara and Svarvīthi.

**Puṣpaśekhara** (S) (M) flower crested; a chaplet of flowers.

**Puṣpaśrīgarbha** (S) (M) **1.** filled with the beauty of flowers. **3.** a Bodhisattva.

**Puṣpavāhana** (S) (M) carrier of flowers.

**Puṣpāvakirṇa** (S) (M) **1.** strewn with flowers. **3.** a prince of the kinnaras (*H. Purāṇa*)

**Puṣpavallī** (S) (F) flower vine.

**Puṣpavān** (S) (M) **1.** possessing flowers. **2.** perfumed; flowering. **3.** a king who once ruled the 3 worlds (*M. Bh.*)

**Puṣpavata** (S) (M) **1.** possessing flowers. **2.** flowery; blossoming; decorated with flowers. **3.** a daitya (*M. Bh.*)

**Puṣpaveṇī** (S) (F) **1.** garland or braid of flowers. **3.** a river (*M. Bh.*)

**Puṣpāyudha** (S) (M) **1.** flower armed. **3.** another name for Kāma.

**Puṣpendra** (S) (M) lord of flowers.

**Puṣpendū** (S) (F) the moon of flowers; the white lotus.

**Puṣpeśa** (S) (M) lord of flowers.

**Puṣpeṣu** (S) (M) **1.** flower arrow. **3.** another name for Kāma.

**Puṣpī** (S) (F) 1. flower like. 2. tender; soft; beautiful; fragrant; flower; blossom.

**Puṣpin** (S) (M) 1. blossoming. 2. rich in flowers.

**Puṣpita** (S) (M) 1. flowered; bearing flowers; blooming. 3. a Buddha.

**Puṣpotkaṭā** (S) (F) 1. bearing flowers. 3. a rākṣasī, the mother of Rāvaṇa and Kumbhakarṇa (*M. Bh.*)

**Pushṭi** (S) (F) 1. fatness; growth; increase; prosperity; comfort; opulence; fullness. 3. the mother of Lobha (*Mā. Purāṇa*); a daughter of Dhruva (*V. Purāṇa*); a daughter of Paurṇamāsa; (*V. Purāṇa*); one of the 16 divine Matris; a digit of the moon (*Br. Purāṇa*); a wife of Gaṇeśa (*Br. Purāṇa*); form of Dākṣāyaṇī (*M. Purāṇa*); a form of Sarasvatī (*Br. Purāṇa*); the daughter of Dakṣa and Prasūti and the wife of Dharma (*V. Purāṇa*); a Śakti (*H.Ć. Ćintāmaṇi*)

**Puṣya** (S) (M) 1. nourishment; the blossom. 2. the best of anything. 3. one of the 24 mythical Buddhas; an asterism (*Ṛg Veda*)

**Puṣyamitra** (S) (M) friend of blossoms.

**Pūtā** (S) (F) 1. purified; clear; bright. 2. Durva grass. 3. another name for Durgā.

**Pūtadakṣa** (S) (M) pure minded.

**Pūtakratu** (S) (M) 1. pure minded. 3. another name for Indra.

**Pūtamali** (S) (M) 1. pure minded. 3. another name for Śiva.

**Pūtanā** (S) (F) 1. blowing hard. 3. a demon killed by infant Kṛṣṇa; a yoginī; an attendant of Skanda (*M. Bh.*)

**Pūti** (S) (F) purity.

**Putra** (S) (M) 1. son. 2. child. 3. a son of Brahmiṣṭha (*K. Granthāvali*); a son of Priyavrata (*V. Purāṇa*)

**Putrī** (S) (F) daughter.

**Putrikā** (S) (F) doll; puppet; daughter; small statue.

**Pūtrima** (S) (M) purified; pure; clean.

**Puttala** (S) (M) pure; made of soil; doll.

# R

**Rā** (S) (M) **1.** fire. **2.** strength. **3.** another name for Indra.

**Rabhasa** (S) (M) **1.** impetuous; shining. **2.** vehemence; passion; zeal; rapid; fierce; wild; strong. **3.** a monkey in Rama's army (*V. Rāmāyaṇa*); a rākṣasa of Rāvaṇa (*V. Rāmāyaṇa*); the son of Rambhā (*Bhā. Purāṇa*)

**Rabhoda** (S) (M) bestowing strength.

**Rābhu** (S) (M) messenger.

**Rabhya** (S) (M) **1.** pleasant; agreeable; a kind of śruti in music. **3.** a king who was known for his justice.

**Raćanā** (S) (F) **1.** accomplishment; creation; production; literary work. **3.** the wife of Tvaṣṭṛ (*Bhā. Purāṇa*)

**Raćita** (S) (M) produced; fashioned; prepared.

**Rāddhi** (S) (M) accomplishment; completion; perfection; success.

**Rādhā** (S) (F) **1.** full moon day in the month of Vaiśākha; prosperity; success; lightning. **3.** the cowherdess who was the reincarnation of Lakṣmī as the daughter of Vṛṣabhānu and Kalāvatī of Gokula, the beloved of Kṛṣṇa and his mental power, is considered one of the 5 forces which help Viṣṇu in the process of creation (*Bhā. Purāṇa*); the foster mother of Karṇa and the wife of Adhiratha (*M. Bh.*); the 21st Nakṣatra of 4 stars (*Panćatantra*)

**Rādhaka** (S) (M) liberal; bountiful.

**Rādhākānta** (S) (M) **1.** beloved of Rādhā. **3.** another name for Kṛṣṇa.

**Rādhākṛṣṇa** (S) (M) Rādhā and Kṛṣṇa conjoined.

**Rādhanā** (S) (F) speech.

**Rādhanī** (S) (F) worship.

**Rādhāramaṇa** (S) (M) **1.** beloved of Rādhā. **3.** another name for Kṛṣṇa.

**Rādhāsuta** (S) (M) **1.** son of Rādhā. **3.** another name for Karṇa.

**Rādhātanaya** (S) (M) **1.** son of Rādhā. **3.** another name for Karṇa.

**Rādheśa** (S) (M) **1.** lord of Rādhā. **3.** another name for Kṛṣṇa.

**Rādheya** (S) (M) **1.** of Radha. **3.** another name for Karṇa.

**Rādhikā** (S) (F) **1.** successful; prosperous. **3.** another name for Rādhā.

**Rādhika** (S) (M) **1.** successful; prosperous. **3.** the son of King Jayasena (*Bhā. Purāṇa*)

**Rāgā** (S) (F) **1.** the act of colouring; feeling; beauty; harmony; melody; loved of all beings; passionate. **3.** a daughter of Bṛhaspati (*M. Bh.*); a daughter of Aṅgiras (*M. Bh.*); a mode of Indian classical music.

**Rāga** (S) (M) **1.** love; to colour; to tinge with emotion; loveliness; passion; harmony; king; sun; moon. **3.** a musical mode personified and wedded to a rāgiṇī (*R. Taraṅginī*)

**Rāgaććhana** (S) (M) **1.** love covered. **3.** anotner name for Kāma and Rāma.

**Rāgalatā** (S) (F) **1.** passion creeper. **3.** another name for Rati.

**Rāgamaya** (S) (M) (F) **1.** red; full of passion; full of colour; full of love. **2.** beloved; dear.

**Rāgavatī** (S) (F) **1.** full of love; coloured; impassioned. **2.** beloved.

**Rāgavṛnta** (S) (M) **1.** passion stem. **3.** another name for Kāma.

**Rāgayuj** (S) (M) **1.** attached to; coloured; attached to love. **2.** ruby.

**Rāghava** (S) (M) **1.** descendant of Raghu. **3.** another name for Rāma.

**Rāghavendra** (S) (M) **1.** chief of the Raghus. **3.** another name for Rāma.

**Rāghaveśvara** (S) (M) **1.** chief of the Raghus. **3.** another name for Rāma; a linga of Śiva.

**Raghu** (S) (M) **1.** fleet; rapid. **2.** light; fleet. **3.** a celebrated king of the solar race who was the son of Dilīpa and Sudakṣinā and father of Aja, the great-grandfather of Rāma, described as the ideal monarch, the dynasty was called after his name, it is believed that the Kṣatriyas who praise Raghu will not be defeated in war, he is among the kings to be remembered at dawn and dusk (*M. Bh.*); a son of Gautama Buddha.

**Raghukara** (S) (M) **1.** inspirer; accelerater. **3.** another name for Kālidāsa the author of *Raghuvaṅśa*.

**Raghukumāra** (S) (M) **1.** son of Raghu.

3. another name for Rāma.

**Raghumaṇi** (S) (M) 1. jewel of the Raghus. 3. another name for Rāma.

**Raghumanyu** (S) (M) quick tempered; eager; zealous.

**Raghunandana** (S) (M) 1. descendant of Raghu. 3. another name for Rāma.

**Raghunātha** (S) (M) 1. lord of the Raghus. 3. another name for Rāma.

**Raghunāyaka** (S) (M) 1. chief of the Raghus. 3. another name for Rāma.

**Raghupati** (S) (M) 1. lord of the Raghus. 3. another name for Rāma.

**Raghurāma** (S) (M) Rāma of the Raghu clan.

**Raghutilaka** (S) (M) 1. ornament of the Raghus. 3. another name for Rāma.

**Raghuttama** (S) (M) 1. the best of the Raghus. 3. another name for Rāma.

**Raghuvaṅśa** (S) (M) 1. of the family of Raghu. 3. a poem by Kālidāsa.

**Raghuvanśi** (S) (M) 1. of the family of Raghu. 3. another name for Rāma.

**Raghuvīra** (S) (M) 1. hero of the Raghus. 3. another name for Rāma.

**Rāgi** (S) (M) 1. full of love; coloured; affectionate; delighting. 3. a prominent king of the Purū dynasty (*M. Bh.*)

**Rāgiṇī** (S) (F) 1. melody; attachment; love. 3. an apsarā who was the daughter of Himavān and elder sister of Pārvatī (*Mā. Purāṇa*); a form of Lakṣmī; a musical mode in Indian classical music.

**Rāgyula** (S) (M) coloured; ruby.

**Rahovādī** (S) (M) 1. speaking guardedly. 3. a king of the Purū dynasty who was the son of Saṁyāti and the father of Bhadrāśva (*A. Purāṇa*)

**Rāhu** (S) (M) 1. seizer. 3. a demon son of Kaśyapa or Vipraćitti and Siṁhikā supposed to devour the sun and moon hence being responsible for their eclipses, he is also a member of the court of Brahmā (*M. Bh.*); a daitya.

**Rāhubhedin** (S) (M) 1. severing Rahu. 3. another name for Viṣṇu.

**Rahūgaṇa** (S) (M) 1. an attendant of Rāhu (*A. Veda*). 3. the son of Suddhodana (*V. Purāṇa*); son of Gautama Buddha.

**Rāhula** (S) (M) 1. able; efficient; given by Rāhu. 2. fetter. 3. the son of Śuddhodana (*V. Purāṇa*); a son of Gautama Buddha.

**Rāhuratna** (S) (F) 1. jewel of Rāhu. 2. the hyacinth.

**Rāhuśatru** (S) (M) 1. the foe of Rāhu. 3. another name for Viṣṇu and the moon.

**Rāhusuta** (S) (M) 1. son of Rāhu. 2. comet.

**Raibhya** (S) (M) 1. of praisers; praising; ritualistic verses. 3. a famous hermit of Yudhiṣṭhira's palace who was the son of Aṅgiras and the father of Arvāvasu and Parāvasu (*M. Bh.*); the father of King Duṣyanta and the son of Sumati (*Bhāgavata*); a son of Brahmā (*Var. Purāṇa*)

**Raikva** (S) (M) 1. place of wealth. 3. a king of ancient India who was the son-in-law of King Janaśruti (*Ć. Upaniṣad*)

**Raivata** (S) (M) 1. wealthy; descended from a rich family. 3. one of the 11 rudras; the 5th Manu (*H. Purāṇa*); the son of King Revata of Anarta and a king who should be praised at dawn and dusk; a son of Amṛtodana and Revatī; a mountain (*M. Bh.*); a daitya; another name for Śiva.

**Raivataka** (S) (M) 1. abounding in wealth. 2. very rich. 3. the son of Priyavrata and Surūpā who became a lord of a Manvantara (*H. Purāṇa*); another name for the Girnār mountain near Junāgarh in Gujarat.

**Raja** (S) (M) 1. sand; silvery; shining; pollen; emotion; affection. 3. a warrior of Skanda (*M. Bh.*); a sage who was the son of Vasiṣṭha and Ūrjā, he and his 6 brothers became the Saptarṣis of the 3rd Manvantara; a son of Viraja (*V. Purāṇa*); one of the 2 gatekeepers of Sūrya (*Bh. Purāṇa*)

**Rājā** (S) (M) king; lord.

**Rājabījin** (S) (M) of royal descent.

**Rājadharman** (S) (M) 1. the duty of a king. 3. a king of storks who was the son of Kaśyapa and a friend of Brahmā (*M. Bh.*)

**Rājādhidevī** (S) (F) 1. goddess of the kings. 2. queen. 3. a daughter of the solar King Śūra and Māriṣā and the wife of King Jayasena of Avantī (*Bhāgavata*)

**Rājadīpa** (S) (M) 1. lamp of kings. 2. lamp

among the kings.

**Rājahansa** (S) (M) 1. royal swan. 2. an excellent king; the Barheaded Goose (*Anser indicus*)

**Rājaka** (S) (M) illuminating; splendid; king; prince.

**Rājakalā** (S) (F) 1. a royal piece. 3. a digit of the moon.

**Rājakanyā** (S) (F) princess.

**Rājakarṇa** (S) (M) 1. with royal ears; an elephant's tusk. 2. an elephant.

**Rājakesarī** (S) (F) shining gold; lion among kings.

**Rājakumāra** (S) (M) 1. son of a king. 2. prince.

**Rājakumārī** (S) (F) 1. daughter of a king. 2. princess.

**Rājakuñjara** (S) (M) 1. elephant among kings. 2. powerful monarch.

**Rājalakṣmana** (S) (M) 1. with marks of royalty. 3. another name for Yudhiṣṭhira.

**Rājamahiṣī** (S) (F) queen of a state.

**Rājamaṇī** (S) (F) crown jewel; royal gem.

**Rajamukha** (S) (M) with a king's face.

**Rajamukhī** (S) (F) 1. with a shining silvery face. 3. an apsarā (*Sk. Purāṇa*)

**Rājan** (S) (M) 1. king. 2. ruler; Kṣatriya. 3. a yakṣa; one of the 18 attendants of the sun; another name for Yudhiṣṭhira, Indra, the moon and Pṛthu.

**Rājana** (S) (M) 1. belonging to a royal family. 3. the teacher mentioned in the *Yajur Veda* who was the son of Kuṇiya and the father of Ugradeva (*Ṛg Veda*)

**Rājanandana** (S) (M) 1. son of a king. 2. prince.

**Rajanī** (S) (F) 1. the dark one. 2. night; turmeric; queen. 3. a holy river in ancient India (*M. Bh.*); the wife of Vivasvata and mother of Revata; an apsarā; another name for Durgā.

**Rajanīćara** (S) (M) 1. night rover. 3. another name for the moon and a rakṣasa.

**Rajanīgandhā** (S) (F) 1. scented at night. 2. the tuberose (*Polianthes tuberosa*)

**Rajanīkānta** (S) (M) 1. beloved of the night. 3. another name for the moon.

**Rajanīkara** (S) (M) 1. night maker. 3. another name for the moon.

**Rājanīla** (S) (M) royal blue; emerald.

**Rajanīmukha** (S) (F) 1. night faced. 2. the evening.

**Rajanīpati** (S) (M) 1. lord of night. 3. another name for the moon.

**Rajanīramaṇa** (S) (M) 1. beloved of the night. 3. another name for the moon.

**Rajanīśa** (S) (M) 1. lord of the night. 3. another name for the moon.

**Rājanvatī** (S) (F) 1. abode of kings. 3. another name for the earth.

**Rājanya** (S) (M) 1. kingly. 3. a Vedic designation of the Kṣatriya class (*M. Bh.*); another name for Agni.

**Rājapati** (S) (M) 1. master of kings. 3. another name for Soma.

**Rājapuṣpā** (S) (F) 1. royal flower. 3. the tree *Mesua roxburghii*.

**Rājaputra** (S) (M) 1. son of a king. 2. prince. 3. a noted writer on *Kāma Śāstra*; another name for the planet Mercury.

**Rājarāj** (S) (M) 1. king of kings. 3. another name for the moon and Kubera.

**Rājarāma** (S) (M) King Rāma.

**Rajas** (S) (M) 1. silvery; the region between heaven and earth; vapour; mist; dust; pollen; passion; autumn. 3. a son of Vasiṣṭha (*V. Purāṇa*)

**Rajasānu** (S) (M) 1. of silvery or misty hue. 2. soul; heart; cloud.

**Rājaśekhara** (S) (M) 1. crown of a king. 3. a Sanskṛt dramatist who was also the preceptor of a king of Kannauj (7th century); a Sanskṛt commentator and author of *Kāvya Mimāmsa*; a poet who was the son of Durdaka and Śīlāvatī and the tutor of King Mahendrapāla of Kānyakubja (10th century)

**Rājasi** (S) (M) 1. passionate. 3. another name for Durgā.

**Rājasiṁha** (S) (M) lion among kings.

**Rājaśrī** (S) (F) 1. royalty; grandeur. 3. a gandharvī.

**Rājasūya** (S) (M) 1. the royal oblation. 3. a Vedic ceremony of royal consecration (*M. Bh.*)

**Rājasvāmin** (S) (M) **1.** lord of kings. **3.** another name for Yudhiṣṭhira and Viṣṇu.

**Rajasvaṇaja** (S) (M) **1.** of passionate sound. **3.** the father-in-law of Kakṣivān.

**Rajata** (S) (M) **1.** silver; pearl bright; pleasing. **2.** mind; pearl; ivory. **3.** a constellation.

**Rajatadanṣṭra** (S) (M) **1.** silver toothed. **3.** a son of King Vajradanṣṭra of the vidyādharas (*K. Sāgara*)

**Rajatādri** (S) (M) **1.** silver mountain. **3.** another name for Mount Kailāśa.

**Rajatadyuti** (S) (M) **1.** shining like silver. **3.** another name for Hanumān.

**Rajatakūṭa** (S) (M) **1.** silver mountain. **3.** a peak of the Malaya mountains (*K. Sāgara*)

**Rajatanābha** (S) (M) **1.** silver navelled. **3.** a yakṣa who was the husband of Maṇivarā and the father of Maṇivara and Maṇibhadra (*Ṛg Veda*)

**Rajatanābhi** (S) (M) **1.** silver navelled. **2.** very rich. **3.** a descendant of Kubera; another name for Kubera.

**Rajataprastha** (S) (M) **1.** silver place. **2.** place where silver is found; place with a silvery lustre. **3.** another name for Mount Kailāśa.

**Rājavāhana** (S) (M) **1.** royal steed. **3.** the vehicle on which Soma is carried; the son of King Rājahaṅsa (*V.D. Ćaritam*)

**Rājāvarta** (S) (M) **1.** of various colours. **2.** Lapis lazuli.

**Rājavata** (S) (M) **1.** royal fragrance. **3.** an ascetic of the Bhṛgu dynasty and son of Dyutimān (*V. Purāṇa*)

**Rājavi** (S) (F) **1.** royal bird. **2.** the Blue Jay (*Coracias benghalensis*)

**Rājendra** (S) (M) **1.** lord of kings; emperor. **2.** a Ćakravartin.

**Rājeśvara** (S) (M) lord of kings.

**Rājeśvarī** (S) (F) **1.** goddess of a state. **2.** princess.

**Raji** (S) (M) **1.** silvery; shining. **3.** a prominent king of the Purū dynasty and the son of Āyus by Svarbhānu (*M. Bh.*); a demon subdued by Indra.

**Rāji** (S) (M) **1.** streak; line; stripe. **3.** a son of Āyu (*M. Bh.*)

**Rājin** (S) (M) **1.** moonlight. **2.** light considered as a horse of the moon.

**Rājindu** (S) (M) **1.** moon among kings. **2.** an excellent king.

**Rajiṣṭha** (S) (M) straightest; most honest and upright.

**Rajita** (S) (M) affected; captivated; allured.

**Rājitā** (S) (F) illuminated; resplendent; bright; brilliant.

**Rājīva** (S) (M) **1.** living at a king's expense; streaked; striped. **2.** elephant; deer; Blue Lotus (*Nymphaea stellata*); Indian crane. **3.** a pupil of Viśvanātha (*M. Bh.*)

**Rājīvaloćanā** (S) (F) **1.** lotus eyed; with eyes as blue as the blue lotus. **3.** a daughter of King Jarāsandha (*Bhā. Purāṇa*)

**Rājīviṇī** (S) (F) a collection of blue lotuses.

**Rājju** (S) (M) **1.** rope like; cord like. **2.** plain; simple. **3.** a son of Vasudeva and Devakī (*Bhā. Purāṇa*)

**Rajju** (S) (M) **1.** rope; cord. **3.** a constellation (*V's. B. Samhitā*)

**Rajjukaṇṭha** (S) (M) **1.** rope necked. **2.** one who wears a cord round his neck. **3.** a grammarian who was a sage with great knowledge of the Vedas.

**Rājñī** (S) (F) **1.** queen. **3.** the western quarter or that which contains the soul of the universe; the wife of the Sun.

**Rajogātra** (S) (M) **1.** with an illuminated body. **3.** a son of Vasiṣṭha (*M. Bh.*)

**Rājyadevī** (S) (F) **1.** goddess of state; royal woman. **3.** the mother of Bāṇa.

**Rājyalakṣmī** (S) (F) **1.** wealth of a state; royal Lakṣmī. **2.** with the fortune and glory of a king.

**Rājyasena** (S) (M) **1.** commander of state. **2.** leader of the kingdom. **3.** a king of Nandipura.

**Rājyaśrī** (S) (F) **1.** grace of the kingdom; goddess of the kingdom. **2.** royal grace. **3.** the sister of King Harśa and the daughter of King Prabhākaravardhana.

**Rājyavardhana** (S) (M) **1.** enhancer of kingdom. **2.** increasing the glory of the kingdom. **3.** a king of Vaiśālī who could tell the past and future (*Mā. Purāṇa*); the brother of King Harśavardhana; a son of Dama.

**Rājyavatī** (S) (F) 1. possessing a kingdom. 2. princess.

**Rākā** (S) (F) the day of the full moon personified as a goddess who is his consort, she is the daughter of Aṅgiras and Smṛtī (*V. Purāṇa*); a rākṣasi who was the mother of Śūrpaṇakhā and Khara by sage Viśrāvas (*M. Bh.*); a daughter of Sumālin; daughter of Aṅgiras and Śraddhā; the wife of Dhātṛ and the mother of Prātṛ; a river (*Bh. Purāṇa*)

**Raka** (S) (M) the sun gem; crystal; the Arakan silver pheasant.

**Rākāćandra** (S) (M) 1. lord of the Rākā. 3. another name for the full moon.

**Rākāniśa** (S) (M) 1. lord of night. 3. another name for the full moon.

**Rākāniṣā** (S) (F) the night of the full moon.

**Rākendra** (S) (M) 1. lord of Rākā. 2. the full moon.

**Rākeśa** (S) (M) 1. lord of the full moon. 3. another name for Śiva.

**Rākiṇī** (S) (F) 1. night. 3. a tāntra goddess.

**Rakṣā** (S) (F) 1. protection. 2. an amulet; a charm that protects.

**Rakṣa** (S) (M) 1. protector. 2. to guard; protect; ashes.

**Rakṣābhūṣaṇa** (S) (M) an ornament of protection; an amulet.

**Rakṣahpati** (S) (M) 1. lord of rākṣasas. 3. another name for Rāvaṇa.

**Rakṣaka** (S) (M) 1. protector. 2. guard; amulet; tutelary deity; lac.

**Rakṣāmalla** (S) (M) 1. warrior who protects. 3. a king.

**Rakṣāmaṇī** (S) (F) 1. a jewel of protection. 2. a jewel worn as an amulet against evil.

**Rakṣamantra** (S) (M) 1. a hymn of protection. 2. a collection of Vedic hymns chanted to protect one from malefic forces.

**Rakṣaṇa** (S) (M) 1. protector. 3. another name for Viṣṇu.

**Rakṣaṇā** (S) (F) protection; guarding.

**Rakṣapāla** (S) (M) protector; guard.

**Rākṣasa** (S) (M) 1. guarding; watching; annihilator of protection; demonical. 3. a particular set of demons who were the offspring of Kāśyapa and Muni (*A. Purāṇa*), in the *Uttar Rāmāyaṇa* they are the forms that have arisen from the anger of Brahmā or his foot.

**Rākṣasādhipa** (S) (M) 1. lord of the rākṣasas. 3. another name for Ghaṭotkaća and Rāvaṇa.

**Rākṣasādhipati** (S) (M) 1. lord of the rākṣasas. 3. another name for Kubera.

**Rākṣasakaṇṭaka** (S) (M) 1. destroyer of rākṣasas. 3. another name for Bhīma.

**Rākṣasamaheśvara** (S) (M) 1. lord of the rākṣasas. 3. another name for Rāvaṇa.

**Rākṣasapuṅgava** (S) (M) 1. bull of the rākṣasas; chief of the rākṣasas. 3. another name for Ghaṭotkaca.

**Rākṣasendra** (S) (M) 1. lord of the rākṣasas. 3. another name for Ghaṭotkaća.

**Rākṣaseśvara** (S) (M) 1. lord of the rākṣasas. 3. another name for Ghaṭotkaća.

**Rākṣeśvara** (S) (M) 1. lord of the rākṣasas. 3. another name for Kubera.

**Rakṣikā** (S) (M) guard; protector.

**Rakṣitā** (S) (F) 1. protected. 3. an apsarā who was the daughter of Kaśyapa and Prādhā (*M. Bh.*)

**Rakṣitṛ** (S) (F) guardian; protector.

**Rakṣohan** (S) (M) destroying rakṣasas.

**Rakṣovikṣobhinī** (S) (F) 1. agitating rākṣasas. 3. a goddess.

**Rakta** (S) (M) 1. blood; painted; reddened; excited; beloved; dear; pleasant; lovely; safflower; lac; vermilion. 3. the son of Mahiṣāsura and the father of Bala and Atibala; another name for Śiva and Mars.

**Raktā** (S) (F) 1. painted; red; beloved; dear; pleasant. 2. Rosary Pea (*Abrus precatorius*) 3. one of the 7 tongues of fire.

**Raktagandhaka** (S) (M) pleasant perfume; myrrh.

**Raktagrīva** (S) (M) 1. iron necked. 3. a rākṣasa.

**Raktahaṅsā** (S) (F) 1. red swan; happy soul. 3. a rāgiṇī.

**Raktahaṅsa** (S) (M) 1. red swan. 3. a rāga.

**Raktaja** (S) (M) 1. born red; born of blood. 2. saffron; copper. 3. Arjuna in his previous incarnation as a thousand handed being that emerged from the blood of wounded Viṣṇu (*P. Purāṇa*)

**Raktakamala** (S) (M) Red Lotus (*Nymphea rubra*)

**Raktakañćana** (S) (F) 1. red gold. 2. *Bauhinia variegata*.

**Raktakanda** (S) (M) 1. red root. 2. coral.

**Raktakeśara** (S) (M) red saffron; Coral tree.

**Raktakumuda** (S) (F) Red Lotus (*Nymphaea rubra*)

**Raktamaṇḍala** (S) (M) 1. with a red disc. 3. another name for the moon.

**Raktāṅga** (S) (M) 1. red bodied. 2. the sun and moon on rising. 3. a nāga of Dhṛtarāṣṭra's dynasty; another name for Mars.

**Raktāṅka** (S) (M) 1. red marked. 2. coral.

**Raktapa** (S) (F) 1. blood drinking. 3. a Dākinī.

**Raktapadma** (S) (F) Red Lotus (*Nymphaea rubra*)

**Raktapakṣa** (S) (M) 1. red winged. 3. another name for Garuḍa.

**Raktapallava** (S) (F) 1. red leaf; with red leaves. 2. the Aśoka tree (*Saraca indica*)

**Raktapuṣpā** (S) (F) 1. red flowered. 3. the pomegranate blossom; *Nerium odorum*; *Rottleria tinctoria*; *Bombax heptaphyllus*; *Hibiscus rosa sinensis*.

**Raktasūryāya** (S) (M) to be like the red sun.

**Raktavīja/Raktabīja** (S) (M) 1. a seed of blood. 2. pomegranate tree. 3. another name for the giant asura Rambhāsura, father of Mahiṣāsura, who fought Ćāmuṇḍa and whose every drop of blood became a warrior.

**Rakti** (S) (F) redness; pleasing; loveliness; affection; devotion.

**Ramā** (S) (F) 1. enchanting; beautiful; charming; vermilion; red earth; good luck; fortune; opulence; splendour. 3. the mother of the 9th Arhat of the present Avasarpinī; an apsarā; a daughter of Saśidhvaja and wife of Kalki; another name for Mahālakṣmī; the Aśoka tree.

**Rāma** (S) (M) 1. causing rest; enchanting; all pervading; omnipresent; pleasing; charming; lovely; pleasant; pleasure; joy; delight; dark. 3. the 7th avatara of Viṣṇu, son of sage Jamadagni and Reṇukā; one of the 7 ṛṣis of the 8th Manvantara (*H. Purāṇa*); a king of Mallapura; a king of Śrngavera, a patron of Nāgeśa (*Ṛg Veda*); another name for Balarāma, elder brother of Kṛṣṇa; another name of Rāmachandra, a descendant of Raghu, son of Daśaratha and Kauśalyā, husband of Sītā of Mithilā, father of Lava and Kuśa; another name for Varuṇa.

**Rāmabhakta** (S) (M) devotee of Rāma.

**Rāmaćandra** (S) (M) Rāma, the excellent one.

**Rāmaćaraṇa** (S) (M) 1. the feet of Rāma. 2. a devotee of Rāma.

**Rāmadāsa** (S) (M) devotee of Rāma.

**Rāmadatta** (S) (M) 1. given by Rāma. 3. a minister of King Nṛsinha of Mithilā.

**Ramādevī** (S) (F) 1. goddess of beauty. 2. lovely woman. 3. the mother of Jayadeva.

**Ramādhipa** (S) (M) 1. lord of Rāma. 3. another name for Viṣṇu.

**Rāmadūta** (S) (M) 1. messenger of Rāma. 3. another name for Hanumān.

**Rāmagaṅgā** (S) (F) 1. the Gaṅgā that pleases and refreshes. 3. a river.

**Rāmagiri** (S) (M) 1. Rāma's mountain. 3. the mountain in Ramtek near Nāgpur (*K. Granthāvali*)

**Rāmagopāla** (S) (M) Rāma and Kṛṣṇa conjoined.

**Rāmaharṣaṇa** (S) (M) 1. pleasing to Rāma. 2. thrilling; inspiring. 3. a disciple of Vyāsa (*M. Bh.*)

**Rāmahṛdaya** (S) (M) the heart of Rāma.

**Rāmajīvana** (S) (M) 1. one whose life is Rāma. 3. a king who was the son of Rudrarāya.

**Rāmaka** (S) (M) 1. sporting; dallying; lover; delighting; gratifying. 3. a mountain conquered by Sahadeva (*M. Bh.*)

**Ramākānta** (S) (M) 1. beloved of Rāma. 3. another name for Viṣṇu.

**Rāmakavaća** (S) (M) Rama's breastplate.

**Rāmakelī** (S) (F) 1. sport of Lakṣmī. 3. a rāgiṇī.

**Ramākha** (S) (M) 1. lover of Lakṣmī. 3. another name for Viṣṇu.

**Rāmakinkara** (S) (M) servant of Rāma.

**Rāmakirī** (S) (F) 1. of omnipresent nature. 2. all pervading. 3. a rāgiṇī.

**Rāmakṛṣṇa** (S) (M) Rāma and Kṛṣṇa conjoined.

**Rāmakṛt** (S) (F) 1. causing rest. 3. a rāga.

**Rāmala** (S) (M) 1. lover. 3. another name for Kāma.

**Rāmalā** (S) (F) bestower of pleasure; lover.

**Rāmaliṅga** (S) (M) the mark of Rāma.

**Rāmamanohara** (S) (M) attracting Rāma.

**Rāmamohana** (S) (M) attracting Rāma; Rāma and Kṛṣṇa conjoined.

**Rāmamūrti** (S) (M) 1. the idol of Rāma. 2. the sign; the symbol of Rāma.

**Ramaṇā** (S) (F) 1. enchanting; worthy of being loved. 2. charming; beloved. 3. Dākṣāyaṇī in Rāmatīrtha.

**Ramaṇa** (S) (M) 1. pleasing; delightful; charming. 2. lover; husband. 3. the son of the vasu named Soma and Manoharā (*M. Bh.*); another name for an island near Dvārakā; another name for Aruṇa the charioteer of the sun; another name for Kāma; the Curry Leaf tree (*Murraya koenigii*)

**Ramaṇaka** (S) (M) 1. devotee of love. 3. a son of Yajñabāhu (*Bh. Purāṇa*); a son of Vitihotra and grandson of Priyavrata (*Bhāgavata*)

**Rāmānanda** (S) (M) 1. pleasure of Rāma. 3. a disciple of Rāmānuja and founder of a subdivision of the sect.

**Rāmanārāyaṇa** (S) (M) Rāma and Viṣṇu con joined.

**Ramānātha** (S) (M) 1. lord of Ramā. 3. another name for Viṣṇu.

**Ramaṇī** (S) (F) 1. loving; delighting; pleasure; joy; sexual union; beautiful; charming. 3. a nāgakanyā (*R. Taraṅginī*)

**Ramaṇikā** (S) (F) loving; pleasing; joyful; beautiful; charming.

**Ramaṇika** (S) (M) 1. worth loving. 2. pleasing; attractive.

**Rāmanivāsa** (S) (M) the dwelling of Rāma.

**Rāmānuja** (S) (M) 1. younger brother of Rāma. 3. a celebrated Vaiṣnava reformer and founder of the doctrine of Viśiṣtādvaita, he lived at Kanchipuram in South India and was thought to be an incarnation of Śeṣa (12th century); another name for Kṛṣṇa and Lakṣmaṇa.

**Ramāpati** (S) (M) 1. lord of Ramā. 3. another name for Viṣṇu.

**Rāmaphala** (S) (M) 1. the fruit of Rāma. 2. given by Rāma.

**Rāmaprakāśa** (S) (M) the glory of Rāma.

**Rāmaprasāda** (S) (M) the blessing of Rāma.

**Rāmapraveśa** (S) (M) one into whom Rāma has access.

**Ramāpriyā** (S) (F) 1. dear to Rāma. 2. lotus.

**Ramāpriya** (S) (M) 1. beloved of Ramā. 3. another name for Viṣṇu.

**Rāmarati** (S) (M) the jewel of Rāma; dwelling in Rāma; devotee of Rāma.

**Rāmarūpa** (S) (M) with the form of Rāma.

**Rāmasakha** (S) (M) 1. friend of Rāma. 3. another name for Sugrīva.

**Ramāśankara** (S) (M) Lakṣmī and Viṣṇu con· joined.

**Rāmaśeṣa** (S) (M) Rāma and Śeṣa conjoined.

**Rāmasetu** (S) (M) 1. the bridge of Rāma. 3. the bridge between India and Lankā, built by Rāmā's army (*Rāmāyaṇā*)

**Rāmasinha** (S) (M) 1. the lion of Rāma; Rāma the lion. 3. a king who was the son of Jayasinha.

**Rāmāśrama** (S) (M) the refuge of Rāma.

**Ramāśraya** (S) (M) 1. refuge of Ramā. 3. another name for Viṣṇu.

**Rāmasvarupa** (S) (M) incarnation of Rāma.

**Ramatārā** (S) (F) 1. the star of fortune; the best Lakṣmī. 3. the Sacred Basil plant.

**Ramati** (S) (M) 1. lover. 2. paradise; time. 3. another name for Kāma.

**Rāmavallabha** (S) (M) 1. dear to Rāma. 2. cinnamon. 3. an author of a commentary on *Rāmāyaṇa*.

**Rāmāvatāra** (S) (M) 1. incarnated as Rāma. 3. Viṣṇu in his incarnation as Rāma.

**Rāmavilāsa** (S) (M) the pleasure of Rāma; pleasing Rāma.

**Rāmāyaṇi** (S) (F) the mirror of Rāma; one well versed in the *Rāmāyaṇa*.

**Rambhā** (S) (F) 1. lovable; pleasing; agreeable; staff; plantain (*Musa sapientum*); the lowing of the cow. 3. the daughter of Kaśyapa and Prādhā she was the wife of Nalakūbara considered the most beautiful of apsarās; the wife of Mayāsura (*Br. Purāṇa*); Dākṣāyaṇī in the Malaya mountains.

**Rambha** (S) (M) **1.** prop; support; a bamboo. **3.** the father of asura Mahiṣa and brother of Karambha; a nāga (*V. Purāṇa*); son of Āyu (*H. Purāṇa*); a son of Viviṅśati (*Bh. Purāṇa*); a son of Purūravas and brother of Nahuṣa (*Bh. Purāṇa*)

**Rambhiṇī** (S) (F) **1.** the staff of a spear. **3.** spear of the maruts (*Ṛg Veda*)

**Rambhoru** (S) (F) **1.** with thighs like a plantain tree. **2.** with lovely thighs; a beautiful woman. **3.** another name for a beautiful woman.

**Ramendra** (S) (M) **1.** lord of Ramā. **3.** another name for Viṣṇu.

**Rameśa** (S) (M) **1.** lord of Ramā. **3.** another name for Viṣṇu.

**Rāmeśvara** (S) (M) **1.** lord Rāma. **3.** a sacred pilgrimage centre in South India where Rāma is supposed to have crossed to Lankā and which has the Śiva temple built by Rāma; a sacred island in the Bay of Bengal.

**Rāmeśvarī** (S) (F) consort of Rāma.

**Rāmī** (S) (M) right.

**Rāmila** (S) (M) **1.** lover. **3.** another name for Kāma.

**Rāmilā** (S) (F) bestower of pleasure; lover.

**Ramita** (S) (M) loved; gladdened; delighted.

**Ramra** (S) (M) **1.** beauty; splendour. **3.** another name for Aruṇa.

**Ramyā** (S) (F) **1.** enchanting; enjoyable. **3.** a daughter of Mount Meru (*Bh. Purāṇa*); another name for night; a river.

**Ramya** (S) (M) **1.** enjoyable. **2.** pleasing; delightful; beautiful. **3.** a son of Agnīdhra (*V. Purāṇa*)

**Ramyaka** (S) (M) **1.** lover. **3.** the son of Āgnidhra who was the king of Ramyaka Varśa near the Nīlgiris and the husband of Pūrvacitti (*Bhāgavata*); Persian Lilac (*Melia azedarach*)

**Ramyarūpā** (S) (F) with a lovely form.

**Ramyaśrī** (S) (M) **1.** most desired. **3.** another name for Viṣṇu.

**Raṇa** (S) (M) **1.** delight; pleasure; joy; battle; sound; the joy of battle; mother. **3.** a rākṣasa (*P. Purāṇa*)

**Rāṇā** (S) (F) **1.** murmuring. **3.** a goddess.

**Raṇacoḍa** (S) (M) **1.** one who leaves the battlefields. **3.** another name for Kṛṣṇa, who left the battlefield in the war with Jarāsandha, so as to save his army from massacre and went to Dvārakā.

**Raṇadā** (S) (F) making a sound; bestower of battles.

**Raṇadeva** (S) (M) lord of battle.

**Raṇadhīra** (S) (M) **1.** patient in battle. **2.** one who does not lose control in a battle; steady warrior.

**Raṇadurgā** (S) (F) Durgā, as the goddess of battle.

**Raṇādya** (S) (M) **1.** beginning of a battle; beginning of a sound. **2.** delightful. **3.** another name for Dāmodara.

**Raṇahastin** (S) (M) best warrior.

**Raṇajīt** (S) (M) victorious in battle.

**Raṇajitā** (S) (F) victorious in battle.

**Raṇaka** (S) (M) warrior; king.

**Raṇakauśala** (S) (M) master of battle.

**Raṇalakṣmī** (S) (F) goddess of war; the fortunes of war.

**Raṇañjaya** (S) (M) victor in war.

**Raṇapriya** (S) (M) warlike; interested in war; falcon.

**Raṇaśūra** (S) (M) hero of war.

**Raṇasvāmin** (S) (M) **1.** lord of water. **3.** an idol of Śiva as lord of the battlefield.

**Raṇavijaya** (S) (M) victor in war.

**Raṇavikrama** (S) (M) victorious warrior.

**Raṇavīra** (S) (M) hero of the battle; warrior.

**Rāṇāyanī** (S) (M) **1.** knowing the art of battle. **3.** a preceptor in the line of disciples of Vyāsa.

**Randhra** (S) (M) **1.** opening; aperture. **3.** the 8th astrological mansion; a son of Manu Bhautya.

**Raṇecara** (S) (M) **1.** moving in the field of battle. **3.** another name for Viṣṇu.

**Raṇeśa** (S) (M) **1.** lord of battle. **3.** another name for Śiva.

**Raṅga** (S) (M) **1.** colour; love; music; amusement; arena; a field of battle. **3.** another name for Viṣṇu and Kṛṣṇa.

**Raṅgabhūtī** (S) (F) 1. born of love. 3. the night of full moon in the month of Āṣvina.

**Raṅgadāsa** (S) (M) 1. devotee of Kṛṣṇa. 3. a great scholar and devotee of Viṣṇu who built temples around Venkatāćala (*Sk. Purāṇa*)

**Raṅgadeva** (S) (M) 1. god of happiness. 3. a tutelary god supposed to preside over sport, diversion and pleasure.

**Raṅgadevatā** (S) (F) 1. goddess of pleasure. 3. a goddess who presides over sports and diversions.

**Raṅgadhara** (S) (M) bearer of love; devotee of Viṣṇu; musician.

**Raṅgajā** (S) (F) vermilion; born of love.

**Raṅgalāla** (S) (M) beloved of Viṣṇu; lover of music.

**Raṅgamāṇikya** (S) (F) 1. coloured stone. 2. ruby.

**Raṅgaṇa** (S) (M) loving; dancing; merrymaking.

**Raṅganātha** (S) (M) 1. lord of love. 3. Viṣṇu on the serpent.

**Raṅganāyakī** (S) (F) 1. beloved of Kṛṣṇa. 3. Rukmiṇī as consort of Kṛṣṇa.

**Raṅgarāja** (S) (M) Viṣṇu on his serpent; royal Kṛṣṇa.

**Raṅgatī** (S) (F) 1. coloured; lovable. 2. agreeable; excited; passionate. 3. a rāga.

**Raṅgavatī** (S) (M) 1. full of colour; full of love; loving; happy. 3. the wife of Rantideva.

**Raṅgavidyādhara** (S) (M) 1. knowing music. 2. knowing music; dance; drama and art. 3. a gandharva (*H. Purāṇa*)

**Raṅgavihārī** (S) (M) 1. abode of happiness; pervading in pleasure. 3. another name for Kṛṣṇa.

**Raṅgeśa** (S) (M) 1. hero of the play. 3. a king who was the patron of Pārāśarabhatta.

**Raṅgita** (S) (M) 1. well coloured. 2. handsome.

**Rangitā** (S) (F) charmed; delighted; painted; coloured.

**Raṅhitā** (S) (F) swift; quick; rapid.

**Rāṇī** (S) (F) queen.

**Rañjanā** (S) (F) 1. pleasing; exciting; charming; pleasing. 2. the *Nyctantes arbor tristis* tree; turmeric; saffron; perfume.

**Rañjana** (S) (M) colouring; pleasing; entertaining; delighting; contenting.

**Rāñjhā** (S) (M) lover.

**Rañjideva** (S) (M) 1. lord of entertainers. 3. a king of the lunar race who was a descendant of King Bharata.

**Rañjikā** (S) (F) 1. one who pleases; exciting love; charming; pleasing. 2. Red Sandalwood (*Pterocarpus satalinus*)

**Rañjinī** (S) (F) 1. colouring; entertaining; delighting; amusing; pleasing; charming. 2. the *Nyctantes arbor tristis*; turmeric; saffron.

**Rañjitā** (S) (F) coloured; pleased; made happy; delighted.

**Rañjula** (S) (M) 1. bestower of entertainment. 2. charming; handsome.

**Rāno** (S) (F) a peacock's tail.

**Raṇotkaṭa** (S) (M) 1. furious in battle. 3. a warrior of Skanda (*M. Bh.*); a daitya (*H. Purāṇa*)

**Ransu** (S) (M) cheerful; delighting.

**Rantideva** (S) (M) 1. lord of pleasure; best warrior; best fighter; lord of devotion. 3. a king of the lunar race who was a son of Saṁkṛti (*M. Bh.*); the kindest and most liberal king of ancient India who was a descendant of Viṣṇu and the son of Nara, he is one of the kings to be remembered at dawn and dusk (*M. Bh.*); another name for Viṣṇu.

**Rantināra** (S) (M) 1. warrior. 3. father of Apratiratha (*V. Purāṇa*)

**Rantū** (S) (F) way; road; river.

**Rantu** (Malayalam) (M) two.

**Raṇvā** (S) (F) pleasant; delightful; agreeable; lovely; joyous; gay.

**Raṇvitā** (S) (F) joyous; gay.

**Raṇvita** (S) (M) pleasant; lovely; joyous; gay.

**Raṇyā** (S) (F) delectable; pleasant; war like.

**Raphenaka** (S) (M) 1. tormentor. 2. injurer; wretched. 3. a nāga of the Takṣaka dynasty (*M. Bh.*)

**Rasā** (S) (F) 1. juice; water; nectar; essence; sentiment; taste; passion; milk; a chemical; quicksilver; the tongue; grapes; love; delight; charm; sentiment. 3. a mythological stream personified as a goddess of the *Ṛg Veda* and said to flow round the world; another name for the earth.

**Rāsa** (S) (F) 1. noise; sport; play; full of essence; full of sentiments. 3. the dance of Kṛṣṇa and the gopīs (*H. Purāṇa*)

**Rasajñā** (S) (F) 1. one who knows the sentiment. 2. knowledgeable about different arts. 3. another name for Gaṅgā.

**Rāsamaṇi** (S) (M) 1. jewel of the Rāsa. 3. another name for Kṛṣṇa.

**Raśanā** (S) (F) rope; cord; a ray of light; beam.

**Rasanā** (S) (F) 1. knower of taste. 2. tongue; taste; perception.

**Rasanāyaka** (S) (M) 1. lord of feelings. 3. another name for Kāma and Śiva.

**Rasanikā** (S) (F) impassioned; full of feeling.

**Rāsapriyā** (S) (F) 1. fond of the Rāsa. 3. another name for a gopī.

**Rasasirā** (S) (M) 1. stream of nectar. 3. another name for Soma.

**Rasavantī** (S) (F) delighting; charming; sentimental; emotional.

**Rasavatī** (S) (F) delighting; full of nectar; sentimental; emotional.

**Rāsavihāri** (S) (M) 1. immersed in the Rāsa. 3. another name for Kṛṣṇa.

**Rasāyana** (S) (M) 1. the vehicle of essence. 3. another name for Garuḍa.

**Raseśa** (S) (M) 1. lord of the Rāsa; lord of sentiments. 3. another name for Kṛṣṇa.

**Rāseśvara** (S) (M) 1. lord of the Rāsa. 3. another name for Kṛṣṇa.

**Rāśi** (S) (M) wealth; quantity; number; zodiac sign.

**Rasikā** (S) (F) with discrimination; aesthetic; sentimental; full of passion; passionate; tasteful; elegant.

**Rasika** (S) (M) passionate; one who appreciates the sentiment; graceful; elegant; beautiful; discriminating; delighting; humourous; tasteful.

**Rasikeśvara** (S) (M) 1. lord of a passionate wife. 3. another name for Kṛṣṇa.

**Rasilā** (S) (M) with taste; covered with gold; gilded.

**Rasindra** (S) (M) lord of chemicals; mercury; the philosopher's stone.

**Rasīśvari** (S) (F) 1. goddess of the Rasa. 3. another name for Rādhā.

**Raśmi** (S) (F) 1. rope; cord; ray. 2. sunbeam; moonbeam.

**Raśmikā** (S) (F) a tiny ray of light.

**Raśmiketu** (S) (M) 1. beam bannered. 3. a comet; a rākṣasa who fought on the side of Rāvaṇa (*Rāmāyaṇa*); another name for the sun.

**Raśmimālin** (S) (M) 1. garlanded with rays. 3. another name for the sun.

**Raśmin** (S) (M) 1. bearer of rays. 3. another name for the sun and moon.

**Raśmiprabhāsa** (S) (M) 1. illuminated by rays. 3. a Buddha.

**Raśmivān** (S) (M) 1. bearer of rays. 3. a viśvadeva (*M. Bh.*); another name for the sun and moon.

**Rāṣtra** (S) (M) 1. realm; kingdom. 3. a son of Kāśī (*Bh. Purāṇa*)

**Rāṣtrabhṛt** (S) (M) 1. holding sway. 3. a son of Bharata (*Bh. Purāṇa*)

**Rāṣtradevī** (S) (F) 1. queen of the kingdom. 3. a wife of Ćitrabhanu.

**Rāṣtrapāla** (S) (M) 1. guardian of the kingdom. 3. a son of Ugrasena (*H. Purāṇa*)

**Raśtravardhana** (S) (M) 1. increasing the kingdom. 3. a minister of Daśaratha (*A. Purāṇa*)

**Rāṣtrī** (S) (F) ruler.

**Rasyā** (S) (F) with essence; emotional; sentimental; full of feelings; juicy.

**Rathabhṛt** (S) (M) 1. possessing a chariot. 3. a yakṣa (*V. Purāṇa*)

**Rathaćitrā** (S) (F) 1. like a multicoloured chariot. 3. a Purāṇic river (*Bhā. Purāṇa*)

**Rathaćitra** (S) (M) 1. with a multicoloured chariot. 3. a yakṣa (*V. Purāṇa*)

**Rathadhvaja** (S) (M) 1. chariot bannered. 3. the father of King Kuśadhvaja of Videha and the grandfather of Vedavatī (*Bhā. Purāṇa*)

**Rathadhvana** (S) (M) 1. making the sound of the chariot. 3. another name for Vīrāgni the son of Śaṁyu.

**Rathagraṇi** (S) (M) 1. one who makes the

sound of the chariot. 3. a warrior who accompanied Śatrughna during Rāma's Aśvamedha Yajña (*P. Purāṇa*)

**Rathajit** (S) (M) 1. conquering chariots. 2. winning affection; charming; level. 3. a yakṣa.

**Rathakṛćra** (S) (M) 1. wheel of a chariot; designer of a chariot. 3. a yakṣa (*V. Purāṇa*)

**Rathakṛta** (S) (M) 1. chariot maker. 3. a yakṣa (*V. Purāṇa*)

**Rathākṣa** (S) (M) 1. the axle of the chariot. 3. a warrior of Skanda (*M. Bh.*)

**Rathamaṇi** (S) (M) 1. with a jeweled chariot. 3. another name for the moon.

**Rathamitra** (S) (M) 1. protector of the chariot; friend of the warrior. 3. a yakṣa.

**Rathāngin** (S) (M) 1. possessing a discus. 3. another name for Viṣṇu.

**Rathantarā** (S) (F) 1. one who sits inside the chariot. 3. the daughter of Tansu.

**Rathantara** (S) (M) 1. dweller of the chariot. 3. son of the agni called Pañćajanya (*M. Bh.*)

**Rathāntarī** (S) (F) 1. dweller of the chariot. 3. a daughter of King Īlina and the mother of King Duśyanta (*M. Bh.*)

**Rathaprabhu** (S) (M) 1. lord of the chariot. 3. another name for Vīrāgni the son of Śaṁyu (*M. Bh.*)

**Ratharāja** (S) (M) 1. lord of the chariot. 2. king of warriors. 3. an ancestor of Gautama Buddha.

**Ratharvi** (S) (M) 1. moving like a chariot. 3. a nāga mentioned in the *Atharva Veda*.

**Rathasena** (S) (M) 1. warrior on the chariot. 3. a warrior who fought on the side of the Pāṇḍavas (*M. Bh.*)

**Rathaspati** (S) (M) 1. lord of chariots. 3. a deity presiding over pleasure and enjoyment.

**Rathasthā** (S) (M) 1. on the chariot. 3. one of the 7 tributaries of the Gaṅgā (*M. Bh.*)

**Rathastha** (S) (M) 1. on the chariot. 3. a yakṣa (*Bhāgavata*)

**Rathavāhana** (S) (M) 1. one who draws the chariot. 2. horse. 3. the brother of the king of Virāta who fought against the Pāṇḍavas (*M. Bh.*)

**Rathavara** (S) (M) 1. best chariot; best warrior. 3. a king (*V. Purāṇa*)

**Rathāvarta** (S) (M) 1. harness of the chariot. 3. a holy place that grants salvation to those who visit it (*M. Bh.*)

**Rathavīthī** (S) (M) 1. path of a chariot. 2. highway. 3. a sage (*Ṛg Veda*)

**Rathavīti** (S) (F) 1. the horse of the carriage. 3. wife of Arćanānas.

**Rathika** (S) (M) one who rides a chariot.

**Rathin** (S) (M) one who moves in a chariot.

**Rathīndra** (S) (M) lord of the chariot.

**Rathītara** (S) (M) 1. good charioteer. 3. a sage of the Bhṛhadevata; a king of the solar dynasty who was the son of Pṛṣatāśva (*Bhāgavata*)

**Rathyā** (S) (F) highway; crossroad; a group of chariots.

**Rāti** (S) (M) 1. generous; favourable. 3. the giver personified as a deity.

**Rati** (S) (F) 1. pleasure; enjoyment; desire; passion; love. 3. a daughter of Dakṣa and wife of Kāma (*M. Bh.*); an apsarā of Alakāpurī (*M. Bh.*); the wife of Vibhu and mother of Pṛthuseṇā (*Bhā. Purāṇa*); the 6th digit of the moon.

**Ratiguṇa** (S) (M) 1. with a passionate disposition. 2. loving; desirous. 3. a gandharva who was the son of Kaśyapa and Prādhā (*M. Bh.*)

**Ratik** (S) (M) satisfied; joyful; delighted; loved.

**Ratikarā** (S) (F) 1. causing pleasure. 3. an apsarā.

**Ratimadā** (S) (F) 1. intoxicated with love. 3. an apsarā (*K. Sāgara*)

**Ratināyaka** (S) (M) 1. lord of Rati. 3. another name for Kāma.

**Ratipati** (S) (M) 1. lord of Rati. 3. another name for Kāma.

**Ratiprīti** (S) (F) 1. love, pleasure and passion conjoined. 2. Rati and Prīti conjoined.

**Ratiramana** (S) (M) 1. beloved of Rati. 3. another name for Kāma.

**Ratiśa** (S) (M) 1. lord of Rati. 3. another name for Kāma.

**Rativara** (S) (M) 1. consort of Rati. 3. another name for Kāma.

**Rativardhana** (S) (M) increasing love.

**Ratna** (S) (M) gift; present; wealth; desirable; jewel; the best of its kind; magnet.

**Ratnā** (S) (F) jewel.

**Ratnabāhu** (S) (M) 1. with jewelled arms. 3. another name for Viṣṇu.

**Ratnaćandra** (S) (M) 1. moon among jewels. 2. the best jewel. 3. a tutelary deity who is the guardian of jewel mines; a Bodhisattva; a son of Bimbisāra.

**Ratnaćchattra** (S) (M) 1. jewelled umbrella. 3. a Buddha.

**Ratnaćūḍa** (S) (M) 1. jewelled forehead. 3. a Bodhisattva.

**Ratnadhā** (S) (M) possessing jewels; distributing riches.

**Ratnadhara** (S) (M) possessing jewels.

**Ratnādhipati** (S) (M) 1. supreme lord of jewels. 2. guardian of treasures. 3. another name for sage Agastya.

**Ratnadhvaja** (S) (M) 1. jewelled banner. 3. a Bodhisattva.

**Ratnadīpa** (S) (M) jewelled lamp; a jewel that illuminates.

**Ratnagarbhā** (S) (F) 1. womb of jewels. 3. another name for the earth.

**Ratnagarbha** (S) (M) 1. womb of jewels. 2 filled with jewels. 3. a Bodhisattva; another name for Kubera and the ocean.

**Ratnagrīva** (S) (M) 1. jewel necked. 3. a king of Kānchananagarī who was a great devotee of Viṣṇu (*P. Purāṇa*); another name for the earth, Kubera and the sea.

**Ratnahasta** (S) (M) 1. possessing jewels. 3. another name for Kubera.

**Ratnakalā** (S) (F) piece of a jewel.

**Ratnākara** (S) (M) 1. jewel mine. 2. the ocean. 3. a Buddha; a Bodhisattva; another name for Kubera.

**Ratnaketu** (S) (M) 1. jewel bannered. 3. name common to 2000 future Buddhas; a Bodhisattva.

**Ratnakiriṭin** (S) (M) 1. with a jewelled crown; with jewel like fame. 3. a king of the kinnaras (*K. Vyuha*)

**Ratnakīrti** (S) (M) 1. with jewel like glory. 3. a Buddha.

**Ratnakūṭā** (S) (F) 1. jewelled peak. 3. a wife of sage Atri (*P. Purāṇa*)

**Ratnakūṭa** (S) (M) 1. jewelled peak. 3. a mountain; a Bodhisattva; the future Buddha.

**Ratnam** (S) (M) jewel; precious object.

**Ratnamālā** (S) (F) 1. jewelled necklace. 3. a gandharvī.

**Ratnamālāvatī** (S) (F) 1. with a necklace of jewels. 3. an attendant of Rādhā (*Panćatantra*)

**Ratnamañjari** (S) (F) 1. jewel blossom. 3. a vidyādharī.

**Ratnamatī** (S) (M) 1. jewelled intellect; jewel among intellectuals. 3. a Sanskṛt grammarian.

**Ratnāmbarī** (S) (F) clad in jewels.

**Ratnamukhya** (S) (M) 1. chief of jewels. 2. diamond.

**Ratnamukuṭa** (S) (M) 1. jewelled crown. 3. a Bodhisattva.

**Ratnanābha** (S) (M) 1. with a jewelled navel. 3. another name for Viṣṇu.

**Ratnanātha** (S) (M) lord of jewels; a diamond.

**Ratnānga** (S) (M) coral.

**Ratnāṅgi** (S) (F) with jewelled limbs.

**Ratnanidhī** (S) (M) 1. treasure of jewels; treasure of pearls. 3. another name for Viṣṇu, Mount Meru and the ocean.

**Ratnāṅka** (S) (M) vehicle of Viṣṇu.

**Ratnapāṇi** (S) (M) 1. holding jewels. 3. a Bodhisattva (*B. Literature*)

**Ratnapāra** (S) (M) 1. one who is beyond jewels. 3. a Bodhisattva.

**Ratnaparvata** (S) (M) 1. jewelled mountain. 3. another name for the mountain Meru.

**Ratnapīṭhā** (S) (F) 1. the seat of jewels. 3. a gandharvī (*K. Vyuha*)

**Ratnaprabhā** (S) (F) 1. the shine of jewels. 3. a nāga maiden (*K. Sāgara*); an apsarā; another name for the earth.

**Ratnarāj** (S) (M) 1. king of jewels. 2. the ruby.

**Ratnarāśī** (S) (F) 1. collection of jewels. 3. another name for the sea.

**Ratnārćis** (S) (M) 1. shining like a jewel. 3. a Buddha.

**Ratnarekhā** (S) (F) 1. a line of jewels; ornamented; embellished. 2. very precious; very gracious.

**Ratnasambhava** (S) (M) **1.** born of jewels. **3.** one of the 5 Dhyāni Buddhas; a Bodhisattva (*L. Vistara*)

**Ratnasānu** (S) (M) **1.** mountain of jewels. **3.** another name for Mountain Meru.

**Ratnaśekhara** (S) (M) **1.** jewelled crown. **3.** a Jaina author (15th century) (*J.S. Koṣa*)

**Ratnaśikhaṇḍa** (S) (M) **1.** jewel crested. **3.** a mythical bird considered to be a companion of Jaṭāyu (*V. Rāmāyaṇa*)

**Ratnaśikhara** (S) (M) **1.** jewelled peak. **3.** a Bodhisattva.

**Ratnaśikhin** (S) (M) **1.** with a jewelled plait. **3.** a Buddha.

**Ratnasū** (S) (F) **1.** producing jewels. **2.** the earth.

**Ratnāvalī** (S) (F) **1.** a necklace of jewels. **3.** a Sanskṛt play written by King Harṣavardhana.

**Ratnavara** (S) (F) **1.** best among all precious things. **2.** gold.

**Ratnavardhana** (S) (M) increasing jewels; bestower of wealth.

**Ratnavatī** (S) (F) **1.** abounding in jewels. **3.** another name for the earth.

**Ratnayaṣṭi** (S) (M) **1.** jewelled pillar. **3.** a Buddha.

**Ratnendra** (S) (M) chief of jewels.

**Ratneśa** (S) (M) **1.** lord of jewels. **2.** the diamond.

**Ratneśvara** (S) (M) **1.** lord of jewels. **2.** the diamond.

**Ratnin** (S) (M) possessing o receiving gifts.

**Ratnojjvala** (S) (M) shining with pearls.

**Ratnolkā** (S) (F) **1.** jewelled meteor. **3.** a tāntric deity.

**Ratnottama** (S) (M) **1.** best jewel. **3.** a Buddha.

**Ratnottamā** (S) (F) **1.** best jewel. **3.** a tāntric deity.

**Rātri** (S) (F) **1.** night. **3.** the sister of Uṣā and a divine mother.

**Rātridevī** (S) (F) goddess of the night; the presiding deity of the night.

**Rātrihāsa** (S) (M) **1.** laughing night; the white lotus opening at night. **2.** another name for the moon.

**Rātrija** (S) (M) **1.** born at night. **2.** star.

**Rātrikā** (S) (F) night.

**Rātrināthа** (S) (M) **1.** lord of the night. **3.** the moon.

**Ratū** (S) (F) **1.** truthful; true speech. **3.** another name for the celestial Gaṅgā.

**Ratujā** (S) (F) daughter of truth.

**Ratujit** (S) (M) conqueror of truth.

**Rātula** (S) (M) **1.** truth seeking. **2.** interested; desiring. **3.** the son of Śuddhodana (*V. Purāṇa*)

**Raubhya** (S) (M) **1.** misty; foggy. **3.** a sage (*U. Rāmāyaṇa*)

**Raućya** (S) (M) **1.** a staff of Bilva wood (*Aegle marmelos*). **3.** the 13th Manu.

**Raudra** (S) (M) wild; impetuous; fierce; coming from Rudra or Śiva.

**Raudrakarman** (S) (M) **1.** fierce in action. **2.** a magic rite performed for a terrible purpose. **3.** a son of Dhṛtarāṣṭra (*M. Bh.*)

**Raudranetrā** (S) (F) **1.** fierce eyed. **3.** a Buddhist goddess.

**Raudraśa** (S) (M) **1.** violent; impetuous; fierce; wild. **3.** the constellation Ārdrā when it passes through Rudra; another name for Kārttikeya and Yama.

**Raudrāśva** (S) (M) **1.** abode of Rudra. **3.** a son of Emperor Pṛthu and Pauśṭī and the husband of the apsarā Miśrakeśī.

**Rauhiṇa** (S) (M) **1.** red; born under the constellation of Rohiṇī. **3.** a demon who was Indra's enemy (*Ṛg Veda*)

**Rauhita** (S) (M) **1.** coming from Manu Rohita. **3.** a son of Kṛṣṇa (*H. Purāṇa*)

**Raumya** (S) (M) **1.** salty. **3.** attendants of Śiva.

**Raupya** (S) (F) **1.** made of silver; silvery. **3.** a Purāṇic river of ancient India where the holy bath of sage Jamadagni was situated (*M. Bh.*)

**Raurava** (S) (M) **1.** unsteady; dishonest. **3.** a hell personified as a husband of Vedanā and father of Duhkha (*Ma. Purāṇa*)

**Rauśadaśva** (S) (M) **1.** angry horse. **3.** another name for Vaśumanas, part author of *Ṛg Veda* (x)

**Rava** (S) (M) sound; noise; roar; song; hum.

**Rāvaṇa** (S) (M) **1.** making a noise; making others weep. **3.** the rākṣasa king of Lankā who was the son of Viśravas and Kaikaśi or Keśinī and the half-brother of Kubera (*K. Rāmāyaṇa*), he was killed by the Ayodhyā prince Rāma who was the 7th avatāra of Viṣṇu (*Rāmāyaṇa*)

**Rāvaṇi** (S) (M) 1. son of Rāvaṇa. 3. another name for Indrajit.

**Ravatha** (S) (M) 1. humming; calling out. 3. the Indian cuckoo (*Cuculus varius*)

**Ravi** (S) (M) 1. sun. 2. Arka plant; the number 12. 3. a prince of Sauvīra (*M. Bh.*); a son of Dhṛtarāṣṭra (*M. Bh.*); a mountain.

**Ravićandra** (S) (M) 1. the sun and moon conjoined. 3. an author of a commentary on the *Amaru Śataka*.

**Ravićandrikā** (S) (F) 1. glory of sun. 2. moonlight. 3. a rāga.

**Ravidāsa** (S) (M) 1. devotee of the sun. 3. a poet.

**Ravideva** (S) (M) 1. lord of the sun. 3. another name for Sūrya.

**Ravidhvaja** (S) (M) 1. sun bannered. 2. the day.

**Ravidīpta** (S) (M) lit by the sun.

**Ravijā** (S) (F) 1. born of the sun. 3. another name for Yamunā.

**Ravija** (S) (M) 1. born of the sun. 3. another name for Karṇa, Yama and the planet Saturn.

**Ravikānta** (S) (M) 1. beloved of the sun. 2. sunstone (*A. Koṣa*)

**Ravikiraṇa** (S) (M) ray of the sun.

**Ravikīrti** (S) (M) 1. with fame as bright as the sun. 2. renowned. 3. a Sanskṛt poet (7th century)

**Raviloćana** (S) (M) 1. with eyes as bright as the sun. 2. with fiery eyes. 3. another name for Śiva.

**Ravinandana** (S) (M) 1. son of the sun. 3. another name for Karṇa, Sugrīva and Manu Vaivasvata.

**Ravināthā** (S) (M) 1. whose lord is the sun. 2. Lotus (*Nelumbo speciosum*)

**Ravīndra** (S) (M) 1. lord of the sun; sun and Indra conjoined. 3. another name for Sūrya.

**Ravinetra** (S) (M) 1. with eyes as bright as the sun. 3. another name for Viṣṇu.

**Ravipriya** (S) (F) 1. beloved of the sun. 3. Dākṣayāṇi in Gangadvāra.

**Raviputra** (S) (M) 1. son of the sun. 3. another name for the planet Saturn.

**Avirāja** (S) (M) king of the sun.

**Ravirathā** (S) (M) chariot of the sun.

**Raviratna** (S) (M) 1. jewel of the sun. 2. ruby.

**Raviśa** (S) (M) 1. one who desires the sun. 3. another name for Kāma.

**Raviśankara** (S) (M) 1. lord of the sun. 3. another name for Sūrya.

**Ravisārathi** (S) (M) 1. charioteer of the sun. 3. another name for Aruṇa.

**Raviśekhara** (S) (M) one whose crest is the sun; with sun as the crest; sun crested.

**Raviṣṭā** (S) (F) 1. loved by the sun. 3. another name for the orange tree; *Polanisia Icosandra*.

**Raviśu** (S) (M) 1. desired by the sun; as inflammatory as the sun. 3. another name for Kāma.

**Ravisūnu** (S) (M) 1. son of the sun. 3. another name for Karṇa.

**Ravisuta** (S) (M) 1. son of the sun. 3. another name for Sugrīva and Saturn.

**Ravitanaya** (S) (M) 1. son of the sun. 3. another name for Karṇa and Yama and Saturn.

**Raya** (S) (M) 1. flow of a river; zeal; ardour; quickness; force; velocity. 2. king; prince. 3. a king of the Lunar dynasty who was the son of Purūravas and Urvaśī (*Bhāgavata*)

**Rāyāṇa** (S) (M) 1. ever moving. 2. forceful. 3. a brother of Yaśoda.

**Rayidā** (S) (M) bestowing wealth.

**Rayipati** (S) (M) lord of wealth.

**Rayiṣṭha** (S) (M) 1. very swift. 3. another name for Agni, Kubera and Brahmā.

**Ṛbhava** (S) (M) skilled; an intensely glowing ray of the sun.

**Ṛbhu** (S) (M) 1. skilful; prudent. 3. one of the 3 sons of Sudhanvān who obtained divinity through good deeds; a sage who was the son of Brahmā and a brilliant scholar (*V. Purāṇa*), the god who is worshipped by other gods; another name for Agni, Indra and the ādityas.

**Ṛbhukṣa** (S) (M) 1. most prudent. 3. another name for Indra's heaven; heaven; the thunderbolt of Indra.

**Rbhvan** (S) (M) 1. clever; skilful; wise.

3. another name for Indra, Tvaṣṭṛ and Agni.

**Ṛbhyā** (S) (F) worshipped.

**Ṛćā** (S) (F) the collected body of the Vedas; splendour; praise; hymn.

**Ṛćaka** (S) (M) effected by a hymn; desire; wish.

**Ṛćeyu** (S) (M) 1. knower of the hymns. 3. a king of the Purū dynasty who was the son of Raudrāśva (*H. Purāṇa*)

**Ṛćīka** (S) (M) 1. knower of hymns; praiser. 3. a sage who was the father of Jamadagni and the grandfather of Paraśurāma, one of the 12 ādityas (*A. Veda*); a king who was the grandson of Emperor Bharata and the son of Dyumanyu (*M. Bh.*)

**Ṛćīkaputra** (S) (M) 1. son of Ṛćīka. 3. another name for Jamadagni.

**Ṛddhi** (S) (F) 1. prosperity; success; wealth; abundance; supremacy; supernatural power. 3. a wife of Gaṇeśa; a wife of Kubera; Varuṇa's wife (*M. Bh.*); another name for Lakṣmī and Pārvatī.

**Ṛddhinātha** (S) (M) 1. lord of prosperity. 3. another name for Śiva and Gaṇeśa.

**Ṛddhimā** (S) (F) full of prosperity; spring; love.

**Ṛddhimān** (S) (M) 1. prosperous; successful. 3. a great serpent which was killed by Garuḍa (*M. Bh.*)

**Ṛdū** (S) (F) pleasant; soft; charming.

**Rebha** (S) (M) 1. singer of praise. 3. a protégé of the aśvins.

**Rebhā** (S) (F) singer of praise.

**Reem** (S) (F) hṛm, seed name of goddess Durgā, i.e. a mantra considered to be very potent in effecting riches.

**Rejākṣī** (S) (F) with eyes of fire; fiery eyes.

**Rekhā** (S) (F) 1. line; streak. 3. a servant of Bhānumatī the wife of Duryodhana (*M. Bh.*)

**Reneśa** (S) (M) 1. lord of love. 3. another name for Kāma.

**Reṇu** (S) (M) 1. dust; sand; pollen; an atom. 3. a sage who was the son of Viśvāmitra and the author of a Ṛg Vedic Sūkta (*A. Brāhmaṇa*); a king of the Ikṣvāku dynasty, who was the father of Reṇukā the wife of sage Jamadagni (*M. Bh.*); a son of Vikukṣi (*V. Rāmāyaṇa*)

**Reṇukā** (S) (F) 1. born of dust. 3. the mother of sage Paraśurāma and wife of Jamadagni; a wife of Viśvāmitra (*H. Purāṇa*)

**Reṇuka** (S) (M) 1. born of dust. 3. a formula recited over weapons (*V. Rāmāyaṇa*); a yakṣa; a mythical elephant (*M. Bh.*)

**Reṇumat** (S) (M) 1. full of sand; sandy. 3. a son of Viśvāmitra and Reṇu (*H. Purāṇa*)

**Reṇumatī** (S) (F) 1. with pollen. 3. wife of Nakula and mother of Śatānīka.

**Repha** (S) (M) 1. having low thoughts; cruel. 3. a Ṛg Vedic hermit.

**Reśaman** (S) (F) silk; soothing.

**Reṣman** (S) (M) storm; whirlwind.

**Retasvat** (S) (M) 1. possessed of seed. 2. prolific. 3. another name for Agni.

**Revā** (S) (F) 1. one that moves; agile. 2. swift; quick. 3. the wife of Kāma; a rāga; another name for the river Narmadā and Kali.

**Reva** (S) (M) to go; to move.

**Revanta** (S) (M) 1. killer of speed. 2. speed-breaker; retarder. 3. a son of Sūrya and Saṁjñā who is the lord of guhyakas or forest spirits and is considered the ideal horseman (*V. Purāṇa*)

**Revata** (S) (M) 1. wealthy; rich. 2. prosperous; brilliant, splendid, beautiful. 3. a son of king Ānarta and the father of Revatī (*Bhāgavata*)

**Revatī** (S) (F) 1. prosperity; wealth. 2. the 27th constellation of 32 stars; cow. 3. the daughter of King Revata and the wife of Balarāma (*Bhāgavata*); the wife of King Vikramaśila's son and the mother of Manu Raivata the lord of the 5th Manvantara; the wife of Mitra (*Bh. Purāṇa*); a yoginī identified with Aditi; the 5th Nakṣatra; a rāgiṇī; a wife of Amṛtodana.

**Revatīramaṇa** (S) (M) 1. beloved of Revatī. 3. another name for Balarāma and Viṣṇu.

**Ṛgmin** (S) (M) jubilant with praise.

**Rićatka** (S) (M) 1. removing armour. 3. father of Śara.

**Rīṇā** (S) (F) melted; dissolved.

**Ripu** (S) (M) 1. foe; enemy. 2. deceiver. 3. a grandson of Dhruva and son of Śliṣṭi and

Sućchāyā (*H. Purāṇa*); a son of Yadu and Bābhru (*Bhā. Purāṇa*)

**Ripughna** (S) (M) 1. one who destroys his enemies. 3. another name for Gaṇeśa.

**Ripuñjaya** (S) (M) 1. vanquisher of foes. 3. a son of Suratha lord of Kuṇḍala city (*P. Purāṇa*); a Brāhmin who was reborn as King Divodāsa of Kāśi (*Sk. Purāṇa*)

**Ripusūdana** (S) (M) destroyer of enemies.

**Ripuvarjita** (S) (M) free from enemies.

**Riṣṭa** (S) (M) 1. one that cuts; pushed; thrust. 2. a sword. 3. a king who worshipped Yama in his assembly (*M. Bh.*); a daitya; a son of Manu (*Mā. Purāṇa*)

**Riṣṭā** (S) (F) 1. sword. 3. another name for the mother of the apsarās.

**Rīti** (S) (F) motion; course; streak; stream; prosperity; remembrance; protection; auspiciousness.

**Rītikā** (S) (F) of a stream; brass.

**Riyā** (S) (F) one who sings; singer.

**Ṛjīṣa** (S) (M) 1. expeller of enemies. 3. another name for Indra.

**Ṛjrāśva** (S) (M) 1. with quick horses; with red horses. 3. a celebrated sage of the *Ṛg Veda* who was an ally of Indra (*V. Purāṇa*)

**Ṛju** (S) (M) 1. straight; honest; sincere. 3. a son of Vasudeva (*Bh. Purāṇa*)

**Ṛjuda** (S) (M) bestowed by truth; honesty; sincerity; righteousness.

**Ṛjukratu** (S) (M) 1. whose works are right. 3. another name for Indra.

**Ṛjula** (S) (M) simple; honest; innocent.

**Ṛjuta** (S) (M) simplicity; honesty.

**Ṛjuvani** (S) (F) 1. granting liberally. 3. the earth.

**Ṛkṣā** (S) (F) 1. female bear; the best; a star. 3. the wife of solar dynasty King Ajamīdha (*M. Bh.*); a follower of Skanda (*M. Bh.*)

**Ṛkṣa** (S) (M) 1. bear; ape; the best; the most excellent; the Pleiades. 3. a king of the Purū dynasty and the father of Saṁvaraṇa (*M. Bh.*); the son of King Ariha and Sudevā and the husband of Jvālā and father of Matināra (*H. Purāṇa*)

**Ṛkṣadeva** (S) (M) 1. lord of the stars; the Great Bear; ape. 3. a son of Śikhaṇḍī (*M. Bh.*); another name for the moon.

**Ṛksambikā** (S) (F) 1. mother of the bears; mother of the stars. 3. a follower of Skanda (*M. Bh.*)

**Ṛkṣanātha** (S) (M) 1. lord of the stars. 3. another name for the moon.

**Ṛksaputra** (S) (M) 1. son of Ṛkṣa. 3. another name for Saṁvarana.

**Ṛkṣarāja** (S) (M) 1. lord of the stars; lord of the bears; lord of the apes. 3. the king of Kiṣkindhā and foster father of Bāli and Sugrīva (*V. Rāmāyaṇa*)

**Ṛkṣavala** (S) (M) 1. forest of the apes; forest of the bears. 3. one of the 7 mountains of India (*M. Bh.*)

**Ṛkta** (S) (M) 1. of true nature. 2. simple; innocent; truthful.

**Ṛkthan** (S) (M) heir; gold.

**Ṛkvan** (S) (M) jubilant with praise.

**Ṛmā** (S) (M) emancipated; released.

**Roća** (S) (M) one who enlightens; shining; radiant.

**Roćaka** (S) (M) brightening; enlightening; of taste; agreeable.

**Roćamānā** (S) (F) 1. consisting of light. 2. shining; bright; splendid; agreeable. 3. an attendant of Skanda (*M. Bh.*)

**Roćamāna** (S) (M) 1. shining; bright. 3. a Kṣatriya king of Aśvamedha who fought on the side of the Pāṇḍavas (*M. Bh.*)

**Roćanā** (S) (F) 1. bright; light; brightness. 2. bright sky; handsome woman; beautiful; blossom of the Śālmali tree. 3. the daughter of King Devaka and the wife of Vasudeva, she was the mother of Hema and Hemāngada (*Bhā. Purāṇa*); a grand daughter of Rukmin the king of Vidarbha and the wife of Aniruddha the grandson of Kṛṣṇa (*Bhā. Purāṇa*); Drumstick tree (*Moringa oleifera*); Sour Lime (*Citrus acida*); White Cotton tree (*Ceiba Pentadra*); Red Lotus (*Nymphaea rubra*); Indian Laburnum (*Cassia fistula*)

**Roćana** (S) (M) 1. shining; radiant; giving pleasure; agreeable; charming. 3. an arrow of Kāma (*A. Koṣa*); a son of Viṣṇu and Dakṣiṇā; (*Bhā. Purāṇa*); a viśvadeva (*V. Purāṇa*); a son of Vasudeva (*V. Purāṇa*); Indra under Manu

Svāroćiṣa (*Bh. Purāṇa*)

**Roćanāmukha** (S) (M) **1.** red faced. **3.** an asura of the *Mahābhārata*.

**Roćanī** (S) (F) delighting; agreeable.

**Roći** (S) (F) light; beam; ray.

**Roćiras** (S) (F) light; aura; glow.

**Roćiṣa** (S) (M) **1.** light; brightness; splendour. **3.** a son of Vibhāvasu (*Bhā. Purāṇa*).

**Roćiṣmat** (S) (M) **1.** possessing light. **3.** a son of Manu Svāroćiṣa (*Bh. Purāṇa*)

**Roćita** (S) (M) glorious; delighting.

**Roćukā** (S) (F) causing pleasure; one who gives pleasure; delighting.

**Rodas** (S) (M) heaven and earth.

**Rodasī** (S) (F) **1.** heaven and earth conjoined. **3.** a Vedic goddess who personifies lightning as the wife of Rudra and the mother of the maruts, she is considered immortal, heroic and the bestower of wealth (*Ṛg Veda*); the earth (*V. Rāmāyaṇa*)

**Rodhasvatī** (S) (F) **1.** with high embankments. **3.** a holy river in India (*Bhā. Purāṇa*)

**Rohaka** (S) (M) rising.

**Rohaṇa** (S) (M) **1.** ascending; climbing. **2.** blossom. **3.** a mountain (Ādam's Peak in Śri Lankā); Indian Redwood tree (*Soymida febrifuga*); another name for Mount Sumerū and Viṣṇu.

**Rohanta** (S) (M) ascending; tree.

**Rohantī** (S) (F) climbing; vine.

**Rohī** (S) (F) **1.** rising up; red. **2.** a doe.

**Rohil** (S) (M) risen; ascended.

**Rohiṇ** (S) (M) **1.** rising; ascending. **2.** born under the asterism Rohiṇī; Banyan tree (*Ficus indica*) and the Sandalwood tree. **3.** another name for Viṣṇu.

**Rohiṇī** (S) (F) **1.** ascending; tall; increasing. **2.** the mother of all cows; the Sandalwood tree; red cow. **3.** the most beloved of all the 27 wives of the moon (*T. Samhitā*); the daughter of the agni called Manu and Niśā and the wife of Hiraṇyakaśipu (*M. Bh.*); the mother of sage Utathya; the constellation Tauri which has 5 stars one of which is Aldebaran; a wife of Kṛṣṇa (*Bhā. Purāṇa*); the wife of Mahādeva (*Purāṇas*); one of the 16 vidyādevīs (*A. Koṣa*); a river between Kapilavastu and Kol (*V. Purāṇa*); a daughter of Dakṣa and Surabhi and mother of Vimalā, Analā and Kāmadhenu the celestial cow, she is the feminine counterpart of the rising sun personified as Rohita and is the divinity of cattle; a wife of Vasudeva and the mother of Balarāma (*M. Bh.*)

**Rohiṇībhava** (S) (M) **1.** son of Rohiṇī. **3.** another name for planet Mercury.

**Rohiṇīkānta** (S) (M) **1.** beloved of Rohinī. **3.** another name for the moon.

**Rohiṇīramaṇa** (S) (M) **1.** beloved of Rohiṇī. **3.** another name for the moon.

**Rohiṇīśa** (S) (M) **1.** lord of Rohiṇī. **3.** another name for the moon.

**Rohitā** (S) (F) **1.** red. **3.** daughter of Brahmā.

**Rohita** (S) (M) **1.** red. **2.** the sun; an ornament made of precious stones; a rainbow; blood; Saffron (*Crocus sativus*). **3.** a son of King Hariśćandra (*Bhā. Purāṇa*); a son of Kṛṣṇa (*Bhā. Purāṇa*); a son of King Vapuṣmat of Śālmala (*V. Purāṇa*); a class of gandharvas (*V. Rāmāyaṇa*); a river; a Manu (*H. Purāṇa*) another name for Sūrya and Agni.

**Rohitaka** (S) (M) **1.** of red hue. **3.** a mountain mentioned in the Purāṇas.

**Rohitāśva** (S) (M) **1.** red horse; one who possesses red horses. **3.** a son of Hariśćandra (*V. Purāṇa*); another name for Agni.

**Rohtākṣa** (S) (M) **1.** red eyed. **3.** another name for the sun.

**Rola** (S) (M) painting.

**Roladeva** (S) (M) lord of painting.

**Romā** (S) (F) full of hair.

**Roma** (S) (M) hair.

**Romaharṣa** (S) (M) **1.** goose flesh. **3.** the father of Ugrāśrava; the father of Sūta (*Bhā. Purāṇa*)

**Romaharṣaṇa** (S) (M) **1.** causing goose flesh. **2.** causing the hair to stand erect. **3.** a famous disciple of Vyāsa (*Bhā. Purāṇa*)

**Romaśā** (S) (F) **1.** having thick hair; hairy. **3.** daughter of Bṛhaspati.

**Romika** (S) (M) salt; magnet.

**Romir** (S) (M) causing goose flesh; interesting; pleasant.

**Romolā** (S) (F) hairy; charming.

**Ropanā** (S) (F) causing to grow; healing.

**Rośāna** (S) (M) passionate; touchstone; quicksilver.

**Rośansā** (S) (F) wish; desire.

**Roṣāvaroha** (S) (M) **1.** diminisher of anger. **3.** a warrior on the side of the gods against the asuras.

**Royinā** (S) (F) rising; growing.

**Ṛpin** (S) (M) deceitful; injurer.

**Ṛṣabha** (S) (M) **1.** bull. **2.** most excellent; the 2nd note of the musical septet. **3.** a king of the Lunar dynasty who was the grandson of Uparićaravasu; a sage who was the grandson of King Agnīdhra and the husband of Jayantī; a nāga of the family of Dhṛtarāṣṭra (*M. Bh.*); an asura (*M. Bh.*)

**Ṛṣabhadeva** (S) (M) **1.** god of bulls; the best god. **2.** best; most excellent. **3.** the 8th incarnation of Viṣṇu as the son of King Nābhi and Merudevī, he was the husband of Jayantī and the father of Bharata; the husband of Devananda and the father of Mahāvira (*J.S. Koṣa*)

**Ṛṣabhaketu** (S) (M) **1.** bull bannered. **3.** another name for Śiva.

**Ṛsal** (S) (M) angry; injured.

**Ṛṣi** (S) (M) singer of sacred hymns; seer; sage; author of the Vedic hymns; circle of light.

**Ṛṣigiri** (S) (M) **1.** mountain of the ṛṣis. **3.** a mountain near Girivraja (*M. Bh.*)

**Ṛṣika** (S) (M) **1.** belonging to seers. **2.** holy; sacred. **3.** a sage who was the reincarnation of Arkka the asura (*M. Bh.*)

**Ṛṣikulyā** (S) (F) **1.** of the family of ṛṣis. **3.** a sacred river of the *Mahābhārata* (*M. Bh.*)

**Ṛṣirāja** (S) (M) lord of the ṛṣis.

**Ṛṣmā** (S) (F) moonbeam.

**Ṛṣṭāśva** (S) (M) **1.** with moving horses. **3.** husband of Bhadrā (*M. Bh.*)

**Ṛṣu** (S) (M) great; powerful; wise; a ray of the sun; strong; a ṛṣi; firebrand; glowing fire.

**Ṛṣvā** (S) (F) elevated; high; great; noble.

**Ṛṣvanjas** (S) (M) **1.** with sublime power. **3.** another name for Indra.

**Ṛśyaketu** (S) (M) **1.** flag of the hermits; best among the ascetics. **3.** another name for Aniruddha and Kāma.

**Ṛśyaśṛṅga** (S) (M) **1.** deer horned. **3.** the son of the hermit Vibhāndaka and husband of Śāntā, daughter of King Daśaratha, he is the sage who performed the sacrifice by which Daśaratha begot his 4 sons (*V. Rāmāyaṇa*)

**Ṛta** (S) (M) **1.** truth. **3.** a rudra (*M. Bh.*)

**Ṛta** (S) (M) **1.** proper; right; respected; luminous; fit; promise; truth. **3.** one of the 11 rudras (*M. Bh.*); a son of Manu Cākṣuṣa (*Bh. Purāṇa*)

**Ṛtadhāma** (S) (M) **1.** house of truth. **2.** ray of light. **3.** a Manu (*V. Purāṇa*); Indra in the 12th Manvantara (*Bh. Purāṇa*); another name for Kṛṣṇa.

**Ṛtadhvaja** (S) (M) **1.** having the banner of truth. **2.** upholding the values of truth. **3.** a king of the Ikṣvāku dynasty who was the son of Adri; a sage who was the father of Jābāli; a rudra (*Bh. Purāṇa*); another name for Śiva.

**Ṛtajit** (S) (M) **1.** gaining truth. **3.** a yakṣa (*V. Purāṇa*)

**Ṛtam** (S) (M) **1.** truth like. **2.** fixed; settled; law; sacred action; divine truth; right; duty; custom personified as an object of worship. **3.** a son of Dharma.

**Ṛtambhara** (S) (M) **1.** bearing the truth in oneself. **3.** another name for Viṣṇu.

**Ṛtapa** (S) (M) guarding divine truth.

**Ṛtapsu** (S) (M) **1.** whose appearance is truth. **3.** another name for the aśvins.

**Ṛtasena** (S) (M) **1.** leader of truth. **3.** a gandharva (*Bh. Purāṇa*)

**Ṛtaspati** (S) (M) **1.** lord of pious works. **3.** another name for Vāyu.

**Ṛtastubha** (S) (M) **1.** propounder of truth. **3.** a ṛṣi (*Ṛg Veda*)

**Ṛtavasu** (S) (M) whose wealth is piety.

**Ṛtayu** (S) (M) **1.** truthful. **3.** a king of the Lunar dynasty; a sage who was Varuṇa's priest (*M. Bh.*)

**Ṛtayus** (S) (M) **1.** observing the sacred law. **3.** son of Purūravas.

**Ṛteśa** (S) (M) lord of truth.

**Ṛtīṣā** (S) (M) subduing enemies.

**Ṛtodaya** (S) (M) true speech.

**Ṛtu** (S) (F) any fixed time; period; fixed

order; season.

**Rtumbharā** (S) (F) **1.** of divine truth; filled with season. **3.** another name for the earth.

**Ṛtunātha** (S) (M) **1.** lord of the seasons. **3.** spring.

**Ṛtuñjaya** (S) (M) one who conquers the seasons; one who conquers truth.

**Ṛtuparṇa** (S) (M) **1.** fertile; fruitful; truth-winged. **3.** a king of the Ikṣvāku dynasty who was the son of Ayutāyus, he provided shelter to King Nala; a king of Ayodhyā (*M. Bh.*)

**Ṛtupati** (S) (M) **1.** lord of the seasons. **2.** spring. **3.** another name for Agni.

**Ṛturāja** (S) (M) **1.** king of the seasons. **3.** another name for spring.

**Ṛtuśri** (S) (F) splendour of the seasons; queen of the seasons.

**Ṛtusthalā** (S) (F) **1.** abode of light; abode of seasons. **3.** an apsarā (*M. Bh.*)

**Ṛtva** (S) (M) **1.** belonging to season. **3.** a gandharva (*M. Bh.*)

**Ṛtvik** (S) (M) **1.** sacrificing at the proper time. **2.** present.

**Ruća** (S) (F) light; splendour; brightness; desire; the voice of the Mynah.

**Ruća** (S) (M) bright; brilliant; radiant; good; beautiful.

**Rućaka** (S) (M) **1.** large; agreeable; golden; ornamental. **2.** any object that brings good luck; dove; a sweet voice. **3.** a son of Uśanas; a mountain; a son of Dharma.

**Rućeru** (S) (M) pleasing; beautiful; charming.

**Rućeyu** (S) (M) **1.** delightful; shining. **3.** a son of Yayāti (*M. Bh.*)

**Rući** (S) (M) **1.** beauty; lustre; light; desire; zest; pleasure. **3.** a prajāpati; a son of Viśvāmitra (*M. Bh.*); a son of Brahmā who married Ākūti and was the father of a reincarnation of Viṣṇu called Yajña and a daughter named Dakṣiṇā who was an incarnation of Mahālakṣmī.

**Rući** (S) (F) **1.** beauty; lustre; light; desire; taste; pleasure. **3.** an apsarā of Alakāpurī who danced at the court of Kubera (*M. Bh.*); the wife of sage Devaśarman (*M. Bh.*)

**Rućidhaman** (S) (M) abode of light.

**Rućikā** (S) (F) shining; of taste; desirable; ornament.

**Rućikara** (S) (M) causing desire.

**Rućiparva** (S) (M) **1.** festival of lights; filled with beauty. **3.** the son of King Ākṛti who fought on the side of the Pāṇḍavas and was killed while trying to save Bhīma (*M. Bh.*)

**Rućipati** (S) (M) lord of light; master of desires.

**Rućiprabha** (S) (M) **1.** lustrous; shining. **3.** a daitya (*M. Bh.*)

**Rućirā** (S) (F) desirable; charming; winsome; pleasing; dainty.

**Rućira** (S) (M) **1.** bright; brilliant; radiant; splendid; beautiful; golden; agreeable. **2.** handsome; shining. **3.** a son of Senajit (*H. Purāṇa*); Garden Radish (*Raphanus sativus*); Saffron (*Crocus sativus*)

**Rućīraketu** (S) (M) **1.** with a golden banner. **3.** a Bodhisattva.

**Rućiraśrīgarbha** (S) (M) **1.** the womb of light. **2.** the origin of illumination; enlightenment; origin of light. **3.** a Bodhisattva.

**Rućirāśva** (S) (M) **1.** shining horse. **3.** a king of the Lunar dynasty (*Bhāgavata*); a son of Senajit.

**Rućitā** (S) (F) bright; brilliant; delighted; glittering; sweet; dainty.

**Rućita** (S) (M) delighted; bright; shining; pleasant; sweet; dainty.

**Rućya** (S) (M) bright; radiant; of taste; desirable; beautiful; pleasing; a lover.

**Rucyavāhana** (S) (M) **1.** carrying glory; happiness. **3.** one of the 7 ṛṣis under Manu Rohita (*H. Purāṇa*)

**Rūdhī** (S) (F) rise; ascent; birth; fame.

**Rudhikrā** (S) (M) **1.** rising; ascending; famous. **3.** an asura conquered by Indra (*Ṛg Veda*)

**Rudhira** (S) (M) **1.** red; blood. **2.** the planet Mars.

**Rudita** (S) (M) crying.

**Rudrā** (S) (F) **1.** crying; howling. **3.** consort of Śiva; a wife of Vasudeva (*Vā. Purāṇa*); a daughter of Raudrāśva (*V. Purāṇa*); another name for Pārvatī.

**Rudra** (S) (M) **1.** crying; howling; roaring; terrific; roarer. **2.** angry; thunder and lightning;

red and flashing. 3. a form of Śiva considered to have originated from the eyebrows of Brahmā when they curved with fury, Rudra divided himself into 11 male parts and 11 female parts who became the wives (*V. Purāṇa*); Vedic god of the tempest and father of the rudras or maruts he is identified with Indra and Agni and later with Śiva in his terrible aspect.

**Rudrabhairavī** (S) (F) 1. angry and frightening. 3. another name for Pārvatī.

**Rudraćaṇḍī** (S) (F) 1. the roaring goddess. 3. a form of Durgā.

**Rudradaman** (S) (M) 1. conquering Rudra; subduing passion. 3. a Vallabhi king of Saurāṣṭra.

**Rudradeva** (S) (M) 1. the divine Rudra. 3. one of the 9 kings of Āryāvarta.

**Rudragarbha** (S) (M) 1. offspring of Rudra. 3. another name for Agni.

**Rudraja** (S) (M) 1. produced from Rudra. 2. quicksilver; mercury.

**Rudraka** (S) (M) 1. a small rudra. 2. horrible; terrible. 3. a Brāhmin teacher of Buddha (*B. Literature*)

**Rudrakālī** (S) (F) 1. black and angry; roaring and deadly. 2. roarer. 3. a form of Durgā (*D. Purāṇa*)

**Rudraketu** (S) (M) 1. fierce bannered. 3. an asura who was the husband of Śāradā and the father of Devāntaka and Narāntaka who were killed by Gaṇeśa (*G. Purāṇa*)

**Rudrakrīḍā** (S) (F) pleasure ground of Rudra; display of Rudra.

**Rudrākṣa** (S) (M) 1. fierce eyed. 3. the fruit of the tree *Elaeocarpus ganitrus* which is said to have originated from the tears of Rudra and is used to make rosaries.

**Rudramārga** (S) (M) 1. fearful path. 3. a holy place at which if one fasts for a day and a night one attains the kingdom of Indra (*M. Bh.*)

**Rudrāmbā** (S) (F) 1. the angry mother. 3. Pārvatī the consort of Rudra.

**Rudrāmbikā** (S) (F) 1. the angry mother. 2. the consort of Rudra. 3. another name for Pārvatī.

**Rudrāṇī** (S) (F) 1. wife of Rudra. 3. the wife of Rudra; another name for Pārvatī.

**Rudrapatnī** (S) (M) 1. wife of Rudra. 3. another name for Pārvatī.

**Rudraprayāga** (S) (M) 1. confluence of sound. 3. the sacred place where the Mandākinī river joins the Gaṅgā (*Bhā. Purāṇa*)

**Rudrapriyā** (S) (F) 1. dear to Rudra. 3. another name for Pārvatī; Black Myrobalan (*Terminalia chebula*)

**Rudrapuṣpa** (S) (F) red blossom; the China Rose (*Hibiscus rosa sinensis*)

**Rudraputra** (S) (M) 1. son of Rudra. 3. another name for the 12th Manu.

**Rudrāri** (S) (M) 1. the enemy of Rudra. 3. another name for Kāma.

**Rudrarodana** (S) (M) 1. the tears of Rudra. 3. another name for gold.

**Rudraroman** (S) (M) 1. with frightful hair. 3. an attendant of Skanda (*M. Bh.*)

**Rudrasakha** (S) (M) 1. friend of Rudra. 3. another name for Kubera.

**Rudrasāvarṇi** (S) (M) 1. resembling Rudra. 3. a Manu (*Bhā. Purāṇa*)

**Rudrasena** (S) (M) 1. with a terrifying army. 3. a king who was a helper of Yudhiṣṭhira (*M. Bh.*)

**Rudrasī** (S) (F) Rudra like; red.

**Rudrasundarī** (S) (F) 1. beloved of the terrible; beloved of Rudra. 3. a form of Goddess Durgā.

**Rudrasuta** (S) (M) 1. son of Rudra. 3. another name for Skanda.

**Rudrata** (S) (M) 1. roaring; howling. 3. a Sanskṛt critic of Kāśmira who wrote *Kāvyālaṅkāra* (9th century)

**Rudratanaya** (S) (M) 1. son of Rudra personified as punishment. 3. the 3rd Jaina Black Vasudeva (*Bhā. Purāṇa*)

**Rudrāyaṇa** (S) (M) 1. in favour of Rudra. 3. a king of Roruka.

**Ruhā** (S) (F) 1. grown; risen; mounted. 3. the daughter of Surasā (*M. Bh.*); Couch Grass (*Cynodon dactylon*)

**Ruhānī** (S) (M) (F) of higher values; spiritual.

**Rūhī** (S) (F) ascending; of higher value; soul.

**Ruhikā** (S) (F) one that rises; longing; desire.

**Rukma** (S) (M) 1. radiant; gold; sun; ornament. 3. a son of Rućaka (*Bh. Purāṇa*)

**Rukmabāhu** (S) (M) 1. golden armed. 3. a son of Bhīṣmaka (*M. Bh.*)

**Rukmābha** (S) (M) shining like gold.

**Rukmadhara** (S) (M) 1. possessing gold. 3. a king (*V. Purāṇa*)

**Rukmakavaća** (S) (M) 1. with golden armour. 3. a grandson of Uśanas (*H. Purāṇa*)

**Rukmakeśa** (S) (M) 1. golden haired. 3. the youngest son of King Bhīṣmaka of Vidarbha (*Bhāgavata*)

**Rukmamālin** (S) (M) 1. garlanded with gold. 3. a son of Bhīṣmaka.

**Rukmāṅgada** (S) (M) 1. golden ornament. 3. son of King Śalya of Madra (*M. Bh.*)

**Rukmaratha** (S) (M) 1. golden chariot. 3. the chariot of Dronāćārya; a son of King Śalya of Madra (*M. Bh.*); another name for Dronāćarya (*M. Bh.*)

**Rukmarekhā** (S) (F) 1. golden line. 3. the wife of King Raibhya and the mother of Ekāvalī (*Bhā. Purāṇa*)

**Rukmaśukra** (S) (M) 1. with golden power; with golden virility. 3. a son of Priyavrata (*D. Bh. Purāṇa*)

**Rukmat** (S) (M) 1. bright; shining. 3. another name for Agni.

**Rukmavat** (S) (M) 1. possessing gold. 3. the eldest son of King Bhīṣmaka (*H. Purāṇa*)

**Rukmavatī** (S) (F) 1. possessing gold. 2. golden; as beautiful as gold. 3. the daughter of Rukmin and the wife of Pradyumna, she was the mother of Aniruddha (*Bhā. Purāṇa*)

**Rukmeṣu** (S) (M) golden arrowed.

**Rukmidarpa** (S) (M) 1. one who overcame Rukmin. 3. another name for Balarāma.

**Rukmin** (S) (M) 1. wearing golden ornaments. 3. the eldest son of King Bhīṣmaka of Vidarbha.

**Rukmineśa** (S) (M) 1. lord of Rukmiṇī. 3. another name for Kṛṣṇa.

**Rukmiṇī** (S) (F) 1. the sister of Rukmin and the chief queen of Kṛṣṇa, she mothered Pradyumna and is supposed to have been an incarnation of Lakṣmī (*M. Bh.*). 3. Dākṣāyāṇī in Dvārāvatī (*M. Bh.*)

**Rumā** (S) (F) 1. salty; salt mine. 3. a hymn of *Ṛg Veda* which is a favourite of Indra; a woman who sprang from the Ocean of Milk (*K. Rāmāyaṇa*); the daughter of the monkey Panasa and wife of Sugrīva (*V. Rāmāyaṇa*); a river.

**Rumāṅgada** (S) (M) 1. born of the salt lake. 3. the incarnation of Indra as a king on earth.

**Rumanvata** (S) (M) 1. possessing salt. 3. the son of Supratīpa a captain of Udayana's army; the eldest son of sage Jamadagni and Renukā (*M. Bh.*)

**Rumata** (S) (M) 1. salt like. 2. bitter; biting; bright; shining. 3. another name for Agni.

**Rumra** (S) (M) tawny; beautiful.

**Rūpā** (S) (F) 1. bearer of form. 2. silver. 3. a river (*V. Purāṇa*); another name for the earth.

**Rūpa** (S) (M) form; shape; figure; beauty; mark.

**Rūpadhara** (S) (M) shapely; slender; handsome.

**Rūpaka** (S) (M) form; sign; figure.

**Rūpala** (S) (M) made of silver.

**Rūpālī** (S) (F) excellent in form; beautiful.

**Rūpam** (S) (M) beauty; form.

**Rūpamatī** (S) (F) 1. possessing beauty. 3. a queen of Mandu who was the wife of Bāz Bahādur.

**Rūpanārāyaṇa** (S) (M) with the form of Viṣṇu.

**Rūpanga** (S) (M) with a beautiful body.

**Rūpāṅgī** (S) (F) with a beautiful body.

**Rūpapati** (S) (M) 1. lord of forms. 3. another name for Tvaṣṭṛ.

**Rūpasena** (S) (M) 1. handsome leader. 3. a vidyādhara (*K. Sāgara*)

**Rūpasī** (S) (F) beautiful.

**Rūpaśikhā** (S) (F) 1. crest of beauty; most beautiful. 3. a daughter of the rākṣasa Agniśikha (*K. Sāgara*)

**Rūpāśraya** (S) (M) a receptacle of beauty.

**Rūpaśrī** (S) (F) divinely beautiful.

**Rūpāstra** (S) (M) 1. having beauty as a weapon. 3. another name for Kāma.

**Rūpaśvin** (S) (M) handsome; beautiful.

**Rūpavajrā** (S) (F) 1. with powerful beauty;

one whose beauty strikes like a thunderbolt. 3. a Buddhist goddess.

**Rūpavāna** (S) (M) possessed with beauty; handsome.

**Rūpāvata** (S) (M) possessed with beauty; handsome.

**Rūpavatī** (S) (F) 1. possessed with beauty; beautiful. 3. a river (*Bh. Purāṇa*)

**Rūpavidyā** (S) (F) 1. form of knowledge. 3. the figure of the 12 handed Devī in a sitting position.

**Rūpendra** (S) (M) 1. lord of form. 3. another name for the eye.

**Rūpeśa** (S) (M) lord of form.

**Rūpeśvara** (S) (M) lord of form.

**Rūpeśvarī** (S) (F) goddess of beauty.

**Rūpikā** (S) (F) possessing a form; figure; shape; appearance; coin of gold or silver.

**Rūpiṇa** (S) (M) 1. having a beautiful form. 3. the son of Emperor Ajamīḍha and Keśinī and brother of Jahnu and Praja (*M. Bh.*)

**Rūpiṇikā** (S) (F) possessing a beautiful form; embodied; corporeal.

**Rūpyāćala** (S) (M) 1. silver mountain. 3. another name for Mount Kailāsa.

**Ruru** (S) (M) 1. antelope. 3. a famous sage of the Bhṛgu dynasty who was the son of sage Pramati and Pratāpi or Ghṛtāćī and the husband of Pramadvarā the daughter of Menakā by Viśvavasu (*D. Bhāgavata*); an asura who was killed by the devī (*P. Purāṇa*); a son of Ahīnagu (*V. Purāṇa*); a son of one of the viśvadevas; one of the 7 ṛṣis under Manu Sāvarṇi; a daitya slain by Durgā (*K. Sāgara*)

**Ruruka** (S) (M) 1. deer like; wild. 3. a king of the Ikṣvāku dynasty who was a scholar of economics and administration (*H. Purāṇa*)

**Ruṣabhānu** (S) (F) 1. the angry sun. 3. the wife of the asura Hiraṇyākṣa (*Bhāgavata*)

**Ruṣadratha** (S) (M) 1. with a white chariot. 3. a king of the Aṅga family who was the son of Titikṣu and the father of Paila (*A. Purāṇa*)

**Ruṣadru** (S) (M) 1. remover of anger; one who eliminates anger. 3. a king of ancient India who stayed in the palace of Yama (*M. Bh.*)

**Ruśamā** (S) (F) 1. angerless; calm. 3. a learned priest of the Vedas and a protégé of Indra.

**Rūsaṇā** (S) (F) 1. covering; adorning; decoration. 3. a wife of Rudra.

**Ruśangu** (S) (M) 1. with white cattle. 3. a hermit called Viśvāmitra obtained salvation by doing penances in his āśrama (*M. Bh.*)

**Ruśat** (S) (M) brilliant; shining; white; bright.

**Ruśatī** (S) (F) white; fair in complexion.

**Ruśeku** (S) (M) 1. with a bright chariot. 3. a son of Śvahi and father of Ćitraratha.

**Ṛutva** (S) (M) 1. speech; intensity. 3. a gandharva.

S

**Sabala** (S) (M) 1. accompanied by strength. 2. full of strength; strong. 3. a son of Manu Bhautya; a son of Vasiṣṭha; one of the 7 ṛṣīs under Manu Rohita (*V. Purāṇa*); son of Bhṛgu; fire (*M. Bh.*)

**Śabalā** (S) (M) 1. spotted; vareigated. 3. a nāga son of Kaśyapa and Kadru (*M. Bh.*); another name for Kāmadhenu.

**Śabalākṣa** (S) (M) 1. with vareigated eyes. 3. a divine mahāṛṣi (*M. Bh.*)

**Śabalāśva** (S) (M) 1. with a dappled horse. 3. a son of Avīkṣit (*M. Bh.*); a child of Dakṣa and Vairaṇī (*H. Purāṇa*)

**Śabalodara** (S) (M) 1. having a spotted belly. 3. a demon.

**Sabar** (S) (M) milk; nectar.

**Śabarā** (S) (F) 1. variegated; spotted; brindled. 3. a yoginī.

**Śabarī** (S) (F) 1. vareigated; belonging to the Śabara tribe. 3. a gandharvī who was changed into a forest woman and then saved by Rāma (*K. Rāmāyaṇa*)

**Śabasta** (S) (M) 1. born with armour. 3. a son of Yuvanāśva.

**Śabdabhedin** (S) (M) 1. aiming an arrow by listening to the sound. 3. another name for Arjuna.

**Śabdarāśimaheśvara** (S) (M) 1. great lord of the alphabet. 3. another name for Śiva.

**Śabdavedhin** (S) (M) 1. piercer of sound. 2. aiming an arrow by listening to the sound. 3. another name for Arjuna.

**Sabhājit** (S) (M) honoured; praised; celebrated.

**Sabhānara** (S) (M) 1. man of the council. 2. chairman of the senate. 3. a king of the Bharata dynasty who was the son of Anudruhyu and father of Kālanara (*Bhāgavata*); a son of Kakṣeyu (*H. Purāṇa*)

**Sabhāpati** (S) (M) 1. master of the assembly; president of the assembly. 3. a prince on the Kaurava side (*M. Bh.*)

**Sabhāsinha** (S) (M) 1. lion of the assembly. 3. a king of Bundelkhand.

**Sabhāvana** (S) (M) 1. effecting welfare. 3. another name for Śiva.

**Sābhramatī** (S) (F) 1. full of water; cloudy. 3. a river flowing through Ahmedabad.

**Sabhya** (S) (M) 1. fit for an assembly. 2. polite courteous; refined; of honourable parentage. 3. one of the 5 sacred fires.

**Saćana** (S) (M) ready to befriend; kindly disposed.

**Sāćāra** (S) (M) well conducted; well behaved.

**Saćāru** (S) (M) very beautiful.

**Saććandrikā** (S) (F) splendid moonlight.

**Saććidānanda** (S) (M) 1. consisting of existence and thought and joy. 3. a conjoining of Brahmā and Viṣṇu.

**Saććila** (S) (M) consisting of good character; virtuous.

**Saććinmaya** (S) (M) consisting of existence and thought.

**Saććit** (S) (M) 1. pure existence and thought. 3. another name for Brahmā.

**Śaćī** (S) (F) 1. might; aid; kindness; favour; grace; skill; dexterity. 3. the daughter of Puloman and wife of Indra, one aspect of her was reborn as Draupadī (*M. Bh.*); the mother of Ćaitanya.

**Sāći** (S) (M) 1. following; accompanying. 3. another name for Agni.

**Śāćigu** (S) (M) with strong rays.

**Śaćikā** (S) (F) 1. kind; graceful; skilled; dextrous. 3. the wife of Indra.

**Saćin** (S) (M) 1. pure existence; affectionate. 3. another name for Śiva.

**Śaćinandana** (S) (M) 1. son of Śaći. 3. another name for Viṣṇu.

**Śaćinara** (S) (M) 1. like Indrāṇī. 3. a king of Kāśmīra (*R. Taraṅginī*)

**Saćinta** (S) (M) thoughtful.

**Śaćīpati** (S) (M) 1. lord of might and aid; husband of Śaćī. 3. another name for Indra.

**Śaćīramaṇa** (S) (M) 1. beloved of Śaćī. 3. another name for Indra.

**Śaćīśa** (S) (M) 1. lord of Śaćī. 3. another name for Indra.

**Śaćiṣṭha** (S) (M) most powerful; helpful.

**Saćita** (S) (M) wise.

**Saćitta** (S) (M) endowed with reason.

**Sadā** (S) (M) always; ever.

**Sadā** (S) (M) 1. fruit. 3. a son of Dhṛtarāṣṭra (*M. Bh.*)

**Sadābhū** (S) (M) fellow; companion; friend.

**Ṣaḍabhujā** (S) (F) 1. 6 armed. 3. another name for Durgā.

**Ṣaḍabindu** (S) (M) 1. with 6 drops. 3. another name for Viṣṇu.

**Ṣaḍabindu** (S) (M) 1. with 6 spots. 3. another name for Viṣṇu.

**Sadāćandra** (S) (M) the eternal moon.

**Sadāćaraṇa** (S) (M) good moral conduct.

**Sadāćārin** (S) (M) with pure and good conduct.

**Sadāćārya** (S) (M) good teacher.

**Sadādīna** (S) (M) always liberal.

**Sadāgati** (S) (M) 1. always in motion. 3. another name for the sun and Vāyu; the universal spirit.

**Sadājit** (S) (M) 1. eternally victorious. 3. a Bharata dynasty king who was the son of Kuntī and the father of Māhiṣmān (*Bhā. Purāṇa*)

**Sadājyotī** (S) (F) eternal lamp.

**Sadākāntā** (S) (F) 1. always loved. 3. a river in Purāṇic India (*M. Bh.*)

**Sadala** (S) (M) 1. with petals. 2. a flower.

**Saḍānana** (S) (M) 1. 6 faced. 3. another name for Skanda.

**Sadānanda** (S) (M) 1. perpetual bliss. 3. another name for Śiva.

**Sadānīrā** (S) (M) 1. always full of water. 3. a river of Purāṇic India (*M. Bh.*)

**Sadāparibhūta** (S) (M) 1. always in fear. 3. a Bodhisattva.

**Sadāpriṇa** (S) (M) 1. always munificent. 3. a ṛṣi and part author of *Ṛg Veda* (v)

**Sadara** (S) (M) 1. fearful. 3. an asura (*H. Purāṇa*)

**Sādara** (S) (M) showing respect; considerate; attentive; devoted.

**Sadāśiṣa** (S) (F) a good blessing.

**Sadāśivā** (S) (F) 1. always belonging to Śiva; always kind happy and prosperous. 3. another name for Durgā.

**Sadāśiva** (S) (M) eternal Śiva; always kind, happy and prosperous.

**Sadaspati** (S) (M) 1. lords of the sacrificial assembly. 3. Indra and Agni conjoined (*Ṛg Veda*)

**Sadaśva** (S) (M) 1. possessing good horses. 3. a son of Samara (*H. Purāṇa*); a king in Yama's court (*M. Bh.*)

**Sadasyormi** (S) (M) 1. member of an assembly. 3. a king in Yama's court (*M. Bh.*)

**Sadātanaja** (S) (M) 1. always young. 3. another name for Viṣṇu.

**Ṣaḍavaktra** (S) (M) 1. 6 faced. 3. another name for Skanda.

**Sadāvīra** (S) (M) eternally brave.

**Sadāyogin** (S) (M) 1. always practicing yoga. 3. another name for Viṣṇu.

**Saddhan** (S) (M) 1. with money; prosperous. 3. a gandharva (*M. Bh.*)

**Saddhī** (S) (M) wise; a sage.

**Sadguṇa** (S) (M) good qualities; virtuous.

**Sadguru** (S) (M) good teacher.

**Sādhakā** (S) (F) 1. effective; efficient; productive; magical. 3. another name for Durgā.

**Sadhan** (S) (M) possessing; money; rich.

**Sādhanā** (S) (F) accomplishment; performance; worship; adoration.

**Sadhanī** (S) (M) companion; comrade.

**Sadhī** (S) (M) endowed with reason.

**Sādhikā** (S) (F) 1. accomplished; skilful; worshipper; efficient. 3. another name for Durgā.

**Sādhilā** (S) (M) accomplished; perfected; mastered; subdued.

**Sadhīman** (S) (M) full of intelligence.

**Sādhiman** (S) (M) goodness; perfection; excellence.

**Sādhin** (S) (M) accomplishing; performing.

**Sādhri** (S) (F) conqueror.

**Sadhri** (S) (M) 1. with the same goal. 3. ṛṣi and part author of *Ṛg Veda* (x); another name for Agni.

**Sādhu** (S) (M) 1. straight; right. 2. unerring; peaceful; excellent; good; virtuous; classical; pure; noble; sage; seer. 3. an incarnation of Śiva (*Br. Purāṇa*)

**Sādhuja** (S) (M) wellborn; good conduct.

**Sādhumatī** (S) (F) 1. virtuous minded. 3. a tāntra deity (*B. Literature*)

**Sadhūmavarṇā** (S) (F) 1. enveloped in smoke. 3. one of the 7 tongues of fire.

**Sādhupuṣpa** (S) (M) 1. beautiful flower. 2. *Hibiscus mutabilis*.

**Sadhvaṁsa** (S) (M) 1. destroyer. 3. a ṛṣi and part author of *Ṛg Veda* (viii)

**Sādhvī** (S) (F) chaste; virtuous; faithful; honest; righteous; pious; noble; unerring; peaceful.

**Sādhyā** (S) (F) 1. accomplishment; perfection. 3. a daughter of Dakṣa and wife of Dharma and mother of the Sādhyas (*H. Purāṇa*)

**Sādhya** (S) (M) 1. conquerable; achievable; feasible. 3. demigods and attendants of Śiva who are celestial beings of the middle region between the sun and earth (*Ṛg Veda*)

**Sādi** (S) (M) having a beginning.

**Sadīva** (S) (M) eternal like the truth.

**Sadman** (S) (M) abode; temple.

**Śadri** (S) (M) 1. cloud. 2. hovering over the enemies like a thundercloud. 3. another name for Arjuna.

**Śadru** (S) (M) 1. falling. 3. another name for Viṣṇu.

**Sadvatī** (S) (F) 1. righteous; truthful; pious. 3. a daughter of Pulastya and wife of Agni.

**Sādyanta** (S) (M) 1. from beginning to end. 2. complete; entire.

**Sadyojāta** (S) (M) 1. a newly born calf. 3. a form of Śiva.

**Sagaṇa** (S) (M) 1. with troops; attended by followers. 2. a leader; a chieftain. 3. another name for Śiva.

**Sagara** (S) (M) 1. full of moisture; accompanied by praise; containing poison. 2. atmosphere; air. 3. a solar dynasty king of Ayodhyā who was the son of Bāhuka and Yādavī and the husband of Sumati and Keśinī, he fathered Asamañjasa and 60,000 other sons, he is an auspicious king who should be remembered at dawn and dusk (*M. Bh.*)

**Sāgara** (S) (M) 1. of Sagara. 2. ocean. 3. a nāga; the 3rd Arhat of the past Utsarpinī.

**Sāgaradatta** (S) (M) 1. given by the ocean. 3. a king of the gandharvas (*K. Sāgara*)

**Sāgaragāsuta** (S) (M) 1. son of the river. 3. another name for Bhīṣma.

**Sāgarakukṣi** (S) (F) 1. living in the whirlpools of the oceans. 3. a nāga maiden.

**Sāgarālaya** (S) (M) 1. living in the ocean. 3. another name for Varuṇa.

**Sāgaramati** (S) (M) 1. with an ocean of knowledge. 3. a Bodhisattva; a nāga king.

**Sāgarāmbarā** (S) (F) 1. ocean clad. 2. the earth.

**Sāgaranemī** (S) (F) 1. encircled by the ocean. 2. the earth.

**Sāgarapāla** (S) (M) 1. guardian of the ocean. 3. a nāga king.

**Sāgaraśaya** (S) (M) 1. resting on the ocean. 3. another name for Viṣṇu.

**Sāgarasūnu** (S) (M) 1. son of the ocean. 3. another name for the moon.

**Sāgaravīra** (S) (M) hero of the ocean.

**Sāgaravyūhagarbha** (S) (M) 1. carrying the body of the ocean. 3. a Bodhisattva.

**Sāgarī** (S) (F) of the ocean.

**Sāgarikā** (S) (F) of the ocean.

**Śagmā** (S) (M) 1. powerful; mighty. 2. elephant; mountain; strong; effective, kind, friendly.

**Sāgni** (S) (M) maintaining a sacred fire, connected with fire.

**Śagun** (S) (M) auspicious; a lucky omen; a prognostic.

**Saguṇa** (S) (M) 1. complete with virtues. 2. virtuous.

**Sāguṇya** (S) (M) excellence; superiority.

**Śāgurikā** (S) (M) capable; energetic.

**Sahā** (S) (F) 1. tolerant. 3. an apsarā (*M. Bh.*); another name for the earth; *Aloe vera; Rosa alba*.

**Saha** (S) (M) 1. tolerant; powerful; mighty; defying; causing; equal to. 3. a son of Manu (*H. Purāṇa*); a son of Prāṇa and Ūrjasvatī (*Bh. Purāṇa*); a son of Dhṛtarāṣṭra (*M. Bh.*); a son of Kṛṣṇa and Mādrī (*Bh. Purāṇa*); an Agni (*M. Bh.*)

**Sahadeva** (S) (M) 1. with the gods; protected by the gods; mighty god. 3. the 5th Pāṇḍava brother who was the son of Pāṇḍu and Mādrī and the twin brother of Nakula, he was the father of Śrutasena by Pāñćālī and of Suhotra by Vijayā (*M. Bh.*); a mahārṣi in the court of Indra (*M. Bh.*); a king in the court of Yama (*M. Bh.*); a son of Jarāsandha who fought on the side of the Pāṇḍavas (*M. Bh.*); a rākṣasa son of Dhumrākṣa and father of Kṛśāśva (*Bhāgavata*); a solar dynasty king who was the son of Dharmanandana and father of Jayatsena (*Bhāgavata*); a solar dynasty king who was the son of Sudāsa and father of Somaka (*Bhāgavata*); a son of Haryaśvat (*H. Purāṇa*); a son of Harṣavardhana (*V. Purāṇa*); a son of Somadatta (*H. Purāṇa*); a son of Divākara (*V. Purāṇa*); a son of Devapi (*Bhāgavata*); an uncle of Gautama Buddha (*B. Literature*); Jelly Leaf (*Sida rhombofolia*); Ash Coloured Heabane (*Vernonia cinerea*)

**Sahadevī** (S) (F) 1. protected by the goddesses; mighty goddess. 3. a daughter of Devaka and wife of Vasudeva (*H. Purāṇa*)

**Sahaja** (S) (M) 1. simple innate; hereditary; original; natural. 3. a Ćedi king (*M. Bh.*)

**Sahājananda** (S) (M) 1. getting happiness easily. 3. founder of a Vaiṣnava sect.

**Sahajanya** (S) (M) 1. produced together. 3. a yakṣa.

**Sahajanyā** (S) (F) 1. produced together. 3. an apsarā (*H. Purāṇa*)

**Śāhaji** (S) (M) 1. king. 3. the father of Śivaji.

**Sahajit** (S) (M) 1. victorious at once. 3. a Bharata dynasty king and son of Mahābhoja (*Bhā. Purāṇa*)

**Sahamāna** (S) (M) conquering; victorious.

**Sahāmpati** (S) (M) 1. always uttering the sacred sound. 3. a Bodhisattva; a serpent demon; another name for Brahmā.

**Sāhañja** (S) (M) 1. easily won. 3. a king (*H. Purāṇa*)

**Sahānya** (S) (M) mighty mountain.

**Sahāpati** (S) (M) 1. lord of the world of man. 3. another name for Brahmā.

**Sahara** (S) (M) 1. like Hara; Śiva like. 3. another name for Śiva; a dānava (*H. Purāṇa*)

**Sahari** (S) (M) 1. like Hari. 2. a bull; a lion. 3. another name for the sun.

**Saharṣa** (S) (M) joyful; glad.

**Sahasāna** (S) (M) powerful; mighty; a sacrifice; peacock.

**Sahasānu** (S) (M) patient; enduring.

**Sahásin** (S) (M) powerful; mighty.

**Sahaskṛt** (S) (M) bestowing strength or power.

**Sahaskṛta** (S) (M) 1. produced by strength. 3. another name for Agni.

**Sahasrabāhu** (S) (M) 1. 1,000 armed. 3. an at tendant of Skanda (*M. Bh.*); another name foı Śiva and Arjuna Kārtavīrya and Bāṇa.

**Sahasrabhānu** (S) (M) 1. 1000 rayed. 3. another name for the Sun.

**Sahasrabhujā** (S) (F) 1. 1000 armed. 3. another name for Durgā.

**Sahasrabhuja** (S) (M) 1. 1000 armed. 3. a gandharva; another name for Viṣṇu (*M. Bh.*)

**Sahasraćaksus** (S) (M) 1. 1000 eyed. 3. another name for Indra.

**Sahasraćarana** (S) (M) 1. 1000 footed. 3. another name for Viṣṇu.

**Sahasraćitya** (S) (M) 1. making a 1000 cremation grounds. 3. a Kekaya king who was the grandfather of King Śatayūpa (*M. Bh.*)

**Sahasrada** (S) (M) 1. giver of a 1000 cows. 3. another name for Śiva.

**Sahasradhāman** (S) (M) 1. with a 1000 fold splendour. 3. another name for the Sun.

**Sahasradīdhiti** (S) (M) 1. 1000 rayed. 3. another name for the Sun.

**Sahasradoṣ** (S) (M) 1. having a 1000 arms. 3. another name for Arjuna Kārtavīrya.

**Sahasradṛśa** (S) (M) 1. 1000 eyed. 3. another name for Indra and Viṣṇu.

**Sahasragu** (S) (M) 1. possessing a 1000 cows; 1000 rayed; 1000 eyed. 3. another name for the sun and Indra.

**Sahasrahasta** (S) (M) 1. 1000 handed. 3. another name for Śiva.

**Sahasrajit** (S) (M) 1. conqueror of the thousands. 3. a Bharata dynasty king who was a son of Mahābhoja (*Bhāgavata*); a son of Bhajamana; a son of Kṛṣṇa (*Bh. Purāṇa*); another name for Viṣṇu.

**Sahasrajyoti** (S) (M) 1. with a 1000 flames. 2. very glorious. 3. a son of King Samrāt who had a million sons (*M. Bh.*)

**Sahasrajyotis** (S) (M) 1. with a 1000 stars. 2. a galaxy of stars. 3. a son of Śubhrāja (*M. Bh.*)

**Sahasrakara** (S) (M) 1. thousand rayed. 3. another name for the Sun.

**Sahasrākṣa** (S) (M) 1. 1000 eyed. 3. another name for Indra, Viṣṇu and Śiva.

**Sahasrākṣajit** (S) (M) 1. conqueror of Indra. 3. a son of Rāvaṇa.

**Sahasralоćana** (S) (M) 1. 1000 eyed. 3. another name for Indra and Viṣṇu.

**Sahasramauli** (S) (M) 1. 1000 crested. 3. another name for Viṣṇu.

**Sahasramukharāvaṇa** (S) (M) 1. 1000 headed demon king. 3. a daitya king of Trilokapuri island who possessed a 1000 heads, he was the husband of Indumukhī and the father of Vajrabāhu, he was killed by Sītā (*K. Rāmāyaṇa*)

**Sahasramūrdhan** (S) (M) 1. 1000 headed. 3. another name for Viṣṇu and Śiva.

**Sahasrānana** (S) (M) 1. 1000 faced. 3. another name for Viṣṇu.

**Sahasranayana** (S) (M) 1. 1000 eyed. 3. another name for Indra and Viṣṇu.

**Sahasranetra** (S) (M) 1. 1000 eyed. 3. another name for Indra and Viṣṇu.

**Sahasrānīka** (S) (M) 1. with an army of thousands. 3. a lunar king who was the father of Udayana (*K. Sāgara*)

**Sahasrānśu** (S) (M) 1. 1000 rayed. 3.another name for the Sun.

**Sahasrānśuja** (S) (M) 1. son of the Sun. 3. another name for Saturn.

**Sahasrapāda** (S) (M) 1. 1000 footed. 3. a maharṣi (*M. Bh.*); another name for Puruṣa, Viṣṇu, Śiva and Brahmā.

**Sahasrārćis** (S) (M) 1. 1000 rayed. 3. another name for the Sun.

**Sahasrāsya** (S) (M) 1. 1000 headed. 3. another name for Ananta.

**Sahasravāk** (S) (M) 1. with a 1000 mouths. 2. very knowledgeable. 3. a son of Dhṛtarāṣṭra (*M. Bh.*)

**Sahasravīra** (S) (M) with the strength of a 1000 men.

**Sahasrāyu** (S) (M) living a 1000 years.

**Sahasvat** (S) (M) 1. full of valour. 2. powerful; mighty; victorious.

**Sahasya** (S) (M) 1. mighty; strong. 3. the month of Pausa (December/January)

**Sahasyaćandra** (S) (M) the winter moon.

**Sahat** (S) (M) mighty; strong.

**Sahaujas** (S) (M) endowed with strength or power.

**Sahāvan** (S) (M) possessing strength; mighty.

**Sahāya** (S) (M) 1. one who goes along with. 2. companion; helper. 3. another name for Śiva.

**Sahelī** (S) (F) a friend; attached with; small minaret.

**Sahendra** (S) (M) 1. with Indra. 2. Indra like; resembling Indra in power.

**Sahima** (S) (F) with snow.

**Sahira** (S) (M) mountain.

**Sahiṣṇu** (S) (M) 1. patient; forebearing; enduring. 3. a ṛṣi under the 6th Manu; a son of Prajāpati Pulaha and Kṣamā (*V. Purāṇa*); another name for Viṣṇu.

**Sahiṣṭha** (S) (M) strongest; most powerful.

**Sahitā** (S) (F) 1. being near. 3. a river (*V. Purāṇa*)

**Sahitrā** (S) (F) full of patience; enduring.

**Sāhlāda** (S) (M) having joy; cheerful.

**Sahodara** (S) (M) 1. born from the same womb. 2. brother.

**Sahoja** (S) (M) full of strength; produced by strength.

**Sahojit** (S) (M) victorious by strength.

**Sahora** (S) (M) good; excellent; pious; a saint.

**Sahovan** (S) (M) mighty; superior.

**Śahughātin** (S) 1. killing enemies. 3. a son of Śatrughna (*Rāmāyaṇa*)

**Sahurī** (S) (F) 1. full of heat; mighty; strong; victorious. 2. the earth.

**Sahuri** (S) (M) 1. full of heat; mighty; strong; victorious. 3. another name for the sun.

**Sahvan** (S) (M) powerful; mighty.

**Sahya** (S) (M) 1. able to bear; powerful; strong; agreeable. 3. one of the principal ranges of mountains in India; a son of Vivasvat.

**Sahyu** (S) (M) conquering; victorious.

**Śaibya** (S) (M) 1. belonging to the Śibis; belonging to Śiva. 3. a king who was the father of Sṛñjaya (*M. Bh.*); a Śibi king who was the grandson of Uśīnara and a father-in-law of Yudhiṣṭhira (*M. Bh.*); a horse of Kṛṣṇa (*M. Bh.*); a Vṛṣṇi hero in Yudhisthira's court (*M. Bh.*); a warrior of the Kauravas (*M. Bh.*); a Sauvīra king and father of Ratnā who married Akrūra (*M. Purāṇa*); one of the 4 horses of Viṣṇu.

**Śaibyā** (S) (F) 1. belonging to the Śibis. 3. a wife of King Sagara who was also known as Keśinī; wife of King Dyumatsena of Śālva and mother of Satyavān; a wife of Kṛṣṇa (*M. Bh.*)

**Śaikhāvatya** (S) (M) 1. has plaited hair. 2. an ascetic; king of the Śailehavatas. 3. a ṛṣi who gave refuge to Ambā (*M. Bh.*)

**Śailā** (S) (F) 1. dwelling in the mountains. 3. Pārvati's mother.

**Śailabāhu** (S) (M) 1. strong armed. 3. a nāga.

**Śailābha** (S) (M) 1. like a mountain. 2. massive; stout; tall; highly esteemed; as high as a mountain. 3. a viśvadeva (*M. Bh.*)

**Śailadhara** (S) (M) 1. mountain holder. 3. another name for Kṛṣṇa.

**Śailādhipa** (S) (M) 1. king of mountains. 3. the Himālaya.

**Śailajā** (S) (F) 1. daughter of the mountain. 3. another name for Pārvatī.

**Śailakampin** (S) (M) 1. shaking mountains. 2. very powerful. 3. an attendant of Skanda (*M. Bh.*); a dānava (*H. Purāṇa*)

**Śailakanyā** (S) (F) 1. daughter of the mountain. 3. another name for Pārvatī.

**Śailālaya** (S) (M) 1. abode of rocks. 2. mountain. 3. a king who was the grandfather of Bhagadatta (*M. Bh.*)

**Śailapati** (S) (M) 1. lord of mountains. 3. another name for Himavān.

**Śailaputrī** (S) (F) 1. daughter of a mountain. 3. another name for Pārvatī.

**Śailarāja** (S) (M) lord of mountains.

**Śailarājasutā** (S) (F) 1. daughter of the king of mountains. 3. another name for Pārvatī and Gaṅgā.

**Śailāsā** (S) (F) 1. dweller of mountains. 3. another name for Pārvatī.

**Śailendra** (S) (M) 1. lord of the mountain. 3. another name for Śiva and Himavān.

**Śailendrajā** (S) (F) 1. daughter of the mountain lord. 3. another name for the Gaṅgā.

**Śaileśa** (S) (M) 1. lord of the mountains. 3. another name for the Himālaya.

**Śailī** (S) (F) carved in rock; style; custom; visage; habit.

**Śailūṣa** (S) (M) 1. actor; dancer. 3. a gandharva who serves Kubera in his assembly (*M. Bh.*); Bengal Quince (*Aegle marmelos*)

**Saindhava** (S) (M) 1. lord of the Sindhus. 3. another name for Jayadratha.

**Saindhavaka** (S) (M) 1. lord of the Sindhus. 3. another name for Jayadratha.

**Saindhavāyana** (S) (M) 1. from the sea. 3. a son of Viśvāmitra (*M. Bh.*)

**Sainhika** (S) (M) leonine.

**Sainika** (S) (M) 1. soldier; martial. 3. a son of Śambara (*H. Purāṇa*)

**Sairandhrī** (S) (F) 1. maid. 2. a maid servant in the women's apartments. 3. Draupadī in King Virāṭa's court (*M. Bh.*)

**Śaiśirāyaṇa** (S) (M) 1. belonging to winter. 2. cold; of a temper. 3. a mahaṛṣi who was the husband of Gopālī and the father of Kālayavana (*H. Purāṇa*)

**Śaiśireya** (S) (M) 1. related to winter. 2. cold; of a cool temper. 3. a disciple of Śākalya and author of the authoritative *Śākalya* treatise.

**Śaiśupāla** (S) (M) 1. son of Śiśupāla. 3. another name for Dhṛṣṭaketu.

**Śaiva** (S) (M) 1. sacred to Śiva; follower of Śiva. 3. a sect of the Hindus; the 5th Jaina Black Vasudeva (*J. Literature*)

**Śaivala** (S) (M) 1. *Blyxa octandra*. 3. a nāga.

**Śaivasutā** (S) (M) 1. daughter of Śiva. 3. another name for Gaṅgā.

**Śaivī** (S) (F) 1. prosperity; auspiciousness. 3. another name for the goddess Manasā.

**Śaivya** (S) (M) the cult of Śiva; prosperous; auspicious.

**Śaivyasugrīvavāhana** (S) (M) 1. with Śaivya and Sugrīva as horses. 3. another name for Kṛṣṇa.

**Sajanī** (S) (F) 1. a woman worth keeping company with. 2. sweetheart.

**Sajiṣṇu** (S) (M) accompanied by Arjuna.

**Sajitvan** (S) (M) victorious; superior.

**Sajīva** (S) (M) full of life; living; alive.

**Sajjambhava** (S) (M) 1. ready. 3. the author of *Daśavaikālika Sutra*, he succeeded Prabhava as the head of the Jaina church (*J.S. Koṣa*)

**Sajjana** (S) (M) wellborn; respectable; nobleman; gentleman; guard; sentry.

**Sajvara** (S) (M) 1. heat. 3. another name for Agni.

**Śāka** (S) power; might; help; aid; herb; vegetation.

**Śakadala** (S) (M) fragment of power.

**Śakāditya** (S) (M) 1. sun of the Śakas. 3. another name for King Śālivāhana.

**Sakala** (S) (M) 1. all; whole; complete; full. 2. perfect; universe.

**Śakalā** (S) (M) 1. cart. 3. the 5 stars forming the asterism Rohiṇī; a demon slain by child Kṛṣṇa.

**Sakalādhāra** (S) (M) 1. receptacle of all. 3. another name for Śiva.

**Sakaladīpa** (S) (M) illuminator of all.

**Sakalasiddhi** (S) (F) possessing all perfection.

**Sakalendu** (S) (M) the full moon.

**Śakalendu** (S) (M) the half moon.

**Sakaleśvara** (S) (M) lord of all.

**Śākalya** (S) (M) 1. an amulet of woodchips. 3. a maharṣi who systematized the *Veda Saṁhitās*.

**Śākambharī** (S) (F) 1. herb nourishing. 2. the tutelary goddess of vegetation. 3. another name for Durgā.

**Śakara** (S) (M) piece; bit; fragment; chip.

**Sākāra** (S) (M) having form; beautiful.

**Sākāśa** (S) (M) with the light shining on.

**Śakata** (S) (M) 1. cart; weapon. 3. a demon slain by child Kṛṣṇa.

**Śakaṭāri** (S) (M) 1. enemy of Śakata. 3. another name for Kṛṣṇa.

**Śākaṭāyana** (S) (M) 1. belonging to the cart. 3. a grammarian and author of *Unādisūtrapatha*.

**Śākavaktra** (S) (M) 1. vegetable faced. 3. a soldier of Skanda (*M. Bh.*)

**Śākayanya** (S) (M) 1. belonging to vegetables or herbs; a mendicant. 3. a maharṣi.

**Sāketa** (S) (M) 1. city of people. 3. another name for Ayodhyā.

**Saketa** (S) (M) 1. with the same intention. 3. an āditya.

**Śākha** (S) (M) 1. branch of a tree. 3. the son of Subrahmaṇya born from his face (*K. Sāgara*), also regarded as Subrahmaṇya's younger brother and the son of the vasu Anala (*M. Bh.*)

**Śākin** (S) (M) helpful; powerful.

**Śākin** (S) (M) 1. of herbs. 2. god of herbs.

**Śākinī** (S) (F) 1. goddess of herbs; helpful; powerful. 3. another name for Pārvatī as the procurer of plants; an attendant of Durgā.

**Śākman** (S) (M) 1. capability; power; strength; capacity. 3. another name for Indra.

**Śakra** (S) (M) 1. strong; powerful; mighty. 3. an āditya; the number 14; another name for Indra; *Terminalia arjuna*.

**Śakradeva** (S) (M) 1. lord Indra. 3. a Kaliṅga king who fought on the Kaurava side (*M. Bh.*); a son of Śṛgāla.

**Śakrāditya** (S) (M) 1. sun among the strong; sun and Indra conjoined. 2. as powerful as sun and Indra conjoined; most capable; as radiant as the sun. 3. another name for Indra.

**Śakradyumna** (S) (M) 1. with powerful splendour. 3. a king of Rāma's dynasty.

**Śakraja** (S) (M) son of Indra.

**Śakrajit** (S) (M) 1. conqueror of Indra. 3. another name for Meghanāda.

**Śakraketu** (S) (M) Indra's banner.

**Śakranandana** (S) (M) 1. son of Indra. 3. another name for Arjuna.

**Śakrāṇi** (S) (F) 1. consort of Śakra. 3. another name for Śacī.

**Śakrāri** (S) (M) 1. Indra's enemy. 3. another name for Kṛṣṇa.

**Śakrasārathi** (S) (M) 1. Indra's charioteer. 3. another name for Mātali.

**Śakrasuta** (S) (M) 1. son of Indra. 3. another name for Vālin and Arjuna.

**Śakrātmaja** (S) (M) 1. son of Indra.

3. another name for Arjuna.

**Śakravāpin** (S) (M) 1. pond of the powerful; living in Indra's pond. 3. a nāga (*M. Bh.*)

**Sākrī** (S) (F) 1. of Indra. 2. consort of Indra.

**Śakri** (S) (M) cloud; thunderbolt; elephant; mountain.

**Sakṣam** (S) (M) able; powerful.

**Sakṣaṇi** (S) (M) conquering; vanquishing; comrade; companion.

**Sākṣī** (S) (F) 1. with eyes. 2. witness.

**Śakta** (S) (M) 1. competent; capable. 3. a son of Manasyu (*M. Bh.*); the son of Manasvī and Sauvirī of the Purū dynasty (*M. Bh.*)

**Śakti** (S) (F) 1. power; ability; strength; might; energy. 3. the energy of a deity personified as his wife, the 8 primary Śaktis are Indrāṇī, Vaiṣṇavī, Śāntā, Brahmāṇī, Kaumārī, Nārasiṇhī, Vārāhī, Māheśvarī also Ćāmuṇḍā and Ćāṇḍikā, another sect includes Kārttikī and Pradhānā, some sects count 50 different forms of the Śakti of Viṣṇu and 50 of Śiva, those counted as white Śaktis or those of a mild nature are Lakṣmī, Sarasvatī, Gaurī etc., the dark or fierce Śaktis includes Durgā, Kālī (*K. Sāgara*)

**Śakti** (S) (M) 1. help; assistance; the force of a magic formula. 2. sword; spear; gift. 3. the son of Vasiṣṭha and Arundhatī he was the husband of Adṛśyantī and the father of Parāśaramuni (*V. Purāṇa*); the weapon of Skanda made by Viśvakarman (*V. Purāṇa*)

**Śaktibhadra** (S) (M) 1. holding a spear. 3. Sanskṛt dramatist of Kerala (7th century A.D.)

**Śaktibhṛt** (S) (M) 1. spearholder. 2. powerful. 3. another name for Skanda.

**Śaktidhara** (S) (M) 1. holding a spear. 2. powerful. 3. another name for Skanda.

**Śaktika** (S) (M) 1. powerful; mighty. 3. another name for Kārttikeya.

**Śaktimatī** (S) (F) powerful.

**Śaktinātha** (S) (M) 1. lord of Śakti; lord of power. 3. another name for Śiva.

**Śaktipāṇi** (S) (M) 1. spear handed. 3. another name for Skanda.

**Śaktirakṣita** (S) (M) 1. protected by power. 3. a king of the Kirātas (*K. Sāgara*)

**Śaktisena** (S) (M) with a powerful spear carrying army.

**Śaktivega** (S) (M) 1. power motivated; speedy and energetic. 3. a vidyādhara (*K. Sāgara*)

**Śaktiyaśas** (S) (F) 1. with powerful fame. 3. a vidyādharī.

**Śakunī** (S) (F) auspicious object; lucky omen.

**Śakuni** (S) (M) 1. large bird. 2. peacock. 3. a son of Duhsaha (*Mā. Purāṇa*); an asura who was the son of Hiraṇyākṣa and father of Vṛka (*H. Purāṇa*); a son of Vikukṣi and grandson of Ikṣvāku (*H. Purāṇa*); a son of Daśaratha (*Bhā. Purāṇa*); the great grandfather of Aśoka (*R. Taraṅginī*); a serpent of Dhṛtarāṣṭra dynasty (*M. Bh.*); a king of the Bharata dynasty who was the son of Bhīmaratha and father of Urudbhī (*Bhāgavata*); a son of Ikṣvāku; a maharṣi (*P. Purāṇa*); the son of King Subala of Gāndhāra and brother of Gāndhāri who was supposed to be the incarnation of Dvāpara (*M. Bh.*)

**Śakunikā** (S) (F) 1. bird. 3. a mother in Skanda's retinue (*M. Bh.*)

**Śakunīśvara** (S) (M) 1. lord of birds. 3. another name for Garuḍa.

**Śakunta** (S) (M) 1. bird; blue jay. 3. a son of Viśvāmitra (*M. Bh.*)

**Śakuntalā** (S) (F) 1. bird; protected by birds. 3. the daughter of Menakā by Viśvāmitra, she was adopted by the sage Kaṇva, she married King Duṣyanta of the Lunar dynasty and became the mother of the Emperor Bharata.

**Śakunti** (S) (F) bird.

**Śakuntikā** (S) (F) a small bird.

**Śākvara** (S) (M) might; powerful; strong.

**Śakvarī** (S) (M) 1. a finger; girdle. 3. a river.

**Śakya** (S) (M) possible; within reach.

**Śākyaketu** (S) (M) 1. banner of the Śākyas. 3. another name for Gautama Buddha.

**Śākyakīrti** (S) (M) 1. glory of the Śakas; a tribe from Kapilavastu. 3. another name for Gautama Buddha.

**Śākyamitra** (S) (M) friend of the Śākya tribe.

**Śākyamunī** (S) (M) 1. Śākya sage. 3. another name for Gautama Buddha.

**Śākyapuṅgava** (S) (M) 1. bull among the

Śākyas. 3. another name for Gautama Buddha.

**Śākyasinha** (S) (M) 1. lion of the Śākyas. 3. another name for Gautama Buddha.

**Śākyavardhana** (S) (M) 1. accomplisher of the possible. 3. a temple (*Divyāvadāna*)

**Sāl** (S) (M) 1. water; dog; moving. 3. the king of Pṛṣṭaćampa who was the follower of Mahāvira.

**Śāla** (S) (M) 1. rampart; wall; fence; the tree *Vatica robusta*. 3. a son of Vṛka.

**Śala** (S) (M) 1. dart; spear; staff. 3. an attendant of Śiva; a son of Śunahotra (*H. Purāṇa*); a wrestler of Kansa killed by Kṛṣṇa (*Bhāgavata*); a serpent of the Vāsuki dynasty (*M. Bh.*); a son of Dhṛtarāṣṭra (*M. Bh.*); a son of King Somadatta of the Kuru dynasty who fought on the side of the Kauravas (*M. Bh.*); a son of King Parīkṣit and Suśobhanā (*M. Bh.*); a son of Śunahotra.

**Śalabhā** (S) (F) 1. grasshopper. 3. the wife of sage Atri (*Br. Purāṇa*)

**Śalabha** (S) (M) 1. grasshopper. 3. locust fabled to be the children of Pulastya or of Tārkṣya and Yāminī; a gandharva (*M. Bh.*); a warrior of the Pāṇḍavas (*M. Bh.*); an asura son of Kaśyapa and Danu (*M. Bh.*)

**Śalabhī** (S) (F) 1. grasshopper; locust. 3. a mother in Skanda's retinue (*M. Bh.*)

**Sālaćandra** (S) (M) moon of the house.

**Śaladā** (S) (F) 1. procurer of the spear. 3. a daughter of Raudrāśva.

**Śalāgraja** (S) (M) 1. elder brother of Śala. 3. another name for Bhūriśravas.

**Śālagrāma** (S) (M) 1. the fence around a village; the protector; belonging to a village near Sāl trees. 3. an ammonite stone worshipped by the Vaiṣṇavas as being pervaded by Viṣṇu, it is found in the Sālagrāma village on the Gaṇḍakī river (*Purāṇas*); another name for Viṣṇu.

**Śalākā** (S) (F) 1. small stick; a needle. 3. the wife of sage Dhanañjaya.

**Śalakara** (S) (M) 1. staff handed. 3. a nāga of the Takṣaka dynasty (*M. Bh.*)

**Śālakāṭaṅka** (S) (M) 1. the thorn of the Śāl tree. 3. a rākṣasa.

**Sālakatāṅkaṭā** (S) (F) 1. fire of the house. 3. a rākṣasī who was the daughter of Sandhyā the wife of Vidyutkeśa and the mother of Sukeśa (*V. Rāmāyaṇa*)

**Śalālu** (S) (M) perfume.

**Śalanga** (S) (M) king.

**Sālaṅkāyana** (S) (M) 1. with a large quantity. 3. a son of Viśvāmitra (*M. Bh.*)

**Śālankāyana** (S) (M) 1. tree marked. 2. living in the woods; an ascetic. 3. a ṛṣi and son of Viśvāmitra (*M. Bh.*); an attendant of Śiva.

**Salatā** (S) (F) a plant yielding Soma juice.

**Śālāvatī** (S) (F) 1. owning a house; housewive; lady of the house. 3. a wife of Viśvāmitra (*H. Purāṇa*)

**Śalendrarāja** (S) (M) 1. lord of the Śal trees. 3. a Buddha.

**Śālihotra** (S) (M) 1. receiving oblations of rice. 3. a muni whose āśrama was visited by the Pāṇḍavas (*M. Bh.*)

**Sālikā** (S) (F) flute.

**Śālika** (S) (M) 1. rice flour. 3. a divine maharṣi (*M. Bh.*)

**Salila** (S) (M) 1. flowing. 2. water.

**Salīla** (S) (M) playing; sporting; sportive.

**Salilapati** (S) (M) 1. lord of water. 2. the ocean. 3. another name for Varuṇa (*V's B. Samhitā*)

**Salilarāja** (S) (M) 1. lord of water. 3. another name for Varuṇa.

**Salileśa** (S) (M) 1. lord of the waters. 3. another name for Varuṇa.

**Salileśvara** 1. lord of water. 3. another name for Varuṇa.

**Śālin** (S) (M) 1. possessing a house; praiseworthy. 2. rice; civet cat. 3. a yakṣa; a maharṣi (*Vā. Purāṇa*)

**Śālinā** (S) (F) 1. courteous. 2. Fennel (*Foeniculum capillaceum*)

**Śālinī** (S) (F) 1. with a fixed abode. 2. settled; established; domestic; shy; bashful; modest.

**Śālipiṇḍa** (S) (M) 1. rice serpent. 3. a nāga son of Kaśyapa and Kadru (*M. Bh.*)

**Śāliśiras** (S) (M) 1. with a tree like head; with high intellect; confident. 3. a gandharva son of Kaśyapa and Muni (*M. Bh.*)

**Śālivāhana** (S) (M) 1. with a chariot made of

Śāla wood. **3.** a celebrated sovereign of India who instituted the Śāka era and whose capital was Prathiṣṭhāna on the Godāvarī (*S. Dvatrinśikā*)

**Śālmalī** (S) (F) **1.** garlanded with Sālmali trees. **3.** a river of the lower regions; a Śakti of Viṣṇu.

**Śālmali** (S) (M) **1.** the Semul tree (*Bombax ceiba*) **3.** a lunar king who was the son of Avīkṣit and grandson of Kuru (*M. Bh.*)

**Śālmalin** (S) (M) **1.** living in the Śālmali tree. **3.** Garuḍa.

**Śālmālinī** (S) (F) the Red Silkcotton tree (*Bombax celba*)

**Saloni** (H) (F) beautiful.

**Śālu** (S) (M) frog; perfume; lotus root.

**Sālva** (S) (M) **1.** dynamic people. **3.** the ruler of Śubha who was the beloved of princess Ambā of Kāśī and is considered a partial incarnation of Ajaka (*M. Bh.*)

**Śalvāyana** (S) (M) **1.** belonging to the Śālvas. **3.** a king of ancient India who escaped to South India in fear of Jarāsandha (*M. Bh.*)

**Śalya** (S) (M) **1.** dart; javelin; spear; arrow. **2.** porcupine; fence; boundary. **3.** an asura (*H. Purāṇa*); a king of Madra and brother of Mādrī the wife of Pāṇḍu, he fought on the side of the Kauravas (*M. Bh.*)

**Śalyāri** (S) (M) **1.** enemy of Śalya. **3.** another name for Yudhiṣṭhira.

**Sama** (S) (M) **1.** equal. **2.** even; smooth; flat; honest; just; peace. **3.** a son of Dharma (*V. Purāṇa*); a son of Dhṛtarāṣṭra (*M. Bh.*)

**Śāma** (S) (M) **1.** equanimity; calmness. **3.** the dog that followed Yudhiṣṭhira and was a son of Saramā (*Br. Purāṇa*)

**Samā** (S) (F) of a peaceful nature; equanimity; similarity; a year.

**Śamā** (S) (F) **1.** tranquil; peaceful; calm; lamp. **3.** an apsarā.

**Śama** (S) (M) **1.** tranquillity; calmness; quietude; equanimity. **3.** peace personified as a son of Dharma and husband of Prāpti (*M. Bh.*); a son of Andhaka (*H. Purāṇa*); the son of the vasu Aah (*M. Bh.*)

**Samabuddhi** (S) (M) **1.** esteeming all things alike. **3.** a muni.

**Samādara** (S) (M) great respect; veneration.

**Samadu** (S) (F) daughter.

**Samadyuti** (S) (M) equal in radiance.

**Sāmagarbha** (S) (M) **1.** destroying sin. **3.** another name for Viṣṇu.

**Samagrendu** (S) (M) full moon.

**Samaja** (S) (M) **1.** forest; multitude. **3.** another name for Indra.

**Samajyā** (S) (F) fame; reputation.

**Śamaka** (S) (M) peacemaker; pacifier.

**Samakarṇa** (S) (M) **1.** with equal ears. **3.** another name for Buddha and Śiva.

**Samākhyā** (S) (F) name; fame; celebrity.

**Samālī** (S) (F) a collection of flowers; a nosegay.

**Samālya** (S) (M) garlanded; crowned.

**Sāman** (S) (M) calming; tranquillizing; destroying sin; a song of praise; chanted hymn.

**Samāna** (S) (M) **1.** similar; equal; identical; possessing honour. **3.** one of the 5 vital airs of the body personified as a son of Sādhya (*A. Veda*)

**Sāmana** (S) quiet; calm; rich; affluent; abundant; universal.

**Samaṅga** (S) (M) **1.** with balanced features. **3.** a cowherd of Duryodhana (*M. Bh.*); a hermit (*M. Bh.*); Sensitive Plant (*Mimosa pudica*)

**Samaṅgala** (S) (M) full of happiness; auspicious.

**Samangini** (S) (F) **1.** complete in all parts. **3.** a deity of the Bodhi tree.

**Śāmani** (S) (F) tranquillity; peace.

**Śamanī** (S) (F) **1.** the calming one. **2.** night.

**Samañjasa** (S) (M) **1.** proper; right; fit; correct; sound; good; excellent. **3.** another name for Śiva.

**Sāmanta** (S) (M) **1.** bordering; limiting; chief of a district. **2.** leader; general; champion.

**Samanta** (S) (M) contiguous; being on every side; universal; whole; entire.

**Samantabhadra** (S) (M) **1.** wholly auspicious. **3.** a Bodhisattva.

**Samantabhuj** (S) (M) **1.** all devouring. **3.** another name for Agni.

**Samantaćāritamati** (S) (M) **1.** with an even mind. **3.** a Bodhisattva.

**Samantadarśin** (S) (M) 1. seeing all. 3. a Buddha.
**Śamantaka** (S) (M) 1. destroyer of tranquillity. 3. another name for Kāma.
**Samantanetra** (S) (M) 1. universal eye. 3. a Bodhisattva.
**Samantaprabha** (S) (M) 1. universal light. 3. a Bodhisattva.
**Samantaprabhāsa** (S) (M) 1. universal illumination. 3. a Buddha.
**Samantaprasādika** (S) (M) 1. offering help on all sides. 3. a Bodhisattva.
**Samantaraśmi** (S) (M) 1. composed of rays of light; all-illuminating. 3. a Bodhisattva.
**Samantra** (S) (M) accompanied by sacred verses.
**Samanyu** (S) (M) 1. wrathful. 3. another name for Śiva.
**Samara** (S) (M) 1. concourse; confluence. 3. a king of the vidyādharas (*K. Sāgara*); a king of Kāmpīlya (*H. Purāṇa*); a brother of King Avantivarman (*R. Taranginī*); a son of King Pṛthuśena of the Bharata dynasty (*Bhāgavata*)
**Sāmara** (S) (M) with the immortals; accompanied by the gods.
**Samarajit** (S) (M) victorious in war.
**Samaramardana** (S) (M) 1. destroying in battle. 3. another name for Śiva.
**Samarañjaya** (S) (M) victorious in a battle.
**Samarasinha** (S) (M) lion in battle.
**Samaratha** (S) (M) 1. with a smooth chariot. 3. a brother of King Virāṭa who fought on the side of the Pāṇḍavas (*M. Bh.*)
**Samaravijaya** (S) (M) victorious in battle.
**Samaravīra** (S) (M) 1. hero of the battle. 3. the father of Yaśodā.
**Samarćaka** (S) (M) worshipping.
**Samarćita** (S) (M) worshipped; adored.
**Samardhana** (S) (M) causing to prosper.
**Samardhukā** (S) (F) 1. prospering; succeeding. 2. daughter.
**Samarendra** (S) (M) lord of war.
**Samasaurabha** (S) (M) 1. with an even fragrance. 2. with a delightful fragrance. 3. a Brāhmin who was a guest of Janamejaya (*M. Bh.*)
**Samastī** (S) (F) 1. all that is reaching; attaining; totality. 2. the universe.
**Samatā** (S) (F) equality; sameness; fairness; benevolence.
**Samatā** (S) (F) 1. equality. 2. peaceful.
**Śamatha** (S) (M) 1. residing in peace; tranquil; calm. 3. a Brāhmin at Yudhiṣṭhira's court (*M. Bh.*)
**Śamavāna** (S) (M) 1. tranquil; calm. 3. a son of Viśvāmitra (*M. Bh.*)
**Samāvarta** (S) (M) 1. turning back; returning. 3. another name for Viṣṇu.
**Samavartin** (S) (M) 1. of fair and impartial disposition. 3. another name for Yama.
**Sāmavat** (S) (M) 1. connected with a Sāma. 3. a son of Sārasvata.
**Samaya** (S) (M) 1. coming together. 2. covenant; understanding; rule; order; direction; time; season; limit; speech; end of trouble. 3. a son of Dharma (*V. Purāṇa*)
**Samayānanda** (S) (M) happy time.
**Sāmba** (S) (M) 1. with the mother. 3. the son of Kṛṣṇa and Jāmbavatī (*M. Bh.*)
**Śambara** (S) (M) 1. made of iron; war; fight; cloud; best; excellent. 3. a demon who was slain by Indra (*Ṛg Veda*); and in the Mahabhārāta by Kāma (*Ṛg Veda*); a leader of the asuras who was the son of Kaśyapa and Danu and was killed by Śiva; a son of Hiraṇyākṣa and the husband of Māyāvatī; a Jīna (*L. Vistara*); Ceylon Leadwort (*Plumbago zeylanica*); California Cinchona (*Symplocos racemosa*); White Murdah (*Terminalia citrina*)
**Śambarāghna** (S) (M) 1. Śambara slayer. 3. another name for Kāma.
**Śambarāri** (S) (M) 1. enemy of Śambara. 3. another name of Kāma.
**Sāmbaśiva** (S) (M) 1. with Pārvatī. 3. another name for Śiva.
**Sambhā** (S) (M) to shine fully; to be visible; to be very bright.
**Sambhara** (S) (M) supporter; bestower; bringing together.
**Śambhava** (S) (M) 1. peacefully born. 3. the 3rd Arhat of the present Avasarpinī.

**Śāmbhava** (S) (M) coming from Śiva; sacred to Śiva.

**Sambhava** (S) (M) 1. meeting; union; birth; origin; ability intimacy; manifestation, creation. 3. a Purū king who was the son of Ūrjā and father of Jarāsandha (*A. Purāṇa*)

**Sambhavanātha** (S) (M) 1. lord of creation. 3. the 3rd Jaina Tīrthaṅkara who was the son of King Jitāri and queen Senā of Śrāvastī.

**Śāmbhavī** (S) (F) 1. a kind of blue flowering sacred grass (*Cynodon dactylon*). 3. another name for Durgā.

**Sambhāvya** (S) (M) 1. honoured; respected; well treated; suited; fit. 3. a son of Manu Raivata (*V. Purāṇa*)

**Sambhogayakṣiṇī** (S) (F) 1. deity of enjoyment. 3. a yoginī.

**Sambhrama** (S) (M) 1. whirling round; agitation; activity; zeal; awe; respect. 3. a class of beings attendant on Śiva.

**Śambhu** (S) (F) 1. helpful; benevolent; kind. 3. the wife of Dhruva and mother of Sliṣṭi and Bhavya (*V. Purāṇa*)

**Śambhu** (S) (M) 1. causing happiness. 2. existing for welfare and happiness; helpful; benevolent; kind. 3. a son of Viṣṇu (*M. Bh.*); Indra in the 10th Manvantara (*Bhā. Purāṇa*); one of the 11 rudras (*M. Bh.*); a king of the daityas (*Rāmāyaṇa*); an Arhat; a son of Śuka (*H. Purāṇa*); a son of Viśvarūpa and the grandson of Tvaṣṭā (*A. Purāṇa*); a son of Ambarīṣa (*Bhāgavata*); a rākṣasa son of Vidyujjīhva and Śurpaṇakhā (*K. Rāmāyaṇa*); a son of Kṛṣṇa and Rukmiṇī (*M. Bh.*); a Bharata dynasty king who was a son of Ugrasena (*Bhāgavata*); another name for Śiva, Brahmā and Viṣṇu.

**Śambhubhairava** (S) (M) 1. Śiva the terrible. 3. a form of Śiva.

**Śambhukāntā** (S) (F) 1. wife of Śiva. 3. another name for Durgā.

**Śambhukumāra** (S) (M) 1. son of the daitya Śambhu. 3. a son of Śūrpaṇakhā.

**Śambhunandana** (S) (M) 1. son of Śiva. 3. another name for Skanda and Gaṇeśa.

**Śambhunātha** (S) (M) 1. lord Śiva. 3. a temple of Śiva in Nepāl.

**Śambhupriyā** (S) (F) 1. dear to Śiva. 3. another name for Durgā.

**Sambhūta** (S) (M) 1. born; originated; manifested; capable; equal. 3. a king who was the son of Trasadasyu and the father of Anaraṇya (*Vā. Purāṇa*)

**Śambhutanaya** (S) (M) 1. son of Śiva. 3. another name for Skanda and Gaṇeśa.

**Sambhūtī** (S) (F) 1. birth; origin; manifestation of might. 3. fitness personified as the daughter of Dakṣa and wife of Marīci (*Purāṇas*); a wife of Jayadratha and mother of Vijaya (*Bhāgavata*)

**Sambhūti** (S) (M) 1. born; manifested. 3. a son of Duhsaha (*V. Purāṇa*); a brother of Trasadasyu (*V. Purāṇa*)

**Sambhūtivijaya** (S) (M) 1. victorious over birth. 2. one who has achieved bliss and shall therefore not be reborn. 3. the monk who succeeded Yaśobhadra as the head of the Jaina church (*J. Literature*)

**Śambhuvallabha** (S) (M) beloved of Śiva; the white lotus (*Nelumbium speciosum*)

**Sambodha** (S) (M) perfect knowledge.

**Sambuddha** (S) (M) wide awake; clever; wise; prudent.

**Sambuddha** (S) (M) eternally wise.

**Sambuddhi** (S) (F) perfect knowledge; perception.

**Śambūka** (S) (M) 1. small conchshell. 3. a Śūdra muni (*K. Rāmāyaṇa*)

**Samedha** (S) (M) full of strength.

**Sameḍī** (S) (F) 1. moving one. 3. a mother attending on Skanda (*M. Bh.*)

**Śamen** (S) (M) happy; prosperous; blessing; protection.

**Samendra** (S) (M) lord of equality; like the god.

**Śamendu** (S) (M) Viṣṇu as conferring happiness.

**Sameśa** (S) (M) lord of equality; like the gods.

**Saṁgharṣaṇa** (S) (M) 1. rubbing together. 2. ointment. 3. another name for Balarāma.

**Śamī** (S) (M) 1. toil; work; effort. 2. legume; the Śami tree supposed to contain fire (*Prosopis spicigera*). 3. a son of Andhaka (*H. Purāṇa*); a king who was the son of Uśīnara (*Bhāgavata*)

**Samića** (S) (M) the ocean; sea.

**Samići** (S) (F) **1.** praise; eulogy. **2.** a doe. **3.** an apsarā.

**Samiddha** (S) (M) perfect; full; complete; inflamed; ignited.

**Samīhā** (S) (F) wish; desire.

**Samīka** (S) (M) **1.** vanquisher of peace. **2.** conflict; fight. **3.** a son of Śurā; a ṛṣi (*M. Bh.*)

**Śamīka** (S) (M) **1.** peaceful. **2.** self restrained. **3.** a muni who was the father of Sṛṅgi; a great warrior of the Vṛṣṇi dynasty (*M. Bh.*); a son of Śūra and brother of Vasudeva.

**Śamīkā** (S) (F) **1.** peaceful. **3.** a daughter of Aurva and wife of Mandara (*G. Purāṇa*)

**Śāmilī** (S) (F) of the Śami tree (*Prosopis spicigera*); containing fire; chaplet; garland.

**Samin** (S) (M) **1.** accomplisher of peace; tranquil; pacific. **2.** consoler. **3.** a son of Rājādhideva (*H. Purāṇa*)

**Śamin** (S) (M) **1.** tranquil; pacific. **2.** one who has subdued his passions; self-controlled. **3.** a son of Rājādhideva (*H. Purāṇa*); a son of Śūra (*V. Purāṇa*); a son of Andhaka (*V. Purāṇa*)

**Samīra** (S) (M) **1.** set in motion; to create; to urge on. **2.** wind; air. **3.** another name for Vāyu and Śiva; *Prosopis spicigera*.

**Śamīrā** (S) (F) a chameli flower.

**Samīraṇsuta** (S) (M) **1.** son of the wind. **3.** another name for Bhīma.

**Samiṣa** (S) (F) dart; javelin.

**Samitī** (S) (F) **1.** committee; senate; herd. **3.** society personified as a daughter of Prajāpati.

**Samitiñjaya** (S) (M) **1.** victorious in battle; eminent in an assembly. **3.** one of the 7 great heroes of the Yādava clan (*M. Bh.*); another name for Yama and Viṣṇu.

**Śamitṛ** (S) (M) one who keeps his mind calm.

**Śammad** (S) (M) **1.** one who has conquered his ego. **3.** an aṅgiras.

**Sammada** (S) (M) **1.** joy; happiness; exhilaration. **3.** a king of the fish (*V. Purāṇa*)

**Sammardana** (S) (M) **1.** crushing; rubbing; trampling. **3.** a king of the vidyādharas (*K. Sāgara*); a son of Vasudeva and Devakī (*Bhāgavata*)

**Sammata** (S) (M) **1.** agreed; consented; thought highly of; highly honoured. **3.** a son of Manu Sāvarna (*H. Purāṇa*)

**Sammati** (S) (F) **1.** harmony; agreement; respect; homage; wish; desire; self knowledge; love; order. **3.** a river (*V. Purāṇa*)

**Sammiśla** (S) (M) **1.** universal mingler. **3.** another name for Indra.

**Sammita** (S) (M) **1.** symmetrical; measured. **3.** a son of Vasiṣṭha.

**Sammiteyu** (S) (M) **1.** with balanced thoughts. **3.** a Purū king who was a son of Bhadrāśva (*A. Purāṇa*)

**Sammoda** (S) (M) fragrance.

**Sammohana** (S) (M) **1.** bewildering; bewitching. **3.** one of the 5 arrows of Kāma.

**Sammud** (S) (M) joy; delight.

**Sāmoda** (S) (M) full of joy; joyful; pleased; fragrant.

**Śampā** (S) (F) lightning.

**Sampad** (S) (F) perfection; attainment; success; accomplishment; blessing; glory; fate.

**Sampadin** (S) (M) **1.** perfect; accomplisher. **3.** a grandson of Aśoka.

**Sampadvasan** (S) (M) **1.** perfectly dressed. **3.** one of the 7 principal rays of the sun.

**Sampadvasu** (S) (M) **1.** god of success. **3.** one of the 7 principal rays of the sun.

**Śampaka** (S) (M) **1.** created by thunderbolts. **2.** shining as lightning. **3.** a pious Brāhmin (*M. Bh.*)

**Sampāṅgi** (S) (F) possessed with a balanced body.

**Sampāra** (S) (M) **1.** conveyed to the other side; accomplished; fulfilled. **3.** a king and son of Samara and brother of Pāra (*V. Purāṇa*)

**Sampata** (S) (M) fortune; wealth; prosperity; welfare.

**Sampāti** (S) (M) **1.** flying; confluence; encounter. **3.** the eldest son of Garuḍa and brother of Jaṭāyu (*M. Bh.*); a son of Bahugava and father of Ahaṁyati (*H. Purāṇa*); a rākṣasa who was the son of Kumbhīnāḍī (*Rāmāyaṇa*); a Kaurava warriors (*M. Bh.*)

**Sampatkumāra** (S) (M) **1.** son of wealth; prosperous youth. **3.** a form of Viṣṇu.

**Sampatpradā** (S) (F) **1.** bestowing fortune. **3.** a form of Bhairavī.

**Sampatti** (S) (F) **1.** prosperity; welfare; accomplishment; concord; being. **3.** a form of Prākṛtī and wife of Īṣāṇa.

**Sampāvana** (S) (M) perfect purification.

**Sampraṇīta** (S) (M) brought together; composed as poetry.

**Samprati** (S) (M) **1.** in the right way; righteous; now; just at present. **3.** a grandson of Aśoka who helped in spreading Buddhism; the 24th Arhat of the past Utsarpinī.

**Samprīta** (S) (M) completely satisfied; pleased; delighted.

**Samprīti** (S) (F) complete satisfaction; joy, delight.

**Sampriyā** (S) (F) **1.** fully loved; dear; beloved. **3.** the wife of Vidura and mother of Anaśva (*M. Bh.*)

**Sampūjā** (S) (F) reverence; esteem.

**Sampūjan** (S) (M) treating with great respect.

**Sampūrṇa** (S) (M) **1.** complete; full; whole; entire; fulfilled; accomplished. **3.** one of the 4 wagtails employed for augury.

**Sampuṣṭi** (S) (F) perfect prosperity.

**Samrāj** (S) (F) **1.** ruling over all. **3.** a daughter of Priyavrata (*V. Purāṇa*)

**Samrāj** (S) (M) **1.** universal ruler. **3.** the son of Ćitraratha and Ūrṇā and the husband of Utkalā, he was the father of Marīći (*Bhā. Purāṇa*); a grandson of Kāmya (*H. Purāṇa*)

**Samrāṭ** (S) (F) **1.** universal queen. **3.** a daughter of Priyavrata (*V. Purāṇa*)

**Samrāṭ** (S) (M) universal; supreme ruler.

**Samṛddha** (S) (M) **1.** accomplished; perfect; complete; whole; abundant; rich. **3.** a nāga of Dhṛtarāṣṭra's family (*M. Bh.*)

**Samṛddhī** (S) (F) prosperity; welfare; fortune; perfection; excellence; wealth.

**Samṛddhin** (S) (F) **1.** accomplished; perfect; happy; blessed; full of riches. **3.** another name for the Gaṅgā.

**Sāmṛta** (S) (M) provided with nectar.

**Samṛti** (S) (F) coming together; meeting.

**Saṁsāraguru** (S) (M) **1.** lord of the universe. **3.** another name fo Kāma.

**Samud** (S) (M) **1.** full of joy. **2.** joyful; glad.

**Samudra** (S) (M) **1.** full of water. **2.** ocean; sea; the number 4.

**Samudradeva** (S) (M) **1.** lord of the waters. **3.** another name for Varuṇa.

**Samudragupta** (S) (M) **1.** hidden ocean. **3.** a king (345-380 A.D.)

**Samudramahiṣī** (S) (F) **1.** chief wife of the ocean. **3.** another name for the Gaṅgā.

**Samudranemī** (S) (F) **1.** surrounded by the ocean. **2.** the earth.

**Samudrasāra** (S) (M) **1.** essence of the sea. **2.** pearl.

**Samudrasena** (S) (M) **1.** leader of the waters. **3.** a king who was a rebirth of the asura Kāleya (*M. Bh.*)

**Samudraśrī** (S) (F) **1.** beauty of the ocean. **2.** mermaid.

**Samudrasubhagā** (S) (F) **1.** favourite of the ocean. **3.** another name for the Gaṅgā.

**Samudravega** (S) (M) **1.** with the passion or speed of the sea. **3.** a warrior of Skanda (*M. Bh.*)

**Samudravijaya** (S) (M) **1.** conqueror of the ocean. **3.** the king of Dvārakā and the father of Neminātha Jaina Tīrthaṅkara.

**Sāmudrī** (S) (F) **1.** born of the ocean. **3.** the daughter of Samudra and wife of Praćīnabarhis.

**Samudronmādana** (S) (M) **1.** with the passion of the ocean. **3.** an attendant of Skanda (*M. Bh.*)

**Samūha** (S) (M) **1.** collection; sum; essence; group; assembly. **3.** a viśvadeva (*M. Bh.*)

**Samunnada** (S) (M) **1.** roaring; shouting. **3.** a rākṣasa (*Rāmāyaṇa*)

**Samvara** (S) (M) **1.** satisfied; contended; fulfilled. **2.** best in every aspect. **3.** a king of Ayodhyā and father of Abhinandana Jaina Tīrthaṅkara (*J. Literature*)

**Śamvat** (S) (M) auspicious; prosperous.

**Sana** (S) (M) **1.** lasting long; old. **3.** one of the 4 spiritual sons of Brahmā.

**Sanadvāja** (S) (M) **1.** bestowing wealth. **3.** a son of Śući (*Bh. Purāṇa*)

**Sānaga** (S) (M) **1.** beautiful mountain. **3.** a preceptor.

**Śanaisćara** (S) (M) **1.** moving slowly.

3. another name for Saturn.

**Sanaj** (S) (M) ancient.

**Sanaka** (S) (M) **1.** former; old; ancient. **3.** a ṛṣi who was a mindborn son of Brahmā and described as one of the counsellers of Viṣṇu along with Sana, Saṇatkumāra and Sanandana (*M. Bh.*)

**Śanaka** (S) (M) **1.** slow walker. **3.** a son of Śambara.

**Sānala** (S) (M) **1.** containing fire. **2.** fiery; vigorous; powerful.

**Sanana** (S) (M) gaining; acquiring.

**Sānandā** (S) (F) **1.** full of pleasure. **2.** pleasant; joyful. **3.** a form of Lakṣmī.

**Sānanda** (S) (M) **1.** full of pleasure. **2.** joyful; glad; delighted. **3.** an attendant of Rādhā.

**Sanandana** (S) (M) **1.** joyful. **3.** a son of Brahmā who was born of his mind (*M. Bh.*); a disciple of Śaṅkarāćārya.

**Sanasa** (S) (M) laughing; smiling.

**Sānasi** (S) (M) bringing wealth or blessings.

**Sanaśruta** (S) (M) famous of old.

**Sanat** (S) (M) **1.** eternal. **2.** always; ever. **3.** another name for Brahmā.

**Sanātana** (S) (M) **1.** eternal; perpetual; permanent; ancient. **3.** a hermit in the court of Yudhiṣṭhira (*M. Bh.*); another name for Brahmā, Viṣṇu and Śiva.

**Sanātanī** (S) (F) **1.** eternal; ancient; permanent. **3.** another name for Durgā, Lakṣmī and Sarasvatī.

**Sanātha** (S) (M) with a protector.

**Sanatkumāra** (S) (M) **1.** eternal youth; son of Brahmā. **3.** one of the 4 sons of Brahmā said to be the oldest of the progenitors of mankind, with Jainas he is one of the 12 ćakravartins.

**Sanatsujāta** (S) (M) **1.** always beautiful. **3.** one of the 7 mindborn sons of Brahmā; another name for Sanatkumāra.

**Śaṇavāsika** (S) (M) **1.** wearing flax/hemp. **3.** an Arhat (*L. Vistara*)

**Sanćāraka** (S) (M) **1.** one who delivers. **2.** leader; guide; messenger. **3.** a warrior of Skanda (*M. Bh.*)

**Sanćāranī** (S) (F) **1.** conveying; bringing near; delivering a message. **3.** one of the 6 Buddhist goddesses of magic.

**Sanćārin** (S) (M) **1.** transitory. **2.** the smoke rising from burnt incense.

**Sanćitta** (S) (M) evenminded; equable.

**Śāṇḍa** (S) (M) **1.** son of the collector. **3.** the father of Lakṣmidhara.

**Śaṇḍa** (S) (M) **1.** curd. **3.** an asurá priest who was the son of Śukra; a yakṣa.

**Ṣaṇḍa** (S) (M) **1.** neuter; impotent. **3.** a son of Dhṛtarāṣṭra.

**Sandarśana** (S) (M) gazing; sight; vision; manifestation; appearance.

**Sandeśa** (S) (M) message; gift.

**Sandhā** (S) (M) compact; promise; ultimate union.

**Sandhātṛ** (S) (M) **1.** one who joins. **3.** Śiva and Viṣṇu conjoined.

**Sandhyā** (S) (F) **1.** holding together; union; juncture of day and night. **2.** religious acts performed at the 3 divisions of the day; reflection; meditation. **3.** twilight personified as a daughter of Brahmā and consort of Śiva, the sun, Kāla, Pulastya, and Pūṣan; the deity presiding over the divisions of the day; the mother of the rākṣasī Śālakataṅkā who married Vidyutkeśa (*U. Rāmāyaṇa*); a river whose goddess sits in Varuṇa's assembly (*M. Bh.*); the goddess of dusk (*M. Bh.*); Arundhatī in her previous birth; a river (*M. Bh.*)

**Sandhyābali** (S) (M) **1.** twilight oblation. **3.** the bull of Śiva.

**Sāndhyakusumā** (S) (F) flower of the twilight (*Hibiscus rosa sinensis*)

**Sandhyānāṭin** (S) (M) **1.** dancing at twilight. **3.** another name for Śiva.

**Sandhyānśu** (S) (M) twilight ray.

**Sandhyārāgā** (S) (F) **1.** the colour of twilight. **3.** the red colour in the evening sky personified as a daughter of Himavān.

**Sandhyārama** (S) (M) **1.** delighting in the Sandhyā. **3.** another name for Brahmā.

**Sandhyāvalī** (S) (F) **1.** period of twilight. **3.** the wife of King Rukmāṅgada.

**Śāṇḍilī** (S) (F) **1.** collector. **3.** a Brāhmaṇī worshipped as the mother of Agni; a daughter of Dakṣa and wife of Dharma and mother of Vasu Anala (*M. Bh.*); a yoginī famous in the Purāṇas.

**Śāṇḍilī** (S) (F) 1. goddess of curd. 3. another name for Pārvatī.

**Śāṇḍilya** (S) (M) 1. son of Śāṇḍilī, derived from fire. 3. a sage and author of a law book and doctrine of *Bhaktisūtra*; a maharṣi who was a member of Yudhiṣṭhira's court (*M. Bh.*); a maharṣi in the dynasty of Kaśyapa (*M. Bh.*); another name for Agni; Bengal Quince (*Aegle marmelos*)

**Sandīpa** (S) (M) blazing; burning; glowing.

**Sandīpana** (S) (M) 1. inflaming; exciting; arousing. 3. one of Kāma's 5 arrows.

**Sāndīpani** (S) (M) 1. illuminator. 2. preceptor. 3. the preceptor of Kṛṣṇa and Balabhadrarāma.

**Sanemi** (S) (M) 1. with a felly. 2. complete; perfect.

**Saṅgal** (S) (M) ductile; melting together.

**Saṅgamana** (S) (M) 1. gatherer. 3. another name for Yama.

**Saṅganī** (S) (F) companion.

**Saṅgata** (S) (M) 1. come together; proper; fit; suitable; consistent; compatible. 3. a Maurya dynasty king who was the son of King Suyaśas and the father of Śāliśūraka (*Bhāgavata*)

**Saṅgava** (S) (M) 1. afternoon. 3. the supervisor of Duryodhana's cattleshed (*M. Bh.*)

**Saṅghamitra** (S) (M) sun of the assembly; friend of society.

**Sanghamitrā** (S) (F) 1. sun of the assembly; friend of society; period of the Buddhist order. 3. the daughter of Emperor Aśoka.

**Saṅghānanda** (S) (M) delighting people; delight of the society.

**Saṅgir** (S) (F) assent; promise.

**Saṅgīta** (S) (M) chorus; concert; symphony.

**Saṅgīti** (S) (F) concert; symphony.

**Saṅgoda** (S) (M) 1. with water. 2. pond; lake; ocean.

**Saṅgraha** (S) (M) 1. holding together; collecting; check; control; protection. 2. guardian; ruler. 3. an attendant given to Skanda by the sea (*M. Bh.*); another name for Śiva.

**Saṅgrāma** (S) (M) host; troop; army; battle; war; combat.

**Saṅgrāmaćandra** (S) (M) 1. the moon of battle. 2. one who excels in battle.

**Saṅgrāmadeva** (S) (M) god of battle.

**Saṅgrāmajit** (S) (M) 1. victorious in battle. 3. a son of Kṛṣṇa and Bhadrā (*M. Bh.*)

**Saṅgrāmapāla** (S) (M) protector in battle.

**Saṅgrāmasinha** (S) (M) 1. lion in battle. 2. a fierce and courageous warrior.

**Saṅgupta** (S) (M) perfectly hidden.

**Sanhadana** (S) (M) 1. chariot. 3. Yudhiṣṭhira's chariot.

**Sanhanana** (S) (M) 1. compact; firm; solid. 3. a son of Manasyu (*M. Bh.*)

**Sanhara** (S) (M) 1. drawing together; destroying. 3. an asura (*H. Purāṇa*)

**Sanhārabhairava** (S) (M) 1. Bhairava as world destroyer. 3. one of the 8 forms of Bhairava.

**Sanhāta** (S) (M) 1. conciseness. 3. an attendant of Śiva.

**Saṅhatāśva** (S) (M) 1. with closely joined horses. 3. a Purū king who was the son of Nikumbha and grandson of Haryāśva (*Br. Purāṇa*)

**Saṅhitāśva** (S) (M) 1. with horses; close together. 3. a Bhṛgu dynasty king who was the son of Nikumbha (*Br. Purāṇa*)

**Saṅhlāda** (S) (M) 1. shouter. 3. a rākṣasa son of Sumāli and Ketumatī (*U. Rāmāyaṇa*); a son of Hiraṇyakaśipu (*M. Bh.*)

**Saṅhrāda** (S) (M) 1. shouter. 3. an asura son of Hiraṇyakaśipu (*M. Bh.*)

**Sani** (S) (M) gain; gift; reward; a quarter of the sky.

**Śani** (S) (M) 1. slow moving. 3. Saturn and its regent fabled as the offspring of Sūrya and Ćhāyā; a son of Atri.

**Sanīhāra** (S) (M) bestowing gifts; liberal.

**Sānikā** (S) (F) a flute.

**Sanil** (S) (M) gifted; rewarded.

**Śaniprasū** (S) (F) 1. mother of Saturn. 3. another name for Ćhāyā.

**Śanipriya** (S) (M) 1. dear to Śani. 2. emerald; sapphire.

**Saniṣṭha** (S) (M) gaining most.

**Saniti** (S) (F) acquisition; obtainment.

**Sanitrā** (S) (F) gift; oblation.

**Sāniya** (S) (M) beyond comparison.

**Saṅja** (S) (M) 1. universal creator. 3. another name for Brahmā and Śiva.

**Sānjali** (S) (F) with hands hollowed and joined in prayer.

**Sañjanā** (S) (F) one who joins; creator.

**Sañjana** (S) (M) one who joins; creator.

**Sañjaya** (S) (M) 1. completely victorious. 2. triumphant. 3. a chief of the yakṣas; a minister of Dhṛtarāṣṭra who was the son of Sūta and a partial incarnation of Gavalgaṇa and was blessed with divine sight through which he was able to witness in great detail the battle of Mahābhārata without actually being present at Kurukṣetra (*M. Bh.*); a Sauvīra prince (*M. Bh.*); a son of Dhṛtarāṣṭra (*M. Bh.*); a son of Supārśva (*V. Purāṇa*); a son of Raṇañjaya (*Bh. Purāṇa*)

**Sañjit** (S) (M) perfectly victorious.

**Sañjiti** (S) (F) complete victory.

**Sañjīva** (S) (M) possessed with life; living; existing.

**Sañjīvin** (S) (M) 1. rendering alive; enlivening. 3. a minister of Meghavarṇa the king of crows.

**Saṅjñā** (S) (F) 1. well known; perfect knowledge; noun. 2. agreement; harmony; consciousness; clear understanding; sign; token; gesture. 3. a daughter of Tvaṣṭṛ or Viśvakarman and the wife of the sun, she was the mother of Manu, Yama and Yamī, the aśvins and Revanta.

**Sañjogitā** (S) (F) 1. attached; related; conjoined. 3. a wife of King Prithvīrāja.

**Saṅjvala** (S) (M) well-lit; blazing brightly.

**Saṅkalpā** (S) (F) 1. will; vow; resolution; determination. 3. a daughter of Dakṣa and the wife of Dharma, she was the mother of Saṅkalpa (*Bhāgavata*); Manu's wife (*H. Purāṇa*)

**Saṅkalpa** (S) (M) 1. conception; notion; conviction; vow. 3. will personified as a son of Sankalpā and Brahmā or Dharma (*Bhāgavata*)

**Saṅkalpaja** (S) (M) 1. born of resolution; mindborn; heartborn; love. 3. another name for Kāma.

**Śaṅkana** (S) (M) causing awe.

**Śaṅkarā** (S) (F) 1. causer of tranquillity; auspicious, causing prosperity. 3. Śankara's wife; a rāga.

**Śaṅkara** (S) (M) 1. causer of tranquillity; causing prosperity; auspicious. 3. a son of Kaśyapa and Danu (*V. Purāṇa*); a nāga; another name for Śiva and Rudra.

**Śaṅkarābharaṇa** (S) (M) 1. pleasing Śankara. 3. a rāga.

**Śaṅkarāćārya** (S) (M) 1. Śiva the teacher; preceptor of the auspicious. 3. a celebrated teacher of the Vedānta and reviver of Brāhmaṇism, might have lived between A.D. 788 and 820, according to tradition he lived in 200 B.C., was the son of Śivaguru and Āryāmbā was born in the village of Kalāti and also supposed to have lived 32 years, considered an incarnation of Śiva.

**Śaṅkaradāsa** (S) (M) servant of Śiva.

**Śaṅkaradeva** (S) (M) 1. lord Śiva. 3. a form of Śiva.

**Śaṅkaragaṇa** (S) (M) servant of Śiva.

**Śaṅkarānanda** (S) (M) 1. pleasing Śankara. 3. a philosopher and guru of Sāyana; a commentator on the Upanishads.

**Śaṅkaranārāyaṇa** (S) (M) Śiva and Viṣṇu conjoined.

**Śaṅkarapriya** (S) (M) 1. dear to Śiva. 2. Francoline Partridge.

**Saṅkaraṣaṇānuja** (S) (M) 1. younger brother of Śiva. 3. another name for Kṛṣṇa.

**Śaṅkarāsvāmin** (S) (M) 1. auspicious lord. 3. the father of Upavarṣa.

**Śaṅkaravardhana** (S) (M) increasing prosperity.

**Śaṅkarī** (S) (F) 1. the wife of Śiva. 2. *Mimosa suma; Prosopis spicigera.*

**Sankarṣaṇa** (S) (M) 1. one who ploughs. 2. ploughing; making rows. 3. the father of Nīlāsura; another name for Balarāma.

**Sāṅkāsin** (S) (M) full visibility or appearance.

**Sāṅkāsya** (S) (M) 1. unstable. 3. a king in Yama's court (*M. Bh.*)

**Saṅkaṭā** (S) (F) 1. goddess who removes dangers. 3. a yoginī; a goddess worshipped in Benaras.

**Sankaṭa** (S) (M) 1. brought together; dense; impassable; dangerous, critical. 3. a son of Kakubh (*Bh. Purāṇa*)

**Sankaṭanāśana** (S) (M) one who removes difficulties and eliminates dangers.

**Sankaṭanātha** (S) (M) lord of dangers; lord who removes dangers.

**Śaṅkhā** (S) (F) a kind of flute.

**Śaṅkha** (S) (M) 1. conch shell. 2. the bone of the forehead. 3. one of the Kubera's treasures and its guardian (*M. Bh.*); one of the 8 chiefs of the nāgas (*M. Bh.*); a daitya conquered by Viṣṇu (*H. Purāṇa*); a son of Vajranābha (*H. Purāṇa*); the son of King Virāṭa and brother of Uttarā (*M. Bh.*); a maharṣi who was the elder brother of Likhita maharṣi; a Kekaya prince on the side of the Pāṇḍavas (*M. Bh.*); a nāga son of Kaśyapa and Kadru (*M. Bh.*)

**Śaṅkhabhṛt** (S) (M) 1. conch bearer. 3. another name for Viṣṇu.

**Śaṅkhaćakragadādhara** (S) (M) 1. holding the conch, disc and mace. 3. another name for Kṛṣṇa.

**Śaṅkhaćakragadāhasta** (S) (M) 1. holding the conch, disc and mace. 3. another name for Kṛṣṇa.

**Śaṅkhaćakragadāpāṇi** (S) (M) 1. holding the conch and disc. 3. another name for Kṛṣṇa.

**Śaṅkhaćakrāsipāni** (S) (M) 1. holding the conch and disc. 3. another name for Kṛṣṇa.

**Śaṅkhaćari** (S) (M) a sandalwood mark of the shape of a conch shell, on the forehead.

**Śaṅkhaćūḍa** (S) (M) 1. crested with a conchshell. 3. a gandharva; an attendant of Kubera (*Bh. Purāṇa*); a nāga (*Bhā. Purāṇa*); an asura who was an incarnation of Sudāmā.

**Śaṅkhadhara** (S) (M) 1. bearer of a conchshell. 3. another name for Kṛṣṇa.

**Śaṅkhadhavala** (S) (F) as white as a conchshell; Jasmine flower (*Jasminum auriculatum*)

**Śaṅkhakarṇa** (S) (M) 1. shell eared. 3. an attendant of Śiva.

**Śaṅkhakumbhaśravas** (S) (F) 1. producing the sound of conchshell and a pitcher. 2. loud-voiced. 3. a mother in Skanda's retinue (*M. Bh.*)

**Śaṅkhalikā** (S) (F) 1. as perfect as a conchshell. 2. flawless. 3. a mother in Skanda's retinue (*M. Bh.*)

**Śaṅkhamaṇi** (S) (M) jewel among conches.

**Śaṅkhamekhala** (S) (M) 1. girdled with shells. 3. a maharṣi (*M. Bh.*)

**Śaṅkhamuktā** (S) (F) conchshell and pearl conjoined; mother of pearl.

**Śaṅkhana** (S) (M) 1. with a conchshell. 3. father of Sudaṛṣaṇa.

**Śaṅkhanābha** (S) (M) 1. shell navelled. 3. a son of Vajranābha (*V. Purāṇa*)

**Śaṅkhanakha** (S) (M) 1. with nails of conch. 3. a nāga in the court of Varuṇa (*M. Bh.*)

**Śaṅkhapā** (S) (M) 1. one who drinks from a conchshell. 3. a son of Kardama (*V. Purāṇa*)

**Śaṅkhapada** (S) (M) 1. with feet of shells. 3. a viśvadeva (*H. Purāṇa*); a son of Kardama; a son of Manu Svāroćiṣa and the father of Suvarṇābha (*M. Bh.*)

**Śaṅkhapāla** (S) (M) 1. protector of the conch. 3. a son of Kardama (*V. Purāṇa*); a nāga (*H. Purāṇa*)

**Śaṅkhapāṇi** (S) (M) 1. with a shell in the hand. 3. another name for Viṣṇu.

**Śaṅkhapiṇḍa** (S) (M) 1. made of shell. 3. a nāga son of Kaśyapa and Kādru (*M. Bh.*)

**Śākhariṇī** (S) (F) 1. one that has branches; supreme among the branches; *Jasminum sambac*. 2. best; excellent.

**Śaṅkhaśiras** (S) (M) 1. shell headed. 3. a nāga son of Kaśyapa and Kadru (*M. Bh.*)

**Śaṅkhaśīrṣa** (S) (M) 1. shell headed. 3. a nāga son of Kaśyapa and Kadru (*M. Bh.*)

**Śaṅkhaśravas** (S) (F) 1. shell eared. 3. an attendant of Skanda (*M. Bh.*)

**Śankhāvatī** (S) (M) 1. full of shells. 3. a river (*Mā. Purāṇa*)

**Śānkhāyana** (S) (M) 1. belonging to a conchshell. 3. a teacher and author of a Brāhmaṇa and 2 sūtras.

**Śaṅkhayūthikā** (S) (F) a collection of conchshells; a garland of jasmine flowers (*Jasminum auriculatum*)

**Śaṅkhin** (S) (M) 1. possessor of a conch; possessor of pearls; bearer of shells. 3. another name for the ocean and Viṣṇu.

**Śaṅkhinī** (S) (F) 1. mother of pearls. 3. a Śakti worshipped by the Buddhists; a kind of semi divine being or fairy.

**Śankhukarnanaga** (S) (M) 1. peaked mountain. 3. a son of Janamejaya.

**Sankhya** (S) (F) welfare; comfort; health; happiness; felicity.

**Sānkhyāyana** (S) (M) 1. calculating; reasoning. 3. a preceptor who was a prominent disciple of Sanatkumāra (*Bhāgavata*)

**Saṅkila** (S) (M) 1. possessed with fire. 2. a burning torch; a firebrand.

**Saṅkoća** (S) (M) 1. contraction; withdrawal. 3. a rākṣasa who ruled the earth in ancient days (*M. Bh.*)

**Saṅkrama** (S) (M) 1. progress; transition. 2. bridge; a shooting star. 3. a son of Vasu and king of the vidyādharas (*M. Bh.*); an attendant of Skanda given to him by Viṣṇu (*M. Bh.*)

**Saṅkrandana** (S) (M) 1. calling; shouting; roaring. 3. a king who was the father of Vapuṣmat (*Mā. Purāṇa*); a son of Manu Bhautya (*H. Purāṇa*); another name for Indra.

**Saṅkṛti** (S) (M) 1. arranger. 3. a king in the court of Yama (*M. Bh.*); a muni of the Atri dynasty (*M. Bh.*); a son of Viśvāmitra; a king of the Bharata dynasty who was the son of King Naraka and father of Rantideva (*Bhāgavata*)

**Śanku** (S) (M) 1. arrow; dart; spear; spike; javelin; weapon. 3. a son of Hiraṇyakṣa (*A. Purāṇa*); a Yādava king (*M. Bh.*); a gandharva attendant of Śiva; a nāga; a son of Kṛṣṇa (*H. Purāṇa*); a son of Ugrasena (*M. Bh.*); another name for Śiva and Kāma.

**Śaṅku** (S) 1. sharp. 3. a son of Hiraṇyākṣa (*A. Purāṇa*); a Yādava king (*M. Bh.*)

**Śankuka** (S) (M) 1. a small nail. 3. a son of Mayūra (*R. Taraṅginī*)

**Śaṅkukarṇa** (S) (M) 1. with pointed ears. 3. a muni mentioned in *Padma Purāṇa*; a nāga in Dhṛtarāṣṭra's dynasty (*M. Bh.*); an attendant of Śiva (*M. Bh.*); an attendant given to Skanda by Pārvatī (*M. Bh.*); a dānava (*H. Purāṇa*); a son of Janamejaya (*M. Bh.*); a rākṣasa (*Rāmāyaṇa*)

**Śāṅkukarṇeśvara** (S) (M) 1. lord with the pointed ears. 3. a form of Śiva (*M. Bh.*)

**Śaṅkura** (S) (M) 1. frightful; formidable. 3. a dānava (*V. Purāṇa*)

**Sāṅkura** (S) (M) budding; possessing shoots.

**Śankura** (S) (M) 1. causing fear. 3. a dānava (*V. Purāṇa*)

**Śaṅkuroma** (S) (M) 1. with needlelike hair. 3. a nāga son of Kaśyapa and Kadru (*M. Purāṇa*)

**Śaṅkuśiras** (S) (M) 1. spear headed. 3. an asura (*H. Purāṇa*)

**Saṅmaṇi** (S) (M) genuine jewel.

**Saṅmati** (S) (F) nobleminded.

**Ṣaṇmātura** (S) (M) 1. having 6 mothers. 3. another name for Kārttikeya.

**Ṣaṇmukha** (S) (M) 1. 6 faced. 3. a Bodhisattva; another name for Skanda.

**Ṣaṇmukhapriya** (S) (M) 1. beloved of Kārttikeya. 3. another name for Śiva; a rāga.

**Saṅnam** (S) (F) favour; kindness.

**Saṅnateyu** (S) (M) 1. bowing evenly. 2. respectful. 3. a son of Raudrāśva and Miśrakeśī (*M. Bh.*)

**Saṅnatī** (S) (F) 1. bending down; humility. 3. humility personified as a daughter of Dakṣa and wife of Kratu and mother of Bālakhilyas (*A. Purāṇa*); wife of King Brahmadatta (*P. Purāṇa*)

**Saṅnati** (S) (M) 1. sound; noise; humility. 3. a son of Sumati (*H. Purāṇa*); a son of Alarka (*H. Purāṇa*)

**Saṅnihatī** (S) (F) 1. destroying easily. 3. a river.

**Sannihita** (S) (M) 1. pervading. 2. absorbed; hidden. 3. an agni who was the 3rd son of Manu (*M. Bh.*)

**Sannimitta** (S) (M) a good omen.

**Sannivāsa** (S) (M) 1. staying with the good; dwelling in truth. 3. another name for Viṣṇu.

**Saṅniveśa** (S) (M) 1. seat; abode; appearance; form; composition; construction. 3. personified as a son of Tvaṣṭṛ and Raćanā (*Bhāgavata*)

**Sanojā** (S) (F) eternal.

**Sanolī** (S) (F) possessed with self penance; introspective.

**Sanrādhya** (S) (M) acquired by perfect

meditation.

**Saṅrāga** (S) (M) 1. redness; passion. 2. vehemence.

**Sanrāj** (S) (M) to reign universally.

**Saṅraktā** (S) (F) 1. full of blood; red coloured. 2. coloured; red; charming; beautiful.

**Sanrañjana** (S) (M) 1. full of charm. 2. gratifying; charming; pleasant.

**Śansā** (S) (F) praise; invocation; charm; blessing; recitation; wish.

**Śānśapāyana** (S) (M) 1. who removes all doubts. 3. an ancient teacher.

**Saṅsāra** (S) (M) 1. course; passage. 2. the world.

**Saṅśati** (S) (F) 1. doubting. 3. the wife of the agni Pavamāna and the mother of Sabhya and Āvasathya (*M. Purāṇa*)

**Sansiddhi** (S) (F) perfection; success; complete accomplishment.

**Śansitā** (S) (F) 1. wished; desired; longed for. 2. praised; celebrated.

**Sanskṛti** (S) (M) 1. making ready; preparation; perfection; consecration; determination. 3. another name for Kṛṣṇa.

**Sanśraya** (S) (M) 1. connection; association; aim; alliance; asylum; shelter. 3. a prajāpati (*Rāmāyaṇa*)

**Saṅśrutya** (S) (M) 1. hearsay; thoroughly heard. 3. a son of Viśvāmitra (*M. Bh.*)

**Sanstubh** (S) (M) a shout of joy.

**Sanśubh** (S) (M) radiant; beautiful.

**Santa** (S) (M) 1. calm. 2. ascetic; hermit. 3. a son of Satya of the family of King Vītahavya and the father of Śravas (*M. Bh.*)

**Śāntā** (S) (F) 1. peaceful; calm. 3. a daughter of Daśaratha and wife of Ṛṣyaśṛnga (*M. Bh.*); a Jaina goddess who executes the orders of the 7th Arhat (*J. Literature*); a Śakti.

**Śānta** (S) (M) 1. tranquil; calm; free from passions; mild; gentle; friendly. 3. a son of day (*M. Bh.*); son of Manu Tāmasa (*Mā. Purāṇa*); son of Śambara (*H. Purāṇa*); son of Idhmajihva (*Bhā. Purāṇa*); son of the vasu Āpa (*V. Purāṇa*); a king who was the son of Priyavrata (*Bhāgavata*)

**Śāntabhaya** (S) (M) 1. fearless. 3. a son of Medhātithi (*V. Purāṇa*)

**Śantāći** (S) (M) beneficient; auspicious.

**Śāntahaya** (S) (M) 1. calm horse. 3. a son of Manu Tāmasa (*V. Purāṇa*)

**Śaṅtama** (S) (M) most beneficient.

**Śāntamati** (S) (M) composed in mind.

**Santāna** (S) (M) 1. continued succession; connection. 3. one of the 5 trees of Indra's heaven; a son of Rudra (*Mā. Purāṇa*)

**Saṅtanagaṇapati** (S) (M) 1. ever spreading lord of people; omnipresent lord of people. 3. a form of Gaṇeśa as the giver of progeny.

**Saṅtānaka** (S) (M) 1. stretching; spreading. 2. that which stretches. 3. one of the 5 trees of Indra's heaven; the Kalpa tree.

**Śāntanava** (S) (M) 1. patronymic of Bhīṣma. 3. a son of Medhātithi (*V. Purāṇa*); a grammarian and author of *Phit Sūtra*.

**Saṅtani** (S) (F) continuing; forming an uninterrupted line; harmony; music.

**Saṅtānikā** (S) (F) 1. stretching. 2. cobweb; cream; foam; the blade of a sword. 3. an attendant of Skanda (*M. Bh.*)

**Śāntānika** (S) (M) 1. auspicious. 3. a king of Vatsya and follower of Mahāvīra.

**Santāniki** (S) (F) made from the flowers of the Kalpa tree.

**Saṅtanitanu** (S) (M) 1. a body of music. 3. a youth attending on Rādhā.

**Śāntāntakara** (S) (M) 1. destroyer of peace. 3. a son of Śambara (*H. Purāṇa*)

**Śantanu** (S) (M) 1. wholesome. 3. the Lunar dynasty Kuru king who was the son of King Pratīpa and Sunandā, he was the father of Bhīṣma by Gaṅgā and of Vićitravīrya and Ćitrāṅgada by Satyavatī, he is one of the kings who should be remembered at dawn and dusk (*M. Bh.*)

**Śantanuja** (S) (M) 1. son of Śantanu. 3. another name for Bhīṣma.

**Śantanuputra** (S) (M) 1. son of Śantanu. 3. another name for Bhīṣma.

**Śantanusuta** (S) (M) 1. son of Śantanu. 3. another name for Bhīṣma.

**Santāpa** (S) (M) 1. heat. 3. another name for Agni.

**Saṅtāpana** (S) (M) 1. one that heats. 2. increasing passion; burning. 3. an attendant of Śiva; an arrow of Kāma.

**Śāntarajas** (S) (M) 1. without anger; one whose desires have been quenched. 3. a king of Kāśī who was the son of King Trikakalpava and father of King Raji (*Bhāgavata*)

**Santarakṣita** (S) (M) 1. protected by the saints. 3. a teacher of the Madhyamika-Svātantrika school of Buddhism in Nālandā (705-762 A.D.)

**Śāntaraya** (S) (M) 1. slackened in speed. 3. a son of Dharmasārathi (*Bhā. Purāṇa*)

**Santardana** (S) (M) 1. connecting; fastening together. 3. a son of Kekaya King Dhṛṣṭaketu (*Bhāgavata*)

**Santarjana** (S) (M) 1. threatening. 3. a warrior of Skanda (*M. Bh.*)

**Śāntasena** (S) (M) 1. with a tranquil army. 3. a son of Subāhu.

**Santateya** (S) (M) continuous; extended.

**Santati** (S) (M) 1. continuous line; multitude; lineage; race. 3. a son of Alarka (*Bh. Purāṇa*)

**Santatī** (S) (F) 1. continuity; race; progeny; offspring. 3. a daughter of Dakṣa and wife of Kratu.

**Santavīra** (S) (M) courageous saint; a saintly warrior.

**Santhānam** (S) (M) to spread.

**Śānti** (S) (F) 1. tranquillity; peace. 3. quiet personified as a daughter of Śraddhā and the wife of Atharvan or as a daughter of Dakṣa and Prasūti and wife of Dharma (*V. Purāṇa*)

**Śānti** (S) (M) 1. peace; tranquillity. 3. a Bharata dynasty king who was the son of Nīla and father of Suśānti (*V. Purāṇa*); the Indra of the 4th Manvantara (*M. Bh.*); a son of Aṅgiras (*M. Bh.*); a son of Indra (*M. Bh.*); Indra in the 10th Manvantara (*Purāṇas*); a son of Viṣṇu and Dakṣiṇā; a son of Kṛṣṇa and Kālindī; a ṛṣi (*M. Bh.*); a Jaina Arhat and Ćakravartin.

**Śāntideva** (S) (M) 1. lord of peace. 3. a teacher of the Mādhyamika-Prāsaṅgika school of Buddhism at Nālandā (691-743 A.D.)

**Śāntidevī** (S) (F) 1. goddess of peace. 3. a daughter of King Devaka and a wife of Vasudeva (*Vā. Purāṇa*)

**Śāntinātha** (S) (M) 1. lord of peace. 3. the 16th Jaina Tīrthaṅkara and the son of Viśvasena and Aćirā of Hastināpur (*J. Literature*)

**Śāntivā** (S) (F) 1. bearer of peace. 2. beneficient; friendly; kind. 3. a deity.

**Śāntiva** (S) (M) 1. bearer of piece. 2. beneficient; friendly; kind.

**Santoṣā** (S) (F) 1. content; satisfied. 3. the mother of Gaṅgādāsa.

**Santoṣa** (S) (M) 1. satisfaction. 3. satisfaction personified as a son of Dharma and Tuṣṭi and considered to be a Tuṣita.

**Santoṣī** (S) (F) satisfied; contented.

**Śāntṛ** (S) (M) reciter; praiser.

**Santurodha** (S) (M) 1. with obstacle; waves pressing together. 3. a Purū king who was the son of Matināra (*A. Purāṇa*)

**Santuṣṭi** (S) (F) complete satisfaction; contentment.

**Santya** (S) (M) bestowing gifts; bountiful; kind.

**Sānuga** (S) (M) having attendants; with followers.

**Sānumatī** (S) (F) 1. mountain. 3. an apsarā.

**Sānurāga** (S) (M) affectionate; feeling passion.

**Saṅvaha** (S) (M) 1. carrying along. 2. bearing. 3. one of the 7 tongues of fire; one of the 7 winds.

**Saṅvara** (S) (M) 1. stopping. 2. dam; bridge. 3. 2 Jaina Arhats (*J. Literature*)

**Saṅvaraṇa** (S) (M) 1. covering; enclosing. 2. resisting; containing. 3. a lunar dynasty king who was the son of Ṛkṣa and husband of Tapatī, and father of Kuru and is one of those kings who should be remembered at dawn and dusk.

**Saṅvarta** (S) (M) 1. meeting; destruction; a rain cloud. 3. a son of Aṅgiras (*M. Bh.*)

**Saṅvartaka** (S) (M) 1. rolling up; the end of the world; a submarine fire. 3. a nāga son of Kaśyapa and Kadru (*M. Bh.*); an eternal fire on Mount Mālyavān (*M. Bh.*); another name for Balarāma.

**Saṅvatsara** (S) (M) 1. the year personified. 3. another name for Śiva.

**Saṅvegadhāriṇī** (S) (F) **1.** bearer of passion; passionate. **3.** a kinnarī.

**Sanvitti** (S) (F) knowledge; intellect; understanding; harmony.

**Saṅvṛta** (S) (M) **1.** happened; occurred. **3.** a nāga of the Kaśyapa dynasty (*M. Bh.*); another name for Varuṇa.

**Saṅvṛttī** (S) (F) **1.** fulfilment. **2.** being; existing; becoming; happening. **3.** fulfilment personified as a devī in Brahmā's court (*M. Bh.*)

**Saṅyadvara** (S) (M) **1.** chief in battle. **2.** a king.

**Sanyadvasu** (S) (M) **1.** with continuous wealth; god of wealth. **3.** one of the 7 rays of the sun.

**Saṅyama** (S) (M) **1.** effort; control; self restraint. **3.** the son of the rākṣasa Śataśṛṅga (*M. Bh.*); a son of Dhūmrākṣa and father of Kṛśāśva (*Bh. Purāṇa*)

**Saṅyamana** (S) (M) **1.** effort; self restraint. **3.** a king of Kāśī (*M. Bh.*); the city of Yama (*Bh. Purāṇa*)

**Saṅyāti** (S) (M) **1.** coming; following. **3.** a son of Nahuṣa (*M. Bh.*); a Purū king who was the son of Praćinvān and Aśmakī and the husband of Vārāṅgī, he was the father of Ahaṅyāti (*M. Bh.*)

**Saṅyodhakaṇṭaka** (S) (M) **1.** a thorn in battle. **3.** a yakṣa attendant of Kubera (*V. Rāmāyaṇa*)

**Śanyu** (S) (M) **1.** benevolent; beneficient. **2.** happy; fortunate. **3.** eldest son of Bṛhaspati and the husband of Satyā (*M. Bh.*)

**Śaṅyu** (S) (M) **1.** benevolent; beneficient; happy; fortunate. **3.** the eldest son of Bṛhaspati.

**Saṅyuktā** (S) (F) relating to; conjoined; united; a kind of metre.

**Saparyā** (S) (F) worship; homage; adoration.

**Saparyu** (S) (M) honouring; devoted; faithful.

**Sapatnajit** (S) (M) **1.** conquering rivals. **3.** a son of Kṛṣṇa and Sudattā.

**Sapatniśa** (S) (M) **1.** lord of co-wives. **3.** another name for Śiva.

**Saprabha** (S) (M) possessing splendour; brilliant.

**Saprathas** (S) (M) **1.** extensive; wide; effective. **3.** another name for Viṣṇu.

**Saptadhiti** (S) (M) **1.** with 7 rays of light. **3.** another name for Agni.

**Saptagu** (S) (M) **1.** with 7 cows. **3.** an aṅgiras ṛṣi and part author of *Ṛg Veda* (x)

**Saptajihva** (S) (M) **1.** 7 tongued. **3.** another name for Agni.

**Saptajit** (S) (F) **1.** winning the 7 elements namely, earth, water, fire, air, ether, mind and ego. **3.** a daughter of Kaśyapa and Danu (*M. Purāṇa*)

**Saptakṛt** (S) (M) **1.** one who performs 7 deeds; created by the 7. **3.** a viśvadeva (*M. Bh.*)

**Saptamarići** (S) (M) **1.** 7 rayed. **3.** another name for Agni.

**Saptānśu** (S) (M) **1.** 7 rayed. **2.** fire.

**Saptapattra** (S) (M) **1.** 7 leaved; drawn by 7 horses. **2.** the Devil's tree (*Alstonia scholaris*); Jasmine. **3.** another name for the sun.

**Saptaraśmi** (S) (M) **1.** 7 rayed. **3.** another name for Agni.

**Saptarāva** (S) (M) **1.** one who makes 7 sounds; singer of 7 notes. **3.** a son of Garuḍa (*M. Bh.*)

**Saptarćis** (S) (M) **1.** 7 rayed. **3.** another name for Saturn and Agni.

**Saptarṣi** (S) (M) the 7 ṛṣis; the 7 stars of the constellation Ursa Major; Ceÿlon Leadwort (*Plumbago zeylanica*)

**Saptarući** (S) (M) 7 rayed; Agni.

**Saptaśīrṣa** (S) (M) **1.** 7 headed. **3.** another name for Viṣṇu.

**Saptāśva** (S) (M) **1.** with 7 horses. **3.** another name for the sun.

**Saptātman** (S) (M) **1.** with 7 essences. **3.** another name for Brahman.

**Saptavāra** (S) (M) **1.** 7 days of the week. **3.** a son of Garuḍa.

**Sapti** (S) (M) **1.** horse; steed. **3.** a ṛṣi and part author of *Ṛg Veda* (x)

**Śara** (S) (M) **1.** arrow; reed; the number 5. **3.** a son of Rićatka (*Ṛg Veda*); an asura.

**Sārā** (S) (F) hard; firm; solid; precious; valuable; best; excellent.

**Sarā** (S) (M) wandering about; brook; cascade; waterfall.

**Śarabendra** (S) (M) 1. lord of animals. 2. lion.

**Śarabha** (S) (M) 1. an animal; a kind of fabulous animal; a deer said to be stronger than a lion or elephant. 3. an asura; a son of Śiśupāla (*M. Bh.*); a brother of Śakuni (*M. Bh.*); a monkey in Rāma's army (*Rāmāyaṇa*); a king of the Aśmakas; a nāga of the Takṣaka dynasty (*M. Bh.*); a nāga of the Airāvata dynasty (*M. Bh.*); a son of Kaśyapa and Danu (*M. Bh.*); a maharṣi in Yama's court (*M. Bh.*); the brother of King Dhṛṣṭaketu of Ćedi who fought on the Pāṇḍava side (*M. Bh.*); a brother of Śakuni (*M. Bh.*); an incarnation of Vīrabhadra (*Ś. Purāṇa*); another name for Viṣṇu.

**Śarabhaṅga** (S) (M) 1. an arrow breaker; destroyer of reeds. 3. a maharṣi in the Daṇḍaka forest (*V. Rāmāyaṇa*)

**Śarabhava** (S) (M) 1. bowman; born of arrows. 3. another name for Kārttikeya.

**Śarabhoji** (S) (M) 1. reed eater. 3. a king of Tanjore and a writer (1798-1833)

**Śarabhū** (S) (M) 1. the bowman. 3. another name for Kārttikeya.

**Śarada** (S) (M) autumn.

**Śāradā** (S) (F) 1. a vīṇa or lute bearer. 3. a Sarasvatī; a daughter of Devaratha; another name for Durgā.

**Śaradaćandra** (S) (M) the autumnal moon.

**Śaradaćandrikā** (S) (F) autumnal moonshine.

**Śaradajyoti** (S) (M) autumn moonlight.

**Śāradāmaṇi** (S) (F) 1. jewel among the lutes. 2. the best lute. 3. the wife of Rāmākṛṣṇa Paramahaṇsa.

**Śāradambā** (S) (M) 1. lute handed mother. 3. another name for Sarasvatī.

**Śāradandāyani** (S) (M) a Kekaya king whose wife was the younger sister of Kuntī (*M. Bh.*)

**Śaradapadma** (S) (M) an autumnal lotus; white lotus (*Nelumbium speciosum*)

**Śaradaśrī** (S) (F) 1. beauty of autumn. 3. a wife of Kuṇala.

**Śaradavasu** (S) (M) 1. autumn treasure. 3. a muni.

**Śaradayāminī** (S) (F) a night in autumn.

**Sāradhātṛ** (S) (M) 1. bestower of strength. 3. another name for Śiva.

**Śāradī** (S) (F) autumn; modest; sky; the day of full moon in the month of Kārtika.

**Śaradī** (S) (F) as lovely as autumn.

**Śaradija** (S) (M) produced in autumn.

**Śāradikā** (S) (F) autumnal.

**Śaradindu** (S) (M) moon of the autumn season.

**Śaradvān** (S) (M) 1. full of years. 2. old. 3. a muni who was the son of Gautama and the father of Kṛpa and Kṛpī by the apsarā Janapadī.

**Śaradvat** (S) (M) 1. full of years. 2. aged. 3. a descendant of Gotama (*M. Bh.*)

**Śāradvata** (S) (M) 1. autumn like; cool. 3. another name for Kṛpa.

**Śāradvatī** (S) (F) 1. with a lute; autumnal. 3. an apsarā (*H. Purāṇa*); another name for Kṛpī.

**Sarāga** (S) (M) having colour; impassioned; passionate.

**Sāragandha** (S) (M) 1. with perfection of scent. 2. sandalwood.

**Saraghā** (S) (F) 1. Indian beech tree (*Pongamia glabra*). 3. wife of Bindumat and mother of Madhu (*Bh. Purāṇa*)

**Sāragrīva** (S) (M) 1. strong necked. 3. another name for Śiva.

**Śaragulma** (S) (M) 1. collection of arrows. 3. a monkey in Rāma's army (*V. Rāmāyaṇa*)

**Saraja** (S) (M) 1. born in water. 2. lotus (*Nelumbo speciosum*)

**Sarajanmā** (S) (M) 1. born in water. 3. another name for Kārttikeya.

**Śarajanman** (S) (M) 1. reed born. 3. another name for Kārttikeya.

**Śarajjyotsnā** (S) (F) autumnal moonshine.

**Śaraka** (S) (M) 1. born in reeds. 3. a son of King Kuśāmba (*Br. Purāṇa*)

**Saralā** (S) (F) 1. straight. 2. right; correct; honest; simple; *Pinus longifolia*; fire. 3. a river.

**Śaraloman** (S) (M) 1. reed haired. 3. a maharṣi who was the father of Dāśūra.

**Saramā** (S) (F) 1. the fleet footed one. 3. the bitch of the gods and the mother of Syāma and Śabala who are the messengers of Yama;

the daughter of the gandharva Śailūṣa and wife of Vibhīṣana (*V. Rāmāyaṇa*); a daughter of Dakṣa and Asiknī and the wife of Kaśyapa, she is considered the mother of ferocious animals (*Bhāgavata*)

**Sāramaya** (S) (M) exceedingly firm; the best of anything.

**Sārameya** (S) (M) 1. the fleet one. 2. dog. 3. a Bharata dynasty king who was the son of Śvaphalka (*Bhāgavata*)

**Sāramiti** (S) (M) measure of all truth.

**Śarana** (S) (M) 1. injuring. 3. an arrow of Kāmadeva.

**Sāraṇa** (S) (M) 1. cracked; split. 2. the autumn wind. 3. a son of Vasudeva and Devakī and brother of Kṛṣṇa (*M. Bh.*); a minister of Rāvaṇa (*Rāmāyaṇa*)

**Śaraṇa** (S) (M) 1. protecting; guarding; defending. 3. a nāga of the Vāsuki dynasty (*M. Bh.*)

**Sarana** (S) (M) moving; running.

**Śaraṇāgata** (S) (M) seeking refuge.

**Sāraṅga** (S) (M) 1. dappled. 2. musical instrument; ornament; jewel; a bow; sandalwood; gold; the earth; light; night; a peacock; a Rājahans; a bee; a spotted antelope; swan. 3. a rāga; another name for Śiva and Kāma.

**Sāraṅgī** (S) (F) 1. a spotted doe. 3. a rāgini.

**Śārañgin** (S) (M) 1. bowman; archer. 3. another name for Viṣṇu-Kṛṣṇa.

**Śaraṇī** (S) (F) 1. protecting. 2. guarding; defending; housing. 3. another name for the earth; *Paederia foetida*.

**Saraṇi** (S) (F) a road; path.

**Śarañjita** (S) (M) protected.

**Śaranmegha** (S) (M) autumn cloud.

**Śaraṇyā** (S) (F) 1. defender; protectress; giving shelter. 3. another name for Durgā.

**Śaraṇya** (S) (M) 1. affording shelter. 2. yielding help. 3. another name for Śiva.

**Śaraṇyu** (S) (M) 1. protector; defender. 2. wind; cloud.

**Saraṅyū** (S) (F) 1. quick; nimble; fleet footed. 3. a daughter of Tvaṣṭṛ represented in the *Ṛg Veda* as the wife of Vivasvat and mother of the 2 aśvins.

**Saraṇyu** (S) (M) 1. moving fast; quick; nimble; fleet footed. 2. wind; cloud; water; spring.

**Śarāri** (S) (M) 1. destroying forests; an enemy of arrows. 3. a monkey who accompanied Hanumān (*V. Rāmāyaṇa*)

**Sārasa** (S) (M) 1. coming from a lake. 2. the Indian Crane (*Ardea sibirica*); the moon. 3. a son of Garuḍa (*M. Bh.*); a son of Yadu (*H. Purāṇa*)

**Sārasākṣī** (S) (F) lotus eyed.

**Sārasam** (S) (M) lotus (*Nelumbo speciosum*)

**Śarāsana** (S) (M) 1. shooting arrows. 3. a son of Dhṛtarāṣṭra (*M. Bh.*)

**Sarasāpati** (S) (M) 1. lord of lakes; a buffalo. 3. another name for Brahmā.

**Sarasavāṇī** (S) (F) 1. sweet voiced. 3. the wife of Maṇḍanmiśra.

**Sarasija** (S) (M) 1. that which originates in water. 2. lotus (*Nelumbo speciosum*)

**Sarasijamukhī** (S) (F) lotus faced.

**Sarasijanman** (S) (M) 1. lotus born. 3. another name for Brahmā.

**Saraśmi** (S) (M) with rays; radiant.

**Sarasvat** (S) (M) 1. abounding in lakes. 2. connected with water; juicy; sapid. 3. a deity considered as the offspring of the water and which acts as guardian of the waters and bestower of fertility.

**Sārasvata** (S) (M) 1. blessed by Sarasvatī; eloquent; learned. 3. an ancient hermit who was the son of Dadhīca and the river Sarasvatī (*M. Bh.*); a son of sage Atri (*M. Bh.*)

**Sarasvatī** (S) (F) 1. region abounding in pools; full of essences. 3. a river celebrated in the *Ṛg Veda*; the river goddess who is the mother of streams, the best among the mothers of rivers and of goddesses, in the earlier hymns she formed a triad with the goddesses Iḍā and Bhāratī; in the Brāhmaṇas she is connected with speech and later becomes the goddess of learning and eloquence identified with Durgā, considered the wife and daughter of Brahmā born from his face and also his consort she is the mother of Svāyambhuva; according to the Purāṇas she assumed the form of the river Sarasvatī (*Ṛg Veda*); the wife of Manu (*M. Bh.*); the wife of sage Dadhīca and the mother of

Sarasvata (*Br. Purāṇa*); Intellect tree (*Celastrus paniculata*)

**Śarat** (S) (M) autumn; wind; cloud.

**Śaratakāntimaya** (S) (M) as lovely as autumn.

**Śaratpadma** (S) (M) autumn lotus; white lotus (*Nelumbium speciosum*)

**Śaravaṇa** (S) (M) a clump of reeds.

**Śaravāni** (S) (M) archer; foot soldier.

**Śarāvara** (S) (M) quiver; shield.

**Śarāvatī** (S) (F) 1. full of reeds. 3. a river (*M. Bh.*)

**Śaravindu** (S) (M) 1. genius. 3. a king of the Bharata dynasty who was the son of Ćitraratha (*Bhāgavata*)

**Śaravṛṣti** (S) (M) 1. a shower of arrows. 3. a marutvat.

**Sarayū** (S) (F) 1. moving fast. 2. air; wind. 3. a Purāṇic river which is considered the source of Agni and in which Rāma drowned himself; the wife of Agni Vīra and the mother of Siddhi (*M. Bh.*)

**Sārći** (S) (M) flaming; burning.

**Sarddvīpa** (S) (M) 1. island in the river. 3. a son of Garuḍa (*M. Bh.*)

**Śardhanīti** (S) (M) acting boldly; leading the host of maruts.

**Śardhat** (S) (M) defiant; bold; daring.

**Śardhya** (S) (M) bold; strong.

**Sārdūla** (S) (M) 1. lion; tiger. 2. best; eminent. 3. a spy of Rāvaṇa (*V. Rāmāyaṇa*)

**Śārdula** (S) (M) 1. tiger. 3. another name for Bhūriśravas.

**Sārdūlakarṇa** (S) (M) 1. tiger eared. 3. a son of Triśaṅku.

**Śārdūlī** (S) (F) 1. tigress. 3. a daughter of Kaśyapa and Krodhavaśā who is the mother of tigers and leopards (*V. Rāmāyaṇa*)

**Śareṣṭa** (S) (M) 1. desired by arrows. 2. the mango tree.

**Sargam** (S) (M) 1. going smoothly. 2. notes of music.

**Sargiṇī** (S) (F) composed of parts.

**Śarī** (S) (F) 1. bird; arrow. 3. a daughter of Māthara and wife of Tiṣya and mother of the 1st disciple of Gautama Buddha (*B. Literature*)

**Sarvāmbha** (S) (M) 1. omnipresent; liked by all. 3. another name for Kārttikeya.

**Sariddvīpa** (S) (M) 1. island in the river. 3. a son of Garuḍa (*M. Bh.*)

**Saridvarā** (S) (F) 1. best of rivers. 3. the Gaṅgā.

**Sarikā** (S) (F) a string of pearls; jewel; pond; lake; the sky.

**Sārikā** (S) (F) 1. the Mynah bird (*Turdus salica*). 2. confidante; the bridge of a stringed instrument; a form of Durgā (*K. Sāgara*) 3. a rākṣasī.

**Sārika** (S) (M) 1. the Mynah bird (*Turdus salica*). 3. a hermit in Yudhiṣṭhira's court (*M. Bh.*)

**Sarikānātha** (S) (M) lord of Durgā.

**Sarila** (S) (M) 1. one that brings essence. 2. water.

**Sāriman** (S) (M) 1. going. 2. wind.

**Sārimejaya** (S) (M) 1. together with. 3. an ancient king (*M. Bh.*)

**Sarin** (S) (M) 1. approaching. 2. helpful. 3. another name for Balarāma.

**Sarinnātha** (S) (M) 1. river lord. 2. the ocean.

**Śāriputra** (S) (M) 1. son of a bird. 3. the 1st disciple of Gautama Buddha.

**Śarīraja** (S) (M) 1. produced from the body. 2. a son. 3. another name for Kāma.

**Sarit** (S) (F) 1. river; stream. 3. another name for Durgā.

**Saritā** (S) (F) 1. moving. 2. stream; river.

**Saritpati** (S) (M) 1. lord of rivers. 2. the ocean.

**Saritsuta** (S) (M) 1. son of the river. 3. another name for Bhīṣma.

**Sarju** (S) (F) lightning.

**Sarjū** (S) (M) 1. going; following. 2. a necklace; a merchant.

**Sarjura** (S) (M) a day.

**Śarka** (S) (M) 1. creeping. 3. a son of King Kuśāmba (*Br. Purāṇa*)

**Sarka** (S) (M) 1. wind, air, mind. 3. another name for Prajāpati.

**Śarmada** (S) (M) conferring happiness; making prosperous; propitious.

**Śarmakāma** (S) (M) desirous of happiness.

**Śarman** (S) (M) 1. shelter; protection. 2. joy; bliss; delight; happiness.

**Śarmaṇya** (S) (M) 1. giving shelter. 2. a protector.

**Śarmilā** (S) (F) shy.

**Śarmin** (S) (M) 1. lucky; auspicious; possessing happiness. 3. a ṛṣi (*M. Bh.*)

**Śarmiṣṭhā** (S) (F) 1. most fortunate. 3. a daughter of Vṛṣaparvan and wife of Yayāti and mother of Druhyu, Anu and Purū.

**Śārṅga** (S) (M) 1. made of horn; bow. 3. the bow of Kṛṣṇa made by Brahmā (*M. Bh.*)

**Śārṅgadhanurdhara** (S) (M) 1. holding the bow. 3. another name for Kṛṣṇa.

**Śārṅgadhanus** (S) (M) 1. armed with a bow. 3. another name for Viṣṇu and Kṛṣṇa.

**Śārṅgadhanvā** (S) (M) 1. armed with a bow. 3. another name for Kṛṣṇa.

**Śārṅgagadāpāṇi** (S) (M) 1. holding the bow and mace. 3. another name for Kṛṣṇa.

**Śārṅgagasipāṇi** (S) (M) 1. holding the bow. 3. another name for Kṛṣṇa.

**Śārṅgapāṇi** (S) (M) 1. holding the Śāraṅga bow. 3. another name for Viṣṇu-Kṛṣṇa.

**Sāraṅgapāṇi** (S) (M) holding a musical intrument.

**Śāraṅgarava** (S) (M) 1. making a noise like a deer. 3. a ṛṣi (*M. Bh.*)

**Śārṅgāyudha** (S) (M) armed with a bow.

**Śārṅgi** (S) (M) 1. bowman; archer. 3. another name for Kṛṣṇa.

**Sārñjaya** (S) (M) 1. most powerful. 3. a son of Sahadeva; a *Ṛg Veda* king.

**Saroja** (S) (M) 1. produced or found in lakes. 2. lotus (*Nelumbo speciosum*)

**Sarojin** (S) (M) 1. abounding in lotuses; living in a lotus. 3. another name for Brahmā.

**Sarojinī** (S) (F) abounding in lotuses.

**Saroṣa** (S) (M) 1. with anger. 2. angry.

**Śarottama** (S) (M) the best arrow.

**Sarpa** (S) (M) 1. creepy. 2. a snake; serpent; nāga. 3. one of the 11 rudras; a son of Tvaṣṭā (*A. Purāṇa*); a son of Sthāṇu (*M. Bh.*)

**Sarpamālin** (S) (M) 1. garlanded with snakes. 3. a maharṣi in Yudhiṣṭhira's court (*M. Bh.*); another name for Śiva.

**Sarpānta** (S) (M) 1. destroyer of serpents. 3. a child of Garuḍa (*M. Bh.*)

**Sarparāja** (S) (M) 1. lord of snakes. 3. another name for Vāsuki (*Rāmāyaṇa*)

**Sarpārāti** (S) (M) 1. enemy of snakes. 3. another name for Garuḍa.

**Sarpāri** (S) (M) 1. enemy of serpents. 2. peacock. 3. another name for Garuḍa.

**Sarparṣi** (S) (M) 1. the sage among serpents. 3. another name for Arbuda (*A. Brāhmaṇa*)

**Sarpāsyā** (S) (F) 1. snake faced. 2. one who eats snakes. 3. a yoginī.

**Sarpāsya** (S) (M) 1. snake faced. 2. serpent eater. 3. a rākṣasa who was the commander-in-chief of Khara's army (*Rāmāyaṇa*)

**Sarpeśvara** (S) (M) 1. the king of snakes. 2. snake king. 3. another name for Vāsuki.

**Sarpī** (S) (F) 1. crawling. 2. snake. 3. the wife of a rudra.

**Sārthaka** (S) (M) having meaning; important; significant.

**Sārthavāha** (S) (M) 1. leader of caravans. 3. a son of Māra; a Bodhisattva.

**Śaru** (S) (M) 1. missile; dart arrow. 2. passion; a partridge. 3. a gandharva (*M. Bh.*); a son of Vasudeva; another name for Viṣṇu.

**Saruci** (S) (M) possessing splendour; splendid.

**Saruha** (S) (M) attainer; achiever; prosperous.

**Sarūpā** (S) (F) 1. uniform; similar; embodied; beautiful; handsome. 3. a wife of Bhūta and mother of many rudras (*Bh. Purāṇa*)

**Sarūpa** (S) (M) uniform; similar; embodied; beautiful; handsome.

**Sarura** (S) (M) 1. heart of the pond. 2. lotus (*Nelumbo speciosum*)

**Śarvā** (S) (F) 1. consort of Śiva. 3. another name for Umā.

**Śarva** (S) (M) 1. killing with an arrow. 3. a god who is mentioned with Bhava and Rudra-Śiva; one of the 11 Rudras (*Bhāgavata*); a son of Dhanuṣa; another name for Śiva.

**Sarvā** (S) (F) 1. while; complete; perfect. 3. a

Purāṇic river (*M. Bh.*)

**Sarva** (S) (M) 1. whole entire; various manifold. 3. another name for Kṛṣṇa and Śiva (*M. Bh.*)

**Sārvabhauma** (S) (M) 1. universal; monarch; emperor. 3. a king of the Bharata dynasty who was the son of Vidūratha and the father of Jayatsena (*Bhāgavata*); a lunar dynasty king who was the son of King Ahaṅyāti and Bhānumatī and the husband of Sunandā (*M. Bh.*); an incarnation of Sāvarṇi Manu as the son of Devaguhya and Sarasvatī (*Bhāgavata*); the elephant of Kubera (*Rāmāyaṇa*)

**Sarvabhāvakara** (S) (M) 1. causer of all being. 3. another name for Śiva.

**Sarvabhāvana** (S) (M) 1. all creating. 3. another name for Śiva.

**Sarvabhibhū** (S) (M) 1. enlightening all. 3. a Buddha.

**Sarvaćakra** (S) (M) 1. possessing all the facets of yoga. 3. a tāntra deity (*B. Literature*)

**Sarvaćārin** (S) (M) 1. all pervading. 3. another name for Śiva.

**Sarvada** (S) (M) 1. all bestowing. 3. another name for Śiva.

**Sarvadamana** (S) (M) 1. all subduing. 3. an asura (*K. Sāgara*); another name for Bharata the son of Śakuntalā (*M. Bh.*)

**Sarvadarśi** (S) (M) 1. seeing everywhere; seen everywhere. 3. a sage who was the son of Kuśika.

**Sarvadāśārhaharta** (S) (M) 1. universal bearer of the Dāśārhas. 3. another name for Kṛṣṇa.

**Sarvadeva** (S) (M) 1. god of all. 3. another name for Śiva.

**Sarvadhā** (S) (M) all pleasing; all containing; all yielding.

**Sarvadhārin** (S) (M) 1. holding all. 3. another name for Śiva.

**Sarvādhikārin** (S) (M) master of all; all administering.

**Sarvaga** (S) (M) 2. all pervading; omnipresent. 2. spirit; soul. 3. a son of Paurṇamāsa (*V. Purāṇa*); a son of Manu Dharma- Sāvarṇika (*V. Purāṇa*); a son of Bhīmasena and Balandharā (*M. Bh.*); another name for Śiva.

**Sarvagata** (S) (M) 1. all that exists. 3. a son of Bhīmasena (*Bh. Purāṇa*)

**Sarvagjñā** (S) (F) 1. knower of all. 2. omnicient. 3. a yoginī; another name for Durgā.

**Sarvaguṇin** (S) (M) possessing all excellences.

**Sarvahara** (S) (M) 1. appropriating all; all destroying. 3. another name for Yama.

**Sarvahita** (S) (M) 1. useful to all. 3. another name for Sākyamuni.

**Sarvajit** (S) (M) all conquering.

**Sarvajña** (S) (M) 1. all knowing. 3. another name for Śiva.

**Sarvaka** (S) (M) all; whole; universal.

**Sarvakāma** (S) (M) 1. whose desires are fulfilled. 2. possessing everything wished for. 3. a son of Ṛtuparṇa (*Bhāgavata*); an Arhat; another name for Śiva.

**Sarvakāmadughā** (S) (F) 1. fulfiller of all desires. 3. a daughter of Surabhi (*M. Bh.*)

**Sarvakara** (S) (M) 1. maker of all. 3. another name for Śiva.

**Sarvakarmā** (S) (M) 1. performer of all acts. 3. a son of King Saudāsa (*M. Bh.*)

**Sarvakarman** (S) (M) 1. one who performs all acts. 3. a son of Kalmāṣapāda (*M. Bh.*); another name for Śiva.

**Sarvalakṣana** (S) (M) 1. with all auspicious marks. 3. another name for Śiva.

**Sarvalālasa** (S) (M) 1. desired by all. 3. another name for Śiva.

**Sarvaloćana** (S) (M) the all seeing eye.

**Sarvalokeśvara** (S) (M) 1. lord of all the worlds. 3. another name for Brahmā.

**Sarvamaṅgalā** (S) (F) 1. universally auspicious. 3. another name for Durgā and Lakṣmī.

**Sarvāmbha** (S) (M) 1. omnipresent; liked by all. 3. another name for Kārttikeya.

**Sarvamitra** (S) (M) friend of all.

**Sarvamohana** (S) (M) attracting all.

**Sarvamūrti** (S) (M) the idol of all; possessed with infinite forms.

**Sarvanāgaripudhvaja** (S) (M) 1. universal banner of Garuḍa. 3. another name for Kṛṣṇa.

**Sarvānanda** (S) (M) making all happy.
**Sarvaṅdama** (S) (M) 1. all subduing. 3. another name for Shakuntalā's son Bharata.
**Sarvanga** (S) (M) 1. perfect in limb; complete. 3. another name for Śiva.
**Sarvāṇī** (S) (F) 1. omnipresent. 2. perfect. 3. another name for Śiva's wife or Durgā.
**Śarvāṇī** (S) (F) Śiva's wife.
**Śarvāṇīramaṇa** (S) (M) 1. Śarvāṇī's husband. 3. another name for Śiva.
**Sarvanivaraṇaviṣkambhin** (S) (M) 1. doing away with all that is poisonous; destroyer of pains and troubles. 2. possessed with an enlightenment. 3. a Bodhisattva.
**Sarvānubhuti** (S) (M) 1. all perceiving. 3. 2 Jaina Arhats.
**Sarvapā** (S) (F) 1. drinking everything. 3. the wife of the daitya Bali.
**Sarvapati** (S) (M) lord of all.
**Śarvapatnī** (S) (F) 1. the wife of Śiva. 3. another name for Pārvatī.
**Sarvapāvana** (S) (M) 1. all purifying. 3. another name for Śiva.
**Sarvapayañjaha** (S) (M) 1. remover of all miseries. 3. a Boddhisatva.
**Sarvaprabhu** (S) (M) lord of all.
**Sarvaprada** (S) (M) all bestowing.
**Sarvapriya** (S) (M) beloved of all.
**Sarvapūjita** (S) (M) 1. worshipped by all. 3. another name for Śiva.
**Sarvapuṇya** (S) (M) full of all merits; perfectly beautiful.
**Sarvapūta** (S) (M) perfectly pure.
**Śarvara** (S) (M) 1. vareigated. 3. another name for Kāma.
**Sarvarājendra** (S) (M) chief of all kings.
**Sarvaratna** (S) (M) 1. having all gems; a gem among all. 3. a minister of Yudhiṣṭhira.
**Sarvaratnaka** (S) (M) 1. complete with jewels. 3. one of the 9 Jaina treasures and the deity who guards it.
**Śārvarī** (S) (F) night.
**Śarvarī** (S) (F) 1. the star spangled night; evening; twilight. 3. the wife of Doṣa and mother of Śiśumāra.
**Śarvarīpati** (S) (M) 1. lord of night. 3. another name for the moon and Śiva.
**Śarvarīśa** (S) (M) 1. lord of night. 3. another name for the moon.
**Śarvarīśvara** (S) (M) 1. lord of the night. 3. another name for the moon.
**Sarvasādhana** (S) (M) 1. accomplishing all. 3. another name for Śiva.
**Sarvasahā** (S) (F) 1. one who endures all. 2. all enduring. 3. another name for the earth; *Commiphora mukul.*
**Sarvasākṣin** (S) (M) 1. witness of all. 3. wind; fire. 3. the Supreme Being.
**Sarvasaṅgā** (S) (F) 1. going with all. 3. a river (*M. Bh.*)
**Sarvasāraṅga** (S) (M) 1. spotted all over. 3. a nāga of Dhṛtarāṣṭra's dynasty (*M. Bh.*)
**Sarvasattvapriyadarśana** (S) (M) 1. with the most beautiful face. 3. a Buḍdha; a Bodhisattva.
**Sarvaśaya** (S) (M) 1. refuge of all. 3. another name for Śiva.
**Sarvasena** (S) (M) 1. leader of all armies. 3. a king of Kāśi whose daughter Sunandā married Emperor Bharata (*M. Bh.*)
**Sarvaśokatamonirghātamatī** (S) (M) 1. destroyer of all grief and darkness. 3. a Bodhisattva.
**Sarvāstrā** (S) (F) 1. with all weapons. 3. one of the 16 Jaina vidyādevis.
**Sarvaśubhaṅkara** (S) (M) 1. auspicious to all. 3. another name for Śiva.
**Śarvata** (S) (M) bearer of arrows.
**Sarvatāpana** (S) (M) 1. all inflaming. 3. another name for Kāma.
**Sarvatejas** (S) (M) 1. universal splendour; universally powerful; omnipresent. 3. a king in Dhruva's dynasty who was the son of Vyuṣṭa (*Bhāgavata*)
**Sarvātman** (S) (M) 1. the whole person; the universal soul. 3. another name for Śiva.
**Sarvatomukha** (S) (M) 1. facing in all directions; complete; unlimited. 2. soul; spirit. 3. another name for Brahmā, Śiva and Agni.
**Sarvatraga** (S) (M) 1. all pervading; omnipresent. 2. wind; air. 3. a son of a Manu (*H. Purāṇa*); a son of Bhīmasena (*V. Purāṇa*)
**Sarvavādin** (S) (M) 1. spokesman of all;

knower of all the doctrines. 3. another name for Śiva.

**Sarvavāsa** (S) (M) 1. all abiding. 3. another name for Śiva.

**Sarvayādavanandana** (S) (M) 1. universal son of the Yādavas. 3. another name for Kṛṣṇa.

**Sarvayaśā** (S) (F) 1. famous among all. 3. a queen of Ayodhyā who was the mother of Anantanātha Jaina Tirthaṅkara (*J. Literature*)

**Sarvayogeśvareśvara** (S) (M) 1. lord of all lords of ascetics. 3. another name for Śiva.

**Sarvayogin** (S) (M) 1. the sage among all. 3. another name for Śiva.

**Sarvendra** (S) (M) universal deity; lord of all.

**Sarveśā** (S) (F) goddess of all.

**Sarveśa** (S) (M) lord of all.

**Sarveśī** (S) (F) desired by all.

**Sarveśvara** (S) (M) 1. lord of all. 3. another name for Śiva.

**Sarvikā** (S) (F) 1. universal. 2. all; whole; entire.

**Sarvavīra** (S) (M) all heroic; accompanied by heroes.

**Sarvayudha** (S) (M) 1. armed with every weapon. 3. another name for Śiva.

**Sarvodaya** (S) (M) upliftment of everyone.

**Sarvottama** (S) (M) best among all; supreme; the best.

**Śaryāti** (S) (M) 1. an arrow shooter. 3. a son of Vaivasvata Manu and the father of Ānarta and Sukanyā (*M. Bh.*); a Purū king who was the son of Prāćinvān and father of Ahaṁyāti; a son of Nahuṣa.

**Śaśabhṛt** (S) (M) 1. hare bearer. 3. another name for the moon.

**Śaśabindu** (S) (M) 1. hare spotted. 3. a king who was the son of Ćitraratha; another name for the moon.

**Śaśāda** (S) (M) 1. hare eater. 3. a son of King Vikukṣi of Ayodhyā and father of Purañjaya (*Br. Purāṇa*); a son of Ikṣvāku.

**Śaśadhara** (S) (M) 1. bearer of hare marks. 3. another name for the moon.

**Śaśalakṣana** (S) (M) 1. hare marked. 3. another name for the moon.

**Śaśalakṣmāna** (S) (M) 1. hare marked. 3. another name for the moon.

**Śaśaloman** (S) (M) 1. with hare's hair. 3. a Purāṇic king.

**Sasaṅga** (S) (M) adhering; attached.

**Śaśāṅka** (S) (M) 1. hare marked. 3. another name for the moon.

**Śaśāṅkaja** (S) (M) 1. son of the moon. 3. another name for Mercury.

**Śaśāṅkamukuta** (S) (M) 1. moon crested. 3. another name for Śiva.

**Śaśāṅkaśatru** (S) (M) 1. foe of the moon. 3. another name for Rāhu.

**Śaśāṅkaśekhara** (S) (M) 1. moon crested. 3. another name for Śiva.

**Śaśāṅkavatī** (S) (F) like the moon.

**Śaśāṅkopala** (S) (M) moonstone.

**Sasāra** (S) (M) possessing strength and ener gy.

**Sasatya** (S) (M) accompanied by truth.

**Sasena** (S) (M) commanding an army.

**Sāsi** (S) (M) armed with a sword.

**Śaśī** (S) (F) 1. hare marked. 3. an apsarā.

**Śaśibhās** (S) (F) moonbeam.

**Śaśibhūṣaṇa** (S) (M) 1. moon decorated. 3. another name for Śiva.

**Śaśideva** (S) (M) lord of the moon.

**Śaśidhāman** (S) (M) the moon's splendour.

**Śaśidhvaja** (S) (M) 1. moon bannered. 3. an asura (*H. Purāṇa*)

**Śaśikalā** (S) (F) 1. digit of the moon. 3. the daughter of King Subāhu of Kāśī and the wil of Emperor Sudarśana.

**Śaśikāntā** (S) (F) 1. beloved of the moon. 2. the white lotus flower (*Nelumbium speciosum*) 3. a river.

**Śaśikānta** (S) (M) moon loved; moonstone.

**Śaśikara** (S) (M) moonbeam.

**Śaśikhaṇḍa** (S) (M) 1. crescent moon. 3. a vidyādhara.

**Śaśikiraṇa** (S) (M) moonbeam.

**Śaśilekhā** (S) (F) 1. a digit of the moon. 3. an apsarā (*Brah. Purāṇa*); *Psoralia corylifolia*.

**Śaśin** (S) (M) 1. hare marked. 3. the moon.

**Śaśimaṇi** (S) (M) moonstone.

**Śaśimauli** (S) (M) **1.** having the moon as a diadem. **3.** another name for Śiva.

**Śaśimukhī** (S) (F) moon faced.

**Śaśinī** (S) (F) containing the moon; a digit of the moon.

**Sāsipāṇi** (S) (M) with sword in hand.

**Śaśiprabhā** (S) (M) **1.** as radiant as the moon. **2.** the White Water Lily (*Nymphaea alba*); a pearl; moonlight.

**Śaśiprabhā** (S) (F) moonlight.

**Śaśipriya** (S) (M) **1.** beloved of the moon. **2.** pearl.

**Śaśiraśmī** (S) (F) moon beam.

**Śaśirekhā** (S) (M) **1.** moon crowned. **3.** another name for Buddha and Śiva.

**Śaśīśa** (S) (M) **1.** lord of the moon. **3.** another name for Śiva.

**Śaśiśekhara** (S) (M) **1.** moon crested. **3.** a Buddha; another name for Śiva.

**Śaśitanaya** (S) (M) **1.** son of the moon. **3.** another name for Mercury.

**Śaśitejas** (S) (M) **1.** power of the moon. **3.** a vidyādhara.

**Śasman** (S) (M) invocation; praise.

**Śaśmān** (S) (M) exerting oneself; zealous.

**Sasmita** (S) (M) accompanied with smiles; smiling.

**Śaśokūlamukhī** (S) (F) **1.** with a face like a sweetmeat. **3.** an attendant of Skanda.

**Saśrīkā** (S) (F) possessed with beauty, grace and fortune; lovely; splendid.

**Śāsta** (S) (M) **1.** one who rules. **2.** a ruler; punisher; chastiser. **3.** the idol of the Sabarimala temple which is considered the offspring of Śiva and Mahāviṣṇu in his form as Mohini; Śāsta was the husband of Pūrṇa and Puṣkalā and father of Sātyaka.

**Ṣaṣṭhī** (S) (F) **1.** a praise; a hymn. **3.** another name for Durgā.

**Ṣaṣṭhidevī** (S) (F) **1.** protectress of a 6 day-child. **3.** folk goddess form of Durgā.

**Ṣaṣṭhīdevī** (S) (F) **1.** one sixth. **3.** a goddess who is the patron of children and is considered the wife of Subrahmaṇya and the daughter of Brahmā (*D. Bhāgavata*)

**Ṣaṣṭhikā** (S) (F) the 6th day after a child's birth personified as a divine mother regarded as a form of Durgā supposed to protect children.

**Ṣaṣṭhipriya** (S) (M) **1.** beloved of Durgā. **3.** another name for Skanda.

**Śāstī** (S) (F) praise; hymn.

**Śasti** (S) (F) praise; hymn.

**Ṣaṣṭibhāga** (S) (M) **1.** 60 parts. **3.** another name for Śiva.

**Śastradevatā** (S) (F) **1.** weapon. **3.** deity of weapons personified as the daughter of Kṛśāśva.

**Śāstri** (S) (M) chastiser; punisher; ruler; teacher; the sword personified.

**Saśūka** (S) (M) a believer in the existence of god.

**Sasura** (S) (M) with the gods.

**Sāśva** (S) (M) **1.** with horses. **3.** a king in the court of Yama (*M. Bh.*)

**Śaśvat** (S) (M) perpetual; endless; numerous.

**Śāśvata** (S) (M) **1.** eternal; constant; perpetual. **3.** a son of Śruta and father of Sudhanvan (*V. Purāṇa*); another name for Śiva and Vyāsa.

**Śāśvatānanda** (S) (M) eternal bliss.

**Sasyahan** (S) (M) **1.** destroying crops. **3.** son of Duhsaha (*Mā. Purāṇa*)

**Sasyaka** (S) (M) **1.** possessed of good qualities; perfect. **2.** sword; precious stone.

**Sata** (S) (M) lasting; enduring; being; existing; real; a truth; good; honest; a sage.

**Sāta** (S) (M) **1.** pleasure; delight; handsome; bright. **3.** a yakṣa friend of Vaiśravaṇa.

**Śaṭa** (S) (M) **1.** sour. **2.** astringent. **3.** a son of Vasudeva (*H. Purāṇa*)

**Śatabāhu** (S) (M) **1.** 100 armed. **3.** an asura (*Bhā. Purāṇa*)

**Śatabāhu** (S) (F) **1.** 100 armed. **3.** a goddess.

**Śatabali** (S) (M) **1.** as strong as 100. **2.** very strong; a kind of fish. **3.** a monkey in the army of Sugrīva (*V. Rāmāyaṇa*)

**Śatābdi** (S) (M) centenary; century.

**Śatabhīru** (S) (M) **1.** extremely shy. **3.** Arabian Jasmine (*Jasminum sambac*)

**Śataćandra** (S) (M) **1.** as beautiful as a 100

moons; adorned with a hundred moons. 3. a brother of Śakuni (*M. Bh.*)

**Sataćita** (S) (M) 1. existence and thought. 3. another name for Brahmā.

**Śatadalā** (S) (F) 1. with a 100 petals. 2. the Indian White Rose (*Rosa alba*)

**Satadeva** (S) (M) the true god; god of existence.

**Śatadhāman** (S) (M) 1. with a 100 forms. 3. another name for Viṣṇu.

**Śatadhanus** (S) (M) 1. with a 100 bows. 3. a Yādava king.

**Śatadhanvan** (S) (M) 1. with a hundred bows. 3. father of Avidānta; father of Bhīṣaj.

**Śatadhṛti** (S) (M) 1. with a 100 sacrifices. 3. another name for Indra and Brahmā.

**Śatadrū** (S) (M) 1. flowing in 100 branches. 3. the Purāṇic name of the river now called Sutlej (*H. Purāṇa*)

**Śatadrutī** (S) (F) 1. flowing in branches. 3. a daughter of Varuṇa and wife of Barhiṣada (*Bhā. Purāṇa*)

**Śatadyumna** (S) (M) 1. with the glory of 100's. 3. a son of Manu Ćākṣusa and Naḍvalā (*V. Purāṇa*)

**Śataghantā** (S) (F) 1. with a 100 spears. 3. a mother attending on Skanda (*M. Bh.*)

**Śataghnī** (S) (M) 1. a deadly weapon. 3. another name for Śiva.

**Śatahaya** (S) (M) 1. with a 100 horses. 3. a son of Manu Tāmasa (*V. Purāṇa*)

**Śatahradā** (S) (F) 1. containing a 100 sounds. 2. thunderbolt. 3. a daughter of Dakṣa and wife of Bahuputra; the mother of the rākṣasa Virādha (*V. Rāmāyaṇa*)

**Śatahrada** (S) (M) 1. thunderbolt. 3. an asura.

**Śatajīhva** (S) (M) 1. 100 tongued. 3. another name for Śiva.

**Śatajit** (S) (M) 1. vanquisher of 100. 3. a Yādava king who was the son of Sahasrajit and the father of Mahāhaya, Veṇuhaya and Hehaya (*Bhāgavata*); a son of Kṛṣṇa and Jāmbavatī (*Bhāgavata*); a son of Viraja (*Purāṇas*); a son of Bhajamāna (*Bhā. Purāṇa*); a yakṣa (*Bhā. Purāṇa*)

**Śatajyoti** (S) (M) 1. with a 100 flames. 2. the moon. 3. a son of King Subhrāj (*M. Bh.*)

**Śatakapāleśa** (S) (M) 1. lord of a 100 skulls. 3. another name for Śiva.

**Śatakārā** (S) (F) 1. knower of a 100 skills. 3. a gandharvī.

**Śātakarṇi** (S) (M) 1. with sharp ears. 3. a son of King Pūrṇotsangha (*M. Purāṇa*)

**Śatakīrti** (S) (M) 1. with the fame of 100s. 3. the 10th Arhat of the future Utsarpinī.

**Śatakratu** (S) (M) 1. with a 100 fold power. 3. another name for Indra.

**Śatākṣi** (S) (F) 1. 100 eyed. 2. the night. 3. another name for Durgā; Dill (*Peucedanum graveolens*)

**Śatakumbhā** (S) (F) 1. with a 100 pitchers. 3. a sacred river (*M. Bh.*)

**Śātakumbha** (S) (M) gold.

**Śataloćana** (S) (M) 1. 100 eyed. 3. an asura (*H. Purāṇa*); a warrior of Skanda (*M. Bh.*)

**Śatāmagha** (S) (M) 1. distributing a 100 rewards. 3. another name for Indra.

**Śatamakha** (S) (M) 1. with a 100 sacrifices. 3. another name for Indra.

**Śatamanyu** (S) (M) 1. with a 100 fold wrath. 3. another name for Indra.

**Śatamukha** (S) (M) 1. with a 100 mouths. 3. a king of the kinnaras; the father-in-law of Śahasramukha Rāvaṇa; an asura devotee of Śiva (*M. Bh.*)

**Śatamukhī** (S) (F) 1. with a 100 faces. 3. another name for Durgā.

**Satanāma** (S) (M) the name of truth.

**Śatananā** (S) (F) 1. 100 faced. 3. a goddess.

**Ṣatānana** (S) (M) 1. 6 faced. 3. another name for Skanda.

**Śatānanda** (S) (M) 1. delighting 100s. 3. the vehicle of Viṣṇu; the family priest of Janaka who was a son of Gautama and Ahalyā (*Bhāgavata*); another name for Viṣṇu and Kṛṣṇa.

**Śatānandā** (S) (F) 1. delighting 100s. 3. an attendant of Skanda.

**Śatānīka** (S) (M) 1. with an army of hundreds. 3. a king of the Yayāti dynasty who was the son of Bṛhadratha and the father of Durdama (*Bhāgavata*); the son of Nakula and Draupadī (*M. Bh.*); a son of Janamejaya and

Vapuṣṭamā and the father of Aśvamedhadatta and Sahasrānīka (*M. Bh.*); a royal ṛṣi of the Kuru dynasty after whom Nakula named his son (*M. Bh.*); a brother of King Virāṭa of Matsya (*M. Bh.*)

**Śatapadmā** (S) (F) **1.** a lotus with a 100 petals; consisting of hundred lotuses. **2.** very beautiful; tender; soft; loving. **3.** the wife of Śukra.

**Satapāla** (S) (M) good protector.

**Śataparvā** (S) (F) **1.** with a 100 portions. **3.** the wife of Śukraćārya (*M. Bh.*)

**Sataprabhā** (S) (F) radiant; brilliant lustre.

**Śatapuṣkarā** (S) (F) consisting of a 100 blue lotus flowers.

**Śatapuṣpā** (S) (F) **1.** consisting of 100 flowers. **2.** extremely beautiful; having a fragrant body.

**Śataratha** (S) (M) **1.** with 100s of chariots. **3.** a king in Yama's court (*M. Bh.*)

**Śatarati** (S) (M) **1.** loved by a 100; attached to 100s. **3.** another name for Indra, Brahmā and heaven.

**Satarūpa** (S) (M) with true beauty; really beautiful.

**Śatarūpā** (S) (F) **1.** with a 100 forms. **3.** the daughter of Brahmā and sister and wife of Svāyambhuva Manu and the mother of Priyavrata, Uttānapāda, Prasūti and Ākūti (*V. Purāṇa*)

**Śataśīrṣā** (S) (F) **1.** 100 headed. **3.** the wife of Vāsuki (*M. Bh.*)

**Śataśīrṣa** (S) (M) **1.** 100 headed. **3.** a king of the nāgas.

**Śataśṛṅga** (S) (M) **1.** with a 100 horns. **3.** the muni who cursed Pāṇḍu; a rākṣasa and father of Saṅyama, Viyama and Suyama (*M. Bh.*); a mountain (*M. Bh.*)

**Sātavāha** (S) (M) **1.** with 7 chariots. **3.** a king.

**Śatavāhana** (S) (M) **1.** with a 100 chariots. **3.** a king of whom Guṇāḍhya was a minister.

**Śatavāṇi** (S) (M) **1.** knowing 100s of arts and sciences. **3.** a royal ṛṣi (*Ṛg Veda*)

**Satavānt** (S) (M) **1.** possessed with truth. **2.** true; faithful; pious; sacred.

**Śatavapuṣ** (S) (M) **1.** with a 100 bodies. **3.** a son of Uṣanas.

**Śatāvarta** (S) (M) **1.** with a 100 curls on the head. **3.** another name for Śiva and Viṣṇu.

**Śatavartin** (S) (M) **1.** 100 locked. **3.** another name for Viṣṇu.

**Satavīra** (S) (M) a true warrior.

**Śatavīra** (S) (M) **1.** warrior among 100s. **3.** another name for Viṣṇu

**Śatāyudha** (S) (M) wielding a 100 weapons.

**Śatayūpa** (S) (M) **1.** with a 100 pillars; well equipped with every type of weapon. **3.** a Kekaya royal sage (*M. Bh.*)

**Śatayuṣ** (S) (M) **1.** a 100 years old. **2.** elderly. **3.** a son of Purūravas and Urvaśī (*M. Bh.*)

**Śatāyus** (S) (M) **1.** fighting 100 battles. **3.** a son of Purūravas and Urvaśī (*M. Bh.*); a Kaurava warrior (*M. Bh.*)

**Satejas** (S) (M) full of power; full of splendour.

**Śateśa** (S) (M) lord of 100s.

**Śaṭha** (S) (M) **1.** dishonest; depraved; wicked. **3.** an asura son of Kaśyapa and Danu (*M. Bh.*); a son of Vasudeva (*H. Purāṇa*)

**Satī** (S) (F) **1.** truthful. **2.** a virtuous and faithful wife; a female ascetic. **3.** the wife of Viśvāmitra; the goddess Durgā described as truth personified or as a daughter of Dakṣa and wife of Bhava; a wife of Aṅgiras; a wife of Viśvāmitra (*Ṛg Veda*)

**Sāti** (S) (F) gaining; obtaining; gift; oblation.

**Satina** (S) (M) real; essential.

**Satīnātha** (S) (M) **1.** husband of Satī. **3.** another name for Śiva.

**Satīndra** (S) (M) **1.** lord of Satī. **3.** another name for Śiva.

**Satīśa** (S) (M) **1.** lord of Satī. **3.** another name for Śiva.

**Sātiśaya** (S) (M) superior; better; best; eminent.

**Satkāra** (S) (M) **1.** a virtuous deed. **2.** honour; respect.

**Satkārī** (S) (M) respectful; doer of virtuous deeds.

**Satkarman** (S) (M) **1.** a virtuous act; doing virtuous deeds. **3.** a son of Dhṛtavrata (*Bh. Purāṇa*)

**Satkartṛ** (S) (M) **1.** doing good. **2.** a benefactor. **3.** another name for Viṣṇu.

**Satkṛta** (S) (M) 1. doer of virtuous deeds; honoured; respected; adored. 3. another name for Śiva.

**Satkṛti** (S) (M) 1. doing good. 2. virtuous. 3. a solar dynasty king who was the son of Jayatsena (*Bhāgavata*)

**Ṣaṭkūtā** (S) (F) 1. eater of 6. 3. a form of Bhairavī.

**Sātman** (S) (M) with a soul; united with the Supreme Spirit.

**Śātodara** (S) (F) slender waisted.

**Śatodara** (S) (M) 1. with a 100 bellies. 3. an attendant of Śiva.

**Śatodarī** (S) (F) 1. with a 100 bellies. 3. an attendant of Skanda (*M. Bh.*)

**Satpati** (S) (M) 1. a true lord; leader; champion; a good lord. 3. another name for Indra.

**Satprītikā** (S) (F) beloved of truth.

**Śatrajit** (S) (M) 1. always victorious. 3. a Yādava king who was the son of Nimna and the brother of Prasena, he fathered Satyabhāmā who married Kṛṣṇa (*Bhāgavata*)

**Satrasaha** (S) (M) irresistable.

**Sātrāsāha** (A) (M) 1. all subduing. 3. a nāga (*A. Veda*)

**Śatrudamana** (S) (M) subduing enemies.

**Śatruddha** (S) (M) making enemies run away.

**Śatrugha** (S) (M) slaying enemies.

**Śatrughna** (S) (M) 1. destroying enemies. 3. a son of Daśaratha and Sumitrā and twin brother of Lakṣmaṇa and the husband of Śrutakīrtī (*Rāmāyaṇa*); a son of Devaśravas (*H. Purāṇa*)

**Śatruhan** (S) (M) 1. destroyer of enemies. 3. a son of Śvaphalka (*H. Purāṇa*)

**Śatrujaya** (S) (M) conquering an enemy.

**Śatrujit** (S) (M) 1. conquering enemies. 3. a son of Rājādhideva (*H. Purāṇa*); the father of Kuvalayāsva (*Purāṇas*); a son of Dhruvasandhi and Līlāvatī; another name for Śiva.

**Śatrumardana** (S) (M) 1. crushing enemies. 3. a son of Daśaratha; a son of Kuvalayāśva (*Mā. Purāṇa*); a king of Videha; a son of King Ṛtadhvaja and Madālasā (*Mā. Purāṇa*)

**Śatruñjayā** (S) (F) 1. conquering enemies. 3. a mother in Skanda's retinue (*M. Bh.*)

**Śatruñjaya** (S) (M) 1. enemy conquering. 3. a son of Dhṛtarāṣṭrą (*M. Bh.*); a brother of Karṇa (*M. Bh.*); a son of Drupada (*M. Bh.*); a king of Sauvīra (*M. Bh.*)

**Śatruntapa** (S) (M) 1. tormentor of enemies. 3. a king in Duryodhana's army (*M. Bh.*)

**Śatrusaha** (S) (M) 1. tolerating enemies. 3. a son of Dhṛtarāṣṭra (*M. Bh.*)

**Śatrutāpana** (S) (M) 1. tormentor of enemies. 3. an asura son of Kaśyapa and Danu (*M. Bh.*); another name for Śiva.

**Śatruvināśana** (S) (M) 1. destroying enemies. 3. another name for Śiva.

**Satsahāya** (S) (M) good companion; with virtuous friends.

**Sattrāyaṇa** (S) (M) 1. course of sacrifices; follower of truth; moving in the Soma sac. 3. the father of Bṛhadbhānu (*Bh. Purāṇa*)

**Sattva** (S) (M) 1. being; existence; reality; true essence; life; resolute; energy; courage. 3. a tāntra deity (*B. Literature*); a son of Dhṛtarāṣṭra.

**Sattvapati** (S) (M) lord of creatures.

**Sattvavatī** (S) (F) 1. pregnant. 3. a tāntric deity.

**Sāttvikī** (S) (F) 1. of true essence. 2. spirited; vigorous; energetic; pure; true; honest. 3. another name for Durgā.

**Satvadanta** (S) (M) 1. having a wisdom tooth. 2. very wise. 3. a son of Vasudeva and Bhadrā (*Vā. Purāṇa*)

**Satvantī** (S) (F) 1. full of truth. 2. faithful.

**Śatvarī** (S) (F) night.

**Satvat** (S) (M) 1. truthful. 2. faithful. 3. a son of Madhu (*H. Purāṇa*); a son of Mādhava and Anśa (*V. Purāṇa*); another name for Kṛṣṇa.

**Sātvata** (S) (M) 1. full of truth. 2. delighted; pleasant; sacred to Kṛṣṇa. 3. a Yadu king who was the son of Devakśatra (*M. Bh.*); a son of Āyu (*Purāṇas*)

**Sātvatī** (S) (F) 1. pleasant. 2. delighted. 3. princess of the Satvata tribe; the mother of Śiśupāla (*M. Bh.*)

**Satvatī** (S) (F) truthful; faithful.

**Satvī** (S) (F) 1. existent; real. 3. a daughter of Vainateya and wife of Bṛhanmanas

(*H. Purāṇa*)

**Sātvika** (S) (M) real; virtuous; essential; good.

**Satvindra** (S) (M) lord of virtue.

**Satyā** (S) (F) 1. truthful; sincere. 3. the wife of Manthu and mother of Bhauvana (*Bh. Purāṇa*); a daughter of Nagnajit and the wife of Kṛṣṇa, the daughter of Dharma who was the wife of the agni Śanyu and mother of Bharadvāja (*M. Bh.*); another name for Durgā and Sītā.

**Satya** (S) (M) 1. true; real; pure; virtuous. 3. a viśvadeva; a son of Havirdhāna; a hermit in the court of Yudhiṣṭhira (*M. Bh.*); an agni who was the son of Agni Niśćyavana and the father of Svana (*M. Bh.*); a warrior of Kalinga (*M. Bh.*); a son of Vitatya and the father of Śānta; another name for Viṣṇu, Kṛṣṇa and the Aśvattha tree.

**Satyabelā** (S) (F) time of truth.

**Satyabhāmā** (S) (F) 1. having true lustre. 3. a daughter of Śatrajit and one of the 8 wives of Kṛṣṇa (*M. Bh.*)

**Satyadarśin** (S) (M) 1. seer of truth. 3. a ṛṣi in the 13th Manvantara (*H. Purāṇa*)

**Satyadeva** (S) (M) 1. lord of truth. 3. a Kaliṅga warrior (*M. Bh.*)

**Satyadevī** (S) (F) 1. goddess of truth; shining with truth. 3. a daughter of King Devaka and a wife of Vasudeva (*M. Purāṇa*)

**Satyadhara** (S) (M) 1. bearer of truth. 2. truthful; honest; virtuous.

**Satyadharma** (S) (M) 1. moral-law; abiding by the moral law. 2. the law of eternal truth. 3. a son of the 13th Manu (*Bh. Purāṇa*); a lunar dynasty king (*M. Bh.*); a brother of King Suśarman of Trigarta (*M. Bh.*); Bengal Quince (*Aegle marmelos*)

**Satyadhṛta** (S) (M) 1. abode of truth. 3. a son of Puṣpavata (*V. Purāṇa*)

**Satyadhṛti** (S) (M) 1. bearer of truth. 3. a son of Satānanda (*A. Purāṇa*); a prominent warrior on the side of the Pāṇḍavas (*M. Bh.*); a son of King Kṣemaka who fought on the side of Pāṇḍavas (*M. Bh.*)

**Satyadhvaja** (S) (M) 1. true fire. 2. eternal fire. 3. another name for Agastya.

**Satyahita** (S) (M) 1. eternal welfare. 3. a Purū dynasty king who was the son of Ṛṣabha and the father of Sudhanvā (*A. Purāṇa*)

**Satyaja** (S) (M) 1. born of truth. 2. of a true nature.

**Satyajit** (S) (M) 1. conquering by truth. 3. a dānava (*H. Purāṇa*); Indra in the 3rd Manvantara; the son of Bṛhaddharman; the son of Kṛṣṇa; the son of Anaka; the son of Amitrajit (*H. Purāṇa*); a yakṣa; a Yayāti dynasty king who was the son of Sunītha and the father of Kṣema (*Bhāgavata*); a brother of Drupada of Pañćāla.

**Satyajyota** (S) (M) 1. lamp of truth. 2. leading others on to the path of truth.

**Satyajyoti** (S) (M) having real splendour; having a real beauty.

**Satyaka** (S) (M) 1. ratification of a bargain. 3. a son of Śini (*M. Bh.*); a son of Manu Raivata (*Mā. Purāṇa*); a son of Kṛṣṇa and Bhadrā (*Bh. Purāṇa*); a Yādava king who was the father of Sātyakī.

**Satyakāma** (S) (M) 1. desirer of truth. 2. seeker of truth. 3. a noble hermit (*Ć. Upaniṣad*)

**Satyakarman** (S) (M) 1. a true act. 2. doer of truthful acts; doing pious deeds. 3. a Bharata dynasty king who was the son of Dhṛtavrata and the father of Aṇuvrata (*Bhāgavata*); a brother of King Śuśarmā of Trigarta (*M. Bh.*)

**Satyakarṇa** (S) (M) 1. listener of truth. 3. a son of Ćandrapīḍa (*H. Purāṇa*)

**Satyaketu** (S) (M) 1. one whose banner is truth. 2. standing by the values of truth. 3. a Pāñćāla king (*Br. Purāṇa*); a Purū dynasty king who was the son of Śukumāra (*A. Purāṇa*); a solar dynasty king who was the son of Dharmaketu and father of Dhṛṣṭaketu (*Bhāgavata*); a son of Akrūra; a Buddha (*L. Vistara*)

**Sātyakī** (S) (M) 1. truthful; faithful. 3. a Yādava warrior of the Vṛṣṇi dynasty who was the son of Satyaka and a great friend of Kṛṣṇa, he is supposed to have been a partial incarnation of the maruts (*M. Bh.*)

**Satyam** (S) (M) 1. the truth. 2. truthful; honest; virtuous.

**Satyamedhas** (S) (M) 1. with true intelligence. 3. another name for Viṣṇu.

**Satyamoti** (S) (M) 1. pearl of truth. 2. jewel

among the truthful.

**Satyamūrti** (S) (M) symbol of truth.

**Satyānanda** (S) (M) true bliss.

**Satyanārāyaṇa** (S) (M) 1. controller of truth. 3. a divinity called Satyapīr in Bengal; another name for Viṣṇu.

**Satyanetra** (S) (M) 1. truth eyed. 2. seer of truth. 3. a son of Atri.

**Satyapāla** (S) (M) 1. protector of truth. 3. a hermit in the court of Yudhiṣṭhira (*M. Bh.*)

**Satyapriya** (S) (M) lover of truth; one who likes truthful people.

**Satyaratā** (S) (F) 1. devoted to truth. 3. a Kekaya princess who married King Triśaṅku of Ayodhya (*Vā. Purāṇa*)

**Satyarata** (S) (M) 1. devoted to truth. 3. a son of Satyavrata (*M. Purāṇa*); another name for Vyāsa.

**Satyarathā** (S) (F) 1. with a chariot of truth. 2. truthful; honest; pious; virtuous. 3. a wife of Triśanku (*H. Purāṇa*)

**Satyaratha** (S) (M) 1. with a chariot of truth. a brother of King Suśarma of Trigarta (*M. Bh.*); a king of Vidarbha; a son of Mīnaratha (*V. Purāṇa*)

**Satyasāgara** (S) (M) 1. ocean of truth. 2. best among the truthful.

**Satyasāhas** (S) (M) 1. with true courage. 2. truly courageous. 3. the father of Svadhāman.

**Satyasandhā** (S) (F) 1. true in promise. 3. another name for Draupadī.

**Satyasandha** (S) (M) 1. true in promise. 2. keeping one's promise. 3. a son of Dhṛtarāṣṭra (*M. Bh.*); an attendant given to Skanda by the god Mitra (*M. Bh.*); another name for Rāma, Bharata, Bhīsma and Janamejaya.

**Satyasangara** (S) (M) 1. true to a promise. 3. another name for Kubera.

**Satyasāra** (S) (M) the essence of truth.

**Satyasena** (S) (M) 1. with a virtuous army. 3. a brother of King Suśarmā of Trigarta (*M. Bh.*); a son of Karṇa (*M. Bh.*)

**Satyaśīla** (S) (M) 1. of a virtuous disposition. 2. very virtuous; pious.

**Satyāśiṣā** (S) (F) a realized wish or prayer.

**Satyaśravas** (S) (M) 1. listener of truth; truly famous. 3. a warrior on the Kaurava side (*M. Bh.*); a son of sage Mārkaṇḍeya (*M. Bh.*)

**Satyaśrī** (S) (M) 1. glory of truth; best among the truthful. 3. a son of Satyahita.

**Satyatapas** (S) (M) the true sage; practising true austerity; following the true path of penance.

**Satyātman** (S) (M) 1. true soul. 2. with a truthful soul; virtuous.

**Satyavāća** (S) (M) 1. speaking the truth. 3. a gandharva (*M. Bh.*); a son of Manu Ćākṣuṣa (*H. Purāṇa*); a son of Manu Sāvarṇa (*Mā. Purāṇa*)

**Satyavādinī** (S) (F) 1. always speaking the truth. 3. a form of Dākṣāyāṇī; a goddess of the Bodhi tree (*L. Vistara*)

**Satyavāha** (S) (M) 1. carrying the truth. 3. teacher of Aṅgiras.

**Satyavāka** (S) (M) 1. truth speaking. 3. a son of Manu Ćākṣuṣa and Nadvalā (*A. Purāṇa*); a gandharva son of Kaśyapa and Muni (*M. Bh.*)

**Satyavara** (S) (M) adopter of truth; best among the truthful.

**Satyavarmā** (S) (M) 1. warrior of truth; wearing the armour of truth. 3. a brother of King Suśarmā of Trigarta (*M. Bh.*)

**Satyavarman** (S) (M) wearing the armour of truth.

**Satyavat** (S) (M) 1. truthful. 2. veracious. 3. a son of Manu Raivata (*H. Purāṇa*); a son of Manu Ćākṣuṣa (*Bhā. Purāṇa*); a son of Dyumatsena of Śālva and husband of Sāvitrī.

**Satyavatī** (S) (F) 1. truthful. 3. the daughter of the apsarā Ādrikā who became the mother of Vyāsa by sage Parāśara, she married King Śantanu of the lunar dynasty and became the mother of Vićitravīrya and Ćitrāṅgada (*M. Bh.*); a sister of Viśvāmitra; a Kekaya princess who married Triśaṅku and was the mother of Hariśćandra (*M. Bh.*); a wife of Nārada (*M. Bh.*); a daughter of Gādhi and wife of Rćika who is fabled to have become the Kauśikī river (*M. Bh.*)

**Satyavrata** (S) (M) 1. devotee to the vow of truth. 3. a son of Dhṛtarāṣṭra (*M. Bh.*); a son of Devadatta; a son of Trayyāruṇa (*H. Purāṇa*); a brother of King Suśarmā of

Trigarta (*M. Bh.*)

**Satyāyu** (S) (M) **1.** with a true life. **2.** one who has had a pious life. **3.** a son of Purūravas and Urvaśī (*Bhāgavata*)

**Satyendra** (S) (M) best among the truthful.

**Satyeṣu** (S) (M) **1.** desirer of truth. **2.** seeker of truth. **3.** a brother of King Suśarmā of Trigarta (*M. Bh.*); a rākṣasa who ruled the earth in ancient times (*M. Bh.*)

**Satyeyu** (S) (M) **1.** striving for truth. **3.** a Purū dynasty king who was a son of Raudrāśva and Ghṛtāćī (*Bhāgavata*)

**Saubala** (S) (M) **1.** full of power. **2.** very powerful. **3.** the father of Saubalī who married Dhṛtarāṣṭra (*M. Bh.*); another name for Śakuni.

**Saubalā** (S) (M) **1.** belonging to Subala. **3.** patronymic of Gāndhārī.

**Saubālī** (S) (F) **1.** daughter of the powerful. **3.** a wife of Dhṛtarāṣṭra (*D. Bhāgavata*)

**Saubhadra** (S) (M) **1.** of Subhadrā. **3.** matronymic of Abhimanyu.

**Saubhaga** (S) (M) **1.** full of fortunes. **2.** auspicious.

**Saubhāgyā** (S) (F) **1.** welfare; success; good fortune. **2.** beauty; charm; happiness.

**Saubhāgya** (S) (M) welfare; success; luck; happiness; beauty; grace; affection.

**Saubhāgyagaurī** (S) (F) **1.** goddess of fortune. **3.** a form of Pārvatī (*A. Purāṇa*)

**Saubhāgyamanjarī** (S) (F) beautiful blossom.

**Saubhāgyasundarī** (S) (F) **1.** beautiful maiden of fortune. **3.** the feminine form of Nārada.

**Saubhara** (S) (M) **1.** born of vitality; son of vigour. **3.** an agni born from a portion of Varćas (*M. Bh.*); Saffron (*Crocus sativus*)

**Saubhari** (S) (M) **1.** born of vigour. **3.** a hermit who married the 50 daughters of Māndhātā (*Bhāgavata*)

**Saubhīki** (S) (M) **1.** surrounded by people of the Saubha city. **3.** another name for Drupada.

**Śaućin** (S) (M) pure.

**Saućuka** (S) (M) **1.** made of sacred threads; sharp witted. **3.** the father of Bhutirāja.

**Saudāmanī** (S) (F) **1.** lightning. **3.** a daughter of Kaśyapa and Vinatā (*V. Purāṇa*); a daughter of the gandharva Hāhā (*K. Sāgara*); the consort of Indra's elephant Airāvata; an apsarā; a yakṣiṇī (*K. Sāgara*)

**Saudāsa** (S) (M) **1.** son of a great devotee; son of Sudāsa. **3.** an Ikṣvāku king and son of Sudāsa (*T. Samhitā*)

**Saudeva** (S) (M) **1.** of Sudeva. **3.** another name for Divodāsa.

**Saudevatanaya** (S) (M) **1.** descendant of Sudeva. **3.** another name for Divodāsa.

**Saudhākara** (S) (M) belonging to the moon.

**Saugandhaka** (S) (M) **1.** fragrant. **2.** blue waterlily.

**Saugandhikā** (S) (F) **1.** fragrant. **3.** the flower garden of Kubera (*M. Bh.*); Blue Lotus (*Nymphaea stellata*); Geranium grass (*Cymbopogon schoenanthus*)

**Saugata** (S) (M) **1.** gone into everything; knowing everything; an enlightened person. **2.** a Buddhist. **3.** a son of Dhṛtarāṣṭra (*M. Bh.*)

**Sauharda** (S) (M) goodheartedness; affection.

**Saujanyā** (S) (F) good; kind; generosity; gentle; friend; compassionate; loving.

**Saujas** (S) (M) full of energy; strong; powerful.

**Śaulkāyani** (S) (M) **1.** with a spearlike body. **3.** a hermit disciple of Vyāsa.

**Saumaki** (S) (M) **1.** of Somaka. **3.** another name for Drupada.

**Sauman** (S) (M) flower; blossom.

**Saumanasa** (S) (M) **1.** made of flowers. **2.** comfort; benevolence; satisfaction; pleasure. **3.** one of the 8 elephants supporting the globe.

**Saumanasya** (S) (M) **1.** causing gladness. **3.** a son of Yajñabahu (*Bh. Purāṇa*)

**Saumendra** (S) (M) belonging to Soma and Indra.

**Saumila** (S) (M) easily available; substance.

**Saumitra** (S) (M) **1.** son of Sumitrā. **3.** another name for Lakṣmaṇa.

**Saumedhika** (S) (M) **1.** possessed with supernatural wisdom. **2.** a sage.

**Saumyā** (S) (F) **1.** related to the moon. **2.** calm; tranquil; beautiful; pleasing; gentle; a pearl. **3.** the 5 stars in Orions head; another name for Durgā; Arabian Jasmine (*Jasminum* *sambac*)

**Saumya** (S) (M) 1. related to the moon. 2. handsome; pleasing; gentle; soft; mild; auspicious; brilliant. 3. a division of the earth; *Desmodium gangeticum*; *Hedychium specatum*; Couch grass (*Cynodon dactylon*)

**Saumyī** (S) (F) moonshine.

**Śaunaka** (S) (M) 1. of Śunaka. 3. a celebrated grammarian and teacher of Kātyāyana; according to the *Viṣṇu Purāṇa* he was the son of Gṛtsamada and created the 4 castes; a renowned āćarya of the Bhṛgu family who was the son of Śunaka (*M. Bh.*); a Brāhmin who went to the forest with Yudhiṣṭhira (*M. Bh.*)

**Saunandā** (S) (F) 1. sweet natured. 3. the wife of Vatsaprī (*Mā. Purāṇa*)

**Saunanda** (S) (M) 1. born of a good milkman. 3. the club of Balarāma.

**Saunandin** (S) (M) 1. possessing Saunanda. 3. another name for Balarāma.

**Saura** (S) (M) 1. sacred to the sun; celestial; divine. 3. another name for the planet Saturn.

**Saurabha** (S) (M) fragrant; *Zanthoxylum alatum*.

**Saurabheyī** (S) (F) 1. of Surabhī. 3. an apsarā (*M. Bh.*)

**Saurabhī** (S) (F) 1. possessing fragrance. 3. the cow daughter of Surabhi and one of the 4 cows that protect the 4 directions, her's being the east (*M. Bh.*)

**Saurama** (S) (M) the Vedic mantra of Sūrya.

**Saurati** (S) (F) 1. always pleasing. 3. a rāgiṇi.

**Saurava** (S) (M) sweet sounding.

**Śaurava** (S) (M) belonging to the brave.

**Śauri** (S) (M) 1. heroic; of the brave. 3. patronymic of Vasudeva the son of Śūrasena (*Bhā. Purāṇa*); another name for the sun, Balarāma and Viṣṇu-Kṛṣṇa.

**Sauri** (S) (M) 1. son of the Sun. 3. another name for Saturn.

**Saurika** (S) (M) 1. heavenly; celestial. 3. another name for Saturn.

**Sauriratna** (S) (M) 1. Saturn stone. 2. sapphire.

**Śaurya** (S) (M) heroism; might; prowess; valour.

**Śausā** (S) (M) praise; wish; eulogium; desire.

**Sauśruti** (S) (M) 1. born of scriptures. 2. pious. 3. the brother of King Suśarmā of Trigarta (*M. Bh.*)

**Sausthava** (S) (M) excellence; superior goodness; cleverness.

**Sauti** (S) (M) 1. son of a charioteer. 3. the son of sage Romaharṣana and the arranger of the Mahābhārata; another name for Karṇa (*M. Bh.*)

**Śauṭīra** (S) (M) liberal; munificent; hero; ascetic; proud.

**Sautraman** (S) (M) belonging to Indra.

**Sauvāna** (S) (M) 1. celestial; heavenly. 3. the grandson of Buddha and son of Rāhula.

**Sauvarṇa** (S) (F) made of gold.

**Sauvasa** (S) (F) a fragrant species of Tulasi (*Ocimum sanctum*)

**Sauvīra** (S) (M) 1. of Sauvīra. 3. another name for Jayadratha.

**Sauvīraja** (S) (M) 1. son of Sauvīra. 3. another name for Jayadratha.

**Sauvīrarāja** (S) (M) 1. lord of Sauvīra. 3. another name for Jayadratha.

**Sauvīrī** (S) (F) 1. daughter of a hero; princess of the Sauvīras. 3. the wife of King Manasyu of the Purū dynasty (*M. Bh.*)

**Savadammā** (S) (F) goddess of the weavers in Coimbatore who is regarded as an incarnation of Pārvatī.

**Savai** (S) (M) an instigator; stimulator.

**Śavakrit** (S) (M) 1. corpse maker. 3. another name for Kṛṣṇa.

**Sāvana** (S) (M) 1. institutor of a sacrifice. 3. another name for Varuṇa.

**Savana** (S) (M) 1. fire. 3. a son of Vasiṣṭha (*V. Purāṇa*); a son of Manu Svāyambhuva (*H. Purāṇa*); a son of Priyavrata and Surūpā and the husband of Suvedā (*D. Bhāgavata*); a son of Bhṛgu Muni (*M. Bh.*)

**Sāvanta** (S) (M) 1. employer. 3. a king in the Pṛthu dynasty who was the son of Yuvanāśva and father of Bṛhadaśva (*D. Bhāgavata*)

**Savarammā** (Kannada) (F) 1. mother of weavers; goddess who rides on horseback. 3. another name for Maheśvarammā or Pārvatī.

**Savarṇā** (S) (F) 1. similar in colour; of the

same appearance. 3. the woman substituted by Saraṇyū for herself as the wife of Sūrya and later called Ćhāyā; the daughter of Samudra and wife of sage Prāćinabarhis, she was the mother of the Praćetas (*V. Purāṇa*)

**Sāvarṇa** (S) (M) 1. belonging to the same colour, tribe or caste. 3. the 8th Manu who was the son of Sūrya and Suvarṇā; a hermit in the court of Yudhiṣṭhira (*M. Bh.*)

**Sāvarṇi** (S) (M) 1. of the same colour. 3. a hermit in the council of Indra (*M. Bh.*); the 8th Manu.

**Śavas** (S) (M) strength; power; might; prowess; valour; heroism.

**Savāsa** (S) (M) scented; perfumed.

**Śavasāna** (S) (M) 1. strong; vigorous; powerful. 2. road.

**Śavasī** (S) (M) 1. the strong one. 3. Indra's mother.

**Sāverī** (S) (F) 1. with saffron. 3. a rāgiṇī.

**Savibhāsa** (S) (M) 1. having great lustre. 3. one of the 7 suns (*V. Purāṇa*)

**Sāvinī** (S) (F) 1. one who prepares soma; nectar giving. 3. a river.

**Savīra** (S) (M) 1. possessed with many warriors; having followers. 2. a leader.

**Śāvirī** (S) (M) 1. moving, motivating. 3. a rāga.

**Savīrya** (S) (M) full of strength; powerful; mighty.

**Savitā** (S) (M) 1. the sun. 3. a son of Kaśyapa and Aditi who is an āditya and the husband of Pṛṣṇī, he is the father of the 3 great sacrifices Agnihotra, Paśusoma and Ćāturmāsya (*V. Purāṇa*)

**Savitara** (S) (M) resembling the sun.

**Savitṛ** (S) (M) 1. rouser; stimulator. 3. a sun deity personified in the Vedas as the vivifying power of the sun, also reckoned as one among the ādityas and worshipped as lord of all creatures delivering his votaries from sin, he is the husband of Pṛṣṇi (*M. Bh.*)

**Sāvitra** (S) (M) 1. belonging to the sun. 2. fire; oblation; embryo. 3. one of the 11 rudras (*M. Bh.*); one of the 8 Vasus (*M. Bh.*); a peak of Mount Sumeru adorned with gems (*M. Bh.*); another name for Karṇa.

**Savitrī** (S) (F) 1. producer. 2. mother.

**Sāvitrī** (S) (F) 1. solar power. 2. a hymn addressed to the sun; ray of light; solar ray; the ring finger. 3. a prayer dedicated to Savitṛ or Sūrya (*Ṛg Veda*); the daughter of the sun married to Brahmā in some Purāṇas, Sāvitrī, Gāyatrī and Sarasvatī are the same; a handmaid of Devī Umā (*M. Bh.*); the daughter of King Aśvapati and Mālatī of Madra and the wife of Satyavān of Śālva, she is considered a model of devotion (*M. Bh.*); a wife of Śiva; a form of Prākṛti; a daughter of Dakṣa and the wife of Dharma (*V. Purāṇa*); a wife of Kaśyapa; the wife of King Bhoja of Dhārā; the daughter of Aṣṭāvakra (*K. Sāgara*)

**Sāvitrikā** (S) (F) 1. solar power. 3. a Śakti.

**Savya** (S) (M) 1. left-handed. 3. Indra incarnated as a son of Aṅgiras (*Ṛg Veda*); another name for Viṣṇu.

**Savyasāćin** (S) (M) 1. able to aim with the left hand; ambidextrous. 3. another name for Arjuna (*M. Bh.*); White Murdah (*Terminalia citrina*)

**Savyasivya** (S) (M) 1. stitching with the left hand. 3. an asura son of Vipraćitti and Siṅhikā (*Br. Purāṇa*)

**Sāya** (S) (M) 1. close of the day. 3. evening personified as the son of Puṣpārṇa and Doṣā or a son of Dhātṛ and Kuhū (*Bh. Purāṇa*)

**Sāyaka** (S) (M) 1. fit to be hurled. 2. missile; arrow; 5 *saccharum sara*, the latitude of the sky.

**Śāyamā** (S) (F) 1. sleeping goddess. 3. a form of Durgā worshipped by the tāntrikas; a daughter of Meru considered an incarnation of Gaṅgā; a goddess who executes the commands of the 6th Arhat; another name for Yamunā.

**Sayana** (S) (M) 1. binding. 3. a son of Viśvāmitra (*M. Bh.*)

**Sāyaṇa** (S) (M) 1. possessing arrows. 2. companion. 3. a commentator of the Vedas in the court of Bukka I of Vijayanagara (14th century A.D.)

**Sayanti** (S) (M) controlling.

**Sāyasūrya** (S) (M) 1. brought by the evening sun. 2. guest.

**Śayu** (S) (M) 1. sleeping; resting. 3. a person protected by the aśvins; a ṛṣi (*Ṛg Veda*)

**Sayuj** (S) (M) **1.** united. **2.** companion; comrade.

**Sećaka** (S) (M) **1.** sprinkler. **2.** cloud. **3.** a nāga of the family of Dhṛtarāṣṭra (*M. Bh.*)

**Seduka** (S) (M) **1.** existent. **3.** a king of ancient India (*M. Bh.*)

**Śekhara** (S) (M) crown of the head; diadem; crest; chaplet; peak; best; chief.

**Śelvamaṇi** (S) (M) beautiful jewel.

**Śelvarāj** (S) (M) most handsome.

**Semantī** (S) (F) the Indian White Rose (*Rosa alba*)

**Semantikā** (S) (F) the Indian White Rose (*Rosa alba*)

**Śemuśī** (S) (F) intellect; understanding; wisdom.

**Sena** (S) (M) **1.** army. **2.** leader; body. **3.** the son of King Ṛṣabha (*Bhāgavata*)

**Senā** (S) (F) **1.** missile; dart. **2.** spear; army. **3.** Indra's wife personified as his thunderbolt (*T. Samhitā*); Kārttikeya's wife personified as armed force (*Ṛg Veda*); a queen of Śrāvasti and mother of Śambhavanātha Jaina Tīrthaṅkara (*J. Literature*)

**Senābindu** (S) (M) **1.** pivot of the army. **3.** a Kṣatriya king who was a partial incarnation of the asura Tuhuṇḍa (*M. Bh.*); a warrior of the Pāṇḍavas (*M. Bh.*)

**Senaćitta** (S) (M) **1.** war minded. **3.** a Bharata dynasty king who was the son of Viśada and the father of Rućirāśva (*Bhāgavata*)

**Senāhan** (S) (M) **1.** destroying armies. **3.** a son of Śambara (*H. Purāṇa*)

**Senajit** (S) (M) **1.** vanquishing armies. **3.** a son of Kṛśāśva (*Bh. Purāṇa*); a son of Kṛṣṇa (*H. Purāṇa*); a son of Viśvajit (*V. Purāṇa*); a son of Bṛhatkarman (*V. Purāṇa*); a son of Kṛśāśva (*Bhā. Purāṇa*); a son of Viśāda (*Bh. Purāṇa*)

**Senajitā** (S) (F) **1.** vanquishing armies. **3.** an apsarā.

**Senaka** (S) (M) **1.** soldier. **3.** a son of Śambara (*H. Purāṇa*)

**Senānī** (S) (M) **1.** leader; general; chief. **3.** a rudra (*H. Purāṇa*); a son of Śambara (*H. Purāṇa*); a son of Dhṛtarāṣṭra (*M. Bh.*); another name for Kārttikeya.

**Senapāla** (S) (M) protector of the army.

**Senāpati** (S) (M) **1.** leader of an army. **3.** a son of Dhṛtarāṣṭra; another name for Kārttikeya and Śiva.

**Senāskandha** (S) (M) **1.** company of an army; a battalion. **3.** a son of Śambara (*H. Purāṇa*)

**Senika** (S) (M) soldier.

**Sephalendu** (S) (M) moon among the brave.

**Śephālī** (S) (F) **1.** with drowsy bees. **2.** very fragrant; the Coral Jasmine tree (*Nyctanthes arbor-tristis*)

**Śephālikā** (S) (F) the fruit of *Nyctanthes arbor-tristis.*

**Śephara** (S) (M) charming; delightful.

**Śeṣa** (S) (M) **1.** remainder. **2.** the rest. **3.** a 1000 headed serpent regarded as the emblem of eternity and represented as forming the couch of Viṣṇu, also known as Ananta, he was partially incarnated as Balabhadrarāma; a prajāpati (*Rāmāyaṇa*); one of the mythical elephants that support the earth.

**Śeṣabhūṣaṇa** (S) (M) **1.** having Śeṣa as an ornament. **3.** another name for Viṣṇu.

**Śeṣadeva** (S) (M) lord of serpents; the god Śeṣa.

**Śesādri** (S) (M) the mountain of Śeṣa.

**Śeṣagiri** (S) (M) the mountain of Śeṣa.

**Śeṣaka** (S) (M) Śeṣa.

**Śeṣānanda** (S) (M) **1.** delighting Śeṣa. **3.** another name for Viṣṇu.

**Śeṣānanta** (S) (M) Śeṣa, the lord of serpents.

**Śeṣanārāyaṇa** (S) (M) Viṣṇu and Śeṣa conjoined.

**Seśvara** (S) (M) believing in god; attaining the favour of gods; theist.

**Setu** (S) (M) **1.** bond; dam; mound; dike. **2.** Rāma's bridge; an established institution; the sacred symbol Om. **3.** a son of Druhyu and brother of Babhru (*H. Purāṇa*); a Bharata dynasty king who was the son of Babhru and the father of Anārabdha (*Bhāgavata*)

**Setuprada** (S) (M) **1.** one who binds. **2.** bridge builder. **3.** another name for Kṛṣṇa.

**Sevā** (S) (F) worship; homage; reverence; devotion.

**Śevā** (S) (F) prosperity; happiness; homage.

**Śevadhi** (S) (M) 1. treasure receptacle; wealth; jewel. 3. one of the 9 treasures of Kubera.

**Śevalinī** (S) (F) 1. with a moss like surface. 3. a river.

**Śevāra** (S) (M) treasury.

**Sevatī** (S) (F) the Indian White Rose (*Rosa alba*)

**Seya** (S) (M) 1. obtaining; achieving. 3. a son of Viśvāmitra (*M. Bh.*)

**Seyana** (S) (M) 1. obtainer; achiever. 3. a son of Viśvāmitra (*M. Bh.*)

**Śībhara** (S) (M) fine rain.

**Śībhya** (S) (M) 1. moving quickly. 2. bull. 3. another name for Śiva.

**Śibi** (S) (M) 1. palanquin. 3. a country; a ṛṣi and part author of *Ṛg Veda* (x); a king renowned for his liberality (*M. Bh.*); a son of Indra (*M. Bh.*); Indra in the 4th Manvantara (*V. Purāṇa*); a son of Manu Ćākṣuṣa (*Bhā. Purāṇa*); a daitya who was the son of Sanhrāda and grandson of Hiraṇyākaśipu (*A. Purāṇa*); a king in the Uśīnara dynasty who was the father of Bhadra, Suvīra, Kekaya and Vṛṣadarbha (*Bhāgavata*); an ancient rājarṣi who was the son of Uśīnara and Mādhavī and the father of Kapotaroma.

**Śići** (S) (F) flame; glow.

**Siddhā** (S) (F) 1. one who has attained power in penance. 3. a form of the devī; a yoginī.

**Siddha** (S) (M) 1. accomplished; successful; perfected; sacred; divine; effective; pure; one who has attained power in penance. 3. semi-divine beings who occupy the sky north of the sun (*V. Purāṇa*); a gandharva son of Kaśyapa and Prādhā (*M. Bh.*); another name for Śiva; *Altingia excelsa*.

**Siddhadeva** (S) (M) 1. perfected deity. 3. another name for Śiva.

**Siddhaheman** (S) (M) perfected gold.

**Siddhalakṣmī** (S) (F) 1. perfect fortune. 3. a form of Lakṣmī.

**Siddhambā** (S) (F) 1. blessed mother. 3. another name for Durgā.

**Siddhānanda** (S) (M) one who has achieved happiness.

**Siddhanātha** (S) (M) lord of power.

**Siddhāṅganā** (S) (F) an accomplished woman; a female siddha.

**Siddhānta** (S) (M) 1. established end. 2. principle; moral; doctrine.

**Siddhapati** (S) (M) lord of perfection; lord of power.

**Siddhapātra** (S) (M) 1. accomplished devotee. 3. a warrior of Skanda (*M. Bh.*)

**Siddharāja** (S) (M) lord of perfection; lord of power.

**Siddhārtha** (S) (M) 1. one who has accomplished his aim. 3. a king who was a partial incarnation of the asura Krodhavaśa (*M. Bh.*); a warrior of Skanda (*M. Bh.*); a minister of Daśaratha (*V. Rāmāyaṇa*); Gautama Buddha in his childhood; the father of the 24th Arhat of the present Avasarpinī (*K. Sāgara*); Wild Turnip (*Brassica campestris*)

**Siddharthā** (S) (F) 1. attainer of meaning; attainer of wealth. 3. the queen of Ayodhyā and mother of Abhinanda Jaina Tīrthaṅkara (*J. Literature*)

**Siddhasena** (S) (M) 1. with a divine army. 3. another name for Kārttikeya.

**Siddhasevita** (S) (M) 1. honoured by Siddhas. 3. a form of Bhairava.

**Siddhavatī** (S) (F) 1. achieving perfection. 3. a goddess.

**Siddhavīrya** (S) (M) possessing perfect strength.

**Siddhayogin** (S) (M) 1. the perfect yogi. 3. another name for Śiva.

**Siddhayoginī** (S) (F) 1. perfect yoginī. 3. another name for Manasā.

**Siddheśa** (S) (M) lord of the blessed.

**Siddheśvara** (S) (M) 1. lord of the blessed. 3. another name for Śiva; Peacock flower (*Caesalpinia pulcherrima*)

**Siddheśvarī** (S) (F) goddess of accomplishment.

**Siddhi** (S) (F) 1. accomplishment; performance; fulfilment; prosperity; luck; the acquisition of magical powers; success personified. 3. the wife of Bhaga and mother of Mahiman (*Bhā. Purāṇa*); a daughter of Dakṣa and wife of Dharma (*V. Purāṇa*); a wife of Gaṇeśa; a goddess worshipped for the attainment of any object, she is believed to have been reborn as Kuntī the mother of the Pāṇḍavas (*M. Bh.*); another name for Durgā.

**Siddhi** (S) (M) 1. accomplishment; power; performance; prosperity. 3. the son of the agni Vīra and Sarayū (*M. Bh.*); another name for Śiva (*M. Bh.*)

**Siddhida** (S) (M) 1. conferring felicity. 3. another name for Śiva.

**Siddhidātrī** (S) (F) 1. giver of perfection. 3. a form of Durgā.

**Siddhirūpinī** (S) (F) goddess of achieving all.

**Siddhiśvara** (S) (M) 1. lord of magical power. 3. another name for Śiva.

**Siddhyāyikā** (S) (F) 1. accomplisher; fulfiller; effector. 3. one of the 24 goddesses who execute the commands of the Arhats.

**Sidhra** (S) (M) perfect; good; successful; efficacious.

**Sidhya** (S) (M) auspicious.

**Śīghra** (S) (M) 1. quick; speedy; swift. 3. a son of Agnivarṇa; a solar dynasty king who was the son of Agnipūrṇa and the father of Maru (*Bhāgavata*); another name for Vāyu.

**Śīghraga** (S) (M) 1. moving quickly. 3. a son of Agnivarṇa (*Rāmayaṇa*); another name for the sun; a son of Sampāti (*M. Purāṇa*)

**Śīghriya** (S) (M) 1. quick; fleet. 3. another name for Viṣṇu and Śiva.

**Sikata** (S) (M) 1. sand; gravel. 3. an ancient hermit (*M. Bh.*)

**Śikhā** (S) (F) crest; plume; topknot; flame; ray of light; pinnacle; peak.

**Śikha** (S) (M) 1. crest; pinnacle; peak. 3. a serpent demon.

**Śikhādhara** (S) (M) 1. with a topknot. 2. peacock. 3. another name for Manjuśrī.

**Śikhāmaṇi** (S) (M) 1. crest jewel. 2. chief; best.

**Śikhaṇḍī** (S) (F) 1. crested. 2. Rosary Pea (*Abrus precatorius*); Yellow Jasmine (*Jasminum humile*)

**Śikhaṇḍiketu** (S) (M) 1. with a peacock emblem. 3. another name for Skanda.

**Śikhaṇḍin** (S) (M) 1. tufted; crested; peacock; arrow. 2. attaining a certain degree of emancipation. Rosary Pea (*Abrus precatorius*); Yellow Jasmine (*Jasminum bignoniaceum*); a ṛṣi who is one of the stars of the Great Bear; a son of Drupada born as a female but changed into a male who was the reincarnation of Ambā (*M. Bh.*); another name for Viṣṇu-Kṛṣṇa.

**Śikhaṇḍinī** (S) (F) 1. peahen. 3. an apsarā daughter of Kaśyapa; the wife of King Antardhāna and the mother of Havirdhāna (*V. Purāṇa*)

**Śikharavāsinī** (S) (F) 1. dwelling on a peak. 3. another name for Durgā.

**Śikharin** (S) (M) 1. pointed; peaked; crested. 2. resembling the buds of the Arabian Jasmine; mountain.

**Śikharīndra** (S) (M) the chief of mountains.

**Śikharinī** (S) (F) 1. eminent; excellent. 2. Arabian Jasmine.

**Śikhāvān** (S) (M) 1. with a topknot of hair; crested. 3. a maharṣi in the court of Yudhiṣṭhira (*M. Bh.*); another name for Agni.

**Śikhāvarta** (S) (M) 1. surrounded by peaks. 3. a yakṣa in the court of Kubera (*M. Bh.*)

**Śikhidhvaja** (S) (M) 1. peacock marked. 3. a king of Mālavā and husband of Ćūḍālā; another name for Kārttikeya.

**Śikhin** (S) (M) 1. crested; reaching the summit of knowledge; the number 3. 2. peacock; arrow; a religious mendicant. 3. a nāga of the Kaśyapa dynasty (*M. Bh.*); Indra under Manu Tāmasa (*Mā. Purāṇa*); the 2nd Buddha (*L. Vistara*); another name for Kāma.

**Śikhivāhana** (S) (M) 1. with a peacock as vehicle. 3. another name for Kārttikeya.

**Sikkarī** (S) (M) 1. sprinkler. 2. the peacock.

**Śikra** (S) (F) skilful; clever; artistic; able.

**Śikṣa** (S) (M) 1. education; knowledge. 2. training 3. a king of the gandharvas (*Rāmāyaṇa*)

**Śikṣaka** (S) (M) 1. one who bestows knowledge; teacher; preceptor. 3. a warrior of Skanda (*M. Bh.*)

**Śikṣākara** (S) (M) 1. instruction causing. 2. teacher. 3. another name for Vyāsa.

**Śikṣitā** (S) (M) docile; skilfull; clever; modest; studied.

**Śikṣu** (S) (M) helpful; liberal.

**Śikvas** (S) (M) mighty; powerful; able.
**Śīlā** (S) (F) 1. calm; tranquil; good natured; good character. 3. the wife of Kauṇḍinya.
**Śilā** (S) (F) 1. rock. 3. a daughter of Dharma and wife of Marīći (*Vā. Purāṇa*)
**Śila** (S) (M) 1. gathering corn. 3. a son of Pāryātra.
**Śīla** (S) (M) moral conduct; disposition; custom; character; piety; virtue.
**Śīlabhadra** (S) (M) eminent in virtue.
**Śīladhara** (S) (M) virtuous; honourable.
**Śilādhara** (S) (M) 1. carrying stone. 3. the chamberlain of Himavata.
**Śīladhārin** (S) (M) 1. virtue possessor. 3. another name for Śiva.
**Śīlāditya** (S) (M) sun of virtue.
**Śīlakīrti** (S) (M) glory of virtue.
**Śīlaṅga** (S) (M) with virtuous features.
**Śīlanidhi** (S) (M) treasury of virtue.
**Śilaukas** (S) (M) 1. dwelling in rock. 3. another name for Garuḍa.
**Śīlavān** (S) (M) 1. virtuous; moral. 3. a divine maharṣi (*M. Bh.*)
**Śīlavatī** (S) (F) 1. virtuous; moral. 3. the wife of Ugraśravas renowned for her fidelity and chastity.
**Śilāyūpa** (S) (M) 1. high mountain. 3. a son of Viśvāmitra (*M. Bh.*)
**Śilin** (S) (M) 1. rocky; mountain like. 3. a nāga in the Takṣaka dynasty (*M. Bh.*)
**Śīlin** (S) (M) 1. virtuous. 2. moral; honest.
**Śilīśa** (S) (M) lord of the mountain; with a rocklike will.
**Śilpā** (S) (F) vareigated.
**Śilparāja** (S) (M) 1. king of artisans. 3. another name for Viśvakarman.
**Śilpī** (S) (F) artisan.
**Śilpikā** (S) (F) skilled in art.
**Śilūṣa** (S) (M) 1. *Aegle marmelos*. 3. ṛṣi who was an early teacher of dancing.
**Sīmā** (S) (F) boundary; boundary of a field; bank; shore; horizon; summit; rule of morality.
**Sīmanta** (S) (M) 1. boundary; limit; parting of the hair. 3. a son of King Bhadrasena.
**Sīmantinī** (S) (F) 1. with hair parted. 3. a wife of King Ćitratāngada (*M. Bh.*)
**Simbala** (S) (F) 1. a small pod. 2. the flower of the Śālmali tree (*Bombax malabaricum*); the preparer of sacrificial food.
**Śimidā** (S) (F) 1. giving work. 3. a demon.
**Śimyu** (S) (M) vigorous; aggressive.
**Sindhū** (S) (F) 1. ocean; sea; river. 3. a river famous in the Purāṇas whose goddess sits in the court of Varuṇa.
**Sindhu** (S) (M) 1. river; ocean; sea. 2. number 4. 3. a rāga; a king of the gandharvas (*Rāmāyaṇa*); another name for Varuṇa and Viṣṇu.
**Sindhudvīpa** (S) (M) 1. island in the ocean. 3. a solar dynasty king who was the son of Jahnu and the father of Balākāṣva (*M. Bh.*)
**Sindhujā** (S) (F) 1. ocean born. 3. another name for Lakṣmī.
**Sindhuka** (S) (M) 1. marine. 3. a king (*V. Purāṇa*)
**Sindhukanyā** (S) (F) 1. daughter of the ocean. 3. another name for Lakṣmī.
**Sindhula** (S) (M) 1. procurer of ocean; one who brings the streams. 3. the father of Bhoja.
**Sindhumātṛ** (S) (F) 1. mother of streams. 3. another name for Sarasvatī.
**Sindhunandana** (S) (M) 1. son of the ocean. 3. another name for the moon.
**Sindhunātha** (S) (M) 1. lord of rivers. 2. the ocean.
**Sindhupati** (S) (M) 1. lord of the waters. 3. another name for Jayadratha.
**Sindhuputra** (S) (M) 1. son of the ocean. 3. another name for the moon.
**Sindhurāja** (S) (M) 1. king of rivers. 2. the ocean. 3. another name for Jayadratha.
**Sindhusauvīrabhartā** (S) (M) 1. chief of Sindhu-Sauvīra. 3. another name for Jayadratha.
**Sindhuvīrya** (S) (M) 1. warrior of the Sindhus. 3. a king of the Madras (*Mā. Purāṇa*)
**Sindhuvṛṣa** (S) (M) 1. drinking the ocean. 3. another name for Viṣṇu.
**Śineyu** (S) (M) 1. white coloured. 2. shining. 3. a son of Uśat (*H. Purāṇa*)
**Siṅha** (S) (M) 1. the powerful one. 2. lion; the zodiac sign of Leo; hero; chief. 3. a son of Kṛṣṇa (*Bhā. Purāṇa*); a king of the

vidyādharas (K. Sāgara)

Siṅhabāhu (S) (M) 1. with the arms of a lion. 2. very powerful. 3. the father of Vijaya the founder of the first Buddhist dynasty in Sri Lanka (B. Literature)

Siṅhabala (S) (M) with the strength of a lion.

Siṅhaćandra (S) (M) 1. moon amongst the lions. 2. most courageous. 3. a king who helped Yudhiṣṭhira (M. Bh.)

Siṅhadanṣṭra (S) (M) 1. lion toothed. 2. an arrow. 3. another name for Śiva.

Siṅhadatta (S) (M) 1. lion given. 3. an asura (K. Sāgara)

Sinhadhvaja (S) (M) 1. lion bannered. 3. a Buddha.

Siṅhaga (S) (M) 1. going like a lion. 3. another name for Śiva.

Siṅhagāminī (S) (F) 1. walking with a lion's gait. 3. a gandharva maiden (K. Vyuha)

Siṅhaghoṣa (S) (M) 1. the roar of a lion. 3. a Buddha.

Siṅhagiri (S) (M) 1. the lion-mountain; an elevated lion. 3. the monk who succeeded Dinna as the head of the Jaina church (J. Literature)

Siṅhagupta (S) (M) 1. lion guarded. 3. the father of Vāgabhaṭa.

Siṅhahanu (S) (M) lion jawed.

Siṅhakarman (S) (M) 1. behaving like a lion. 2. achieving lion like deeds.

Siṅhakeli (S) (M) 1. sporting like a lion. 3. a Bodhisattva.

Sinhaketu (S) (M) 1. lion bannered. 3. a warrior of the Pāṇḍava army (M. Bh.); a Bodhisattva.

Sinhamati (S) (F) lion hearted; brave.

Siṅhamukha (S) (M) 1. lion faced. 3. an attendant of Śiva (H. Purāṇa)

Siṅhanāda (S) (M) 1. lion roar. 3. an asura (K. Śagara); a son of Rāvaṇa (B. Rāmāyaṇa); a king of Malaya; another name for Śiva.

Siṅhasena (S) (M) 1. with an army of lions. 3. a commander of the army of Kārtavīryārjuna (Br. Purāṇa); a Pāñćāla warrior (M. Bh.); a king of Ayodhyā and father of Jaina Tīrthaṅkara Anantanātha (J. Literature)

Siṅhavāhana (S) (M) 1. drawn by lions. 3. another name for Śiva.

Sinhavāhinī (S) (F) 1. drawn by lions. 3. another name for Durgā.

Siṅhavakra (S) (M) 1. lion faced. 3. a rākṣasa (Rāmāyaṇa)

Sinhavikrama (S) (M) 1. horse. 3. a king of the vidyādharas (K. Sāgara)

Siṅhayānā (S) (F) 1. with a car drawn by lions. 3. another name for Durgā.

Siṅhendra (S) (M) mighty lion.

Siṅhī (S) (F) lioness.

Siṅhika (S) (F) 1. lioness. 3. a daughter of Dakṣa and wife of Kaśyapa and mother of Rāhu (M. Bh.); a form of Dakṣāyaṇī; a rākṣasī who was the daughter of Kaśyapa and Diti and the wife of Vipraćitti and the mother of Rāhu and Ketu (M. Bh.)

Siṅhinī (S) (F) 1. lioness. 3. a Buddhist goddess.

Siṅhīya (S) (M) small lion.

Śini (S) (M) 1. bright. 2. of the race of bright people. 3. a king of the Yādava dynasty (M. Bh.); a son of Sumitra (M. Bh.); a son of Garga (H. Purāṇa); the father of Sātyaka (Purāṇas)

Sinivāk (S) (M) 1. illustrious preacher. 3. a hermit in the council of Yudhiṣṭhira (M. Bh.)

Sinīvāli (S) (M) 1. the first day of the new moon. 3. a goddess presiding over fecundity who in later Vedic texts is the presiding deity of the first day of the new moon; daughter of Aṅgiras (M. Bh.); the wife of Dhātṛ and mother of Darśa (Bh. Purāṇa)

Sinīvāli (S) (F) 1. the day before the new moon. 2. goddess of easy birth; goddess of fecundity. 3. a daughter of Aṅgiras and Smṛtī, she is invoked in the Ṛg Veda with Sarasvatī and Rākā; in later Vedic texts she is the deity of the 1st day of the new moon and a wife of Viṣṇu; the wife of Dhātṛ and mother of Darśa (Bhā. Purāṇa); a river (Mā. Purāṇa); a daughter of Bṛhaspatī and Śubhā given in marriage to Kardama but abandoned him and lived with Soma the moon (Vā. Purāṇa)

Śiñja (S) (F) 1. tinkle; jingle. 2. the tinkling of

silver ornaments.

**Śinśapā** (S) (F) 1. the Sheesham tree (*Dalbergia sissoo*); Aśoka tree (*Saraca indica*). 3. a daughter of a king of Gāndhāra and a wife of Kṛṣṇa.

**Śinśumar** (S) (F) 1. porpoise. 3. a daughter of a Gāndhāra king and wife of Kṛṣṇa.

**Śiphā** (S) (F) 1. the lash of a whip. 2. a tuft of hair on the crown of the head. 3. a river extolled in the *Ṛg Veda*

**Śiphālikā** (S) (F) the Coral Jasmine tree (*Nyctantes arbor tristis*)

**Śipi** (S) (M) a ray of light.

**Śipiviṣṭa** (S) (M) 1. pervaded by rays of light. 3. another name for Rudra-Śiva and Viṣṇu.

**Śiprā** (S) (F) 1. cheeks. 2. the visor of a helmet; the nose. 3. a holy river.

**Śipraka** (S) (M) 1. full cheeked. 3. the 1st king of the Āndhrakas.

**Sīradhvaja** (S) (M) 1. plough bannered. 3. a son of Hrasvaroman (*V. Purāṇa*); another name for Janaka and Balarāma.

**Sīraka** (S) (M) 1. plough. 2. the sun.

**Sīrapāṇi** (S) (M) 1. plough handed. 3. another name for Balarāma.

**Sīrāyudha** (S) (M) 1. plough handed. 3. another name for Balarāma.

**Sīrin** (S) (M) 1. holding a plough. 3. another name for Balarāma.

**Śirin** (S) (M) Kuśa grass.

**Śiriṇā** (S) (F) night.

**Śiriṣa** (S) (M) Sizzling tree (*Albizzia lebbeck*)

**Śiriṣaka** (S) (M) 1. a serpent residing in the *Acacia sirissa*. 3. a nāga of the Kaśyapa dynasty (*M. Bh.*)

**Śiriśeṣa** (S) (M) 1. with only the head left. 3. another name for Rāhu.

**Śiriṣin** (S) (M) 1. *Acacia sirissa.* 3. a son of Viśvāmitra (*M. Bh.*)

**Śirṇapāda** (S) (M) 1. with shrivelled feet. 3. another name for Yama.

**Śirobhūṣana** (S) (M) head ornament.

**Śirohārin** (S) (M) 1. wearing a garland of heads. 3. another name for Śiva.

**Śiromālin** (S) (M) 1. garlanded with skulls. 3. another name for Śiva.

**Śiromaṇi** (S) (M) crest jewel.

**Śiromauli** (S) (M) crest jewel; eminent; best.

**Śiroratna** (S) (M) crest jewel.

**Sīsara** (S) (M) 1. flown from a straight line. 3. husband of Saramā the dog.

**Śiśaya** (S) (M) liberal; munificent.

**Śiśira** (S) (M) 1. cool; cold; frost; dew; the cold season. 3. a mountain; son of Dhara and Manoharā (*M. Bh.*); son of Medhātithi (*Mā. Purāṇa*); son of the vasu Soma and Manoharā (*M. Bh.*); Velvet Leaf (*Cissampelos pareira*)

**Śiśiraghna** (S) (M) 1. cold destroying. 3. another name for Agni.

**Śiśirakara** (S) (M) 1. cold rayed. 3. another name for the moon.

**Śiśirānśu** (S) (M) 1. having cold rays. 3. another name for the moon.

**Siṣṇu** (S) (M) ready to give.

**Śiṣṭha** (S) (M) 1. polite; modest; taught; commanded; disciplined; cultured; eminent. 3. son of Dhruva and Dhānyā, husband of Succhāyā and father of Kṛpa, Ripuñjaya, Vṛtta and Vṛka (*M. Purāṇa*)

**Śiṣṭi** (S) (M) 1. direction; order; command; punishment. 3. a son of Dhruva and Śambhu (*V. Purāṇa*)

**Śiśu** (S) (M) 1. child; infant. 3. a son of Sāraṇa (*V. Purāṇa*); a son born to the Saptamātṛs due to the blessing of Subrahmaṇya (*M. Bh.*); a descendant of Aṅgiras; another name for Skanda.

**Śiśubhūpati** (S) (M) young prince.

**Śisugandha** (S) (F) 1. with a youthful fragrance. 2. Double Jasmine.

**Śiśukumāra** (S) (M) 1. young prince. 3. a ṛṣi who lived in the form of a crocodile (*P. Brāhmaṇa*); a constellation said to be a starry form of Viṣṇu (*V. Purāṇa*)

**Śiśukumāramukhī** (S) (F) 1. with a face like a young prince. 3. a mother in Skanda's retinue (*M. Bh.*)

**Śiśula** (S) (M) infant; child.

**Śiśumāra** (S) (M) 1. porpoise (*Delphinus gangeticus*); child killer. 3. a collection of stars supposed to represent a dolphin and personified as a son of Doṣa and Śarvarī or as father of Brāhmī the wife of Dhruva (*M. Bh.*)

**Śiśumāramukhī** (S) (F) 1. dolphin faced. 3. a mother in Skanda's retinue.

**Śiśunāga** (S) (M) 1. young snake; young elephant. 3. the first king of the Śiśunāga dynasty and the father of Kākavarṇa (*Vā. Purāṇa*); a king of Magadha (*Bhā. Purāṇa*)

**Śiśunandi** (S) (M) young bull.

**Śiśupāla** (S) (M) 1. child protector. 3. the king of Ćedi who was an incarnation of Jaya, the gatekeeper of Viṣṇu, born as the son of King Damaghoṣa and Śrutaśravas, he was killed by Kṛṣṇa (*Bhāgavata*)

**Śiśupalātmaja** (S) (M) 1. son of Śiśupala. 3. another name for Dhṛṣṭaketu.

**Śiśupriya** (S) (M) 1. dear to children. 2. treacle; the White Waterlily (*Nymphaea alba*)

**Śiśuroman** (S) (M) 1. having hair like that of a child. 3. a nāga in the family of Takṣaka (*M. Bh.*)

**Śita** (S) (M) 1. good natured. 3. a son of Viśvāmitra (*M. Bh.*)

**Sita** (S) (M) 1. bright; white; candid; pure. 3. an attendant of Skanda (*M. Bh.*); another name for the planet Venus.

**Sītā** (S) (F) 1. furrow; the track of a ploughshare. 3. a form of Dākṣāyaṇī; the eastern branch of the 4 mythical branches of the heavenly Gaṅgā; the wife of Rāma who is considered the incarnation of Māhālakṣmī, found in a field by King Janaka of Mithilā, she married Rāma of Ayodhyā and was the mother of Lava and Kuśa (*Rāmāyaṇa*)

**Sitā** (S) (F) 1. white. 2. white sugar; moonlight; handsome woman; Durvā Grass; Arabian Jasmine; the Gaṅgā river. 3. one of the 8 Buddhist devīs.

**Śītabhānu** (S) (M) 1. cool rayed. 3. another name for the moon.

**Sitābja** (S) (M) White Lotus (*Nelumbium speciosum*)

**Sitakamala** (S) (M) White Lotus (*Nelumbium speciosum*)

**Śītakara** (S) (M) 1. cool rayed. 3. another name for the moon.

**Sitakara** (S) (M) 1. white rayed. 3. another name for the moon.

**Sitakarman** (S) (M) pure in deed.

**Sitakeśa** (S) (M) 1. whitehaired. 3. a dānava (*H. Purāṇa*)

**Śītakiraṇa** (S) (M) 1. cool rayed. 3. another name for the moon.

**Śītalā** (S) (F) 1. of cold disposition. 2. sand. 3. the goddess of smallpox.

**Śītala** (S) (M) 1. cool; cold. 2. calm; gentle; free from passion; the wind. 3. *Michelia champaka*; the 10th Arhat of the present Avasarpiṇī; another name for the moon.

**Sītālakṣmī** (S) (F) Sītā and Lakṣmī as one; purity of fortune.

**Sītalammā** (T) (F) 1. mother of purity. 3. village goddess of water.

**Śītalanātha** (S) (M) 1. lord of the gentle. 3. the 10th Jaina Tīrthaṅkara, he was the son of King Dṛḍharatha and Sunandā of Bhādilpura (*J. Literature*)

**Śītalaprasāda** (S) (M) given in the cold season.

**Śītalatā** (S) (F) cooling power.

**Sitamanas** (S) (M) pure hearted.

**Sitamaṇi** (S) (M) crystal.

**Śītamanjarī** (S) (F) 1. blossom of the cold. 3. the Coral Jasmine tree (*Nyctantes arbor tristis*)

**Sitāmbara** (S) (M) 1. clothed in white. 2. one of the 2 divisions of Jaina monks.

**Sitāmbuja** (S) (M) White Lotus (*Nelumbium speciosum*)

**Sitānana** (S) (M) 1. white faced. 3. an attendant of Śiva; another name for Garuḍa.

**Sītānātha** (S) (M) 1. lord of Sītā. 3. another name for Rāma.

**Sitānṣu** (S) (M) 1. white rayed. 3. another name for the moon.

**Śītanśu** (S) (M) 1. cool rayed. 3. another name for the moon.

**Śītapāṇi** (S) (M) 1. cold handed; cool rayed. 3. another name for the moon.

**Sītāpati** (S) (M) 1. lord of Sītā. 3. another name for Rāma.

**Sitaprabha** (S) (M) white crystal.

**Sītārāma** (S) (M) Sītā and Rāma conjoined.

**Sitarañjana** (S) (M) yellow.

**Sitaraśmi** (S) (M) 1. white rayed. 3. another name for the moon.

**Sitarući** (S) (M) 1. bright. 3. another name for the moon.

**Śītāṣī** (S) (F) 1. cold eater. 3. a river famous in the *Purāṇas* (*M. Bh.*)

**Sitasindhu** (S) (F) 1. pure river. 3. another name for the Gaṅgā.

**Śītaśman** (S) (M) moonstone.

**Sitāśva** (S) (M) 1. with white horses. 3. another name for Arjuna.

**Sitaturaga** (S) (M) 1. white horsed. 3. another name for Arjuna.

**Sitavājin** (S) (M) 1. with white horses. 3. another name for Arjuna.

**Sītāvallabha** (S) (M) 1. beloved of Sītā. 3. another name for Rāma.

**Sitavarman** (S) (M) armoured in purity.

**Sitayāminī** (S) (F) moonlight.

**Sīteśa** (S) (M) 1. lord of Sītā. 3. another name for Rāma.

**Śītikā** (S) (F) coldness.

**Śitikaṇṭha** (S) (M) 1. white necked; blue necked. 3. a nāga (*M. Bh.*); another name for Śiva.

**Sitikanṭha** (S) (M) 1. dark throated. 3. another name for Śiva.

**Śitikeśa** (S) (M) 1. white haired. 3. a warrior of Skanda (*M. Bh.*)

**Śitīkṣu** (S) (M) 1. striving for the earth. 3. a son of Uśanas (*V. Purāṇa*)

**Sitiman** (S) (M) whiteness.

**Śitipṛṣṭha** (S) (M) 1. white backed. 3. a serpent priest.

**Śitiratna** (S) (M) 1. blue gem. 2. sapphire.

**Sitivāsas** (S) (M) 1. dark clothed. 3. another name for Balarāma.

**Sitodara** (S) (M) 1. white bellied. 3. another name for Kubera.

**Sītormilā** (S) (F) Sīta and her sister Ūrmilā conjoined.

**Śītoṣṇā** (S) (F) 1. cold and hot. 3. a demon.

**Śivā** (S) (F) 1. auspicious power; goddess of grace; final emancipation. 3. the wife of Aṅgiras (*M. Bh.*); the wife of the vasu Anila and mother of Manojava and Avijñātagati (*M. Bh.*); the mother of the 22nd Arhat of the present Avasarpinī; a river (*M. Bh.*); a Purāṇic river (*M. Bh.*); the energy of Śiva personified as his wife, Pārvatī, Durgā, Kālī, Umā, and Gaurī.

**Śiva** (S) (M) 1. in whom all things lie; auspicious; propitious; gracious; favourable; benign; kind; friendly; dear. 2. the auspicious one. 3. the destroying and reproducing deity who constitutes the 3rd god of the triad, in his destructive character he is Kāla often identified with time, as reproducer his symbol is the phallus or liṅga, he has three eyes, the middle one in the forehead bears the crescent moon; his thickly matted and coiled hair bears the Gaṅgā, his throat is dark blue, around his neck are garlands of snakes and skulls and in his hand he holds a trident, his consort is Durgā or Pārvatī, Umā, Gaurī, Kālī and his sons are Gaṇeṣa and Kārttikeya, his heaven is Kailāsa mountain in the Himālayas, his ferocious form is Rudra, he is considered the father of the 11 rudras; a son of Medhātithi (*Mā. Purāṇa*); a son of Idhmajīhva (*Bhā. Purāṇa*); *Commiphorra mukul*; *Curcuma longa*; Couch Grass (*Cynodon dactylon*); Prosopis spicigera; Black Myrobalan (*Terminalia chebula*)

**Śivabhadra** (S) (M) an auspicious person; servant of Śiva.

**Śivabhāskara** (S) (M) Śiva compared to the sun.

**Śivadāsa** (S) (M) servant of Śiva.

**Śivadatta** (S) (M) given by Śiva.

**Śivadeva** (S) (M) lord of grace; prosperity and welfare.

**Śivadevī** (S) (F) 1. goddess of grace; prosperity and welfare. 3. a queen of Dvārakā and mother of Nemīnātha Jaina Tīrthaṅkarạ (*J. Literature*)

**Śivadīna** (S) (M) devotee of Śiva.

**Śivadūtī** (S) (F) 1. Śiva's messenger. 3. a form of Durgā (*Mā. Purāṇa*); a yoginī.

**Śivadūtikā** (S) (F) 1. messenger of Śiva. 3. a mother in Skanda's retinue.

**Śivagāmi** (S) (M) follower of Śiva.

**Śivagaṇa** (S) (M) attendant of Śiva.
**Śivagaṅgā** (S) (F) the Gaṅgā flowing through Śiva's hair.
**Śivagati** (S) (M) 1. auspicious; happy; prosperous. 3. a Jaina Arhat of the past Utsarpinī.
**Śivaguru** (S) (M) 1. Śiva the preceptor. 3. the son of Vidyādhirāja and father of Śankarāćārya.
**Śivajī** (S) (M) 1. the auspicious one. 3. a Marāṭhā king.
**Śivakāntā** (S) (F) 1. beloved of Śiva. 3. another name for Durgā.
**Śivakara** (S) (M) 1. causing happiness; auspicious. 3. a Jaina Arhat of past Utsarpinī.
**Śivakāriṇī** (S) (F) 1. doer of benevolent deeds. 2. goddess of welfare. 3. a form of Durgā.
**Śivakarṇī** (S) (F) 1. procurer of prosperity. 3. a mother in Skanda's retinue (*M. Bh.*)
**Śivakeśava** (S) (M) Śiva and Kṛṣṇa conjoined.
**Śivakiṅkara** (S) (M) servant of Śiva.
**Śivakīrtana** (S) (M) 1. Śiva praiser. 3. another name for Viṣṇu.
**Śivakumāra** (S) (M) son of Śiva.
**Śivalāla** (S) (M) son of Śiva.
**Śivālī** (S) (F) 1. beloved of Śiva. 3. another name for Pārvatī.
**Śivam** (S) (M) 1. of Śiva. 2. prosperous; auspicious; graceful.
**Śivamūrti** (S) (M) idol of Śiva.
**Śivānanda** (S) (M) Śiva's joy.
**Śivanārāyaṇa** (S) (M) Śiva and Viṣṇu conjoined.
**Śivanātha** (S) (M) lord Śiva.
**Śivānī** (S) (F) Pārvatī the wife of Śiva.
**Śivāṅka** (S) (M) mark of Śiva.
**Śivaṅkara** (S) (M) 1. punishment personified as an attendant of Śiva. 3. a demon causing illness (*H. Purāṇa*)
**Śivapattra** (S) (M) 1. leaf of prosperity. 2. Red Lotus flower (*Nymphaea rubra*)
**Śivaprakāśa** (S) (M) light of prosperity; light of Śiva.
**Śivaprasāda** (S) (M) 1. given by Śiva. 3. the father of Gaṅgādhara.
**Śivapriyā** (S) (F) 1. beloved of Śiva. 3. another name for Durgā; Rudrakśa tree (*Eleocarpus ganitrus*)
**Śivaputra** (S) (M) 1. son of Śiva. 3. another name for Gaṇeśa.
**Śivarāja** (S) (M) Śiva the lord.
**Śivarāma** (S) (M) pervaded by Śiva; Śiva and Rāma conjoined.
**Śivaratha** (S) (M) the chariot of Śiva.
**Śivarūpa** (S) (M) the form or image of Śiva.
**Śivasahāya** (S) (M) companion of Śiva.
**Śivaśakti** (S) (M) Śiva and his Śakti conjoined.
**Śivaśankara** (S) (M) Śiva the prosperous.
**Śivaśaraṇa** (S) (M) protected by Śiva.
**Śivaśekhara** (S) (M) 1. Śiva's crest. 3. another name for the moon.
**Śivasinha** (S) (M) 1. lion of prosperity and grace. 3. a king of Mithilā.
**Śivaśrī** (S) (M) glory of Śiva.
**Śivasundarī** (S) (F) 1. wife of Śiva. 3. another name for Pārvatī.
**Śivasūnu** (S) (M) 1. son of Śiva. 3. another name for Gaṇeśa and Kārttikeya.
**Śivasvāmin** (S) (M) 1. considering Śiva as master; benign lord. 3. a Sanskṛt poet in the court of the King of Kāśmīra, King Avantivarman (854-888 A.D.)
**Śivatama** (S) (M) most fortunate.
**Śivātmikā** (S) (F) soul of Śiva; consisting of the essence of Śiva.
**Śivavallabhā** (S) (F) 1. loved by Śiva; the Indian white rose (*Rosa alba*). 3. another name for Pārvatī.
**Śivavarman** (S) (M) prosperous protector; protected by Śiva.
**Śivendra** (S) (M) Śiva and Indra conjoined.
**Śiveśvara** (S) (M) god of welfare.
**Śivikā** (S) (F) palanquin.
**Skambha** (S) (M) 1. support; prop. 3. the fulcrum of the universe identified with the Supreme Being.
**Skanda** (S) (M) 1. hopper; attacker. 2. king; clever; quicksilver. 3. Kārttikeya as the god of war (*M. Bh.*); another name for Śiva.
**Skandaguru** (S) (M) 1. father of Skanda.

3. another name for Śiva.

**Skandajit** (S) (M) 1. conqueror of Skanda. 3. another name for Viṣṇu.

**Skandha** (S) (M) 1. shoulder. 3. a nāga of the family of Dhṛtarāṣṭra (*M. Bh.*)

**Skandhākṣa** (S) (M) 1. with eyes like quicksilver. 3. a warrior of Skanda (*M. Bh.*)

**Śliṣṭhi** (S) (M) 1. adherence; connection; embrace. 3. a son of Dhruva and Śambhu and the husband of Sućchāyā and the father of Ripu, Ripuñjaya, Puṇya, Vṛkala and Vṛkatejas (*H. Purāṇa*)

**Smadibha** (S) (M) having followers.

**Smarabhū** (S) (M) arisen from love.

**Smaradhvajā** (S) (F) a bright moonlit night.

**Smaradūtī** (S) (F) 1. messenger of love. 3. a maid of Vṛndā the wife of Jalandhara (*P. Purāṇa*)

**Smaraguru** (S) (M) 1. love preceptor. 3. another name for Viṣṇu.

**Smarahara** (S) (M) 1. destroying Kāma. 3. another name for Śiva.

**Smaranī** (S) (F) 1. act of remembering. 2. a rosary of beads.

**Smarapriyā** (S) (F) 1. dear to Kāma. 3. another name for Rati.

**Smarasakha** (S) (M) 1. love's friend. 2. the spring; the moon.

**Smarodgitha** (S) (M) 1. love song. 3. a son of Devakī (*Bh. Purāṇa*)

**Śmaśānabhairavī** (S) (F) 1. terrible goddess of crematoriums. 3. a form of Durgā.

**Śmaśānakālikā** (S) (F) 1. black goddess of crematoriums. 3. a form of Durgā.

**Śmaśānavāsī** (S) (M) 1. residing in burning grounds. 3. another name for Śiva.

**Smayana** (S) (M) smile; gentle laughter.

**Smerā** (S) (F) smiling; friendly; blossomed; evident; apparent.

**Smita** (S) (M) smiling; blossomed.

**Smiti** (S) (F) a smile; laughter.

**Smṛta** (S) (M) recorded; regarded; remembered.

**Smṛtī** (S) (F) 1. remembrance. 2. a code of laws; desire; wish; understanding. 3. memory personified as the daughter of Dakṣa and wife of Aṅgiras and the mother of Sinīvālī, Kūhū, Rākā and Anumatī (*V. Purāṇa*); in later texts she is the daughter of Dharma and Medhā.

**Smṛtīmālā** (S) (F) garland of memories.

**Sneha** (S) (M) oiliness; affection; tenderness; love.

**Snehakānta** (S) (M) lord of love; beloved of love.

**Snehala** (S) (F) full of affection.

**Snehalatā** (S) (F) vine of love.

**Snehamayī** (S) (F) loving.

**Snehana** (S) (M) 1. anointing; lubricating; affectionate; a friend. 3. another name for the moon and Śiva.

**Snehaprabha** (S) (M) light of love.

**Snehu** (S) (M) 1. moist. 3. another name for the moon.

**Snigdhā** (S) (F) adhesive; tender; friendly; charming; agreeable; loving; attached; glossy; shining; intent; resplendant.

**Śobhā** (S) (F) splendour; brilliance; lustre; beauty; grace; loveliness.

**Śobhaka** (S) (M) brilliant; beautiful.

**Śobhana** (S) (M) 1. handsome; excellent. 3. the son-in- law of Mućukuṇḍa; another name for Śiva and Agni; *Curcuma longa*.

**Śobhanā** (S) (F) 1. beautiful. 2. turmeric. 3. an attendant of Skanda.

**Śobhikā** (S) (F) brilliant; beautiful.

**Śobhin** (S) (M) brilliant; splendid; beautiful.

**Śobhinī** (S) (F) graceful; splendid.

**Śobhiṣṭhā** (S) (F) most beautiful; splendid.

**Śobhita** (S) (M) splendid; beautiful; adorned; embellished.

**Sobodhinī** (S) (F) waking the gods.

**Śoćayantī** (S) (F) 1. inflaming. 3. an apsarā (*T. Brāhmaṇa*)

**Śoći** (S) (F) flame.

**Śoćiṣkeśa** (S) (M) flame haired; another name for Agni and the sun.

**Śoćiṣṭha** (S) (M) most brilliant.

**Śoḍaṣī** (S) (F) 1. 16 year old; having the length of one sixteenth of a man. 3. one of the 12 forms of Durgā; one of the 10 mahāvidyās.

**Sohan** (H) (M) handsome.

**Sohanā** (H) (F) graceful; beautiful.

**Sohanī** (H) (F) 1. beautiful. 3. a rāga.

**Sohelā** (H) (F) beautiful.

**Sohinī** (S) (F) splendid; adorned; beautiful.

**Śoka** (S) (M) 1. flame; glow; heat; sorrow. 3. sorrow personified as the son of death or of Droṇa and Abhimatī (*Purāṇas*)

**Śokarahitā** (S) (F) 1. griefless; without troubles. 3. a form of Durgā.

**Śokī** (S) (F) the night.

**Sollasa** (S) (M) rejoicing; delighted.

**Somā** (S) (F) 1. the Soma plant; moon-like. 2. beautiful. 3. an apsarā (*M. Bh.*)

**Soma** (S) (M) 1. juice. 2. juice of the Soma plant offered in libations to the gods. 3. personified as an important Vedic god identified with Ćandra, the moon and ray of light; water; a son of Agni Bhānu and Niśā (*M. Bh.*); one of the 8 vasus (*V. Purāṇa*); a son of Jarāsandha (*Bhāgavata*); another name for Kubera, Śiva, Yama and Sugrīva.

**Somabandhu** (S) (M) friend of the moon; the white esculent Water Lily (*Nymphaea alba*)

**Somābhā** (S) (F) like the moon.

**Somābhojana** (S) (M) 1. eating Soma. 3. a son of Garuḍa (*M. Bh.*)

**Somabhu** (S) (M) 1. Somaborn; belonging to the family of the moon. 3. the 4th Jaina Vasudeva; another name for Mercury.

**Somaćandra** (S) (M) the tranquil moon.

**Somadā** (S) (F) 1. like a moon. 2. giver of tranquility; procurer of nectar. 3. a gandharvī (*Rāmāyaṇa*)

**Somadatta** (S) (M) 1. given by the moon. 3. an Ikṣvāku dynasty king of Pāñćāla who was the son of Kṛśāśva and the grandson of Sahadeva (*V. Rāmāyaṇa*); a Kuru dynasty king who was the son of Bālhīka and the father of Bhūri, Bhūriśravas, and Śala.

**Somadeva** (S) (M) 1. god of the moon. 3. the author of the *Kathāsaritsāgara*.

**Somadevī** (S) (F) 1. goddess of nectar. 3. the wife of Kāmapāla.

**Somadhara** (S) (M) moon bearing; the sky; heaven.

**Somadhārā** (S) (F) 1. stream of Soma. 3. the Milky Way.

**Somāditya** (S) (M) the sun and moon conjoined.

**Somagarbha** (S) (M) 1. creator of nectar. 3. another name for Viṣṇu.

**Somāhuti** (S) (F) a Soma sacrifice.

**Somaja** (S) (M) 1. son of the moon. 3. another name for the planet Mercury.

**Somaka** (S) (M) 1. little moon. 3. a Pāñcāla king who was the son of Sahadeva and the grandson of Subhāsa (*M. Bh.*); a ṛṣi (*V. Samhitā*); a son of Kṛṣṇa (*Bhā. Purāṇa*)

**Somakānta** (S) (M) as lovely as the moon; beloved of the moon; the moonstone.

**Somākhya** (S) (M) 1. as virtuous as the moon. 2. the Red Lotus (*Nymphaea rubra*)

**Somakīrti** (S) (M) 1. as famous as the moon. 3. a son of Dhṛtarāṣṭra (*M. Bh.*)

**Somāla** (S) (M) soft; placid.

**Somalaka** (S) (M) topaz.

**Somalatā** (S) (F) 1. the creeper from which Soma is extracted. 3. another name for the river Godāvarī; Common Rue (*Ruta graverlens*)

**Somāli** (S) (M) 1. soft; bland. 3. father of Anuśrutaśravas (*V. Purāṇa*)

**Somālī** (S) (F) beloved of the moon.

**Soman** (S) (M) 1. Soma sacrificer. 3. the moon.

**Somanandin** (S) (M) 1. delighted by the moon. 3. an attendant of Śiva.

**Somanātha** (S) (M) 1. lord of the moon. 3. a liṅga of Śiva.

**Somānśu** (S) (M) moonbeam; a shoot of the Soma plant.

**Somapa** (S) (M) 1. one who drinks Soma juice; Soma sacrificer. 3. a viśvadeva (*M. Bh.*); an attendant of Skanda (*M. Bh.*); an asura (*H. Purāṇa*); one of the 7 Pitṛs who dwells in the palace of Brahmā.

**Somapāla** (S) (M) 1. guardian of the Soma. 3. another name for the gandharvas.

**Somapati** (S) (M) 1. lord of Soma. 3. another name for Indra.

**Somapatnī** (S) (F) wife of Soma; wife of the moon.

**Somapī** (S) (M) 1. drinker of Soma. 3. a son of Sahadeva.

**Somaputra** (S) (M) **1.** son of the moon. **3.** another name for the planet Mercury.

**Somarāga** (S) (M) **1.** nectar rāga. **3.** a rāga.

**Somarāja** (S) (M) **1.** lord of Soma. **3.** another name for the moon.

**Somaraśmi** (S) (M) **1.** moonlight. **3.** a gandharvā.

**Somaśekhara** (S) (M) **1.** moon crested. **3.** another name for Śiva.

**Somasena** (S) (M) **1.** with an army of moons; lord of the moon. **3.** a son of Śambara (*H. Purāṇa*)

**Somasindhu** (S) (M) **1.** ocean of Soma. **3.** another name for Viṣṇu.

**Somaśravas** (S) (M) **1.** as famous as the moon. **3.** a hermit who was the son of Śrutaśravas.

**Somaśrī** (S) (F) divine nectar.

**Somasundara** (S) (M) beautiful moon.

**Somasutā** (S) (F) daughter of the moon; the river Narmadā.

**Somavarćas** (S) (M) **1.** with the splendour of the moon. **3.** a viśvadeva (*M. Bh.*); a gandharva (*H. Purāṇa*)

**Somavat** (S) (M) like the moon; containing Soma.

**Somavatī** (S) (F) containing Soma.

**Somendra** (S) (M) **1.** belonging to Soma and Indra; lord of Soma. **3.** another name for the moon.

**Somendu** (S) (M) the moon.

**Someśa** (S) (M) **1.** lord of Soma. **3.** another name for the moon.

**Someśvara** (S) (M) **1.** lord of the moon. **3.** a liṅga of Śiva set up by Soma; another name for Kṛṣṇa.

**Somilā** (S) (F) **1.** moonlike. **2.** calm.

**Somin** (S) (M) **1.** lord of Soma; possessing Soma. **3.** another name for the moon.

**Somodbhava** (S) (M) **1.** sprung from the moon; moon producer. **3.** another name for Kṛṣṇa.

**Śoṇā** (S) (F) **1.** redness; blooded; fiery. **3.** a Purāṇic river supposed to be a source of Agni (*M. Bh.*)

**Śoṇa** (S) (M) **1.** redness; fire. **3.** a Pāñćāla prince (*Ś. Brāhmaṇa*); a river.

**Sonā** (H) (F) gold.

**Śoṇāhaya** (S) (M) **1.** with red horses. **3.** another name for Droṇa.

**Sonākṣi** (H) (F) **1.** golden eyed. **3.** another name for Pārvatī.

**Sonala** (H) (M) golden.

**Sonāli** (H) (F) Indian laburnum; golden.

**Sonālikā** (H) (F) golden.

**Sonam** (H) (F) **1.** gold-like. **2.** beautiful; lucky.

**Sonam** (H) (M) **1.** gold-like. **2.** beautiful; lucky.

**Śoṇamaṇī** (S) (F) **1.** red gem. **2.** ruby.

**Śoṇapadma** (S) (M) red lotus (*Nymphaea rubra*)

**Śoṇaratna** (S) (M) **1.** red gem. **2.** ruby.

**Śoṇaśman** (S) (M) ruby.

**Śonāśva** (S) (M) **1.** with red horses. **3.** a son of Rājādhideva (*H. Purāṇa*); another name for Droṇa.

**Śonāśvavāha** (S) (M) **1.** borne by red horses. **3.** another name for Droṇa.

**Soni** (H) (F) golden; beautiful.

**Sonikā** (H) (F) with golden beauty.

**Śoṇitā** (S) (F) **1.** blooded; red. **2.** Saffron (*Crocus sativus*)

**Śoṇitapriyā** (S) (F) **1.** lover of blood. **3.** a goddess (*S. Dvatrinśikā*)

**Śoṇitoda** (S) (M) **1.** blood and water. **3.** a yakṣa in Kubera's assembly (*M. Bh.*)

**Śoṇopala** (S) (M) ruby.

**Śoṣana** (S) (M) **1.** absorption; drying up; draining; parching. **3.** an arrow of Kāma.

**Soṣman** (S) (M) having heat; warm; hot.

**Sotpala** (S) (M) possessing lotuses.

**Sotṛ** (S) (M) **1.** generating. **2.** one who extracts Soma.

**Sovā** (S) (F) one's own.

**Sovala** (S) (M) powerful.

**Soven** (S) (M) beautiful.

**Spandanā** (S) (F) throbbing; heart throb; pulsating beauty.

**Sparśānanda** (S) (F) **1.** delighting the touch. **3.** an apsarā.

**Sphaṭikayaśas** (S) (M) **1.** crystal-like flame.

3. a vidyadhara (*K. Sāgara*)

**Sphuliṅga** (S) (M) 1. sparks. 3. another name for Agni.

**Śraddhā** (S) (F) 1. faith; confidence; reverence; trust; loyalty. 3. reverence personified as a daughter of Dakṣa and Prasūtī and wife of Dharma and mother of Kāma (*V. Purāṇa*); daughter of Sūrya also known as Sāvitrī (*Ś. Brahmaṇa*); wife of Vaivasvata Manu; a daughter of Prajāpati Kardama and Devahūtī who married Aṅgiras and was the mother of Utathya and Bṛhaspati (*Bhāgavata*)

**Sragviṇī** (S) (F) 1. wearing a wreath of flowers. 3. a goddess.

**Sraja** (S) (M) 1. garland. 3. a viśvadeva (*M. Bh.*)

**Śrama** (S) (M) 1. labour. 2. toll; exertion; weariness. 3. a son of the vasu Āpa (*V. Purāṇa*); a son of Vasudeva (*Bh. Purāṇa*)

**Śrānta** (S) (M) 1. tired; calmed; tranquil. 3. a son of Āpa (*V. Purāṇa*)

**Śrāntha** (S) (M) 1. tying; binding; stringing together. 3. another name for Viṣṇu.

**Śrāva** (S) (M) 1. hearing; listening. 3. a son of King Yuvanāśva and the father of King Śrāvasta (*M. Bh.*)

**Śravā** (S) (M) 1. loud praise; glory; fame; renown. 3. a son of maharṣi Santa and the father of Tāmasa (*M. Bh.*)

**Śravaṇa** (S) (M) 1. ear; to hear; lame. 3. a nakṣatra presided over by Viṣṇu and which contains 3 stars; a son of Naraka (*Bh. Purāṇa*); a son of Murāsura (*Bhāgavata*); *Sphaeranthus indicus*.

**Śrāvaṇa** (S) (M) 1. the rainy season of July/August. 3. son of Murāsura (*Bhāgavata*); one of the 27 constellations (*M. Bh.*)

**Śrāvaṇī** (S) (F) the day of the fullmoon in the month of Śrāvaṇa (July/August)

**Śravaṇīya** (S) (M) worthy to listen.

**Sravantī** (S) (F) 1. flowing. 2. a river.

**Śrāvasta** (S) (M) 1. much heard; famous. 3. the son of King Srāva (*M. Bh.*)

**Śraviṣṭhā** (S) (F) 1. most famous. 3. a nakṣatra (*V's B. Samhitā*); the daughter of Ćitraka (*H. Purāṇa*)

**Śraviṣṭha** (S) (M) most famous.

**Śraviṣṭhāramaṇa** (S) (M) 1. lover of Śravisthā. 3. another name for the moon.

**Śravojit** (S) (M) winning renown; glorious.

**Śreṇi** (S) (M) line; row; troop; necklace; garland; chain.

**Śreṇika** (S) (M) 1. front tooth. 3. a king of Magadha and follower of Mahāvīra.

**Śreṇimān** (S) (M) 1. having followers. 3. a rājarṣi who fought on the side of the Pāṇḍavas (*M. Bh.*)

**Śreṣṭha** (S) (M) 1. excellent; best; chief; foremost. 3. another name for Viṣṇu and Kubera.

**Śreṣṭhapāla** (S) (M) the best guardian.

**Śreyā** (S) (F) best; beautiful; excellent.

**Śreyānśanātha** (S) (M) 1. lord of fortune; lord of bliss; master of welfare. 3. the 11th Jaina Tīrthaṅkara and the son of King Viṣṇu and Queen Viṣṇu of Sinhapur.

**Śreyas** (S) (M) 1. best; most beautiful; excellent; auspicious; fortunate. 3. the deity of the Bodhi tree (*L. Vistara*)

**Śṛgāla** (S) (M) 1. jackal. 3. a king (*M. Bh.*)

**Sṛgalavadana** (S) (M) 1. jackal-faced. 3. an asura (*H. Purāṇa*)

**Śrī** (S) (F) 1. diffusing radiance. 2. prosperity; beauty and grace conjoined; light; grace; splendour; glory; welfare; power; majesty. 3. Lakṣmī as goddess of prosperity (*Ś. Brāhmaṇa*); a Buddhist goddess; another name for Sarasvatī; a daughter of King Suśarman (*K. Sāgara*); Indian Lotus (*Nelumbium nucifera*)

**Śrī** (S) (M) 1. diffusing light. 2. adorning; sacred; holy. 3. a rāga.

**Śrībālā** (S) (F) divine maiden.

**Śrībandhu** (S) (M) 1. brother of Lakṣmī. 3. another name for the moon.

**Śrībhadrā** (S) (F) 1. best among people. 3. a goddess; a wife of Bimbisāra (*B. Literature*)

**Śrībhadra** (S) (M) 1. best among men. 3. a nāga.

**Śrībhānu** (S) (M) 1. divine sun. 3. a son of Kṛṣṇa and Satyabhāmā (*Bhā. Purāṇa*)

**Śrībhartṛ** (S) (M) 1. husband of Śrī. 3. another name for Viṣṇu.

**Śrībinda** (S) (M) 1. knower of fortune. 3. a

demon slain by Indra.

**Śrībindu** (S) (M) mark of fortune.

**Śrīćanda** (S) (M) divine moon.

**Śrīćandra** (S) (M) divine moon.

**Śrīdā** (S) (F) 1. given by Lakṣmī; bestowing fortune. 3. another name for Rādhā.

**Śrīda** (S) (M) 1. bestowing prosperity. 3. another name for Kubera.

**Śrīdāman** (S) (M) 1. tied by fortune. 3. a playmate of Kṛṣṇa.

**Śrīdatta** (S) (M) 1. fortune giver. 3. a son Kālanemi (*K. Sāgara*)

**Śrīdayita** (S) (M) 1. Śrī's husband. 3. another name for Viṣṇu.

**Śrīdevā** (S) (F) 1. fortune giver. 3. a daughter of King Devaka and wife of Vasudeva and mother of Nandaka (*Bhāgavata*)

**Śrīdevī** (S) (F) 1. goddess of prosperity. 3. another name for Lakṣmī; a queen of Ayodhyā.

**Śrīdhara** (S) (M) 1. possessor of fortune. 3. a form of Viṣṇu (*M. Bh.*); the 7th Arhat of the past Utsarpinī.

**Śrīgaṇeśa** (S) (M) divine Gaṇeśa; divine master of the horde.

**Śrīgarbhā** (S) (F) 1. having welfare as the inner nature. 3. another name for Rādhā.

**Śrīgarbha** (S) (M) 1. having welfare as the inner nature. 3. a Bodhisattva; another name for Viṣṇu.

**Śrīgupta** (S) (M) 1. possessing a hidden treasure; possessed with an inner glory. 3. a teacher of the Mādhyamika-Svātantrika school of Buddhism at Nālandā (8th century)

**Śrīhara** (S) (F) 1. excelling all in beauty. 3. another name for Rādhā.

**Śrīhari** (S) (M) 1. lion of prosperity. 3. another name for Viṣṇu.

**Śrīharṣa** (S) (M) 1. delighting in prosperity. 3. author of *Naiṣadhaćarita* (12th century A.D.)

**Śrīhastinī** (S) (F) 1. in the hands of fortune. 2. the sunflower (*Heliotropium indicum*) supposed to be held by Śrī.

**Śrīja** (S) (M) 1. born of Śrī. 3. another name for Kāma.

**Śrīkā** (S) (F) prosperity; fortune; wealth; beauty.

**Śrīkalā** (S) (F) a portion of Lakṣmī.

**Śrīkāma** (S) (F) 1. desirous of glory. 3. another name for Rādhā.

**Śrīkānta** (S) (M) 1. beloved of Śrī. 3. another name for Viṣṇu.

**Śrīkaṇṭha** (S) (M) 1. beautiful throated. 3. another name for Śiva.

**Śrīkaṇṭhasakha** (S) (M) 1. friend of Śiva. 3. another name for Kubera.

**Śrīkaṇṭhikā** (S) (F) 1. graceful voiced. 3. a rāga.

**Śrīkara** (S) (M) 1. causing prosperity. 3. another name for Viṣṇu.

**Śrīkeśava** (S) (M) the divine Kṛṣṇa.

**Śrīkīrtana** (S) (M) chanting for prosperity.

**Śrīkriyārūpiṇī** (S) (F) 1. incarnation of goddess of fortune. 3. another name for Rādhā.

**Śrīkṛṣṇa** (S) (M) divine Kṛṣṇa.

**Śrīlā** (S) (F) given by Lakṣmī; prosperous; happy; beautiful; eminent.

**Śrīlakṣmī** (S) (F) divine Lakṣmī.

**Śrīlalitā** (S) (F) graceful; prosperous.

**Śrīlatā** (S) (F) divine vine.

**Śrīmahādevī** (S) (F) 1. divine Pārvatī. 3. the mother of Śankara.

**Śrīmālā** (S) (M) blossom of the Parijāta tree (*Nyctantes arbor tristis*)

**Śrīman** (S) (M) 1. bearer of prosperity, beauty and grace. 2. fortunate. 3. a son of Nimi and grandson of Dattātreya.

**Śrīmaṅgalā** (S) (F) goddess of prosperity.

**Śrīmaṇī** (S) (F) 1. best among the jewels. 2. beautiful jewel. 3. a rāga.

**Śrīmanta** (S) (M) pleasant; charming; glorious; royal; wealthy.

**Śrīmat** (S) (M) 1. bearer of prosperity. 2. beautiful; charming; pleasant; glorious; auspicious; royal; wealthy. 3. a son of Nimi (*M. Bh.*); another name for Viṣṇu, Kubera and Śākyamitra.

**Śrīmātā** (S) (F) 1. divine mother. 3. a form of the devī (*Sk. Purāṇa*)

**Śrīmatī** (S) (F) 1. bearer of prosperity; beauty and grace. 2. pleasant; royal; divine; beautiful. 3. a gandharva maid; a mother in

Skanda's retinue (*M. Bh.*); Spanish Jasmine (*Jasminum grandiflorum*)

**Śrīmohana** (S) (M) 1. seducer of grace; lover of Lakṣmī or Rādhā. 3. divine Kṛṣṇa.

**Śrīmukha** (S) (M) a beautiful face.

**Śrīmukhī** (S) (F) with a radiant face.

**Śrīmūrti** (S) (M) divine image; idol.

**Śrīṇā** (S) (F) night.

**Śrīnanda** (S) (M) 1. delighting Śrī. 3. another name for Viṣṇu.

**Śrīnandana** (S) (M) 1. son of Śrī. 3. another name for Kāma and Rāma.

**Śrīnandinī** (S) (F) daughter of prosperity.

**Śrīnātha** (S) (M) 1. lord of Śrī. 3. another name for Viṣṇu.

**Śrīnidhi** (S) (M) 1. receptacle of beauty. 3. another name for Viṣṇu.

**Śrīniketa** (S) (M) 1. abode of beauty; abode of Śrī. 2. lotus flower (*Nelumbo speciosum*)

**Śrīniketana** (S) (M) 1. dwelling with Śrī. 3. another name for Viṣṇu.

**Śrīnitambā** (S) (F) 1. with beautiful hips. 3. another name for Rādhā.

**Śrīnivāsa** (S) (M) abode of Śrī.

**Śrīpāda** (S) (M) divine feet.

**Śrīpadma** (S) (M) 1. divine lotus. 3. another name for Kṛṣṇa.

**Śrīpāla** (S) (M) 1. protector of prosperity. 3. another name for Viṣṇu.

**Śrīpati** (S) (M) 1. lord of Śrī; lord of fortune. 3. another name for Viṣṇu-Kṛṣṇa as worshipped on the hill Venkaṭa.

**Śrīputra** (S) (M) 1. son of Śrī. 3. another name for Kāma.

**Śrīrāma** (S) (M) the divine Rāmaćandra.

**Śrīrāmakṛṣṇa** (S) (M) a great Hindu philospher born in 1836 who was the son of Khudīrāma Ćattopādhyāya and Ćandrādevī.

**Śrīraṅga** (S) (M) 1. divine Viṣṇu. 3. a Vaiṣṇava temple near Trićinopoly.

**Śrīraṅgam** (S) (M) divine Kṛṣṇa.

**Śrīraṅgeśa** (S) (M) 1. lord of Śrīraṅga. 3. another name for Viṣṇu.

**Śrīraṅgeśvarī** (S) (M) consort of Śrīraṅga.

**Śrīrañjana** (S) (M) 1. amusing Lakṣmī. 3. another name for Viṣṇu.

**Śrīrūpā** (S) (M) 1. with the form of Lakṣmī. 3. another name for Rādhā.

**Śrīśa** (S) (M) 1. lord of fortune; lord of Śrī. 3. another name for Viṣṇu and Rāma.

**Śrīsahodara** (S) (M) 1. brother of Śrī. 3. another name for the moon.

**Śrīśaila** (S) (M) divine rock.

**Śrīsvāmin** (S) (M) 1. lord of Śrī. 3. the father of Bhaṭṭi.

**Śrīsvarūpa** (S) (M) 1. with the form of Śrī. 3. a disciple of Ćaitanya.

**Śrīsvarūpiṇī** (S) (M) 1. with the form of Śrī. 3. another name for Rādhā.

**Śrītejas** (S) (M) 1. extremely glorious. 3. a Buddha (*L. Vistara*)

**Śrīvaha** (S) (M) 1. bringing fortune. 3. a nāga son of Kaśyapa and Kadru (*M. Bh.*)

**Śrīvallabha** (S) (M) favourite of fortune.

**Śrīvāṇī** (S) (F) divine speech.

**Śrīvarāha** (S) (M) 1. divine boar. 3. another name for Viṣṇu.

**Śrīvardhana** (S) (M) 1. increaser of fortune. 3. another name for Śiva and Viṣṇu.

**Śrīvāsa** (S) (M) 1. abode of Śrī. 3. another name for Viṣṇu.

**Śrīvatsa** (S) (M) 1. favourite of Srī. 3. a mole on Viṣṇu's chest (*M. Bh.*); another name for Viṣṇu.

**Śrīvatsalāñćana** (S) (M) 1. marked by a white curl of hair on the chest. 3. another name for Kṛṣṇa.

**Śrīvidyā** (S) (F) 1. divine knowledge. 3. a form of Durgā.

**Śrīvṛddhī** (S) (F) 1. increasing fortune. 3. a Buddhist goddess; the mother of the 17th Arhat; a deity of the Bodhi tree (*L. Vistara*)

**Śriyā** (S) (F) prosperity and happiness personified as the wife of Śrīdhara.

**Śriyāditya** (S) (M) divine sun.

**Śriyaśas** (S) (M) desirous of splendour and glory.

**Sṛjavāna** (S) (M) 1. wearing a garland. 3. a son of Dyutimat (*V. Purāṇa*)

**Sṛmala** (S) (M) 1. wrestler. 3. an asura.

**Śṛnga** (S) (M) 1. horn; peak; summit of a mountain; highest point; perfection. 3. a muni who is worshipped in some parts of India in times of drought; the musical instrument of Śiva (*M. Bh.*)

**Śṛṅgapriya** (S) (M) **1.** fond of hornblowing. **3.** another name for Śiva.

**Śṛṅgāra** (S) (M) **1.** horned one. **2.** love; passion; elegant dress; dainty; gold; powder.

**Śṛṅgārajanman** (S) (M) **1.** born from desire. **3.** another name for Kāma.

**Śṛṅgārāvalli** (S) (F) **1.** garland of love. **3.** the mother of the Tamil poet Kambar.

**Śṛṅgārikā** (S) (F) **1.** horned. **2.** love.

**Śṛṅgavān** (S) (M) **1.** with horns. **3.** a sage who was the son of Gālava (*M. Bh.*)

**Śṛṅgavera** (S) (M) **1.** full of horns; dried ginger. **3.** a nāga of the Kaurava family (*M. Bh.*)

**Śṛṅgaviśa** (S) (M) **1.** one who stays on a peak. **3.** a sage from whose stomach Indra was born (*Ṛg Veda*)

**Śṛṅgeśa** (S) (M) **1.** lord of peaks. **3.** another name for Śiva.

**Śṛṅgi** (S) (M) **1.** horned; crested peaked. **2.** bull; mountain. **3.** a mythical mountain chain encirling the earth; the sage who cursed Parīkṣit (*M. Bh.*)

**Śṛṅginī** (S) (F) **1.** horned; crested. **2.** cow; *Jasminum sambac.*

**Śṛṅgotpādinī** (S) (F) **1.** producer of horns. **3.** a yakṣinī who changes men into animals.

**Śṛñjaya** (S) (M) **1.** giving victory. **3.** an Ikṣvāku king who was the son of Śviti and also the father of Sućismitā and Suvarṇaṣṭhīvī (*M. Bh.*); a royal hermit who was the grandfather of Ambā of Kāśī (*M. Bh.*); a son of Devavata (*Ṛg Veda*)

**Sṛnjayī** (S) (F) **1.** giving victory. **3.** a wife of Bhajamāna (*H. Purāṇa*)

**Srotasya** (S) (M) **1.** flowing in streams. **2.** a thief. **3.** another name for Śiva.

**Sṛṣta** (S) (M) **1.** creator. **3.** another name for Brahmā.

**Sṛtañjaya** (S) (M) **1.** conquering the running one. **3.** a son of Karamjit (*Bh. Purāṇa*)

**Sṛti** (S) (F) road; path.

**Śruṣṭhigu** (S) (M) **1.** obedient. **3.** a ṛṣi.

**Śrutā** (S) (F) **1.** famous; glorious; celebrated. **2.** heard; known. **3.** a daughter of Dīrghadanṣtra (*K. Sāgara*); sacred knowledge personified as a daughter of Dharma and Medhā (*Purāṇa*)

**Śruta** (S) (M) **1.** heard; known; famous; celebrated; knowledge; scriptures. **3.** a son of Bhagīratha (*H. Purāṇa*); a son of Kṛṣṇa and Kālindī (*Bhā. Purāṇa*); a son of Upagu (*V. Purāṇa*); a son of Bhīmasena (*A. Purāṇa*); a solar dynasty king who was the son of Subhāṣaṇa and father of Jaya (*Bhāgavata*); a Bharata dynasty king who was the son of Dharmanetra and father of Dṛḍhasena (*Bhāgavata*)

**Śrutabandhu** (S) (M) **1.** companion of knowledge. **3.** a ṛṣi.

**Śrutadevā** (S) (F) **1.** with divine knowledge. **3.** a daughter of Śūra (*H. Purāṇa*)

**Śrutadeva** (S) (M) **1.** the well known god; with god like knowledge. **3.** a son of Kṛṣṇa; a servant of Kṛṣṇa.

**Śrutadevī** (S) (F) **1.** goddess of knowledge. **3.** name of a sister of Vasudeva and aunt of Kṛṣṇa (*Bhāgavata*); another name for Sarasvatī.

**Śrutadharman** (S) (M) **1.** follower of scriptures. **3.** a son of Udāpi (*H. Purāṇa*)

**Śrutadhī** (S) (M) receptacle of knowledge.

**Śrutadhvaja** (S) (M) **1.** characterized by knowledge. **3.** a brother of King Virāṭa (*M. Bh.*)

**Śrutāhva** (S) (M) **1.** known to be firm. **3.** a king on the side of the Pāṇḍavas (*M. Bh.*)

**Śrutakakṣa** (S) (M) **1.** abode of scriptures. **3.** a ṛṣi.

**Śrutakarman** (S) (M) **1.** according to the scriptures. **3.** a son of Sahadeva (*M. Bh.*); a son of Arjuna (*M. Bh.*); a son of Somapi (*V. Purāṇa*)

**Śrutakīrtī** (S) (F) **1.** of well known glory. **2.** famous. **3.** a wife of Śatrughna and daughter of Kuśadhvaja (*K. Rāmāyaṇa*); a sister of Vasudeva and aunt of Kṛṣṇa (*Bhāgavata*)

**Śrutakīrti** (S) (M) **1.** one whose fame is heard about. **3.** a son of Arjuna and Draupadī (*M. Bh.*)

**Śrutanābha** (S) (M) **1.** centre of the scriptures. 3. a solar dynasty king who was the son of Bhagīratha and father of Sindhudvīpa (*Bhāgavata*)

**Śrutānīka** (S) (M) 1. with a celebrated army. 3. a brother of King Virāṭa (*M. Bh.*)

**Śrutañjaya** (S) (M) 1. with celebrated victory. 3. a brother of King Suśarmā of Trigarta (*M. Bh.*); a son of Senajit (*V. Purāṇa*); a son of Satyāyu (*Bhā. Purāṇa*); a son of Karmajit.

**Śrutānta** (S) (M) 1. the limit of fame. 2. most famous. 3. a son of Dhṛtarāṣṭra (*M. Bh.*)

**Śrutapāla** (S) (M) guardian of knowledge.

**Śrutārva** (S) (M) 1. with known resistance. 3. a son of Dhṛtarāṣṭra (*M. Bh.*)

**Śrutārya** (S) (M) 1. knower of the scriptures; learned; famous. 3. a hermit mentioned in the *Ṛg Veda*.

**Śrutaśarman** (S) (M) 1. celebrated protector; protector of knowledge; armoured with knowledge. 3. a son of Udāyus (*V. Purāṇa*); a prince of the vidyādharas (*K. Sāgara*)

**Śrutasenā** (S) (F) 1. with a famous army. 3. a wife of Kṛṣṇa (*H. Purāṇa*)

**Śrutasena** (S) (M) 1. with a famous army. 3. a brother of King Janamejaya (*Ś. Brāhmaṇa*); the younger brother of the serpent Takṣaka (*M. Bh.*); an asura; a warrior on the Kaurava side (*M. Bh.*); a son of Sahadeva (*M. Bh.*); a son of Parīkṣit (*M. Bh.*); a son of Śatrughna (*Bh. Purāṇa*); a son of Bhīma (*Bhā. Purāṇa*); a son of Śambara (*H. Purāṇa*); a prince of Gokarṇa (*K. Sāgara*)

**Śrutasomā** (S) (F) 1. of the moon. 3. a wife of Kṛṣṇa (*H. Purāṇa*)

**Śrutasoma** (S) (M) 1. moon. 3. a son of Bhīma (*V. Purāṇa*)

**Śrutaśravas** (S) (M) 1. listener of scriptures. 3. a king of Magadha (*Bhāgavata*); a maharṣi who was the father of Somaśravas and a priest of Janamejaya (*M. Bh.*); a rājarṣi in the palace of Yama (*M. Bh.*)

**Śrutaśravas** (S) (F) 1. listener of the scriptures. 3. a sister of Vasudeva and aunt of Kṛṣṇa (*Bhāgavata*); a wife of King Damaghoṣa of Ćedi and mother of Śiśupāla.

**Śrutaśrī** (S) (M) 1. with wellknown wealth. 3. an asura (*M. Bh.*)

**Śrutavat** (S) (M) 1. learned; pious. 3. a son of Somapi (*Bhā. Purāṇa*)

**Śrutavatī** (S) (F) 1. favourably known. 3. a daughter of sage Bharadvāja and Ghṛtāćī (*M. Bh.*)

**Śrutavindā** (S) (F) 1. knower of the scriptures. 3. a river (*Bhā. Purāṇa*)

**Śrutayajña** (S) (M) 1. acting according to the scriptures. 3. a Bharata dynasty king who was the son of Karmajit and grandson of Vivanava (*Bhāgavata*)

**Śrutāyudha** (S) (M) 1. possessor of famous weapons. 3. a king of Kaliṅga who was the son of Varuṇa by Parṇāśā (*M. Bh.*)

**Śrutāyus** (S) (M) 1. with a celebrated life. 3. a son of Purūravas (*M. Bh.*); a Kṣatriya king who was a partial incarnation of the daitya Krodhavaśa (*M. Bh.*); a brother of Ayutāyus who fought on the Kaurava side (*M. Bh.*); a Solar dynasty king and descendant of Kuśa.

**Śrutī** (S) (F) hearing; ear; knowledge of the Vedas.

**Śruti** (S) (M) 1. knowledge of scriptures. 3. a king of ancient India (*M. Bh.*)

**Śrutibuddhī** (S) (F) 1. with knowledge of scriptures. 3. a daughter of Atri and wife of Kardama (*V. Purāṇa*)

**Śrutirañjana** (S) (M) delighting in knowledge.

**Śrutya** (S) (M) to be famous; glorious.

**Stambamitra** (S) (M) 1. friend of grass. 3. a bird child of sage Mandapāla and Jaritā (*M. Bh.*)

**Stambha** (S) (M) 1. pillar. 2. mountain; shrub. 3. one of the 7 sages of the Manu Svāroćiṣa age (*V. Purāṇa*)

**Stambhaka** (S) (M) 1. post; pillar. 3. an attendant of Śiva (*K. Sāgara*)

**Stambhakī** (S) (F) 1. post; pillar. 3. a goddess.

**Stanayitnu** (S) (M) thunder personified as a child of Vidyota or lightning.

**Stāvā** (S) (F) 1. praiser. 3. an apsarā.

**Stava** (S) (M) praise; eulogy.

**Staveyya** (S) (M) 1. who can be stolen. 3. another name for Indra.

**Stavitṛ** (S) (M) praiser; singer.

**Sthāga** (S) (M) 1. dead body. 3. an attendant of Śiva.

**Sthala** (S) (M) **1.** place; spot. **2.** chapter. **3.** son of Bala.

**Sthaleyu** (S) (M) **1.** terrestrial. **3.** a son of Raudrāśva (*H. Purāṇa*)

**Sthāman** (S) (M) strength; power.

**Sthandileya** (S) (M) **1.** belonging to a sacrificial ground. **3.** son of Raudrāśva and Miśrakeśī (*M. Bh.*)

**Sthāṇu** (S) (M) **1.** immobile; firm; fixed. **2.** a trunk of a tree. **3.** a prajāpati (*Rāmāyaṇa*); a nāga; a rākṣasa; Śiva as the son of Brahmā and the father of the 11 rudras (*M. Bh.*); one of the 11 rudras (*M. Bh.*); a hermit in the palace of Indra (*M. Bh.*)

**Sthapati** (S) (M) **1.** place lord. **2.** best; eminent; chief; king; architect; guard. **3.** another name for Kubera and Bṛhaspati.

**Sthāvarā** (S) (F) **1.** stable; immovable; standing still; firm; constant. **3.** a Buddhist goddess (*L. Vistara*)

**Sthavira** (S) (M) **1.** broad; thick; solid; old; venerable. **3.** another name for Brahmā.

**Sthira** (S) (M) **1.** sure; immovable; permanent; certain; fixed. **3.** an attendant given to Skanda by Meru (*M. Bh.*)

**Sthirā** (S) (F) **1.** strong minded. **3.** another name for the earth.

**Sthirabuddhi** (S) (M) **1.** noble; steadfast. **3.** an asura (*K. Sāgara*)

**Sthitivarman** (S) (M) **1.** living in armour. **3.** a king.

**Sthūla** (S) (M) **1.** dense; large; thick; massive; big. **3.** an attendant of Śiva.

**Sthūlabhadra** (S) (M) **1.** a strong opponent; a stout person. **3.** a son of Śakadala and Laććhadevī he succeeded Bhadrabāhu as the head of the Jaina church (*J. Literature*)

**Sthūlabhuja** (S) (M) **1.** strong armed. **3.** a vidyādhara (*K. Sāgara*)

**Sthūlakarna** (S) (M) **1.** large eared. **3.** a ṛṣi (*M. Bh.*)

**Sthūlakeśa** (S) (M) **1.** with thick hair. **3.** a hermit who was the foster father of Pramadvarā (*M. Bh.*)

**Sthūlākṣa** (S) (M) **1.** large eyed. **3.** a rākṣasa (*V. Rāmāyaṇa*); a hermit (*M. Bh.*)

**Sthūlaśiras** (S) (M) **1.** strong headed. **3.** a hermit in the court of Yudhiṣṭhira (*M. Bh.*); a rākṣasa (*K. Sāgara*)

**Sthūna** (S) (M) **1.** post; pillar. **2.** beam of a house. **3.** a son of Viśvāmitra (*M. Bh.*); a yakṣa (*M. Bh.*)

**Sthūṇākarṇa** (S) (M) **1.** with marked ears. **2.** cattle. **3.** a hermit in the court of Yudhiṣṭhira (*M. Bh.*); a yakṣa who helped Śikhaṇḍī (*M. Bh.*)

**Stīrṇa** (S) (M) **1.** spread; strewn. **3.** an attendant of Śiva (*Ś. Purāṇa*)

**Stotra** (S) (M) praise; hymn of praise.

**Stotri** (S) (M) **1.** praising. **3.** another name for Viṣṇu.

**Strīratna** (S) (F) **1.** jewel of a woman. **3.** another name for Lakṣmī.

**Strītamā** (S) (F) a complete woman.

**Stubha** (S) (M) **1.** uttering a joyful sound; humming; chanting hymns. **2.** goat. **3.** a son of Agni Bhānu (*M. Bh.*)

**Stuti** (S) (F) **1.** praise; eulogy; adulation. **3.** the wife of Pratihartṛ; another name for Durgā.

**Stutyavrata** (S) (M) **1.** one who praises; a devotee. **3.** a son of Hiraṇyaretas (*Bhā. Purāṇa*)

**Stuvat** (S) (M) praiser; worshipper.

**Stuvi** (S) (M) praiser; worshipper.

**Subāhū** (S) (F) **1.** with beautiful arms. **3.** an apsarā daughter of Kaśyapa and Prādhā (*M. Bh.*)

**Subāhu** (S) (M) **1.** with strong arms. **3.** a nāga son of Kaśyapa and Kadru (*M. Bh.*); a Kṣatriya king who was the incarnation of the asura Hara (*M. Bh.*); a Kṣatriya king who was the partial incarnation of the asura Krodhavaśa (*M. Bh.*); a son of Dhṛtarāṣṭra (*M. Bh.*); a king of Kāśi and father of Śaśikalā (*M. Bh.*); a rākṣasa who was a son of Tāṭaka (*M. Bh.*); a king of Ćedi who was a son of Vīrabāhu (*M. Bh.*); a Kulinda king who fought on the side of the Pāṇḍavas (*M. Bh.*); a warrior of the Kauravas (*M. Bh.*); a warrior of Skanda (*M. Bh.*); the father of Sagara of the Solar dynasty (*H. Purāṇa*); a Ćola king and worshipper of Viṣṇu (*P. Purāṇa*); a dānava (*H. Purāṇa*); a yakṣa (*V. Purāṇa*); a son of Matināra (*H. Purāṇa*); a king of Videhā

(*B. Literature*); a son of Ćitraka (*H. Purāṇa*); a son of Kṛṣṇa (*Bhā. Purāṇa*); son of Śatrughna (*Rāmāyaṇa*); a son of Kuvalayāśva (*Mā. Purāṇa*); a son of Pratibāhu (*B. Literature*); a brother of Alarka (*Mā. Purāṇa*); a Bodhisattva.

**Subāhuka** (S) (M) **1.** possessing strong arms. **3.** a yakṣa (*V. Purāṇa*)

**Subala** (S) (M) **1.** very powerful. **3.** a mythical bird who was the son of Vainateya (*M. Bh.*); a son of Manu Bhautya; a son of Sumati (*V. Purāṇa*); a Gāndhārā king who was the father of Śakuni and Gāndhārī (*M. Bh.*); an Ikṣvāku king (*M. Bh.*); a son of Garuḍa (*M. Bh.*); another name for Śiva.

**Subāla** (S) (M) **1.** good boy. **2.** a god.

**Subalaja** (S) (M) **1.** son of Subala. **3.** another name for Śakuni.

**Subalī** (S) (F) very strong; very powerful.

**Śubana** (S) (M) shining brightly; brilliant.

**Subāndhava** (S) (F) **1.** good friend. **3.** another name for Śiva.

**Subandhu** (S) (M) **1.** good friend. **3.** the author of the *Vāsavadattā* (7th century A.D.); the main priest of King Asamāti (*Ṛg Veda*)

**Subarmā** (S) (M) strong warrior.

**Subbālakṣmī** (S) (F) divine fortune.

**Subbārao** (S) (M) **1.** divine leader. **3.** another name for Kārttikeya.

**Subbāratna** (S) (M) **1.** auspicious jewel. **2.** the white jewel of Kārttikeya.

**Śubhā** (S) (F) **1.** splendour; beauty; ornament; decoration; light; lustre; desire. **2.** an assembly of the gods. **3.** a companion of the goddess Umā; another name for Dhruva's mother.

**Śubha** (S) (M) **1.** splendid; bright; beautiful; auspicious; prosperous; good; virtuous. **3.** a son of Dharma (*Bhā. Purāṇa*); Himalayan Cherry (*Prunus cerasoides*)

**Subhā** (S) (F) **1.** prosperous; auspicious. **3.** a wife of Aṅgiras and mother of Bṛhatkirti (*M. Bh.*)

**Śubhadantī** (S) (F) **1.** with good teeth. **3.** the elephant consort of Puṣpadanta.

**Subhadrā** (S) (F) **1.** glorious; splendid; auspicious. **3.** a form of Durgā (*H. Ć. Ćintāmaṇi*); a wife of Durgama (*Mā. Purāṇa*); a daughter of Balin and wife of Avīkṣit; a grand daughter of Rukmin and wife of Aniruddha (*V. Purāṇa*); a daughter of the asura Sumāya (*K. Sāgara*); the daughter of Vasudeva and Devakī and the sister of Kṛṣṇa and the wife of Arjuna and the mother of Abhimanyu (*M. Bh.*); a daughter of Surabhi and guardian of the western region (*M. Bh.*)

**Subhadra** (S) (M) **1.** glorious; splendid; fortunate; auspicious. **3.** a son of Kṛṣṇa (*Bh. Purāṇa*); a son of Vasudeva (*Bhā. Purāṇa*); a son of Idhmajīhva (*Bh. Purāṇa*); the last man converted by Gautama Buddha (*S. Puṇḍarikā*); another name for Viṣṇu; Neem tree (*Azadirachta indica*)

**Subhāgā** (S) (F) **1.** fortunate; rich. **3.** a daughter of Raudrāśva.

**Subhagā** (S) (F) **1.** good fortune. **2.** wild Jasmine; Sacred Basil (*Ocimum sanctum*); honoured mother; beloved by husband. **3.** a daughter of Kaśyapa and Prādhā (*M. Bh.*); a mother in Skanda's retinue.

**Subhāga** (S) (M) fortunate; rich; wealthy.

**Subhaga** (S) (M) **1.** very fortunate; lucky; prosperous; blessed; lovely; charming; beloved; dear. **3.** a son of Subala and brother of Śakuni (*M. Bh.*); another name for Śiva; *Michelia champaka*; *Saraca indica*; red amaranth.

**Śubhagā** (S) (F) **1.** going well. **2.** gracious; elegant. **3.** a Śakti (*H. Ć. Ćintāmaṇi*)

**Śubhagābhirī** (S) (F) **1.** deep and virtuous. **3.** a rāgiṇī.

**Subhagarbha** (S) (M) **1.** centre of virtue and prosperity. **3.** a Bodhisattva.

**Śubhakarman** (S) (M) **1.** acting nobly. **3.** an attendant of Skanda (*M. Bh.*)

**Śubhākṣa** (S) (M) **1.** auspicious eyed. **3.** another name for Śiva.

**Śubhalakṣaṇa** (S) (M) with auspicious marks.

**Śubhalakṣmī** (S) (F) radiant Lakṣmī.

**Śubhaloćana** (S) (M) fair eyed.

**Śubhaloćanā** (S) (F) fair eyed.

**Śubhamālā** (S) (F) **1.** with a splendid garland. **3.** a gandharvī (*K. Vyuha*)

**Śubhamaya** (S) (M) full of splendour; splendid; beautiful.

**Śubhamayī** (S) (F) 1. full of splendour. 2. splendid; beautiful.

**Śubhamitra** (S) (M) auspicious friend.

**Śubhāna** (S) (M) shining; bright; brilliant.

**Śubhānana** (S) (M) 1. with a beautiful face. 2. handsome; good looking.

**Śubhānandā** (S) (F) 1. beauty and pleasure conjoined. 2. delighting in virtues. 3. a goddess said to be a form of Dākṣāyāṇī.

**Śubhāṅga** (S) (M) 1. handsome limbed. 3. another name for Śiva.

**Śubhāṅgada** (S) (M) 1. of beautiful form; handsome. 3. a king at Draupadī's svayamvara (*M. Bh.*)

**Śubhāṅgī** (S) (F) 1. handsome limbed. 3. the daughter of Rukmin and wife of Pradyumna (*H. Purāṇa*); a wife of Kubera; a wife of Kuru of the lunar dynasty and the mother of Vidura (*M. Bh.*); another name for Rati.

**Śubhāñjana** (S) (M) decorated with beauty.

**Śubhaṅkara** (S) (M) 1. doer of good deeds; virtuous. 3. an asura (*K. Sāgara*); another name for Śiva.

**Śubhaṅkarī** (S) (F) 1. doer of good deeds; virtuous. 3. another name for Pārvatī.

**Subhānu** (S) (M) 1. shining brightly. 3. a son of Kṛṣṇa and Satyabhāmā (*Bhāgavata*)

**Subhāryā** (S) (F) 1. prosperous lady. 2. graceful lady. 3. a daughter of Śvaphalka and sister of Akrūra (*Bhāgavata*)

**Subhāsa** (S) (M) 1. shining beautifully. 3. a dānava (*K. Sāgara*); a son of Sudhanvan (*V. Purāṇa*)

**Subhāṣa** (S) (M) well spoken; eloquent.

**Subhāṣaćandra** (S) (M) moon among the eloquent.

**Subhaṣana** (S) (M) 1. speaking well. 3. a solar dynasty king who was the son of Yuyudhāna and father of Śruta (*Bhāgavata*)

**Śubhāṣaṇa** (S) (M) good speaker.

**Subhāṣaṇī** (S) (F) soft spoken.

**Śubhaśīla** (S) (M) with a good disposition.

**Śubhāśiṣa** (S) (M) blessings.

**Subhaṣitā** (S) (F) spoken well of.

**Śubhaspati** (S) (M) 1. lord of splendour. 3. another name for the 2 aśvins.

**Śubhasūćanī** (S) (F) 1. indicating good. 3. a deity worshipped by women in times of calamity.

**Subhāsvara** (S) (M) radiant; splendid.

**Subhaṭa** (S) (M) great soldier; champion.

**Subhaṭṭa** (S) (M) learned; wise.

**Śubhavaktrā** (S) (F) 1. of auspicious face. 3. a mother in Skanda's retinue (*M. Bh.*)

**Subhavimalagarbha** (S) (M) 1. with pure and bright garment. 2. centre of splendour and cleanliness. 3. a Bodhisattva.

**Śubhāya** (S) (M) to be bright and beautiful; to become a blessing.

**Śubhendra** (S) (M) lord of virtue.

**Śubhikā** (S) (F) a garland of auspicious flowers.

**Subhīmā** (S) (F) 1. very dreadful or terrible. 3. a wife of Kṛṣna (*H. Purāṇa*)

**Subhīma** (S) (M) 1. terrible; dreadful; bewildering. 3. a son of the agni Tapa (*M. Bh.*)

**Subhojita** (S) (M) well fed.

**Śubhrā** (S) (F) 1. radiant. 3. another name for the Gaṅgā.

**Śubhra** (S) (M) 1. radiant; shining; beautiful; clear; white. 2. heaven; sandal. 3. the husband of Vikuṇṭhā and father of Vaikuṇṭha (*Bhā. Purāṇa*)

**Śubhrabhānu** (S) (M) 1. white rayed. 3. another name for the moon.

**Śubhrāja** (S) (M) 1. shining brightly. 3. a son of Devabhrāja (*M. Bh.*); an attendant given to Skanda by Sūrya (*M. Bh.*)

**Śubhraraśmi** (S) (M) 1. white rayed. 3. another name for the moon.

**Subhrata** (S) (M) a good brother.

**Śubhrāvatī** (S) (F) 1. fair complexioned. 3. a river (*H. Purāṇa*)

**Śubhri** (S) (M) 1. bright; beautiful; shining. 2. a Brāhmin. 3. the sun.

**Śubhrū** (S) (F) 1. lovely browed woman. 3. an attendant of Skanda (*M. Bh.*)

**Śubhū** (S) (M) of an excellent nature; good; strong; powerful.

**Subhūma** (S) (M) 1. possessed with good

land. 2. a king. 3. another name for Kārtavirya as the 8th Jaina Ćakravartin.

**Subhūmi** (S) (M) 1. a good place. 3. a son of Ugrasena; the 9th Jaina Tīrthaṅkara and the son of King Sugrīva and Queen Ramā of Kakanādī (*J. Literature*)

**Subirāja** (S) (M) well decorated.

**Subodha** (S) (M) right intelligence.

**Subrahmaṇya** (S) (M) 1. good hermit. 2. good devotee; kind to hermits. 3. the son of Śiva and Pārvatī born to destroy the demon Tārakāsura, delivered by Gaṅgā from Agni and fostered by the 6 kṛttikās, he has 6 faces and is known by the names Kārttikeya, Kumāra, Skanda, Guha, Mahāsena and Śravāna according to his various parents, he is the husband of Devasenā.

**Subrāṅgsu** (S) (M) having beautiful limbs; born of a beautiful person.

**Śubrānśu** (S) (M) 1. with white rays. 3. another name for the moon.

**Subuddhi** (S) (F) 1. of good intellect. 2. understanding; wise; clever.

**Sućakra** (S) (M) 1. a good chariot. 3. an attendant of Skanda (*M. Bh.*); a son of Vatsaprī and Sunandā (*Mā. Purāṇa*)

**Sućakṣus** (S) (M) 1. with beautiful eyes. 3. one of the 7 tributaries of the Gaṅgā; another name for Śiva.

**Sućandra** (S) (M) 1. beautiful moon. 3. a gandharva (*M. Bh.*); an Ikṣvāku king and the son of Hemaćandra and the father of Dhūmrāśva (*V. Rāmāyaṇa*); an asura son of Siṁhikā (*M. Bh.*); a gandharva son of Kaśyapa and Prādhā (*M. Bh.*); a king of Vaiśālī; a Bodhisattva.

**Śućanti** (S) (M) 1. in continuous grief. 3. a person under the protection of the aśvins (*Ṛg Veda*)

**Sućārā** (S) (F) 1. very skilful. 2. a good performer. 3. a daughter of Śvaphalka.

**Sućarā** (S) (F) 1. with a beautiful gait. 3. an apsarā (*V. Purāṇa*)

**Sućāru** (S) (M) 1. very lovely; handsome; pleasing; delightful. 3. a son of Viśvakṣena (*H. Purāṇa*); a son of Pratiratha; a son of Bāhu (*V. Purāṇa*); a son of Dhṛtarāṣṭra (*M. Bh.*); a son of Kṛṣṇa and Rukmiṇī (*M. Bh.*)

**Sućchāyā** (S) (F) 1. throwing a beautiful shadow. 2. beautiful; shining brightly; splendid. 3. the wife of Śliṣṭi (*V. Purāṇa*)

**Sućendra** (S) (M) lord of piousness.

**Sućetana** (S) (M) very concious; very notable; distinguished.

**Sućetas** (S) (M) 1. extremely wise; intelligent; benevolent. 3. a son of Praćetas (*H. Purāṇa*); a son of Gṛtsamada and father of Varćas (*M. Bh.*)

**Sūći** (S) (M) 1. needle; magnet. 2. a military array; sight. 3. a son of Niṣāda.

**Śući** (S) (F) 1. shining; bright; clean; holy; virtuous. 3. a daughter of Tāmrā and wife of Kaśyapa regarded as the mother of waterfowl (*H. Purāṇa*)

**Śući** (S) (M) 1. shining; radiant; pure; bright; clean; holy; innocent; honest; virtuous. 2. a ray of light; a true friend. 3. a fire personified as the son of Agni Abhimānin and Svāhā (*V. Purāṇa*) or as a son of Antardhāna and Śikhaṇḍinī and brother of Pavamāna and Pāvaka (*Purāṇas*); a son of Bhṛgu (*M. Bh.*); a son of Gada (*H. Purāṇa*); a son of the 3rd Manu; Indra in the 14th Manvantara (*Purāṇas*); a son of Śatadyumna (*M. Bh.*); a son of Andhaka; a son of Vipra; a son of Manu Ćākṣuṣa and Nadvalā (*V. Purāṇa*); a solar dynasty king who was the son of Śakradyumna and father of Vanadvāja (*Bhāgavata*); a king in Yama's assembly (*M. Bh.*); a son of Viśvāmitra (*M. Bh.*); a son of sage Bhṛgu (*M. Bh.*); a maharṣi of Aṅgiras' family who was reborn as the son of King Vijitāśva (*Bhāgavata*); the son of Śuddha and the father of Trikālpava (*Bhāgavata*); a son of Kaśyapa and Tāmrā; another name for the sun, the moon, wind, Śiva and the planet Venus.

**Śućikā** (S) (F) 1. puritan; sacred. 3. an apsarā (*M. Bh.*)

**Śućikāma** (S) (M) of pure desires; one who loves purity.

**Śućikarṇika** (S) (M) White Lotus (*Nelumbium speciosum*)

**Śućimallikā** (S) (F) 1. the white vine. 2. Arabian Jasmine.

**Śućimaṇi** (S) (M) 1. pure jewel. 2. crystal.

**Śućimukhī** (S) (F) 1. pure faced. 3. the maid of princess Prabhāvatī the daughter of Vajranābha.

**Śućindra** (S) (M) lord of purity.

**Sućintā** (S) (F) deep thought.

**Śućipati** (S) (M) 1. lord of purity. 2. fire.

**Sućira** (S) (M) 1. of long duration. 2. eternity.

**Śućiratha** (S) (M) 1. with a virtuous chariot. 3. a king of the Bharata dynasty who was a son of Ćitraratha and Dhṛṣaman's father (*Bhāgavata*)

**Śućirońis** (S) (M) 1. white rayed. 3. another name for the moon.

**Sućiroṣita** (S) (M) 1. long lived. 3. a minister of Daśaratha (*V. Rāmāyaṇa*)

**Śućiṣmat** (S) (M) 1. shining; radiant. 3. a son of Kardama.

**Śućiṣmatī** (S) (F) 1. shining; radiant. 3. the mother of Agni; an apsarā in Kubera's assembly (*M. Bh.*)

**Śućismitā** (S) (F) 1. with a pious smile. 3. an apsarā in Kubera's assembly (*M. Bh.*)

**Śućiśravas** (S) (M) 1. with bright renown. 3. a prajāpati (*V. Purāṇa*); another name for Viṣṇu.

**Sućitā** (S) (F) sacred; propitious.

**Sućitra** (S) (M) 1. well marked; having auspicious marks. 2. distinguished; manifold; vareigated. 3. a nāga in the family of Dhṛtarāṣṭra (*M. Bh.*); the father of King Sukumāra of Pulinda; a son of Dhṛtarāṣṭra (*M. Bh.*); a king on the side of the Pāṇḍavas (*M. Bh.*)

**Śućivaktra** (S) (M) 1. with a needle like mouth. 3. a warrior of Skanda (*M. Bh.*); an asura (*H. Purāṇa*)

**Śućivarćas** (S) (M) having pure splendour.

**Śućivrata** (S) (M) 1. pious; follower of purity. 3. an ancient Indian king (*M. Bh.*)

**Sūdā** (S) (M) munificent.

**Sudakṣiṇa** (S) (M) 1. with an excellent right hand. 2. dextrous; courteous; polite; sincere; liberal. 3. the son of King Pauṇḍraka (*Bhāgavata*); a king of Kāmboja who fought cn the side of the Kauravas (*M. Bh.*); a warrior on the side of the Pāṇḍavas (*M. Bh.*)

**Sudāmā** (S) (F) 1. bountiful. 3. a mother in Skanda's retinue; a river (*Rāmāyaṇa*)

**Sudāman** (S) (M) 1. bountiful. 2. cloud; mountain. 3. a King Daśārṇa whose daughters married Bhīma of Vidarbha and Vīrabāhu of Ćedi (*M. Bh.*); a minister of King Janaka (*V. Rāmāyaṇa*); an attendant of Skanda (*M. Bh.*); a cowherd reborn as an asura because of the curse of Rādhā; a warrior on the side of the Pāṇḍavas (*M. Bh.*); the keeper of the garden of Kaṅsa (*Bhāgavata*); a childhood friend of Kṛṣṇa; a gandharva (*Rāmāyaṇa*); another name for Airāvata.

**Sudāmana** (S) (M) 1. good donor. 2. mythical weapon. 3. a councillor of Janaka (*Rāmāyaṇa*)

**Sudāminī** (S) (F) 1. as bright as lightning. 2. bright; light; wealthy. 3. a wife of Śamīka (*Bhā. Purāṇa*)

**Sudanṣṭra** (S) (M) 1. with beautiful teeth. 3. a rākṣasa (*Rāmāyaṇa*); a son of Kṛṣṇa (*H. Purāṇa*); a son of Śambara (*H. Purāṇa*); a son of Asamañjasa.

**Sudantā** (S) (F) 1. with good teeth. 3. an apsarā.

**Sudantī** (S) (F) 1. with good teeth. 3. the female elephant of the northwest quarter.

**Sudānu** (S) (M) bounteous; munificent.

**Sudaralakṣmī** (S) (F) goddess of beauty.

**Sudarśa** (S) (M) 1. lovely in appearance; pleasing to eyes. 2. easily seen; conspicuous; beautiful; lovely.

**Sudarśanā** (S) (F) 1. lovely in appearance; pleasing to eyes. 3. a gandharva maiden, the daughter of Ikṣvāku dynasty king, Duryodhana and Narmadā and wife of the god Agni, she is said to have been the most beautiful woman born (*M. Bh.*)

**Sudarśana** (S) (M) 1. lovely in appearance; pleasing to eyes; easily seen; keen sighted. 3. the discus of Viṣṇu (*M. Bh.*); a king rescued by Kṛṣṇa (*M. Bh.*); a king on the side of the Kauravas (*M. Bh.*); a Mālava king on the side of the Pāṇḍavas (*M. Bh.*); a son of Dhṛtarāṣṭra (*M. Bh.*); a son of King Dhruvasaṅdhi and Manoramā of Kosala; a son of Bharata and Pañćajanī (*Bhāgavata*); the son of Agni and Sudarśanā and the husband of Oghavatī; a vidyādhara (*Bhāgavata*); a son of Dīrghabāhu (*Bh. Purāṇa*); the chariot of Indra (*M. Bh.*); a Buddha (*L. Vistara*); a nāga; a ćakravartin; a king of Ujjayinī; a son of Śaṅkhana (*Rāmāyaṇa*); a son of Arthasiddhi (*H. Purāṇa*); a son of Dadhīći; a son of Ajamīdha (*H. Purāṇa*); a son-in-law of Pṛatīka (*Bh. Purāṇa*); a king of Hastināpur and father of Tīrthaṅkara Aranātha; a son of Śaṅkhana (*Rāmāyaṇa*)

**Sudarśi** (S) (M) **1.** easily seen; conspicuous. **3.** a sage who was the son of Kuśika.

**Sudarśinī** (S) (F) **1.** lovely in appearance; pleasing to eyes. **2.** a lotus pond.

**Sudāsa** (S) (M) **1.** a good servant. **2.** worshipping the gods well. **3.** a king of the Tṛtsus and son of Divodāsa; a king of Kosala who is among those that should be remembered at dawn and dusk (*M. Bh.*); a king of Ayodhyā who was the son of Sarvakāma and the father of Kalmāṣapāda (*Bhāgavata*); the grandson of Ṛtuparṇa (*H. Purāṇa*); a son of Ćyavana; a son of Bṛhadratha (*H. Purāṇa*); the father of Mitrasaha.

**Sudattā** (S) (F) **1.** well given. **3.** a wife of Kṛṣṇa (*M. Bh.*)

**Sudatta** (S) (M) **1.** well given. **3.** a son of Śatadhanvan (*H. Purāṇa*)

**Sudāvan** (S) (M) bounteous; munificent.

**Sudāya** (S) (M) good and auspicious gift.

**Śuddhā** (S) (F) **1.** clean; pure; holy; sacred. **3.** a daughter of Sinhahanu (*B. Literature*)

**Śuddha** (S) (M) **1.** clean; clear; pure; bright; white; blameless; right; correct; genuine; true. **3.** one of the 7 sages under the 14th Manu (*Bhā. Purāṇa*); a Bhṛgu dynasty king who was the son of Anenas and father of Sūći (*Bhāgavata*); another name for Śiva.

**Śuddhābha** (S) (M) consisting of pure light.

**Śuddhabhairava** (S) (M) **1.** pure. **3.** a rāga.

**Śuddhakarman** (S) (M) pure; honest.

**Śuddhakirti** (S) (M) having pure renown.

**Śuddhamati** (S) (M) **1.** pure minded. **3.** the 21st Arhat of the past Utsarpinī.

**Śuddhānanda** (S) (M) pure joy.

**Śuddhātman** (S) (M) **1.** pure minded. **3.** another name for Śiva.

**Śuddhī** (S) (F) **1.** purification; holiness; truth; clearness. **3.** a Śakti of Viṣṇu; Dākṣāyāṇī in Kapālamoćanạ; another name for Durgā.

**Śuddhodana** (S) (M) **1.** having pure food. **3.** a king of Kapilavastu and father of Gautama Buddha (*B. Literature*)

**Sudeśa** (S) (M) good place.

**Sudeṣṇā** (S) (F) **1.** born in a good place. **3.** the daughter of the king of Kekaya and wife of King Virāṭa of Matsya and the mother of Uttarā (*M. Bh.*); the wife of King Bali and the mother of Aṅga, Vaṅga, Kaliṅga, Puṇḍra and Suhma by the hermit Dīrghatamas (*Bhāgavata*)

**Sudeṣṇa** (S) (M) **1.** born in a good place. **3.** a son of Kṛṣṇa and Rukmiṇī (*H. Purāṇa*); a son of Asamañjas.

**Sudevā** (S) (F) **1.** a real goddess. **3.** the daughter of King Ariha of Aṅga and the father of King Ṛkṣa (*M. Bh.*); the wife of King Vikuṇṭha of the Purū dynasty and the mother of King Ajamīdha (*M. Bh.*); the daughter of King Devarāta of Kāśī and the wife of Ikṣvāku, she is supposed to have been an incarnation of Lakṣmī (*P. Purāṇa*)

**Sudeva** (S) (M) **1.** a real god. **3.** a captain of the army of King Ambarīṣa (*M. Bh.*); a son of King Haryaśva of Kāśī (*M. Bh.*); a king whose daughter married Nābhāga; a son of Akrūra (*H. Purāṇa*); a son of Ćañcu (*H. Purāṇa*); a son of Devaka (*V. Purāṇa*); a son of Viṣṇu (*Bh. Purāṇa*)

**Sudevī** (S) (F) **1.** real goddess. **3.** the wife of Nābhi and mother of Ṛṣabha (*Bhā. Purāṇa*)

**Sudhā** (S) (F) **1.** good drink; welfare; ease, comfort. **2.** nectar; lightning; honey, Soma, water. **3.** the wife of a rudra; another name for the Gaṅgā; *Desmodium gangeticum*; Prickly Pear (*Opuntia dillenii*); Black Myrobalan (*Terminalia chebula*)

**Sudhābhuja** (S) (M) **1.** eating nectar. **2.** a deity.

**Sudhādhāra** (S) (M) **1.** nectar receptacle. **3.** another name for the moon.

**Sudhākara** (S) (M) **1.** receptacle of nectar. **3.** another name for the moon.

**Sudhāman** (S) (M) **1.** a holy place; belonging to a holy place; living in a sacred house. **3.** a son of King Ghṛtapṛṣṭha (*Bhāgavata*); a mountain.

**Sudhāmṛta** (S) (M) nectar and honey conjoined.

**Sudhāmukhī** (S) (F) 1. nectar mouthed. 3. an apsarā.

**Sudhana** (S) (M) very rich.

**Sudhāṅga** (S) (M) 1. nectar bodied. 3. another name for the moon.

**Sudhānidhi** (S) (M) 1. treasure of nectar. 3. another name for the moon.

**Sudhānśu** (S) (M) 1. nectar rayed. 3. another name for the moon.

**Sudhānśuratna** (S) (F) 1. jewel of the moon. 2. pearl.

**Sudhanuṣ** (S) (M) 1. good archer. 2. with a good bow. 3. a Purū king who was the son of King Kuru (*A. Purāṇa*); the father of Suhotra (*Bhāgavata*); a Pānćāla warrior who was the son of King Drupada and the brother of Vīraketu and who fought on the side of the Pāṇḍavas (*M. Bh.*); an ancestor of Gautama Buddha.

**Sudhanvan** (S) (M) 1. with an excellent bow. 3. a son of Vairāja (*H. Purāṇa*); a son of Sambhūta (*H. Purāṇa*); a son of Ahīnagu; a son of Kuru (*H. Purāṇa*); a son of Śāśvata (*V. Purāṇa*); a son of Satyadhṛta; the guard at the end of the eastern quarter of the world (*A. Purāṇa*); son of sage Aṅgiras and the father of Ṛbhū, Vibhvan and Vāja (*Ṛg Veda*); a warrior on the side of the Kauravas (*M. Bh.*); king of Saṅkāśya (*V. Rāmāyaṇa*); another name for Viṣṇu, Ananta and Tvaṣṭṛ.

**Sudhanya** (S) (M) overtly blessed; good archer; much praised.

**Sudhapāṇi** (S) (M) 1. bearing nectar in his hands. 3. another name for Dhanvantari.

**Sudhara** (S) (M) 1. abode of the good. 3. an Arhat.

**Sudharmā** (S) (F) 1. of right path; follower of law. 3. the assembly hall of the gods (*Bhāgavata*); the wife of Mātali and the mother of Guṇakeśī (*M. Bh.*)

**Sudharma** (S) (M) 1. maintaining law or justice. 3. one of the 10 disciples of Mahāvira; a king of the kinnaras; a Vṛṣṇi prince who was a member of Yudhiṣṭhira's assembly (*M. Bh.*); a king of Dāśārṇa (*M. Bh.*); a Kaurava army warrior (*M. Bh.*); the son of Dhammilla and Bhaddalā, he became the head of the Jaina church after Mahāvira's death (*J. Literature*)

**Sudharman** (S) (M) 1. of right path; the maintainer of a family. 3. a viśvadeva (*H. Purāṇa*); a son of Dṛḍhanemi (*H. Purāṇa*); a son of Ćitraka (*H. Purāṇa*)

**Sudharmiṣṭha** (S) (M) most virtuous.

**Sudhāsū** (S) (M) 1. nectar producer. 3. another name for the moon.

**Sudhāsūti** (S) (M) 1. producing nectar. 2. a lotus flower (*Nelumbo speciosum*). 3. another name for the moon.

**Sudhavāsa** (S) (M) 1. abode of nectar. 3. another name for the moon.

**Sudhendra** (S) (M) 1. lord of nectar. 3. another name for the moon.

**Sudhendu** (S) (M) nectar and moon conjoined.

**Sudhī** (S) (F) good sense; intelligence.

**Sudhibhūṣaṇa** (S) (M) with knowledge as his ornament.

**Sudhīra** (S) (M) very considerate or wise; firm; resolute.

**Sudhita** (S) (M) well disposed; kind; benevolent; nectarlike.

**Sudhṛti** (S) (M) 1. very patient; very tolerant. 3. a king of Videha who was the son of Mahāvīrya and the father of Dhṛṣṭaketu (*Bhāgavata*)

**Sudīkṣā** (S) (F) 1. beautiful consecration. 3. another name for Lakṣmī.

**Sudīpa** (S) (M) very bright.

**Sudīpta** (S) (M) shining brightly.

**Suditi** (S) (F) bright flame.

**Sudiva** (S) (M) shining brightly.

**Śudrā** (S) (F) 1. a woman of the 4th caste. 3. a daughter of Raudrāśva.

**Śūdraka** (S) (M) 1. of the 4th caste. 3. Sanskṛt dramatist and author of *Mrcćhākaṭikā* (2nd century A.D.)

**Sudṛś** (S) (M) 1. pleasing to the eye. 2. handsome; with beautiful eyes.

**Sudṛśī** (S) (F) 1. pleasing to the eye. 2. pretty; with beautiful eyes.

**Sudurjaya** (S) (M) 1. very difficult to overcome. 3. a son of Suvīra (*M. Bh.*); one of the 13 stages of a Bodhisattva.

**Sudya** (S) (M) 1. shining brightly; very well illuminated. 3. a Yayāti dynasty king who was the son of Ćārupāda and the father of Bahugava (*Bhāgavata*)

**Sudyotman** (S) (M) shining brightly.

**Sudyumna** (S) (M) 1. very glorious. 2. with an illuminating beauty. 3. a son of Manu Ćākṣuṣa and Nadvalā (*V. Purāṇa*); a son of Manu Vaivasvata (*M. Bh.*); a son of Abhayada (*H. Purāṇa*)

**Sudyut** (S) (M) shining beautifully.

**Sugaṇā** (S) (F) 1. good attendant. 3. a mother in Skanda's retinue (*M. Bh.*)

**Sugandhā** (S) (F) 1. fragrant; Sacred Basil (*Ocimum sanctum*) 3. a form of Dākṣāyāṇī; an apsarā (*M. Bh.*); Fleabane (*Artemisia vulgaris*); Caraway (*Carum carvi*); *Hiptage madoblata*.

**Sugandha** (S) (M) 1. fragrance. 3. a rākṣasa killed by Agni (*P. Purāṇa*)

**Sugandhī** (S) (F) 1. fragrant. 2. the small banana; the blue lotus (*Nymphaea stellata*); sandal. 3. a wife of Vasudeva and mother of Puṇḍra (*Vā. Purāṇa*); *Elettaria cardomomum*.

**Sugandhi** (S) (M) 1. sweet smelling. 2. fragrance; lion; virtuous; pious. 3. Supreme Being.

**Sugandhikā** (S) (F) fragrant.

**Sugandhimukha** (S) (M) 1. one who has a fragrant mouth. 3. a Bodhisattva.

**Sugata** (S) (M) 1. going well; well bestowed. 3. a Buddha.

**Sugatī** (S) (F) welfare; happiness; bliss.

**Sugati** (S) (M) 1. welfare; bliss; happiness. 3. a Bharata dynasty king who was the son of Gaya (*M. Bh.*); an Arhat.

**Sugātra** (S) (M) fair limbed; graceful.

**Sugātrī** (S) (F) fair limbed; graceful; beautiful.

**Sugātu** (S) (M) welfare; prosperity.

**Sugavi** (S) (M) 1. with a beautiful; gait; possessing good cattle. 3. a son of Prasuśruta (*V. Purāṇa*)

**Sugeṣṇā** (S) (F) 1. singing well. 3. a kinnarī.

**Sughosa** (S) (M) 1. making a pleasant sound. 3. the conch of Nakula (*M. Bh.*); a Buddha (*L. Vistara*)

**Sugopta** (S) (M) 1. well protected. 3. a viśvadeva (*M. Bh.*)

**Sugrīva** (S) (M) 1. handsome necked. 2. hero; swan; a type of weapon. 3. the father of the 9th Arhat of the present Avasarpinī; a conch; the monkey son of Sūrya and Aruṇī and the brother of Bāli and king of Kiṣkindhā after Rāma killed Bāli (*Rāmāyaṇa*); an asura minister of Śumbha (*D. Bhāgavata*); a horse of Kṛṣṇa (*M. Bh.*)

**Sugrīveśa** (S) (M) 1. lord of Sugrīva. 3. another name for Rāma.

**Sugrīvī** (S) (F) 1. beautiful necked. 3. a daughter of Kaśyapa and Tāmrā and mother of horses, camels and donkeys (*H. Purāṇa*); an apsarā (*H. Purāṇa*)

**Suguṇa** (S) (M) with good qualities.

**Suhā** (S) (F) 1. rejoicing. 3. a rāga.

**Suhala** (S) (M) with an excellent plough.

**Suhanu** (S) (M) 1. with beautiful jaws. 3. an asura in Varuṇa's assembly (*M. Bh.*)

**Suhara** (S) (M) 1. seizing well. 3. an asura (*M. Bh.*)

**Suhāsa** (S) (M) with a beautiful smile.

**Suhāsinī** (S) (F) smiling beautifully.

**Suhasta** (S) (M) 1. with beautiful hands. 2. skilled; dextrous. 3. a son of Dhṛtarāṣṭra (*M. Bh.*)

**Suhastin** (S) (M) 1. a good elephant. 3. the successor of Mahāgiri as the head of the Jaina church (*J. Literature*)

**Suhastya** (S) (M) 1. with beautiful hands; possessing nice elephants. 3. a muni extolled in the *Ṛg Veda* who was the son of Ghoṣā.

**Suhava** (S) (M) 1. invoking well. 2. performer of rites; devout; pious; performing oblation.

**Suhavis** (S) (M) 1. offering many oblations. 2. devout. 3. a Bharata dynasty king who was the son of Bhūmanyu and Puṣkariṇī (*M. Bh.*)

**Suhelā** (S) (F) easily accessible.

**Suhitā** (S) (F) 1. beneficial. 2. suitable. 3. one of the 7 tongues of fire.

**Suhita** (S) (M) 1. beneficial. 2. very fit; suitable.

**Suhma** (S) (M) 1. measuring happiness. 3. a son of Dīrghatamas and Sudeṣṇā.

**Suhotṛ** (S) (M) 1. sacrificer. 3. a son of

Bhumanyu (*M. Bh.*); a son of Vitatha (*H. Purāṇa*)

**Suhotra** (S) (M) **1.** good priest. **3.** a son of Bhumanyu (*M. Bh.*); a son of Kañćanaprabha (*H. Purāṇa*); a son of Bṛhatkṣatra (*H. Purāṇa*); a son of Bṛhadīkṣu (*H. Purāṇa*); a son of Sudhanus; a daitya; sage Jamadagni and Reṇukā (*Br. Purāṇa*); a Ćandra dynasty king who was a grandson of Emperor Bharata and the husband of Suvarnā and the father of Ajamīdha, Sumīdha and Purumīdha (*M. Bh.*); a son of Sahadeva and Vijayā (*M. Bh.*); a Kuru dynasty king; a rākṣasa who once ruled the world (*M. Bh.*)

**Suhṛda** (S) (M) **1.** kind hearted. **2.** friend; another name for Śiva.

**Suhu** (S) (M) **1.** invoking. **3.** a Yādava king who was a son of Ugrasena (*Bhāgavata*)

**Suhva** (S) (M) **1.** cordially invited. **3.** a king of the Bharata dynasty who was a son of Bali's wife and the sage Dīrghatamas (*Bhāgavata*)

**Sujala** (S) (M) **1.** of good water. **2.** the Indian Lotus (*Nelumbium nucifera*)

**Sujana** (S) (M) **1.** a nice person; good; virtuous; kind; benevolent; a gentlemen. **3.** another name for Indra's charioteer.

**Sujantu** (S) (M) **1.** good animal. **3.** a son of Jahnu (*V. Purāṇa*)

**Sujānu** (S) (M) **1.** with beautiful knees. **3.** a hermit (*M. Bh.*)

**Sujasā** (S) (F) **1.** of good fame. **3.** mother of Anantanātha.

**Sujāta** (S) (M) **1.** well-born; noble; fine; beautiful. **3.** a son of Dhṛtarāṣṭra (*M. Bh.*); a monkey king who was the son of Pulaha and Śvetā (*Br. Purāṇa*); a son of Bharata (*V. Purāṇa*)

**Sujātā** (S) (F) **1.** well born. **2.** noble; beautiful. **3.** a daughter of Uddālaka and wife of Kahoda (*M. Bh.*)

**Sujāti** (S) (M) **1.** of good tribe. **3.** a son of Vitihotra.

**Sujaya** (S) (M) a great triumph.

**Sujita** (S) (M) great conqueror.

**Sujīthava** (S) (M) related to a great triumph.

**Sujyeṣtha** (S) (M) **1.** great noble. **3.** a king who was the son of Agnimitra and the father of Vasumitra (*Bhāgavata*)

**Suka** (S) (M) **1.** arrow; air; wind; lotus (*Nelumbo speciosum*) **3.** a son of Hrāda (*H. Purāṇa*)

**Śuka** (S) (M) **1.** the bright one. **2.** parrot. **3.** a son of sage Vyāsa and apsarā Ghṛtāći and husband of Pīvarī and father of Kṛṣṇa, Gauraprabhā, Bhūri and Devaśruta and a daughter named Kīrtī (*Bhāgavata*); a messenger of Rāvaṇa (*V. Rāmāyaṇa*); a lunar dynasty king (*Bhāgavata*); a king of the Śaryāti dynasty who was the son of Pṛṣata (*M. Bh.*); a son of King Subala of Gāndhāra (*M. Bh.*); a son of the monkey Śarabha and the husband of Vyāghrī and father of Ṛkṣa (*Br. Purāṇa*); an asura (*H. Purāṇa*); a king of the gandharvas (*Rāmāyaṇa*); a minister of Rāvaṇa (*Rāmāyaṇa*)

**Śukadeva** (S) (M) **1.** lord of parrots. **3.** a son of Vyāsa; a son of Harihara; another name for Kṛṣṇa.

**Sukakṣa** (S) (M) **1.** abode of good. **3.** a ṛṣi and author of *Ṛg Veda* (viii)

**Sukalā** (S) (F) a good part; very skilled.

**Sukalya** (S) (M) perfectly sound.

**Sukāma** (S) (M) having good desires; much desired; lovely.

**Sukamala** (S) (M) **1.** beautiful lotus flower. **3.** a yakṣa who was the son of Manivara and Devajanī (*Br. Purāṇa*)

**Śukanābha** (S) (M) **1.** parrot navelled. **3.** a rākṣasa in the army of Rāvaṇa (*V. Rāmāyaṇa*)

**Sukānta** (S) (M) very handsome.

**Sukaṇṭha** (S) (M) sweet voiced.

**Sukaṇṭhi** (S) (F) **1.** sweet voiced. **2.** the female Indian cuckoo. **3.** an apsarā (*B. Rāmāyaṇa*)

**Sukānti** (S) (M) full of glory; very handsome.

**Sukanyā** (S) (F) **1.** beautiful maiden. **3.** the daughter of Śaryāti and wife of ṛṣi Ćyavana (*H. Purāṇa*); the wife of sage Mātariśvan and the mother of Maṅkaṇa.

**Sukarmā** (S) (M) **1.** doer of good; virtuous. **3.** an attendant given to Skanda by Vidhātā (*M. Bh.*); a teacher of the *Sāma Veda*.

**Sukarman** (S) (M) **1.** doer of good; virtuous; good; good architect. **3.** another name for Viśvakarman; a class of deities.

**Sukarṇa** (S) (M) 1. beautiful eared. 3. a rākṣasa (*Rāmāyaṇa*)

**Śukasangīti** (S) (M) 1. singing like a parrot. 3. a gandharva.

**Śukavāṇi** (S) (F) with a voice like the note of a parrot.

**Śukāyana** (S) (M) 1. resembling a parrot. 2. with a bright path. 3. an Arhat (*B. Literature*)

**Sukendu** (S) (M) the Tāmala tree; like the moon.

**Sukeśa** (S) (M) 1. with beautiful hair. 3. a rākṣasa son of Vidyutkeśa and Śālakaṭaṅkā who married Devavatī and the father of Māli, Sumāli and Mālyavān (*U. Rāmāyaṇa*)

**Sukesara** (S) (M) of saffron colour; beautiful orange; the Citron tree (*Citrus medica*)

**Sukeśī** (S) (F) 1. with beautiful hair. 3. the daughter of the king of Gāndhāra and a wife of Kṛṣṇa (*M. Bh.*); an apsarā (*M. Bh.*); a daughter of King Ketuvīrya of Magadha and wife of Marutta (*Mā. Purāṇa*)

**Suketa** (S) (M) 1. having good intentions; benevolent. 3. an āditya.

**Suketana** (S) (M) 1. with a good banner. 3. a Bhṛgu dynasty king who was the son of Sunīthā and father of Dharmaketu (*Bhāgavata*)

**Suketu** (S) (M) 1. very bright. 3. a king of the yakṣas; a solar dynasty king who was the son of Nandivardhana and father of Devarāta (*Bhāgavata*); a Purū dynasty king who was a son of Bharata (*A. Purāṇa*); a son of Śiśupāla (*M. Bh.*); a king on the side of the Pāṇḍavas who was the son of Ćitraketu (*M. Bh.*); the son of the Gandharva king, Surākṣaka and the father of Tāṭakā (*K. Rāmāyaṇa*); another name for Viṣṇu.

**Sukhā** (S) (F) 1. piety; virtue; ease; comfort; pleasure. 3. one of the 9 Śaktis of Śiva.

**Sukha** (S)*(M) happiness personified as the son of Dharma and Siddhi.

**Sukhadā** (S) (F) 1. bestower of happiness. 3. an apsarā; another name for the Gaṅgā; *Mimosa suma*; *Prosopis spicigera*.

**Sukhadarśina** (S) (M) seer of happiness.

**Sukhadeva** (S) (M) lord of happiness.

**Sukhadīpa** (S) (M) lamp of happiness.

**Sukhagandha** (S) (M) sweet smelling; fragrant.

**Sukhajammā** (Kannada) (F) 1. the mother who grants happiness. 3. the village goddess of smallpox.

**Sukhājāta** (S) (M) 1. happy. 3. another name for Śiva.

**Sukhajīt** (S) (M) conquering happiness.

**Sukhakara** (S) (M) 1. causing happiness. 3. another name for Rāma.

**Sukhaleśa** (S) (M) a little pleasure.

**Sukhamaṇi** (S) (M) jewel of happiness.

**Sukhamaya** (S) (M) filled with happiness.

**Sukhamitra** (S) (M) friend of happiness.

**Sukhamukha** (S) (M) 1. happy faced. 3. a yakṣa.

**Sukhānanda** (S) (M) the joy of happiness.

**Sukhanātha** (S) (M) 1. lord of happiness. 3. a deity worshipped in Mathurā.

**Sukhaṅkara** (S) (M) giving pleasure.

**Sukhapāla** (S) (M) protecting happiness.

**Sukhaprada** (S) (M) giving happiness.

**Sukharāja** (S) (M) lord of happiness.

**Sukharañjana** (S) (M) delighting in happiness; coloured with pleasure.

**Sukharūpa** (S) (M) with a pleasant appearance.

**Sukhasāgara** (S) (M) ocean of happiness.

**Sukhāśakta** (S) (M) 1. devoted to happiness. 3. another name for Śiva.

**Sukhavanta** (S) (M) happy.

**Sukhavarman** (S) (M) warrior of happiness.

**Sukhavatī** (S) (F) 1. happy. 3. the paradise of Amitābha (*B. Literature*); the wife of Sūryaprabhā (*K. Sāgara*)

**Sukhayitrī** (S) (M) one who gladdens.

**Sukheśa** (S) (M) lord of happiness.

**Sukheśin** (S) (M) desirer of happiness; desiring others happiness; wishing well.

**Sukheṣṭha** (S) (M) 1. living in joy. 3. another name for Śiva.

**Sukhin** (S) (M) 1. happy; glad; joyful. 2. a religious ascetic.

**Sukhinala** (S) (M) 1. carrier of joy. 3. a son of

Sućakṣus (*Bhā. Purāṇa*)

**Sukhodaya** (S) (M) 1. resulting in happiness; the realization of pleasure. 3. an intoxicating honey drink. 3. a son of Medhātithi (*Mā. Purāṇa*)

**Sukhsam** (S) (M) delicate.

**Sukhyāta** (S) (M) very renowned.

**Śukī** (S) (F) 1. parrot. 2. bright; talkative; quickwitted. 3. a daughter of Kaśyapa and Tāmrā and the mother of Natā (*V. Rāmāyaṇa*); the mythical mother of parrots and wife of Kaśyapa; the wife of Saptarṣi (*Bh. Purāṇa*)

**Sukīrtī** (S) (F) well praised; hymn of praise.

**Sukīrti** (S) (M) 1. well praised. 3. a ṛṣi and author of *Ṛg Veda* (x)

**Śuklā** (S) (F) 1. white; bright; pure; white cow. 3. another name for Sarasvatī.

**Śukla** (S) (M) 1. white; bright; light; pure; unsullied. 3. a Pānćāla warrior on the side of the Pāṇḍavas (*M. Bh.*); the month Vaiśākha; a son of Havirdhāna (*H. Purāṇa*); another name for Śiva and Viṣṇu.

**Śuklāćāra** (S) (M) pure in conduct.

**Śuklodana** (S) (M) 1. pure water. 3. a brother of Śuddhodana.

**Śukra** (S) (M) 1. bright; resplendent; clear; pure; white; spotless. 3. the month of Jyeṣṭha (May/June), personified as the guardian of Kubera's treasure (*M. Bh.*); a marutvat (*H. Purāṇa*); the 3rd Manu (*H. Purāṇa*); one of the 7 sages under Manu Bhautya (*Mā. Purāṇa*); a son of Bhava (*V. Purāṇa*); the planet Venus and its regent regarded as the preceptor of the asuras who was a son of Bhṛgu and Pulomā, he married Jayantī the daughter of Indra, Ūrjāṣvatī and Sataparvā and was the father of Devayānī, Arā, Devī and 4 sons (*M. Bh.*); a son of Vasiṣṭha and Ūrjjā and a saptarṣi of the 3rd Manvantara (*V. Purāṇa*); a king of the Pṛthu dynasty who was a son of Havirdhāna and Dhīṣaṇā (*V. Purāṇa*); another name for Agni (*Rāmāyaṇa*)

**Śukrāćārya** (S) (M) 1. preceptor of purity. 3. the regent of the planet Venus and the preceptor of the daityas.

**Sukratu** (S) (M) 1. one who does virtuous deeds. 2. benevolent; virtuous; pious. 3. another name for Agni, Śiva, Indra, Mitra, Varuṇa, Sūrya, and Soma.

**Sukrīḍā** (S) (F) 1. sporting. 3. an apsarā.

**Śukriman** (S) (M) brightness; purity.

**Sukṛṣa** (S) (M) 1. very thin. 3. a hermit (*Mā. Purāṇa*)

**Sukṛtā** (S) (F) 1. a pious deed; doing good; pious. 3. a river (*V. Purāṇa*)

**Sukṛta** (S) (M) 1. a pious deed; doing good; virtuous; pious; wise; benevolent. 2. lucky; well made. 3. another name for Tvaṣṭṛ and fire; a prajāpati (*V. Purāṇa*); a son of Pṛthu (*H. Purāṇa*)

**Sukṛtī** (S) (F) kindness; good conduct; virtue; kindness; auspiciousness.

**Sukṛtin** (S) (M) 1. righteous; virtuous. 3. a son of Manu Svārocisa (*H. Purāṇa*); a ṛṣi in the 10th Manvantara (*Bhā. Purāṇa*)

**Sukṣa** (S) (F) with good eyes.

**Sukṣatra** (S) (M) 1. great warrior; ruling well; powerful. 3. a son of the king of Kosala who fought on the side of the Pāṇḍavas (*M. Bh.*); a son of Niramitra (*V. Purāṇa*)

**Sukṣetra** (S) (M) 1. sprung from a good womb. 2. noble. 3. a son of the 10th Manu (*Mā. Purāṇa*)

**Sūkṣma** (S) (M) 1. thin; subtle. 3. a dānava son of Kaśyapa and Danu and who was reborn as King Jayadratha (*M. Bh.*)

**Sūkṣmanābha** (S) (M) 1. mystical navelled. 3. another name for Viṣṇu.

**Sūktā** (S) (M) 1. well recited. 2. the Sārika bird.

**Śukta** (S) (M) 1. astringent; sour. 3. a son of Vasiṣṭha (*Mā. Purāṇa*)

**Sūkti** (S) (F) beautiful verse; a wise saying.

**Śukti** (S) (F) 1. shining; bright. 2. an oyster shell.

**Śuktikarṇa** (S) (M) 1. shell eared. 3. a serpent demon (*H. Purāṇa*)

**Śuktimatī** (S) (F) 1. having oyster shells. 3. a river (*M. Bh.*)

**Sukukṣī** (S) (F) 1. born from a good womb. 2. noble. 3. a gandharva maiden (*K. Vyuha*)

**Sukula** (S) (M) sprung from a noble family.

**Sukumāra** (S) (M) 1. very tender; very delicate. 2. the wild Ćampaka flower (*Michelia champaka*). 3. a Pulinda king who was the son of King Sumitra (*M. Bh.*); a nāga in the family of Takṣaka (*M. Bh.*); a Purū dynasty king who was a son of Vibhu and the father of Satyaketu (*A. Purāṇa*); a son of King Bhavya of Śāka island (*M. Bh.*); banana (*Musa sapientum*); Blackeye Pea (*Vigna catiang*); Yellow Ćampa (*Michelia champaka*)

**Sukumāraka** (S) (M) 1. very tender. 3. a son of Jāmbavat (*V. Purāṇa*)

**Sukumārī** (S) (F) 1. very tender; very delicate; with soft and delicate skin. 2. *Jasminum sambac*. 3. a river (*M. Bh.*); a daughter of King Sṛñjaya and a wife of sage Nārada.

**Sukuṇḍala** (S) (M) 1. with beautiful earrings. 3. a son of Dhṛtarāṣṭra (*M. Bh.*)

**Sukusumā** (S) (F) 1. ornamented with beautiful flowers. 3. a mother in Skanda's retinue (*M. Bh.*)

**Sulabhā** (S) (F) 1. easily available. 2. attainable; *Jasminum sambac*; *Ocimum sanctum*. 3. an ascetic who held discourse with King Janaka (*M. Bh.*)

**Sulabhalalitā** (S) (F) easily obtainable pretty woman.

**Śūlabhṛt** (S) (M) 1. bearing a spear. 3. another name for Śiva and Kṛṣṇa.

**Śūladhara** (S) (M) 1. bearing a spear. 3. another name for Rudra-Śiva.

**Śūladharā** (S) (F) 1. consort of Śiva. 3. another name for Durgā.

**Śūladhāriṇī** (S) (F) 1. holding a spear. 3. another name for Durgā.

**Śūladhṛk** (S) (M) 1. bearing a spear. 3. another name for Śiva.

**Śūlahasta** (S) (M) 1. holding a spear. 3. another name for Śiva.

**Sulakṣa** (S) (M) 1. having auspicious marks. 2. fortunate.

**Sulakṣaṇā** (S) (F) 1. with auspicious marks. 2. fortunate; with good qualities. 3. a wife of Kṛṣṇa; a friend of Umā; a wife of Ćaṇḍaghoṣa.

**Sulakṣmī** (S) (F) 1. divine Lakṣmī. 3. one of the 4 divine women who rose out of the Ocean of Milk (*P. Purāṇa*)

**Śūlāṅka** (S) (M) 1. marked by a spear. 3. another name for Śiva.

**Śūlapāṇi** (S) (M) 1. with a spear in hand. 3. another name for Rudra-Śiva.

**Suleka** (S) (M) 1. the sun. 3. the āditya having beautiful rays.

**Sulekhā** (S) (F) 1. having auspicious lines. 2. fortunate.

**Śūlī** (S) (M) 1. spear carrier. 3. another name for Kṛṣṇa.

**Śūlin** (S) (M) 1. armed with a spear. 3. another name for Rudra-Śiva.

**Śūlinī** (S) (F) 1. armed with a spear. 3. another name for Durgā.

**Suloćanā** (S) (F) 1. with beautiful eyes. 3. a wife of Indrajit; an apsarā (*H. Purāṇa*); a yakṣiṇī (*K. Sāgara*); the wife of King Mādhava (*P. Purāṇa*)

**Suloćana** (S) (M) 1. having beautiful eyes. 2. deer. 3. a son of Dhṛtarāṣṭra (*M. Bh.*); the father of Rukmiṇī; a Buddha (*L. Vistara*)

**Sulohitā** (S) (F) 1. very red. 3. one of the 7 tongues of fire.

**Sulomā** (S) (F) 1. with beautiful hair. 2. Indian Redwood (*Soymida febrifuga*)

**Suma** (S) (M) the moon; the sky; camphor; flower.

**Sūma** (S) (M) milk; water.

**Sumada** (S) (M) 1. joyful; delighting. 3. a ṛṣi.

**Sumadātmajā** (S) (F) 1. daughter of passion. 3. an apsarā.

**Sumadhura** (S) (M) sweet speech.

**Sumadhyā** (S) (F) 1. graceful woman; slender waisted. 3. daughter of Madirākṣa (*M. Bh.*)

**Sumaha** (S) (M) 1. glorious. 3. the charioteer of Paraśurāma (*M. Bh.*)

**Sumahasvana** (S) (M) 1. very loud sounding. 3. another name for Śiva.

**Sumahu** (S) (M) with glory.

**Sumāla** (S) (M) nice garland.

**Sumālin** (S) (M) 1. well garlanded. 3. a rākṣasa who was the son of Sukeśa; a son of Patālarāvaṇa (*K. Rāmāyaṇa*); an asura son of Praheti (*Br. Purāṇa*)

**Sumālinī** (S) (F) 1. well garlanded. 3. a gandharvī (*K. Vyuha*)

**Sumāllikā** (S) (F) a special kind of geese; a

beautiful shuttle.

**Sumālya** (S) (M) **1.** wearing a nice garland. **3.** a son of Nanda.

**Sumanā** (S) (F) **1.** charming; lovely; beautiful; wheat; Spanish Jasmine (*Jasminum grandiflorum*); *Rosa glandulifera*. **3.** a wife of Dama (*Mā. Purāṇa*); the wife of Madhu and mother of Vīravrata.

**Sumana** (S) (M) **1.** of nice disposition; of a great heart; extremely thoughtful; charming; handsome. **3.** a nāga.

**Sumanas** (S) (M) **1.** of high intellect; pure-hearted. **2.** benevolent; gracious; favourable; agreeable; cheerful; easy; a god. **3.** a son of Ūru and Āgneyī; a dānava (*H. Purāṇa*); a son of Ulmuka (*Bhā. Purāṇa*); a son of Haryaśva (*V. Purāṇa*); a king in Yudhiṣṭhira's court (*M. Bh.*); a king in Yama's court (*M. Bh.*); a son of Purū and Atrī (*A. Purāṇa*)

**Sumanda** (S) (M) **1.** well decorated; watchful; very slow. **3.** son of Santurodha and brother of King Duṣyanta (*A. Purāṇa*)

**Sumaṇḍala** (S) (M) **1.** charmed circle; halo round the moon or sun. **3.** a king.

**Sumangalā** (S) (F) **1.** auspicious. **3.** an apsarā; a mother in Skanda's retinue (*M. Bh.*); a river (*K. Purāṇa*); a queen of Ayodhyā and mother of Sumatīnātha Jaina Tīrthaṅkara (*J. Literature*)

**Sumangala** (S) (M) auspicious.

**Sumangalī** (S) (F) **1.** auspicious. **3.** another name for Pārvatī.

**Sumaṇi** (S) (M) **1.** adorned with jewels; a nice jewel. **3.** an attendant given to Skanda by the moon (*M. Bh.*)

**Sumanomukha** (S) (M) **1.** with a nice face and heart. **3.** a nāga in the Kaśyapa dynasty (*M. Bh.*)

**Sumanta** (S) (M) easily known; a friendly sentiment.

**Sumantra** (S) (M) **1.** good advisor; following good advice. **3.** a minister and charioteer of Daśaratha (*V. Rāmāyaṇa*); a son of Antarīkṣa (*V. Purāṇa*)

**Sumantraka** (S) (M) **1.** following good advice. **3.** an elder brother of Kalki (*K. Purāṇa*)

**Sumantu** (S) (M) **1.** well known. **2.** invocation. **3.** a son of Jahnu (*V. Purāṇa*); a disciple of Vyāsa (*M. Bh.*)

**Sumanyu** (S) (M) **1.** liberal. **3.** a gandharva (*M. Bh.*)

**Sumat** (S) (M) **1.** of a good nature; highly intellectual. **2.** benevolent; wise.

**Sumatī** (S) (F) **1.** good mind; benevolence; kindness; devotion. **3.** a daughter of Kratu (*V. Purāṇa*); a wife of Viṣṇuyaśas and mother of Kalkin (*K. Purāṇa*); a wife of Lava.

**Sumati** (S) (M) **1.** good mind; benevolence; kindness; devotion. **3.** a daitya (*M. Bh.*); a ṛṣi under Manu Sāvarṇa (*M. Bh.*); a son of Bharata (*Bh. Purāṇa*); a son of Somadatta (*Bh. Purāṇa*); a son of Janamejaya (*V. Purāṇa*); a son of Nṛga (*Bh. Purāṇa*); a son of Ṛteyu; a son of Viduratha.

**Sumatinātha** (S) (M) **1.** lord of wisdom. **2.** master of a better intellect. **3.** the 5th Jaina Tīrthaṅkara who was the son of King Megharatha and Queen Maṅgalā of Ayodhyā.

**Sumāvalī** (S) (F) a garland of flowers.

**Sumāyā** (S) (F) **1.** with excellent plans. **3.** a daughter of Maya.

**Sumāya** (S) (M) **1.** with excellent plans; very wise. **3.** a king of the asuras (*K. Sāgara*); a vidyādhara (*K. Sāgara*)

**Śumbha** (S) (M) **1.** killer; tormentor. **3.** an asura who was the son of Gaveṣṭhin and grandson of Prahlāda and who was slain by Durgā (*H. Purāṇa*)

**Sumbha** (S) (M) **1.** killer; destroyer; attacker. **3.** an asura who was the son of Kaśyapa and Danu and the brother of Niśumbha.

**Śumbhamathanī** (S) (F) **1.** Śumbha destroying. **3.** another name for Durgā.

**Śumbhana** (S) (M) purifying.

**Sumedhas** (S) (M) **1.** of high intellect. **2.** sensible; intelligent; wise. **3.** a ṛṣi under Manu Ćākṣuṣa; a son of Vedamitra.

**Sumeru** (S) (M) **1.** very exalted. **2.** excellent. **3.** a mountain; a vidyādhara (*K. Sāgara*); another name for Śiva.

**Sumeṣa** (S) (M) good ram.

**Sumīḍha** (S) (M) **1.** good sacrificer. **3.** a son of King Suhotra and Aikṣvākī of the Solar dynasty (*M. Bh.*)

**Sumīndra** (S) (M) lord of nectar.

**Sumirā** (S) (F) much remembered; overtly praised.

**Sumitā** (S) (F) well measured; having a balanced form; one who has a beautiful body.

**Sumita** (S) (M) well measured.

**Sumitrā** (S) (F) 1. a nice friend; having many friends. 3. a wife of Daśaratha and mother of Lakṣmaṇa and Śatrughna (*Rāmāyaṇa*); a wife of Kṛṣṇa (*M. Bh.*); a yakṣiṇī (*K. Sāgara*); the mother of Mārkaṇḍeya; the mother of Jayadeva.

**Sumitra** (S) (M) 1. a nice friend; having many friends. 3. a king of the Sauvīras (*M. Bh.*); a king of Mithilā (*B. Literature*); a son of Gada (*H. Purāṇa*); a son of Śyāma (*H. Purāṇa*); son of Śamīka (*Bhā. Purāṇa*); son of Vṛṣṇi (*Bh. Purāṇa*); son of Agnimitra; a Yādava king who was the son of Vṛṣṇi and the brother of Yudhajit (*Bhāgavata*); a Sauvīra king who was a partial incarnation of the asura Krodhavaśa and a supporter of the Pāṇḍavas (*M. Bh.*); a maharṣi who was a member of Yudhiṣṭhira's court (*M. Bh.*); a son of Kālindanagara who was the father of Sukumāra (*M. Bh.*); a son of the agni Tapa (*M. Bh.*); a charioteer of Abhimanyu (*M. Bh.*); a Hehaya dynasty king (*M. Bh.*); a son of King Suratha and the last king of the Ikṣvāku dynasty (*Bhāgavata*); a son of Kṛṣṇa and Jāmbavatī (*Bhāgavata*); a king of Rājagṛha and father of Munisuvrata Jaina Tīrthaṅkara (*J. Literature*); a son of Kṛṣṇa (*Bh. Purāṇa*)

**Sumitrābhū** (S) (M) 1. born of Sumitrā. 3. the 20th Arhat of the present era; Sāgara as a Ćakravartin.

**Sumnāvarī** (S) (F) 1. bringing joy. 3. another name for Uṣās (*Ṛg Veda*)

**Sumonā** (S) (F) calm; quiet.

**Sumukha** (S) (M) 1. bright faced. 2. fair; handsome. 3. a son of Droṇa (*Mā. Purāṇa*); a king of the kinnaras (*K. Vyuha*); an asura (*H. Purāṇa*); a ṛṣi (*M. Bh.*); a nāga son of Kaśyapa and Kadru who married Guṇakeśī (*M. Bh.*); a son of Garuḍa (*M. Bh.*); another name for Śiva and Gaṇeśa.

**Sumukhī** (S) (F) 1. bright faced; lovely; pleasing; learned; mirror. 3. the mother of a serpent called Aśvasena on the arrow of Karṇa (*M. Bh.*); an apsarā (*M. Bh.*)

**Sumuṇḍika** (S) (F) 1. with a good head. 3. an asura.

**Śuna** (S) (M) 1. the auspicious one. 3. another name for Vāyu and Indra.

**Sunābha** (S) (M) 1. having deep navel. 2. with a stable centre. 3. a son of Dhṛtarāṣṭra (*M. Bh.*); a minister of Varuṇa (*M. Bh.*); a dānava who was the brother of Vajranābha and the father of Ćandrāvatī and Guṇavatī (*H. Purāṇa*); a son of Garuḍa; a mountain (*M. Bh.*)

**Sunaha** (S) (M) 1. well dressed. 3. a son of Jahnu.

**Śunahotra** (S) (M) 1. offering auspicious sacrifices. 3. a son of Bharadvāja.

**Śunahśepa** (S) (M) 1. dog tailed. 3. a vedic ṛṣi son of Ajīgarta (*A. Brāhmaṇa*)

**Śunaka** (S) (M) 1. young dog. 3. a solar dynasty king who is the son of Kṛta and the father of Vītihotra (*Bhāgavata*); a rājaṛṣi who is a partial incarnation of the asura Ćandrahantā (*M. Bh.*); a maharṣi who was the son of King Ruru and Pramadvarā (*M. Bh.*); a son of Ṛćīka (*Rāmāyaṇa*); a son of Ṛta (*Bhā. Purāṇa*); a son of Gṛtsamadā (*H. Purāṇa*); the father of Pradyota (*Bhā. Purāṇa*)

**Sunakṣatrā** (S) (F) 1. born under an auspicious constellation. 3. a mother in Skanda's retinue.

**Sunakṣatra** (S) (M) 1. born under an auspicious nakṣatra. 3. the son of Marudeva (*Bhā. Purāṇa*); a Bharata dynasty king who was the son of Niramitra and father of Bṛhatsena (*Bhāgavata*)

**Sunāman** (S) (M) 1. well named. 3. the son of King Suketu (*M. Bh.*); a son of King Ugrasena and brother of Kansa (*M. Bh.*); a son of Garuḍa (*M. Bh.*); a warrior of Skanda (*M. Bh.*); a daitya; a son of Suketu (*M. Bh.*); a son of Vainateya (*M. Bh.*)

**Sunāmī** (S) (F) 1. well named. 3. a daughter of Devaka and wife of Vasudeva (*H. Purāṇa*)

**Sunandā** (S) (F) 1. pleasing; delighting. 3. a wife of Kṛṣṇa (*H. Purāṇa*); the mother of Bāhu and Vālin; a river (*Bhā. Purāṇa*); a club made by Tvaṣṭṛ (*Mā. Purāṇa*); a Kekaya princess who was married to King Sārvabhauma of the Kuru dynasty and the mother of Jayatsena (*M. Bh.*); a daughter of King Sarvasena of Kāśī and a wife of King Bharata and the mother of Bhaumanyu (*M. Bh.*); a princess of Śibi who married King Pratīpa and was the mother of Devāpi, Sāntanu and Bālhīka (*M. Bh.*); a daughter of Vīrabāhu and sister of King Subāhu of Ćedi (*M. Bh.*); another name for Umā.

**Sunanda** (S) (M) **1.** pleasing; delighting. **3.** a son of Pradyota (*Bhā. Purāṇa*)

**Sunandī** (S) (F) pleasing; delighting.

**Śunaṅkari** (S) (M) **1.** causing growth and prosperity. **3.** a rural deity.

**Sūnara** (S) (M) glad; joyous; merry; delightful.

**Sunartaka** (S) (M) **1.** good dancer. **3.** name assumed by Śiva.

**Sūnaśara** (S) (M) **1.** flower arrowed. **3.** another name for Kāma.

**Śunāsīra** (S) (M) **1.** share and plough. **3.** 2 rural deities favourable to the growth of grain identified with Indra and Vāyu.

**Śunasśepha** (S) (M) **1.** dogtailed. **3.** a vedic ṛṣi who was the son of Ajīgarta.

**Śunassakha** (S) (M) **1.** with a dog. **3.** another name for Indra.

**Sunayā** (S) (F) **1.** very just; well conducted. **3.** the mother of Jaina Tīrthaṅkara Sitalanatha and queen of Bhadrikapuri (*J. Literature*)

**Sunaya** (S) (M) **1.** very just; well conducted. **3.** a king who was the son of the king of Pāriplava and the father of Medhāvi (*Bhāgavata*); a son of Ṛta (*Purāṇas*); a son of Khaninetra.

**Sunayaka** (S) (M) wise leader.

**Sunayanā** (S) (F) with beautiful eyes.

**Sunda** (S) (M) **1.** one who shines. **3.** a daitya who was the son of Niśumbha; the brother of Upasunda and son of Nisunda (*M. Bh.*); another name for Viṣṇu.

**Sundara** (S) (M) **1.** beautiful; handsome; charming; agreeable; noble. **3.** a son of Pravilasena (*V. Purāṇa*); a gandharva son of Vīrabāhu (*Sk. Purāṇa*); an Āndhra monarch who was the son of Pulindasena and the father of King Śātakarṇi (*V. Purāṇa*); another name for Kṛṣṇa and Kāma.

**Sundaravatī** (S) (F) **1.** having beauty. **3.** a river.

**Sundareśvara** (S) (M) **1.** lord of beauty. **3.** a form of Śiva.

**Sundarī** (S) (F) **1.** beautiful. **3.** a yoginī; an apsarā (*B. Rāmāyaṇa*); a daughter of Śvaphalka (*H. Purāṇa*); a daughter of Vaiśvānara (*V. Purāṇa*); a rākṣasi who was the wife of Mālyavat (*Rāmāyaṇa*)

**Sundarīvallī** (S) (F) **1.** beautiful vine. **3.** a daughter of Mahāviṣṇu (*Sk. Purāṇa*)

**Śundhyu** (S) (M) **1.** pure; bright; radiant; beautiful; purified. **3.** another name for Agni.

**Śuṇḍu** (S) (M) **1.** elephant. **3.** a Purū king who was the son of Vītabhaya and the father of Bahuvidha (*A. Purāṇa*)

**Sunehrī** (H) (F) golden.

**Sunetra** (S) (M) **1.** fair eyed; a good leader. **3.** a son of Vainateya (*M. Bh.*); a son of the 13th Manu (*H. Purāṇa*); a son of Dhṛtarāṣṭra (*M. Bh.*); a son of Garuḍa (*M. Bh.*)

**Śungī** (S) (M) **1.** *Ficus infectoria*; the sheath of a bud. **3.** the mother of Garuḍa.

**Śuni** (S) (M) **1.** dog. **3.** a Solar dynasty king who was the son of Vivanava and father of Śruta (*Bhāgavata*)

**Sunīlā** (S) (F) of blue colour; very blue; dark.

**Sunīla** (S) (M) **1.** very blue; dark. **2.** the pomegranate tree (*Punica granatum*); sapphire; Common Flax (*Linum Usitatissimum*); Blue grass (*Cymbopogon jwarancusa*)

**Sunīlimā** (S) (F) bright blue; dark.

**Suniṣkā** (S) (F) with beautiful ornaments.

**Sunītā** (S) (F) **1.** well conducted; well behaved. **2.** polite; civil.

**Sunīta** (S) (M) **1.** well conducted. **2.** prudent. **3.** a son of Subala (*V. Purāṇa*)

**Sunīthā** (S) (F) **1.** well disposed; righteous; virtuous; moral. **3.** the firstborn mental daughter of Mṛtyu or death who became the wife of King Aṅga and was the mother of Veṇa (*H. Purāṇa*)

**Sunītha** (S) (M) **1.** well disposed; righteous; virtuous; moral. **2.** a good leader; well conducted; righteous. **3.** a maharṣi in the court of

Indra (*M. Bh.*); a king in the court of Yama (*M. Bh.*); a Vṛṣṇi dynasty king (*M. Bh.*); a Bharata dynasty king who was the son of Suṣeṇa and father of Nṛkṣuṣ (*M. Bh.*); a son of Kṛṣṇa (*H. Purāṇa*); a son of Saṁtati (*H. Purāṇa*); a son of Subala (*H. Purāṇa*)

**Sunīti** (S) (F) **1.** good conduct. **2.** wisdom; discretion. **3.** the wife of Uttānapāda and mother of Dhruva (*Bhā. Purāṇa*)

**Suniti** (S) (M) **1.** guiding well. **3.** a son of Vidūratha (*Mā. Purāṇa*); another name for Śiva.

**Suṅkalammā** (Kannada) (F) **1.** mother of diseases. **3.** the village goddess of smallpox.

**Śunolāṅgūla** (S) (M) **1.** dog tailed. **3.** a son of Ṛćīka (*A. Brāhmaṇa*)

**Sunṛta** (S) (M) **1.** one who dances very well. **3.** a constellation.

**Sūnṛtā** (S) (F) **1.** gladness; joy; exultation; song of joy; kindness. **3.** the daughter of Dharma and wife of Uttānapāda (*H. Purāṇa*); an apsarā; truth personified as a goddess (*Ṛg Veda*)

**Śuṇṭhaćārya** (S) (M) **1.** small white bull. **2.** teacher. **3.** a great Śaiva sage.

**Sūnu** (S) (M) **1.** son; child; offspring; inciter. **3.** another name for the sun.

**Sunvat** (S) (M) **1.** offerer of the Soma sacrifice. **3.** son of sage Sumantu (*Bh. Purāṇa*)

**Śūnyabandhu** (S) (M) **1.** with no friend; friend of dogs. **3.** a son of Tṛṇabindu.

**Śūnyapāla** (S) (M) **1.** preceptor of the cypher. **3.** a divine maharṣi (*M. Bh.*)

**Supadma** (S) (M) as lovely as a lotus; having beautiful lotuses.

**Suparṇā** (S) (F) **1.** with beautiful leaves. **2.** a lotus plant. **3.** the mother of Garuḍa (*Bhā. Purāṇa*); another name for Pārvatī.

**Suparṇa** (S) (M) **1.** with beautiful wings; with beautiful leaves. **2.** a ray of the sun. **3.** a gandharva son of Kaśyapa and Muni (*M. Bh.*); a gandharva son of Kaśyapa and Prādhā (*M. Bh.*); an asura who was the brother of Mayūra and was reborn as King Kālakīrti (*M. Bh.*); a mythical bird often identified with Garuḍa (*Ṛg Veda*); the sun and moon as having beautiful rays; a son of Antarīkṣa (*V. Purāṇa*); another name for Mahāviṣṇu.

**Suparṇaketu** (S) (M) **1.** bird bannered. **3.** another name for Viṣṇu.

**Suparṇi** (S) (M) **1.** with beautiful wings. **2.** personification of the mother of metres. **3.** one of the 7 tongues of fire.

**Supārśva** (S) (M) **1.** with beautiful sides. **2.** good looking. **3.** the son of Sampāti and elder brother of Jaṭāyu (*V. Rāmāyaṇa*); a son of Rukmaratha (*H. Purāṇa*); a son of Śrutāyu (*V. Purāṇa*); the 7th Arhat of the present Avasarpiṇī; a mountain (*M. Bh.*); a king who was an incarnation of the asura Kapaṭa (*M. Bh.*); a king in the Yayāti dynasty who was a son of Dṛdhanemi and father of Sumati (*Bhāgavata*); a rākṣasa brother of Prahasta (*Rāmāyaṇa*)

**Supārśvaka** (S) (M) **1.** with beautiful sides. **2.** good looking. **3.** a Yādava king who was the son of Akrūra and Aśvinī (*M. Purāṇa*); a son of Vasudeva and Rohiṇī (*Vā. Purāṇa*); a son of Ćitraka (*H. Purāṇa*); a son of Śrutāyu (*Bhā. Purāṇa*); the 3rd Arhat of the future Utsarpiṇī.

**Supārśvanātha** (S) (M) **1.** the neighbouring god. **2.** the guardian angel. **3.** the 7th Jaina Tīrthaṅkara and son of King Pratiṣṭha and Queen Prithvī of Benāras.

**Suparvan** (S) (M) **1.** with beautiful sections. **2.** arrow; a god; a deity. **3.** a viśvadeva (*H. Purāṇa*); son of the 10th Manu (*Mā. Purāṇa*); a son of Antarīkṣa (*V. Purāṇa*)

**Supāśa** (S) (M) **1.** with a good noose. **3.** another name for Gaṇeśa.

**Supeśas** (S) (M) **1.** well adorned. **2.** beautiful; handsome.

**Suphala** (S) (M) good result; good fruit.

**Suphulla** (S) (F) with beautiful blossoms.

**Supiś** (S) (M) with fine ornaments; graceful.

**Supoṣa** (S) (M) prosperous.

**Suprabhā** (S) (F) **1.** very bright. **2.** beautiful; splendid. **3.** a wife of Kṛṣṇa (*M. Bh.*); an asura who was the daughter of Kaśyapa and Svarbhānu (*A. Purāṇa*); the river Sarasvatī when it flows through Puṣkara; a daughter of sage Vadānya and wife of Aṣṭāvakra; a daughter of Dakṣa and mother of arrows; a daughter of King Suratha and wife of

Nābhāga and the mother of Bhalandana (*Mā. Purāṇa*); one of the 7 tongues of fire; a mother in Skanda's retinue (*M. Bh.*); *Psoralia corylifolia*.

**Suprabhāta** (S) (F) illuminated by dawn; a morning prayer.

**Suprabuddha** (S) (M) 1. completely enlightened. 3. a king of the Śākyas.

**Suprajā** (S) (F) 1. with many children. 3. a wife of the agni Bhānu (*M. Bh.*)

**Suprakāśa** (S) (M) well illuminated.

**Supraketa** (S) (M) very bright; conspicuous; notable; wise.

**Suprasādā** (S) (F) 1. auspicious; propitious; gracious. 3. a mother in Skanda's retinue (*M. Bh.*)

**Suprasāda** (S) (M) 1. auspicious; gracious. 3. an asura (*H. Purāṇa*); an attendant of Skanda (*M. Bh.*); another name for Śiva.

**Suprasanna** (S) (M) 1. very clear; gracious; serene; very happy. 3. another name for Kubera.

**Suprāta** (S) (M) beautiful dawn.

**Supratardana** (S) (M) 1. deity of the beautiful dawn. 3. an ancient king and companion of Indra (*M. Bh.*)

**Supratīka** (S) (M) 1. with a beautiful form. 2. handsome; lovely. 3. one of the 8 elephants that support the earth and ancestor of Airāvata (*M. Bh.*); a yakṣa (*K. Sāgara*); a sage and brother of Vibhāvasu; another name for Śiva and Kāma.

**Supratīkinī** (S) (F) 1. with a beautiful form. 3. the wife of the elephant Supratīka.

**Supratima** (S) (M) 1. beautiful idol. 3. a king referred to as chief among those in ancient India (*M. Bh.*)

**Supratiṣṭhā** (S) (F) 1. well established. 2. famous; glorious; installation; consecration. 3. a mother in Skanda's retinue (*M. Bh.*)

**Supratiṣṭha** (S) (M) 1. standing firm; well established. 2. famous; glorious. 3. a king of Benaras and father of Supārśvanātha Jaina Tīrthaṅkara (*J. Literature*)

**Supratiṣṭhitā** (S) (F) 1. standing firm; consecrated; celebrated; with beautiful legs. 3. an apsarā (*V. Purāṇa*)

**Supravṛddha** (S) (M) 1. well extended; full grown. 3. a Sauvīra prince (*M. Bh.*)

**Suprayogā** (S) (F) 1. well practised. 2. well managed; dextrous. 3. a sacred river believed to be a source of Agni (*M. Bh.*)

**Supremā** (S) (F) very loving.

**Suprīta** (S) (M) 1. very dear. 2. lovely; cherished; kind; friendly.

**Suprīti** (S) (F) great joy or delight.

**Suprītikara** (S) (M) 1. causing great joy or delight. 3. a king of the kinnaras (*B. Literature*)

**Supritīkara** (S) (M) 1. causing delight. 3. a king of the kinnaras.

**Supriyā** (S) (F) 1. very dear. 2. lovely. 3. an apsarā daughter of Kaśyapa and Prādhā (*M. Bh.*); Indian Pennywort (*Hydrocotyle asiatica*)

**Suptāghna** (S) (M) 1. killer of sleeping persons. 3. a son of the rākṣasa Mālyavat and Sundarī (*Rāmāyaṇa*)

**Supuñjika** (S) (M) 1. well knit. 3. a son of Vipraćitti and Siṁhikā (*Br. Purāṇa*)

**Supuṇyā** (S) (F) 1. bearer of good deeds; of great religious merit. 3. a river (*M. Bh.*)

**Supuṣpā** (S) (F) with beautiful flowers; Indian Coral tree (*Erythrina indica*)

**Supuṣya** (S) (M) 1. blossom. 3. a Buddha (*L. Vistara*)

**Surā** (S) (F) 1. spirituous liquor. 3. wine personified as a daughter of Varuṇa.

**Sura** (S) (M) 1. god; divinity; idol; sage. 2. the sun.

**Sūra** (S) (M) 1. wise; learned. 2. the sun. 3. father of the 17th Arhat of the present Avasarpiṇī.

**Śūra** (S) (M) 1. powerful; brave; valiant. 2. lion; tiger; a warrior. 3. a lunar dynasty king who was the son of Vidūratha and father of Śini (*Bhāgavata*); a son of Kārtavīrya (*Br. Purāṇa*); a son of King Ilina and Rathāntarī (*M. Bh.*); a Sauvira prince (*M. Bh.*); a Yādava king who was the husband of Māriṣā and father of Vasudeva (*Vā. Purāṇa*); the father of Daśaratha's wife Sumitrā (*V. Rāmāyaṇa*); a son of Devamīḍhuṣa (*H. Purāṇa*); son of Bhajamāna (*H. Purāṇa*); a son of Vasudeva (*Bh. Purāṇa*);

a son of Vatsaprī (*Mā. Purāṇa*)

**Surabhi** (S) (F) 1. sweet smelling; agreeable; shining; charming; pleasing; famous; good; beautiful; beloved; wise; virtuous. 2. Campaka tree; nutmeg; Kadamba tree; spring; Sacred Basil (*Ocimum sanctum*); Jasmine. 3. a fabulous cow who was the daughter of Dakṣa and wife of Kaśyapa and the mother of Kāmadhenu, cattle and of the rudras (*M. Bh.*); cow of the gods formed from a syllable of Brahmā whose daughters Surūpā, Hansikā, Subhadrā and Sarvakāmadughā are protectors of the 4 regions (*M. Bh.*); another name for the earth; Curryleaf tree (*Murraya koenigii Mimusops elengi*); *Prosopis spicigera*.

**Surabhibāṇa** (S) (M) 1. with fragrant arrows. 3. another name for Kāma.

**Surabhimān** (S) (M) 1. virtuous; fragrant. 3. an agni (*M. Bh.*)

**Surabhivatsa** (S) (M) 1. a calf. 3. a vidyādhara (*K. Sāgara*)

**Surabhū** (S) (F) 1. born of the gods. 3. a daughter of Ugrasena and sister of Kansa (*Bhāgavata*)

**Surabhūṣaṇa** (S) (M) ornament of the gods.

**Surāćārya** (S) (M) 1. preceptor of the gods. 3. another name for Bṛhaspati.

**Sūradāsa** (S) (M) 1. devotee of the sun. 3. a commentator on *Harivamśa Purāṇa*.

**Śūradeva** (S) (M) 1. lord of heroes. 3. a son of King Vīradeva; the 2nd Arhat of the future Utsarpiṇī.

**Surādevī** (S) (F) 1. goddess of wine. 3. a daughter of Varuṇa and Devī and who is the presiding goddess of liquor (*M. Bh.*)

**Suradhāman** (S) (M) a piece of the gods.

**Suradhas** (S) (M) 1. liberal; bountiful. 3. a ṛṣi and part author of *Ṛg Veda* (i)

**Surādhipa** (S) (M) 1. lord of the gods. 3. another name for Indra.

**Surādhipati** (S) (M) 1. lord of the gods. 3. another name for Nahuṣa.

**Surādhīśa** (S) (M) 1. lord of the gods. 3. another name for Indra.

**Suradhunī** (S) (M) 1. river of the gods. 3. another name for the Gaṅgā.

**Suradhvaja** (S) (M) banner of the gods.

**Suragaṇa** (S) (M) 1. with servants of god. 3. another name for Śiva.

**Suragiri** (S) (M) the mountain of the gods.

**Suragrāmaṇi** (S) (M) 1. chief of the gods. 3. another name for Brahmā.

**Suraguru** (S) (M) 1. preceptor of the gods. 3. another name for Bṛhaspati.

**Surahanta** (S) (M) 1. destroyer of gods. 3. a son of the agni Tapa (*M. Bh.*)

**Śūraja** (S) (M) son of a hero.

**Surajā** (S) (F) 1. born of gods. 3. an apsarā daughter of Kaśyapa and Prādhā (*M. Bh.*)

**Surājan** (S) (M) well illuminated; divine; a good king.

**Surajana** (S) (M) the race of gods.

**Surajanī** (S) (F) beautiful night.

**Sūrajaprakāśa** (S) (M) the light of the sun.

**Surajit** (S) (M) victorious over the gods.

**Surājīva** (S) 1. livelihood of the gods. 3. another name for Viṣṇu.

**Surajyeṣṭha** (S) (M) 1. oldest of the gods. 3. another name for Brahmā.

**Surakāminī** (S) (F) 1. desired by the gods. 3. an apsarā.

**Surakāru** (S) (M) 1. artificer of the gods. 3. another name for Viśvakarman.

**Suraketu** (S) (M) the banner of the gods.

**Surakṛt** (S) (M) 1. act of god. 3. a son of Viśvāmitra (*M. Bh.*)

**Sūrakṛta** (S) (M) procured by the sun.

**Sūrakṣaka** (S) (M) 1. protecting well; protector; defender. 3. a gandharva king who was the grandfather of Tāṭaka.

**Suralā** (S) (F) 1. one who brings the gods. 3. another name for the Gaṅgā.

**Suralokasundarī** (S) (M) 1. celestial woman. 3. an apsarā; another name for Durgā.

**Śūrama** (S) (M) a great warrior.

**Suramitra** (S) (M) friend of the gods.

**Suramohinī** (S) (F) attracting the gods.

**Suramukha** (S) (M) with a divine face.

**Suramyā** (S) (F) 1. very beautiful. 3. a queen of Kāmpīlya and mother of Vimalanātha Jaina Tīrthaṅkara (*J. Literature*)

**Suraṇā** (S) (F) 1. joyous; gay; making a pleasing sound. 3. a river.

**Suraṇa** (S) (M) joyous; gay; a pleasing sound.

**Surānandā** (S) (F) 1. joy of the gods. 3. a river.

**Surānāyaka** (S) (M) 1. leader of the gods. 3. another name for Indra.

**Suraṅga** (S) (M) 1. good colour; vermilion. 2. Sweet Orange (*Citrus aurantium*)

**Suraṅgama** (S) (M) 1. with a beautiful body; according to the rhythm. 2. musical; rhyming with music. 3. a Bodhisattva.

**Surāṅganā** (S) (F) celestial woman.

**Suranimnagā** (S) (M) 1. river of the gods. 3. another name for Gaṅgā.

**Surañjana** (S) (M) delighting greatly; Arecanut Palm (*Areca catechu*)

**Śūrapadma** (S) (M) 1. lotus among heroes. 3. an asura (*Sk. Purāṇa*)

**Surapānsulā** (S) (M) 1. covered with celestial dust. 3. an apsarā.

**Surapati** (S) (M) 1. leader of the gods. 3. another name for Indra.

**Surapravīra** (S) (M) 1. best among the gods. 3. a son of the agni Tapa (*M. Bh.*)

**Surapriya** (S) (M) 1. beloved of the gods. 3. another name for Indra and Bṛhaspati.

**Surapriyā** (S) (F) 1. dear to the gods. 3. an apsarā (*Bh. Purāṇa*)

**Surapuṣpa** (S) (M) celestial flower.

**Śūraputrā** (S) (F) 1. with a heroic son. 3. another name for Aditi.

**Surarāja** (S) (M) 1. king of the gods. 3. another name for Indra.

**Surāraṇī** (S) (F) 1. mother of the gods. 3. another name for Aditi.

**Surāri** (S) (M) 1. enemy of the gods. 3. an ancient king (*M. Bh.*)

**Surārihan** (S) (M) 1. destroyer of the enemy of the gods. 3. another name for Śiva.

**Surarṣi** (S) (M) 1. ṛṣi of the gods. 3. another name for Nārada.

**Surasā** (S) (F) 1. of good essence. 2. well flavoured; lovely; sweet; elegant; Sacred Basil (*Ocimum sanctum*). 3. a rāgiṇī; a daughter of Raudrāśva (*H. Purāṇa*); a daughter of Kaśyapa and Krodhavaśā and the mother of serpents who was reborn as Rohiṇī the wife of Vasudeva (*Bhāgavata*); an apsarā (*M. Bh.*); another name for Durgā; Indian Snakeroot (*Ophiorrhiza mungos*)

**Surasakha** (S) (M) friend of the gods.

**Surasena** (S) (M) with an army of gods.

**Śūrasena** (S) (M) 1. with a heroic army. 3. a king of Mathurā (*M. Bh.*); a son of Śatrughna (*V. Purāṇa*); a Yadu king and father of Vasudeva; son of Kārtavīrya (*H. Purāṇa*); a king who fought on the Kaurava side (*M. Bh.*)

**Śūrasenī** (S) (F) 1. with an army of warriors. 3. the wife of Pravīra and mother of Manasyu of the Purū dynasty (*M. Bh.*)

**Suraskandha** (S) (M) 1. divine shoulder. 3. a demon.

**Suraśreṣṭha** (S) (M) 1. best of the gods. 3. another name for Viṣṇu, Śiva, Indra, Brahmā, Dharma and Gaṇeśa.

**Surastrī** (S) (F) celestial woman.

**Surasū** (S) (F) mother of gods.

**Surasū** (S) (M) father of gods.

**Surasundarī** (S) (F) 1. celestial beauty. 3. a yoginī; another name for Durgā.

**Śūrasūnu** (S) (M) 1. son of Śūra. 3. another name for Vasudeva.

**Śūrasūta** (S) (M) 1. charioteer of the sun. 3. another name for Aruṇa.

**Surata** (S) (M) well disposed; tender; tranquil; calm.

**Śūratara** (S) (M) 1. better warrior. 3. a king on the Pāṇḍava side (*M. Bh.*)

**Surathā** (S) (F) 1. with a good chariot. 3. an apsarā daughter of Kaśyapa and Prādhā (*M. Bh.*); a river (*Mā. Purāṇa*); the mother of Emperor Śibi (*M. Bh.*)

**Suratha** (S) (M) 1. having a good chariot. 3. son of Sudeva (*Rāmāyaṇa*); a son of Ādiratha; son of Kuṇḍaka; a son of Raṇaka (*Bh. Purāṇa*); son of Ćaitra; a Purū dynasty king who was a son of Jahnu (*V. Purāṇa*); a son of Janamejaya and father of Vidūratha (*H. Purāṇa*); husband of Ćitrāṅgadā the daughter of Viśvakarmā; a king who was a partial incarnation of the asura Krodhavaśa (*M. Bh.*); father of King Koṭikāśya of Śibi (*M. Bh.*); a king of Trigarta (*M. Bh.*); a warrior on the Kaurava side (*M. Bh.*); a son of Drupada (*M. Bh.*); a son of Jayadratha and

Duśśalā (*M. Bh.*); a king of Kundalānagari (*P. Purāṇa*)

**Suratnā** (S) (F) possessing rich jewels.

**Suratna** (S) (M) possessing rich jewels.

**Suravāhinī** (S) (F) 1. river of the gods. 3. another name for the heavenly Gaṅgā.

**Suravallī** (S) (F) 1. vine of the gods. 2. Sacred Basil (*Ocimum sanctum*)

**Surāvān** (S) (M) 1. intoxicater. 3. a horse of Agastya's chariot.

**Suravāni** (S) (F) earth as the mother of the gods.

**Suravara** (S) (F) 1. best among the gods. 3. another name for Indra.

**Suravarćas** (S) (M) 1. glory of the gods. 3. an agni who was the son of Tapas (*M. Bh.*)

**Suravarman** (S) (M) armoured by the gods.

**Surāvi** (S) (M) divine sun.

**Suravilāsinī** (S) (F) heavenly nymph; apsarā.

**Surayuvatī** (S) (F) celestial maiden; apsarā.

**Surebha** (S) (M) fine voiced.

**Surejyā** (S) (F) worshipped by the gods; the Sacred Basil (*Ocimum sanctum*); bow-thread of the gods.

**Surejya** (S) (M) 1. preceptor of the gods. 3. another name for Bṛhaspati.

**Surekhā** (S) (F) 1. having beautiful lines; a beautiful line. 2. fortunate; auspicious.

**Surendra** (S) (M) 1. chief of the gods. 3. another name for Indra.

**Surendrajit** (S) (M) 1. conqueror of Indra. 3. another name for Garuḍa.

**Sureṇū** (S) (F) 1. very small. 2. dust particle; an atom. 3. a daughter of Tvaṣṭṛ and wife of Vivaśvat; a river regarded as one of the 7 Sarasvatīs (*M. Bh.*)

**Sureśa** (S) (M) 1. lord of the gods. 3. a viśvadeva (*M. Bh.*); a son of the agni Tapa (*M. Bh.*); another name for Indra and Śiva.

**Sureśi** (S) (F) 1. supreme goddess. 3. another name for Durgā.

**Sureṣṭa** (S) (M) beloved of the gods.

**Sureśvara** (S) (M) 1. lord of the gods. 3. one of the 11 rudras (*M. Bh.*); another name for Brahmā, Śiva and Indra.

**Surgati** (S) (M) being born as a god.

**Sūrī** (S) (F) 1. consort of the sun. 3. another name for Kuntī as being married to the Sun before her marriage of Pāṇḍu.

**Sūri** (S) (M) 1. learned man. 2. worshipper. 3. another name for the Sun and Kṛṣṇa.

**Suri** (S) (F) goddess.

**Suri** (S) (M) 1. sage. 3. another name for Bṛhaspati.

**Surīlā** (H) (F) melodious.

**Sūrin** (S) (M) 1. wise; learned. 2. scholar.

**Surīndra** (S) (M) Indra the god.

**Suriśvarī** (S) (F) 1. goddess of the gods. 2. pious; pure. 3. another name for the celestial Gaṅgā.

**Sūrmya** (S) (M) 1. channelled. 3. a wife of Anuhrāda (*Bh. Purāṇa*)

**Surośanā** (S) (F) 1. much liked. 2. enlightening beautifully. 3. a son of Yajñabāhu (*Bh. Purāṇa*); an attendant of Skanda (*M. Bh.*)

**Surośis** (S) (M) 1. much liked. 3. son of Vasiṣṭha and Arundhatī (*Bhāgavata*)

**Surodha** (S) (M) 1. good growth; well-stopped. 3. a son of Tanṣu (*H. Purāṇa*)

**Surohiṇī** (S) (F) beautifully red.

**Suroman** (S) (M) 1. with beautiful hair. 3. a nāga of the Takṣaka dynasty (*M. Bh.*)

**Surottamā** (S) (F) 1. best among the goddesses. 3. an apsarā (*V. Purāṇa*)

**Surottama** (S) (M) chief of the gods.

**Śūrpaka** (S) (M) 1. with a winnowing fan. 3. a gandharva; a demon enemy of Kāma.

**Śūrpaṇakhā** (S) (F) 1. with fingernails like winnowing fans. 3. the daughter of Viśravas and Kaikasī and sister of Rāvaṇa and wife of Vidyujjīhva and mother of Śambhukumāra (*K. Rāmāyaṇa*)

**Surtā** (S) (F) divine truth.

**Suru** (S) (M) excellent; with fine tastes.

**Surućā** (S) (F) bright light; with fine tastes.

**Surućа** (S) (M) 1. fine taste. 2. glorious; taking great delight. 3. son of Garuḍa (*M. Bh.*)

**Surućī** (S) (F) 1. taking great delight in. 3. a wife of Uttānapāda and mother of Uttama (*Purāṇas*)

**Surući** (S) (M) 1. with fine tastes; taking great delight in. 3. a gandharva king

(*H. Purāṇa*); a yakṣa (*Bhā. Purāṇa*)

**Surudha** (S) (M) very prominent.

**Surukhī** (S) (F) having a beautiful face.

**Surūpā** (S) (F) 1. well formed. 2. lovely; beautiful. 3. a daughter of Viśvakarman and wife of Priyavrata; an apsarā (*H. Purāṇa*); Spanish Jasmine (*Jasminum grandiflorum*)

**Surūpa** (S) (M) 1. well formed. 2. handsome; wise; learned. 3. another name for Śiva.

**Surūpikā** (S) (F) 1. well formed. 2. beautiful.

**Surūṣa** (S) (M) shining.

**Suruttama** (S) (M) 1. best among the gods. 3. another name for Viṣṇu, the Sun and Indra.

**Sūryā** (S) (F) wife of Sūrya.

**Sūrya** (S) (M) 1. the sun. 3. the sun is said to be born of sage Kaśyapa and Aditi as an āditya, is regarded as part of the original Vedic triad with Agni and Indra, in later mythology identified with Savitṛ as one of the 12 ādityas, also called Vivasvān and founder of the solar race through his son Vaivasvata Manu, married Sañjñā and Ćhāyā and was the father of Manu, Yama, Yamī, the Aśvinīkumāras, Revanta, Sanaiścara and Tapatī, on other occasions he became the father of Sugrīva, Kālindī and Karṇa (*Ṛg Veda*); a king of Ayodhyā and father of Tīrthaṅkara Kuntanātha.

**Sūryabali** (S) (M) as powerful as the sun.

**Sūryabhā** (S) (F) as bright as the sun.

**Sūryabhānu** (S) (M) 1. with the heat and light of the sun; reflector of the sun; as bright as the sun. 3. gatekeeper of Kubera's city Alakapuri (*V. Rāmāyaṇa*); a Yakśa (*Rāmāyaṇa*)

**Sūryabhrāj** (S) (M) radiant as the sun.

**Sūryaćakṣus** (S) (M) 1. the eye of the sun. 3. a rākṣasa (*Rāmāyaṇa*)

**Sūryaćandra** (S) (M) the sun and moon conjoined.

**Sūryadāsa** (S) (M) devotee of the sun.

**Sūryadatta** (S) (M) 1. given by the sun. 3. a brother of King Virāṭa (*M. Bh.*)

**Sūryadeva** (S) (M) the god Sūrya.

**Sūryadhvaja** (S) (M) 1. sun bannered. 3. a king of ancient India (*M. Bh.*)

**Sūryāditya** (S) (M) Surya, the son of Aditi.

**Sūryagarbha** (S) (M) 1. the band of the sun; having sun as the navel; sun centred. 3. a Boddhisattva (*K. Vyuha*)

**Sūryahasta** (S) (M) 1. the hands of the sun. 2. ray of the sun.

**Sūryajā** (S) (F) 1. born of the sun. 3. another name for the river Yamunā.

**Sūryaja** (S) (M) 1. sun born. 3. another name for Sugrīva, the planet Saturn and Karṇa.

**Sūryakalā** (S) (F) a portion of the sun.

**Sūryakamala** (S) (M) the sunflower (*Helianthus anuus*); heliotrope.

**Sūryakānta** (S) (M) 1. sun loved. 2. the sun stone; sun crystal.

**Sūryakānti** (S) (F) sunshine; sunlight.

**Sūryaketu** (S) (M) 1. having the sun for a banner. 3. a daitya killed by King Purañjaya (*K. Rāmāyaṇa*)

**Sūryakīrti** (S) (M) sunlight; the Sesamum flower (*Sesamum indicum*)

**Sūryākṣa** (S) (M) 1. the eye of the sun; sun eyed. 3. a king who was an incarnation of King Kratha (*M. Bh.*)

**Sūryaloćanā** (S) (F) 1. eye of the sun. 2. one whose eyes are as bright as the sun. 3. a gandharvī.

**Sūryamālā** (S) (M) 1. garlanded by the sun. 3. another name for Śiva.

**Sūryamaṇi** (S) (M) sunstone.

**Sūryamāsa** (S) (M) 1. the solar month. 3. a warrior of the Kauravas (*M. Bh.*)

**Sūryamukhī** (S) (F) 1. sun faced. 2. with a face as bright as the sun; *Helianthus annuus*.

**Sūryanābha** (S) (M) 1. sun navelled. 3. a dānava (*H. Purāṇa*)

**Sūryānana** (S) (M) sun faced.

**Sūryanandana** (S) (M) 1. son of the sun. 3. another name for Saturn.

**Sūryanārāyaṇa** (S) (M) the lord of the sun; the sun and Viṣṇu conjoined.

**Sūryanetra** (S) (M) 1. sun eyed. 3. son of Garuḍa (*M. Bh.*)

**Sūryāṇī** (S) (F) the wife of the sun.

**Sūryanśu** (S) (M) sunbeam.

**Sūryapati** (S) (M) the god Sūrya.

**Sūryapīḍa** (S) (M) 1. tormentor of the sun.

3. a son of Parīkṣit.

**Sūryaprabhā** (S) (F) as bright as the sun.

**Sūryaprabha** (S) (M) 1. bright as the sun. 3. a nāga; a Bodhisattva.

**Sūryaprakāśa** (S) (M) light of the sun.

**Sūryaputra** (S) (M) 1. son of the sun. 3. patronymic of the aśvins, Yama, the planet Saturn, Varuṇa, Karṇa and Sugrīva.

**Sūryaputrī** (S) (F) 1. daughter of the sun. 3. patronymic of the Yamunā river; lightning.

**Sūryaraśmi** (S) (M) sunbeam.

**Sūryasambhava** (S) (M) 1. son of the sun. 3. another name for Karṇa.

**Sūryasārathi** (S) (M) 1. charioteer of the sun. 2. dawn.

**Sūryasāvitra** (S) (M) 1. sun, the pious; Sūrya and Sāvitra conjoined. 3. a viśvadeva (*M. Bh.*)

**Sūryasnāta** (S) (M) devotee of the sun; the sun worshipper.

**Sūryaśobhā** (S) (F) sunshine.

**Sūryaśrī** (S) (M) 1. divine sun. 3. a viśvadeva.

**Sūryatapas** (S) (M) 1. heat of the sun. 3. a muni (*K. Sāgara*)

**Sūryatejas** (S) (M) 1. with the power of the sun. 3. sunshine.

**Sūryavarćas** (S) (M) 1. as splendid as the sun. 3. a gandharva son of Kaśyapa (*M. Bh.*)

**Sūryavarma** (S) (M) 1. as powerful as the sun. 3. a king of Trigarta (*M. Bh.*)

**Sūryavarman** (S) (M) 1. protected or armoured by the sun. 3. a king of Trigarta.

**Sūryavighna** (S) (M) 1. destroyer of the sun. 3. another name for Viṣṇu.

**Sūryodaya** (S) (M) sunrise.

**Suṣāḍha** (S) (M) 1. 6 good faces. 3. another name for Śiva.

**Susaha** (S) (M) 1. bearing well. 3. another name for Śiva.

**Suṣamā** (S) (F) exquisite beauty; splendour.

**Suṣama** (S) (M) very beautiful; very even.

**Susāman** (S) (M) 1. a beautiful song. 3. a Brāhmin in Yudhiṣṭhira's court (*M. Bh.*)

**Susambhāvya** (S) (M) 1. knower of the sacred texts; singer of *Sāma Veda* hymns. 3. son of Manu Raivata (*V. Purāṇa*)

**Susandhi** (S) (M) 1. fully reconciled; a good treaty. 3. a son of Māndhātṛ (*Rāmāyaṇa*); a son of Prasuśruta (*V. Purāṇa*)

**Susangatā** (S) (F) a good companion; easily attainable.

**Suśansa** (S) (M) saying good things; blessing.

**Suśānta** (S) (M) very calm; placid.

**Suśāntā** (S) (F) 1. very calm; placid. 3. a wife of Śaśidhvaja.

**Suśānti** (S) (F) perfect calm.

**Suśānti** (S) (M) 1. perfect calm. 3. Indra under the 3rd Manu; a son of Ajamīḍha; a son of Śānti (*V. Purāṇa*)

**Suśaraṇya** (S) (M) 1. offering secure protection. 3. another name for Śiva.

**Suśarman** (S) (M) 1. granting secure refuge. 3. a king of Trigarta who was the son of Vṛddhakṣema (*M. Bh.*); a Pānćāla warrior of the Pāṇḍavas (*M. Bh.*); the last king of the Kanva dynasty (*Bhāgavata*)

**Susatyā** (S) (F) 1. always truthful; nice and truthful. 3. wife of Janaka (*K. Purāṇa*)

**Suṣeṇa** (S) (M) 1. with a good missile. 3. a nāga of the Dhṛtarāṣṭra family (*M. Bh.*); a son of Dhṛtarāṣṭra (*M. Bh.*); a Purū dynasty king who was son of Parīkṣit (*M. Bh.*); a son of sage Jamadagni (*M. Bh.*); son of Varuṇa and father-in- law of the monkey king, Bāli and father of Tārā (*V. Rāmāyaṇa*); a son of Karṇa (*M. Bh.*); a Bharata dynasty king who was the son of Dhṛṣa and father of Sunītha (*Bhāgavata*); a king who married Rambhā the apsarā; a gandharva; a yakṣa (*V. Purāṇa*); a son of the 2nd Manu (*H. Purāṇa*); a son of Kṛṣṇa; a son of Śūrasena; a son of Viśvagarbha (*H. Purāṇa*); son of Vasudeva (*Bh. Purāṇa*); a son of Śambara (*H. Purāṇa*); a son of Vṛṣṇimat (*V. Purāṇa*); a vidyādhara (*K. Sāgara*); another name for Viṣṇu and Śiva; Chair bottom Cane (*Calamus rotang*)

**Suśenta** (S) (M) ray of the sun.

**Suśeva** (S) (M) very dear; auspicious; kind; favourable.

**Suṣinandi** (S) (M) 1. good pleasure. 3. a king (*V. Purāṇa*)

**Suśira** (S) (M) with a good head.

**Suśita** (S) (M) very bright; white.

**Suśīlā** (S) (F) 1. well disposed; good

tempered. 3. a wife of Kṛṣṇa (*H. Purāṇa*); a female attendant of Rādhā; wife of Yama; a daughter of Harisvāmin; daughter of the gandharva named Suśīla; a cow sister of Surabhi.

**Suśīla** (S) (M) 1. good tempered; amiable. 3. a gandharva.

**Śuśila** (S) (M) air; wind.

**Suśīlikā** (S) (F) of a good character; a bird.

**Susīmā** (S) (F) 1. with the hair well parted. 3. mother of the 6th Arhat.

**Suśīma** (S) (M) 1. cold. 2. moonstone.

**Susīma** (S) (M) 1. with the hair well parted. 3. a son of Bindusāra.

**Suśivendra** (S) (M) 1. lord of divine welfare. 3. Siva and Indra conjoined.

**Śuṣka** (S) (M) 1. dry. 3. a maharṣi of the Gokarṇa temple.

**Suska** (S) (M) 1. dry. 3. a mahārṣi of Gokarṇa.

**Śuṣma** (S) (M) 1. hissing; roaring; fragrant; strength; vigour; courage; valour; fire; flame. 3. another name for the sun.

**Śuṣmi** (S) (M) 1. wind. 3. another name for Vāyu.

**Śuṣmiṇa** (S) (M) 1. strong; fiery; courageous; bold. 3. a king of the Śibis.

**Susmitā** (S). (F) with a pleasant smile.

**Susmita** (S) (M) with a pleasant smile.

**Śuṣṇa** (S) (M) 1. hisser. 2. the sun; fire. 3. a demon slain by Indra (*Ṛg Veda*)

**Suśobhanā** (S) (F) 1. very charming; very graceful. 3. a wife of King Parīkṣit and the mother of Śala, Dala and Bala.

**Suśoka** (S) (M) shining beautifully.

**Suśona** (S) (M) dark red.

**Suśrama** (S) (M) 1. hard work. 3. a son of Dharma (*V. Purāṇa*)

**Suśravā** (S) (F) 1. much heard of; abounding in fame. 3. a wife of King Jayatsena of the Purū dynasty and the mother of Arvaćina (*M. Bh.*)

**Suśravas** (S) (M) 1. much heard of. 2. abounding in fame and glory. 3. a prajāpati (*V. Purāṇa*); a nāga (*R. Taraṅginī*); a spy of the gods.

**Suśrī** (S) (F) very splendid; very rich.

**Suśroṇī** (S) (F) 1. with beautiful hips. 3. a goddess.

**Suśruta** (S) (M) 1. much heard of; very famous. 3. the grandson of King Gādhi and son of Viśvāmitra and the reputed master of the science of surgery (*M. Bh.*); a son of Subhāṣa (*V. Purāṇa*); a son of Padmodbhava.

**Susthīla** (S) (M) 1. fortunate. 2. well off; firm; unshaken. 3. the monk who succeeded Suhasti as the head of the Jaina church (*J. Literature*)

**Sustuta** (S) (M) 1. overtly praised. 3. a son of Supārśva.

**Suśubhā** (S) (F) very beautiful; very auspicious.

**Śuśukvāna** (S) (M) shining; resplendent;brilliant.

**Suṣumna** (S) (M) 1. very gracious; kind. 3. one of the 7 main rays of the sun (*V. Purāṇa*)

**Susvarā** (S) (F) 1. sweet voiced. 3. a gandharvī.

**Susvara** (S) (M) 1. a beautiful voice. 3. a son of Garuḍa (*M. Bh.*)

**Suśyāmā** (S) (F) 1. very beautiful; very dark. 3. an apsara who married Ṛtadhvaja and became the mother of Vṛddhā (*Br. Purāṇa*)

**Sūta** (S) (M) 1. charioteer. 3. a hermit son of sage Lomaharṣa and pupil of Vyāsa (*Bhāgavata*); a son of Viśvāmitra (*M. Bh.*)

**Sutā** (S) (F) 1. begotten. 2. daughter.

**Suta** (S) (M) 1. begotten. 2. son. 3. son of the 10th Manu (*H. Purāṇa*)

**Sutama** (S) (M) best among the virtuous.

**Sutambhara** (S) (M) 1. carrying away Soma. 3. a ṛṣi and part author of *Ṛg Veda* (v)

**Sūtanandana** (S) (M) 1. son of a charioteer. 3. another name for Karṇa.

**Sutanjaya** (S) (M) 1. winning. 2. son.

**Sutantu** (S) (M) 1. with fair offspring. 3. a dānava (*K. Sāgara*); another name for Śiva and Viṣṇu.

**Sutanu** (S) (F) 1. possessing a slender body. 2. delicate; slender; lovely woman. 3. a daughter of Āhuka (*M. Bh.*); a concubine of Vasudeva (*H. Purāṇa*); a daughter of Ugrasena (*H. Purāṇa*); a daughter of Yudhiṣṭhira and wife of King Aśvasuta of Vajra (*Vā. Purāṇa*); wife of Akrūra.

**Sutanu** (S) (M) **1.** with a beautiful body. **3.** a gandharva (*Rāmāyaṇa*); a son of Ugrasena (*H. Purāṇa*)

**Sutapa** (S) (M) **1.** drinking Soma juice. **3.** a class of deities.

**Sutapas** (S) (M) **1.** one who has done a lot of penance; very hot. **2.** ascetic. **3.** a Bharata dynasty king who was the son of Homa and father of Bala (*Bhāgavata*); a prajāpati and the husband of Pṛṣṇi and the father of Pṛṣṇigarbha who was supposed to be a partial incarnation of Mahāviṣṇu; a son of Vasiṣṭha; father of the hermit Upamanyu (*Br. Purāṇa*); a hermit of the Bhṛgu family; a sage of the Bharadvāja family whose wife became the mother of Aśvinīsuta by the sun.

**Sūtaputra** (S) (M) **1.** son of a charioteer. 3. another name for Karṇa.

**Sutārā** (S) (F) **1.** very bright. **2.** shining star; cat's eye. **3.** a daughter of Śvaphalka (*V. Purāṇa*); an apsarā; a gandharvī.

**Sutārā** (S) (M) divine star.

**Sutārakā** (S) (F) **1.** with beautiful stars. 3. one of the 24 goddesses who executes the commands of the 24 Arhats.

**Sutasomā** (S) (F) **1.** offerer of Soma. **3.** a wife of Kṛṣṇa.

**Sutasoma** (S) (M) **1.** offerer of Soma. **3.** a son of Bhīmasena and Draupadī (*M. Bh.*)

**Sutasravas** (S) (M) born of fame.

**Sūtasūnu** (S) (M) **1.** son of a charioteer. 3. another name for Karṇa.

**Sūtasuta** (S) (M) **1.** son of a charioteer. 3. another name for Karṇa.

**Sūtatanaya** (S) (M) **1.** son of a charioteer. 3. another name for Karṇa.

**Sutejana** (S) (M) **1.** well pointed; a sharpened arrow. **3.** a king who was a friend of Yudhiṣṭhira (*M. Bh.*)

**Sutejas** (S) (M) **1.** very bright. **2.** splendid; mighty; a worshipper of the sun. **3.** the 10th Arhat of the past Utsarpinī; a son of Gṛhatsamada (*M. Bh.*); *Cleome viscosa*.

**Sutīkṣṇa** (S) (M) **1.** very sharp. **3.** a hermit who was a brother of Agastya (*V. Rāmāyaṇa*)

**Śutīra** (S) (M) a hero.

**Sutīrtha** (S) (M) **1.** a good preceptor. 3. another name for Śiva.

**Sutoyā** (S) (F) **1.** with beautiful water. **2.** a river.

**Sutrāmā** (S) (F) **1.** protecting well. **3.** another name for the earth.

**Sutrāman** (S) (M) **1.** protecting well. 3. another name for Indra.

**Sutrāvan** (S) (M) guarding well.

**Sutṛpta** (S) (M) fully satisfied.

**Suvaćā** (S) (F) **1.** speaking well. **3.** a gandharvī.

**Suvāća** (S) (M) **1.** praiseworthy; sounding good; keeper of the Soma. **3.** a son of Dhṛtarāṣṭra.

**Suvaćanī** (S) (F) **1.** always speaking well. **3.** a goddess.

**Suvah** (S) (M) patient; enduring.

**Suvaha** (S) (M) **1.** carrying well; bearing well. **2.** lute.

**Suvāha** (S) (M) **1.** easily carried away. **2.** a good stallion. **3.** a warrior of Skanda (*M. Bh.*)

**Suvāk** (S) (M) **1.** soft spoken; with a sweet voice; very learned. **3.** a maharṣi (*M. Bh.*)

**Suvaktra** (S) (M) **1.** handsome faced. **3.** a son of Dantavaktra (*H. Purāṇa*); a warrior of Skanda (*M. Bh.*)

**Suvalī** (S) (F) graceful.

**Suvāmā** (S) (F) **1.** beautiful woman. **3.** a famous river of the Purāṇas (*M. Bh.*)

**Suvana** (S) (M) the sun; fire; the moon.

**Suvanśa** (S) (M) **1.** with a good pedigree. **3.** a son of Vasudeva (*Bh. Purāṇa*)

**Suvapus** (S) **1.** with a handsome body. **3.** an apsarā (*V. Purāṇa*)

**Suvara** (S) (M) the sun; light; heaven.

**Suvarćalā** (S) (F) **1.** abode of a glorious life. 3. daughter of sage Devala and the wife of Śvetaketu (*M. Bh.*); a wife of Sūrya (*M. Bh.*); wife of Pratīha (*Bh. Purāṇa*); wife of Parameṣṭhin and mother of Pratīha (*Bh. Purāṇa*)

**Suvarćas** (S) (F) **1.** full of life; very glorious. 3. wife of sage Dadhīći and the mother of Pippalāda.

**Suvarćas** (S) (M) **1.** full of life; fiery; very glorious; splendid. **3.** a son of the 10th Manu;

a brother of Bhūti (*Mā. Purāṇa*); a son of Dhṛtarāṣṭra (*M. Bh.*); a son of Suketu (*M. Bh.*); a son of the agni Tapa (*M. Bh.*); a son of Garuḍa (*M. Bh.*); an attendant given to Skanda by Himavān (*M. Bh.*); a son of King Khanīnetra (*M. Bh.*); another name for Śiva.

**Suvarman** (S) (M) 1. having good armour. 2. a great warrior. 3. a son of Dhṛtarāṣṭra (*M. Bh.*)

**Suvarṇā** (S) (F) 1. of beautiful colour. 2. gold; turmeric. 3. one of the 7 tongues of fire; daughter of Ikṣvāku and wife of King Suhotra and the mother of Hastī (*M. Bh.*); Prickly Poppy (*Argemone mexicana*); Ironwood tree (*Mesua ferrea*); *Curcuma longa*.

**Suvarṇa** (S) (M) 1. of beautiful colour; gold. 2. famous; of noble birth. 3. a gandharva (*M. Bh.*); a minister of Daśaratha; a son of Antarīkṣa (*V. Purāṇa*); a king of Kāśmīra (*R. Taraṅginī*); another name for Śiva.

**Suvarṇābha** (S) (M) 1. having a golden shine. 3. a king who was a grandson of Manu Svāroćiṣa and son of Śaṅkhapāda (*M. Bh.*)

**Suvarṇabhāsa** (S) (F) 1. golden glitter. 3. a gandharva maiden.

**Suvarṇabindu** (S) (M) 1. golden spot. 3. another name for Viṣṇu.

**Suvarnaćūḍā** (S) (M) 1. gold crested. 3. a son of Garuḍa (*M. Bh.*)

**Suvarṇagarbha** (S) (M) 1. golden womb. 2. bringing forth gold. 3. a Bodhisattva.

**Suvarṇaka** (S) (M) golden.

**Suvarṇakeśa** (S) (M) 1. golden haired. 3. a nāga.

**Suvarṇakṣa** (S) (M) 1. golden eyed. 3. another name for Śiva.

**Suvarṇamekhalī** (S) (F) 1. golden girdled. 3. an apsarā.

**Suvarṇapadma** (S) (M) golden lotus.

**Suvarṇaprabhāsa** (S) (M) 1. with golden radiance. 3. a yakṣa.

**Suvarṇarekhā** (S) (F) 1. golden line. 3. a river.

**Suvarṇaretas** (S) (M) 1. with golden semen. 3. another name for Śiva.

**Suvarṇaroman** (S) (M) 1. golden haired. 3. a son of Mahāroman (*V. Purāṇa*)

**Suvarṇaśiras** (S) (M) 1. golden headed. 3. a sage who was the son of Piṅgalavarman (*M. Bh.*)

**Suvarṇasthīvī** (S) (M) 1. residing in gold. 3. son of King Śṛñjaya (*M. Bh.*)

**Suvarṇavarman** (S) (M) 1. golden warrior. 3. a king of Kāśi whose daughter Vapustamā married Janamejaya.

**Suvārtā** (S) (F) 1. good news. 2. one who brings good news. 3. a wife of Kṛṣṇa (*H. Purāṇa*)

**Suvasa** (S) (M) 1. perfume. 3. another name for Śiva.

**Suvāsa** (S) (M) 1. well clad. 3. another name for Siva.

**Suvāsaraka** (S) (M) 1. well clad; very fragrant. 3. a son of Kaśyapa.

**Suvāstuka** (S) (M) 1. an efficient architect. 3. a king in ancient India (*M. Bh.*)

**Suvāsu** (S) (F) 1. fragrant. 3. an apsarā.

**Suvavrata** (S) (M) acting for welfare.

**Suvedā** (S) (F) 1. very intelligent; knower of scriptures; very knowledgeable. 3. wife of Priyavrata's son Savana.

**Suvela** (S) (M) tranquil; still; quiet.

**Suveṇā** (S) (F) 1. with a beautiful plait of hair. 3. a Purāṇic river which sage Mārkaṇḍeya saw in the stomach of child Kṛṣṇa (*M. Bh.*)

**Suvibhu** (S) (M) 1. very bright. 3. a son of Vibhu (*H. Purāṇa*)

**Suvidha** (S) (M) of a kind nature.

**Suvidhinātha** (S) (M) 1. lord of the right manner. 3. the 8th Jaina Tīrthaṅkara.

**Suvidyut** (S) (M) 1. with the brilliance of lightning. 3. an asura.

**Suvikrama** (S) (M) 1. great valour. 3. a son of Vatsaprī (*Mā. Purāṇa*)

**Suvimala** (S) (M) perfectly pure.

**Suvipra** (S) (M) very learned.

**Suvīra** (S) (M) 1. very brave; hero. 3. a king who was a partial incarnation of the asura Krodhavaśa (*M. Bh.*); a son of King Dyutimān (*M. Bh.*); a son of Kṣemya (*H. Purāṇa*); a son of Śibi (*H. Purāṇa*); a son of Devaśravas (*Bh. Purāṇa*); another name for Śiva and Jayadratha.

**Suviraja** (S) (M) free from all passion.

**Suvīrya** (S) (M) **1.** with heroic strength; chivalrous. **2.** White Emetic Nut (*Gardenia lucida*)

**Suviśālā** (S) (F) **1.** very large. **3.** an attendant of Skanda (*M. Bh.*)

**Suviśāla** (S) (M) **1.** very large. **3.** an asura (*K. Sāgara*)

**Suvita** (S) (M) easy to traverse; a good path; welfare; prosperity; good luck.

**Suvitti** (S) (F) **1.** good knowledge. **3.** a divine being.

**Suvratā** (S) (F) **1.** very religious; a virtuous wife. **3.** a queen of Ratnapuri and mother of Dharmanātha Jaina Tīrthaṅkara; a daughter of Dakṣa and Vīraṇī (*Br. Purāṇa*); an apsarā.

**Suvrata** (S) (M) **1.** ruling well; very religious. **3.** a Bharata dynasty king who was the son of Kṣema and father of Viśvajit (*Bhāgavata*); an Aṅga king who was the son of King Uṣīnara and Daśa (*A. Purāṇa*); a famous muni (*M. Bh.*); an attendant given to Skanda by Mitra (*M. Bh.*); an attendant given to Skanda by Vidhātā (*M. Bh.*); a prajāpati (*Rāmāyaṇa*); a son of Manu Raućya (*Mā. Purāṇa*); a son of Nābhāga (*Rāmāyaṇa*); a son of Priyavrata; the 20th Arhat of the present Avasarpinī.

**Suvṛddha** (S) (M) **1.** very ancient. **3.** an elephant of the southern quarter.

**Suvṛtta** (S) (M) **1.** well behaved. **2.** virtuous; good.

**Suvṛttā** (S) (F) **1.** well conducted. **2.** virtuous. **3.** an apsarā (*H. Purāṇa*)

**Suvyūhā** (S) (F) **1.** halo. **3.** an apsarā.

**Suyajñā** (S) (F) **1.** good sacrificer. **3.** a daughter of King Prasenajit of the Purū dynasty and wife of King Mahābhauma and the mother of Ayutanāyī (*M. Bh.*)

**Suyajña** (S) (M) **1.** a good sacrifice. **3.** a son of Rući and Ākūti who is considered an incarnation of Viṣṇu (*Bhā. Purāṇa*); a son of Vasiṣṭha (*Rāmāyaṇa*); a son of Antara (*H. Purāṇa*); a king of the Uśīnaras (*Bhā. Purāṇa*)

**Suyajus** (S) (M) **1.** worshipping well. **3.** a son of Bhūmanyu (*M. Bh.*)

**Suyama** (S) (M) **1.** easily controlled. **3.** son of the rākṣasa Śataśṛṅga (*M. Bh.*)

**Suyāmuna** (S) (M) **1.** a palace. **2.** belonging to a mountain; a kind of cloud. **3.** another name for Viṣṇu.

**Suyaśā** (S) (F) **1.** very famous. **3.** a daughter of King Bahudā and wife of Parīkṣit who was the son of Anaśva (*M. Bh.*); an apsarā (*V. Purāṇa*)

**Suyaśas** (S) (M) **1.** glorious fame; very famous. **3.** a son of Aśokavardhana (*Purāṇas*)

**Suyaśas** (S) (F) **1.** very famous. **3.** a wife of King Divodāsa (*H. Purāṇa*)

**Suyaṣṭavya** (S) (M) a son of Raivata.

**Suyati** (S) (M) **1.** one who has controlled his passion. **3.** a son of Nahuṣa; another name for Viṣṇu.

**Suyodhana** (S) (M) **1.** good warrior. **3.** another name for Duryodhana.

**Svābhāsa** (S) (M) very illustrious.

**Svabhīla** (S) (M) very formidable.

**Svabhirāma** (S) (M) very delightful.

**Śvabhra** (S) (M) **1.** chasm; hole. **3.** a son of Vasudeva (*H. Purāṇa*); a king of Kampana (*R. Taraṅginī*)

**Svabhū** (S) (M) **1.** self born. **3.** another name for Brahmā, Śiva and Viṣṇu.

**Svabhūmi** (S) (M) **1.** one's proper place; own land. **3.** a son of Ugrasena (*V. Purāṇa*)

**Svadhā** (S) (F) **1.** self power. **3.** the offerings to the gods and ancestors personified as the daughter of Dakṣa and wife of the Pitṛs or Manes and the mother of Menā and Dhāraṇī (*V. Purāṇa*)

**Svadhādhipa** (S) (M) **1.** lord of the Svadhā. **3.** another name for Agni.

**Svadhāman** (S) (M) **1.** self radiant. **3.** a son of Satyasahas and Sūnṛtā (*Bh. Purāṇa*)

**Svadhi** (S) (F) well minded; thoughtful.

**Svādhīna** (S) (M) self willed; free.

**Svadhita** (S) (M) firm; solid.

**Svadhīta** (S) (M) well read.

**Svāditya** (S) (M) befriended by the ādityas.

**Svādman** (S) (M) sweetness.

**Svāgata** (S) (M) **1.** welcome. **3.** a Buddha (*L. Vistara*)

**Svāhā** (S) (F) **1.** oblation personified as the daughter of Dakṣa and wife of Agni and supposed to be the goddess presiding over burnt offerings, also represented as the wife of the rudra Paśupati. 3. a daughter of Bṛhaspati (*M. Bh.*)

**Svāhādevī** (S) (F) 1. goddess of oblation. 3. wife of Agni and the mother of Pāvaka, Pavamāna and Śući.

**Svāhi** (S) (M) 1. sacrificer. 3. the son of Vṛjinīvat (*H. Purāṇa*)

**Śvaitreya** (S) (M) 1. son of white; brilliancy of lightning; fiery. 3. the son of Śvitra (*Ṛg Veda*)

**Svaketu** (S) (M) 1. self bannered. 3. a king (*V. Purāṇa*)

**Svākṛti** (S) (F) good looking.

**Svakṣa** (S) (M) handsome eyed.

**Svaladā** (S) (F) 1. giving a little. 3. a daughter of Raudrāśva.

**Svalīna** (S) (M) 1. absorbed in oneself. 3. a dānava.

**Svāmikumāra** (S) (M) 1. son of the lord. 2. young prince. 3. another name for Kārttikeya.

**Svāmin** (S) (M) 1. owner; master; lord; chief. 3. the 11th Arhat of the past Utsarpini; another name for Viṣṇu, Śiva, Garuḍa and Skanda.

**Svāmināthа** (S) (M) 1. lord of lords. 2. lord of ascetics. 3. another name for Gaṇeśa.

**Svāminī** (S) (F) lady of the house.

**Svana** (S) (M) 1. sound; noise. 3. the son of the agni Satya (*M. Bh.*)

**Svanaya** (S) (M) 1. self carried; self judgement. 3. a son of King Bhāvayavya whose daughter married sage Kakṣivān.

**Svaṅga** (S) (M) with a handsome body.

**Svani** (S) (M) 1. noisy; turbulent. 3. son of Āpa.

**Svanīka** (S) (M) with a radiant countenance.

**Śvānta** (S) (M) tranquil; placid.

**Śvaphalka** (S) (M) 1. fruit of a citron tree. 3. the son of Vṛṣṇi and husband of Gandinī and father of Akrūra (*H. Purāṇa*)

**Svāpi** (S) (M) good friend.

**Svapnā** (S) (F) dream.

**Svapna** (S) (M) dream; sleep.

**Svapnas** (S) (M) wealthy; rich.

**Svapnasundarī** (S) (F) dream girl.

**Svarā** (S) (F) 1. goddess of sound or a musical note. 3. the chief wife of Brahmā.

**Svara** (S) (M) 1. sound; a musical note. 3. one of the 7 rays of the sun; another name for Viṣṇu.

**Svaradhīta** (S) (M) 1. reaching heaven. 3. another name for Mount Meru.

**Svārāj** (S) (M) 1. king of heaven. 3. another name for Indra.

**Svarāja** (S) (M) 1. self rule. 3. one of the 7 rays of the sun (*V. Purāṇa*); another name for the Supreme Being, Brahmā, Viṣṇu and Indra.

**Svārājya** (S) (M) sovereignty; union with Brahmā; self effulgence.

**Svarapurañjaya** (S) (M) 1. victor of music. 3. a son of śE3a (*V. Purāṇa*)

**Svaravedī** (S) (F) 1. knower of music. 3. an apsarā.Śeṣa (*V. Purāṇa*)

**Svarbhānavī** (S) (F) 1. daughter of the divine. 3. daughter of the sun; daughter of Svarbhānu who married Āyus and was the mother of Nahuṣa (*M. Bh.*)

**Svarbhānu** (S) (M) 1. light of heaven. 2. the divine sun. 3. a dānava son of Kaśyapa and Danu who was reborn as Ugrasena the father of Kaṁsa (*M. Bh.*); a son of Kṛṣṇa and Satyabhāmā (*Bhāgavata*); a demon supposed to eclipse the sun and moon, later identified with Rāhu (*Ṛg Veda*)

**Svarćanas** (S) (M) pleasing to heaven; as lovely as light.

**Svarćis** (S) (M) flashing beautifully.

**Svardā** (S) (M) bestowing heaven.

**Svardhāman** (S) (M) abiding in light.

**Svareṇū** (S) (F) 1. beautiful note. 3. wife of the sun.

**Svarga** (S) (M) 1. leading to light or heaven; heaven. 3. Indra's paradise; son of the rudra Bhīma (*V. Purāṇa*)

**Svargaṅgā** (S) (F) the celestial Gaṅgā; the Milky Way.

**Svargapati** (S) (M) 1. lord of heaven. 3. another name for Indra.

**Svargiri** (S) (M) 1. the mountain of light. 3. another name for Sumeru.

**Svarhat** (S) (M) very honourable.

**Svarjit** (S) (M) winning heaven.

**Svarmaṇi** (S) (M) 1. sky jewel. 3. another name for the sun.

**Svarṇā** (S) (F) 1. golden. 3. an apsara and mother of Vṛndā (*P. Purāṇa*)

**Svarṇa** (S) (M) 1. gold. 3. a form of Gaṇapati the lord of the ganas.

**Svarṇabindu** (S) (M) 1. golden spot. 3. a warrior of Skanda (*M. Bh.*); another name for Viṣṇu.

**Svarṇaćūḍa** (S) (M) gold crested; the blue jay.

**Svarṇadāmā** (S) (F) 1. gold girdled. 3. a tutelary goddess.

**Svarṇagaṇapati** (S) (M) 1. golden lord of the ganas. 3. a form of Gaṇeśa.

**Svarṇagrīva** (S) (M) 1. golden necked. 3. an attendant of Skanda (*M. Bh.*)

**Svarṇajit** (S) (M) gold winner.

**Svarṇakalā** (S) (M) a piece of gold.

**Svarṇakāya** (S) (M) 1. gold bodied. 3. another name for Garuḍa.

**Svarṇalatā** (S) (F) 1. golden vine. 2. Climbing Staff Plant (*Celastrus paniculata*)

**Svarṇamālā** (S) (F) golden necklace.

**Svarṇambha** (S) (F) white light; golden light.

**Svarṇapadmā** (S) (F) 1. bearing golden lotuses. 3. another name for the celestial Gaṅgā.

**Svarṇaprabha** (S) (M) shining like gold.

**Svarṇapuṣpa** (S) (M) 1. golden flower. 2. the Ćampaka tree (*Michelia champaka*); *Cassia fistula*.

**Svarṇapuṣpikā** (S) (F) 1. golden flower. 2. jasmine.

**Svarṇarekhā** (S) (F) 1. golden streak. 3. a river (*V. Purāṇa*); a vidyādharī (*Hitopadeśa*)

**Svarṇaroman** (S) (M) 1. golden haired. 3. a solar dynasty king who was the son of Mahāromā and the father of Prastharomā.

**Svarnetṛ** (S) (M) guide to heaven.

**Svarnīta** (S) (M) led to heaven.

**Svaroćas** (S) (M) self shining.

**Svaroćis** (S) (M) 1. self shining. 3. a son of King Dyutimān and Varūthinī who married Manoramās, Vibhāvā and Kalāvatī and was the father of Śvāroćiṣa who became an emperor (*Mā. Purāṇa*); the son of the apsarā Varūthinī (*Mā. Purāṇa*)

**Svāroćiṣa** (S) (M) 1. self shining. 3. Manu as the son of Svāyambhuva's daughter Ākūti.

**Svarpati** (S) (M) lord of light.

**Svārṣā** (S) (F) celestial; winning heaven; bestowing light.

**Svarūpa** (S) (M) 1. having one's own form. 2. pleasing; handsome; wise. 3. a son of Sunandā (*Mā. Purāṇa*); a daitya (*M. Bh.*); an asura in the palace of Varuṇa (*M. Bh.*)

**Svarūptā** (S) (F) beautiful.

**Svarvadhū** (S) (F) celestial woman; apsarā.

**Svarvīthī** (S) (F) 1. heavenly path; abode of music. 3. a wife of Vatsara (*Bhā. Purāṇa*)

**Svaryoṣit** (S) (F) celestial woman.

**Svaryu** (S) (M) desirous of light or splendour.

**Svāsa** (S) (M) the breath.

**Śvāsā** (S) (F) 1. the breath; hissing; panting; breathing. 3. the mother of Śvasana (*M. Bh.*); a daughter of Dakṣa and wife of Dharma and mother of Anila (*M. Bh.*)

**Śvasana** (S) (M) 1. breathing; panting; blowing; hissing. 2. air; wind. 3. a vasu and son of Śvāsā (*M. Bh.*); a nāga.

**Svasti** (S) (F) well being; fortune; success sometimes personified as a goddess.

**Svastibhāva** (S) (M) 1. god of fortune. 3. another name for Śiva.

**Svastidevī** (S) (F) 1. goddess of welfare. 3. a goddess represented as the wife of Vāyu and said to have sprung from the essence of Prākṛtī; a mystical cross.

**Svastika** (S) (M) 1. any lucky or auspicious object or mark; a mystical cross. 3. a dānava (*H. Purāṇa*); a nāga in the palace of Varuṇa (*M. Bh.*); a warrior of Skanda (*M. Bh.*)

**Svastikṛt** (S) (M) 1. causing prosperity. 3. another name for Śiva.

**Svastimatī** (S) (M) 1. auspicious. 3. an attendant of Skanda (*M. Bh.*)

**Svastyātreya** (S) (M) 1. auspicious ascetic. 3. an ancient hermit of South India (*M. Bh.*)

**Svāśū** (S) (M) very swift.

**Svasū** (S) (F) 1. self created. 3. the earth.

**Svaśva** (S) (M) 1. with excellent horses; good

rider. 3. a king praised in the *Ṛg Veda*.

**Śvāśva** (S) (M) 1. with a dog as steed. 3. another name for Bhairava.

**Svāti** (S) (F) 1. the star Arcturus. 3. a wife of the Sun; one of the 27 constellations.

**Svāti** (S) (M) 1. born under the Svāti star. 3. a son of Meghasvāti; a grandson of Ćākṣuṣa Manu and son of Ūru and Āgneyi (*A. Purāṇa*)

**Svaujas** (S) (M) having natural energy.

**Svayambhoja** (S) (M) 1. self made. 3. son of Pratikṣatra (*H. Purāṇa*); a son of Śini (*Bhā. Purāṇa*)

**Svāyambhū** (S) (M) 1. self existent. 3. another name for Brahmā, Śiva, Viṣṇu, Buddha, Kāla and Kāma; the Jaina 3rd Black Vasudeva.

**Svāyambhūta** (S) (M) 1. self created. 3. another name for Śiva.

**Svāyambhuva Manu** (S) (M) 1. selfborn Manu. 3. the 1st Manu and son of Brahmā and husband of Śātarūpa and father of Priyavrata and Uttānapāda, he is considered the ancestor of human beings.

**Svayamhārikā** (S) (F) 1. self seizing. 3. a daughter of Nirmārṣṭi and Dusśaha (*Mā. Purāṇa*)

**Svāyamīśvara** (S) (M) one's own lord; absolute sovereign.

**Svāyamprabhā** (S) (F) 1. self shining. 3. an apsarā (*M. Bh.*); the daughter of Hemasāvarṇi (*Rāmāyaṇa*); a daughter of the asura Maya (*K. Sāgara*)

**Svayamprabha** (S) (M) 1. self shining. 3. the Jaina 4th Arhat of the future Utsarpini.

**Svāyus** (S) (M) full vigour.

**Svedaja** (S) (M) 1. born of sweat. 3. an asura.

**Śvenī** (S) (F) white.

**Śvetā** (S) (F) 1. white. 3. one of the 7 tongues of fire; a mother in Skanda's retinue (*M. Bh.*); the mother of the elephant Śveta (*M. Bh.*); a daughter of Dakṣa and Krodhavaśā (*V. Rāmāyaṇa*); *Aconitum heterophyllum*; Blue Pea (*Clitoria ternatea*)

**Śveta** (S) (M) 1. white; white horse; white shell; white cloud. 3. an ancient king who is considered among those who should be remembered at dawn and dusk (*M. Bh.*); a son of King Virāṭa and Surathā (*M. Bh.*); a warrior of Skanda (*M. Bh.*); the elder brother of King Sudeva; a nāga; a daitya and son of Vipraćitti (*H. Purāṇa*); an incarnation of Śiva; a pupil of Śiva; a manifestation of Viṣṇu in his Varāha incarnation; a son of King Sudeva (*Rāmāyaṇa*); a son of Vapuṣmat (*Mā. Purāṇa*); a mythical elephant (*M. Bh.*); another name for the planet Venus.

**Śvetābha** (S) (M) white shine.

**Śvetabhadra** (S) (M) 1. white gentleman; having a fair complexion. 3. a guardian of Kubera's treasury.

**Śvetabhānu** (S) (M) 1. white rayed. 3. the moon.

**Śvetadvipa** (S) (M) 1. white elephant. 3. another name for Airāvata.

**Śvetaka** (S) (M) 1. white. 2. cowry; silver. 3. a nāga.

**Śvetakamala** (S) (M) white lotus (*Nelumbium speciosum*)

**Śvetakarṇa** (S) (M) 1. white eared. 3. a son of Satyakarṇa (*H. Purāṇa*)

**Śvetaketu** (S) (M) 1. white bannered. 3. a comet; a son of Senajit (*H. Purāṇa*); Gautama Buddha as a Bodhisattva (*L. Vistara*); another name for maharṣi Auddālaki who was the son of sage Āruṇi.

**Śvetakī** (S) (M) 1. fair complexioned. 3. a king who spent his whole life performing yajñas (*M. Bh.*)

**Śvetāmbarā** (S) (F) clad in white.

**Śvetāmbara** (S) (M) 1. clad in white. 3. the 2nd great Jaina sect (*J. Literature*); a form of Śiva.

**Śvetāṅka** (S) (M) 1. having a white mark. 2. bright.

**Śvetānśu** (S) (M) 1. white rayed. 3. another name for the moon.

**Śvetapāda** (S) (M) 1. white footed. 3. an attendant of Śiva.

**Śvetapadma** (S) (M) white lotus (*Nelumbium speciosum*)

**Śvetaparṇa** (S) (M) 1. of white leaves; of white glory; glorious; famous. 3. the king of Bhadrāvatī (*M. Bh.*)

**Śvetapingala** (S) (M) 1. pale yellow; tawny. 2. lion. 3. another name for Śiva.

**Śvetaraśmi** (S) (M) 1. white rayed. 3. the white elephant of King Ratnādhipa

(*K. Sāgara*); a gandharva (*K. Sāgara*); another name for the moon.

**Śvetārćis** (S) (M) 1. white rayed. 3. another name for the moon.

**Śvetarohita** (S) (M) 1. white and red. 3. another name for Garuḍa.

**Śvetasiddha** (S) (M) 1. with bright accomplishments. 3. a warrior of Skanda (*M. Bh.*)

**Śvetaśīrṣa** (S) (M) 1. white headed. 3. a daitya (*H. Purāṇa*)

**Śvetāśvā** (S) (F) 1. with a white horse. 3. a goddess.

**Śvetavāha** (S) (M) 1. borne by white horses. 3. another name for Indra.

**Śvetavāhana** (S) (M) 1. with a white chariot. 3. a son of Rājādhideva (*H. Purāṇa*); a son of Śūra (*V. Purāṇa*); another name for the moon, Śiva and Arjuna.

**Śvetavāhin** (S) (M) 1. borne by white horses. 3. another name for Arjuna.

**Śvetavājin** (S) (M) 1. with white horses. 3. another name for the moon and Arjuna.

**Śvetavaktra** (S) (M) 1. white faced. 3. a warrior of Skanda (*M. Bh.*)

**Śvetī** (S) (F) 1. silver. 3. a river.

**Śvetyā** (S) (F) 1. white; brilliant as the dawn. 3. a river.

**Svīkṛtī** (S) (F) acceptance.

**Sviṣṭakṛt** (S) (M) 1. offering a correct sacrifice. 3. a son of Bṛhaspati (*M. Bh.*)

**Sviṣṭi** (S) (F) a successful sacrifice.

**Śviti** (S) (F) whiteness.

**Śvitrā** (S) (F) white.

**Svojas** (S) (M) very strong or powerful.

**Śyāmā** (S) (F) 1. blue; black; dark; beautiful. 2. consort of Śyāma. 3. a goddess who executes the commands of the 6th Jaina Arhat; a daughter of Meru and wife of Agnīdhra (*Bhāgavata*); another name for Yamunā; *Aglaia odoratissima*; *Curcuma longa*; Common Indigo (*Indigofera hinctoria*); Couch grass (*Cynodon dactylon*); Rādhā as the beloved of the dark one.

**Śyāma** (S) (M) 1. black; darkblue; dark complexioned; cloud; the kokila bird. 3. a rāga; a son of Śūra and brother of Vasudeva (*H. Purāṇa*); a sacred figtree at Prayāga (*Rāmāyaṇa*); another name for Kṛṣṇa.

**Śyāmaka** (S) (M) 1. dark. 3. a brother of Vasudeva and a son of Śūra and Māriṣā (*Bhāgavata*)

**Śyāmakaṇṭha** (S) (M) 1. black throated. 3. another name for Śiva.

**Śyāmalā** (S) (F) 1. dark. 3. a form of Durgā.

**Śyāmala** (S) (M) dark; Black Plum (*Eugenia Jambolana*)

**Śyāmāṅga** (S) (M) dark bodied; the planet Mercury.

**Syamantaka** (S) (M) 1. destroyer of dangers. 3. the celebrated jewel worn by Kṛṣṇa on his wrist described as yielding gold and preserving from all danger (*H. Purāṇa*)

**Śyāmasundara** (S) (M) 1. dark and beautiful. 3. another name for Kṛṣṇa.

**Śyāmavihāri** (S) (M) Kṛṣṇa the wanderer.

**Śyāmāyana** (S) (M) 1. very dark coloured or darkness personified. 3. a son of Viśvamitra.

**Syandana** (S) (M) 1. moving on swiftly. 2. chariot; air; wind. 3. the 23rd Arhat of the past Utsarpinī.

**Śyavaka** (S) (M) 1. brown. 3. the horses of the sun.

**Śyāvāśva** (S) (M) 1. dark house. 3. the son of sage Arćanānas.

**Śyena** (S) (M) 1. eagle; falcon; hawk. 3. a sage in Indra's assembly (*M. Bh.*)

**Śyenagāmī** (S) (M) 1.moving like an eagle. 2. as fast as an eagle. 3. a commander of Khara's army (*V. Rāmāyaṇa*)

**Śyenajit** (S) (M) 1. conqueror of the falcon. 3. a son of the Ikṣvāku king, Dala (*M. Bh.*); the uncle of Bhīmasena (*M. Bh.*)

**Śyenī** (S) (F) 1. female hawk. 3. the daughter of Kaśyapa regarded as the mother of hawks (*M. Bh.*)

**Śyetī** (S) (F) white.

**Syona** (S) (M) 1. mild; soft; gentle; pleasing; auspicious. 2. ray of light; the sun.

**Syūma** (S) (M) ray of light; happiness; water.

**Syūmaraśmi** (S) (M) 1. ray of light. 3. an ancient hermit.

**Syūnā** (S) (M) a ray of light.

T

**Tāḍakā** (S) (F) 1. beater; murderer. 3. a fierce rākṣasī who was the daughter of the yakṣa Suketu and the wife of Sunda and mother of Marīci and Subāhu, she was killed by Rāma whereupon she was restored to being a gandharvī (*V. Rāmāyaṇa*)

**Taḍitprabhā** (S) (F) 1. a flash of lightning. 3. a mother attending on Skanda (*M. Bh.*)

**Taittiri** (S) (M) 1. sprung from a partridge. 3. a sage and elder brother of Vaiśampāyana (*M. Bh.*); a son of Kapotaroman (*H. Purāṇa*)

**Takṣa** (S) (M) 1. cutting through. 3. a son of Bharata and Māṇḍavī (*Vā. Purāṇa*)

**Takṣaka** (S) (M) 1. cutter; carpenter. 3. the architect of the gods; a son of Prasenajit (*Bhā. Purāṇa*); a deity worshipped in Bengal as the bestower of rain; a serpent lord who is the son of Kaśyapa and Kadru and is one of the 8 snakes worn by Śiva, he lives in the court of Varuṇa; the son of Lakṣmaṇa and Ūrmilā and the king of Agati (*U. Rāmāyaṇa*)

**Tāladhvaja** (S) (M) 1. palm bannered. 3. the husband of Nārada when the latter became the woman Saubhāgyasundarī; a mountain; another name for Balarāma and Bhīṣma.

**Tālajangha** (S) (M) 1. with legs as long as a palm tree. 3. a descendant of Śaryāti; a son of Jayadhvaja and grandson of Kārtavīrya (*Br. Purāṇa*); a rākṣasa (*Rāmāyaṇa*); a tribe (*M. Bh.*)

**Tālākākṣi** (S) (F) with green eyes.

**Tālaketu** (S) (M) 1. palm bannered. 3. a dānava killed by Kṛṣṇa (*M. Bh.*); another name for Bhīṣma and Balarāma.

**Tālākhyā** (S) (F) perfume; with the scent of a palm tree.

**Tālanka** (S) (M) 1. endowed with every auspicious sign. 3. another name for Balarāma and Śiva.

**Talava** (S) (M) musician.

**Tālikā** (S) (F) 1. the palm of the hand. 2. nightingale (*Curculigo orchioides*)

**Tālin** (S) (M) 1. furnished with cymbals. 3. another name for Śiva.

**Talinodarī** (S) (F) slender waisted.

**Talīśa** (S) (M) 1. lord of the earth. 2. mountain.

**Tallaja** (S) (M) excellent.

**Tallī** (S) (F) 1. youthful; boat. 3. a wife of Varuṇa.

**Taluna** (S) (M) young; youth; wind.

**Talunī** (S) (F) maiden.

**Tālūra** (S) (M) whirlpool.

**Tama** (S) (M) 1. darkness. 3. a king who was the son of Śravā of the race of Ghṛtasamada (*M. Bh.*)

**Tamā** (S) (F) night.

**Tamahariṇī** (S) (F) 1. remover of darkness. 3. a deity who destroys darkness.

**Tamāla** (S) (M) 1. dark barked; mark on the forehead. 2. *Xanthochymos pictorius*.

**Tamas** (S) (M) 1. darkness; gloom. 3. a son of Pṛthuśravas (*V. Purāṇa*); a son of Dakṣa.

**Tamasā** (S) (F) 1. dark coloured. 3. a river that merges with the Gaṅgā and on whose banks was the āśrama of Vālmiki (*V. Rāmāyaṇa*)

**Tāmasa** (S) (M) 1. dark; malignant. 3. the 4th Manu who was the son of Priyavrata and Barhiśmatī (*Bh. Purāṇa*); an attendant of Śiva.

**Tāmasī** (S) (F) 1. night; sleep. 3. a river (*M. Bh.*); another name for Durgā.

**Tamasvinī** (S) (F) night.

**Tamī** (S) (F) night.

**Tamisrahā** (S) (M) 1. destroying darkness. 3. another name for Sūrya.

**Tamiśvara** (S) (M) 1. lord of the darkness. 3. another name for the moon.

**Tamoghna** (S) (M) 1. destroying darkness. 3. another name for the sun, the moon, Agni, Viṣṇu, Śiva and Buddha.

**Tamohara** (S) (M) 1. one who removes darkness. 3. another name for the moon.

**Tamontakṛt** (S) (M) 1. exterminating darkness. 3. an attendant of Skanda.

**Tamonud** (S) (M) 1. dispersing darkness. 2. fire; lamp; the sun and moon.

**Tamori** (S) (M) 1. enemy of darkness. 3. another name for the sun.

**Tāmrā** (S) (F) 1. copper crested. 3. a follower of Skanda.

**Tāmra** (S) (M) 1. of a coppery red colour; made of copper. 3. a son of the demon Murāsura and the minister of Mahiṣāsura who was killed by Kṛṣṇa (*D. Bh. Purāṇa*); a son of Naraka Bhauma (*Bh. Purāṇa*)

**Tāmrajākṣa** (S) (M) 1. copper eyed. 3. a son of Kṛṣṇa and Satyabhāmā (*H. Purāṇa*)

**Tāmraka** (S) (M) 1. copper. 3. a gandharva; Redwood (*Adenanthera pavonina*)

**Tāmrakarṇī** (S) (F) 1. copper eared. 3. the consort of Añjana the elephant of a quarter.

**Tāmrākhya** (S) (M) a red pearl.

**Tāmralipta** (S) (M) 1. surrounded by copper. 3. an ancient king who was crowned by Sahadeva (*M. Bh.*)

**Tāmrapakṣa** (S) (M) 1. copperclad. 3. a son of Kṛṣṇa.

**Tāmrapakṣā** (S) (F) 1. copper coloured. 3. a daughter of Kṛṣṇa (*H. Purāṇa*)

**Tāmraparṇī** (S) (F) 1. with red leaves. 3. a holy river of Kerala on whose banks the devas did penance (*M. Bh.*)

**Tāmrarasā** (S) (F) 1. of red juice. 3. a daughter of Raudrāśva (*Vā. Purāṇa*)

**Tāmrasa** (S) (M) day lotus; gold; copper.

**Tāmratapta** (S) (M) 1. redhot like copper. 3. a son of Kṛṣṇa (*Bhā. Purāṇa*)

**Tāmrāvatī** (S) (F) 1. coppery. 3. an ancient river which is supposed to have generated fire (*M. Bh.*)

**Tāmrikā** (S) (F) 1. coppery. 2. Rosary Pea (*Abrus precatorius*); Indian Madder (*Rubia cordifolia*)

**Tāmroṣṭha** (S) (M) 1. red lipped. 3. a yakṣa in the court of Kubera (*M. Bh.*)

**Tana** (S) (M) offspring.

**Tanaka** (S) (M) a reward.

**Tanamaya** (S) (M) embodied.

**Tanas** (S) (M) offspring.

**Tanavīra** (S) (M) strong; robust.

**Tanaya** (S) (M) 1. belonging to one's family. 2. son.

**Tanayuta** (S) (M) wind; night; thunderbolt.

**Tāṇḍa** (S) (M) 1. dance. 3. an attendant of Śiva skilled in dance and inventor of the Taṇḍava nṛtya.

**Tāṇḍavapriya** (S) (M) 1. fond of the Tāṇḍava dance. 3. another name for Śiva.

**Tāṇḍi** (S) (M) 1. the art of dancing. 3. a celebrated sage who repeated to Brahmā the 1000 names of Śiva (*M. Bh.*)

**Tāṇḍya** (S) (M) 1. of dance. 3. a sage and friend of Indra (*M. Bh.*)

**Taniṣṭha** (S) (M) smallest.

**Tañjala** (S) (M) the Ćataka bird.

**Tankā** (S) (M) 1. leg. 3. a rāgiṇī.

**Tansu** (S) (M) 1. decorative. 3. a Purū dynasty king who was the son of Matīnāra and the father of Īlina (*M. Bh.*)

**Tāntava** (S) (M) 1. made of threads. 2. a son.

**Tantipāla** (S) (M) 1. guardian of the cows. 3. name assumed by Sahadeva at Virāta's court (*M. Bh.*)

**Tantrāyin** (S) (M) 1. drawing out threads of light. 3. another name for the sun.

**Tantripāla** (S) (M) 1. guardian of the calves. 3. another name for Sahadeva.

**Tantu** (S) (M) 1. thread. 2. propogator of the family. 3. a son of Viśvāmitra (*M. Bh.*)

**Tantuvardhana** (S) (M) 1. procreator; propagator; increaser of the race. 3. another name for Viṣṇu and Śiva.

**Tanu** (S) (M) 1. slender; little; minute; delicate. 3. a sage in the court of King Vīradyumna (*M. Bh.*)

**Tanūbhava** (S) (M) son.

**Tanūbhavā** (S) (F) daughter.

**Tanūjā** (S) (F) 1. born of the body. 2. daughter.

**Tanūja** (S) (M) 1. born of the body. 2. son.

**Tanulatā** (S) (F) 1. with a vine like body. 2. slender; flexible; elastic.

**Tanūna** (S) (M) 1. bodiless. 3. the wind.

**Tanūnapāt** (S) (M) 1. self generated. 2. the sacred name of fire (*Ṛg Veda*). 3. another name for Śiva.

**Tanūrja** (S) (M) 1. with heat in the body. 3. a son of the 3rd Manu (*H. Purāṇa*)

**Tanuśrī** (S) (F) with a divine body.

**Tanūvaśin** (S) (M) 1. having power over the person; ruling. 3. another name for Agni and Indra.

**Tanuvī** (S) (F) a slender woman.

**Tanvangī** (S) (F) slender limbed.

**Tanvī** (S) (F) 1. slender; beautiful; delicate; fine. 2. *Desmodium gangeticum*; *Uraria lagopoides*.

**Tanvin** (S) (M) 1. possessed of a body. 3. a son of Manu Tāmasa (*H. Purāṇa*)

**Tapā** (S) (F) 1. consuming by heat; one who performs penance. 2. doer of penance. 3. one of the 8 deities of the Bodhi tree (*L. Vistara*)

**Tapa** (S) (M) 1. consuming by heat; warming; burning; shining. 2. the sun. 3. a deva with fire like splendour who was born of the penance of 5 sages and is therefore also known as Pāñćajanya; an attendant of Śiva; a fire that generated the 7 mothers of Skanda (*M. Bh.*)

**Tapana** (S) (M) 1. illuminating; burning. 2. the sun; the hot season; the sunstone. 3. one of Kāma's arrows; a Pāñćala soldier in the Mahābhārata battle (*M. Bh.*); a rākṣasa (*Rāmāyaṇa*); a yakṣa (*M. Bh.*); another name for Agastya; Common Marking Nut tree (*Semecarpus anacardium*)

**Tapanaććhada** (S) (M) 1. to please the sun. 2. sunflower.

**Tapanadyuti** (S) (M) as brilliant as the sun.

**Tapanakara** (S) (M) sunbeam; the ray of the sun.

**Tapanamaṇi** (S) (M) 1. gem of the sun. 2. the sunstone.

**Tapanāśman** (S) (M) sunstone.

**Tapanasutā** (S) (F) 1. daughter of the sun. 3. another name for the Yamunā river.

**Tapanatanaya** (S) (M) 1. son of the sun. 3. another name for Karṇa.

**Tapanatanayā** (S) (F) 1. daughter of the sun. 3. the rivers Yamunā and Godāvarī conjoined.

**Tapanātmajā** (S) (F) 1. daughter of the sun. 3. another name for the Yamunā river.

**Tāpanī** (S) (F) 1. heat. 3. a river.

**Tapanīyaka** (S) (M) 1. purified through fire. 2. gold.

**Tapanopala** (S) (M) sunstone.

**Tapantī** (S) (F) 1. warming. 3. a river.

**Tapas** (S) (M) 1. penance; warmth; heat; fire; meditation; merit; bird; ascetic; potential power. 3. the 9th lunar mansion; another name for the sun, Agni and the moon.

**Tāpasanidhi** (S) (M) 1. store of ascetism. 3. the Supreme Spirit.

**Tapasarāja** (S) (M) 1. lord of ascetics. 3. another name for the moon.

**Tapasomūrti** (S) (M) 1. an example of austerity. 3. a ṛṣi of the 12th Manvantara (*H. Purāṇa*)

**Tapasvat** (S) (M) hot; ascetic; devout; pious.

**Tapasvin** (S) (M) 1. hermit; ascetic. 3. a son of Manu Ćākṣusa and Nadvalā (*V. Purāṇa*); seer of the 12th Manvantara (*Bhā. Purāṇa*); another name for Nārada; Indian Beech (*Pongamia glabra*)

**Tapasvinī** (S) (F) 1. ascetic. 2. Spikenard (*Nardostachys jatamansi*)

**Tāpasya** (S) (M) 1. produced by heat; belonging to austerity. 2. the Phālguna season. 3. a son of Manu Tāmasa (*H. Purāṇa*); the flower *Jasminum multiflorum*; another name for Arjuna.

**Tapatī** (S) (F) 1. warming. 3. the daughter of Sūrya and Saṁjñā and goddess of the river Tāpati, she is the wife of Saṁvaraṇa and the mother of Kuru, she was transformed into the river Narmadā (*Bh. Purāṇa*)

**Tāpatī** (S) (F) 1. of Tapatī. 3. a river.

**Tapeśa** (S) (M) 1. lord of penances. 3. another name for the divine trinity (Brahmā, Viṣṇu and Śiva) and the sun.

**Tapeśvara** (S) (M) 1. lord of penances. 3. another name for Śiva and the sun.

**Tāpī** (S) (F) 1. heat; glow. 3. another name for the Tāpatī river.

**Tāpīja** (S) (M) a gem found near the Tāpatī river.

**Tapiṣṇu** (S) (M) warming; burning.

**Tapiṣṇudeva** (S) (M) 1. lord of heat. 3. another name for the sun.

**Tapita** (S) (M) refined gold.

**Tapodhana** (S) (M) 1. rich in religious austerities. 3. son of Manu Tāmasa (*V. Purāṇa*); a ṛṣi of the 12th Manvantara (*V. Purāṇa*)

**Tapodharma** (S) (M) 1. religious ascetic. 3. a son of the 13th Manu (*H. Purāṇa*)

**Tapodhika** (S) (M) 1. menacing the sun. 3. a

sage who was the son of Kuśika.

**Tapodhriti** (S) (M) 1. observing religious austerities. 3. a son of the 12th Manu.

**Tapodyuti** (S) (M) 1. brilliant with religious merit. 3. the ṛṣi of the 12th Manvantara (*V. Purāṇa*)

**Tapoja** (S) (M) 1. born from heat. 2. to become a saint through religious austerities.

**Tapomūla** (S) (M) 1. founded on austerities. 3. a son of Manu Tāmasa (*H. Purāṇa*)

**Tapomūrti** (S) (M) an incarnation of religious austerities.

**Taponidhi** (S) (M) 1. a treasure of austerities. 3. a seer of the 12th Manvantara.

**Taporāja** (S) (M) 1. lord of austerities. 3. another name for the moon.

**Taporati** (S) (M) 1. rejoicing in religious austerities. 3. a son of Manu Tāmasa (*H. Purāṇa*); a seer of the 12th Manvantara.

**Taporavi** (S) (M) 1. the sun of ascetics. 3. a ṛṣī of the 12th Manvantara (*H. Purāṇa*)

**Taposana** (S) (M) 1. one whose food is austerity. 3. a ṛṣi of the 12th Manvantara (*H. Purāṇa*); a son of Manu Tāmasa.

**Tapurmūrdhan** (S) (M) 1. fire headed. 3. the son of Bṛhaspati and part author of *Ṛg Veda* (x); another name for Agni.

**Tapuṣi** (S) (F) a burning weapon.

**Tārā** (S) (F) 1. star. 2. the pupil of the eye; meteor; perfume. 3. Dākṣāyāṇī worshipped in Kiskindha (*M. Purāṇa*); wife of Buddha Amoghasiddha; a female monkey who was the daughter of Suṣeṇa and the wife of Bāli, she was the mother of Aṅgada (*M. Bh.*); the wife of Bṛhaspati who eloped with Ćandra and became the mother of Budha or Mercury who became the ancestor of the lunar race of kings (*Bhāgavata*); a tāntric goddess who figures predominantly in the Jaina and Buddhist traditions as the great mother goddess and one of the 10 mahāvidyas; a yoginī (*H. Ć. Cintamaṇi*); a Śakti (*J. Literature*); a rāga.

**Tāra** (S) (M) 1. carrying across. 2. saviour; protector; shining; radiant; good; excellent; silver; star. 3. one of Rāma's monkey generals who was the son of Bṛhaspati and the husband of Tārā; a daitya (*H. Purāṇa*)

**Tārābhūṣā** (S) (F) 1. decorated with stars. 2. the night.

**Tārāćandra** (S) (M) the stars and moon conjoined.

**Tārādatta** (S) (F) 1. given by the stars. 3. the wife of King Kalingadatta of Takṣaśila and mother of an incarnation of the apsarā Surabhidattā.

**Tārādhipati** (S) (M) 1. lord of the stars. 3. another name for the moon.

**Tārādhīśa** (S) (M) 1. lord of the stars. 3. another name for the moon.

**Tārahemābha** (S) (M) shining like silver and gold.

**Tārakā** (S) (F) 1. star; falling star; meteor; the eye. 3. Bṛhaspati's wife (*V. Purāṇa*)

**Tāraka** (S) (M) 1. rescuing; liberating; saving; helmsman. 2. belonging to the stars. 3. an asura chief who fathered Tārakākṣa, Kamalākṣa and Vidyunmālikā and was killed by Skanda (*M. Bh.*); a minister of King Bhadrasena of Kāśmira and a great devotee of Śiva (*Ś. Purāṇa*)

**Tārakajit** (S) (M) 1. conqueror of Tāraka. 3. another name for Skanda.

**Tārakākṣa** (S) (M) 1. star eyed. 3. a son of Tārakāsura and lord of the golden city of Tripura (*M. Bh.*)

**Tārakānātha** (S) (M) 1. lord of the stars. 3. another name for the moon.

**Tārakārāja** (S) (M) 1. lord of the stars. 3. another name for the moon.

**Tārakeśvara** (S) (M) 1. lord of the stars. 3. another name for the moon.

**Tārakiṇī** (S) (F) 1. starry. 2. night.

**Tārakita** (S) (M) star spangled.

**Tārākṣa** (S) (M) 1. star eyed. 3. a king of the Niṣadhas; a mountain.

**Tārakṣya** (S) (M) the sun as a white horse.

**Taralā** (S) (F) 1. spirituous liquor. 2. a bee. 3. a yoginī (*H. Ć. Cintāmaṇi*)

**Tarala** (S) (M) 1. tremulous; glittering. 2. the central gem of a necklace; a wave; ruby; iron.

**Taralalekhā** (S) (F) a tremulous line.

**Tārāmati** (S) (F) 1. with a glorious mind. 3. the wife of Hariśćandra and the mother of Rohita.

**Tārāmbā** (S) (F) mother star (*Br. Purāṇa*)

**Tarānā** (S) (F) song.

**Taraṅga** (S) (M) **1.** goes across. **2.** wave; billow.

**Taraṅgabhīru** (S) (M) **1.** afraid of the waves. **3.** a son of the 14th Manu (*H. Purāṇa*)

**Taraṅgiṇī** (S) (F) **1.** full of waves; restless; moving. **3.** a river.

**Taraṇī** (S) (F) raft; boat.

**Taraṇi** (S) (M) **1.** moving forward; quick; untired; energetic; helping. **3.** another name for the sun.

**Taraṇiratna** (S) (M) **1.** jewel of the sun. **2.** ruby.

**Taraṇitanaya** (S) (F) **1.** daughter of the sun. **3.** another name for the river Yamunā.

**Taranta** (S) (M) the ocean.

**Tarantuka** (S) (M) **1.** boat. **3.** a yakṣa installed on the boundary of Kurukṣetra (*M. Bh.*)

**Tārāpati** (S) (M) **1.** lord of Tārā. **3.** another name for Bṛhaspati, Śiva and the monkey Bālin.

**Tārāpuṣpa** (S) (F) star blossom; jasmine.

**Tārāramaṇa** (S) (M) **1.** beloved of the stars. **3.** another name for the moon.

**Tārāsaṅkara** (S) (M) the stars and Śiva conjoined.

**Tarasvat** (S) (M) **1.** quick; violent; energetic; bold. **3.** a son of the 14th Manu (*H. Purāṇa*)

**Tarasvin** (S) (M) **1.** quick; energetic; violent; bold. **2.** courier; hero; falcon; the wind. **3.** another name for Śiva and Garuda.

**Tārāvalī** (S) (F) **1.** a multitude of stars. **3.** the daughter of the yakṣa prince Maṇibhadra.

**Tārāvatī** (S) (F) **1.** surrounded by stars. **3.** a daughter of Kakutstha and wife of King Ćandraśekhara; the wife of Dharmadhvaja; a form of Durgā.

**Tārendra** (S) (M) star prince; the prince of stars.

**Tāreya** (S) (M) **1.** son of Tārā. **3.** another name for Aṅgada.

**Tārikā** (S) (F) belonging to the stars.

**Tāriṇī** (S) (F) **1.** enabling to cross over; saving. **3.** another name for Durgā.

**Tāriṇićaraṇa** (S) (M) **1.** the feet that enable one to cross over. **3.** another name for Viṣṇu.

**Tāriṇirā** (S) (F) **1.** having the quality of liberation; crossing over the water. **3.** a Buddhist goddess.

**Tariśa** (S) (M) **1.** raft; boat. **2.** a competent person; the ocean.

**Tarit** (S) (M) one who has crossed over.

**Taritā** (S) (F) **1.** the forefinger; the leader. **3.** another name for Durgā.

**Tārkṣya** (S) (M) **1.** amulet; creeper; bird. **3.** a mythical bird who was the son of Kaśyapa and Vinatā and who with Garuḍa formed a class of demigods (*M. Bh.*); a sage and member of Indra's court (*M. Bh.*); another name for Garuḍa; another name for Śiva.

**Tārkṣyadhvaja** (S) (M) **1.** Garuḍa symboled. **3.** another name for Viṣṇu.

**Tārkṣyarakṣaṇa** (S) (M) **1.** protecting Garuda. **3.** another name for Kṛṣṇa.

**Tarpaṇa** (S) (M) satiating; refreshing; gladdening.

**Tarpiṇī** (S) (F) **1.** satisfying; offering oblations. **2.** *Hibiscus mutabilis*.

**Tarṣa** (S) (M) **1.** with a fine shape. **2.** raft; ocean; sun.

**Taru** (S) (M) **1.** quick; protecting; a tree. **3.** a son of Manu Ćākṣuṣa (*M. Purāṇa*)

**Tarulatā** (S) (F) vine.

**Taruṇa** (S) (M) **1.** young; tender; fresh; new. **3.** a ṛṣī of the 11th Manvantara (*H. Purāṇa*)

**Taruṇaka** (S) (M) **1.** youthful. **3.** a serpent of the family of Dhṛtarāṣṭra (*M. Bh.*)

**Taruṇapat** (S) (M) **1.** with new attire. **3.** another name for Agni.

**Taruṇendu** (S) (M) the waxing moon; the new moon.

**Taruṇī** (S) (F) **1.** young girl. **2.** *Rosa alba*.

**Taruṣa** (S) (M) conqueror.

**Taruṣī** (S) (F) victory.

**Tarutṛ** (S) (M) conqueror.

**Tarutra** (S) (M) triumphant; conquering; superior.

**Tāspandra** (S) (M) **1.** one who discloses secrets. **3.** a ṛṣī.

**Tāṭanka** (S) (M) **1.** earring. **3.** King Sinhadhvaja in his previous incarnation.

**Tathāgata** (S) (M) 1. being such; he who goes and comes in the same way (as the Buddhas before him). 3. another name for Gautama Buddha.

**Tathavādin** (S) (M) telling the exact truth.

**Taṭinī** (S) (F) 1. with banks. 2. a river.

**Tātṛpi** (S) (F) intensely satisfying.

**Tattvadarśin** (S) (M) 1. knower of substance; perceiving truth. 3. a seer of the 13th Manvantara; a son of Manu Raivata (*H. Purāṇa*)

**Taturi** (S) (M) conquering.

**Taṭya** (S) (M) 1. living on slopes. 3. another name for Śiva.

**Taukṣika** (S) (M) 1. balance. 2. the zodiac sign of Libra.

**Taulika** (S) (M) painter.

**Tauṭeśa** (S) (M) 1. guardian of the banks; guard of the banks. 3. a kṣetrapāla.

**Tautika** (S) (M) the pearl oyster; pearl.

**Tavalīna** (S) (M) 1. absorbed in god. 2. one with god in meditation.

**Tavaṣya** (S) (M) strength.

**Taviṣa** (S) (M) 1. strong; energetic; courageous. 2. the ocean; heaven; gold.

**Taviṣī** (S) (F) 1. power; strength; violence; courage; river; heavenly virgin. 3. a daughter of Indra; another name for the earth.

**Tāvura** (S) (M) the zodiac sign of Taurus.

**Tāyin** (S) (M) protector.

**Teja** (S) (M) lustre; glow; effulgence; sharpness; protection.

**Tejala** (S) (M) 1. bringing light. 2. the Francoline Partridge.

**Tejapāla** (S) (M) controller of power.

**Tejas** (S) (M) fiery energy; spiritual and moral power; glory; majesty; authority; the sharp edge of a knife; the point of a flame; splendour; brilliance; light; clearness of the eyes; energy; power; spirit; essence; gold; marrow; dignity.

**Tejasāmrāśi** (S) (M) 1. a heap of splendour. 3. another name for Sūrya.

**Tejaścaṇḍa** (S) (M) 1. very bright; sharp and powerful. 3. a deity who adorns the god Sūrya with a garland daily.

**Tejasinha** (S) (M) 1. lion of power. 3. a son of Raṇadāra.

**Tejaśrī** (S) (F) with divine power and grace.

**Tejasvat** (S) (M) sharp edged; splendid; bright; glorious; beautiful; energetic; spirited.

**Tejasvatī** (S) (F) 1. splendid; bright; glorious; energetic. 3. the daughter of King Vikramasena of Ujjayinī and the wife of Somadatta (*K. Sāgara*); the wife of King Ādityasena of Ujjayinī; *Zanthoxylum budrunga*.

**Tejasvin** (S) (M) 1. brilliant; bright; strong; heroic; dignified; famous; sharp; powerful; splendid; energetic; noble; inspiring respect. 3. a son of Indra (*M. Bh.*); one of the 5 Indras.

**Tejeyu** (S) (M) 1. one who is possessed with splendour. 3. a son of Raudrāśva and Miśrakeśī (*M. Bh.*)

**Tejindra** (S) (M) glorious chief.

**Tejini** (S) (F) 1. sharp; bright; energetic. 2. touchstone; whetstone.

**Tejiṣṭha** (S) (M) very sharp; very hot; very bright.

**Tejita** (S) (M) sharpened; whetted.

**Tejomayī** (S) (F) consisting of light and splendour.

**Tejomūrti** (S) (M) consisting totally of light.

**Tejonidhi** (S) (M) abounding in glory.

**Tejorāśi** (S) (M) 1. mass of splendour. 3. another name for Mount Meru.

**Tejorūpa** (S) (M) 1. consisting of splendour. 3. another name for Brahmā.

**Tejovatī** (S) (F) 1. sharp; bright; splendid. 3. the city of Agni (*D. Bhāgavata*)

**Tevana** (S) (M) sport; a pleasure garden.

**Thanavelu** (Tamil) (M) the youthful Balarāma.

**Thangam** (Tamil) (M) full of joy; gold.

**Thirumāla** (S) (M) the hills of Tirupati.

**Tidiri** (S) (M) the Shoveller bird.

**Tigma** (S) (M) 1. sharp; pointed; hot; scorching; violent; intense; weapon; fame; ray of light. 3. Indra's thunderbolt.

**Tigmaketu** (S) (M) 1. flame bannered. 3. a son of Vatsara and Svarvīthi (*Bh. Purāṇa*)

**Tigmamanyu** (S) (M) 1. of violent wrath.

3. another name for Śiva.

**Tigmānśu** (S) (M) 1. hot rayed. 2. fire.

**Tigmaraśmi** (S) (M) 1. hot rayed. 3. the sun.

**Tijila** (S) (M) the moon.

**Tīkam** (S) (M) moving.

**Tīkamćandra** (S) (M) the moving moon.

**Tīkṣnakantā** (S) (F) 1. fond of cruelty. 3. a form of Ćaṇdikā (*K. Purāṇa*)

**Tīkṣṇānśu** (S) (M) 1. sharp rayed. 3. another name for the sun.

**Tilabhāvanī** (S) (F) 1. beautiful dot. 3. jasmine.

**Tilakā** (S) (F) a type of necklace.

**Tilaka** (S) (M) 1. a freckle compared to a sesamum seed. 2. a mark on the forehead made either as an ornament or as a distinction; the ornament of anything; California Cinchona (*Symplocos racemosa*)

**Tilakalatā** (S) (F) 1. ornamental vine. 2. the *Chlerodendron phlomoides*.

**Tilakarāja** (S) (M) the best king; an ornament to kings.

**Tilakāśraya** (S) (M) 1. one that receives the tilaka. 2. the forehead.

**Tilakāvatī** (S) (F) 1. decorated. 3. a river.

**Tilakottara** (S) (M) 1. the supreme tilaka. 3. a vidyādhara.

**Tilikā** (S) (F) a small mark of sandalwood.

**Tillā** (S) (F) 1. one who has gone before. 3. a deity.

**Tilottamā** (S) (F) 1. one of the guardians of the sun; the best sesamum seed. 3. a form of Dākṣāyānī (*M. Purāṇa*); an apsarā who was the daughter of Kaśyapa and Prādhā and was created by Viśvakarmān from small particles of all the best things in the world, Śiva developed his 4 heads and Indra his 1000 eyes in order to see her beauty always (*M. Bh.*)

**Timi** (S) (F) 1. fish. 3. a daughter of Dakṣa and wife of Kaśyapa and the mother of the sea monsters.

**Timī** (S) (M) 1. a whale or mythical fish of an enormous size. 3. a son of Dūrva and father of Bṛhadratha (*Bhā. Purāṇa*); the zodiac sign of Pisces.

**Timidhvaja** (S) (M) 1. whale bannered. 3. a son of asura Śambara who made King Daśaratha faint, the latter was helped by Kaikeyī and promised her 2 boons (*Rāmāyaṇa*)

**Timikoṣa** (S) (M) 1. receptacle of Timi. 2. the ocean.

**Timilā** (S) (F) a musical instrument.

**Timiṁgila** (S) (M) 1. a large fabulous fish. 3. a king defeated by Sahadeva (*M. Bh.*)

**Timirānud** (S) (M) 1. darkness destroyer. 3. another name for the sun.

**Timirāri** (S) (M) 1. enemy of darkness. 3. another name for the sun.

**Timiraripu** (S) (M) 1. the enemy of darkness; darkness destroyer. 3. another name for the sun.

**Timita** (S) (M) calm; tranquil; steady; quiet; fixed.

**Tiraśćī** (S) (M) 1. striped across. 3. a ṛṣi who was a descendant of Aṅgiras (*Ṛg Veda*)

**Tīrtha** (S) (F) passage; way; ford; stairs for descent into a river; a place of pilgrimage; sacred object; a worthy person.

**Tīrthadeva** (S) (M) 1. lord of the pilgrimage. 3. another name for Śiva.

**Tīrthaka** (S) (M) sanctified.

**Tīrthakara** (S) (M) 1. creating a passage through life. 2. a term used to denote the head of a sect. 3. another name for Viṣṇu and Śiva.

**Tīrthakīrti** (S) (M) one whose fame carries on through life.

**Tīrthamayī** (S) (F) containing pilgrimage centres.

**Tīrthanemi** (S) (F) 1. encircling the sacred place; carrying sacred objects. 3. an attendant of Skanda (*M. Bh.*)

**Tīrthankara** (S) (M) 1. creating a passage; ascetic. 2. a term used to denote a sanctified teacher and saint of the Jainas. 3. another name for Viṣṇu.

**Tīrthapad** (S) (M) 1. with sanctifying feet. 3. another name for Kṛṣṇa.

**Tīrthapūjā** (S) (F) the washing of Kṛṣṇa's statue in water.

**Tīrtharāma** (S) (M) resting in a holy place.

**Tīrthasenī** (S) (F) 1. with an army of sanctified ones. 3. a mother in Skanda's retinue (*M. Bh.*)

**Tīrthatama** (S) (M) an object of the highest sanctity.

**Tīrthavatī** (S) (F) 1. holy; pious; flowing through a sacred place. 3. a river (*Bhā. Purāṇa*)

**Tīrtheśvara** (S) (M) 1. maker of the passage. 3. a Jaina Arhat.

**Tirujnānasambandha** (S) (M) 1. connoisseur of learning. 3. one of the 4 southern Śaivaite teachers who was born in Thanjāvūr and is supposed to have merged with the Śiva statue at the Ćidambara temple (7th century)

**Tirunavukkarasa** (S) (M) 1. knower of the divine. 3. Śaivaite and a disciple of Tirujñanasambandha who acquired divine knowledge.

**Tiryagīśa** (S) (M) 1. lord of the animals. 3. another name for Kṛṣṇa.

**Tiṣya** (S) (M) 1. auspicious; fortunate. 3. a heavenly archer; the 8th Nakṣatra, the month Pauṣa.

**Tiṣyagupta** (S) (M) 1. auspicious; fortunate; protected by the Tiṣya Nakṣatra. 3. the founder of schism 2 of the Jaina community.

**Tiṣyaketu** (S) (M) 1. with the banner of fortune. 3. another name for Śiva.

**Tiṣyarakṣitā** (S) (F) 1. protected by luck. 3. Aśoka's 2nd wife.

**Titha** (S) (M) 1. fire; love; time; autumn. 3. another name for Kāma.

**Titikṣā** (S) (F) 1. patience; endurance. 3. patience personified as the daughter of Dakṣa and Prasūti and the wife of Dharma, she was the mother of Kshema (*Skandha Bhagāvata*)

**Titikṣu** (S) (M) 1. enduring patiently. 3. a king who was the son of Uśīnara and the father of Ruṣadratha (*A. Purāṇa*); a son of Mahāmanas.

**Titlī** (S) (F) butterfly.

**Tittirī** (S) (M) 1. partridge. 3. a sage who was a member of the council of Yudhiṣṭhira (*M. Bh.*); a nāga (*M. Bh.*); a pupil of Yāska.

**Tīvradyuti** (S) (M) 1. hot rayed. 3. another name for the sun.

**Tīvrānanda** (S) (M) 1. eternally intense and sharp. 3. another name for Śiva.

**Toḍara** (S) (M) 1. removing fear. 3. a minister of Akbar who was one of his Navratnas.

**Toḍikā** (S) (F) 1. splitting; breaking. 3. a rāgiṇī.

**Tola** (S) (Malayalam) (M) 1. with a deer skin belt. 3. a Sanskṛt scholar who was a great satirical poet of Malayālam literature and a minister of King Bhāskara Ravi Varmā of Kerala (11th century)

**Tomara** (S) (M) lance; javelin.

**Tomaradhara** (S) (M) 1. lance bearer. 2. fire.

**Torāmana** (S) (M) a Hūṇ king and father of Mihirākula.

**Toraṇa** (S) (M) 1. arch; a triangle supporting a large balance. 3. another name for Śiva.

**Toṣa** (S) (M) 1. satisfaction; contentment; pleasure; joy. 3. the son of Bhāgavata and one of the 12 tuśitas (*Bhā. Purāṇa*)

**Toṣaṇī** (S) (F) 1. satisfying; gratifying; appeasing; pleasing. 3. another name for Durgā.

**Toṣin** (S) (M) satisfied.

**Toṣita** (S) (M) satisfied; pleased.

**Totalā** (S) (F) 1. repeating. 3. another name for Gaurī and Durgā.

**Toya** (S) (F) 1. water. 2. *Pavonia odoralā*.

**Toyadhī** (S) (M) 1. containing water; water receptacle. 2. the ocean.

**Toyanīvī** (S) (F) 1. ocean girdled. 2. the earth.

**Toyarāj** (S) (M) 1. the king of waters. 2. the ocean.

**Toyeśa** (S) (M) 1. lord of water. 3. another name for Varuṇa.

**Trailokyabandhu** (S) (M) 1. friend of the 3 worlds. 3. another name for the sun.

**Trailokyadevī** (S) (F) 1. goddess of the 3 worlds. 3. the wife of King Yaśakara (*R. Taraṅginī*)

**Trailokyanātha** (S) (M) 1. lord of the 3 worlds. 3. another name for Rāma and Kṛṣṇa.

**Trailokyaprabhā** (S) (F) 1. splendour; grace; light of the 3 worlds. 3. the daughter of a dānava.

**Trailokyavikramin** (S) (M) 1. striding through the 3 worlds. 3. a Bodhisattva.

**Traiṣāṇi** (S) (M) 1. desirer of the trinity of

gods. 3. a king of the family of Turvasu who was the father of Karaṁdhāma.

**Traivali** (S) (M) 1. with 3 lines on the stomach. 3. a sage at the court of Yudhiṣṭhira (*M. Bh.*)

**Trāman** (S) (M) protection.

**Trāṇana** (S) (M) protecting.

**Trasadasyu** (S) (M) 1. before whom the dasyus tremble; tormentor of the demons. 3. a king of the Ikṣvāku dynasty who was the son of Purukutsa and is one of the kings who should be remembered in the morning (*M. Bh.*)

**Trasareṇu** (S) (F) 1. the mote in the sunbeam. 3. a wife of the sun.

**Trāta** (S) (M) protected.

**Trātṛ** (S) (M) 1. protector; defender. 3. another name for Indra.

**Trayī** (S) (F) 1. intellect; understanding. 3. the 3 Vedas.

**Trayitanu** (S) (M) 1. with the 3 vedas for a body. 3. another name for Sūrya.

**Trayyāruṇa** (S) (M) 1. the sun as depicted in the 3 Vedas. 3. a king of the solar dynasty who was the son of Tridhanvan and the father of Triśanku (*Br. Purāṇa*)

**Trayyāruṇi** (S) (M) 1. knowing the sun of the 3 Vedas. 3. a sage in the line of disciples of Vyāsa.

**Tṛbhi** (S) (M) a ray.

**Treyā** (S) (F) walking in 3 paths.

**Triakṣa** (S) (M) 1. 3 eyed. 3. another name for Śiva.

**Triambaka** (S) (M) 1. 3 eyed. 3. a rudra; another name for Śiva.

**Triambikā** (S) (F) 1. consort of the 3 eyed Śiva. 3. another name for Pārvatī.

**Tribandhana** (S) (M) 1. the 3 bonds. 2. bonded 3 ways to the parents and the preceptor. 3. a son of Aruṇa (*Bh. Purāṇa*)

**Tribandhu** (S) (M) 1. a friend of the 3 worlds. 3. another name for Indra.

**Tribhānu** (S) (M) 1. the sun of the 3 Vedas; the sun of the morning, noon and evening. 3. a descendant of Yayāti and father of Karaṁdhama (*Bhāgavata*)

**Tribhuvana** (S) (M) the 3 worlds.

**Tribhuvanaprabhā** (S) (F) 1. glory and grace; light of the 3 worlds. 3. a daughter of a dānava (*K. Sāgara*)

**Tribhuvaneśvara** (S) (M) 1. lord of the 3 worlds. 3. another name for Indra.

**Tribhuvaneśvarī** (S) (M) 1. wife of Tribhuvaneśvara. 3. another name for Pārvatī.

**Tricakṣus** (S) (M) 1. 3 eyed. 3. another name for Śiva.

**Tridaśendra** (S) (M) 1. chief of the gods. 3. another name for Indra.

**Tridaśeśvara** (S) (M) 1. lord of the gods. 3. another name for Śiva, Indra, Agni, Varuṇa and Yama.

**Tridaśeśvarī** (S) (F) 1. chief of the gods. 3. an attendant of Durgā; another name for Durgā.

**Tridasyu** (S) (M) 1. with the qualities of 3 dasyus. 3. a sage who was the son of Agastya and Lopāmudrā.

**Trideśvara** (S) (M) 1. lord of heaven. 2. a god.

**Tridhāma** (S) (M) 1. shining in the 3 worlds. 3. the 10th incarnation of Śiva.

**Tridhāman** (S) (M) 1. shining in the 3 worlds. 3. another name for Viṣṇu, Brahmā, Śiva and Agni.

**Tridhanvan** (S) (M) 1. with the 3 bows (Sāma, Dāma, Daṇḍa) of power. 3. a king of the solar dynasty who was the grandfather of Triśanku (*Bh. Purāṇa*)

**Tridhārā** (S) (F) 1. 3 streamed. 3. another name for the Gaṅgā river.

**Tridharman** (S) (M) 1. follower of 3 paths. 3. another name for Śiva.

**Tridhātu** (S) (M) 1. consisting of 3 parts. 3. another name for Gaṇeśa.

**Tridīpa** (S) (M) with 3 lights (Jñāna, Karma, Bhakti)

**Tridivā** (S) (F) 1. heaven; cardamoms. 3. a river of ancient Bhārata (*M. Bh.*)

**Trigarta** (S) (M) 1. king of Trigarta. 3. another name for Suśarman.

**Trigartā** (S) (F) woman; a pearl.

**Trihāyaṇī** (S) (F) 1. returning in 3 years. 3. Svargalakṣmī who was reborn 3 times as Draupadī, Vedavatī and Sītā.

**Trijagatī** (S) (F) 1. mother of the 3 worlds. 3. another name for Pārvatī.

**Trijaṭa** (S) (M) 1. with 3 locks of hair (i.e. having desire, anger and lust). 3. a son of Viśvāmitra who was a poor sage and was granted cattle by Rāma (*V. Rāmāyaṇa*); another name for Śiva.

**Trijaṭā** (S) (F) 1. with 3 locks of hair. 3. a rākṣasī who was friendly to Sītā (*Rāmāyaṇa*)

**Trijña** (S) (M) 1. omniscient; seer; deity. 3. a Buddha.

**Trikakalpava** (S) (M) 1. of the 3rd Kalpa. 3. a king (*Bhāgavata*)

**Trikakubdhāmā** (S) (M) 1. abode of the 3 worlds. 3. another name for Mahāviṣṇu.

**Trikakubha** (S) (M) 1. triply pronged; triply distinguished. 3. Indra's thunderbolt.

**Trikakud** (S) (M) 1. having 3 peaks. 2. thrice excelling one's equals. 3. a mountain (*Ś. Brāhmaṇa*); a prince (*Bhā. Purāṇa*)

**Trikakup** (S) (M) 1. 3 peaked. 3. son of Āyus and Svarbhānu.

**Trikalā** (S) (F) 1. 3 pieces. 3. a goddess produced by the union of 3 gods for the destruction of Andhaka.

**Trikālajña** (S) (M) 1. knower of 3 times (past, present and future). 2. omniscient. 3. a Buddha.

**Trikālavid** (S) (M) 1. omniscient. 3. a Buddha; an Arhat of the Jainas.

**Trikāya** (S) (M) 1. with 3 bodies. 3. a Buddha.

**Trikha** (S) (M) 1. sharp. 2. nutmeg.

**Trikṣā** (S) (M) 1. destroying in 3 ways. 3. another name for Kaśyapa.

**Trilocanā** (S) (F) 1. consort of Śiva; the 3 eyed one. 3. another name for Pārvatī.

**Trilocana** (S) (M) 1. 3 eyed. 3. another name for Śiva.

**Trilocanapāla** (S) (M) defender of Śiva.

**Trilokacandra** (S) (M) 1. the moon of the 3 worlds; providing light to the 3 worlds. 3. another name for the moon.

**Trilokanātha** (S) (M) 1. lord of the 3 worlds. 3. another name for Indra and Śiva.

**Trilokātman** (S) (M) 1. soul of the 3 worlds. 3. another name for Śiva.

**Trilokavīra** (S) (M) 1. hero of the 3 worlds. 3. a Buddhist deity.

**Trilokeśa** (S) (M) 1. lord of the 3 worlds. 3. another name for Śiva, Viṣṇu and the sun.

**Trilokījit** (S) (M) conquering the 3 worlds.

**Trilokīnātha** (S) (M) 1. lord of the 3 worlds. 3. another name for Viṣṇu.

**Trimadhura** (S) (M) made of sugar, ghee and honey.

**Trimukhā** (S) (F) 1. 3 faced. 3. Śākyamuni's mother.

**Trimukha** (S) (M) 1. 3 faced. 3. the 3rd Arhat of the present Avasarpiṇī.

**Trimūrti** (S) (M) 1. with 3 forms. 3. Brahmā, Viṣṇu and Śiva conjoined; a Buddha; one of the 8 Vidyeśvaras.

**Trinābha** (S) (M) 1. one whose navel supports the 3 worlds. 3. another name for Viṣṇu.

**Trinayana** (S) (M) 1. 3 eyed. 3. another name for Śiva.

**Trinetra** (S) (M) 1. 3 eyed (the eyes represent the sun, moon and fire). 3. a minister of Mahiṣāsura (*Bh. Purāṇa*); another name for Śiva; Bulb bearing Yam (*Dioscorea bulbifera*)

**Tripād** (S) (M) 1. 3 footed. 3. a rākṣasa slain by Skanda (*M. Bh.*)

**Tripan** (S) (M) pleasing; refreshing.

**Tripanna** (S) (M) 1. follower of 3 types of knowledge; thrice worthy of admiration. 3. a horse of the moon.

**Tripat** (S) (M) 1. with pleasure; to one's satisfaction. 3. another name for the moon.

**Tripathagā** (S) (F) 1. flowing through 3 regions. 3. another name for the Gaṅgā.

**Tripathagaminī** (S) (F) 1. flowing through three regions. 3. another name for Gaṅgā.

**Tripṛṣṭha** (S) (M) 1. with 3 spines; 3 backed. 3. the 1st Black Vasudeva of the Jainas; another name for Viṣṇu.

**Tripurā** (S) (F) 1. triply fortified. 2. kind of cardomom. 3. another name for Durgā.

**Tripuraghātī** (S) (M) 1. destroyer of Tripurā. 3. another name for Śiva.

**Tripuraghna** (S) (M) 1. destroyer of Tripurā. 3. another name for Śiva.

**Tripurahartā** (S) (M) 1. destroyer of Tripurā. 3. another name for Śiva.

**Tripurajit** (S) (M) 1. conqueror of Tripurā. 2. conqueror of the city Tripurā of the asuras. 3. another name for Śiva.

**Tripuranāśana** (S) (M) 1. destroyer of Tripurā. 3. another name for Śiva.

**Tripurāntaka** (S) (M) 1. destroyer of Tripurā. 3. another name for Śiva.

**Tripurāntakara** (S) (M) 1. destroyer of Tripurā. 3. another name for Śiva.

**Tripurāri** (S) (M) 1. enemy of the city Tripurā. 3. another name for Śiva.

**Tripurasundari** (S) (F) 1. damsel of gold, silver and iron. 3. another name for Durgā.

**Tripurmardana** (S) (M) 1. destroyer of Tripura. 3. another name for Śiva.

**Tripuṣkara** (S) (M) decorated with 3 lotus flowers

**Triputā** (S) (F) 1. 3 fold. 2. Arabian Jasmine (*Jasminum sambac*). 3. another name for Durgā.

**Trirāva** (S) (M) 1. making 3 types of sound. 3. a son of Garuḍa.

**Triśalā** (S) (F) 1. 3 pointed. 3. the mother of Mahāvīra also known as Priyakarṇi.

**Triśaṅku** (S) (M) 1. sacrificing for the 3 (Dharma, Artha, Kāma). 3. an Ayodhya king of the dynasty of Māndhātā who was the son of Tribandhana and the father of Hariśćandra (*Bhā. Purāṇa*); a famous Solar dynasty king who was the son of Trayyāruṇa and who remains suspended in mid air between heaven and earth forming the southern cross constellation (*Ṛg Veda*); a son of Pṛthu (*H. Purāṇa*); a mythical river.

**Trisara** (S) (M) a triple pearl string.

**Triṣavana** (S) (M) 1. connected with 3 Soma libations. 3. a sage (*M. Bh.*)

**Triśikha** (S) (M) 1. trident; 3 pointed. 3. Indra in Manu Tāmasa's Manvantara (*Bh. Purāṇa*); Bengal Quince (*Aegle marmelos*)

**Triśiras** (S) (M) 1. 3 headed. 3. a rākṣasa who was a friend of Rāvaṇa; a son of the prajāpati Tvaṣṭā who was killed by Indra and from each of whose heads birds were born; another name for Kubera.

**Triṣnāri** (S) (M) 1. removing thirst. 2. satisfying; fulfilling. 3. Fine leaved Fumitory (*Fumaria parviflora*)

**Triśoka** (S) (M) 1. 3 types of grief. 2. physical, emotional and spiritual grief. 3. a sage who was the son of Kaṇva (*Ṛg Veda*)

**Trisrotā** (S) (M) 1. with 3 streams. 3. another name for Gaṅgā.

**Triṣṭup** (S) (M) 1. stopping 3 times. 3. a Vedic metre; a horse of the sun (*V. Purāṇa*)

**Triśukra** (S) (M) triply pure.

**Triśūla** (S) (M) 1. 3 pronged. 3. Śiva's trident. (*H. Purāṇa*)

**Triśūlagaṅgā** (S) (F) 1. coming from Śiva's trident 3. the trifurcated streams of the Gaṅgā; a river.

**Triśūlahasta** (S) (M) 1. holding the Triśūla. 3. another name for Śiva.

**Triśūlāṅka** (S) (M) 1. marked by the Triśula. 3. another name for Śiva.

**Triśūlapāṇi** (S) (M) 1. holding the Trisula. 3. another name for Śiva.

**Triśulin** (S) (M) 1. bearing the Triśula. 3. another name for Śiva.

**Triśulinī** (S) (F) 1. consort of Triśulin. 3. another name for Durgā.

**Trisuvarćaka** (S) (M) triply splendid.

**Trita** (S) (M) 1. 3rd. 3. an inferior Vedic deity associated with the maruts, Vāyu and Indra who conquered the demons with the help of Indra, he is also the keeper of nectar. In the epics Ekata, Dvita and Trita are the sons of Gautama or Prajāpati or Brahmā, he is also described as one of the 12 sons of Manu Ćākṣuṣa and Nadvalā.

**Trivakrā** (S) (F) 1. bent at 3 places. 3. a hunch backed woman who gave her scents to Kṛṣṇa and was cured by him (*Bhāgavata*)

**Trivarćaka** (S) (M) 1. shining in 3 ways. 3. a sage who was the son of Aṅgiras and who joined with 4 others to produce Pāñćajanya.

**Trivāstapa** (S) (M) 1. the sky as the abode of the 3 worlds. 3. another name for Dyaus the god of the sky.

**Triveṇī** (S) (F) 1. triple braided. 3. the confluence point of the 3 rivers Gaṅgā, Yamunā and Sarasvatī.

**Trividyā** (S) (M) a Brāhmin versed in 3 Vedas.

**Trivikrama** (S) (M) the 3 steps of Viṣṇu; possessed with 3 types of power.

**Trivṛṣan** (S) (M) 1. with 3 bulls. 3. a father of

Trayyaruṇa.

**Triyā** (S) (F) young woman.

**Triyuga** (S) (M) 1. appearing in the first 3 yugas. 3. another name for Kṛṣṇa.

**Tṛṇabindu** (S) (M) 1. water drops on grass; pieces of grass; a mortal. 3. a sage who was the father of Māninī and grandfather of Viśravas (*U. Rāmāyaṇa*)

**Tṛṇaka** (S) (M) 1. a blade of grass; mortal. 3. a king in the court of Yama (*M. Bh.*)

**Tṛṇamaṇi** (S) (M) 1. a jewel that attracts grass when rubbed. 2. sapphire; amber.

**Tṛṇaṅku** (S) (M) 1. fragrant grass. 3. a sage (*Ṛg Veda*)

**Tṛṇapa** (S) (M) 1. grass swallower. 3. a gandharva (*M. Bh.*)

**Tṛṇapāṇi** (S) (M) 1. holding grass in his hand. 3. a ṛṣi.

**Tṛṇasomāṅgiras** (S) (M) 1. accepting nectar made from grass. 3. a sage who lived in South India (*M. Bh.*)

**Tṛṇāvarta** (S) (M) 1. surrounded by straw. 2. tornado. 3. the son of Tārakāsura who was killed by Kṛṣṇa (*Bhāgavata*)

**Trotaki** (S) (F) 1. angry speech. 3. a rāgiṇī.

**Tṛptā** (S) (F) 1. satiety; contentment. 3. the wife of Kālu and the mother of Guru Nānak who founded the Sikh religion; another name for the Gaṅgā.

**Tṛpta** (S) (M) satiated; satisfied with.

**Tṛptātman** (S) (M) with a contented soul.

**Tṛptī** (S) (F) 1. satisfaction; contentment; water. 3. a gandharvī.

**Tṛṣā** (S) (F) 1. thirst. 3. desire personified as the daughter of Kāma.

**Tṛṣlā** (S) (F) making thirsty; desiring.

**Tṛṣṇā** (S) (F) 1. thirst; desire. 3. avidity personified as the mother of Dambha and the daughter of Mṛtyu.

**Tṛtīya** (S) (F) 1. the 3rd. 3. a river personified as a goddess who sits in the court of Varuṇa (*M. Bh.*)

**Truṭi** (S) (F) 1. atom; a minute period of time. 3. an attendant of Skanda (*M. Bh.*)

**Tryaksa** (S) (M) 1. 3 eyed. 3. an asura; another name for Śiva.

**Tryambaka** (S) (M) 1. born of 3 mothers; 3 eyed. 3. one of the 11 rudras; another name for Rudra.

**Tuḍi** (S) (F) 1. satisfying. 3. a rāgiṇī.

**Tugra** (S) (M) 1. water. 3. a king and father of Bhujyu who was once saved by the aśvins (*Ṛg Veda*); an enemy of Indra.

**Tuhara** (S) (M) 1. remover of darkness. 3. a soldier of Skanda (*M. Bh.*)

**Tuhi** (S) (F) a cuckoo's cry.

**Tuhina** (S) (M) 1. frost; cold; mist; dew. 3. moonlight; camphor.

**Tuhinakara** (S) (M) 1. cold rayed. 3. another name for the moon.

**Tuhināṅśu** (S) (M) 1. cold rayed. 3. another name for the moon.

**Tuhuṇḍa** (S) (M) 1. destroyer of darkness; causing pain. 2. an iron rod that keeps darkness away. 3. a dānava who was the son of Kaśyapa and Danu (*M. Bh.*); a son of Dhṛtarāṣṭra (*M. Bh.*)

**Tuja** (S) (F) thunderbolt.

**Tuka** (S) (M) 1. young; youthful; boy. 3. an astronomer.

**Tukarāma** (S) (M) 1. youthful Rama. 3. a saint and poet (17th century)

**Tula** (S) (M) 1. balance; scale. 2. the zodiac sign of Libra.

**Tuladhara** (S) (M) 1. scale holder. 2. the zodiac sign of Libra.

**Tulaka** (S) (M) ponderer.

**Tulakuci** (S) (M) 1. balanced. 2. with a good heart. 3. a prince and son of Śalin.

**Tulāpurusa** (S) (M) 1. a gift of gold equivalent to a man's weight. 3. another name for Viṣṇu/Kṛṣṇa.

**Tulasāriṇī** (S) (F) a quiver.

**Tulasī** (S) (F) 1. matchless. 2. Sacred Basil (*Ocimum sanctum*) produced from the ocean when churned (*P. Purāṇa*) or from the hair of the goddess Tulasī (*Brahma Purāṇa*); the Basil plant is held sacred by the Hindus as it is regarded as an incarnation of Mahālakṣmī who was born as the daughter of King Dharmadhvaja and Mādhavī, she prayed for many thousand years to obtain Māhāviṣṇu as her husband, she became the wife of the demon Śankhaćuḍa who was an incarnation of Sudāmā and ascended to Vaikunṭha with Mahāviṣṇu.

**Tulasidāsa** (S) (M) 1. devotee of Tulasī. 3. the author of *Rāmaćaritamānas*.

**Tūlinī** (S) (F) the Cotton tree.

**Tulya** (S) (M) equal to; of the same kind.

**Tulyabala** (S) (M) compare; equal in strength.

**Tulyatejas** (S) (M) equal in splendour.

**Tulyavīrya** (S) (M) of equal strength.

**Tumbavīṇā** (S) (M) 1. having the gourd for a lute. 3. another name for Śiva.

**Tumburu** (S) (M) 1. fruit of the Tumba gourd (*Lagenaria vulgaris*). 3. a pupil of Kalāpin; the attendant of the 5th Arhat of the present Avasarpinī; the best musician of the gandharvas who was the son of Kaśyapa and Prādhā and a member of Kubera's court (*M. Bh.*); a sage (*U. Rāmāyaṇa*)

**Tūṇava** (S) (M) a flute.

**Tuṇḍa** (S) (M) 1. mouth; trunk; the point of an arrow. 3. a king invited by the Pāṇḍavas to take part in the Mahābhārata (*M. Bh.*); a rākṣasa who fought on the side of Rāvaṇa (*M. Bh.*); another name for Śiva.

**Tundi** (S) (M) 1. with a prominent navel. 3. a gandharva.

**Tuṇḍin** (S) (M) the bull of Śiva.

**Tuṅga** (S) (M) 1. prominent; erect; lofty; high; chief; strong; peak. 2. *Prosopis spicigera*.

**Tungā** (S) (F) 1. strong; elevated; high. 3. a river in Mysore.

**Tuṅgabala** (S) (M) very strong.

**Tuṅgabhadrā** (S) (F) 1. very noble; sacred. 3. the river in Mysore which is formed by the junction of the Tuṅgā and Bhadrā.

**Tuṅgadhanvan** (S) (M) 1. with a lofty bow. 3. a king of Suhmā.

**Tuṅganātha** (S) (M) lord of height; lord of mountains.

**Tuṅgaśaila** (S) (M) 1. with high words; rocks. 3. a mountain with a temple of Śiva.

**Tuṅgaśekhara** (S) (M) 1. high peaked. 2. mountain.

**Tuṅgaveṇā** (S) (F) 1. loving heights. 3. a river in the Deccan.

**Tuṅgeśvara** (S) (M) 1. lord of mountains. 3. a temple of Śiva.

**Tungī** (S) (F) night; turmeric.

**Tungīpati** (S) (M) 1. lord of the night. 3. another name for the moon.

**Tungīśa** (S) (M) 1. lord of the night. 3. another name for Śiva, Kṛṣṇa, the sun and the moon.

**Tungīśvara** (S) (M) 1. lord of the night. 3. another name for Śiva.

**Tūṇi** (S) (M) 1. quiver bearer. 3. Yugandhara's father.

**Turaga** (S) (M) 1. moving swiftly; going quickly. 2. the mind; horse; thought; the number 7. 3. the white horse that emerged from the churning of the ocean and was claimed by Sūrya (*M. Bh.*)

**Turaṇya** (S) (M) 1. to be swift. 3. a horse of the moon.

**Turaṇyu** (S) (M) swift; zealous.

**Turāṣāt** (S) (M) 1. overpowering the mighty. 3. another name for Indra.

**Turī** (S) (F) 1. a painter's brush. 3. a wife of Vasudeva (*H. Purāṇa*)

**Tūrṇi** (S) (M) 1. quick; clever; zealous; expeditious. 2. the mind.

**Turṣārasuvra** (S) (M) as white as snow.

**Turvaṇi** (S) (M) victorious.

**Turvaśa** (S) (M) 1. overpowering; victorious. 3. a hero king extolled in the *Ṛg Veda* and ancestor of the Āryan race.

**Turvasu** (S) (M) 1. victorious. 3. a son of Yayāti by Devayānī and the brother of Yadu (*M. Bh.*)

**Tūrvayāṇa** (S) (M) 1. overpowering. 3. a king extolled in the *Ṛg Veda*.

**Tūrvi** (S) (M) superior.

**Turvīti** (S) (M) 1. superior; overpowering; fast moving. 3. a sage protected by Indra.

**Turyā** (S) (F) superior powers.

**Tuṣāra** (S) (M) cold; frost; snow; mist; dew.

**Tuṣāradyuti** (S) (M) 1. cold rayed. 3. another name for the moon.

**Tuṣāragiri** (S) (M) 1. snow mountain. 3. another name for the Himālaya.

**Tuṣārakānti** (S) (M) 1. beloved of the snow

mountains. 3. another name for Śiva.

**Tuṣārakara** (S) (M) 1. cold rayed. 3. another name for the moon.

**Tuṣārakiraṇa** (S) (M) 1. cold rayed. 3. another name for the moon.

**Tuṣārānśu** (S) (M) 1. cold rayed. 3. another name for the moon.

**Tuṣāraraśmi** (S) (M) 1. cold rayed. 3. another name for the moon.

**Tuṣitā** (S) (F) 1. satisfied; pleased. 3. the wife of Vedaśiras and mother of the tuśitas.

**Tuṣita** (S) (M) 1. satisfied; contented. 3. Viṣṇu in the 3rd Manvantara; another name for 12 devas in the Ćākṣuṣa Manvantara.

**Tuṣṭa** (S) (M) satisfied; pleased.

**Tuṣṭi** (S) (F) 1. satisfaction. 3. contentment personified as a daughter of Dakṣa, wife of Dharma and mother of Santoṣa or Mudā (*V. Purāṇa*) or as daughter of Paurnamāsa (*Vā. Purāṇa*) or as a deity sprung from Prakṛtī (*Brahma Purāṇa*) or as a mātrika or a Śakti; a digit of the moon.

**Tuṣṭimān** (S) (M) 1. satisfied. 3. a king of the Yayāti dynasty (*Bhāgavata*)

**Tuṣya** (S) (M) 1. satisfied. 3. another name for Śiva.

**Tuvideṣṇa** (S) (M) 1. giving much. 3. another name for Indra.

**Tuvidyumna** (S) (M) 1. very glorious; powerful. 3. another name for Indra, the maruts and Agni.

**Tuvigra** (S) (M) 1. swallowing much. 3. another name for Agni.

**Tuvijāta** (S) (M) 1. of powerful nature. 3. another name for Indra and Varuṇa.

**Tuvikṣa** (S) (M) 1. powerful. 3. Indra's bow.

**Tuvikṣatra** (S) (F) 1. ruling powerfully. 3. another name for Aditi.

**Tuvikūrmi** (S) (M) 1. powerful in working. 3. another name for Indra.

**Tuvimanyu** (S) (M) 1. very zealous. 3. another name for the maruts.

**Tuviśravas** (S) (M) 1. highly renowned. 3. another name for Agni.

**Tuviṣṭama** (S) (M) strongest.

**Tuviśuṣma** (S) (M) 1. high spirited. 3. Indra and Varuṇa conjoined.

**Tūyam** (S) (M) 1. strong; quick. 2. water.

**Tvakṣas** (S) (M) energy; vigour.

**Tvaritā** (S) (F) 1. hasty; quick; swift; expeditious. 3. another name for Durgā and a magical formula named after her.

**Tvaṣṭṛ, Tvaṣṭā** (S) (M) 1. carpenter; maker of carriages; creator of living beings; heavenly builder. 3. a prajāpati who was the maker of divine implements including Indra's thunderbolt, teacher of the Ṛbhus, supposed author of the *Ṛg Veda*, the father of Śaraṇyū, Triśiras or Viśvarūpa by Rećana and the grandfather of Yama, Yamī and the aśvins; a king of the Bharata dynasty who was the son of Bhauvana and father of Viraja; one of the ādityas (*M. Bh.*); a son of Manasyu; a rudra (*Bh. Purāṇa*); another name for Viśvakarman.

**Tvaṣṭādhara** (S) (M) 1. abode of creation. 3. one of the 2 sons of Śukrāćārya.

**Tveṣā** (S) (F) brilliant; glittering; impetuous; vehement.

**Tveṣin** (S) (M) impetuous.

**Tviṣā** (S) (F) 1. light; splendour. 3. a daughter of Marīći and Sambhūti (*Vā. Purāṇa*)

**Tviṣāmpati** (S) (M) 1. lord of light. 3. another name for Sūrya.

**Tviṣi** (S) (F) vehemence; impetuousity; splendour; light; brilliance; energy.

**Tyāgarāja** (S) (M) 1. lord of renunciation. 3. the deity at Tiruvarun (*Thaurajana*) temple; a Bhakti saint of a high order and a great composer of Carnatic music.

**Tyāgin** (S) (M) ascetic; sacrificing; donor; liberal; hero.

# U

**Ućatha** (S) (M) verse; praise.
**Ućathya** (S) (M) **1.** deserving praise. **3.** a muni and disciple of Vyāsa (*Bhāgavata*) and the father of Śibi and Veṇa by Mādhavī; a king of the Yādavas.
**Uććadeva** (S) (M) **1.** superior god. **3.** another name for Viṣṇu and Kṛṣṇa.
**Uććadevatā** (S) (F) **1.** superior god. **2.** time personified.
**Uććadhvaja** (S) (M) **1.** with a lofty banner. **2.** highly eminent. **3.** another name for Śākyāmuni.
**Uććaghana** (S) (M) laughter in the mind.
**Uććaihpaurṇamāsi** (S) (F) **1.** the lofty full moon day. **2.** a particular full moon day when the moon appears before sunset.
**Uććaihśravas** (S) (M) **1.** having lifted ears. **2.** long eared; neighing loudly. **3.** Indra's horse who emerged from the churning of the Ocean of Milk (*M. Bh.*); a king of the Purū dynasty who was the son of Avīkṣit (*M. Bh.*)
**Uććairdhāman** (S) (M) with intense rays.
**Uććairmanyu** (S) (M) highly placed.
**Uććaka** (S) (M) **1.** to look fearlessly. **2.** a king. **3.** a king of the Solar dynasty (*Bhāgavata*)
**Uććala** (S) (M) going up; the mind; understanding.
**Uććalalāṭa** (S) (M) with a high forehead; proud; lucky.
**Uććaṇḍa** (S) (M) rising fervour; very passionate; violent; terrible; mighty.
**Uććandras** (S) (M) **1.** the high moon; the moon that has gone high i.e. moon that has gone beyond vision. **2.** the moonless period of the night; the last watch of the night.
**Uććārya** (S) (M) to be spoken; to be pronounced; having spoken; uttered.
**Uććāryamāna** (S) (M) being uttered or pronounced.
**Uććatā** (S) (F) height; superiority; the apex of the orbit of a planet.
**Uććāṭana** (S) (M) **1.** ruining. **3.** one of the 5 arrows of Kāma (*S. Purāṇa*)
**Uććataru** (S) (M) lofty tree; the Coconut tree (*Cocos nucifera*)
**Uććedin** (S) (M) resolving difficulties.
**Uććharāyin** (S) (M) high; raised; lofty.
**Uććhikha** (S) (M) **1.** with an upright comb. **2.** flaming; blazing; radiant; high crested. **3.** a serpent of the family of Takṣaka (*M. Bh.*); another name for Nārada.
**Uććhikhaṇḍa** (S) (M) **1.** high crested. **3.** another name for Nārada.
**Uććhiras** (S) (M) **1.** high headed. **2.** with the head held high. **3.** a mountain.
**Uććhirayata** (S) (M) **1.** rising up. **2.** standing erect; ambitious. **3.** a rākṣasa who was the son of Mālyavān (*V. Rāmāyaṇa*)
**Uććhiṣṭabhojana** (S) (M) **1.** eating remains of someone else's food. **3.** the attendant upon an idol (whose food is the leavings of offerings)
**Uććhiṣṭaćāṇḍālinī** (S) (F) **1.** the fierce goddess of the eater of remains. **3.** Durgā as worshipped by Uććhiṣṭas; a goddess.
**Uććhiṣṭagaṇapati** (S) (M) Gaṇeśa as worshipped by the Uććhiṣṭas (or men who leave the remains of food in their mouth during prayer); a form of tāntric worship for early success.
**Uććhrayopeta** (S) (M) possessing height; high; lofty; elevated.
**Uććhreya** (S) (M) high; lofty.
**Uććhṛta** (S) (M) (F) raised; lifted up; erect; arising; growing powerful.
**Uććhuṣma** (S) (M) **1.** with rising heat. **2.** one whose crackling becomes manifest. **3.** a deity (*B. Literature*); another name for Agni.
**Uććṛṅga** (S) (M) **1.** with erect horns. **3.** one of the 2 attendants given to Skanda by Vindhya (*M. Bh.*)
**Uććūda** (S) (M) the rising cloth; the flag or pennon of a banner; an ornament tied on top of a banner.
**Ućita** (S) (M) delightful; pleasurable; agreeable; proper; fit; right.
**Udadhi** (S) (M) **1.** receptacle of water. **2.** cloud; river; sea; ocean.
**Udadhirāja** (S) (M) **1.** lord of the ocean. **3.** another name for Varuṇa (*V. Rāmāyaṇa*)
**Udadhisutā** (S) (F) **1.** daughter of the ocean. **3.** another name for Lakṣmī and Kṛṣṇa's capi-

tal Dvārakā (*Bhā. Purāṇa*)

**Udaja** (S) (M) 1. born in water. 2. lotus (*Nelumbo speciosum*)

**Udakapati** (S) (M) 1. lord of water. 3. another name for Varuṇa.

**Udalākāśyapa** (S) (F) 1. giving water to the earth. 3. a tutelary goddess of agriculture.

**Udamaya** (S) (M) 1. made of water. 3. a ṛṣi (*A. Brāhmaṇa*)

**Udanćita** (S) (M) raised up; worshipped.

**Udankanyā** (S) (F) 1. daughter of the ocean. 3. another name for Lakṣmī and Dvārakā the capital of Kṛṣṇa.

**Udanta** (S) (M) good; virtuous; end of work; rest; news; message; folktale.

**Udantikā** (S) (F) satiety; satisfaction.

**Udanvata** (S) (M) 1. abounding in water. 2. the ocean. 3. a ṛṣi.

**Udāpekṣī** (S) (M) 1. requiring water. 3. a son of Viśvāmitra.

**Udāpi** (S) (M) 1. one who attains. 2. successful. 3. a son of Sahadeva (*M. Bh.*)

**Udāra** (S) (M) high; lofty; exalted; great; best; noble; generous; liberal; gentle; munificent; dignified; illustrious; splendid; kind; distinguished.

**Udāradhī** (S) (M) with an exalted intellect; wise; sagacious.

**Udāraka** (S) (M) 1. excellent person. 3. a minister of Mahiṣāsura.

**Udārākṣa** (S) (M) 1. with generous eyes; merciful. 3. a warrior of Skanda (*M. Bh.*)

**Udāramatī** (S) (F) noble minded; highly intelligent; wise; virtuous; chaste.

**Udāraśāṇḍilya** (S) (M) 1. benevolent fire. 3. a hermit of the court of Indra (*M. Bh.*)

**Udārathi** (S) (M) 1. rising; arising. 3. another name for Viṣṇu.

**Udarćiṣ** (S) (M) 1. shining upwards. 2. flaming; brilliant; resplendent. 3. another name for Śiva.

**Udarśa** (S) (M) overflowing.

**Udātta** (S) (M) 1. lofty; elevated; high; great; illustrious; dear; beloved; gift; ornament; generous; gentle. 2. the raised tone of the Vedic chant.

**Udāvasu** (S) (M) 1. treasure of nobility. 3. a son of King Janaka of Videha (*V. Rāmāyaṇa*)

**Udaya** (S) (M) 1. ascending; prosperity; accomplishment. 2. splendour; the rising of the sun; the mountains of the east behind which the sun is supposed to rise; coming forth; appearance; development; production; creation; success. 3. the 1st lunar mansion (*V. Rāmāyaṇa*)

**Udayāditya** (S) (M) sunrise.

**Udayagiri** (S) (M) mountain of ascent; mountain of sunrise; the eastern mountain from behind which the sun rises.

**Udayajit** (S) (M) conqueror of the rising sun.

**Udayana** (S) (M) 1. rising up. 2. rising of the sun; result; conclusion. 3. a renowned king of the lunar dynasty of Vatsa who was the son of Śahasrānīka and Mṛgāvatī and the husband of princess Vāsavadattā of Ujjayanī and Padmāvatī and the father of Naravāhanadatta who became king of the vidyādharas; another name for King Vatsa of Kausambhi and sage Agastya.

**Udayanta** (S) (M) risen; end of sunrise.

**Udayantī** (S) (F) risen; virtuous; excellent.

**Udayāśva** (S) (M) 1. horse of development; progressing horse. 2. fast and progressing; strong and swift. 3. a grandson of Ajātaśatru (*V. Purāṇa*)

**Udayatī** (S) (F) 1. of Udaya. 2. daughter of the mountain. 3. the daughter of Udayatuṅga.

**Udayatuṅga** (S) (M) 1. lofty among the mountains. 2. lord of the mountains. 3. a king (*Ś. Brāhmaṇa*)

**Udayavīra** (S) (M) emerging as a hero.

**Udāyin** (S) (M) 1. rising; ascending; coming forward. 2. prosperous; flourishing. 3. a grandson of Ajātaśatru (*A. Brāhmaṇa*); another name for Viṣṇu.

**Udāyus** (S) (M) 1. to stir up. 3. father of Śrutaśarman.

**Udbala** (S) (M) highly strong; powerful.

**Udbhāsa** (S) (M) radiance; splendour.

**Udbhāsita** (S) (M) come forth; lit up; splendid; ornamented; beautiful.

**Udbhāsura** (S) (M) highly shining; radiant.

**Udbhaṭa** (S) (M) high gentry; excellent;

eminent; exalted; magnanimous; passionate; extraordinary; invincible.

**Udbhava** (S) (M) **1.** originate from. **2.** existence; origin; birth. **3.** a son of Nahuṣa (*Bhā. Purāṇa*)

**Udbhida** (S) (M) **1.** sprouting; germinating. **3.** a son of Jyotiṣmat (*V. Purāṇa*)

**Udbhrama** (S) (M) **1.** whirling. **2.** excitement; intoxication. **3.** a class of deities attendant on Śiva.

**Udbhūti** (S) (F) coming forth; existence; appearance; fortune giver.

**Uddālaka** (S) (M) **1.** burnt open; a kind of honey. **3.** son of sage Aruṇa and a prominent teacher of the Vedas (*Ṛg Veda*); *Bauhinia vareigata*.

**Uddāma** (S) (M) **1.** flaring up. **2.** unrestrained; free; extraordinary; unlimited; large; great; violent; impetuous. **3.** another name for Yama and Varuṇa.

**Uḍḍāmara** (S) (M) excellent; respectable; of high rank

**Uḍḍāmarin** (S) (M) making an extraordinary noise.

**Uddaṇḍaśāstrī** (S) (M) **1.** extraordinary scholar. **3.** one of the 18 famous poets of Kerala.

**Uddānta** (S) (M) humble; energetic; elevated; pure; virtuous.

**Uddarśana** (S) (M) **1.** with clear vision. **3.** a king of the nāgas

**Uddarśita** (S) (M) made visible; appearing; come forth.

**Uddātta** (S) (M) high; lofty; noble; exalted; generous; famous; beloved.

**Uddeśa** (S) (M) exemplification; illustration.

**Uddhara** (S) (M) **1.** freed from burdens. **2.** wild; lively; cheerful; unrestrained.

**Uddharaṇa** (S) (M) **1.** rescuing; final emancipation; raising; delivering. **3.** the father of King Śantanu (*M. Bh.*)

**Uddharṣa** (S) (M) courage to undertake anything.

**Uddhas** (S) (M) **1.** to break into laughter. **2.** lightning.

**Uddhava** (S) (M) **1.** lifting up; lifting up the spirits of others. **2.** sacrificial fire; festival; joy; pleasure. **3.** a Yādava who was a friend and minister of Kṛṣṇa and a disciple of Bṛhaspati (*Bhā. Purāṇa*)

**Uḍḍīnam** (S) (M) flying up; soaring.

**Uddīpa** (S) (M) inflaming; lighting up; illuminating.

**Uddīpaka** (S) (M) stimulating; inflaming.

**Uddīpti** (S) (F) excited; inflamed.

**Uddīrṇa** (S) (M) **1.** created; formed; blossomed; progressed; secret. **3.** another name for Viṣṇu.

**Uḍḍīśa** (S) (M) **1.** lord of the flying ones. **2.** lord of divine beings. **3.** a tāntra work (containing charms and incantations); another name for Śiva.

**Uḍḍīyakavi** (S) (M) a lofty poet.

**Uḍḍīyamāna** (S) (M) one who soars; flying up; soaring.

**Uḍḍīyana** (S) (M) soaring; flying up.

**Uddṛṣṭa** (S) (M) **1.** seen properly. **2.** the appearance of the moon.

**Uddyota** (S) (M) shining; flashing.

**Udgama** (S) (M) the rising of a star; the elevation of a mountain.

**Udgandhi** (S) (M) giving forth perfume; fragrant.

**Udgata** (S) (M) **1.** risen; ascended; coming forth. **2.** leader; priest; preceptor. **3.** one of the 7 chief priests of the Vedas (*Ṛg Veda*)

**Udgātṛ** (S) (M) **1.** chanter. **2.** priest.

**Udgīta** (S) (F) **1.** sung; announced; celebrated; highly praised. **2.** hymn of glory; ultimate song.

**Udgītha** (S) (M) **1.** chanting of the *Sāma Veda*. **3.** the syllable Om; a son of Bhuva (*V. Purāṇa*)

**Udgīti** (S) (F) singing.

**Udīćya** (S) (M) **1.** living in the north. **3.** a disciple of Vyāsa (*Bhāgavata*)

**Udīṣita** (S) (M) risen; elevated.

**Udita** (S) (M) **1.** risen; ascended; high; lofty; tall; born; produced; apparent; visible. **2.** the sunrise.

**Uditi** (S) (F) rising of the sun.

**Uditvara** (S) (M) risen; surpassed; extraordinary.

**Udojas** (S) (M) exceedingly powerful; effective.

**Udraka** (S) (M) **1.** of the water. **3.** a ṛṣi (*Ṛg Veda*)

**Udrapāraka** (S) (M) **1.** helping to cross the water. **3.** a serpent of the family of Dhṛtarāṣṭra (*M. Bh.*)

**Udreka** (S) (M) blossoming of a thought; passion; preponderance; superiority; predominance.

**Udrodhana** (S) (M) rising; growing.

**Udu** (S) (F) water; star.

**Uḍugaṇādhipa** (S) (M) **1.** the lord of the stars. **3.** another name for the moon and the Nakṣatra Mṛgaśiras.

**Udumbala** (S) (M) of wide reaching power.

**Udumbara** (S) (M) **1.** the ultimate tree; the essence of all trees. **3.** *Ficus glomerata*.

**Uḍunātha** (S) (M) **1.** lord of the stars. **3.** another name for the moon.

**Uḍūpa** (S) (M) protecting from water; drinking water; a raft or float; a kind of drinking vessel covered with leather.

**Uḍupas** (S) (M) **1.** boat shaped. **2.** the crescent moon.

**Uḍupatha** (S) (M) the path of the stars; firmament; the ether.

**Uḍupati** (S) (M) **1.** lord of the stars. **3.** another name for the moon and Soma

**Uḍurāj** (S) (M) **1.** king of the stars. **3.** another name for the moon.

**Udvahā** (S) (F) **1.** continuing; carrying on. **2.** daughter.

**Udvaha** (S) (M) **1.** carrying up; continuing. **2.** eminent; best; son. **3.** the 4th of the 7 winds or courses of air and the one that supports the lunar constellations (*H. Purāṇa*); one of the 7 tongues of fire; a Kṣatriya king born of the family of the asura Krodhavaśa (*M. Bh.*)

**Udvahni** (S) (F) gleaming; sparkling.

**Udvanśa** (S) (M) of noble descent.

**Udyat** (S) (M) **1.** rising. **2.** astar.

**Udyati** (S) (F) raised; elevation.

**Udyota** (S) (M) shining forth; light; lustre.

**Udyotana** (S) (M) to enlighten; to make manifest; illuminated.

**Ugāgra** (S) (M) high peak.

**Ugam** (S) (M) rising upwards.

**Ugaṇa** (S) (M) **1.** consisting of extended troops. **2.** an army.

**Ugra** (S) (M) **1.** powerful; violent; mighty; impetuous; strong; huge; formidable; terrible; high; noble; cruel; fierce; ferocious; savage; angry; passionate; wrathful; hot; sharp; pungent; acrid; rude. **3.** a military captain of Sūrapadmāsura the chief of asuras (*H. Purāṇa*); a son of Dhṛtarāṣṭra (*M. Bh.*); a Yādava prince (*M. Bh.*); the son of Prajāpati Kavi (*M. Bh.*); another name for Rudra (*M. Bh.*)

**Ugrabāhu** (S) (M) one whose arms are large or powerful.

**Ugrabhairava** (S) (M) **1.** powerful and fierce. **2.** terrible; frightful; horrible. **3.** a Kāpālika (*K. Sāgara*)

**Ugrabhata** (S) (M) **1.** powerful soldier. **2.** mighty soldier. **3.** a king (*K. Sāgara*)

**Ugraćaṇḍā** (S) (F) **1.** powerful and fierce. **3.** a violent form of Durgā (*K. Purāṇa*)

**Ugraćārin** (S) (M) **1.** moving impetuously. **3.** another name for the moon.

**Ugraćāriṇī** (S) (F) **1.** moving impetuously. **3.** another name for Durgā.

**Ugrāćārya** (S) (M) **1.** powerful teacher. **3.** an author.

**Ugraćaya** (S) (M) strong desire.

**Ugradaṇḍa** (S) (M) stern in punishment; stern sceptred; holding a terrible rod.

**Ugradanṣṭrī** (S) (F) **1.** with terrible teeth; with sharp teeth. **3.** a daughter of Mahāmeru and wife of a son of Agnīdhra (*J.S. Koṣa*)

**Ugradeva** (S) (M) **1.** mighty deity. **2.** worshiping mighty deities. **3.** a ṛṣi (*Ṛg Veda*)

**Ugradhanvan** (S) (M) **1.** with a powerful bow. **3.** another name for Indra.

**Ugraduhitṛ** (S) (F) daughter of a powerful man; daughter of Śiva.

**Ugragandha** (S) (M) **1.** strong smelling. **2.** garlic; *Michelia champaca*; Wild Turnip (*Brassica campestris*)

**Ugrajit** (S) (F) **1.** victor of passion. **3.** an apsarā (*A. Veda*)

**Ugraka** (S) (M) **1.** brave; powerful. **3.** a

serpent (*M. Bh.*)

**Ugrakālī** (S) (F) 1. fierce and black. 3. goddess Durgā in her dreadful form (*D. Bh. Purāṇa*)

**Ugrakarman** (S) (M) 1. fierce in action. 2. violent; one who does cruel deeds. 3. a king of Śālva (*M. Bh.*); the military chief of the Kekaya prince Viśoka (*M. Bh.*)

**Ugrakarṇikā** (S) (M) (F) with large earrings.

**Ugramaya** (S) (M) 1. with a violent image. 3. a demon causing diseases (*H. Purāṇa*)

**Ugranarasiṁha** (S) (M) 1. ferocious manlion. 3. Viṣṇu in his lion incarnation (*Bhā. Purāṇa*)

**Ugrapaśyā** (S) (F) 1. frightful; hideous; fierce looking; malignant. 3. an apsarā (*A. Veda*)

**Ugraputra** (S) (M) 1. son of the ferocious; son of Śiva; son of a powerful man; having mighty sons. 3. another name for Kārttikeya.

**Ugraravas** (S) (M) 1. speaking violently. 3. a muni.

**Ugraretas** (S) (M) 1. possessor of a horrible weapon. 3. a form of Rudra (*Bhā. Purāṇa*)

**Ugraśakti** (S) (M) 1. of terrible might. 3. a son of King Amaraśakti.

**Ugraśāsana** (S) (M) severe in command; strict in orders.

**Ugraśekharā** (S) (F) 1. crest of the ferocious. 3. the Gaṅgā as the crest of Ugra or Śiva (*Ś. Purāṇa*)

**Ugrasena** (S) (M) 1. formidable leader. 2. fierce; high; noble; powerful. 3. the Yādava king of Mathurāpuri who was the son of Āhuka and the father of Kaṇsa (*Bhā. Purāṇa*); a brother of King Janamejaya (*M. Bh.*); a son of Kaśyapa and Muni (*M. Bh.*); a king who was the incarnation of the asura Svarbhānu; a son of Dhṛtarāṣṭra (*M. Bh.*); a son of King Parīkṣit (*M. Bh.*)

**Ugrasenānī** (S) (M) 1. the mighty warrior; with a mighty army. 3. another name for Kṛṣṇa.

**Ugrasenī** (S) (F) 1. wife of a powerful leader. 3. wife of Akrūra.

**Ugraśravas** (S) (M) 1. with enormous fame. 2. very famous. 3. the son of ṛṣi Lomaharṣa (*M. Bh.*); a son of Dhṛtarāṣṭra (*M. Bh.*); the husband of Śīlāvatī.

**Ugratā** (S) (F) violence; passion; anger; pungency; acrimony.

**Ugratapas** (S) (M) 1. mighty ascetic. 2. doing terrible penances. 3. the son of ṛṣi Sutapas of the Bhṛgu dynasty who was reborn as a gopi (*P. Purāṇa*)

**Ugratārā** (S) (F) 1. ferocious star. 2. having terrible eyes. 3. a tāntric goddess (*K. Purāṇa*)

**Ugratejas** (S) (M) 1. with violent energy. 2. fiercely worthy; noble and passionate. 3. a serpent (*M. Bh.*); a Buddha (*L. Vistara*); another name for Śiva.

**Ugratīrtha** (S) (M) 1. visiting places of violence. 3. a Kṣatriya king who was an incarnation of the asura Krodhavaśa (*M. Bh.*)

**Ugratyās** (S) (M) terribly energetic; endowed with great or terrible energy.

**Ugravega** (S) (M) with terrible velocity; very fast; very active; very swift.

**Ugravīra** (S) (M) violent hero.

**Ugravīrya** (S) (M) terrible in might.

**Ugravyaghra** (S) (M) 1. violent tiger. 3. a dānava (*H. Purāṇa*)

**Ugrāyudha** (S) (M) 1. with terrible weapons. 3. a son of Dhṛtarāṣṭra (*M. Bh.*); a Pāñćāla king who fought on the side of the Pāṇḍavas (*M. Bh.*); a warrior of the Kauravas (*M. Bh.*); an emperor killed by Bhīṣma (*M. Bh.*)

**Ugreśa** (S) (M) 1. the mighty or terrible lord. 3. another name for Śiva (*A. Veda*)

**Ugrī** (S) (F) 1. angry. 3. a being belonging to a class of demons (*A. Veda*)

**Ujāsa** (S) (M) light before dawn.

**Ujjāgara** (S) (M) excited.

**Ujjaya** (S) (M) 1. archer whose bow string is open; archer ever ready to win. 3. a son of Viśvāmitra (*M. Bh.*)

**Ujjayana** (S) (M) conqueror.

**Ujjayanta** (S) (M) 1. having conquered. 3. a mountain (*M. Bh.*)

**Ujjayatī** (S) (F) 1. one who has won. 2. winner; conquerer; victorious.

**Ujjendra** (S) (M) victor.

**Ujjeṣā** (S) (F) victorious.

**Ujjeṣa** (S) (M) victorious.

**Ujjeṣin** (S) (M) **1.** victorious. **3.** one of the 7 maruts.

**Ujjhaka** (S) (M) cloud; devotee.

**Ujji** (S) (M) to win; to conquer.

**Ujjiti** (S) (F) victory.

**Ujjīvati** (S) (F) brought to life; full of life; jubilant; optimist; to return to life.

**Ujjīvayatī** (S) (F) restored to life; animated.

**Ujjīvin** (S) (M) **1.** revival. **2.** one who has revived; having the power of correcting one's self. **3.** a counsellor of Meghavarṇa the king of crows (*Panćatantra*)

**Ujjṛmbhitā** (S) (F) opened; stretched; expanded; blown.

**Ujjūṭitā** (S) (M) (F) with upgoing hair; wearing the hair twisted together and coiled upwards.

**Ujjvala** (S) (M) highly inflamed; bright; illuminated; splendid; light; burning; clean; clear; lovely; beautiful; sunshine; the sentiment of love.

**Ujjvalā** (S) (F) brightness; clearness; splendour.

**Ujjvaladatta** (S) (M) **1.** bestowed with brightness. **2.** bright; intelligent. **3.** the author of a commentary on the *Unadi Sūtras* (*K. Sāgara*)

**Ujjvalanam** (S) (M) **1.** burning; shining; lighting up. **2.** fire; gold.

**Ujjvalas** (S) (M) inflamed; love; passion.

**Ujjvalatā** (S) (F) splendour; radiance; beauty; clarity.

**Ujjvalitā** (S) (F) lighted; shining; flaming.

**Ukha** (S) (M) **1.** boiler; cauldron; vessel; a part of the upper leg. **3.** a pupil of Tittiri (*P. Ratra*)

**Ukhya** (S) (M) **1.** being in a cauldron. **3.** a grammarian (*Ṛg Veda*)

**Ukṣaṇ** (S) (M) **1.** sprinkling; consecrating. **2.** an ox or bull as impregnating the flock. **3.** in the Vedas the ox or bull draw the chariot of the dawn; another name for Soma, the maruts, the sun and Agni.

**Ukṣasena** (S) (M) **1.** having an army of bulls; commander of bulls; one who possesses bulls; chief of the bulls. **3.** a king (*M. Upaniṣad*)

**Ukṣatara** (S) (M) a young bull; a strong bull.

**Ukṣita** (S) (M) sprinkled; moistened; strong; of full growth.

**Ukta** (S) (M) uttered; said; spoken.

**Uktapratyukta** (S) speech and reply; discourse; conversation; a kind of anthem or alternate song.

**Uktatva** (S) (M) spoken speech.

**Uktavākya** (S) (M) spoken sentence; one who has given an opinion; a dictum; decree.

**Uktavat** (S) (M) one who has spoken.

**Uktha** (S) (M) **1.** saying; sentence; verse; eulogy; praise; hymn; ritual recitation. **2.** Sāman verses which are sung or muttered as sacrificial formula; treasure; a special beat. **3.** an agni and the father of Parāvāṇī (*M. Bh.*); another name for the sun, *Sāma Veda*, *Yajur Veda* and Brāhmā.

**Ukthabhṛt** (S) (M) offering verses.

**Ukthāmada** (S) praise and rejoicing conjoined.

**Ukthamukha** (S) (M) preface of the recitation; the beginning of an Uktha recitation.

**Ukthapātra** (S) (M) **1.** vessel of praise. **2.** vessels of libation offered during the recitation of an Uktha.

**Ukthapattra** (S) (M) having verses as wings; one who flies with praise.

**Uktharkā** (S) (F) recitation and hymn conjoined; praise of the sun; hymn of the sun.

**Ukthasampadā** (S) (F) **1.** wealth of hymns. **2.** a particular concluding verse of a Śāstra (*A. Araṇyaka*)

**Ukthaśansin** (S) (M) (F) reciter of hymns; praising; uttering the Ukthas.

**Ukthaśāstra** (S) (M) discipline of recital; recitation and praise according to the Śāstras.

**Ukthasuṣma** (S) (M) beauty of the hymn; loudly resonant with verses; moving on with the sound of verses (as with the roaring of waters); accompanied by sound of verses; one whose strength is praise.

**Ukthavardhana** (S) (M) **1.** having hymns as a cause of refreshment. **2.** one who is refreshed or delighted by praise.

**Ukthāvī** (S) (M) fond of hymns.

**Ukthavid** (S) (M) knower of hymns; conversant with hymns of praise.

**Ukthavidha** (S) (M) verse like; knower of the

verse.

**Ukthavīrya** (S) power of the verse; a particular part of Śāstra, conversant in speech.

**Ukthāyu** (S) (M) eager for praise.

**Ukthīn** (S) (F) uttering verses; lauding; accompanied by praise or in ritual by Ukthas.

**Ukthyasthālī** (S) (F) place of Uktha; a place for the preparation of an Uktha libation.

**Ukti** (S) (F) sentence; proclamation; speech; expression; word; a worthy speech; idiom.

**Uktopaniṣatka** (S) (M) one to whom the Upaniṣads have been spoken; one who has been taught the Upaniṣads.

**Ulanda** (S) (M) 1. throwing out. 3. a king (*P. Ratra*)

**Ulapa** (S) (M) 1. spreading. 2. a species of soft grass; a spreading vine. 3. a pupil of Kalāpin.

**Ulapya** (S) (M) 1. abiding in or belonging to the Ulapa grass. 3. a rudra (*M. Samhitā*)

**Ulbaṇa** (S) (M) 1. abundant; excessive; immense; strong; powerful. 3. a son of Vasiṣṭha (*Bh. Purāṇa*)

**Ulkā** (S) (F) meteor; fire; falling from heaven; firebrand; torch.

**Ulkāmukha** (S) (M) 1. with a fiery mouth. 3. a son of Agni (*A. Koṣa*); a rākṣasa (*Rāmāyaṇa*)

**Ulkuśi** (S) (F) a brilliant phenomenon in the sky; a meteor; firebrand.

**Ullāgha** (S) (M) 1. to be able. 2. dextrous; clever; pure; happy.

**Ullāsa** (S) (M) light; splendour; appearance; joy; delight; increase; growth.

**Ullāsin** (S) (M) playing; sporting; dancing.

**Ullāsit** (S) (M) shining; brilliant; splendid; happy.

**Ulmuka** (S) (M) 1. firebrand. 3. a son of Balarāma (*M. Bh.*); a son of Manu Ćākṣuṣa; a king of the Vṛṣṇi dynasty (*V. Purāṇa*)

**Ulūka** (S) (M) 1. owl; tip of a needle; a kind of grass. 3. another name for Indra; a muni (*V. Purāṇa*); a nāga (*M. Bh.*); the son of Śakuni (*M. Bh.*); a yakṣa (*M. Bh.*); a son of Viśvāmitra (*M. Bh.*)

**Ulūkajit** (S) (M) 1. conqueror of Indra. 3. another name for Indrajit (*V. Purāṇa*)

**Ulūkī** (S) (F) 1. she owl. 3. a daughter of Kaśyapa and Tāmrā (*H. Purāṇa*)

**Ululi** (S) (F) 1. loud. 2. a cry indicative of prosperity.

**Ulūpī** (S) (F) 1. with a charming face. 2. a species of soft grass; one who lives in water. 3. the daughter of the nāga Kauravya and the wife of Arjuna and mother of Irāvān (*M. Bh.*)

**Ulūpya** (S) (M) 1. with a charming face. 3. another name for Rudra.

**Ulūtī** (S) (F) 1. she falcon. 3. a wife of Garuḍa (*M. Bh.*)

**Umā** (S) (F) 1. O, do not! splendour; light; fame; reputation; quiet; tranquillity; night. 3. Pārvatī born as the daughter of Himavat and Menā who became the wife of Śiva and is also known as Pārvatī and Durgā, the name is derived from the exclamation 'O Child, do not practice austeries' supposed to have been said to Pārvatī by her mother (*Ś. Purāṇa*); Turmeric (*Curcuma longa*); Flax (*Linum usitatissimum*)

**Ūma** (S) (M) helper; friend; companion.

**Umāguru** (S) (M) 1. father of Umā. 3. another name for Himavat.

**Umākānta** (S) (M) 1. beloved of Umā. 2. lord of night; moonlight. 3. another name for Śiva and the moon.

**Umāmaheśvarī** (S) (F) 1. Umā, the consort of Maheśvara. 3. another name for Pārvatī.

**Umāmaṇi** (S) (M) 1. gem of Umā; gem of fame. 2. a special kind of gem that attracts men.

**Umānātha** (S) (M) 1. lord of Umā. 3. another name for Śiva.

**Umāpati** (S) (M) 1. lord of Umā. 3. another name for Śiva.

**Umāprasāda** (S) (M) given by Umā; gift of Umā; gift of splendour; light; fame.

**Umāśahāya** (S) (M) 1. companion of Umā. 3. another name for Śiva.

**Umāśankara** (S) (M) Parvatī and Śiva conjoined.

**Umāsuta** (S) (M) 1. son of Umā. 3. another name for Skanda.

**Umbara** (S) (M) 1. lintel of a door. 3. a gandharva (*H. Purāṇa*)

**Umeśa** (S) (M) 1. lord of Umā. 3. Umā and

Śiva conjoined; another name for Śiva.

**Umeśvara** (S) (M) 1. lord of Umā. 3. another name for Śiva.

**Umloćā** (S) (F) 1. with questioning eyes. 3. an apsarā in the court of Śiva (*S. Purāṇa*)

**Unćādi** (S) (M) 1. gathering grains. 3. a gaṇa (*Ś. Purāṇa*)

**Ūṇi** (S) (M) a Soma vessel.

**Uṅkara** (S) (M) 1. bestower of pleasure. 3. companion of Viṣṇu (*Ṛg Veda*)

**Unma** (S) (M) joy.

**Unmadā** (S) (F) 1. with intoxicating beauty; passionate. 3. an apsarā who was reborn as Hariṇī the daughter of King Videha (*V. Rāmāyaṇa*)

**Unmādana** (S) (M) 1. intoxicating; causing madness. 3. one of the 5 arrows of Kāma (*Ś. Purāṇa*)

**Unmādinī** (S) (F) betwitching; intoxicating.

**Unmaj** (S) (M) rising upwards; emerging; progressing.

**Unmanda** (S) (M) cheerful; delighted; amused.

**Unmaṇi** (S) (M) superior gem; a gem lying on the surface.

**Unmātha** (S) (M) 1. shaking; killing. 2. a trap. 3. an attendant given to Skanda by Yama (*M. Bh.*); an attendant given to Skanda by Pārvatī (*M. Bh.*)

**Unmatta** (S) (M) 1. disordered; furious; frantic. 3. a rākṣasa (*Rāmāyaṇa*); one of the 8 forms of Bhairava (*V. Rāmāyaṇa*)

**Unmayūkha** (S) (M) shining forth; radiant.

**Unmeṣa** (S) (M) opening the eyes; flashing; blossoming of a flower; coming forth; visible.

**Unmīla** (S) (M) becoming visible; to appear.

**Unmuktī** (S) (F) deliverance.

**Unnābha** (S) (M) 1. as high as the sky. 3. a king (*Bhā. Purāṇa*)

**Unnāda** (S) (M) 1. crying out. 2. clamour. 3. a son of Kṛṣṇa (*Bhā. Purāṇa*)

**Unnamana** (S) (M) raising; lifting up; increase; prosperity.

**Unnata** (S) (M) 1. elevated. 2. raised; high; tall; prominent; great; noble. 3. a Buddha (*L. Vistara*); a ṛṣi in the Manu Ćākṣuṣa Manvantara (*V. Purāṇa*); a mountain (*V. Purāṇa*)

**Unnati** (S) (F) 1. prosperity; progress; dignity. 2. rising; ascending. 3. a daughter of Dakṣa and wife of Dharma (*Bhā. Purāṇa*); the wife of Garuḍa.

**Unnatīśa** (S) (M) 1. lord of progress; desiring prosperity; lord of Unnati. 3. another name for Garuḍa.

**Unnī** (S) (M) to lead up; help; rescue; free; redeem; set up; promote; raise.

**Unnidra** (S) (M) beyond sleep; sleepless; awake; blossomed; shining as the rising sun or the moon.

**Upabarhaṇa** (S) (M) 1. cushion; pillow. 3. another name for the gandharvā Nārada.

**Upabhukti** (S) (F) enjoyment; the daily course of a star (*P. Ratra*)

**Upaćārumat** (S) (M) 1. civil; polite. 3. father of Bhadra.

**Upaćitra** (S) (M) 1. variegated; coloured. 3. a son of Dhṛtarāṣṭra (*M. Bh.*)

**Upāćyutam** (S) (M) near Kṛṣṇa.

**Upaḍā** (S) (F) present; offering; benevolent.

**Upadānavī** (S) (F) 1. near a dānava. 3. a daughter of the dānava Vṛṣaparvaṇ (*H. Purāṇa*); a daughter of Vaiśvānara (*Bhā. Purāṇa*)

**Upadeśa** (S) (M) sermon; teaching; advice.

**Upadeva** (S) (M) 1. a secondary deity. 3. a king of the Purū dynasty (*Bhā. Purāṇa*)

**Upadevaka** (S) (M) 1. minor god. 3. son of Akrūra.

**Upadevī** (S) (F) 1. a secondary deity. 3. a wife of Vasudeva.

**Upādeya** (S) (M) useful; to be chosen; excellent; admirable; not to be refused.

**Upadhṛtī** (S) (F) ray of light.

**Upādhyāya** (S) (M) 1. nearing knowledge. 2. teacher; preceptor.

**Upādiśa** (S) (M) 1. suggested; pointing out; showing. 2. teacher. 3. a son of Vasudeva (*Bhā. Purāṇa*)

**Upādya** (S) (M) 2nd.

**Upagahana** (S) (M) 1. nearing a forest or cave. 2. a person with a depth of character; serious person. 3. a ṛṣi (*M. Bh.*)

**Upagraha** (S) (M) **1.** a secondary planet. **2.** satellite; comet; meteor. **3.** a son of Viśvāmitra (*M. Bh.*)

**Upagu** (S) (M) **1.** near a teacher; assistant teacher. **3.** a king.

**Upagupta** (S) (M) **1.** secret; hidden. **3.** a king of the lunar dynasty.

**Upaguru** (S) (M) **1.** assistant teacher; near teachers. **3.** a king (*Bhā. Purāṇa*)

**Upahāra** (S) (M) offering; gift; oblation to a deity.

**Upahūta** (S) (M) called; invited; summoned; invoked.

**Upajas** (S) (M) **1.** produced; coming from. **3.** a deity.

**Upajaya** (S) (M) **1.** to help; to support. **3.** a hermit who performed the sacrifice for King Drupada to bear children (*M. Bh.*)

**Upajīka** (S) (M) **1.** living near water plants. **3.** a Vedic water deity (*A. Veda*)

**Upajit** (S) (M) to acquire by victory.

**Upakāla** (S) (M) **1.** almost black. **2.** dark. **3.** a king of nāgas.

**Upakāra** (H) (M) favour; kindness; ornament; decoration; embellishment.

**Upakārikā** (S) (F) protectress.

**Upakāśa** (S) (M) wearing the sky; aurora; dawn.

**Upakośā** (S) (F) **1.** like a treasure. **3.** a daughter of Upavarṣa and wife of Vararući (*K. Sāgara*)

**Upakṛṣṇaka** (S) (M) **1.** almost black. **3.** a warrior of Skanda (*M. Bh.*)

**Upakṣatra** (S) (M) **1.** with a small domain. **3.** a king (*V. Purāṇa*)

**Upakṣaya** (S) (M) **1.** secondary destruction. **3.** the destroyer of the world; another name for Śiva.

**Upakuśa** (S) (M) **1.** near Kuśa. **3.** son of Kuśa (*V. Rāmāyaṇa*)

**Upāli** (S) (M) **1.** friend of a friend. **3.** one of Buddha's most eminent pupils and the 1st propounder of Buddhist law (*B. Literature*)

**Upamā** (S) (F) resemblance; similarity; equality.

**Upama** (S) (M) highest; best; nearest; 1st.

**Upamanyu** (S) (M) **1.** striving for knowledge. **2.** zealous; knowing; intelligent. **3.** a hermit son of Sutapas (*Br. Purāṇa*); the son of Vyāsa; a Śaiva sage whose hermitage in the Himālayas became a sanctuary for all the animals; a ṛṣi who received the Ocean of Milk from Śiva (*L. Purāṇa*)

**Upamaśravas** (S) (M) **1.** highly renowned. **3.** a son of Kuruśravana and grandson of Mitratithi.

**Upamātiṣ** (S) (M) **1.** granting wealth. **3.** another name for Agni.

**Upananda** (S) (M) **1.** approaching happiness; pleasant; mythical. **3.** a son of Dhṛtarāṣṭra (*M. Bh.*); a serpent (*M. Bh.*); a warrior of Skanda (*M. Bh.*)

**Upanandaka** (S) (M) **1.** giving or nearing pleasure. **3.** a son of Dhṛtarāṣṭra (*M. Bh.*)

**Upanandana** (S) (M) **1.** like a son. **3.** a form of Śiva (*A. Koṣa*)

**Upanara** (S) (M) offering; present; gift.

**Upanāya** (S) (M) leader.

**Upaṇāyika** (S) (F) fit for an offering.

**Upanetṛ** (S) (M) **1.** bringing near. **2.** spiritual preceptor.

**Upāṅga** (S) (M) **1.** the act of anointing; secondary part of the body; additional work; mark of sandalwood on the forehead. **3.** the secondary Vedas.

**Upanibha** (S) (M) similar; equal.

**Upanidhi** (S) (M) **1.** a deposit. **2.** pledge; a ray of light. **3.** a son of Vasudeva (*V. Purāṇa*)

**Upanīti** (S) (F) initiation.

**Upānśu** (S) (M) a prayer uttered in a low voice.

**Upapati** (S) (M) gallant.

**Uparatna** (S) (M) a secondary gem.

**Uparićaravasu** (S) (M) **1.** a deity who travels above. **2.** guardian angel. **3.** a descendant of Viṣṇu he was the son of Kṛti and the father of Bṛhadratha, Kuśāmbha, Mavella, Yadu and Rājanya (*M. Bh.*)

**Upāsanā** (S) (F) devotion; worship; homage.

**Upaśloka** (S) (M) **1.** secondary verse. **3.** the father of the 10th Manu (*Bh. Purāṇa*); a son of Kṛṣṇa and Sairindhrī.

**Upaśobhin** (S) (M) acquiring beauty; beautiful; brilliant; bright.

**Upaśruti** (S) (F) 1. listening attentively. 3. a goddess of the sun's progress towards the north in the first half of the year (*M. Bh.*); the secondary Vedas.

**Upastava** (S) (M) praise.

**Upāsti** (S) (F) adoration; worship.

**Upastu** (S) (M) to invoke; celebrate in song; praise.

**Upastuta** (S) (M) 1. invoked; praised. 3. a ṛṣi (*Ṛg Veda*)

**Upaśubha** (S) (M) nearing auspiciousness; to be beautiful and brilliant.

**Upasunda** (S) (M) 1. younger brother of Sunda. 3. a daityā (*M. Bh.*)

**Upatiṣyam** (S) (M) 1. near the asterism Tiṣya. 2. asterisms called Āśleṣā and Punarvasu (*T. Brāhmaṇa*)

**Upavarṣa** (S) (M) 1. acquiring knowledge. 2. possessed of extraordinary knowledge. 3. the younger brother of Varṣa and son of Śankarasvāmin, author of the Mīmānsā philosophy.

**Upavaṭa** (S) (M) 1. similar to the Vata tree. 2. pious; sacred; *Buchnania latifolia*.

**Upaveṇā** (S) (F) 1. with small tributaries. 3. a river who is considered the mother of Agni (*M. Bh.*)

**Upāvi** (S) (M) cherishing; pleasing.

**Upavīta** (S) (M) invested with the sacred thread; the sacred thread worn over the left shoulder.

**Upayāma** (S) (M) 1. with restraint; a ladle used in the Soma sacrifice. 3. a deity (*V. Samhitā*)

**Upayuta** (S) (M) 1. performing sacrifices. 3. a king (*V. Purāṇa*)

**Upekṣa** (S) (M) 1. to wait on patiently; to expect; to neglect; to connive. 3. a son of Śvaphalka.

**Upendrā** (S) (F) 1. younger sister of Indra. 3. a river (*M. Bh.*)

**Upendra** (S) (M) 1. younger brother of Indra. 3. another name for Viṣṇu/Kṛṣṇa born after Indra in his dwarf incarnation.

**Upendrabala** (S) (M) 1. with Viṣṇu's power. 3. the son of a minister of King Śrīdatta (*V. Purāṇa*)

**Upodayam** (S) (M) at the time of sunrise.

**Upoditi** (S) (M) 1. advancing. 3. a ṛṣi (*T. Samhitā*)

**Uppala** (S) (M) precious stone; jewel; cloud; lotus (*Nelumbo speciosum*)

**Uragabhūṣaṇa** (S) (M) 1. decorated or ornamented with serpents. 3. another name for Śiva.

**Uragarāja** (S) (M) 1. king of snakes. 3. another name for Vāsuki.

**Uragāri** (S) (M) 1. enemy of snakes. 3. another name for Garuḍa.

**Uragīndra** (S) (M) 1. lord of serpents. 3. another name for Vāsuki and Śeṣa.

**Urasila** (S) (M) broadchested.

**Ūrdhvabāhu** (S) (M) 1. with lifted hands. 2. devotee. 3. a son of Vasiṣṭha and Ūrjā (*A. Purāṇa*)

**Ūrdhvabhāk** (S) (M) 1. going up. 3. the agni who was the 5th son of Bṛhaspati (*M. Bh.*)

**Ūrdhvabhās** (S) (M) rising splendour; one whose splendour rises.

**Ūrdhvadeva** (S) (M) 1. upper god. 2. god of the upper regions. 3. another name for Viṣṇu.

**Ūrdhvaga** (S) (M) 1. ascending. 3. a son of Kṛṣṇa (*Bh. Purāṇa*)

**Ūrdhvakeśā** (S) (F) 1. with erect hair. 3. a goddess.

**Ūrdhvāsana** (S) (M) sitting high; high superior; victorious.

**Ūrdhvaveṇīdharā** (S) (F) 1. with hair tied at the top of the head. 3. an attendant of Skanda (*M. Bh.*)

**Ūrjā** (S) (F) 1. energy; strength; vigour. 2. food; water; power; breath; heartborn; loving daughter. 3. a daughter of Dakṣa and wife of sage Vasiṣṭha and the mother of the 7 ṛṣis of the 2nd Manvantara (*V. Purāṇa*); the month of Kārttika; another name for Pārvatī.

**Ūrjamedha** (S) (M) strong intelligence; very wise.

**Ūrjānī** (S) (F) 1. belonging to energy; energy personified. 3. a daughter of the sun (*Ṛg Veda*); goddess of strength.

**Ūrjasani** (S) (M) 1. granting strength. 3. another name for Agni.

**Ūrjastambha** (S) (M) 1. pillar of strength. 3. a ṛṣi of the 2nd Manvantara (*Bhā. Purāṇa*)

**Ūrjasvala** (S) (M) 1. powerful; strong; mighty. 3. a ṛṣi in the 2nd Manvantara (*V. Purāṇa*)

**Ūrjasvatī** (S) (F) juicy; vigorous; powerful; strong.

**Ūrjaśvin** (S) (M) powerful; strong; mighty.

**Ūrjayoni** (S) (M) 1. originator of energy. 3. a son of Viśvāmitra (*M. Bh.*)

**Ūrjita** (S) (M) possessed with power; powerful; distinguished; excellent; beautiful; noble; strong; mighty; great; important; gallant.

**Ūrjitāśraya** (S) (M) 1. abode of strength. 2. a hero.

**Ūrjja** (S) (M) 1. powerful. 3. a king of the Hehaya dynasty who was the grandfather of Jarāsandha (*A. Purāṇa*); a ṛṣi of the Svāroćiṣa Manvantara (*V. Purāṇa*)

**Ūrjjaketu** (S) (M) 1. with a strong (victorious) flag. 3. a king of the dynasty of King Janaka (*Bhāgavata*)

**Ūrjjasvatī** (S) (F) 1. full of energy; energetic; strong. 3. a daughter of Priyavrata and Surūpā she became the wife of Śukra and the mother of Devayānī (*Bhāgavata*)

**Ūrmī** (S) (F) wave; ripple; light.

**Ūrmikā** (S) (F) wave; finger ring; humming of bees.

**Ūrmilā** (S) (F) 1. of the waves of passion; beautiful; enchanting. 3. the daughter of King Janaka and the sister of Sītā, she married Lakṣmaṇa and was the mother of Takṣaka and Ćitraketu (*U. Rāmāyaṇa*)

**Ūrmyā** (S) (F) 1. wavy. 2. night. 3. a Vedic goddess of light (*V. Rāmāyaṇa*)

**Ūrṇā** (S) (F) 1. woollen. 2. warm; ever excited. 3. a wife of Ćitraratha; a wife of Marīći (*D. Bhāgavata*)

**Ūrṇa** (S) (M) 1. wool. 3. a yakṣa (*Bhā. Purāṇa*)

**Ūrṇanābha** (S) (M) 1. with a woolly navel. 2. spider; a particular position of the hands. 3. a son of Dhṛtarāṣṭra (*M. Bh.*); a dānava.

**Ūrnāvatī** (S) (F) 1. rich in sheep. 3. a tributary river of the Indus (*Ṛg. Veda*)

**Ūrṇāyu** (S) (M) 1. wool carder. 3. a gandharva who fell in love with Menakā (*M. Bh.*)

**Ūru** (S) (M) 1. wide; broad; spacious; great; excellent; large; thigh. 3. a son of the 14th Manu (*Bh. Purāṇa.*); the son of Manu Ćākṣusa and Naḍvalā and the husband of Ātreyī (*A. Veda*)

**Ūrubilvā** (S) (F) 1. broad leaved. 3. the place to which the Buddha retired for meditation and obtained supreme knowledge, it was later known as Bodhagayā (*B. Literature*)

**Urućakri** (S) (M) 1. doing great work; the circle of evolution. 3. a descendant of Atri (*Ṛg Veda*)

**Urućakṣas** (S) (M) 1. far seeing. 3. another name for Varuṇa, Sūrya and the ādityas.

**Urūćī** (S) (M) far reaching; capacious; extending far.

**Urudbhī** (S) (M) 1. terrifying in many ways. 3. son of Śakuni.

**Urudhiṣṇya** (S) (M) 1. exceedingly thoughtful. 3. a sage of the 11th Manvantara.

**Urugāya** (S) (M) 1. wide striding; much praised. 3. another name for Indra, Viṣṇu, Kṛṣṇa, Soma and the aśvins.

**Ūruja** (S) (M) 1. born from the thigh. 3. another name for the ṛṣi Aurva.

**Urukīrti** (S) (F) of far reaching fame.

**Urukrama** (S) (M) 1. far stepping; with wide strides. 3. another name for Vāmana.

**Urukṣaya** (S) (M) 1. occupying spacious dwellings. 3. another name for Varuṇa and the maruts.

**Uruloka** (S) (M) ample; vast.

**Urunjirā** (S) (F) 1. pleaser of heart; heart winning. 3. another name of the river Vipās.

**Uruṣā** (S) (F) granting much; producing abundantly.

**Uruśaṇsa** (S) (M) 1. of far reaching praise; praised by many. 3. another name for Varuṇa; Pūṣan, Indra, the Soma and the ādityas.

**Urusattva** (S) (M) of a generous or noble nature.

**Uruśravas** (S) (M) of wide reaching fame; an ardent listener.

**Urutā** (S) (F) greatness; vastness.

**Uruvalka** (S) (M) 1. well dressed. 3. a son of Vasudeva (*Bhā. Purāṇa*)

**Uruvī** (S) (F) 1. great; large; spacious; excellent; broad. 3. another name for the earth.

**Ūrva** (S) (M) 1. of the thigh. 3. a renowned hermit of the Bhṛgu family who was the son of Ćyavana and the father of Ṛćīka (*V. Samhitā*)

**Urvāṅga** (S) (M) 1. large bodied. 2. a mountain; ocean.

**Urvarā** (S) (F) 1. fertile soil. 2. the earth. 3. an apsarā in the palace of Kubera (*M. Bh.*)

**Urvarāpati** (S) (M) 1. lord of the cultivated soil. 3. another name for Indra.

**Urvarīyān** (S) (M) 1. fertile. 3. the son of Prajāpati Pulaha and Kṣamā (*V. Purāṇa*)

**Urvaśī** (S) (F) 1. widely extending. 3. an apsarā considered the most beautiful in the 3 worlds who was born from the thigh of Nārāyaṇa and married Purūravas and had 6 sons; another name for Gaṅgā as she sat on the thigh of Bhagīratha (*M. Bh.*)

**Urvī** (S) (F) 1. the wide one. 2. the earth; river; heaven and earth conjoined.

**Urvībhuj** (S) (M) 1. earth enjoyer. 2. king.

**Urvīdhara** (S) (M) 1. earth bearer. 2. king.

**Urvīpati** (SS) (M) 1. master of the earth. 2. king.

**Urvīśa** (S) (M) 1. lord of the earth. 2. king.

**Urvīśvara** (S) (M) 1. god of the earth. 2. king.

**Uṣā/Uṣas** (S) (F) 1. daybreak. 2. dawn. 3. morning light personified as the daughter of heaven and sister of the ādityas and night; the evening light; night; the period between the setting of the stars and the rising of the sun; a wife of Rudra or Bhava; a daughter of Bāṇa and wife of Aniruddha (*A. Purāṇa*)

**Uṣadgu** (S) (M) 1. remover of darkness. 3. a son of Svāhi (*V. Purāṇa*)

**Uṣadratha** (S) (M) 1. chariot of the sun. 3. a son of Titikṣu (*V. Purāṇa*)

**Uṣākara** (S) (M) 1. night maker. 3. another name for the moon.

**Uṣākiraṇa** (S) (M) the 1st ray of dawn.

**Uṣalākṣī** (S) (F) dawn eyed; large eyed; with piercing eyes.

**Uśanā** (S) (F) 1. with desire. 3. a wife of Rudra (*H. Purāṇa*); Ceylon Leadwort (*Plumbago zeylanica*)

**Uśānā** (S) (F) 1. wish; desire. 2. the plant from which the Soma juice is produced.

**Uśanas** (S) (M) 1. with desire. 3. a sage later identified with Śukra the son of Bhṛgu and the regent of the planet Venus (*Ṛg Veda*); a Vedic ṛṣi who was associated with the fire ritual in the *Ṛg Veda*; a son of Kavi, he was the friend of Indra.

**Uṣaṅgava** (S) (M) 1. one who rises at dawn. 2. early riser. 3. a king in the court of Yama (*M. Bh.*)

**Uṣaṅgu** (S) (M) 1. one who gets up at dawn. 2. early riser. 3. a hermit (*M. Bh.*); a king of the Yadu family who was the son of Vṛjinivān and the father of Ćitraratha (*M. Bh.*); a sacred cow; another name for Śiva.

**Uṣāpati** (S) (M) 1. master of Uṣā. 3. another name for Aniruddha and the moon.

**Uṣāramaṇa** (S) (M) 1. beloved of Uṣā. 3. another name for Aniruddha.

**Uṣarbhudha** (S) (M) 1. waking with the morning light. 3. another name for Agni.

**Uṣasī** (S) (F) twilight.

**Uṣasti** (S) (M) 1. true dawn. 3. a ṛṣi who was the husband of Ātikī.

**Uśenya** (S) (M) to be wished for; desirable.

**Uṣeśa** (S) (M) 1. lord of Uṣā. 3. another name for the moon.

**Uśī** (S) (F) wish.

**Uśijā** (S) (F) 1. desire born. 2. wishing; desiring; zealous; lovely; charming; amiable; desirable. 3. the mother of Kakṣīvat (*V. Purāṇa*)

**Uśija** (S) (M) 1. desire born; wishing; desiring; zealous; amiable; desirable; fire; ghee. 3. the father of Kakṣīvat; a son of Ūru (*V. Purāṇa*)

**Uṣikā** (S) (F) 1. dawn worshipper. 3. a wife of Dīrghatamas and the mother of Kakṣīvān.

**Uṣika** (S) (M) 1. dawn worshipper; early riser. 3. a hermit mentioned in the *Ṛg Veda*.

**Uśīnara** (S) (M) 1. most desired. 3. a famous king of the lunar dynasty who was the son of Sṛñjaya and the husband of Mādhavī and father of Śibi and Veṇa; a Yādava king (*M. Bh.*)

**Ūṣmā** (S) (M) 1. heat. 2. spring; passion; anger; ardour; the hot season. 3. a son of the agni Pāñćajanya (*M. Bh.*)

**Ūṣman** (S) (M) heat; glow; ardour.

**Uṣṇa** (S) (M) hot; passionate; ardent; sharp; active.

**Uṣṇagu** (S) (M) 1. hot rayed. 3. another name for the sun.

**Uṣṇakara** (S) (M) 1. hot rayed; creator of heat. 3. another name for the sun.

**Uṣṇaraṣmi** (S) (M) 1. hot-rayed. 3. another name for Sūrya.

**Uśṇih** (S) (M) 1. attached. 2. metre of poetry. 3. one of the 7 horses of the sun (*V. Purāṇa*)

**Uśṇinābha** (S) (M) 1. fire navelled. 3. a viśvadeva (*M. Bh.*)

**Uṣṇiṣa** (S) (M) anything worn on the head; turban; diadem; crown.

**Uṣṇiṣin** (S) (M) 1. wearing a crown. 3. another name for Śiva.

**Uṣojala** (S) (M) 1. water of dawn; the dawn's tears. 2. dew.

**Uṣorāga** (S) (M) morning light; the dawn.

**Usṛ** (S) (F) morning light; daybreak; day.

**Usrā** (S) (F) morning light; daybreak; brightness personified as a red cow; earth as the source of all good things.

**Usra** (S) (M) morning light; sun; bright; shining; morning; dawn; the 2 aśvins; flame; bull.

**Uśrāyus** (S) (M) 1. with a bright life. 3. a son of Purūravas (*Ṛg Veda*)

**Uṣṭrajihva** (S) (M) 1. buffalo tongued. 3. an attendant of Skanda (*M. Bh.*)

**Utanka** (S) (M) 1. stretching out. 3. a ṛṣi (*M. Bh.*)

**Utathya** (S) (M) 1. deliberation. 2. intensity. 3. elder brother of Bṛhaspati (*V. Purāṇa*); Viṣṇu born as the son of Aṅgiras and Śraddhā who married Soma's daughter Bhadrā and was the advisor to King Māndhāta (*M. Bh.*)

**Utathyānuja** (S) (M) 1. Utathya's younger brother. 3. another name for Bṛhaspati (*M. Bh.*)

**Ūti** (S) (F) help; protection; kindness; enjoyment.

**Utī** (S) (F) wish; enjoyment; desire.

**Utkala** (S) (M) 1. glorious. 2. glorious country; a porter; carrying a burden or load; a fowler; a bird catcher. 3. a son of Dhruva (*Bhā. Purāṇa*); the son of Vaivasvata Manu (*Br. Purāṇa*); a country now called Orissa; another name for Sudyumna.

**Utkalā** (S) (F) 1. coming from Utkala. 3. a wife of Samrāj (*Bh. Purāṇa*)

**Utkalikā** (S) (F) longing for glory; a bud; ungrown flower; a wave.

**Utkalitā** (S) (F) unbound; loosened; opened; blossoming; brilliant.

**Utkaṇikā** (S) (F) desire; longing.

**Utkānti** (S) (F) excessive splendour.

**Utkarikā** (S) (F) made of precious material; made of milk treacle and ghee.

**Utkarṣa** (S) (M) superior; eminent; much; excessive; attractive; pulling upwards; drawing; elevation; increase; prosperity; rising to something better; excellence; eminence; progress; development.

**Utkārthinī** (S) (F) 1. fulfilling one's ambitions. 3. an attendant of Skanda (*M. Bh.*)

**Utkāśa** (S) (M) to shine forth; flash; coming forth.

**Utkāśaṇā** (S) (F) giving orders; commanding.

**Utkaṭa** (S) (M) (F) exceeding the usual measure; immense; gigantic; richly endowed with; abounding in; superior; high; uneven; difficult.

**Utkhalā** (S) (F) perfume.

**Utkhalin** (S) (M) 1. perfumed. 3. a Buddhist deity.

**Utkīla** (S) (M) 1. excited. 2. opened. 3. ṛṣi (*Ṛg Veda*)

**Utkroṣa** (S) (M) 1. loud speaker. 3. one of the 2 attendants given to Skanda by Indra (*M. Bh.*)

**Utkṛṣṭa** (S) (M) excellent; eminent; superior; best.

**Utkṣiptikā** (S) (F) lifted; a crescent shaped ornament worn on the upper ear.

**Utkūjā** (S) (F) a cooing note as of the Kokila.

**Utkumuda** (S) (M) with lotus flowers on the surface.

**Utpaksha** (S) (M) 1. with up turned wings. 3. a son of Śvaphalka (*H. Purāṇa*)

**Utpalā** (S) (F) 1. filled with lotuses. 3. a river (*H. Purāṇa*)

**Utpala** (S) (M) 1. to burst open. 2. the blossom of the Blue Lotus (*Nymphaea stellata*)

**Utpalābha** (S) (M) glory of a lotus; lotus like; soft; tender; precious.

**Utpalāćārya** (S) (M) **1.** master of the Blue Lotus. **3.** a pupil of Somanada who wrote the *Iśvara-Pratyabijña- Kārikā*.

**Utpalākṣa** (S) (M) **1.** lotus eyed. **3.** another name for Viṣṇu.

**Utpalākṣī** (S) (F) **1.** lotus eyed. **3.** a goddess (*M. Purāṇa*); another name for Lakṣmī.

**Utpalamālā** (S) (F) a garland of lotus flowers.

**Utpalaśrigarbha** (S) (M) **1.** divine womb of lotus. **3.** a Bodhisattva.

**Utpalāvatī** (S) (F) **1.** made of lotuses. **3.** an apsarā; a river (*M. Bh.*)

**Utpalin** (S) (M) abounding in lotus flowers.

**Utpalinī** (S) (F) **1.** an assemblage of lotuses; **3.** a river flowing near the Naimiṣāraṇya forest (*M. Bh.*)

**Utpāra** (S) (M) boundless; endless.

**Utprabhas** (S) (M) flashing forth; bright fire; shining.

**Utsāha** (S) (M) courage; courageous; powerful; energetic; perseverance; firmness; determination; happiness.

**Utsarga** (S) (M) **1.** emission; setting free; delivering; gift; donation; oblation. **3.** excretion personified as a son of Mitra and Revatī.

**Utsmaya** (S) (M) **1.** open; blooming. **2.** a smile.

**Uttāla** (S) (M) great; strong; roaring; formidable; swift; excellent; tall; high; abundant.

**Uttamā** (S) (F) best; excellent; affectionate.

**Uttama** (S) (M) **1.** best; excellent; greatest. **2.** highest; chief. **3.** a son of Uttānapāda and Surući and brother of Dhruva (*V. Purāṇa*); a son of Priyavrata and Barhiṣmatī (*Bhā. Purāṇa*)

**Uttamabala** (S) (M) strongest.

**Uttamāha** (S) (M) a fine day; a lucky day.

**Uttamamaṇi** (S) (M) the best gem.

**Uttamatejas** (S) (M) extremely glorious; of excellent glory.

**Uttamaujas** (S) (M) **1.** of excellent valour. **3.** a warrior of the Mahābhārata.

**Uttamaveśa** (S) (M) **1.** excellently dressed; with the best dress. **3.** another name for Śiva.

**Uttambha** (S) (M) upholding; supporting; propping.

**Uttamikā** (S) (F) best worker.

**Uttana** (S) (M) **1.** to stretch out and upwards. **3.** a deity who is a form of the earth (*A. Brāhmaṇa*)

**Uttānabarhis** (S) (M) **1.** with a high tail. **2.** peacock. **3.** the son of Śaryāti of the family of Vaivaśvata Manu (*Bhāgavata*)

**Uttānahaya** (S) (M) **1.** with a flying horse. **2.** fast thinker. **3.** a son of Śatājit.

**Uttānapāda** (S) (M) **1.** with a high position. **3.** the star called Little Bear personified as the king who was the son of Svāyambhuva Manu and the brother of Priyavrata and the husband of Surući and Sunītī and father of Dhruva (*V. Purāṇa*)

**Uttaṅka** (S) (M) **1.** high cloud. **2.** a type of cloud. **3.** a disciple of Āpodadhaumya who prompted the snake sacrifice of Janamejaya (*M. Bh.*)

**Uttanśa** (S) (M) a crest; chaplet; ornament.

**Uttansika** (S) (M) **1.** adorned with a crest. **3.** a nāga (*M. Bh.*)

**Uttarā** (S) (F) **1.** upper; higher; northern. **2.** future; result. **3.** daughter of King Virāṭa of Matsya and wife of Abhimanyu, she was the mother of Parīkṣit (*M. Bh.*)

**Uttara** (S) (M) **1.** north; higher; upper. **2.** superior. **3.** the son of King Virāṭa of Maṭsya (*M. Bh.*); a fire (*M. Bh.*); a king of nāgas; a mountain (*K. Sāgara*); another name for Śiva.

**Uttāraka** (S) (M) **1.** deliverer. **3.** another name for Śiva.

**Uttarikā** (S) (F) **1.** crossing over. **2.** coming out; delivering; conveying; a boat. **3.** a river (*Rāmāyaṇa*)

**Uttejinī** (S) (F) **1.** exciting; animating. **3.** a follower of Skanda (*M. Bh.*)

# V

**Vabhravāyani** (S) (M) 1. weaver. 3. a son of Viśvāmitra (*M. Bh.*)

**Vāća** (S) (F) 1. speech. 2. word; voice; oath; sacred text. 3. language personified in the Vedas as having been created by Prajāpati and married to him, she is also represented as the mother of the Vedas and wife of Indra and as the daughter of Dakṣa and wife of Kaśyapa, she is most frequently identified with Sarasvatī (*A. Brāhmaṇa*)

**Vāćaknavī** (S) (F) 1. with the power of speech. 2. an orator; a speaker; eloquent. 3. a preceptress of the family of Gārgi (*Ṛg Veda*)

**Vaćaknu** (S) (M) eloquent.

**Vaćana** (S) (M) declaration; oath; command; order.

**Vāćasāmpati** (S) (M) 1. master of speech. 3. another name for Bṛhaspati.

**Vāćaspati** (S) (M) 1. lord of speech. 3. another name for Bṛhaspati.

**Vaćasya** (S) (M) well spoken of; praiseworthy; celebrated.

**Vaćchacārya** (S) (M) 1. teacher of children. 3. the grandfather of Nīlakanṭha.

**Vāćispati** (S) (M) 1. lord of speech. 3. another name for Bṛhaspati; an author of *Tattvakāumudi*; the constellation Puṣya.

**Vāćyā** (S) (F) 1. blamed. 3. another name for Sītā.

**Vaḍabā** (S) (F) 1. mare. 3. the apsarā Aśvinī in her form as mare-wife of Vivasvān; a wife of Vasudeva (*V. Purāṇa*)

**Vaḍabāsuta** (S) (M) 1. son of a mare; son of Vaḍabā. 3. another name for the aśvins.

**Vadānya** (S) (M) 1. bountiful; liberal; munificent; eloquent. 3. a ṛṣi (*Ṛg Veda*)

**Vadha** (S) (M) 1. murder. 2. killer; slayer; a deadly weapon. 3. the son of giant Yātudhāna and the father of Vighna and Śama (*Br. Purāṇa*)

**Vadhrimatī** (S) (F) 1. with an impotent husband. 3. a Ṛg Vedic princess and devotee of the aśvins and mother of Hiraṇyahasta (*Ṛg Veda*)

**Vadhryaśva** (S) (M) 1. with a castrated horse. 3. a king in the court of Yama (*M. Bh.*)

**Vadhūsarā** (S) (F) 1. roaming woman. 3. a river made of the tears of Pulomā that flowed through the hermitage of Ćyavana (*M. Bh.*)

**Vādin** (S) (M) 1. speaker; disputant; propounder of a theory. 3. a son of Emperor Pṛthu (*V. Purāṇa*)

**Vādindra** (S) (M) excellent disputant.

**Vādirāj** (S) (M) 1. king among disputants. 3. a Baudhya sage; another name for Mañjuśrī.

**Vādiśa** (S) (M) lord of disputants; one who resolves disputes, peace maker; learned; virtuous; seer; sage.

**Vādisinha** (S) (M) 1. lion among disputants; resolver of disputes; one who dispels doubts. 3. another name for Buddha.

**Vādīśvara** (S) (M) god of disputants; peace maker.

**Vādrmatī** (S) (F) with Viṣṇu.

**Vāduli** (S) (M) 1. orator; logician. 3. a son of Viśvāmitra (*V. Rāmāyaṇa*)

**Vāgabali** (S) (M) possessing the power of speech.

**Vāgabhaṭa** (S) (M) 1. scholar of speech. 3. a Sanskṛt scholar of rhetorical science (12th century)

**Vāgadevī** (S) (F) 1. goddess of speech. 3. another name for Sarasvatī.

**Vāgadhīpa** (S) (M) 1. lord of speech. 3. another name for Bṛhaspati.

**Vāgaduṣṭa** (S) (M) 1. vile in speech; sophistry. 3. a son of sage Kauśika (*M. Purāṇa*)

**Vagalā** (S) (F) 1. slow; limping. 3. a tāntric goddess.

**Vāgara** (S) (M) 1. ascertainment. 2. scholar; hero.

**Vāgavādinī** (S) (F) 1. disputing speech. 2. one who takes part in discussion. 3. a goddess (*Pañćatantra*)

**Vāghat** (S) (M) institutor of a sacrifice.

**Vāgindra** (S) (M) 1. lord of speech. 2. lord of cranes. 3. the son of King Prakāśaka of the family of Gṛtsamada and the father of King Pramiti (*M. Bh.*)

**Vāgīśa** (S) (M) 1. lord of speech; master of language. 3. another name for Bṛhaspati and Brahmā.

**Vāgīśvara** (S) (M) 1. master of language. 2. a deified sage. 3. a Jina; another name for Brahmā.

**Vāgīśvarī** (S) (F) 1. goddess of speech. 3. another name for Sarasvatī.

**Vāgmin** (S) (M) 1. eloquent. 3. a son of King Manasyu and Sauvīrī (*M. Bh.*); another name for Bṛhaspati.

**Vahati** (S) (M) 1. friend. 2. wind. 3. a river.

**Vāhi** (S) (M) 1. carrying; bearing. 3. a devil living in the Vipāśā river (*M. Bh.*)

**Vāhika** (S) (M) vehicle drawn by oxen; one who carries; one who bears along; an inhabitant of Punjab.

**Vāhin** (S) (M) 1. driving; bearing; bringing; causing; carrying. 3. Śiva as one who carries the world.

**Vāhinara** (S) (M) 1. drawn by men. 3. a king in the palace of Yama (*M. Bh.*)

**Vāhinī** (S) (F) 1. army; body of force. 3. the wife of King Kuru (*M. Bh.*)

**Vahni** (S) (M) 1. conveying. 2. a draught animal. 3. an asura who was a lokapāla (*M. Bh.*); a son of Turvasu (*Bh. Purāṇa*); a son of Kṛṣṇa and Mitravindā (*Bhāgavata*)

**Vāhni** (S) (M) 1. one who carries; one who conveys or bears along or is borne along. 2. draught animal; charioteer. 3. a son of Kukura (*M. Bh.*); an asura who was once a Lokapāla (*M. Bh.*); the son of King Turvasu and the father of Bharga (*Bhāgavata*); a son of Kṛṣṇa and Mitravindā (*Bhāgavata*); another name for Agni, Indra, the maruts and Soma.

**Vahnigarbha** (S) (M) 1. with fire in the womb; bamboo. 3. a gaṇa of Śiva (*Ś. Purāṇa*)

**Vahnih** (S) (M) 1. bearing along; carrying oblations. 3. another name for Agni.

**Vahṇijāyā** (S) (F) 1. conqueror of fire. 3. the wife of the agni Vahni (*Ṛg Veda*)

**Vahnikanyā** (S) (F) 1. daughter of fire. 2. air; wind.

**Vahnimitra** (S) (M) 1. friend of fire. 2. air; wind.

**Vahninetra** (S) (M) 1. fiery eyed. 3. another name for Śiva.

**Vahnipriyā** (S) (F) 1. beloved of fire. 3. the wife of Vahni (*M. Bh.*)

**Vahnīśvarī** (S) (F) 1. goddess of fire. 3. another name for Lakṣmī.

**Vahnivadhū** (S) (F) 1. wife of fire. 3. the wife of Agni (*Ṛg Veda*)

**Vahnīvallabha** (S) (F) 1. beloved of fire. 3. another name for Svāhā.

**Vāhūka** (S) (M) 1. with strong arms. 3. name assumed by King Nala (*M. Bh.*)

**Vāhuli** (S) (M) 1. leader. 3. a son of Viśvāmitra (*V. Rāmāyaṇa*)

**Vāhyakā** (S) (F) 1. chariot. 2. venomous insect. 3. the 2 daughters of King Sṛnjaya who were married to the Yādava king Bhajamāna and became the mothers of Nimi, Vṛṣṇi and Kṛmila (*M. Purāṇa*)

**Vaibhātika** (S) (M) of the dawn.

**Vaibhava** (S) (M) might; power; greatness; grandeur; glory.

**Vaibhrāja** (S) (M) garden of the gods.

**Vaibudha** (S) (M) belonging to the gods; divine.

**Vaićitravīrya** (S) (M) 1. son of Vićitravīrya. 3. another name for Dhṛtarāṣṭra.

**Vaidagdhī** (S) (F) grace; beauty.

**Vaidarbhī** (S) (F) 1. of Vidarbha. 3. a wife of King Sagara and the mother of 60,000 sons; the wife of King Kuśa and the mother of Kuśāmba, Kuśanābha, Asūrtarajas and Vasu (*V. Rāmāyaṇa*); the wife of Agastya; another name for Ḍamayantī; another name for Rukmiṇī.

**Vaidarbhi** (S) (M) 1. belonging to Vidarbha. 3. a king who was the father of Lopāmudrā (*M. Bh.*)

**Vaidat** (S) (M) knowing.

**Vaideha** (S) (M) 1. belonging to the Videhas; with a handsome body. 3. another name for Janaka.

**Vaidehī** (S) (F) 1. princess of the Videhas. 3. another name for Sītā.

**Vaidehībandhu** (S) (M) 1. consort of Sītā. 3. another name for Rāma.

**Vaidhava** (S) (M) 1. son of the moon. 3. another name for Mercury.

**Vaidhṛta** (S) (M) 1. lying on the same side. 3. a particular position of the sun and moon;

Indra in the 11th Manvantara (*Bhā. Purāṇa*)
**Vaidhṛtī** (S) (F) 1. with a similar disposition. 2. properly adjusted. 3. the wife of Āryaka and mother of Dharmasetu (*Bhā. Purāṇa*)
**Vaidhyata** (S) (M) 1. supporter of law. 3. Yama's door-keeper.
**Vaiḍūrya** (S) (M) 1. anything excellent of its kind. 2. a cat's eye jewel.
**Vaiḍūryakānti** (S) (M) with the lustre of the cat's eye jewel.
**Vaiḍūryamaṇi** (S) (M) the cats eye jewel.
**Vaiḍūryaprabhā** (S) (M) 1. with the light of the cat's eye jewel. 3. a nāga.
**Vaidya** (S) (M) 1. versed in medical science; learned; physician. 3. a ṛṣi (*M. Bh.*); a son of Varuṇa and Suṇādevī and the father of Ghṛṇi and Muni (*Vā. Purāṇa*)
**Vaidyalingam** (S) (M) knowing the secrets of medicine; emblem of learning.
**Vaidyanātha** (S) (M) 1. lord of physicians. 3. a form of Śiva; another name for Dhanvantari.
**Vaidyarāja** (S) (M) 1. king among physicians. 3. another name for Dhanvantari.
**Vaidyuta** (S) (M) 1. coming from lightning. 2. flashing; brilliant. 3. a son of Vapuṣmat (*Mā. Purāṇa*)
**Vaijayanta** (S) (M) 1. bestower of victory. 2. banner; flag. 3. the flag of Indra (*M. Bh.*); a mountain in the Sea of Milk visited daily by Brahmā for meditation (*M. Bh.*); the palace of Indra (*B. Literature*); a Jaina group of deities (*J. S. Koṣa*); another name for Skanda (*M. Bh.*)
**Vaijayantī** (S) (F) 1. gift of victory. 2. flag; banner; garland of victory. 3. the necklace of Viṣṇu; the bells of Airāvata presented by Indra to Subrahmaṇya (*M. Bh.*)
**Vaijayantikā** (S) (F) 1. bestowing victory. 2. flag; banner; pearl necklace.
**Vaijayantimālā** (S) (F) 1. garland of victory. 3. the 5 gemmed garland worn by Viṣṇu (*Bhā. Purāṇa*)
**Vaijayī** (S) (M) 1. victor. 3. the 3rd ćakravartin of Bhārata (*M. Bh.*)
**Vaijayika** (S) (M) conferring victory.
**Vaikartana** (S) (M) 1. belonging to the sun. 3. another name for Karṇa.
**Vaikhāna** (S) (M) 1. abode of the absolute. 3. another name for Viṣṇu.
**Vaikuṇṭhā** (S) (F) 1. without hindrance; abode of the absolute. 3. consort of Viṣṇu (*Bhā. Purāṇa*)
**Vaikuṇṭha** (S) (F) 1. abode of the absolute. 2. without hindrance. 3. another name for Mahāviṣṇu and the name of his dwelling place on the eastern peak of Mount Meru.
**Vaikunṭhanātha** (S) (M) 1. lord of Vaikunṭha. 3. another name for Viṣṇu.
**Vaimitrā** (S) (F) 1. friend of the universe. 3. one of the Saptamātṛs or 7 mothers of Skanda (*M. Bh.*)
**Vaimṛdhī** (S) (F) consecrated to Indra.
**Vainateya** (S) (M) 1. humble; modest. 3. a son of Garuḍa (*M. Bh.*); another name for Garuḍa.
**Vaiṇavī** (S) (F) 1. of Veṇu. 2. gold from the Veṇu river.
**Vaiṇavīka** (S) (M) flautist.
**Vaiṇavīn** (S) (M) 1. possessing a flute. 3. another name for Śiva.
**Vainya** (S) (M) 1. of Vena. 3. another name for Emperor Pṛthu.
**Vairāga** (S) (M) freedom from passions and desires.
**Vairāgī** (S) (F) 1. free from passions. 3. a rāgiṇī.
**Vairāgya** (S) (M) 1. loss of colour. 2. asceticism. 3. a son of Bhakti.
**Vairāja** (S) (M) 1. divine glory. 2. belonging to Brahmā. 3. the father of Ajita (*Bhā. Purāṇa*); one of the Saptapitṛs or 7 manes (*M. Bh.*); another name for the Manus, Puruṣa and sage Ṛsabha.
**Vairaṅgika** (S) (M) free from passions and desires.
**Vairaṇī** (S) (F) 1. of Vīraṇa. 3. a wife of Dakṣa (*H. Purāṇa*)
**Vairāta** (S) (M) 1. a precious stone; an earthworm. 3. a son of Dhṛtarāṣṭra (*M. Bh.*)
**Vairatha** (S) (M) 1. without chariot. 3. a son of Jyotiṣmat (*V. Purāṇa*)
**Vairinćya** (S) (M) 1. son of the creator. 3. a son of Brahmā (*Ṛg Veda*)

**Vairivīra** (S) (M) 1. triumphing over enemies. 3. a son of Daśaratha (*V. Purāṇa*)

**Vairoćana** (S) (M) 1. belonging to the sun. 3. a son of the sun; a son of Viṣṇu; a son of Agni; patronymic of Bali (*M. Bh.*); one of the 5 Dhyāni Buddhas; the consort of Loćana and father of Bodhisattva Samantabhadra.

**Vaiśākā** (S) (F) lioness.

**Vaiṣākhī** (S) (F) 1. the day of full moon in the month of Vaiṣākha. 3. a wife of Vasudeva (*H. Purāṇa*)

**Vaiśālī** (S) (F) 1. the great. 2. princess of Viśālā. 3. a wife of Vasudeva (*V. Purāṇa*); an east Indian kingdom where the Buddha lived.

**Vaiśālinī** (S) (F) 1. daughter of the great. 3. the daughter of King Viśāla and the wife of Avikṣit and the mother of Marutta (*Mā. Purāṇa*)

**Vaiśampāyana** (S) (M) 1. connoisseur of a cup of nectar. 3. a sage who was a pupil of Vyāsa and the narrator of the *Mahābhārata* to Janamejaya (*G. Sutra*); a son of Śukanāsa; the compiler of *Yajur Veda* and the preceptor of Yājñavalkya (*M. Bh.*)

**Vaiṣṇavī** (S) (F) 1. worshipper of Viṣṇu. 3. the Śakti of Viṣṇu; the Nakṣatra Śravana; *asparagus racemosus*; another name for Manasā.

**Vaiśrambhaka** (S) (M) 1. awakening. 2. inspiring confidence. 3. a celestial grove (*Bhā. Purāṇa*)

**Vaiśravaṇa** (S) (M) 1. widely known; belonging to Viśravas. 3. another name for Kubera and Rāvaṇa.

**Vaiṣṭra** (S) (M) the world.

**Vaiśvānara** (S) (M) 1. belonging to all men. 2. omnipresent; worshipped everywhere. 3. an agni (*Ṛg Veda*); a hermit in the palace of Indra (*M. Bh.*); a son of the agni called Bhānu (*M. Bh.*); a son of Kaśyapa and Manu (*Bhāgavata*)

**Vaiśyaputra** (S) (M) 1. son of a Vaiśya woman. 3. another name for Yuyutsu.

**Vaitālin** (S) (M) 1. possessed with ghostly power; magician. 3. a warrior of Skanda (*M. Bh.*)

**Vaitaṇḍa** (S) (M) 1. disputatious; captious. 3. a son of the vasu Āpa (*V. Purāṇa*)

**Vaitaraṇī** (S) (F) 1. crossing over the world. 2. one who helps in crossing over the world; one who takes the devotees up to the other world. 3. the river Gaṅgā when it flows through the world of the manes (*M. Bh.*); a river which gives the lustre of the moon to bathers (*M. Bh.*); a river in Orissa (*M. Bh.*)

**Vaitrāsura** (S) (M) 1. a demon who resides in cane. 2. reed dweller. 3. an asura (*Bhā. Purāṇa*)

**Vaivasvata** (S) (M) 1. belonging to the sun. 3. a rudra (*V. Purāṇa*); the 7th Manu also called Satyavrata who was the son of Vivasvān and the husband of Śraddhā (*Ṛg Veda*), their most prominent children were Yama, Yamī, Aśvinīkumāras, Revanta, Ikṣvāku, Nṛga, Sudyumna, Śaryāti, Kavi, Nabhāga Karūṣa and Pṛśadhra (*M. Bh.*)

**Vaivasvatī** (S) (F) 1. belonging to the sun. 3. another name for the Yamunā river (*M. Bh.*)

**Vāja** (S) (M) 1. strength; vigour; energy; speed. 2. contest; battle; booty; gain; reward; wing; feather; wing. 3. one of the 3 Ṛbhus (*Ṛg Veda*); a son of Laukya; a son of Manu Sāvarṇa; a son of Sudhanvā and grandson of Aṅgiras (*Ṛg Veda*)

**Vājaćandra** (S) (M) moon among the strong.

**Vājajit** (S) (M) reward winner; winning the reward in a contest.

**Vājapati** (S) (M) 1. the lord of reward. 3. another name for Agni.

**Vājapeya** (S) (M) 1. the drink of strength. 3. one of the 7 forms of sacrifice offered by kings or Brāhmins (*A. Veda*)

**Vājaratna** (S) (M) gem of rewards; rich in treasure as the Ṛbhus.

**Vājasaneya** (S) (M) 1. steadfast; vigorous; mighty; awarded; honoured. 3. another name for Yājñavalkya, the author of the *Vajasaneyi Saṃhitā* or the *Śukla Yajur Veda*.

**Vājasani** (S) (M) 1. winning reward; victorious; granting strength. 3. another name for Viṣṇu.

**Vājaśravas** (S) (M) 1. famous for wealth. 3. a son of Naćiketas (*Br. Upaniṣad*)

**Vājin** (S) (M) swift; spirited; heroic; war like; strong; manly; hero; the number 7; arrow; steed.

**Vājineya** (S) (M) son of a hero.

**Vājinīvasu** (S) (M) giving strength and power.

**Vajrā** (S) (F) 1. mighty; strong; hard. 3. another name for Durgā; a daughter of Vaiśvānara (*Ṛg Veda*)

**Vajra** (S) (M) 1. the hard or mighty one; thunderbolt. 2. lightning; diamond; pillar. 3. a mountain (*Rāmāyaṇa*); an asura; a son of Manu Sāvarṇa; a son of Bhūti; a son of Viśvāmitra (*M. Bh.*); the son of Aniruddha who was appointed by Kṛṣṇa to be the king of the remaining Yādavas after the Mausala fight; the monk who succeeded Sinhagiri as the head of the Jaina church (*J. S. Koṣa*); Prickly Pear (*Opuntia dillenii*); *Pavonia odorata*.

**Vajrabāhu** (S) (M) 1. thunderbolt armed. 2. with hard arms. 3. an asura who was the son of the vidyādharī Ćanćalākṣī (*K. Rāmāyaṇa*); another name for Indra, Agni, Rudra.

**Vajrābha** (S) (M) 1. diamond like. 2. opal.

**Vajrabhṛkuti** (S) (F) 1. with a thunderous frown. 3. one of the 6 Buddhist goddesses of magic.

**Vajradakṣiṇa** (S) (M) 1. with a thunderbolt in the right hand. 3. another name for Indra.

**Vajradanṣtra** (S) (M) 1. with adamantine teeth. 2. lion. 3. an asura captain of Tripurāsura (*G. Purāṇa*); a rākṣasa in Rāvaṇa's army (*V. Rāmāyaṇa*); the king of the vidyādharas (*K. Sāgara*)

**Vajradatta** (S) (M) 1. born of a mighty one. 3. the king of Prāgjyotiṣapura who was the son of Bhāgadatta (*M. Bh.*); a king of Puṅḍarikinī (*M. Bh.*)

**Vajradehā** (S) (F) 1. hard bodied. 2. diamond bodied. 3. a goddess.

**Vajradhara** (S) (M) 1. holding a thunderbolt. 3. a Bodhisattva (*B. Literature*); a primordial monotheistić god of Vajrayāna Buddhism; another name for Indra.

**Vajradhātṛ** (S) (F) 1. bearer of the thunderbolt. 3. a Buddhist Śakti.

**Vajradhridhanetra** (S) (M) 1. with thunderous eyes. 3. a king of the yakṣas (*Ṛg Veda*)

**Vajragarbha** (S) (M) 1. the matrix of the thunderbolt. 3. a Bodhisattva.

**Vajraghoṣa** (S) (M) sounding like a thunderbolt.

**Vajrahastā** (S) (F) 1. thunderbolt handed; mighty. 2. diamond handed. 3. a Buddhist goddess.

**Vajrahasta** (S) (M) 1. thunderbolt handed. 3. another name for Indra, the maruts, Agni and Śiva.

**Vajrajit** (S) (M) 1. conquerer of the thunderbolt. 2. powerful. 3. another name for Indra.

**Vajrajvālā** (S) (F) 1. illuminated by a thunderbolt. 2. shining like lightning. 3. a granddaughter of Vairoćana (*Rāmāyaṇa*)

**Vajrakālī** (S) (F) 1. black goddess of lightning. 3. a Jina Śakti (*V. Purāṇa*)

**Vajrakālikā** (S) (F) 1. black goddess of lightning. 3. the mother of Gautama Buddha (*B. Literature*)

**Vajrakāmā** (S) (F) 1. wishing for thunderbolts. 3. a daughter of Maya (*V. Purāṇa*)

**Vajrakaṅkata** (S) (M) 1. with adamantine armour. 3. another name for Hanumān.

**Vajrakarṣana** (S) (M) 1. ploughing with the thunderbolt. 3. another name for Indra.

**Vajraketu** (S) (M) 1. thunderbold bannered. 3. another name for the demon Naraka.

**Vajrakīla** (S) (M) hard nail; thunderbolt.

**Vajramālā** (S) (F) 1. with a diamond necklace. 3. a gandharvī (*K. Vyuha*)

**Vajramaṇi** (S) (M) 1. hard jewel. 2. diamond.

**Vajramati** (S) (M) 1. with diamond like intelligence. 3. a Bodhisattva.

**Vajrāmbujā** (S) (F) 1. thunderbolt of Indra. 3. a goddess (*D. Purāṇa*)

**Vajramitra** (S) (M) friend of Indra.

**Vajramukuṭa** (S) (M) diamond crowned.

**Vajramuṣṭi** (S) (M) 1. grasping a thunderbolt; hard fisted. 3. a gaṇa of Śiva; a rākṣasa son of Mālyavān and Sundarī (*U. Rāmāyaṇa*); another name for Indra.

**Vajranābha** (S) (M) 1. diamond navelled. 3. Kṛṣṇa's discus; a son of Uktha; a dānava (*H. Purāṇa*); a son of Unnābha (*Bhā. Purāṇa*); a warrior of Skanda (*M. Bh.*); a king of the line of Rāma who was the son of Vinda and the father of Khagaṇa (*Bhāgavata*); an asura whose daughter

Prabhāvatī was the wife of Pradyumna (*H. Purāṇa*); a king of Mathurā (*Bhā. Purāṇa*)

**Vajranetra** (S) (M) 1. diamond eyes. 3. a king of the yakṣas.

**Vajrānga** (S) (M) 1. hard limbed; with a curved body. 3. an asura son of Kaśyapa and Diti and the husband of Varāngī and the father of Tarakāsura (*M. Bh.*)

**Vajrāṅkuśī** (S) (F) 1. diamond hooked. 2. stern controller. 3. a goddess.

**Vajrānśu** (S) (M) 1. diamond rayed. 2. as bright as a diamond. 3. a son of Kṛṣṇa (*M. Bh.*)

**Vajrapāṇi** (S) (M) 1. thunderbolt handed. 3. a Bodhisattva; another name for Indra.

**Vajraprabha** (S) (M) 1. as shiny as a diamond. 3. a vidyādhara (*H. Purāṇa*)

**Vajraprabhava** (S) (M) 1. diamond born. 2. bright as a diamond. 3. a king of the Karūṣas.

**Vajraprastāriṇī** (S) (F) 1. extender of the thunderbolt. 3. a tāntric goddess (*Ṛg Veda*)

**Vajrapuṣpam** (S) (M) 1. diamond flower; valuable flower. 2. the blossom of the Sesamum plant.

**Vajrasamhata** (S) (M) 1. attacking like thunderbolts. 3. a Buddha (*B. Literature*)

**Vajrasāra** (S) (M) the essence of a diamond; bright; precious.

**Vajrasattva** (S) (M) 1. with an adamantine soul. 3. another name for a Dhyāni Buddha.

**Vajrasena** (S) (M) 1. diamond armied. 3. a Bodhisattva (*K. Vyuha*); a king of Śrāvastī.

**Vajraśīrṣa** (S) (M) 1. diamond headed. 3. a son of Bhṛgu (*M. Bh.*)

**Vajraśrī** (S) (F) 1. divine diamond. 3. a gandharvī (*K. Vyuha*)

**Vajraśṛnkhalā** (S) (F) 1. diamond chain. 3. one of the 16 Jaina vidyādevīs.

**Vajrasūrya** (S) (M) 1. thunderbolt and sun conjoined. 3. a Buddha.

**Vajraṭa** (S) (M) 1. severe; hard; impregnable. 3. the father of Uvata.

**Vajraṭīka** (S) (M) 1. diamond like. 3. a Buddha.

**Vajratulya** (S) (M) resembling a diamond.

**Vajratuṇḍa** (S) (M) 1. hard beaked; hard tusked. 3. another name for Garuḍa and Gaṇeśa.

**Vajravālā** (S) (F) 1. stern maiden; a maiden with diamonds. 3. a daughter of Mahābalī and wife of Kumbhakarṇa (*U. Rāmāyaṇa*)

**Vajravallī** (S) (F) valuable vine; Sunflower (*Heliotropium indicum*)

**Vajravārāhī** (S) (F) 1. as strong as a boar. 3. a tāntric goddess.

**Vajravega** (S) (M) 1. as swift as lightning. 3. a giant brother of Khara and the attendant of Kumbhakarṇa (*M. Bh.*); a vidyādhara (*H. Purāṇa*)

**Vajravelu** (S) (M) 1. with a diamond hard plough. 3. another name for Balarāma.

**Vajravidrāviṇī** (S) (F) 1. defeating with a thunderbolt. 3. a Buddhist goddess.

**Vajravīra** (S) (M) 1. strong warrior. 3. another name for Mahākāla.

**Vajraviṣkambha** (S) (M) 1. hurling the thunderbolt; a hard support. 3. a son of Garuḍa (*M. Bh.*)

**Vajrayoginī** (S) (F) 1. stern meditator. 3. a goddess.

**Vajrāyudha** (S) (M) 1. thunderbolt armed. 3. another name for Indra and the weapon of Indra.

**Vajrendra** (S) (M) 1. lord of the thunderbolt. 3. another name for Indra.

**Vajreśvarī** (S) (F) 1. goddess of the thunderbolt. 3. a Buddhist goddess.

**Vajrijit** (S) (M) 1. conqueror of Indra. 3. another name for Garuḍa.

**Vajrin** (S) (M) 1. holding a thunderbolt; wielder of the Vajra weapon. 3. another name for Indra; a viśvadeva (*M. Bh.*)

**Vajrodarī** (S) (F) 1. hard bellied. 3. a rākṣasī (*Bhā. Purāṇa*)

**Vākā** (S) (F) 1. word; speech. 2. text; recitation. 3. the daughter of Mālyavān and the wife of Viśravas she was the mother of Triśiras, Dūṣana, Vidyujjihvā and Anupālikā.

**Vakanakha** (S) (M) 1. with crooked nails. 3. a son of Viśvāmitra (*M. Bh.*)

**Vākapati** (S) (M) 1. lord of speech. 3. another name for Bṛhaspati.

**Vākaprada** (S) (F) 1. giver of speech. 3. another name for the river Sarasvatī

(*V. Rāmāyaṇa*)

**Vākasiddha** (S) (M) perfection in speech.

**Vākinī** (S) (F) 1. one who recites. 3. a tāntric deity.

**Vakman** (S) (M) utterance; speech; hymn of praise.

**Vākmya** (S) (M) to be worthy of praise.

**Vakra** (S) (M) 1. crooked; curled. 2. cunning; cruel. 3. another name for the planets Mars and Saturn, Rudra, the asura Bāṇa.

**Vakrabhuja** (S) (M) 1. crooked armed. 3. another name for Gaṇeśa.

**Vakradanta** (S) (M) 1. crooked teeth. 3. a prince of the Karūṣas (*M. Bh.*)

**Vakrapāda** (S) (M) 1. crooked legged. 3. another name for Gaṇeśa.

**Vakratu** (S) (M) 1. crooked. 3. a deity (*Mā. Purāṇa*)

**Vakratuṇḍa** (S) (M) 1. with a curved trunk. 3. another name for Gaṇeśa.

**Vakṣa** (S) (M) chest; breast; strength giving; nourishing.

**Vakṣanā** (S) (F) the nourisher; the bed of a river; refreshment; oblation; flame.

**Vakṣana** (S) (M) nourishing; strengthening; refreshing; invigorating.

**Vakṣani** (S) (F) strengthening.

**Vakṣī** (S) (F) strength; nourishment; flame.

**Vakṣogrīva** (S) (M) 1. ox necked. 2. proud and strong. 3. a son of Viśvāmitra (*M. Bh.*)

**Vakṣomaṇi** (S) (M) a jewel worn on the breast.

**Vakṣu** (S) (M) 1. refreshing. 3. the Oxus river.

**Vakti** (S) (F) speech.

**Vaktṛ** (S) (M) speaker; eloquent; learned; wise.

**Vaktraja** (S) (M) 1. born of the mouth of Brahmā. 2. a Brāhmin.

**Vaktrāmbuja** (S) (M) with a lotus like face.

**Vaktrayodhin** (S) (M) 1. fighting with the mouth. 3. an asura (*H. Purāṇa*)

**Vaktrendu** (S) (M) with a moonlike face.

**Vakula** (S) (M) crooked; curved.

**Vala** (S) (M) 1. enclosure; cave; beam; pole. 3. an asura killed by Indra (*P. Purāṇa*)

**Valabhi** (S) (M) 1. the pinnacle of a house. 3. a 7th century king.

**Valāka** (S) (M) 1. beam; pole. 3. a sage under Manu Tāmasa (*Rg Veda*)

**Valārāti** (S) (M) 1. enemy of Vala. 3. another name for Indra.

**Valāsaka** (S) (M) 1. handsome. 3. the Koel or Indian Cuckoo (*Cuculus varius*)

**Valaśiphā** (S) (F) 1. curled hair. 3. a yoginī (*D. Purāṇa*)

**Valayā** (S) (F) 1. coiled. 2. bracelet; armlet; ring.

**Valgu** (S) (M) 1. handsome; beautiful; attractive. 3. one of the 4 tutelary deities of the Bodhi tree (*L. Vistara*)

**Valgujangha** (S) (M) 1. handsome legged. 3. a son of Viśvāmitra (*M. Bh.*)

**Valguka** (S) (M) very handsome.

**Vālgukī** (S) (F) very beautiful.

**Vālihantri** (S) (M) 1. slayer of Vāli. 3. another name for Rāma.

**Valīmukha** (S) (M) 1. with a wrinkled face. 3. a monkey in Rāma's army (*V. Rāmāyaṇa*)

**Vālin** (S) (M) 1. hairy; tailed. 3. a monkey who was the son of Indra and elder brother of Sugrīva (*Rāmāyaṇa*)

**Vālinī** (S) (F) 1. tailed. 3. the constellation Aśvinī (*M. Bh.*)

**Vāliśikha** (S) (M) 1. with a crest of hair. 3. a nāga (*M. Bh.*)

**Valkala** (S) (M) 1. the bark of a tree. 3. a daitya (*M. Bh.*)

**Vallabhā** (S) (F) beloved.

**Vallabha** (S) (M) 1. beloved. 2. above all; favourite; desired; cowherd. 3. a son of Balākāśva and the father of Kuśika (*V. Rāmāyaṇa*)

**Vallabhāćārya** (S) (M) 1. beloved teacher. 3. a celebrated Vaiṣṇava teacher and author of commentaries on the Purāṇas and Vedānta (15th century)

**Vallabhānanda** (S) (M) rejoicing in being loved.

**Vallabhendra** (S) (M) Indra among the beloved; best beloved.

**Vallabheśvara** (S) (M) most beloved; god among the beloved.

**Vallakī** (S) (F) a lute.

**Vallarī** (S) (F) 1. cluster of blossoms. 2. creeper. 3. another name for Sītā.

**Vallārī** (S) (F) 1. vine. 3. a rāgiṇī.

**Vallarikā** (S) (F) vine.

**Vallava** (S) (M) 1. cowherd. 3. another name for Bhīma in the court of king Virāta.

**Vallī** (S) (F) 1. creeper; vine. 2. lightning. 3. a daughter of Ira and mother of vines; another name for the earth.

**Vallikā** (S) (F) 1. covered with vines; covered with plants, greenery. 3. diminutive for the earth; Velvet Leaf (*Cissampelos pareira*)

**Vallikāgra** (S) (M) 1. tip of a vine. 2. coral.

**Vallura** (S) (M) arbour; bower; a cluster of blossoms.

**Vālmīki** (S) (M) 1. from a white anthill. 3. a hermit who is 1st among poets and the author of the *Valmiki Rāmāyaṇa* and is said to have been the 10th son of Varuṇa, from dacoity he turned to religion and built a hermitage in Bāṇḍā in Bundelkhand where he received Sītā when banished by Rāma, he is now a member of the palace of Indra (*M. Bh.*); a son of Garuḍa (*M. Bh.*)

**Vāmā** (S) (F) 1. beautiful. 3. a form of Durgā; a mother in Skanda's retinue; a queen of Kāśī and mother of Jaina Tirathankara Pārśvanātha; a village goddess who represents a fierce class of yoginīs (*Purāṇas*); another name for Lakṣmī and Sarasvatī.

**Vāma** (S) (M) 1. lovely; dear; pleasant; splendid; noble. 3. a rudra (*Bhā. Purāṇa*); a son of Ṛćika; a son of Kṛṣṇa and Bhadrā; a son of Dharma (*Bhā. Purāṇa*); a horse of the moon (*V. Purāṇa*); an attendant of Skanda (*M. Bh.*); another name for Śiva, Kāma and Varuṇa.

**Vāmadatta** (S) (M) given by Śiva.

**Vāmadeva** (S) (M) 1. noble lord. 3. one of the 5 faces of Śiva; a hermit who was the son of King Parīkṣit and Suśobhanā (*M. Bh.*); a son of Manu and Śatarūpā who was an incarnation of Śiva (*M. Purāṇa*); a ṛṣi and part author of *Rg Veda* (iv); a minister of Daśaratha; a son of Nārāyaṇa (*Ṛg Veda*); father of Viśvanātha (*H. Purāṇa*); another name for Śiva.

**Vāmaka** (S) (M) 1. hard; cruel; rough; left; contrary. 3. a king of Kāśī (*M. Bh.*); a son of Bhajamāna (*V. Purāṇa*); a ćakravartin.

**Vāmākṣī** (S) (F) fair eyed.

**Vāmaloćanā** (S) (F) 1. fair eyed. 3. a daughter of Vīraketu (*V. Ćaritam*)

**Vāmanā** (S) (F) 1. short. 3. an apsarā (*M. Bh.*)

**Vāmana** (S) (M) 1. small; short; dwarf. 3. the 5th incarnation of Mahāviṣṇu who was born as the dwarf son of Kaśyapa and Aditi to defeat the asura Mahābali (*Bhāgavata*); one of the 8 elephants supporting the universe and the son of Irāvatī (*M. Bh.*); a nāga; a son of Garuḍa (*M. Bh.*); a son of Hiraṇyagarbha (*H. Purāṇa*); one of the 18 attendants of the sun (*H. Purāṇa*); a dānava (*H. Purāṇa*)

**Vāmanabhattabāṇa** (S) (M) 1. the arrow of the noble dwarf. 2. subtle. 3. a Sanskṛt poet (15th century)

**Vāmanī** (S) (F) 1. bringing wealth; short; dwarf. 3. a yoginī (*H. C. Ćintāmaṇi*)

**Vāmanikā** (S) (F) 1. dwarfish; small. 3. an attendant of Skanda (*M. Bh.*)

**Vāmikā** (S) (F) 1. situated on the left side; consort of Vāma. 3. another name for Durgā (*D. Purāṇa*)

**Vana** (S) (M) 1. forest; cluster of plants; water; fountain; spring; longing; desire. 3. a son of Uśīnara (*Bhā. Purāṇa*)

**Vāna** (S) (M) 1. intelligent. 3. another name for Yama.

**Vanaćampaka** (S) (M) the wild Ćampaka tree (*Michelia champaka*)

**Vanaćandana** (S) (M) the sandalwood of the forest; the Devadāru tree (*Pinus deodora*)

**Vanaćandrikā** (S) (F) 1. moon rays of the jungle. 2. *Jasminum Sambac*.

**Vanada** (S) (M) 1. bestowing; longing; desire; desirable; rain giving. 2. a cloud.

**Vanadeva** (S) (M) forest god.

**Vanadurgā** (S) (F) 1. goddess of the forest; dweller of the forest. 3. a form of Durgā (*D. Purāṇa*)

**Vanadvāja** (S) (M) 1. desiring strength and energy. 3. son of Śući.

**Vanahāsa** (S) (M) 1. smile of the forest. 3. Musk Jasmine (*Jasminum pubescens*)

**Vanajā** (S) (F) 1. forest born; sylvan; wild; water born. 3. Blue Lotus flower (*Nymphaea* *stellata*)

**Vanajākṣī** (S) (F) blue lotus eyed.

**Vanajam** (S) (M) Blue Lotus (*Nymphaea stellata*)

**Vanajāyata** (S) (F) resembling a lotus.

**Vanajyotsnī** (S) (F) 1. light of the jungle. 2. Jasmine.

**Vanakapīvat** (S) (M) 1. resembling a wild monkey. 3. a son of Pulaha (*M. Bh.*)

**Vanalakṣmī** (S) (F) 1. ornament of the forest; fortune of the forest; treasure of the forest. 2. Banana (*Musa sapientum*)

**Vanalatā** (S) (F) creeper of the forest; vine.

**Vanalikā** (S) (F) 1. of forest. 3. Sunflower (*Heliotrope indicum*)

**Vanamālā** (S) (F) garland of the forest; a garland of wild flowers; flower braid.

**Vanamālikā** (S) (F) 1. garland of the forest. 2. garland of wild flowers. 3. a friend of Rādhā; a river (*H. Purāṇa*); *Michelia champaka*.

**Vanamālin** (S) (M) 1. wearing a garland of wild flowers. 3. another name for Kṛṣṇa.

**Vanamālīśā** (S) (F) 1. desired by the gardener of forest. 2. lady of the forest gardener; with Kṛṣṇa as consort. 3. another name for Rādhā.

**Vanamallī** (S) (F) wild Jasmine.

**Vanamallikā** (S) (F) *Jasminum sambac*.

**Vanāmbikā** (S) (F) 1. mother of forest. 3. the tutelary deity of the family of Dakṣa (*K. Sāgara*)

**Vanana** (S) (M) longing; desire.

**Vananātha** (S) (M) 1. controller of forest. 2. a lion.

**Vananitya** (S) (M) 1. with an eternal longing. 3. a son of Raudrāśva (*H. Purāṇa*)

**Vanapāla** (S) (M) 1. protector of forest. 3. a son of Devapāla.

**Vanapriya** (S) (M) 1. beloved of forest. 2. the Indian cuckoo; the Cinnamon tree.

**Vanapuṣpā** (S) (F) flower of the forest; wild flower.

**Vanarāja** (S) (M) 1. lord of the forest. 2. lion; *Bauhinia racemosa*.

**Vānaraketu** (S) (M) 1. monkey bannered. 3. another name for Arjuna.

**Vanaraśmi** (S) (F) light of forest; a ray of light.

**Vānarendra** (S) (M) 1. lord of monkeys. 3. another name for Hanumān.

**Vanas** (S) (M) loveliness; longing; desire.

**Vanasarojinī** (S) (F) lotus of the forest; the wild cotton plant; collection of wild lotuses.

**Vanaśobhana** (S) (F) 1. water; beautifying. 2. lotus (*Nelumbo speciosum*)

**Vanaspatī** (S) (F) 1. protector of the forest. 2. plants; trees; vegetables. 3. a gandharvī (*K. Vyuha*)

**Vanaspati** (S) (M) 1. king of the forest. 2. the Indian Fig tree (*Ficus indica*); the Soma plant; wooden beam; ascetic. 3. a son of King Ghṛtapṛṣṭha (*Bhāgavata*); another name for Kṛṣṇa.

**Vanastamba** (S) (M) 1. pillar of the forest. 2. a bunch of wild flowers; a wild thicket. 3. a son of Gaḍa (*H. Purāṇa*)

**Vanathi** (S) (F) of the forest.

**Vanāyu** (S) (M) 1. long lived; like a forest. 3. a son of Kaśyapa and Dānu (*M. Bh.*); a son of Urvaśī and Purūravas (*M. Bh.*)

**Vānća** (S) (F) wish; desire.

**Vanćita** (S) (M) wished; desired; beloved.

**Vanćula** (S) (M) 1. a cow that gives a lot of milk. 3. a bird whose cry forbodes victory (*V. Rāmāyaṇa*)

**Vandanā** (S) (F) 1. praise; worship; adoration. 3. a river famous in the Purāṇas (*M. Bh.*)

**Vandana** (S) (M) 1. praise; worship; adoration. 3. a hermit saved from an asura by the Aśvinikumāras (*Ṛg Veda*)

**Vandanavāra** (S) (M) a sequence of adorations; a wreath of green leaves hung on auspicious occasions.

**Vandāru** (S) (M) praising; celebrating; respectful; polite.

**Vandatha** (S) (M) deserving praise.

**Vandin** (S) (M) 1. one who praises. 2. one who honours; a class of poets and scholars who sing songs of praise in the royal courts. 3. a scholar in King Janaka's court (*V. Rāmāyaṇa*)

**Vandinikā** (S) (F) 1. honoured; praised. 3. another name for Dākṣāyanī.

**Vanditā** (S) (F) praised; worshipped.

**Vandita** (S) (M) praised; extolled; celebrated.

**Vanditṛ** (S) (M) one who praises.

**Vandra** (S) (M) worshipping.

**Vandyā** (S) (F) 1. praiseworthy; adorable. 3. a yakṣi.

**Vaneyu** (S) (M) 1. residing in the forest. 2. hermit; ascetic. 3. a king who was the son of Raudrāśva and Miśrakeśī (*M. Bh.*)

**Vaṅga** (S) (M) 1. Bengal. 3. a king of the lunar race who was a son of Dīrghatamas and who is regarded as the ancestor of the people of Bengal (*M. Bh*); a mountain.

**Vāṅgāla** (S) (M) 1. of Vaṅga. 3. a rāga.

**Vāṅgālī** (S) (F) 1. belonging to Bengal. 3. a rāgiṇī.

**Vāṇī** (S) (F) 1. speech; praise; sweet in voice. 2. sound; voice; music. 3. another name for Sarasvatī (*Ṛg Veda*)

**Vānī** (S) (F) wish; desire.

**Vāṇići** (S) (F) speech.

**Vāṇija** (S) (M) 1. merchant; trader; submarine fire. 3. the zodiac sign of Libra; another name for Śiva.

**Vāṇimayī** (S) (F) 1. goddess of speech. 3. another name for Sarasvatī.

**Vāṇinī** (S) (F) soft voiced; a clever and intriguing woman.

**Vāṇīśrī** (S) (F) 1. divine speech. 3. another name for Sarasvatī.

**Vaniṣṭha** (S) (M) very munificent; very generous.

**Vanitā** (S) (F) wished for; desired; loved; woman.

**Vanita** (S) (M) wished for; desired; loved.

**Vanjula** (S) (M) 1. of the beauty of the forest. 2. the Aśoka tree (*Saraca indica*); *Hibiscus mutabilis*; Chairbottom Cane (*Calamus rotang*); Chariot tree (*Ougeinia oojeinensis*)

**Vanjulā** (S) (F) 1. a cow that has an abundance of milk. 3. a river (*Ma. Purāṇa*)

**Vankālakāćārya** (S) (M) 1. crooked teacher. 3. an astronomer who wrote in Prakṛt.

**Vaṅksu** (S) (F) 1. arm. 2. a tributary of the Gaṅgā.

**Vaṅmali** (S) (M) 1. eloquent. 3. a sacred river.

**Vanmayī** (S) (F) 1. goddess of speech. 3. another name for Sarasvatī.

**Vanśā** (S) (F) 1. offspring; daughter; bamboo; lineage. 3. an apsarā daughter of Kaśyapa and Prādhā (*M. Bh.*); Indian Dammer tree (*Shorea robusta*); Solid Bamboo (*Dendrocalamus strictus*)

**Vanśadhārā** (S) (F) 1. perpetuating the race. 3. a river rising from the Mahendra mountain.

**Vanśaja** (S) (M) from a good family.

**Vanśakara** (S) (M) perpetuating a race; son.

**Vanśalakṣmī** (S) (F) the family fortune.

**Vanśapota** (S) (M) bamboo shoot; offspring of a good family.

**Vanśarāja** (S) (M) lord of the race.

**Vanśavardhana** (S) (M) bringing prosperity to the family; son.

**Vanśī** (S) (F) flute; pipe; artery.

**Vanśīdhara** (S) (M) 1. holding a flute. 3. another name for Kṛṣṇa.

**Vanśikā** (S) (F) flute.

**Vanu** (S) (F) 1. zealous; eager. 2. friend. 3. a river of heaven (*Ṛg Veda*)

**Vānyā** (S) (F) 1. sylvan. 3. Rosary Pea (*Arbus precatorius*)

**Vanyavid** (S) (M) 1. knower of the forest. 3. a ṛṣi. (*M. Bh.*)

**Vapodara** (S) (M) 1. corpulent. 3. another name for Indra (*Ṛg Veda*)

**Vaprā** (S) (F) 1. garden bed. 3. the mother of the Arhat Nimi (*J. S. Koṣa*)

**Vapra** (S) (M) 1. rampart; shore; bank; father. 3. a son of the 14th Manu (*H. Purāṇa*)

**Vapu** (S) (F) 1. body. 3. an apsarā (*M. Bh.*)

**Vapuna** (S) (M) 1. bodyless; formless. 2. a god; knowledge.

**Vapunandana** (S) (M) son of the body.

**Vapurdhara** (S) (M) embodied; handsome; with a beautiful form.

**Vapuṣā** (S) (F) 1. embodied. 2. wonderfully beautiful; handsome; beauty; nature. 3. a daughter of Dakṣa and wife of Dharma (*V. Purāṇa*); an apsarā who was reborn as the daughter of Kundhara and Menakā (*Mā. Purāṇa*)

**Vapuṣa** (S) (M) embodied; wonderful; admirable.

**Vapuṣī** (S) (F) **1.** embodied. **2.** wonderfully beautiful. **3.** beauty personified as a daughter of Dakṣa (*V. Purāṇa*); an apsarā (*V. Purāṇa*)

**Vapuṣmān** (S) (M) **1.** possessing a body; embodied; possessing a beautiful body. **3.** the son of King Sankrandana of Vidarbha (*Mā. Purāṇa*)

**Vapuṣmat** (S) (M) **1.** embodied. **2.** handsome. **3.** a viśvadeva (*H. Purāṇa*); a son of Priyavrata (*Purāṇas*); a ṛṣi in the 11th Manvantara (*V. Purāṇa*); a king of Kuṇḍina (*V. Purāṇa*)

**Vapuṣmatī** (S) (F) **1.** having a form. **2.** beautifully formed. **3.** a mother attending on Skanda; the daughter of the king of Sindhu and wife of Mārutta (*Mā. Purāṇa*)

**Vapuṣṭamā** (S) (F) **1.** best among the embodied. **2.** wonderfully beautiful. **3.** the daughter of King Suvarṇavarmā of Kāśī and wife of Janamejaya and the mother of Śatānika and Śankukarṇa (*M. Bh.*); *Hibiscus mutabilis*.

**Vapuṣṭama** (S) (M) best in form; most beautiful; most wonderful.

**Vapusya** (S) (M) possessing a form; wonderfully beautiful or handsome.

**Varā** (S) (F) **1.** boon; choice; gift; reward; benefit; blessing. **3.** a river; another name for Pārvatī and Ćhāyā.

**Vara** (S) (M) **1.** boon; choice; gift; reward; benefit; blessing. **2.** choosing; best; valuable; excellent; royal. **3.** a son of Svaphalka (*V. Purāṇa*); *Curcuma longa*.

**Varadā** (S) (F) **1.** giver of boons. **2.** girl; maiden. **3.** a deity; a river (*M. Bh.*); a yoginī (*H. Ć. Ćintāmaṇi*)

**Varada** (S) (M) **1.** granting wishes. **3.** a ṛṣi in the 4th Manvantara (*V. Purāṇa*); a Dhyāni Buddha (*B. Literature*); a warrior of Skanda (*M. Bh.*); another name for Agni.

**Varadarāja** (S) (M) **1.** lord of boons. **3.** another name for Viṣṇu.

**Varadhā** (S) (M) granter of a boon.

**Varadharmin** (S) (M) noble; very religious.

**Varādi** (S) (M) **1.** group of excellence; cause of excellence. **3.** a rāga.

**Varagātra** (S) (M) fair limbed; beautiful.

**Varaghaṇṭa** (S) (M) **1.** gift of Śiva. **3.** another name for Skanda.

**Varāha** (S) (M) **1.** boar. **2.** superiority; preeminence. **3.** a hermit in the palace of Yudhiṣṭhira (*M. Bh.*); one of the 10 incarnations of Mahāviṣṇu who was born of the nose of Brahmā to destroy Hiraṇyākṣa and Hiraṇyakaṣipu.

**Varāhadatta** (S) (M) given by Viṣṇu.

**Varāhadeva** (S) (M) Viṣṇu as the boar.

**Varāhaka** (S) (M) **1.** boar like. **3.** a serpent born in the family of Dhṛtarāṣṭra (*M. Bh.*)

**Varāhakarṇa** (S) (M) **1.** boar eared. **3.** a yakṣa (*M. Bh.*)

**Varāhāmba** (S) (M) **1.** making others bow down. **3.** an asura (*M. Bh.*)

**Varāhamihira** (S) (M) **1.** Viṣṇu and the sun conjoined. **3.** an astrologer who was one of the 9 gems at King Vikramādityā's court (*K. Granthāvali*)

**Varāhaśṛnga** (S) (M) **1.** boar horned. **3.** another name for Śiva.

**Vārāhī** (S) (F) **1.** consort of boar. **2.** sow. **3.** the female energy of the boar form of Viṣṇu; a mother attending on Skanda (*M. Bh.*); Bulb bearing Yam (*Dioscorea bulbifera*); Nut Grass (*Cyperus rotundis*)

**Varajākṣi** (S) (F) with lotus eyes.

**Varajānuka** (S) (M) **1.** preceptor of the noble. **2.** disciple of a noble preceptor. **3.** a ṛṣi (*M. Bh.*)

**Varakratu** (S) (M) **1.** doer of good deeds; granter of boons. **3.** another name for Indra.

**Varāli** (S) (M) **1.** friend of the noble. **2.** the moon. **3.** a rāga.

**Varālikā** (S) (F) **1.** goddess of power. **2.** controller of the army. **3.** another name for Durgā.

**Varaṇā** (S) (F) **1.** surrounding; enclosing **2.** rampart. **3.** a holy river flowing past north Benaras now called Barnā (*M. Bh.*)

**Varānanā** (S) (F) **1.** beautiful faced. **3.** an apsarā (*M. Bh.*)

**Varanārī** (S) (F) best woman.

**Vārāṇasī** (S) (F) **1.** granting boons. **3.** holy place of pilgrimage between the rivers Varaṇā and Asi, it was also known as Prayāga and Kāśi.

**Vāranātha** (S) (M) **1.** lord of the waters. **2.** ocean; cloud. **3.** another name for Varuṇa.

**Varanganā** (S) (F) beautiful.

**Vārāṅgī** (S) (F) **1.** having a beautiful body. **3.** the wife of Vajrāṅga and mother of Tārakāsura; the wife of King Saṁyati of the lunar dynasty and the mother of Ahaṁyati (*M. Bh.*)

**Varāṅgī** (S) (F) **1.** with an elegant form. **2.** turmeric. **3.** the daughter of Dhṛṣadvata; the wife of the asura Vajrānga.

**Varapakṣiṇī** (S) (F) **1.** well feathered. **3.** a tāntric goddess.

**Varaprabha** (S) (M) **1.** of best brightness. **2.** brightest. **3.** a Bodhisattva.

**Varapradā** (S) (F) **1.** granting wishes. **3.** a yoginī (*H. Ć. Ćintāmaṇi*); another name for Lopāmudrā.

**Vārarāja** (S) (M) **1.** lord of the waters. **3.** another name for Varuṇa.

**Varāraka** (S) (M) **1.** magnificent stone. **2.** diamond.

**Varārohā** (S) (F) **1.** handsome; elegant; fine rider; fine hipped. **3.** Dākṣāyānī in Someśvara.

**Varāroha** (S) (M) **1.** an excellent rider; with fine hips. **3.** another name for Viṣṇu.

**Vararući** (S) (M) **1.** taking pleasure in boons. **3.** an ancient scholar of astronomy and astrology who is supposed to have been the incarnation of an attendant of Śiva called Puṣpadanta born to Somadatta; a grammarian, poet and author of the *Varttikas*, who is placed among the 9 gems of Vikramāditya (*Panćatantra*)

**Vararūpa** (S) (M) **1.** with an excellent form. **3.** a Buddha (*L. Vistara*)

**Varaśikha** (S) (M) **1.** well crested. **3.** an asura (*Ṛg Veda*)

**Varastrī** (S) (F) **1.** noble woman. **3.** a sister of Bṛhaspati and wife of the vasu Prabhāsa (*M. Bh.*)

**Varasyā** (S) (F) request; wish; desire.

**Varatama** (S) (M) **1.** best among excellent. **2.** most preferable.

**Varatantu** (S) (M) **1.** well clad. **3.** the preceptor of the hermit Kautsa (*H. Ć. Ćintāmaṇi*)

**Varatanu** (S) (M) **1.** with an excellent body. **3.** a Kuru dynasty king.

**Varatara** (S) (M) most excellent.

**Varatri** (S) (M) **1.** desiring. **2.** chooser; wooer. **3.** a son of Śuka.

**Varavarṇinī** (S) (F) **1.** with a beautiful complexion. **3.** another name for Durgā, Lakṣmī and Sarasvatī.

**Varavṛddha** (S) (M) **1.** eldest among the best. **3.** another name for Śiva.

**Varayoṣita** (S) (F) a beautiful woman.

**Varayu** (S) (M) **1.** best born. **3.** a king of the family of Mahaujas (*M. Bh.*)

**Varćas** (S) (M) **1.** vigour; energy; brilliance; lustre; light; colour; form; figure; shape. **3.** the son of the vasu Soma and Manoharā, he was reborn as Abhimanyu; the son of the hermit Sućetas and the father of Vihavya (*M. Bh.*); a son of Sutejas; a rākṣasa.

**Varćasvin** (S) (M) **1.** vigorous; energetic. **2.** active. **3.** a son of Varćas and grandson of Soma.

**Varćāvasu** (S) (M) **1.** sun-beam. **3.** a gandharva (*V. Purāṇa*)

**Vārddhakṣatrī** (S) (M) **1.** descended from Vṛddhakṣhatra. **3.** another name for Jayadratha.

**Vārdhakṣemi** (S) (M) **1.** looking after elders. **3.** a king of the Vṛṣṇi dynasty who fought on the side of the Pāṇḍavas (*M. Bh.*)

**Vardhamāna** (S) (M) **1.** striving to prosper; crescent moon; increasing; growing; prosperous. **3.** another name for Viṣṇu (*Bhā. Purāṇa*); the 24th Arhat; one of the 8 elephants that support the world (*J.S. Koṣa*)

**Vardhamānamati** (S) (M) **1.** with a growing intellect. **3.** a Bodhisattva.

**Vardhana** (S) (M) **1.** increasing; growing. **2.** animator; bestower of prosperity. **3.** a son of Kṛṣṇa and Mitravindā (*Bhā. Purāṇa*); an attendant of Skanda (*M. Bh.*); another name for Śiva (*M. Bh.*)

**Vardhanasūrī** (S) (M) **1.** prosperous sun. **3.** a Jaina preceptor (*J.S. Koṣa*)

**Vardhin** (S) (M) increasing; augmenting.

**Vardhita** (S) (M) **1.** increased. **2.** augmented; strengthened; gladdened.

**Varendra** (S) (M) **1.** lord of the nobles. **2.** chief; sovereign.

**Vareṇyā** (S) (F) **1.** desirable. **3.** Śiva's wife

(*Ś. Purāṇa*); Saffron (*Crocus sativus*)

**Vareṇya** (S) (M) 1. to be wished for; desirable. 3. a son of Bhṛgu (*M. Bh.*)

**Vareśa** (S) (M) presiding over boons.

**Vareśvara** (S) (M) 1. god of boons. 2. able to grant all wishes. 3. another name for Śiva.

**Vargā** (S) (F) 1. belonging to a division; belonging to a set or group. 3. an apsarā changed into a crocodile who was released from her curse by Arjuna.

**Vārī** (S) (F) 1. rich in gifts; goddess of speech; water. 3. another name for Sarasvatī (*Ṛg Veda*)

**Varī** (S) (F) stream; river.

**Varīdāsa** (S) (M) 1. devotee of water. 3. the father of the gandharva Nārada (*K. Sāgara*)

**Vāridhi** (S) (M) 1. treasure of water. 2. ocean.

**Vārija** (S) (M) 1. born of water. 2. lotus (*Nelumbo speciosum*)

**Vārijākṣā** (S) (F) lotus eyed.

**Varīman** (S) (M) best; expanse; width; breadth.

**Varin** (S) (M) 1. rich in gifts. 3. a viśvadeva (*M. Bh.*)

**Varīndra** (S) (M) lord of the chosen.

**Vāripa** (S) (M) 1. lord of water. 3. another name for Varuṇa.

**Variṣā** (S) (F) the rainy season.

**Vāriśa** (S) (M) 1. sleeping on the ocean. 3. another name for Viṣṇu.

**Vārīṣa** (S) (M) 1. lord of the waters. 2. ocean. 3. another name for Varuṇa.

**Varīṣāpriya** (S) (M) 1. friend of the rains. 3. the Ćātaka bird (*Clamator jacobinus serratus*) (*T. Brāhmaṇa*)

**Vārisena** (S) (M) 1. lord of water. 3. a king in the palace of Yama (*M. Bh.*)

**Variṣṭha** (S) (M) 1. most excellent. 2. best; chief. 3. a son of Manu Ćākṣuṣa (*H. Purāṇa*)

**Variṣu** (S) (M) 1. chooser of the best. 3. another name for Kāma.

**Varītākṣa** (S) (M) 1. with wooing eyes. 3. an asura (*M. Bh.*)

**Varivasyā** (S) (F) service; devotion; obedience; honour.

**Varīyas** (S) (M) 1. excellent; best. 3. a son of Manu Sāvarṇa (*H. Purāṇa*); a son of Pulaha and Gati (*Bh. Purāṇa*); another name for Śiva.

**Varjā** (S) (F) 1. water born. 2. lotus (*Nelumbo speciosum*)

**Vārkṣī** (S) (M) 1. relating to trees; arboreous. 3. the daughter of sage Kaṇḍu and the wife of the 10 Praćetases she was the mother of Dakṣa (*Bhāgavata*)

**Varmaćit** (S) (M) 1. protected by the mind. 3. a king of the Lunar dynasty (*Bhāgavata*)

**Varṇakavi** (S) (M) 1. arranger of verse. 3. a son of Kubera.

**Varṇamātṛkā** (S) (F) 1. mother of speech. 3. another name for Sarasvatī.

**Varṇapuṣpī** (S) (F) 1. the coloured flower. 2. Amaranth Lily (*Echinops echinatus*)

**Varṇikā** (S) (F) of fine colour; fine gold; the purity of gold.

**Varṇu** (S) (M) 1. coloured. 2. the sun.

**Varpeyu** (S) (M) 1. master of forms. 2. designer. 3. a son of Raudrāśva (*V. Purāṇa*)

**Varṣā** (S) (F) rain; the rainy season.

**Varṣa** (S) (M) 1. year; cloud. 3. the teacher of Vararući.

**Vārṣagaṇya** (S) (M) 1. whose years are counted. 3. a hermit and preceptor of the gandharva King Viśvāvasu (*M. Bh.*)

**Varṣaketu** (S) (M) 1. cloud bannered. 3. a son of Ketumat (*H. Purāṇa*); a Purū king who was the son of Kṣemaka and the father of Vipu (*A. Purāṇa*)

**Varṣāmada** (S) (M) 1. rejoicing in the rain. 2. peacock.

**Varṣandhara** (S) (M) 1. bearer of rain; cloud. 3. a ṛṣi.

**Vārṣikī** (S) (F) 1. belonging to the rainy season; yearly. 2. *Jasminum sambac*.

**Varṣman** (S) (M) 1. body. 2. auspicious; handsome; great.

**Vārṣṇeya** (S) (M) 1. of the Vṛṣṇi clan. 3. patronymic of Kṛṣṇa; a charioteer of King Nala; another name for Mahāviṣṇu (*M. Bh.*)

**Vārtta** (S) (M) 1. healthy; right; with means of subsistance. 3. a king in the palace of Yama (*M. Bh.*)

**Vārttā** (S) (F) news; intelligence; tidings.

**Vartula** (S) (M) 1. round; circular. 2. a pea.

3. an attendant of Śiva.

**Varuṇa** (S) (M) **1.** all enveloping sky. **3.** an āditya who is one of the oldest Vedic gods and was regarded as the supreme deity, he is described as fashioning and upholding heaven and earth and the guardian of immortality (*Ṛg Veda*); one of the 8 guardians of the quarters, he is the guardian of the west, prominent among his wives are Gaurī, Varuṇānī, Ćārṣaṇī, Devī Jyeṣṭhā, among his children are Susena, Vandī, Vasiṣṭha, Vāruṇī, the sage Bhṛgu, Vālmīki, Puśkara, Bala, Sūrā, Adharmaka, the name of his city is Śraddhāvatī, in later Vedic literature he is regarded as the god of the waters in the *Mahābhārata*, he is the son of Kardama and father of Puṣkara and is variously represented as a gandharva son of Kaśyapa and Muni, a nāga, as a Lokapāla (*Ṛg Veda*), the Jainas consider him the servant of the the 20th Arhat of the present Avasarpinī (*J.S. Koṣa*); *Crataeva nurvala*.

**Varuṇānī** (S) (F) **1.** goddess of water. **3.** wife of Varuṇa (*Ṛg Veda*)

**Varuṇaśarman** (S) (M) **1.** commander of the waters; commander of the navy. **3.** a warrior of the gods in their battle with the daityās (*K. Sāgara*)

**Varuṇavegā** (S) (F) **1.** with the speed of Varuṇa. **3.** another name for a kinnarī.

**Varuṇāvī** (S) (F) **1.** water born. **3.** another name for Lakṣmī.

**Varuṇeśa** (S) (M) with Varuṇa as the lord.

**Vāruṇī** (S) (F) **1.** of water; resembling water; liquor; wine. **3.** the daughter of Varuṇa who married the devas (*P. Purāṇa*); a river (*V. Rāmāyaṇa*) the Śakti or female energy of Varuṇa said to have been produced from the churning of the Ocean of Milk and is regarded as the mother of spirituous liquor (*Ṛg Veda*)

**Vāruṇi** (S) (M) **1.** of Varuna. **3.** sage Bhṛgu when reborn as the son of Varuṇa (*M. Bh.*)

**Varūtha** (S) (M) **1.** protection; defence; abode; shelter. **3.** an Aṅga king (*A. Purāṇa*)

**Varūthinī** (S) (F) **1.** multitude; troop; army. **3.** an apsarā (*M. Bh.*)

**Varūtṛ** (S) (M) protector; guardian; deity.

**Varūtrī** (S) (F) **1.** protectress. **3.** a tutelary goddess (*Ṛg Veda*)

**Varyā** (S) (F) treasure; wealth; chosen; valuable.

**Varya** (S) (M) **1.** chosen. **2.** treasure; excellent; eminent; chief. **3.** another name for Kāma (*M. Bh.*)

**Vaśa** (S) (M) **1.** authority; dominion personified as a god (*A. Veda*). **3.** a hermit praised in the *Ṛg Veda*.

**Vaśā** (S) (F) obedient; willing.

**Vāsaka** (S) (M) **1.** dweller; populating. **3.** a nāga.

**Vāsanā** (S) (F) **1.** knowledge derived from past perception; fancy; imagination; notion; idea; desire; inclination. **3.** the wife of the vasu Arka (*Bhāgavata*); another name for Durgā.

**Vasanta** (S) (M) **1.** bestower of desires. **3.** brilliant spring personified as a companion of Kāma (*K. Granthāvali*); Arabian Manna plant (*Alhagi Camelorum*); Custard Apple (*Annona reticulata*); Musk Jasmine (*Jasminum pubescens*); Bedda Nut (*Terminalia belerica*)

**Vasantabandhu** (S) (M) **1.** friend of spring. **3.** another name for Kāma.

**Vasantadeva** (S) (M) **1.** the lord of spring. **3.** another name for Kāma.

**Vasantadūta** (S) (M) **1.** the messenger of spring; the Indian Cuckoo (*Cuculus varius*); the Mango tree (*Mangifera indica*). **3.** a rāga.

**Vasantagandhi** (S) (M) **1.** the fragrance of spring. **3.** a Buddha (*L. Vistara*)

**Vasantajā** (S) (F) **1.** born in spring. **2.** Jasmine; the Mādhavi creeper.

**Vasantaka** (S) (M) spring.

**Vasantakusuma** (S) (F) spring flower.

**Vasantalatā** (S) (F) the vine of spring.

**Vasantalekhā** (S) (F) written by spring; spring born.

**Vasantapuṣpa** (S) (M) **1.** spring blossom. **2.** Kadamba flower (*Anthocephalus cadamba*)

**Vasantarāja** (S) (M) king of spring.

**Vasantarañjana** (S) (M) delight of spring.

**Vasantasahāya** (S) (M) **1.** supporter of spring. **3.** another name for Kāma.

**Vasantasakha** (S) (M) **1.** companion of spring. **3.** the wind blowing from the Malaya mountains (*K. Granthāvali*)

**Vasantaśekhara** (S) (M) **1.** crested with the spring. **2.** best among the charming. **3.** a kinnara.

**Vasantasenā** (S) (F) **1.** with spring as the commander. **2.** as charming as the spring.

**Vasantasena** (S) (M) with spring as the commander; loving; with the charms of spring.

**Vasantaśrī** (S) (F) the beauty of spring.

**Vasantatilaka** (S) (M) the ornament of spring.

**Vasantaviṭṭhala** (S) (M) **1.** god of the spring. **3.** a form of Viṣṇu (*Bhā. Purāṇa*)

**Vasantayodha** (S) (M) **1.** warrior of spring. **2.** spring combatant. **3.** another name for Kāma.

**Vāsantī** (S) (F) **1.** of the spring season; vernal; light yellow; saffron. **3.** a rāgiṇī; a sylvan deity; the Navamallikā Jasmine (*Jasminum officianale*); a daughter of King Bhūmiśukla; another name for the mother of Vyāsa (*M. Bh.*); *Hiptage Madoblata*.

**Vasantikā** (S) (F) **1.** goddess of the spring. **3.** a forest deity; *Gaertnera racemosa*.

**Vāsara** (S) (M) **1.** day. **3.** a nāga.

**Vāsarādhīśa** (S) (M) **1.** lord of the day. **3.** another name for the sun.

**Vāsaramaṇi** (S) (M) **1.** jewel of the day. **3.** another name for the sun.

**Vasātī** (S) (F) **1.** dawn. **3.** a son of Ikṣvāku (*H. Purāṇa*); a lunar dynasty king and son of Janamejaya (*M. Bh.*); a king on the side of the Kauravas (*M. Bh.*)

**Vasātika** (S) (M) **1.** as bright as the dawn; belonging to the dawn. **3.** a warrior on the side of the Kauravas (*M. Bh.*)

**Vāsava** (S) (M) **1.** descended from or relating to the vasus. **3.** a son of King Vasu (*Bhā. Purāṇa*); another name for Indra.

**Vāsavadattā** (S) (F) **1.** enticing; fragrance born; given by Indra. **3.** the wife of King Udayana (*K. Granthāvali*)

**Vāsavadatta** (S) (M) **1.** given by Indra. **3.** a king of Bijoypuri and follower of Mahāvira (*J.S. Koṣa*)

**Vāsavaja** (S) (M) **1.** son of Indra; son of the omnipresent. **3.** another name for Arjuna.

**Vasavāna** (S) (M) preserver of wealth.

**Vasavānuja** (S) (M) **1.** younger brother of Indra. **3.** another name for Upendra.

**Vasavartin** (S) (M) **1.** having power over gods. **3.** another name for Viṣṇu.

**Vāsavavarāja** (S) (M) **1.** Indra's younger brother. **3.** another name for Viṣṇu.

**Vāsavī** (S) (F) **1.** daughter of the all pervading. **3.** the mother of Vyāsa who was the daughter of King Vasu and the apsarā Adrikā (*M. Bh.*)

**Vasāvī** (S) (F) treasury.

**Vāsavi** (S) (M) **1.** son of Indra. **3.** another name for Arjuna and Vālin.

**Vāsavopama** (S) (M) resembling Indra.

**Vaśāyu** (S) (M) **1.** one who controls his age. **3.** a son of Purūravas and Urvaśī (*P. Purāṇa*)

**Vaśendriya** (S) (M) **1.** controller of senses. **2.** one who controls his senses.

**Vāśi** (S) (M) **1.** roaring. **3.** another name for Agni.

**Vaśin** (S) (M) **1.** having will or power. **2.** ruler; lord; master of one's passions. **3.** a son of Kṛti (*Bhā. Purāṇa*)

**Vasiṣṭha** (S) (M) **1.** most excellent; best; richest; master of every vasu or desirable object. **3.** a celebrated sage who was a mindborn son of Brahmā born of his breath, he was reborn as the son of Mitravarunas, he was the husband of Arundhatī or Ūrjā who was reborn with him as Akṣamālā and the father of 7 sons who became the saptarṣis in the 1st Manvantara, both are now stars and Vasiṣṭha shines in the assembly of Brahmā, he was the owner of Nandinī or the cow of plenty which granted all desires (*K. Granthāvali*), he is enumerated among the 10 prajāpatis produced by Manu Svāyambhuva, he was the family priest of the Ikṣvāku clan and is also regarded as one of the arrangers of the Vedas (*M. Bh.*); an agni (*M. Bh.*)

**Vasordhārā** (S) (F) **1.** stream of wealth. **3.** the celestial Gaṅgā (*M. Bh.*); the wife of the vasu named Agni (*Bhā. Purāṇa*)

**Vāstoṣpati** (S) (M) **1.** house protector. **3.** a deity who presides over the foundation of a house; another name for Indra and Rudra.

**Vastṛ** (S) (F) shining; illumining.

**Vastu** (S) (F) dawn; morning.

**Vastu** (S) (M) 1. site or foundation of a dwelling; a thing; the real; matter; property; whatever exists. 3. one of the 8 vasus; a rākṣasa (*Bhā. Purāṇa*)

**Vāstunara** (S) (M) deity who protects the house.

**Vāstupāla** (S) (M) tutelary deity of a house.

**Vāstupati** (S) (M) master of the house; a deity who protects the house.

**Vāstupuruṣa** (S) (M) 1. lord of architecture. 3. the deity of all that is built on earth (*A. Purāṇa*)

**Vastuvṛtta** (S) (M) the actual fact; real matter; beautiful creature.

**Vasu** (S) (F) 1. light; radiance. 3. a daughter of Dakṣa and mother of the vasus (*H. Purāṇa*)

**Vasu** (S) (M) 1. dwelling in all beings; divine; existing; precious; god; gem; gold; water; wealthy; ray of light; excellent; good; beneficient. 3. a particular class of 8 demi-gods or ganadevatas who were personifications of natural phenomena who were born of Dharma and Vasu (*M. Bh.*); in some Purāṇas they are the children of Kaśyapa, they are the lords of the elements, the 1st vasu Āpa was reborn as Bhīsma, the others are the first 7 sons of Gaṅgā; a son of Kuśa and Vaidarbhī (*V. Rāmāyaṇa*); a son of Jamadagni and Reṇukā and brother of Paraśurāma (*Br. Purāṇa*); a son of Murāsura (*Bhāgavata*); a mighty king of the Kṛmi dynasty (*M. Bh.*); a son of King Īlina and Rathāntari (*M. Bh.*); a hermit and father of Paila (*M. Bh.*); a king who was the son of Uttānapāda and Sūnṛtā (*M. Purāṇa*); a son of Manu (*H. Purāṇa*); a son of Vasudeva (*Bh. Purāṇa*); a son of Kṛṣṇa (*Bh. Purāṇa*); a son of Vatsara; a son of Hiraṇyaretas; a son of Bhūtajyotis (*Bh. Purāṇa*); a son of Naraka (*Bhā. Purāṇa*); the Supreme Soul of the universe (*Ṛg Veda*); another name for the Sun, Kubera, Śiva, Bhīṣma, Viṣṇu and Agni.

**Vasubandhu** (S) (M) 1. friend of the gods. 3. a celebrated Buddhist scholar (*B. Literature*)

**Vāsubhadra** (S) (M) 1. best of the deities. 3. another name for Kṛṣṇa.

**Vasubhāga** (S) (M) 1. share of the gods. 2. offering to the gods.

**Vasubhṛdyāna** (S) (M) 1. chariot carried by the gods; led by the gods. 3. a son of Vasiṣṭha (*V. Rāmāyaṇa*)

**Vasubhūta** (S) (M) 1. born of Vasu; embodied wealth. 3. a gandharva (*H. Purāṇa*)

**Vasućandra** (S) (M) 1. moon among the gods. 2. most beautiful. 3. a king who was a supporter of Yudhiṣṭhira and as mighty as Indra (*M. Bh.*)

**Vasudā** (S) (F) 1. granting wealth. 3. another name for the earth; a mother in Skanda's retinue (*M. Bh.*); a gandharvī (*M. Bh.*)

**Vasuda** (S) (M) 1. granting wealth. 3. another name for Kubera.

**Vasudāmā** (S) (F) 1. controlling the divine beings. 3. an attendant of Skanda (*M. Bh.*)

**Vasudāman** (S) (M) 1. controller of divine beings. 3. a son of Bṛhadratha.

**Vasudāna** (S) (M) 1. gift of the divine. 2. donor of the earth. 3. a king of Pānśu who was a member of Yudhiṣṭhira's council (*M. Bh.*); a prince of Panćala who fought for the Pāṇḍavas (*M. Bh.*)

**Vasudānaputra** (S) (M) 1. son of the donor of wealth. 3. a king on the Kaurava side (*M. Bh.*)

**Vasudattā** (S) (F) 1. given by the gods. 3. the mother of Vararući (*K. Sāgara*)

**Vasudatta** (S) (M) gift of the divine.

**Vasudevā** (S) (F) 1. goddess of wealth. 3. a daughter of Śvaphalka (*V. Purāṇa*)

**Vasudeva** (S) (M) 1. lord of living beings; god of wealth; god of earth. 3. a son of Śurā of the line of Yadu and the brother of Kuntī and the husband of Rohiṇī, Devakī, Upadevī, Saptamīdevī, Vṛkadevī, Jani, Śrutandharā, Śraddhādevī and the father of Kṛṣṇa, Subhadrā, Balarāma, he is regarded as an incarnation of sage Kaśyapa and is now a viśvadeva; a king of the Kaṇva dynasty (*M. Bh.*)

**Vāsudeva** (S) (M) 1. son of Vasudeva. 3. another name for Kṛṣṇa; a king of the Puṇḍras (*M. Bh.*)

**Vasudevabhattatiri** (S) (M) 1. worshipper of

the omnipresent. 3. a Sanskṛt poet of Kerala.

**Vasudevaputra** (S) (M) 1. son of Vasudeva. 3. another name for Kṛṣṇa.

**Vasudevatā** (S) (F) 1. goddess of wealth. 3. a goddess granting wealth (*Bhā. Purāṇa*); the lunar mansion Dhaniṣṭha.

**Vasudevya** (S) (M) 1. granting wealth. 3. 9th day of a fortnight (*Ṛg Veda*)

**Vasudhā** (S) (F) 1. producing wealth. 3. the daughter of gandharvī Narmadā (*M. Bh.*); another name for the earth and Lakṣmī.

**Vasudharā** (S) (F) 1. bearing wealth. 3. a Buddhist goddess (*B. Literature*); a Jaina Śakti; a river (*J.S. Koṣa*)

**Vasudhāra** (S) (M) 1. holding treasure. 3. a mountain.

**Vasudhāriṇī** (S) (F) 1. bearer of treasures. 3. another name for the earth.

**Vasudhitī** (S) (F) possessing wealth.

**Vasuhoma** (S) (M) 1. one who sacrifices to the gods. 3. a king of Aṅga (*M. Bh.*)

**Vasujit** (S) (M) conqueror of wealth.

**Vasujyeṣṭha** (S) (M) 1. the best wealth; 1st among the gods. 3. a king and son of Puṣyamitra (*M. Purāṇa*)

**Vasukarṇa** (S) (M) 1. with divine ears. 3. a ṛṣi and part author of *Ṛg Veda*.

**Vāsukeśvarī** (S) (F) 1. sister of Vāsukī. 3. another name for Manasā.

**Vāsuki** (S) (M) 1. one who resides under earth. 3. the eldest serpent son of Kaśyapa and Kadrū and one of the 7 nāgas that hold up the earth, he is the bracelet of Śiva and in the burning of Tripura acted as his bowstring and the axle of his chariot, he is the king of the nāgas and was used by the gods and demons as a rope for twisting Mount Mandāra to churn the ocean (*Bhā. Purāṇa*)

**Vasukra** (S) (M) 1. knower of the gods. 3. a ṛṣi and a part author of *Ṛg Veda* (x)

**Vasukṛt** (S) (M) 1. one who behaves like the gods. 2. with a pious conduct; act of the gods. 3. a ṛṣi and an author of *Ṛg Veda* (x)

**Vasula** (S) (M) a god.

**Vasulakṣmī** (S) (F) 1. divine goddess of wealth. 3. a sister-in-law of Agnimitra (*K. Granthāvali*)

**Vasumanas** (S) (M) 1. with a rich mind; knower of all. 3. an Ikṣvāku king who was the son of Haryaśva and Mādhavī (*M. Bh.*); a king in the council of Yudhiṣṭhira (*M. Bh.*); an agṇi; a king of the Janaka family (*M. Bh.*); a king of Kosala (*M. Bh.*)

**Vasumat** (S) (M) 1. possessing treasure; attended by the Vasus. 3. a son of Manu Vaivasvata (*Purāṇas*); another name for Kṛṣṇa.

**Vasumatī** (S) (F) 1. possessing treasure. 3. another name for the earth.

**Vasumitra** (S) (M) 1. friend of the gods. 2. friend of treasure. 3. a Kṣatriya king who was a partial incarnation of the asura Vikṣara (*M. Bh.*); a Śuṅga dynasty king who was the father of Udaṅka (*Bhāgavata*)

**Vasunanda** (S) (M) delighting the gods.

**Vasundharā** (S) (F) 1. abode of wealth. 2. containing wealth. 3. a portion of the goddess Prakṛti; a daughter of Śvaphalka (*Ṛg Veda*); another name for the earth.

**Vasundhareśā** (S) (F) 1. consort of the lord of the earth. 3. another name for Rādhā.

**Vasundhareyī** (S) (F) 1. daughter of the earth. 3. another name for Sītā.

**Vasunemi** (S) (M) 1. felly of the gods. 3. a nāga.

**Vasunītha** (S) (M) bringing wealth.

**Vasunīti** (S) (M) bringing wealth.

**Vaṣupāla** (S) (M) 1. protector of wealth. 2. king.

**Vasupati** (S) (M) 1. lord of wealth and good things; lord of the vasus. 3. another name for Kṛṣṇa, Agni, Indra, Kubera.

**Vasupātṛ** (S) (M) 1. protector of the vasus. 3. another name for Kṛṣṇa.

**Vasuprabhā** (S) (F) 1. divine light. 3. one of the 7 tongues of fire (*M. Bh.*)

**Vasuprabha** (S) (M) 1. with divine glory. 3. a warrior of Skanda (*M. Bh.*)

**Vasuprada** (S) (M) 1. bestowing wealth. 3. an attendant of Skanda (*M. Bh.*)

**Vasuprāṇa** (S) (M) 1. breath of the vasus. 2. fire.

**Vasupūjyarāj** (S) (M) 1. honoured by the gods. 3. the father of the 12th Arhat of the present Avasarpiṇī (*J.S. Koṣa*)

**Vāsurā** (S) (F) 1. valuable. 2. night; the earth; woman.
**Vasura** (S) (M) 1. valuable. 2. rich.
**Vasuratha** (S) (M) 1. chariot of the gods. 2. led by gods.
**Vasuretas** (S) (M) 1. with divine power. 3. another name for Agni (*Ṛg Veda*)
**Vasurući** (S) (M) 1. with divine glory; having divine tastes. 3. a gandharva (*A. Veda*)
**Vasurūpa** (S) (M) 1. of a divine form; with the nature of the vasus. 3. another name for Śiva.
**Vasuśakti** (S) (M) 1. divine power. 2. with the power of the vasus (*P. Ratra*)
**Vasusena** (S) (M) 1. divine army; divine commander; distributer of wealth. 3. Karṇa in his boyhood; another name for Viṣṇu (*M. Bh.*)
**Vasuśravas** (S) (M) famous for wealth; flowing with wealth.
**Vasuśreṣṭha** (S) (M) 1. best of the vasus. 2. silver; wrought gold. 3. another name for Kṛṣṇa.
**Vasuśrī** (S) (F) 1. divine grace. 3. a mother in Skanda's retinue (*M. Bh.*)
**Vasuttama** (S) (M) 1. best of the vasus. 3. another name for Bhīṣma (*Bh. Purāṇa*)
**Vasuvāha** (S) (M) 1. bringing wealth; preceptor of the divine. 3. a ṛṣi (*M. Bh.*)
**Vasuvāhana** (S) (M) bringing wealth.
**Vasuvinda** (S) (M) gaining wealth.
**Vasuvīrya** (S) (M) with the power of the vasus.
**Vasvānanta** (S) (M) 1. infinite wealth; external divinity; eternal wealth. 3. a king of Videha who was the son of Upagupta and the father of Yuyudha (*Bhāgavata*)
**Vasvī** (S) (F) the divine night.
**Vasvoksārā** (S) (F) 1. essence of the divine waters. 3. one of the 7 branches of the Gaṅgā (*M. Bh.*)
**Vaśyā** (S) (M) 1. dutiful; humble; tamed; obedient. 3. a son of Āgnīdhra (*Mā. Purāṇa*)
**Vaṭa** (S) (M) 1. the Indian Fig or Banyan tree (*Ficus indica*); cowrie shell (*Cypraea moneta*); pawn in chess. 3. one of the 5 attendants given to Skanda by the god Anśa (*M. Bh.*)
**Vāta** (S) (M) 1. wind; the god of wind. 3. a rākṣasa (*V. Purāṇa*); a son of Śūra; a Saptaṛṣi of the Manvantara of Manu Svāroćisa (*V. Purāṇa*)
**Vāṭadhāna** (S) (M) 1. an officer who knows his army. 3. a king who was a partial incarnation of the asura Krodhāvaśa (*M. Bh.*)
**Vātādhipa** (S) (M) 1. lord of wind. 3. a famous Purāṇic king (*M. Bh.*)
**Vātaghna** (S) (M) 1. vanquisher of the wind. 3. a son of Viśvāmitra (*M. Bh.*)
**Vātajava** (S) (M) 1. swift as the wind. 3. a rākṣasa.
**Vātansā** (S) (F) garland; crest; ring.
**Vātāpi** (S) (M) 1. with the wind as an ally; swollen by the wind. 3. an asura who was the son of Hṛāda (*M. Bh.*); an asura born of Kaśyapa and Danu (*M. Bh.*)
**Vātaputra** (S) (M) 1. son of the wind. 3. another name for Hanumān and Bhīma.
**Vātarūpā** (S) (F) 1. with the form of the wind. 2. subtle; transparent. 3. a rākṣasi who was the daughter of Līkā (*Mā. Purāṇa*)
**Vātaskandha** (S) (M) 1. the direction from where the wind blows. 3. a hermit in the palace of Indra (*M. Bh.*)
**Vatāśraya** (S) (M) 1. dwelling in the fig tree. 3. another name for Kubera.
**Vātātmaja** (S) (M) 1. son of the wind. 3. another name for Hanumān and Bhīma (*M. Bh.*)
**Vātavega** (S) (M) 1. with the speed of wind. 2. as fast as wind; very swift. 3. a son of Dhṛtarāṣṭra (*M. Bh.*); a son of Garuḍa (*M. Bh.*); another name for Garuḍa.
**Vaṭeśa** (S) (M) 1. lord of the Banyan tree. 3. the father of Śiśu (*A. Purāṇa*)
**Vaṭeśvara** (S) (M) 1. lord of the Banyan tree. 3. the father of Pṛthu (*Ṛg Veda*)
**Vāti** (S) (M) air; wind; sun; moon.
**Vātika** (S) (M) 1. airy. 2. a talker; the Ćataka bird. 3. a warrior of Skanda (*M. Bh.*)
**Vatśā** (S) (F) calf; daughter; breast.
**Vatsa** (S) (M) 1. calf; child; darling; son; boy. 3. a descendant of Kaṇva (*Ṛg Veda*); a son of Senajit (*H. Purāṇa*); a son of Akṣamālā; a son of Urukṣepa (*V. Purāṇa*); the son of King Pratardana of Kāśi (*M. Bh.*); a king of the Śaryāti family who was the father of Tālajangha and Hehaya (*M. Bh.*)
**Vatsabālaka** (S) (M) 1. loving child. 3. a

brother of Vasudeva (*M. Bh.*)

**Vatsahanu** (S) (M) 1. with a calflike chin. 3. a son of Senajit (*V. Purāṇa*)

**Vatsaka** (S) (M) 1. young calf. 2. a term of endearment. 3. a son of Śūra (*Bh. Purāṇa*); an asura (*Bh. Purāṇa*)

**Vatsala** (S) (M) 1. child loving; affectionate towards offspring. 3. a son of Bhūmi.

**Vatsalā** (S) (F) 1. child loving. 2. affectionate; tender; devoted. 3. an attendant of Skanda (*M. Bh.*)

**Vatsamitrā** (S) (F) 1. friend of children; friend of calves. 3. an apsarā (*H. Purāṇa*)

**Vatsanābha** (S) (M) 1. with a loving navel; aconite. 3. a hermit once saved by Dharma in the form of a she-buffalo (*M. Bh.*)

**Vatsapāla** (S) (M) 1. keeper of calves; protector of children. 3. another name for Kṛṣṇa and Balarāma.

**Vatsapati** (S) (M) 1. lord of calves; lord of the Vatsa tribe. 3. another name for Udayana.

**Vatsaprīti** (S) (M) 1. affectionate to children; calf loving. 3. a hermit and author of *Ṛg Veda* (ix)

**Vatsara** (S) (M) 1. a year; the 5th year in a cycle of 5 years. 3. the year personified as a son of Dhruva and Bhrami who was the husband of Svarvīthi and the father of Puṣpārṇa, Tigmaketu, Īśa, Vasu, Ūrja and Jaya (*Bhāgavata*); another name for Viṣṇu (*M. Bh.*); a son of Kaśyapa (*M. Bh.*)

**Vatsavat** (S) (M) 1. having many calves. 2. rich in cattle. 3. a son of Śūra (*Bhā. Purāṇa*)

**Vatsavṛddha** (S) (M) 1. veterinary physician. 3. a son of Urukriya (*Bhā. Purāṇa*)

**Vatsin** (S) (M) 1. with many children. 3. another name for Viṣṇu.

**Vātsyāyana** (S) (M) 1. loving. 2. preceptor of the art of love. 3. a hermit who wrote the famous *Vātsyāyana Sūtra* or Science of Love.

**Vatū** (S) (F) 1. who speaks the truth. 3. a river of heaven.

**Vatyā** (F) gale; storm; hurricane.

**Vavri** (S) (M) 1. a cover; vesture; the body. 3. a hermit and supposed part author of *Ṛg Veda* (v)

**Vayā** (S) (F) 1. a branch; twig. 2. child; vigour; strength; power.

**Vayasya** (S) (M) 1. contemporary; friend; companion. 3. a brother of Bṛhaspati.

**Vāyava** (S) (M) sacred to the god of wind.

**Vāyavyā** (S) (F) the northwest presided over by Vayu.

**Vayodhā** (S) (F) strengthening; invigorating.

**Vāyu** (S) (M) 1. wind. 3. air personified as a deity of equal rank though not as prominent as Indra, he is one of the 8 guardians of the world being the guardian of the north west, he was born from the breath of Viśvapuruṣa (*Ṛg Veda*), he is the father of Bhīma, Hanumān and Agni and is the father-in-law of Tvaṣṭā, his palace is known as Gandhavatī, he is the messenger of the gods; a vasu (*H. Purāṇa*); a daitya; the king of the gandharvas (*V. Purāṇa*); a marut (*V. Purāṇa*)

**Vāyubala** (S) (M) 1. as mighty as the wind. 3. one of the 7 ṛṣis said to have been the fathers of the maruts (*V. Purāṇa*)

**Vāyubhakṣa** (S) (M) 1. one who lives on wind. 3. a hermit in the palace of Yudhiṣṭhira (*M. Bh.*)

**Vāyubhūti** (S) (M) 1. born of wind. 3. a main disciple of Mahāvira (*V. Rāmāyaṇa*)

**Vāyućakra** (S) (M) 1. discus of the wind. 3. a pot born hermit son of Maṅkanaka (*M. Bh.*); one of the 7 ṛṣis said to have been the fathers of the maruts (*M. Bh.*)

**Vāyuhan** (S) (M) 1. friend of wind. 3. a pot-born hermit son of Maṅkanaka (*M. Bh.*); one of the 7 ṛṣis said to have been the fathers of the maruts.

**Vāyujāta** (S) (M) 1. wind born. 3. another name for Hanumān.

**Vāyujvāla** (S) (M) 1. inflamer of the wind. 2. cause of the wind. 3. a pot born hermit son of Maṅkanaka (*M. Bh.*); one of the 7 ṛṣis said to have been the fathers of the maruts (*M. Bh.*)

**Vāyukeśa** (S) (M) 1. with windswept hair. 3. another name for the gandharvas.

**Vāyumaṇḍala** (S) (M) 1. atmosphere. 3. a pot born hermit son of Maṅkanaka (*M. Bh.*); one of the 7 ṛṣis said to have been the father of the maruts.

**Vayunā** (S) (F) 1. moving; active; alive; mark;

aim; goal; knowledge; wisdom. 3. a daughter of Svadhā (*Y. Veda*)

**Vayuna** (S) (M) 1. moving; active; alive; clear. 3. a son of Kṛṣāśva and Dhīṣaṇā (*Bhā. Purāṇa*)

**Vāyuna** (S) (M) god; a deity.

**Vāyunandana** (S) (M) 1. son of the wind. 3. another name for Hanumān and Bhīma.

**Vāyupatha** (S) (M) 1. the path of the wind. 3. a king (*K. Sāgara*)

**Vāyuputra** (S) (M) 1. son of the wind. 3. another name for Hanumān and Bhīma.

**Vāyuretas** (S) (M) 1. power of wind; as powerful as wind; as subtle as wind; as pervading as wind. 3. a pot born hermit son of Maṅkanaka (*M. Bh.*); one of the 7 ṛṣis said to have been the father of the maruts.

**Vāyusakha** (S) (M) 1. friend of the wind; with the wind as ally. 3. another name for Agni.

**Vāyusuta** (S) (M) 1. son of Vāyu. 3. another name for Bhīma.

**Vāyuvāhana** (S) (M) 1. travelling with the wind. 3. another name for Viṣṇu and Śiva.

**Vāyuvegā** (S) (F) 1. swift as the wind. 3. a yoginī; a kinnarī; a sister of Vāyupatha (*K. Sāgara*)

**Vāyuvega** (S) (M) 1. with the speed of wind. 3. a pot born hermit son of Maṅkanaka (*M. Bh.*); a king who was a partial incarnation of the asura Krodhavaśa (*M. Bh.*); a son of Dhṛtarāṣṭra; one of the 7 ṛṣis said to have been the fathers of the maruts (*M. Bh.*)

**Vayya** (S) (M) 1. friend; companion. 3. an asura (*Ṛg Veda*)

**Vedā** (S) (F) 1. well known; meritorious; pious; famous. 3. a river (*Ṛg Veda*)

**Veda** (S) (M) 1. knowledge; wealth; obtaining; weaving together; all that is to be known. 3. four books that constitute the basis for the Hindu religion.

**Vedabāhu** (S) (M) 1. armed with the Vedas. 3. a ṛṣi under Manu Raivata (*H. Purāṇa*); a son of Pulastya (*V. Purāṇa*); a son of Kṛṣṇa (*Bhā. Purāṇa*)

**Vedabhā** (S) (F) obtained from knowledge; a magic charm which brings jewels from the sky.

**Vedāćārya** (S) (M) teacher of the Vedas.

**Vedadharma** (S) (M) 1. devotee of the sacred text. 3. a son of Paila (*Ṛg Veda*)

**Vedādhideva** (S) (M) 1. deity of the Vedas. 3. another name for Brahmā.

**Vedādhyakṣa** (S) (M) 1. protector of the Vedas. 3. another name for Kṛṣṇa.

**Vedadiṣa** (S) (M) 1. point or precept with the Vedas. 3. a son of King Bṛhadratha of Ćedi (*Bhāgavata*)

**Vedagarbhā** (S) (F) 1. womb of the Vedas. 3. another name for Durgā (*A. Purāṇa*) and Sarasvatī (*Bhā. Purāṇa*)

**Vedagarbha** (S) (M) 1. womb of the Vedas. 3. another name for Brahmā and Viṣṇu.

**Vedagātha** (S) (M) 1. singer of the texts. 3. a ṛṣi (*H. Purāṇa*)

**Vedaghoṣa** (S) (M) 1. the voice of Vedas. 2. sound caused by the recitation of the Vedas.

**Vedāgraṇī** (S) (M) 1. leader of the Vedas. 3. another name for Sarasvatī.

**Vedagupta** (S) (M) 1. preserver of the Vedas. 3. another name for Kṛṣṇa the son of Parāśara.

**Vedajananī** (S) (F) 1. mother of the Vedas. 2. the Gāyatrī mantra.

**Vedakartṛ** (S) (M) 1. author of the Vedas. 3. another name for the Sun, Śiva and Viṣṇu.

**Vedakumbha** (S) (M) master of Vedas; pitcher of the Vedas.

**Vedamātṛ** (S) (F) 1. mother of the Vedas. 3. another name for Sarasvatī, Sāvitrī and Gāyatrī.

**Vedamitra** (S) (M) 1. friend of the Vedas. 3. father of Sumedhas.

**Vedamūrti** (S) (M) embodiment of the Vedas.

**Vedanā** (S) (F) 1. knowledge; perception; pain. 3. the goddess of pain who is the daughter of Nirṛti and the mother of Duhkha (*A. Purāṇa*)

**Vedāṅgarāya** (S) (M) 1. scholar of the Vedic school. 3. an author who wrote the *Shrāddhadīpikā* for Shahjahān (17th century)

**Vedanidhi** (S) (M) storehouse of the Vedas.

**Vedaprakāśa** (S) (M) light of the Vedas.

**Vedasāra** (S) (M) 1. essence of the Vedas. 3. another name for Viṣṇu.

**Vedaśarmā** (S) (M) 1. protector of the Vedas. 3. the son of the hermit Śivaśarmā.

**Vedāsinī** (S) (F) 1. carrying wealth. 3. a river.

**Vedaśiras** (S) (M) 1. head of the Vedas. 3. a son of Prāṇa; a hermit of the Bhṛgu clan, son of Mārkaṇḍeya and Mūrdhanyā or Dhūmrā and husband of Pīvarī (*Vā. Purāṇa*); a hermit and son of Kṛśāśva and Dhīṣaṇā who learnt the *Viṣṇu Purāṇa* from the nāgas in Pātāla (*V. Purāṇa*)

**Vedasmṛtā** (S) (F) 1. remembrance of the scriptures. 3. a river (*M. Bh.*)

**Vedasparśa** (S) (M) 1. touched by the sacred text. 3. a disciple of the hermit Kabandha (*Vā. Purāṇa*)

**Vedaśravas** (S) (M) listener of the scriptures; famous in the scriptures.

**Vedaśrī** (S) (M) 1. beauty of the Vedas. 3. a ṛṣi (*Mā. Purāṇa*)

**Vedaśrutī** (S) (F) 1. heard about in the Vedas; famous in Vedas. 3. a famous river of the Purāṇas (*Purāṇas*)

**Vedāśva** (S) (M) 1. horse of the scriptures. 2. famous carrier. 3. a river (*M. Bh.*)

**Vedātman** (S) (M) 1. soul of the Veda. 3. another name for Viṣṇu (*Ṛg Veda*)

**Vedavatī** (S) (F) 1. familiar with the Vedas. 3. a daughter of Kuśadhvaja who was reborn as Sītā; an apsarā (*V. Rāmāyaṇa*)

**Vedavṛddha** (S) (M) learned in the Vedas.

**Vedavyāsa** (S) (M) 1. arranger of the Vedas. 3. another name for Vyāsa.

**Vedeśa** (S) (M) lord of the Vedas.

**Vedeśvā** (S) (F) 1. born of the sacred texts. 3. a river.

**Vedeśvara** (S) (F) lord of the Vedas.

**Vedha** (S) (M) 1. breaking through; piercing; pious; faithful. 3. a son of Ananta (*Vah. Purāṇa*)

**Vedhagupta** (S) (M) 1. with an inner penetration; possessing a hidden disturbance. 3. a rāga.

**Vedhas** (S) (M) 1. pious; religious; virtuous; good; brave; arranger; disposer; creator. 3. the father of Hariśćandra; part of the hand at the root of the thumb considered sacred to Brahmā; a ṛṣi of the family of Aṅgiras (*Ṛg Veda*)

**Vedhasyā** (S) (F) worship; piety.

**Vedī** (S) (F) 1. knowledge; science; altar. 3. the wife of Brahmā (*M. Bh.*)

**Vedi** (S) (M) wise man; teacher.

**Vedijā** (S) (M) 1. altar born. 3. another name for Draupadī.

**Vedikā** (S) (F) 1. a seal ring; making known; restoring to consciousness. 3. an apsarā.

**Vedin** (S) (M) 1. knowing; feeling. 3. another name for Brahmā.

**Vedinī** (S) (F) 1. knowing; feeling; proclaiming. 3. a river (*Rāmāyaṇa*)

**Vedīśa** (S) (M) 1. lord of the wise. 3. another name for Brahmā.

**Vedodaya** (S) (M) 1. origin of the Vedas. 3. another name for Sūrya.

**Veduka** (S) (M) 1. striving for knowledge. 2. acquiring; obtaining.

**Vedyā** (S) (F) knowledge.

**Vedya** (S) (M) well known; famous; celebrated.

**Vegavāhinī** (S) (F) 1. flowing fast. 3. a river whose deity lives in the court of Varuṇa (*M. Bh.*)

**Vegavān** (S) (M) 1. fast; violent; rapid; swift. 2. leopard. 3. a nāga of the family of Dhṛtarāṣṭra (*M. Bh.*); an asura son of Kaśyapa and Danu who was reborn as the prince of Kekaya (*M. Bh.*); a daitya killed by Sāmba the son of Kṛṣṇa (*M. Bh.*); a son of Kṛṣṇa (*Bhā. Purāṇa*); a vidyādhara (*K. Sāgara*); an asura (*M. Bh.*); a king and son of Bandhumat (*Ṛg Veda*)

**Vegavatī** (S) (F) 1. rapid. 3. a river (*V. Rāmāyaṇa*); an apsarā.

**Vegin** (S) (M) 1. swift. 2. hawk; falcon. 3. another name for Vāyu.

**Veginī** (S) (F) 1. going swiftly. 3. a river (*M. Bh.*)

**Vekā** (S) (F) 1. offspring of a bird. 3. a rākṣasi who was the sister of Puṣpotkaṭa and Kaikaśī.

**Vekata** (S) (M) a youth.

**Velā** (S) (F) 1. limit; coast; shore. 3. boundary of sea and land personified as the daughter of Meru and Dhāriṇī and the wife of Samudra (*M. Bh.*); the wife of the Buddha (*L. Vistara*); a princess (*K. Sāgara*)

**Velan** (S) (M) 1. pungent. 3. a son of Śiva.

**Velumaṇi** (S) (M) 1. strong willed. 2. diamond.

**Vemaćitra** (S) (M) 1. woven picture. 3. an asura king.

**Veṇā** (S) (F) 1. yearning; longing; to go; to move; discern; to play on an instrument. 3. a famous Purāṇic river which is among those where fire originated and worthy of being mentioned morning and evening (*M. Bh.*)

**Veṇa** (S) (M) 1. yearning; loving; longing; eager. 3. a notorious king of the Manu Ćākṣuṣa family who was the son of Aṅga and Sunīthā the daughter of Yama and the father of Pṛthu (*Vām. Purāṇa*); a son of Vaivasvata Manu (*M. Bh.*)

**Veṇavin** (S) (M) 1. furnished with a flute. 3. another name for Śiva

**Veṇī** (S) (F) 1. a braid of hair; stream; the confluence of rivers. 3. *Luffa echinata*.

**Veṇikā** (S) (F) 1. flowing. 2. a continuous stream. 3. a holy river of the Purāṇas (*H. Purāṇa*)

**Veṇimādhava** (S) (M) 1. god with braided hair. 3. a 4 handed idol at Prayāga (*Mā. Purāṇa*)

**Veṇin** (S) (M) 1. with a hood like braided hair. 3. a serpent in the family of Dhṛtarāṣṭra (*M. Bh.*)

**Veṇiprasāda** (S) (M) gift of braided hair.

**Veṇirāma** (S) (M) with braided hair.

**Veṇiskandha** (S) (M) 1. with braided shoulders. 3. a serpent of the Kaurava family (*M. Bh.*)

**Veṅkaṭa** (S) (M) 1. self born. 2. naturally manifest; divine. 3. a sacred hill in the Draviḍa country near Madras, on its summit is a temple dedicted to Viṣṇu/Kṛṣṇa as Lord Veṅkata or Śrīpati or Thirupati; a king of Vijayanagara (*Bhā. Purāṇa*)

**Veṅkaṭāćala** (S) (M) the Veṅkaṭa mountain.

**Veṅkaṭāćaleśa** (S) (M) 1. lord of the Veṅkaṭa mountain. 3. another name for Viṣṇu.

**Veṅkatadhvari** (S) (M) 1. performing sin destroying sacrifices. 3. a Sanskṛt poet and author of *Yādavarāghaviya* (17th century)

**Veṅkaṭagiri** (S) (M) the Veṅkaṭa mountain.

**Veṅkaṭanātha** (S) (M) 1. lord of the Veṅkaṭa hill. 3. a poet and philospher venerated now as divine (14th century); another name for Viṣṇu/Kṛṣṇa.

**Veṅkaṭarāghavana** (S) (M) 1. Veṅkaṭa, the Rāghava. 3. Viṣṇu in his incarnation as Rāma (*A. Koṣa*)

**Veṅkaṭaraman** (S) (M) 1. Veṅkaṭā, the Rāma. 3. Viṣṇu in his incarnation as Rāma (*A. Koṣa*)

**Veṅkatasvāmin** (S) (M) 1. lord of the Veṅkata mountain. 3. another name for Viṣṇu/Kṛṣṇa (*V. Koṣa*)

**Veṅkatavaradāna** (S) (M) the boon of Viṣṇu.

**Veṅkateśa** (S) (M) 1. lord of Veṅkata. 3. another name for Viṣṇu/Kṛṣṇa.

**Veṅkaṭeśvara** (S) (M) lord of Veṅkaṭa.

**Veṇu** (S) (M) 1. bamboo; reed; flute; fife; pipe. 3. a deity of the Bodhi tree (*L. Vistara*); a king of the Yādavas (*M. Bh.*); a son of Śatajita (*V. Purāṇa*); a mountain (*Mā. Purāṇa*); a river; Solid Bamboo (*Dendrocalamus strictus*)

**Veṇudāri** (S) (M) 1. tearing the flute. 3. a Yādava warrior (*M. Bh.*)

**Veṇugopāla** (S) (M) 1. the flute bearing cowherd. 3. another name for Kṛṣṇa.

**Veṇuhaya** (S) (M) 1. resounding like a flute. 3. a king of the lunar dynasty who was the son of Śatajita and the brother of Mahāhaya and Hehaya (*Bhāgavata*)

**Veṇujangha** (S) (M) 1. bamboo thighed. 3. a hermit in the assembly of Yudhiṣṭhira (*M. Bh.*)

**Veṇukā** (S) (M) flute; pipe.

**Veṇumanta** (S) (M) 1. possessing bamboos. 3. a white mountain on par, in the Purāṇas, with Mandāra.

**Veṇumat** (S) (M) 1. with bamboo. 3. a mountain (*Bhā. Purāṇa*); a son of Jyotiṣmat (*V. Purāṇa*)

**Veṇuvīṇādharā** (S) (F) 1. bearer of flute and lute. 3. an attendant of Skanda (*M. Bh.*)

**Veṇya** (S) (F) to be loved; desirable.

**Verāćarya** (S) (M) 1. master of the body. 3. a prince (*B. Literature*)

**Vetāla** (S) (M) 1. ghost; spirit; phantom; goblin. 3. a ghost in *Kathāsarit Sāgara* (*K. Sāgara*); an attendant of Śiva (*K. Purāṇa*)

**Vetālajananī** (S) (F) 1. mother of the phantom. 3. an attendant of Skanda (*M. Bh.*)

**Vetrāsura** (S) (M) 1. the reed demon; a large reed. 3. an asura (*M. Bh.*)
**Vetravat** (S) (M) 1. made of reeds. 3. a son of Pūṣan (*K. Sāgara*)
**Vetravatī** (S) (F) 1. full of reeds. 3. a form of Durgā (*H. Purāṇa*); a river now called Betwā (*Bha. Purāṇa*); the mother of Vetrāsura (*M. Bh.*)
**Vettṛ** (S) (M) 1. one who knows. 2. sage.
**Vibalī** (S) (F) 1. young. 3. a river.
**Vibhā** (S) (F) light; lustre; splendour; glory.
**Vībhā** (S) (M) to become visible; to glitter; shining; bright.
**Vibhākara** (S) (M) 1. light maker; creator of brightness. 2. sun; fire; moon; king; Ceylon Leadwort (*Plumbago zeylanica*)
**Vibhāṇḍaka** (S) (M) 1. without any possessions. 3. a hermit of the Kaśyapa family and father of Ṛṣyaśṛṅga (*M. Bh.*)
**Vibhānu** (S) (M) shining; beaming; radiant.
**Vibhāsa** (S) (M) 1. brightness; splendour. 3. a rāga; a deity (*Mā. Purāṇa*); one of the 7 suns (*T. Āraṇyaka*)
**Vibhāsita** (S) (M) illuminated.
**Vibhāsvatī** (S) (F) brilliant; resplendant.
**Vibhāta** (S) (M) 1. shining forth; appearing. 2. dawn.
**Vibhava** (S) (M) power; riches; omnipresence; might; magnanimity; loftiness.
**Vibhāva** (S) (M) 1. friend; acquaintaince. 3. another name for Śiva.
**Vibhāvā** (S) (F) 1. cause of emotion. 3. a wife of Svaroćis.
**Vibhāvarī** (S) (F) 1. brilliant; bright. 2. dawn; most illuminated. 3. a mindborn daughter of Brahmā considered a personification of a star filled night (*M. Bh.*)
**Vibhāvarīśa** (S) (M) 1. lord of the night. 3. another name for the Moon.
**Vibhāvasu** (S) (M) 1. abounding in light. 2. garland. 3. one of the 8 vasus; a son of Naraka; a dānava (*Bh. Purāṇa*); a gandharva; a hermit and brother of Supratīka (*M. Bh.*); a son of Kaśyapa and Danu; another name for Agni, Soma, Kṛṣṇa, the sun and the moon.
**Vibhī** (S) (M) fearless.
**Vibhīndu** (S) (M) 1. fearless moon; moon among the fearless. 3. a king famous for his liberality (*Ṛg Veda*)
**Vibhīṣaṇa** (S) (F) 1. terrifying. 3. an attendant of Skanda (*M. Bh.*); the son of Viśravas and Mālinī and the brother of Rāvaṇa and the husband of Saralā, he joined the side of Rāma and was made king of Laṅkā after the battle (*U. Rāmāyaṇa*)
**Vibhrāja** (S) (M) 1. shining; splendid; luminous. 3. a king who was a descendant of Yayāti the son of Kṛti and the father of Anuha and father-in-law of Kīrtī the daughter of Śuka (*Bhāgavata*)
**Vibhrāṣṭi** (S) (F) radiance; flame; blaze.
**Vibhu** (S) (M) 1. all pervading; omnipresent; eternal; mighty; powerful; excellent; great; strong; effective. 2. king; lord. 3. a god who was the son of Vedaśiras and Tuṣitā (*Bhā. Purāṇa*); a son of Viṣṇu and Dakṣiṇā (*Bhā. Purāṇa*); a son of Bhaga and Siddhī (*Bhā. Purāṇa*); a son of Śambara (*H. Purāṇa*); a son of Satyaketu and father of Suvibhu; a son of Dharmaketu and father of Sukumāra; a son of Bhṛgu; father of Ānarta (*H. Purāṇa*); a king of the Bharata family who was the son of Prastotā and the father of Pṛthuseṇa (*Bhā. Purāṇa*); Indra in the 5th Manvantara (*Bh. Purāṇa*); the brother of Śakuni (*M. Bh.*); another name for Brahmā, Viṣṇu, Śiva, Buddha, and Kubera.
**Vibhudharāja** (S) (M) 1. king of the gods. 3. another name for Indra.
**Vibhumat** (S) (M) 1. omnipresent; extending everywhere; omnipotent; appearing in many forms. 3. another name for Kṛṣṇa.
**Vibhūrasi** (S) (M) 1. highly powerful. 3. son of the agni called Adbhuta (*M. Bh.*)
**Vibhūṣā** (S) (F) 1. ornament; decoration. 2. light; splendour; beauty.
**Vibhūṣanā** (S) (F) decorated; ornamented; splendour; beauty.
**Vibhūṣana** (S) (M) 1. ornament; adorning. 3. another name for Manjuśrī.
**Vibhūṣita** (S) (F) decorated; adorned.
**Vibhūṣṇu** (S) (M) 1. omnipresent. 3. another name for Śiva.
**Vibhūti** (S) (F) 1. expansion; abundance; splendour; fortune; welfare; plenty. 3. another

name for Lakṣmī.

**Vibhūti** (S) (M) 1. pervading. 2. penetrating; abundant; plentiful; mighty; powerful; ash. 3. a son of Viśvāmitra (*M. Bh.*)

**Vibhūtibhūṣaṇa** (S) (M) 1. full of powers; adorned by ash. 3. another name for Śiva.

**Vibhūvas** (S) (M) powerful.

**Vibhvan** (S) (M) 1. far-reaching; penetrating; all pervading. 3. a semi-divine being and son of Sudhanvan a descendant of Aṅgiras who became divine due to his good works; a ṛbhu (*Ṛg Veda*)

**Vibodha** (S) (M) intelligence; awakening; perception.

**Vibuddha** (S) (M) awakened; expanded; clever; skilful.

**Vibudha** (S) (M) 1. wise; learned. 2. sage; god; teacher. 3. the son of Devamīdha (*Rāmāyaṇa*); another name for the moon.

**Vibudhāćārya** (S) (M) 1. teacher of the gods; preceptor of the wise. 3. another name for Bṛhaspati.

**Vibudhaguru** (S) (M) 1. teacher of the gods. 3. another name for Bṛhaspati.

**Vibudhapati** (S) (M) 1. king of the gods. 3. another name for Indra.

**Vibudhendra** (S) (M) best of the wise.

**Vibudheśvara** (S) (M) king of the gods.

**Vićakṣaṇa** (S) (M) conspicuous; visible; sagacious; far-sighted.

**Vićakṣṇu** (S) (M) 1. perceiver; observer. 3. an ancient king and propounder of vegetarianism (*M. Bh.*)

**Vićakṣus** (S) (M) 1. eyeless; blind. 3. a king (*H. Purāṇa*)

**Vićāru** (S) (M) 1. thoughtful; charming; handsome; ever-moving; traveller. 3. a son of Kṛṣṇa and Rukmiṇī (*Bhāgavata*)

**Vićintana** (S) (M) thought.

**Vićitrā** (S) (F) 1. strange; variegated; wonderful. 2. a white deer. 3. a river (*V. Purāṇa*)

**Vićitra** (S) (M) 1. strange; variegated; motley; brilliant; manifold; various; wonderful; diverse; charming; lovely; beautiful. 3. a son of Manu Raućya (*H. Purāṇa*); a Kṣatriya king born from a portion of the asura Krodhavaśa (*M. Bh.*); *Curcumis trigonus*; Aśoka tree (*Saraca indica*)

**Vićitrabhūṣana** (S) (M) wonderful brilliant ornament.

**Vićitravīrya** (S) (M) 1. of marvellous heroism. 3. the son of Śāntanu and Satyavatī and half-brother of Bhīṣma, he married Ambikā and Ambālikā of Kāśi but died childless (*M. Bh.*)

**Vidalla** (S) (M) 1. split; expanded; divided; a fragment; pomegranate bark. 3. a minister of King Dhruvasandhi (*M. Bh.*)

**Vidaṇḍa** (S) (M) 1. door-keeper; door. 3. an ancient king (*M. Bh.*)

**Viḍanga** (S) (M) clever; skilful; able.

**Vidarbha** (S) (M) 1. without darbhā grass. 3. a son of Ṛṣabha and brother of Bharata and the father of Nimi (*Bhāgavata*); a son of Jyāmagha; a country and its people (*H. Purāṇa*)

**Vidarbhā** (S) (F) 1. without darbhā grass. 3. a daughter of Ugra and wife of Manu Ćākṣuṣa (*Mā. Purāṇa*)

**Vidarśanā** (S) (F) right knowledge; right perception; true philosophy.

**Videha** (S) (M) 1. bodyless. 2. one who doesn't care for the body; one who is ever involved in the divine pursuits. 3. another name for the Emperor Nimi and the king of Mithilā (*V. Rāmāyaṇa*)

**Vidhalingām** (S) (M) the mark of creation.

**Vidhātā** (S) (M) 1. disposer; arranger; creator. 3. a son of Bhṛgu and Khyāti and husband of Niyati and father of Mṛkaṇḍu (*V. Purāṇa*); another name for Brahmā.

**Vidhātṛ** (S) (M) 1. disposer; arranger. 2. creator; maker; author; granter; giver. 3. the son of Brahmā or Bhṛgu and brother of Dhātṛ; another name for Brahmā, Viṣṇu, Śiva, Kāma and Viśvakarman.

**Vidhatru** (S) (M) 1. maker; creator. 3. another name for Brahmā.

**Vidhava** (S) (M) resembling the moon.

**Vidhi** (S) (M) 1. method; precept; creation; law; system; worshipper. 3. another name for Brahmā.

**Vidhisāra** (S) (M) 1. essence of law. 3. a king and father of Ajātaśatru (*V. Purāṇa*)

**Vidhivadhū** (S) (F) 1. wife of Brahmā.

3. another name for Sarasvatī.

**Vīdhra** (S) (M) 1. clean; clear; pure. 2. sunshine; wind; fire.

**Vidhṛti** (S) (M) 1. separation; division; partition; arrangement. 3. father of Hiraṇyanābha (*Bhāgavata*)

**Vidhu** (S) (M) 1. solitary; alone. 3. a rākṣasa; another name for Brahmā, Viṣṇu and the moon.

**Vidhūma** (S) (M) 1. smokeless. 3. a vasu (*K. Sāgara*)

**Vidhumukhi** (S) (F) moon faced.

**Vidhupriyā** (S) (F) 1. dear to the moon. 2. a lunar mansion.

**Vidīp** (S) (M) shining forth; illuminating.

**Vidīpaka** (S) (M) 1. one that illuminates. 2. lamp.

**Vidīpitā** (S) (F) 1. illuminated. 2. bright.

**Vidipta** (S) (M) shining; bright.

**Vidiśā** (S) (F) 1. an intermediate region. 3. a river whose deity lives in the palace of Varuṇa (*M. Bh.*)

**Vidita** (S) (M) known; learnt; understood.

**Viditā** (S) (F) 1. known; understood; perceived. 3. a Jaina goddess (*J.S. Koṣa*)

**Vidman** (S) (M) knowledge; intelligence; wisdom.

**Vidojas** (S) (M) 1. with well-known power. 3. another name for Indra.

**Vidrāvaṇa** (S) (M) 1. putting to flight. 3. a son of Kaśyapa and Danu (*M. Purāṇa*)

**Vidruta** (S) (M) 1. with great speed. 3. a king in the family of Yayāti who is the son of Rućaka (*Bhāgavata*)

**Vidu** (S) (M) 1. intelligent; wise. 3. a deity of the Bodhi tree (*B. Literature*)

**Vidujjvalā** (S) (F) flash of lightning.

**Vidulā** (S) (F) 1. wise; intelligent. 3. a heroic Kṣatriya woman who sent her fleeing son back into the battlefield (*M. Bh.*); the mother of Sanjaya the narrator of the battle to Dhṛtarāṣṭra (*M. Bh.*); *Calamus rotang; Acacia rugata.*

**Vidura** (S) (M) 1. knowing; wise; intelligent; learned; skilled. 3. half-brother of Dhṛtarāṣṭra and Pāṇḍu who was advisor to the former and a man of collosal intelligence, known for his righteousness, he was a partial incarnation of Dharma born of Vyāsa and a Śudra woman (*M. Bh.*)

**Vidūra** (S) (M) 1. very remote or distant; far removed from. 3. a Kuru king who was the son of Kuru and Śubhāṅgī and the husband of Saṁpriyā and the father of Anaśvā (*M. Bh.*)

**Viduraja** (S) (M) 1. son of the wise. 2. the cat's-eye jewel.

**Vidūrastha** (S) (M) 1. thrown far. 3. father of Māninī (*Ma. Purāṇa*)

**Vidūratha** (S) (M) 1. distant. 3. a king of the Vṛṣṇi dynasty who became a viśvadeva after death; a Purū king (*M. Bh.*); a king who was the father of Sunīti, Sumati and Mudāvatī (*Mā. Purāṇa*); a king of the Bharata family who was the son of Suratha and the father of Sārvabhauma (*Bhāgavata*); the brother of Dantavaktra (*Bhāgavata*); a muni; a son of the 12th Manu; a descendant of Vṛṣṇi; a son of Kuru (*M. Bh.*); a son of Bhajamana and father of Śūra; a son of Suratha and father of Ṛkṣa; a son of Ćitraratha (*Bhā. Purāṇa*)

**Vidurya** (S) (M) 1. belonging to the wise. 2. Lapiz lazuli.

**Viduṣa** (S) (M) 1. wise. 3. a king of the Aṅga dynasty who was the son of King Ghṛta and father of Praćetas (*A. Purāṇa*)

**Viduṣī** (S) (F) wise.

**Vidvala** (S) (M) clever.

**Vidvattama** (S) (M) 1. most wise. 3. another name for Śiva.

**Vidvattara** (S) (M) very wise.

**Vidveśi** (S) (F) 1. having resentment. 3. a rākṣasī daughter of Duhsaha (*Mā. Purāṇa*)

**Vidyā** (S) (F) 1. knowledge; learning; science; philosophy. 3. a maid of Devī Umā (*M. Bh.*); a deity of the 3 Vedas (*Ṛg Veda*); another name for Durgā.

**Vidyābhūṣana** (S) (M) ornament of knowledge.

**Vidyaćandra** (S) (M) 1. moon of knowledge; most knowledgeable. 3. a sage who was the son of Kuśika.

**Vidyādevī** (S) (F) 1. goddess of learning. 3. a Jaina divinity (*J.S. Koṣa*)

**Vidyādhara** (S) (M) 1. possessed of science

and spells. 3. attendants of Śiva dwelling in the Himālayas (*H. Purāṇa*)

**Vidyādhāra** (S) (M) receptacle of knowledge.

**Vidyādharī** (S) (F) 1. bearing knowledge. 3. a daughter of Śūrasena (*Bhā. Purāṇa*); attendants of Śiva.

**Vidyādhidevatā** (S) (F) 1. presiding god of knowledge. 3. Sarasvatī as the tutelary deity of science.

**Vidyādhipa** (S) (M) 1. lord of knowledge. 3. another name for Śiva.

**Vidyāgaurī** (S) (F) goddess of knowledge.

**Vidyākara** (S) (M) mine of learning.

**Vidyānanda** (S) (M) delight in knowledge.

**Vidyānātha** (S) (M) 1. lord of knówledge. 3. a Sanskṛt writer of rhetoric and the member of the court of Warangal (14th century)

**Vidyāpati** (S) (M) master of knowledge.

**Vidyāraṇya** (S) (M) 1. taking pleasure in knowledge. 3. an authority on medical diagnosis (14th century A.D.)

**Vidyāratna** (S) (M) jewel of learning.

**Vidyāsāgara** (S) (M) 1. ocean of knowledge. 3. the father of Bhartṛhari.

**Vidyāvadhū** (S) (F) a goddess presiding over learning.

**Vidyāvatansa** (S) (M) 1. perfect in learning. 3. a vidyādhara.

**Vidyāvati** (S) (F) 1. learned. 3. an apsarā (*V. Purāṇa*)

**Vidyeśa** (S) (M) 1. lord of learning. 3. another name for Śiva.

**Vidyotā** (S) (F) 1. consisting of lightning; shining; glittering. 3. an apsarā (*M. Bh.*)

**Vidyota** (S) (M) 1. shining; glittering. 3. a son of Dharma and Lambā and the father of Sthanayitnu (*Bhā. Purāṇa*)

**Vidyudakṣa** (S) (M) 1. with glittering eyes. 3. a daitya (*H. Purāṇa*)

**Vidyudambhas** (S) (F) 1. shining water. 3. a river (*V. Purāṇa*)

**Vidvuddhara** (S) (M) 1. bearer of lightning; cloud. 3. a gandharva.

**Vidyuddhvaja** (S) (M) 1. lightning bannered. 3. an asura (*K. Sāgara*)

**Vidyudrūpa** (S) (M) 1. of the form of lightning. 2. with a shining form. 3. a yakṣa who was a favourite of Kubera and the husband of Madanikā the daughter of Menakā (*Mā. Purāṇa*)

**Vidyudvallī** (S) (F) a flash of lightning.

**Vidyudvarćas** (S) (M) 1. flashing like lightning. 3. a viśvadeva (*M. Bh.*)

**Vidyudvarṇā** (S) (F) 1. lightning coloured. 3. an apsarā (*V. Purāṇa*)

**Vidyudyotā** (S) (F) with the brightness of lightning.

**Vidyujjihvā** (S) (F) 1. lightning tongued. 3. a mother attending on Skanda (*M. Bh.*)

**Vidyujjihva** (S) (M) 1. with a lightning like tongue. 3. a rākṣasa who was a friend of Ghaṭotkaća (*M. Bh.*); the husband of Śūrparṇakhā and the father of Śambhukumāra (*K. Rāmāyaṇa*); a rākṣasa follower of Rāvaṇa (*V. Rāmāyaṇa*); a son of Viśravas and Vākā (*Vā. Purāṇa*); a yakṣa (*K. Sāgara*)

**Vidyullatā** (S) (F) creeper of lightning.

**Vidyullekhā** (S) (F) a streak of lightning.

**Vidyunmālā** (S) (F) 1. a wreath of lightning. 3. a yakṣi; a daughter of Suroha (*K. Sāgara*)

**Vidyunmālin** (S) (M) 1. garlanded with lightning. 3. a son of Tārakāsura; a rākṣasa friend of Rāvaṇa (*Rāmāyaṇa*); a vidyādhara (*H. Purāṇa*)

**Vidyut** (S) (M) 1. flashing; glittering. 3. an asura; a rākṣasa (*V. Purāṇa*)

**Vidyutā** (S) (F) 1. lightning; a flashing thunderbolt; the dawn. 3. the 4 daughters of Prajāpati Bahuputra; an apsarā (*M. Bh.*)

**Vidyutākṣa** (S) (M) 1. lightning eyed. 2. with glittering eyes. 3. a warrior of Skanda (*M. Bh.*)

**Vidyutapuñjā** (S) (F) 1. heap of lightning. 3. the daughter of the dānava Vidyutprabha (*M. Bh.*)

**Vidyutapuñja** (S) (M) 1. heap of lightning. 3. a vidyādhara.

**Vidyutkeśin** (S) (M) 1. with glittering hair. 3. a rākṣasa king and father of Sukeśa (*M. Bh.*)

**Vidyutparṇā** (S) (F) 1. bearing lightning as wings. 3. an apsarā daughter of Kaśyapa and Prādhā (*H. Purāṇa*)

**Vidyutprabhā** (S) (F) 1. flashing like lightning. 3. a daughter of the king of the rākṣasas; a daughter of the king of the yakṣas (*K. Sāgara*); a nāga maiden; an apsarā (*M. Bh.*); the granddaughter of Māhābali (*K. Sāgara*)

**Vidyutprabha** (S) (M) 1. flashing like lightning. 3. a king of the daityas; a hermit (*M. Bh.*); a dānava who was a devotee of Rudradeva (*M. Bh.*)

**Vigāhana** (S) (M) 1. plunger; penetrator; diver; obtainer; practicer. 3. a king of Mukuṭa Vanśa (*M. Bh.*); another name for fire.

**Vigataśoka** (S) (M) 1. griefless. 3. a grandson of Aśoka.

**Vigatoddhava** (S) (M) 1. free from levity. 3. another name for Buddha.

**Vighana** (S) (M) 1. cloudless; best attacker. 3. a rākṣasa on the side of Rāvaṇa (*V. Rāmāyaṇa*)

**Vighnahantṛ** (S) (M) 1. destroyer of obstacles. 3. another name for Gaṇeśa.

**Vighnahārin** (S) (M) 1. vanquisher of obstacles. 3. another name for Gaṇeśa.

**Vighnajit** (S) (M) 1. overcoming obstacles. 3. another name for Gaṇeśa.

**Vighnanāśaka** (S) (M) 1. destroyer of obstacles. 3. another name for Gaṇeśa.

**Vighnanāyaka** (S) (M) 1. lord of obstacles. 2. one who removes obstacles. 3. another name for Gaṇeśa.

**Vighnapati** (S) (M) 1. master of obstacles. 3. another name for Gaṇeśa.

**Vighnarāja** (S) (M) 1. king of obstacles. 3. another name for Gaṇeśa.

**Vighnavināyaka** (S) (M) 1. vanquisher of obstacles. 3. another name for Gaṇeśa.

**Vighneśvara** (S) (M) 1. god of obstacles. 3. another name for Gaṇeśa.

**Vigraha** (S) (M) 1. separate; independent; idol; image. 3. one of the 2 attendants given to Skanda by the ocean (*M. Bh.*); another name for Śiva.

**Vihā** (S) (F) heaven.

**Vihān** (S) (M) morning; dawn.

**Vihaga** (S) (M) 1. sky goer. 2. arrow; bird. 3. another name for the sun and moon.

**Vihagapati** (S) (M) 1. king of birds. 3. another name for Garuḍa.

**Vihagavega** (S) (M) 1. as swift as a bird. 3. a vidyādhara (*H. Purāṇa*)

**Vihanga** (S) (M) 1. flying; sky going. 2. bird; arrow. 3. a serpent of the family of Airāvata (*M. Bh.*); another name for the sun and moon.

**Vihangama** (S) (M) 1. moving in the sky. 3. soldier of the army of Khara (*V. Rāmāyaṇa*); another name for the sun, and Garuḍa as the incarnation of Viṣṇu.

**Vihārin** (S) (M) 1. wandering. 2. a wanderer for pleasure. 3. another name for Kṛṣṇa.

**Vihasatikā** (S) (F) gentle laughter; smiling.

**Vihava** (S) (M) invocation.

**Vihavya** (S) (M) 1. to be invoked; to be desired. 3. a ṛṣi of the Aṅgiras family (*Ṛg Veda*); the son of Varćas of the Gṛtsamada dynasty and the father of Vitatya (*M. Bh.*)

**Vihuṇḍa** (S) (M) 1. not a tiger. 3. an asura who was the son of Huṇḍa and who was killed by Pārvatī (*P. Purāṇa*)

**Vijarā** (S) (F) 1. never growing old. 3. a river in Brahmā's world.

**Vijayā** (S) (F) 1. victorious; triumphant. 3. a friend of Durgā (*M. Bh.*); Kṛṣṇa's birthday (*H. Purāṇa*); the wife of Yama (*M. Bh.*); a yoginī (*H. Koṣa*); a daughter of Dakṣa (*Rāmāyaṇa*); Kṛṣṇa's garland (*M. Bh.*); the daughter of King Dāśārha and wife of Emperor Bhumanyu (*M. Bh.*); the daughter of Dyutimān and the wife of the Pāṇḍava Sahadeva and the mother of Suhotra (*M. Bh.*); the queen of Ćampāpuri and mother of Jaina Tirathaṅkara Vusupūjya (*J.S. Koṣa*); another name for Durgā.

**Vijaya** (S) (M) 1. victory; conquest; triumph. 3. the hour of Kṛṣṇa's birth; a kind of flute (*Bh. Purāṇa*); a chariot of the gods; a son of Jayanta (*H. Purāṇa*); a son of Vasudeva (*H. Purāṇa*); a son of Kṛṣṇa (*Bh. Purāṇa*); an attendant of Viṣṇu; an attendant of Padmapāṇi; a warrior on the Pāṇḍava side (*M. Bh.*); a son of Svarociṣ (*Mā. Purāṇa*); a councillor of Daśaratha (*Rāmāyaṇa*); a son of Jaya (*H. Purāṇa*); a son of Canću; a son of Bṛhanmānas (*H. Purāṇa*); a son of Yajñaśrī; the founder of Buddhist civilization in Ceylon (*B. Literature*); the 20th Arhat of the future and the father of the 21st Arhat of the present Avasarpiṇī; an attendant of the 8th Arhat of the present Avasarpiṇī (*J.S. Koṣa*); a son of Kalki (*K. Purāṇa*); a lance of Rudra; a son of Sanjaya (*V. Purāṇa*); a son of Sudeva (*Bh. Purāṇa*); a gatekeeper of Vaikuṇṭha (*Bh. Purāṇa*); a son of Purūravas and Urvaśī (*Bh. Purāṇa*); a Kosala king (*V. Rāmāyaṇa*); secret name given to Arjuna by Yudhiṣṭhira (*M. Bh.*); a son of Dhṛtarāṣṭra (*M. Bh.*); a king of Vārāṇasī (*Bh. Purāṇa*); the trident of Śiva (*M. Bh.*); a bow of Indra (*M. Bh.*); the divine bow of Karṇa (*M. Bh.*); Sweet Flag (*acorus calamus*); Couch Grass (*Cynodon dactylon*); Common Indigo (*Indigofera tinctoria*); Indian Madder (*Rubia cordifolia*); Black Myrobalan (*Terminalia chebula*); another name for Yama, Arjuna, Śiva and Viṣṇu.

**Vijayaćandra** (S) (M) moon of victory.

**Vijayadatta** (S) (M) 1. bestowed by victory. 3. the hare in the moon (*P. Ratra*)

**Vijayāditya** (S) (M) sun of victory.

**Vijayakānta** (S) (M) beloved of victory.

**Vijayaketu** (S) (M) 1. victory bannered. 3. a vidyādhara (*V. Samhitā*)

**Vijayalakṣmī** (S) (F) 1. goddess of victory. 3. one of the 8 Lakṣmīs who keeps the treasury of Brahmā and was reborn as Laṅkalakṣmī guarding Rāvaṇa until hit by Hanumān when she resumed her original form (*V. Rāmāyaṇa*); the mother of Venkaṭa (*R. Taraṅginī*)

**Vijayanandana** (S) (M) 1. delighting in victory; son of victory. 3. a ćakravartin.

**Vijayanātha** (S) (M) lord of victory.

**Vijayāṅka** (S) (M) with a mark of victory.

**Vijayanta** (S) (M) 1. victorious in the end. 3. another name for Indra.

**Vijayantikā** (S) (F) 1. victorious in the end. 3. a yoginī (*A. Koṣa*)

**Vijayarāja** (S) (M) king of victory.

**Vijayarāma** (S) (M) victorious Rāma; abode of victory; consisting of victory.

**Vijayaśrī** (S) (F) 1. glory of victory. 3. the goddess of victory; a kinnarī (*K. Vyuha*)

**Vijayavatī** (S) (F) 1. victorious. 3. the daughter of the nāga Gandhamālin (*K. Sāgara*)

**Vijayavega** (S) (M) 1. with a passion for victory. 3. a vidyādhara (*K. Sāgara*)

**Vijayendra** (S) (M) lord of victory.

**Vijayeśa** (S) (M) 1. lord of victory. 3. another name for Śiva.

**Vijayin** (S) (M) victor.

**Vijeṣakṛt** (S) (M) bestowing victory.

**Viji** (S) (M) to conquer; win; to excel; to defeat.

**Vijita** (S) (M) 1. conquered. 2. defeated; won.

**Vijitāśva** (S) (M) 1. with subdued horses. 3. a son of Emperor Pṛthu (*Bhāgavata*)

**Vijitātman** (S) (M) 1. self subdued. 3. another name for Śiva.

**Vijiti** (S) (F) 1. victory; triumph. 3. a goddess (*M. Bh.*)

**Vijittāri** (S) (F) 1. vanquisher. 3. a rākṣasa (*V. Rāmāyaṇa*)

**Vijitvarā** (S) (F) 1. best among the conquerors. 3. a goddess (*Ć. Upaniṣad*)

**Vijña** (S) (M) knowing; intelligent; wise.

**Vijñāna** (S) (M) understanding; intelligence; knowledge.

**Vijñānaprasāda** (S) (M) with the blessing of knowledge; gift of science.

**Vijñati** (S) (F) knowledge; understanding.

**Vijṛmbhaka** (S) (M) 1. blossoming; yawning; expanding. 3. a vidyādhara (*H. Purāṇa*)

**Vijula** (S) (M) the Silkcotton tree (*Bombax heptaphyllum*)

**Vijvala** (S) (M) 1. blessing of knowledge. 3. the son of the bird Kunjala and a famous scholar.

**Vika** (S) (M) bird; wind.

**Vikaća** (S) (M) 1. hairless; shining; brilliant; radiant; opened. 3. a dānava (*H. Purāṇa*)

**Vikaćalambā** (S) (F) 1. radiant mother. 3. another name for Durgā (*D. Purāṇa*)

**Vikaćānana** (S) (M) with a radiant face.

**Vikaćaśrī** (S) (F) with radiant beauty.

**Vikadru** (S) (M) 1. tawny complexioned. 3. a Yādava warrior (*M. Bh.*)

**Vikala** (S) (M) 1. crippled; imperfect. 3. a son of Śambara; a son of Lambodara (*Bh. Purāṇa*); a son of Jīmūta (*V. Purāṇa*)

**Vikāla** (S) (M) twilight.

**Vikalaṅka** (S) (M) spotless; bright as the moon.

**Vikāma** (S) (M) free from desire.

**Vikarālā** (S) (F) 1. formidable; terrible. 3. another name for Durgā.

**Vikarṇa** (S) (M) 1. large eared. 3. a kind of arrow (*M. Bh.*); a son of Karṇa; a son of Dhṛtarāṣṭra (*M. Bh.*); a hermit and devotee of Śiva (*M. Bh.*)

**Vikarṣaṇa** (S) (M) 1. distractor. 3. an arrow of Kāma.

**Vikartaṇa** (S) (M) 1. dividing; cutting as under. 3. a solar dynasty king (*P. Purāṇa*); another name for the sun.

**Vikāsa** (S) (M) brightness; light; lustre; budding; cheerfulness; expansion; serenity; to appear; to become visible; to shine forth; radiance; development; growth.

**Vikāśini** (S) (F) 1. shining. 2. radiant; illuminating. 3. a mother in Skanda's train (*H. Purāṇa*)

**Vikaṭā** (S) (F) 1. huge; large; great; terrible; ugly; dreadful. 3. the mother of Gautama Buddha (*B. Literature*); a Buddhist divinity (*B. Literature*); a rākṣasi in the harem of Rāvaṇa (*V. Rāmāyaṇa*)

**Vikaṭa** (S) (M) 1. huge; large; great; terrible; ugly; dreadful. 3. an attendant of Skanda (*M. Bh.*); a rākṣasa (*H. Purāṇa*); a brother of Prahasta; a son of Dhṛtarāṣṭra (*M. Bh.*)

**Vikaṭābha** (S) (M) 1. of terrible appearance. 3. an asura (*H. Purāṇa*)

**Vikaṭākṣa** (S) (M) 1. with dreadful eyes. 3. an asura (*H. Purāṇa*)

**Vikaṭānana** (S) (M) 1. ugly faced. 3. a son of Dhṛtarāṣṭra (*K. Sāgara*)

**Vikaṭavadana** (S) (M) 1. monstrous faced. 3. an attendant of Durgā (*M. Bh.*)

**Vikāthinī** (S) (F) 1. boasting. 3. an attendant of Skanda (*M. Bh.*)

**Vikeśī** (S) (F) 1. hairless; with dishevelled hair. 3. the wife of Śiva manifested in the form of Mahī or the earth (*Purāṇas*)

**Vikheda** (S) (M) free from weariness.

**Vikhyāti** (S) (F) fame; celebrity.

**Vikoka** (S) (M) 1. detached from sex. 3. the son of the asura Vṛka and the younger brother of Koka (*K. Purāṇa*)

**Vikrama** (S) (M) 1. step; stride; pace; valour; strength; heroism; power. 3. a son of Vasu (*K. Sāgara*); a son of Vatsaprī; a son of Kanaka (*Mā. Purāṇa*); another name for Viṣṇu.

**Vikramaćandra** (S) (M) moon among heroes.

**Vikramāditya** (S) (M) 1. son of valour. 3. a mighty emperor of Bhārata who was the king of Ujjayinī and the son of King Mahendrāditya of Ujjayinī and Saumyadarśanā and was considered an incarnation of Mālyavān, he was the founder of the Vikrama era, a great patron of literature, he was supposed to have been killed by King Śālivāhana of the Deccan.

**Vikramaka** (S) (M) 1. petty hero. 3. an attendant of Skanda (*M. Bh.*)

**Vikramakesarin** (S) (M) 1. strong like a lion. 3. a king of Pāṭaliputra (*K. Sāgara*)

**Vikramaśīla** (S) (M) 1. strong in character. 3. a king who was the husband of Kālindī and the father of Durgama (*Mā. Purāṇa*)

**Vikrameśa** (S) (M) 1. lord of valour. 3. a Buddhist saint.

**Vikramin** (S) (M) 1. striding; courageous; gallant. 3. another name for Viṣṇu.

**Vikrānta** (S) (M) 1. courageous; bold; taking wide strides; victorious. 3. a prajāpati (*V. Purāṇa*); a son of Kuvalayāśva and Madālasā (*Mā. Purāṇa*); a king who was the son of Sudhṛti and the father of King Dama (*Vā. Purāṇa*); *Adiantum lunulatum; Cleome viscosa.*

**Vikrānti** (S) (F) 1. all pervading power. 2. heroism; prowess; strength; might.

**Vikrīta** (S) (M) 1. sold. 3. a prajāpati.

**Vikrodha** (S) (M) free from anger.

**Vikṛtā** (S) (F) 1. deformed; changed; strange. 3. a yoginī (*H. Koṣa*)

**Vikṛta** (S) (M) 1. deformed; altered; strange. 3. a prajāpati (*V. Rāmāyaṇa*); a demon son of Parivarta (*Mā. Purāṇa*); Kāma in his form as a Brāhmin (*M. Bh.*)

**Vikṛtadanṣtra** (S) (M) 1. with strange teeth. 3. a vidyādhara (*H. Purāṇa*)

**Vikṛti** (S) (M) 1. change; alteration. 3. a king

of the Yayāti family who was the son of Jīmūta and the father of Bhīmaratha (*Bhāgavata*)

**Vīkṣā** (S) (F) knowledge; intelligence.

**Vīkṣara** (S) (M) 1. to flow out. 3. an asura son of Kaśyapa and Danu who was reborn as King Vasumitra (*M. Bh.*); another name for Viṣṇu/Kṛṣṇa.

**Vīkukṣi** (S) (M) 1. with a prominent belly. 3. a son of Ikṣvāku and the father of Kakutstha (*D. Bhāgavata*)

**Vikuṇṭhā** (S) (F) 1. inward glance; mental concentration; penetration. 3. the mother of the devatas or minor gods of the Raivata Manvantara (*Br. Purāṇa*)

**Vikuṇṭha** (S) (M) 1. not blunt. 2. sharp; keen; penetrating; irresistable. 3. another name for Viṣṇu.

**Vikuṇṭhāna** (S) (M) 1. sharpening; penetration. 3. a son of King Hastin of the lunar dynasty and Yaśodharā who was the husband of Sudevā and the father of Ajamīdha (*M. Bh.*)

**Vikuṇṭhānana** (S) (M) 1. with an irresistible face. 2. very attractive. 3. a son of Hastin (*M. Bh.*)

**Vikusra** (S) (M) 1. crying out. 2. the moon.

**Vilāpana** (S) (M) 1. causing moaning. 3. an attendant of Śiva.

**Vilāsa** (S) (M) 1. shining forth; appearance; grace; beauty; liveliness; play; sport. 3. a hermit.

**Vilāsamayī** (S) (F) playful; full of grace; charming.

**Vilāsantī** (S) (F) flashing; shining; glittering.

**Vilāsin** (S) (M) 1. shining; radiant; sportive; playful. 2. lover. 3. another name for Kṛṣṇa, Śiva, Kāma, and the moon.

**Vilāsinī** (S) (F) 1. radiant; shining; playful; charming; lively. 3. another name for Lakṣmī.

**Vilasita** (S) (M) gleaming; glittering; shining forth; appearing.

**Vilohitā** (S) (F) 1. deep red. 3. one of the 7 tongues of fire (*M. Upaniṣad*)

**Vilohita** (S) (M) 1. deep red. 3. a rākṣasa son of Kaśyapa (*Vā. Purāṇa*); another name for Śiva, Rudra and Agni.

**Viloman** (S) (M) 1. opposite; inverse; hair-less. 3. a king who is the son of King Vahni (*Bhāgavata*) or Kapotaromā (*V. Purāṇa*)

**Vimada** (S) (M) 1. sober; free from intoxication. 3. a king known for his truthfulness (*Ṛg Veda*)

**Vimahat** (S) (M) very great; immense.

**Vimalā** (S) (F) 1. stainless. 2. clean; pure; bright; spotless; sacred. 3. a calf who was the daughter of Rohiṇī and the granddaughter of Surabhi (*M. Bh.*); Dākṣāyaṇī in Puruṣottama; a yoginī; a daughter of Gandharvī (*M. Bh.*)

**Vimala** (S) (M) 1. stainless; spotless. 2. clean; bright; pure; clear; transparent; white. 3. the brother of Yaśas; an asura (*K. Sāgara*); the 5th Arhat of the past Utsarpiṇī and the 13th in the present Avasarpiṇī (*J.S. Kośa*); a king of South India who was the son of Sudyumna (*Bhāgavata*); a king of Ratnatāṭa and ally of Śatrughna's (*P. Purāṇa*); one of the 13 stages of a Bodhisattva (*B. Literature*); *Acacia rugata*.

**Vimalabhadra** (S) (M) spotless person.

**Vimalabodha** (S) (M) pure intelligence.

**Vimalaćandra** (S) (M) spotless moon.

**Vimaladatta** (S) (M) given by purity.

**Vimalagarbha** (S) (M) 1. womb of purity. 2. originator of purity. 3. a Bodhisattva.

**Vimalakīrti** (S) (M) of spotless fame.

**Vimalamati** (S) (F) pure in heart.

**Vimalanātha** (S) (M) 1. lord of the pure ones. 3. the 13th Jaina Tirathankara son of King Kṛtavarmā and Queen Śyāmā of Kāmpilapur (*J.S. Kośa*)

**Vimalanetra** (S) (M) 1. pure eyed. 3. a Buddha.

**Vimalapiṇḍaka** (S) (M) 1. spotless snake. 3. a nāga son of Kaśyapa and Kadru (*M. Bh.*)

**Vimalaprabha** (S) (M) 1. pure light. 3. a Buddha.

**Vimalaśrīgarbha** (S) (M) 1. divine womb of purity. 3. a Boddhisattva.

**Vimalavegaśrī** (S) (M) 1. master of pure emotions. 3. a gandharva.

**Vimaleśa** (S) (M) lord of purity.

**Vimanyu** (S) (M) free from anger.

**Vimardana** (S) (M) 1. pressing; squeezing; destroying. 2. fragrance; perfume. 3. a rākṣasa (*V. Rāmāyaṇa*); a vidyādhara (*K. Sāgara*)

**Vimarśa** (S) (M) 1. deliberation; examination; test; discussion; knowledge; intelligence. 3. another name for Śiva.

**Vimarśana** (S) (M) 1. discussion; discourse. 3. the king of the Kirātas.

**Vimba** (S) (M) 1. an illuminated point. 2. an intensely glowing ray of the sun.

**Vimoćana** (S) (M) 1. unyoking; loosening; delivering. 3. another name for Śiva.

**Vimoćanī** (S) (F) 1. liberation; emancipation; freedom. 3. a river.

**Vimṛdha** (S) (M) 1. averter of enemies. 3. another name for Indra.

**Vimuća** (S) (M) 1. freed; liberated. 3. a south Indian hermit (*M. Bh.*)

**Vimukha** (S) (M) 1. with the face averted. 3. a hermit in Indra's court (*M. Bh.*)

**Vimuktaćandra** (S) (M) 1. moon among the free. 2. liberated. 3. a Bodhisattva.

**Vimuktāćarya** (S) (M) liberated teacher; preceptor of the liberated.

**Vimuktasena** (S) (M) 1. commander of the liberated. 3. a teacher of the Mādhyamika-Svātantrika school of Buddhism at Nālandā.

**Vīṇā** (S) (F) 1. lightning; lute. 3. the Indian lute supposed to have been invented by Nārada (*Bhā. Purāṇa*); a yoginī (*A. Koṣa*); a river (*M. Bh.*)

**Vīṇadatta** (S) (M) 1. bestowed by lute. 2. musician. 3. a gandharva (*K. Sāgara*)

**Vinadī** (S) (F) 1. noisy. 3. a river (*M. Bh.*)

**Vīṇāhasta** (S) (M) 1. holding a lute. 3. another name for Śiva.

**Vinamratā** (S) (F) politeness; gentleness; modesty.

**Vinanda** (S) (M) to rejoice.

**Vīṇāpāṇi** (S) (M) 1. lute handed. 3. another name for Nārada.

**Vināśana** (S) (M) 1. destroyer; killer; murderer. 3. an asura born to Kaśyapa and Kālā (*M. Bh.*)

**Vinatā** (S) (F) 1. humble; one who bows. 2. hunchback. 3. a daughter of Dakṣa and wife of Kaśyapa and mother of Aruṇa, Garuḍa, Sumati (*M. Bh.*); a rākṣasī (*Ś. Purāṇa*)

**Vinata** (S) (M) 1. inclined; bowing. 2. humble. 3. a son of Sudyumna; a son of Śveta and a captain of Rāma's monkey army (*V. Rāmāyaṇa*)

**Vinatānandavardhana** (S) (M) 1. increasing the joy of Vinatā. 3. another name for Garuḍa.

**Vinatāsūnu** (S) (M) 1. son of Vinatā. 3. another name for Garuḍa.

**Vinatāsuta** (S) (M) 1. son of Vinatā. 3. another name for Garuḍa.

**Vinatāśva** (S) (M) 1. with modest horses. 3. a son of Ilā or Sudyumna and grandson of Vaivaśvata Manu (*V. Purāṇa*)

**Vinatātmaja** (S) (M) 1. son of Vinatā. 3. another name for Garuḍa.

**Vinati** (S) (F) prayer; entreaty; humility; modesty.

**Vīṇāvinoda** (S) (M) 1. lute player; amusing with the lute. 3. a vidyādhara (*B. Rāmāyaṇa*)

**Vinaya** (S) (M) 1. taking away; leading; guidance; decency; modesty; control. 3. mildness personified as the son of Kriyā or Lajjā; a son of Sudyumna (*Mā. Purāṇa*)

**Vināyaka** (S) (M) 1. remover; leader; guide; lord of prayer. 3. a deity of the gaṇas or attendants of Śiva (*M. Bh.*); another name for Gaṇeśa.

**Viṇāyavatī** (S) (F) 1. polite; gentle; modest. 3. a queen of Kāmarūpa and wife of Bhūtivarman.

**Vināyikā** (S) (F) the consort of Gaṇeśa.

**Vinda** (S) (M) 1. finding; getting; gaining. 3. a son of Dhṛtarāṣṭra (*M. Bh.*); a prince of Avanti who fought on the side of the Kauravas; a Kekaya prince on the side of the Kauravas (*M. Bh.*)

**Vindhya** (S) (M) 1. gaining height. 3. a low range of hills connecting the Western and Eastern Ghāts which form the southernmost portion of the middle region of Indra, they are personified by a deity who elevated himself to bar the progress of the sun and moon and was stopped by Agastya (*M. Bh.*)

**Vindhyaketu** (S) (M) 1. mountain bannered. 3. a king of the Pulindas (*K. Sāgara*)

**Vindhyānilayā** (S) (F) 1. wind of the Vindhyas; resident of the Vindhyas. 3. a form of Durgā (*A. Koṣa*)

**Vindhyapāra** (S) (M) 1. beyond the

Vindhyas; higher than the Vindhyas. 3. a king of the vidyādharas (*K. Sāgara*)

**Vindhyaṭana** (S) (M) 1. conqueror of Vindhya; as high as Vindhya. 2. a great scholar. 3. another name for sage Agastya.

**Vindhyāvalī** (S) (F) 1. row of Vindhya mountains. 3. the wife of Mahābali and the mother of Bāṇa and Kumbhīnāśī (*M. Purāṇa*)

**Vindhyavāsinī** (S) (F) 1. dwelling in the Vindhyas. 3. a form of Durgā (*D. Purāṇa*)

**Vīndu** (S) (F) dot; point; intelligent; wise.

**Vindu** (S) (M) knowing; familiar with; finding; getting; acquiring.

**Vindumān** (S) (M) 1. knower; scholar; wise. 3. a king in the dynasty of Bharata who was the son of Marīći and the father of Madhu (*Bhāgavata*)

**Vinetṛ** (S) (M) leader; guide; teacher.

**Vinetra** (S) (M) teacher; preceptor.

**Vinīla** (S) (M) very blue.

**Vinimeṣa** (S) (M) a twinkle; twinkling of the eye.

**Vinirjaya** (S) (M) complete victory; conquest.

**Viniśćala** (S) (M) immovable; firm; steady.

**Vinīta** (S) (M) 1. tamed; trained. 2. well behaved; humble; modest; educated; handsome; neat. 3. a son of Pulastya (*V. Purāṇa*)

**Vinīti** (S) (F) modesty; good behaviour; training.

**Vinna** (S) (M) known; understood.

**Vinoda** (S) (M) diversion; sport; pastime; pleasure.

**Vinoditā** (S) (F) diverted; amused; delighted.

**Vinśa** (S) (M) 1. the number 20. 3. the eldest son of Ikṣvāku and the father of Vivinśa (*M. Bh.*)

**Vinśabāhu** (S) (M) 1. 20 armed. 3. another name for Rāvaṇa.

**Vinu** (S) (M) to spread in different directions.

**Vipā** (S) (F) speech.

**Vipanći** (S) (F) 1. remover of troubles. 2. the Indian lute.

**Vipāpman** (S) (M) 1. free from suffering. 3. a viśvadeva (*M. Bh.*)

**Viparṣi** (S) (M) 1. wise sage. 3. another name for Mārkaṇḍeya.

**Vipāśā** (S) (F) 1. fetterless; unbound. 3. a river, famous in the Purāṇas for having saved sage Vasiṣṭha, now known as Beas (*H. Purāṇa*)

**Vipaśćit** (S) (M) 1. inspired. 2. wise; learned. 3. Indra in the Manvantara of Manu Svārociṣa; the husband of Pīvarī (*M. Purāṇa*); another name for Buddha.

**Vipaśyin** (S) (M) 1. discerning. 2. seeing in detail. 3. a Buddha mentioned as the 1st of the 7 Tathāgatas or principal Buddhas (*B. Literature*)

**Vipāta** (S) (M) 1. shooting arrows; melting; killing. 3. a brother of Karṇa killed by Arjuna (*M. Bh.*)

**Vipina** (S) (M) jungle; wood.

**Vipinavihārī** (S) (M) 1. wanderer of the jungle. 2. one who roams the forest. 3. another name for Kṛṣṇa.

**Vipodhā** (S) (F) giving inspiration.

**Vipra** (S) (M) 1. stirred; excited; inspired. 2. wise; sage; seer. 3. a son of Śrutanjaya; a son of Dhruva; a king of the family of Dhruva who was the son of Śliṣṭi and Suććhaya (*V. Purāṇa*); another name for the moon.

**Vipraćitti** (S) (F) 1. sagacious. 3. an apsarā (*V. Purāṇa*)

**Vipraćitti** (S) (M) 1. sagacious. 3. a dānava son of Kaśyapa and Danu and the husband of Siṁhikā who was reborn as Jarāsandha (*M. Bh.*); a dānava and father of Rāhu (*M. Bh.*)

**Vipraćūḍāmaṇi** (S) (M) crest jewel among the sages; an excellent Brāhmin.

**Viprādhipa** (S) (M) 1. lord of the wise. 3. another name for the moon.

**Vipratama** (S) (M) wisest.

**Viprayogi** (S) (M) 1. wise ascetic. 3. another name for Pulastya.

**Vipṛṣṭha** (S) (M) 1. with a solid back. 2. warrior. 3. a son of Vasudeva (*Bhā. Purāṇa*)

**Vipṛthu** (S) (M) 1. not fat. 2. slender; sharp. 3. a member of the Vṛṣṇi clan who was a member of Yudhiṣṭhira's court (*M. Bh.*); an ancient emperor (*M. Bh.*); a son of Ćitraka and younger brother of Pṛthu (*M. Bh.*)

**Vipsā** (S) (F) succession; repitition.

**Vipulā** (S) (F) 1. large; great; abundant.

3. another name for the earth.

**Vipula** (S) (M) 1. large; great; wide; thick; abundant. 3. a prince of the Sauvīras (*M. Bh.*); a pupil of Devaśarman (*M. Bh.*); a mountain; a son of Vasudeva and Rohiṇī and a brother of Balarāma (*Bhā. Purāṇa*)

**Vipulamati** (S) (M) 1. abounding in intelligence. 3. a Bodhisattva.

**Vipulekṣaṇā** (S) (F) large eyed.

**Vīrā** (S) (F) 1. brave; wise; heroic; strong; powerful; excellent. 3. the wife of the Agni named Bharadvāja and the mother of the agni Vīra (*M. Bh.*); a famous river of the Purāṇas (*M. Bh.*); the wife of King Karandhama and mother of Avikṣit (*Mā. Purāṇa*)

**Vīra** (S) (M) 1. brave; hero. 2. son. 3. an asura born of Kaśyapa and Danu (*M. Bh.*); a son of Dhṛtarāṣṭra (*M. Bh.*); an agni born of Bharadvāja and his wife Vīrā who was the husband of Sarayū and the father of Siddhi (*M. Bh.*); a son of the agni called Pāṅćajanya (*M. Bh.*); a king of the Purū dynasty who was the son of Girīka (*A. Purāṇa*); a son of Puruṣa and Vairāja and the father of Priyavrata and Uttānapāda (*H. Purāṇa*); a son of Gṛnjima (*H. Purāṇa*); 2 sons of Kṛṣṇa; a son of Kṣupa and father of Vivinṣa; the father of Līlāvatī; the last Arhat of the present Avasarpiṇī (*J.S. Koṣa*); *Aconitum heterophyllum*; *Costus speciosus*; Saffron (*Crocus sativus*)

**Vīrabāhu** (S) (M) 1. strong armed. 3. a son of Dhṛtarāṣṭra; a brother of Subrahmanya (*Sk. Purāṇa*); a Ćedi king who protected Damayanti (*M. Bh.*); another name for Viṣṇu.

**Vīrabālā** (S) (F) brave maiden.

**Vīrabhadra** (S) (M) 1. distinguished hero. 3. a form of Śiva said to have emerged from his mouth with a 1000 heads, eyes and feet for the destruction of the sacrifice of Dakṣa and the protection of the devas, after that he became the Mangala planet in the sky and one portion was reborn as Ādiśankara or Śankarāćarya (*P. Purāṇa*); Khuskhus grass (*Vetiveria zizanioides*)

**Vīrabhānu** (S) (M) brave sun; sun among the brave; best warrior.

**Vīrabhūpati** (S) (M) 1. brave king. 2. king of the brave.

**Vīrāćārya** (S) (M) preceptor of the brave.

**Virādha** (S) (M) 1. thwarter. 3. a rākṣasa who was an incarnation of the gandharva Tumburu, he was killed by Rāma and Lakṣmaṇa and regained his old form (*V. Rāmāyaṇa*)

**Virādhahan** (S) (M) 1. slayer of Virādha. 3. another name for Indra or Viṣṇu.

**Vīradhanvan** (S) (M) 1. brave archer; with a strong bow. 3. a Trigarta warrior who fought on the side of the Kauravas (*M. Bh.*); a gandharva; another name for Kāma.

**Vīradharmā** (S) (M) 1. following the path of bravery. 3. an ancient king (*M. Bh.*)

**Vīradyumna** (S) (M) 1. shining with bravery; with the glory of strength. 3. a king and father of Bhūridyumna (*M. Bh.*)

**Virajā** (S) (F) 1. free from dust; clean. 2. pure. 3. the wife of Nahuṣa (*H. Purāṇa*); Durvā grass (*Panicum dactylon*); a rākṣasi (*H. Purāṇa*); a gopi or cowherdess who melted due to Rādhā's anger and became a river (*D. Bhāgavata*)

**Virāja** (S) (M) 1. ruling far and wide; shining; brilliant; splendid. 2. king; excellence; pre-eminence; dignity; majesty. 3. the 1st son of Brahmā who then produced the 1st Manu, he is also identified with Prajāpati, Brahmā, Agni, Puruṣa and later Viṣṇu/Kṛṣṇa (*Ṛg Veda*); a son of Priyavrata and Kāmyā (*H. Purāṇa*); a son of Nara (*V. Purāṇa*); a son of Rādhā (*V. Purāṇa*); a Kuru king who was the son of Avīkṣit (*M. Bh.*); another name for Agni, the sun and Buddha.

**Viraja** (S) (M) 1. free from dust; clean; pure. 3. a marut, a son of Tvaṣṭṛ (*Bh. Purāṇa*); a son of Purṇiman (*Bhā. Purāṇa*); a nāga son of Kaśyapa and Kadru (*M. Bh.*); a son of Dhṛtarāṣṭra (*M. Bh.*); a son born of the radiance of Mahāviṣṇu who was the father of Kīrtimān (*M. Bh.*); a sage under Manu Ćākṣuṣa (*H. Purāṇa*); a son of Manu Sāvarṇi (*Mā. Purāṇa*); a son of Nārāyaṇa; a son of Kavi; a son of Vasiṣṭha (*Bh. Purāṇa*); a son of Paurṇamāsa.

**Virajaprabha** (S) (M) 1. pure light. 3. a Buddha.

**Virajāśka** (S) (M) 1. clear eyed. 2. one whose

perception is pure and clean. 3. a son of Manu Sāvarṇī (*Ṛg Veda*)

**Virajeśvarī** (S) (F) 1. goddess of the pure. 3. another name for Rādhā.

**Virājin** (S) (M) splendid; brilliant.

**Virājinī** (S) (F) brilliant; splendid; queen.

**Vīrājit** (S) (M) conquering heroes; eminent; illustrious; brilliant; glorious; splendid.

**Vīraka** (S) (M) 1. petty warrior. 3. a king of the Aṅga dynasty who was the son of Śibi (*A. Purāṇa*); the adopted son of Śiva and Pārvatī; a sage under Manu Ćākṣuṣa (*Bh. Purāṇa*)

**Vīraketu** (S) (M) 1. with a flag of bravery. 3. a son of King Drupada of Panćāla (*M. Bh.*); a king of Ayodhyā (*K. Sāgara*)

**Virala** (S) (M) rare.

**Vīramaṇi** (S) (M) 1. jewel among the brave. 3. a king and husband of Śrutāvatī who was a devotee of Śiva.

**Vīraṇa** (S) (M) 1. tuft of Khus grass. 3. a prajāpati and preceptor of sage Ṛaibhya (*M. Bh.*); and father of Aśikni or Vīraṇī (*M. Bh.*)

**Vīraṇaka** (S) (M) 1. made of khus grass. 3. a nāga born in the family of Dhṛtarāṣṭra (*M. Bh.*)

**Vīranārāyaṇa** (S) (M) 1. divine hero. 3. another name for Viṣṇu.

**Vīranātha** (S) (M) lord of the brave.

**Virańća** (S) (M) 1. heavenly; celestial. 3. another name for Brahmā.

**Vīrandhara** (S) (M) peacock; possessor of the brave; the mount of the bravest.

**Vīraṇī** (S) (F) 1. brave woman. 3. a daughter of Brahmā born of his left thumb who married Dakṣa and was the mother of Nārada (*D. Bhāgavata*); a disciple of Yājñavalkya (*Vā. Purāṇa*); the daughter of Vīraṇa and mother of Manu Ćākṣuṣa (*Bhā. Purāṇa*)

**Vīrarāghava** (S) (M) Rāma among the warriors; Rāma the hero.

**Vīraratha** (S) (M) bearer of bravery; with a powerful chariot.

**Virasa** (S) (M) 1. tasteless; insipid; essenceless. 3. a nāga son of Kaśyapa (*M. Bh.*)

**Vīraśekhara** (S) (M) 1. best of heroes; best among heroes. 3. a vidyādhara; a brother of Subrahmanya (*Sk. Purāṇa*); a son of Dhṛtarāṣṭra (*M. Bh.*); a Ćedi king who protected Damayantī (*M. Bh.*)

**Vīrasena** (S) (M) 1. having an army of heroes. 3. a dānava; a Niśāda king who was the father of Nala; a king of Kanyakubjā; a king of Kalinga; a king of Murala; a king of Kosala (*M. Bh.*)

**Vīrasiṁha** (S) (M) 1. brave lion; lion among the brave. 3. a captain of the army of the asura Vyālīmukha who fought with Skanda (*Sk. Purāṇa*); a son of King Vīramaṇi (*M. Bh.*)

**Vīrasvāmibhaṭṭa** (S) (M) 1. bravest warrior. 3. the father of Medhātithi (*Ṛg Veda*)

**Vīrasvāmin** (S) (M) 1. lord of the brave. 3. a dānava.

**Virāt** (S) (M) 1. shining; brilliant. 3. the grandson of Priyavrata and the son of sage Kardama (*A. Purāṇa*); the 1st incarnation of Brahmā (*Ṛg Veda*)

**Virāṭa** (S) (M) 1. majestic; magnificent. 3. the king of Matsya country who sheltered the Pāṇḍavās and was the father-in-law of Arjuna, he is supposed to have been an incarnation of the Marudgaṇas (*M. Bh.*); he was the husband of Suratha and Sudeṣṇā and the father of Śveta, Śankha, Uttarā and Uttara (*D. Purāṇa*)

**Vīratara** (S) (M) stronger hero.

**Virāva** (S) (M) 1. resounding; roaring. 3. the horse of sage Agastya (*M. Bh.*)

**Vīravarman** (S) (M) 1. protector of the brave. 3. the son of King Tāladhvaja by Nārada in his female form; a son of Sārasvata and Mālinī and the father of Subhāla, Sulabha, Lola, Kuvala and Sarasa.

**Viravin** (S) (M) 1. shouting; roaring; resounding. 3. a son of Dhṛtarāṣṭra (*M. Bh.*)

**Viraviṇī** (S) (F) 1. crying; weeping. 3. a river.

**Vīravrata** (S) (M) 1. keeping to one's purpose. 3. a king of the family of Bharata who was the son of Madhu and the father of Manthu and Amanthu (*Bhāgavata*)

**Vīrendra** (S) (M) chief of heroes.

**Vīrendrī** (S) (F) 1. goddess of the brave. 3. a yoginī (*A. Koṣa*)

**Virepas** (S) (M) blameless; faultless.

**Vīreśa** (S) (M) 1. lord of heroes. 3. another name for Śiva and Vīrabhadra.

**Vīreśvara** (S) (M) 1. god of heroes. 3. another name for Śiva and Vīrabhadra.

**Vīresvarānanda** (S) (M) 1. delight of the god of heroes; delighting the brave. 2. victory; success; achievement.

**Vīrikā** (S) (F) 1. possessed with bravery. 3. a wife of Harṣa.

**Virinća** (S) (M) 1. illuminating. 3. another name for Brahmā, Viṣṇu and Śiva.

**Vīriṇī** (S) (F) 1. of whom the brave are born. 2. a mother of sons. 3. a wife of Dakṣa also called Aśikni and mother of a 1000 sons (*M. Bh.*)

**Viroćanā** (S) (F) 1. shining upon; illuminating. 3. an attendant of Skanda (*M. Bh.*); a daughter of Prahlāda the asura king and the wife of Tvaṣṭā and the mother of Viraja (*Bhāgavata*) and Tṛśiras (*Vā. Purāṇa*)

**Viroćana** (S) (M) 1. illuminating; shining upon. 3. an asura who was the son of Prahlāda and Dhṛti and the husband of Viśālākṣi and Devi and the father of Mahābali, Bala and Yaśodharā; a son of Dhṛtarāṣṭra (*M. Bh.*); another name for Sūrya, the moon and Viṣṇu.

**Viroćiṣṇu** (S) (M) shining; bright; illuminating.

**Viroha** (S) (M) 1. causing to heal. 3. a nāga (*M. Bh.*)

**Virohaṇa** (S) (M) 1. growing out; budding. 3. a nāga of the family of Takṣaka (*M. Bh.*)

**Virohin** (S) (M) sprouting; shooting forth.

**Viroka** (S) (M) shining; gleaming; a ray of light; effulgence.

**Virūdhā** (S) (F) 1. sprouting; grown; formed. 3. a daughter of Ira or of Surasā the mother of the serpents and who became the mother of vines.

**Virūdhaka** (S) (M) 1. sprouted grain. 3. the guardian of the south; a son of Ikṣvāku; a son of Prasenajit.

**Viruj** (S) (M) 1. healthy; free from disease. 3. a submarine agni (*Ṛg Veda*)

**Virukmat** (S) (M) 1. shining; brilliant; bright. 2. a bright weapon or ornament.

**Virūpā** (S) (F) 1. manifold; variegated; changed. 3. the wife of Yama; a tāntric deity.

**Virūpa** (S) (M) 1. many coloured; manifold; vareigated; altered; changed; different from. 3. an asura; a son of the demon Parivarta (*Mā. Purāṇa*); a sage of the Āṅgiras family; a solar dynasty king who was the father of Pṛṣadāśva and son of Ambarīṣa (*Ṛg Veda*); a son of Kṛṣṇa (*Bhā. Purāṇa*); a descendant of Manu Vaivaśvata; a son of King Ambarīṣa of the solar dynasty (*Bhāgavata*); Krodha in its human form (*M. Bh.*); an asura killed by Kṛṣṇa (*M. Bh.*); a son of Aṅgiras (*M. Bh.*); *Aconitum heterophyllum; Fagonia cretica.*

**Virūpaćakṣus** (S) (M) 1. diversely eyed. 3. another name for Śiva.

**Virūpaka** (S) (M) 1. disfigured. 3. an asura who once ruled the world (*M. Bh.*)

**Virūpākṣa** (S) (M) 1. diversely eyed. 3. an elephant that holds up the earth and who causes earthquakes by the shaking of his head; a rākṣasa son of Mālyavān and Sundarī who was a captain of Rāvaṇa's army; one of the 33 dānavas born to Kaśyapa and Danu who was reborn as King Ćitravarmā (*M. Bh.*); a rākṣasa friend of Ghaṭotkaća (*M. Bh.*); one of the 11 rudras; an asura who was a follower of Narakāsura (*M. Bh.*); the Buddhist guardian of the east (*B. Literature*); one of Śiva's attendants (*K. Sāgara*); a yakṣa (*K. Sāgara*); a nāga (*J.S. Koṣa*); another name for Śiva.

**Virūpaśakti** (S) (M) 1. with manifold powers. 3. a vidyādhara (*K. Sāgara*)

**Virūpāśva** (S) (M) 1. with variegated horses. 3. a king famed for his vegetarianism (*M. Bh.*)

**Vīryā** (S) (F) 1. vigour; energy; strength. 3. a nāga maiden.

**Vīryaćandra** (S) (M) 1. moon among the brave. 3. the father of Vīrā.

**Vīryaja** (S) (M) 1. produced from manliness. 2. son.

**Vīryamitra** (S) (M) friend of the brave.

**Vīryasaha** (S) (M) 1. famous for bravery. 3. a son of Saudāsa.

**Vīryavat** (S) (M) 1. strong; powerful. 2. efficacious. 3. a viśvadeva (*M. Bh.*); a son of the 10th Manu (*H. Purāṇa*)

**Vīryavatī** (S) (F) 1. powerful. 3. a mother in Skanda's retinue (*M. Bh.*)

**Viśada** (S) (M) 1. conspicuous. 2. bright; brilliant; shining; splendid; white; spotless; pure; calm; easy; cheerful; tender. 3. a son of King Jayadratha and the father of King Senajit (*Bhāgavata*)

**Viśadānana** (S) (M) radiant faced.

**Viśadaprabha** (S) (M) shedding pure light.

**Viśadātman** (S) (M) pure hearted; pure soul.

**Viṣadhātrī** (S) (M) 1. venom preserver. 3. another name for Manasā.

**Viṣāgnipā** (S) (M) 1. drinker of burning poison. 3. another name for Śiva.

**Viṣaharā** (S) (F) 1. removing venom. 3. another name for Manasā.

**Viṣahara** (S) (M) 1. removing venom. 3. a son of Dhṛtarāṣṭra (*M. Bh.*)

**Viṣakaṇṭha** (S) (M) 1. poison necked. 3. another name for Śiva.

**Viśākha** (S) (M) 1. branched. 3. one of the 3 brothers of Skanda who was born of his body (*H. Purāṇa*); a hermit in the palace of Indra (*M. Bh.*); born under the Viśākha constellation (*M. Bh.*); a dānava (*K. Sāgara*); another name for Śiva.

**Viśākhadatta** (S) (M) 1. given by Viśākha. 3. a Sanskṛt playright who was the son of King Bhāskaradatta and the grandson of Vaṭeśvaradatta and the author of *Mudrā Rākṣasa* (5th century A.D.)

**Viṣākṣa** (S) (M) with venomous eyes.

**Viśālā** (S) (F) 1. large; spacious; extensive; wide. 3. the wife of the lunar dynasty king Ajamīḍha (*M. Bh.*); the wife of Bhīma the son of Mahāvirya and the mother of Trayyāruṇi, Puṣkarī and Kapi (*Vā. Purāṇa*); the city Ujjayinī (*K. Granthāvali*); an apsarā (*V. Purāṇa*); a daughter of Dakṣa and wife of Aristhanemi (*Mā. Purāṇa*)

**Viśāla** (S) (M) 1. spacious; extensive; wide; great; important; mighty; illustrious; eminent. 3. the father of Takṣaka (*S.G. Sutra*); an asura (*K. Sāgara*); a son of Tṛṇabindu; a son of Ikṣvāku by the apsarā Alambusā and the father of Hemaćandra; a son of Abja.

**Viśālaka** (S) (M) 1. *Feronia elephantum*. 3. a yakṣa (*M. Bh.*); a king whose daughter Bhadrā married Vasudeva; a yakṣa in the palace of Kubera (*M. Bh.*); another name for Garuḍa.

**Viśālākṣa** (S) (M) 1. large eyed. 3. a nāga (*H. Purāṇa*); a son of Dhṛtarāṣṭra (*M. Bh.*); a younger brother of King Virāṭa also known as Madirākṣa (*M. Bh.*); a son of Garuḍa (*M. Bh.*); a king of Mithilā (*Bhāgavata*); another name for Śiva and Garuḍa.

**Viśālākṣī** (S) (F) 1. large eyed. 3. a mother in Skanda's retinue (*M. Bh.*); a yoginī (*A. Koṣa*); a daughter of Śāndilya; a subordinate female deity of Trichinopoly; another name for Durgā.

**Viśālanetra** (S) (M) 1. large eyed. 3. a Bodhisattva.

**Viśalyā** (S) (F) 1. freed from pain. 3. a wife of Lakśmaṇa (*V. Rāmāyaṇa*); a holy river whose deity lives in the palace of Varuṇa (*M. Bh.*); *Tinospora cordifolia*.

**Viṣamākṣa** (S) (M) 1. with an odd number of eyes; 3 eyed. 3. another name for Śiva.

**Viṣamāyudha** (S) (M) 1. with an odd number of arrows; 5 arrowed. 3. another name for Kāma

**Viṣambāṇa** (S) (M) 1. with an odd number of arrows; 5 arrowed. 3. another name for Kāma.

**Viṣamekṣaṇa** (S) (M) 1. with an odd number of eyes; 3 eyed. 3. another name for Śiva.

**Viṣameśu** (S) (M) 1. with an odd number of arrows; 5 arrowed. 3. another name for Kāma.

**Viśampa** (S) (M) protecting people.

**Viṣamśara** (S) (M) 1. with an odd number of arrows; 5 arrowed. 3. another name for Kāma.

**Viṣamśīla** (S) (M) 1. with an unequable disposition. 2. rough; difficult; cross tempered. 3. another name for Vikramāditya.

**Viṣāṇa** (S) (M) 1. peak; summit; the best of its kind. 3. the tuft on Śiva's head.

**Viśanka** (S) (M) fearless.

**Viṣāntaka** (S) (M) 1. poison destroying. 3. another name for Śiva.

**Viṣāpaha** (S) (M) 1. vanquisher of poison. 2. antidotal. 3. another name for Garuḍa.

**Viṣaparvan** (S) (M) 1. with poison in every part. 3. a daitya (*K. Sāgara*)

**Viśārada** (S) (M) 1. proficient. 2. *Fagonia cretica*; *Mimusops elengi*.

**Viśasta** (S) (M) praised; celebrated.

**Viśātana** (S) (M) 1. destroying; setting free;

delivering. 3. another name for Viṣṇu.

**Visaṭha** (S) (M) 1. holding the stalk of a lotus. 3. a son of Balarāma and Revatī (*M. Bh.*)

**Viśaujas** (S) (M) ruling people.

**Viṣavidya** (S) (M) 1. knower of poison. 2. antidote. 3. a child of Garuḍa.

**Viṣayin** (S) (M) 1. sensual; material. 2. prince; king. 3. another name for Kāma.

**Viśeṣa** (S) (M) special; excellent; superior; distinguished.

**Viśikha** (S) (M) 1. bald; unfeathered. 2. arrow. 3. a king of the birds born of Garuḍa and Śukī.

**Viśirā** (S) (F) 1. with no prominent veins. 3. an attendant of Skanda (*M. Bh.*)

**Viṣita** (S) (M) 1. released. 2. the sun just before setting.

**Viṣkambhin** (S) (M) 1. the bolt of a door. 3. a Bodhisattva; another name for Śiva.

**Viṣkara** (S) (M) 1. bolt of a door. 3. an asura who once ruled the world (*M. Bh.*)

**Vismāpana** (S) (M) 1. conjurer; illusion. 3. another name for Kāma.

**Viṣṇāpu** (S) (M) 1. as pure as Viṣṇu. 3. a hermit son of Viśvaka helped by the aśvins (*Ṛg Veda*)

**Viṣṇu** (S) (F) 1. omnipresent. 3. the queen of Simhapuri and mother of Jaina Tiranthakara Śreyansanātha (*J.S. Koṣa*)

**Viṣṇu** (S) (M) 1. all pervader. 3. the preserver in the Hindu triad or Trimurti, he is the sustainer and whenever there is injustice in the world he incarnates himself to restore righteousness, hermits, Manus, devas, sons of Manus, prajāpatis all these are portions of Viṣṇu, of the 21 incarnations the most prominent are of Rāma, Kṛṣṇa and Buddha (*B. Literature*), in the Vedic period he is a personification of light and the sun, later he was given the foremost position among the ādityas (*Ṛg Veda*); in the epics he rises to supremacy and is described as having 22 incarnations, he is identified with Nārāyana the primeval living spirit, the god Brahmā is described as emerging from his navel, the wives of Viṣṇu are Aditi and Śinivali, later Lakṣmī or Srī, his son is Kāmadeva and his paradise Vaikuṇṭha, he is worshipped under a 1000 names (*Ṛg Veda*); the king of Simhapuri and father of Jaina Tirathankara Śreyansanātha (*J.S. Koṣa*); a son of Manu Sāvarna.

**Viṣṇućakra** (S) (M) discus of Viṣṇu.

**Viṣṇućandra** (S) (M) 1. moon and Viṣṇu conjoined. 3. the calm form of Viṣṇu.

**Viṣṇućitta** (S) (M) 1. with an omnipresent mind. 3. a Vaiṣṇavite devotee of Tamil Nadu who was supposed to have been the incarnation of Garuḍa and was the father of Āṇḍāl.

**Viṣṇudāsa** (S) (M) 1. devotee of Viṣṇu. 3. a Vaiṣṇavite devotee of the Ćola court who was rewarded by Viṣṇu for his devotion (*P. Purāṇa*)

**Viṣṇudatta** (S) (M) 1. given by Viṣṇu. 3. another name for Parīkṣit.

**Viṣṇudeva** (S) (M) lord of Viṣṇu; the omnipresent god.

**Viṣṇudharman** (S) (M) 1. acting like Viṣṇu. 3. a son of Garuḍa (*M. Bh.*)

**Viṣṇugangā** (S) (F) 1. the river of the omnipresent. 3. a river (*Bhā. Purāṇa*)

**Viṣṇugopa** (S) (M) 1. protected by Viṣṇu, the cattle keeper. 3. a Pallava king of Kāñći; another name for Kṛṣṇa.

**Viṣṇugupta** (S) (M) 1. hidden by Viṣṇu. 3. another name for Vātsyāyana and sage Kaundinya.

**Viṣṇumatī** (S) (F) 1. with omnipresent intelligence. 3. the wife of King Śatānīka and the mother of Sahaśrānīka (*K. Sāgara*)

**Viṣṇumāyā** (S) (F) 1. the illusion of Viṣṇu. 3. a form of Durgā (*K. Purāṇa*)

**Viṣṇumitra** (S) (M) 1. a friend of Viṣṇu. 3. son of Devamitra (*M. Bh.*)

**Viṣṇupada** (S) (M) 1. footmark of Viṣṇu. 2. lotus (*Nelumbo speciosum*); the sky; the Sea of Milk.

**Viṣṇupadī** (S) (F) 1. emerging from the foot of Viṣṇu. 3. the Gaṅgā river which flows from Viṣṇu's foot (*V. Purāṇa*)

**Viṣṇupatnī** (S) (F) 1. wife of Viṣṇu. 3. another name for Aditi and Lakṣmī.

**Viṣṇuprasāda** (S) (M) gift of Viṣṇu.

**Viṣṇupriyā** (S) (F) 1. beloved of Viṣṇu. 2. Sacred Basil (*Ocimum sanctum*); Wax Flower (*Ervatomia coronaria*). 3. another name for Lakṣmī.

**Viṣṇuputra** (S) (M) son of Viṣṇu.

**Viṣṇurāta** (S) (M) 1. given by Viṣṇu. 3. another name for Parīkṣit (*Bh. Purāṇa*)

**Viṣṇuratha** (S) (M) 1. vehicle of Viṣṇu. 3. another name for Garuḍa.

**Viṣṇuśakti** (S) (F) 1. power of Viṣṇu. 3. another name for Lakṣmī.

**Viṣṇuvāhana** (S) (M) 1. vehicle of Viṣṇu. 3. another name for Garuḍa.

**Viṣṇuvallabhā** (S) (F) 1. beloved of Viṣṇu. 3. another name for Lakṣmī and Tulasī.

**Viṣṇuvṛddha** (S) (M) 1. knower of the omnipresent. 3. a king who was the son of Trasadasyu.

**Viṣṇuyaśas** (S) (M) 1. with the fame of Viṣṇu. 3. another name of Kalki (*M. Bh.*)

**Viśobhaginā** (S) (F) 1. prosperous. 3. another name for Sarasvatī.

**Viśodhana** (S) (M) 1. cleansing; purifying; washing away. 3. the capital of Brahmā (*M. Bh.*); another name for Viṣṇu.

**Viśokā** (S) (F) 1. exempted from grief. 3. a wife of Kṛṣṇa (*M. Bh.*); a mother in Skanda's train (*M. Bh.*)

**Viśoka** (S) (M) 1. griefless. 3. the charioteer of Bhīma (*M. Bh.*); a prince of Kekaya on the side of the Pāṇḍavas (*M. Bh.*); a son of Kṛṣṇa and Trivakrā; a spiritual son of Brahmā (*V. Purāṇa*); a ṛṣi (*S. Veda*); a dānava.

**Viśpati** (S) (M) lord of the house.

**Viśrama** (S) (M) tranquillity; calm; composure; rest.

**Viśrānta** (S) (M) reposed; rested.

**Viśravaṇa** (S) (M) much heard of; very famous.

**Viśravas** (S) (M) 1. much heard of. 2. great fame. 3. a ṛṣi who was the son of Pulastya and Havirbhū and the father of Rāvaṇa and Kumbhakarṇa by his wife Kaikasī and of Vaiśravaṇa or Kubera by his wife Īlabīla and Khara and Surpaṇakhā by his wife Rākā and Vibhīṣaṇa by Mālinī (*M. Bh.*)

**Viśruta** (S) (M) 1. much heard of. 2. famous; celebrated; pleased; delighted; happy. 3. a son of Vasudeva (*Bhā. Purāṇa*)

**Viśrutī** (S) (F) celebrity; fame.

**Viṣṭap** (S) (M) top; summit; highest.

**Viṣṭāraśravas** (S) (M) 1. far famed. 3. another name for Viṣṇu/Kṛṣṇa and Śiva.

**Viṣṭārāśva** (S) (M) 1. having a well travelled horse. 3. a son of Pṛthu.

**Viṣṭāriṇī** (S) (F) 1. extensive; spreading; mighty; large. 3. a goddess (*Mā. Purāṇa*)

**Viṣṭi** (S) (M) 1. compulsory work. 3. a ṛṣi in the 11th Manvantara.

**Viśuddha** (S) (M) clean; clear; pure; virtuous; honest.

**Viśuddhī** (S) (F) purity; holiness; virtue; perfect knowledge.

**Viśuddhira** (S) (M) pure and grave.

**Viśuṇḍī** (S) (M) 1. with an excessively long neck. 3. a nāga of the family of Kaśyapa (*M. Bh.*)

**Viṣupa** (S) (M) the equinox.

**Viśvā** (S) (F) 1. the earth. 3. a tongue of Agni (*Mā. Purāṇa*); a daughter of Dakṣa and the wife of Dharmā and mother of the viśvadevas (*M. Bh.*)

**Viśva** (S) (M) 1. whole; entire; all; universe; world. 2. the number 13. 3. a king who was a partial incarnation of the asura Mayūra (*M. Bh.*)

**Viśvabandhu** (S) (M) a friend of the world.

**Viśvabhānu** (S) (M) all illuminating; sun of the world.

**Viśvabhāvana** (S) (M) 1. abode of universe. 3. a spiritual son of Brahmā; another name for Viṣṇu.

**Viśvabhraj** (S) (M) all illuminating.

**Viśvabhū** (S) (M) 1. creator of the universe. 3. a Buddha.

**Viśvabhuj** (S) (M) 1. all enjoying. 3. another name for Indra.

**Viśvabhuk** (S) (M) 1. one who eats everything. 3. a son of Bṛhaspati who is the digestor of all food as he sits in the lining of all living things, he is supposed to have been the husband of the river Gomatī (*M. Bh.*)

**Viśvabhūta** (S) (M) being everything; born of universe.

**Viśvabodha** (S) (M) 1. knower of universe. 3. a Buddha.

**Viṣvāć** (S) (M) 1. universally present. 3. an

asura killed by the aśvins (*Ṛg Veda*)

**Viśvaćandra** (S) (M) moon of the universe; all radiant; all brilliant; illuminator of the universe.

**Viśvāćarya** (S) (M) universal teacher.

**Viśvāći** (S) (F) **1.** universal. **3.** an apsarā in the palace of Kubera (*M. Bh.*)

**Viśvaćyvas** (S) (M) **1.** moving the universe. **3.** one of the 7 principal rays of the sun.

**Viśvadāni** (S) (M) all giving; donor of universe.

**Viśvadanṣtra** (S) (M) **1.** with all eating teeth. **3.** an asura (*M. Bh.*)

**Viśvadāsā** (S) (F) **1.** servant of the world. **3.** one of the 7 tongues of fire (*T. Samhitā*)

**Viśvadeva** (S) (M) **1.** all divine; god of universe. **3.** a class of deities who are the sons of Dharmā and Viśva who are supposed to be offered to daily – a boon bestowed by Brahmā in return for their austerities (*V. Purāṇa*); *Sida spinosa*; Ash coloured Fleabane (*Vernonia cinerea*)

**Viśvadhara** (S) (M) **1.** abode of the universe. **2.** preserving all things. **3.** a son of Medhātithi (*Bh. Purāṇa*); another name for Viṣṇu.

**Viśvadhārin** (S) (M) **1.** abode of the universe. **2.** all maintaining. **3.** another name for Viṣṇu.

**Viśvadhāriṇī** (S) (F) **1.** abode of the universe. **2.** all maintaining. **3.** another name for the earth.

**Viśvadhenā** (S) (F) **1.** cow of the universe. **2.** all feeding. **3.** another name for the earth

**Viśvadhriśṭa** (S) (M) seer of the universe; all seeing.

**Viśvadīpa** (S) (M) light of the universe.

**Viśvaga** (S) (M) **1.** going everywhere. **3.** a son of Pūrṇiman; another name for Brahmā.

**Viśvagandhā** (S) (F) **1.** fragrance of the universe. **2.** giving out fragrance everywhere. **3.** another name for the earth (*A. Koṣa*)

**Viśvagandhi** (S) (M) **1.** with an all pervading fragrance. **3.** a son of Pṛthu (*Bhā. Purāṇa*)

**Viśvagarbha** (S) (M) **1.** womb of the universe. **2.** containing all things. **3.** a son of Raivata (*H. Purāṇa*)

**Viśvagāśva** (S) (M) **1.** one whose horses go everywhere. **3.** a king who was the son of the Emperor Pṛthu and the father of King Adri (*M. Bh.*); a Purū king.

**Viśvagoptṛ** (S) (M) **1.** preserver of the universe. **3.** another name for Viṣṇu, Śiva and Indra.

**Viśvaguru** (S) (M) father of the universe; preceptor of the universe.

**Viśvahetu** (S) (M) **1.** cause of the universe. **3.** another name for Viṣṇu.

**Viśvajayin** (S) (M) conquerer of the universe.

**Viśvajit** (S) (M) **1.** conquerer of the universe. **2.** all conquering. **3.** the noose of Varuṇa; a dānava (*M. Bh.*); a son of Gādhi (*H. Purāṇa*); an Aṅga king who was the son of Jayadratha (*A. Purāṇa*); a king of the Yayāti dynasty who was the son of Suvrata and the father of Ripuñjaya (*Bhāgavata*); a son of Bṛhaspati who has the intelligence of all the living beings of the universe (*M. Bh.*); an asura who was ruler of the world for a short while (*M. Bh.*)

**Viśvajyotis** (S) (M) **1.** one whose light spreads everywhere; illuminator of universe. **3.** the eldest son of Śatajit.

**Viśvaka** (S) (M) **1.** all pervading. **2.** all containing. **3.** a hermit who was the father of Viṣṇāpū (*Ṛg Veda*)

**Viśvakāraka** (S) (M) **1.** creator of the universe. **3.** another name for Śiva.

**Viśvakarman** (S) (M) **1.** creator of the world. **2.** accomplishing or creating everything; all doer. **3.** the divine architect and weapon maker and chariot maker of the devas said to be a son of Brahmā, earlier mythology identified him with Prajāpati (*Ṛg Veda*); later he was identified with Tvaṣṭṛ, he presides over the 64 mechanical arts; variously the son of Bhuvana, the vasu Prabhāsa and Yogasiddhā or Varastrī he was the father of 5 sons – Ajaikapāt, Ahirbudhnya, Tvaṣṭā, Rudra and the monkey Nala, the daughters are Saṁjñā, Ćitrāṅgadā, Surūpā and Barhiśmatī (*Ṛg Veda*)

**Viśvakartṛ** (S) (M) creator of the world.

**Viśvakāru** (S) (M) **1.** architect of the universe. **3.** another name for Viśvakarman (*Ṛg Veda*)

**Viśvakārya** (S) (M) **1.** architect of the universe; effector of the universe. **3.** one of the 7 principal rays of the sun (*V. Purāṇa*)

**Viśvakāyā** (S) (F) 1. the universal form. 2. one whose body is the universe. 3. a form of Dākṣāyāṇī (*D. Purāṇa*)

**Viśvaketu** (S) (M) 1. one whose banner is the universe. 3. another name for Kāma and Aniruddha.

**Viśvakṛt** (S) (M) 1. creator of the universe. 2. creating all. 3. a viśvadeva (*M. Bh.*); a son of Gādhi (*H. Purāṇa*); another name for Viśvakarman.

**Viṣvakṣeṇa** (S) (M) 1. one whose powers go everywhere. 3. a hermit in the palace of Indra (*M. Bh.*); an attendant of Viṣṇu (*Bhā. Purāṇa*); the 14th Manu (*V. Purāṇa*); a son of Brahmadatta (*H. Purāṇa*); a son of Śambara (*H. Purāṇa*); a ṛṣi (*Bhā. Purāṇa*); *Aglaia odoratissima*; another name for Viṣṇu/Kṛṣṇa and Śiva.

**Viśvamadā** (S) (F) 1. enchanting the universe; all delighting; all consuming. 3. one of the 7 tongues of fire (*A. Koṣa*)

**Viśvamahas** (S) (M) most powerful in universe; all powerful; all pleasant.

**Viśvamahat** (S) (M) 1. great principle of the universe. 3. a son of Viśvaśarman (*V. Purāṇa*)

**Viśvamanas** (S) (M) with a universal mind; perceiving all.

**Viśvambhara** (S) (M) 1. feeding the universe; all bearing; all sustaining. 2. Supreme Being; fire; another name for Kṛṣṇa.

**Viśvambharī** (S) (F) 1. feeding the universe. 2. all bearing. 3. another name for the earth.

**Viśvamitra** (S) (M) 1. friend of all. 3. a celebrated sage of the lunar race who was the son of Gādhi and the father of Śakuntalā by Menakā.

**Viśvamukhī** (S) (F) 1. of the universe. 3. Dākṣāyāṇī in Jalandhara (*D. Purāṇa*)

**Viśvamūrti** (S) (M) idol of the universe; having all forms.

**Viśvanābha** (S) (M) 1. navel of the universe. 3. another name for Viṣṇu.

**Viśvananda** (S) (M) 1. delighting the universe. 2. pleasing all. 3. a son of Brahmā (*V. Purāṇa*)

**Viśvānara** (S) (M) 1. man of the universe. 2. dear to all men. 3. a king who was the husband of Śućismitā and the father of Gṛhapati (*Sk. Purāṇa*); the father of Agni.

**Viśvanātha** (S) (M) 1. lord of the universe. 3. the form of Śiva worshipped in Benaras (*Mā. Purāṇa*); a Sanskṛt literary critic of Orissa (14th century)

**Viśvāntara** (S) (M) 1. subduing the universe. 2. all subduing. 3. the Buddha in a former existence; a son of Suṣadmān (*B. Literature*)

**Viśvapā** (S) (M) 1. protector of the universe. 2. all protecting. 3. another name for the sun, the moon and fire.

**Viśvapāla** (S) (M) protector of the universe; all protecting.

**Viśvapāṇi** (S) (M) 1. palm of the universe. 3. a Dhyāni Bodhisattva.

**Viśvapati** (S) (M) 1. master of the universe. 3. a son of the agni called Manu (*M. Bh.*); another name for Mahāpuruṣa and Kṛṣṇa.

**Viśvapāvanī** (S) (F) 1. pious in the world. 2. Sacred Basil (*Ocimum sanctum*)

**Viśvapūjitā** (S) (F) 1. worshipped by all. 2. Sacred Basil (*Ocimum sanctum*)

**Viśvārādhya** (S) (M) 1. granting all. 3. an ascetic and a founder of the Vara-Śaiva sects.

**Viśvarāj** (S) (M) universal sovereign.

**Viśvarandhi** (S) (M) 1. conqueror of the universe. 3. the son of King Pṛthu of the solar dynasty who was the father of King Ćandra and the grandfather of Yuvanāśva (*D. Bhāgavata*)

**Viśvaratha** (S) (M) 1. with the universe as his chariot; chariot of the universe. 3. the father of Gādhi (*H. Purāṇa*)

**Viśvaretas** (S) (M) 1. seed of the universe. 3. another name for Brahmā and Viṣṇu.

**Viśvarući** (S) (F) 1. illuminator of the universe. 2. all glittering. 3. one of the 7 tongues of fire (*M. Upaniṣad*)

**Viśvarući** (S) (M) 1. all glittering; enjoyer of the universe. 3. a gandharva king (*M. Bh.*)

**Viśvarūpā** (S) (F) 1. with the form of the universe. 2. many coloured. 3. a wife of sage Dharma and the mother of Dharmavratā (*Vā. Purāṇa*)

**Viśvarūpa** (S) (M) 1. with the form of the

universe. 2. many coloured; variegated; the body that fills the universe. 3. a rākṣasa in the palace of Varuṇa (*M. Bh.*); the son of Tvaṣṭṛ and Raćanā and brother of Sanniveśa (*Ṛg Veda*); another name for Viṣṇu/Kṛṣṇa and Hanumān.

**Viśvarūpī** (S) (F) 1. of the form of universe. 2. multicoloured. 3. one of the 7 tongues of fire.

**Viśvarūpikā** (S) (F) 1. with the form of the universe. 3. a yoginī (*H. Koṣa*)

**Viśvarūpiṇī** (S) (F) 1. with the form of the universe; creator of universe. 3. a goddess (*A. Koṣa*)

**Viśvāsa** (S) (M) confidence; trust.

**Viśvasahā** (S) (F) 1. enduring all. 3. one of the 7 tongues of fire (*M. Upaniṣad*); another name for the earth.

**Viśvasāhvan** (S) (M) 1. companion of the world. 3. a son of Mahasvat (*Bhā. Purāṇa*)

**Viśvasakha** (S) (M) friend of all.

**Viśvaśambhu** (S) (M) 1. benefactor of all. 3. a submarine fire (*Ṛg Veda*)

**Viśvasāra** (S) (M) 1. essence of the universe. 3. a son of Kṣatraujas.

**Viśvaśarman** (S) (M) 1. honoured by all; best in the universe. 3. the father of Viśvamahat (*V. Purāṇa*)

**Viśvasćandra** (S) (M) moon of the universe; all glittering.

**Viśvaśrī** (S) (M) 1. treasure of the universe. 2. useful to all. 3. another name for Agni.

**Viśvasvāmin** (S) (M) lord of the universe.

**Viśvatanu** (S) (M) one whose body is the universe; omnipresent.

**Viśvātman** (S) (M) universal soul.

**Viśvatrayarćas** (S) (M) 1. honoured by the 3 worlds namely the earth, the heaven and the netherworld. 3. one of the 7 principal rays of the sun (*V. Purāṇa*)

**Viśvavārya** (S) (M) containing all good things.

**Viśvāvasu** (S) (M) 1. beneficient to all. 3. a gandharva regarded as the author of several Ṛg Vedic hymns; a marutvata (*H. Purāṇa*); a son of Purūravas; a prince of the Siddhas; a son of Jamadagni; a brother of Paraśurāma (*Br. Purāṇa*); a gandharva king who was the son of Kaśyapa and Prādhā and the father of Pramadvarā by the apsarā Menakā (*M. Bh.*)

**Viśvāvatī** (S) (F) 1. possessing the universe. 2. universal. 3. another name for the Gaṅgā.

**Viśvavedi** (S) (M) 1. knower of the universe. 3. a son of Prajāpati and a minister of King Śauri (*Ma. Purāṇa*)

**Viśvavṛkṣa** (S) (M) 1. tree of the universe. 3. another name for Viṣṇu.

**Viśvavyaćas** (S) (M) 1. absorbing all things. 3. another name for Aditi.

**Viśvayoni** (S) (M) 1. womb of the universe. 3. another name for Brahmā and Viṣṇu.

**Viśvāyu** (S) (M) 1. universally known. 3. a son of Purūravas (*M. Bh.*); a viśvadeva (*M. Bh.*)

**Viśveśā** (S) (F) 1. lady of the universe; desired by all. 3. a daughter of Dakṣa and wife of Dharma (*Mā. Purāṇa*)

**Viśveśa** (S) (M) 1. lord of the universe; desired by all. 3. another name for Brahmā, Viṣṇu and Śiva.

**Viśveśvara** (S) (M) 1. the lord of the universe. 3. a form of Śiva worshipped in Benaras (*M. Bh.*)

**Viśveśvaraya** (S) (M) lord of the universe.

**Vītā** (S) (F) wish; desire.

**Vītabhaya** (S) (M) 1. fearless. 3. a Purū king who was the son of King Manasyu and the father of King Śuṇḍu (*A. Purāṇa*); another name for Śiva and Viṣṇu.

**Vītabhī** (S) (M) fearless.

**Vītabhīti** (S) (M) 1. fearless. 3. an asura (*K. Sāgara*)

**Vīṭabhūta** (S) (M) 1. free from the past; fearless. 3. an asura in the palace of Varuṇa (*M. Bh.*)

**Vītadhvaja** (S) (M) 1. without a banner. 3. a king of the Janaka dynasty who was the son of Dharmadhvaja and the father of Khāndikya (*Bhāgavata*)

**Vītadru** (S) (M) 1. motionless. 3. a Yādava king (*M. Bh.*)

**Vītahavya** (S) (M) 1. one whose offerings are acceptable. 3. a son of Śunaka and father of Dhṛti; another name for King Ekavīra and Kṛṣṇa.

**Vītamala** (S) (M) free from darkness.

**Vītamanyu** (S) (M) free from anger.

**Vitamas** (S) (M) free from darkness.

**Vitana** (S) (F) 1. extension; heap; performance; oblation; plenty; abundance. 3. the wife of Sattrāyana (*Bhā. Purāṇa*)

**Vitanu** (S) (M) 1. thin; slender; with no essence or reality. 3. another name for Kāma.

**Vītarāga** (S) (M) free from passion; calm.

**Vitarka** (S) (M) 1. guess; fancy; imagination; conjecture; opinion. 3. a son of Dhṛtarāṣṭra (*M. Bh.*)

**Vītaśanka** (S) (M) fearless; without doubt.

**Vītaśoka** (S) (M) free from sorrow.

**Vitastā** (S) (F) 1. a measure of length which is form the wrist to the tip of the fingers. 3. a river now known as the Jhelum whose deity was once an advisor to Pārvatī and stays in the palace of Varuṇa (*M. Bh.*)

**Vitatha** (S) (M) 1. false. 3. another name for the hermit Dīrghatamas who was the foster son of Bharata (*Ṛg Veda*)

**Vitatya** (S) (M) 1. to stretch; expand. 3. the son of the Gṛtsamada dynasty king Vihavya and the father of King Satya (*H. Purāṇa*)

**Vīti** (S) (F) enjoyment; light; lustre; fire.

**Vītihotra** (S) (M) 1. invited to a feast. 2. a god; king. 3. a son of Priyavrata (*Bhā. Purāṇa*); a son of Indrasena (*Bhā. Purāṇa*); a son of Sukumāra; a son of Tālajangha; the husband of Śabari in her previous life; another name for the sun and Agni (*R. Taraṅgiṇī*)

**Vitolā** (S) (F) 1. very calm. 3. a river (*R. Taraṅgiṇī*)

**Vittadā** (S) (F) 1. wealth giver. 3. a mother attending on Skanda. (*M. Bh.*)

**Vittadha** (S) (M) wealth possessing.

**Vittagoptā** (S) (M) 1. hiding wealth. 3. another name for Kubera.

**Vittaka** (S) (M) very wealthy; very famous.

**Vittanātha** (S) (M) 1. lord of wealth. 3. another name for Kubera.

**Vittapa** (S) (M) 1. guarding wealth. 3. another name for Kubera.

**Vittapati** (S) (M) 1. lord of wealth. 3. another name for Kubera.

**Vitteśa** (S) (M) 1. lord of wealth. 3. another name for Kubera.

**Viṭṭhala** (S) (M) 1. fortune giver. 2. ascetic; homeless; without any desire for shelter. 3. a god worshipped in Pandharpur stated to be an incarnation of Viṣṇu/Kṛṣṇa who visited the city to reward a pious Brāhmin.

**Vitti** (S) (F) consciousness; understanding; intelligence.

**Vitti** (S) (F) finding; acquisition; gain.

**Vitula** (S) (M) 1. large; wide; thick; long; loud. 3. one of the 7 winds; one of the 7 tongues of fire (*H. Purāṇa*); a Sauvira king (*M. Bh.*)

**Vivandiṣā** (S) (F) the wish to worship.

**Vivardhana** (S) (M) 1. augmenting; increasing; promoting. 3. a king in the assembly of Yudhiṣṭhira (*M. Bh.*)

**Vivāsa** (S) (M) shining forth; dawning.

**Vivāsana** (S) (M) illuminating.

**Vivasvata** (S) (M) 1. the brilliant one. 2. shining forth; diffusing light. 3. the sun born as one of the 12 ādityas of Kaśyapa and Aditi (*V. Purāṇa*); also known as Mārtaṇḍa he was the husband of Saṁjñā and the father of Vaivaśvata Manu from whom the Solar dynasty begins, he was also the father of Yama and Yamī and the Aśvinidevas, Nasatya and Dasra from his wife Ćhāyā he was the father of Manu Sāvarṇi, Śani and Tapatī (*M. Bh.*); an asura killed by Garuḍa (*M. Bh.*); a viśvadeva (*M. Bh.*); the 1st human being who offered sacrifice who is supposed to have been the son of Kaśyapa and Dākṣāyāṇī, the father of Manu and Yama and the ancestor of all the people on earth (*Ṛg Veda*)

**Vivasvatī** (S) (F) 1. shining forth; diffusing light. 3. a city of the sun.

**Viveka** (S) (M) discrimination; distinction; true knowledge.

**Vivekānanda** (S) (M) rejoicing in knowledge.

**Vivekin** (S) (M) discriminating; judicious; prudent; discreet; wise.

**Viviċi** (S) (M) 1. discriminating; discerning. 3. another name for Agni and Indra.

**Vivida** (S) (M) 1. knowing. 3. an asura follower of Kaṅsa (*Bhāgavata*)

**Vivikta** (S) (M) 1. distinguished; solitary;

pure; neat; clear; profound. 3. a king of Kuṣadvīpa who was the son of Hiraṇyaretas (*Bhāgavata*)

**Viviktanāman** (S) (M) 1. sign of discrimination. 3. one of the sons of Hiraṇyaretas (*Ṛg Veda*)

**Vivikvas** (S) (M) 1. discerning; discriminating. 3. another name for Indra (*Ṛg Veda*)

**Vivindhya** (S) (M) 1. frightening. 3. an asura killed by Ćārudeṣṇa (*M. Bh.*)

**Vivinśa** (S) (M) 1. of a group of 20. 3. the son of King Vinśa of the solar dynasty and the father of Khaninetra and 14 others (*M. Bh.*)

**Vivinśati** (S) (M) 1. best of 20. 3. a king who sat in the dice game of Duryodhana and Yudhiṣṭhira; a son of Dhṛtarāṣṭra (*M. Bh.*)

**Vivitsā** (S) (F) desire for knowledge.

**Vivitsu** (S) (M) 1. desirous of knowledge. 3. a son of Dhṛtarāṣṭra (*M. Bh.*)

**Viyadgangā** (S) (F) the celestial Gaṅgā; the galaxy.

**Viyama** (S) (M) 1. to stretch out; to extend. 3. a son of the hermit Śataśṛṅga (*M. Bh.*)

**Viyanmaṇi** (S) (M) 1. sky jewel. 3. another name for the sun.

**Viyāsa** (S) (M) 1. tormentor; divider. 3. a demon who inflicts torment in Yama's world.

**Viyati** (S) (M) 1. stretched out. 3. a son of Nahuṣa (*Bhāgavata*)

**Vopadeva** (S) (M) 1. walking like a demi-god. 3. a grammarian who was the son of Keśava and pupil of Dhaneśvara and who lived at the court of King Hemādri of Devagiri (13th century)

**Vraja** (S) (M) 1. cowpen; cattleshed; host; multitude. 3. the district around Āgra and Mathurā and the abode of young Kṛṣṇa (*Bhā. Purāṇa*); a king of the Manu Svāyambhuva dynasty who was the son of Havirdhāna and Dhīṣaṇā (*A. Purāṇa*)

**Vrajabhuṣaṇa** (S) (M) 1. ornament of Vraja. 3. another name for Kṛṣṇa.

**Vrajakiśora** (S) (M) 1. adolescent of Vraja. 3. another name for Kṛṣṇa.

**Vrajalāla** (S) (M) 1. son of Vraja. 3. another name for Kṛṣṇa.

**Vrajamohana** (S) (M) 1. fascinator of Vraja. 3. another name for Kṛṣṇa.

**Vrajana** (S) (M) 1. travelling. 2. a road. 3. a son of Ajamīdha and Keśinī and brother of Jahnu (*M. Bh.*)

**Vrajanandana** (S) (M) 1. son of Vraja. 3. another name for Kṛṣṇa

**Vrajanātha** (S) (M) 1. lord of Vraja. 3. another name for Kṛṣṇa.

**Vrajarāja** (S) (M) 1. king of Vraja. 3. another name for Kṛṣṇa.

**Vrajaspati** (S) (M) 1. master of the cattle. 3. another name for Kṛṣṇa.

**Vrajavallabha** (S) (M) 1. beloved of Vraja. 3. another name for Kṛṣṇa.

**Vrajavara** (S) (M) 1. best in Vraja. 3. another name for Kṛṣṇa.

**Vrajendra** (S) (M) 1. lord of Vraja. 3. another name for Kṛṣṇa.

**Vrajeśa** (S) (M) 1. lord of Vraja. 3. another name for Kṛṣṇa.

**Vrajeśvara** (S) (M) 1. lord of Vraja. 3. another name for Kṛṣṇa.

**Vrajīravan** (S) (M) 1. the noise of the hard. 3. a Yadu king who was the son of Kroṣṭu and the father of Kuṣanku (*Bhāgavata*)

**Vrata** (S) (M) 1. law; obedience; service; pious austerity; holy practice; vow. 3. a son of Manu and Naḍvalā.

**Vrateśa** (S) (M) 1. lord of observances. 3. another name for Śiva.

**Vrateyu** (S) (M) 1. follower of law; keeper of promises. 3. a son of Raudrāśva (*Purāṇas*)

**Vratin** (S) (M) observing vows; worshipping.

**Vratya** (S) (M) obedient; faithful.

**Vrayas** (S) (M) with superior power.

**Vrćayā** (S) (F) 1. searching. 3. a woman given by Indra to Kakṣīvat.

**Vṛddhā** (S) (F) great; large; wise; learned; experienced; eldest.

**Vṛddhakanyā** (S) (F) 1. daughter of a preceptor. 3. the daughter of the hermit Kuṇigarga.

**Vṛddhakṣatra** (S) (M) 1. eminent warrior. 3. ancestor of Jayadratha.

**Vṛddhakṣema** (S) (M) 1. giving security to elders by the learned. 2. desiring the welfare of all. 3. the king of Trigarta and father of

Suśarmā (*M. Bh.*)

**Vṛddhaśarma** (S) (M) 1. great preceptor. 3. a son of King Ayus and Svarbhānū (*M. Bh.*)

**Vṛddhasenā** (S) (F) 1. with mighty hosts. 3. a wife of Sumalin (*Bh. Purāṇa*)

**Vṛddhaśravas** (S) (M) 1. possessed of great swiftness. 3. another name for Indra.

**Vṛja** (S) (M) 1. strength. 3. a hermit of the family of Emperor Pṛthu who was the son of Havirdhāna and Dhīṣaṇā (*V. Purāṇa*)

**Vṛjabala** (S) (M) strong.

**Vṛjinīvān** (S) (M) 1. wicked; deceitful. 3. a son of Kroṣṭa and the father of Uṣaṅgu (*M. Bh.*)

**Vṛka** (S) (M) 1. tearer. 2. wolf; cow; Kṣatriya; plough; thunderbolt. 3. a son of Bharuka (*H. Purāṇa*); a son of Pṛthu (*Bhā. Purāṇa*); a son of Vatsaka; a son of the Kekaya King Dhṛṣṭaketu and Dūrvā (*Bhāgavata*); a son of Kṛṣṇa and Mitravindā (*Bhā. Purāṇa*); an asura (*Bhāgavata*); a warrior on the Pāṇḍava's side (*M. Bh.*); a son of Śūra and Māriṣā who was the husband of Dūrvākṣi and the father of Takṣa and Puṣkara (*Bhāgavata*); another name for the moon, the sun.

**Vṛkadeva** (S) (M) 1. lord of the wolves. 3. a son of Vasudeva (*H. Purāṇa*)

**Vṛkadevi** (S) (M) 1. goddess of the plough. 3. a daughter of Devaka (*V. Purāṇa*)

**Vṛkadīpti** (S) (M) 1. shining like lightning. 3. a son of Kṛṣṇa. (*H. Purāṇa*)

**Vṛkakarman** (S) (M) 1. acting like a wolf; wolf like. 3. an asura.

**Vṛkala** (S) (M) 1. a garment made of bark. 3. the grandson of Dhruva and the son of Śliṣṭi and Sućchāyā (*V. Purāṇa*)

**Vṛkanirvṛti** (S) (M) 1. free from thunderbolts. 3. a son of Kṛṣṇa (*H. Purāṇa*)

**Vṛkāsya** (S) (M) 1. wolfmouthed. 3. a son of Kṛṣṇa.

**Vṛkatejas** (S) (M) 1. with the power of the thunderbolt. 3. a grandson of Dhruva and the son of Śliṣṭi and Sućchāyā (*V. Purāṇa*)

**Vṛkati** (S) (M) 1. murderer; one who tears. 3. a son of Kṛṣṇa; a son of Jīmūta (*H. Purāṇa*)

**Vṛkodara** (S) (M) 1. wolf bellied. 3. a class of attendants of Śiva (*M. Bh.*); another name for Bhīma and Brahmā.

**Vṛndā** (S) (F) 1. heap; swarm; flocks; cluster of flowers; many; much; all; a chorus of singers; Sacred Basil (*Ocimum sanctum*). 3. the wife of the asura Jalandhara (*Bhā. Purāṇa*); another name for Rādhā.

**Vṛndāra** (S) (M) 1. surrounded by a group. 2. deity; a god.

**Vṛndāraka** (S) (M) 1. surrounded by a group. 2. chief; head; eminent; most beautiful; a god. 3. a son of Dhṛtarāṣṭra (*M. Bh.*); a warrior on the side of the Kauravas (*M. Bh.*)

**Vṛndāvana** (S) (M) 1. forest of Vṛnda; forest of Tulasī; forest of Rādhā. 3. the forest near Gokula where Kṛṣṇa spent his early years (*Bhā. Purāṇa*)

**Vṛndāvaneśa** (S) (M) 1. lord of Rādhā's forest. 3. another name for Kṛṣṇa.

**Vṛndāvaneśvarī** (S) (F) 1. goddess of Vṛndāvan. 3. consort of Kṛṣṇa; another name for Rādhā.

**Vṛṣa** (S) (M) 1. bull. 2. man; male; the zodiac sign of Taurus; chief; best. 3. justice or virtue personified as Śiva's bull; Indra in the 11th Manvantara; 2 sons of Kṛṣṇa (*Bhā. Purāṇa*); a son of Vṛṣasena and grandson of Karṇa (*H. Purāṇa*); a Yādava and son of Madhu (*H. Purāṇa*); the son of Śṛnjaya (*H. Purāṇa*); one of the 10 horses of the moon; a warrior of Skanda (*M. Bh.*); an asura (*M. Bh.*); a king of the family of Bharata who was the son of Duṣyanta and Śakuntalā (*Bhā. Purāṇa*); the incarnation of Śiva as an ox (*Ś. Purāṇa*); a son of Kārtavīryārjuna (*Br. Purāṇa*); another name for Viṣṇu/Kṛṣṇa, Indra, the sun and Kāma.

**Vṛṣabha** (S) (M) 1. the bull. 2. manly; mighty; strong; chief; excellent; eminent. 3. an asura killed by Viṣṇu (*H. Purāṇa*); a son of the 10th Manu (*Mā. Purāṇa*); a son of Kuśāgra; a son of Kārtavīrya (*J. S. Koṣa*); the Jaina 1st Arhat of the present Avasarpinī; a mountain; the son of King Subala of Gāndhāra and the brother of Śakuni (*M. Bh.*); a Yādava king who was the son of Anāmitra and the husband of Jayantī (*M. Purāṇa*); the zodiac sign of Taurus.

**Vṛṣabhadhvaja** (S) (M) 1. bull bannered. 3. an attendant of Śiva (*M. Bh.*)

**Vṛṣabhagati** (S) (M) 1. going on a bull. 3. another name for Śiva.

**Vṛṣabhaketu** (S) (M) 1. bull bannered. 3. another name for Śiva.

**Vṛṣabhāṅka** (S) (M) 1. marked by a bull. 3. another name for Śiva.

**Vṛṣabhānu** (S) (M) 1. best bull. 3. a king who was the son of Śūrabhanu and father of Rādhā (*Brah. Purāṇā*)

**Vṛṣabhasvāmin** (S) (M) 1. lord of the bulls. 3. another name for Śiva; a king who was the founder of the family of Ikṣvāku and the father of Draviḍa (*H. Purāṇa*)

**Vṛṣabhavāhana** (S) (M) 1. bull vehicled. 3. another name for Śiva.

**Vṛṣabhekṣaṇa** (S) (M) 1. bull eyed. 3. another name for Viṣṇu/Kṛṣṇa.

**Vṛṣadarbha** (S) (M) 1. grass for the bull. 3. a son of Śibi (*H. Purāṇa*); a saintly king in the palace of Yama (*M. Bh.*); another name of King Uśīnara of Kāśī.

**Vṛṣādarbhi** (S) (M) 1. bull feeder. 3. a king of Kāśī also known as Yuvanāśva who was the son of Vṛṣadarbha (*M. Bh.*); a son of Śibi (*H. Purāṇa*)

**Vṛṣadarpa** (S) (M) 1. as proud as a bull. 3. a son of Emperor Śibi (*Bhāgavata*)

**Vṛṣadevā** (S) (F) 1. goddess of the bulls. 3. a wife of Vasudeva (*Bhā. Purāṇa*)

**Vṛṣadhara** (S) (M) 1. bull bearer. 3. another name for Śiva.

**Vṛṣadhvajā** (S) (F) 1. bull bannered. 3. another name for Durgā.

**Vṛṣadhvaja** (S) (M) 1. rat bannered. 3. a king of the line of Pravīra (*M. Bh.*); another name for Gaṇeśa.

**Vṛṣaga** (S) (M) 1. going on a bull. 3. another name for Śiva.

**Vṛṣāgir** (S) (M) 1. strong voiced. 3. a hermit and father of Ṛjrāśva.

**Vṛṣakā** (S) (F) 1. cow. 3. a yakṣī who is the tutelary divinity of fertility.

**Vṛṣaka** (S) (M) 1. poisonous. 3. a son of King Subala of Gāndhāra (*M. Bh.*); a Kaliṅga prince.

**Vṛṣākapi** (S) (M) 1. bull and monkey conjoined. 3. a semi-divine being; one of the 11 rudras (*A. Purāṇa*); a hermit (*M. Bh.*); another name for Viṣṇu.

**Vṛṣaketana** (S) (M) 1. having a bull for a sign. 3. another name for Śiva.

**Vṛṣaketu** (S) (M) 1. bull bannered. 3. a son of Karṇa; another name for Paraśurāma.

**Vṛṣakrātha** (S) (M) 1. killing bulls. 3. a Kaurava warrior (*M. Bh.*)

**Vṛṣakrātu** (S) (M) acting like a bull; manly.

**Vṛṣalākṣa** (S) (M) 1. horse eyed. 3. a king in the line of Bharata who was the son of Ćaturaṅga and the grandson of Romapāda (*Bhāgavata*)

**Vṛṣāmitra** (S) (M) 1. a friend of bulls. 3. a hermit and devotee of Yudhiṣṭhira (*M. Bh.*)

**Vṛṣaṇa** (S) (M) 1. sprinkling; fertilizing. 3. a son of Madhu (*H. Purāṇa*); a son of Kārtavīrya; another name for Śiva.

**Vṛṣaṇāśva** (S) (M) 1. drawn by stallions; fertilized by stallions. 3. a Ṛg Vedic king who was the father of Indra as the girl Menā (*Ṛg Veda*); a gandharva; another name for Indra.

**Vṛṣāṇḍa** (S) (M) 1. bull testicled. 3. an asura (*M. Bh.*)

**Vṛṣaṅgan** (S) (M) 1. not to be doubted. 3. another name for Śiva.

**Vṛṣāṅka** (S) (M) 1. bull marked. 3. another name for Śiva.

**Vṛṣaṅku** (S) (M) 1. without any sin. 3. a hermit (*U. Rāmāyaṇa*)

**Vṛṣaparvan** (S) (M) 1. with joints as strong as that of a bull. 2. strong jointed. 3. a son of Kaśyapa and Danu who was reborn as the King Dīrghaprajña and was the father of Śarmiṣṭhā (*M. Bh.*); a hermit; another name for Indra, Viṣṇu and Śiva.

**Vṛṣapati** (S) (M) 1. lord of the bull. 3. another name for Śiva.

**Vṛṣasena** (S) (M) 1. with an army of bulls. 3. a son of the 10th Manu (*H. Purāṇa*); a son of Karna; a great-grandson of Aśoka; another name for Karṇa.

**Vṛṣaskandha** (S) (M) 1. bull shouldered. 3. another name for Śiva.

**Vṛṣātmaja** (S) (M) 1. son of the Sun. 3. another name for Karṇa.

**Vṛṣavāhana** (S) (M) 1. whose vehicle is a bull. 3. another name for Śiva.

**Vṛśćika** (S) (M) 1. scorpion. 2. the zodiac sign of Scorpio.

**Vṛśćikeśa** (S) (M) 1. lord of scorpions. 2. ruler of the sign of Scorpio. 3. another name for the planet Mercury.

**Vṛṣin** (S) (M) 1. fond of rain. 2. a peacock.

**Vṛṣṇī** (S) (M)) 1. strong; manly; powerful; mighty; passionate; a ram; bull; ray of light; air; wind. 3. a famous king of the Yadu dynasty who was the son of Madhu and the husband of Mādrī and Gāndhārī, he was the founder of the dynasty and Kṛṣṇa was born in it (*M. Bh.*); another name for Śiva, Viṣṇu/Kṛṣṇa, Indra and Agni.

**Vṛṣṇigarbha** (S) (M) 1. born in the Vṛṣṇi family. 3. another name for Kṛṣṇa.

**Vṛṣṇijīva** (S) (M) 1. soul of the Vṛṣṇis. 3. another name for Kṛṣṇa.

**Vṛṣṇikulodvaha** (S) (M) 1. elevating the Vṛṣṇi family. 3. another name for Kṛṣṇa.

**Vṛṣṇinandana** (S) (M) 1. son of the Vṛṣṇis. 3. another name for Kṛṣṇa.

**Vṛṣṇipati** (S) (M) 1. lord of the Vṛṣṇis. 3. another name for Kṛṣṇa.

**Vṛṣṇipravara** (S) (M) 1. chief of the Vṛṣṇis. 3. another name for Kṛṣṇa.

**Vṛṣṇipuṅgava** (S) (M) 1. bull of the Vṛṣṇis. 3. another name for Kṛṣṇa.

**Vṛṣṇiśārdula** (S) (M) 1. tiger of the Vṛṣṇis; noblest of the Vṛṣṇis. 3. another name for Kṛṣṇa.

**Vṛṣṇisattama** (S) (M) 1. best of the Vṛṣṇis. 3. another name for Kṛṣṇa.

**Vṛṣṇisiṁha** (S) (M) 1. lion of the Vṛṣṇis. 3. another name for Kṛṣṇa.

**Vṛṣṇiśreṣtha** (S) (M) 1. first of the Vṛṣṇis. 3. another name for Kṛṣṇa.

**Vṛṣṇivareṇya** (S) (M) 1. best of the Vṛṣṇis. 3. another name for Kṛṣṇa.

**Vṛṣṇyandhakapati** (S) (M) 1. lord of the mighty. 3. another name for Kṛṣṇa.

**Vṛṣṇyandhakottama** (S) (M) 1. best of the mighty. 3. another name for Kṛṣṇa.

**Vṛṣtimat** (S) (M) 1. rainy. 3. a son of Kaviratha (*Bhā. Purāṇa*)

**Vṛtra** (S) (M) 1. coverer; restrainer; enemy; foe. 3. the Vedic personification of a demon of darkness and drought which takes possession of clouds causing them to keep back the waters; an asura who was an incarnation of the Emperor Ćitraketu created by Kaśyapa (*P. Purāṇa*) or Tvaṣṭa (*D. Purāṇa*) and was killed by Indra.

**Vṛtrāghnī** (S) (M) 1. killing enemies; destroyer of Vṛta. 3. another name for Indra.

**Vṛtrahā** (S) (M) 1. killer of Vṛtra. 3. another name for Indra.

**Vṛtta** (S) (M) 1. circle; fixed; firm character; conduct. 3. a nāga son of Kaśyapa and Kadru (*M. Bh.*)

**Vṛttamallikā** (S) (F) 1. the encircling creeper. 2. *Jasminum sambac*.

**Vṛttī** (S) (F) 1. being; existence; state; moral conduct. 3. a wife of Rudra (*Bhā. Purāṇa*)

**Vūrnā** (S) (F) chosen; selected.

**Vyābhāsa** (S) (M) to illuminate beautifully.

**Vyādhi** (S) (F) 1. disease; trouble; epidemic. 3. the daughter of Mṛtyu (*V. Purāṇa*)

**Vyadvan** (S) (M) 1. having various paths. 3. another name for Agni.

**Vyāgheśvarī** (S) (F) goddess of a tiger; goddess who rides a tiger.

**Vyāghra** (S) (M) 1. tiger. 3. the tiger offspring of Śārdūlī or Kaśyapa and Danṣṭrā (*A. Veda*)

**Vyāghrabala** (S) (M) with the strength of the tiger.

**Vyāghrabhaṭa** (S) (M) 1. as powerful as the tiger. 3. an asura (*K. Sāgara*); a minister of King Śṛdatta (*K. Sāgara*)

**Vyāghradatta** (S) (M) 1. given by a tiger. 3. a Magadha prince who fought on the side of the Kauravas (*M. Bh.*)

**Vyāghraketu** (S) (M) 1. tiger bannered. 3. a Pāñcāla warrior on the Pāṇḍava side (*M. Bh.*)

**Vyāghrākṣa** (S) (M) 1. tiger eyed. 3. a follower of Skanda (*M. Bh.*); an asura (*H. Purāṇa*)

**Vyāghramukha** (S) (M) 1. tiger faced. 3. a king; a mountain (*Mā. Purāṇa*)

**Vyāghrapad** (S) (M) 1. tiger footed. 3. a hermit and father of Upamanyu (*M. Bh.*)

**Vyāghrasena** (S) (M) one who fights like a

tiger.

**Vyāghrāsyā** (S) (F) 1. tiger faced. 3. a Buddhist goddess.

**Vyāghravadhū** (S) (F) tigress.

**Vyāghravaktra** (S) (M) 1. tiger faced. 3. an attendant of Śiva (*H. Purāṇa*)

**Vyāghrī** (S) (F) 1. tigress. 3. a Buddhist being attending on the mātṛs.

**Vyāhṛti** (S) (F) 1. utterance; speech. 2. declaration. 3. mystical utterances personified as the daughters of Sāvitṛ and Pṛṣṇi.

**Vyakta** (S) (M) 1. manifest; distinguished; wise; adorned; embellished; beautiful. 3. one of the main disciples of Mahāvira (*J.S. Koṣa*); another name for Viṣṇu.

**Vyaktarūpa** (S) (M) 1. with a manifested form. 3. another name for Viṣṇu.

**Vyālimukha** (S) (M) 1. snake faced. 3. an asura killed by Skanda (*M. Bh.*)

**Vyāna** (S) (M) 1. vital air. 2. one of the 5 vital airs of the body personified as the son of Udāna and the father of Apāna.

**Vyanśa** (S) (M) 1. with wide shoulders; broad shouldered. 3. a son of Vipraćitti; a demon killed by Indra (*Ṛg Veda*)

**Vyāpti** (S) (F) accomplishment; attainment; omnipresence.

**Vyāsa** (S) (M) 1. separation; division. 2. distributing; arranging; compiling. 3. a celebrated sage regarded as the original compiler of the Vedas, he was the son of sage Pārāśara and Satyavatī and half-brother of Vićitravīrya and Bhīṣma, he is also called Bādarāyaṇa and Kṛṣṇa Dvaipayana, he became the father of Dhṛtarāṣṭra and Pāṇḍu by Vićitravīrya's widows, he was also the father of Vidura by a servant girl and of Śuka the narrator of the *Bhāgavata Purāṇa*, he was the spiritual preceptor of the Kauravas and Pāṇḍavas; towards the close of his life he dictated the story of the *Mahābharata* to Gaṇapati, he was reborn as Apāntaratamas.

**Vyāsamātṛ** (S) (M) 1. mother of Vyāsa. 3. another name for Satyavatī.

**Vyāsamūrti** (S) (M) 1. idol of the compiler. 3. another name for Śiva.

**Vyaṣṭi** (S) (F) attainment; success; singleness; individuality.

**Vyaśva** (S) (M) 1. horseless. 3. a ṛṣi; a king in the palace of Yama (*M. Bh.*)

**Vyatibhā** (S) (F) shining forth.

**Vyavasāya** (S) (M) 1. effort; resolve; purpose; act; strategem. 3. resolution personified as a son of Dharmā and Vapus; another name for Viṣṇu and Śiva.

**Vyenī** (S) (F) 1. variously tinted. 2. the dawn.

**Vyomabha** (S) (M) 1. heaven like. 3. another name for a Buddha.

**Vyomadeva** (S) (M) 1. lord of the sky. 3. another name for Śiva.

**Vyomādhipa** (S) (M) 1. lord of the sky. 3. another name for Śiva.

**Vyomagaṅgā** (S) (F) the celestial Gaṅgā.

**Vyomakeśa** (S) (M) 1. sky haired. 3. another name for Śiva.

**Vyomamṛga** (S) (M) 1. the animal of the sky. 3. one of the 10 horses of the moon (*M. Bh.*)

**Vyoman** (S) (M) 1. heaven; sky; atmosphere; wind; air. 3. a temple sacred to the sun (*Bhā. Purāṇa*); the year personified; a king in the dynasty of Bharata who was the son of Dāśārha and father of Jīmūta (*Bhāgavata*)

**Vyomaratna** (S) (M) 1. sky jewel. 3. another name for the sun.

**Vyomāri** (S) (M) 1. shining in the sky. 3. a viśvadeva (*M. Bh.*)

**Vyomasad** (S) (M) 1. dwelling in the sky. 2. a god; a gandharva (*Ṛg Veda*)

**Vyomāsura** (S) (M) 1. demon of the sky. 3. a son of Māyāsura killed by Kṛṣṇa (*Bhā. Purāṇa*)

**Vyomeśa** (S) (M) 1. lord of the sky. 3. another name for the sun.

**Vyomin** (S) (M) 1. travelling in space. 3. one of the 10 horses of the moon (*A. Koṣa*)

**Vyominī** (S) (F) celestial; apsarā.

**Vyūdhoru** (S) (M) 1. with thick thighs. 3. a son of Dhṛtarāṣṭra (*M. Bh.*)

**Vyuharāja** (S) (M) 1. lord of reason. 3. a Bodhisattva.

**Vyuṣa** (S) (M) dawn; daybreak.

**Vyuśitāśva** (S) (M) 1. with the horses of dawn. 3. a Purū king and husband of Bhadrā considered the most beautiful woman in India; she was the mother of the 3 Satvas and

4 Madras (*M. Bh.*); a king and descendant of Daśaratha.

**Vyuṣṭa** (S) (M) 1. dawned; grown bright and clear. 3. daybreak personified as a son of Kalpa or as a son of Puṣpārṇa and Doṣā or as a son of Vibhāvasu and Uṣas (*Bhā. Purāṇa*); a king of the Dhruva dynasty who was the son of King Puṣpārṇa and Prabhā and the father of Sarvatejas (*Bhāgavata*)

**Vyuṣṭi** (S) (F) the 1st gleam of dawn; grace; beauty; fruit; reward; prosperity; felicity

# Y

**Yādasāmbhartā** (S) (M) 1. chief of marine animals. 3. another name for Varuṇa.
**Yādaspati** (S) (M) 1. lord of marine animals. 3. another name for Varuṇa.
**Yādava** (S) (M) 1. descended from Yadu. 3. another name for Kṛṣṇa.
**Yādavāgrya** (S) (M) 1. first of the Yādavas. 3. another name for Kṛṣṇa.
**Yādavaprakāśa** (S) (M) 1. light of the Yādavas. 3. another name for Kṛṣṇa.
**Yādavaputra** (S) (M) 1. son of Yadu. 3. another name for Kṛṣṇa.
**Yādavarāya** (S) (M) 1. king of the Yādavas. 3. another name for Kṛṣṇa.
**Yadavaśārdūla** (S) (M) 1. tiger or chief of the Yādavas. 3. another name for Kṛṣṇa.
**Yādavaśreṣṭha** (S) (M) 1. first of the Yādavas. 3. another name for Kṛṣṇa.
**Yādavendra** (S) (M) 1. lord of the Yādavas. 3. another name for Kṛṣṇa.
**Yādaveśvara** (S) (M) 1. lord of the Yādavas. 3. another name for Kṛṣṇa.
**Yādavī** (S) (F) 1. woman of the Yādava tribe. 3. wife of Subāhu and mother of Sagara; another name for Durgā.
**Yādīśa** (S) (M) lord of marine animals.
**Yādonātha** (S) (M) 1. lord of sea animals. 3. another name for Varuṇa.
**Yadu** (S) (M) 1. cowherd. 3. an ancient hero in the Vedas and the founder of the Yādava Vanśa, he was the son of Yayāti and Devayānī and the brother of Turvasu, he was the father of Sahasrajit, Kroṣṭā, Nala and Ṛpu; a son of Uparićara Vasu who was considered invincible (*M. Bh.*) .
**Yadūdvaha** (S) (M) 1. supporter of the Yadus. 3. another name for Kṛṣṇa and Vasudeva.
**Yadukumāra** (S) (M) 1. youth of the Yadu tribe. 3. another name for Kṛṣṇa.
**Yadumaṇi** (S) (M) 1. jewel of the Yadus. 3. the father of Parama.
**Yadunandana** (S) (M) 1. son of Yadu. 3. another name for Akrūra (*V. Purāṇa*)
**Yadunandinī** (S) (F) daughter of the Yadus.
**Yadunātha** (S) (M) 1. lord of the Yadus. 3. another name for Kṛṣṇa.
**Yadupati** (S) (M) 1. lord of the Yadus. 3. another name for Kṛṣṇa.
**Yadupuṅgava** (S) (M) 1. bull of the Yadus; chief of the Yadus. 3. another name for Kṛṣṇa.
**Yadurāj** (S) (M) 1. lord of the Yadus. 3. another name for Kṛṣṇa.
**Yaduśreṣṭha** (S) (M) 1. best of the Yādus. 3. another name for Kṛṣṇa.
**Yadusukhāvaha** (S) (M) 1. bringing pleasure to the Yadus. 3. another name for Kṛṣṇa.
**Yaduttama** (S) (M) 1. best of the Yadus. 3. another name for Kṛṣṇa.
**Yaduvaṅśavivardhana** (S) (M) 1. dividing the Yadu family. 3. another name for Kṛṣṇa.
**Yaduvīra** (S) (M) 1. hero of the Yadus. 3. another name for Kṛṣṇa.
**Yadvā** (S) (F) perception; mind; intelligence.
**Yahu** (S) (M) offspring; child; restless; swift; mighty; strong.
**Yahvā** (S) (F) heaven and earth; the flowing water.
**Yahva** (S) (M) 1. restless; swift. 2. active. 3. another name for Agni, Soma, Indra.
**Yahvat** (S) (F) the everflowing waters.
**Yahvī** (S) (F) heaven and earth conjoined.
**Yajā** (S) (F) 1. worshipper. 2. sacrificer. 3. a tutelary goddess.
**Yāja** (S) (M) 1. sacrificer. 2. worshipper. 3. a sage born in the Kaśyapa gotra.
**Yajāka** (S) (M) worshipping; liberal.
**Yajamāna** (S) (M) 1. sacrificing; worshipping. 2. patron of priests.
**Yajana** (S) (M) act of sacrificing or worshipping.
**Yajanīya** (S) (M) to be worshipped.
**Yajata** (S) (M) 1. holy; divine; dignified; worthy of worship. 2. adorable. 3. another name for Śiva, the moon and the officiating priest of a sacrifice.
**Yajatra** (S) (M) worthy of worship; deserving adoration.
**Yajin** (S) (M) worshipper.
**Yajiṣṇu** (S) (M) worshipping the gods.
**Yajña** (S) (M) 1. worship; devotion; oblation;

sacrifice; worshipper; sacrificer. 3. an incarnation of Viṣṇu as the son of Prajāpati Ruci and Ākūti and the twin of Dakṣiṇā, they married each other and their 12 children were the demigods known as the Yāmas in the Svāyambhuva Manvantara (*Bhāgavata*); a sage who was an author of *Ṛg Veda* (x)

**Yajñabāhu** (S) (M) 1. arm of sacrifice. 2. fire. 3. a sage who was the son of Priyavrata and Barhiṣmatī and grandson of Svāyambhuva Manu (*Bhāgavata*)

**Yajñadatta** (S) (M) 1. given by sacrifice. 3. the *Agni Purāṇa* name for the youthful sage otherwise known as Śravaṇa who was shot by Daśaratha.

**Yajñodaya** (S) (M) risen from the sacred fire.

**Yajñadhara** (S) (M) 1. the bearer of the sacrifice. 3. another name for Viṣṇu.

**Yajñagamya** (S) (M) 1. accessible through worship. 3. another name for Viṣṇu/Kṛṣṇa.

**Yajñaguhya** (S) (M) 1. lord of the sacrifice. 3. another name for Viṣṇu/Kṛṣṇa.

**Yajñahotri** (S) (M) 1. a priest at a sacrifice. 3. a son of Manu Uttama (*Bhā. Purāṇa*)

**Yajñakṛt** (S) (M) 1. worshipping; causing sacrifice. 3. another name for Viṣṇu.

**Yajñamaya** (S) (M) containing the sacrifice.

**Yajñamūrti** (S) (M) 1. the idol of sacrifice. 3. another name for Viṣṇu.

**Yajñanemi** (S) (M) 1. surrounded by sacrifices. 3. another name for Kṛṣṇa.

**Yajñapati** (S) (M) 1. lord of sacrifice. 3. another name for Viṣṇu and Soma.

**Yajñapātra** (S) (M) a sacrificial vessel.

**Yajñaphala** (S) (M) the fruit of worship.

**Yajñapriya** (S) (M) 1. fond of sacrifice. 3. another name for Kṛṣṇa.

**Yajñapuruṣa** (S) (M) 1. soul of the sacrifice. 3. another name for Viṣṇu.

**Yajñarāj** (S) (M) 1. king of the sacrifice. 3. another name for the moon.

**Yajñāri** (S) (M) 1. enemy of the sacrifice. 3. another name for Śiva.

**Yajñarupa** (S) (M) 1. the form of a sacrifice. 3. another name for Kṛṣṇa.

**Yajñaśarman** (S) (M) 1. protector of the sacrifice. 3. a Brāhmin made famous in the Purāṇas.

**Yajñaśatru** (S) (M) 1. enemy of the sacrifice. 3. another name for Rāma and Lakṣmaṇa; a rākṣasa (*Rāmāyaṇa*)

**Yajñasena** (S) (M) 1. leader of the sacrifice. 3. a king of Vidarbha; a dānava (*K. Sāgara*); another name for Viṣṇu and Drupada of Pāñćāla (*M. Bh.*)

**Yajñaseni** (S) (M) 1. son of Drupada. 3. another name for Dhṛṣṭadyumna.

**Yājñasenī** (S) (F) 1. sister of Dhṛṣṭadyumna. 3. another name for Draupadī.

**Yajñasenisuta** (S) (M) 1. son of Drupada. 3. another name for Dhṛṣṭadyumna.

**Yajñaśila** (S) (M) performing the sacrifice diligently.

**Yajñātman** (S) (M) 1. the soul of sacrifice. 3. another name for Viṣṇu.

**Yajñatrātṛ** (S) (M) 1. protector of the sacrifice. 3. another name for Viṣṇu.

**Yajñavāha** (S) (M) 1. conducting the sacrifice to the gods. 3. an attendant of Skanda; another name for the aśvins.

**Yajñavāhana** (S) (M) 1. having sacrifice as a vehicle. 3. another name for Śiva and Viṣṇu.

**Yājñavalkya** (S) (M) 1. clad in oblation. 2. surrounded or covered by the sacrifice. 3. an ancient sage and the first teacher of the white *Yajur Veda* said to have been revealed to him by the sun, he was also the author of a code of laws secondary in importance only to Manu and the author of *Vājasaneyī Saṃhitā*, he was King Janaka's priest (*A. Purāṇa*)

**Yajñavarāha** (S) (M) 1. deity of oblation. 3. Viṣṇu in his boar incarnation.

**Yajñavardhana** (S) (M) increasing sacrifice.

**Yajñavatī** (S) (F) 1. worshipping. 3. a queen of Kāmarupa.

**Yajñavīrya** (S) (M) 1. one whose might is sacrifice. 3. another name for Viṣṇu.

**Yajñayoga** (S) (M) 1. worthy of sacrifice. 3. another name for Viṣṇu.

**Yajñeśa** (S) (M) 1. lord of the sacrificial fire. 3. another name for Viṣṇu and the sun.

**Yajñeśvara** (S) (M) 1. lord of sacrifice. 3. another name for Viṣṇu, Vāyu and the moon.

**Yajñeśvarī** (S) (F) 1. lord of the sacrifice. 3. a goddess.

**Yājñikā** (S) (F) 1. used in an oblation. 2. Flame of the Forest (*Butea frondosa*); Bastard Teak (*Butea monosperma*); Black Catechu tree (*Acacia catechu*)

**Yājñikadeva** (S) (M) lord of sacrifices.

**Yājñikāśraya** (S) (M) 1. refuge of sacrificers. 3. another name for Viṣṇu.

**Yājñīya** (S) (M) 1. worthy of worship and sacrifice; sacred; godly; divine. 3. *Ficus glomerata*.

**Yajñu** (S) (M) worshipping; pious; worthy of worship.

**Yaju** (S) (M) 1. a sacrificial prayer. 3. one of the 10 horses of the moon.

**Yajuṣpati** (S) (M) 1. lord of the sacrifice. 3. another name for Viṣṇu.

**Yajvin** (S) (M) worshipper.

**Yakṣa** (S) (M) 1. protector of forests; quick; speedy; living supernatural being. 3. a class of semi-divine beings who are attendants of Kubera and sometimes of Viṣṇu, they are variously descibed as the sons of Pulastya, Pulaha, Kaśyapa and Krodha and also produced from the feet of Brahmā, they are generally regarded as beings of a benevolent and inoffensive disposition and they live in trees; a son of Śvaphalka (*V. Purāṇa*); Indra's palace; the attendants of the Jaina Tīrthaṅkaras (*J. Literature*)

**Yakṣādhipa** (S) (M) 1. lord of the yakṣas. 3. another name for Kubera.

**Yakṣanāyaka** (S) (M) 1. lord of the yakṣas. 3. the servant of the 4th Arhat of the present Avasarpinī.

**Yakṣāṅgī** (S) (F) 1. alive; speedy. 3. a river.

**Yakṣapati** (S) (M) 1. king of the yakṣas. 3. another name for Kubera (*H. Purāṇa*)

**Yakṣapravara** (S) (M) 1. chief of the yakṣas. 3. another name for Kubera.

**Yakṣarāj** (S) (M) 1. king of the yakṣas. 3. another name for Kubera and Maṇibhadra.

**Yakṣarakṣodhipa** (S) (M) 1. leader of the yakṣas and rākṣasas. 3. another name for Kubera.

**Yakṣarāṭ** (S) (M) 1. giving yakṣas. 3. another name for Kubera.

**Yakṣataru** (S) (M) 1. tree of the yakṣas. 3. the Indian Fig tree (*Ficus indica*)

**Yakṣendra** (S) (M) 1. lord of the yakṣas. 3. another name for Kubera.

**Yakṣeśa** (S) (M) 1. lord of the yakṣas. 3. the servants of the 11th and 18th Arhats of the present Avasarpinī.

**Yakṣeśvara** (S) (M) 1. lord of the yakṣas. 3. an incarnation of Siva (*Ś. Purāṇa*); another name for Kubera.

**Yakṣī** (S) (F) 1. a female yakṣa. 3. Kubera's wife.

**Yakṣin** (S) (M) having life; living.

**Yakṣiṇī** (S) (F) 1. a female yakṣa. 3. attendants of Durgā; another name for Kubera's wife.

**Yama** (S) (M) 1. rein; curb; bridle; restraint; number. 2. driver; charioteer; twin born. 3. the god who rules over the spirits of the dead, he is regarded as the first of men and the son of Vivasvat the sun and Śaraṇyū, his twin sister is Yamī, his abode is a nether region called Yamapura, he is also one of the 8 guardians of the world and the regent of the southern quarter, he is the regent of the constellation Bharaṇī and the supposed author of *Ṛg Veda* (x); one of Skanda's attendants.

**Yamabhaginī** (S) (F) 1. sister of Yama. 3. another name for the river Yamunā.

**Yamadanṣṭra** (S) (M) 1. with restraining teeth. 3. a rākṣasa (*K. Sāgara*); a warrior on the side of the gods.

**Yamadevatā** (S) (M) 1. having Yama for one's deity. 3. another name for the lunar constellation Bharaṇī.

**Yamadruma** (S) (M) 1. Yama's tree. 3. *Bombax heptaphyllum*.

**Yamadūta** (S) (M) 1. Yama's messenger sent to bring the departed spirit to the seat of judgement. 3. a son of Viśvāmitra (*M. Bh.*)

**Yamaghna** (S) (M) 1. one who destroys Yama. 3. another name for Viṣṇu.

**Yamahārdikā** (S) (F) 1. heart piercing. 3. one of Durgā's attendants.

**Yamaja** (S) (M) twin born.

**Yamajihvā** (S) (F) 1. Yama's tongue. 3. a

yoginī.

**Yamajit** (S) (M) 1. conqueror of Yama. 3. another name for Śiva.

**Yāmaka** (S) (M) 1. restraint; a watch on 3 hours or one-eighth of a day. 3. the constellation Punarvasu.

**Yamakālindī** (S) (F) 1. blossoming. 3. another name for Saṁjñā the mother of Yama.

**Yamakīla** (S) (M) 1. self restrained. 3. another name for Viṣṇu.

**Yamalā** (S) (F) 1. a twin; a hiccough. 3. a tāntric deity; a river.

**Yamala** (S) (M) 1. a twin. 3. a magic tree identified with the sons of Kubera; the Arjuna tree (*Terminalia arjuna*)

**Yāman** (S) (M) motion; course; flight; invocation; prayer; march.

**Yamaṇa** (S) (M) 1. restraining; governing; managing. 3. a rāga; another name for Yama.

**Yamanetra** (S) (M) having Yama as the leader.

**Yamāṅgikā** (S) (F) 1. destroyer of Yama. 3. a yoginī.

**Yamantaka** (S) (M) 1. destroyer of Yama. 3. another name for Śiva.

**Yamānućara** (S) (M) a servant of Yama.

**Yamapriya** (S) (M) 1. loved by Yama. 3. *Ficus indica*.

**Yamarāja** (S) (M) King Yama.

**Yamāri** (S) (M) 1. enemy of Yama. 3. another name for Viṣṇu.

**Yamasū** (S) (M) 1. bringing forth twins. 3. another name for the sun.

**Yamasvasṛ** (S) (F) 1. Yama's sister. 3. another name for the river Yamunā and Durgā.

**Yamavat** (S) (M) one who governs himself; self restrained.

**Yameśa** (S) (M) 1. having Yama as ruler. 3. another name for the constellation Bharaṇī.

**Yamī** (S) (F) 1. the elder twin sister; brace; pair; couple. 3. a daughter of Sūrya and Saṁjñā and the twin sister of Yama who is identified in post Vedic mythology with the river Yamunā (*V. Purāṇa*)

**Yāmī** (S) (F) 1. motion; course; progress; road; path; carriage. 3. a daughter of Dakṣa and wife of Dharma (*V. Purāṇa*); an apsarā (*H. Purāṇa*)

**Yamin** (S) (M) one who has curbed his passions.

**Yaminemi** (S) (M) 1. felly of a chariot wheel. 2. bearer of motion. 3. another name for Indra.

**Yāminī** (S) (F) 1. consisting of watches. 2. night. 3. daughter of Prahlāda (*K. Sāgara*) wife of Tārakṣa and the mother of Śalabha (*Bh. Purāṇa*); a daughter of Dakṣa and wife of Kaśyapa (*Bhāgavata*)

**Yāmininātha** (S) (M) 1. lord of night. 3. another name for the moon.

**Yāminīpati** (S) (M) 1. the beloved of night. 3. another name for the moon.

**Yāmīra** (S) (M) 1. lord of night. 3. another name for the moon.

**Yamita** (S) (M) restrained; checked.

**Yamunā** (S) (F) 1. a river commonly called Jamunā which is identified with Yamī, it rises in the Himālayas among the Jamnotri peaks and flows down to join the Gaṅgā in Allahabad. 3. the daughter of sage Mataṅga (*K. Sāgara*); another name for the Kālindī river which is personified as a black goddess on a tortoise with a water-pot in her hand (*M. Bh.*)

**Yāmuna** (S) (M) 1. growing in the Yamuna. 3. a mountain standing between the rivers Gaṅgā and Yamunā (*M. Bh.*)

**Yāmunāćārya** (S) (M) 1. preceptor from the Yamunā. 3. a principal teacher of the Vaiṣṇava cult.

**Yamunājanaka** (S) (M) 1. father of Yamunā. 3. another name for the sun.

**Yamunāpati** (S) (M) 1. lord of Yamunā. 3. another name for Viṣṇu.

**Yāmya** (S) (M) 1. southern; the right hand; belonging to Yama. 3. another name for Śiva, Viṣṇu and Agastya; the Sandalwood tree.

**Yāmyā** (S) (F) night.

**Yantri** (S) (M) restraining; establishing; granting; bestowing; charioteer; ruler; governor; guide.

**Yantur** (S) (M) ruler; guide.

**Yaśaćandra** (S) (M) as famous as the moon.

**Yaśahketu** (S) (M) 1. with a famous banner. 3. a king of a city called Śobhāvatī (*K. Sāgara*)

**Yaśakāya** (S) (M) with a body of fame and glory.

**Yaśapāla** (S) (M) lord of fame.

**Yaśapāṇi** (S) (M) 1. holding fame. 2. renowned. 3. a Buddhist king of Benaras.

**Yaśas** (S) (M) 1. beauty; splendour; worth; glory; fame. 3. renown personified as a son of Kāma and Rati or of Dharma and Kīrti; the father of Kalki the 10th incarnation who will come at the end of time.

**Yaśaskāma** (S) (M) 1. desiring fame. 3. a Bodhisattva.

**Yaśaskara** (S) (M) 1. conferring glory; causing renown; glorious. 3. a king of Kāśmira.

**Yaśastara** (S) (M) more renowned and resplendent.

**Yaśasvat** (S) (M) glorious; famous; honourable; splendid; magnificent; excellent.

**Yaśasvatī** (S) (F) illustrious; famous.

**Yaśasvinī** (S) (F) 1. beautiful; splendid; illustrious; famous. 3. a mother of Skanda's retinue; a sister of Draupadī (*Bhāgavata*)

**Yāska** (S) (M) 1. desiring heat; exerting. 3. a Sanskṛt grammarian of ancient times who composed the Nirukta in 500 B.C. (*M. Bh.*)

**Yaśo** (S) (M) beauty; fame; splendour; glory; honour.

**Yaśobhadra** (S) (M) 1. famous for one's gentleness. 3. son of King Manobhadra (*P. Purāṇa*)

**Yaśobhagin** (S) (M) rich in glory.

**Yaśobhāgya** (S) (M) one whose destiny is glory.

**Yaśobhṛt** (S) (M) conferring fame; possessing fame.

**Yaśodā** (S) (F) 1. conferring fame. 3. the wife of the cowherd Nanda and the foster mother of Kṛṣṇa she is considered the incarnation of Dharā; the wife of Mahāvīra and the daughter of Samaravīra; another name for Durgā.

**Yaśodeva** (S) (M) 1. lord of fame and beauty. 3. a son of Rāmaćandra.

**Yaśodevī** (S) (F) 1. goddess of fame and beauty. 3. a wife of Bṛhanmanas (*H. Purāṇa*)

**Yaśodhā** (S) (F) conferring splendour and fame.

**Yaśodhāman** (S) (M) abode of glory.

**Yaśodhana** (S) (M) one whose wealth is fame.

**Yaśodharā** (S) (F) 1. maintaining fame or glory. 3. the wife of Tvaṣṭṛ and the mother of Tṛśiras and Viśvarupa; the 4th night of the month; a daughter of King Trigarta and married to King Hasti of the Purū dynasty, she was the mother of Vikaṇṭha (*M. Bh.*); wife of Gautama Buddha and mother of Rāhula.

**Yaśodhara** (S) (M) 1. maintaining or preserving glory. 3. the 18th Jaina Arhat of the preceding and 19th Arhat of the coming Utsarpiṇī; the son of Durmukha who fought on the side of the Pāṇḍavas (*M. Bh.*); a son of Kṛṣṇa and Rukmiṇī (*M. Bh.*)

**Yaśolekhā** (S) (F) a narrative of glorious deeds.

**Yaśomādhava** (S) (M) 1. excellent and famous descendant of Madhu. 3. a form of Viṣṇu.

**Yaśomatī** (S) (F) 1. having fame. 3. the foster-mother of Kṛṣṇa; the 3rd lunar night.

**Yaśomitra** (S) (M) a friend of fame.

**Yaśonandi** (S) (M) with happy fame.

**Yaśonidhi** (S) (M) one whose wealth is fame.

**Yaśorāja** (S) (M) lord of fame.

**Yaśorāśi** (S) (M) a mass of glory.

**Yaśovara** (S) (M) 1. reputed. 3. a son of Kṛṣṇa and Rukmiṇī.

**Yaśovarman** (S) (M) 1. armoured by fame. 3. a king of Kanyākubjā (720 A.D.)

**Yaśovat** (S) (M) possessing glory and fame.

**Yaśovatī** (S) (F) 1. possessing glory and fame. 3. a mythical city on Mount Meru of Īśāna's the ruler of the north eastern part (*D. Bh. Purāṇa*)

**Yaśoyuta** (S) (M) possessing fame; renowned.

**Yaṣṭi** (S) (M) 1. anything slender. 2. support; staff; pillar; rod; mace; stem; sugarcane.

**Yaṣṭikā** (S) (F) a string of pearls.

**Yaṣṭṛ** (S) (M) worshipper.

**Yāśu** (S) (M) embrace.

**Yataćetas** (S) (M) with a controlled mind.

**Yatagir** (S) (M) one who restrains his speech.

**Yatakṛta** (S) (M) restrained; governed; subdued.

**Yatamanyu** (S) (M) subduing anger.

**Yātanā** (S) (F) 1. torment; agony. 3. the pains of hell personified as the daughter of Bhaya and Mṛtyu.

**Yatamkara** (S) (M) subduer; conqueror.

**Yatendriya** (S) (M) chaste; pure; of controlled passions.

**Yathāvāsa** (S) (M) 1. in the manner of perfume. 3. a sage (*M. Bh.*)

**Yati** (S) (F) restraint; control; guidance.

**Yati** (S) (M) 1. ascetic; devotee; one who has renounced his possessions. 3. a son of Brahmā; a king who was the eldest son of Nahuṣa and the brother of Yayāti (*M. Bh.*); a son of Viśvāmitra (*M. Bh.*); another name for Śiva.

**Yatidharman** (S) (M) 1. follower of an ascetic path. 3. a son of Śvaphalka.

**Yatin** (S) (M) ascetic; devotee.

**Yatinātha** (S) (M) 1. lord of ascetics. 3. an incarnation of Śiva as a forest sage.

**Yatīndra** (S) (M) 1. lord of the yatis or ascetics. 3. another name for Indra.

**Yatirāja** (S) (M) 1. king of ascetics. 3. another name for Rāmānuja.

**Yatīśa** (S) (M) lord of ascetics.

**Yatīśvara** (S) (M) lord of ascetics.

**Yatīyasa** (S) (M) silver.

**Yatna** (S) (M) activity of will; performance; effort; energy; zeal.

**Yātnika** (S) (M) making efforts.

**Yātu** (S) (M) 1. going. 2. traveller; wind; time.

**Yātudhāna** (S) (M) 1. creating obstacles for others. 2. sorcerer; magician. 3. a rākṣasa who was the son of Kaśyapa and Surasā.

**Yātudhānī** (S) (F) 1. magician; conjurer. 3. a rākṣasī born from a sacrificial fire who was killed by Indra (*M. Bh.*)

**Yātughna** (S) (M) 1. destroyer of Yatus or evil spirits. 3. the Balsamodendron plant whose gum is said to protect one from curses; bdellium.

**Yātuvid** (S) (M) one who knows magic; skilful in sorcery.

**Yaudheya** (S) (M) 1. warrior. 3. a son of Yudhiṣṭhira and Devikādevī (*M. Bh.*); a king who was the son of Prativindhya (*M. Purāṇa*)

**Yaudhiṣṭhira** (S) (M) 1. son of Yudhiṣṭhira. 3. another name for Prativindhya.

**Yaugandharāyaṇa** (S) (M) 1. lord of the strong ones. 3. a minister of Prince Udayana who is celebrated in the Purāṇas.

**Yaugāndharī** (S) (M) 1. descendant of Yugandhara. 3. a king of the Śalvas.

**Yauvanobheda** (S) (M) 1. the ardour of youthful passion. 3. another name for Kāma.

**Yauyudhāni** (S) (M) 1. son of a warrior. 3. son of King Sātyaki of the Yādavas (*M. Purāṇa*)

**Yavakṛta** (S) (M) 1. purchased with barley. 3. a son of Aṅgiras; a son of Bharadvāja who practiced austerities to gain the knowledge of the Vedas without studying them and was granted his wish by Indra (*M. Bh.*)

**Yavakṣā** (S) (F) 1. with barley in abundance. 3. a river (*M. Bh.*)

**Yavana** (S) (M) 1. quick; swift; a Greek; mixing; mingling; keeping aloof; averting. 2. wheat (*Triticum aestivum*)

**Yavāśira** (S) (M) 1. mixed with barley. 3. another name for Soma.

**Yavayaśa** (S) (M) 1. controller of anger; self restrained. 3. a son of Idhmajihva and the country ruled by him.

**Yavīnara** (S) (M) 1. young. 3. a king of the Purū dynasty who was the son of Bāhyāśva (*A. Purāṇa*); a son of Ajamīdha (*H. Purāṇa*)

**Yaviṣṭha** (S) (M) 1. youngest; last born. 3. another name for Agni.

**Yavīyas** (S) (M) 1. younger. 3. a preceptor.

**Yavya** (S) (M) 1. a stock of barley and fruit. 3. a family of ṛṣis.

**Yavyavatī** (S) (F) 1. to have barley and fruit in abundance. 3. a river (*Ṛg Veda*)

**Yayāti** (S) (M) 1. wanderer; traveller; mover; goer. 3. a monarch of the lunar race who was the son of Nahuṣa, from his 2 wives came the 2 lines of the lunar race, Yadu the son of Devayānī and Purū of Śarmiṣṭhā, Yayāti is also represented as an author of *Ṛg Veda* (ix) and a member of Yama's court.

**Yayin** (S) (M) 1. quick; hastening. 3. another name for Śiva.

**Yayu** (S) (M) 1. going; moving; swift. 3. a horse of the moon.

**Yelemelā** (T) (F) 1. wealthy. 3. Rukmiṇi as an

incarnation of Lakṣmī.

**Yodhaka** (S) (M) fighter; soldier.

**Yodheya** (S) (M) warrior; combatant.

**Yodhin** (S) (M) fighter; warrior; soldier; conqueror.

**Yogā** (S) (F) 1. total; conjunction; meditation. 3. a Śakti; another name for Pīvari daughter of the Pitṛs called Barhiṣads (*H. Purāṇa*)

**Yoga** (S) (M) 1. the act of harnessing; yoke; application; means; charm; remedy; union; junction; connection; arrangement; fitness; zeal; concentration; meditation; devotion. 2. abstract meditation; practised as a philosophy taught by Pātañjali. 3. yoga personified as a son of Dharma and Kriyā or Śraddhā and the grandson of Manu Svāyambhuva (*Bhāgavata*)

**Yogaćakṣus** (S) (M) 1. one whose eye is contemplation. 3. another name for Brahmā.

**Yogaćandra** (S) (M) moon among zealots.

**Yogaćara** (S) (M) 1. one who performs meditation. 3. another name for Hanumān.

**Yogadeva** (S) (M) 1. lord of meditation. 3. a Jaina author (*J. Literature*)

**Yogadīpikā** (S) (F) light of meditation.

**Yogaja** (S) (M) arising from meditation.

**Yogakanyā** (S) (F) 1. born of meditation. 3. the infant daughter of Yaśodā who was substituted for Kṛṣṇa and killed by Kaṅsa.

**Yogamāyā** (S) (F) 1. the magical power of abstract meditation. 3. another name for Durgā.

**Yogamāyādevī** (S) (F) the form of Devī in the state of yoga, she transferred the 7th child of Devakī, Balarāma, from her womb to that of Rohiṇī (*D. Bh. Purāṇa*)

**Yogāmbara** (S) (M) 1. ever in meditation; clad in meditation. 3. a Buddhist deity.

**Yogānanda** (S) (M) delighting in meditation.

**Yoganātha** (S) (M) 1. lord of yoga. 3. another name for Śiva

**Yoganidrā** (S) (F) 1. meditation sleep. 3. Viṣṇu's sleep personified as a goddess said to be a form of Durgā.

**Yoganidrālu** (S) (M) 1. in the sleep of meditation. 3. another name for Viṣṇu.

**Yoganilaya** (S) (M) 1. in impenetrable meditation. 3. another name for Śiva.

**Yogapāraṁga** (S) (M) 1. expert in yoga. 3. another name for Śiva.

**Yogapati** (S) (M) 1. lord of yoga. 3. another name for Viṣṇu.

**Yogapatnī** (S) (F) 1. wife of Yoga. 3. another name for Pīvarī.

**Yogarāja** (S) (M) lord of medicines; lord of meditation.

**Yogaraṅga** (S) (M) the Sweet Orange tree (*Citrus aurantium*)

**Yogaratna** (S) (F) a magical jewel.

**Yogasiddhā** (S) (F) 1. perfected through yoga. 3. a sister of Bṛhaspati.

**Yogatārā** (S) (F) the chief star of any constellation.

**Yogātman** (S) (M) one whose essence is yoga.

**Yogavatī** (S) (F) 1. united; joined. 2. one who is versed in yoga. 3. the 3rd daughter of Menā who was the wife of the sage Jaigīṣavya (*P. Purāṇa*)

**Yogayuj** (S) (M) one who has given himself to yoga.

**Yogendra** (S) (M) 1. lord of yoga. 3. another name for Śiva.

**Yogeśa** (S) (M) 1. lord of yoga. 3. the city of Brahmā; another name for Yājñavalkya and Śiva.

**Yogeśanandana** (S) (M) 1. son of the lord of yoga. 3. another name for Kārttikeya.

**Yogeśvara** (S) (M) 1. master of yoga. 2. deity; object of devout contemplation. 3. a son of Devahotra (*Bh. Purāṇa*); another name for Kṛṣṇa and Yājñavalkya.

**Yogeśvarī** (S) (F) 1. adept in yoga. 3. a form of Durgā (*H. Ć. Ćintāmaṇi*); a vidyādharī (*K. Sāgara*); *Mimordica balsamina*.

**Yogī** (S) (M) 1. contemplative saint; devout; ascetic. 3. a Buddha; another name for Yājñavalkya, Arjuna, Viṣṇu and Śiva.

**Yogin** (S) (F) meditator; devotee; ascetic.

**Yoginī** (S) (F) 1. a being endowed with magical power. 2. fairy; witch; sorceress. 3. attendants created by Durgā (*H. Purāṇa*)

**Yogīśa** (S) (M) 1. lord of yogis. 3. another name for Kṛṣṇa.

**Yogitā** (S) (F) bewitched; enchanted; wild.

**Yojaka** (S) (M) 1. yoker; employer; user; arranger. 3. another name for Agni.

**Yojanabāhu** (S) (M) 1. with long arms like a Yojana. 3. another name for Rāvaṇa.

**Yojanagandhā** (S) (F) 1. diffusing fragrance to the distance of a Yojana (about 9 miles). 3. another name for Satyāvatī and Sītā.

**Yoktṛ** (S) (M) one who excites or rouses; one who yokes; charioteer.

**Yūpaketana** (S) (M) 1.flag of victory. 3. another name for Bhūriśravas.

**Yūpaketu** (S) (M) 1. flag of victory. 3. another name for Bhūriśravas.

**Yoṣā** (S) (F) young woman; maid.

**Yoṣaṇā** (S) (F) girl; young woman.

**Yoṣidratnā** (S) (F) a jewel among women.

**Yoṣitā** (S) (F) woman; wife.

**Yoṭaka** (S) (M) a combination of stars; a constellation.

**Yotimastaka** (S) (M) 1. with a bright forehead. 3. a king who was asked by the Pāṇḍavas to take part in the great war (*M. Bh.*)

**Yotu** (S) (M) cleaning; purifying.

**Yuddha** (S) (M) 1. fought; conquered; subdued. 3. a son of Ugrasena (*V. Purāṇa*)

**Yuddhāćārya** (S) (M) one who teaches the art of war.

**Yuddhakīrti** (S) (M) 1. famous in war. 3. a pupil of Śankarāćārya.

**Yuddhamuṣṭi** (S) (M) 1. one who fights with his fists. 3. a son of Ugrasena (*V. Purāṇa*)

**Yuddhānivartin** (S) (M) heroic; valiant.

**Yuddhapravīṇa** (S) (M) skilled in war.

**Yuddharaṅga** (S) (M) 1. one whose arena is battle; battlefield. 3. another name for Kārttikeya.

**Yuddhavīra** (S) (M) hero; warrior.

**Yudhājit** (S) (M) 1. victorious in battle. 3. a son of Kroṣṭu and Mādrī (*H. Purāṇa*); a son of Vṛṣṇi (*V. Purāṇa*); a king of Ujjayinī; a Kekaya king who was the brother of Kaikeyī, Daśaratha's wife, and the uncle of Bharata (*V. Rāmāyaṇa*); a king of Avantī who was the brother of Śatrujita; a Yādava king who was the son of Pṛthvī and Anamitra (*P. Purāṇa*)

**Yudhāmanyu** (S) (M) 1. young warrior. 3. a Pāñćāla warrior who fought the war on the side of the Pāṇḍavas (*M. Bh.*)

**Yudhaśālin** (S) (M) warlike; valiant.

**Yudhiṣṭhira** (S) (M) 1. firm or steady in battle. 3. the eldest son of the 5 sons of Pāṇḍu, he was actually the child of Kuntī and Dharma, he succeeded Pāṇḍu as king, first reigning over Indraprastha and then Hastināpura, he was known for his unswerving dedication to truth (*M. Bh.*); a son of Kṛṣṇa. (*H. Purāṇa*)

**Yudhma** (S) (M) warrior; hero; battle; arrow; bow.

**Yudhvan** (S) (M) martial; warrior.

**Yugādhyakṣa** (S) (M) 1. superintendant of a yuga or cycle of time. 3. another name for Śiva.

**Yugādikṛt** (S) (M) 1. creator of the beginning of the world. 3. another name for Śiva.

**Yugala** (S) (F) 1. pair. 2. a double prayer to Lakṣmī and Nārāyaṇa.

**Yugandharā** (S) (F) 1. bearing an era. 3. another name for the earth.

**Yugandhara** (S) (M) 1. bearing the yoke; the pole of a carriage; bearer of an era; strongest person of the era. 3. a warrior who fought on the side of the Pāṇḍavas (*H. Purāṇa*); a mountain (*M. Bh.*)

**Yugapa** (S) (M) 1. best of the era. 3. a gandharva (*M. Bh.*)

**Yugavāha** (S) (M) one who directs the age.

**Yugavarta** (S) (M) one who changes the eras.

**Yugma** (S) (M) 1. even; twins. 2. the zodiac sign of Gemini.

**Yujya** (S) (M) connected; related; allied; equal in power; proper; capable.

**Yukta** (S) (M) 1. yoked; absorbed; attentive; skilful; clever; fit; prosperous. 3. a son of Manu Raivata (*H. Purāṇa*); a ṛṣi under Manu Bhautya.

**Yuktāśva** (S) (M) 1. with yoked horses. 2. having wealth. 3. a sage and scholar in the Vedas.

**Yuktimat** (S) (M) ingenious; clever; inventive.

**Yuñjāna** (S) (M) uniting; suitable; proper; successful; prosperous.

**Yūpākṣa** (S) (M) 1. the eye of victory. 3. a

military commander of Rāvaṇa who was killed by Hanumān; a rākṣasa killed by the monkey Mainda (*V. Rāmāyaṇa*)

**Yutajit** (S) (M) 1. accompanied by victory; victorious. 3. a son of King Bhoja of the Yadu clan (*Bhāgavata*)

**Yūthanātha** (S) (M) the chief of a troop.

**Yūthikā** (S) (F) 1. multitude. 2. Common White Jasmine (*Jasminum officianale)*

**Yuvana** (S) (M) 1. young; strong; healthy. 3. another name for the moon.

**Yuvanāśva** (S) (M) 1. young horse. 3. a king of the Ikṣvāku dynasty who was the son of Prasenajit and the father of Māndhātā (*M. Bh.*); another king of the Ikṣvāku dynasty who was the son of Adri and the father of King Śrāva; a son of Vṛṣadarbha; an Ikṣvāku king who was the grandson of Māndhātā.

**Yuvarāja** (S) (M) young king; crown prince.

**Yuvatī** (S) (F) young girl applied as an adjective in the *Ṛg Veda* to Uṣās; night; morning; heaven and earth; the zodiac sign of Virgo; *Curcuma longa*.

**Yuvatiṣṭā** (S) (F) Yellow Jasmine (*Jasminum humile*)

**Yuvikā** (S) (F) young girl.

**Yuyudhāna** (S) (M) 1. Kṣatriya; warrior. 3. a son of Sātyaka and an ally of the Pāṇḍavas (*M. Bh.*); a king of Mithila (*Bh. Purāṇa*); another name for Indra.

**Yuyudhi** (S) (M) warlike; martial.

**Yuyutsu** (S) (M) 1. combative; pugnacious. 3. a son of Dhṛtarāṣṭra by a Vaiśya woman who joined the Pāṇḍavas, he was an honest and mighty hero; a son of Dhṛtarāṣṭra and Gāndhārī (*M. Bh.*)

# LIST OF THE SOURCES

| | | |
|---|---|---|
| Āśvālayam Gṛhyasūtra | – | *A. Gṛhyasūtra.* |
| Āpasthambha Srantasūtra | – | *Ā. Śrantasūtra.* |
| Atma Prabodha | – | *A. Prabodha.* |
| Āryabhatiya | – | *Āryabhṭiya.* |
| | | |
| Bāla Bhārata | – | *B. Bhārata.* |
| Buddhist Jatakas | – | *B. Jatakas.* |
| Bhartṛhari Śatakam | – | *B. Śatakam.* |
| Devi Bhāgavata | – | *D. Bhāgavata.* |
| Mahādevi Bhāgavata | – | *M. Bhāgavata.* |
| Aitareya Brāhmaṇa | – | *A. Brāhmaṇa.* |
| Kauśtiki Brāhmaṇa | – | *K. Brāhmaṇa.* |
| Pañćavimśa Brāhmaṇa | – | *P. Brāhmaṇa.* |
| Śatapatha Brāhmaṇa | – | *Ś. Brāhmaṇa.* |
| Tāṇḍya Brāhmaṇa | – | *Tā. Brāhmaṇa.* |
| Vanśa Brāhmaṇa | – | *V. Brāhmaṇa.* |
| Bhāva Prakāśa | – | *B. Prakāśa.* |
| | | |
| Ćaitya Vandana | – | *Ć. Vandana.* |
| Ćandrāloka | – | *Ćandraloka.* |
| Naisadha Ćarita | – | *N. Ćarita.* |
| Mahāvira Ćarita | – | *M. Ćarita.* |
| Buddha Ćarita | – | *B. Ćarita.* |
| Bhadrabāhu Ćarita | – | *Bha. Ćarita.* |
| Vīra Ćarita | – | *V. Ćarita.* |
| Chandraswamy Ćarita | – | *Ć. Ćarita.* |
| | | |
| Divyāvadāna | – | *Divyāvadāna.* |
| Datta Ćandrika | – | *D. Ćandrikā.* |
| Durgāsaptaśati | – | *D. Saptaśati.* |
| | | |
| Gaṇaratna Mahodadhi | – | *G. Mahodadhi.* |

| | | |
|---|---|---|
| Gautam's Dhaı maśastra | – | *G's. Dharmaśastra.* |
| Gobhilas Śraddhā Kalpa | – | *G's Ś. Kalpa.* |
| Gṛhya Samigraha | – | *G. Samigraha.* |
| Gṛhya Sūtra | – | *G. Sūtra.* |
| | | |
| Hitopadeśa | – | *Hitopadeśa.* |
| Hemendrīya Ćaturvarga Ćintāmaṇi | – | *H.Ć. Ćintāmaṇi.* |
| | | |
| Īśa Tantra | – | *I. Tantra.* |
| | | |
| Jaimini Aśvamedha | – | *J. Aśvamedha.* |
| Jaimuni Bhārata | – | *J. Bhārata.* |
| Jātākam | – | *Jātakam.* |
| Jaina Sāhitya | – | *J. Literature.* |
| | | |
| Kāvya Prakāśa | – | *K. Prakāśa.* |
| Kalpa Sūtra | – | *K. Sūtra.* |
| Kālidasa Granthāvali | – | *K. Granthāvali.* |
| Kaṇvādi | – | *Kaṇvādi.* |
| Kādambari | – | *Kadambari.* |
| Kathārṇava | – | *Kathārṇava.* |
| Kharatara Gaccha | – | *K. Gaccha.* |
| Kathāsaritasāgara | - | *K. Sāgara.* |
| Karaṇḍvyuha | – | *K. Vyuha.* |
| Amaṛ Koṣa | – | *A. Koṣa.* |
| Hatayudha Koṣa | – | *H. Koṣa.* |
| Hemaćandra Koṣa | – | *He. Koṣa.* |
| Jainendra Siddhānta Koṣa | – | *J. S. Koṣa.* |
| | | |
| Lalita Vistara | – | *L. Vistara.* |
| Buddha Sahitya | – | *B. Literature.* |
| | | |
| Maskāra stava | – | *M. Stava.* |
| Mṛcchakaṭikam | – | *M. Katikam.* |
| Manu Smṛti | – | *M. Smṛti.* |
| Mahābhārata | – | *M. Bh.* |
| | | |
| Naćiketupākhyana | – | *N. Pākhyāna.* |

| | | |
|---|---|---|
| Nirukta | — | *Nirukta.* |
| Nalopākhyāna | — | *Nalopākhyāna.* |
| Niti Śataka | — | *N. Śataka.* |
| | | |
| Panćdaṇḍa Ćatraprabandha | — | *P. Ćatraprabandha.* |
| Agni Purāṇa | — | *A. Purāṇa.* |
| Bhāgavata Purāṇa | — | *Bhā. Purāṇa.* |
| Bhaviṣya Purāṇa | — | *Bh. Purāṇa.* |
| Bhiṣma Purāṇa | — | *Bhi. Purāṇa.* |
| Brahmāṇḍa Purāṇa | — | *Br. Purāṇa.* |
| Brahmavaivarta Purāṇa | — | *Brah. Purāṇa.* |
| Brahma Purāṇa | — | *Brahma Purāṇa.* |
| Devi Purāṇa | — | *D. Purāṇa.* |
| Ganeśa Purāṇa | — | *G. Purāṇa.* |
| Garuḍa Purāṇa | — | *Gar. Purāṇa.* |
| Harivamśa Purāṇa | — | *H. Purāṇa.* |
| Harivanśa Purāṇa | — | *H. Purāṇa.* |
| Kalki Purāṇa | — | *K. Purāṇa.* |
| Linga Purāṇa | — | *L. Purāṇa.* |
| Matsya Purāṇa | — | *M. Purāṇa.* |
| Mārkaṇḍeya Purāṇa | — | *Mā. Purāṇa.* |
| Nārada Purāṇa | — | *N. Purāṇa.* |
| Nahni Purāṇa | — | *Nah. Purāṇa.* |
| Padma Purāṇa | — | *P. Purāṇa.* |
| Śiva Purāṇa | — | *Ś. Purāṇa.* |
| Skanda Purāṇa | — | *Sk. Purāṇa.* |
| Subāhu Purāṇa | — | *Su. Purāṇa.* |
| Vāṣist Purāṇa | — | *V. Purāṇa.* |
| Viṣṇu Purāṇa | — | *V. Purāṇa.* |
| Vāyu Purāṇa | — | *Vā. Purāṇa.* |
| Vāmana Purāṇa | — | *Vam. Purāṇa.* |
| Varāha Purāṇa | — | *Var. Purāṇa.* |
| Varuṇa Purāṇa | — | *Varuṇa Purāṇa.* |
| Purāṇas | — | *Purāṇas.* |
| Prabhodha Ćandrodaya | — | *P. Ćandrodaya.* |
| Pāṇinī | — | *Pāṇinī.* |
| Panćatantra | — | *Panćatantra.* |
| Pārśavanatha Ćaritra | — | *P. Ćaritra.* |
| | | |
| Ānanda Rāmāyaṇa | — | *A. Rāmāyaṇa.* |
| Bāla Rāmāyaṇa | — | *B. Rāmāyaṇa.* |

| | | |
|---|---|---|
| Kamba Rāmāyaṇa | – | *K. Rāmāyaṇa.* |
| Uttar Rāmāyaṇa | – | *U. Rāmāyaṇa.* |
| Valmiki Rāmāyaṇa | – | *V. Rāmāyaṇa.* |
| Rāja Taraṅginī | – | *R. Taraṅginī.* |
| Rasa Gaṅgādhara | – | *R. Gangādhara.* |
| Raghuvanśa | – | *Raghuvanśa.* |
| Ṛg Veda Ankuramaṇikā | – | *R. Ankuramaṇikā.* |

| | | |
|---|---|---|
| Āpastamba Samhitā | – | *Ā. Samhitā.* |
| Pārāśara Samhitā | – | *P. Samhitā.* |
| Suśruta Samhita | – | *S. Samhitā.* |
| Taittarīya Samhita | – | *T. Samhitā.* |
| Vājasaneyī Samhita | – | *V. Samhitā.* |
| Varāhamihira's Bṛhat Samhitā | – | *V's B. Samhita.* |
| Yajurveda Samhitā | – | *Y. Samhitā.* |
| Śiva Rāja Vijaya | – | *Ś. R. Vījaya.* |
| Suvarṇa Prābhāsa | – | *S. Prābhāsa.* |
| Saddharma Puṇḍarikā | – | *S. Puṇḍarikā.* |
| Sinhāsanadvatrinśika | – | *S. Dvatrinśika.* |
| Śatruñjaya Mahātmya | – | *Ś. Mahātmya.* |
| Śankaravijaya | – | *Ś. Vījaya.* |
| Svapna Vāsavadattam | – | *S. Vāsavadattam.* |
| Sarvadarśana Samgraha | – | *S. Samgraha.* |
| Śankhayan Śrauta Sutra | – | *Ś. Ś. Sutra.* |
| Tantra Śāstra | – | *T. Śāstra.* |
| Dharma Śāstra | – | *D. Śāstra.* |
| Jyotiṣa Śāstra | – | *J. Śāstra.* |

| | | |
|---|---|---|
| Tithyāditya | – | *Tithyāditya.* |
| Taittarīya Prātiśākya | – | *T. Prātiśākhya.* |
| Taittarīya Āraṇyaka | – | *T. Āraṇyaka.* |

| | | |
|---|---|---|
| Bṛhadāraṇyaka Upaniṣad. | – | *Br. Upaniṣad.* |
| Ćandogya Upaniṣad | – | *Ć. Upaniṣad.* |
| Kaṭhopaniṣad | – | *K. Upaniṣad.* |
| Kauśtiki Upaniṣad | – | *Kau. Upaniṣad.* |
| Maitryupaniṣad | – | *M. Upaniṣad.* |
| Muṇḍaka Upaniṣad | – | *Mu. Upaniṣad.* |
| Rāmatapaniya Upaniṣad | – | *Rā. Upaniṣad.* |
| Vetāla Pañćavinśatikā | – | *V. Pañćavinśatika.* |

| | | |
|---|---|---|
| Vikramorvaśiyam | – | *Vikramorvaśīyam.* |
| Vićaramṛta Samgraha | – | *V. Samgraha.* |
| Vikramāṅka Deva Ćaritam | – | *V.D. Ćaritam.* |
| Atharva Veda | – | *A. Veda.* |
| Ṛg Veda | – | *Ṛg. Veda.* |
| Sāma Veda | – | *S. Veda.* |
| Yajur Veda | – | *Y. Veda.* |
| Yogavaśiṣtha | – | *Yogavaśiṣtha.* |